CONTEMPORARY
advertising
and Integrated Marketing Communications

fifteenth edition

William F. Arens
Michael F. Weigold

CONTEMPORARY ADVERTISING AND INTEGRATED MARKETING COMMUNICATIONS, FIFTEENTH EDITION

Published by McGraw-Hill Education, 2 Penn Plaza, New York, NY 10121. Copyright © 2017 by McGraw-Hill Education. All rights reserved. Printed in the United States of America. Previous editions © 2013, 2011, and 2009. No part of this publication may be reproduced or distributed in any form or by any means, or stored in a database or retrieval system, without the prior written consent of McGraw-Hill Education, including, but not limited to, in any network or other electronic storage or transmission, or broadcast for distance learning.

Some ancillaries, including electronic and print components, may not be available to customers outside the United States.

This book is printed on acid-free paper.

1 2 3 4 5 6 7 8 9 DOW 21 20 19 18 17 16

ISBN 978-1-259-92126-1
MHID 1-259-92126-3

mheducation.com/highered

To Debbie

My partner in everything
MFW

the preface

What's New?

As with every communications discipline, digital media are disrupters in the advertising world. The 15th edition of *Contemporary Advertising and Integrated Marketing Communications* incorporates many changes designed to ensure it is relevant and essential for your students.

We provide a chapter-by-chapter breakdown of what is new for our returning adopters later in this introduction. But here we introduce our biggest changes to the book: the addition of significantly more information about digital media throughout the text, and the a fuller realization of the book itself as a digital product, incorporating McGraw-Hill's latest digital learning technologies such as LearnSmart and Connect.

In our last edition we introduced the topic of social media. The wisdom of that decision has become more clear with time as Facebook, Twitter, Instagram, and Snapchat are major ad platforms. Digital interactive advertising expenditures already exceed those of newspapers and magazines combined. Moreover, Internet budgets are growing at a far greater pace than other media. Within the category of digital interactive, social media, mobile and search are growing at far faster rates than other forms (banner ads, e-mail, etc.). If expenditures are a sign of importance, then social media is significant today, and will be more so tomorrow.

Perhaps most importantly, generalizations concerning effective use of other media types do not always hold for social media. It really is a new way of engaging consumers. This is a point we stress in our new opening vignette on Shakira's amazing World Cup viral video. In fact, many of the vignettes have been updated or completely rewritten to continue the fresh approach students and instructors have always valued in the book. We believe that your students will have a better sense of the value, and the challenge, of social media by giving it it's own coverage. We are proud to be the first advertising and IMC text to cover social media this way.

The IMC concept remains front and center in this edition. As with other texts, changing the focus from advertising to IMC has been a gradual evolution, until now. Our adopters tell us that the broader focus is the one they prefer, and we endorse that perspective. What does this mean for you and your students? It means we encourage message creators to begin with an audience and message in mind rather than a media platform. It means solving communications problems rather than working through advertising tactics. It means stressing relationship development rather than executing a sale. Advertising remains a uniquely powerful way to address brand messaging, but not the only way, and sometimes not the best way. We've ensured the text will continue to help you guide your students toward an audience-focused approach to brand communications. We think this reflects how companies think about their messaging, and how you think about the topics your course should cover.

McGraw-Hill's Connect and LearnSmart technologies, for educators who've not used them in the past, are amazing online platforms for enriching your students' learning. Created by the authors of the text, Connect and LearnSmart bring advertising and IMC practice alive and help reinforce key learning objectives from the text. Instructors can assign students a variety of exercises that include case studies, video cases, and concept reinforcement. The experience is completely customizable, so that instructors can use as much or as little of the Connect content as they wish. The exercises can be done strictly for student study or set up as online homework. Instructors can even add their own exercises to the ones created by the authors.

Best of all, both technologies scale easily to the size of your class. One of us (Weigold) regularly teaches advertising and IMC to over 200 students a semester. Reaching large numbers of students in an engaging and exciting way has never been easier. We think that you and your students will love having these resources.

As always, we want to know what you think. Drop us a line about what you like and don't like. Write Mike at mweigold@gmail.com, I'd love to hear from you. Also follow the text on Facebook (McGraw-Hill Contemporary Advertising) to get regular resources, updates, news items, and news relevant for your students and your course.

The Audience for This Book

Every one of us exists as a member of the target audience for thousands of brands. That alone would make the study of advertising and IMC worthwhile. In addition, at some point in their lives, most people will probably become creators of advertising—whether they design a flier for a school car wash, write a classified ad for a garage sale, post a YouTube message advocating for a cause or idea, create a LinkedIn profile for professional advancement, or develop a whole campaign for some business, charitable event, or political cause.

That makes the study of IMC and advertising more important today than ever before, not only for students of business or journalism—who may be contemplating a career in the field—but also for students of sociology, psychology, political science, economics, history, language, science, or the arts. Many of these people will create some form of advertising; all will be lifetime consumers of it.

The study of IMC gives students, regardless of their major field of study, valuable tools to use in any subsequent profession. It teaches them to think and plan strategically; gather and analyze research data; compute and evaluate alternative courses of action; cooperate with a team in developing creative solutions; analyze competitive proposals; understand why people behave the way they do; express themselves and their ideas with clarity and simplicity; defend their point of view with others; appreciate and assess the quality of different creative endeavors; and use powerful ideas to speak with knowledge, confidence, and conviction.

In addition, students of business, journalism, and communications gain several specific benefits. The study of IMC can help students to

- Understand the real economic, social, and cultural role of advertising and, conversely, the impact of a society's values on advertising.
- Realize how advertising supports journalism and relates to the whole field of communications.
- Appreciate the global effect of IMC on business, industry, and national economies.
- Comprehend the strategic function of IMC within the broader context of business and marketing.
- Evaluate and even apply the impressive artistic creativity and technical expertise required in IMC.
- Discover what people in advertising and related disciplines do, how they do it, and what the expanding career opportunities in these fields now offer.

Student-Oriented Features for the Twenty-First Century

Our mission in *Contemporary Advertising and Integrated Marketing Communications* continues to be presenting advertising as it is actually practiced. Now, as we introduce the 15th edition, our purpose remains the same. We also believe advertising and IMC should be taught in an intelligible manner and lively style relevant to college and university students of the 21st century.

Award-Winning Graphic Design

Among the many benefits this text brings to instructors and students of IMC are an elegant feel and award-winning graphic design—an important feature for a book that professes to educate students about the aesthetics of advertising design and production. The open, airy look contributes to learning by making the text material colorful, inviting, and accessible to students. Throughout the book, chapter overviews, chapter learning objectives, and key terms printed in boldface type all work together to make the text material as reader-friendly as possible.

Chapter-Opening Vignettes

To capture and hold student interest, each chapter begins with a story. Each vignette depicts an actual situation that illustrates a basic concept. Wherever possible, the opening story is then woven throughout the chapter to demonstrate how textbook concepts actually come to life in real-world situations. For example, throughout Chapter 1, we examine how Activia responded to changes in the practice of global IMC with an innovative music viral. In Chapter 4, the story of McDonald's advertising is complemented with numerous examples that range from global to local. In Chapter 7 we examine the actual media plan of an organization dedicated to eradicating HIV. And in Chapter 16 we look at how social media helped grow donations at one nonprofit nearly 1000 percent. The integration continues in Connect, where the opening vignettes are featured in many of the video cases.

Extensive Illustration Program

The best way to teach is to set a good example. So each of the 19 chapters features beautiful full-color illustrations of recent award-winning ads, commercials, and campaigns that demonstrate the best in the business. In fact, *Contemporary Advertising and Integrated Marketing Communications* is one of the most heavily illustrated textbooks on the market, with all the major media represented—print, electronic, digital, social, and out-of-home—in a balanced manner. We carefully selected the examples and illustrations for both their quality and their relevance to students. Nearly half of the ads are new to this edition.

Furthermore, we feature a mix of local, national, and international ads from both business-to-business and consumer campaigns. In-depth captions tell the stories behind many of the ads and explain how the ads demonstrate the concepts discussed in the text.

The book is liberally illustrated with models, charts, graphs, and tables. Some of these encapsulate useful information on advertising concepts or the advertising industry. Others depict the processes employed in account management, research, account planning, media planning, and production.

Full-Color Portfolios

In addition to the individual print ads and actual frames from TV commercials, the book contains several multipage portfolios of outstanding creative work. These include "Strategic Use of the Creative Mix," "Outstanding Magazine Ads," "Advertising on the Internet," "Corporate Advertising," and others. Accompanying captions and questions tie the ads to topics germane to the chapter in which they appear.

Ad Lab

Active participation enhances learning, so Ad Labs play a significant role in virtually every chapter. These unique sidebars to the world of advertising introduce students to topics of current interest or controversy and then involve them in the subject by posing questions that stimulate critical thinking. Some of the many topics presented in Ad Labs include government regulation, bottom-up marketing, creativity, the psychological impact of color, advertising on the Internet, "green" advertising, sales promotion, and direct-response advertising.

Ethical Issues

Students face new and challenging ethical issues, and they need to exercise even greater sensitivity than their 20th-century counterparts. Therefore, in *every* chapter of the book, we introduce a current ethical issue—to focus attention on the most critical social questions facing marketers today. These include the debate over puffery, marketing to children, comparative advertising, the targeting of ethnic minorities, consumer profiling, privacy, negative political advertising, visual and statistical manipulation, and others.

My IMC Campaign

For instructors who offer students semester-long projects as a way of getting their hands dirty, we've included this valuable resource. In each chapter students receive practical advice on developing a real campaign, culminating with tips on developing a plans book and a client presentation.

My IMC Campaign is a chapter-by-chapter guide for students enrolled in classes that involve semester-long campaign projects. From our conversations with dozens of professors, we know that semester-long projects are a major component of many advertising and IMC courses. These projects help students gain their first experience with the practice of marketing communications. We applaud instructors who make the effort to offer their students this opportunity, and we are proud to provide a chapter-by-chapter project guide.

The My IMC Campaign feature offers students practical advice for developing their projects. The advice ranges from frameworks for developing creative strategy, media plans, and situation analyses, to practical tips on using collaborative software, developing presentations, and working in teams. We believe professors who incorporate team projects in their classes will find this new feature greatly assists their efforts to give students real-world experience in advertising.

People behind the Ads

Behind the thousands of ads we see and hear are real human beings—the writers, designers, programmers, executives, and media specialists. In the final analysis, the marketing communications industry is more than a collection of concepts, processes, and activities. It is an industry of people, some of the smartest, most creative, and most interesting people in the world. Your students will meet some of the most interesting right here, many offering insights provided uniquely for this text. The feature presents students contemporary practioners who are already industry legends (Bogusky, Steele), enduring legends (Bernbach, Gallup, Lasker) and new individuals changing the industry every day.

Additional Learning Aids

Each chapter concludes with a summary followed by questions for review and discussion. These pedagogical aids help students review chapter contents and assimilate what they have learned. Throughout the text, key ideas and terms are highlighted with boldface type and defined when introduced. The definitions of all these terms are collected at the end of the book in a thorough and extensive glossary.

The Advertising Experience Exercises

True to the text's agency approach, the 15th edition of *Contemporary Advertising and Integrated Marketing Communications* continues hands-on application exercises that place students in the advertisers' shoes to help them see how advertising is done in the real world. Effective as outside assignments or in-class discussion starters, the Advertising Experience allows students to effectively apply their knowledge of each chapter.

Many exercises also require students to access the Web and perform research on questions relevant to the chapter topic.

This edition deepens our commitment to our IMC core. The need to consider advertising within an IMC framework is no longer debated in either industry or academia. The focus on the message receiver, as compared to the message creator, has improved the practice of marketing communications. While advertising remains an important part of the book, we give greater coverage to other promotional elements. You will find that in choosing between the words *advertising* versus *IMC,* we emphasize the former when the practices we describe are largely those of advertising agencies. When practices are used across broader or more integrated messaging platforms, we use *IMC.* Some marketers may still pine for the days of complete control over brand messages (if such days ever truly existed) but savvy organizations have embraced the new world of "conversations" with customers. In a recent *Ad Age* article, writer Jack Neff noted that "Managing a brand has always been a slightly odd concept, given that consumers are the real arbiters of brand meaning, and it's become increasingly outmoded in today's two-way world." Neff writes that companies such as P&G and Unilever are going so far as to rename brand managers "brand advocates."

For the Professor: The 15th Edition Has Been Strategically Revised

Our continuing goal has been to bring clarity to the often-murky subject of advertising. Our method has been to personally involve students as much as possible in the practical experiences of advertising, while simultaneously giving them a clear understanding of advertising's dynamic role in both marketing management and the human communication process. In the pursuit of this objective, we have included numerous modifications and improvements in the 15th edition of *Contemporary Advertising and Integrated Marketing Communications.*

Current and Concise

As with every new edition, our first effort was to update all statistics and tables and to document the most recent academic and professional source material to give *Contemporary Advertising and Integrated Marketing Communications* the most current and relevant compendium of academic and trade citations in the field. We've referenced important recent research on topics ranging from the effects of advertising and sales promotion on brand building to relationship marketing, integrated communications, and Internet advertising. And, where appropriate, we've redesigned the building-block models that facilitate student comprehension of the often-complex processes involved in human communication, consumer behavior, marketing research, and IMC.

In this edition we introduce a new, simpler organization scheme for the chapters. Part One, which covers chapters 1 through 4, is titled "What are Advertising and Integrated Marketing Communications?" The focus of these chapters is to introduce students to the practice of advertising and to the role advertising plays in the United States and the world. In Part Two, "Planning the Campaign," covering Chapters 5–10, we present detailed information about research and the development of strategy for markets, media, and creative. Finally, Part Three, "Executing and Evaluating the Campaign," explains how the strategic decisions of a campaign are realized in the creation of copy and art and decisions about IMC platforms, including major media. This part of the book covers Chapters 11–19. The book concludes with an epilogue, "Repositioning a Brand." Original author Bill Arens' choice of Mastercard as the subject of the book's epilog is another testament to his genius. For nearly 20 years the "Priceless" campaign has epitomized the big idea. Just before this book went to print, Mastercard collaborated with its agency on a repositioning process, keeping important elements of "Priceless" and abandoning others. The update will provide a perfect capstone for students looking to see how the processes described in the text are applied in support of a global brand.

As always, we have prudently governed the length of the text material. The illustrations, graphics, sidebar information, and overall design are all aimed at keeping the text open, airy, and inviting while sharpening *clarity*—the hallmark of *Contemporary Advertising and Integrated Marketing Communications*.

Compared to the true length of other comprehensive course books, *Contemporary Advertising and Integrated Marketing Communications* is one of the most concise texts in the field.

Fresh, Contemporary, Relevant Examples

For the 15th edition, we added many new, real-world examples, selected for their currency and their relevance to students. Likewise, many of the chapter-opening stories are new, such as the advertising success stories of Activia, Lance Armstrong, the ALS Foundation "Ice Bucket Challenge," the Banner ads for Psychopaths campaign, and the Dumb Ways to Die campaign. Others document marketing or communication misfires such as the Tiger Woods fiasco. All of the full-color portfolios have been updated, expanded, or replaced with more recent examples and all of the Ad Labs and Ethical Issues have been updated and edited for currency and accuracy.

Global Orientation Integrated Throughout

In light of the increasing globalization of business, we introduce the subject of global advertising early in the book in Chapter 4, "The Scope of Advertising: From Local to Global." We've also added more examples of international advertising throughout the book. All the international data have been extensively revised and updated to reflect the increased importance of advertising in the new economic and marketing realities of Asia, especially China, Europe, and Latin America.

CASE STUDY: Epilogue: Repositioning a Brand

So that students can see how many of the principles taught in the text come together in the real world, we have included an updated Epilogue, immediately following Chapter 19, on the complete story behind the highly successful "Priceless" branding campaign for MasterCard, created by McCann Worldwide in New York. We are greatly indebted to both McCann and MasterCard for authorizing us to share the details of this interesting, student-relevant campaign and for the tremendous assistance they gave us in the creation of this outstanding Epilogue.

Local and Business-to-Business Advertising Coverage

Throughout the book, *Contemporary Advertising and Integrated Marketing Communications* addresses the needs of both small and large consumer and business-to-business advertisers with its many examples, case histories, Ad Labs, and advertisements. Moreover, this is one of the few texts to devote adequate attention to the needs of the small retail advertiser by discussing how local advertisers can integrate their marketing communications.

Highlights of This Revision

Each chapter of *Contemporary Advertising and Integrated Marketing Communications* has been thoroughly updated to reflect the most recent trends, facts, and statistics available. We have created several new chapter-opening vignettes for this edition and have rewritten significant portions of the remaining vignettes to ensure they are up-to-date and current. As with previous editions, many of these vignettes are referenced within their corresponding chapters and in chapter-concluding review questions.

Chapters 1, "Advertising Today"

A new opening vignette helps ready students for the changes that new media and globalization are presenting to brands. It introduces a spectacular viral spot produced by Activia and featuring world star Shakira. The "Greenthreads" story that begins the chapter is refreshed to incorporate social media. The chapter has been extensively reworked to focus on defining advertising before exploring the broader dimensions of IMC.

Chapters 2, "The Big Picture: The Evolution of IMC"

This chapter has long featured Coke as a way to illustrate the history of advertising. Our discussion is updated to reflect Coke's most recent IMC efforts including some much-discussed Super Bowl efforts. We've also greatly expanded our definition and discussion of branding, and the importance of brands to marketers. We've updated the "Global Interactive" portion of the history of advertising to review the most recent industry trends.

Chapters 3, "The Big Picture: Economic and Regulatory Aspects"

The opener is updated to include information about Lance Armstrong and his difficulties following his admission of cheating in his sport. The history timeline includes new milestones, including the founding of Google and Facebook. These developments are more fully explored in the text as well. The history discussion is also updated to include the recent economic recovery and its impact on IMC. Industry statistics are updated throughout. The discussion of tobacco now includes some of the controversy surrounding e-cigs.

Chapters 4, "The Scope of Advertising: From Local to Global"

The chapter updates the McDonald's vignette and more information about McDonald's global IMC campaigns are included. Our "My IMC Campaign" box helps students familiarize themselves with their semester client.

Chapters 6, "Market Segmentation and the Marketing Mix: Determinants of Advertising Strategy"

We've retained the spectacular "The man your man could smell like" campaign for Old Spice and referenced its lessons more often throughout the Chapter. Students love these ads, and those interested in IMC will love the impressive results of the campaign.

Demographics discussion in the chapter contains significantly more material on Millenials and Hispanics.

Chapters 7, "Research: Gathering Information for Advertising Planning"

For the second straight year Budweiser was recognized as having the best Super Bowl spot with its revisit of a lost puppy and some brave Clydesdales. The new opening vignette demonstrates how research guided the development and evaluation of such great creative work. New material examines pretesting in digital media, including discussions of Google's Keyword Planner and Analytics. UX testing for Websites is also described.

Chapters 9, "Planning Media Strategy: Disseminating the Message"

The chapter is substantially revamped, starting with a new opener describing the media planning of Aids.gov, one of the important Federal agencies fighting against the ravages of the disease. New material discusses planning in the digital age, and introduces programmatic advertising.

Chapters 11, "Creative Execution: Art and Copy"

A new opener illustrates the power of art and copy with the story of the popular "Dumb ways to Die" and we continue to expand on execution in digital media.

Chapters 12, "Print, Electronic, and Digital Media Production"

We've expanded coverage of digital production which, in most cases now, represents the way even small shops produce messages.

Chapters 13, "Using Print Media"

The impact of the digital revolution has been felt in legacy media, but none more than newspapers. The new chapter opener brings that message home with telling statistics. A new People Behind the Ads star, Nancy Cardone Berger, is introduced. Berger, an advertising leader at Marie Claire, was an Ad Age Publisher of the Year in 2012.

Chapters 14, "Using Electronic Media: Television and Radio"

Even in the digital age television remains a powerful advertising medium. The text suggests ways TV complements rather than competes with social media and how it can be used to target desirable market segments. The latter point is driven home with a new People behind the Ads that describes the dynamic leadership of Univision's Randy Falco.

Chapters 15, "Using Digital Interactive Media"

Our new opener suggests an innovative use of the lowly banner ad. Readers will find the latest statistics and updates on every aspect of digital media. In addition, almost every ad has been replaced with new examples. The "My IMC Campaign" box directs students toward effectively using online media for their clients.

Chapters 16, "Using Social Media"

The chapter has been substantially revised, beginning with a new opener about the famous "Ice Bucket Challenge," and its remarkable impact on the fight against ALS. The vast changes in the social media world that have occurred since our last edition are captured with new material describing Pinterest, Instagram, and Snapchat. The section on social media advertising has been broadened to include details about Facebook, Twitter, and other social media programs.

Chapters 17, "Using Out-of-Home, Exhibitive, and Supplementary Media"

The chapter has been updated to include the latest on new technologies in Out-of-Home advertising and the section on directory advertising has been eliminated.

Chapters 18, "Relationship Building: Direct Marketing, Personal Selling, and Sales Promotion"

A new People Behind the Ads features an interview with CEO and Founder of MecLabs Flint McLaughlin. McGloughlin's company gathers data from countless tests to improve both understanding and execution of the best ways to communicate value.

Chapters 19, "Relationship Building: Public Relations, Sponsorship, and Corporate Advertising"

An update shows how Netflix founder Reed Hasting's proactive response to a potential crisis has created a foundation for the enormous success of the company in reorienting to the digital age.

Uses for This Text

Contemporary Advertising and Integrated Marketing Communications was written for undergraduate students in liberal arts, journalism, mass communication, and business schools. However, because of its practical, hands-on approach, depth of coverage, and marketing management emphasis, it is also widely used in independent schools, university extension courses, and courses on advertising management. The wealth of award-winning advertisements also makes it a resource guide to the best work in the field for students in art and graphic design courses and for professionals in the field.

Many of the stories, materials, and techniques included in this text come from the authors' personal experiences in marketing communications and in higher education. Others come from the experiences of friends and colleagues in the business. We believe this book will be a valuable resource guide, not only in the study of advertising but later in the practice of it as well. In all cases, we hope readers will experience the feel and the humanness of the advertising world—whether they intend to become professionals in the business, to work with practitioners, or simply to become more sophisticated consumers.

Our goal with each new edition is to produce a finer book. We think instructors and students alike will approve of many of the changes we've made to this one. We would love to hear from you—what you like, what you don't, what we should look to add in the future. E-mail Mike Weigold at mweigold@gmail.com.

Michael F. Weigold

I would like to thank all of the wonderful people at Fallon Worldwide who agreed to be interviewed for the video that accompanies this text, especially Fred Senn, Michael Buchner, Ritchie Emslie, and Joel Rodriguez. Thanks also to Rosemary Abendroth and Brenna Brelie for their incredible assistance and patience setting up our visit. I am grateful to Verchele Wiggins and Steve Ekdahl of InterContinental Hotels Group for their insightful observations about Holiday Inn Express advertising. My thanks to the video's producer and editor, Rick Armstrong, for his patience and encouragement throughout the process.

We are grateful to all of the individuals who serve as the focus of our People behind the Ads feature. I am especially grateful to Flint McLaughlin, Alex Bogusky, Ken Cervantes, Cliff Marks, Samantha Avivi, John Posey, Jon Steel, and Tere and Joe Zubi for the extra time and energy that they spent sharing their thoughts about their advertising and marketing careers.

This edition benefited from the abilities and efforts of some great people at McGraw-Hill/Irwin. Kelly I. Pekelder served as the Product Developer of the text and always works to make the product better. She is a delight to work with. The book benefited greatly from their skills. Kim Leistner, Executive Brand Manager, was our Editor and helped further the book's evolution to a complete digital learning platform for students of advertising and IMC. I am also grateful to our Marketing Manager and our Senior Project Manager. Thanks are also due to our wonderful photo researcher.

I am appreciative to my department chair, Tom Kelleher, and to my wonderful colleagues in the Department of Advertising at the University of Florida, for their support and encouragement and for making Florida a special place to work. Go Gators!

My coauthor Chris Arens brings an enormous wealth of knowledge to this book as a working professional and enormous talent as a book author. It is a privilege to work with him.

Finally, thanks to Debbie Treise for her support, encouragement, and love.

M. F. W.

Required=Results

McGraw-Hill Connect®
Learn Without Limits

Connect is a digital teaching and learning environment that improves student performance over a variety of critical outcomes; it is easy to use; and it is proven effective.

Connect empowers students by continually adapting to deliver precisely what they need, when they need it and how they need it, so your class time is more engaging and effective.

88% of instructors who use **Connect** require it; instructor satisfaction **increases** by 38% when **Connect** is required.

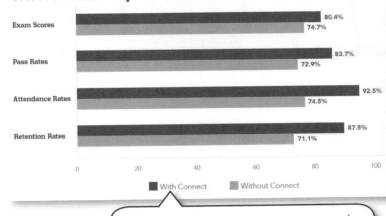

Course outcomes improve with Connect.

	With Connect	Without Connect
Exam Scores	80.4%	74.7%
Pass Rates	83.7%	72.9%
Attendance Rates	92.5%	74.5%
Retention Rates	87.5%	71.1%

Using **Connect** improves passing rates by **10.8%** and retention by **16.4%**.

Analytics

Connect Insight®

Connect Insight is Connect's new one-of-a-kind visual analytics dashboard—now available for both instructors and students—that provides at-a-glance information regarding student performance, which is immediately actionable. By presenting assignment, assessment, and topical performance results together with a time metric that is easily visible for aggregate or individual results, Connect Insight gives the user the ability to take a just-in-time approach to teaching and learning, which was never before available. Connect Insight presents data that empowers students and helps instructors improve class performance in a way that is efficient and effective.

Connect helps students achieve better grades

	A	B	C	D	F
With Connect	36%	29.5%	22%	4.3%	
Without Connect	22.2%	22.3%	25.6%	9.8%	

Based on McGraw-Hill Education Connect Effectiveness Study 2013

Students can view their results for any **Connect** course.

Mobile

Connect's new, intuitive mobile interface gives students and instructors flexible and convenient, anytime–anywhere access to all components of the Connect platform.

Adaptive

THE FIRST AND ONLY **ADAPTIVE READING EXPERIENCE** DESIGNED TO TRANSFORM THE WAY STUDENTS READ

More students earn **A's** and **B's** when they use McGraw-Hill Education **Adaptive** products.

SmartBook®

Proven to help students improve grades and study more efficiently, SmartBook contains the same content within the print book, but actively tailors that content to the needs of the individual. SmartBook's adaptive technology provides precise, personalized instruction on what the student should do next, guiding the student to master and remember key concepts, targeting gaps in knowledge and offering customized feedback, driving the student toward comprehension and retention of the subject matter. Available on smartphones and tablets, and fully accessible offline, SmartBook puts learning at the student's fingertips—anywhere, anytime.

Over **4 billion questions** have been answered, making McGraw-Hill Education products more intelligent, reliable, and precise.

STUDENTS WANT

SMARTBOOK®

95% of students reported **SmartBook** to be a more effective way of reading material

100% of students want to use the Practice Quiz feature available within **SmartBook** to help them study

100% of students reported having reliable access to off-campus wifi

90% of students say they would purchase **SmartBook** over print alone

95% reported that **SmartBook** would impact their study skills in a positive way

Mc Graw Hill Education

*Findings based on a 2015 focus group survey at Pellissippi State Community College administered by McGraw-Hill Education

Tegrity Campus: Lectures 24/7

Tegrity Campus is a service that makes class time available 24/7 by automatically capturing every lecture in a searchable format for students to review when they study and complete assignments. With a simple one-click start-and-stop process, you capture all computer screens and corresponding audio. Students can replay any part of any class with easy-to-use browser-based viewing on a PC or Mac.

Educators know that the more students can see, hear, and experience class resources, the better they learn. In fact, studies prove it. With patented Tegrity "search anything" technology, students instantly recall key class moments for replay online, or on iPods and mobile devices. Instructors can help turn all their students' study time into learning moments immediately supported by their lecture. To learn more about Tegrity, watch a 2-minute Flash demo at http://tegr itycampus.mhhe.com.

AACSB Tagging

McGraw-Hill Education is a proud corporate member of AACSB International. Understanding the importance and value of AACSB accreditation, this text recognizes the curricula guidelines detailed in the AACSB standards for business accreditation by connecting selected questions in the test bank to the six general knowledge and skill guidelines in the AACSB standards.

The statements contained in this text are provided only as a guide for the users of this textbook. The AACSB leaves content coverage and assessment within the purview of individual schools, the mission of the school, and the faculty. While Contemporary Advertising Behavior and the teaching package make no claim of any specific AACSB qualification or evaluation, we have within Organizational Behavior labeled selected questions according to the six general knowledge and skills areas.

Blackboard Partnership

McGraw-Hill and Blackboard have teamed up to simplify your life. Now you and your students can access Connect and Create right from within your Blackboard course—all with one single sign-on. The grade books are seamless, so when a student completes an integrated Connect assignment, the grade for that assignment automatically (and instantly) feeds your Blackboard grade center. Learn more at www.domorenow.com.

McGraw-Hill Campus

McGraw-Hill Campus is a new one-stop teaching and learning experience available to users of any learning management system. This institutional service allows faculty and students to enjoy single sign-on (SSO) access to all McGraw-Hill materials, including the award-winning McGraw-Hill Connect platform, from directly within the institution's website. With McGraw-Hill Campus, faculty receive instant access to teaching materials (e.g., e-textbooks, test banks, PowerPoint slides, learning objects, etc.), allowing them to browse, search, and use any instructor ancillary content in our vast library at no additional cost to instructor or students. In addition, students enjoy SSO access to a variety of free content and subscription-based products (e.g., McGraw-Hill Connect). With McGraw-Hill Campus enabled, faculty and students will never need to create another account to access McGraw-Hill products and services. Learn more at www.mhcampus.com.

Create

Create Craft your teaching resources to match the way you teach! With McGraw-Hill Create, www.mcgrawhillcreate.com, you can easily rearrange chapters, combine material from other content sources, and quickly upload content you have written, like your course syllabus or teaching notes. Find the content you need in Create by searching through thousands of leading McGraw-Hill textbooks. Arrange your book to fit your teaching style. Create even allows you to personalize your book's appearance by selecting the cover and adding your name, school, and course information. Order a Create book and you'll receive a complimentary print review copy in three to five business days or a complimentary electronic review copy (eComp) via e-mail in about one hour. Go to www.mcgrawhillcreate.com today and register. Experience how McGraw-Hill Create empowers you to teach your students your way.

McGraw-Hill Customer Eperience Group Contact Information

At McGraw-Hill, we understand that getting the most from new technology can be challenging. That's why our services don't stop after you purchase our products. You can e-mail our Product Specialists 24 hours a day to get product training online. Or you can search our knowledge bank of Frequently Asked Questions on our support website. For Customer Support, call 800-331-5094, or visit www.mhhe.com/support. One of our Technical Support Analysts will be able to assist you in a timely fashion.

contents in brief

Part One   What are Advertising and Integrated Marketing Communications?

1. Advertising and IMC Today 2
2. The Big Picture: The Evolution of Advertising and IMC 32
3. The Big Picture: Economic and Regulatory Aspects 60
4. The Scope of Advertising: From Local to Global 102

Part Two   Planning the Campaign

5. Marketing and Consumer Behavior: The Foundations of Advertising 142
6. Market Segmentation and the Marketing Mix: Determinants of Campaign Strategy 172
7. Research: Gathering Information for IMC Planning 208
8. Marketing and IMC Planning 238
9. Planning Media Strategy: Disseminating the Message 270
10. Creative Strategy and the Creative Process 304

Part Three   Executing and Evaluating the Campaign

11. Creative Execution: Art and Copy 336
12. Print, Electronic, and Digital Media Production 374
13. Using Print Media 400
14. Using Electronic Media: Television and Radio 428
15. Using Digital Interactive Media 458
16. Social Media 492
17. Using Out-of-Home, Exhibitive, and Supplementary Media 514
18. Relationship Building: Direct Marketing, Personal Selling, and Sales Promotion 544
19. Relationship Building: Public Relations, Sponsorship, and Corporate Advertising 578

Epilogue   Repositioning a Brand 610
Appendix A   Marketing Plan Outline 622
Appendix B   Advertising Plan Outline 629
Important Terms 633
Endnotes 656
Name Index 673
Company Index 679
Subject Index 689

detailed contents

The Preface, vi

Part One What are Advertising and Integrated Marketing Communications?

1. Advertising and IMC Today 2

   What Is Advertising? 7

   Relationship Marketing 9

   The Importance of Relationships 9

   Levels of Relationships 10

   The Dimensions of IMC 14

   Communication: What Makes Advertising Unique 14

   The Human Communication Process 14

   Applying the Communication Process to Advertising 15

   Marketing: Determining the Type of IMC Message to Use 18

   What Is Marketing? 18

   Advertising and the Marketing Process 19

   Identifying Target Markets and Target Audiences 19

   Implementing Marketing Strategy 21

   Why Integrated Marketing Communications? 28

   MY IMC CAMPAIGN 1
   Overview 6
   AD LAB 1–A
   Advertising as a Literary Form 17
   ETHICAL ISSUES
   Ethics in Advertising: An Overview 19
   PORTFOLIO REVIEW 22
   PEOPLE BEHIND THE ADS
   Albert Lasker and Claude Hopkins Advertising Legends 28

2. The Big Picture: The Evolution of Advertising and IMC 32

   Economics: The Functions of Advertising and IMC in Free Markets 34

   Principles of Free-Market Economics 35

   Functions and Effects of Advertising in a Free Economy 35

   The Brand 37

   The Evolution of Advertising as an Economic Tool 38

   The Global Interactive Age: Looking at the 21st Century 52

   Society and Ethics: The Effects of Advertising 54

   PORTFOLIO REVIEW
   The Modern History of Advertising 40
   ETHICAL ISSUES
   Ethical Dilemma or Ethical Lapse? 45
   MY IMC CAMPAIGN 2
   Tools for Teamwork 50
   AD LAB 2–A
   What Kills Bugs Dead? 53
   PEOPLE BEHIND THE ADS
   William Bernbach Advertising Legend 56

3. The Big Picture: Economic and Regulatory Aspects 60

The Many Controversies about Advertising 62

The Economic Impact of Advertising   64

  Effect on the Value of Products   65

  Effect on Prices   65

  Effect on Competition   66

  Effect on Consumer Demand   66

  Effect on Consumer Choice   67

  Effect on the Business Cycle   67

  The Abundance Principle: The Economic Impact of Advertising in Perspective   67

The Social Impact of Advertising 68

  Deception in Advertising   68

  The Effect of Advertising on Our Value System   69

  The Proliferation of Advertising   70

  The Use of Stereotypes in Advertising   71

  Offensiveness in Advertising   72

  The Social Impact of Advertising in Perspective   73

Social Responsibility and Advertising Ethics 73

  Advertisers' Social Responsibility   74

  Ethics of Advertising   75

How Government Regulates Advertising 78

Government Restraints on International Advertisers 78

Current Regulatory Issues Affecting U.S. Advertisers 80

  Freedom of Commercial Speech   80

  Consumer Privacy   83

Federal Regulation of Advertising in North America 84

  The U.S. Federal Trade Commission   84

  The Food and Drug Administration (FDA)   87

  The Federal Communications Commission (FCC)   89

  The Patent and Trademark Office and the Library of Congress   89

State and Local Regulation   90

  Regulation by State Governments   90

  Regulation by Local Governments   91

Nongovernment Regulation   91

  The Better Business Bureau (BBB)   91

  The National Advertising Review Council (NARC)   92

  Regulation by the Media   93

  Regulation by Consumer Groups   95

  Self-Regulation by Advertisers   95

  Self-Regulation by Ad Agencies and Associations   96

The Ethical and Legal Aspects of Advertising in Perspective 98

AD LAB 3–A
Unfair and Deceptive Practices in Advertising 70

ETHICAL ISSUES
The First Amendment and Commercial Speech 76

MY IMC CAMPAIGN 3
Your Assignment 78

AD LAB 3–B
The Importance of Good Legal Counsel in Advertising 80

AD LAB 3–C
Editorial or Advertising: It's Adversarial 94

PEOPLE BEHIND THE ADS
Edward Boyd Advertising Legend 96

4. The Scope of Advertising: From Local to Global 102

The Advertising Industry 104

The Organizations in Advertising   104

The People in Advertising   105

The Advertisers (the Clients) 105

Local Advertising: Where the Action Is   105

Regional and National Advertisers   110

Transnational Advertisers   114

The Advertising Agency 116

The Role of the Advertising Agency   116

Types of Agencies   116

What People in an Agency Do   120

How Agencies Are Structured   123

How Agencies Are Compensated   125

The In-House Agency   126

The Client–Agency Relationship   127

How Agencies Get Clients   127

Stages in the Client–Agency Relationship   128

Factors Affecting the Client–Agency Relationship   130

The Suppliers in Advertising 132

Art Studios and Web Designers   132

Printers and Related Specialists   132

Film and Video Houses   132

Research Companies   132

The Media of Advertising 134

Print Media   134

Electronic Media   135

Digital Interactive Media   135

Social Media   135

Out-of-Home Media   135

Direct Response   138

Other Media   138

Media around the World   138

MY IMC CAMPAIGN 4-A
Understanding Your Client 106
MY IMC CAMPAIGN 4-B
Creating Local Advertising 110
AD LAB 4-A
The Co-op Marriage 111
AD LAB 4-B
How Big Is the Agency Business? 117
ETHICAL ISSUES
Accounting for Account Reviews 126
MY IMC CAMPAIGN 4-C
Agency Review 129
MY IMC CAMPAIGN 4-D
Ways to Be a Better Client 131
PEOPLE BEHIND THE ADS
Nancy Hill, CEO, American Association of Advertising Agencies 136

Part Two   Planning the Campaign

5. Marketing and Consumer Behavior: The Foundations of Advertising 142

Marketing: Creating Satisfying Exchanges by Creating Utility 144

The Relationship of Marketing to IMC   144

Customer Needs and Product Utility   145

Exchanges, Perception, and Satisfaction   145

The Key Participants in the Marketing Process 148

Customers   148

Markets 149

Marketers   151

Consumer Behavior: The Key to IMC Strategy 151

The Importance of Knowing the Consumer   151

The Consumer Decision Process: An Overview   151

Psychological Processes in Consumer Behavior   152

The Consumer Perception Process   152

Learning and Persuasion: How Consumers Process Information   154

A Theory of Persuasion: The Elaboration Likelihood Model   155

The Consumer Motivation Process   158

Interpersonal Influences on Consumer Behavior 161

Family Influence   161

Societal Influence   161

Cultural and Subcultural Influence   164

Nonpersonal Influences on Consumer Behavior 165

Time   165

Place   165

Environment   165

The Purchase Decision and Postpurchase Evaluation 166

6. Market Segmentation and the Marketing Mix: Determinants of Campaign Strategy 172

Market Segmentation   174

Segmenting the Consumer Market   174

Psychographic Segmentation   180

Segmenting Business and Government Markets: Understanding Organizational Buying Behavior   184

Aggregating Market Segments   187

The Target Marketing Process 188

Target Market Selection   188

The Marketing Mix: A Strategy for Matching Products to Markets   189

IMC and the Product Element 191

Product Life Cycles   191

Product Classifications   193

Product Positioning   193

AD LAB 5–A
The Context of Choice: How a Product's Perceived Value Varies by the Products It is Compared With 146

MY IMC CAMPAIGN 5
Understanding What Consumers Look for in a Product 159

ETHICAL ISSUES
Helping an Industry Look Like America 163

AD LAB 5–B
Applying Consumer Behavior Principles to Ad Making 167

PEOPLE BEHIND THE ADS
Jon Steel Advertising Legend 168

ETHICAL ISSUES
The Youngest Target Market 182

AD LAB 6–A
Market Segmentation: A Dog of a Job 184

AD LAB 6–B
Understanding the Product Element: Starbucks Coffee 189

MY IMC CAMPAIGN 6
Segmenting the Audience 190

AD LAB 6–C
Starbucks and the Place Element 200

AD LAB 6–D
Price and Promotion 203

PEOPLE BEHIND THE ADS
Tere and Joe Zubi, Zubi Advertising 204

Product Differentiation   194

Product Branding   195

Product Packaging   196

IMC and the Price Element 197

Key Factors Influencing Price   198

IMC and the Distribution (Place) Element 199

Direct Distribution   199

Indirect Distribution   199

Vertical Marketing Systems: The Growth of Franchising   202

IMC and the Communication (Promotion) Element 202

Personal Selling   202

Advertising   202

Direct Marketing   203

Public Relations   205

Collateral Materials   205

Sales Promotion   205

The Marketing Mix in Perspective 205

7.   Research: Gathering Information for IMC Planning 208

The Need for Research in Marketing
and IMC 210

What Is Marketing Research?   210

What Is IMC Research?   211

Applying Research to
IMC Decision Making 212

Message Strategy Research   212

Developing Creative Concepts   215

Pretesting and Posttesting   215

Steps in the Research Process   217

*Step 1: Analyzing the Situation and
Defining the Problem   218*

Step 2: Conducting Informal (Exploratory) Research   218

Step 3: Establishing Research Objectives   219

Step 4: Conducting Primary Research   220

Step 5: Interpreting and Reporting the Findings   220

Understanding Qualitative and Quantitative Research Approaches 221

Message Testing before and after a Campaign 224

Pretesting Methods   224

The Challenge of Pretesting   226

Posttesting Methods   226

The Challenge of Posttesting   227

MY IMC CAMPAIGN 7–A
Research 221

MY IMC CAMPAIGN 7–B
Methods for Pretesting 225

MY IMC CAMPAIGN 7–B
Methods for Posttesting 226

ETHICAL ISSUES
Research Statistics Can Be
Friends or Foes 228

MY IMC CAMPAIGN 7–C
Developing an Effective
Questionnaire 232

PEOPLE BEHIND THE ADS
George Gallup Advertising
Legend 234

Important Issues in IMC Research 228

    Considerations in Conducting Primary Quantitative Research   229

    Collecting Primary Data in International Markets   232

8.   Marketing and IMC Planning 238

Strategic Planning: The Marketing
Plan 240

    The Mission Statement   240

    The Situation Analysis 241

    The Marketing Objectives   241

    The Marketing Strategy   243

Tactical Planning: Small Company
"Bottom-Up" Marketing 247

The IMC Approach to Marketing and
Campaign Planning 248

    *The Importance of IMC to the Study of
Advertising   251*

The IMC Plan 252

    Reviewing the Marketing Plan   253

    Setting Objectives   253

    IMC Strategy and the Creative Mix   256

    The Secret to Successful Planning   258

IMC Budgeting Approaches 259

    IMC: An Investment in Future Sales 259

    Developing an IMC Budget   264

    The Bottom Line   268

MY IMC CAMPAIGN 8-A
Developing the Situation
Analysis 242

AD LAB 8-A
The Strategies of Marketing
Warfare 245

ETHICAL ISSUES
Subliminal Persuasion 248

MY IMC CAMPAIGN 8-B
Developing IMC Objectives 255

PORTFOLIO REVIEW
Strategic Use of the
Creative Mix 260

AD LAB 8-B
The Economic Effect of
Advertising on Sales 263

MY IMC CAMPAIGN 8-C
Ways to Set IMC Budgets 264

PEOPLE BEHIND THE ADS
Samantha Avivi, Marketing
Director for Residential Business
at ADT, former Global Marketing
Director at Kimberly-Clark 266

9.   Planning Media Strategy: Disseminating the Message 270

Media Planning: Integrating Science with Creativity
in Advertising 272

    The Challenge   272

    The Role of Media in the Marketing Framework   279

    The Media-Planning Framework   279

Defining Media Objectives 281

    Audience Objectives   281

    Message-Distribution Objectives   282

    *Optimizing Reach, Frequency, and
Continuity: The Art of Media Planning   285*

Developing a Media Strategy: The
Media Mix 287

    *Elements of the Media Mix:
The Five Ms   287*

    *Factors That Influence
Media Strategy Decisions   288*

    Stating the Media Strategy   294

AD LAB 9-A
Off-the-Wall Media That Pull
Customers Off the Fence 275

ETHICAL ISSUES
The Ethical Dilemmas of Agency
Compensation 278

MY IMC CAMPAIGN 9
Developing Media Objectives
and Strategies 293

AD LAB 9-B
Media Selection: A Quicklist of
Advantages 295

PEOPLE BEHIND THE ADS
Ken Cervantes, Senior Partner
at Moroch Brothers 300

Media Tactics: Selecting and Scheduling Media Vehicles 294

   Criteria for Selecting Individual Media Vehicles   294

   Economics of Foreign Media   297

   The Synergy of Mixed Media 297

   Methods for Scheduling Media 298

   Computers in Media Selection and Scheduling   299

10.   Creative Strategy and the Creative Process 304

What Makes for Great Creative? 306

   The Impact Dimension   307

   The Relevance Dimension   308

Developing and Implementing the
Creative Strategy 308

   *Writing the Creative Brief (Copy
Platform)   309*

   Elements of Message Strategy   310

How Creativity Enhances IMC 311

   What Is Creativity?   311

   *The Role of Creativity
in IMC Campaigns   311*

   Understanding Creative Thinking   314

The Creative Process   316

   *The Explorer Role:
Gathering Information   316*

   *The Artist Role: Developing and
Implementing the Big Idea   317*

   The Judge Role: Decision Time   326

   The Warrior Role: Overcoming Setbacks and Obstacles   326

AD LAB 10–A
The Psychological Impact
of Color 313

MY IMC CAMPAIGN 10
The Creative Brief 318

ETHICAL ISSUES
Does Sex Appeal? 322

AD LAB 10–B
Applying the Creative
Pyramid 325

AD LAB 10–C
The Creative Gymnasium 327

PORTFOLIO REVIEW
The Creative Director's
Greatest Ads 328

PEOPLE BEHIND THE ADS
Tim Piper, Writer/Director for PiRo,
former Associate Creative Director,
Ogilvy & Mather, Toronto 332

Part Three   Executing and Evaluating the Campaign

11.   Creative Execution: Art and Copy 336

Designing Print Layouts 339

   The Use of Layouts   339

   *Design and Production: The Creative and
Approval Process   339*

   *Creating Effective Layouts: Tools and
Formats   343*

   The Use of Visuals in Print   346

Creating Great Copy in Print 351

   Headlines   351

   Headlines in Search ads   354

   Subheads   354

   Body Copy   354

   Slogans   357

   Seals, Logos, and Signatures   357

MY IMC CAMPAIGN 11–A
Product Facts for
Creatives 340

AD LAB 11–A
The Role of the Artist 342

MY IMC CAMPAIGN 11–B
Creating Great Headlines
and Copy 344

MY IMC CAMPAIGN 11–C
Design Principles 345

PORTFOLIO REVIEW
The Art Director's Guide to
Layout Styles 348

ETHICAL ISSUES
Imitation, Plagiarism, or
Flattery? 353

MY IMC CAMPAIGN 11–D
Writing Effective Copy 355

Writing for Radio and TV 357

Writing Radio Copy 358

Writing Television Copy 359

Developing Great Spots in Radio
and TV 360

*Developing the Artistic Concept for
Commercials 360*

*Formats for Radio and TV
Commercials 361*

*Basic Mechanics of Storyboard
Development 365*

Writing Effectively for Websites and Social Media 366

Creating Ads for International Markets 367

Translating Copy 367

Art Direction for International Markets 371

Legal Restraints on International Marketers 371

12. Print, Electronic, and Digital Media
Production 374

Managing the Production Process 376

Planning and Organizing 376

Directing and Controlling 376

Managing Production Costs 377

The Print Production Process 379

*The Preproduction Phase: Planning the
Project 379*

*The Production Phase: Creating the
Artwork 380*

The Prepress Phase: Stripping, Negs, and Plates 384

*The Duplication and Distribution Phase: Printing,
Binding, and Shipping 385*

Quality Control in Print Production 385

Production Phase Quality Issues 386

Prepress Quality Issues 386

The Radio Commercial Production Process 387

Preproduction 387

Production: Cutting the Spot 388

Postproduction: Finishing the Spot 389

The Television Commercial
Production Process 389

The Role of the Commercial Producer 389

The Preproduction Phase 390

Production: The Shoot 391

Postproduction 393

MY IMC CAMPAIGN 11–E
Creating Effective Radio
Commercials 359

MY IMC CAMPAIGN 11–F
Creating Effective TV
Commercials 360

AD LAB 11– B
Creative Ways to Sell
on Radio 362

PEOPLE BEHIND THE ADS
Alex Bogusky, Former Cochair,
Crispin Porter + Bogusky 368

AD LAB 12–A
The Characteristics of Type 382

MY IMC CAMPAIGN 12
Producing Ads 386

AD LAB 12–B
The Film versus Digital Video
Decision 392

PEOPLE BEHIND THE ADS
John Posey Actor, Director,
Producer and Scriptwriter 394

Producing Advertising for Social Media and the Web 393

   The People Who Produce Digital Media 395

   Producing a WebSite 395

13. Using Print Media 400

The Role of the Print Media Buyer 402

Using Magazines in the Creative
Mix 402

   *The Pros and Cons of Magazine
   Advertising 402*

   *Special Possibilities
   with Magazines 402*

   How Magazines Are Categorized 405

   Geography 409

Buying Magazine Space 410

   Understanding Magazine Circulation 410

   Reading Rate Cards 412

   Software for Buying Print Media 413

Using Newspapers in the
Creative Mix 413

   Who Uses Newspapers? 414

   *The Pros and Cons of Newspaper
   Advertising 414*

   How Newspapers Are Categorized 414

   Types of Newspaper Advertising 416

How Advertisers Buy Newspaper Space 417

   Understanding Readership and Circulation 418

   Co-ops and Networks 420

   Insertion Orders and Tearsheets 421

Print: A Worldwide Medium 422

Print Media and New Technologies 424

14. Using Electronic Media: Television and Radio 428

The Medium of Television 430

   Broadcast TV 430

   Cable TV 431

   DTV 431

   TV Audience Trends 432

   The Use of Television in IMC 435

   Types of TV Advertising 435

   Defining Television Markets 441

   Dayparts 441

   Audience Measures 443

   Gross Rating Points 444

MY IMC CAMPAIGN 13–A
The Pros and Cons of Magazine
Advertising 403

AD LAB 13–A
Magazines and the Creative
Mix 404

AD LAB 13–B
Innovations in Magazine
Advertising 405

PORTFOLIO REVIEW
Outstanding Magazine Ads 406

MY IMC CAMPAIGN 13–B
The Pros and Cons of
Newspaper Advertising 416

AD LAB 13–C
Newspapers and the Creative
Mix 417

ETHICAL ISSUES
What's at Stake with
Sweepstakes? 421

MY IMC CAMPAIGN 13–C
Planning and Evaluating Print
Media 423

PEOPLE BEHIND THE ADS
Nancy Cardone Berger, VP/
Publisher and CRO at Marie
Claire 425

MY IMC CAMPAIGN 14–A
Planning and Buying TV and
Radio 432

MY IMC CAMPAIGN 14–B
The Pros and Cons of
Broadcast TV Advertising 433

MY IMC CAMPAIGN 14–C
The Pros and Cons of Cable TV
Advertising 436

ETHICAL ISSUES
Advertising to Children:
Child's Play? 439

AD LAB 14–A
Where Do Those Infamous TV
Ratings Come From? 442

Buying Television Time 444

Requesting Avails   444

Selecting Programs for Buys   445

Negotiating Prices and Contracts   446

Electronic Media Buying Software   446

Other Forms of Television 446

The Medium of Radio 447

Who Uses Radio?   447

The Use of Radio in IMC   447

Radio Programming and Audiences   448

Buying Radio Time 450

Types of Radio Advertising   450

Radio Terminology   451

The Seven Steps in Preparing a Radio Schedule   453

15. Using Digital Interactive Media 458

Digital Interactive Media 460

The Internet as a Medium 461

A Brief History of the Internet and the World Wide Web   464

The Internet Audience   464

Measuring the Internet Audience 466

How People Access the Internet   466

How People Use the Internet   466

Media Planning Tools   466

The Promise of Enhanced Tracking   467

Seeking Standardization   469

Buying Time and Space on the Internet 470

Pricing Methods   470

The Cost of Targeting   471

Stretching Out the Dollars   471

Types of Internet Advertising   471

Search Engine Marketing   473

Problems with the Internet as an Advertising Medium   485

Using the Internet in IMC   485

The Global Impact of the Internet 486

Other Interactive Media 486

Interactive TV   487

Mobile Advertising   488

16. Social Media 492

Introducing Social Media 494

Our Social Media Peronas   495

Social Is More Than Media   496

AD LAB 14–B
Getting "You're Out" on TV 445
MY IMC CAMPAIGN 14–D
The Pros and Cons of Radio Advertising 450
AD LAB 14–C
The Reports That Make or Break Radio Stations 451
PEOPLE BEHIND THE ADS
Randy Falco, CEO, Univision 454

AD LAB 15–A
Internet Ratings: A Call for Standards 468
ETHICAL ISSUES
Who's watching you? 472
PORTFOLIO REVIEW
Advertising on the Internet 476
MY IMC CAMPAIGN 15–A
Using Interactive Media 485
PEOPLE BEHIND THE ADS
Brian Green Senior Director, Property and Advertiser Solutions, Yahoo 489

ETHICAL ISSUES
It's Not Always Nice to Share 500
MY IMC CAMPAIGN
Using Social Media 508
PEOPLE BEHIND THE ADS
Mark Zuckerberg Founder and CEO, Facebook 511

The Rise of Social Media 496

Adoption of Social Media   496

Social Trends   498

Who Uses Social Media   499

Types of Social Media   499

Managing Social Media 502

Owned Media and Fragmentation   503

Building Social Authority 503

Transparency and Authenticity   504

Two-Way Brand Communication   504

Customer Service in Social Media   505

Social Media by the Numbers   506

Application of Social Media   507

Common Uses of Social Media   507

17. Using Out-of-Home, Exhibitive, and Supplementary Media 514

Out-of-Home Media 516

Out-of-Home (OOH) Advertising 518

*Standardization of the Outdoor
Advertising Business   518*

Types of Outdoor Advertising   519

Buying OOH Advertising   520

Regulation of Outdoor Advertising   528

Transit Advertising   528

Types of Transit Advertising   528

Buying Transit Advertising   530

Other Out-of-Home Media 531

Mobile Billboards   531

Electronic Signs and Display Panels   531

Parking Meters and Public Phones   531

Exhibitive Media   531

Product Packaging   532

Trade-Show Booths and Exhibits   535

Supplementary Media   537

Specialty Advertising   537

Emerging Media   537

**18. Relationship Building: Direct
Marketing, Personal Selling,
and Sales Promotion 544**

Understanding Direct Marketing 546

The Role of Direct Marketing in IMC   548

Types of Direct Marketing Activities   553

AD LAB 17–A
How to Use Color and Type in
Out of Home Advertising
PORTFOLIO REVIEW
Out-of-Home Advertising 522
ETHICAL ISSUES
Does Spillover Need Mopping
Up? 529
MY IMC CAMPAIGN 17–A
Using Out-of-Home, Exhibitive,
and Supplementary Media 532
PEOPLE BEHIND THE ADS
Cliff Marks, CineMedia 538

ETHICAL ISSUES
Political Advertising: Positively
Negative 552
MY IMC CAMPAIGN18–A
Developing a Plans Book 555
AD LAB 18–A
Developing Effective Direct-Mail
Packages 558
AD LAB 18–B
Applying Push–Pull Strategies to
Sales Promotion 569
PEOPLE BEHIND THE ADS
Flint McGlaughlin Founder and
CEO, MecLabs 572

Understanding Personal Selling 560

  Types of Personal Selling   561

  Advantages of Personal Selling 561

  Drawbacks of Personal Selling   561

  The Role of Personal Selling in IMC   562

Understanding Sales Promotion 564

  The Role of Sales Promotion in IMC   565

  Sales Promotion Strategies and Tactics   565

19. Relationship Building: Public Relations, Sponsorship, and Corporate Advertising 578

Public Relations: IMC and More 580

  The Difference between Advertising and Public Relations   581

  Advertising and PR in the Eyes of Practitioners   582

The Public Relations Job 584

  PR Planning and Research   584

  Reputation Management   585

  Other Public Relations Activities   587

  Public Relations Tools   589

Sponsorships and Events 592

  The Growth of Sponsorship   592

  Benefits of Sponsorship   593

  Drawbacks of Sponsorship   594

  Types of Sponsorship   594

  Methods of Sponsorship   598

  Measuring Sponsorship Results   598

Corporate Advertising 599

  Public Relations Advertising   599

  Corporate/Institutional Advertising   599

  Corporate Identity Advertising   608

  Recruitment Advertising   608

ETHICAL ISSUES
Public Relations—Meet Social Media and the Web 582

AD LAB 19–A
"Green" Advertising 587

MY IMC CAMPAIGN 19–A
Corporate Blogging 589

MY IMC CAMPAIGN 19–B
The Client Presentation 591

PEOPLE BEHIND THE ADS
Bill Imada Chair and Chief Connectivity Officer, the IW Group 600

PORTFOLIO REVIEW
Corporate Advertising 602

AD LAB 19–B
David Ogilvy on Corporate Advertising 607

Epilogue   Repositioning a Brand 610

Appendix A   Marketing Plan Outline 622

Appendix B   Advertising Plan Outline 629

  Important Terms 633

  Endnotes 656

  Name Index 673

  Company Index 679

  Subject Index 689

CONTEMPORARY
advertising
and Integrated Marketing Communications

CHAPTER

Advertising and IMC Today

Learning Objectives

This chapter introduces you to some important themes of the text, including integrated marketing communications (IMC), and the importance of IMC to relationship marketing. The chapter also introduces one of the most important components of IMC, advertising, and distinguishes it from other forms of marketing communications.

 After studying this chapter, you will be able to:

LO1-1   Define integrated marketing communications.

LO1-2   Clarify what advertising is and how it differs from other kinds of marketing communications.

LO1-3   Explain the importance of relationship marketing.

LO1-4   Depict the human communication process and demonstrate its usefulness in understanding how advertising communicates.

LO1–5   Define marketing and identify the four elements of marketing strategy.

LO1-6   Illustrate IMC's role in marketing strategy.

LO1-7   Identify important categories under promotion: the communication element of strategy.

© Mediablitzimages/Alamy

Search Twitter 🔍 Have an account? Log

Ad Age Ad Age ✓
@adage

+ Follow

Shakira vanquishes Darth Vader: Pop star's Activia-sponsored music video becomes most-shared ad of all time bit.ly/1ogx9UW

Ad Age

Shakira's Activia-Sponsored Music Video Vanquishes 'The Force' as...

Music video for Shakira sponsored by Activia tops Volkswagens "The Force" as most shared of all time.

View on web

RETWEETS	FAVORITES
22	10

6:04 AM - 3 Aug 2014

↩ ♻ ★ •••

Source: Advertising Age

What kind of commercial barely mentions the brand, focuses most of its attention on a pop star, and only occasionally runs on TV? ■ One answer is yogurt brand Activia's commercial featuring Shakira. And on first blush, it doesn't seem much like an ad at all (watch it for yourself here: https://www.youtube.com/watch?v=7-7knsP2n5w). With a driving beat, a distinct multicultural ambiance, and one of the most popular musical stars today, it seems more like a music video. Watching one sees soccer, dancing, eagles, elephants, babies, and Shakira. Yogurt? Not so much. What is going on here? ■ If your idea of an advertisement is a 30-second TV spot encouraging you to use a new laundry detergent or to test* drive a new car, you may find Activia's approach puzzling. And you would not be alone. One prominent blog focused on Latino lifestyles boldly stated that "Shakira's Activia ad is confusing everyone."[1] ■ The Shakira ad certainly contrasts with Activia's previous campaign, which featured American actress Jamie Lee Curtis discussing in frank terms the benefits of eating the yogurt (some research suggests that Activia aids digestion). Given that Activia achieved respectable global sales in 2013 of nearly $3.5 billion, why change what isn't broken? ■ The answer is that the Shakira Activia spot is a response to a number of distinct, important trends that are rocking the modern world of advertising. These include a global rather than national perspective for large consumer firms, surging interest in millennials as a target audience (individuals between 18 and 30 years of age),[2] the fragmentation of media audiences,[3] and the power of social media.[4] ■ A global perspective and the focus on young consumers can explain the decision to stop the ads featuring Jamie Lee Curtis and replace them with the Shakira spot. Shakira is a global pop icon adored by young audiences. She is especially popular in the fast growing markets of Latin and South America, where Activia sees big opportunities for growth. Curtis, known largely to American audiences for her roles in popular films from the 1980s and 1990s, has nowhere near the global influence of the singer. ■ Why the musical, soft-sell format? Why not just let Shakira eat the yogurt and smile? ■ Start with the suspicion young people have for "advertising." Millennials expect to watch content they like, not sit through advertising messages that they don't. ■ In addition, Activia's parent company, Dannon, didn't just want consumers to watch the ad. They wanted them to share it. Who is more credible to you than your friends? When a good friend sends you a video link and writes "You've got to watch this!" you probably do. ■ Activia's approach is really an interesting blend of "old" advertising and "new." The "old" was Dannon's decision to run the spot during the immensely popular World Cup finals in 2014. But that was just the tease, intended to get consumers online to go and share the ad with friends. That's the "new" element of the campaign. ■ Did it work? As with every advertising effort, all the preparation and strategic planning in the world does not guarantee success. Would consumers like the ad?

Would fans share the spot on their social media accounts? And would sales of Activia, which were flat the previous year, climb again? Or would the shift in approach from the old spots be so dramatic that users would be alienated? And would the video prove so subtle that people would miss the brand message entirely? ■ Viewers loved the ad. One survey suggested audiences believed it was the best commercial run during the World Cup. And fans did go online to watch the ad and they did, as hoped, share it in social media. In fact the spot became the single most shared advertisement in history,[5] with nearly five and a half million shares across Facebook, Twitter, and other social platforms. As for sales, Dannon reported better than expected earnings in 2015 on growing sales.[6] ■ As this story suggests, advertising is in transition. But the new approach to advertising hasn't replaced the old. Instead, campaigns borrow elements of both old and new. Hoping an expensive commercial run during a popular sporting event will be seen and liked is a strategy that dates to the early days of television. Hoping audiences will love the ad enough to seek it out and share it with friends online, that's pretty new. Mastering both approaches is helping Activia find the sweet spot with young audiences.

Look around. If your TV or radio is on, if you've sorted through your mail, or if you've checked in on Instagram, it is likely that you've just seen a brand. In fact, you've probably been exposed to many brand messages today.

Brand messages seem to be everywhere because marketers spend lots of money trying to reach you. Every year, expenditures on advertising alone amount to hundreds of dollars for every man, woman, and child living in the United States. Perhaps you think that the money spent trying to reach you is largely wasted. When was the last time, after all, that you bought something just because it was advertised? Answering that question is difficult because many things influence your buying decisions.

One way to demonstrate how brand messages, or more broadly, **marketing communications,** work, and at the same time introduce some important concepts, is to tell a story about an ordinary person, perhaps someone similar to yourself. The story is about a woman who sees an ad and ultimately buys a product. As you read, think about all the factors that influence her decision. In addition, try to identify which influences conform to your definition of "advertising," and which do not.

Sharon, a college student, decides it is finally time to buy some clothes. Normally she would head to the local mall, but a Facebook ad for a new clothing store catches her eye. The ad features photos of women Sharon's age wearing attractive jackets, hats, sweaters, and cotton jeans. Connecting the pictures and running through the company's logo are two thin, bright green lines. The store is called Green Threads.

The ad says that Green Threads clothing is made exclusively from natural materials and that all of their products are "workshop free." Sharon isn't quite sure what that means, but it calls to mind an article she once read describing terrible conditions at the factory of one of her favorite mall brands. After reading that article, she had decided never to buy from that brand again.

Grabbing her bike Sharon sets off for the store. When she arrives she notices a sturdy bike rack near the attractive, naturally lit entrance. How thoughtful, she thinks (it bothers her that so many retailers cater only to drivers). Inside she is pleased to find clothing in the bright colors and the natural fabrics that she loves. Sharon selects a pair of jeans and a beautiful sweater and considers whether she should buy them.

The clothes are not exorbitantly expensive, but they list for at least 20 percent over their mall equivalents. Sharon asks a clerk whether the store ever runs sales. He smiles and shakes his head no. To reduce excess inventory, he explains, Green Threads donates clothes to local charities. Sensing Sharon's concern about the prices, he hands her a pamphlet titled "Our Philosophy" and encourages her to learn more about the company's business practices on the Web. He admits that Green Threads clothes are not the cheapest available, but points out that all the store's products are made from natural fibers and stitched in the United States. The cotton used in the clothes is grown organically and all wool comes from farms that treat livestock humanely.

Sharon is not sure what to do. She is very impressed with Green Threads' corporate philosophy and she loves the clothes. But she also hates spending extra money. After going back and forth she finally decides to buy the jeans and the sweater.

Over the next few months Sharon concludes that she made the right choice. She loves the compliments that she gets when she wears them. She believes that wearing Green Threads clothes helps let other people see that she supports socially responsible companies. In fact, Sharon thinks that she is being socially responsible by spending a bit more to get her clothes at Green Threads. Eventually she posts a positive Google review of Green Threads. She's happy to see other five-star reviews there as well.

Sharon also begins receiving e-mails from Green Threads announcing new arrivals at the store. She also notices that Green Threads display ads begin showing up in her Facebook newsfeed. She much prefers the social media posts to a paper catalog, thinking it is one less thing for her to recycle. Each feed has a link to the company's Website where she can find everything sold at Green Threads and learn more about the company's business practices.

Sharon's story helps introduce the modern practice of marketing communications. In this case, the Facebook ad helped make Sharon *aware* of Green Threads and allowed her to *comprehend* what the store offered and how it differed from its competition. The ad sparked a series of events that ultimately resulted in a purchase. But the ad wasn't the sole, or even the most important, reason that Sharon became a customer. Much of what she learned about Green Threads came from other sources—for example, her own assessment of the look and feel of the store, the clothing, the helpful sales clerk, and the corporate brochure. Even the thoughtfully placed bike rack helped Sharon form an impression of the company. The fact that all of the marketing communications reinforced an image of Green Threads as a socially aware, socially responsible retailer was no accident. Smart organizations ensure that all company—or brand-related messages reinforce a strategically designed idea. The point of the Sharon's story is to introduce you to a central idea of this book: Companies do not create ads or other promotional messages in isolation. Instead, they strive to reinforce core ideas about who they are and what their products are like. Smart companies they spend a lot of time providing evidence to consumers that this core idea is credible. Such evidence can come in advertising messages, but from a broader perspective, it comes from everything a consumer learns about the company. When a company deliberately coordinates and integrates messages from a variety of sources about its products or brands, it is practicing **integrated marketing communications**, or **IMC.**

How much did all of this information matter in Sharon's purchase decision? Recall that she was conflicted about buying clothes at Green Threads because they were pricey. Cost was a serious consideration for Sharon because she is on a limited budget. But the information Sharon learned that day helped create a *conviction* that Green Threads was a company with both great clothes and a socially responsible way of doing business. That unique combination of attributes helped Sharon decide that, even at a higher price, Green Threads clothes were a better value than clothes at the mall. No other retailer offered her both important qualities.

My IMC Campaign 1

Overview

Welcome to My IMC Campaign, an important feature of this text. My IMC Campaign should be useful in any of the following situations:

■ Your instructor has asked students in your class to work on part or all of an ad campaign, either individually or in groups.

■ You are doing an internship and want practical advice on how to help your company advertise.

■ You want to try to apply the concepts and ideas that you are reading about in this book in the real world.

Professors approach advertising projects differently. Some assign students to create ads for a real product, although you never actually contact the company that makes the product. Some assign a fictional brand in a real product category. Perhaps your professor has offered your talents to a client, such as a small local business or firm. You may even have to find a client yourself by making inquiries in your community. Finally, your professor may ask you to help a charity or non-profit with its advertising. No matter which of these things is true, the good news is that developing an advertising campaign follows a similar path. And the My IMC Campaign feature is designed to help you do it well.

Let's begin with a definition. An IMC campaign involves the creation and placement of a series of strategic communications that are unified by an underlying theme or core message. The communications are intended to help promote a brand, product, service, organization, or idea. The messages are typically designed to resonate with a group called a target audience. Campaigns usually have specific objectives, such as increasing product awareness or persuading people to try a service or donate money to a cause. And to ensure that the target audience receives them, messages appear in various media, such as newspapers, radio commercials, or Web pages. You may not do all of these activities, especially placing ads in real media. But you will get a chance to do some serious thinking, planning, and brainstorming.

We can make our definition of a campaign a bit more concrete by thinking back to the opening vignette of this chapter.

Hopefully you've inferred from all of this that brand messages are very strategic. Lots of planning takes place long before messages are created. For that reason, while you may be itching to create some advertisements for your client, you have lots of work to do before you begin brainstorming ideas. ?????? was successful not only because they created great ads, but because they understood their candidate, his

opponents, the audiences that were important to reach, the media that could be used to reach them, and the objectives that were crucial to success. On a much smaller scale and with far fewer resources, you face similar challenges. My IMC Campaign is designed to help you meet that challenge.

In subsequent chapters, we'll help you learn to develop a deeper understanding of your brand or client, develop a plan for marketing and advertising activities, conduct research so that you can better understand your target audience, formulate media strategy, and design effective advertisements. Finally, we'll teach you how to implement evaluation programs to test whether your ads have been successful. By the end of the semester, you won't be a top advertising professional, but you'll have some real experience in the art and science of developing an ad campaign.

The My IMC Campaign topics are listed below. You may find it useful or necessary to jump around as you develop your own campaign.

1. Overview
2. Tools for Teamwork
3. Your Assignment
4. Understanding Your Client
5. Understanding How Consumers Respond to Advertising
6. Segmenting the Audience
7. Research
8. The Situation Analysis; the SWOT Analysis; Developing Advertising Objectives
9. Media Strategy
10. The Creative Brief
11. Product Facts for Creatives; Creating Great Headlines, Copy, and Visuals; Design Principles
12. Producing Ads
13. Evaluating Print Media
14. Evaluating Electronic Media
15. Evaluating Digital and Other Media
16. Evaluating Social Media
17. Proposing Evaluation Programs
18. Creating a Plan Book
19. Creating Your Client Presentation

The uniqueness of the offerings at Green Threads led Sharon to form a *desire* to buy from the store. And, after thinking carefully about her clothes budget, she took *action* and made a purchase.

Why do companies practice IMC? Because IMC helps companies adopt a consumer-centric, rather than marketer-centric, perspective in creating brand messages. And in today's marketing environment, nothing is more important than understanding and effectively communicating with consumers. IMC reminds companies that the images people have about

In relationship marketing and IMC, companies don't just advertise to customers, they listen too.
Source: Southwest Airlines Co.

Some airlines run ads that talk to business travelers.
We're running an ad that says

WE LISTEN
to them.

1. **INTRODUCING A WHOLE NEW, BETTER BOARDING PROCESS**
It's a calmer, more relaxed way to board. There is no need to line up early because your boarding pass number holds your place in line. So you are free to work, relax, or do whatever.

2. **INTRODUCING SOUTHWEST AIRLINES® BUSINESS SELECT**
You deserve Southwest Airlines Business Select. For just a little extra, you can be part of the select group that's guaranteed to be one of the first to board and get a free drink and extra Rapid Rewards® credit. Plus, your fare is fully refundable.

3. **INTRODUCING MORE NONSTOP FLIGHTS FOR YOUR NONSTOP BUSINESS**
Fly long without the stops. Southwest offers over 3,400 daily nonstop flights, which lets you fly nonstop to more places you do business.

SOUTHWEST.COM®

brands don't come just from advertising, but from many different sources. And perhaps most importantly, IMC helps companies to initiate, develop, and nurture relationships with important groups, especially customers.

What Is Advertising?

Now that you know what IMC is, let's focus on one important element in many IMC campaigns: advertising. Many of the most vivid and memorable IMC messages you will encounter are advertisements. But not all. Think of the hundreds of commercial messages you encounter in an average day. They may appear in many forms—commercials, Websites, and text messages—or in the form of product placements in TV shows, coupons, sales letters, event sponsorships, telemarketing calls, or e-mails. These are just a few of the many communication tools that companies and organizations use to initiate and maintain contact with their customers, clients, and prospects. You may refer to them all as "advertising." But, in fact, the correct term for these tools is **marketing communications.** And advertising is just one type of marketing communications.

So, then, what is advertising?

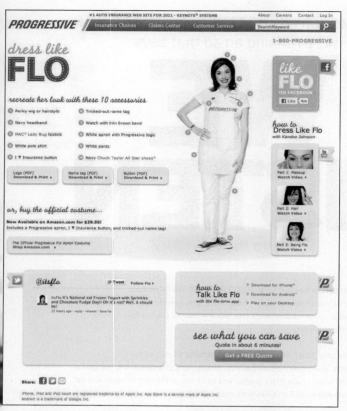

Companies use ads to differentiate their brands from those of competitors. But guided by an IMC philosophy, ads are just one part of an overall message strategy. Progressive finds a humorous way to remind consumers of its iconic spokesperson "Flo" by encouraging people to dress like her on Halloween. When people do so, it turns parties into yet another way of encountering and developing attitudes about the Progressive brand.
Source: Progressive Casualty Insurance Company

At the beginning of the 20th century, Albert Lasker, who today is generally regarded as the father of modern advertising (see People behind the Ads on page 28), defined advertising as "salesmanship in print, driven by a reason why."[7] But that was long before the advent of radio, television, or the Web. The nature and scope of the business world, and advertising, were quite limited. A century later, our planet is a far different place. The nature and needs of business have changed, and so have the concept and practice of advertising.

Definitions of advertising sometimes reflect the functions that it serves a person in their professional life. Journalists, for example, might define it as a communication, public relations, or persuasion process; businesspeople see it as a marketing process; economists and sociologists tend to focus on its economic, societal, or ethical significance. And some consumers might define it simply as a nuisance. Interestingly, scholars and professionals also disagree somewhat about how to define advertising, as scholars Jeff Richards and Catharine Curran discovered in a research study intended to build consensus for a definition. Their multi-wave panel study suggested the following definition comes closest to a consensus of experts:

> **Advertising** is a paid, mediated form of communication from an identifiable source, designed to persuade the receiver to take some action, now or in the future.[8]

Let's take a closer look at this definition. Advertising is, first of all, a type of *communication,* which is commonly defined as the process through which meaning or information is exchanged between individuals using some system of symbols, signs, or behavior. It is actually a very *structured* form of applied communication, employing both verbal and nonverbal elements that are *composed* to fill specific space and time formats determined by the sponsor.

Second, advertising is directed to message receivers, or groups of people, usually referred to as audiences, rather than to individuals. These people could be **consumers,** who buy products like cars, deodorant, or food for their personal use. Or they might be businesspeople, who buy fleets of cars for commercial or government use. The messages are delivered via media, such as television or the Internet, rather than through direct, personal contact between a seller and a buyer. Advertising is, therefore, a kind of nonpersonal, or mass, communication.

Most advertising is *paid for* by sponsors. GM, Walmart, the Obama campaign, and your local fitness salon pay the newspaper or the radio or TV station to carry the ads you read, see, and hear. But some sponsors don't have to pay for their ads. The American Red Cross, United Way, and American Cancer Society are among the many organizations whose **public service messages** are carried at no charge because of their nonprofit status.

Of course, most advertising is intended to be *persuasive*—to make audiences more favorably disposed toward a product, service, or idea. Some ads, such as legal announcements, are intended merely to inform, not to persuade. But they are still ads because they satisfy all the other requirements of the definition.

In addition to promoting tangible **goods** such as oranges, oatmeal, and olive oil, advertising helps publicize the intangible **services** of bankers, beauticians, bike repair shops, and bill collectors. Advertising is also used to advocate a wide variety of **ideas,** whether economic, political, religious, or social. In this book, the term **product** encompasses goods, services, and ideas.

An ad *identifies* its sponsor. This seems obvious. Typically the sponsor wants to be identified, or why pay to advertise? One of the basic differences between advertising and *public*

Transactional Marketing	Relationship Marketing
Product focus	Partner and customer focus
Customer acquisition	Customer retention and growth
Department-level work	Cross-functional teams
Talking	Listening and learning

Exhibit 1-1

A comparison of Transactional and Relationship marketing. Adapted from Kotler[9]

relations is that many PR activities (for example, publicity) aren't openly sponsored. We'll discuss the differences between advertising and other forms of marketing communications later in this chapter.

Finally, advertising reaches us through a channel of communication referred to as a **medium.** An advertising medium is any nonpersonal means used to present an ad to a large audience. Thus, we have radio advertising, television advertising, newspaper ads, Google ads, and so on. When you tell somebody how much you like a product, that's sometimes called *word-of-mouth (WOM)* advertising. Although WOM is a communication medium, it has not generally been considered an advertising medium. However, the popularity of social media, such as Facebook and Twitter, is forcing advertisers to reconsider this belief. Historically, advertisers have used the traditional **mass media** (the plural of *medium*) to deliver their messages. But today technology enables advertising to reach us efficiently through a variety of *addressable media* (for example, direct mail) and *digital media* (like the Web). Advertisers also use an increasing variety of *nontraditional media* such as shopping carts, blimps, and DVDs to find their audience. A thorough understanding of the strengths, weaknesses, and capabilities of different media is important and we devote several chapters to the subject.

Now that you better understand the types of messages do and do not qualify as advertising, let's focus a bit more deeply on the concept as it is practiced today. You will first learn that modern advertising, at least as used by the world's biggest brands, focuses less on making a single sale, and more on helping companies develop relationships with their customers and other stakeholders. We also show that for advertising to work best, it must be thoroughly integrated into the marketing communications efforts of a business.

Looking ahead to the other chapters in Part One, we will trace the evolution of IMC from its earliest practice, delve more deeply into the role of marketing messages in a free economy, review the most important regulatory and legal considerations practitioners must keep in mind, and consider the scope of advertising from local to global. Finally, we will consider the audiences for advertising messages.

Relationship Marketing

LO 1-3

As companies have become less advertising-centric and more IMC-centric, they've shifted their focus from an exclusive concern with sales to one that embraces building relationships with consumers. This shift has important implications for brand messages.

A market-driven firm's overriding purpose is to profitably create happy, loyal customers. Customers, not products, are the lifeblood of the business. This realization has created a trend away from simple *transactional marketing* to **relationship marketing**—creating, maintaining, and enhancing long-term relationships with customers and other stakeholders that result in exchanges of information and other things of mutual value.[10] As can be seen in Exhibit 1-1, the shift from a transactional to a relationship focus has broad implications for the goals of marketing and the focus of advertising and IMC. None of these changes is more significant than the elevation of listening as a corporate value. Southwest's ad on this page is a great example of this principle in action.

Consumers can choose from a wide variety of products and services. As a result, the customer relationship—in which the sale is only the beginning—is the key strategic resource of the successful 21st-century business. Companies that commit to relationship marketing are generally trying to accomplish three things: (1) identify, satisfy, retain, and maximize the value of profitable customers; (2) manage the contacts between the customer and the company to ensure their effectiveness; and (3) develop a full view of the customer by acquiring useful data.

The Importance of Relationships

To succeed, companies must focus on managing loyalty among carefully chosen customers and **stakeholders** (employees, centers of influence, stockholders, the financial community, and the press).[11] This is important for a number of reasons:

1. *The cost of lost customers.* Great marketing will not win back a customer lost from shoddy products or poor service. The real profit lost is the **lifetime customer value (LTCV)**

Most business is conducted with repeat customers. This places a premium on customer retention. Retention can be achieved by offering special benefits to loyal customers, effectively rewarding and thanking them for business, and providing an incentive for a continued relationship in the future. Retail food giant Kroger successfully retains their customers with their community rewards program. The more a customer spends, the more Kroger gives back to a customer's preferred nonprofit organization.

Source: The Kroger Co.

to a firm. For example, the average customer of one major transportation firm represented a lifetime value of $40,000. The company had 64,000 accounts and lost 5 percent of them due to poor service. That amounted to loss of $128 million in revenue and $12 million in profits![12] Moreover, negative word of mouth can have a terrible snowballing effect. And if one lost customer influences only one other customer not to patronize the business, the LTCV loss doubles. With the pervasiveness of social media, this is more important today than ever before.

2. *The cost of acquiring new customers.* Defensive marketing, which attempts to retain loyal customers, typically costs less than offensive marketing, which seeks new customers, because it isn't easy to lure satisfied customers away from competitors.[13] In fact, it costs five to eight times as much in marketing, advertising, and promotion to acquire a new customer as it does to keep an existing one.

3. *The value of loyal customers.* Repeat customers keep a company profitable even in tough economic times.[14] Retention is enormously profitable because acquiring new customer is almost five times as expensive as retaining old ones. In addition, long-term customers are less sensitive to the marketing efforts of other companies.[15] The bottom line is a company that makes a small increase in customer retention may be rewarded with big profits in return.[16]

Thus, a company's first market should always be its current customers. Successful marketers are shifting their resources to *postsale* activities, making customer retention their first line of defense. They have discovered the primary benefit of focusing on relationships: increasing retention and optimizing lifetime customer value.[17]

Levels of Relationships

Kotler and Keller distinguish five levels of relationships that can develop between a company and its stakeholders, depending on their mutual needs:

- *Basic transactional relationship.* The company sells the product but does not follow up in any way (Target).
- *Reactive relationship.* The company (or salesperson) sells the product and encourages customers to call if they encounter any problems (Men's Wearhouse).
- *Accountable relationship.* The salesperson phones customers shortly after the sale to check whether the product meets the expectations and asks for product improvement suggestions and any specific disappointments. This information helps the company continuously improve its offering (Acura dealers).
- *Proactive relationship.* The salesperson or company contacts customers from time to time with suggestions about improved product use or helpful new products (Verizon).
- *Partnership.* The company works continuously with customers (and other stakeholders) to discover ways to deliver better value (Nordstrom's Personal Shopper).[18]

Different stakeholders require different types of relationships. The relationship a company seeks with a customer is different from the one it seeks with its suppliers. However, there is often significant overlap in stakeholder roles. An employee may also be a customer and a stockholder.

The number of stakeholders is also important. The more there are, the more difficult it is to develop an extensive personal relationship with each. Some customers may not want anything more than a transactional relationship.[19] Most people wouldn't want a phone call from a store-label soft drink company. But Mtn Dew believes its customers *do* want a relationship with the brand. As a result, the company has encouraged users to design new flavors

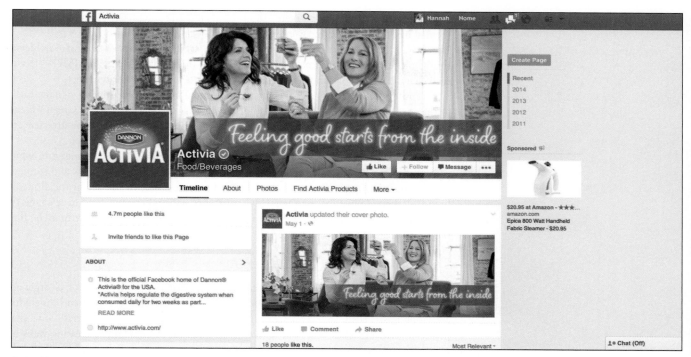

Activia, like many contemporary brands, stays close to its customers by maintaining a friendly and helpful Facebook page. How does the use of social media change the relationship between a brand like Activia and its consumers?

Source: The Dannon Company, Inc.

and bottle designs. This is because of the potential for **interactive customer relationships** which makes it easy for companies and customers to communicate in digital media. In such relationships, companies encourage consumers to "feel like they're a part of your brand in a unique way."[20]

Mtn Dew also places a great deal of emphasis on creating a "Dew-x-perience" for its customers. Using guerilla marketing tactics (guerilla marketing involves using unconventional, inexpensive marketing tactics) to reach out to urban youth, it employs a variety of hip-hop and Latin recording artists in various "street marketing" efforts to distribute bottles of Dew. It also sponsors extreme athletes and appears at sporting events such as the Gravity Games and ESPN's X Games with vans full of merchandise and giveaways.[21]

The final consideration is the profit margin. High-profit product or service categories make deeper, personal relationships more desirable (see Exhibit 1-2). Low profit margins per

Exhibit 1-2

Relationship levels as a function of profit margin and number of customers.

	Profit margins		
	High	Medium	Low
Many	Accountable	Reactive	Basic
Medium	Proactive	Accountable	Basic
Few	Partnership	Accountable	Reactive

Number of customers

customer suggest that the marketer should pursue basic transactional relationships augmented by brand image advertising.[22]

IMC is both a concept and a process. The *concept* of integration is *wholeness*. Achieving this wholeness in communications creates *synergy*—the principal benefit of IMC—because each element of the communications mix reinforces the others for greater effect.

This idea of wholeness and synergy was illustrated in the Green Threads vignette earlier in the chapter. Sharon perceived that all of the messages she received about Green Threads reinforced one another. This made credible the big idea that the brand is both attractive and socially responsible.

Tom Duncan, an IMC scholar, has pointed out that IMC is also a *process* in which communication becomes the driving, integrating force in the marketing mix and throughout the organization. Consumers are part of that process too. In the age of social media, brand marketers must "assess their IMC capability and understand how to leverage the consumer's voice."[23] In other words, for IMC to retain value, it's capability must be fluid rather than static.

The Evolution of the IMC Concept

Glen Nowack and Joe Phelps, advertising professors from the Universities of Georgia and Alabama, argue that IMC developed as a consequence of several important trends, including escalating media costs, splintering consumer markets, and skepticism about traditional mass media advertising. These have led marketers to question the wisdom of creating walls between disciplines such as public relations, direct-response advertising, and sales promotion.[24]

The IMC approach, according to Nowak and Phelps, focuses on four related tactics: (1) less emphasis on advertising relative to other promotional tools, (2) heavier reliance on targeted messages and on reaching smaller segments, (3) increased use of consumer data, and (4) changed expectations for marketing communications suppliers.

Although IMC is considered crucial to any contemporary marketing effort, it has proven surprisingly difficult to define. Nowak and Phelps noted that IMC is used by some to mean *"one voice"* (i.e., ensuring all elements of the marketing mix converge on a single idea), by others to mean *integrated communications* (that advertising can and should achieve both action and awareness objectives simultaneously), and by still others to mean *coordinated marketing communications* (ensuring the various marketing mix elements such as advertising direct-response, sales promotions, and the like, work together).[25]

One scholar's review suggests that a complete definition would include four elements: first, that IMC refers both to a concept (or idea) and process (a sequence of steps); second that IMC draws on management skill at strategic planning; third, that IMC, as compared with traditional promotional approaches, places greater emphasis on audiences, channels, and results; and finally that IMC represents a broadened view of brand promotion. He concludes that IMC is best defined as "the concept and process of strategically managing audience-focused, channel-centered, and results-driven brand communication programs over time."[26]

How the Customer Sees Marketing Communications

Clearly, to understand IMC, we have to look through the customer's eyes. Customers develop perceptions of the company or brand through a variety of sources: news reports, word of mouth, gossip, experts' opinions, financial reports, Websites, blogs, and even the CEO's personality.

All these communications or brand contacts, sponsored or not, create an *integrated product* in the consumer's mind.[27] In other words, customers automatically integrate all the brand-related messages that they encounter. The way they integrate those messages determines their perception of the company. IMC gives companies a better opportunity to manage or influence those perceptions and create a superior relationship with those stakeholders.

The Four Sources of Brand Messages

To influence customers' perceptions, marketers must understand one of the basic premises of IMC: that *everything we do (and don't do) sends a message.* That is to say, every corporate activity has a message component. Duncan and Moriarty describe four sources of company/brand-related messages stakeholders receive: *planned, product, service,* and *unplanned.* Each of these influences a stakeholder's relationship decision, so marketers must know where these messages originate, what effect they have, and the costs to influence them.

1. *Planned messages.* These are the traditional promotional messages—advertising, sales promotion, personal selling, merchandising materials, publicity releases, event sponsorships. These often have the *least* impact because they are seen as self-serving. Planned messages should be coordinated to work toward a predetermined set of communications objectives.

2. *Product messages.* In IMC theory, every element of the marketing mix sends a message. Messages from the product, price, or distribution elements are typically referred to as *product* (or *inferred*) *messages.* For example, customers and other stakeholders receive one product message from a $25,000 Rolex watch and a different one from a $30 Timex. Product messages also include packaging, which communicates about the product through the use of color, type, imagery, design, layout, and materials.

     Product messages have great impact. When a product performs well, it reinforces the purchase decision. However, a gap between the product's performance and advertised promises creates violated expectations.

3. *Service messages.* Employee interactions also send messages to customers. In many organizations, customer service people are supervised by operations, not marketing. Yet the service messages they send have greater marketing impact than the planned messages. With IMC, marketing people work with operations to minimize negative messages and maximize positive ones.

4. *Unplanned messages.* Companies have little control over the unplanned messages that emanate from employee gossip, unsought news stories, comments by the trade or competitors, word-of-mouth rumors, or major disasters. Unplanned messages may affect customers' attitudes dramatically, but they can sometimes be anticipated and influenced, especially by managers experienced in public relations.[28]

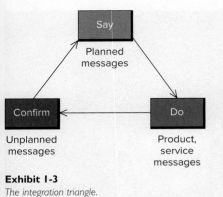

Exhibit 1-3
The integration triangle.

The Integration Triangle

The integration triangle developed by Duncan and Moriarty is a simple illustration of how perceptions are created from the various brand message sources (see Exhibit 1-3). Planned messages are *say* messages—what companies say about themselves. In the story of Sharon and Green Threads, the Facebook ad was an example of this. Product and service messages are *do* messages because they represent what a company does. The bike rack, socially aware business practices, and helpful clerk were examples of this in the Green Threads story. Unplanned messages are *confirm* messages because that's what others say and confirm (or not) about what the company says and does. The positive posts on Google and any positive (or negative) news articles that Sharon might encounter about Green Threads are examples of this. Constructive integration occurs when a brand does what its maker says it will do and then others confirm that it delivers on its promises.[29]

The Dimensions of IMC

To maximize the synergy benefits of IMC, Duncan suggests three priorities for an organization's integration process. It should first ensure consistent positioning, then facilitate purposeful interactivity between the company and its customers or other stakeholders, and finally actively incorporate a socially responsible mission in its relationships with its stakeholders.

As Duncan's IMC model shows in Exhibit 1-3, the cross-functional planning and monitoring of IMC activities result in an enhanced relationship with customers and other stakeholders, which leads to stakeholder loyalty and ultimately to greater brand equity.

The interest in IMC is global.[30] The campaign that opened this chapter from Activia ran globally. In fact, it launched in over 50 countries including the United States.

In short, IMC offers accountability by maximizing resources and linking communications activities directly to organizational goals and the resulting bottom line.[31]

While this text deals with most major facets of IMC and brand messages, one particular kind, advertising, has a central role. Why? Because advertising is typically the element of marketing communications over which a company has greatest control. As such, it remains an important component of almost every great IMC campaign. And it is likely to remain so for the foreseeable future. Moreover, a full appreciation of what advertising can and cannot do is vital for grasping the bigger picture of IMC.

Communication: What Makes Advertising Unique

First and foremost, advertising is communication—a special kind of communication. McCann Worldgroup, the ad agency for MasterCard, claims that advertising is "truth well told." This means that ethical advertisers and the agencies they employ work together to discover the best methods possible to tell their story truthfully and creatively. To succeed, they must understand the advertising communication process, which derives from the basic human communication process.

The Human Communication Process

Success in life depends on our ability to inform others or persuade them to do something (or stop doing something). The first scholars to study human communication formulated a model like the one in Exhibit 1-4. The process begins when one party, called the **source,** formulates an idea, **encodes** it as a **message,** and sends it via some **channel** to another party, called the **receiver.** The receiver must **decode** the message in order to understand it. To respond, the receiver formulates a new idea, encodes it, and then sends the new message back through some channel. A message that acknowledges or responds to the original message constitutes **feedback,** which also affects the encoding of a new message.[32] And, of course, all this takes place in an environment characterized by **noise**—the distracting cacophony of many other messages being sent at the same time by other sources.

Applying this model to advertising, the source is the sponsor, the message is the ad, the channel is the medium, the receiver is the consumer or prospect, and the noise is the din of competing messages, including other ads. But this model oversimplifies the process that

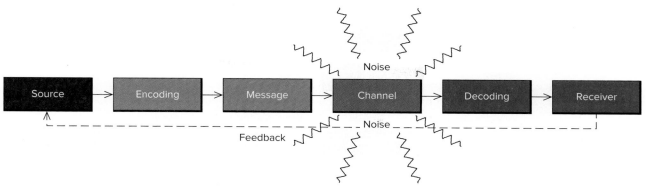

Exhibit 1-4
The traditional human communication process.

occurs in advertising or other sponsored marketing communications. It doesn't take into account either the structure or the creativity inherent in composing the advertising message. We need to consider some of the many complexities involved, especially with the advent of *interactive media,* which let consumers participate in the communication by extracting the information they need, manipulating what they see, and responding in real time. The realization that much contemporary communication, especially in marketing, is better characterized as dialogue has led many scholars to revise the communication model to reflect interactivity, as depicted in Exhibit 1-5.

Exhibit 1-5 presents an interactive model of communication. In this model, no single entity operates as a source or receiver. Instead, two entities serve both roles in an ongoing process. This model better represents marketers' understanding of their relationships with consumers today. Marketers no longer dominate the exchange of messages. Rather, they are engaged in a conversation with consumers who send their own messages, both to the marketer and to other consumers. The interactive model helps remind companies that they do not have as much control over messages as the traditional model seems to suggest. It also reminds companies that the reputation of brands is not just a function of what the company says, but what consumers and other say as well.

Applying the Communication Process to Advertising

Communications scholar Barbara Stern proposes a more sophisticated communication model, one that views advertising as *composed commercial text* rather than informal speech. The Stern model helps remind us that in advertising, sources, messages, and receivers have multiple dimensions. Some of these dimensions exist in the real world; others exist on a different level of reality—a virtual world within the text of the advertising message itself.

Source Dimensions: The Sponsor, the Author, and the Persona

In oral communication, the source is typically one person talking to another person or a group. But in advertising, identifying the source of a message is not so simple. Certainly the real-world **sponsor,** that is, the company that is advertising a product or idea, is legally responsible for the communication and has a message to communicate to actual consumers. But as the Stern model in Exhibit 1-6 shows, the path from sponsor to consumer can be long and circuitous. To begin with, the sponsor does not usually produce the message. That is the typical role of the sponsor's ad agency. So the **author** of the communication is actually a creative team at an ad agency. Commissioned by the sponsor to create the advertising message, these people exist in the real world but are unknown to the reader or viewer.

At the same time, *within the text* of the ad is a real or imaginary spokesperson (a **persona**) who lends some voice or tone to the ad. To the consumer, this persona, who represents the sponsor, is the source of the within-text message. But the persona's discourse is composed and crafted by the ad's authors solely for the purposes of the text; it is not a part of real life. It exists only in the virtual world of the ad. As an example, the Garnier ad shown in Ad Lab 1–A, presents a living person, a woman whose daily

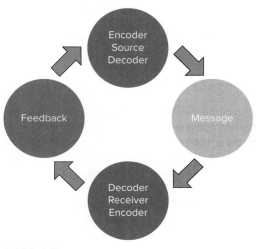

Exhibit 1-5
The interactive model of communication.

Exhibit 1-6
The Stern model of the advertising communication process.

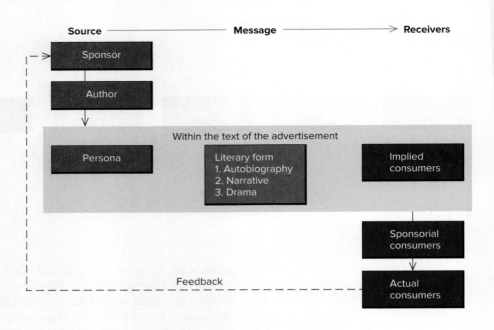

stresses cause people to see her as older at night than when she first wakes. Although her experiences seem spontaneous, the entire "day" has been planned by ad agency creatives. (See Ad Lab 1–A, "Advertising as a Literary Form.")

Message Dimensions: Autobiography, Narrative, and Drama

Advertising messages may also be multi dimensional. As artful imitations of life, they typically use one or a blend of three literary forms: autobiography, narrative, or drama. In **autobiographical messages,** "I" tell a story about myself to "you," the audience eavesdropping on my personal experience. Other ads use **narrative messages** in which a third-person persona tells a story about others to an imagined audience. Finally, in the **drama message,** the characters act out events as though in a play. The audience is an invisible observer of the actions in the ad.

The creators of ads make important decisions about what kind of persona and which literary form to use to express the message. Key considerations are the emotions, attitudes, and motives that drive customers in their target audience. Words and visuals are placed in the structured format most suitable to the medium selected for delivering the message. The format may be a dramatic 30-second TV commercial; an autobiographical, full-page, black-and-white magazine ad; a colorful, narrative brochure; or a multipage Website that employs a variety of message styles. In all cases, though, the message exists only within the text of the ad. Doing all this effectively requires great skill, but it's this creativity that distinguishes advertising from all other forms of communication.

Receiver Dimensions: Implied, Sponsorial, and Actual Consumers

The receivers of advertising are also multidimensional. First, *within the text,* every ad or commercial presumes an audience. These **implied consumers,** who are addressed by the ad's persona, are not real. They are imagined by the ad's creators to be ideal consumers who accept uncritically the arguments made by the ad. These are the people imagined by the copywriter as he or she composes the words that will appear on paper or in electronic or digital form. They are, in effect, part of the ad's drama.

When we move outside the text of the ad, though, the first audience is, in fact, a group of decision makers at the sponsor or advertiser. These **sponsorial consumers** are the gatekeepers who decide if the ad will run or not. So, before an ad ever gets a chance to persuade a real consumer, the ad's authors must first persuade the sponsor's executives and managers who pay for the campaign and must approve it.

AD Lab 1-A

Advertising as a Literary Form

These four ads show how advertising messages typically come in one or a blend of three literary forms: autobiography, narrative, or drama.

Autobiography tells its story from a first-person point of view and may often use the word I. In the screenshot for a Garnier ad, a woman is followed throughout her busy day, demonstrating the toll that life's stresses take on youthful beauty. The narrative form typically uses a third-person voice, which often exudes a well-informed, authoritative quality to tell the reader about the product. In the next example, a narrator describes the heroic efforts to save a white lion in desperate need of treatment for his deteriorating teeth. The video, and the treatment, is sponsored by Fixodent. The drama form uses the style of theater to create or perform a scene, so the reader receives the message by implication rather than by direct telling. The ad for Wilkenson Sword blades depicts a sensual "battle" between two sultry characters.

Two other key elements are the persona, which usually represents the advertiser, and the implied consumer. Sometimes a character may represent the implied consumer. The persona may be a trade character, such as the Pillsbury Doughboy, or a real person, such as Eminem, shown below in the Brisk Iced Tea Ad. A logo may even be a form of persona. Ads may also employ a number of literary forms simultaneously.

1. Autobiography.
Source: L'Oréal International

2. Narrative.
Source: Procter & Gamble

3. Drama.
Source: Wilkinson Sword

4. Mixture of literary forms and elements.
Source: Pepsi Cola Company

The **actual consumers**—equivalent to the receiver in oral communications—are people in the real world who make up the ad's target audience. They are the people to whom the sponsor's message is ultimately directed. But they will get to see, hear, or read it only with the sponsor's approval.[33]

Actual consumers do not usually think or behave the same as the implied consumer or even the sponsorial consumer. Thus, the advertiser (and the creative team) must be concerned about how the actual consumer will decode, or interpret, the message. The last thing an advertiser wants is to be misunderstood.

Unfortunately, message interpretation is only partially determined by the words and symbols in the ad. The medium used has an effect as well. As Marshall McLuhan said, "The medium is the message." Communications professionals are very interested in how different media affect the way people receive and interpret promotional messages.

The characteristics of the receivers are also very important, and in Chapter 5, we'll see how attitudes, perceptions, personality, self-concept, and culture are important influences that affect the way people receive and respond to messages.

Finally, the sponsor's messages must vie with hundreds of competing commercial and noncommercial messages every day. They are referred to as **noise.** So the sender doesn't know *how* the message is received, or even *if* it's received, until a consumer acknowledges it.

Feedback and Interactivity

That's why feedback is so important. It completes the cycle, verifying that the message was received. Feedback employs a sender-message-receiver pattern, except that it is directed from the receiver back to the source.

In advertising, feedback can take many forms: redeemed coupons, Website visits, phone inquiries, visits to a store, tweets, Facebook posts, increased sales, responses to a survey, or e-mail inquiries. Dramatically low responses to an ad indicate a break in the communication process. Questions arise: Is the product wrong for the market? Is the message unclear? Have the right media been chosen? Without feedback, these questions cannot be answered.

Long gone are the days when audiences could be considered passive receivers of impersonal mass messages. They are active decision makers who control what communications they receive and choose the information they want about a particular product. Social media allow for instantaneous, real-time feedback on the same channel used by the message sender.

This offers companies the chance to nourish relationships with their customers, ones that will be more fruitful for both sponsors and consumers.

Marketing: Determining the Type of IMC Message to Use

LO I-5

Now that you have a better understanding of the communication dimension, let's consider the marketing dimension because that's what defines IMC's role in business. Every business performs a number of diverse activities, typically classified into three broad functional divisions:

- Operations (production/manufacturing)
- Finance/administration
- Marketing

Of all the business functions, marketing is the only one whose primary role is to bring in revenue. Without revenue, of course, a company cannot recover its initial investment, pay its employees, grow, or earn a profit. So marketing is very important.

What Is Marketing?

Over the years, the concept of marketing has evolved based on the supply of and demand for products. Because we need to understand marketing as it relates to IMC, we define the term as follows:

> **Marketing** is the activity, set of institutions, and processes for creating, communicating, delivering, and exchanging offerings that have value for customers, clients, partners, and society at large.[34]

Companies that exist to make a profit are not the only organizations that use marketing principles. Charities also apply these ideas in their quest to increase donations. The "crack" in the pavement is part of an unusual outdoor ad in San Francisco that reminds city residents of how important the Red Cross would be in an earthquake.
Source: American Red Cross

We devote much of this text to the subject of developing marketing and IMC strategies. What's important to understand now is that marketing is a **process**—a sequence of actions or methods—aimed at satisfying customer needs profitably. This process includes developing products, pricing them strategically, making them available to customers through a distribution network, and promoting them through sales and advertising activities. The ultimate goal of the marketing process is to earn a profit for the firm by consummating the exchange of products or services with those customers who need or want them. And the role of advertising is to inform, persuade, and remind groups of customers, or markets, about the need-satisfying value of the company's goods and services. Today even many nonprofit organizations use the marketing process to develop and promote services that will satisfy their constituents' needs.

Ethical Issues

Ethics in Advertising: An Overview

Advertising is fun. It can also be exciting, creative, and entertaining. And sometimes it's not.

Without question, though, advertising is invariably criticized—both for what it is and for what it is not. One of the most frequent criticisms of advertising concerns ethics, either the ethics of the marketer or the ethics of a particular ad. As a student of advertising, and possibly a future practitioner, you should be aware of the major ethical issues related to marketing and advertising. Awareness of the issues is the first step in learning about and practicing ethical behavior.

One could successfully argue that advertising's lack of credibility is due in large part to the cumulative effect of poor ethical behavior on the part of some advertisers during the last century. Deception, misrepresentation, false advertising, exaggerated promises, unfair comparisons—all these are injurious to consumers and competitors as well as people's perception of advertisers in general. In other words, any advertisers that

engage in unethical behavior are damaging not only the fragile relationship they have with their customers, but also the whole profession of advertising. Unfortunately, not all advertisers have figured this out.

We believe that ethical behavior is so important to building customer relationships in the 21st century that we've included a current Ethical Issues feature in advertising in every chapter of this book. Our aim is to focus attention on the most critical social issues facing advertisers today. These include the debate over puffery, advertising to children, comparative advertising, the targeting of ethnic minorities, consumer profiling, privacy, negative political advertising, and statistical manipulation.

Part of being a good student is learning to question what you are taught. As you read each Ethical Issues feature, try to examine all sides of the issues presented to see if you can better understand the motivations and reasoning of the people involved. You might even try debating some of these issues with your classmates.

Advertising and the Marketing Process

Companies and organizations use many different types of advertising, depending on their particular marketing strategy. The marketing strategy will determine who the targets of advertising should be, where ads should appear, what media should be used, and what advertising should accomplish. (Exhibit 1-7 shows some of the ways advertising can be classified, based on these strategic marketing elements.) These criteria will also determine what different advertising skills are required.

Identifying Target Markets and Target Audiences

A firm's marketing activities are always aimed at a particular segment of the population—its **target market.** Likewise, advertising is aimed at a particular group called the **target audience.** When we see an ad that doesn't appeal to us, it may be because the ad is not aimed at any of the groups we belong to. For example, a TV commercial for denture cream isn't meant to appeal to teens. They're not part of either the target market or the target audience. There are two main types of target markets, *consumers* and *businesses.*

By Target Audience	By Geographic Area	By Purpose
Consumer advertising: Aimed at people who buy the product for their own or someone else's use.	*Local (retail) advertising:* Advertising by businesses whose customers come from only one city or local trading area.	*Product advertising:* Promotes the sale of products and services.
Business advertising: Aimed at people who buy or specify products and services for use in business.	*Regional advertising:* Advertising for products sold in one area or region but not the entire country.	*Nonproduct (corporate or institutional) advertising:* Promotes the organization's mission or philosophy rather than a specific product.
• *Trade:* Aimed at wholesalers and retailers of products and services who buy for resale to their customers.	*National advertising:* Advertising aimed at customers in several regions of the country.	*Commercial advertising:* Promotes products, services, or ideas with the expectation of making a profit.
• *Professional:* Aimed at people licensed under a code of ethics or set of professional standards.	*International advertising:* Advertising directed at foreign markets.	*Noncommercial advertising:* Sponsored by or for a charitable or nonprofit institution, civic group, or religious or political organization.
• *Agricultural:* Aimed at people in farming or agribusiness.	**By Medium**	*Action advertising:* Attempts to stimulate immediate action by the reader.
	Print advertising: Newspapers, magazines.	*Awareness advertising:* Attempts to build the image of a product or familiarity with the product's name and package.
	Broadcast (electronic) advertising: Radio, TV.	
	Out-of-home advertising: Outdoor, transit.	
	Direct mail advertising: Advertising sent through the Postal Service and by e-mail.	
	Interactive advertising: Web, social media, mobile, etc.	

Exhibit 1-7
The classifications of advertising.

This ad for Nivea helps to identify the target audience and convey a "personality" of the brand. The ad resonates with the company's target audiences.

Source: Beiersdorf AG

Consumer Markets

Most ads you encounter fall under the broad category of **consumer advertising.** Usually sponsored by the producer (or manufacturer) of the product or service, these ads are typically directed at **consumers,** people who buy the product for their own or someone else's personal use. One example is **retail advertising,** advertising sponsored by retail stores and businesses. Consumer advertising also includes noncommercial *public service announcements (PSAs)* from organizations such as the American Cancer Society or the Partnership for a Drug-Free America.

To create messages that are persuasive, advertising professionals try to understand how people act and think—and why they buy, what they buy. This area of study is the province of *consumer behavior,* our focus in Chapter 5. The better an advertiser understands the buying behavior of people, the better it can bring its products into the collective consciousness of prospective customers.

Industrial/Business Markets

Companies use **business advertising** to reach people who buy or specify goods and services for business use. It tends to appear in specialized business publications or professional journals, in direct-mail pieces sent to businesses, or in trade shows. Since business advertising (also called **business-to-business,** or **B2B, advertising**) rarely uses consumer mass media, it is typically invisible to consumers. However, some business-to-business ads, by firms such as FedEx, do appear on TV and in consumer magazines.

Trade advertising is aimed not at consumers but at people who buy or influence business purchases. This website encourages businesses to consider using glass for packaging their products. The award-winning campaign can be seen here: https://www.doremus.com/work/case-studies/a-day-made-of-glass/

Source: Corning Incorporated

Professional advertising targets audiences in fields such as accounting, medicine, and education. Law firms are the intended target of this ad.

Source: Wells & Drew Companies, Jacksonville, FL

In addition to general business advertising, there are three specialized types of business advertising: trade, professional, and agricultural. Companies aim **trade advertising** at resellers (wholesalers, dealers, and retailers) to obtain greater distribution of their products. For example, Sunkist places trade advertising in publications such as *California Grocer* to develop more grocery outlets and to increase sales to existing outlets.

Advertising aimed at teachers, accountants, doctors, dentists, architects, engineers, lawyers, and the like is called **professional advertising** and typically appears in official publications of professional societies (such as the *Archives of Ophthalmology*). Professional advertising has three objectives: to convince professionals (people with specialized training who work under a code of ethics) to recommend or prescribe a specific product or service to their clients, to buy brands of equipment and supplies for use in their work, or to use the product personally.

Companies use **agricultural** (or **farm**) **advertising** to promote products and services used in agriculture to farmers and others employed in agribusiness. FMC Corp., a large agricultural chemical company, for example, might advertise its plant nutrition products to growers using *California Farmer* magazine. Agricultural advertising typically shows farmers how the advertised product will increase efficiency, reduce risks, and widen profit margins.

Business customers tend to be very knowledgeable and sophisticated, and they may require extensive technical information before making the purchase decision. So people who work in business-to-business advertising often require more specialized product knowledge and experience than their consumer advertising colleagues.

Implementing Marketing Strategy

LO **1-6**

After selecting a target market for its products, a firm designs a strategy to serve that market profitably. As we'll discuss in Chapter 6, marketing strategy is the particular blend, or *mix,* of strategic elements over which the marketer has control: product concept, pricing, distribution, and communication. For ease of memory, marketers often refer to these elements as the 4Ps: product, price, place, and promotion. Each of these elements also influences the type of message used.

Product: Features and Benefits

Products have multiple features and solve a variety of problems. Advertising typically focuses on those features (product or brand components) or benefits (problems the brand can solve or ways the brand can provide desired rewards) of greatest relevance to the target audience. Consider automobiles. All have tires, a steering wheel, and windshields, and all will get you from one location to another. However a Prius, with its hybrid engine, will do so in an environmentally friendly way. A BMW Z4 will draw admiring looks from others. And a Ford F150 will complement an outdoor lifestyle. Part of the way we know these things is because advertising messages remind us why a brand is special.

Price: Strategies for Emphasizing Value

Consumers view value as the ratio of a brand's quality to its price. If two brands are priced similarly, the one highest in quality is the better value. If two brands are equal in quality, the one with the lowest price is the best value. The implications for advertising strategy are straightforward. Some products (Suave personal care brands, No-Ad lotions) are publicized using **price advertising,** in which an ad claims the product is equal in quality to higher priced brands. Other goods and services, which do not attempt to compete on price, emphasize product quality. **Image advertising,** which creates a perception of a company or a personality for a brand, is rarely explicit about price. Apple's iPods and Macs generally sell for more than competing brands, so Apple emphasizes how "cool" its technologies are and almost never mentions price. **Sale advertising** is used most often by retailers, dealers, and shops to call attention to a recent drop in the price of a brand or service. Such advertising allows retailers to match competitor price drops, move inventory, or increase retail traffic. However, when a brand is frequently put on sale, consumers may believe it is not worth its regular price. For this reason, some manufacturers prohibit retailers from discounting their products.

(continued on page 26)

Portfolio Review

Great advertising is both time-less and contemporary. This Portfolio Review presents some of the best recent work by agencies around the world. Examine the ads both as you would as a consumer and as an advertising professional. Train your eye to notice how art, copy, and color make ads grab the attention of consumers. Don't be afraid to critique the ads as well. Given your understanding of the target audience and the brand, what approach would you have taken?

"Never Hide" is the slogan for this great Ray-Ban campaign. What elements of the ads ensure continuity across the different spots? Great ads speak to the consumer in a way that helps the consumer see the value of the brand. Brands may solve simple problems (quench your thirst) or help consumers let others know how they see themselves. Ray-Ban uses powerful images and a bold slogan to connect with audiences.

Source: Luxottica Group S.p.A.

Shakira's viral, which became the most shared ad-sponsored viral in history, is an example of content marketing. Content marketing consists of creating shareable content that entertains, engages, and garners positive attention for a brand.

Source: World Food Programme

Activia also markets to consumers using the more traditional approach of an informative Website. How would you account for the differences in tone, color, and approach of the creative work featured in Activia's Website and in the Shakira's viral video?

Source: The Dannon Company, Inc.

Like many global brands, Activia adjusts its marketing to include national customs, norms, and values. This Facebook page specifically targets Russian consumers.

Source: The Dannon Company, Inc.

Activia, like many global brands, understands that there are important markets developing all over the world. Latin and South American consumers will represent a growing percentage of the brand's consumers over the next decade.

Source: The Dannon Company, Inc.

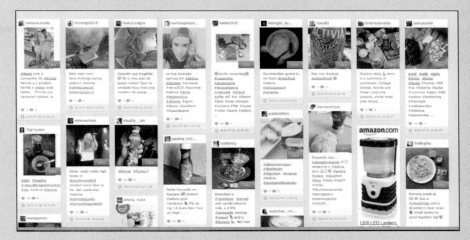

Instagram is a relatively new social media platform. Its highly graphical design makes it a perfect place for consumers and brands to exchange ideas. As seen in the above Activia Instagram page, consumers of Activia from around the world have posted photos of their favorite Activia product along with recipes and meal ideas.

Source: The Dannon Company, Inc.

Twitter is yet another social media platform. What marketing goals do you believe differentiate Activia's presence on Twitter from its presence on Instagram?

Source: The Dannon Company, Inc.

(continued from page 21)

Place: The Distribution Element

The third element of marketing strategy, place (or more accurately, distribution), also affects the type of advertising used. Global marketers such as Coca-Cola, Toyota, and IBM may use **global advertising,** in which messages are consistent in ads placed around the world. Other firms may promote their products in foreign markets with **international advertising,** which may contain different messages and even be created locally in each geographic market. The field of international marketing is so important that we discuss global advertising issues in every chapter of this book.

Companies that market in several regions of the United States and use the major mass media are called *national advertisers,* and their promotion is called **national advertising.** Some companies sell in only one part of the country or in two or three states. They use **regional advertising,** placing their ads in local media or regional editions of national media. Finally, businesses and retailers that sell within one small trading area typically use **local advertising** placed in local media or direct mail. We'll explore this topic further in Chapter 4.

Promotion: The Communication Element

The final element of marketing strategy is communication. As we mentioned at the beginning of this chapter, advertising is just one of the tools in the marketing communications tool kit. **Marketing communications** typically refers to all the *planned messages* that companies and organizations create and disseminate to support their marketing objectives. In addition to advertising, major marketing communication tools include *personal selling, sales promotion, public relations activities,* and *collateral materials.* The extent to which an organization uses any or all of these tools again depends on its marketing needs, objectives, and strategy.

Each marketing communication tool offers particular opportunities and benefits to the marketer. **Personal selling,** for example, in which salespeople deal directly with customers either face-to-face or via telemarketing, offers the flexibility possible only through human interaction. Personal selling is ideal for conveying information, giving demonstrations, and consummating the sale (or exchange), especially on high-ticket items such as cars, real estate, and furniture as well as most business-to-business products. The drawback to personal selling is its high cost, so companies that emphasize personal selling in their marketing mix often spend a lower percentage of sales on advertising than other firms. We'll discuss personal selling in greater detail in Chapter 18.

As a marketing communications tool, advertising enables marketers to reach more prospects at lower cost than a salesperson could ever do. Further, the creativity inherent in advertising allows the marketer to create an image or personality, full of symbolic meaning and benefits, for the company's brand. No salesperson can do this. However, advertising does suffer from credibility gaps, a topic we'll discuss in Chapter 3.

Advertising can be used to satisfy a variety of sponsor objectives. Some advertising is meant to help generate profits for the advertiser; some is sponsored by nonprofit groups. Some ads try to spur the target audience to immediate action, others to create awareness or understanding of the advertiser's offering.

To promote their goods and services, companies use **product advertising.** To sell ideas, though, organizations use **nonproduct advertising.** An ExxonMobil ad that touts a new gasoline additive as a way of encouraging consumers to fuel up at an ExxonMobile service station is a product ad. But an ExxonMobile ad promoting the company's mission or philosophy (for example, how the company develops new technologies to conserve energy and protect the environment) is called *nonproduct, corporate,* or *institutional advertising.* Why do companies communicate their good works or activities to consumers? We'll answer that question in Chapter 19.

Similarly, while commercial advertising seeks profits, **noncommercial advertising** is used around the world by governments and nonprofit organizations to seek donations, volunteer support, or changes in consumer behavior.

Some ads are intended to bring about immediate action by the reader; others have a longer term goal. The objectives of **awareness advertising,** for example, are to create an

Global companies must advertise not only in their home country but also overseas to cover the distribution element of their marketing strategies. This ad for Kentucky Fried Chicken targets consumers through a purely illustrative advertisement, overcoming any language barriers.

© Vincent Thian/AP Images

image for a product and to position it competitively with the goal of getting readers or viewers to select the brand the next time they shop.

A direct mail ad, on the other hand, exemplifies **action** (or **direct-response**) **advertising** because it seeks an immediate, direct response from the reader. Most ads on TV and radio are awareness ads, but some are a mixture of awareness and action. For example, a 60-second TV commercial may devote the first 50 seconds to image building and the last 10 to a toll-free phone number for immediate information.

Sales promotion is a communication tool that offers special incentives to motivate people to act right away. The incentives may be coupons, free samples, contests, or rebates on the purchase price. By offering added value, sales promotion accelerates sales. So it is a very effective tool. It is often used in conjunction with advertising—to promote the promotion. However, like personal selling, it is very expensive; it suffers from other drawbacks as well, as we'll discuss in Chapter 10. While ad agencies create and place media advertising, most sales promotion efforts are created by firms that specialize in that field.

Public relations (PR) is an umbrella process—much like marketing—responsible for managing the firm's relationships with its various *publics*. These publics may include customers but are not limited to them. Public relations is also concerned with employees, stockholders, vendors and suppliers, government regulators, interest groups, and the press. So PR is much larger than just a tool of marketing communications. However, as part of their marketing mix, marketers use a number of **public relations activities** because they are so good at creating awareness and credibility for the firm at relatively low cost. These activities (often referred to as **marketing public relations [MPR]**) include publicity, press agentry, sponsorships, special events, and a special kind of advertising called **public relations advertising,** which uses the structured, sponsored format of media advertising to accomplish public relations goals. While PR is closely aligned with advertising, it requires very different skills and is usually performed by professionals in PR firms rather than ad agency people. However, advertising people need to understand how important PR activities are, so we'll discuss the topic in some detail in Chapter 19.

Companies use a wide variety of promotional tools other than media advertising to communicate information about themselves and their brands. These **collateral materials** include flyers, brochures, catalogs, posters, sales kits, product specification sheets, instruction booklets, and so on. These materials may be very inexpensive or frightfully costly. But because they contribute so much information to customers and prospects, they are very important to both closing sales and reinforcing prior sales decisions. The people who produce collateral materials may work for the company's advertising agency, but often they work for outside graphic design firms, packaging specialists, and independent film and video producers.

People BEHIND the Ads

Albert Lasker and Claude Hopkins Advertising Legends

© Everett Collection Historical/Alamy Stock Photo

Albert Lasker didn't start out wanting an advertising career at all. His dream was to become a great newspaper reporter. One of eight children, Lasker began writing a weekly newsletter at 12 and working for his hometown paper while still in high school.

In his teens, he set his sights on New York, home of the country's biggest dailies. But, as he later recalled, there was just one problem:

My father had a dread of my becoming a newspaperman, because in those days (and this is no exaggeration) almost every newspaperman was a heavy drinker. . . . I was very devoted to my father, and he proposed instead that I go to a firm in what he considered a kindred field—Lord & Thomas in Chicago, an advertising agency.

Just 19 when he arrived in Chicago, Lasker was given only menial office tasks around the agency. His plan was to stay for a short while and then eventually move on to become a reporter. But a gambling loss equivalent to nearly his entire annual salary dashed those prospects. In an early display of his persuasive abilities, Lasker convinced agency owner Thomas to cover his debt in exchange for a portion of his weekly pay.

If he proved to be a poor gambler, Lasker quickly showed other talents. He convinced his bosses to "temporarily" assign him a sales territory vacated by a departing employee and soon brought in thousands of dollars more business each month than the man he replaced. Reflecting on his predecessor, Lasker later wrote: "He was a fine man, but he wasn't a 'closer.'"

"So far as I know, no ordinary human being has ever resisted Albert Lasker," Claude Hopkins once observed. Lasker's persuasive talents were rooted in his gifts as both a leader and a visionary. Impressing everyone he worked with, Lasker was quickly promoted through the agency ranks. He was still in his early twenties when he bought Lord & Thomas and began creating the first true "modern" ad agency.

Lasker's assumption as leader at Lord & Thomas corresponded with a change in what ad agencies did for clients. Once considered to

Why Integrated Marketing Communications?

In recent years, as new media have proliferated and the cost of competition has intensified, sophisticated marketers have searched for new ways to get more bang (and accountability) from their marketing communications buck. The result has been a growing understanding on the part of corporate management that (1) the efficiencies of mass media advertising are not what they used to be; (2) consumers are more sophisticated, cynical, and distrusting than ever before; (3) tremendous gaps exist between what companies say in their advertising and what they actually do; and (4) in the long run, nourishing good customer relationships is far more important than making simple exchanges.[35] As we've emphasized in this chapter, this has led to a growing movement toward integrating all the messages created by an advertiser's various communication agencies and sent out by various departments within the company to achieve consistency. IMC is not only an important marketing trend, it is *the* business imperative for the 21st century.

In many ways, IMC represents a continuation of the kind of strategic thinking that has evolved with the growth and sophistication of advertising. To see that more clearly, the next chapter presents an overview of the development of advertising, illustrated through the history of Coca-Cola.

be media brokers, agencies were just beginning to provide creative services for advertisers. Lasker embraced this change and Lord & Thomas soon became famous for its creative work. This was due in no small part to Lasker's willingness to pay top dollar for talent and for his lifelong fascination with "how advertising works." It was his interest in the latter that led to one of Lasker's two most famous hires, John E. Kennedy. Kennedy, a former Canadian police officer, was toiling in relative anonymity as a freelance copywriter when, as legend has it, he sat at a bar beneath the famous ad agency and wrote on a piece of paper:

I am in the saloon downstairs. I can tell you what advertising is. I know you don't know. It will mean much to me to have you know what it is and it will mean much to you. If you wish to know what advertising is, send the word "yes" down by the bell boy. Signed— John E. Kennedy

Lasker, intrigued, invited Kennedy up. Like many in his day, Lasker believed that advertising was best thought of as a kind of news. But Kennedy's deceptively simple idea was that advertising was "salesmanship in print." This philosophy helped shape and define the work produced by Lord & Thomas for many years and proved influential not only with Lasker, but with generations of advertising professionals such as Rosser Reeves, Claude Hopkins, John Orr Young (cofounder of Young & Rubicam), and David Ogilvy.

While the salesmanship in print notion was Kennedy's, the man who put the idea into practice was Kennedy's successor, Claude Hopkins. Hopkins believed advertising had one function: selling. A man of amazing energy, curiosity, and talent, Hopkins believed that there were basic principles that could be discovered through repeated testing and that these principles would guarantee success. Hopkins even claimed these

principles were understood and he set them out in a book, *Scientific Advertising*.

As we will see in Chapter 2, later generations of advertising professionals such as Bill Bernbach eventually rejected the idea that advertising is a science, and few today would call it that. Thus many of the "principles" that Hopkins described now appear quaint and simplistic.

But if Hopkins was wrong about some things, he was remarkably prescient about others. For example, he believed that agency people should develop a deep understanding of the product and the consumer. He also understood the value of research both before and after a campaign (he especially liked the use of coupons as a way of gauging advertising effectiveness, foreshadowing the popularity of direct-response advertising today). Finally, Hopkins advocated finding a "preemptive claim" for each brand, an attribute that could be used to distinguish the brand from its competitors. One famous example was Hopkins's claim for Schlitz that the brand's bottles were "washed with live steam." The fact that all beer bottles were sterilized with steam did nothing to diminish, in the minds of consumers, the association of Schlitz with purity, cleanliness, and safety. Hopkins eventually became one of the ad industry's highest paid talents, earning a six-figure salary.

The Lord & Thomas agency endured after Lasker and Hopkins ended their careers, eventually becoming Foote, Cone, & Belding, now part of the Interpublic empire. And while Albert Lasker never did become a reporter, he lived a rich, full life. In his retirement, he donated much of his wealth to charities. Especially noteworthy was his creation of the Albert and Mary Lasker Foundation, named for the executive and his wife. The foundation has helped fund and reward groundbreaking clinical and basic medical research since 1945 (www.laskerfoundation.org/index .html).

Chapter Summary

Advertising is a paid, mediated form of communication from an identifiable source, designed to persuade the receiver to take some action, now or in the future. To maximize advertising effectiveness, most companies work to ensure that their advertisements complement other messaging efforts. This practice is called integrated marketing communications.

Integrated marketing communications involves strategically managing and coordinating the sources of information consumers have about brands. IMC is both a concept and a process that offers the synergy of various communications media, strategically managed to enhance the relationship between the customer and the brand or company. Starting with the customer, the IMC planning model uses seven steps to segment the customer database by product and purchase-related attributes: determine the best place,

situation, and time to reach the prospect; develop behavior-related marketing and communications objectives and strategies; and develop specific communications tactics to implement the plan. In the IMC model, all marketing becomes communications and all communications become marketing.

Advertising is often a critically important component of IMC. Looking at four important dimensions of advertising (communication, marketing, economic, and social) helps clarify what advertising is and how it has evolved.

Advertising is first and foremost communication. The basic human communication process begins when a source formulates an idea, encodes it as a message, and sends it via some channel or medium to a receiver. The receiver must decode the message in order to understand it. To respond, the receiver formulates a new idea, encodes that concept, and then sends a new message back through some channel. A message that acknowledges or responds to the original message is feedback, and it affects the encoding of a new message. In advertising, the communication process is complex because of the multidimensional nature of the source, the message, and the recipient. Traditionally, advertising has been a one-way process, but interactive technology allows consumers to give feedback in real time using the same channels as the sender.

Marketing's primary role is to attract revenues, so advertising is important. The targets of a firm's marketing will determine the targets of its advertising. Marketers address two major types of audiences with their advertising: consumers and businesses. Within each of these categories, though, are special forms of advertising, such as retail, trade, professional, and agricultural.

A firm's marketing mix—or strategy—establishes the type of advertising needed and the skills required to implement it. The marketing mix

includes those elements over which the marketer has control: product, price, distribution, and communication. Depending on the product marketed, the advertiser may use packaged-goods advertising, professional services advertising, or some other type such as high-tech advertising. Likewise, the firm's pricing strategy will determine if it should use sale advertising.

The distribution strategy dictates the firm's use of local, regional, national, or international advertising. The communication element determines the mix of marketing communications tools to be used. These include advertising, personal selling, sales promotion, public relations activities, and collateral materials.

To achieve consistency in all the organization's messages, sophisticated companies seek to integrate their marketing communications with all other corporate activities through a process called integrated marketing communications.

Important Terms

action advertising, *26*

actual consumers, *17*

advertising, *8*

agricultural advertising, *21*

author, *15*

autobiographical messages, *16*

awareness advertising, *26*

business advertising, *20*

business-to-business (B2B) advertising, *20*

channel, *14*

collateral materials, *27*

consumer advertising, *20*

consumers, *8, 20*

decode, *14*

direct-response advertising, *27*

drama message, *16*

encodes, *14*

farm advertising, *21*

feedback, *14*

global advertising, *26*

goods, *8*

ideas, *8*

image advertising, *21*

implied consumers, *16*

integrated marketing communications (IMC), *5*

international advertising, *26*

interactive customer relationships, *11*

lifetime customer value (LTCV), *9*

local advertising, *26*

marketing, *19*

marketing communications, *7, 26*

marketing public relations (MPR), *27*

mass media, *9*

medium, *9*

message, *14*

narrative messages, *16*

national advertising, *26*

noise, *14, 18*

noncommercial advertising, *26*

nonproduct advertising, *26*

persona, *15*

personal selling, *26*

price advertising, *21*

process, *19*

product, *8*

product advertising, *26*

professional advertising, *21*

public relations (PR), *27*

public relations activities, *27*

public relations advertising, *27*

public service messages, *8*

receiver, *14*

regional advertising, *26*

relationship marketing, *9*

retail advertising, *20*

sale advertising, *21*

sales promotion, *27*

services, *8*

source, *14*

sponsor, *15*

sponsorial consumers, *16*

stakeholders, *9*

target audience, *19*

target market, *19*

trade advertising, *21*

Review Questions

1. What is IMC and how is it different from advertising?
2. What kinds of relationships do brands have with consumers?
3. What are the advantages of the interactive communications model over the traditional one?
4. In the marketing communications process, what are the various dimensions of the source, the message, and the receiver?
5. Who else besides consumers do brands sometimes seek to develop relationships with?
6. What are the two broad categories of target markets?
7. In addition to consumer advertising, what specific form of business advertising would a pharmaceutical company be likely to employ?
8. What are the four elements that comprise a company's marketing strategy and how do they affect the type of advertising a company uses?
9. What is the purpose of awareness advertising?
10. What important activities does a company engage in under the heading of "promotions"?

The Advertising Experience

1. **Ad Action: Strategy and the Marketing Mix**

   This chapter has emphasized building relationships as an important objective for IMC. Think about your favorite brands. Do you feel as though you have a "relationship" with any? What do the companies that support these brands do to ensure you are happy in the relationship? And are you an advocate for any brand? How and when do you communicate to others your positive feelings or excitement about the brand?

2. **Role of Advertising**

   In Chapter 1, you learned about the standard definition of advertising and the various roles and forms that advertising can take. Browse through the following Websites and discuss what type of advertising each uses and what the purpose of the advertising is:

   a. American Cancer Society: www.cancer.org

   b. Amazon: www.amazon.com

   c. Nike: www.nike.com

   d. Ford: www.ford.com

   e. McDonald's: www.mcdonalds.com

   f. MINI: www.MINIUSA.com

   g. United Parcel Service: www.ups.com

3. **Literary Forms in Television Ads**

   Watch three television ads and examine them for literary form. Do they take the form of autobiography, narrative, or drama? For each ad, discuss why you think its creator chose this particular form over another.

4. Reread the brief account of Sharon and her discovery of a new clothing store. How do you think Green Threads used IMC in its communications with consumers like Sharon? What kind of message would threaten the brand image of Green Threads? How might the retailer deal with such a message?

5. Activia's brilliant video featuring Shakira has generally drawn praise. What made this video effective given the realities of advertising as it is practiced today? Based on what you know about IMC, what other messaging activities should Activia be engaging in to ensure the success of the video?

The Big Picture: The Evolution of Advertising and IMC

Learning Objectives

Advertising and IMC play a large role in the economic vitality of a nation. Both consumers and sellers gain from the information about brands contained in IMC messages. To demonstrate this the chapter introduces the basic principles of free-market economics, the functions and effects of advertising in a free economy, the evolution of advertising as an economic tool, and advertising's overall impact on society. The chapter will help you understand why the practice of advertising began, how it has changed, and why it will continue to evolve in the future.

 studying this chapter, you will be able to:

LO2-1 Explain the role of competition in free-market economics.

LO2-2 Discuss the functions advertising performs in a free market.

LO2-3 Understand the importance of branding, including the benefits that strong brands offer companies.

LO2-4 Identify important milestones in the history of advertising.

LO2-5 Discuss how the role of advertising has changed in recent years.

LO2-6 Explore the impact of advertising on society yesterday, today, and tomorrow.

Agency: Peter Gregson, Client: The Coca-Cola Europe, Creative director: Jovan Trkulja, Art director: Marijana Zaric, Copywriter: Nikola Skoric

Source for both: The Coca-Cola Company

John Pemberton's original recipe included coca leaves and kola nuts, stimulants intended to relieve headaches. The storied traces of cocaine are long gone from the Coca-Cola formula, but today's logo is still based on the heading of the original recipe.[1] Like the swirls of the logo, urban legend and myth surround the world's most valuable brand. Although the company cultivates the mystique, especially by guarding the "secret formula," Coke's advertising has been nothing but straightforwardly charming and positive from the very beginning. ■ In 1886, Pemberton began selling his new remedy for five cents a glass in an Atlanta drugstore. The first Coca-Cola advertisement ran in the patent medicine section of the *Atlanta Journal* that same month. ■ But Pemberton was an inventor, not a visionary marketer, and the company was still quite small when in 1892 Asa Candler secured the rights to the beverage from Pemberton's family for $2,300. ■ Candler

incorporated the Coca-Cola Company and gave birth to the brand. He aggressively expanded the company's customer base with novel promotions, such as handing out coupons for free samples. Candler also placed advertising in the new media of the era, on wall murals and on fixtures in apothecary shops, such as scales, calendars, clocks, and soda fountains. ■ In 1906, agency head William D'Arcy convinced Candler to start a newspaper advertising campaign. During the early years, Coke advertising paired the beverage with a variety of appealing images, from fresh-faced young women to Santa Claus. D'Arcy believed that "Coca-Cola advertising should create scenes that drew people in and made them a part of the pleasant interludes of everyday life."[2] Ads of the 1920s and 1930s showed people enjoying Coke during activities such as boating that many aspired to—perhaps realistically during the boom years but wistfully during the Depression. ■ D'Arcy handled the

Coke account until 1956, when the agency faltered in the face of a new medium, television. It gracefully passed the account to fresh talent McCann-Erickson, but not without commemorating its 50-year relationship with Coca-Cola in a *Wall Street Journal* ad. ■ McCann-Erickson's Coke campaigns of the 1950s, 1960s, and 1970s hooked into the popular culture spreading through TV by featuring performers and their music. For some of the most memorable spots in TV history, see the Portfolio Review on page 40. ■ Coke experimented with a new recipe and in 1985 pulled out all the stops to introduce New Coke. The public's reaction to New Coke was harsh, loud, and immediate: Some people began hoarding Old Coke, while others lobbied the company and prepared to sue. The company soon realized that it was the brand—not its taste—that customers were loyal to. As Coca-Cola's president noted in a later press conference, "All the time and money and skill poured into consumer research on the new Coca-Cola could not measure or reveal the deep and abiding emotional attachment to original Coca-Cola. . . . Some cynics will say we planned the whole thing. The truth is we are not that dumb and we are not that smart."[3] The company pulled the plug on New Coke in the early 1990s. ■ Coca-Cola recovered market share with the help of the seven-year "Always Coca-Cola" advertising campaign. The Creative Edge agency contributed a whimsical series of computer-generated TV spots, bringing Coke advertising into the digital age and showing simple, Coke-worthy moments in the lives of animated polar bears. ■ At the start of the new millennium, critics suggested that Coca-Cola advertising was adrift. Investors wanted the company to divert more energy into the growing sports drink sector instead: "Why pump money into marketing for a slowing brand when you should be coming up with a better Powerade or Dasani?" asked one major shareholder.[4] ■ Why indeed? The classic formula still represents 41 percent of the company's U.S. volume. Through 120 years of cultural change, new technologies, and market trends, the Coca-Cola Company's careful stewardship of the brand's value has made Coke not only the world's best-selling carbonated beverage but also the world's most venerable brand. ■ In the 2014 Super Bowl, Coke debuted "It's Beautiful," a spot showing Americans from varied backgrounds and languages singing "America the Beautiful." The ad proved controversial and generated negative backlash in social media. Perhaps in response, Coke's effort for the 2015 game played it safer with "Make it Happy," an ad that harkens to recurring Coke themes that personal divisions melt in our united love of Coca Cola. Was this return to the company's tried and true approach smart or too cautious[5]? Time will tell. ■ No recent series has popularized the advertising world as well as "Mad Men," which broadcast its final episode in early 2015. Producer Mathew Weiner chose to end his celebrated series with one of Coke's iconic advertisements, "Hilltop Singers." The ad was a huge success for Coke and McCann, and made clear the shift of Coke from national to global brand. The music featured in the spot was so well liked that it was even re-recorded and turned into a top-selling single. Weiner used this ending to call attention to the evolution of the agency world at the dawn of the 1970s and to call attention to the power of great advertising. ■ There is no question that great advertising is central to Coke's global dominance for more than one hundred years. In fact, the history of advertising and the history of Coca Cola are inseparable, and no other advertiser has engaged in a cultural dialog with consumers for so long, or as well. What is Coke's "secret formula" for advertising success? Since the nineteenth century, Coke's ads have spoken to consumers in a variety of media and using varied approaches. What unites all of their best ads is that while Coke ads may not show us as we are, they appeal to our hopes for how we would like to be. Whether we are looking for "the real thing," "the pause that refreshes," or world peace, Co

Economics: The Functions of Advertising and IMC in Free Markets

In Chapter 1, we looked at the communication dimension of advertising to get a sense of what advertising is and how it works. The marketing dimension, then, showed us some of the many types of advertising that companies use to help them succeed, and it showed us where advertising fits in a company's overall marketing strategy. Now we consider a broader dimension—economics, which created the need for advertising and has made it a staple of the free enterprise system. As English historian Raymond Williams wrote, advertising is "the official art of capitalist society."

Have you ever wondered what a world without ads would be like? For some, that world sounds attractive. Is advertising really necessary for anything important? In this chapter, we'll explain how the economic, cultural, and social developments influenced the evolution of advertising through the centuries. Then, in Chapter 3, we'll look at how advertising in turn influences the economy and society and, as a result, often becomes an object of controversy and criticism.

Principles of Free-Market Economics

In the United States and in many, but not most, countries of the world, a market economy determines what and how much is produced and consumed. Harvard economist N. Gregory Mankiw defines a market economy as one in which "Firms decide whom to hire and what to make. Households decide . . . what to buy with their incomes. These firms and households interact in the marketplace, where prices and self-interest guide their decisions."[6] A market economy is characterized by four assumptions:

1. *Self-interest.* People and firms pursue their own goals. By nature, people are acquisitive. They always want more—for less. Open competition between self-interested sellers marketing to self-interested buyers naturally leads to greater product availability at more competitive prices.

2. *Complete information.* Buyers make better decisions when they have more information about the products they can choose from. Sellers can also more efficiently find consumers of their goods by providing information about what they sell.

3. *Many buyers and sellers.* Having many sellers ensures that if one does not meet customer needs, another will capitalize on the situation by producing a better product. Similarly, a wide range of buyers ensures that sellers can find customers interested in the unique products they are able to produce at a fair price.

4. *Absence of externalities (social costs).* Sometimes the sale or consumption of products may benefit or harm other people who are not involved in the transaction and didn't pay for the product. For example, in March 2009, India's Tata Group introduced the world's cheapest car, Nano, which retails for just $2,000. This will give millions of poor Indians access to affordable transportation. But it may also contribute significantly to health problems and climate change through increases in air pollution and carbon emissions. In these cases, government may use taxation and/or regulation to compensate for or eliminate the externalities.

These assumptions describe an *ideal* economy, not one that actually exists. For example, you almost never have complete information about products that you buy. But the assumption tells us that the more information you have about a product before you buy it, the more satisfied you will probably be with your purchase. Free-market economists believe that the closer an economy comes to satisfying the four assumptions, the better for everyone. To see why advertising and IMC can benefit society, let's consider how they contribute to furthering these economic values.

Functions and Effects of Advertising in a Free Economy

Advertising performs a variety of functions and, when executed correctly, its effects may be dramatic. To see how this works, let's go back to the beginnings of Coca-Cola, when druggist John Pemberton was still mixing the syrup in his lab. (For a chronology of the evolution of the Coca-Cola brand and company, see Exhibit 2-1.)

Pemberton's business partner and bookkeeper, Frank Robinson, suggested the name "Coca-Cola" to identify the two main flavors and because he thought that "the two Cs would look well in advertising."[7] Robinson wrote down the name in his flowing script, creating the logo that is now instantly recognizable around the world. Later, a distinctive bottle shape became the standard throughout the company. The proprietary curvy bottle helped customers differentiate Coca-Cola from other drinks. The creation of the Coca-Cola logo and contour bottle illustrates one of the most basic functions of **branding** as well as advertising: *to identify products and their source and to differentiate them from others.* (The functions and effects discussed here are listed in Exhibit 2-2.)

When Pemberton first began selling Coca-Cola at Jacobs' Pharmacy, he needed to let people know what it was—although we associate the word *cola* with a cold, dark, bubbly beverage, the people of Atlanta didn't automatically make the same connection. Therefore,

1880s and 1890s

1884 John Pemberton develops "Pemberton's French Wine Coca," an alcoholic headache remedy.

1885 Prohibition laws are passed in Atlanta; Pemberton reformulates his drink into a nonalcoholic version and calls it "Coca-Cola."

1886 Coca-Cola goes on sale in an Atlanta drugstore.

1887 A dying Pemberton sells stakes in his company to four businessmen.

1888 Asa Candler secures sole rights to make and sell Coca-Cola.

1894 Coca-Cola is first sold in bottles.

1900s and 1910s

1901 Candler begins the first free drink coupon campaign.

1906 D'Arcy creates a newspaper ad campaign for Coca-Cola.

1906 The first international syrup plant opens in Havana, Cuba.

1911 Coca-Cola's advertising budget reaches $1 million.

1912 Copycat colas abound.

1915 The "contour" Coke bottle is designed and becomes the standard.

1916 Candler resigns from Coca-Cola and is elected mayor of Atlanta.

1919 Coca-Cola introduces the six-pack to encourage buying enough to take home.

1920s and 1930s

1923 Robert Woodruff becomes company president.

1928 More people drink Coca-Cola from bottles than from the fountain.

1928 Coca-Cola sponsors the Olympic Games in Amsterdam.

1930 Bottlers go door-to-door installing Coke-branded bottle openers in homes.

1931 Haddon Sundblom's classic Santa Claus appears in Coca-Cola ads.

1935 Coin-operated vending machines become widely available.

1940s, 1950s, and 1960s

1941 After years of battling the short form, the company begins to use the word "Coke" in ads.

1942 Coca-Cola avoids sugar rationing by supplying the army with Coke.

1943 General Eisenhower sends a telegram asking for 10 Coca-Cola bottling plants to be set up in war zones.

1950 Coke is the first product to appear on the cover of *Time* magazine.

1955 Coca-Cola introduces family-size bottles.

1964 First pop-tab cans introduced.

1970s and 1980s

1971 Coca-Cola teaches the world to sing with the "hilltop" TV spot.

1978 The People's Republic of China allows Coca-Cola, and no other drink company, to operate in the country.

1982 Diet Coke is born.

1985 New Coke is released with much fanfare in April but is rejected by consumers.

1985 Classic Coke returns to the shelves in July, sweetened entirely with high-fructose corn syrup.

1985 Astronauts use a special "space can" to drink Coca-Cola aboard the shuttle.

1990s and 2000s

1993 Polar bears appear in ads as part of the "Always Coca-Cola" campaign. Advertising annual spending reaches $1 billion.

2002 Coca-Cola begins high-visibility sponsorship of *American Idol*.

2005 Coke Zero, sweetened with aspartame, is developed and marketed.

2011 Coke introduces special white cans to partner with the World Wildlife Fund and protect polar bears.

2014 Coke sparks controversy with "It's beautiful" Super Bowl ad.

2015 Coke is served 1.8 billion times each day. Coke global advertising expenditures nearly $3 billion each year.

Exhibit 2-1

Coca-Cola chronology: the story of Coke and its parent company.

Exhibit 2-2

Functions and effects of advertising as a marketing tool.

- To identify products and differentiate them from others.
- To communicate information about the product, its features, and its place of sale.
- To induce consumers to try new products and to suggest reuse.
- To stimulate the distribution of a product.
- To increase product use.
- To build value, brand preference, and loyalty.
- To lower the overall cost of sales.

Pemberton and Robinson added the suggestion *drink* before *Coca-Cola* on the signs that they had painted and placed in front of the drugstore.[8] Ads in the *Atlanta Journal* let readers know why they should drink it (because it is "delicious, exhilarating, refreshing, and invigorating,"), how much it cost, and where they could get it. This demonstrates another basic function of advertising: *to communicate information about the product, its features, and its location of sale.*

After Asa Candler gained control of the Coca-Cola Company, he began to develop the drink's market on a grander scale. He mailed thousands of coupons for free drinks to Atlanta residents. Thousands more were handed out on the street and inserted in magazines. To cover the costs of the samples, the company gave free syrup to the soda fountains that offered the beverage. The free sample campaign accompanied Coca-Cola's introduction in new markets. This campaign illustrates another function of advertising: *to induce consumers to try new products and to suggest reuse.*

Through the early part of the 20th century, Coca-Cola wasn't the dominant force we know today. Competitors such as Pepsi and the now-defunct Moxie cut into Coca-Cola's market share. Outside forces also threatened the entire industry; sugar rationing during wartimes was especially damaging. Prior to the entry of the United States in World War II, Coca-Cola executives persuaded the government to give Coke to troops to boost their morale.

To accomplish this, the D'Arcy advertising agency gathered endorsements from U.S. officers in training camps to support Coke's bid to become an official military supplier—and therefore to be exempt from rationing. The War Department agreed to the plan, and Coca-Cola borrowed $5.5 million to establish 64 bottling plants near the front lines. The risky investment had great returns. Surveys found returning vets preferred Coke by eight to one over Pepsi.[9] Coca-Cola masterfully blended patriotism with another of the most important functions of advertising: *to increase product use.*

As soft drinks became a staple in convenience stores, restaurants, and homes throughout the United States, Coca-Cola began campaigns outside the country. The first international bottling plants were established in Canada, Cuba, and Panama in 1906; today, the company bottles Coke in more than 200 countries. Coca-Cola franchise bottlers around the world can tweak the recipe to match local tastes by altering the amount of sweetener they add to the base syrup. Bottlers and distributors also supplement the company's advertising with their own promotions and event sponsorships—from a community clean-up day in Armenia to a major film festival in Korea. Through various activities, Coca-Cola has succeeded in accomplishing yet another function of advertising: *to stimulate the distribution of a product*—in this case, on a global level.

In a free-market economy, when one company starts to make significant profits, other companies immediately jump in to compete. Over the years, to battle the constant competitive threat, Coca-Cola has funded ongoing marketing communications campaigns to accomplish yet another function of advertising: *to build value, brand preference, and loyalty.* Although the taste test wars of the 1980s showed that many people liked the taste of Pepsi better than that of Coke, such blind preference has never knocked Coca-Cola out of the top spot. A century of consistently upbeat messages has made its mark. Coca-Cola advertising, such as its current campaign, "Make it Happy," has always promoted a common voice and a common theme: Coca-Cola makes life's relaxing moments even better.

For more than 120 years, the Coca-Cola Company has used a variety of media to communicate this message to diverse audiences. Why? To achieve the most significant function of advertising: *to lower the overall cost of sales.* For the cost of reaching just one prospect through personal selling, companies can reach thousands of people through media advertising. The average cost to make a face-to-face field sales call is about $170. Multiply that $170 by the more than 15 million people who watch a network TV show, and the cost comes to a mind-boggling $2.55 billion. However, for only $500,000, Coca-Cola can buy a 30-second TV commercial during a top-rated show and reach the same 15 million people. Through television, advertisers can talk to a thousand prospects for only $30—less than 20 percent of what it costs to talk to a single prospect through personal selling.[10]

Now, considering this brief synopsis of Coca-Cola history, how does Coke's advertising fit with the basic assumptions of a free-market economy? Has Coke's advertising helped make the soft drink available to more people at lower cost? Has it informed them about where they can buy Coke? Has the freedom to advertise contributed to the competitive environment? What externalities might have had a positive or negative impact on the Coca-Cola Company's efforts to market its beverages?

The Brand

The history of Coca-Cola provides a useful introduction to a powerful marketing idea: branding. The vast majority of IMC activities are devoted to branding. Consider each of these pairings: soft drink—Coca-Cola; coffee—Starbucks; digital music player—iPod; wireless service—Verizon. In each case, a generic product category is paired with a strong brand. To the extent that you found yourself having clearer, stronger, and more positive responses to the brands than to the categories, you are experiencing the power of brands.

But what is a **brand**? Scott M. Davis and Michael Dunn define the concept as follows:

> Promises made to customers . . . based on multiple experiences over time . . . delivered with consistently high level of quality and value . . . that are perceived to be unparalleled relative to the competition, . . . ultimately resulting in deep, trust-based relationships . . ., which in turn [garner] great amounts of loyalty and profits over time.[11]

Let's unpack this definition to highlight the following important elements: A brand is a promise about a product. It allows consumers to have an expectation that a product will do something valuable or desirable, and that this will happen each time you buy or use the product. Your next hamburger at McDonald's will taste like the last one. Your next Toyota Camry will offer reliability and comfort just like the last one.

Additionally, the brand's value to a loyal user is unmatched. People who prefer Coke do not accept that other cola brands are just as good. Instead, they believe that Coke is the best. Because of this perception, customers form trust-based relationships with the brand. So if Apple introduces a new product, such as the Apple Watch, millions will buy one sight unseen. Apple has earned their trust and they believe the product will provide satisfaction.

Finally, because a brand is considered to be unique and to consistently deliver desired benefits, companies can charge more for their product. Any consumer can find cheaper substitutes for Coke and Apple products. But the cheaper alternatives are not attractive to loyal users because of the value attached to the Coke and Apple brands.

To understand the power of a brand, think back to the big advertisers of the 19th century. You may recall that these were manufacturers, companies that made textiles, or equipment, or canned goods. Compare that with two of the biggest advertisers of the present day: Apple and Nike. Neither of these companies manufactures anything. Their products are produced at independent factories, typically located overseas. But each company stands for an important idea in the mind of consumers. The financial worth of most modern companies that serve consumers is directly related to the strength of their brands.

Among the more specific benefits provided to a company by strong brands are these:

1. They allow companies to charge more for their products.
2. They afford protection against price wars.
3. They allow for a greater chance a new product will succeed.
4. They afford leverage in negotiating with channel partners.
5. They make companies more attractive to co-branding partners.
6. They help companies more effectively deal with a brand crisis.
7. They help companies recruit top talent.
8. They garner consumer loyalty.[12]

Each of these benefits has been enjoyed by Coca-Cola over its long history. For example, item 6 in the list suggests that strong brands help companies deal with a crisis. Coke experienced such a crisis when it introduced New Coke. Loyal Coke drinkers rejected the brand's reformulation, but quickly forgave the company when it brought back the old formula. Or consider item 3. When Coke introduced Diet Coke, the brand extension was an immediate hit.

Today Coca-Cola is one of the largest, most successful, and best-known companies in the world. And a good deal of that success can be traced to the outstanding advertising and IMC campaigns that have built the Coke brand. But a bit of luck was involved too. Had Coke been invented 20 years earlier, no one might know of it today. This is because, as we'll see in the next section, Coca-Cola was introduced to the marketplace just as advertising was becoming an important social force in the United States. To see an overview of important milestones in advertising history, see Exhibit 2-3.

The Evolution of Advertising as an Economic Tool

Thousands of years ago, people spent most of their time meeting basic survival needs: food, clothing, shelter. They lived in small, isolated communities where artisans and farmers bartered products and services. Distribution was limited to how far vendors could walk and "advertising" to how loud they could shout. Because goods weren't produced in great quantity, there was no need for advertising to stimulate mass purchases. There were also no mass media available for possible advertisers to use. Nevertheless, archaeologists have found evidence of messages meant to encourage trade among the Babylonians dating back as far as 3000 BC.

(continued on page 44)

3000 BC–AD 1	AD 500–1599	1600–1799	1800–1899
3000 BC Written advertisement offering "Whole gold coin" for runaway slave "Shem." **500 BC** Political and trade graffiti on Pompeii walls. **AD 1** First uppercase lettering appears on Greek buildings.	**1455** First printed Bible. **1472** First printed ad in English tacked on London church doors. **1544** Claude Garamond, first "typefounder," perfects a roman typeface that bears his name and is still used today.	**1650** First newspaper ad offers reward for stolen horses. **1662** *London Gazette* offers first advertising supplement. **1704** First ads in America published in the *Boston Newsletter.* **1729** Ben Franklin is first to use "white space" and illustration in ads. **1785** Widespread use of advertising and long print runs become possible.	**1841** Volney B. Palmer becomes first "newspaper agent" (advertising agent) in America. **1844** First magazine ad runs. **1869** Francis W. Ayer founds ad agency bearing his father's name, N. W. Ayer & Sons, in Philadelphia. He initiates first "for commission" ad contract (1876), first market survey for an ad (1879), and first on-staff creative services (art in 1890, copywriting in 1892). **1888** *Printers' Ink* is first U.S. publication for ad profession.

1900–1919	1920–1939	1940–1959	1960–1969
1900 Psychologists study the attention-getting and persuasive qualities of advertising. **1900** Northwestern University is first to offer advertising as a discipline. **1903** Scripps-McRae League of Newspapers appoints ad censor, rejects $500,000 in ads in first year. **1905** First national ad plan is for the "Gillette Safety Razor." **1911** First "truth in advertising" codes are established by what is now called the American Advertising Federation (AAF).	**1920s** Albert Lasker, father of modern advertising, calls advertising "salesmanship in print." First ad testimonials by movie stars appear. Full-color printing is available in magazines. **1922** First radio ad solves radio's need for financing. **1924** N. W. Ayer produces first sponsored radio broadcast, the "Eveready Hour." **1930** *Advertising Age* magazine is founded. **1938** Wheeler-Lea amendments to FTC Act of 1938 grant FTC further power to curb false ad practices.	**1946** America has 12 TV stations broadcasting to the public. **1947** Lanham Trademark Act protects brand names and slogans. **1948** 46 TV stations are operating and 300 others are awaiting FCC approval. **1950** First political ads, by Gov. Dewey of New York, appear on TV. **1950s** David Ogilvy's "Hathaway man" and "Commander Whitehead" become popular ad personae.	**1960s** Doyle Dane Bernbach's "Think small" ad for American Volkswagen becomes one of the most famous ads of the decade, establishing a strong market position for the smallest European import. The agency's slogan for Avis, "We're only No. 2, so we try harder," is also very successful. New York's Madison Avenue becomes known worldwide as the center of the advertising world and features the best in advertising creativity.

1970–1979	1980–1989	1990–2000	2001–2010
1971 Armed services begin first advertising for the new "all-volunteer" military ("Be all that you can be in the Army"). **1972** The *Ad Age* article "Positioning: The Battle for Your Mind" by Al Ries and Jack Trout details the strategy of positioning that dominates the 1970s. **1973** Oil shortages begin period of "demarketing," ads aimed at slowing demand.	**1980s** Ad agency megamergers take place worldwide. **1982** First edition of *Contemporary Advertising* is published. **1984** The Internet (government controlled since 1973) is turned over to the private sector. **1986** *Marketing Warfare* by Al Ries and Jack Trout portrays marketing in terms of classic warfare manual written by General Clausewitz in 1831.	**1990s** A recession leads marketers to shift funds from advertising to sales promotion. **1994** Media glut leads to market fragmentation; network TV is no longer sole medium for reaching total marketplace. Ad professions adopt integrated marketing communications (IMC) as the new strategy to build market relationships. **1995** Google founders Larry Page and Sergey Brin meet at Stanford. **2000** The Internet is the fastest-growing new ad medium since TV, with 400 million users. Google introduces AdWords.	**2002** Following 9-11 attacks and financial crisis, a general economic slump hammers ad spending. **2004** Mark Zuckerburg launches Facebook. **2005** Online advertisers spend $8.32 billion to reach the 170 million wired U.S. residents. **2006** Advertisers begin creating HDTV spots (shooting digitally instead of on analog tape). **2007** U.S. ad agency revenue surges 8.6% to $31 billion, led by double-digit growth in digital advertising. **2008 to 2010.** Broad global recession leads to cutbacks in ad expenditures. Two major advertisers, GM and Chrysler, are guided through restructuring after a government takeover. **2010**-present **2013** Internet ad spending greater than radio, magazine, and out-of-home combined. **2014** Growth of spending on mobile advertising tops all other ad categories. **2015** Snapchat annoucnes 3V, a new native video ad product. **2015** Total US programmatic ad spending tops $15 billion.

Exhibit 2-3
Timetable of advertising history.

:: The Modern History of Advertising

While advertising is thousands of years old, it has come into its own only in the last 100 years, thanks to a growing population hungry for goods and services and a rapidly changing technology that could make these products available.

If we look back at the ad campaigns of 30, 50, 70, and even 100 years ago, we get a fascinating indication of how life was lived back then, and we can also see how the development of modern advertising parallels the development of our own standard of living. As British writer and diplomat Norman Douglas said in 1917, "You can tell the ideals of a nation by its advertisements."

• Study the array of historical ads in this Portfolio Review and consider how well each relates to the seven functions and effects of advertising discussed in this chapter.

Coca-Cola was first served at a small pharmacy in Atlanta in 1886. Coca-Cola's inventor, John S. Pemberton, placed an ad in the *Atlanta Journal* proclaiming that the soft drink was "delicious and refreshing."

Source: Library of Congress Prints and Photographs, LC-USZ62-39705

This full-color ad from the 1920s would have been considered very modern at the time of publication. Then as now, Coke combines a contemporary image with a timeless message.

© The Image Works Archives/The Image Works

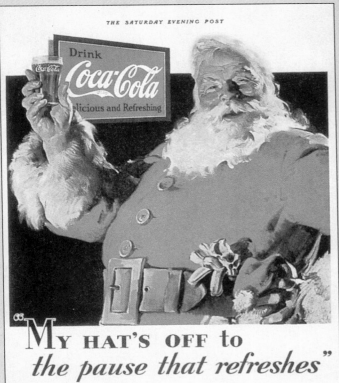

Appearing in publications across the country, this 1930s print ad for Coca-Cola was one of the first to incorporate Santa Claus. Interestingly, it was not until the mid-19th century that Santa Claus began to be portrayed in this rotund, jolly manner, and in fact, artists working for Coca-Cola played a major role in popularizing the Santa Claus we know today.

Source: The Coca-Cola Company

McCann-Erickson art designer Phil Messina and director Harvey Gabor shot three versions—one in England and two in Italy, each with a cast of hundreds—before they found gold with the classic 1971 "Hilltop" TV spot. Young, modern people from around the world throng on a hillside to drink Coca-Cola and sing, "I'd like to teach the world to sing in perfect harmony/I'd like to buy the world a Coke and keep it company." The commercial flopped in Europe, but U.S. audiences embraced the spot and the music, deluging the company and radio stations with requests for it.

Source: The Coca-Cola Company

Do polar bears and penguins really get along? Since they live on different continents, we may never really know. However, Coca-Cola's playful depiction of polar bears and penguins sharing a Coke as an ice-breaker is another great example of how Coca-Cola continues to build value, brand preference, and loyalty with their advertisements.

Source: The Coca-Cola Company

Coke's "Arctic Explorer," which ran in 2011 and 2012, illustrated the plight of real polar bears. Do you think that Coca-Cola's decision to issue the beverage in all-white cans helped consumers to associate with and relate to the plight of the polar bears?

Source: The Coca-Cola Company

Coke has been advertising for well over a century. As you can see here, youthful vibrant ads keep the brand's image fresh and attractive to a new generation of consumers.

Source: The Coca-Cola Company

An early form of advertising. Until the advent of public schooling, most people couldn't read—so signs featured symbols of the goods or services for sale, such as the chair on this cabinetmaker's sign in Williamsburg, Virginia.

© Pat & Chuck Blackley/Alamy

wasn't until 1729 that Ben Franklin, innovator of dvertising art, made ads more readable by using larger eadlines, changing fonts, and adding art. This 1767 ad nnounces the availability of Stage Waggons to carry assengers from Powles Hook Ferry to Philadelphia.

(continued from page 38)

Early Advertising

Civilizations began emerging approximately 5,000 years ago as people mastered agriculture. A stable food supply meant people could settle, and soon cities began forming in Europe, Asia, and South America. Trade among cities led to the development of merchant classes and markets.

During this **preindustrial age,** several important events contributed to the eventual development of modern advertising. The Chinese invented paper, and Europe had its first paper mill by 1275. Around 1439, Johannes Gutenberg invented the movable-type printing press in Germany. The press was not only the most important development in the history of advertising, and indeed communication, but it also revolutionized the way people lived and worked.

The introduction of printing allowed information to be established, substantiated, recorded, and transported. People no longer had to rely on their memories. Movable letters provided the flexibility to print in local dialects. The slow hand transcription of monks and scholars gave way to more rapid volume printing by a less select group. Some entrepreneurs bought printing presses, mounted them in wagons, and traveled from town to town selling printing. This new technology made possible the early instances of advertising—posters, handbills, and signs—and, eventually, the first mass medium—the newspaper.

In 1472, the first ad in English appeared: a handbill tacked on church doors in London announcing a prayer book for sale. Two hundred years later, the first newspaper ad was published, offering a reward for the return of 12 stolen horses. Soon newspapers carried ads for coffee, chocolate, tea, real estate, medicines, and even personal ads. These early ads were still directed to a very limited number of people: the customers of the coffeehouses where most newspapers were read.

By the early 1700s, the world's population stood at about 600 million people, and some cities were big enough to support larger volumes of advertising. Samuel Johnson, a famous English literary figure, observed in 1758 that advertisements were now so numerous they were "negligently perused," and it had become necessary to gain attention "by magnificence of promise." This was the beginning of *puffery* in advertising.

In the colonies, the *Boston Newsletter* began carrying ads in 1704. About 25 years later, Benjamin Franklin, the father of advertising art, made ads more readable by using large headlines and considerable white space. In fact, Franklin was the first American known to use illustrations in ads.

In the mid-1700s, the Industrial Revolution began in England, and by the early 1800s, it had reached North America. Machinery began to replace animal power. By using machines to mass-produce goods with uniform quality, large companies increased their productivity. It now costs people less to buy a product than to make it themselves. As people left the farm to work in the city, mass urban markets began to emerge, further fueling market development and the growth of advertising.

The Industrial Age and the Birth of Ad Agencies

The **industrial age** started during the second half of the 19th century and lasted well into the 20th. As we have seen, ads were created prior to the industrial age, but it was not until this period that it can be said that an advertising industry existed anywhere in the world. It was a period marked by tremendous growth and maturation of the country's industrial base. As U.S. industry met the basic needs of much of the population, commodity markets became saturated. Fresh mass markets then developed for the new, inexpensive brands of consumer luxury and convenience goods called **consumer packaged goods.**

By the mid-1800s, the world's population had doubled to 1.2 billion. Producers needed mass consumption to match the high levels of manufactured goods. Fortunately, breakthroughs in bulk transportation—the railroad and steamship—facilitated distribution of products beyond the manufacturer's local market. But with the need for mass consumption came the increasing need for mass marketing techniques to inform consumers of the availability of products.

During the 1800s, manufacturers were principally concerned with production. The burden of marketing fell on wholesalers, who used advertising primarily as an information vehicle.

Ethical Issues

Ethical Dilemma or Ethical Lapse?

False and misleading advertising—and all the damage it can create—begins with unethical judgments. Hence, it pays to understand the differences between ethical dilemmas and ethical lapses.

An *ethical dilemma* arises from an unresolved interpretation of an ethical issue. To begin, there is a distinction between "legal" and "ethical." For example, should advertisers attempt to persuade poor, inner-city youths to buy sneakers priced at more than $200 a pair? There's no law against it, but the responsible action (both socially and morally) may be to refrain. And so we have an ethical dilemma.

How are such ethical dilemmas resolved? The late University of Wisconsin professor Ivan L. Preston believed that advertising professionals often find ethics largely synonymous with legality. But as Preston wrote, "You can be ethical only when you have the option of being unethical. You can't choose to be ethical when you can't choose at all, so ethics begins only where the law ends."

The prospect of a serious protest from watchdog groups, civic leaders, and clergy generally eliminates an advertiser's hesitancy to resolve an ethical dilemma. For small companies, a hostile public reaction can even lead to bankruptcy. In contrast, a strong market leader may have the goodwill and deep pockets to survive an ethically borderline advertising campaign—and go forward to stimulate greater name awareness from the ensuing publicity. Calvin Klein's jeans campaign, for example, depicted models who looked 15, were dressed skimpily, and posed suggestively. The huge outcry against those "kiddie porn" ads that emerged from all sectors, including trade publications and the national press, prompted Klein to discontinue the campaign. However, the press continued carrying the story for weeks.

Ethical dilemmas can occur because advertisers typically sell brands, not just products. Because each brand must be presented as being different from other brands—even though functionally it may not be—advertisers are tempted to create false differences. Incomplete information is another breeding ground for ethical dilemmas. Advertisers tend to highlight the good things about their brands and omit the neutral and bad. Nothing that's said is false, yet the ad does not tell the whole truth. The use of technology to distort images to portray the product most favorably can create new ethical dilemmas. Models, for example, can be made to appear slimmer than they really are, a consequence that some have linked to a rise in eating disorders in young women. Feminist lawmakers in Europe believe consumers should be warned when commercial images have been digitally altered. And Dartmouth digital forensics professor Hany Farid may have the tool to help lawmakers enforce such laws. Farid's software can analyze digital images and determine the degree to which they've been changed with software such as Photoshop.

In contrast, an *ethical lapse* is a clear case of unprincipled conduct and, in many cases, may even include illegal behavior. The Federal Trade Commission (FTC) is the enforcement agency against such lapses in the United

© Evan Agostini/Liaison/Getty Images

States. It brings lawsuits against companies that have engaged in illegal advertising claims—and it can even name advertising agencies as defendants.

A myriad of federal, state, and local laws govern what is legal in advertising, but laws ultimately reflect ethical judgments. As for self-regulation, the creative code of the American Association of Advertising Agencies also reflects legalities rather than philosophies. However, the eternal question remains: When, how, and by whom are these laws to be enforced in resolving ethical dilemmas and lapses?

Exploring the Internet

In addition to consumer and government regulation, the advertising industry itself is concerned about ethics in advertising. One of the industry's most prestigious organizations, the American Advertising Federation (AAF), sponsors the annual Vance L. Stickell Memorial Student Internship Program. Established in 1989 in honor of the former executive vice president, marketing, for the *Los Angeles Times*, the program is intended to further the awareness and understanding of the advertising process and business ethics among students. Visit the AAF Website (www.aaf.org) and learn more about how you may qualify for this prestigious award.

Sources: Ivan Preston, *The Tangled Web They Weave: Truth, Falsity and Advertisers* (Madison, WI: University of Wisconsin Press, 1996); FTC News Release, "FTC Charges Marketers of Foot Pads with Deceptive Advertising; Seeks Funds for Consumer Redress," January 28, 2009, accessed on March 23, 2009, at www.casewatch.org/ftc/news/2009/kinoki.shtml. Steve Lohr, "Photoshopped or not? A tool to tell." *New York Times*, November 29, 2011.

Ads appeared in publications called *price currents* that informed retailers about the sources of supply and shipping schedules for commodities. Montgomery Ward and Sears Roebuck produced the earliest catalogs, bringing a wide variety of products to new, rural markets. Only a few innovative manufacturers (mostly of patent medicines, soaps, tobacco products, and canned foods) foresaw the usefulness of mass media advertising to stimulate consumer demand.

This full page of advertising from an 1894 Scientific American (www.scientificamerican.com) is historically telling. The ads feature unbranded commodities such as soap, paper, paint, or services. Advertising focused on persuading consumers to prefer specific brands was still decades away.

The American *profession* of advertising began when Volney B. Palmer set up business in Philadelphia in 1841. Palmer was essentially a mediator, buying large volumes of discounted newspaper advertising space and reselling to advertisers at a profit. The advertisers usually prepared the ads themselves.

In 1869, Francis Ayer formed an ad agency in Philadelphia and named it after his father. N. W. Ayer & Sons was the first agency to charge a commission based on the "net cost of space" and the first to conduct a formal market survey. Ayer became the first ad agency to operate as agencies do today—planning, creating, and executing complete ad campaigns in exchange for media-paid commissions or fees from advertisers. In 1892, Ayer set up a copy department and hired the first full-time agency copywriter.

The telegraph, telephone, typewriter, phonograph, and, later, motion pictures all let people communicate as never before. With the development of the nationwide railroad system, the United States entered a period of spectacular economic growth. In 1896, when the federal government inaugurated rural-free mail delivery, direct mail advertising and mail-order selling flourished. Manufacturers now had an ever-increasing variety of products to sell and a new way to deliver their advertisements and products to the public.

With the advent of public schooling, the nation reached an unparalleled 90 percent literacy rate. Manufacturers gained a large reading public that could understand print ads. The United States thus entered the 20th century as a great industrial state with a national marketing system propelled by advertising. With the end of World War I, the modern period in advertising emerged.

During the 19th century, wholesalers controlled the marketing process because they distributed the manufacturers' unbranded commodity products. When those markets became saturated, though, the wholesalers started playing one manufacturer off against another. This hurt manufacturers' profits dramatically, so they started looking for ways to wrest back control. The manufacturers changed their focus from a *production* orientation to a *marketing* orientation. They dedicated themselves to new product development, strengthened their own sales forces, packaged and branded their products, and engaged in heavy national brand advertising. Early brands included Wrigley's spearmint gum, Coca-Cola, Jell-O, Kellogg's corn flakes, and Campbell's soup.

In the 1920s, the era of salesmanship had arrived and its bible was *Scientific Advertising*, written by the legendary copywriter Claude Hopkins at Albert Lasker's agency, Lord & Thomas (see People behind the Ads at the end of this chapter). Published in 1923, it claimed that "Advertising has reached the status of a science. It is based on fixed principles." Hopkins outlawed humor, style, literary flair, and anything that might detract from his basic copy strategy of a preemptive product claim repeated boldly and often.[13]

Radio was born at about the same time and rapidly became a powerful new advertising medium. World and national news now arrived direct from the scene, and a whole new array of family entertainment—music, drama, and sports—became possible. Suddenly, national advertisers could quickly reach huge audiences. In fact, the first radio shows were produced by their sponsors' ad agencies.

On October 29, 1929, the stock market crashed, the Great Depression began, and advertising expenditures plummeted. In the face of declining sales and corporate budget cutting, the advertising industry needed to improve its effectiveness. It turned to research. Daniel Starch, A. C. Nielsen, and George Gallup founded research groups to study consumer attitudes and preferences. By providing information on public opinion, the performance of ad messages, and sales of advertised products, these companies started the marketing research industry.

During this period, each brand sought to convince the public of its own special qualities. Wheaties was the "Breakfast of Champions" not because of its ingredients but because of its advertising. Manufacturers followed this strategy of *product differentiation* vigorously, seeking to portray their brands as different from and better than the competition by offering consumers quality, variety, and convenience.

The Depression ended in 1941 with America's involvement in World War II. The ad industry did its part in aiding with the war effort, as demonstrated in the ad shown below.

The Golden Age of Advertising

The postwar period from 1946 through the 1970s is sometimes referred to as advertising's "Golden Age." This is because the introduction of television helped make the advertising industry a focus of great attention, which led to both acclaim and criticism.

Postwar prosperity of the late 1940s and early 1950s seemed to many to create a culture in which consumers tried to climb the social ladder by buying more and more modern products. A creative revolution ensued in which ads focused on product features that implied social acceptance, style, luxury, and success. Giants in the field emerged—people such as Leo Burnett, David Ogilvy, and Bill Bernbach, who built their agencies from scratch and forever changed the way advertising was planned and created.[14]

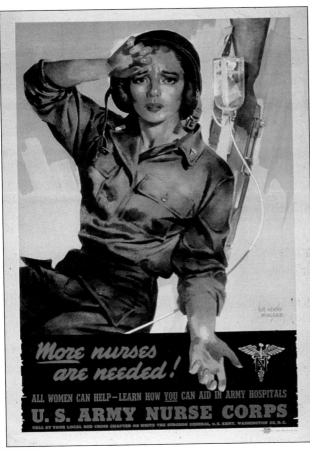

Advertisers and agencies pitched in to do their part during World War II. Shortages of many basic consumer goods reduced ad expenditures during the war.

Artwork by Henry McAlear, Image from the History of Medicine (NLM)

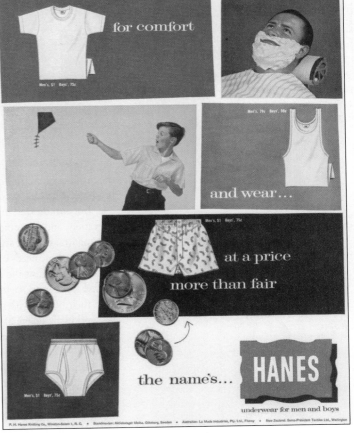

By the middle of the 20th century, advertisers knew it was important to tell consumers why they should prefer a particular brand over its competitors. This 1958 ad for Hanes gives consumers several benefits to think about.

© Vintage Skivvies

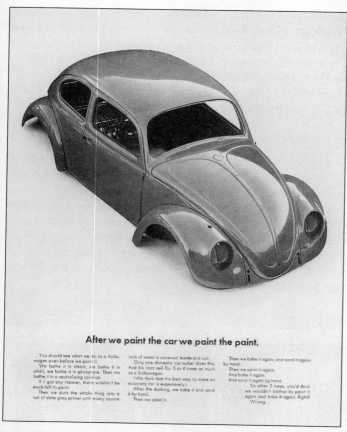

After we paint the car we paint the paint.

Some shapes are hard to improve on.

Dealer Name

Doyle Dane Bernbach's "Think small" ad for Volkswagen was named the greatest ad of all time by Advertising Age. These clever, simple, and elegant ads from the same campaign offer further proof of the brilliance of William Bernbach's creative talent. Learn more about Bernbach in People behind the Ads at the end of Chapter 2.
Source: Volkswagen of America, Inc.

Rosser Reeves of the Ted Bates Agency introduced the idea that every ad must point out the product's USP *(unique selling proposition)*—features that differentiate it from competitive products. The USP was a logical extension of the Lasker and Hopkins "reason why" credo.

But as more and more imitative products showed up in the marketplace, all offering quality, variety, and convenience, the effectiveness of this strategy wore out. Companies turned to a new mantra: **market segmentation,** a process by which marketers searched for unique groups of people whose needs could be addressed through more specialized products. The image era of the 1960s was thus the natural culmination of the creative revolution. Advertising's emphasis shifted from product features to brand image or brand personality as advertisers sought to align their brands with particularly profitable market segments. Cadillac, for example, became the worldwide image of luxury, the consummate symbol of success.

Just as me-too product features killed the product differentiation era, me-too images eventually killed the market segmentation era. With increased competition, a new kind of advertising strategy evolved in the 1970s, in which competitors' strengths became just as important as the advertiser's. Jack Trout and Al Ries insisted that what really mattered was how the brand ranked against the competition in the consumer's mind—how it was positioned.

Positioning strategy proved to be an effective way to separate a particular brand from its competitors by associating that brand with a particular set of customer needs that ranked high on the consumer's priority list. Thus, it became a more effective way to use product differentiation and market segmentation. The most famous American ads of the positioning era were Volkswagen ("Think small"), Avis ("We're only no. 2"), and 7UP ("The uncola"). Product failures of the period, such as Life Savers gum and RCA computers, were blamed on flawed positioning.

Demarketing is used to dampen demand for products, especially those that create unwanted costs for society. This public service message created for France's ANPAA (National Association for Prevention of Alcoholism and Addiction) uses the metaphor of a fish hook and the tagline: "It's your choice to keep off the hook" to convey the dangerous addictive qualities of alcohol.

Source: CGSS/ANPAA

Product differentiation, market segmentation, and positioning are all important strategies to understand, and you'll learn more about them in Chapter 6.

While this was all going on in the United States, across the Atlantic, a new generation of advertising professionals had graduated from the training grounds of Procter & Gamble (P&G) and Colgate-Palmolive and were now teaching their clients the secrets of mass marketing. Lagging somewhat behind their U.S. counterparts due to the economic ravages of World War II, European marketers discovered the USP and the one-page strategic brief, or summary statement, that P&G had popularized to bring focus to ad campaigns. Immediately following the war, French advertising pioneer Marcel Bleustein-Blanchet waged a frustrating battle to introduce U.S. research techniques to his country; a decade or two later, in-depth attitude and behavioral research was all the rage.[15] Because commercial TV was not yet as big as in the United States, European advertisers divided their media money between newspapers and outdoor media, along with a healthy dose of cinema advertising. Germany, the Netherlands, and Scandinavia wouldn't get commercial TV for another decade.[16]

In the 1970s, though, the European Common Market already offered untapped opportunities. Following the American example, agencies and clients began to think multinationally to gain economies of scale. But it was not easy. While physically close, the countries of Europe were still separated by a chasm of cultural diversity that made the use of single Europe-wide campaigns nearly impossible.[17]

The Postindustrial Age

Beginning around 1980, the **postindustrial age** has been a period of cataclysmic change. Citizens became increasingly aware of the sensitive environment in which we live and alarmed by our dependence on vital natural resources. Acute energy shortages of the 1970s and 1980s introduced a new marketing term, **demarketing.** Producers of energy and energy-consuming goods used advertising to *slow* the demand for their products. Ads asked people to refrain from operating washers and dryers during the day when the demand for electricity peaked. In time, demarketing became a more aggressive strategic tool for advertisers to use against competitors, political opponents, and social problems. The California Department of Health Services, for example, is one of many organizations today that actively seek to demarket the use of tobacco.

Then, following a period of unprecedented boom in the West and bust in the East, the Berlin Wall and the Iron Curtain came tumbling down. This finally ended the Cold War. Newly freed nations in the former Warsaw Pact states offered millions of underserved consumers. To expand globally, big multinational companies and their advertising agencies went on a binge, buying other big companies and creating a new word in the financial lexicon: *megamerger.*

By now European and Asian advertising had caught up with the United States. TV was the hot medium, and agencies focused on growth, acquisitions, and superior creative executions. For several years, Young & Rubicam in New York and Dentsu in Japan alternated as the largest advertising agency in the world. Two brothers in London, Charles and Maurice Saatchi, started acquiring agencies globally. In rapid succession, a number of high-profile U.S. agencies disappeared under the Saatchi & Saatchi umbrella—big companies such as Ted Bates Worldwide and Dancer, Fitzgerald, Sample. Saatchi & Saatchi was suddenly the largest agency in the world. More buyouts followed as the big agencies from Europe, the United States, and Japan emulated the merger mania of their huge multinational clients. Names of agency founders disappeared from the doors, replaced by initials and acronyms: WPP Group, RSCG, TBWA, FCA, DDB Needham, and FCB, to mention just a few.

The European agencies fueled their growth by establishing huge bulk-media-buying conglomerates, although their now-sophisticated clients stopped looking to the agencies for research and marketing advice. Rather, they expected extraordinary creative executions to give their brands an edge, and the agencies delivered. Awards at the Cannes International

My IMC Campaign 2

Tools for Teamwork

Advertising agencies look for at least three qualities in the people they hire: talent, knowledge, and the ability to work well with others. If you are working on your campaign in a group, you'll find those qualities—especially the third—to be important as well.

Your campaign assignment may be the first time you've worked on a group project. If so, you'll discover that working in a team is very different from doing a project on your own.

First, you will need to coordinate everything that you do. That means each person must create schedules that accommodate not only his or her own obligations, but also those of the group. Second, you will be sharing work. Tools that help you share documents, calendars, and other files will help you produce better work and do it faster. Third, you should consider the importance of leadership in a group. Your group will usually perform better if someone is formally appointed as leader, at least in the sense of organizing meetings, maintaining a calendar, and keeping track of what has to be done. Finally, everyone is accountable. Talk to your professor about whether he or she expects peer evaluations or some other means to assess differences in group member effort and performance.

Many Internet tools are now available to help improve the coordination of teams. Best of all, they are free. The ones I prefer are those created by Google because they are easy to use, powerful, and integrated (both with each other and with mobile devices). If you would prefer not to use a Google product, I've tried to find equivalents where possible.

Staying Connected

E-mail, of course, remains an essential tool. You may have a university e-mail account, but these can be problematic because (1) your inbox space is limited, (2) spam filters in these accounts are often very aggressive (too much useful mail is moved to the spam folder), and (3) they lack many useful tools for organizing and labeling your mail. Gmail (www.gmail.com) is an excellent free mail service that you will most likely never fill up (which means you never have to delete e-mails and your inbox never gets too full). You can use "labels" to quickly identify mail from people in your group. And with "contacts" you can set up groups of e-mail addresses to message easily and quickly. Use "tasks" to create a to-do list right in your e-mail list. These programs also work well with many mobile devices. Yahoo! Mail offers similar functions (http://mail.yahoo.com).

Creating Documents

If you already own Microsoft Office, you have a strong suite of tools for collaboration in the Cloud (https://www.office.com/). Google docs (http://docs.google.com) is a free suite of simple yet powerful document creation tools that includes a word processor, a spreadsheet program, and a presentation creator. You can share some or all of the documents you create with others and edit them simultaneously. So if a group member is working on a creative brief, he or she can share it

immediately with everyone else for edits and comments. If you would prefer a non-Google solution, Thinkfree "My Office" is similar to Google docs (www.thinkfree.com).

Staying Organized

Many people find that calendars and to-do lists are essential. Google has an excellent calendar program (www.google.com/calendar) that everyone in the team can edit. You can also sync the calendar with many mobile devices. As I indicated before, Google's "task" program is built into gmail.

Conducting Research

Powerful tools for doing research are also available for free on the Web. For secondary research purposes, it is great to have a program that allows you to copy and store documents, Web pages, photos, charts, and other kinds of information. A powerful and popular program is Evernote (www.evernote.com). Your group may also find itself collecting primary data. If you need to administer a survey, consider a useful component of Google docs called "forms." With forms you can easily create a Web-based survey and have your data set up in a Google spreadsheet as it comes in. A non-Google program that does the same thing is SurveyMonkey (www.surveymonkey.com).

Working Well and Staying Accountable

Learning to adapt to group projects is not easy for everyone. Knowing what to expect and developing the skills to work well with others are essential. For guidance, consider these thoughts from experts:

- MIT: http://hrweb.mit.edu/learning-development/learning-topics/teams/articles/basics
- Susan Heathfield: http://humanresources.about.com/od/workrelationships/a/play_well.htm
- Analytic Tech: http://www.analytictech.com/mb021/teamhint.htm

If you volunteer to be a team leader (or are appointed one), some helpful tips can be found here:

- www.cooper.com/journal/2008/11/habits_of_effective_teams.html
- Stephen Covey: www.stephencovey.com/blog/?p=6
- Jack Welch, former CEO of GE (this is an hour-long video filmed at the MIT School of Management) http://mitworld.mit.edu/video/260/

If you are doing peer evaluations in your class, your professor will likely have a form that you should use. These types of forms can be found throughout the Web. Some examples include these:

- https://courses.worldcampus.psu.edu/public/faculty/PeerEvalForm.html
- www.utexas.edu/courses/kincaid/peerevaltips.html

This ad for the Department of Tourism, Philippines is considered comparative advertising because it makes claims about both the sponsoring brand and a competitor.

Source: The Philippine Department of Tourism

Advertising Festival disclosed the blossoming of creative advertising from Spain and confirmed the creative leadership of the British, who were only slightly ahead of the French.[18]

Two related economic factors characterized the marketing world of this period: (1) the aging of traditional products, with a corresponding growth in competition, and (2) the growing affluence and sophistication of the consuming public, led by the huge baby boomer generation.[19]

The most important factor was competition, intensified by lower trade barriers and growing international trade. As high profits lured imitators into the marketplace, each offering the most attractive product features at lower cost, consumers benefited from more choices, higher quality, and lower prices.

On the demand side, newly affluent consumers concerned themselves more with the quality of their lives. With their basic commodity needs already met, baby boomers were interested in saving time and money to spend on leisure-time activities or on products, services, and social causes that represented their aspirations.

As the 1990s unfolded, the traditional advertising industry found itself threatened on all sides and suffering from overpopulation.[20] Clients demanded better results from their promotional dollars; small, imaginative, upstart agencies competed for (and won) some big accounts that had never been available to them; TV viewers appeared immune to conventional commercials; and media options based on new technologies promised to reinvent advertising. In three short years, the advertising agency business lost more than 13,500 jobs. Major clients such as Coca-Cola defected from Madison Avenue, giving various portions of their business to specialists in small, regional creative shops and media-buying services. But the setback went far beyond the agency business. Throughout the media world, newspapers, magazines, and TV networks all lost advertising dollars.[21]

By the mid-1990s, U.S. marketers began shifting dollars back from sales promotion to advertising to rebuild value in their brands. In 1994, ad budgets surged ahead by 8.1 percent to $150 billion nationally. And throughout the rest of the 1990s, ad spending increased about 7 percent every year until the year 2000, when U.S. advertisers spent $247.5 billion, a whopping 11.3 percent increase over the previous year.[22] Consumers began discovering the benefits of "going online," as personal computers became commonplace. Advertisers, enthralled with the potential of the Internet, began exploring ways to take advantage of this new medium.

But then the bubble burst. In 2001, the combination of a mild recession, a stock market decline, and the bust of the dot-coms contributed to a record decline in advertising activity. On September 11 of that year, terrorists attacked the United States and suddenly all marketing and advertising seemed to stop—not just in North America but also around the world.[23] The end result: spending in the United States declined 6.5 percent to $231 billion, and overseas spending dropped 8.6 percent to $210 billion.[24]

A year later, though, the economy seemed to be turning around and marketers were again starting to spend money on advertising. By 2005, U.S. advertising expenditures had reached $264 billion, more than completely recovering from the 2001 decline.[25] But the old days were gone for good. Technology, evolving lifestyles, new fears over security, and the rising cost of reaching consumers had changed the advertising business forever. Two developments from the early 2000s were little noticed then, but in time would shake up the marketing world. Larry Page and Sergey Brin, two Stanford grad students, developed AdWords, an advertising program for their search engine, Google, that eventually generated billions in profits. And Mark Zuckerberg dropped out of Harvard, headed west, and named his new social media company Facebook. By tapping into a strong consumer desire to connect with others, Zuckerberg created what may well be the greatest word-of-mouth

Exhibit 2-4
Top Global Marketers

2013	Marketer	Headquarters	WW Spend (billions)	2012-2013 Chg
1.	Procter & Gamble	U.S.A.	$11.5	10%
2.	Unilever	Netherlands	7.9	9.2
3.	L'Oreal	France	5.6	6.4
4.	Toyota	Japan	3.0	1.7
5.	General Motors	U.S.A.	3.3	5.1
6.	Voikswagen	Germany	3.2	7.9
7.	Nestle	Switzerland	3.1	4.1
8.	Coca Cola	U.S.A.	2.9	0.5
9.	Mars	U.S.A.	2.9	22.1
10.	Pepsi	U.S.A.	2.7	9.4

Source: Advertising Age Datacenter, retrieved at: http://adage.com/datacenter/datapopup.php?article_id=295216

marketing platform in history. The Internet had created an electronic frontier—what Tom Cuniff, VP/creative director at Lord, Dentsu & Partners, calls "the second creative revolution."[26]

The Global Interactive Age: Looking at the 21st Century

In the new millennium, the rest of the world has in many respects caught up to North America, thanks to improved economic conditions and a desire for expansion. Recent estimates of worldwide advertising expenditures exceed $600 billion per year.[27] The importance of advertising in individual countries depends on the country's level of development and national attitude toward promotion. Typically, advertising expenditures are higher in countries with higher personal incomes. As Exhibit 2-4 shows, the top 10 global marketers are based in many different countries.

Although the Communist countries once condemned advertising as an evil of capitalism, eastern European countries now encourage private enterprise and realize the benefits of advertising. And the United States now looks elsewhere to find its biggest economic rival. Some estimates suggest the Chinese economy, which is growing at more than 10 percent a year, will surpass that of America in the near future. Indeed, by some measures it already has.[28]

Widespread availability of cable TV and satellite receivers allows viewers to watch channels devoted to single types of programming, such as news, home shopping, sports, or comedy. This shift transformed television from the most widespread of mass media to a more specialized, "narrowcasting" medium. Small companies and product marketers that appeal to a limited clientele use TV to reach audiences with unique interests.

But increasingly, consumers are cutting their cables to watch TV via the Web on such popular services as Netflix, Hulu, and Amazon Prime. This trend has proven so strong that as of 2015, both HBO and Showtime, which have operated as premium cable channels since their inceptions, have made their services available outside of cable to Internet viewers.[29]

In September of 2008, the global economy began an economic slowdown. Many companies, faced with declining sales and lower revenue, cut back on advertising expenditures.

Particularly hard hit was the newspaper industry. Through late 2011, newspapers saw 20 consecutive quarters of ad revenue decline, and the total decline through 2012 was 48.8 percent.[30] Even worse, as the U.S. economy slowly improved heading into 2015, newspaper advertising revenue has failed to recover.

In truth, despite strong government intervention on behalf of banks, insurers, and auto manufacturers, and despite scattered

Modern advertisers understand that ads should explain a brand benefit in a clear, compelling, and creative way. Amundsen's agency, Ogilvy & Mather, Ukraine, uses a clever metaphor to demonstrate why "six times distilled" is worth purchasing in a vodka.

Source: Amundsen Premium Vodka

AD Lab 2-A

What Kills Bugs Dead?

Successful marketing communications sometimes take on a life of their own. Over the years, advertising agencies have created many successful product slogans for their clients, which have become part of our popular culture. Here are some of the most famous. Test your knowledge and see how many advertisers you can identify.

1. "Think different."
2. "_____ kills bugs dead."
3. "Don't leave home without it."
4. "Diamonds are forever."
5. "Good to the last drop."
6. "Just Do It."
7. "When it rains, it pours."
8. "We bring good things to life."
9. "M'm! M'm! Good!"
10. "Let your fingers do the walking."

Laboratory Applications

1. Now that you know a little about slogans, create one for yourself personally or for your (real or imagined) company. Which qualities and characteristics do you want your slogan to highlight? Share your slogan with your classmates and gauge their reactions.

2. Business cards serve a higher purpose than simply providing information for a Rolodex. They are mini-advertisements. Create a business card for yourself using your slogan.

Internet Exercise

1. Need help getting started on your slogan assignment? Adslogans.com has step-by-step instructions that lead you through the process (www.adslogans.co.uk/general/students.html). For more ideas, look at slogans and ad campaigns past and present at www.adflip.com.

Answers

1. Apple
2. Raid
3. American Express
4. DeBeers
5. Maxwell House Coffee
6. Nike
7. Morton Salt
8. General Electric (GE)
9. Campbell Soup Co.
10. Yellow Pages

"occupy" protests around the country, capitalism is likely to remain the greatest influence on markets in the United States. By 2015, the U.S. economy was growing again, but at a very slow rate.

Advertising has come a long way from the simple sign on the bootmaker's shop. Today it is a powerful influence that announces the availability and location of products, describes

New technology has meant new media, manifested largely in the Internet. This has opened new avenues of exposure for advertisers. This site for Coke shows that beautiful layout and design are not confined to the traditional medium of print.

Source: The Coca-Cola Company

their quality and value, imbues brands with personality, and simultaneously defines the personalities of the people who buy them while entertaining us. More than a reflection of society and its desires, advertising can start and end fads, trends, and credos—sometimes all by itself.

The endless search for competitive advantage and efficiency has made advertising's journey in the last 100-plus years fascinating. Now companies are realizing that their most important asset is not capital equipment, or research capability, or their line of products. In the global marketplace, their most important asset is their customer and the relationship they have with that person or organization. Protecting that asset is the marketing imperative for the 21st century. In an effort to do a better job of *relationship marketing,* companies understand that they must be consistent in both what they say and what they do. It's not enough to produce outstanding advertising anymore. They must integrate all their marketing communications with everything else they do, too. That's what *integrated marketing communications* really means.

Society and Ethics: The Effects of Advertising

Advertising has been a major factor in improving the standard of living in the United States and around the world. By publicizing the material, social, and cultural opportunities of a free enterprise society, advertising has encouraged increased productivity by both management and labor.

With just a small amount of money, for instance, you can buy a car. It may be secondhand, but advertising lets you know it's available. If you earn more money, you can buy a new car or one with more luxury features. You can also make a statement about yourself as an individual with the vehicle you purchase. As it does for many products, advertising has created a personality for each automobile model on the market, in part by informing you of the options, benefits, performance, look, and style available for purchase. You, as a free individual, have the opportunity to select the brand that best matches your functional, financial, or social needs and aspirations.

Ads are not just used to sell products. They are also used to promote ideas and causes. This Website for the American Heart Association encourages people to "go red" to help fight heart disease in women.

Source: The American Heart Association

The Ad Council works with agency talent to tackle difficult social issues and causes. In the ad above for Adoptuskids.org, the Ad Council uses the clever imagery of a lopsided birthday cake to convey the message that "you don't have to be perfect to be a perfect parent."

Source: U.S. Department of Health and Human Services' Administration for Children and Families, AdoptUSKids and The Advertising Council

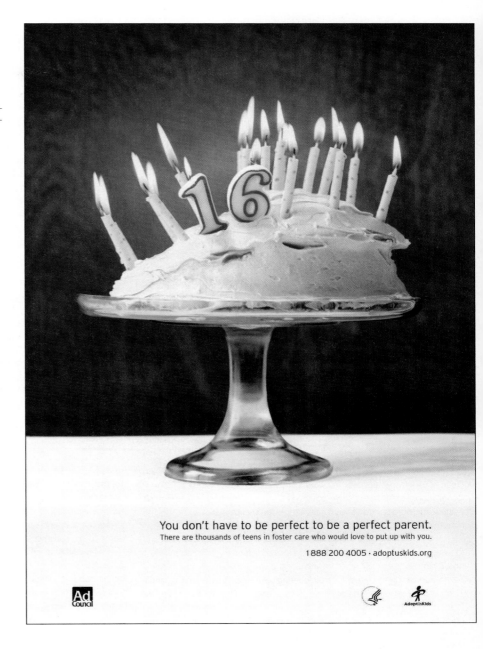

You don't have to be perfect to be a perfect parent.
There are thousands of teens in foster care who would love to put up with you.

1 888 200 4005 · adoptuskids.org

Advertising serves other social needs besides simply stimulating sales. Free media are not really "free"; newspapers must pay for paper, ink, and energy, and radio stations require equipment, buildings, and towers. All media organizations must pay salaries and benefits for reporters, engineers, and management. Facebook, magazines, radio, television, and many Websites all receive their primary income from advertising. This facilitates freedom of the press and promotes more complete information.

Some advertising organizations also foster growth and understanding of important social issues and causes through public service. The Red Cross, United Way, and other noncommercial organizations receive continuous financial support and volunteer assistance due in large part to the power of advertising.

However, advertising is certainly not without its shortcomings. Since its beginnings, the profession has had to struggle with issues of honesty and unethical. In fact, in the early

People **BEHIND** the Ads

© Bettmann/Corbis

Apple's famous campaign of the early 1980s asked consumers to "Think different." The ads used icons such as Einstein, Gandhi, and Picasso. They should have included Bill Bernbach.

The modern stereotype is that ad agencies are unconventional places populated with quirky visionaries. But that notion would have surprised professionals in the early 1960s. Back then agencies tended to be every bit as corporate as their clients. The stars were the account executives, not the creative directors. The agencies of that earlier age preferred safe, cautious campaigns developed through careful testing.

For most of the 1950s creativity carried little currency. After all, Claude Hopkins had dismissed the role of creativity by declaring that "scientific principles" were the key to effective advertising. Hopkins famously opened his book *Scientific Advertising* by noting:

The causes and effects [of advertising] have been analyzed until they are well understood. The correct methods of procedure have been proved and established. We know what is most effective, and we act on basic laws.

But by 1959, a creative revolution was brewing, led by the founder and creative leader of an upstart New York agency, Doyle Dane Bernbach. Contradicting Hopkins's claim that advertising was a science, Bernbach wrote: "I don't want academicians. I don't want scientists. I don't want people who do the right things. I want people who do inspiring things. . . . Let us blaze new trails."

There is little doubt that by the end of the 1950s advertising was ready for a revolution. It seemed that every ad looked like every other. To take just one example, every car ad from the decade used brilliant, almost blinding color, showcasing the latest Detroit offering surrounded by a smiling family. The car itself would be bigger, faster, longer, and more elaborate than last year's model. The copy would go on about new luxuries, comforts, and technologies. The ad would almost scream "American Dream" to consumers enjoying the postwar boom. And every car ad looked like every other car ad. Why stand out? Why take a risk?

Then came Bernbach. DDB's car client was a new German import: Volkswagen. The agency's unenviable task: market the decidedly unsexy "people's car" imported from a country against whom America had just concluded a world war. And the brand itself was everything Detroit's offerings were not: tiny, unusual, and humble.

Yet almost overnight Volkswagen entered the collective consciousness of American consumers. DDB placed it there by creating brilliant, even outrageous, "anti-advertising," that looked like nothing

Americans had ever seen. Instead of bright colors, outdoor scenes, and smiling families, DDB's ads were black and white, stark, and simple. Audacious, punchy headlines encouraged people to reconsider everything they usually thought about when buying a car. "Think small," read one, putting a tiny photo of the car in the top left portion of the ad. "Lemon," read another. Why would an ad use a headline that seemed to insult the brand? Consumers were drawn into the body copy to find out. There they discovered that the lemon in question had been pulled from the assembly line because of stringent quality controls.

Bernbach developed copy that encouraged consumers to reject groupthink, the mass society, and the idea that everyone should be like everyone else. The appeals were simple, straightforward, clean, and specific. For those tiring of the "keep up with your neighbors" treadmill, Bernbach wrote the manual for getting off. One Volkswagen ad from 1963 showed readers "How to do a Volkswagen ad." "Speak to the reader," the copy noted, "Don't shout. He can hear you. Especially if you talk sense."

Bernbach's efforts for other clients were just as brilliant, unusual, and fresh. Ads for Levy's bread featured people of many ethnicities enjoying the product. The message: "You don't have to be Jewish" to like rye bread. Client Avis was the number two car company in the United States. Why not choose number one? Because the people at Avis "work harder." Unstated, but just as clear, was the notion that employees at industry leader Hertz took customers for granted.

The culture at DDB was a reflection of Bernbach himself. Thomas Frank notes that Bernbach "was an ideologue of disorder, an untiring propagandist for the business value of the principles of modern art." Front and center was his insistence that agency culture respect creative talent. Copywriter Phyllis Robinson recalled it this way, "we just felt very free, as if we had broken our shackles, gotten out of jail, and were free to work the way we wanted to work."

The new culture fostered by Bernbach also extended to the relationship of client and agency. In the old days, agencies knuckled under if a client demanded advertising be done a certain way. DDB clients were expected to respect the agency's creative ideas. If they could not, Bernbach was prepared to walk.

DDB and its leader took the advertising business by storm. Created in 1949, the agency rocketed from obscurity to international prominence in a mere 10 years. Soon every ad agency was playing catch-up by transforming its own culture.

Bernbach passed away in 1982 after a fabled career, but his legacy is intact. *Harper's Magazine*, noting his passing, wrote that Bernbach had made "a greater impact on American culture than any of the distinguished writers and artists" appearing in the magazine during its 133 years. And when *Advertising Age* published a top-100 list of the greatest advertising campaigns (http://adage.com/century/campaigns.html) and individuals (http://adage.com/century/people001.html) of the 20th century, the number one spots went to DDB's Volkswagen ads and Bill Bernbach.

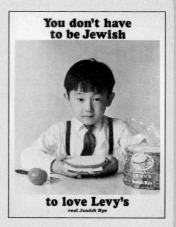

You don't have to be Jewish

to love Levy's
real Jewish Rye

Source: DDB Worldwide Communications Group Inc.

Avis is only No.2 in rent a cars. So why go with us?

We try harder.
(When you're not the biggest, you have to.)
We just can't afford dirty ashtrays. Or half-empty gas tanks. Or worn wipers. Or unwashed cars. Or low tires. Or anything less than seat-adjusters that adjust. Heaters that heat. Defrosters that defrost.
Obviously, the thing we try hardest for is just to be nice. To start you out right with a new car, like a lively, super-torque Ford, and a pleasant smile. To know, say, where you get a good pastrami sandwich in Duluth.
Why?
Because we can't afford to take you for granted.
Go with us next time.
The line at our counter is shorter.

Source: DDB Worldwide Communications Group Inc.

1900s, the advertising profession was forced to mend its unethical ways. Consumers suffered for years from unsubstantiated product claims, especially for patent medicines and health devices. The simmering resentment finally boiled over into a full-blown consumer movement, which led to government regulation and ultimately to industry efforts at self-regulation.

In 1906, Congress responded to public outrage by passing the Pure Food and Drug Act to protect the public's health and control drug advertising. In 1914, it passed the Federal Trade Commission Act to protect the public from unfair business practices, including misleading and deceptive advertising.

Advertising practitioners formed groups to improve advertising effectiveness and promote professionalism and started vigilance committees to safeguard the integrity of the industry. The Association of National Advertisers (ANA), the American Advertising Federation (AAF), and the Better Business Bureau (BBB) are today's outgrowths of those early groups. These organizations are the result of a fundamental truth: the biggest opponents of unethical advertisers are advertisers who embrace ethical and truthful communication practices.

But in times of economic crisis, false and misleading advertising invariably reappears, perhaps out of advertiser desperation. During the Depression years, several best-selling books exposed the advertising industry as an unscrupulous exploiter of consumers, giving birth to a new consumer movement and further government regulation.

In the 1970s, a new American consumer movement grew out of the widespread disillusionment following the Kennedy assassination, the Vietnam War, the Watergate scandals, and the sudden shortage of vital natural resources—all communicated instantly to the world via new satellite technology. These issues fostered cynicism and distrust of the establishment and tradition and gave rise to a new twist in moral consciousness. On the one hand, people justified their personal irresponsibility and self-indulgence in the name of self-fulfillment. On the other, they attacked corporate America's quest for self-fulfillment (profits) in the name of social accountability.

Today, corporate America has generally cleaned up many of the inequities in advertising. But now attention has shifted to more subtle problems of puffery, advertising to children, advertising legal but unhealthy products, concerns about wealth inequality and climate change, and other concerns regarding advertisers' ethics and social responsibilities. We believe ethics in IMC is such an important issue that we have included a feature on this topic in every chapter.

In short, advertising has had a pronounced effect on society as well as the economy. It has also fostered a host of social attitudes and laws that have dramatically affected advertising itself. We'll take a closer look at these issues in Chapter 3.

Chapter Summary

Economic theory includes four fundamental assumptions of free-market economics: self-interest, complete information, many buyers and sellers, and absence of externalities. Given these principles, advertising has a number of functions and effects in a free economy. It identifies and differentiates products; communicates information about them; induces nonusers to try products and users to repurchase them; stimulates products' distribution; increases product use; builds value, brand preference, and loyalty; and lowers the overall cost of sales.

The greatest impact on the evolution of advertising has been economic. In ancient times when most people could not read or write, there was little need for advertising. Marketers used symbols on signs to advertise

their products. As the world expanded, urban populations soared, and manufacturing and communication technologies developed, as did advertising. Printing was the first major technology to affect advertising; cable TV and the Internet are the most recent.

With changing economies and increased competition, advertising has evolved from the preindustrial age through the industrializing and industrial ages to the postindustrial age. Since World War II, advertisers have used a variety of strategies, such as product differentiation, market segmentation, and positioning, to set their products apart. Recently the advertising industry experienced a period of retrenchment and reevaluation, but the future offers new opportunities for advertisers and agencies that can harness the interactive revolution and develop deep relationships with their customers. Economic hardships in 2008 and 2009 led to cutbacks in ad budgets, but smart companies continue to advertise and will emerge with gains in market share.

As a social force, advertising has helped improve the standard of living in the United States and around the world. Advertising makes us aware of the availability of products, imbues products with personality, and enables us to communicate information about ourselves through the products we buy. Through its financial support, advertising also fosters the free press and the growth of many nonprofit organizations.

However, advertising has also been severely criticized over the years for its lack of honesty and ethics. This has given rise to numerous consumer movements and laws that regulate the practice of advertising.

Important Terms

brand, *38*

branding, *35*

consumer packaged goods, *44*

demarketing, *49*

industrial age, *44*

market segmentation, *47*

positioning strategy, *48*

postindustrial age, *49*

preindustrial age, *44*

Review Questions

1. What are the four fundamental assumptions of free-market economics?
2. What are the primary functions of advertising in a free economy?
3. What has had the greatest impact on the way advertising has evolved?
4. How does advertising lower the cost of sales?
5. How would you differentiate the advertising used in the industrializing age and the industrial age?
6. What has been the most important influence on advertising in the postindustrial age?

7. What are three examples of companies or organizations that use a demarketing strategy?
8. What companies can you think of that are engaged in marketing warfare?
9. As a consumer, are you likely to save money buying at a store that doesn't advertise? Explain.
10. What effects do you believe advertising has had on society in general? Explain.

The Advertising Experience

1. **Ad Action: Demarketing**

   Identify a social problem at your school that has had an effect on your life in the past few months. Then create a print demarketing advertisement that addresses this problem. The ad should have a visual element as well as a slogan.

2. **Economic Perspectives of Advertising**

   Visit the Websites that follow for readings on the economics of advertising. After studying them, do you believe advertising primarily promotes monopoly or does it foster many buyers and sellers? Support your argument with points from the articles.

   a. "The Economics of Advertising" (Introduction), 2001—introductory essay to a volume edited by Columbia University economist Kyle Bagwell: http://web.stanford.edu/~kbagwell /Bagwell_Web/advertisingintrofv2.pdf

   b. "Advertising," The Library of Economics and Liberty: *The Concise Encyclopedia of Economics*—an interesting primer by Prof. George Bittlingmayer, University of Kansas: www.econlib .org/library/Enc/Advertising.html

3. **Advertising History**

   Visit the following Websites to see what else you can learn about the early advertising efforts of companies here and abroad. Can you find some early ads for Kodak? Coca-Cola? Sunkist? Who are some of the other major advertisers listed? What specific characteristics in art and copy styles do you notice that make these ads different from advertising today?

   a. The Emergence of Advertising in America section of the John W. Hartman Center for Sales, Advertising, and Marketing History at Duke University: http://scriptorium.lib.duke.edu/eaa

   b. Archives of the History of Advertising Trust: http://www.hatads .org.uk/

   c. History Matters: http://historymatters.gmu.edu/mse/ads/amadv .html

   d. The Museum of Broadcast Communications (Chicago):

   e. Nineteenth-century advertising in *Harper's Weekly* magazine: http://advertising.harpweek.com

f.   USATVADS (a large—more than 1 million examples—pay-site collection of American television commercials): www.usatvads.net

g.   Advertising, marketing, and commercial imagery collections of the National Museum of American History at the Smithsonian: http://americanhistory.si.edu/collections/subjects/advertising

4.   Volkswagen's advertising from the early 1960s was clearly quite different from that of its competitors—perhaps because of its decision to pair copywriters with art directors, a partnership that is now all but standard in the advertising industry. But did other automakers sit up and take notice? Find some examples of American auto advertising in the years since that could potentially have been influenced by DDB's VW work.

5.   Some Coca-Cola investors want the company to spend more on advertising products in growing categories, such as sports drinks, and less on trying to revive consumer interest in full-calorie soft drinks. How would you respond to these shareholders?

6.   After stirring up consumers' emotions and shaking their faith in the company by introducing New Coke, company executives have been treading somewhat lightly for the last 20 years. Do you think their efforts to conserve and protect the brand have stifled the creativity of Coca-Cola advertising? Why or why not?

The Big Picture: Economic and Regulatory Aspects

Learning Objectives

To identify and explain the economic, social, ethical, and legal issues advertisers must consider. The basic economic principles that guided the evolution of advertising also have social and legal effects. These effects can lead governments to take corrective measures. Society determines what is offensive, excessive, and irresponsible; governments determine what is deceptive and unfair. To be law-abiding, ethical, socially responsible, and economically effective, advertisers must understand these issues.

 studying this chapter, you will be able to:

LO3-1 Relate advertising activities to the workings of a free-market economy.

LO3-2 Identify and give examples of the two main types of social criticisms of advertising.

LO3-3 Explain the difference between social responsibility and ethics in advertising.

LO3-4 Describe how governments regulate advertising here and abroad.

LO3-5 Discuss regulatory issues that affect U.S. advertisers and commercial speech.

LO3-6 Classify ways that federal agencies regulate advertising to protect both consumers and competitors.

LO3-7 Define the roles state and local governments play in advertising regulation.

LO3-8 List the ways that private organizations help reduce fraudulent and deceptive advertising.

© Shawn Thew/EPA/Newscom

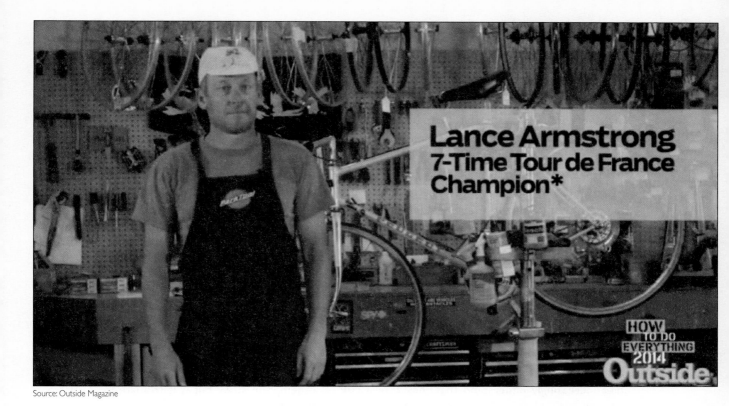

Would you be more likely to buy a watch brand if you knew that Jeff Gordon wears it? What if it was the preferred brand of Maria Sharapova or Leonardo DiCaprio? Swiss luxury watchmaker TagHeuer must think so, since it pays these stars to appear in ads. And shoe company Nike spends millions on endorsement contracts. The company has long partnered with Michael Jordan and has exclusive deals with many other athletes, including Chris Paul and Serena Williams. The athletes agree to wear Nike clothes and use Nike gear during competitions. Many also appear in Nike ads. ■ Are celebrity endorsements worth the big bucks that TagHeuer and Nike spend on them? Business professors Jagdish Agrawal and Wagner Kamakura argue that celebrities help make ads believable, enhance ad recall, increase brand recognition, and ultimately influence consumers to choose an endorsed brand.[1] So it should be no surprise that as many as one of five TV commercials features someone famous. ■ Former world champion cyclist Lance Armstrong made tens of millions of dollars from endorsements and in return helped companies like Nike become dominant global brands. So has elite golfer Tiger Woods. Woods has said that "if you are given a chance to be a role model, I think you should always take it because you can influence a person's life in a positive light, and that's what I want to do. That's what it's all about." ■ Unfortunately, as virtually everyone knows, both Amstrong and Woods went through embarrassing public scandals. The resulting furors were more than personal tragedies for these men. Millions of people were crushed by the upsetting news about their heroes. And the companies that made Tiger and Lance highly paid endorsers were suddenly faced with a public relations disaster. ■ It happens all the time. The long list of famous individuals who have lost endorsement deals because of controversy includes Madonna (Pepsi), Ludacris (Pepsi), Jose Canseco (California Egg Commission), Kobe Bryant (McDonald's), Mary Kate Olsen (milk), Eminem (Ford), and Kate Moss (Chanel). ■ The dilemma for companies that sponsor celebrities was highlighted in a series of events that led Nike to stop its sponsorship of Atlanta Falcons quarterback Michael Vick after he confessed to criminal activities that included cruelty to animals. Nike signed a major sponsorship deal with Vick as a rookie in the NFL. When news broke that the quarterback was being investigated for acts involving animal cruelty, the company faced a quandary. The quarterback initially argued that the illegal acts were done by associates. No matter how implausible that claim might have seemed, many believed that Vick was entitled to a presumption of innocence before trial. Nike had to determine whether to drop its support of Vick before his day in court or stand by the athlete. As the experiences of Kobe Bryant and the Duke lacrosse team made clear, being accused of a crime is not the same as being guilty. Nike decided to suspend sales of Vick's product lines shortly after the story broke. But it did not break its endorsement contract until Vick admitted guilt. The marketing community generally applauded this approach as one that acknowledged both the seriousness of the crime and Vick's right to a presumption of innocence before trial. ■ Companies increasingly understand that they take a risk when they associate their brands too closely with a single endorser. Jeremy Mullman, writing for *Advertising Age,* says that Nike has been recently moving toward an "ensemble approach" to endorsements.

Translation: Nike uses a pool of athletes to promote its wares rather than one big star. Risk to the brand is reduced, therefore, should any of the athletes stumble. Under Armour, a Nike competitor, uses a similar approach. A company VP notes that Under Armour doesn't "let any one person get bigger than the brand."[2] ■ Lessons? Tiger Woods, Lance Armstrong, and Michael Vick earned big endorsement contracts because of the things they do as athletes. And yet, for all three, the journey from endorsement superstar to marketing disaster happened with lightning speed. For brands, the lesson is caution in aligning a product's image too closely with real and potentially flawed human beings. *Outside* magazine recently took a gamble and decided to play on Lance Armstrong's flaws and his fall from public grace and and used Armstrong to promote a clip online called "How to Fix a Flat Tire." Will this be the first step in getting Lance back in the endorsement game? Although people usually love a redemption story, but is it too late for Armstrong, Woods, Vick, and others? Or is it worth pondering whether the uncritical adoration we offer celebrities and stars is in some way a catalyst for the very behaviors that we ultimately find so disappointing.

This chapter also focuses most specifically on the advertising dimension of IMC. While other kinds of promotional messages are relevant to the themes we develop here, advertising is most often associated with offences that attract attention from critics and regulators alike.

The Many Controversies about Advertising

Advertising is perhaps the most visible of business activities. Companies risk public criticism if their advertising offends the audience or if their products don't measure up. For this reason, defenders of advertising say advertised products are safer because a company tries harder to fulfill its promises when its name and reputation are on the line.

Advertising is both applauded and criticized not only for its role in selling products but also for its influence on the economy and on society. For years, critics have associated advertising with a wide range of sins—some real, some imagined.

John O'Toole, former chair of Foote, Cone & Belding and president of the American Association of Advertising Agencies, believed that many critics attack advertising because it *isn't something else.* Advertising isn't journalism, education, or entertainment—although it often performs the functions of all three. In our definition of advertising, we emphasized that ads are meant to be persuasive, to tell one side of a story. They are not intended to be a neutral perspective on a brand or service. As a form of communication, advertising shares certain characteristics with journalism, education, and entertainment, but it shouldn't be judged by their standards. Sponsors advertise because they hope it will help them sell some product, service, or idea.[3]

Views of offensiveness vary a great deal. This ad for Shoebaloo created by agency Kessels Kramer entitled "Amputee" uses a handicap model to get its message across. Does this ad make you feel uncomfortable? Or is it empowering?

Source: Shoebaloo Advertisement by KesselsKramer

Notwithstanding O'Toole's articulate defense, many controversies still swirl around the whole field of advertising. Some focus on advertising's *economic* role. For example, how does advertising affect the value of products? Does it cause higher prices? Does it promote competition or discourage it? How does advertising affect overall consumer demand? What effect does it have on consumer choice and on the overall business cycle?

Other controversies focus on the *societal* effects of advertising. For instance, does advertising make us more materialistic? Does it tempt us into buying things we don't need? Does it affect us subliminally in ways we can't control? (For more on this topic, see the Ethical Issues box in Chapter 8, "Advertising and Subliminal Persuasion.") How does it affect the art and culture of our society? Does advertising debase our language? How much do advertisers know about us and how safe is our privacy?

From these economic and social controversies, questions arise concerning where to locate responsibility for advertising. How much latitude should marketers have in the kinds of products they promote and how they advertise them? And what about consumers? Don't they have some responsibility in the process? Finally, what is the proper role of government? What laws should we have to protect consumers? And what laws go too far and violate the marketer's freedom of speech?

Such complex questions have no simple answers. But the process of raising the issues and considering them in a thoughtful way helps advertisers better understand the effects of their messages. It also helps government better evaluate the tradeoffs of commercial speech policies. This chapter addresses some of the major questions and criticisms about advertising, both the pros and the cons, and delves into the regulatory methods used to remedy advertisers' abuses.

Recall from Chapter 2 the underlying principle of free-market economics—that a society is best served by empowering people to make their own decisions and act as free agents, within a system characterized by four fundamental assumptions: *self-interest, many buyers and sellers, complete information,* and *absence of externalities* (social costs).

This fundamentally utilitarian framework, derived from the idea that society should promote behaviors that foster the greatest good for the most people, offers a system of economic activity—capitalism—that has raised living standards better than any other economic system in history. This is why societies around the world are increasingly adopting free-enterprise economics.

By using this framework for our discussion of advertising controversies, we have a basis for understanding how advertising may contribute to, or detract from, the basic goal of free enterprise: "the most good for the most people."

Exhibit 3-1

Advertising spending per capita (excluding direct mail) worldwide is correlated with GDP per capita.

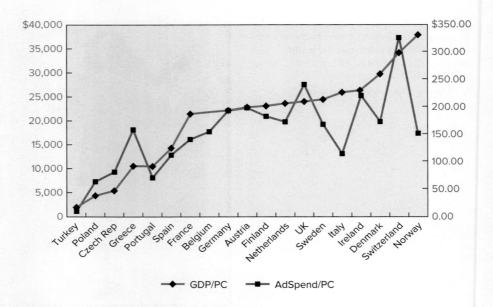

The Economic Impact of Advertising

LO 3-1

Advertising expenditures historically average between 1 and 2 percent of the U.S. gross domestic product (GDP).[4] In relation to the total U.S. economy, this percentage is small. Still, the United States has the highest per capita spending in the world, approximately $567 per person in 2014. By comparison, spending is only $362 per capita in the UK and a mere $35 per capita in China. And, as illustrated in Exhibit 3-1, worldwide there is a positive relationship between per capita spending on advertising and personal wealth.[5]

The economic effect of advertising is like the break shot in billiards or pool. The moment a company begins to advertise, it sets off a chain reaction of economic events, as shown in Exhibit 3-2. The extent of the chain reaction, although hard to predict, is related to the force of the shot and the economic environment in which it occurred. Let's consider the economic questions we posed earlier.

Exhibit 3-2

The economic effect of advertising is like the opening break shot in billiards.

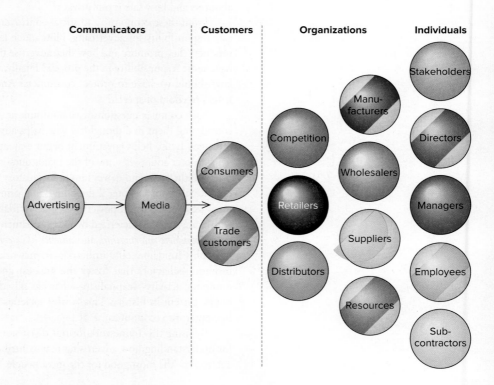

Effect on the Value of Products

Why do most people prefer Coca-Cola to some other cola? Why do some people prefer iPods to an unadvertised brand? Are the advertised products functionally better? Not necessarily. Advertising has given these brands *added value.*

Some believe that a product's *image,* created in part by advertising and promotion, is *an inherent feature of the product itself.*[6] While an ad may not address a product's quality directly, the positive image conveyed by advertising implies quality. By simply making the product better known, advertising can make the product more desirable. In this way, advertising adds value to the brand.[7] That's why people pay more for Bufferin than an unadvertised brand displayed right next to it—even though all buffered aspirin, by law, are (referring to all types) functionally the same.

Advertising also adds value to a brand by educating customers about new uses for a product. Kleenex was originally advertised as a makeup remover, later as a disposable handkerchief. AT&T first promoted the telephone as a necessity and later as a convenience. Apple ads for the iPhone regularly explain how apps give the device greater functionality.

In a free-market system, consumers can choose the qualities they want in products they buy. For example, a car buyer who considers low price to be important can buy an economy car. If status and luxury are important, he or she can buy an SUV or a sports car, and if environmental concerns are paramount, a hybrid. Many of our wants are emotional, social, or psychological rather than functional. One way we communicate who we are (or want to be) is through the products we purchase and display. By associating the product with some desirable image, advertising offers people the opportunity to satisfy those symbolic wants and needs. So, for example, buying a hybrid car is not just a way to help protect the environment, it is also a way to show others that being environmentally friendly is important to how you see yourself.

In terms of our economic framework, by adding value to products, advertising helps both the consumer and the advertiser. It also contributes to the number of sellers. That increases competition, which also serves the consumer's self-interest.

Effect on Prices

If advertising adds value to products, it follows that advertising also increases prices, right? And if companies stopped advertising, products would cost less, right?

Not necessarily. Economists have argued about the impact of advertising on prices and in some cases still disagree.

Some advertised products do cost more than unadvertised products, but the opposite is also true. Both the Federal Trade Commission and the Supreme Court have ruled that, by encouraging competition, advertising has the effect of keeping prices down. That again serves the consumer's self-interest.

Sweeping statements about advertising's positive or negative effect on prices are almost always simplistic. We can make some important points, though:

- As a cost of doing business, advertising is paid for by the consumer. In most product categories, though, the amount spent on advertising is small compared with the total cost of the product. One estimate suggests that advertising costs as a percentage of sales range from nearly 10 percent for packaged goods to just 0.4 percent for retailer Walmart.[8]

- Advertising is one element of the mass distribution system that enables many manufacturers to engage in mass production, which in turn lowers the unit cost of products. These savings can then be passed on to consumers in the form of lower prices. In this indirect way, advertising helps lower prices.

- In industries subject to government price regulation (agriculture, utilities), advertising has historically had no effect on prices. When the government deregulated many of these industries in an effort to restore free-market competition, advertising has affected price—usually downward, but not always.

- Price is a prominent element in many retail ads, which tends to hold down prices. On the other hand, national manufacturers use advertising to stress features that make their brands better; in these cases advertising may support higher prices.

Does advertising lead to higher prices? Economists believe that in many cases ads can actually contribute to lower prices for products. This ad for Darty, a French retailer, is designed to attract price-sensitive consumers to the savings they can get at the store.

Source: Darty France

Prix bas.

Prix bas tout compris.

Effect on Competition

Some believe advertising restricts competition because small companies can't compete with the immense advertising budgets of large firms. Conversely, small firms often rely on advertising to inform consumers about their brands' unique benefits. If new brands could not be promoted, how would consumers learn about choices that might better serve their needs and wants?

Intense competition can reduce the number of businesses in an industry. However, some of the firms eliminated by competition may be those that served customers least effectively. In other cases, competition is reduced because of mergers and acquisitions (big companies working in their own self-interest).

High costs may inhibit the entry of new competitors in industries that spend heavily on advertising. In some markets, the original brands probably benefit greatly from this barrier. However, the investments needed for plants, machinery, and labor are of far greater significance. These are typically the real barriers to entry, not advertising.

Advertising by big companies often has only a limited effect on small businesses because a single advertiser is rarely large enough to dominate the whole country. Regional oil companies, for example, compete very successfully with national oil companies on the local level. In fact, the freedom to advertise encourages more sellers to enter the market. And we've all seen nonadvertised store brands of food compete very effectively with nationally advertised brands on the same grocery shelves.

Effect on Consumer Demand

The question of advertising's effect on total consumer demand is complex. Many studies show that promotional activity affects aggregate consumption, but they disagree as to the extent. Social and economic forces, including technological advances, the population's educational level, increases in population and income, and changes in lifestyle, are more significant. For example, the demand for flat-panel TVs and smartphones expanded at a tremendous rate, thanks in part to advertising but more to favorable market conditions. At the same time, advertising hasn't reversed declining sales of such items as DVDs, outsized SUVs, or newspapers.

The famous "Got Milk" campaign promotes primary rather than selective demand because the goal of the campaign is to have consumers drink more milk, not a particular brand of milk. The "Got Milk?" campaign created by agency Goodby Silverstein & Partners for the California Milk Processor Board has been around for over 20 years, and its memorable two-word slogan is undoubtedly one of the most famous taglines in advertising history.

Source: The California Milk Advisory Board

In Chapter 6 we'll see that marketing promotions can help get new products off the ground by giving more people more complete information, thereby stimulating **primary demand**—demand for the entire product class. In declining markets, when the only information people want is price information, advertising can influence **selective demand**—demand for a particular brand. But the only effect it will have on primary demand is to slow the rate of decline. In growing markets, advertisers generally compete for shares of that growth. In mature, static, or declining markets, they compete for each other's shares—*conquest sales.*

Effect on Consumer Choice

The best way for a manufacturer to beat the competition is to make a unique product. For example, look at the long list of car models, sizes, colors, and features designed to attract different buyers. And grocery shelves may carry more than 100 different brands of breakfast cereals—something for everybody.

The freedom to advertise encourages businesses to create new brands and improve old ones. When one brand reaches market dominance, smaller brands may disappear for a time. But the moment a better product comes along and is advertised skillfully, the dominant brand loses out to the newer, better product. Once again, the freedom to advertise promotes the existence of more sellers, and that gives consumers wider choices.

Effect on the Business Cycle

The relationship between advertising and gross domestic product has long been debated. John Kenneth Galbraith, a perennial critic of advertising, concedes that by helping maintain the flow of consumer demand (encouraging more buyers), advertising helps sustain employment and economic growth.[9] Consumer demand is considered a pillar of a strong economy by some economists. When President Obama championed a billion dollar stimulus act in 2008, his purpose was to create demand by putting more money in consumers' pockets. The failure of the stimulus to restore healthy growth in the economy was due, in part, to its failure to create demand. Consumers used the money to pay off debt or increase savings, rather than using it to buy products.

Historically, in hard economic times, companies cut promotional expenditures. That may help short-term profits, but studies prove that businesses that continue to advertise during a recession are better able to protect, and sometimes build, market shares.[10] However, if everybody just keeps advertising, it is unlikely that the recessionary cycle will turn around. We conclude that when business cycles are up, advertising contributes to the increase. When business cycles are down, advertising may act as a stabilizing force by encouraging more buyers to buy. In the current recession, even when companies are not cutting marketing dollars, they are looking to spend their IMC budgets more efficiently (i.e., on less expensive promotional tools) and they are looking for ways to measure the return on investment (ROI) of their message options.

The Abundance Principle: The Economic Impact of Advertising in Perspective

To individual businesses such as Quaker Oats, the local car dealer, or the convenience store on the corner, advertising pays back more than it costs. If advertising didn't pay, no one would use it. And the various news and entertainment media that depend on advertising for financial support would go out of business.

To the economy as a whole, the importance of advertising may best be demonstrated by the *abundance principle.* It states that in an economy that produces more goods and services than can be consumed, advertising serves two important purposes: It keeps consumers informed of their alternatives *(complete information),* and it allows companies to compete more effectively for consumer dollars *(self-interest).* In North America alone, the U.S. and Canadian economies produce an enormous selection of products. Most supermarkets carry more than 30,000 different items. Each carmaker markets dozens of models. This competition generally results in more and better products at similar or lower prices.

Advertising stimulates competition *(many buyers and sellers).* In countries where consumers have more income to spend after their physical needs are satisfied, advertising also stimulates innovation and new products. However, no amount of advertising can achieve long-term acceptance for products that do not meet consumer approval. Despite massive advertising expenditures, fewer than a dozen of the 50 best-known cars developed in the 20th Century are still sold today. Or to take a more recent example, advertising expeditures on 3-D TV sets have thus far failed to create large consumer demand.

Advertising stimulates a healthy economy. It also results in consumers who are more informed, better educated, and more demanding. As a result, consumers now insist that manufacturers be held accountable for their advertising. This has led to an unprecedented level of social criticism and legal regulation, the subject of our next sections.

The Social Impact of Advertising

LO 3-2

Because it's so visible, advertising is frequently criticized, both for what it is and for what it isn't. Many of the criticisms focus on the *style* of advertising, saying it's deceptive or manipulative. Collectively we might refer to these as **short-term manipulative criticisms.** Other criticisms focus on the *social or environmental impact* of advertising. These are **long-term macro criticisms.**[11] A short-term criticism is one that suggests that a particular ad has harmed a particular consumer at a specific point in time. Long-term criticisms are ones that deal with the broad impact of many ads on many people over long periods of time.

In our discussion of the economic impact of advertising, we focused primarily on the first two principles of free-market economics: self-interest and many buyers and sellers. The social aspect of advertising typically involves the last two principles: *complete information* and *absence of externalities*. We can examine many issues from these two perspectives. Some of the most important are deception and manipulation in advertising, the effect of advertising on our value system, commercial clutter, stereotypes, and offensiveness.

Deception in Advertising

A common short-term argument about advertising is that it is often deceptive. The late professor Ivan Preston noted that the essence of a marketplace lies in the willingness of buyers and sellers to enter commercial transactions. Anything that detracts from the satisfaction of the transaction produces a loss of activity that ultimately hurts both parties.[12] If a brand does not live up to its claims, dissatisfaction occurs—and in the long term that is as harmful to the advertiser as to the buyer.

For advertising to be effective, consumers must have confidence in it. So deception not only detracts from the complete information principle of free enterprise but also risks being

This chainsaw doesn't literally have small warriors marching along the blade, of course. Consumers recognize that this is exaggeration, or puffery. Puffery may not be believable at a literal level. But bragging of this sort can serve as a metaphor for the benefits the brand is promoting. What benefits do you think STIHL is promoting for its chainsaw in this ad?

Source: STIHL Inc.

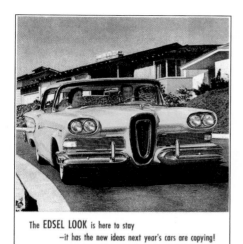

The EDSEL LOOK is here to stay
—it has the new ideas next year's cars are copying!

Less than fifty dollars difference between Edsel and V-8's in the Low-Priced Three

Despite extensive advertising efforts, some products, like the Edsel automobile, will fail simply because they do not meet the expectations of customers at that particular time. Many of the best-known cars developed in the 20th century are no longer sold today.

© Pictorial Press Ltd/Alamy

self-defeating. Even meaningless (but legal) puffery might be taken literally and therefore become deceptive. **Puffery** refers to exaggerated, subjective claims that can't be proven true or false, such as "the best," "premier," or "the only way to fly."

Under current advertising law, the only ads that can be considered deceptive are those that are *factually false* or convey a false impression and therefore have the potential to deceive or mislead reasonable people.[13] Puffery is excluded from this requirement because it is assumed that reasonable people don't believe it. Preston points out that since advertisers regularly use puffery and nonproduct facts to enhance the image of their products, they must think consumers *do* believe it. **Nonproduct facts** are not about the brand but about the consumer or the social context in which the consumer uses the brand. An example is "Pepsi. The choice of a new generation."

While advertising helps society achieve the economic goal of complete information, individual ads typically provide less than complete information. They only tell part of the story, generally a part that is favorable to the advertiser. People expect advertisers to be proud of their products and probably don't mind if they puff a little. But when advertisers cross the line between simply giving their point of view and creating false expectations, people begin to object. Papa John's Pizza no doubt thought it was just puffing when it advertised "Better ingredients. Better pizza." Pizza Hut saw it differently, though, and sued Papa John's for deceptive advertising. A U.S. district judge agreed and awarded Pizza Hut close to half a million dollars in damages. The judge then ordered Papa John's to stop using its "Better ingredients" slogan.[14] This decision was later overturned on appeal, but the case still goes to show that there are limits on what an advertiser can safely puff.[15]

Preston believes these kinds of problems can be avoided if marketers simply improve the kind of information they give in their advertising. He believed advertisers should have a reasonable basis for any claims they make, whether those claims are facts about the product, nonfacts such as "Coke is it," or nonproduct facts.[16] This, he thought, would contribute positively to our free-market system. Ad Lab 3–A lists some other common deceptive practices.

The Effect of Advertising on Our Value System

HARD ROCK IS THE REAL CULTURAL REVOLUTION.

G92 Galaxy FM
www.galaxy92.com   Η μουσική δεν είναι δόγμα

TThis ad for radio station Galaxy G92 FM in Greece uses nonproduct facts to appeal to the rebellious side of its listeners. Who do you think this ad is trying to appeal to?

Source: Galaxy G92 FM Greece

A long-term argument, often voiced by consumer advocates, is that advertising degrades people's value systems by promoting a materialistic way of life. Advertising, they say, encourages us to buy more cars, more DVDs, more clothing, and more junk we don't need. It is destroying the essence of our "citizen democracy," replacing it with a selfish consumer democracy.[17]

Critics claim advertising manipulates us into buying things by playing on our emotions and promising greater status, social acceptance, and sex appeal. It causes people to take up harmful habits, makes impoverished kids buy $300 sneakers, and tempts ordinary people to buy useless products to emulate celebrity endorsers.[18] Advertising, say its detractors, is so powerful that consumers are helpless to defend themselves against it.

Certainly there's no question that advertisers spend millions trying to convince people their products will make them sexier, healthier, and more successful. The volume of advertising seems to suggest that every problem can be solved by a purchase.

However, this argument exaggerates the power of advertising. In fact, most Americans express a healthy skepticism toward it. One study showed that only 17 percent of U.S. consumers see advertising as a source of information to help them decide what to buy.[19] Perhaps that's why more advertised products fail than succeed in the marketplace.

Even if we assume that most people can willingly accept or reject an advertising message, they are still not getting the whole picture. After all, advertising is supported by marketers who want to sell their products, but nobody markets the opposite stance of why we don't need to or shouldn't buy a particular product at all. In this sense, consumers don't have *complete information.* This is an important issue of *externalities,* because the aggregate activities of the nation's advertisers affect many people outside the immediate marketing transaction and create an unexpected cost to society.

AD Lab 3-A

Unfair and Deceptive Practices in Advertising

The courts have held that these acts constitute unfair or deceptive trade practices and are therefore illegal.

False Promises

Making an advertising promise that cannot be kept, such as "restores youth" or "prevents cancer." When Listerine claimed to prevent or reduce the impact of colds and sore throats, the FTC banned the campaign and required the company to run millions of dollars' worth of corrective ads.

Incomplete Description

Stating some but not all of a product's contents, such as advertising a "solid oak" desk without mentioning that only the top is solid oak and the rest is pine.

False and Misleading Comparisons

Making false comparisons, either explicitly or by implication, such as "Like Tylenol, Advil doesn't upset my stomach." That implies that Advil is equal in avoiding stomach upset, though in truth Tylenol is better. To some people, Advil's claim might even suggest that Tylenol upsets the stomach, which is also false.

Bait-and-Switch Offers

Advertising an item at an unusually low price to bring people into the store and then "switching" them to a higher-priced model by claiming that the advertised product is out of stock or poorly made.

Visual Distortions and False Demonstrations

Using trick photography or computer manipulation to enhance a product's appearance—for example, a TV commercial for a "giant steak"

dinner special showing the steak on a miniature plate that makes it look extra large. In one classic case, General Motors and its window supplier, Libby Owens-Ford, rigged a demonstration to show how clear their windows were. The GM cars were photographed with the windows down, the competitor's car with the windows up—and Vaseline smeared on them.

False Testimonials

Implying that a product has the endorsement of a celebrity or an authority who is not a bona fide user, or implying that endorsers have a certain expertise that in fact they don't.

Partial Disclosure

Stating certain facts about the advertised product but omitting other material information. An example is claiming, "Kraft's Singles processed cheese slices are made from five ounces of milk," which gives Singles more calcium than the imitators' without mentioning that processing loses about two ounces of the milk.

Small-Print Qualifications

Making a statement in large print, such as Beneficial's "Instant Tax Refund," only to qualify or retract it in obscure, small, or unreadable type elsewhere in the ad: "If you qualify for one of our loans." To the FTC, if readers don't see the qualification, it's not there.

Laboratory Applications

1. Describe some examples of deception you have seen in advertising.

2. Who is affected by unfair or deceptive advertising practices and what remedies are available to them?

The Proliferation of Advertising

One of the most common long-term complaints about advertising is that there's just too much of it. In the United States, the average person may be exposed to 500 to 1,000 commercial messages a day. With so many products competing for attention, advertisers themselves worry about the impact of excessive advertising. According to Nielsen, ad clutter is still on the rise. In 2005, the amount of nonprogram time on network TV—which includes advertising, public service announcements, and program promotions—ranged from about 16 minutes per hour during prime time to nearly 21 minutes per hour in daytime, a day part that is particularly important to advertisers.[20] And the situation is even worse on some cable networks: Spike TV experimented with commercial breaks lasting as long as 10 minutes.[21] The networks add to the problem by jamming every possible moment with promotions for their shows. Too much advertising creates an externality not only for consumers (nuisance) but also for the advertisers themselves—the more commercials that hit the consumer's brain, the less effective any single one can be. Some of the rise in digital and social media IMC expenditures can be traced to marketer dissatisfaction with clutter in traditional media.

Commercial radio is just as cluttered as TV. Conscious of the negative effects of ad clutter, Clear Channel—the largest radio group in the United States, with over 1,200 stations—introduced the "Less Is More" program. Reduced inventory allowed Clear Channel to raise the price of its scarcer spots.[22] The Federal Communications Commission, which in years

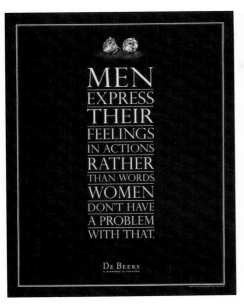

The use of stereotypes is considered unethical by many, even when done in a light-hearted way. Is this attempt by De Beers Diamonds to capitalize on gender stereotypes funny? Or is it offensive?

Source: De Beers Diamond Jewellers US Inc.

past regulated advertising on all broadcast television, now focuses primarily on limiting ads in TV programming aimed at children 12 and under—advertising may not exceed 10.5 minutes per hour on weekends and 12 minutes per hour on weekdays.[23]

Clutter is not so evident in other countries. In the European Union, for example, TV broadcasters can carry no more than 12 minutes of commercials per hour.[24]

In North America we should be so lucky. During election periods, the clutter problem gets worse, seriously devaluing an advertiser's commercial. In 2004, an unexpectedly large number of political ads ran on television in Ohio, a crucial swing state in the presidential election. Ad spending exceeded $20 million, an estimated increase of 50 percent from the previous presidential campaign, and three out of four commercials that aired one weekend were for political candidates.[25] In 2008, another presidential election year, political ad spending set a record of $2.8 billion. That was easily eclipsed by the $4.2 billion spent in 2010, a year without a presidential contest and the $6 billion spent in 2012.[26] And few doubt that new records will be set in the race of 2016.

The Use of Stereotypes in Advertising

Advertising has long been criticized for insensitivity to minorities, women, immigrants, the disabled, the elderly, and other groups."[27] This long-term argument also addresses externalities because advertising affects the nature of our culture and environment, even when we do not want it. This is ironic, because marketing and advertising practitioners are supposed to be professional students of the communication process and consumer behavior. But, in fact, they sometimes lose touch with the very people they're trying to reach.

In recent years, national advertisers have become more sensitive to the concerns of minorities and women. Latinos, African Americans, Asians, Native Americans, and others are now usually portrayed with sensitivity in ads, not only because of pressure from watchdog groups, but also because it's just good business; these consumers represent sizable target markets. Marilyn Kern-Foxworth, a professor and expert on minorities in advertising, believes that positive role portrayal in some mainstream ads has raised the self-esteem of African American youth.[28] As we'll see in Chapter 4, this positive trend has accelerated with the emergence of many ad agencies that specialize in reaching minority markets.

The image of women is also changing from their historic depiction as either homemakers or sex objects. This may be partially due to the growing number of women in executive positions with both advertisers and agencies. Stanford professor Debra Meyerson says "the glass ceiling definitely exists, but at the same time, there are an increasing number of women who are breaking through it."[29] In 2007, about 59 percent of all women were in the workforce, with more than 48 million in managerial and professional careers.[30] Advertisers want to reach, not offend, this sizable market of upwardly mobile consumers. Some agencies now retain feminist consultants to review ads that may risk

Advertising may sometimes perpetuate stereotypes, but it can also help dispel them. In this PSA, The Shelter Pet Project those who believe animals end up in shelters because of behavioral problems are shown that they may often end up there through no fault of their own.

Source: Shelter Pet Project

With tightening markets, advertisers must double their efforts to maintain or expand market share. One way is to expand into minority communities, which have enormous buying power and are growing at a faster rate than the rest of the population. The ad for Bounty Paper Towels targeted at the Spanish community and the ad for Quaker Oats targeted at the African American community are good examples of efforts to expand the market share of these two popular brands.

Bounty: © The Advertising Archives

Quaker: Source: Pepsi Cola Company

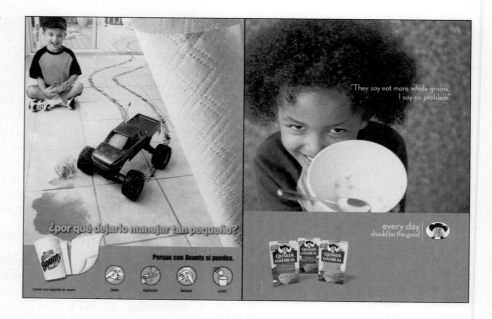

offending women.[31] In 2003, Ann Fudge shattered the glass ceiling when she was named chairperson and CEO of Young and Rubicam and became the first African American woman to head a major U.S. advertising agency. *Forbes* named Fudge one of the 100 most powerful women in America in 2004. And in 2007, Nancy Hill became the first female head of the American Association of Advertising Agencies (AAAA) (see People behind the Ads in Chapter 4). The days when sexist practitioners like Don Draper, the central character of AMC's *Mad Men*, defined the culture of ad agencies, are now far in the past.

However, problems still exist, especially in local and regional advertising and in certain product categories such as beer and sports promotions. Many advertisers are just not sensitive to the externalities that their ads can create, and some may perpetuate male and female stereotypes without even realizing it.

Of course, avoiding negative stereotypes is not the same as embracing cultural diversity. Research evidence suggests that many Americans value their ethnic identities and prefer brands that speak to them. This in turn has led agencies to see the value of diversifying their own ranks to better understand and communicate with their clients' consumers[32] (see Ethical Issues, "Helping an Industry Look Like America," in Chapter 5).

Offensiveness in Advertising

Offensiveness is a short-term style argument that also speaks to externalities. Parents are sometimes upset by ads that embrace provocative or sexual themes, especially when the advertiser targets children or teens. Prominent targets of parental ire include Calvin Klein and Abercrombie & Fitch.[33]

Taste, of course, is highly subjective: What is bad taste to some is perfectly acceptable to others. And tastes change. What is considered offensive today may not be so tomorrow. People were outraged when the first ad for underarm deodorant appeared in a 1927 *Ladies Home Journal;* today no one questions such ads. Yet, even with the AIDS epidemic, many broadcast networks still do not air condom commercials during the day; instead, the "Make a Difference" condom campaign was placed in prime time. Networks known to run condom ads include Fox, MTV, Comedy Central, BET, CNN, TNT, USA, TBS, and NBC (after 10 PM).[34]

Taste is also geographic. A shockingly bloody ad for a small surfwear company in Sydney, Australia, showed a gutted shark lying on a dock. Protruding from its cut-open belly were a human skeleton and an intact pair of surfer shorts. The tagline: "Tough clothes by Kadu—Triple stitched. Strongest materials available. Homegrown and sewn."

While we might consider that ad quite offensive in North America, it won the Grand Prix at the International Advertising Festival in Cannes. In Australia it received wide media

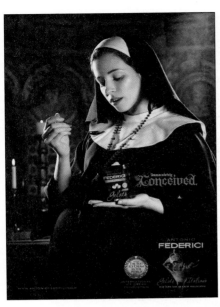

While most advertisers try to avoid controversy at all costs, others seem to positively relish it. This ad is intended to purposely offend some, possibly to attract attention from others. Is it ethical to violate strongly held beliefs in order to promote a brand? Is it responsible?

© Uppa/Zuma Press/Newscom Images

coverage because two surfers were killed by sharks while it was running. Rather than pulling the ad out of respect, the company reveled in its timeliness, and local surfers responded favorably.[35] But roles were reversed with a global campaign to increase Australian tourism that ran in 2006. The campaign tagline, "Where the bloody hell are you?" was viewed as quaint in America, where the term "bloody" is uncontroversial. In Australia and England, where the adjective is considered strong language, consumers and critics complained.

Today, grooming, fashion, and personal hygiene products often use partial nudity in their ads. Where nudity is relevant to the product, people are less likely to regard it as obscene or offensive—except when the advertising targets kids. In Europe, nudity in commercials is commonplace.[36]

Some consumers get so offended by both advertising and TV programming that they boycott sponsors' products. Of course, they also have the option to just change the channel. Both of these are effective strategies for consumers because, ultimately, the marketplace has veto power. If ads don't pull in the audience, the campaign will falter and die.

The Social Impact of Advertising in Perspective

Marketing professionals earnestly believe in the benefits that advertising brings to society. Advertising, they say, encourages the development and speeds the acceptance of new products and technologies. It fosters employment. It gives consumers and business customers a wider variety of choices. By encouraging mass production, it helps keep prices down. And it stimulates healthy competition between producers, which benefits all buyers.[37] Advertising, they point out, also promotes a higher standard of living; it pays for most of our news media and subsidizes the arts; it supports freedom of the press; and it provides a means to disseminate public information about important health and social issues.

Critics of advertising might disagree with many of these points. Some argue that rather than supporting a free press, advertising actually creates an externality that interferes with it. The media, they say, pander to national advertisers to attract ad dollars. In the process, they modify their editorial content to suit their corporate benefactors and shirk their responsibility of presenting news in the public interest.[38]

A balanced perspective might suggest that while advertising may legitimately be criticized for offering less-than-complete information and, in some instances, for creating unwanted externalities, it should also be applauded when it contributes to economic growth and consumer prosperity. In most cases, by being a rich information source (albeit not a complete one), advertising contributes to the existence of many buyers and sellers and, therefore, to the goals of both consumers and marketers. Moreover, while advertising is biased, it is broadly recognized as such by its intended targets. It offers consumers information they are not likely to get anywhere else. And for many, it is a legitimate form of speech in societies that value diverse viewpoints. And while advertisers have been known to pressure news outlets for favorable coverage, there is no easy way for media groups to replace the income advertising provides. Where their interests collide, it is ultimately a news organization's job to determine whether they will serve advertisers or their audience.

Social Responsibility and Advertising Ethics

LO 3-3

When advertising violates one of the basic economic assumptions we've described, some corrective action is needed. As we'll discuss in the next section, laws determine what advertisers can and cannot do, but they also allow a significant amount of leeway. That's where ethics and social responsibility come into play. An advertiser can act unethically or irresponsibly without breaking any laws. If laws did not prevent vodka brands from sponsoring shows aimed at children, that would not mean it was ethical or responsible to do so. As Ivan Presto says, ethics begin where the law ends.[39]

Being **ethical** means doing what is morally right in a given situation. **Social responsibility** means doing what society views as best for the welfare of people in general or for a specific community of people. Together, ethics and social responsibility can be seen as the obligation of advertisers to society, even when there is no legal obligation.

Advertisers' Social Responsibility

The foundation of any human society is peaceful and respectful relationships among its members. Without harmony, societies collapse. So institutions have some responsibility for helping maintain social harmony through proper stewardship of individuals and groups, honesty and integrity in relationships, adherence to accepted ethical standards, willingness to assist various segments of the society, and respect for the privacy of others.

Advertising plays an important role in developed countries. It influences a society's stability and growth. It helps secure large armies, creates entertainment events attracting hundreds of thousands of fans, and often affects the outcome of political elections. Such power places a burden of responsibility on those who sponsor, buy, create, produce, and sell advertising to maintain ethical standards that support the society and contribute to the economic system.

In most countries, for example, the advertising industry is part of a large business community. Like any good neighbor, it has responsibilities: to keep its property clean, participate in civic events, support local enterprises, and improve the community. U.S. advertising professionals have met these challenges by forming local advertising clubs, the American Advertising Federation (AAF), the American Association of Advertising Agencies (AAAA), and the Ad Council. These organizations provide thousands of hours and millions of dollars' worth of pro bono (free) work to charitable organizations and public agencies. They also provide

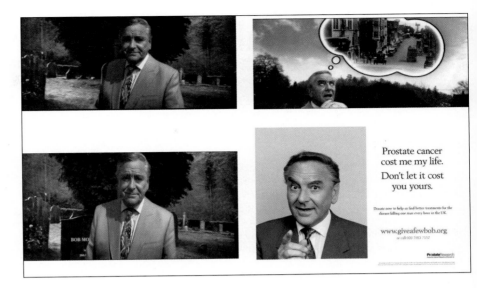

This award-winning ad, called "Give a few Bob," featured British TV celebrity Bob Monkhouse talking about the dangers of prostate cancer. Monkhouse died from the disease four years before the commercial was made. Using computer effects, the ad agency that produced the spot created an ad in which Monkhouse jokes about his own death. Effective or creepy? Or both?

Source: The Communications Agency for the Prostate Cancer Research Foundation and the Monkhouse Family

scholarships and internships, contributions that serve the whole of society. As we discuss later, they even regulate themselves fairly effectively.

Advertisers such as AT&T, IBM, and Honda commit significant dollars to supporting the arts, education, and various charitable causes as well as their local Better Business Bureaus and Chambers of Commerce. Still, advertisers are regularly chided when they fail the social responsibility litmus test. Concerned citizens, consumer advocates, and special-interest groups pressure advertisers when they perceive the public's welfare is at risk. The earliest "green advertising" campaigns, for instance, exemplified a blatant effort by some advertisers to cash in on consumers' desire for a cleaner environment. Some promoted nebulous product qualities, such as "environmental friendliness," that had no basis in fact. Finally, when the state attorneys general got together and defined relevant terms for use in green advertising, marketers cleaned up their act.

Ethics of Advertising

Philosophies of ethics span the centuries since Socrates. We can hardly do them justice here. But for practical purposes, let's consider three levels of ethical responsibility and apply them to advertising.

On one level, ethics comprise two interrelated components: the traditional actions taken by people in a society or community, which are customs, and the philosophical rules that society establishes to justify past actions and decree future actions, which are principles. Customs and principles create the primary rules of ethical behavior in the society and enable us to measure how far an individual or company (or advertiser) strays from the norm.

Every individual also faces a second set of ethical issues: the attitudes, feelings, and beliefs that add up to a personal value system. When these two systems conflict, should the individual act on personal beliefs or on the obligation to serve society? For example, nonsmoking ad agency people may create ads for a tobacco client. At the first societal level of ethics there is some conflict: Smoking has been a custom in the United States for centuries and is not illegal today. However, the U.S. Surgeon General has declared that smoking is a national health problem (harming innocent people violates an important principle). This conflict at the first ethical level passes the responsibility for decision making to the second, individual level. Recognizing this, many agencies give their employees considerable latitude regarding whether they work on a tobacco (or alcohol) account.

When the group or individuals cannot resolve an ethical dilemma, they must redefine the issue in dispute. Thus, the third level of ethics concerns singular ethical concepts such as good, bad, right, wrong, duty, integrity, and truth. Are these concepts absolute, universal, and binding? Or are they relative, dependent on situations and consequences? A person's moral

Ethical Issues

The First Amendment and Commercial Speech

The United States was less than two decades old when, in 1789, the U.S. Congress proposed a set of 10 basic rights to be enjoyed by all citizens. These rights were so strong that they could not be infringed by government.

The first of the amendments, dealing with speech and religious freedom, was thought to be relatively uncontroversial. James Madison, who drafted the amendment, thought that "if we confine ourselves to an enumeration of simple, acknowledge principles," there would be little disagreement about whether it should be passed. Madison's talent as a political thinker and writer clearly did not extend to his ability to forecast the future, as the meaning and scope of the First Amendment has preoccupied the courts ever since.

The amendment reads as follows:

Congress shall make no law respecting an establishment of religion, or prohibiting the free exercise thereof; or abridging the freedom of speech, or of the press; or the right of the people peaceably to assemble, and to petition the government for a redress of grievances.

Americans still struggle with the nature and scope of First Amendment protections in our lives. For example, what does the amendment protect and what does it not? In the former category, the courts have consistently included criticism of the government, including the burning of the U.S. flag. In the latter, they have included harassment, obscenity, and defamation.

And somewhere in a rather gray area is commercial speech. Commercial speech is speech "where the speaker is more likely to be engaged in commerce, where the intended audience is commercial or actual or potential customers, and where the content of the message is commercial in nature."

Historically, court decisions have evolved from the notion that commercial speech enjoys no First Amendment protection (the 1942 *Valentine v. Christensen* case) to a more nuanced approach, as suggested in the *Central Hudson* case. The key idea from *Central Hudson* is that commercial speech may be regulated, but not with impunity. Regulation is permissible only when there is a compelling reason to do it and it is done in the narrowest possible way.

In 2011, the Supreme Court issued a ruling with important implications for commercial speech. The case, *Sorrell v. IMS Inc.*, concerned data mining, a practice whereby companies develop marketing strategies by analyzing sales data. IMS Health, a data-mining company, sold information about large numbers of prescriptions to pharmaceutical companies. The data had no information about the consumers who bought the prescriptions, but they did include the names of the doctors who wrote them. Doctors who were not prescribing branded drugs were identified and then contacted by sales reps for the drug companies.

Vermont passed a law banning the practice. When the case went to the Supreme Court, representatives of the state defended the ban by claiming that the data increased the likelihood that (a) doctors would prescribe branded drugs over less expensive generics, thereby raising state health care costs; (b) drug company marketing campaigns would succeed, resulting in busy doctors relying more heavily on promotional materials for learning about new drugs; (c) companies could tailor their messages to specific doctors; and (d) doctors would be exposed to "harassing" visits from pharmaceutical reps.

As one reviewer noted, "Essentially, Vermont's law attempted to correct what it saw as an unbalanced marketplace of ideas that undermines the state's interests in promoting public health, protecting prescriber privacy, and reducing health care costs."

Before finding out what the Supreme Court decided in the case, you may wish to form your own opinions about this practice, and determine for yourself whether you believe Vermont had the legal authority, and even the ethical responsibility, to ban the use of data mining by the drug companies. On the legal authority side, you may wish to review the four criteria outlined in *Central Hudson* (see page 81). Ethically, you may wish to review the reasons Vermont offered to defend its law. Additionally, you may wish to think about freedom of speech and its value to

and ethical philosophy, influenced by religion, society, and individual values will determine his or her answer (see Exhibit 3-3).

Let's say, for example, the copywriter for a cigarette ad is a smoker, and he writes copy that implies that smoking is a favorable behavior. But the ad's art director, a nonsmoker, complains that the ad is unethical because the copy conflicts with the truth that smoking is unsafe. At this point they reach the third ethical level, and a more senior person, such as the creative director, may step in and lead a discussion aimed at defining the agency's ethical policy on smoking.

As we mentioned before, ethics is such an important topic that we address those issues that pertain to advertising in Ethical Issues sidebars in each chapter. The Ethical Issues box here examines the First Amendment and commercial speech.

Most advertisers today strive to maintain ethical standards and practice socially responsible advertising. Once a free-swinging, unchecked business, advertising is today a closely scrutinized and heavily regulated profession. Advertising's past shortcomings have created society. Do you agree that First Amendment protections should apply to commercial speech? And is data mining an example of "speech"?

The Supreme Court, in a 6–3 opinion, upheld a lower-court ruling that the Vermont ban was unconstitutional because it violated the First Amendment. The majority opinion noted that the law restricted the sale and use of information about prescriptions, but only for the drug companies. Other companies were still legally allowed to purchase the information. The Court also disagreed with Vermont's claim that sharing information gleaned from data mining is "conduct," not "speech." It ruled that "the creation and dissemination of information are speech for First Amendment purposes." Finally, Vermont's effort to protect the privacy of doctors and lower its health costs by limiting speech rights of drug companies was wrong because "the fear that people would make bad decisions if given truthful information cannot justify . . . burdens on speech."

Since this is an ethical analysis, it seems important to return to the notions embodied in the First Amendment. Why protect free speech at all? What if Vermont's assertions are true? What if data mining raises health care costs, skews doctors' decisions in favor of more expensive drugs, and subjects doctors to, if not harassing, then possibly undesired visits from drug company salespeople? Can freedom of commercial speech be more important than serving the public interest, as Vermont asserted its law would do?

Americans, perhaps like Madison, think it uncontroversial that a good society values free speech. And yet Americans are also confronted with expression they find offensive, rude, illogical, and even heretical. In the hometown of one of this book's authors, Gainesville, a local preacher attracted global attention when he threatened to make a political statement by burning the Koran. Confronted with this kind of expression, many people reacted with revulsion.

So why value speech at all? Most countries, even relatively free ones, do not have guarantees of free speech as powerful as the First Amendment. The framers of our Constitution enshrined freedom of speech for several reasons. One was that they believed that people and institutions make better decisions when they are exposed to different points of view, and diverse viewpoints are best encouraged in a climate of free speech. Another was that the framers believed that the right of every citizen to openly criticize government is vital to a free society. The First Amendment was created from a conviction that a virtuous government must answer its critics in society and the press.

At an abstract level, almost everyone agrees with freedom of speech. But moving closer to the issues in our day-to-day lives, people may disagree. As we've seen, the courts have had conflicting views on whether commercial speech is protected by the Constitution. The Supreme Court has, for example, upheld many restrictions on the marketing of cigarettes. In the marketplace of ideas, how important are expressions about the marketplace?

Questions

1. What is your opinion about whether commercial speech should be protected by the First Amendment?

2. If commercial speech is protected, are there still additional burdens that people may place on it to further other goals, such as protecting vulnerable groups (like children) or ensuring privacy (as in do-not-call lists)? If you do not agree commercial speech is protected, are there any limits on the power of government to regulate advertising and IMC you would agree with?

Sources: Legal Information Institute, "First Amendment, Religion and Expression, Freedom of Expression—Speech and Press," retrieved from www.law.cornell.edu/anncon/html/amdt1bfrag1_user.html#amdt1b_hd4, December 10, 2011. Legal Information Institute, "Commercial Speech," retrieved from www.law.cornell.edu/wex/commercial_speech, December 10, 2011. U.S. Supreme Court: Sorrell vs. IMS Inc.—Court Upholds Data Mining," Policy and Medicine, retrieved from www.policymed.com/2011/06/us-supreme-court-sorrell-vs-ims-inc-court-upholds-data-mining.html, December 10, 2011. Mark Cooray, "Freedom of Speech and Expression," retrieved from www.urcivilisation.com/cooray/rights/chap6.htm, December 10, 2011.

Exhibit 3-3
Levels of ethical responsibility.

Level	Influences	Participant(s)	Ethical Outcome
1. The Group	Customs and debate from other two levels	Society (or its component groups)	Custom reinforced or new rules
2. The Individual	Customs, rules, and debate from other two levels	Individual	Personal value system better defined
3. Ethic Definition	Customs and rules established by the other two levels	Groups and individuals (in debate)	Single ethic defined or redefined

My **IMC** Campaign 3

You will be working on an advertising/IMC campaign, or part of one, this semester. Few things are more important for you when preparing for a semester-long project than understanding the final product that is expected of you. It is only when you know what is expected at the end that you can plan what happens in between.

What You May Be Working On

Different classes have different projects, but it is likely that you will work on one or more of the following for a brand, service, or firm:

- A campaign audit.
- A research report.
- A marketing or IMC plan, including a SWOT analysis.
- An advertising or IMC budget.
- A media plan.
- A creative brief or creative platform.
- A plans book.

Below we explain each of these in turn and give you guidance about where you can find information in this text and on the Internet.

Campaign Audit

Many classes begin by having teams audit the plans books from prior semesters. This accomplishes several things. First, it gives you an idea about what you will be doing all semester. Second, it introduces you to the importance of seeing how research, strategy, planning, budgeting, and creative all flow together. If you don't have access to the work of other students, why not look over the work of the very best? Visit the Effie Award Website https://www.effie.org/, where you can find great ads and a lot of background information about the campaigns.

Research Report

You may be asked to conduct formative research for the brand. This may include secondary research, useful for gathering information for your IMC plan; qualitative primary research, in which you conduct a focus group or series of in-depth interviews; and quantitative research, in which you administer a survey. You'll find a lot of information in Chapter 7 about these activities. Your university likely has a web page devoted to secondary marketing research. A useful collection of market research resources can also be found here: http://blog.hubspot.com/marketing/market-research-tools-resources

---

layers of laws, regulations, and regulatory bodies. Consumer groups, governments, special-interest groups, and even other advertisers now review, control, and modify advertising in order to create more *complete information* and reduce the impact of unwanted *externalities*.

How Government Regulates Advertising

LO **3-4**

Many laws govern what advertisers can and cannot do. These laws are passed by legislatures, enforced by the executive branch, and interpreted by the judiciary. This system is repeated at the state and local levels.

On the national level, the president, cabinet departments, and various federal commissions are responsible for executing the laws passed by Congress. On the state level, governors, attorneys general, and state departments administer laws. Locally, mayors, city managers, city attorneys, and police chiefs enforce the laws passed by city councils.

Similarly, local laws are interpreted by municipal courts, while the superior courts and state supreme courts interpret state laws. Federal laws are interpreted by federal district courts and the U.S. Supreme Court. Every day, advertisers from the local copy shop to international soft drink marketers have to deal with the actions and decisions of all these branches of government. We'll discuss shortly some of the most important issues that concern U.S. regulators.

Government Restraints on International Advertisers

The campaigns of global advertisers often use similar themes and even the same ads across frontiers. Other governments often regulate advertising more extensively than either the United States or Canada. And while Europe has moved toward uniformity in marketing activities, the laws governing advertising remain largely national.[40] So advertisers need to keep up with the changing legal environments of the countries in which they advertise.

Europe and the United States have very different perspectives on privacy protection, with Europeans generally favoring stricter controls. As examples, Europeans must give

Marketing or IMC Plan

Many classes require that you create a marketing or IMC plan. We've included lots of information in this text to help. Be sure to read Chapter 8 carefully, as it is your guide to the art and science of planning. Then, to make things more concrete, use the Appendices of the book to create an outline for your plan. Your instructor may have his or her own outline; if so, use that.

Media Plan

A media plan shows the specific allocations of the budget to different media and promotional activities. It will also specify what vehicles will be used for the campaign, as well as when and how often the ads will run. You will most likely want to use a spreadsheet to show the calendar. We have a sample media plan in Chapter 9.

The Creative Brief

The creative brief is a fairly short document that is used to inform and guide the people who create the ads. It contains information that has been distilled from some of the documents that we've just reviewed,

such as the IMC plan. There are as many different outlines for creative briefs as there are ad agencies, but in many instances the differences are superficial. Chapter 11 gives some suggestions for a creative brief and shows you the elements of message strategy. For examples of creative briefs, visit the following sites:

- Emily Cohen: www.graphicdefine.org/issue2/successfulcreativebriefs

- SmileyCat blog (for a brief written for a Web campaign): www.smileycat.com/miaow/archives/000226.php

The Plans Book

If you are doing a plans book it means you are doing almost everything we've reviewed to this point. A typical plans book will include research findings, an IMC plan, a creative brief, media plans, and, in many cases, mock-ups of real ads. But it puts these things together in a seamless, integrated way, so that the reader has a clear understanding of the entire arc of a planned campaign. In many plans books there will also be a section on campaign evaluation (ways of assessing the campaign).

permission for collection of personal data and they have the right to review any data that is collected. Such data cannot be shared between companies unless consumers give permission they may do so. Work e-mail is off limits to employers and retailers may not request a shopper's telephone number at checkout.[41] European courts have ruled people have a "right to be forgotten," mandating that Google eliminate search results for an individual who requests that this information be destroyed.[42]

Many countries prohibit puffery. In Germany, for example, advertisers may use only scientifically provable superlatives. McCann-Erickson once had to retranslate the old Coca-Cola slogan, "Refreshes you best," because it implied a leadership position that was unprovable. The agency substituted "Refreshes you right."[43]

Many European countries also ban coupons, premiums, free tie-in offers, and the like. Companies may advertise price cuts only during "official sales periods," and advertisers often need government approval before publishing a sale ad. Across Europe, advertising on television must be clearly recognizable and kept separate from other programming.[44]

In Singapore, the state-owned broadcasting company yanked a Qantas Airline spot after the Ministry of Information and the Arts criticized the ad's "harmful values." The spot had used the line "last of the big spenders," which the ministry felt encouraged reckless spending by consumers (see Ad Lab 3–B).[45]

With the rapid growth of China's economy and the growth of a prosperous middle class, the country has faced new challenges in regulating advertising. A draft of new regulations were issued by China's National People's Congress that regulate ads for specific products (i.e., tobacco, pharmaceuticals) and provide clarity about penalties for false advertising, the use of paid spokespeople, and government supervision of advertising.[46] But regulation may still only be rough guides to the rules that advertisers must follow, as the Communist Party remains firmly in control and social media censorship is strictly enforced.[47]

In international advertising, the only way to navigate this morass of potential legal problems is to retain firms that specialize in advertising law.

AD Lab 3-B

The Importance of Good Legal Counsel in Advertising

For many years, Jack Russell had dreamed of this opportunity—opening a members-only club for young people who were not yet old enough to drink. He could already taste the success that was about to be his—money, fame, and fortune were all within his reach. He took every avenue possible to promote the new, exclusive club. He ran ads in local entertainment magazines and community newspapers. Local rock radio stations, though, were the mainstay—shouting out the good news for kids all over town, complete with a phone number and address for sending in their charter membership fees. Jack's wonderful idea was about to take flight. But then the local district attorney ripped the magic carpet out from underneath him. You see, Jack Russell was selling memberships to a club that had not opened yet. In fact, he hadn't even signed the lease on the proposed premises. To the DA, it smelled of scam. He figured Jack was taking money from kids for something that didn't exist. The DA charged him with false advertising—and fraud. When Jack answered his ringing doorbell, two uniformed officers were standing there. They handcuffed him, gave him a ride downtown, and threw him in jail. If Jack had just passed his ads by a communications lawyer, he could have avoided a very embarrassing and expensive nightmare. And he'd be a free man.

Ethical and legal problems with advertising seem to pop up constantly. Not only government officials but also competitors and consumer rights groups scrutinize ads carefully—either for their own self-interest or to protect the rights of consumers. As a result, every agency and advertiser needs to have a strong understanding of the laws that govern advertising. They also need to retain the services of a good law firm that specializes in advertising and communication law.

One such firm is Reed Smith's Advertising, Technology, and Media Group. With 77 communications law specialists spread among its 18 offices, Reed Smith is well situated to counsel advertisers throughout the United States, the United Kingdom, and Europe. Its clients come from all levels of the industry—from blue chip advertisers (such as Merck, Pfizer, Sony, and Lancôme) to ad agencies (such as Worldwide Partners, Inc.) to advertising associations (such as the Association of National Advertisers and the Advertising Research Foundation).

Reed Smith routinely provides its clients with a wide array of services: checking advertising copy for legal acceptability; reviewing conventional and online promotional concepts involving sweepstakes, games, and contests; researching comparative advertising and copyright violations; and representing clients before federal and state regulatory bodies and courts. The firm also helps clients in their relationships with the media, Internet service providers, talent, and performers' unions.

The chair of the firm's advertising, technology, and media group, Douglas J. Wood, is the author of *Please Be Ad-Vised* (ANA, 2004), a comprehensive reference written for advertising and marketing professionals.

Reed Smith also publishes a free e-mail newsletter and a sophisticated Website, both under the name of *Adlaw by Request*, which provide clients and prospects with summaries and analyses of new and proposed legislation affecting advertising. The Website (www.adlawbyrequest.com) offers a wide array of regularly updated resources, including downloadable contract forms, sample legal documents, and articles on the legal complexities of all types of advertising and marketing communications.

Laboratory Applications

1. Go to adlawbyrequest.com and explore the Website. Click on the "In the Courts" tab and read about current advertising-related legal cases. Pick one that interests you, read it, and then write a brief report including the title of the case, the names of the parties involved, the issues at stake, and a summary of the decision that was handed down if there has been a judgment.

2. Click "Regulators" in the topics listed on the left side of the page. Summarize one of the posts concerning the actions of a federal regulatory agency (such as the FTC, FCC, FDA, etc.). Then visit the Website of the agency to find out more about its mission. In your opinion, how well does the action of the federal agency described in the post fit with its mission?

3. What ethical, social, or legal issues do you think will be addressed in the next 10 years relative to advertising and the Internet?

Current Regulatory Issues Affecting U.S. Advertisers

Both federal and state courts have made a number of significant rulings pertaining to advertising issues. The most important of these concern First Amendment rights and privacy rights. We'll discuss each of these, paying special attention to the controversy surrounding tobacco advertising as well as the sensitive issue of advertising to children.

Freedom of Commercial Speech

LO 3-5

The Supreme Court historically distinguishes between "speech" and "commercial speech" (speech that promotes a commercial transaction). The Court first ruled on the issue of whether commercial speech is protected by the First Amendment in a 1942 case, *Valentine* v. *Christensen*. Christensen wanted to distribute handbills in New York for his business. When told to stop by the police, who were enforcing an anti-littering ordinance, Christensen turned to the courts to argue he had a right to advertise. After several appeals brought the case before the Supreme Court, the news for advertisers was not good. The justices ruled that government was free to regulate "purely commercial advertising," implying that whatever forms of speech the First Amendment protected, advertising was not among them.[48] While the

Valentine decision concluded there was no constitutionally guaranteed protection for commercial speech, court rulings ever since have suggested otherwise.

The trend started in 1976 when the Supreme Court held in *Virginia State Board of Pharmacy* v. *Virginia Citizens Consumer Council* that truthful ads enjoy protection under the First Amendment as commercial speech.[49] The next year the Court declared that bans by state bar associations on attorney advertising also violated the First Amendment. Now a third of all lawyers advertise, and a few states even permit client testimonials.

In 1980, the Court used *Central Hudson Gas* v. *Public Service Commission* to offer guidance about when commercial speech can be regulated. The four-pronged *Central Hudson* test includes the following parts:

1. *Does the commercial speech at issue concern a lawful activity?* The ad in question must be for a legal product and must be free of misleading claims.

2. *Will the restriction of commercial speech serve the asserted government interest substantially?* The government must prove that the restriction on speech will go a long way toward solving an important problem.

3. *Does the regulation directly advance the government interest asserted?* The government must establish conclusively that cessation of commercial speech would be effective in remedying the problem that government is trying to address.

4. *Is the restriction no more than necessary to further the interest asserted?* The government should show that there are no other means to accomplish the same end without restricting free speech.[50]

In 1982, the Supreme Court upheld an FTC order allowing physicians and dentists to advertise. Since then, advertising for medical and dental services has skyrocketed.

In 2011, a Supreme Court ruling had important implications for commercial speech. The case, *Sorrell v. IMS Inc.*, concerned data mining. In this case the Court invalidated a state law that made the practice illegal, at least for drug companies. Many saw this as a broader protection for commercial speech than the one outlined in the *Central Hudson* case. Decide for yourself by rereading the test proposed in the Central Hudson case, and then applying it to the facts in *Sorrell v. IMS Inc.* You can find these facts in this chapter's Ethics box.[51]

The issue of freedom of commercial speech is far from settled. Allowing greater freedom of commercial speech enhances the "government interests" of many buyers and sellers and complete information. But critics contend that advertising regulations can help reduce externalities related to controversial or unhealthy products.

The Tobacco Advertising Controversy

While all 50 states permit adults to legally use tobacco products, smoking causes diseases that kill or disable more than half a million people annually and costing taxpayers billions of dollars every year in health costs—a major externality. To recover these costs, a majority of states' attorneys general sued the tobacco industry. In 1998, they reached a historic settlement that imposed limits on brand-name promotion at events with young attendees, banned the use of cartoon characters (like Joe Camel) in cigarette ads, and created a fund of over $200 billion to be used by the various signatory states. Much of that money was in fact used to reimburse the various law firms that the states had hired to negotiate the settlement.[52] Today, state budgets rely heavily on the revenues obtained in the suit.[53]

For businesspeople who believe that commercial speech should be afforded protection under the First Amendment, the tobacco case is ominous. Many people are antismoking, antialchohol, antipornography, or antigun. But free speech advocates have First Amendment concerns about efforts to abridge speech, whether it's for any political, social, or religious idea or a legal, commercial product. They warn that this limitation of freedom of commercial speech threatens every legal business in America, especially because restrictions on the freedom to advertise give often a huge, monopolistic advantage to those big brands that are already the category leaders.[54]

Few products arouse greater concern about the effects of advertising than tobacco products. Tobacco is legal in every state but is governed by stringent restrictions on marketing. The emergence of e-cigarettes has prompted a great deal of discussion. Although e-cigs contain a variety of ingredients, including nicotine, they do not have tobacco. What advertising restrictions, if any, should apply to them?

Source: blu™ Electronic Cigarettes

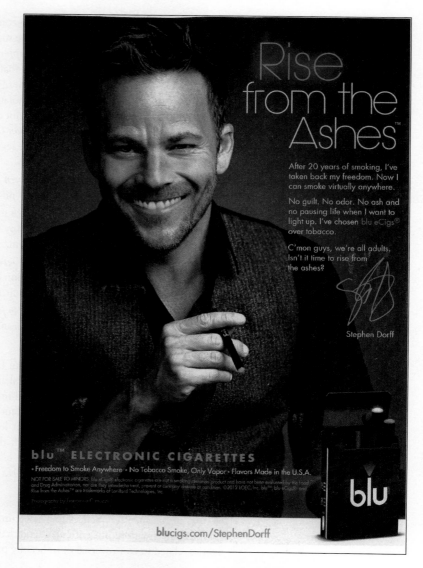

The most recent controversy surrounding "cigarettes" is the marketing of e-cigarettes. According to the FDA, e-cigarettes are "battery-operated products designed to deliver nicotine, flavor, and other chemicals" by turning water and additives into a vapor.[55] While e-cigs do not have tobacco, they do contain nicotine. Are e-cigarettes a dangerous gateway for teens on the path to tobacco use, or a healthier alternative to tobacco products? The debate has yet to be settled.[56]

The Issue of Advertising to Children

Advertising to children presents different challenges. Kids aren't sophisticated consumers. Their conceptions of self, time, and money are immature. Their ability to understand the consequences of some of their choices and behaviors is not as developed as that of an adult. This makes it likely that child-oriented advertising can lead to false beliefs or unrealistic product expectations.

While most children and parents are joint consumers, more children are becoming sole decision makers. To protect them, and their parents, most agree that advertisers should not intentionally deceive children. The central issue is how far advertisers should go to ensure that children are not misled by ads.

To promote responsible children's advertising and to respond to public concerns, the Council of Better Business Bureaus established the **Children's Advertising Review Unit (CARU).** CARU advises advertisers and agencies and also offers informational material for children, parents, and educators. For more than 20 years, CARU's *Self-Regulatory Guidelines for Children's Advertising* has guided marketers in the development of child-directed advertising for all traditional media. In 2009 CARU revised its guidelines, at least partially in response to requests from the FTC and the Department of Health and Human Services. The revisions dealt with new standards for food advertised to children on TV, to food packaging, and to guidelines for marketing via online video games and product placements.

The basic activity of CARU is the review and evaluation of child-directed advertising in all media. When children's advertising is found to be misleading, inaccurate, or inconsistent with the *Guidelines,* CARU seeks changes through voluntary cooperation of the advertisers.[57] For an overview of the basic principles underlying CARU's *Guidelines,* see http://www.caru .org/guidelines/guidelines.pdf.

Many countries are far more strict than the United States about advertising to children. Sweden and Norway, for example, do not permit any television advertising to be directed toward children under 12, and no advertisements at all are allowed during children's programs. Germany and Holland prohibit sponsorship of children's shows, and the Flemish region of Belgium permits no ads five minutes before or after any programs for children. While the highest level of advertising to children is in Australia (an average of 34 ads per hour), that country allows no ads on programs aimed at preschool children.[58]

In the area of television advertising, the government and consumer groups play an important role at both the national and international levels to ensure that adequate consumer protection for children is maintained and strengthened where necessary. For more on child-oriented TV advertising, see the Ethical Issues feature in Chapter 6.

Consumer Privacy

The second major regulatory issue facing advertisers is privacy. With the increased use of wireless devices, mobile phones, and the Internet, all of which can be used for advertising, the issue of **privacy rights** is in the news. The issue deals with people's right to protect their personal information. Privacy is an ethical issue as well as a legal one. It's also a practical issue: Prospective customers who find pop-up ads, telemarketing calls, and e-mail spam annoying and intrusive aren't likely to buy the offending company's products.

Internet users worry about people they don't know, and even businesses they do know, getting personal information about them. And their concern is not without reason. Many Websites create profiles of their visitors to get data such as e-mail addresses, clothing sizes, or favorite books. Some sites also track users' surfing habits, usually without their knowledge, to better target ads for products.

To create these user profiles, Web advertisers store files called **cookies,** on consumer hard drives, that keep a log of Internet activities, allowing sites to track customers' web-surfing habits. The cookies are created when consumers first visit a site or use some feature like a personalized news service or a shopping cart.

Because Internet users access online content on a variety of devices, including phones, tablets, smart TVs, etc., advertisers have turned to new technologies for tracking their behaviors, including methods for obtaining real-time location data from phones.[59] Other privacy worries center on the data collected by giant web companies like Facebook and Google. For example, the search-engine giant's business model focuses on using data that consumers, willingly or not, share during search, while using e-mail, posting photos, texting friends, or scanning Google Maps. This data is helpful for serving targeted ads, but also raises concerns about what happens to the information and to what purposes it is put.[60]

Internet companies argue that such tracking is not personal; it's typically performed anonymously and helps them customize content to match users' interests. However, Double-Click, a leading provider of marketing tools for web advertisers, direct marketers, and web publishers, has acquired Abacus Direct, a direct-mail company with an extensive offline database of retail and catalog purchasers. This enables DoubleClick to combine online profiles with offline names, addresses, demographic information, and purchasing data.[61] In turn, DoubleClick has now been acquired by the largest web advertiser, Google. This means that Google has potential access to an enormous amount of information about web users. Companies like Apple and Facebook do as well.

Advertisers would be wise to take consumer privacy concerns seriously. A Pew opinion survey from 2015 found over 9 out of 10 respondents believe that "being in control of who can get information about them is important." A similar majority indicate that "controlling what information is collected about them is important."[62]

Fortunately, consumers are not completely helpless. They can disable the cookies on their computers. But this may limit their access because some Websites *require* that cookies be accepted. Internet surfers also have the option to "opt in." This feature allows users to set the terms under which they give personal information. Also available is the "opt-out" feature, which allows sites to continuously gather information about visitors unless they specifically inform the site not to by clicking on a button.

Responding to consumer concerns, the Federal Trade Commission together with the Network Advertising Initiative (an organization comprised of leading Internet advertising networks, including AdKnowledge, 24/7, Ad Force, and DoubleClick) have created a framework for self-regulation of online profiling. The Fair Information Practice Principles consist of five core elements:

- *Notice,* which requires that the Website clearly post its privacy policy.
- *Choice,* which relates to consumers' level of control over being profiled and how their information is used.
- *Access,* the ability for consumers to access information collected about them and make amendments to it.
- *Security,* which requires that network advertisers make reasonable efforts to protect the data they collect from loss, misuse, or improper access.
- *Enforcement,* a requirement that all industry members subject themselves to monitoring by an independent third party to ensure compliance with the Fair Information Practice Principles.[63]

Naturally Internet companies would prefer to avoid government intervention and the layers of laws and regulations that would bring. So it's in everybody's interest for self-regulation to work.

Federal Regulation of Advertising in North America

LO 3-6

The U.S. government controls advertisers through laws, regulations, and judicial interpretations. Among the many federal agencies and departments that regulate advertising are the Federal Trade Commission, the Food and Drug Administration, the Federal Communications Commission, the Patent and Trademark Office, and the Library of Congress. Because their jurisdictions often overlap, advertisers may sometimes have difficulty complying with their regulations.

Canada has a similar maze of federal regulators. But the Canadian legal situation is considerably more complex than the United States' due to the separate (but often concurrent) jurisdictions of federal and provincial governments, the broad powers of government regulators, the vast array of self-regulatory codes, and the complexity of a bilingual and bicultural society. One simple example of this is the fact that all packages and labels must be printed in both English and French throughout Canada.[64]

The U.S. Federal Trade Commission

In the United States, the **Federal Trade Commission (FTC)** is the major regulator of advertising for products sold in interstate commerce. Established by an act of Congress, the FTC has a mission of ensuring "that the nation's markets function competitively, and are vigorous, efficient, and free of undue restrictions."[65] The commission enforces a variety of federal anti-trust and consumer protection laws and works to enhance the operation of the marketplace by eliminating acts or practices that are deceptive or unfair. In other words, it is the FTC's responsibility to maintain the existence of *many sellers* in the marketplace, strive to provide more *complete information* to consumers, and keep the marketing process as free of *externalities* as possible.

The FTC's job is complicated by the fact that the definitions of *deceptive* and *unfair* are controversial.

Defining Deception

The FTC defines **deceptive advertising** as any ad that contains a representation, omission, or practice that is likely to mislead the consumer. The mislead consumer should be one who is acting reasonably, and the misrepresentation should be material, i.e., it must be one that changes how the consumer would act.[66]

Take the case of the FTC against Office Depot, Buy.com, and Value America. According to the FTC, the companies were deceptive in advertising "free" and "low-cost" personal computer (PC) systems because they failed to adequately disclose the true costs and important restrictions on the offers. The low cost of the computers was contingent on long-term Internet service contracts. For example, one ad featured a computer for $269. But the purchaser's actual expenses would exceed $1,000 when taking into account the cost of the required three-year Internet service contract.

Without admitting any wrongdoing, the companies all signed consent agreements, agreeing to disclose the information prominently in the future to help consumers easily determine the real costs of such deals.[67]

The FTC is a powerful regulator. The commission cracked down on Exxon and ordered a groundbreaking educational campaign to inform consumers that the right octane for most cars is regular octane, not the more expensive premium grade. The FTC also looks at environmental claims such as biodegradable, degradable, photodegradable, and recyclable. To avoid confusing terminology, the FTC and the Environmental Protection Agency (EPA) worked jointly with attorneys general from many states to develop uniform national guidelines for environmental marketing claims.

Defining Unfairness

According to FTC policy, ads that are not technically deceptive may still be considered unfair to consumers. **Unfair advertising** occurs when a consumer is "unjustifiably injured" or there is a "violation of public policy" (such as other government statutes). In other words, unfair advertising is due to the inadequacy of *complete information* or some other *externality.* For example, practices considered unfair are claims made without prior substantiation, claims that exploit vulnerable groups such as children and the elderly, and cases where the consumer cannot make a valid choice because the advertiser omits important information about the product or about competing products mentioned in the ad.[68]

In one case, the FTC found that an automaker's failure to warn of a safety problem was not deceptive but was unfair. Advertising organizations have argued that the word *unfair* lacks a clear meaning. They have lobbied Congress to eliminate the FTC's power to prosecute on unfairness grounds, and Congress did pass a compromise bill requiring the FTC to show that (1) an alleged unfair practice involves substantial, unavoidable injury to consumers; (2) the injury is not reasonably avoidable by consumers themselves; and (3) the injury is not outweighed by benefits to consumers or competition.[69] This legislation resulted in the FTC becoming more restricted in its effort to regulate unfairness.[70]

Comparative Advertising

Advertisers use **comparative advertising** to claim superiority to competitors in some aspect. In the United States, such ads are legal (and encouraged by the FTC) so long as the

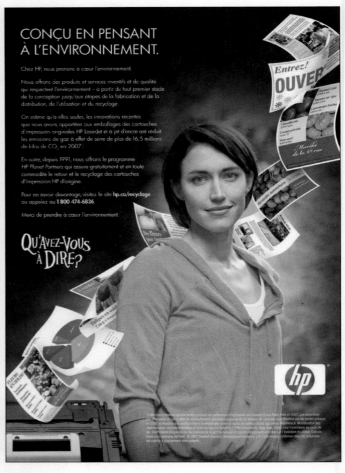

In Canada, all packages and labels must be printed in both English and French, and most major companies also run their ads in both languages.

Courtesy of HP Canada

comparison is truthful. In fact, the FTC cracked down on the Arizona Automobile Dealers Association for restricting truthful, nondeceptive comparative price advertising among its members.[71]

In 1994, the AADA's 199 members constituted 99 percent of the new automobile and truck dealers in Arizona. The FTC challenged the association's Standards for Advertising Motor Vehicles, which, among other things, prohibited members from advertising that prices are equal to or lower than a competitor's, or are the lowest; that the advertiser will match or beat any price; or that the advertiser will offer compensation if it cannot offer an equal or lower price.

These prohibitions, according to the FTC, unreasonably restrained competition among the member dealers and injured consumers by depriving them of truthful information concerning the prices and financing available for new cars and trucks.

The 1988 Trademark Law Revision Act closed a loophole in the Lanham Act, which governed comparison ads but did not mention misrepresenting another company's product. Under current law, any advertiser that misrepresents its own or another firm's goods, services, or activities is vulnerable to a civil action.

In addition to being truthful, comparative ads must compare some objectively measurable characteristic. And great scrutiny must be given to the substantiation. Given the potential for sizable damages—up to millions of dollars—for faulty comparative advertising, the greatest care must be exercised in this area.[72]

This ad for Smart Water relates to several interesting issues in advertising. From a legal perspective, federal law requires that celebrity endorsers actually use the product. From a creative perspective, this ad demonstrates that sexual appeal can indeed be used to market water.

Source: Glacéau SmartWater

The Food and Drug Administration (FDA)

Investigating Suspected Violations

If it receives complaints from consumers, competitors, or its own staff members who monitor ads in various media, the FTC may decide to investigate an advertiser. The agency has broad powers to pursue suspected violators and demand information from them. Typically, the FTC looks for three kinds of information: *substantiation, endorsements,* and *affirmative disclosures.*

If a suspected violator cites survey findings or scientific studies, the FTC may ask for **substantiation.** Advertisers are expected to have supporting data before running an ad, although the FTC sometimes allows postclaim evidence. The FTC does not solicit substantiation for ads it is not investigating.

The FTC also scrutinizes ads that contain questionable **endorsements** or **testimonials.** If a noncelebrity endorser is paid, the ad must disclose this on-screen.[73] The endorsers may not make claims the advertiser can't substantiate. Further, celebrity endorsers must actually use the product or service (if portrayed), and they can be held personally liable if they misrepresent it.[74]

Advertisers must make **affirmative disclosure** of their product's limitations or deficiencies: for example, EPA mileage ratings for cars, pesticide warnings, and statements that saccharin may be hazardous to one's health.

Remedies for Unfair or Deceptive Advertising

When the FTC determines that an ad is deceptive or unfair, it may take three courses of action: negotiate with the advertiser for a consent decree, issue a cease-and-desist order, and/or require corrective advertising.

A **consent decree** is a document the advertiser signs agreeing to stop the objectionable advertising without admitting any wrongdoing. Before signing, the advertiser can negotiate specific directives with the FTC that will govern future advertising claims.

If an advertiser won't sign a consent decree, the FTC may issue a **cease-and-desist order** prohibiting further use of the ad. Before the order is final, it is heard by an administrative law judge. Most advertisers sign the consent decree after the hearing and agree, without admitting guilt, to halt the advertising. Advertisers that violate either a consent decree or a cease-and-desist order can be fined up to $11,000 per showing of the offending ad.

The FTC may also require **corrective advertising** for some period of time to explain and correct offending ads. In 1999, the FTC ruled that pharmaceutical giant Novartis advertised without substantiation that its Doan's Pills brand was more effective against back pain than its rivals. Because the deceptive advertising had gone on for more than nine years, the FTC ordered Novartis to run $8 million worth of corrective advertising. The advertising was to include this statement: "Although Doan's is an effective pain reliever, there is no evidence that Doan's is more effective than other pain relievers for back pain." The FTC also ordered Novartis to place the statement on Doan's packaging for a year.[75]

To help advertisers avoid such expense, the FTC will review advertising before it runs and give "advance clearance" in an advisory opinion. It also publishes *Industry Guides and Trade Regulation Rules,* which gives advertisers, agencies, and the media ongoing information about FTC regulations.

In Canada, the laws are even tougher and the consequences stiffer. It's an offense for any public promotion to be "false or misleading in a material respect." It is not necessary that anyone be misled by the representation, only that it be false. An *offense* is a crime. If convicted, an advertiser or agency executive could go to jail, pay a fine, or both.[76]

A division of the Department of Health and Human Services, the **Food and Drug Administration (FDA)** enforces the Federal Food, Drug, and Cosmetic Act and several other health laws. The agency monitors the manufacture, import, transport, storage, and sale of over $1 trillion worth of products annually, which accounts for about 9 cents of every dollar spent annually by American consumers.[77] And it does so at a cost to taxpayers of about $3 per person.[78]

It's the FDA's job to see that the food we eat is safe, the cosmetics we use won't hurt us, and the medicines and therapeutic devices we buy are safe and effective. With authority over the labeling, packaging, and branding of packaged foods and therapeutic devices, the FDA strives

revolution® (selamectin)

Topical Parasiticide For Dogs and Cats

CAUTION:
U.S. Federal law restricts this drug to use by or on the order of a licensed veterinarian.

INDICATIONS:
Revolution kills adult fleas and prevents flea eggs from hatching for one month and is indicated for the prevention and control of flea infestations (Ctenocephalides felis), prevention of heartworm disease caused by Dirofilaria immitis, and the treatment and control of ear mite (Otodectes cynotis) infestations in dogs and cats. Revolution also is indicated for the treatment and control of sarcoptic mange (Sarcoptes scabiei) and for the control of tick (Dermacentor variabilis) infestations in dogs, and the treatment of intestinal hookworm (Ancylostoma tubaeforme) and roundworm (Toxocara cati) infections in cats. Revolution is recommended for use in dogs and cats six weeks of age and older.

WARNINGS:
Not for human use. Keep out of the reach of children.
May be irritating to skin and eyes. Wash hands after use and wash off any product in contact with the skin immediately with soap and water. If contact with eyes occurs, then flush eyes copiously with water. In case of ingestion by a human, contact a physician immediately. The material safety data sheet (MSDS) provides more detailed occupational safety information. For a copy of the MSDS or to report adverse reactions attributable to exposure to this product, call 1-800-366-5288.

Flammable—Keep away from heat, sparks, open flames or other sources of ignition.

PRECAUTIONS:
Use with caution in sick, debilitated or underweight animals (see SAFETY).
Prior to administration of Revolution, dogs should be tested for existing heartworm infections. At the discretion of the veterinarian, infected dogs should be treated to remove adult heartworms. Revolution is not effective against adult D. immitis and, while the number of circulating microfilariae may decrease following treatment, Revolution is not effective for microfilariae clearance.

Hypersensitivity reactions have not been observed in dogs with patent heartworm infections administered three times the recommended dose of Revolution. Higher doses were not tested.

ADVERSE REACTIONS:
Following treatment with Revolution, transient localized alopecia with or without inflammation at or near the site of application was observed in approximately 1% of 691 treated cats. Other signs observed rarely (≤0.5% of 1743 treated cats and dogs) included vomiting, loose stool or diarrhea with or without blood, anorexia, lethargy, salivation, tachypnea, and muscle tremors.

DOSAGE:
The recommended minimum dose is 2.7 mg selamectin per pound (6 mg/kg) of body weight.

Administer the entire contents of a single dose tube of Revolution topically in accordance with label directions. (See ADMINISTRATION for the recommended treatment intervals.)

For cats over 15 lbs use the appropriate combination of tubes.

For dogs over 85 lbs use the appropriate combination of tubes.
Recommended for use in animals 6 weeks of age and older.

ADMINISTRATION:
Firmly depress the cap to puncture the seal on the Revolution tube; then remove the cap to administer the product.

Part the hair on the back of the animal at the base of the neck in front of the shoulder blades until the skin is visible. Place the tip of the tube on the skin and squeeze the tube to empty its entire contents directly onto the skin in one spot. Do not massage the product into the skin. Due to alcohol content, do not apply to broken skin. Avoid contact between the product and fingers. Do not apply when the hair coat is wet. Bathing or shampooing the animal 2 or more hours after treatment will not reduce the effectiveness of Revolution. Stiff hair, clumping of hair, hair discoloration, or a slight powdery residue may be observed at the treatment site in some animals. These effects are temporary and do not affect the safety or effectiveness of the product. Discard empty tubes in your ordinary household refuse.

Flea Control in Dogs and Cats
For the prevention and control of flea infestations, Revolution should be administered at monthly intervals throughout the flea season, starting one month before fleas become active. In controlled laboratory studies >98% of fleas were killed within 36 hours. Results of clinical field studies using Revolution monthly demonstrated >90% control of flea infestations within 30 days of the first dose. Dogs and cats treated with Revolution, including those with pre-existing flea allergy dermatitis, showed improvement in clinical signs associated with fleas as a direct result of eliminating the fleas from the animals and their environment.

If the dog or cat is already infested with fleas when the first dose of Revolution is administered, adult fleas on the animal are killed and no viable fleas hatch from eggs after the first administration. However, an environmental infestation of fleas may persist for a short time after beginning treatment with Revolution because of the emergence of adult fleas from pupae.

Heartworm Prevention in Dogs and Cats
For the prevention of heartworm disease, Revolution must be administered on a monthly basis. Revolution may be administered year-round or at least within one month after the animal's first exposure to mosquitoes and monthly thereafter until the end of the mosquito season. The final dose must be given within one month after the last exposure to mosquitoes. If a dose is missed and a monthly interval between dosing is exceeded then immediate administration of Revolution and resumption of monthly dosing will minimize the opportunity for the development of adult heartworms. When replacing another heartworm preventive product in a heartworm disease prevention program, the first dose of Revolution must be given within a month of the last dose of the former medication.

At the discretion of the veterinarian, cats ≥6 months of age may be tested to determine the presence of existing heartworm infections before beginning treatment with Revolution. Cats already infected with adult heartworms can safely be given Revolution monthly to prevent further infections.

Ear Mite Treatment in Dogs and Cats
For the treatment of ear mite (O. cynotis) infestations in dogs and cats, Revolution should be administered once as a single topical dose. A second monthly dose may be required in some dogs. Monthly use of Revolution will control any subsequent ear mite infestations. In the clinical field trials ears were not cleaned, and many animals still had debris in their ears after the second dose. Cleansing of the infested ears is recommended to remove the debris.

Sarcoptic Mange Treatment in Dogs
For the treatment of sarcoptic mange (S. scabiei) in dogs, Revolution should be administered once as a single topical dose. A second monthly dose may be required in some dogs. Monthly use of Revolution will control any subsequent sarcoptic mange mite infestations. Because of the difficulty in finding sarcoptic mange mites on skin scrapings, effectiveness assessments also were based on resolution of clinical signs. Resolution of the pruritus associated with the mite infestations was observed in approximately 50% of the dogs 30 days after the first treatment and in approximately 90% of the dogs 30 days after the second monthly treatment.

Tick Control in Dogs
For the control of tick (Dermacentor variabilis) infestations in dogs, Revolution should be administered on a monthly basis. In heavy tick infestations, complete efficacy may not be achieved after the first dose. In these cases, one additional dose may be administered two weeks after the previous dose, with monthly dosing continued thereafter.

Nematode Treatment in Cats
For the treatment of intestinal hookworm (A. tubaeforme) and roundworm (T. cati) infections, Revolution should be applied once as a single topical dose.

NADA 141-152, Approved by FDA.

 Animal Health
Exton, PA 19341, USA
Div. of Pfizer Inc
NY, NY 10017

www.revolutionpet.com

 TAKE TIME ... OBSERVE LABEL DIRECTIONS

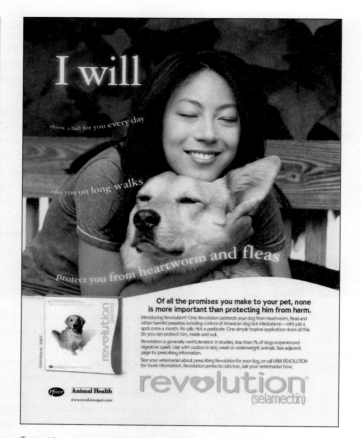

To provide consumers with more complete information, the U.S. Food and Drug Administration regulates the content of pharmaceutical ads. It used to require that advertisers include all the information from the product insert in its ads. This necessitated lengthy commercials with miniscule copy. In 1997, the rule was changed allowing pharmaceutical companies to advertise on TV and radio as long as they mentioned any important side effects and directed consumers to other sources for further information, such as their magazine ads or their Websites. Notice how this magazine ad for Revolution (www.revolutionpet.com) complies with the FDA's disclosure requirements.
Source: Zoetis, Inc.

to give consumers *complete information* by ensuring that products are labeled truthfully with the information people need to use them properly. The FDA requires manufacturers to disclose all ingredients on product labels, in in-store product advertising, and in product literature. The label must accurately state the weight or volume of the contents. Labels on therapeutic devices must give clear instructions for use. The FDA can require warning statements on packages of hazardous products. It regulates "cents off" and other promotions on package labels and has jurisdiction over the use of words such as *giant* or *family* to describe package sizes.

When consumer-oriented drug ads became common in the mid-1980s, the FDA ruled that any ad for a brand-name drug must include all the information in the package insert.[79] That meant advertisers had to run lengthy commercials or use minuscule type in print ads. In 1997, the FDA changed that rule, allowing pharmaceutical companies to advertise their drugs on broadcast media as long as they mentioned any important possible side effects and directed people to their print ads, their Internet sites, or consumers' own doctors for more information.[80] With that ruling, prescription drug advertising soared on television and radio, tripling over the next five years. It's estimated that in 2005, pharmaceutical companies spent some $4 billion in direct-to-consumer advertising.[81] Although the FDA is responsible for ensuring that these ads are fair and accurate, the agency is so understaffed that many questionable and, unfortunately, deceptive or misleading ads do get through. However, any time the FDA has sent a letter to marketers citing false advertising claims, the companies have stopped running the misleading ads.[82]

The **Nutritional Labeling and Education Act (NLEA)** gives the FDA additional muscle by setting stringent legal definitions for terms such as *fresh, light, low fat,* and *reduced calories.*

It also sets standard serving sizes and requires labels to show food value for one serving alongside the total recommended daily value as established by the National Research Council.[83]

The first time the FDA took severe action against a prominent marketer over a labeling dispute, it seized 2,400 cases of Procter & Gamble's Citrus Hill Fresh Choice orange juice. Fresh Choice was made from concentrate, not fresh-squeezed juice as P&G claimed.[84] Due to increased FDA scrutiny, many advertisers are now more cautious about their health and nutritional claims.

The Federal Communications Commission (FCC)

The seven-member **Federal Communications Commission (FCC)** is an independent federal agency with jurisdiction over the radio, television, telephone, satellite, Internet, and cable TV industries. The FCC is responsible for protecting the public interest and encouraging competition. Its control over broadcast advertising is actually *indirect,* stemming from its authority to license broadcasters (or take away their licenses). The FCC stringently controls the airing of obscenity and profanity, and it can restrict both the products advertised and the content of ads. For example, the FCC required stations to run commercials about the harmful effects of smoking even before Congress banned cigarette advertising on TV and radio.

In the 1980s, the FCC decided there were enough buyers and sellers that marketplace forces could adequately control broadcast media, so it deregulated both radio and TV stations. The FCC no longer limits commercial time or requires stations to maintain detailed program and commercial logs. However, stations still keep records of commercial broadcasts to assure advertisers they ran.

The 1992 Cable Television Consumer Protection and Competition Act gave the FCC additional teeth. It placed new controls on the cable TV industry to encourage a more service-oriented attitude and to improve the balance between rates and escalating ad revenues.[85] The FCC can set subscriber rates for cable TV, so subscription revenues should slow while advertising rates rise.

In addition to protecting consumers' interests, the FCC and other government entities can also attempt to regulate to promote the common good. In 2004, for example, the FCC revised its rules to further limit children's exposure to advertising while watching child-oriented TV. More types of ads are now counted toward the maximum 10.5 minutes of nonprogram time per hour on weekends (12 minutes per hour on weekdays). Spots that pointed kids to interactive Websites featuring a show's characters—and selling products and services associated with the characters—were especially on the hot seat. Activist groups applauded and most networks just groaned, but NBC and Disney filed suit in 2005. A federal court of appeals ordered the FCC to open a review of the revised rules.[86]

The Patent and Trademark Office and the Library of Congress

A basic role of government is to promote and protect the economic well-being *(self-interest)* of its citizens. One way the U.S. government does this is by promoting "the progress of science and useful arts, by securing for limited times to authors and inventors the exclusive right to their respective writings and discoveries"—in other words, by registering and protecting their **intellectual property.**[87]

Through the issuance of **patents,** the government provides incentives to invent, invest in, and disclose new technology worldwide. By registering trademarks and copyrights, the government helps businesses protect their investments, promote their goods and services, and safeguard consumers against confusion and deception in the marketplace *(complete information).*

A trademark such as Coca-Cola, AT&T, or Levi's is a valuable asset. According to the Lanham Trade-Mark Act (1947), a **trademark** is "any word, name, symbol, or device or any combination thereof adopted and used by a manufacturer or merchant to identify his goods and distinguish them from those manufactured or sold by others."

Patents and trademarks are registered with and protected by the **U.S. Patent and Trademark Office,** part of the Department of Commerce. Ownership of a trademark may be designated in advertising or on a label, package, or letterhead by the word *Registered,* the symbol®, or the symbol™. If someone persists in using a trademark owned by another or confusingly similar to another's mark, the trademark owner can ask for a court order and sue for trademark infringement.

The Library of Congress protects all copyrighted material, including advertising, in the United States. A **copyright** is a form of protection provided to the authors of "original works of

Coca-Cola's trademark varies from country to country. But the overall look is retained through use of similar letterforms and style, even with different alphabets.

© Imaginechina/Corbis

authorship," including literary, dramatic, musical, artistic, and certain other "intellectual works."[88] A copyright issued to an advertiser grants the exclusive right to print, publish, or reproduce the protected ad for the life of the copyright owner plus 50 years. An ad can be copyrighted only if it contains original copy or illustrations. An idea cannot be copyrighted; nor can slogans, short phrases, and familiar symbols and designs (although the latter may be trademarkable).

Copyright is indicated by the word *Copyright,* the abbreviation *Copr.,* or the symbol © followed by the year of first publication and the name of the advertiser or copyright owner.

State and Local Regulation

Regulation by State Governments

Advertisers are also subject to state or local laws. Since the U.S. federal deregulation trend of the 1980s, state and local governments have taken a far more active role.

State legislation governing advertising is often based on the truth-in-advertising model statute developed in 1911 by *Printer's Ink,* for many years the major trade publication of the industry. The statute holds that any maker of an ad found to contain "untrue, deceptive, or misleading" material is guilty of a misdemeanor. Today most states enforce laws patterned after this statute.

All states also have "little FTC acts," consumer protection laws that govern unfair and deceptive business practices. States can investigate and prosecute cases, and individual consumers can bring civil suits against businesses. To increase their clout, some states team up on legal actions—for example, to challenge deceptive ad promotions in the airline, rental car, and food-making industries. As one observer pointed out, "Many of the food manufacturers could litigate some of the smaller states into the ground, but they might not be willing to fight it out against 10 states simultaneously."[89]

Different states have different regulations governing what can be advertised. Some states prohibit advertising for certain types of wine and liquor, and most states restrict the use of federal and state flags in advertising.

This can present a major problem to national marketers. And in some cases, it actually hurts consumers. For example, many companies trying to conduct environmentally responsible marketing programs feel stymied by the different state laws governing packaging materials and recycling.[90] In the tobacco case discussed earlier, numerous state attorneys general acting together proved a formidable foe for the giant tobacco industry. In the end, facing the prospect of an infinite number of lawsuits from individual states and even municipalities, the industry buckled under, agreeing to settle and pay hundreds of billions of dollars.[91]

Regulation by Local Governments

Many cities and counties also have consumer protection agencies to enforce laws regulating local advertising practices. The chief function of these agencies is to protect local consumers against unfair and misleading practices by area merchants.

In one year alone, the Orange County, California, district attorney's office received more than 1,200 complaint letters from consumers about everything from dishonest mechanics and phony sale ads to a taco stand that skimped on the beef in its "macho" burrito.[92] In a case against Los Angeles–based Closet Factory, Inc., the DA collected $40,000 in fines to settle a false advertising suit. The company was charged with running newspaper ads that gave consumers a false sense of urgency regarding "sales" that actually never end. This type of advertising, known as a *continuous sale,* violates the state's Business and Professions Code. It also advertises a false percentage off the regular price. Because the sale is never really over, the sale price becomes the regular price.[93]

Nongovernment Regulation

Nongovernment organizations also issue advertising guidelines (see Exhibit 3-4). In fact, advertisers face considerable regulation by business-monitoring organizations, related trade associations, the media, consumer groups, and advertising agencies themselves.

The Better Business Bureau (BBB)

The largest of the U.S. business-monitoring organizations is the **Better Business Bureau (BBB),** established in 1916. Funded by dues from more than 100,000 member companies, it operates primarily at the local level to protect consumers against fraudulent and deceptive advertising and sales practices. When local bureaus contact violators and ask them to revise their advertising, most comply.

The BBB's files on violators are open to the public. Records of violators that do not comply are sent to appropriate government agencies for further action. The BBB often works with local law enforcement agencies to prosecute advertisers guilty of fraud and misrepresentation. Each year, the BBB investigates thousands of ads for possible violations of truth and accuracy.

Exhibit 3-4
American Association of Advertising Agencies' policy statement and guidelines for comparative advertising.

The Board of Directors of the American Association of Advertising Agencies recognizes that when used truthfully and fairly, comparative advertising provides the consumer with needed and useful information.

However, extreme caution should be exercised. The use of comparative advertising, by its very nature, can distort facts and, by implication, convey to the consumer information that misrepresents the truth. Therefore, the Board believes that comparative advertising should follow certain guidelines:

1. The intent and connotation of the ad should be to inform and never to discredit or unfairly attack competitors, competing products, or services.
2. When a competitive product is named, it should be one that exists in the marketplace as significant competition.
3. The competition should be fairly and properly identified but never in a manner or tone of voice that degrades the competitive product or service.
4. The advertising should compare related or similar properties or ingredients of the product, dimension to dimension, feature to feature.
5. The identification should be for honest comparison purposes and not simply to upgrade by association.
6. If a competitive test is conducted, it should be done by an objective testing source, preferably an independent one, so that there will be no doubt as to the veracity of the test.
7. In all cases the test should be supportive of all claims made in the advertising that are based on the test.
8. The advertising should never use partial results or stress insignificant differences to cause the consumer to draw an improper conclusion.
9. The property being compared should be significant in terms of value or usefulness of the product to the consumer.
10. Comparatives delivered through the use of testimonials should not imply that the testimonial is more than one individual's thought unless that individual represents a sample of the majority viewpoint.

The Council of Better Business Bureaus is the parent organization of the Better Business Bureau and a sponsoring member of the National Advertising Review Council. One of its functions is to help new industries develop standards for ethical and responsible advertising. The Code of Advertising of the Council of Better Business Bureaus (the BBB Code) has been called the most important self-regulation of advertising.[94] The BBB Code is only a few pages long, but it is supplemented by a monthly publication called *Do's and Don'ts in Advertising Copy*, which provides information about advertising regulations and recent court and administrative rulings that affect advertising.[95] Since 1983, the National Advertising Division of the Council of Better Business Bureaus has published guidelines for advertising to children, a particularly sensitive area.

The National Advertising Review Council (NARC)

The **National Advertising Review Council (NARC)** was established in 1971 by the Council of Better Business Bureaus, the American Association of Advertising Agencies, the American Advertising Federation, and the Association of National Advertisers. Its primary purpose is to promote and enforce standards of truth, accuracy, taste, morality, and social responsibility in advertising.

NARC is one of the most comprehensive and effective mechanisms for regulating American advertising. A U.S. district court judge noted in a 1985 case that its "speed, informality, and modest cost," as well as its expertise, give NARC special advantages over the court system in resolving advertising disputes.[96]

NARC Operating Arms

The NARC has two operating arms: the **National Advertising Division (NAD)** of the Council of Better Business Bureaus and the **National Advertising Review Board (NARB)**. The NAD monitors advertising practices and reviews complaints about advertising from consumers and consumer groups, brand competitors, local Better Business Bureaus, trade associations, and others. The appeals board for NAD decisions is the NARB, which consists of a chairperson and 70 volunteer members (40 national advertisers, 20 agency representatives, and 10 laypeople).[97]

The NAD–NARB Review Process

To encourage consumers to register complaints, the NAD itself runs ads that include a complaint form. Most target untruthfulness or inaccuracy.

When the NAD finds a valid complaint, it contacts the advertiser and requests that any claims be substantiated. If substantiation is inadequate, the NAD requests modification or discontinuance of the claims.

The case of a leather flight jacket shows how well the NAD process works. Neil Cooper LLC manufactures a leather jacket. In its print ads it claims that its A-2 leather flight jackets are the "official battle gear of U.S. Air Force Pilots." Avirex, Ltd., a competing company, complained to the NAD because it manufactures the A-2 jacket currently being purchased by the Department of Defense and worn by U.S. pilots, not Neil Cooper. Neil Cooper explained that, while it was not the current supplier, many pilots preferred its jacket. Notwithstanding, the NAD sided with Avirex and recommended that Neil Cooper make clear that it is selling a reproduction of an authentic A-2 flight jacket. Neil Cooper agreed.[98]

If the NAD and an advertiser reach an impasse, either party can request a review by an NARB panel (consisting of three advertisers, one agency representative, and one layperson). The panel's decision is binding. If an advertiser refuses to comply with the panel's decision (which has never yet occurred), the NARB will refer the matter to an appropriate government body.

To help consumers make informed decisions, scientists at the Good Housekeeping Research Institute evaluate products before they are accepted for publication in Good Housekeeping magazine as well as for the Good Housekeeping Seal. This gives consumers a trustworthy, authoritative voice to listen to when making purchasing decisions.

Source: Hearst Communications, Inc.

Regulation by the Media

Almost all media review ads and reject those they regard as objectionable, even if they aren't deceptive. Many people think the media are more effective regulators than the government.

Internet

Key players in the self-regulation of Internet advertising include the IAB (Interactive Advertising Bureau) and the AAAA (American Association of Advertising Agencies). The groups in 2009 issued guidelines for digital ads in the form of seven principles: education (advertisers should educate consumers about how online advertising works), transparency (advertisers should clearly disclose data collection and use practices), consumer control (consumers should be able to choose whether and what data is collected and shared), data security (information that is collected should be safe), material changes (advertisers should obtain consent from consumers before changing their privacy policies), sensitive data (some data, such as data about children, prescriptions, medical records, etc.) merits special treatment, and accountability (online advertisers should work together to ensure firms follow the principles). The IAB has indicated that the Direct Marketing Association and the Council of Better Business Bureaus have formulated similar guidelines for digital ads.[99]

Television

Of all media, the TV networks conduct the strictest review. Advertisers must submit commercials intended for a network or affiliated station to its *broadcast standards* department. Many commercials (in script or storyboard form) are returned with suggestions for changes or greater substantiation. Ads are rejected outright if they violate network policies. (See Ad Lab 3–C.)

The major U.S. broadcast networks base their policies on the original National Association of Broadcasters Television Code. But network policies vary enough that it's difficult to prepare universally acceptable commercials. Cable networks and local stations tend to be much less stringent. Most observers would agree that in recent years, with increased competition from cable networks, broadcast networks have relaxed their standards considerably, both for content and commercials.

Radio

The U.S. radio networks, unlike TV networks, supply only a small percentage of their affiliates' programming, so they have little or no say in what their affiliates advertise. A radio station is also less likely to return a script or tape for changes. Some stations, such as KLBJ in Austin, Texas, look mainly at whether the advertising is illegal, unethical, or immoral.[100] They don't want spots to offend listeners or detract from the rest of the programming.

Every radio station typically has its own unwritten guidelines. KDWB, a Minneapolis–St. Paul station with a large teenage audience, turned down a psychic who wanted to buy advertising time.[101] KSDO in San Diego, a station with a business and information format, won't air commercials for X-rated movies or topless bars.[102] SiriusXM, or satellite radio, tends to use standards related to its individual channels. Listeners are likely to hear very different spots on the Catholic Channel then they will on Howard Stern's program.

Magazines

National magazines monitor all advertising, especially by new advertisers and for new products. Newer publications eager to sell space may not be so vigilant, but established magazines, such as *Time* and *Newsweek,* are highly scrupulous. Many magazines will not accept advertising for certain types of products. The *New Yorker* won't run discount retail store advertising or ads for feminine hygiene or self-medication products. *Reader's Digest* won't accept tobacco ads.

Some magazines test every product before accepting the advertising. *Good Housekeeping* rejects ads if its tests don't substantiate the advertiser's claims. Products that pass are allowed to feature the Good Housekeeping "Seal of Approval."

Newspapers

Newspapers also monitor and review advertising. Larger newspapers have clearance staffs who read every ad submitted; most smaller newspapers rely on the advertising manager, sales personnel, or proofreaders.

AD Lab 3-C

Editorial or Advertising: It's Adversarial

Pick up a glossy magazine such as *Vogue, Esquire,* or *Sports Illustrated* and you'll find it loaded with ads for cars, liquor, and cigarettes. Advertising agencies like buying space in these upscale publications as long as nothing in the publication directly offends their clients. Agencies are very protective of their clients, so they're careful about where their ads are placed. If an ad runs alongside a story that might reflect badly on the client's product or, even worse, might offend the client's customers, the ad agency will either pull the ad or request that the article be dropped. Moreover, agencies and their clients want to be warned ahead of time when a controversial story will appear. Increasingly, this is becoming a sore point with magazine editors and is creating an ethical stir in the industry. Editors see it as an assault on their independence and integrity. Advertisers see it as their responsibility to sponsor content suitable for, and not offensive to, their customers.

On the other hand, a survey sponsored by the Newspaper Advertising Association and the American Society of Magazine Editors discovered that newspaper ads actually meet consumer expectations better than the quality of news coverage. Consumers told the survey they believe newspaper ads are useful and relevant, saving them both time and money by allowing them to comparison shop at home. As a result, newspaper editors are now looking at expanding their partnerships with advertisers.

"I think we need to have advertising and editorial work more closely together to produce a paper, especially since advertising has this solid local franchise," said *Washington Post* research chief Sharon P. Warden.

In the world of print media, publishers are the businesspeople who worry about the bottom line, and editors worry about editorial content and journalistic integrity. Often their interests collide. To interest more advertisers, magazine publishers now create whole sections, sometime entire issues, devoted to *advertorials*—pages of commercial copy dressed up as news stories. Often it's difficult to differentiate between actual editorial copy and advertising text. *Sports Illustrated (SI)* publishes an annual special issue called *Golf Plus*, figuring that the 500,000-plus copies will generate higher interest from advertisers such as Foot Joy and Titleist golf balls.

Maxim Publications is one of a few remaining publications that separate the editorial and business sides of publications. Even so, advertisers with *Maxim* exert influence over the content that surrounds their ads by reminding editors of revenue loss if certain material is published. *Ms* magazine solved the conflict by going ad-free in 1990.

Print is not the only medium that falls under editorial scrutiny. Radio and TV are also constantly monitored for content. Some advertisers buying time on radio stations that air syndicated personalities such as Rush Limbaugh specify "NO RUSH." Because of the show's controversial content, they simply refuse to allow their ads to be placed there. Except for the news, television is taped in advance. Many advertisers can review

episodes prior to airing and decide to pull the ads if necessary. (See Chapters 15 through 19 for more information on media buying.)

One Michigan homemaker was angered by sexual innuendoes on Fox's TV sitcom *Married . . . with Children*. So she persuaded Procter & Gamble and other leading advertisers not to buy time on the show. Similarly, many blue-chip advertisers shunned the police drama *NYPD Blue* on ABC because of scenes with partial nudity and blunt language—until it did too well in the ratings for them to ignore. During the coming-out episode of *Ellen* in 1997, many advertisers such as Chrysler pulled their spots. The spots, however, were quickly replaced by other sponsors eager to be part of a show that was expected to reach an unusually large audience.

"With TV, it's a case of supply and demand, and right now the demand for commercial time exceeds the supply," said Kevin Goldman, a former advertising columnist for *The Wall Street Journal*.

However, the case is not the same for magazines. "Magazines are different because there's a finite number of advertisers that want in on a particular book. If Chrysler pulls out of an issue, the pool of advertisers that might take its place is shallow," explained Goldman.

Moreover, magazines (especially new specialty magazines) increasingly tailor their editorial focus to reach niche audiences or a particular demographic. This narrows their options for ad dollars to those marketers targeting the same groups—in effect, giving greater influence to fewer advertisers.

Years ago, the American Society of Magazine Editors (ASME) drew up guidelines on how magazines should distinguish advertising from regular editorial pages. The ASME created a three-paragraph "Standard for Editorial Independence" following a few episodes in which editors left magazines as a result of apparent interference from their corporate employers. The standard states, "Editors need the maximum possible protection from untoward commercial or extra-journalistic pressures. The chief editor of any magazine must have final authority over the editorial content, words and pictures, that appear in the publication."

Laboratory Applications

When is it OK for an advertiser to give its "editorial" view in a publication or on a show? Provide data to support your answers to the following questions:

1. To what degree, if at all, should an advertiser exercise control over placement of its ads or content of the publication?

2. What effect, if any, could advertorials have on national problems such as age discrimination, racism, sexism, and teenage pregnancy? Be specific.

The advertising policies set forth in *Newspaper Rates & Data* specify, "No objectionable medical, personal, matrimonial, clairvoyant, or palmistry advertising accepted; no stock promotion or financial advertising, other than those securities of known value." Another rule prohibits ads that might easily be mistaken for regular reading material unless they feature the word *advertisement* or *advt*.

In addition, most papers have their own acceptability guidelines, ranging from one page for small local papers to more than 50 pages for large dailies such as the *Los Angeles Times*. Some codes are quite specific. The *Detroit Free Press* won't accept classified ads containing such words as *affair* or *swinger*. Some newspapers require advertisers that claim "the lowest price in town" to include a promise to meet or beat any price readers find elsewhere within 30 days.

One problem advertisers face is that newspapers' codes are far from uniform. Handgun ads may be prohibited by one newspaper, accepted by another if the guns are antique, and permitted by a third so long as the guns aren't automatic. In addition, newspapers regularly revise their policies.

Regulation by Consumer Groups

Starting in the 1960s, the consumer movement became increasingly active in fighting fraudulent and deceptive advertising. Consumers demanded that products perform as advertised and that more product information be provided for people to compare and make better buying decisions. The consumer movement gave rise to **consumerism,** social action dramatizing the rights of the buying public. It is clear now that the U.S. consumer can influence advertising practices dramatically.

Today, advertisers and agencies pay more attention to product claims, especially those related to energy use and the nutritional value of processed foods. Consumerism fostered the growth of consumer advocacy groups and regulatory agencies and promoted more consumer research by advertisers, agencies, and the media in an effort to learn what consumers want—and how to provide it. Investment in public goodwill pays off in improved consumer relations and sales.

Consumer Information Networks

Organizations such as the Consumer Federation of America (CFA), the National Council of Senior Citizens, the National Consumer League, and the National Stigma Clearinghouse exchange and disseminate information among members. These **consumer information networks** help develop state, regional, and local consumer organizations and work with national, regional, county, and municipal consumer groups.

Consumer interests also are served by private, nonprofit testing organizations such as Consumers Union, Consumers' Research, and Underwriters Laboratories.

Consumer Advocates

Consumer advocate groups investigate advertising complaints received from the public and those that grow out of their own research. If a complaint is warranted, they ask the advertiser to halt the objectionable ad or practice. If the advertiser does not comply, they release publicity or criticism about the offense to the media and submit complaints with substantiating evidence to appropriate government agencies for further action. In some instances, they file a lawsuit to obtain a cease-and-desist order, a fine, or other penalty against the violator.

Today, with so many special-interest advocacy groups, even the most sensitive advertisers feel challenged. To attract attention, advertising must be creative and stand out from competing noise. Yet advertisers fear attention from politically correct activists (the "PC police"). Calvin Klein ads were attacked by the Boycott Anorexic Marketing group. A Nike ad starring Porky Pig was protested by the National Stuttering Project in San Francisco. An animated public service spot from Aetna Insurance drew complaints from a witches' rights group.[103]

When the protests start flying, the ads usually get pulled. Steve Hayden, chair of BBDO Los Angeles, believes it would be possible to get any spot pulled with "about five letters that appear on the right stationery."[104] As Shelly Garcia noted in *Adweek,* "The way things are these days, nothing motivates middle managers like the need to avoid attention." She lamented the fact that "there are fewer and fewer opportunities to have any fun in advertising."[105]

Self-Regulation by Advertisers

Advertisers also regulate themselves. Most large advertisers gather strong data to substantiate their claims. They maintain careful systems of advertising review to ensure that ads meet both their own standards and industry, media, and legal requirements. Many advertisers try to promote their social responsibility by tying in with a local charity or educational organization.

People BEHIND the Ads

Edward Boyd Advertising Legend

Courtesy of The Family of Edward Boyd

Source: Pepsi Cola Company

now it's Pepsi–for those who think young
You see the change—today people are putting more into their leisure, finding more ways to enjoy life. This is thinking young. And this is the life for Pepsi —light, bracing, clean-tasting Pepsi. Think young. Say "Pepsi, please!"

You probably think that there is too much advertising directed at people like you. That can be annoying. But imagine a world in which ads never seem to be directed to you. For African American consumers, that description was not far from the mark until well into the 20th century.

Today, of course, companies spend hundreds of millions of dollars on marketing activities that target blacks, Hispanics, and other ethnic groups. But it was not always so. For most of our country's history, long after the elimination of slavery, blacks encountered many barriers, legal and cultural, to full participation in American life. The most obvious of these barriers were the Jim Crow laws of the South that mandated public separation of the races. But even outside the South, blacks were often denied opportunities taken for granted by whites. From corporate boardrooms to professional sports, only white males were allowed to compete.

The year 1947 proved a watershed for change in both sports and boardrooms. Most famously, it was the year that Jackie Robinson broke the color barrier to become the first black regular in big league baseball. Less well known, but in many ways just as importantly, it

was the year that Ed Boyd was hired to improve Pepsi's marketing efforts with black Americans. Donald Kendall, former chair and CEO at Pepsi, noted, "Jackie Robinson may have made more headlines, but what Ed did—integrating the managerial ranks of corporate America— was equally groundbreaking."

Boyd was a 33-year-old executive at the National Urban League in New York City when he and a small group of black salesmen were hired by Pepsi CEO Walter S. Mack. Mack wanted to increase sales to the country's 14 million African Americans. Boyd and his team were given the charge of figuring out how to do it. Mack had actually had the idea as early at 1940, when he hired the first black executive at Pepsi, Herman T. Smith, and two young black interns. However, World War II put Mack's plans on hold.

By 1947 he was ready to try again, and Boyd's group was given relatively free reign to design the campaign. Their challenge was not easy. Very few ads at that time targeted blacks, and those that did were often demeaning. Boyd noted, "We'd been caricatured and stereotyped," and he set out to change that.

The team decided to create advertising that represented blacks as "normal Americans." For example, one series of ads offered consumers profiles of 20 great black achievers, including Ralph Bunche, the 1950 winner of the Nobel Peace Prize. Another ad featured students at black colleges. Still other ads showed black middle-class families in grocery stores buying Pepsi. The common theme: Blacks shared the American Dream too, and their business was important.

Of course, the reality of America in the late 1940s was nowhere near as perfect as the view depicted in Pepsi's ads. As Boyd and his black sales team traveled around the United States, they regularly encountered discrimination. The group rode on segregated trains and stayed in black-only hotels. They even faced insults and discrimination from co-workers at Pepsi. At one point the men received threats from the Ku Klux Klan.

Many industries maintain advertising codes that companies agree to follow. These codes also establish a basis for complaints. However, industry advertising codes are only as effective as the enforcement powers of the individual trade associations. And because enforcement may conflict with antitrust laws, trade associations usually use peer pressure rather than hearings or penalties.

Self-Regulation by Ad Agencies and Associations

Most ad agencies monitor their own practices. Professional advertising associations also oversee members' activities to prevent problems that might trigger government intervention. Advertising publications report issues and court actions to educate agencies and advertisers and warn them about possible legal infractions.

Source: Pepsi Cola Company

But they persevered. In just a few short years, Boyd and his team produced results that exceeded Mack's expectations for increasing sales of Pepsi to blacks. But helping the brand increase its market share is really just part of the story. Stephanie Capparell, a *Wall Street Journal* reporter who wrote a book about Boyd's history-making team, recounts

> On their way to nudging their country to a better place, the sales team helped define niche marketing some thirty years before it became a widespread business strategy. They gave formal talks to white drivers and salesmen about their role in the company, thereby instigating some of the earliest formalized diversity training. They also helped to instill in African Americans a unique sense of brand loyalty—to products produced by companies with a commitment to social progress as much as to product quality.

When Walter Mack retired from Pepsi in 1950, support for Boyd and his group gradually eroded. He finally left the company in 1951. In the decades that followed, Boyd lived a full, rich, and active life, working in ad agencies, for CARE, as a consultant, and even as a farmer. But memory of his history-making achievements at Pepsi faded until the publication of Capparell's book in 2006.

On April 30, 2007, Boyd passed away, depriving the world of one of its great civil rights pioneers. Through his tireless and frequently underappreciated efforts to bring black consumers into the mainstream of American life, Boyd made history. He was practicing ethnic target marketing years before the business world would embrace such a strategy. He fundamentally altered the image that white Americans had of their black fellow citizens. And he taught corporations an important lesson on the value of embracing diversity, both within the corporate ranks and in choosing customers to serve. Ed Boyd lived a life dedicated to fighting for justice and equality. It is a measure of how much our nation has changed from Boyd's time at Pepsi that just days after his passing, Barack Obama formally announced his own history-making candidacy for president.

Source: Stephanie Capparell, *The Real Pepsi Challenge: The Inspirational Story of Breaking the Color Barrier in American Business.* (New York: Wall Street Journal Books, 2007), p. xi.

Advertising Agencies

Although advertisers supply information about their products or services to their agencies, the agencies must research and verify product claims and comparative product data before using them in advertising. The media may require such documentation before accepting the advertising, and substantiation may be needed if government or consumer agencies challenge the claims.

Agencies can be held legally liable for fraudulent or misleading advertising claims. For this reason, most major advertising agencies have in-house legal counsel and regularly

Exhibit 3-5

Principles and Practices for Advertising this by the American Advertising Federation (AAF).

1. Advertising, public relations, marketing communications, news, and editorial all share a common objective of truth and high ethical standards in serving the public.
2. Advertising, public relations, and all marketing communications professionals have an obligation to exercise the highest personal ethics in the creation and dissemination of commercial information to consumers.
3. Advertisers should clearly distinguish advertising, public relations and corporate communications from news and editorial content and entertainment, both online and offline.
4. Advertisers should clearly disclose all material conditions, such as payment or receipt of a free product, affecting endorsements in social and traditional channels, as well as the identity of endorsers, all in the interest of full disclosure and transparency.
5. Advertisers should treat consumers fairly based on the nature of the audience to whom the ads are directed and the nature of the product or service advertised.
6. Advertisers should never compromise consumer's personal privacy in marketing communications, and their choices as to whether to participate in providing their information should be transparent and easily made.
7. Advertisers should follow federal, state and local advertising laws, and cooperate with industry self-regulatory programs for the resolution of advertising practices.
8. Advertisers and their agencies, and online and offline media, should discuss privately potential ethical concerns, and members of the team creating ads should be given permission to express internally their ethical concerns.

Wally Snyder 2011 All Rights Reserved

Source: Institute for Advertising Ethics, "Principles and Practices for Advertising Ethics," reprinted with permission of the American Advertising Federation.

submit their ads for review. If any aspect of the advertising is challenged, the agency asks its client to review the advertising and either confirm claims as truthful or replace unverified material.

Advertising Associations

Several associations monitor industrywide advertising practices. The **American Association of Advertising Agencies (AAAA),** an association of the largest advertising agencies throughout the United States, controls agency practices by denying membership to any agency judged unethical. The AAAA *Standards of Practice and Creative Code* set advertising principles for member agencies.

The **American Advertising Federation (AAF)** helped establish the FTC, and its early vigilance committees were the forerunners of the Better Business Bureau. The AAF *Advertising Principles of American Business,* adopted in 1984, define standards for truthful and responsible advertising. Since then, the trade association has established the Principles and Practices for Advertising Ethics (see Exhibit 3-5). Because most local advertising clubs belong to the AAF, it is instrumental in influencing agencies and advertisers to abide by these principles.

The **Association of National Advertisers (ANA)** is comprised of 370 major manufacturing and service companies that are clients of member agencies of the AAAA. These companies, pledged to uphold the ANA code of advertising ethics, work with the ANA through a joint Committee for Improvement of Advertising Content.

The Ethical and Legal Aspects of Advertising in Perspective

Unquestionably, advertising offers considerable benefits to marketers and consumers alike. However, there's also no disputing that advertising has been and still is too often misused. As former *Adweek* editor Andrew Jaffe said, the industry should do all it can to "raise its standards and try to drive out that which is misleading, untruthful, or downright tasteless and irresponsible." Otherwise, he warned, the pressure to regulate even more will become overwhelming.[106]

Advertising apologists point out that of all the advertising reviewed by the Federal Trade Commission in a typical year, 97 percent is found to be satisfactory.[107] In the end, advertisers and consumers need to work together to ensure that advertising is used intelligently, ethically, and responsibly for the benefit of all.

Chapter Summary

As one of the most visible activities of business, advertising is both lauded and criticized for the role it plays in selling products and influencing society. Some controversy surrounds advertising's role in the economy. To debate advertising's economic effects, we employ the four basic assumptions of free enterprise economics: self-interest, many buyers and sellers, complete information, and absence of externalities.

The economic impact of advertising can be likened to the opening shot in billiards—a chain reaction that affects the company as well as its competitors, customers, and the business community. On a broader scale, advertising is often considered the trigger on a country's mass distribution system, enabling manufacturers to produce the products people want in high volume, at low prices, with standardized quality. People may argue, though, about how advertising adds value to products, affects prices, encourages or discourages competition, promotes consumer demand, narrows or widens consumer choice, and affects business cycles.

Although controversy surrounds some of these economic issues, few dispute the abundance principle: In an economy that produces more goods and services than can be consumed, advertising gives consumers more complete information about the choices available to them, encourages more sellers to compete effectively, and thereby serves the self-interest of both consumers and marketers.

Social criticisms of advertising may be short-term manipulative arguments or long-term macro arguments. While the economic aspect of advertising focuses on the free enterprise principles of self-interest and many buyers and sellers, the social aspect typically involves the concepts of complete information and externalities.

Critics say advertising is deceptive; it manipulates people into buying unneeded products, it makes our society too materialistic, and there's just too much of it. Further, they say, advertising perpetuates stereotypes, and all too frequently, it is offensive and in bad taste.

Proponents admit that advertising is sometimes misused. However, they point out that despite its problems, advertising offers many social benefits. It encourages the development of new products and speeds their acceptance. It fosters employment, gives consumers and businesses a wider variety of product choices, and helps keep prices down by encouraging mass production. It stimulates healthy competition among companies and raises the overall standard of living. Moreover, sophisticated marketers know the best way to sell their products is to appeal to genuine consumer needs and be honest in their advertising claims.

In short, while advertising can be criticized for giving less than complete information and for creating some unwanted externalities, it also contributes to the free enterprise system by encouraging many buyers and sellers to participate in the process, thereby serving the self-interest of all.

Under growing pressure from consumers, special-interest groups, and government regulation, advertisers have developed higher standards of ethical conduct and social responsibility. Advertisers confront three levels of ethical consideration: the primary rules of ethical behavior in society, their personal value systems, and their personal philosophies of singular ethical concepts.

The federal and state courts are involved in several advertising issues, including First Amendment protection of commercial speech, and infringements on the right to privacy. Advertising is regulated by federal, state, and local government agencies, business-monitoring organizations, the media, consumer groups, and the advertising industry itself. All of these groups encourage advertisers to give more complete information to consumers and eliminate any externalities in the process.

The Federal Trade Commission, the major federal regulator of advertising in the United States, is responsible for protecting consumers and competitors from deceptive and unfair business practices. If the FTC finds an ad deceptive or unfair, it may issue a cease-and-desist order or require corrective advertising.

The Food and Drug Administration (FDA) monitors advertising for food and drugs and regulates product labels and packaging. The Federal Communications Commission (FCC) has jurisdiction over the radio and TV industries, although deregulation has severely limited its control over advertising in these media. The Patent and Trademark Office governs ownership of U.S. trademarks, trade names, house marks, and similar distinctive features of companies and brands. The Library of Congress registers and protects copyrighted materials.

State and local governments also enact consumer protection laws that regulate advertising.

Nongovernment regulators include the Council of Better Business Bureaus and its National Advertising Division. The NAD, the most effective U.S. nongovernment regulatory body, investigates complaints from consumers, brand competitors, or local Better Business Bureaus and suggests corrective measures. Advertisers that refuse to comply are referred to the National Advertising Review Board (NARB), which may uphold, modify, or reverse the NAD's findings.

Other sources of regulation include the codes and policies of the print media and broadcast media. Consumer organizations and advocates also control advertising by investigating and filing complaints against advertisers and by providing information to consumers. Finally, advertisers and agencies regulate themselves.

Important Terms

affirmative disclosure, *87*

American Advertising Federation (AAF), *98*

American Association of Advertising Agencies (AAAA), *98*

Association of National Advertisers (ANA), *98*

Better Business Bureau (BBB), *91*

cease-and-desist order, *87*

Children's Advertising Review Unit (CARU), *82*

comparative advertising, *86*

consent decree, *87*

consumer advocates, *95*

consumer information networks, *95*

consumerism, *95*

cookies, *83*

copyright, *89*

corrective advertising, *87*

deceptive advertising, *85*

endorsements, *87*

ethical, *73*

Federal Communications Commission (FCC), *89*

Federal Trade Commission (FTC), *85*

Food and Drug Administration (FDA), *87*

intellectual property, *89*

long-term macro arguments, *99*

National Advertising Division (NAD), *92*

National Advertising Review Board (NARB), *92*

National Advertising Review Council (NARC), *92*

nonproduct facts, *69*

Nutritional Labeling and Education Act (NLEA), *88*

patent, *89*

primary demand, *67*

privacy rights, *83*

puffery, *69*

selective demand, *67*

short-term manipulative arguments, *99*

social responsibility, *73*

substantiation, *87*

testimonials, *87*

trademark, *89*

unfair advertising, *85*

U.S. Patent and Trademark Office, *89*

Review Questions

1. What role does advertising play in our economic system?
2. What are the two types of social criticisms of advertising?
3. What is puffery? Give some examples. Do you ever feel deceived by puffery in advertising?
4. Does advertising affect our value system? In what ways?
5. What is the difference between an advertiser's ethics and its social responsibility?
6. How does government regulation of advertising in the United States differ from regulation in many foreign countries?

7. How does commercial speech differ from political speech? Do you think advertisers should have the same First Amendment rights as everyone else? Explain.
8. What is the role of the FTC in advertising? Do you think this role should be expanded or restricted?
9. How do regional and local governments affect advertisers?
10. How well do advertisers regulate themselves? In what areas do you think advertisers have done well, and where should they clean up their act?

The Advertising Experience

1. **Ad Action: "I Know It When I See It"**
   Where is the socially accepted line between "erotic suggestiveness" and "explicit sexuality" in advertising? Describe three hypothetical ads: one that is safely suggestive, one that is as suggestive as it is acceptable (say, for a prime-time network TV spot or national newsmagazine), and one that is just over the line of explicitness. Compare your responses with those of others in your study group. How and why do you think your answers differ? What roles might your ages or social backgrounds play in these differences?

2. **Regulation of Advertising**
   The FTC's Division of Advertising Practices protects consumers from deceptive and unsubstantiated advertising. Review what you have learned by exploring the policies and guides available on the division's Website (www.ftc.gov/bcp/menu-ads.htm). Then answer the following:

   a. Give a general description of what the FTC considers to be deceptive and unfair advertising.

   b. Describe the requirements for substantiating advertising and the process advertisers and their agencies must undergo to do so.

   c. Choose another topic covered on the site and discuss its relevance and importance to the advertising industry.
   Be sure to check out the following sites related to the regulation of the advertising industry:
   - Council of Better Business Bureau's National Advertising Division (NAD): www.nadreview.org
   - Consumers International: www.consumersinternational.org
   - European Commission Consumer Protection Directorate-General "Report on Advertising" (2005): http://ec.europa.eu /consumers/overview/report_advertising_en.htm

3. **Responding to Critical Commentary**
   Go to the following Websites that host critical commentaries on advertising and marketing. Using what you have learned in Chapters 1, 2, and 3, analyze the content of the Websites and articles: What kinds of advertising do they target? What are their criticisms? Do they use long-term macro arguments or short-term manipulative arguments?

   - *Stay Free!* magazine archives: www.stayfreemagazine.org /archives/index.html

- Media Watch Hall of Shame—click to read users' comments about ads deemed offensive by the activist group: www .mediawatch.com/gallery/ads
- "The Return of the Hidden Persuaders"—a three-part series by columnist Ruth Shalit (*Salon,* 1999): www.salon.com/media /col/shal/1999/09/27/persuaders/index.html

4. How well do you think Nike handled the Michael Vick controversy? Is a company responsible for the actions of an athlete that endorses its products? Why or why not? Should Nike have fired Vick sooner? Should they have fired him at all?

5. Some believe that Michael Vick and Tiger Woods have been "rehabilitated," in the sense that they've paid for their transgressions. If you made decisions for a sponsor of these athletes, would you agree? What are the varying perspectives that you can identify about whether Vick or Woods should receive lucrative sponsorship dollars, given their behaviors? Can you identify potential sponsors that would make different decisions about paying these athletes for their endorsements?

6. Gather several lingerie catalogs (such as those of Victoria's Secret and Frederick's of Hollywood) and several magazines like *Maxim* and *Stuff.* Compare the photography, themes, amount of skin shown, and purposes of the publications. Based on your findings, do you think that the catalogs, whether they were distributed free or sold, should be regulated differently than magazines?

7. Calvin Klein and Abercrombie & Fitch get free publicity when their advertising campaigns draw protests. At what point does controversy become a negative externality rather than a positive boost? What might be some signs that a campaign has gone too far?

The Scope of Advertising: From Local to Global

Learning Objectives

To introduce the people and groups that sponsor, create, produce, and transmit advertisements here and abroad. Advertising people may serve in a variety of roles. This chapter discusses the basic tasks of both the client and the advertising agency, the roles of suppliers and the media, the ways agencies acquire clients and are compensated, and the overall relationship between the agency and the client.

 After **studying this chapter, you will be able to:**

LO4-1   Identify the various groups in the advertising business and explain their relationships with one another.

LO4-2   Describe what advertisers do and detail the organizational structures they use to manage advertising both here and abroad.

LO4-3   Classify the types of advertising agencies.

LO4-4   Account for the range of tasks people perform in an ad agency and an in-house advertising department.

LO4-5   Discuss how agencies attract new clients and how they make money.

LO4-6   Explain the stages in the agency–client relationship.

LO4-7   List the factors that affect the client/agency relationship.

LO4-8   Indicate how suppliers and the media help advertisers and agencies.

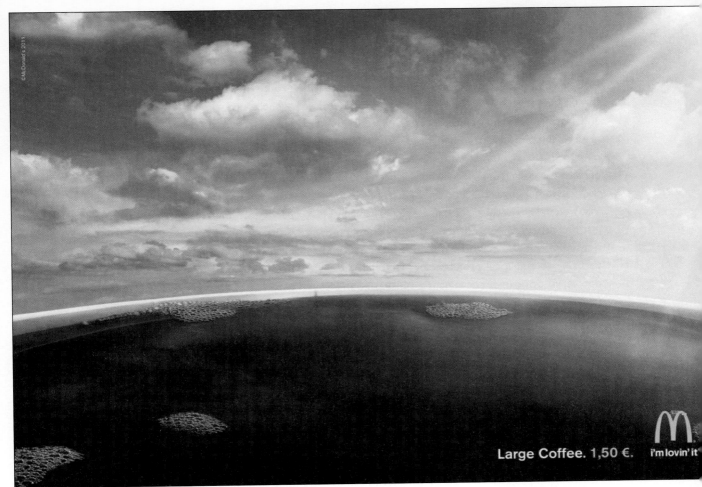

Large Coffee. 1,50 €.   i'm lovin' it

Source: McDonald's

Thomas Friedman once wrote that "No two countries that both had McDonald's had fought a war against each other since each got its McDonald's." Friedman's point was really not about McDonald's per se, but rather that economic development and international trade reduce conflict. Still, who can rule out the possibility that international harmony grows in direct proportion to the availability of Happy Meals? ■ The foods you can get at McDonald's are similar to those sold in thousands of competing restaurants and chains. Its menu item ingredients—ground beef, potatoes, and more recently, salads and yogurt—are widely available. And indeed, there are plenty of competitors out there. But none is so successful. What is McDonald's secret? ■ One could start with the company's dedication to offering value: a tasty, affordable meal served quickly. Add the relentless focus on quality, such as ensuring that meals are freshly prepared and cooked properly and that the restaurants are

clean, attractive, and comfortable. ■ But it's hard to avoid the conclusion that integrated marketing communications (IMC) is part of the equation as well. Throughout its history, McDonald's has invested heavily in marketing, both in the United States and around the world. And that investment has paid dividends by helping make the McDonald's brand one of the most valuable in the world. ■ The slogans are part of advertising lore. "You deserve a break today." "Two all beef patties, special sauce, lettuce, cheese, pickles, onions, on a sesame seed bun." "Have you had your break today?" And, of course, the current global campaign, "i'm lovin' it!" A good example of the far-reaching success of this campaign is depicted in the ad above from Finland, featuring a beautiful McDonald's coffee seascape. ■ Behind the deceptive simplicity of McDonald's ads lies a well-honed IMC strategy that reinforces a core message about the brand, promotes the company's key food offerings, and helps remind audiences that McDonald's is a fun place to get a fast, delicious meal. ■ McDonald's is a global brand, with franchises in over 100 countries. Customers entering a McDonald's franchise can always expect to encounter the Golden Arches, a menu of American food items, and fast, friendly service. Employees will be found dressed in colorful, clean uniforms. The unified brand message is also reinforced with advertising. McDonald's current campaign runs globally, so in dozens of countries customers hear the familiar, "BA DA BA BA BA," followed by "I'm lovin' it". ■ But the global campaign is just one aspect of McDonald's marketing communications efforts. It also customizes its offerings and its advertising to suit local preferences. McDonald's does not serve pork in predominantly Muslim countries (and it refers to hamburgers as "beefburgers"). In countries where beef is not a big part of the regular diet (such as India), the company offers the McVeggie sandwich along with many chicken options. Local soft drink brands are available in Scotland and Brazil and beer is available in Belgium. ■ This willingness to suit local tastes while remaining true to the brand is also

reflected in the company's advertising. McDonald's allocates a substantial portion of its advertising budget to cooperative efforts with franchises. Franchise groups make their own decisions about hiring ad agencies and campaign themes. ■ Even at the national level, McDonald's often runs several campaigns simultaneously. For example, alongside the "I'm lovin it" ads, the company runs ads promoting specific menu items, such as its premium salad offerings. The advertiser also runs ads designed to increase restaurant traffic at a particular time of day, such as breakfast or dinner. Other spots target carefully selected markets, such as Hispanics, African Americans, or working moms. ■ To help with so many different objectives, the company works with a variety of agencies. For example, Burrell has helped with advertising directed at African Americans, and Tribal DDB is the company's U.S. digital agency. ■ It may be true that anyone can make a hamburger. But building one of the world's most iconic global brands is a rare feat. McDonald's success is built on a smart business model and flawless execution. But it is also built on great IMC.

This chapter focuses on the advertising component of IMC, for several reasons. First, advertising agencies remain major players in the creation of IMC campaigns, and advertising typically represents a substantial portion of the IMC budget of firms from small to large. Second, a solid understanding of client-agency relationships in this chapter will serve as a good foundation for understanding how marketers relate to other IMC agencies. Finally, an examination of the advertiser–agency relationship helps set the stage for our later examination in this text of media.

When a business, non-profit, or individual uses advertising to market a product, service, or idea, that entity is frequently called an advertiser. In other chapters we've avoided using the term "advertiser" to better remind you that marketers have a broader communications toolbox than just paid advertising. So elsewhere we use the term "marketer" or "company." But in this chapter we'll view the marketer as a person or organization that has chosen advertising to reach its target audience, and in doing so we'll refer to the marketer as an advertiser.

The Advertising Industry

The simplicity and focus of McDonald's ads hide the great complexity of what happens behind the scenes. This chapter will help you see this as it introduces you to the people who work in the advertising industry.

The Organizations in Advertising

The advertising business has evolved into four distinct groups. The two main ones are the *marketers (or advertisers)* and the *agencies.* The advertisers (or clients) are the companies—like McDonald's, Coca-Cola, or the local shoe store—that sponsor advertising for themselves and their products. Advertisers range in size from small independent businesses to huge multinational firms, and in type from service organizations to industrial manufacturers to local charities and political action committees. The second group, *advertising agencies,* helps the advertisers plan, create, and prepare ad campaigns and other promotional materials.

A third group, the *suppliers,* includes the photographers, illustrators, printers, digital service bureaus, color film separators, video production houses, Web developers, and others who assist both advertisers and agencies in preparing advertising materials. Suppliers also include consultants, research firms, and professional services that work with both advertisers and agencies. The fourth group, the *media,* sell time (on radio and TV) and space (in print, outdoor, or digital media) to carry the advertiser's message to the target audience.

The People in Advertising

When most people think of advertising, they imagine the agency copywriters and art directors. But the majority of people in advertising are actually employed by advertisers. Most companies have an advertising department, even if it's just one person. Many other people work for the suppliers and the media. They're in advertising, too.

The fact is, advertising is a very broad field that employs a wide variety of people in sales, research, management, accounting, computer science, and law, as well as specialists in the communication arts—artists, writers, photographers, musicians, performers, and cinematographers.

In this chapter, we'll see what all these people do. In the process, you'll get a good understanding of how the business operates both in the United States and abroad.

The Advertisers (the Clients)

While most companies have some sort of advertising department, its importance depends on the company's size and industry, the size of the advertising program, the role advertising plays in the company's marketing mix, and most of all, the involvement of top management.

To get a sense of the diversity of companies that advertise, we'll look first at local advertisers to see how they operate. Then we'll examine the regional and national advertisers. Finally, we'll look at the companies that market their products globally.

Local Advertising: Where the Action Is

There are more than 18,000 American firms with 500 or more employees. But there are more than 5 million that employ fewer than 20, according to the Census Bureau.[1] The vast majority of these small firms are local. Local businesses use IMC to grow, flourish, and fulfil the dreams of their owners. Let's see how one small business, Rubio's used IMC to grow from a small start-up to a strong regional food chain. Not long after graduating from San Diego State, Ralph Rubio opened his first Mexican restaurant. He offered an unusual specialty fish tacos—lightly battered and fried whitefish served in soft-shelled corn tortillas with white sauce, salsa, cabbage, and a wedge of lime. At the time, very few other Mexican eateries offered fish tacos, and non featured them. So Rubio found fish tacos hard to sell, even with hi secret batter recipe (which he'd gotten from a street vendor in Sa Felipe, Mexico). The first month's sales at the restaurant averaged onl $163 a day.

Rubio started using small newspaper ads with coupons to lur courageous customers. It worked. As business picked up, he ex panded his advertising to radio and TV, targeting his market furthe with ads on Hispanic stations (whose listeners knew what fish taco were). And he went after younger, venturesome customers aged 1 to 34 by advertising at local movie theaters. Business picked u some more. Rubio soon opened another restaurant, and the another.

With each new opening, Rubio distributed direct-mail flye in the area and took free samples to nearby stores. Working with a artist, he created a cartoon character named Pesky Pescado based o

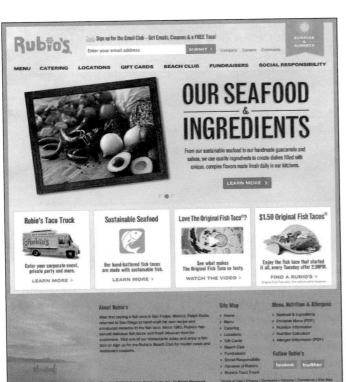

Local advertisers such as Rubio's Baja Grill (www.rubios.com) must find ways to differentiate their products from the competition—and then create awareness through advertising. Rubio's Website touts their use of fresh ingredients and sustainable seafood, which sets them apart from other restaurants.

Source: Rubio's Restaurants, Inc.

My IMC Campaign 4–A

Understanding Your Client

Obtaining a clear understanding of what your client wants from you and what you are prepared to do for your client is essential for a mutually satisfying relationship. From your end it is vital that you be clear about the finished product. In many classes this might be a plans book, which contains research, an advertising plan, a media plan, and even some creative. In other classes you might not provide all of that. In either case, make sure your client knows what to expect. If previous classes have done campaign work for other clients, you might wish to show your client that work.

As important as it is that your client understand you, it is equally crucial that you understand your client's expectations. Recognize that some clients may not have a clear set of expectations at first; these may in fact evolve over time. Even in this instance, asking the right questions can get your client thinking about what they hope advertising will do for them.

Below you will find some questions that might prove useful for getting to know your client better. Dr. Debbie Treise, who regularly teaches advertising campaigns at the University of Florida, uses this form. Sending it to the client in advance of a meeting can make your first interaction more useful and informative.

1. Provide a complete description of your product/service:
   What is its current position?
   What is the brand personality as you perceive it?
   Does it need changing?
   Are there seasonal trends for your product?
   Would you be willing to share annual sales trend information?
2. Do you have information on your company to share? Your mission statement? How would you describe the culture of your organization?
3. Do you have a definite target market in mind? Are you targeting consumers, groups, businesses, or some combination?
4. Is the market local? Regional? National? International?
5. Would you be willing to share:
   Information on your competition?
   Information on your market?
   Information on market trends? Legal trends?
   Advertising that your competition has used?
   Previous advertising efforts you have undertaken?
6. What is the time period of this campaign? Do you have definite start and stop dates in mind?
7. What is the budget?
8. Do you have any specifications on the budget breakdown in terms of promotion versus advertising? Any other specifications?
9. What are your marketing objectives for this campaign?
10. Please list your advertising/communications objectives for this campaign (i.e., to increase knowledge, change attitudes, elicit a specific behavior).
11. Are there media that you would like us to be sure to consider?
12. Are there media that you would prefer we not recommend?
13. Do you have a current, active Website? If so, what is its primary purpose? Who accesses it?
14. Do you have any specifications on creative executions? Are you looking to continue current efforts or to come up with something completely different?
15. Are there any current clients/consumers that we could contact?
16. Are there potential clients/customers that we could contact?
17. Who is the individual in your organization we should contact when we have questions? What is the best time to contact this person? How does he or she prefer to be contacted (e-mail, phone, fax)?

the fish taco. He purchased a 15-foot inflatable Pesky to display at his restaurants. Employee T-shirts sported Pesky's picture, and Rubio sold Pesky T-shirts and sweatshirts to enthusiastic patrons. He also offered bumper stickers and antenna balls to add some fun to his promotions. To further integrate his activities, Rubio took an active part in community affairs, including tie-ins with a blood bank, a literacy program, and fund-raising activities for both a Tijuana medical clinic and a local university's athletic program.

As the popularity of the fish taco grew, so did Rubio's revenues, doubling every year for the first five years. He trademarked the phrase "Rubio's, Home of the Fish Taco," and a local restaurant critic, commenting on things San Diegans couldn't do without, called fish tacos "the food San Diegans would miss the most." After 19 years, Rubio had 137 restaurants in five states. Together they produced more than $112 million in annual sales and helped Rubio's serve more than 50 million fish tacos.[2]

Every year, advertisers spend billions of dollars in the United States. Almost half of that is spent on **local advertising,** ads placed by local businesses in a particular city or county targeting customers in their geographic area.

Issue-oriented organizations such as Mothers Against Drunk Driving (MADD) uses advertising to advance their perspectives, as seen in this ad. By showing a man that lost his arm while drinking and driving, do you feel this MADD advertisement effectively illustrates the perils of drunk driving?

With Permission from MADD Canada

Local advertising is sometimes called *retail advertising* because retail stores account for so much of it. But retail advertising isn't always local; Sears and JCPenney advertise nationally. And many businesses besides retail stores use local advertising: banks, real estate developers, movie theaters, auto mechanics, plumbers, radio and TV stations, funeral homes, museums, and local politicians, to name a few. McDonald's franchises engage in local advertising too. Since many franchises are locally owned and operated, they are good examples of small businesses that use advertising to achieve marketing objectives.

Local advertising is critically important because most consumer sales are made (or lost) locally. McDonald's may spend billions advertising nationwide, but if its franchises don't make a strong effort locally, those dollars are wasted. When it comes to making the sale and dealing with customers, local advertising is where the action is—where relationships often start and truly develop.

Types of Local Advertisers

There are four main types of local advertisers:

1. Dealers or local franchisees of national companies (McDonald's, Mail Boxes Etc., Kinko's, H&R Block).
2. Stores that sell a variety of branded merchandise, usually on a nonexclusive basis (convenience, grocery, and department stores).
3. Specialty businesses and services (banks, insurance brokers, restaurants, music stores, shoe repair shops, remodeling contractors, florists, hair salons, travel agencies, attorneys, accountants).
4. Governmental and nonprofit organizations (municipalities, utility companies, charities, arts organizations, political candidates).

A small, local business—say, a hardware, clothing, or electronics store—may have just one person in charge of advertising. That person, the **advertising manager,** performs the administrative, planning, budgeting, and coordinating functions. He or she may lay out ads, write copy, and select the media. A manager with some artistic talent may even design the ads and produce them on a desktop computer.

A chain store often maintains a completely staffed advertising department to handle production, media placement, and marketing support services. The department needs artists, copywriters, and production specialists. The department head usually reports to a vice president or marketing manager, as shown in Exhibit 4-1.

Types of Local Advertising

Choose lovin' placed in local media are product, institutional, or classified advertising. Each serves a different purpose.

Product Advertising   **Product advertising** promotes a specific product or service and stimulates short-term action while building awareness of the business. When a McDonald's franchise promotes its premium salads, it is engaging in product advertising. Local advertisers use three major types of product ads: regular price-line, sale, and clearance. **Regular price-line advertising** informs consumers about services or merchandise offered at regular prices. An accounting firm might use regular price-line advertising to promote its accounting and tax services.

To stimulate sales of particular merchandise or increase store traffic, local merchants occasionally use **sale advertising,** placing items on sale and offering two-for-one specials or other deals. Local advertisers use **clearance advertising** (a special form of sale advertising) to make room for new product lines or new models and to get rid of slow-moving lines.

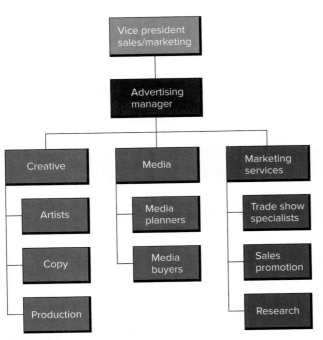

Exhibit 4-1
Typical department structure for small advertisers with high volumes of work, such as grocery store chains.

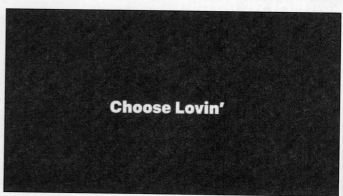

In this campaign McDonald's extends its "I'm lovin' it" slogan to "choose lovin." The ad shows archenemies finding a way to love one another.

Source: McDonald's

floor samples, broken or distressed merchandise, or out-of-season items. Companies going out of business also use clearance advertising.

Institutional Advertising   **Institutional advertising** attempts to create a favorable long-term perception of the business as a whole, not just of a particular product or service. A McDonald's franchise using an ad to let consumers know it uses beef and produce from local farms is a good example of this type. Many types of businesses (stores, restaurants, banks, professional firms, hospitals) use institutional advertising to promote an *idea* about the company and build long-term goodwill. It makes the public aware of what the business stands for and attempts to build reputation and image. An institutional ad might focus on convenient hours, a new credit policy, store expansion, or company philosophy.

Although readership is often lower, effective institutional ads build a favorable image for the business, attract new customers, and encourage customer loyalty.

Classified Advertising   Advertisers use **classified advertising** in the newspaper for many reasons: to locate and recruit new employees, offer services (such as those of an employment agency or business opportunity broker), or sell or lease merchandise (such as cars, real estate, and office equipment). Many McDonald's franchises use classifieds to recruit new employees.

Local Advertisers: Where IMC Began

When Ralph Rubio built his restaurant business, his promotional activities involved a lot more than just running ads. In fact, he did everything he could to develop a *relationship* with his customers and to promote a good word-of-mouth reputation. That meant using publicity, sales promotion, and direct response as well as media advertising—all integrated with consistently good food, reasonable prices, and excellent service. This combination constitutes

integrated marketing communications (IMC)—joining together in a consistent manner everything that communicates with customers. Thanks to IMC, Rubio's fish taco became a local staple.

Local advertisers and the local agencies that serve them are not stuck with the traditional national view that advertising means "ads placed in the media." By necessity, local advertisers wear many hats every day. They tend the cash register, talk with customers, prepare mailers, write and place ads, evaluate suppliers' trade promotions, answer phone inquiries, spruce up the office, talk to media people, and coordinate the graphics for a seasonal promotion. By successfully combining personal selling with media advertising, direct marketing, sales promotion, and public relations, the local advertiser can be the consummate integrator of marketing communications.[3]

Creating Local Advertising

For many years, local advertisers had limited advertising options. Most relied on either newspapers or radio, with some local television in the mix. Many newspaper ads featured what professionals would call a *schlock* approach—heavy bold type, items crowded into ad space, loud headlines, and unsophisticated graphic design. If the message is honest, consistent, and effective and meets the advertiser's objectives, that may be all that matters. To direct and control the creative aspects of their ads and commercials and ensure consistency, local advertisers should develop a checklist of creative do's and don'ts. (See My IMC Campaign 4–B, "Creating Local Advertising.")

In recent years, digital media have expanded the palette of options available for local advertisers. Google and Facebook allow small advertisers to create highly concentrated and efficient campaigns. And "deal-of-the-day" sites such as Groupon allow local advertisers to run sale advertising in e-mails received by thousands of local customers.

Finding big ideas for local ad campaigns can be extremely difficult. Some advertisers look to the merchandise for ideas; others look to the customer. An important goal for local advertisers is to achieve a consistent, distinctive look that makes their ads both appealing and identifiable. We discuss the creative process in depth in Chapters 10–12.

Local advertisers can turn to a number of sources for creative help, including reps from the local media, local ad agencies, freelancers and consultants, creative boutiques, syndicated art services, and the *cooperative advertising programs* of wholesalers, manufacturers, and trade associations. McDonald's offers its franchises considerable help in designing ads and promotional materials.

Cooperative Advertising

As a service to their distributors and dealers, and to ensure proper reproduction of their products, wholesalers, manufacturers, and trade associations often provide local advertisers with ready-made advertising materials and cooperative advertising programs where the costs are shared.

There are two key purposes for **cooperative (co-op) advertising:** to build the manufacturer's brand image and to help its distributors, dealers, or retailers make more sales.[4] Every year, national manufacturers give their local retailers millions for co-op projects. Whereas co-op spending favored newspapers years ago, budgets today increasingly favor digital, mobile, and social media.[5] To take one example, Ford Motor Co. is now requiring that it's local dealers spend a quarter of their co-op dollars on digital.[6]

In **vertical cooperative advertising,** the manufacturer provides the complete ad and shares the cost of the advertising time or space. The local newspaper sets the name and address of the local advertiser, or the radio station adds a tagline with the advertiser's name, address, and phone number. Bridgestone makes vertical co-op advertising even more customizable for its retailers. It developed templates for newspaper ads, flyers, and point-of-sale (POS) materials that retail managers can download and edit to fit their needs. After only a few minutes of training, dealers without any graphic design expertise can create local

My IMC Campaign 4–B

Creating Local Advertising

Is your client a local business or service? Use these time-tested practices to guide your thinking about how local advertising can help.

■ *Stand out from the competition.* Make your ads easily recognizable. Ads with unusual art, layout, and typefaces have higher readership. Make the ads distinctive but keep their appearance consistent.

■ *Use a simple layout.* The layout should carry the reader's eye through the message easily and in proper sequence from headline to illustration to explanatory copy to price to store name. Avoid too many typefaces.

■ *Use a dominant element.* A large picture or headline ensures quick visibility. Photos of real people and action pictures win more readership, as do photos of local people or places. Color attracts more readers.

■ *Stress the benefits.* Present the emotional reason to buy or the tangible performance element customers seek.

■ *Make the headline count.* Use a compelling headline to feature the main benefit.

■ *Watch your language.* Make your writing style active, lively, and involving. Make the readers feel they already own the product. Avoid negativism and profanity.

■ *Let white space work for you.* White space focuses the reader's attention and makes the headline and illustration stand out.

■ *Make the copy complete.* Emphasize the benefits most appealing to customers.

■ *Make your visual powerful and eye-catching.* Focus on the benefit. The main visual is often more important than the headline. Photos work better than artwork.

■ *Specify branded merchandise.* If the item is a known brand, say so.

■ *Include related items.* Make two sales instead of one by offering related items along with a featured one.

■ *Urge readers to buy now.* Ask for the sale. Stimulate prompt action by using "limited supply" or "this week only."

■ *Don't forget the business name and address.* Check every ad to be certain the business name, address, phone number, and hours are included.

■ *Don't be too clever.* Many people distrust or misunderstand cleverness.

■ *Don't use unusual or difficult words.* Everyone understands simple language. Use it.

■ *Don't generalize.* Be specific. Shoppers want all the facts before they buy.

■ *Don't make excessive claims.* Advertisers lose customers when they make claims they can't back up.

■ *Plan ad size carefully.* Attention usually increases with size.

■ *Consider your target customers.* People notice ads more if they are directed at their own gender or age group.

■ *Use tie-ins* with local or special news events.

---

advertising that looks as polished as national advertising.[7] (See Ad Lab 4–A for the pros and cons of co-op advertising.)

With **horizontal cooperative advertising,** firms in the same business (real estate agents, insurance agents, pharmacies, car dealers, or travel agents) or in the same part of town advertise jointly. Competing auto dealers, for example, might pool their dollars to advertise their common retail area as the "Mile of Cars."

Regional and National Advertisers

Regional advertisers operate in one part of the country—in one or several states—and market exclusively within that region. Examples include regional grocery and department store chains, governmental bodies (such as state lotteries), franchise groups (such as the Southern California Honda dealers), telephone companies (such as SBC), and statewide or multistate banks (like Bank of America).

Other companies sell in several regions or throughout the country and are called **national advertisers.** These include consumer packaged-goods manufacturers (such as Procter & Gamble and Johnson & Johnson), national airlines (Delta, American), media and entertainment companies (Disney, Time Warner), electronics manufacturers (Apple, Hewlett-Packard), all the auto companies, and restaurant chains like McDonald's. These firms make up the membership of the **Association of National Advertisers (ANA)** and comprise the largest advertisers in the country (see Exhibit 4-2).

How National and Local Advertisers Differ

The basic principles of advertising are the same in both local and national advertising. However, local advertisers have special challenges stemming from the day-to-day realities

AD Lab 4-A

The Co-op Marriage

On the surface, cooperative advertising seems like a great arrangement for retailers. A manufacturer supplies advertising materials (saving the retailer production costs) and pays a percentage of the media cost. The retailer drops in the store's logo, arranges for the ad to run, and collects the co-op dollars from the manufacturer. The small retail business can stretch its ad budget and associate its business with a nationally advertised product. The retailer receives professionally prepared ads and acquires greater leverage with the local media that carry the co-op ads.

But as with any marriage, there is give and take.

A retailer may have to sell a lot of merchandise to qualify for significant co-op funds. More often, the retailer and manufacturer have different advertising objectives and different ideas about how the ads should be executed.

The manufacturer often wants total control. The manufacturer expects co-op ads to tie in with its national advertising promotions. It wants the right product advertised at the right time. Manufacturers prepare guideline pamphlets specifying when and where the ads should appear, what form they should take, and what uses of the name and logo are not allowed.

Retailers have their own ideas about which products to advertise when. They're more concerned with daily volume and with projecting an image of value and variety. An appliance store might prefer to advertise inexpensive TVs even though the manufacturer wants to emphasize its top-of-the-line models.

Manufacturers worry that retailers will place the product in a cluttered, ugly ad or next to inferior products; that the ad will run in inappropriate publications; and that it will not run at the best time. Retailers counter that they know the local market better. In short, manufacturers think they don't have enough control; retailers think they have too much.

A retailer contemplating co-op funds should consider the following questions:

- What requirements must be met in order for ads to qualify for co-op money?
- What percentage is paid by each party?
- When can ads be run?
- What media can be used?
- Are there special provisions for message content?
- What documentation is required for reimbursement?
- How does each party benefit?
- Do cooperative ads obscure the retailer's image?

Laboratory Applications

1. Look through today's edition of a daily paper in your city. Identify two ads that can qualify as co-op. Do the ads fit both the store's image and the manufacturer's image? Explain.

2. A store may develop its own ad and drop in the manufacturer's logo or it may take an ad created by the manufacturer and simply add the store's location. Which do your two ads do?

---

of running a small business. As a result, local and national advertisers differ in terms of focus, time orientation, and resources (see Exhibit 4-3).

Focus   National companies are concerned about building their brands, so their advertising tends to focus on the competitive features of one brand over another, especially in conquest sales situations. Local merchants or dealers often carry hundreds of different brands or

---

Exhibit 4-2

Ten biggest brands as measured by total U.S. measured-media spending in 2014 (000,000).

Rank		Brand	Total 2014	% Chg from 2013
2014	**2013**			
1	1	AT&T	1,442	−20.0
2	2	Verizon	1,269	4.2
3	3	Geico	1,159	14.2
4	5	McDonald's	953	−4.2
5	4	Chevrolet	888	−10.8
6	8	WalMart	867	1.1
7	9	Sprint	828	8.2
8	10	Macy's	757	−0.5
9	6	Toyota	736	−22.2
10	13	Nissan	703	9.0

Source: Advertising Age Data Center, 2015, retrieved at http://adage.com/datacenter/datapopup.php?article_id=298948

	National	**Local**
Focus	Brand Market share Strategies Markets	Point Volume, gross sales Tactics Customers
Time	Long-term campaigns	Short-term ads
Resources	$5–$10 million+ Many specialists	Less than $1 million A few generalists

Exhibit 4-3

Differences between local and national advertisers.

numerous models of an exclusive brand, so they focus on attracting customers to a particular **point**—their place of business. That's why local car dealers typically advertise their dealerships rather than the make of car. And local grocers often promote only those brands for which they receive co-op advertising or trade allowances from the national manufacturer.

In every product category, big companies battle for market share against a few competitors, and every share point is worth millions of dollars. Local advertisers compete with many companies, so their focus is on gross sales or volume: 60 cars a month, five new insurance policies a week, 55 oil changes a day.

National advertisers plan *strategically* to launch, build, and sustain brands. Local advertisers think *tactically.* Will a new $15,000 sign bring more people into the store? Should we stay open on Labor Day? Can we attract more lunchtime customers by reducing our prices or by offering free refills on soft drinks?

The relationship with the customer may be the greatest difference between national and local advertisers. National advertisers' marketing executives rarely see retail customers; instead, they traditionally think in terms of large groups of people—segments, niches, target markets—with various geographic, demographic, or psychographic descriptions. They design their strategies and campaigns to appeal to these large groups.

But local advertisers deal with individual customers every day. They also interact with customers in nonbusiness ways; they may be neighbors, friends, or schoolmates. The local advertiser gets feedback every day—on the company's advertising, prices, product performance, employee service, store decor, and the new sign out front. The national marketer gets occasional feedback—from surveys and from customer complaint lines.

Time Orientation   National and local advertisers also have different time orientations. National companies think long-term. They develop five-year strategic plans and budget for annual advertising campaigns. Local advertisers worry that this week's ad in the *Pennysaver* didn't *pull* (a term rarely used by national marketers) as well as last week's; a New York advertiser may have months to develop a network TV campaign; the coffeehouse downtown may have to churn out a new newspaper ad every week to reach its local customers.

Resources   Finally, national advertisers have more resources available—both money and people. A local advertiser that spends $100,000 a year has a relatively large budget. A national advertiser needs to spend at least $5 million a year just to get started. (Proctor & Gamble, the largest U.S. advertiser, spends close to $5 billion annually.)[8]

The national advertiser has an army of specialists dedicated to the successful marketing of its brands. The local advertiser may have a small staff or just one person—the owner—to market the business. So the local entrepreneur has to know more about every facet of marketing communications.

How Large Companies Manage Their Advertising

In large companies, many people are involved in advertising. Company owners and top corporate executives make key advertising decisions; sales and marketing personnel often assist in the creative process, help choose the ad agency, and evaluate proposed ad programs; artists and writers produce ads, brochures, and other materials; product engineers and designers give input to the creative process and provide information about competitive products; administrators

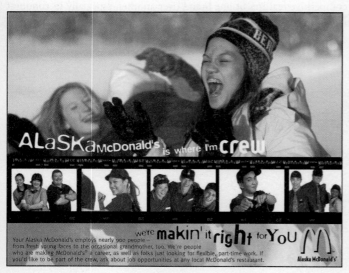

McDonald's franchises help craft campaigns to suit local markets. Here franchises in Alaska advertise to attract new employees.

Source: McDonald's

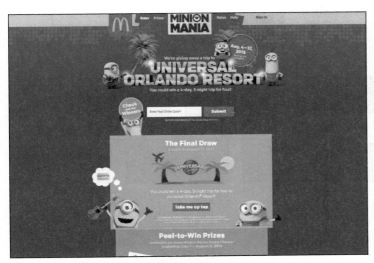

Advertising can help make sales promotions more effective, especially when they are teamed with a summer movie blockbuster, Minions. In this screenshot, McDonald's offers its customers a chance to win prizes, including a trip to Universal Studios Orlando when they buy select food items that have the Minions game piece on them.

Source: McDonald's

evaluate the cost of ad campaigns and help plan budgets; and clerical staff members coordinate various promotional activities, including advertising.

A large company's advertising department may employ many people and be headed by an advertising manager who reports to a marketing director or marketing services manager. The exact department structure depends on many variables. Most large advertisers tend to use some mix of two basic management structures: *centralized* and *decentralized*.

Centralized Organization   Companies are concerned with cost efficiency and continuity in their communications programs. Thus, many embrace the **centralized advertising department** because it gives the greatest *control* and offers both *efficiency* and *continuity* across divisional boundaries. In centralized departments, an advertising manager typically reports to a marketing vice president. In addition, companies may organize the department in any of five ways:

- By product or brand.
- By subfunction of advertising (copy, art, print production, media buying).
- By end user (consumer advertising, trade advertising).
- By media (radio, TV, newspapers, outdoor).
- By geography (southwestern U.S. advertising, European advertising).

The cereal giant General Mills, for example, is one of the nation's largest advertisers. It operates a vast advertising and marketing services department with some 350 employees. It spends more than $894 million annually on advertising alone, along with millions more on other promotional activities.[9]

General Mills's Marketing Services is really many departments within a department. Its centralized structure enables it to administer, plan, and coordinate the promotion of more than 100 brands. It also supervises five outside ad agencies and operates its own in-house agency for new or smaller brands.[10]

Organized around functional specialties (market research, media, graphics), Marketing Services helps General Mills's brand managers consolidate many of their expenditures for maximum efficiency. The media department, for example, prepares all media plans for the marketing divisions. The production and art department designs the packages for all brands and the graphics for the company's in-house agency. From one spot, Marketing Services handles a wide variety of brands efficiently and effectively (see Exhibit 4-4).

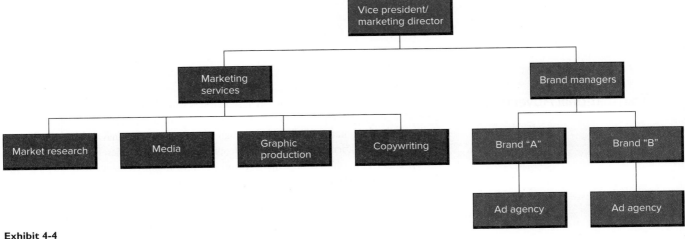

Exhibit 4-4
General Mills has a centralized advertising department like this model.

Exhibit 4-5

In a decentralized system, each division is its own marketing department.

Decentralized Organization   As companies become larger, diversify their product lines, acquire subsidiaries, and establish divisions in different regions or countries, a centralized advertising department can become impractical.

In a **decentralized system,** the company sets up separate ad departments for different divisions, subsidiaries, regions, brands, or other groups. The general manager of each division or brand is responsible for that group's advertising.

For large companies with many divisions, decentralized advertising offers flexibility. Campaigns and media schedules can be adjusted faster. New approaches and creative ideas can be introduced more easily, and sales results can be measured independently of other divisions. In effect, each division is its own marketing department, with the advertising manager reporting to the division head (see Exhibit 4-5).

A drawback, though, is that decentralized departments often concentrate on their own budgets, problems, and promotions rather than the good of the whole company. Across divisions, ads typically lack uniformity, diminishing the power of repetitive corporate advertising. Rivalry among brand managers may even escalate into unhealthy competition.

Transnational Advertisers

Companies advertising abroad typically face markets with different value systems, environments, and languages. Their customers have different purchasing abilities, habits, and motivations. Media customary to U.S. and Canadian advertisers may be unavailable or ineffective. The companies will therefore likely need different advertising strategies. But they face a more basic problem: How should they manage and produce the advertising? Should their U.S. agency or in-house advertising department do it? Should they use a foreign agency or set up a local advertising department?

As advertisers enter international markets, they may start by simply exporting their existing products. At first, the home office controls all foreign marketing and advertising. Everything is centralized. Then, as companies get more involved in foreign markets, they may form joint ventures or invest in foreign facilities. Advertisers typically view such operations as foreign marketing divisions and use a decentralized **international structure,** in which the divisions are responsible for their own product lines, marketing operations, and profits, and create customized advertising for each market.[11]

Procter & Gamble, for example, is a nearly 200-year-old company with annual sales of $83 billion. It sells more than 300 consumer brands to more than 5 billion consumers in 140 countries. These brands include such market leaders as Tide, Ivory soap, Pampers, Folgers, Pringles, and Crest.[12]

P&G is one of the biggest and most influential consumer advertisers in the world; its expenditures in the United States alone exceed $4.9 billion annually. But more than half its sales come from abroad.[13] Each overseas division is set up almost like a separate company with its own research and development department, manufacturing plant, advertising department, sales force, and finance and accounting staff. Every brand within a division has a **brand manager** who oversees a brand group and directs his or her own ad agency to create the brand's media advertising. Brand managers work under a marketing manager, who reports to a *category manager.*[14]

Each division also has an advertising department to help coordinate sales promotion and merchandising programs across brands. The corporate advertising department provides statistical information and guidance.

While the brand manager's primary goal is to use advertising and promotion to build market share, the category manager focuses on sharpening overall strategy and building profits.[15] In recent years, P&G has streamlined the system by eliminating extra layers of management and redundant facilities. This ensures that each brand has the single-minded drive needed for success and gives more authority to the individual responsible for the brand.[16]

As companies continue to grow and prosper around the world, they may invest directly in many countries. True **multinational corporations** strive for full, integrated participation in world markets.[17] Foreign sales often grow faster than domestic sales. Multinationals such as Exxon and IBM earn about 50 percent of their sales abroad; Kodak and Xerox, about 25 percent. Typically, the top 25 U.S. multinational corporations earn more than 40 percent of their revenues and two-thirds of their profits overseas.[18]

A multinational usually exerts strong centralized control over all its marketing activities. Multinational firms such as Microsoft get strong direction and coordination from headquarters and have a standardized product line and marketing structure.

Multinationals that use a *standardized approach* to marketing and advertising in all countries are **global marketers,** and they create global brands. They assume that the way the product is used and the needs it satisfies are universal.[19] Estée Lauder, for example, markets its cosmetics globally. In 2005, Gwyneth Paltrow became the latest in a long line of international actresses to promote the company's products. Estée Lauder's Pleasures is the world's fourth largest fragrance brand.[20] Global advertisers include Coca-Cola, British Airways, British Petroleum, TGI Friday's, FedEx, and of course, McDonald's.[21]

Companies must research extensively before attempting a global advertising strategy. So much depends on the product and where they try to sell it. A "no" answer to any of the following questions means the attempt will probably fail

1. *Has each country's market for the product developed in the same way?* A Ford is a Ford in most markets. On the other hand, many Europeans use clotheslines, so they don't need fabric softeners for dryers.

2. *Are the targets similar in different nations?* Chinese consumers like PCs and Microsoft Windows. The same is true in Europe and the United States. But when Chinese Web users search the Internet, they prefer BAIDU, a home-grown search engine, to Google.

3. *Do consumers share the same wants and needs?* Breakfast in Brazil is usually a cup of coffee. Kellogg's corn flakes won't be served the same way there as in the United States, where people commonly eat cereal for breakfast.[22]

According to J. Walter Thompson, the secret to success in global advertising is knowing how to tap into basic human emotions and uncover universal appeals that don't depend solely

Humor is an important ingredient in McDonald's global messages. Messages like this one resonate in a variety of cultures. In this ad, created by DDB Finland, McDonald's humorosly promotes their real milkshakes by depicting a cow jumping on a trampoline.

Source: McDonald's

on language.[23] Sports competition has broad appeal around the world, which is one reason McDonald's was a major sponsor of the 2008 Olympics.

Ultimately, the advertising direction a company takes depends on many variables: breadth of product line, quality of management, ability to repeat marketing strategies across countries, costs, and the decision to operate internationally, multinationally, or globally. Every organization operates in a slightly different environment. This alters the search for an *ideal structure* into a search for a *suitable structure*.[24] Most companies blend aspects of centralized and decentralized structures to fit their own needs.

The Advertising Agency

LO 4-3

The Role of the Advertising Agency

Why does a company such as McDonald's hire an advertising agency in the first place? Couldn't it save money by hiring its own staff and creating its own ads? How does Leo Burnett win such a large account? Must an agency's accounts be that big for it to make money? This section sheds some light on these issues and gives a clearer understanding of what agencies do and why so many advertisers use agencies.

The American Association of Advertising Agencies (AAAA) defines an **advertising agency** as an independent organization of creative people and businesspeople who specialize in developing and preparing marketing and advertising plans, advertisements, and other promotional tools. The agency also purchases advertising space and time in various media on behalf of different advertisers, or sellers (its clients), to find customers for their goods and services.[25]

This definition offers clues to why so many advertisers hire ad agencies. First, an agency like Leo Burnett is *independent.* The agency isn't owned by the advertiser, the media, or the suppliers, so it can bring an outside, objective viewpoint to the advertiser's business—a state the advertiser can never attain.

Second, like all full service agencies, Leo Burnett employs a combination of *businesspeople* and *creative people,* including administrators, accountants, marketing executives, researchers, market and media analysts, writers, and artists. They have day-to-day contact with outside professional suppliers who create illustrations, take photos, retouch art, shoot commercials, record sound, and print brochures.

The agency provides yet another service by researching, negotiating, arranging, and contracting for commercial space and time with the various print, electronic, and digital media. Because of its *media expertise,* Leo Burnett saves its clients time and money.

Agencies don't work for the media or the suppliers. Their moral, ethical, financial, and legal obligation is to their clients. Just as a well-run business seeks professional help from attorneys, accountants, bankers, or management specialists, advertisers use agencies out of *self-interest* because the agencies can create more effective advertising and select more effective media than the advertisers can themselves. Today, almost all sizable advertisers rely on an ad agency for expert, objective counsel, and unique creative skills—to be the "guardian of their brands."[26] Ad Lab 4–B gives a snapshot of advertising agencies in the United States.

Finally, a good agency serves its clients' needs because of its daily exposure to a broad spectrum of marketing situations and problems both here and abroad. As technology has enabled companies to work across borders with relative ease, the advertising business has boomed worldwide. All the large U.S. agencies, for example, maintain offices in many foreign countries.

Types of Agencies

Advertising agencies are typically classified by their geographic scope, the range of services they offer, and the type of business they handle.

Local Agencies

Every community of any size has reputable small ad agencies that offer expert assistance to local advertisers. A competent **local agency** can help

- Analyze the local advertiser's business and the product or service being sold.
- Evaluate the markets for the business, including channels of distribution.

AD Lab 4-B

How Big Is the Agency Business?

Advertising today is a massive, worldwide business with a strong presence in the United States. All told, the more than 12,000 U.S. agencies employ more than 150,000 people. Agency employment plummeted 15.5 percent between 2000 and 2004, but hiring has been on the rise again since 2005—regrowth that industry analysts chalk up to the hot interactive marketing sector.

1. Agencies need fewer people than businesses in many other industries: about half of all firms employ fewer than 10 people. But about one-third of all people in the industry work in the 10 percent of agencies with 500 or more people. Want to work for a big power player? Visit the Websites of three of the top 10 U.S. agencies and jot down your impressions.

2. What are the advantages and disadvantages that small agencies and boutiques face? Visit *Advertising Age's* "Small Agency Diary" (http://amiga.adage.com/blogs/) to see the world through the eyes of three small fish in the big pond.

World's Top 5 Agency Companies

2014 Rank	Agency	Headquarters	WW Revenue 2014 (000,000)
1	WPP	London	$18,956
2	Omnicom	New York	15,318
3	Publicis Groupe	Paris	9,625
4	Interpublic Group	New York	7,537
5	Dentsu	Tokyo	6,015

Share of U.S. advertising and media market

World's Top 5 Advertising Agencies

Rank 2014	Rank 2013	Network, Parent / Selected Units	Headquarters	Worldwide Revenue 2014	Worldwide Revenue 2013	% CHG
1	1	Young & Rubicam Group*, WPP	New York	$3,670	$3,590	2.2
2	2	McCann Worldgroup*, Interpublic Group of Cos.	New York	3,097	2,909	6.5
3	4	DDB Worldwide Communications Group*, Omnicom Group	New York	2,865	2,729	5
4	3	Dentsu (Japan)*, Dentsu Inc.	Tokyo	2,775	2,848	−2.5
5	5	BBDO Worldwide*, Omnicom Group	New York	2,620	2,513	4.3

All data from Advertising Age Datacenter, 2015

- Evaluate the advertiser's competitive position and offer strategic options.
- Evaluate media alternatives and offer rational recommendations.
- Devise an integrated communications plan and implement it with consistency and creativity.
- Save the advertiser valuable time by taking over media interviewing, analysis, checking, billing, and bookkeeping.
- Assist in other aspects of advertising and promotion by implementing sales contests, publicity, grand openings, and other activities.

Unfortunately, local advertisers use ad agencies less extensively than national advertisers. Many advertisers simply don't spend enough money on advertising to warrant hiring an agency. And some large agencies don't accept local advertisers because their budgets are too low to support the agency's overhead.

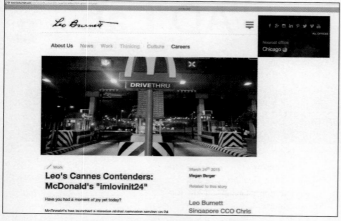

Leo Burnett is one of many McDonald's ad agencies. Visit the agency's Website at www.leoburnett.com to see examples of its work for McDonald's and other advertisers.
Source: Leo Burnett

Regional and National Agencies

Every major city has numerous agencies that can produce and place the quality of advertising suitable for national campaigns. **Regional and national agencies** typically participate in a regional trade group such as the Western States Advertising Agency Association (WSAAA). The *Standard Directory of Advertising Agencies* (the Red Book) lists these agencies geographically, so they're easy to find.

International Agencies

The largest national agencies are also **international agencies.** That is, they have offices or affiliates in major communication centers around the world and can help their clients market internationally or globally as the case may be. Likewise, many foreign-based agencies have offices and affiliates in the United States. For example, the largest advertising agency organization in the world today, WPP Group, is based in London. But it owns several of the top agencies in the United States, such as Ogilvy & Mather and Grey Worldwide.

Full-Service Agencies

The modern **full-service advertising agency** supplies both advertising and nonadvertising services in all areas of communications and promotion. *Advertising services* include planning, creating, and producing ads; performing research; and selecting media. *Nonadvertising functions* run the gamut from packaging to public relations to producing sales promotion materials, annual reports, and trade show exhibits. With the trend toward IMC, many of the largest agencies today are in the forefront of the emerging *interactive media.*[27]

Full-service agencies may specialize in certain kinds of clients. Most, though, can be classified as either *general consumer agencies* or *business-to-business agencies.*

General Consumer Agencies   A **general consumer agency** represents the widest variety of accounts, but it concentrates on *consumer accounts*—companies that make goods purchased chiefly by consumers (soaps, cereals, cars, pet foods, toiletries). Most of the ads are placed in consumer media (TV, radio, magazines, and so on) that pay a *commission* to the agency. General agencies often derive much of their income from these commissions.

General agencies include the international superagency groups headquartered in communication capitals such as New York, London, Paris, and Tokyo, as well as many other large firms in New York, Chicago, Los Angeles, Minneapolis, Montreal, and Toronto. A few of the better-known names in North America are McCann-Erickson; Ogilvy & Mather; BBDO; DDB Worldwide; Y&R; Draft FCB; and Cossette Communications-Marketing (Canada). But general agencies also include the thousands of smaller *entrepreneurial agencies* located in every major city across the country (Crispin Porter + Bogusky, Miami; Rubin/Postaer, Los Angeles; Fallon Worldwide, Minneapolis).

Profit margins in entrepreneurial agencies are often slimmer, but these shops are often more responsive to the smaller clients they serve. They offer the hands-on involvement of the firm's principals, and their work is frequently startling in its creativity. For these very reasons, many large agencies are spinning off smaller subsidiaries. Gotham, Inc., for example, is a hot creative shop in New York that was spun off by the Interpublic Group to do work for a variety of clients its bigger sister agencies couldn't serve.[28] Some entrepreneurial agencies, such as Zubi Advertising in Coral Cables, Florida, carve a niche for themselves by serving particular market segments.

Business-to-business Agencies   A **business-to-business agency** represents clients that market products to other businesses. Examples are electronic components for computer manufacturers, equipment used in oil and gas refineries, and MRI equipment for radiology. High-tech advertising requires some technical knowledge and the ability to translate that knowledge into precise, as well as persuasive, communications.

Most business-to-business advertising is placed in trade magazines or other business publications. These media are commissionable, but their circulation is smaller, so their rates are far lower than those of consumer media. Because commissions usually don't cover the cost of the agency's services, business agencies typically charge their clients service fees. They can be expensive, especially for small advertisers, but failure to obtain a business agency's expertise may carry an even higher price in lost marketing opportunities.

Business and industrial agencies may be large international firms such as MacLaren/ Lintas in Toronto or HCM/New York, or smaller firms experienced in areas of recruitment, biomedical, or electronics advertising.

Specialized Service Agencies

Many agencies assist their clients with a variety of limited services. In the early 1990s the trend toward specialization blossomed, giving impetus to many of the small agency-type groups called *creative boutiques* and other specialty businesses such as *media-buying services* and *interactive agencies.*

Creative Boutiques   Some talented artists—such as graphic designers and copywriters—set up their own creative services, or **creative boutiques.** They work for advertisers and occasionally subcontract to ad agencies. Their mission is to develop exciting creative concepts and produce fresh, distinctive advertising messages. In the 1990s, Creative Artists Agency (CAA), a Hollywood talent agency, caused a stir on Madison Avenue (the collective term for New York agencies) by taking on the role of a creative boutique, using its pool of actors, directors, and cinematographers to create commercials for Coca-Cola. McCann-Erickson Worldwide remained Coke's *agency of record,* but the majority of the creative work came from CAA. Since that time, Coke has allowed numerous other smaller shops to work on its account. At one point, Coke employed more than 20 different agencies, and the company continues to use the multiagency approach.[29]

Advertising effectiveness depends on originality in concept, design, and writing. However, while boutiques may be economical, they usually don't provide the research, marketing, sales expertise, or deep customer service that full-service agencies offer. Thus, boutiques tend to be limited to the role of creative suppliers.

Media-Buying Services   Some years ago, a few experienced agency media people started setting up organizations to purchase and package radio and TV time. The largest **media-buying service** (or *media agency*) is Starcom Mediavest. Based in Chicago, it is owned by the Publicis Group, has offices around the world, and places more than $25 billion worth of advertising annually for a wide variety of clients.[30]

Media time and space are perishable. A 60-second radio spot at 8:00 PM can't be sold later. So radio and TV stations presell as much time as possible and discount their rates for large buys. The media-buying service negotiates a special discount and then sells the time or space to agencies or advertisers.

Media-buying firms provide customers (both clients and agencies) with a detailed analysis of the media buy. Once the media package is sold, the buying service orders spots, verifies performance, sees that stations "make good" for any missed spots, and even pays the media bills. Compensation methods vary. Some services charge a set fee; others get a percentage of what they save the client.

Media agencies have experienced so much growth in the last decade that they have become major players on the advertising stage. We'll discuss them in greater detail in Chapter 9.

Burrell Communications handles McDonald's ads aimed at African American consumers. To see examples of its work, visit www.burrell.com.

Source: Burrell Communications

We built the first
McDonald's in the world
that was entirely
dreamed up...
by kids.

Interactive Agencies   With the stunning growth of the Internet and the heightened interest in integrated marketing communications has come a new breed of specialist—the **interactive agency.** Avenue A/Razorfish and Digitas are just two of the many firms that specialize in designing web pages and creating fun, involving, information-rich, online advertising.[31] When McDonald's introduced a CD-ROM game in its Happy Meals titled "Fairies and Dragons," its advertising partner was the digital shop Fuel Industries.

Other specialists, such as *direct-response* and *sales promotion agencies,* are also growing in response to client demands for greater expertise and accountability. In the IMC era, it is rare that a large company relies on an advertising agency alone for its branding efforts.

McDonald's uses the creative ideas of its partner agencies to come up with clever executions like this challenge for kids to design their own McDonald's. As shown in these stills from the commercial "I'm Amazing", McDonald's worked with their ad agency in Hong Kong and asked local children to answer the question, "if you could build the McDonald's of your dreams-what would it look like?" The result was a McDonald's themed restaurant designed solely by kids and selling only Happy Meals.

Source: McDonald's

What People in an Agency Do   LO 4-4

The American Association of Advertising Agencies (AAAA) is the national trade association of the advertising agency business and the industry's spokesperson with government, media, and the public (see the People behind the Ads box featuring Nancy Hill later in this chapter). Its approximately 450 agency members, representing a wide spectrum of small, medium, and large agencies, place 80 percent of all national advertising handled by agencies in the United States.[32]

The AAAA Service Standards explain that an agency's purpose is to interpret to the public, or to desired segments of the public, information about a legally marketed product or service. How does an agency do this? First, it studies the client's product to determine its strengths and weaknesses. Next, it analyzes the product's present and potential makers. Then, using its knowledge of distribution channels and available media, the agency formulates a plan to carry the advertiser's message to consumers, wholesalers, dealers,

McDonald's uses two-way message channels to share information with customers and respond to their needs. The "Our Food, Your Questions" site is a great example of this. By addressing customer concerns in a proactive way, McDonald's helps protect its brand and build customer loyalty.

Source: McDonald's

or contractors. Finally the agency writes, designs, and produces ads; contracts for media space and time; verifies media insertions; and bills for services and media used.

The agency also works with the client's marketing staff to enhance the advertising's effect through package design, sales research and training, and production of sales literature and displays. To understand these functions, consider the people who were involved, directly or indirectly, in the creation, production, and supervision of the McDonald's campaign created by Leo Burnett.

Account Management

The **account executives (AEs)** at Leo Burnett are the liaisons between the agency and the client. Large agencies typically have many account executives, who report to **management** (or **account**) **supervisors.** They in turn report to the agency's director of account (or client) services.

Account executives are in the middle of the fray; they are responsible for formulating and executing advertising plans (discussed in Chapter 8), mustering the agency's services, and representing the client's point of view to the agency. McDonald's account executive has to be well versed in the extraordinary range of media and demonstrate how her agency's creative work satisfies both her client's marketing needs and the market's product needs. Characteristically, an AE must be able to see things from all points of view. He or she must be not only enterprising, courageous, and demanding, but also tactful, artistic and articulate, meticulous, forgiving, perceptive, ethical, and discreet. And what's more, an AE must always deliver the work on time and within budget.

Research and Account Planning

Agency creatives (artists and copywriters) require a wealth of product, market, and competitive information because, at its core, advertising is based on information. Therefore, before creating any advertising, agencies research the uses and advantages of the product, analyze current and potential customers, and try to determine what will influence them to buy. After the ads are placed, agencies use more research to investigate how the campaign fared. Chapter 7 discusses some of the many types of research ad agencies conduct.

Account planning is a hybrid discipline that uses research to bridge the gap between account management and creatives. The account planner defends the consumer's point of view and the creative strategy in the debate between the agency's creative team and the client.

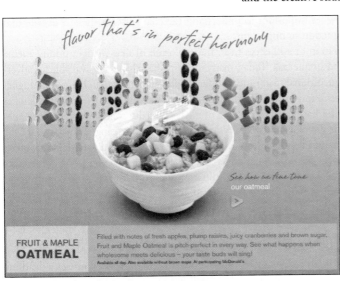

Some McDonald's advertising is devoted to specific menu items. These ads give existing customers a reason to visit the restaurant chain more often, and may attract new customers who are unaware of the variety of offerings at McDonald's. By promoting their Fruit and Maple Oatmeal, do you think McDonald's is attracting a broader base of health-conscious customers that would normally not visit McDonald's?
Source: McDonald's

Account planners study consumer needs and desires through surveys and focus groups, but primarily through personal interviews. They help the creative team translate its findings into imaginative, successful campaigns. Not attached to either account management or creative, the account planner balances both elements to make sure the research is reflected in the ads.[33]

Through good account planning, Del Rivero Messiano DDB, McDonald's Hispanic agency, developed a unique and award-winning spot targeted to Spanish-language consumers. The commercial features a young man who dreams he is playing an ancient Aztec game, *juego de pelotas.* A key element of the spot is the Spanish word "sueño," which means both *dream* and *sleep.* Although his alarm clock rouses him from the wonderful dream, he can hit the snooze button and return to his fantasy because he knows he can pick up a fast breakfast at McDonald's.

By putting the consumer, rather than the advertiser, at the center of the process, account planning changes the task from simply creating an advertisement to nurturing a relationship between consumer and brand. That requires understanding, intuition, and insight. When performed properly, planning provides that mystical leap into the future—the brilliant, simplifying perspective that lights the way for the client and the creatives. For more on one of the greatest planners of all time, see People behind the Ads in Chapter 5.

Creative Concepts

Most ads rely heavily on **copy,** the words that make up the headline and message. The people who create these words, called **copywriters,** must condense all that can be said about a product into a few pertinent, succinct points.

Ads also use nonverbal communication. That is the purview of the **art directors,** graphic designers, and production artists, who determine how the verbal and visual symbols will fit together. (The creative process is discussed in Chapters 10–12.) The agency's copywriters and artists work as a creative team under a **creative director.** Each team is usually assigned a particular client's business.

One award-winning ad for McDonald's focuses on the Ronald McDonald House charity. Titled "First Step," the ad tells the story of a young toddler whose medical care was made more affordable by the organization. The beautiful spot was developed by an experienced DDB Chicago team, including creative director Bill Cimino, copywriter Geoff McCartney, and art director Gordon West.

Advertising Production: Print and Broadcast

Once an ad is designed, written, and approved by the client, it is turned over to the agency's print production manager or broadcast producers.

For print ads, the production department buys type, photos, illustrations, and other components and works with printers, engravers, and other suppliers. For a broadcast commercial, production people work from an approved script or storyboard. They use actors, camera operators, and production specialists (studios, directors, editors) to produce a commercial. The "First Step" commercial described earlier was directed by a famous commercial director named Joe Pytka and was filmed at Pytka's studio.

But production work is not limited to just ads and commercials. Dealer kits and direct mailings are just two examples of other types of media that may be created as part of a campaign.

Media Planning and Buying

Ad agencies provide many media services for their clients: research, negotiating, scheduling, buying, and verifying. Media planning is critical because the only way advertisers can communicate is through some medium. We discuss media extensively in Chapters 9 and 13 through 18, but for now it's important to understand the changes over the last decade that have made the media function so important.

With the fragmentation of audiences from the explosion of new media options, media planning and buying is no simple task. Today, many more media vehicles are available for advertisers to consider, as the traditional major media offer smaller audiences than before—at higher prices. Add to this the trend toward IMC and relationship marketing, and the media task takes on added significance. This has fueled the growth of media specialty companies and simultaneously recast agency media directors as the new rising stars in the advertising business.

Tight budgets demand ingenious thinking, tough negotiating, and careful attention to details. In this age of specialization, what advertisers really need are exceptional generalists who understand how advertising works in coordination with other marketing communication tools and can come up with creative media solutions to tough marketing problems. Today, many products owe their success more to creative media buying than to clever ads.

Traffic Management

One of the greatest sins in an ad agency is a missed deadline. If an agency misses a deadline for a monthly magazine, for example, the agency will have to wait another month before it can run the ad, much to the client's displeasure.

The agency traffic department coordinates all phases of production and makes sure everything is completed before client and/or media deadlines. Traffic is often the first stop for entry-level college graduates and an excellent place to learn about agency operations.

Additional Services

The growth of IMC has caused some agencies to employ specialists who provide services besides advertising. Larger agencies may have a fully staffed **sales promotion department** to produce dealer ads, window posters, point-of-purchase displays, and dealer sales material. Or, depending on the nature and needs of their clients, they may employ public relations people and direct marketing specialists, web page designers, home economics experts, or package designers.

Agency Administration

In small agencies, administrative functions may be handled by the firm's principals. Large agencies often have departments for accounting, human resources, data processing, purchasing, financial analysis, legal issues, and insurance.

How Agencies Are Structured

An ad agency organizes its functions, operations, and personnel according to the types of accounts it serves, its size, and its geographic scope.

In small agencies (annual billings of less than $20 million), each employee may wear many hats. The owner usually supervises daily business operations, client services, and new business development. Account executives generally handle day-to-day client contact. AEs may also do some creative work, such as writing copy. Artwork may be produced by an art director or purchased from an independent studio or freelance designer. Most small agencies have production and traffic departments or an employee who fulfills these functions. They may have a media buyer, but in very small agencies account executives also purchase media time and space. Exhibit 4-6 shows how a typical advertising agency is organized.

Medium and large agencies are usually structured in a *departmental* or *group system.* In the **departmental system,** the agency organizes its various functions—account services, creative services, marketing services, and administration—into separate departments.

Exhibit 4-6
Typical advertising agency organization.

2016 rate card

RATE BASE: 1,250,000 | EFFECTIVE JAN/FEB 2016 ISSUE | ALL RATES ARE GROSS

Volume Discount Page Equivalent	1 Page	5% 3 Pages	7% 6 Pages	10% 9 Pages
Four Color				
1 page	$81,250	$77,188	$75,563	$73,125
⅔ page	69,065	65,612	64,230	62,159
½ page	52,815	50,174	49,118	47,534
⅓ page	40,625	38,594	37,781	36,563
B&W				
1 page	$65,000	$61,750	$60,450	$58,500
⅔ page	55,250	52,488	51,383	49,725
½ page	42,250	40,138	39,293	38,025
⅓ page	32,500	30,875	30,225	29,250
Covers				
Cover 2	$101,565	$96,487	$94,455	$91,409
Cover 3	85,315	81,049	79,343	76,784
Cover 4	101,565	96,487	94,455	91,409

sales offices

New York:	212-649-2963
Chicago:	312-984-5166
Detroit:	248-931-5256
Los Angeles:	310 664 2869
Northwest (San Francisco):	415-828-0908
Southeast (Atlanta):	404-256-3800
Southwest (Dallas):	214-526-3800

Cancellation policy: As stated in the Terms and Conditions, in the event insertion orders are not timely canceled by the applicable cancellation date, advertiser and its agency, if there is one, shall be jointly and severally liable for the cost of such canceled advertisement, including "kill fees" for the premiums on covers not canceled in a timely manner. Closing dates for covers are 45 days prior to space closing dates. Please note that advertisers releasing covers fewer than 45 days before the published close date will be charged a kill fee equal to the cover premium. Hearst guarantees rate base on a 6-month average as reported by AAM.

The 2016 rate card from HGTV magazine. The cards are used by agency media planners to estimate costs for running campaigns in print.

Source: HGTV Magazine

In the **group system,** the agency is divided into a number of "little" agencies or groups. Each group may serve one large account or, in some cases, three or four smaller ones. An account supervisor heads each group's staff of account executives, copywriters, art directors, a media director, and any other necessary specialists. A very large agency may have dozens of groups with separate production and traffic units.

To deal with the economic pressures, many agencies have looked for ways to reorganize. TBWA Chiat/Day in Venice, California, credits its laid-back office design with encouraging creativity throughout the agency. Based on an idealized city, the layout by architect Clive Wilkinson features open workstations clustered into communities and arranged around public gathering places. The idea is to free employees to roam and interact. A black surfboard displays the skull and crossbones of the self-proclaimed "pirates of the industry."[34] In Chicago, Leo Burnett, which was traditionally highly centralized, restructured itself into numerous client-oriented mini-agencies, each meant to function as an agency within an agency.[35] And in France, Y&R encourages employees to spend more time out of the office with clients and to work from home while linked to the agency via laptop.[36]

How Agencies Are Compensated

 LO 4-5

To survive, agencies must make a profit. But recent trends in the business—mergers of super-agencies, shifts in emphasis from advertising to sales promotion and direct marketing, increased production costs, and the fragmentation of media vehicles—have all cut into agency profits.[37] Moreover, different clients demand different services, forcing agencies to develop various compensation methods. Still, there are really only three ways for agencies to make money: *media commissions, markups,* and *fees* or *retainers.*

Media Commissions

As we saw in Chapter 2, when ad agencies first came on the scene more than 100 years ago, they were really space brokers, or reps, for the newspapers. Because they saved the media much of the expense of sales and collections, the media allowed the agencies to retain a 15 percent **media commission** on the space or time they purchased on behalf of their clients. That started a tradition that endures to this day, although it is now changing rapidly. Let's see how it works.

Say a national rate-card price for a full-page color magazine ad is $100,000. The magazine bills the agency, and the agency in turn bills the client for the $100,000. The client pays that amount to the agency, and the agency sends $85,000 to the magazine, keeping its 15 percent commission ($15,000). For large accounts, the agency typically provides extensive services (creative, media, accounting, and account management) for this commission. With dwindling profits, though, and clients negotiating smaller commissions, many agencies now charge a fee for services that used to be free.[38]

Markups

In the process of creating an ad, the agency normally buys a variety of services or materials from outside suppliers—for example, photos and illustrations. The agency pays the supplier's charge and then adds a **markup** to the client's bill, typically 17.65 percent of the invoice (which becomes 15 percent of the new total).

For example, a markup of 17.65 percent on an $8,500 photography bill yields a $1,500 profit. When billing the client, the agency adds the $1,500 to the $8,500 for a new total of $10,000. When the client pays the bill, the agency keeps the $1,500 (15 percent of the total)—which, not coincidentally, is the standard commission agencies normally receive.

$$\$8,500 \times 17.65\% = \$1,500$$
$$\$8,500 + \$1,500 = \$10,000$$
$$\$10,000 \times 15\% = \$1,500$$

Some media—local newspapers, for example—allow a commission on the higher rates they charge national advertisers but not on the lower rates they charge local advertisers. So, to get their commission, local agencies have to use the markup formula above.

Today many agencies find that the markup doesn't cover their costs of handling the work, so they're increasing their markups to 20 or 25 percent. While this helps, agency profits are still under pressure, forcing many agencies to a fee system in place of, or in addition to, commissions and markups.

Fees

Clients today expect agencies to solve problems rather than just place ads, so fees are becoming more common. In fact, very few national advertisers still rely on the 15 percent commission system. An equal number now use some fee-based system. The rest use some reduced commission or incentive system.[39]

There are two pricing methods in the fee system. With the **fee–commission combination,** the agency charges a basic monthly fee for all its services to the client and retains any media

Ethical **Issues**

Accounting for Account Reviews

Periodically, advertisers invite presentations from a variety of agencies. This process is referred to as an *agency* or *account review*. If the client's current agency is invited to participate, and the review is handled responsibly and respectfully, it can serve as a mutually beneficial tool in keeping the relationship between the client and the agency honest and open for both sides. Conversely, when used in an unethical manner, account reviews can be very destructive to the relationship, tarnishing the reputation of the client and/or the agency and damaging the integrity of the brand. How can reviews be unethical. Typically agencies spend a great deal of time and money pitching. Such time and money is not reimbursed. So agencies have a lot to lose. Advertisers extending reviews should be seriously considering changing agencies and should limit reviews to firms they would strongly consider hiring.

Historically, advertisers have been expected to show some allegiance to their current agency, unless that agency has mishandled a campaign through ineptitude, malfeasance, or simple ineffectiveness. Recently, though, client loyalty seems to be on the wane, while agency reviews are on the rise. A survey by the American Association of Advertising Agencies, covering 175 agencies and their 3,700 accounts, shows that the average length of the client–agency relationship has dropped significantly. Several examples illustrate this trend: United Airlines dumped Leo Burnett Chicago after 31 years; Delta Air Lines reviewed its 50-year relationship with BBDO Worldwide; Colgate-Palmolive Co. shifted $200 million in billing from Foote, Cone & Belding to Y&R Advertising.

The increase in account reviews is linked to two recent changes in the traditional client–agency relationship. The first change lies in the very nature of the client–agency bond. The historical, brand-building marriage is on the decline, and vendor-based services are on the rise. Today's advertisers, focused on the bottom line, increasingly settle for a quick fix that will temporarily increase volume sales, as opposed to the long-run investment of working with one agency to create an established brand. Used in this way, agencies are treated like specialized vendors, hired to spur the movement of the product or service desired, and called into review the moment that movement slows. Once a review is called, the chances of an agency keeping the account are slim—an informal survey by *Adweek* revealed that only 1 incumbent agency out of 12 actually survives a review.

The second change in the traditional client–agency relationship is agency consolidation. As the industry transforms from a wide array of agencies into a handful of superpowers, the odds of rival advertisers falling under the services of the same shop have increased. Many clients believe same-house representation creates a conflict of interest, sparking more account reviews.

In addition to the fundamental changes in the structure of the client–agency relationship, many agency people cite other, more questionable motives as the cause for review increases. One such basis for review, tied closely to the bottom-line-oriented approach, is what Roger Lewis, a partner at Hoffman/Lewis, San Francisco, dubs the "BOSS Theory of Marketing—Blame Others, Save Self." Here is the BOSS theory: In the event an advertiser's sales decline, marketing directors look for the quick fix by calling an agency into review to lend the perception that action is being taken to reverse the decline. Although unfair to the agency, the advertiser has the incentive to do so as an immediate means of bolstering management and shareholder confidence.

The lure of free creative work is a second questionable motivation for clients to hold account reviews. In conducting a review, clients ask the participating agencies to create mock presentations as a means of assessing the capabilities and creativity of each in relation to the prospective account campaign. After reviewing these presentations, clients have no financial or legal commitment to pay participating agencies, even though they may later incorporate these ideas into their campaigns.

commissions earned. In the **straight-fee** or **retainer method,** agencies charge for all their services, either by the hour or by the month, and credit any media commissions earned to the client.

Accountability is a major issue in client–agency relationships. With a new type of agency compensation, the **incentive system,** the agency earns more if the campaign attains specific, agreed-upon goals. DDB Needham, for example, offers its clients a "guaranteed results" program. If a campaign meets or exceeds agreed-upon marketing objectives, the agency earns more; if it falls short, the agency earns less. Kraft General Foods rewards its agencies based on their performance. An A grade gets an extra 3 percent commission; C grades are put on review.[40]

The In-House Agency

Some companies set up a wholly owned **in-house agency** (or *house agency*) to save money and tighten control over their advertising. The in-house agency may do all the work of an independent full-service agency, including creative tasks, production, media placement, publicity, and sales promotion.

Advertisers with in-house agencies hope to save money by cutting overhead, keeping the media commission, and avoiding markups on outside purchases. Small, local advertisers in particular seek this goal.

Advertisers also expect more attention from their house agencies, which know the company's products and markets better and can focus all their resources to meet its deadlines. Management is often more involved in the advertising when it's done by company people,

The ethical involvement of agency review consultants has also been questioned. Many within the industry believe that because review consultants are in the business of account reviews, it is in their best interest to see that account reviews happen more often. In an article titled "Conducting an Effective Advertising Agency Review," one marketing strategist suggests that "four agencies should be asked to produce twelve campaigns in total ... [as] an opportunity to look at a vast amount of work built specifically to your needs." By spurring these disputed uses of account reviews, review consultants have aided in the growth of unethical reviews.

Account reviews clearly are important. Yet the growing abuse of the review process for unethical gains will only serve to create an unprofitable rift between the sides. On the agency side, the costs of participating in a review are escalating, as the average per-pitch cost to an agency runs in the range of $60,000 to $75,000! This enormous cost unfairly keeps smaller agencies from competing for accounts. If the frequency of reviews continues to rise, smaller agencies will obtain a lesser and lesser percentage of the business, greatly reducing the competition within the industry over time.

What's more, reviews are extremely damaging to the reputation of the incumbent agency: Other clients can be led to wonder what caused the agency to lose the account. For Peter Drakoulias, director of business development at Interpublic's Deutsch, New York, agencies are "perceived as damaged goods" after losing an account—a status from which an agency may never recover.

On the client side, reviews can be equally damaging in terms of the health of a brand. If a brand is often changing its identity and public perception, it loses its integrity as consumers become skeptical of the product. Loyalty to one agency can create the stable brand recognition that comforts consumers and propels the sales of a brand. Before the rise in account reviews, long-term marriages were believed to give an agency "deep knowledge of the client and product, a deep knowledge of the essence of the brand, a deep knowledge of retail relationships, and a deep knowledge of the customer," all of which are important in creating a strong brand.

If unethical motivations continue to drive the desire for account reviews, the client–agency relationship will suffer severely. Advertisers and agency review consultants have the power to ensure this does not happen by changing the way that account reviews are used and, in doing so, defining a fair and stable role for ad agencies in the years to come.

Questions

1. What degree of loyalty should clients have to agencies and vice versa? Is it ethical for agencies to represent multiple clients within the same industry?

2. What do you think might be done to reduce the amount of account reviews motivated by unethical gains?

3. How can the account review process be structured to more fairly incorporate smaller agencies? What can be done to lower the cost of participating in an agency review?

Sources: "The Bond between an Advertiser and His Client Is Changing," *Escalate*, April 20, 2004 (retrieved from www.escalate.ca); Douglas LaBahn, "Advertiser Perceptions of Fair Compensation, Confidentiality and Rapport: The Influence of Advertising Agency Cooperativeness and Diligence" (retrieved from www.highbeam.com/library/index.asp?refid=ae_org_1); Mark Gleason, "MIA on Madison Ave.: Agency, Client Loyalty," *Advertising Age*, January 27, 1997 (retrieved from www.adage.com); Alice Z. Cuneo, "Agencies Feel Business Pinch, Eye More Cuts," *Advertising Age*, January 29, 2001 (retrieved from www.adage.com); Michael Marsak, "Conducting an Effective Advertising Agency Review," Effective Marketing Strategies, Inc. (retrieved from www.effectivemarketing.com).

especially in "single-business" companies. And some in-house advertising is outstanding, especially in the fashion field. But usually companies sacrifice more than they gain. In-house flexibility is often won at the expense of creativity. Outside agencies typically offer greater experience, versatility, and talent. In-house agencies have difficulty attracting and keeping the best creative people, who tend to prefer the variety and challenge offered by independent agencies.

The biggest problem for in-house agencies is loss of objectivity. In the shadow of internal politics, linear-thinking policymakers, and harangues from management, ads may become insipid contemplations of corporate navels rather than relevant messages to customers. In advertising, that's the kiss of death.

The Client–Agency Relationship

How Agencies Get Clients

Many factors affect the success of a company's advertising program, but one of the most important is the relationship between the advertiser and its agency.

To succeed, advertising agencies need clients. New clients come from personal contact with top management, referrals from satisfied clients or advertising consultants, publicity on recent successful campaigns, trade advertising, direct-mail solicitation, or the agency's general reputation.[41] The three most successful ways to develop new business are having clients who strongly champion the agency, having superior presentation skills, and cultivating a personal relationship with a network of top executives.

While much of McDonald's advertising is instantly recognizable, this print ad shows the company is sometimes prepared to produce edgier ads and often needs assistance to get the job done right. In the ad campaign, "I See Fries," consumers were encouraged to see McDonald's fries in everyday objects and to share a picture using a special Fry Finding Filter in Meitu, a photo sharing app in China. The "I See Fries" ad was actually a collaboration between various McDonald's agencies: Tribal Worldwide Shanghai, DDB Group Sydney, and DDB Asia Pacific. By having multiple McDonald's agencies work together to create this successful campaign, the importance of good relationships between the agencies is evident as the ad proved successful when more than 674,000 customers shared "I See Fries" photos.

Source: McDonald's

Referrals

Most good agencies get clients by referral—from existing clients, friends, review consultants, or even other agencies. The head of one company asks another who's doing her ads, and the next week the agency gets a call. If a prospective client presents a conflict of interest with an existing client, the agency may decline the business and refer the prospect to another agency.[42]

Independent *agency review consultants* often help arrange marriages between agencies and clients. In fact, independent advisers are now involved in most of the important recent account shuffles on Madison Avenue.[43]

Sales reps for media and suppliers frequently refer local advertisers to an agency they know. So it's important for agencies to maintain cordial relations with the media, suppliers, other agencies, and, of course, their existing clients.

Presentations

An advertiser may ask an agency to make a presentation—anything from a simple discussion of the agency's philosophy, experience, personnel, and track record to a full-blown audiovisual presentation of a proposed campaign. Successful agencies, therefore, need excellent presenters.

Some advertisers ask for or imply that they want a **speculative presentation,** meaning they want to see what the agency will do before they sign on. But most agencies prefer to build their presentations around the work they've already done, to demonstrate their capabilities without giving away ideas for a new campaign. Invariably, the larger the client, the bigger the presentation.

The presentation process also allows the agency and the advertiser to get to know each other before they agree to work together. Advertising is a people business, so human qualities— integrity, mutual regard, trust, and communication—play an important role (see the Ethical Issues box, "Accounting for Account Reviews").

Networking and Community Relations

Agencies frequently find that the best source of new business is people their employees know in the community. Some agencies work pro bono (for free) for charities or nonprofit organizations such as the American Indian College Fund. Matt Freeman, the young CEO of Tribal DDB, volunteers his time on behalf of the Ad Council and The Hunger Site. Leo Burnett partners with GlobalGiving, an organization that matches needs with donors.

Agencies may help local politicians (a controversial practice in some areas) or contribute to the arts, education, religion, or the community. Some agencies sponsor seminars; others assist ad clubs or other professional organizations. All these activities help an agency gain visibility and respect in its community.

Soliciting and Advertising for New Business

Lesser-known agencies must take a more aggressive approach. An agency may solicit new business by advertising, writing letters, making cold calls, or even posting a viral video on YouTube. An agency principal usually solicits new business, but staffers help prepare presentations.

Today, more agencies are advertising themselves. Many agencies submit their best ads to competitions around the world to win awards and gain publicity and professional respect for their creative excellence.[44]

Stages in the Client–Agency Relationship

Just as people and products have life cycles, so do relationships. In the advertising business, the life cycle of the agency–client relationship passes through four distinct stages: *prerelationship, development, maintenance,* and *termination.*[45]

My IMC Campaign 4–C

Agency Review

What will your client look for in your agency team? This agency review should give you an idea. To use this scale, an advertiser would rate each agency on a scale from 1 (strongly negative) to 10 (strongly positive). Use the "Creative Abilities" qualities below for this chapter's AdForum exercise.

General Information

____ Size compatible with our needs.

____ Strength of management.

____ Financial stability.

____ Compatibility with other clients.

____ Range of services.

____ Cost of services; billing policies.

Marketing Information

____ Ability to offer marketing counsel.

____ Understanding of the markets we serve.

____ Experience dealing in our market.

____ Success record; case histories.

Creative Abilities

____ Well-thought-out creativity; relevance to strategy.

____ Art strength.

____ Copy strength.

____ Overall creative quality.

____ Effectiveness compared to work of competitors.

Production

____ Faithfulness to creative concept and execution.

____ Diligence to schedules and budgets.

____ Ability to control outside services.

Media

____ Existence and soundness of media research.

____ Effective and efficient media strategy.

____ Ability to achieve objectives within budget.

____ Strength at negotiating and executing schedules.

Personality

____ Overall personality, philosophy, or position.

____ Compatibility with client staff and management.

____ Willingness to assign top people to account.

____ Ability to articulate rationale behind work.

References

____ Rating by current clients.

____ Rating by past clients.

____ Rating by media and financial sources.

The Prerelationship Stage

The **prerelationship stage** occurs before an agency and client officially do business. They may know each other by reputation, by previous ads, or through social contact. Initial perceptions usually determine whether an agency is invited to pitch the account. Through the presentation process, the agency tries to give the best impression it can because it is selling and the client is buying (the My IMC Campaign segment titled "Agency Review" offers guidelines for selecting an agency).

The Development Stage

Once the agency is appointed, the **development stage** begins. During this honeymoon period, the agency and the client are at the peak of their optimism and eager to develop a mutually profitable relationship. Expectations are at their highest, and both sides are most forgiving. During development, the rules of the relationship are established. The respective roles get set quickly, the true personalities of all the players come out, and the agency creates its first work. At this point, the agency's output is eagerly awaited and then judged very thoroughly. The agency also discovers how receptive the client is to new ideas, how easy the client's staff is to work with, and how well the client pays its bills. During the development stage the first problems in the relationship also occur.

The Maintenance Stage

The year-in, year-out, day-to-day working relationship is called the **maintenance stage.** When successful, it may go on for many years. McDonald's and Leo Burnett have partnered since 1981. Other long-lasting relationships include Unilever–JWT, ExxonMobil–McCann-Erickson, and Hammermill Papers–BBDO Worldwide, all more than 80 years. Unfortunately, the average client–agency relationship is much shorter—usually five to six years.

The Termination Stage

At some point, an irreconcilable difference may occur, and the relationship reaches the **termination stage.** Perhaps the agency has acquired a competing account, or the agency's creative work doesn't seem to be working. Or perhaps one party or the other simply decides it is time to move on.

During the nervous 1990s, several long-standing client–agency relationships were terminated. After 75 years, AT&T replaced Ayer as the company's lead agency on its $200 million consumer long-distance account, splitting the business between Y&R and FCB, both in New York.[46] Seagram fired DDB Needham from its $40 million Chivas Regal account after a 32-year marriage. And Anheuser-Busch dropped a bombshell on D'Arcy Masius Benton & Bowles when it pulled the Budweiser account after 79 years.[47] Both Ayer and D'Arcy have since disappeared from the agency landscape.

The way a termination is handled will affect both sides for a long time and is an important factor in whether the two ever get back together. After losing the Apple Computer account in 1986, TBWA Chiat/Day gave Madison Avenue a lesson in class by placing a full-page ad that thanked Apple for their many years together. In 1997, the account came back.[48]

Factors Affecting the Client–Agency Relationship

Many forces influence the client/agency relationship. Generally they can be grouped into the four Cs: *chemistry, communication, conduct,* and *changes.*

The most critical factor is the personal *chemistry* between the client's and the agency's staff. A very nasty (and public) breakup of a partnership between Walmart and Draft FCB that occurred several years ago boiled down to differences in the cultures of the two firms.[49]

Poor *communication,* a problem often cited by both agencies and advertisers, leads to misunderstandings about objectives, strategies, roles, and expectations—and to poor advertising. Constant, open communication and an explicit agreement on mutual contribution for mutual gain are key to a good relationship.[50]

Dissatisfaction with agency *conduct,* or performance, is the most commonly cited reason for agency switches in every country.[51] The service the agency gave two years ago may not be valued by the client in the same way today.[52] Or perhaps the agency doesn't understand the client's marketing problems. And clients change, too. Does the client give the agency timely, accurate information? Does it appreciate good work, or does it treat the agency like a vendor?[53] (For more on how clients hold up their end of the relationship, see the My IMC Campaign segment, "Ways to Be a Better Client.")

Changes occur in every relationship. Unfortunately, some of them damage the agency–client partnership. The client's market position or policies may change, or new management may arrive. Agencies may lose key staff people. Client conflicts may arise if one agency buys another that handles competing accounts. Legally, an ad agency cannot represent a client's competition without the client's consent.[54] Saatchi & Saatchi was forced to resign Helene Curtis under pressure from Saatchi's biggest client, Procter & Gamble.[55]

My IMC Campaign 4–D

Ways to Be a Better Client

These are some ideas your client may wish to keep in mind as they think about working with you.

Relationships

- *Cultivate honesty.* Be truthful in your meetings and in your ads.
- *Be enthusiastic.* When you like the ads, let the agency know.
- *Be frank when you don't like the advertising.* Always cite a reason when turning down an idea.
- *Be human.* React like a person, not a corporation. Laugh at funny ads even if they don't work.
- *Be willing to admit you're unsure.* Don't be pressured. Let your agency know when you need time.
- *Allow the agency to feel responsible.* Tell the agency what you feel is wrong, not how to fix it.
- *Care about being a client.* Creative people work best for clients they like.

Management

- *Don't insulate your top managers from creative people.* Agency creatives work best when objectives come from the top, not filtered through layers.
- *Set objectives.* For timely and quality service from your agency, establish and openly share your marketing objectives.
- *Switch people, not agencies.* When problems arise, agencies often prefer to bring in fresh talent rather than lose you as a client.
- *Be sure the agency makes a profit on your account.* Demanding more services from your agency than fees or commissions can cover hurts relationships.

Production

- *Avoid nitpicking last-minute changes.* Perfection is important, but waiting until the last moment to make minor changes can damage the client–agency relationship. Agencies see such behavior as indecisive and/or arrogant and lose respect for the client.
- *Be aware of the cost of changes (both time and money).* The cost of making major changes at the production stage may be five times greater than in the earlier stages.
- *Don't change concepts during the production stage.* Late changes can inadvertently alter product positioning and image.

Media

- *Understand the economics (and economies) of media.* Be prepared to deal with costs per thousand (CPMs), costs per ratings point (CPP), and other key elements of media planning and buying so that you can evaluate and appreciate your agency's media strategy.
- *Understand the importance of lead time.* Early buys can eliminate late fees, earn discounts, make you eligible for special promotions, strengthen your agency's buying position, and reduce anxiety.
- *Avoid interfering with the agency's media relationship.* The stronger your agency's buying position, the greater the discounts available to you. Refrain from cutting deals with media reps directly and plan media use well in advance.
- *Avoid media arrogance ("they need us").* Some media will deal with clients, and some won't. Misinterpret this relationship and you may either pay more than you should or be too late to get into a medium you need.
- *Avoid insularity.* Be willing to let your mind travel beyond your immediate environment and lifestyle.
- *Suggest work sessions.* Set up informal give-and-take sessions with creatives and strategists.
- *Keep the creative people involved in your business.* Agency creatives do their best work for you when they're in tune with the ups and downs of your business.

Research

- *Share information.* Pool information to create new and bigger opportunities.
- *Involve the agency in research projects.* An agency's creative talent gets its best ideas from knowledge of your environment.

Creative

- *Learn the fine art of conducting the creative meeting.* Deal with the important issues first: strategy, consumer benefits, and reasons why.
- *Look for the big idea.* Concentrate on positioning strategy and brand personality. Don't allow a single ad—no matter how brilliant—to change the positioning or personality of the product.
- *Insist on creative discipline.* The creative process stimulates concepts and actions. Discipline helps keep focus on those that count the most.
- *Don't be afraid to ask for great advertising.* Agencies prefer the high road, but as the client you must be willing to accompany them. If the agency slips, be strong and ask it to try again.

Perhaps the best way to improve understanding between clients and agencies would be to have staff members change places for a while. A Foote, Cone & Belding account executive did just that with great success, filling in temporarily as marketing manager at Levi's Jeans for Women. It gave her a whole new perspective on her agency job and the daily challenges her client was facing.[56]

The Suppliers in Advertising

LO 4-8

Spend a few weeks inside an ad agency, and you are likely to see many different vendors making presentations about the special services they can provide. These service providers are called **suppliers.** Without their services it would be impossible to produce the billions of dollars' worth of advertising placed every year.

Although we can't mention them all, important suppliers include *art studios and web design houses, printers, engravers, film and video production houses,* and *research companies.*

Art Studios and Web Designers

Art studios design and produce artwork and illustrations for advertisements. They may supplement the work of an agency's art department or even take its place for small agencies. Art studios are usually small organizations with as few as three or four employees. Some, though, are large enough to employ several art directors, graphic designers, layout artists, production artists, and sales reps.

Most studios are owned and managed by a graphic designer or illustrator. He or she calls on agencies and advertising managers to sell the studio's services, takes projects back to the office to be produced, and then delivers them for the client's approval. The work is time-consuming and requires organization and management skills as well as a core competency in art direction and computer graphics.

Similar to art studios, **web design houses** employ specialists who understand the intricacies of web-based technologies and can design ads and web pages that are both effective and cost efficient.

Printers and Related Specialists

The printers who produce brochures, stationery, business cards, sales promotion materials, and point-of-purchase displays are vital to the advertising business. Ranging from small instant-print shops to large offset operations, **printers** employ or contract with highly trained specialists who prepare artwork for reproduction, operate digital scanning machines to make color separations and plates, operate presses and collating machines, and run binderies.

Film and Video Houses

Few agencies have in-house TV production capabilities. Small agencies often work with local TV stations to produce commercials. But the large agencies normally work with **independent production houses** that specialize in film or video production or both.

Research Companies

Advertisers are concerned about the attitudes of their customers, the size of potential markets, and the acceptability of their products. Agencies want to know what advertising approaches to use, which concepts communicate most efficiently, and how effective past campaigns have been.

The media are concerned with the reading and viewing habits of their audiences, the desired markets of their advertiser customers, and public perceptions toward their own particular medium.

Research, therefore, is closely allied to advertising and is an important tool for marketing professionals. But most firms do not maintain a fully staffed research department. Instead, they use **independent research companies** or consultants. Research firms come in all sizes and specialties, and they employ statisticians, field interviewers, and computer programmers, as well as analysts with degrees in psychology, sociology, and marketing. We discuss research in Chapter 7.

Most marketers work with web design houses that understand both the intricacies of programming languages and the various elements of good web design. The McDonald's Website provides rich content and a high degree of interactivity. As shown in these screenshots, among the many offerings on the Website, customers can browse the history of McDonald's, learn about promotions and special offers, and even build their own meal and determine its nutritional value.

Source: McDonald's

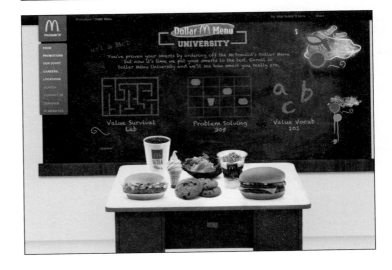

The Media of Advertising

The *medium* that carries the advertiser's message is the vital connection between the company that manufactures a product or offers a service and the customer who may wish to buy it. Although the plural term **media** commonly describes channels of mass communication such as television, radio, newspapers, and magazines, it also refers to other communications vehicles such as direct mail, out-of-home media (transit, billboards, etc.), specialized media (aerial/blimps, inflatables), specialty advertising items (imprinted coffee mugs, balloons), and new communication technologies such as digital media, interactive TV, and satellite networks. (Exhibit 4-7 shows the largest U.S. media companies.)

It's important to understand the various media, their role in the advertising business, and the significance of current media trends. For a person seeking a career in advertising, the media may offer the first door to employment, and for many they have provided great financial rewards.

We classify advertising media into seven major categories: *print, electronic, digital interactive, social media, out-of-home, direct response,* and *other media.* Due to recent media trends, there is some overlap. We shall mention these in passing, along with a brief description of each major category.

Print Media

The term **print media** refers to any commercially published, printed medium—such as newspapers and magazines—that sells advertising space to a variety of advertisers. In the United States in 2007, there were 1.422 daily newspapers and more than 900 weekly newspapers and shoppers' guides.[57] Most are local. However, some national newspapers such as *USA Today, The Wall Street Journal, Barron's,* and trade publications such as *Electronic News* and *Supermarket News* have become quite successful. Once strictly a local newspaper, *The New York Times* is now distributed to more than 916,000 readers nationwide.[58]

Magazines, on the other hand, have long been national, and some periodicals, such as *Elle,* publish editions in many countries. For over a decade, though, the trend has been toward localization and specialization.

Exhibit 4-7

Top media companies.

Newspaper Companies

Rank	Name	# Dailies	Total Circulation (000)
1	Gannett	85	4,896
2	MediaNews	56	2,570
3	News Co.	2	2,562
4	McClatchy Comp.	30	2,078
5	Tribune Co.	13	1,874

Online Companies

Rank	Name	Monthly Unique Visitors (000)	Top News Site
1	Yahoo!	40,459	news.yahoo.com
2	Time Warner	35,658	cnn.com
3	Comcast	31,951	msnbc.com
4	AOL	20,821	news.aol.com
5	New York Times Co.	15,948	nytimes.com

Magazine Companies

Rank	Name	# Magazines	Combined Circulation (000)
1	Time Warner	20	32,478
2	Meredith Co.	29	24,556
3	Hearst Co.	21	22,551
4	Advance Publications	29	17,528
5	Reader's Digest	12	16,694

Multichannel Video Programming Distributers

Rank	Name	Subscribers (000)
1	Comcast	22,360
2	DirecTV	19,760
3	Dish Network	13,945
4	Time Warner Cable	12,109
5	Cox Comm.	4,789

Top Three Search Engines (percentage of searches and percentage change from 2007 to 2008)

1	Google	65.1%
2	Yahoo!	15.9%
3	Bing	13.1%

Sources: http://stateofthemedia.org/media-ownership/newspapers/?srt=3&so=-1&compare=. http://stateofthemedia.org/media-ownership/online/?srt=5&so=-1&compare=. http://stateofthemedia.org/media-ownership/magazines/. http://www.ncta.com/Stats/TopMSOs.aspx.

As of 2008, 19,552 magazines are published in North America, including 6,809 that target consumers.[59] These include national consumer publications such as *Time* and *National Geographic;* national trade publications such as *Progressive Grocer* and *Marketing News;* local city magazines such as *Palm Springs Life* and *Chicago;* regional consumer magazines such as *Sunset;* and local or regional trade or farm publications such as *California Farmer.*

Print media also include directories such as the Yellow Pages; school or church newspapers and yearbooks; and programs used at sporting events and theatrical performances. As we shall see in Chapter 13, the vast array of newspapers and magazines makes it possible for both consumer and business advertisers to pinpoint the delivery of their messages to highly select target markets in a variety of fields or geographic locations.

Electronic Media

The **electronic media** of radio and television used to be called the broadcast media. But with the advent of cable TV, many programs are now transmitted electronically through wires rather than broadcast through the air.

The big four television networks, NBC, CBS, ABC, and Fox, reach in excess of 97% of all households. Each accomplishes this through partnerships with over 200 affiliate stations.[60] Cable television reaches additional tens of millions of people, and features popular channels like USA, the Disney Channel, and ESPN. And despite the advent of new digital technologies, 14,000 radio stations continue to prosper across the United States. We discuss electronic media in more detail in Chapter 14.

Digital Interactive Media

Digital interactive and social media allow the audience to participate actively and immediately. The Internet offers tiny companies with scant resources instant access to customers worldwide.

As we shall see in Chapters 15 and 16, this presents a challenge to advertisers and agencies to learn new forms of creativity. They have to deal with a whole new environment for their ads. It's an environment where customers may spend 20 minutes or more, not just 30 seconds, and where advertising is a dialogue, not a monologue.[61]

Technology and competition for viewers have led to tremendous audience fragmentation. Running a spot on network TV used to cover the majority of a market. Now ad budgets must be bigger to encompass many media. Wherever elusive customers hide, new media forms emerge to seek them out. But for the big, mass-market advertiser, this represents an enormous financial burden.

Social Media

In previous editions we've categorized sites such as Facebook, Twitter, YouTube, LinkedIn, and others as digital interactive media. However, these unique web destinations are so important that they deserve their own category. *Social media* is a term for sites where the prime motivation for audience consumption is audience-created content. This content, from friends, family, business associates, acquaintances, celebrities, and others, is highly credible immediate, and persuasive. Needless to say, advertisers want to participate in social media exchanges. And they are finding more and more ways to do just that. Chapter 16 is a chapter we introduce in this edition that focuses exclusively on social media.

Out-of-Home Media

The major categories of out-of-home media are *outdoor advertising* and *transit advertising*. In the United States, most **outdoor advertising** (billboard) companies are local firms, but most of their revenue comes from national advertisers such as liquor and airline companies. **Transit advertising** (bus, taxi, and subway advertising) is an effective and inexpensive medium to reach the public while they're in the retail neighborhood. Out-of-home media also include posters in bus shelters and train stations, billboards in airport terminals, stadium scoreboards flying banners and lights, skywriting, and kiosk posters. We go into greater detail about these media options in Chapter 17.

This ad titled "First Step" was created to support the Ronald McDonald House. It can be viewed both in electronic media and digital interactive.

© Robin Weiner/WirePix/The Image Works

People **BEHIND** the Ads

BEHIND

Nancy Hill, CEO, American Association of Advertising Agencies

Courtesy of Nancy Hill

In 2008, when the AAAA launched a search to replace O. Burtch Drake, president and CEO since 1994, it knew it needed to find someone special. The AAAA is the national trade association that represents marketing communications companies, including many of the largest agencies, as well as numerous small and mid-sized agencies across the United States. The 1,200 agencies that the AAAA serves employ more than 65,000 people and place 80 percent of all national advertising.

In 2008, to broad acclaim, the organization named Nancy Hill its first-ever female CEO. After 91 years, many thought it was certainly time. But Hill brings much more than a woman's perspective to her job. In the words of *Advertising Age*, "the choice wasn't driven by gender but by Ms. Hill's charisma, energy, and a resume that includes stints at agencies large and small and on both coasts, giving her a broad perspective on the industry. The AAAA's membership ranks are a diverse group of companies that range from sprawling networks with global concerns to tiny shops with comfortable existences crafting ads for local businesses."

Hill's advertising career began in 1983, at Doner, a Baltimore agency. In the years since, she has held a variety of progressively more responsible positions in many different agencies. Prior to joining the AAAA, Hill served as CEO at Lowe Worldwide, New York.

A self-proclaimed tech geek and early adopter of many consumer technologies, Hill's personal and professional interests have long focused on the high-tech sector. She has overseen marketing communications efforts for a wide range of clients, including AOL, Cisco Systems, Motorola, Sony, Sybase, Verizon Wireless, and VISA, among many others.

Hill shared her views about the advertising industry and the challenges she faces as CEO with *Contemporary Advertising*.

CA: How did your career in the ad agency business start?

NH: After college I worked at a company that decided to phase out its consumer division, and my supervisor, who was the head of marketing, told me that he thought advertising would be a good career fit for me. I hadn't considered a career in advertising before that, but the idea intrigued me.

Coming from a small town, I didn't want to drive into the New York market right away, so I looked for an advertising position at an agency in a smaller market, and ended up with my first advertising job at Doner in Baltimore.

I didn't see a clear path at the beginning of my advertising career, but my "no plan" plan turned out to be exactly the right path for me, in an industry that I love.

CA: What were your favorite experiences working in the agency business?

NH: The two things that I have enjoyed the most are the people and the opportunity to be engaged with many types of new technologies.

The types of people who are attracted to careers in advertising tend to be ambitious, smart and fun, and who wouldn't want to be around people like that all of the time?

Early in my career I chose technology as a specialty, and that exposed me to the many ways that technology shapes our culture and society, impacting virtually everything that we do. I've been fortunate to be able to be a cheerleader for new technology, and to work in an industry that prizes creative and technological innovation.

CA: What does the AAAA do on behalf of advertising agencies?

NH: We are a management-oriented association that provides a wide range of products and services to help our member agencies succeed. This includes education and training programs; financial services; employee benefits programs; management consultancy services; information and research services; and diversity programs.

Additionally, the AAAA works tirelessly as the advocate on behalf of advertising companies to local and federal government, the media, and the general public. The AAAA office in Washington, DC, works to ensure that the advertising industry is not subject to unfair legislation and undue regulations. Our government relations initiative is really about working toward achieving desirable and civic goals that effectively convey the value of advertising.

Perhaps most importantly, the AAAA is a resource for our members to help them better understand and respond to the rapid changes taking place in the marketplace, whether that's training for digital technologies or advocacy for diversity.

CA: What excites you about your new challenge as head of the AAAA?

NH: As an association that represents the best, most innovative companies working in marketing communications today, the AAAA has a unique, front-row view to the myriad changes that are occurring in our industry. It's an exciting time to be working in this business, but there are challenges ahead.

One of the big challenges is recruitment of talented, creative employees. The AAAA has many programs in place to help our member agencies identify top talent, and I'm very much looking forward to expanding our education and training programs to support our existing initiatives.

I'm excited to get the message out to students that if you are a liberals arts major who has a double minor in dance and anthropology, you are exactly the kind of out-of-the-box thinker who would thrive in the ad business.

Also, it's important for me to note that the AAAA and the industry are deeply committed to the business case for diversity, and I feel passionately that the challenge for the industry is to further develop the framework in which people from diverse backgrounds—whether we're talking about race/ethnicity, points of view/life experience, or skill sets—can succeed in advertising.

CA: What other challenges do agencies face over the next few years?

NH: Agencies need to compete to find the best talent to work in the industry, especially recruiting employees with digital/interactive expertise.

Today's college students grew up immersed in technology: handheld and online gaming, mobile phones, Internet, digital video recorders . . . the list goes on and on. The challenge is to convey to students that their personal interests are well-suited to careers in advertising. As consumers who don't know a world that's not digital, the next generation is well-equipped to think of new and better ways for marketers to communicate with customers.

Fostering diversity is also incredibly important, and agencies need to be vigilant about supporting their own diversity and multicultural efforts, with the help of the AAAA.

The twin issues of diversity and technology, in many ways, go hand in hand. Emerging markets, both consumer and media, will dictate how agencies work with their clients to create effective marketing communications campaigns. Reaching the right consumer, with the right message, at the right time, in the right medium—when they are willing to accept a message, these are critical issues that agencies deal with each day in trying to create the perfect marketing communications solutions for their clients.

Lastly, with ever-increasing pressure from agencies' clients to justify marketing expenditures, agencies are challenged to better articulate the value that they give in providing business solutions, and not just creating clever television commercials.

CA: What are some of the multicultural initiatives the AAAA is pursuing?

NH: The AAAA's Multicultural Advertising Intern Program (MAIP) is one of the industry's longest, continuously running programs that support students from ethnically and racially diverse backgrounds. Through our 10-week, paid summer internships at AAAA member agencies across the country, participating interns are better prepared to pursue careers in advertising. Founded in 1973, MAIP has since graduated more than 1,600 students, many of them remaining and flourishing in the advertising business.

Also, the AAAA Foundation administers a number of scholarship programs aimed at supporting ethnically and racially diverse undergraduate and graduate students and women. In 2008, the AAAA Foundation has awarded more than $1.7 million in scholarship money. While the focus of our scholarship programs is aimed at diverse students, the ultimate goal is to teach students and educators about the professional and personal rewards that can be gained in a career in advertising.

CA: How can college students best prepare for a career in advertising?

NH: Working in advertising is an excellent career path for anyone who is passionate about communications and likes to work in a fast-paced, creative environment. To me, the kinds of people the industry needs aren't necessarily what the general public may expect. Yes, we want to attract analytical, financial wizards or business majors, who have their sights on a job on Wall Street or at a consultancy, but we're also interested in attracting people who might otherwise work in television, film, or the arts. A little bit of left brain and right brain rolled into one.

Advertising is a great industry for anyone who is creative, curious, and hard-working. The best training to prepare students who are interested in pursuing careers in advertising is to be open, have a great sense of curiosity and creativity, and have a good solid educational foundation. Anyone can work in advertising, and it's an industry that welcomes all with open arms. But those who succeed tend to be driven, analytical, and creative.

McDonald's not only uses out-of-home advertising, it does so in a creative way.
© Outdoor Advertising Association of America

Direct Response

The purpose of much IMC is to create an enduring, positive perception of a brand or company. But some efforts are meant to have a much faster, more immediate impact. These messages are designed to induce a consumer to buy right now, or to take some other desired action. Direct-response advertising is designed to generate an immediate response. For example, when companies mail or e-mail their advertising directly to prospective customers without using one of the commercial media forms, it's called **direct-mail advertising.** The ad may be a simple sales letter, or it may be a complex package with coupons, brochures, samples, or other devices designed to stimulate a response. Direct mail using the Postal Service ("snail mail") is the most expensive medium on a cost-per-exposure basis, but it is also the most effective because marketers can target customers directly without competition from other advertisers. We discuss direct mail in Chapter 18.

Other Media

Technology has spawned a host of new advertising media that can confound even the most knowledgeable media planner and buyer. Advertising appears on DVDs and CDs. Computers dial telephones and deliver messages by simulating speech or playing a prerecorded message. Computers can also put callers on hold and play prerecorded sales messages until a customer service rep answers. Business presentations are copied to CDs that are mailed to prospective customers. As progress continues, so will the proliferation of new media and the opportunities for those seeking careers (or fortunes) in the media.

Media around the World

Many U.S. advertising people get used to foreign styles of advertising faster than they get used to foreign media. In the United States, if you want to promote a soft drink as a youthful, fun refresher, you use TV. In some parts of Europe, Asia, South America, and Africa you may not be able to. Around the world, most broadcast media are owned and controlled by the government, and many governments do not allow commercial advertising on radio or television. In Egypt, the current hot medium used by Coca-Cola and others is the fleet of boats plying the Nile with corporate logos emblazoned on their sails.[62]

Where countries do allow TV advertising, TV ownership is high, cutting across the spectrum of income groups. In less developed countries, though, TV sets may be found only among upper-income groups. This means advertisers may need a different media mix in foreign markets.

Virtually every country has access to radio, television, newspapers, magazines, outdoor media, and direct mail. However, the legalities of different media forms vary from country to country. Generally, the media available to the international advertiser can be categorized as either *international* or *foreign media,* depending on the audience they serve.

International Media

In the past, **international media**—which serve several countries, usually without any change in content—have been limited to newspapers and magazines. Several large American publishers such as Time, McGraw-Hill, and Scientific American circulate international editions of their magazines abroad. Usually written in English, they tend to be read by well-educated, upper-income consumers and are therefore good vehicles for advertising high-end, brand-name products. *Reader's Digest,* on the other hand, is distributed to 126 foreign countries and printed in the local language of each. Today, television is also a viable international medium. And we are beginning to see the emergence of commercial *global media vehicles,* such as CNN.

This ad for McDonald's helps celebrate an Islamic observance. Sensitivity to the infinite diversity of worldwide cultures and beliefs is important for a global advertiser's success.
Source: McDonald's

Foreign Media

Advertisers use **foreign media**—the local media of each country—for large campaigns targeted to consumers or businesses within a single country. Because foreign media cater to their own national audience, advertisers must produce their ads in the language of each country. In countries such as Belgium and Switzerland, with more than one official language, ads are produced in each language.

Unlike the United States, most countries have strong national newspapers that are a good medium for national campaigns. Advertisers also get broad penetration of lower-income markets through radio, which enjoys almost universal ownership. And cinema advertising is a viable alternative to TV in markets with low TV penetration or restricted use of commercial TV.

Chapter Summary

The advertising business comprises four main groups: advertisers (clients), agencies, suppliers, and media. It employs a wide range of artists and businesspeople, sales reps and engineers, top executives, and clerical personnel.

There are four main categories of advertisers based on their geographic activities: local, regional, national, and transnational. Local advertising is placed by businesses in a particular city or county and aimed at customers in the same geographic area. It is important because most sales are made or lost in the local arena.

There are three types of local advertising: product, institutional, and classified. Product advertising can be further divided into regular price-line advertising, sale advertising, and clearance advertising. Institutional advertising creates a long-term perception of the business as a whole by positioning it within the competitive framework. Classified advertising is used to recruit new employees, offer services, and sell or lease new or used merchandise.

Local advertisers are the consummate integrators of marketing communications. Successful local advertisers wear many hats every day, and many of their daily activities help advertise the business. Building relationships is a key element.

Local advertisers can get creative assistance from local ad agencies, media, freelancers and consultants, creative boutiques, syndicated art services, and desktop publishers. Wholesalers, manufacturers, and trade groups often help with cooperative advertising.

Regional advertisers operate in one or several states and market exclusively within that region. National advertisers operate in several regions or throughout the country and comprise the largest advertisers.

Local and national advertisers differ in focus, time orientation, and resources. National advertisers focus on brand building, share of market, grand strategies, and market groups. Local advertisers focus on daily traffic, gross sales or volume, tactical solutions, and the individual customers they see every day. National advertisers have a long-term perspective, local advertisers a short-term one. National advertisers also have more money and more employees.

A large company's advertising department may be centralized or decentralized. Each structure has advantages and disadvantages. The centralized organization is the most typical and may be structured by product, subfunction of advertising, end user, or geography.

Decentralized departments are typical of large, far-flung organizations with numerous divisions, subsidiaries, products, countries, regions, and/or brands.

Transnational advertisers face unique challenges. Their markets have a different value system, environment, and language with customers of different purchasing abilities, habits, and motivations. Media customary in the United States may be unavailable or ineffective. Companies therefore often need different advertising strategies. To manage their advertising, transnational advertisers use an international, multinational, or global marketing structure.

Ad agencies are independent organizations of creative people and businesspeople who specialize in developing and preparing advertising plans, ads, and other promotional tools on behalf of their clients.

Like their clients, ad agencies may be local, regional, national, or international in scope. Agencies can be classified by the range of services they offer and the types of business they handle. The two basic types are full-service agencies and specialized service agencies, such as creative boutiques, media-buying services, and interactive agencies. Agencies may specialize in either consumer or business-to-business accounts. The people who work in agencies may be involved in account management, research, account planning, creative services, production, traffic, media, new business, administration, or a host of other activities.

Agencies may be organized into departments of functional specialties or into groups that work as teams on various accounts. Agencies charge fees or retainers, receive commissions from the media, or mark up outside purchases made for their clients.

Some advertisers develop in-house agencies to save money by keeping agency commissions for themselves. However, they risk losing objectivity and creativity.

Most agencies get clients through referrals, publicity on successful campaigns, advertising, personal solicitation, or networking. The client-agency relationship goes through four stages: prerelationship, development, maintenance, and termination. Numerous factors affect the relationship, including chemistry, communication, conduct, and changes.

The suppliers in advertising are all the people and organizations that assist in the business. Examples are art studios and web designers, printers, photoengravers, film and video houses, talent agencies, research firms, and consultants.

The media of advertising include the traditional mass media of print, electronic, and out-of-home as well as more specialized channels such as direct response, digital interactive media, social media, and specialty advertising.

Print media include magazines and newspapers as well as directories, Yellow Pages, school yearbooks, and special event programs. Electronic media include radio, TV, and cable TV. Out-of-home refers to billboard and transit advertising. Direct-mail advertising is the most expensive medium on a cost-per-exposure basis but also typically is the most effective at generating inquiries or responses. Interactive media let customers participate, turning advertising from a monologue to a dialogue.

In foreign markets, advertisers are faced with different media mixes, different legal constraints, and different economies of advertising.

Important Terms

account executives (AEs), *120*

account planning, *121*

advertising agency, *116*

advertising manager, *107*

art director, *121*

art studio, *132*

Association of National Advertisers (ANA), *110*

brand manager, *115*

business-to-business agency, *118*

centralized advertising department, *113*

classified advertising, *108*

clearance advertising, *107*

cooperative (co-op) advertising, *109*

copy, *121*

copywriter, *121*

creative boutique, *119*

creative director, *121*

decentralized system, *114*

departmental system, *123*

development stage, *129*

digital interactive media, *135*

direct-mail advertising, *138*

electronic media, *135*

fee–commission combination, *125*

foreign media, *139*

full-service advertising agency, *118*

general consumer agency, *118*

global marketers, *115*

group system, *123*

horizontal cooperative advertising, *110*

incentive system, *125*

independent production house, *132*

independent research company, *132*

in-house agency, *126*

institutional advertising, *108*

integrated marketing communications (IMC), *109*

interactive agency, *120*

international agencies, *118*

international media, *138*

international structure, *115*

local advertising, *106*

local agency, *117*

maintenance stage, *130*

management (account) supervisors, *121*

markup, *124*

media, *119*

media-buying service, *119*

media commission, *124*

multinational corporation, *115*

national advertiser, *110*

national agency, *118*

outdoor advertising, *135*

point, *112*

prerelationship stage, *128*

print media, *134*

printer, *132*

product advertising, *107*

regional advertisers, *110*

regional agency, *118*

regular price-line advertising, *107*

sale advertising, *107*

sales promotion department, *122*

speculative presentation, *128*

straight-fee (retainer) method, *125*

supplier, *132*

termination stage, *130*

transit advertising, *135*

vertical cooperative advertising, *109*

Web design houses, *132*

Review Questions

1. What roles do the major organizations involved in the advertising business perform?

2. What is the difference between a local advertiser and a national advertiser?

3. What services might a modern full-service advertising agency offer a large business-to-business advertiser?

4. What are the most important things an advertiser should consider when selecting an agency?

5. How does an agency make money? What is the best way to compensate an agency? Explain your answer.

6. If you owned an ad agency, what would you do to attract new business? Be specific.

7. What are the advantages and disadvantages of an in-house agency?

8. What are the major influences on the client–agency relationship? What can clients and agencies do to maintain a good relationship?

9. What is meant by the term *interactive media*? Give some examples.

10. If you were planning to advertise your brand of computers in Europe, would you likely use foreign or international media? Why?

The Advertising Experience

1. **Advertising Agencies**

   Ad agencies often specialize in a particular type of business or focus on a special market and/or consumer. Visit the Websites for the following agencies:

   - Bates/Lee: www.bates-lee.com
   - BBDO: www.bbdo.com
   - Crispin Porter + Bogusky: www.cpbgroup.com
   - DDB Worldwide Communications Group Inc.: www.ddb.com
   - Fallon: www.fallon.com
   - Foote, Cone & Belding: www.fcb.com
   - GroundZero: www.groundzero.com
   - JWT: www.jwtworks.com
   - Kirshenbaum Bond + Partners: www.kb.com
   - Leo Burnett: www.leoburnett.com
   - McCann-Erickson: www.mccann.com
   - Modem Media: www.modemmedia.com
   - Muse Communications: www.museusa.com
   - Ogilvy & Mather Worldwide: www.ogilvy.com
   - RPA: www.rpa.com
   - Saatchi & Saatchi: www.saatchi-saatchi.com
   - TBWA Chiat/Day: www.tbwachiat.com
   - TeamOne Advertising: www.teamoneadv.com
   - The Phelps Group: www.phelpsgroup.com
   - Webfactory Ltd.: www.webfactory.ie
   - Y+R: www.yr.com

   Answer the following questions for each:

   a. What is the focus of the agency's work (e.g., consumer, business-to-business, ethnic, general market)?

   b. What are the scope and size of the agency's business? Who makes up its clientele?

   c. What is the agency's mission statement or philosophy? How does that affect its client base?

   d. What is the agency's positioning (e.g., creative-driven, strategy [account]-driven, media-driven)?

   e. What is your overall impression of the agency and its work?

2. **Agencies and Clients (Advertisers)**

   The advertising industry is truly vast, and advertisers and their agencies focus on a wide range of businesses in a broad scope of markets. Visit the following Websites and familiarize yourself further with the nature and scope of the advertising world:

   Advertisers

   - Global—International Advertising Association (IAA): www.iaaglobal.org
   - National—Association of National Advertisers (ANA): www.ana.net

   Advertising Agencies

   - National (United States)—American Association of Advertising Agencies (AAAA): www.aaaa.org
   - National (Canada)—Institute of Communications and Advertising (ICA): www.ica-ad.com

   Advertising Practitioners

   - International—Institute of Practitioners in Advertising (IPA): www.ipa.co.uk
   - National—American Advertising Federation (AAF): www.aaf.org
   - Regional—Advertising Federation of Minnesota: www.adfed.org
   - Local—AdClub of Greater Boston: www.adclub.org

   Advertising Publications

   - National—*Advertising Age:* www.adage.com
   - Regional/local—*Adweek:* www.adweek.com

   Answer the following questions for each site:

   a. What advertising group (advertiser, ad agency, practitioner, trade press) sponsors the site? Who is the intended audience?

   b. What are the size and scope of the organization?

   c. What is the organization's purpose? The site's purpose?

   d. What benefit does the organization provide individual members? The advertising community at large?

   e. How is this organization important to the advertising industry? Why?

3. **Developing a Brand Image**

   After visiting at least three of the Websites listed in Exercise 1, develop a mission statement for two hypothetical new advertising agencies. The first agency is small, has an irreverent edge, and is primarily dedicated to working for nonprofit clients. The second agency would like to represent luxury goods companies looking to add young professionals to its clientele.

4. Visit the Lost Ring game at www.thelostring.com. The site has a rather surprising corporate sponsor (you can find it if you look carefully) mentioned frequently in this chapter. What purpose does this site serve for its sponsor?

5. Del Rivero Messianu DDB (see page 119) can be classified as a general consumer agency with an entrepreneurial slant because of its smaller size and the market segments it caters to. How do you think it would classify itself?

CHAPTER

5

Marketing and Consumer Behavior: The Foundations of Advertising

Learning Objectives

To underline the importance of the marketing process in business and to define the role of advertising and other marketing communications tools in presenting the company and its products to the market. The successful advertising practitioner must understand the relationship between marketing activities and the way consumers behave. Ideally, it is this relationship that shapes the creation of effective advertising.

 After studying this chapter, you will be able to:

LO5-1 Define marketing and explain the relationship between consumer needs and product utility.

LO5-2 Identify the key participants in the marketing process.

LO5-3 Explain why consumer behavior is the key to IMC strategy.

LO5-4 Outline the psychological processes in consumer behavior.

LO5-5 Describe the fundamental motives behind consumer purchases.

LO5-6 Elaborate on the interpersonal influences on consumer behavior.

LO5-7 Explain the nonpersonal influences on consumer behavior.

© Justin Sullivan/Getty Images

On January 24th,
Apple Computer will introduce
Macintosh.
And you'll see why 1984
won't be like "1984."

Imagine you've created the most amazing product in the world. Wouldn't you want to introduce it with one of the greatest ads of all time? Steve Jobs thought so, and fought to make it happen. But it almost didn't. ■ Apple's origins date to the late 1970s when Jobs and his engineering buddy Steve (Woz) Wozniak bonded over a shared obsession with building a machine that allowed someone to hack AT&T and make free (illegal) long-distance phone calls.[1] ■ Amazingly, they created a simple device that worked as promised. After a potential "customer" demanded the machine and pointed a gun at Jobs' stomach, he decided to find other things to build. ■ So they turned to the new technology of personal computers. The Apple I was little more than a motherboard sold directly to hobby shops. Realizing the value of a more polished and consumer-friendly product, Jobs and Wozniak created a true computer, the Apple II. The machine was an immediate hit, beloved by technology enthusiasts, and it helped the company attract significant venture capital. ■ But trouble was brewing. Jobs had a unique talent for rubbing people the wrong way. Intense, abrasive, moody, self-absorbed, and thoroughly unconventional, he was thought by many to be too immature to lead a growing firm. ■ Jobs was relegated to a development team. Worse, it was a "B-team" assigned to a secondary product. Apple's hopes rested with a successor to the Apple II named "Lisa." Jobs was given the task of developing a "backup," which came to be called the Macintosh. ■ True to form, Jobs became obsessed with making the Mac a dream computer. Intensely competitive, he wanted a device that would not only outsell the IBM PC, the industry's leader, but that would also crush the Lisa. Jobs believed computers could be instruments of personal liberation and empowerment. So he infused the Mac with an assortment of cutting-edge technologies, including a revolutionary graphical user interface (GUI). The interface was beautiful, incorporating a variety of fonts, colors, and graphics. The machine could even talk. ■ By the end of 1983, the Mac was ready. Apple enlisted a well-known California ad agency, Chiat/Day, to help introduce the machine. Jobs told agency executives that the popular IBM PC represented a bland, almost sinister technology, one that turned individuals into drones. But the beautifully designed Macintosh, he explained, was an instrument of freedom, creativity, and self-expression.[2] ■ Chiat/Day pitched an idea that positioned the Mac against the PC using the metaphor of George Orwell's novel *1984*. If the PC helped to "enslave the masses," the Mac would liberate the individual. Jobs loved it. ■ Film director Ridley Scott (Blade Runner, Alien, Gladiator) was hired to direct the ad. The script depicted a future in which gray drones stare blankly at a giant screen depicting Big Brother (IBM). Suddenly, a young woman with a sledge hammer runs toward the screen, chased by guards. She twirls, tosses her hammer into the screen, and changes the future forever. The ad ends with the tag line "On January 24th, Apple Computer will introduce Macintosh. And you'll see why 1984 won't be like 1984." ■ Jobs, Woz, and everyone at Chiat/Day loved it. But the Apple board was not so sure. Expensive to produce, the ad was supposed to run during the most costly ad buy of the year, the 1984 Super Bowl. A single showing would cost well over a million dollars, big money for a young technology company struggling to generate profits. Getting cold feet at the last minute, Apple's board decided to cancel the buy and Chiat/Day was instructed to sell back the airtime. ■ Jobs was furious, as was Chiat/Day. The agency claimed it could not find a buyer for the ad time, although legend has it that this wasn't true. ■ And so "1984" debuted during the Super Bowl. Audiences and critics alike were awestruck. It became an instant classic, even though it ran on network television just once. In fact the "1984" ad helped to establish the Super Bowl as the place where the very best ads premiere each year.[3] Cannes named the spot the best of the year and *Ad Age* eventually ranked it twelfth in its list of the 100 greatest ads of the century. Best of all, the Macintosh was introduced to broad acclaim and became a big seller for Apple. ■ Unfortunately, even this sweet success could not prevent conflicts between Jobs and Apple execs from boiling over. In 1985, things became so bad that he was asked to leave the company. He would return years later to lead Apple to new heights and oversee the development of amazing products, such as the iPhone and iPad. And Apple would continue to be associated with a variety of great ad campaigns. ■ But no Apple campaign would achieve greater respect than "1984." Beautifully produced, the ad was much more than great entertainment. It communicated in a powerful, almost irresistible way, Jobs' belief that Apple was the future of computing.[4] By vividly comparing IBM to Big Brother, and Apple to a beautiful young rebel, the spot may well have been the greatest example of positioning in advertising history.[5]

Marketing: Creating Satisfying Exchanges by Creating Utility

All marketers face the challenge of how best to present their products, services, and ideas effectively. To do this, they must comprehend the important relationship between the product and the marketplace. This is the task of marketing.

A company prospers only if it can attract and keep customers who are willing to pay for its goods and services. Marketers must be able to locate prospective customers—where they live, work, and play—and then understand their needs, wants, and desires; create products and services that satisfy such desires better than the products of competitors; and finally communicate information about the company's offerings in a powerful, clear, and compelling way.

This chapter will help you better understand IMC's proper role in the marketing function and introduce the human factors that ultimately shape responses to advertising.

The Relationship of Marketing to IMC

In Chapter 1 we noted that **marketing** is used by management to plan and execute the conception, pricing, *promotion,* and distribution of its products. The ultimate purpose of marketing is to create exchanges that satisfy the perceived needs, wants, and objectives of individuals and organizations.

Integrated marketing communications (IMC) is just one of many tools used in the promotional aspect of marketing. But how the IMC is done, and where it is placed, depends largely on the other aspects of the marketing mix and for whom the messages are intended.

Customer Needs and Product Utility

Companies conduct marketing research to discover the needs and wants that exist in the marketplace. The goal is to use this information for *product shaping* and development—designing products, through manufacturing, repackaging, or IMC, to satisfy more fully the customers' needs and wants.

This definition of marketing shows that one of the important elements is the special relationship between a customer's *needs* and a product's *need-satisfying potential.* This is known as the product's utility. **Utility** is the product's ability to satisfy both functional needs and symbolic (or psychological) wants.[6] One of the roles of IMC is to communicate this utility. Thus, some messages suggest how well a product works; others tout glamor, sex appeal, or status.

To woo Gen Xers and Echo Boomers (the children of baby boomers), for example, Ford developed Focus—a low-priced sporty compact car. Optional extras included a sports rack and an unconventional, removable pet holder with a foldable dish, designed to keep Rover from sliding around on the seat. The company also gave buyers the choice of flowers or swirls on the outside and fleece, jersey, or neoprene for the seats.

Aimed at a generation raised on extreme sports such as snowboarding, inline skating, and sky surfing, Ford's commercials were equally cool. They featured a talky, scattered comedienne, Annabelle Gurwitch, demonstrating how fabulous the new Focus is as she drives around the country. And to be even more edgy, the first spots were aired *live* as Ms. Gurwitch, trying to find her way to the MTV music awards, got lost in Manhattan.[7]

Exchanges, Perception, and Satisfaction

Recall that the purpose of marketing is "to create exchanges that satisfy the perceived needs, wants, and objectives of individuals and organizations." Three important ideas are expressed in this definition: *exchanges, perception,* and *satisfaction.* Let's take a brief look at each of these.

Exchanges: The Purpose of Marketing and IMC

Any transaction in which one person or organization trades something of value with someone else is an **exchange.** Exchange is the traditional, theoretical core of marketing. We all engage in exchanges. It's a natural part of our human self-interest. Buyers do it to acquire more things and improve their lives or the lives of others. Sellers do it to grow their businesses and make a profit.

Marketing facilitates these exchanges, thus increasing our potential for satisfaction. How? In a variety of ways: by developing products we might want; by pricing them attractively; by distributing them to convenient locations; and by informing us about them through advertising and other promotional tools. By providing information, advertising makes people aware of the availability of products and of the selection alternatives among different brands. IMC communicates product features and benefits, price options, and locations where the product can be purchased. In the case of *direct marketing,* IMC may even close the sale.

Perception Is Everything

The essence of a successful marketing transaction is that each party come away satisfied with the exchange. Companies must therefore sell their goods at a profit. Customers must feel they received their money's worth. But sometimes the people who are about to engage in a business exchange feel apprehensive. They may worry that the exchange is not equal, even when it is truly fair. This is where *perception* comes in. The perception of inequity is more likely if the customer has little knowledge of the product. In this case, the more knowledgeable party (the seller) must reassure the buyer—perhaps through IMC—that a satisfactory

AD Lab 5-A

The Context of Choice: How a Product's Perceived Value Varies by the Products It is Compared With

How much is something worth? Economists would say "whatever someone is willing to pay for it." But the value of a thing can change based on its context. A fountain cola might cost you a dollar at a convenience store. The same drink will cost four or five dollars in a movie theater. How is that possible? And why would people pay so much more in the theater?

If a convenience store charges you four dollars for a drink, you just drive to the next place soft drinks are sold, where you know it will be cheaper. In the theater your choice is different: pay four dollars or watch the movie without a drink. So context matters.

Interestingly, context can matter even in ads, as is demonstrated by marketing professor Dan Ariely in his fascinating book *Predictably Irrational: The Hidden Forces That Shape Our Decisions*. Ariely describes an experiment in which he asked students to choose the magazine subscription they would prefer.

Economist.com subscription—US $59.00
One-year subscription to Economist.com. Includes online access to all articles from *The Economist* since 1997.

Print subscription—US $125.00
One-year subscription to the print edition of *The Economist*.

Print & Web subscription—US $125.00
One-year subscription to the print edition of *The Economist* and online access to all articles from *The Economist* since 1997.

Assuming you wanted to read *The Economist*, which of these options would be your first choice? Think about it for a moment before reading further.

When Ariely presented the choice to his students, the preferred option was the combined print and Web subscription for $125. In fact 84% of the students chose this option. An additional 16% choose the cheaper Web-only subscription for $59. No one chose the print-only subscription of $125.

In fact, the print-only option seems almost silly. Given that the combined print and Web option costs exactly the same amount as print only, who in their right mind would choose the latter? Why offer consumers an option in an ad that no one would choose?

But if you think the print subscription option is useless in this ad, you would be mistaken. In fact, Ariely labels the print-only option a decoy. What is the purpose of the decoy? To make the print and Web combination offer look particularly enticing. And Ariely proved it.

He created a different version of the ad that mimicked the one you just read, except that option 2, the print-only option, was not included.

Economist.com subscription—US $59.00
One-year subscription to Economist.com. Includes online access to all articles from *The Economist* since 1997.

Print & Web subscription—US $125.00
One-year subscription to the print edition of *The Economist* and online access to all articles from *The Economist* since 1997.

Students who saw the second ad reversed their preferences, with more than two-thirds preferring the Web-only subscription and just 32% preferring the print and Web combination. The preferred option from the first ad became the distant loser in the second. And this happened because "useless" information from the first ad was deleted from the second. How can this be?

Ariely traces the effect to relativity. In the ad that features the decoy, the combination offer looks like a great deal. For the same amount of money as the print subscription, you can get the Web version too. In the second ad, minus the decoy, that combination Web plus print offer looks rather pricey.

The smart IMC professional understands that rational people are influenced by a variety of irrational pieces of information. And as Ariely demonstrates, information in IMC messages can influence perceptions of product value even when that information is "useless."

Laboratory Application

Type up the first version of the *Economist* ads that Ariely used above and give it to your friends. Ask them to choose their preferred options. For those friends who select option 3, point out that they were likely influenced by the "print-only" option. Do you think they will agree? Can you explain the decoy effect to them in a way that will help them understand the importance of context?

---

exchange is possible. If the seller can provide the information and inspiration the buyer seeks, the two may recognize the potential for a *perceived equal-value exchange*. Without this perception, though, an exchange is unlikely. For example, if people don't believe the benefits of a Macbook Air are worth $1,000, they won't buy one, no matter how much Apple spends on IMC.

So marketers must first acquire an understanding of their customers. What do they need? What do they want? How do they see us now? Once marketers develop a deep

Apple advertising fits with Apple products, they are both "cool" and at a deeper level, the ads and the products share other features: simplicity, elegance, and style. As shown in the two Apple ads on this page, both share a similarity in their design and simplicity, yet both are also strikingly different. What are some of the differences in the two ads and despite those differences, why do you think both are effective pieces of advertising?

© The Advertising Archives

understanding of their customers, they can be more effective in adjusting or altering their customers' perception of the product (awareness, attitude, interest) and their customers' belief in the product's ability (value) to satisfy their perceived wants or needs (utility).

IMC can do this in many ways. By using just the right mood lighting or music, for example, a TV commercial can simultaneously capture customers' attention and stimulate their emotions toward the goal of need or want fulfillment. If customers are aware of the product and its value, and if they decide to satisfy the particular want or need the product addresses, they are more likely to act.[8] Since perception is so important to advertisers, we discuss it in greater detail later in this chapter.

Apple's ads succeed because they speak to Apple consumers, and address the needs and desires these consumers want.

© Xinhua/eyevine/Redux

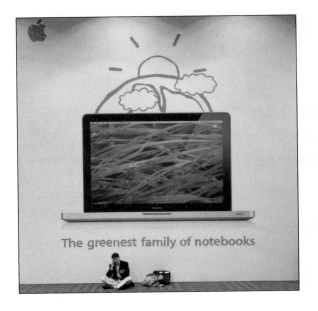

Transnational ads are those that appear in foreign countries. This ad for adidas appeals to the enormous pride felt by the Chinese when they hosted the 2008 Summer Olympics.

Source: adidas

Satisfaction: The Goal of the Customer

Even after an exchange occurs, *satisfaction* remains an issue. Satisfaction must occur every time customers use the product, or people won't think they got an equal-value exchange. Satisfaction leads to more exchanges: Satisfied customers repurchase; and satisfied customers tell their friends. Positive word of mouth creates even more sales and contributes to a good reputation. And while word of mouth has always been important, it is crucial in the new age of social media such as Facebook. Thus, while satisfaction is the goal of the customer, it must also be the fundamental goal of any sophisticated marketer.

IMC *reinforces* satisfaction by reminding customers why they bought the product, helping them defend the purchase against skeptical friends, and enabling them to persuade others to buy it. It should be easy to see why messages founded on false or empty promises won't prove effective. If a product performs poorly, the negative effect will be even more far-reaching. And good campaigns for a poor product can actually hasten the brand's demise. The better the campaign, the more people will try the product—once. And the more who try an unsatisfactory product, the more who will reject it—and tell their friends.

This is why experts define marketing as the process companies use to make a profit by satisfying their customers' needs and desires.

The Key Participants in the Marketing Process

People's needs and wants change daily, and marketers constantly promote a variety of products for customer attention and interest. This makes the marketing process very dynamic. At times, it seems like everybody is searching for an exchange. At other times, it seems nobody is. Marketing exchanges depend on three types of participants: *customers, markets* (groups of customers), and *marketers.*

Customers

Customers are the people or organizations that consume goods and services. They fall into three general categories: *current customers, prospective customers,* and *centers of influence.*

Current customers have already bought something from a business or brand; in fact, they may buy regularly. One way to measure a business's success is by calculating the number of its current customers and their repeat purchases. **Prospective customers** are people about to make

A Value Proposition summarizes why a consumer should buy a product or use a service. How does the above Apple advertisement accomplish this?

Source: Apple Inc.

an exchange or considering it. **Centers of influence** are those people or groups whose ideas and actions others respect. A center of influence is often the link to many prospective customers.

Markets

The second participant in the marketing process is the **market,** which is a group of current customers, prospective customers, and noncustomers who share a common interest, need, or desire; who have the money to spend to satisfy needs or solve problems; and who have the authority to buy.[9] As we discuss more fully in Chapter 6, a market never includes everybody. Companies design messages for four broad classifications of markets:

1. **Consumer markets** comprise people who buy for their own use. Both Nissan and Ford, for example, aim at the consumer market. But they cater to different groups within that market. They promote some vehicles to single women; others to upscale young families; and still others to retired people. The consumer market is huge, accounting for almost two-thirds of all spending in the U.S. economy.[10] Chapter 6 discusses ways to categorize consumer segments.

2. **Business markets** are made up of organizations that buy services, natural resources, and component products that they resell, use to conduct their business, or use to manufacture another product. While you are likely more familiar with consumer promotions, almost half of all marketing is business-to-business. In the United States, business buyers purchase trillions of dollars' worth of manufactured goods every year, billions more of raw materials, and billions more for the services of law firms, accountants, airlines, and advertising agencies.[11] The two most important business markets are *reseller markets* and *industrial markets.*

 Reseller markets buy products to resell them. Ford, for example, distributes cars to consumers through a network of independently owned dealers. Similarly, Sunkist relies on retail grocers to carry its brand of fruits, or they will never be sold to consumers.

 Industrial markets include millions of firms that buy products used to produce other goods and services.[12] Manufacturers of plant equipment and machinery promote to industrial markets, as do office suppliers, computer companies, and telephone companies. Chapter 6 categorizes industrial markets by factors of industry segment, geographic location, and size.

Although the iPad is an expensive technology, Apple uses the "peripheral route" in the above ad. Are they successful with this approach because of the trust the Apple brand has earned with their consumers?

© The Advertising Archives

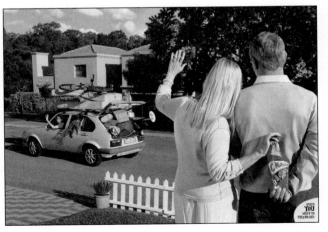

As they enter their later years, Boomers represent an important consumer market for companies. How do you think Boomers would react to the above advertisement? Do you think the ad also appeals to younger consumers?

Source: Mars, Incorporated

For the high-involvement consumer, information is everything. This ad for Charles Schwab offers useful facts to potential investors. The information helps consumers decide if an account with Charles Schwab fits their investment needs.

Source: Charles Schwab & Co.

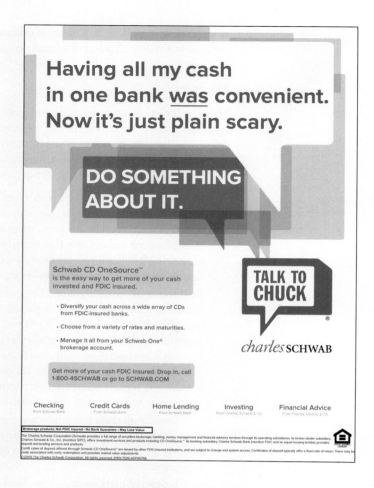

3. **Government markets** buy products for municipal, state, federal, and other government activities. Some firms are immensely successful selling only to government markets. They promote post office vehicles, police and military weapons, and tax collector office equipment to government buyers.

4. **Transnational** (or **global**) **markets** include any of the other three markets located in foreign countries. Every country has consumers, resellers, industries, and governments. So what's the difference between the transnational market and the domestic U.S. or Canadian market for the same product? Environment. The environment in France

Apple's products appeal to many different markets. While consumers view iPads as entertainment devices, the product is also attractive to millions of businesspeople.

© Oleksiy Maksymenko/age fotostock

differs from that in Japan. The environment in Brazil differs from that in Saudi Arabia. Sometimes, as in the case of Switzerland, environments even vary widely within a single country. Targeting markets across national boundaries presents challenges and opportunities for contemporary marketers, so we deal with the subject wherever applicable throughout this book.

Marketers

LO **5-3**

The third participant in the marketing process, **marketers,** includes every person or organization that has products, services, or ideas to sell. Manufacturers market consumer and business products. Farmers market wheat; doctors market medical services; banks market financial products; and political organizations market philosophies and candidates. To be successful, marketers must know their markets intimately—*before* they create messages.

Consumer Behavior: The Key to IMC Strategy

Take a look at your friends, or the people you work with. How well do you know them? Could you describe their lifestyles and the kinds of products they prefer? Do they typically eat out or cook for themselves? Do they ski? Play tennis? If so, what brands do they buy? Do you know which radio stations they listen to? What TV programs they watch? What Websites they frequent? If you were Motorola's advertising manager and wanted to advertise a new tablet to these people, what type of appeal would you use? What media would you use to reach them?

The Importance of Knowing the Consumer

Marketers spend a lot of money to keep individuals and groups of individuals (markets) interested in their products. To succeed, they need to understand what makes potential customers behave the way they do. The goal is to get enough market data to develop profiles of buyers—to find the common ground (and symbols) for communication. This involves the study of **consumer behavior:** the mental and emotional processes and the physical activities of people who purchase and use goods and services to satisfy needs and wants.[13] The behavior of **organizational buyers** (the people who purchase products and services for use in business and government) is also important. We examine this in Chapter 6.

The Consumer Decision Process: An Overview

Social scientists develop many theories of consumer behavior to explain the process of making a purchase decision. Let's look at this information from the viewpoint of the advertiser.

The moment someone recognizes a need that might be satisfied by a purchase, he or she begins the **consumer decision process.** Exhibit 5-1 presents the basic steps of this process. It involves a sequence of activities: *problem recognition* (which may occur as a result of seeing an ad), *information search, evaluation and selection, store choice and purchase,* and finally *postpurchase behavior.* For simple, habitual, everyday purchases, the decision-making process is short. But in those situations where the consumer is highly involved in the purchase, it's not at all unusual for the consumer to substantially extend the decision process.

Whether the process is limited or extended, many factors play a role in the way consumers behave. These include a series of personal subprocesses that are shaped by various influences.

The three **personal processes** govern the way we discern raw sensory information (*stimuli*) and translate it into feelings, thoughts, beliefs, and actions. The personal processes are *perception, learning and persuasion,* and *motivation.*

Second, our mental processes and behavior are affected by two sets of influences. **Interpersonal influences** include *family, society,* and *culture.* **Nonpersonal influences**—factors often outside the consumer's control—include *time, place,* and *environment.*

After engaging these processes and responding to these influences, we face the pivotal decision: to buy or not to buy. Taking that final step requires **evaluation of alternatives,** in which we choose brands, sizes, styles, and colors. If we do decide to buy, our **postpurchase evaluation** will affect whether or not we buy again.

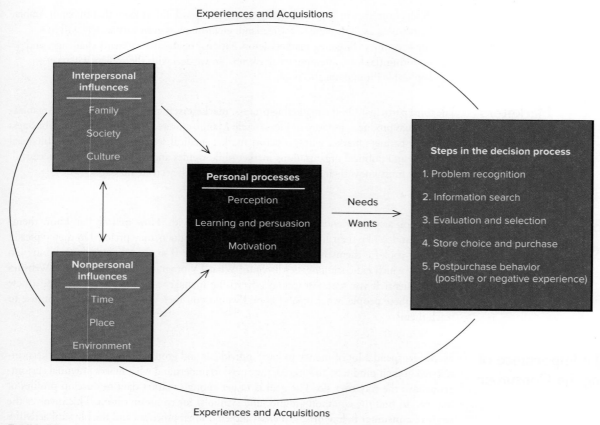

Experiences and Acquisitions

Interpersonal influences
- Family
- Society
- Culture

Nonpersonal influences
- Time
- Place
- Environment

Personal processes
- Perception
- Learning and persuasion
- Motivation

Needs
Wants

Steps in the decision process
1. Problem recognition
2. Information search
3. Evaluation and selection
4. Store choice and purchase
5. Postpurchase behavior (positive or negative experience)

Experiences and Acquisitions

Exhibit 5-1

The basic consumer decision process comprises a set of fundamental steps that the consumer experiences during and after the purchase process. Advertising can affect the consumer's attitude at any point in this process.

Psychological Processes in Consumer Behavior

LO 5-4

Assume you are the brand manager preparing to launch Apple's newest campaign. What's your first objective?

The first task in promoting any new product is to create awareness (*perception*) that the product exists. The second is to provide enough compelling information (*learning and persuasion*) about the product for prospective customers to find interest and make an informed decision. Finally, you want your advertising to stimulate customers' desire (*motivation*) to satisfy their needs and wants by trying the product. If they find the Old Spice body wash satisfying, they likely will continue to purchase it. These three personal processes of consumer behavior—perception, learning and persuasion, and motivation—are extremely important to advertisers. By studying them, advertisers can better evaluate how their messages are perceived.

The Consumer Perception Process

As we mentioned earlier, perception is everything. It guides all our activities from the people we associate with to the products we buy. How a consumer perceives each of the different brands in a category determines which ones he or she uses.[14] The perception challenge, therefore, is the first and greatest hurdle advertisers must cross. Some marketers spend millions of dollars on national advertising, sales promotion, point-of-purchase displays, and other marketing communications only to discover that many consumers don't remember the product or the promotion. The average adult may be exposed to thousands of ads each day but notices only a handful and remembers even fewer.[15] How does this happen? The answer lies in the principle of perception.

The term **perception** refers to the information we receive through our five senses. There are several key elements to the consumer perception process, as shown in Exhibit 5-2.

Exhibit 5-2

This model of the consumer perception process portrays how consumers perceive, accept, and remember an ad or other stimulus to buy.

A **stimulus** is something (light, sound, a scent) we can receive through our senses. It may originate within our bodies, as when we notice that we feel hungry at lunchtime. Or it may originate from outside our bodies, as when we see an ad for an iPhone and decide it looks beautiful.

IMC messages are external stimuli that can appear in a variety of forms: a window display at a local department store, the brightly colored labels on cans of Campbell's tomato soup, or even the red price tag on a pair of skis at REI. These objects are all physical in nature; they stimulate our senses (with varying degrees of intensity) in ways that can be measured.

Physiological Screens

Before a stimulus can be perceived, it must first penetrate a set of **physiological screens,** the subconscious filters that shield us from unwanted messages.

The physiological screens comprise the five senses: sight, hearing, touch, taste, and smell. They detect the incoming data and measure the dimension and intensity of the physical stimuli. A sight-impaired person can't read an ad in *Sports Illustrated*. And if the type in a movie ad is too small for the average reader, it won't be read. Similarly, if the music in a TV commercial for a furniture store is not complementary to the message, the viewer may tune out, change channels, or even turn off the TV. A message is effectively screened out when the viewer can't detect it; perception does not occur, and the furniture goes unsold.[16]

Cognition

The third key element in perception is **cognition:** comprehending the stimulus. Once we detect the stimulus and allow it through our perceptual screens, we can comprehend and accept it.

But each of us has his or her own reality. For example, some people admire Apple products for their simplicity and beauty. Others buy Apple products because they are best sellers and find it comforting to use the same technology as most others. Still others are Apple fanatics, closely monitoring the technology press for any word on new product developments. And some people, perhaps wanting to be seen as different from the masses, would never consider an Apple product, no matter how good. That person's reality is considerably different.

Just as we have screens at the level of perception, so too do screens exist at the level of cognition. Each consumer uses **psychological screens** to evaluate, filter, and personalize information according to subjective emotional standards. These screens evaluate data based on *innate factors,* such as the consumer's personality and instinctive human needs, and *learned*

Screens are the barriers that IMC must penetrate. How does the appearance of Katy Perry in this Super Bowl ad help attract attention and break through perceptual and psychological barriers?

Source: Pepsi Cola Company

factors, such as self-concept, interests, attitudes, beliefs, past experiences, and lifestyle. They help consumers summarize unwieldy or complex data. For example, perceptual screens help us accept or reject symbolic ideas, such as the sexy commercial for Levi's Dockers in which a man and a number of women dance provocatively in a nightclub. Prospective partners pull at the man by grabbing his belt loops. When he finally leaves with one, the voice-over says, "You'll get worn out before they do." The campaign is targeted toward upscale, fashion-forward men in the 25 to 34 age group who critically influence others.

Psychologists in recent years[17] have proposed that people have two systems for thinking, one that is relatively fast, uncontrolled and immediate ("I'm hungry and that burger looks amazing!") and one that is slower and more deliberate ("But remember you are on a diet! Get a salad"). We use the fast, intuitive system to make many decisions and only call on the slower, effortful system when we believe a decision requires deliberation and caution. Advertising, through provocative imagery and powerful copy, is remarkably effective at engaging the fast system. For many low-priced, low-involvement purchases (buying a soft drink) the fast system works fine but for important purchases (e.g., a computer) consumers may find themselves experiencing an internal dialog ("That laptop is gorgeous, I have to have it! But should I really spend that much money?")

Learning and Persuasion: How Consumers Process Information

By definition, **learning** is a relatively permanent change in thought process or behavior. Learning produces our habits and skills. It also contributes to the development of interests, attitudes, beliefs, preferences, prejudices, emotions, and standards of conduct—all of which affect, among other things, our eventual purchase decisions.

Mental Files

Cognition is not just about how we respond to things we perceive, it is also about how we store information for later use. Many promotional messages rely on consumers making a purchase long after they are exposed to a brand message. Information in memory is not stored randomly, but rather in **mental** (or *perceptual*) **files.**

To cope with the complexity of stimuli such as advertising, we rank products and other data in our files by importance, price, quality, features, or a host of other descriptors.

Memory is a limited resource, and one susceptible to some well-known biases. As an example, pause for a moment and consider whether there are more words that begin with the letter *k* (i.e., *kangaroo*) versus words that have *k* in the third position (i.e., *Arkansas*). What is your guess? Many people are surprised to discover there are nearly three times more words (*ask, askance, ark*) with *k* in the third position. But when we search through memory, our mental files make it easier to retrieve words by their first letter. We then confuse this ease of retrieval with the frequency of occurrence. This "availability" heuristic is just one example of how the structure of our cognitive system influences what we recall and how we decide.[18] For another, see Ad Lab 5–A.

Because screens are such a major challenge to advertisers, it's important to understand what's in the consumer's mental files and, if possible, modify them in favor of the advertiser's product. That brings us to the second process in consumer behavior: *learning and persuasion.*

Theories of Learning

Conditioning theories suggest that learning occurs when consumers associate stimuli or behaviors with things they desire. **Classical conditioning** is the theory of learning associated with the Russian psychologist Pavlov. Pavlov knew that dogs salivate when they are presented with food. He wanted to test whether another stimulus, one that had no significant meaning to his dogs, could also elicit salivation if it was paired with the food. Pavlov called food an *unconditioned stimulus* and salivation an *unconditioned* (naturally occurring) *response* for the dogs. When he began sounding a bell just before giving his dogs food, he found that after many occasions the dogs would salivate just from the sound of the bell. The bell was now a *conditioned stimulus.* The dogs associated the bell with something desirable.[19]

The American psychologist B. F. Skinner developed another theory of learned association, which he labeled **operant conditioning**. Operant conditioning involves an organism

"Free" is a word that most people respond to positively. In operant conditioning, people associate rewards with specific behaviors. Pizza Hut uses operant conditioning effectively in the above ad.
© The Advertising Archives

receiving reinforcement for a behavior. Skinner's "subjects" were frequently pigeons who received food when they performed a desired activity, such as pecking a bar. Both *positive reinforcement* (a reward such as food) and *negative reinforcement* (removing a noxious stimulus such as a loud noise) increase the likelihood of a reinforced behavior.

Of course, consumers are not pigeons or dogs, and many people find it hard to believe that what they've learned can be traced to direct experiences. You don't need to smoke to know it is dangerous or practice poor dental hygiene to know it will hurt your teeth. The same thoughts likely influenced Albert Bandura, an American psychologist, to expand on conditioning theories and propose that people can learn in a variety of ways, not just from personal experience. For example, people can watch what happens to other people (my friend Sam studied hard this semester, and as a result made the dean's list) and deduce the implications for themselves. Bandura's **social cognitive theory** provides a richer, cognitive perspective on how people learn. It suggests that consumers pay attention to the rewards and costs experienced by others in response to the things they do. When individuals in our environment (called models by Bandura) experience good outcomes, we are motivated to try the behavior that led to them. When they experience bad outcomes, we are motivated to avoid the behaviors that led to them. This is true whether the models are our friends and neighbors, or people appearing on our TV screens.[20]

Conditioning theories are more applicable to the simple, basic purchases consumers make every day—soap, cereal, toothpaste, paper towels, and so forth. And it is here that reinforcement advertising plays its most important role—along with superior product performance and good service. If learning is reinforced enough and repeat behavior is produced, a purchasing habit may result.

Learning and persuasion are closely linked. **Persuasion** occurs when the change in belief, attitude, or behavioral intention is caused by promotion communication (such as advertising or personal selling).[21] Naturally, advertisers are very interested in persuasion and how it takes place.

A Theory of Persuasion: The Elaboration Likelihood Model

The fact that learning can happen through a relatively thoughtful way (cognition) or a relatively simple way (conditioning) has direct implications for how marketers should try to persuade consumers to try or use a product. This is because, according to theorists, there are two different routes to persuasion: the *central* and the *peripheral routes*. Like learning theory, each depends on the consumer's level of involvement with the product and the message. When the consumer's level of involvement is higher, the central route to persuasion is more likely. On the other hand, the peripheral route to persuasion is more likely when consumer involvement is low.[22]

The two routes are part of the **Elaboration Likelihood Model** in Exhibit 5-3. In the **central route to persuasion,** consumers have a higher level of involvement with the

Exhibit 5-3

The Elaboration Likelihood Model.

product or the message, so they are motivated to pay attention to the central, product-related information, such as product attributes and benefits or demonstrations of positive functional or psychological consequences. Because of their high involvement, consumers tend to learn cognitively and comprehend the ad-delivered information at deeper, more elaborate levels. This can lead to product beliefs, positive brand attitudes, and purchase intention.[23]

Suppose you are in the market for a significant purchase, say, a new camera or a computer. Because the purchase is relatively expensive, your level of involvement is higher. Perhaps you ask for advice from some friends or family members. You may shop different stores to compare models and prices. And you probably read ads for these products thoroughly to understand the variety of product features and benefits. That's central processing. And in that situation, a well-written, informative ad can be very persuasive.

The **peripheral route to persuasion** is very different. People who are not in the market for a product typically have low involvement with the product message. They have little or no reason to pay attention to it or to comprehend the central information of the ad. As a result, consumers form few if any brand beliefs, attitudes, or purchase intentions. However, these consumers might attend to some peripheral aspects—say, the pictures or the colors in an ad or the actors in a commercial—for their entertainment value. And whatever they feel or think about these peripheral, nonproduct aspects might integrate into a positive attitude toward the ad. At some later date, if a purchase occasion does arise and the consumer needs to make some brand evaluation, these ad-related meanings could be activated to form a brand attitude or purchase intention. The Macintosh campaign, described in the opening vignette of this chapter, appears to make heavy use of peripheral cues.

Most mass media are evaluated through peripheral processing. Very few of the messages we see have relevance to our immediate goals or needs, so we pay little attention to them. Our involvement is very low. That's why we also have very little recall of promotions we saw yesterday. In cases where there is little product differentiation, marketers may actually *want* us to engage in peripheral processing. Their campaigns focus more on image or entertainment than product features. This is typical for everyday low-involvement purchases such as soap, cereal, toothpaste, and chewing gum.

Positive motivation offers a bonus to the consumer rather than addressing problem avoidance. This ad for Lamborghini appeals to the sense of power and majesty that goes with owning a high-end sports car, no matter where the driver finds himself or herself.

Source: Automobili Lamborghini S.p.A.

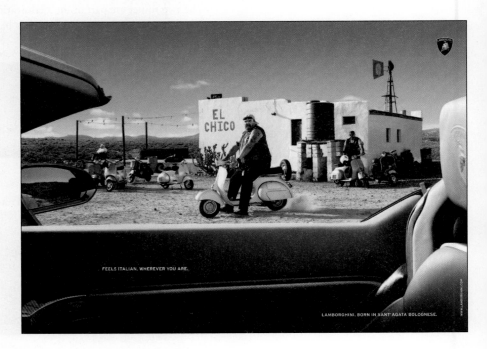

But when a product has a distinct advantage, the company's goal should be to encourage central route processing by increasing consumers' involvement with the message. This is where we see a lot of comparative advertising.[24]

One key to learning and persuasion is repetition. Just as a student prepares for an exam by repeating key information to memorize it, marketers must repeat key information to prospective customers so they remember the product's name and its benefits. Repeat messages penetrate consumer screens by rekindling memories of information from prior messages.

Learning Produces Attitudes and Interest

An **attitude** is our acquired mental position regarding some idea or object. It is the positive or negative evaluations, feelings, or action tendencies that we learn and cling to. For most companies, creating and maintaining positive consumer attitudes are critical to success. Attitudes must be either capitalized on or changed.

In Japan, for instance, dishwashers are not a common household appliance. Not only is there very little space for them, Japanese homemakers feel guilty about using the labor-saving device. As a result, dishwasher manufacturers have designed smaller, space-saving machines and then promoted them using good hygiene themes rather than convenience appeals.[25]

For mature brands in categories with familiar, frequently purchased products, *brand interest* is even more critical for motivating action. **Brand interest** is an individual's openness or curiosity about a brand.[26] Enjoyable, entertaining campaigns can enhance interest in the brand and reduce the variety-seeking tendencies of consumers who become bored with using the same old product.[27]

Learning Leads to Habits and Brand Loyalty

Attitude is the mental side and *habit* the behavioral side of the same coin. **Habit**—the acquired behavior pattern that becomes nearly or completely involuntary—is the natural extension of learning. We really are creatures of habit.

Most consumer behavior is habitual for three reasons: It's safe, simple, and essential. First, regardless of how we learned to make our purchase decision (through either central or peripheral route processing), if we discover a quality product, brand, or service, we feel *safe* repurchasing it through habit.

Second, habit is *simple*. To consider alternatives we must evaluate, compare, and then decide. This is difficult, time-consuming, and risky.

Finally, because habit is both safe and easy, we rely on it for daily living. Imagine rethinking every purchase decision you make. It would be virtually impossible, not to mention impractical. So it's really *essential* to use habit in our lives.

The major objective of all brand marketers is to produce *brand loyalty,* a direct result of the habit of repurchasing and the reinforcement of continuous advertising. **Brand loyalty** is the consumer's conscious or unconscious decision, expressed through intention or behavior, to repurchase a brand continually.[28] It occurs because the consumer *perceives* that the brand offers the right product features, image, quality, or relationship at the right price.

In the quest for brand loyalty, companies have three aims related to habits:

1. *Breaking habits.* Get consumers to unlearn an existing purchase habit and try something new. Marketers frequently offer incentives to lure customers away from old brands or stores. Or they may use comparative advertising to demonstrate their product's superiority.

2. *Acquiring habits.* Teach consumers to repurchase their brand or repatronize their establishment. JetBlue, like many major airlines, offers frequent flyer miles to loyal customers.

Apple seeks to offer users an "end-to-end" experience. In iTunes, this means everything the consumer wants to do with music can be done with Apple technologies. Apple is capitalizing on people's habits: if you know how to use one of the company's technologies, you are comfortable with them all.

© Susan Van Etten/PhotoEdit, Inc.

Superstars like LeBron James ensure an ad is noticed and remembered. Kia expects that the value of his popularity and attractiveness will help not only in attracting new customers, but also in building loyalty among existing users of the brand.

Source: Kia Motors Corporation

3. *Reinforcing habits.* Remind current customers of the value of their original purchase and encourage them to continue purchasing. Many magazines, for example, offer special renewal rates to their regular subscribers.

Developing brand loyalty is difficult due to consumers' sophistication and to the legions of habit-breaking, *demarketing* activities of competitive advertisers.[29] Practitioners of IMC are constantly weighing the costs and benefits of breaking consumer habits (among those who use competing brands) versus encouraging habits (among loyal brand users). One rule of thumb is that sales promotion activities break habits by encouraging consumers to switch brands because of the promotion. Conversely, advertising generally provides consumers with benefit information intended to convince them that they should pay full price for a product or service.

Apple is able to maintain high levels of consumer loyalty and rarely competes on price. Many Apple customers buy its products out of habit. This means there is little to decide when choosing a new technology. They will choose Apple's products every time. In the quest for instant results, Apple shifted much of its advertising budget to sales promotions (deals, coupons, price cuts). Apple believes that IMC activities devoted to brand building, rather than sales promotion are the key to reinforcing loyalty and maintaining market share.[30] We revisit this topic in our discussion of sales promotion in Chapter 10.

Learning Defines Needs and Wants

Learning is both immediate and long term. The moment we file information, some learning takes place. When we see a succulent food ad, we may suddenly feel hungry; we *need* food. This leads to the next personal process, motivation.

The Consumer Motivation Process

Motivation refers to the underlying forces (or motives) that contribute to our actions. These motives stem from the conscious or unconscious goal of satisfying needs and wants. **Needs** are the basic, often instinctive, human forces that motivate us to do something. **Wants** are "needs" that we learn during our lifetime.[31]

Motivation cannot be observed directly. When we see people eat, we assume they are hungry, but we may be wrong. People eat for a variety of reasons besides hunger: They want to be sociable, it's time to eat, or maybe they're nervous or bored.

People are usually motivated to satisfy some combination of needs, which may be conscious or unconscious, functional or psychological. *Motivation research* offers some insights into the underlying reasons for unexpected consumer behavior. The reasons *(motives)* some people buy a hybrid car may be environmental concern, sensitivity to gas prices, or a desire to be seen as progressive and sensitive to carbon emissions. Any or all of these factors might make a car buyer switch to a hybrid, even though he or she may give up many desirable features to do so.

To better understand what motivates people, Abraham Maslow developed the classic model shown in Exhibit 5-4 called the **hierarchy of needs.** Maslow maintained that the lower physiological and safety needs dominate human behavior and must be satisfied

Exhibit 5-4

The hierarchy of needs suggests that people meet their needs according to priorities. Physiological and safety needs carry the greatest priority. In advertising, the message must match the need of the market or the ad will fail. Advertisers use marketing research to understand the need levels of their markets and use this information in determining the marketing mix.

Need	Product	Promotional appeal
Self-actualization	Golf lessons	"Realize your full potential"
Esteem	Luxury car	"Be in control of the road"
Social	Pendant	"Show her you care"
Safety	Tires	"Bounces off hazards"
Physiological	Breakfast cereal	"The natural energy source"

My **IMC** Campaign 5

Understanding What Consumers Look for in a Product

Your client's hope is that you can offer helpful advice on creating promotional messages that will get people to do something. In most cases, that something will be buying the client's product or using the service. If your client is a nonprofit, it might involve donating time and/or money.

This seems like common sense, but in fact persuading people to do something they are not already doing can be quite difficult. To help you organize your approach, it may be useful to review what marketing and psychology scholars have learned about consumers and how they are persuaded.

Your challenge at this point in the campaign is to understand the consumer and to get a sense of how the product or service your client offers relates to the consumer's life. Doing this well will require at least two things: a complete understanding of the product and its possible benefits, and a thorough understanding of the consumer.

Maslow's hierarchy of needs suggests that individuals have a range of needs they seek to satisfy in life.

Here is Maslow's hierarchy and some examples that involve food. Consider whether your client's product or service might have benefits that relate to one or more needs:

Need	Examples Involving Food
Self-actualization	Culinary arts degree
Esteem	Cooking lessons
Social	What everyone is eating
Safety	Healthful, organic foods
Physiological	Something that satisfies your hunger

Informational motives involve eliminating a problem, whereas transformational motives involve getting a reward. Consider the possible informational and transformational motives that exist in your consumers that might be addressed by your product.

Informational Motives	
Motive	**Solution**
Problem removal	"Eliminates your headache fast"
Problem avoidance	"Stay out in the sun—you're protected"
Incomplete satisfaction	"The diet drink that doesn't taste like a diet drink"
Mixed approach–avoidance	"Pain-free dental care"
Normal depletion	"Last gas station for 20 miles"

Transformational Motives	
Sensory gratification	"These headphones sound like you are at the show"
Intellectual stimulation	"Hours of fun with challenging puzzles"
Social approval	"Your spouse will love the way you look"

The Foote, Cone & Belding grid below was developed to classify how consumers learn about different types of products. Although it was originally designed with the idea that different products would fit in different quadrants, some believe that the quadrants can also be used to classify competing brands within a product category (e.g., luxury brands versus discount brands). Where would you place your client's brand? What does that suggest for how you might persuade consumers?

The following guides can help you determine where your client's brand belongs in the FCB grid:

Involvement

1. Is the decision to buy or use the product an important or an unimportant one?
2. Does the consumer stand to lose a great deal or very little if he or she chooses the wrong brand?
3. Does the decision require a great deal of consideration or very little?

Think versus Feel

Think

1. The decision is based on objective criteria.
2. The decision is based primarily on factual information.

Feel

1. The decision is based on a feeling.
2. The decision is closely related to the consumer's personality.
3. The decision is based on the senses (taste, touch, etc.).

FCB Grid

	Think	Feel
High Involvement	I. Informative Learn—Feel—Do (products: major purchases such as insurance, appliances, computers) Strategy: Follow steps of the creative pyramid, beginning with awareness.	II. Affective Feel—Learn—Do (products: expensive car, jewelry, high-end apparel) Strategy: Focus on self-esteem and ego benefits of product purchases.
Low Involvement	III. Habitual Do—Learn—Feel (products: car fuel, detergents, razors) Strategy: Focus on offering samples and creating habits in consumer purchasing.	IV. Satisfaction Do—Feel—Learn (products: experiential products such as beer, chewing gum, greeting cards, pizza) Strategy: Focus on social factors and peer use of the product.

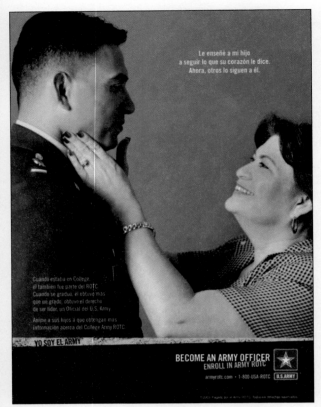

Le enseñé a mi hijo
a seguir lo que su corazón le dice.
Ahora, otros lo siguen a él.

Cuando estaba en College,
él también fue parte del ROTC.
Cuando se graduó, él obtuvo más
que un grado, obtuvo el derecho
de ser líder, un Oficial del U.S. Army.

Anime a sus hijos a que obtengan más
información acerca del College Army ROTC.

YO SOY EL ARMY

BECOME AN ARMY OFFICER
ENROLL IN ARMY ROTC
armyrotc.com • 1-800-USA-ROTC   U.S. ARMY

Advertisers realize that English speakers are not the only market in the United States. Other linguistic and ethnic cultures exist and offer enormous markets for the culturally savvy. Here, the U.S. Army (www.goarmy.com) suggests to the Spanish-speaking audience that the soldier pictured followed his heart, and now "others follow it."

Source: U.S. Army

before the higher, socially acquired needs (or wants) become meaningful. The highest need, self-actualization, is the culmination of fulfilling all the lower needs and reaching to discover the true self.

The promise of satisfying a certain level of need is the basic promotional appeal for many ads. In affluent societies such as the United States, Canada, western Europe, and Japan, most individuals take for granted the satisfaction of their physiological needs. So advertising campaigns often portray the fulfillment of social, esteem, and self-actualization needs, and many offer the reward of satisfaction through personal achievement.

In focus groups for Nabisco SnackWells, for example, it became apparent that middle-aged women today have a high sense of self-worth. Wellness, to them, is no longer about looking good in a bathing suit; rather, it's about celebrating what they do well. The advertiser wondered if it could use women's positive attitude about themselves to change their attitude toward the concept of snacking. Nabisco's agency, Foote, Cone & Belding, capitalized on the idea in a new campaign aimed at boosting women's self-esteem. The message: "Snacking is not about 'filling' yourself, but 'fulfilling' yourself."[32]

We all have needs and wants, but we are frequently unaware of them. Before the advent of the laptop computer, people were completely unaware of any need for it. But the moment a consumer consciously recognizes a product-related want or need, a dynamic process begins. The consumer first evaluates the need and either accepts it as worthy of action or rejects it. Acceptance converts satisfaction of the need into a goal, which creates the dedication (the motivation) to reach a particular result. In contrast, rejection removes the necessity for action and thereby eliminates the goal and the motivation to buy.

Modern researchers have translated Maslow's theory about needs and motives into more strategic concepts for use by marketers and advertisers. Rossiter and Percy, for example, identify eight fundamental purchase and usage motives (see Exhibit 5-5). They refer to the first five as *negatively originated (informational) motives* and the last three as *positively originated (transformational) motives.*[33]

Negatively Originated (Informational) Motives

The most common energizers of consumer behavior are the **negatively originated motives,** such as problem removal or problem avoidance. Whenever we run out of something, for instance, we experience a negative mental state. To relieve those feelings, we actively seek a new or replacement product. Thus, we are temporarily motivated until the time we make the purchase. Then, if the purchase is satisfactory, the drive or motivation is reduced.

These are also called **informational motives** because the consumer actively seeks information to reduce the mental state. In fact, Rossiter and Percy point out, these could also be called "relief" motives because consumers work to find relief from the negative state.

Positively Originated (Transformational) Motives

From time to time, we all want to indulge ourselves by buying some brand or product that promises some benefit or reward. With the **positively originated motives,** a positive bonus is promised rather than the removal or reduction of some negative situation. The goal is to use positive reinforcement to increase the consumer's motivation and to energize the consumer's investigation or search for the new product.

The three positively originated motives—sensory gratification, intellectual stimulation, and social approval—are also called **transformational motives** because the consumer expects to be transformed in a sensory, intellectual, or social sense. They could also be called "reward" motives because the transformation is a rewarding state.[34]

Exhibit 5-5

Rossiter and Percy's eight fundamental purchase and usage motives.

Negatively originated (informational) motives

1. Problem removal
2. Problem avoidance
3. Incomplete satisfaction
4. Mixed approach–avoidance
5. Normal depletion

Positively originated (transformational) motives

6. Sensory gratification
7. Intellectual stimulation or mastery
8. Social approval

For some consumers, the purchase of a particular product (say, a new suit) might represent a negatively originated motive (they don't really want to spend the money on it, but they have to have it for work). But for other consumers, it might be positively originated (they love to shop for new clothes). This suggests two distinct target markets that marketers must understand and that may call for completely different strategies.

Before creating messages, companies must carefully consider the goals that lead to consumer motivations. Chili's restaurants would make a costly mistake if its ads portrayed the reward of a romantic interlude if the real motive of most Chili's customers is simply to satisfy their need to reduce hunger with a filling, low-priced meal.

The issues of high-involvement and low-involvement products and informational and transformational motives are so important that we will revisit them in Chapter 8 when we discuss the planning of IMC strategies.

Interpersonal Influences on Consumer Behavior

For marketers, it's not enough just to know the personal processes of perception, learning and persuasion, and motivation. Important **interpersonal influences** affect—sometimes even dominate—these processes. They also serve as guidelines for consumer behavior. These influences can best be categorized as the *family*, the *society*, and the *cultural environment* of the consumer.

Family Influence

From an early age, family communication affects our socialization as consumers—our attitudes toward many products and our purchasing habits. This influence is usually strong and long lasting. A child who learns that the "right" headache relief is Bayer aspirin and the "right" name for appliances is General Electric has a well-developed adult purchasing behavior.

From 1970 to 1990, married couple households with children declined sharply—from 40 to 26 percent of all households. Since 2004, that decline has been slower. Still, this suggests that family influence has greatly diminished in the United States over the last 30 years as working parents take a less active role in raising their children and youngsters look outside the family for social values.[35] As this happens, the influence of the social and cultural environments intensifies.

Societal Influence

The community we live in exerts a strong influence on all of us. When we affiliate with a particular societal division or identify with some reference group or value the ideas of certain opinion leaders, it affects our views on life, our perceptual screens, and eventually the products we buy.

Societal Divisions: The Group We Belong To

Sociologists traditionally divided societies into **social classes:** upper, upper-middle, lower-middle, and so on. They believed that people in the same social class tended toward similar attitudes, status symbols, and spending patterns.

But today this doesn't apply to most developed countries. U.S. society, especially, is extremely fluid and mobile—physically, socially, and economically. Americans believe strongly in getting ahead, being better than their peers, and winning greater admiration and self-esteem. As the famous Army campaign illustrates, advertisers capitalize on this desire to "be all you can be."

Because of this mobility, increases in immigration, and the high divorce rate, social class boundaries have become quite muddled. Single parents, stockbrokers, immigrant shopkeepers, retired blue-collar workers, and bankers all see themselves as part of the great middle class. So "middle class" doesn't mean anything anymore. From the advertiser's point of view, social class seldom represents a functional or operational set of values.

To deal with these often bewildering changes, marketers seek new ways to classify societal divisions and new strategies for advertising to them. We discuss some of these in Chapter 6. Exhibit 5-6 outlines some of the classifications marketers use to describe society today: for example, Upper Crust, Brite Lites Li'l City, Young Influentials, and Urban Achievers. People in the same group tend to have similar patterns of behavior and product usage.

Upper Crust	Blue-Chip Blues
The nation's most exclusive address, Upper Crust is the wealthiest lifestyle in America—a haven for empty-nesting couples over 55 years old. No segment has a higher concentration of residents earning over $200,000 a year or possessing a postgraduate degree. And none has a more opulent standard of living.	Blue-Chip Blues is known as a comfortable lifestyle for young, sprawling families with well-paying blue-collar jobs. Ethnically diverse—with a significant presence of Hispanics and African Americans—the segment's aging neighborhoods feature compact, modestly priced homes surrounded by commercial centers that cater to child-filled households.
Brite Lites, Li'l City	**Old Glories**
Not all of America's chic sophisticates live in major metros. Brite Lights, Li'l City is a group of well-off, middle-aged couples settled in the nation's satellite cities. Residents of these typical DINK (double income, no kids) households have college educations, well-paying business and professional careers, and swank homes filled with the latest technology.	Old Glories are the nation's downscale suburban retirees, Americans aging in place in older apartment complexes. These racially mixed households often contain widows and widowers living on fixed incomes, and they tend to lead home-centered lifestyles. They're among the nation's most ardent television fans, watching game shows, soaps, talk shows, and newsmagazines at high rates.
Young Influentials	**City Startups**
Once known as the home of the nation's yuppies, Young Influentials reflects the fading glow of acquisitive yuppiedom. Today, the segment is a common address for young, middle-class singles and couples who are more preoccupied with balancing work and leisure pursuits. Having recently left college dorms, they now live in apartment complexes surrounded by ball fields, health clubs, and casual dining restaurants.	In City Startups, young, multiethnic singles have settled in neighborhoods filled with cheap apartments and a commercial base of cafés, bars, laundromats, and clubs that cater to twentysomethings. One of the youngest segments in America—with 10 times as many college students as the national average—these neighborhoods feature low incomes and high concentrations of Hispanics and African Americans.
Urban Achievers	**Low-Rise Living**
Concentrated in the nation's port cities, Urban Achievers is often the first stop for up-and-coming immigrants from Asia, South America, and Europe. These young singles and couples are typically college-educated and ethnically diverse; about a third are foreign-born, and even more speak a language other than English.	The most economically challenged urban segment, Low-Rise Living is known as a transient world for young, ethnically diverse singles and single parents. Home values are low—about half the national average—and even then, less than a quarter of residents can afford to own real estate. Typically, the commercial base of Mom-and-Pop stores is struggling and in need of a renaissance.

Exhibit 5-6

Contemporary social classes. The social groups outlined in this exhibit are just a few of the 66 lifestyle segments defined by Claritas. This division of Equifax wants to know what financial services various consumers, from the wealthiest (Upper Crust) to the poorest (Low-Rise Living), are likely to need.

Reference Groups: The People We Relate To

Most of us care how we appear to people whose opinions matter. We may even pattern our behavior after members of some groups we value. This is the significance of **reference groups**—people we try to emulate or whose approval concerns us. Reference groups can be personal (family, friends, coworkers) or impersonal (political parties, religious denominations, professional associations). A special reference group, our peers, exerts tremendous influence on what we believe and how we behave. They determine which brands are cool and which are not.[36] To win acceptance by our peers (fellow students, coworkers, colleagues), we may purchase a certain style or brand of clothing, choose a particular place to live, and acquire behavioral habits that will earn their approval.

Often an individual is influenced in opposite directions by two reference groups and must choose between them. For example, a college student might feel pressure from some friends to join a Greek house and from others to live independently off campus. In ads targeted to students, a local apartment complex might tap the appeal of reference groups by showing students splashing in the complex's pool.

Opinion Leaders: The People We Trust

An **opinion leader** is some person or organization whose beliefs or attitudes are respected by people who share an interest in some specific activity. All fields (sports, religion, fashion, politics) have opinion leaders. An opinion leader may be a knowledgeable friend or some expert we find credible. We reason, "If Kiera Knightley thinks Chanel is the best perfume, then it must be so." Thus, the purchasing habits and testimonials of opinion leaders are important to advertisers.

Ethical **Issues**

Helping an Industry Look Like America

Advertising agencies have long struggled to represent the diversity of the U.S. population within their ranks. There is no question that the backgrounds of those working in ad agencies have, for many years, differed from those of the broader population. As late as the middle of the 20th century, for example, most jobs and all senior management positions were held by white males. In this respect, agencies were no better (but also perhaps no worse) than most other businesses.

The agency world can even point to some dramatic successes in promoting people from diverse backgrounds. For example, in 1967 Mary Wells Lawrence, a savvy creative head at Doyle, Dane, Bernbach, made history as the first female agency CEO at Wells Rich Greene. With clients like IBM, Procter & Gamble, and Sheraton Hotels, WRG was a major advertising shop. Lawrence eventually became the highest-paid agency head in the business and the first female leader of an NYSE-listed company.

But many, both within and outside the agency business, believe that diversity is still a problem in the world of advertising. Some even contend that agencies have a special obligation to take a leadership role on the issue. After all, they say, how can agencies develop effective and responsible messages for diverse audiences if their own employees lack diversity? According to Rick Milentha, CEO of TenUnited, "It is a travesty that our industry, which is supposed to market to all of America, does not reflect all of America. . . . I think it's incumbent on us to find a way for this not to be the case in the future. The truth is, it's just plain good business. If we're going to do our job for our clients, we can't be predominantly white and male."

Diversity became much more than an abstract issue in the fall of 2006 when the New York City Commission on Human Rights issued a barely veiled threat to the industry: institute-specific practices that can help with minority recruitment or face public humiliation.

To understand what happened between the commission and America's biggest ad agencies, a bit of history is in order. The commission is charged with eliminating discrimination in employment practices. In 1967 it surveyed 40 agencies with branches in New York and discovered that only 634 blacks and about 300 Hispanics could be found among the nearly 18,000 agency employees. That math worked out to a workforce of about 5 percent minorities in a metropolitan labor force that was about 25 percent minority. The commission urged agencies to do a better job in hiring and retaining blacks and Hispanics.

In 1977 the commission once again examined the agency workforce. In seven large agencies, the percentage of black and Hispanic employees was nearly 12 percent. Two other large agencies, both of which had agreed to specific affirmative action plans, had workforces that were almost 14 percent minority. It was progress, but the commission continued to believe agencies could do more. By 2006, the commission had apparently had enough. It announced that it would hold hearings on industry practices in hiring and retaining minorities. Perhaps not coincidentally, the hearings would take place during an annual New York event called Advertising Week. Advertising Week is, according to its own promotional materials, the "largest assembly of advertising and media leaders in North America" (you can find out more at www.advertisingweek.com). The event is a celebration of the ad industry.

But the commission threatened to make Advertising Week anything but a celebration when it issued subpoenas to 16 senior agency executives, including the CEOs of the four big conglomerates: Omnicom, WPP, Interpublic, and Publicis. The subpoenas required that the executives testify regarding their hiring practices and their failures to diversify.

Fearing a humiliating grilling during the most widely publicized event of the year, three of the four conglomerates immediately agreed to the commission's demands, including pledges of money to historically black colleges and setting hiring goals. The goals ranged from 5 to 30 percent for minority hires and promotions. But one conglomerate, Omnicom, held out. Omnicom was not ignoring diversity; indeed, it pledged more than $2 million for its own initiatives, including creating an advertising curriculum at Medgar Evers College, a historically black institution. The group argued that it merely wished to address diversity in its own way, rather than follow dictates from the commission. But after several weeks of bad press, Omnicom buckled and signed.

How much of a difference were these concessions likely to make? Not much, according to *Advertising Age*, which commented "Why do we—along with 93% of those responding [to an industry poll]—get the feeling that we'll be reading something similar in another 30 years?" The magazine argued that "Both sides need to get real. The commission needs to cease grandstanding attempts to embarrass the industry into action . . . and acknowledge the fact that in a supply-demand market, qualified and interested minority applicants can get a lot more out of their degrees in other sectors." Turning to the industry, it noted it could "be a little less defensive and a great deal more proactive. Poaching qualified minority applicants already in the system doesn't boost numbers. And time spent whining that there aren't enough black kids [in ad programs] could be better spent looking for undergraduates in other programs. Training and mentoring would help. As would breaking up the good ol' boy vibe prevalent in many agencies."

But perhaps *Advertising Age* is missing the bigger picture. Nancy Hill, the new CEO of the AAAA, has made diversity a priority (see People behind the Ads, Chapter 4). Even her appointment as president, the first woman in the 90-plus-year history of the organization, suggests a change in perspective. And the AAAA is a sponsor of the Minority Advertising Internship Program (MAIP), which places students of Asian/Asian American, Latino/Hispanic, Black/African American, Native American, multiracial or multiethnic backgrounds in top agency internships where they receive mentoring and develop valuable contacts (find out more about the MAIP and how you might become a participant at www.aaaa-maip.org). These efforts, and many others by ad agencies across the United States, may finally make it more likely that the ad industry begins to look like America.

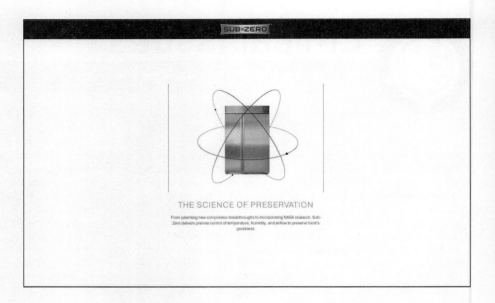

When choosing an opinion leader as a spokesperson for a company or product, advertisers must understand the company's target market thoroughly. Even if executives in the company do not relate to the spokesperson, they must follow market tastes and interests. A spokesperson out of sync with the market undermines his or her credibility—and the company's. On the other hand, an internal person such as Steve Jobs, before he passed away in 2011, turned out to be a highly credible spokesperson without the risks associated with outside celebrities and athletes.[37]

Opinion leaders don't even have to be real people. Even fictional ones will do. That's why it is not surprising that Apple laptops turn up on many highly rated shows and feature films. The fact that key characters in these entertainment media use the brand represents a belief that viewers will notice and be influenced by the choices of their favorite characters.[38]

Cultural and Subcultural Influence

Culture has a tenacious influence on consumers. **Culture** refers to the whole set of meanings, beliefs, attitudes, and ways of doing things that are shared by some homogeneous social group and are typically handed down from generation to generation.[39] Americans love hot dogs, peanut butter, corn on the cob, and apple pie. Canada, Russia, Germany—every country has its own favorite specialties. And companies find it much easier to work with these tastes than try to change them.

Global marketers are especially concerned with the purchase environment. According to Professor Carolyn Lin, of all business functions, marketing activities are the most susceptible to cultural error.[40]

For example, while both demographic and psychographic traits figure importantly in U.S. consumer marketing, age and sex are better indicators of behavior and lifestyles in Japan, where income is largely proportional to seniority and sex roles tend to be standardized.[41] In international markets, companies must consider many environmental factors: cultural trends, social norms, changing fads, market dynamics, product needs, and media channels.[42]

In countries where people earn little income, demand for expensive products is low. So the creative strategy of an automobile advertiser might be to target the small group of wealthy, upper-class consumers. In a country with a large middle class, the same advertiser might be better off mass-marketing the car and positioning it as a middle-class product.

The United States and Canada embrace many subcultures, some of them quite large. They may be based on race, national origin, religion, language, or geographic proximity. The marketer must understand these subcultures because differences among them may affect responses to both products and messages.

The United States, in particular, is a great patchwork of minority subcultures. A **subculture** is a segment within a culture that shares a set of meanings, values, or activities that differ in certain respects from those of the overall culture.[43] According to the U.S. Census, 39 million African Americans, 48 million Hispanics, and 14 million Asians live in the United States. These three minority groups alone account for more than a third of the American population.[44] Canada has two major subcultures, anglophones and francophones, based on language (English and French), plus a mosaic of many other cultures based on ethnic and national origin.

Racial, religious, and ethnic backgrounds affect consumers' preferences for styles of dress, food, beverages, transportation, personal care products, and household furnishings, to name a few. As we saw in Chapter 4, many agencies now specialize in minority markets. Recognizing the rapid growth of the Hispanic population, for example, Procter & Gamble spends more than $153 million per year to understand and promote to this market. Other major Hispanic marketers include Ford Motor Co., AT&T, and Sears.[45]

Global marketers also face cultural challenges. In North America, advertising encourages us to keep our mouths clean, our breath fresh, and our teeth scrubbed. But people in some southern European countries consider it vain and improper to overindulge in toiletries. Consumers in the Netherlands and the United Kingdom use three times as much toothpaste as those in Spain and Greece. To communicate effectively with Spanish consumers, who view toothpaste as a cosmetic product, marketers use chic creative executions rather than dry, therapeutic pitches.[46]

Clearly, many interpersonal factors influence consumers. They have an important effect on our purchase decisions. Awareness of these interpersonal influences helps marketers, both domestic and international, create the strategies on which much IMC is based.

Nonpersonal Influences on Consumer Behavior

Numerous nonpersonal influences affect a consumer's final purchase decision. The most important **nonpersonal influences** are *time, place,* and *environment.*

Time

The old saw "timing is everything" certainly applies to marketing. A special weekend sale may provide just the added incentive to penetrate customers' perceptual screens and bring them into a store. But running an ad for that sale on Sunday evening would be a waste of advertising dollars.

Likewise, the consumer's particular need may be a function of time. Forecasts of an unusually wet winter from the El Niño phenomenon motivated special ads from a variety of national companies as well as many small retailers of linens, boots, snow shovels, and rock salt. Consumers don't need snow tires and rock salt in the summer (although some off-season promotions do work). But if we unexpectedly get a flat on the highway, tire campaigns suddenly become timely. As we will see in our chapters on media, companies must plan all their marketing activities with the consumer's clock in mind.

Place

Once consumers decide to purchase a certain product, they will still hesitate if they don't know where to buy it or if it isn't available in a convenient or preferred location. Similarly, if consumers believe a particular brand is a specialty good but it suddenly appears everywhere, their perception of the product's "specialness" may diminish. Thus, marketers carefully weigh consumer demand when planning distribution strategy, and they devote much of their promotional activities to communicating the convenience of location. Distribution is an important element of the marketing mix and will be discussed further in Chapter 6.

Environment

Many **environments**—ecological, social, political, technical, economic, household, and point-of-sale location, to mention a few—can affect the purchase decision. For example, during a recession, companies can't expect to accomplish much with consumers who don't have enough money to buy. And no matter how good the message or how low the price, memberships in the National Rifle Association aren't likely to be a hot item with members of the Audubon Society. On the other hand, an enticing display next to the cash register can improve sales of low-cost impulse items. Marketers must consider the influence of the purchase environment on the consumer's decision processes.

Likewise, the state of technological development affects economic and social conditions—and the prospects for advertisers of certain products and services. For example, countries that don't manufacture computers might be poor markets for components such as hard drives and microprocessors. On the other hand, campaigns for low-priced, imported computers might do very well.

Finally, some governments exert far greater control over their citizens and businesses than does the U.S. government. For example, for many years, virtually no American-made products could be sold in former Eastern bloc countries or China. It simply wasn't allowed. Political control often extends to which products companies may advertise and sell, which media they use, and what their ads say.

The Purchase Decision and Postpurchase Evaluation

Now that you've learned about the elements in the consumer purchase decision process, let's see how they might work in a typical situation. Ad Lab 5–B demonstrates an advertiser's approach, but it is also important to look through the eyes of a consumer. A hypothetical consumer named Chris is thinking about buying a tablet.

Chris is enrolled at a state university and financed in part by a small scholarship. He also has a part-time job but must act conservatively when it comes to spending money because tuition, books, and other expenses are costly.

One day, thumbing through a consumer electronics magazine, Chris sees an exciting ad for a new top-of-the line tablet. A beautiful photograph shows the product's modern yet understated design. The copy highlights the tablet's special features. They exude high-tech class—it's just the right style. The ad's signature: "Exclusively at TechMart."

In a split second Chris leaps from perception to motivation. Got to have it! He is highly involved and he wants this personal reward for all his hard work.

The next day Chris visits TechMart. While looking for the advertised tablet, he encounters a variety of alternative styles and models by well-known manufacturers.

The ad has already done its work; the purchase decision process is well under way. At the point of making a purchase decision, though, consumers typically search, consider, and compare alternative brands.

Consumers evaluate selection alternatives (called the **evoked set**). To do this, they establish **evaluative criteria,** the standards they use to judge the features and benefits of alternative products. Not all brands make it to the evoked set. In fact, based on their mental files, most consumers usually consider only four or five brands—which presents a real challenge to advertisers. If none of the alternatives meet the evaluative criteria, the consumer may reject the purchase entirely or postpone the decision.

Chris finally finds the advertised product. But it looks larger on the shelf than it did in the ad. Two other good tablets are also displayed; both are attractive, both expensive. While looking over the beautiful screen, Chris considers other unique qualities of style and design. "This one may be a little too bulky." "This one syncs easily with my phone." "This one is less expensive."

Using central route processing, Chris compares the tablets, considering their style, technology, possible advantages, and price. The advertised unit really is the best buy and would be the most satisfying. The purchase decision is complete when Chris uses his debit card to make the purchase.

On the way home, the **postpurchase evaluation** begins. Chris suddenly envisions some friends' possible negative reactions to the purchase. Maybe it wasn't wise to spend so much money on a high-end device. Chris starts to worry—and to plan.

"It's really a great piece of technology. It's excellent quality and worth the money. I'll get a lot of use out of it."

A key feature of the postpurchase evaluation is *cognitive dissonance.* The **theory of cognitive dissonance** (also called **postpurchase dissonance**) holds that people strive to justify their behavior by reducing the dissonance, or inconsistency, between their cognitions (their perceptions or beliefs) and reality.[47] In fact, research shows that, to combat dissonance,

AD Lab 5-B

Applying Consumer Behavior Principles to Ad Making

When Polaroid needed to capture the attention of photo enthusiasts, it turned to the creatives at Leonard/Monahan to design a series of ads that would exhibit the advantages of the instant film over other photo products. The first challenge for the creative design team was to break through the consumers' resistance, the subtle barrier that begins with the perceptual screens. Second, the team had to present the picture as being worth a thousand words while avoiding clichés.

The advertisement's headline—"The victim refuses to speak. The pictures refuse to keep quiet."—commands your attention and expresses the big idea with urgency. The ad's black-and-white visual of a battery victim suggests the subject's grave nature while allowing the color Polaroid pictures to jump out, emoting a raw portrayal of reality. The ad becomes credible by demonstrating the benefits of Polaroid pictures and how they can be successfully used (to investigate, prosecute, and win). The tagline, "Instant evidence," sums up the product's features and helps the prospective consumer recall the product's benefits. These factors show clearly the product's benefits to those who may be critical of their purchase decision.

Source: Polaroid

Laboratory Application

Choose an ad from a popular magazine and explain how the visuals, the words, and the overall design of the ad accomplish the following tasks. Provide specific details to support your answers.

1. Penetrate consumer perceptual screens.
2. Stimulate consumer learning.
3. Use the consumer's existing beliefs.
4. Tap consumer wants and needs to achieve motivation.

---

consumers are more likely to read ads for brands they've already purchased than for new products or competing brands.[48]

> As soon as he leaves the store, Chris begins thinking that the other tablets were pretty attractive too, and some were cheaper or had more features. This begins creating an uneasy feeling in Chris that he might not have made a wise decision. He also knows that the money he used to buy the tablet could have been used for many more practical purchases. Chris is anxious to get confirmation that he made the right choice so that he'll begin feeling better. He decides to go online and find some cool apps he can download. He also visits Facebook to share a photo of the new device. Chris is relieved to see many friends weigh in with "likes" and positive comments. Later, when he sees an ad for the tablet on TV, Chris is proud that he decided to buy one.

During the postpurchase period, the consumer may enjoy the satisfaction of the purchase and thereby receive reinforcement for the decision. Or the purchase may turn out to be unsatisfactory for some reason. In either case, feedback from the postpurchase evaluation updates the consumer's mental files, affecting perceptions of the brand and similar purchase decisions in the future.

This story is common for a high-involvement purchase decision. Of course, if Chris' decision had merely involved the purchase of a pack of gum, the process would have been significantly simpler.

Chris may typify a particular group of consumers, and that is important to marketers. Marketers are interested in defining target markets and developing effective marketing strategies for groups of consumers who share similar characteristics, needs, motives, and buying habits. These are the subjects of market segmentation and the marketing mix, the focus of Chapter 6.

People BEHIND the Ads

Courtesy of Jon Steel

Jon Steel has been named "West Coast Executive of the Year," "Agency Innovator," one of the "100 smartest people in the Bay Area," and a member of the Advertising Federation Hall of Achievement for executives under 40. Lee Clow, the famous CEO of TBWA Chiat/Day, called him "one of the great practitioners in advertising today."

What has Steel done to earn such accolades? The answer, at least in part, is that he helped change the way advertising is done in the United States. During a wildly successful run at Goodby Silverstein & Partners, Steel became both the greatest advocate for and greatest practitioner of account planning.

Steel traces the origins of the planner role to the kind of advertising created by industry legend William Bernbach (see People behind the Ads, Chapter 2). You might remember that Bernbach was a strong critic of the formulaic ads of the 1950s. More than anything, Bernbach believed that advertising should respect rather than pander to the consumer.

And just what is account planning? Some view it as a hybrid of research and strategy that places the consumer front and center. At Steel's first agency, England's Boase Massimi Pollitt (BMP), account planning developed when founder Stanley Pollitt insisted that account managers and researchers work together in teams, much as copywriters and art directors do in creative departments. Pollitt thought the

consumer was often forgotten after researchers handed control of a campaign over to account people and creatives. The account planner would maintain a consumer focus throughout the campaign and serve, in Steel's words, as the "conscience" of the agency.

Would you make a good account planner? Steel believes that great planners share some obvious characteristics such as intellect, curiosity, facility with both left- and right-brain thinking, and well-honed written and oral communication skills. Less obvious but equally important are modesty and humility, an interest in listening rather than speaking, and talent for building relationships with a broad range of people. And least obvious of all, Steel believes that account planners have to be, well, just a little weird. "Almost all of the good planners I have known are a little out of the ordinary. This manifests itself in two main ways: In a somewhat off-center perspective on situations and a rather eclectic mix of background and interests." To prove the point he lists the backgrounds of some of the best: professional chess player, musician, aeronautical engineer, classics scholar, and a killer whale trainer at Sea World.

Jon Steel was born and grew up in England, earning a degree from Nottingham University in geography. He was interviewed for an account management position at BMP, but his interviewer spotted skills that fit better with a planning job. It was Steel's good fortune that BMP had pioneered account planning as early as 1968 and was well known for using the approach.

By the late 1980s, U.S. agencies recognized that the best ads in the world were being done in England, not the United States. A big factor in London's excellence was the widespread use of account planning. But there really wasn't anyone practicing it in the United States.

Goodby Silverstein & Partners, a respected San Francisco agency, went right to the source, and recruited Steel to develop account planning at the agency in 1989. Steel came to America prepared to shake things up. For example, believing that focus groups are often designed more for the comfort of brand managers sitting behind one-way mirrors than for the consumer, Steel insisted that planners venture out into consumers' "native habitats." So to help pitch a campaign for Sega, Steel and his colleagues invaded the bedrooms of kids to watch them playing video games. His book recounts a funny story of a six-year-old bounding out of a closet in a super-hero costume and biting the arm of one of the Goodby planners. Goodby got the account.

Clearly account planning was a different way to do developmental research, and as the Sega work demonstrated, it could even be a bit dangerous! But was it a better way to develop great ads? By almost any measure the answer is yes. During Steel's tenure at Goodby, the agency's billings surged tenfold. The creative work was stunning as well, as the agency produced award-winning ads for clients like Sega, Norwegian

Cruise Lines, Porsche, the Partnership for a Drug-Free America, and the California Fluid Milk Processors Advisory Board (the famous "Got Milk" campaign).

Steel eventually left Goodby and now works for one of the largest advertising companies in the world, the WPP group, where he directs the marketing fellowship program. He has also produced two wonderful books on the advertising business, *Truth, Lies & Advertising,* published in 1998, and more recently *Perfect Pitch.*

Jon Steel graciously answered some questions for students of *Contemporary Advertising:*

CA: How did you help to bring planning to America?

Steel: At the time I joined GS&P, planning was still in its infancy in the United States. Jay Chiat had introduced it a few years before, famously declaring it "the best new business tool ever invented." And with great planners like Jane Newman, M.T. Rainey, and Rob White, Chiat/Day did indeed win a lot of new business. For a while planning was Chiat/Day's Unique Selling Proposition, but planning alone was not responsible for the agency's success. Chiat/Day won new business and produced great work, because of the combination of some very good planners with an excellent creative department.

When I moved from BMP in London to start a planning department in San Francisco, many people assumed that I would be "introducing BMP-style planning to Goodby." That was never my intention, because the most effective planning evolves from an agency culture; it's never the other way around. Goodby Silverstein was founded on the desire to be the best advertising agency in the world ("as judged by our peers and by our effectiveness in the marketplace"). That meant that creative excellence and relevance walked hand-in-hand from the start, and thus it was a fertile environment for planners who shared those beliefs.

I'd like to think that in the time I was responsible for planning at Goodby, I developed a model of planning that was more agile than that traditionally practiced at BMP and other British agencies. If we had six months to develop strategic recommendations then we could take six months, but if we only had six days then we were still capable of delivering something interesting. Our aim was always to create the best possible solution, not to show how clever we were. The planners were there both as an aid to creativity and as a reality check. But most important, the style of planning we practiced was designed solely for that agency. It's not easily transplanted elsewhere, and it was very hard for experienced planners to come in from the outside and ply their trade effectively. (Many of my most successful planners were home-grown, hired straight out of school and trained inside the agency environment.)

CA: Two of your own advertising heroes are Howard Gossage and William Bernbach. What did you admire most about each man? How have they influenced your own career?

Steel: Bill Bernbach changed the face of advertising by putting art directors and copywriters together for the first time. It probably seems ridiculous now, but there was a time when the copy department and the art department were separate, and copy was sent along the corridor or to a different floor for someone else to make it look nice. The idea of the creative team ultimately changed the way all agencies work, and the campaigns that came out of Doyle, Dane, Bernbach inspired generation after generation of creative talent to come into the business.

Even if he never employed anyone in his agency with the word *planner* on their business card, Bill Bernbach valued human insights and substance as much as the artistry and poetry that his "new advertising" embodied. "At the heart of an effective creative philosophy," he once said, "is the belief that nothing is so powerful as an insight into human nature, what compulsions drive a man, what instincts dominate his action, even though his language so often camouflages what really motivates him." For the last 20 years I have found myself searching for such insights, attempting to fuse research and creativity so that my clients don't talk at people but rather *with* them; so that members of our audience don't just hear a message and understand it, but instead *feel* it.

Gossage is a legend in San Francisco, but not as well known and, therefore, less influential than Bernbach in the wider world of advertising. But Jeff Goodby, Andy Berlin, and Rich Silverstein were big fans of Gossage's work and for that reason he probably had the greater direct influence on my career.

"Is advertising worth saving?" he wrote. "From an economic point of view I don't think that most of it is. From an aesthetic point of view I'm damn sure it's not; it is thoughtless, boring, and there is simply too much of it." In his view advertising was an uninvited guest in people's homes, and being uninvited he felt it should not only behave impeccably, but also give something in return for the attention paid to it. Gossage believed in interactive advertising about 40 years before technology made it possible for lesser mortals; he put a coupon on every print ad, not as a simple transactional device but rather as a way of establishing a two-way dialogue with his readers.

CA: What else would you like to share with students of the industry?

Steel: My advice? Always remember: it's only advertising. No one's going to die, so don't take it so seriously. And the less seriously you take it, the better the work will be.

Chapter Summary

Marketing is the process companies use to make a profit by satisfying their customers' needs. Marketing focuses on the special relationship between a customer's needs and a product's utility. The essence of marketing is the perceived equal-value exchange. Need satisfaction is the customer's goal and should be the marketer's goal as well.

Advertising is concerned with the promotion aspect of the marketing process. It is one of several tools marketers use to inform, persuade, and remind groups of customers (markets) about the need-satisfying value of their products and services. Advertising's effectiveness depends on the communication skill of the advertising person. It also depends on the extent to which firms correctly implement other marketing activities, such as market research, pricing, and distribution.

There are three categories of participants in the marketing process: customers, markets, and marketers. To reach customers and markets, advertisers must effectively blend data from the behavioral sciences with the communicating arts. Advertisers study the behavioral characteristics of large groups of people to create advertising aimed at those groups.

Successful advertising people understand the complexity of consumer behavior, which is governed by three personal processes: perception, learning and persuasion, and motivation. These processes determine how consumers see the world around them, how they learn information and habits, and how they actualize their personal needs and motives. Two sets of influences also affect consumer behavior: interpersonal influences (the consumer's family, society, and culture) and nonpersonal influences (time, place, and environment). These factors combine to determine how the consumer behaves, and their influence differs considerably from one country to another. Advertisers evaluate the effect of these factors on groups of consumers to determine how best to create their messages.

Once prospects are motivated to satisfy their needs and wants, the purchase process begins. Based on certain standards, they evaluate various alternative products (the evoked set). If none of the alternatives meet their evaluative criteria, they may reject or postpone the purchase. If they do buy, they may experience cognitive dissonance. The result of the postpurchase evaluation will greatly affect the customer's attitude toward future purchases.

Important Terms

attitude, *157*
brand interest, *157*
brand loyalty, *157*
business markets, *149*
centers of influence, *149*
central route to persuasion, *155*
classical conditioning, *154*
cognition, *153*
consumer behavior, *151*
consumer decision process, *151*
consumer markets, *149*
culture, *164*
current customers, *149*
Elaboration Likelihood Model, *155*
environments, *165*
evaluation of alternatives, *151*
evaluative criteria, *166*
evoked set, *166*
exchange, *145*
government markets, *150*

habit, *157*
hierarchy of needs, *158*
industrial markets, *150*
informational motives, *160*
interpersonal influences, *151*
learning, *154*
market, *144*
marketers, *151*
marketing, *144*
mental files, *154*
motivation, *158*
needs, *158*
negatively originated motives, *160*
nonpersonal influences, *151*
operant conditioning, *154*
opinion leader, *163*
organizational buyers, *151*
perception, *152*
peripheral route to persuasion, *156*

personal processes, *151*
persuasion, *155*
physiological screens, *153*
positively originated motives, *160*
postpurchase dissonance, *166*
postpurchase evaluation, *151*
prospective customers, *149*
psychological screens, *153*
reference groups, *163*
reseller markets, *150*
social classes, *161*
social cognitive theory, *155*
stimulus, *153*
subculture, *165*
theory of cognitive dissonance, *166*
transformational motives, *160*
transnational (global) markets, *150*
utility, *145*
wants, *158*

Review Questions

1. What is marketing, and what is the role IMC plays in the marketing process?

2. How does product utility relate to IMC?

3. Why is the perceived equal-value exchange an important campaign issue?

4. What is the difference between a *customer* and a *market*? What are the different types of markets?

5. What does the term *consumer behavior* refer to, and why is it important to marketers?

6. Which consumer behavior process presents the greatest challenge to marketers?

7. What is the difference between the central route and the peripheral route to persuasion?

8. What is the significance of negatively originated motives and positively originated motives for IMC planners?

9. What are some of the environmental influences on consumer behavior in international markets?

10. How does the theory of cognitive dissonance relate to IMC?

The Advertising Experience

1. Cognitive Dissonance

Describe an incident of cognitive dissonance that you (or someone you interview) felt after a significant purchase. Discuss the feelings generated by this purchase and what happened to those feelings. For example, perhaps the purchaser felt better over time as the quality and value of the product became evident. Finally, discuss what the company could have done to make the buyer feel better during the period of cognitive dissonance.

2. Consumer Behavior

Understanding consumer behavior is essential to the contemporary advertiser. Browse the Websites listed below, keeping in mind what you learned about culture/subculture, social class, reference groups, family/household, and opinion leaders. Identify and describe the major social influences that enable each organization to be successful in reaching its consumers.

- Beechnut: www.beechnut.com
- Ben & Jerry's: www.benjerry.com
- CNN: www.cnn.com
- Motorola: www.motorola.com
- Music Television (MTV): www.mtv.com

- Oprah: www.oprah.com
- PetSmart: www.petsmart.com
- Facebook: www.facebook.com
- See's Candies: www.sees.com
- Google: www.google.com
- Xbox: www.xbox.com

3. Motivation and Interpersonal Influences

Review the Websites in Exercise 2 in terms of Maslow's hierarchy of needs. Find three instances of appeals to each of the five basic needs. Next, discuss what kind of people might seek to satisfy each of these needs with the particular products. Finally, consider opinion leaders whose testimonies could be added to each site. How could these leaders strengthen the appeal of the site for the consumers who have unsatisfied needs?

4. Write narratives for two hypothetical customers (like Chris and the tablet on pages 164, 165): one who wants a Taco Bell chihuahua, and one who needs a chalupa. Use Exhibit 5-1 (page 150) for guidance.

5. Analyze Apple's advertising strategy using theories of learning and the Elaboration Likelihood Model (see Exhibit 5-3, page 153).

6

Market Segmentation and the Marketing Mix: Determinants of Campaign Strategy

Learning Objectives

To describe how marketers use behavioral characteristics to cluster prospective customers into market segments. Because no product or service pleases everybody, marketers need to select specific target markets that offer the greatest sales potential. Thus, they can fine-tune their mix of product-related elements (the four Ps), including IMC, to match the needs or wants of the target market.

 studying this chapter, you will be able to:

LO6-1   Define market segmentation and describe its purposes.

LO6-2   Explain the target marketing process.

LO6-3   Show how IMC is used with the product element in marketing.

LO6-4   Illustrate how IMC is used with the price element in marketing.

LO6-5   Review how IMC is used with the place element in marketing.

LO6-6   Discuss how IMC is used with the communication element in marketing.

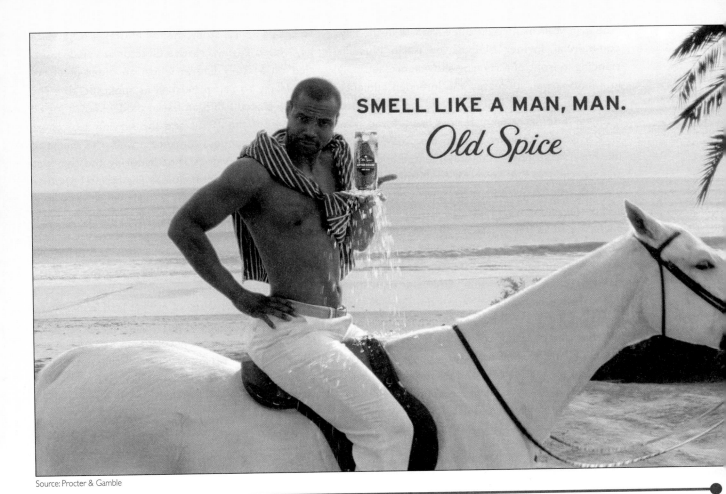

SMELL LIKE A MAN, MAN.

Old Spice

Source: Procter & Gamble

■MC success is not just about what you say, but to whom you say it. Case in point, perhaps the best IMC campaign of 2011, the Old Spice "Man your man could smell like" promotion. A key secret to the campaign's success? Addressing the ads for a male body wash . . . to women. Targeting women for a male brand was certainly not a conventional approach, but then, just about everything about this campaign was unusual. To fully appreciate the ads, let's see why Old Spice needed to produce a game-changing campaign in the first place. ■ Old Spice was first sold in the 1930s. Owned by consumer giant Procter & Gamble (P&G), Old Spice first became a consumer staple as a men's after-shave lotion. Later, as male consumers showed interest in other grooming products, including deodorants and liquid soaps, Old Spice introduced brand extensions to meet those demands. ■ In 1983 P&G's global archrival, Unilever, introduced Axe. As a younger

product, Axe had credibility in positioning itself as a sexy alternative. While Old Spice ads over the years have tended to be safe and conventional, Axe has used provocative spots suggesting the brand makes men irresistible to beautiful women.[1] ■ However implausible the "irresistibility" appeal may seem, it's worked. By the 2000s, Axe established a healthy lead in share of the market. ■ In 2010, Proctor & Gamble had to consider whether to invest in a mature brand or move on. It decided to assign the challenge of reinvigorating Old Spice to one of the world's greatest agencies, Wieden+Kennedy. W+K built its reputation by making Nike a world leader in footwear. Their new challenge would be making Old Spice fresh, relevant, even hip.[2] ■ Before starting, the agency and client made a big decision. They would create ads that appealed to men (who use body wash) but spoke directly to women (who often buy it for them). The campaign slogan would be "the man your man could smell like." ■ In the first commercial, former NFL player Isaiah Mustafa, standing in front of a running shower, dressed only in a bath towel, addressed the intended audience right from the start. "Hello ladies," he confidently intoned, "Look at your man, now back to me, now back at your man, now back to me. Sadly, he isn't me. But if he stopped using lady-scented body wash and switched to Old Spice, he could smell like he's me."[3] ■ The fast-paced and somewhat absurd style and pacing, along with Mustafa's charm and humor, made the ad an immediate hit. Old Spice was back. ■ But now what? Advertising is filled with "one-hit wonder" campaigns that quickly fizzle. So Wieden+ Kennedy changed the game. After the Old Spice campaign drew national attention, the agency began using Mustafa in social media, developing dozens of different, personalized executions for key influencers like Ellen DeGeneres. Naturally Ellen was flattered and invited Mustafa on her show. More buzz for Old Spice. And a Cannes Grand Prix for the campaign.[4] ■ W+K still wasn't done. They decided to create a viral story line for Mustafa's "Old Spice guy." Jason Bagley, creative director at Wieden, settled on a story line in which an older celebrity would try to usurp Mustafa as spokesperson. The agency picked Fabio, an Italian model known for ad work from the 1990s and for serving as a cover model for countless romance novels. The theme of over 100 viral videos shot featuring the two was "Mano a Mano en el Baño." ■ The results? Another win for Old Spice. During a single week the videos were watched more than 20 million times. The number one and four spots for most viewed channels on YouTube were held by Old Spice and New Old Spice Guy Fabio. And the brand attracted nearly 70,000 new fans on Facebook.[5] And best of all, Old Spice regained its share of market lead from Axe as sales increased dramatically. The Old Spice ads have received about as many accolades as a campaign can attract. And W+K have solidified their reputation as an amazing creative shop. And it all started with a decision to tout the benefits of male body wash to women.[6]

Market Segmentation

LO 6-1

Marketing people constantly search for clusters of consumers who might be better satisfied. The process of **market segmentation** involves two steps: *identifying groups of people* (or organizations) with certain shared needs and *aggregating* (combining) these groups into larger market segments according to their interest in the brand's utility. This process should result in market segments large enough to target and reachable through a mix of marketing activities.

Markets often consist of many segments. A company may offer different products and use distinct marketing strategies for every segment, or concentrate its marketing activities on only one or a few segments. Either task is far from simple. Toyota, a company best known for selling cars to middle-class Americans, developed its Scion line to appeal to the 63 million generation Ys. It also markets Lexus to wealthier, older consumers. And Toyota sells these cars around the globe. Catering to all these needs on a global level requires a sophisticated marketing and communications system. In this chapter, we look first at how marketers identify and categorize *consumer markets* and second at the techniques they use to segment *business markets*. Then we discuss various IMC strategies companies use to match their products with markets and create profitable exchanges.

Segmenting the Consumer Market

The concept of *shared characteristics* is critical to market segmentation. Marketing and advertising people know that consumer needs and wants can be identified from consumer "footprints in the sand"—the telltale signs of where they live and work, what they buy, and how they spend their leisure time. By following these footprints, marketers can

Old Spice helped keep the buzz going and fans flocking to its social media by introducing Fabio to the campaign.

Source: Procter & Gamble

locate and define groups of consumers with similar needs and wants, create messages for them, and know how and where to send their messages. The goal is to find that particular niche, or space in the market, where the marketer's product or service will fit. Consider the Old Spice story you read at the beginning of the chapter. For a moment, think about what you can determine about the brand's target market. Old Spice's research has revealed that men will use the product if women buy it for them. The campaign encourages women to help their partner's stop using "lady-scented body wash." The category of "men" is narrowed to men with the following characteristics: they are in relationships and already use liquid soap. This is a much smaller, but presumably more valuable segment than just "men."

Marketers group these shared characteristics into categories (*behavioristic, geographic, demographic,* and *psychographic*) to identify and segment consumer markets (see Exhibit 6-1). Most marketers have two goals: first, to identify people who are likely to be interested in a brand's benefits; and second, to develop a mix of effective messages that can help these consumers understand the benefits.

Behavioristic Segmentation

A straightforward way to segment markets is to group consumers by buying behavior. This is called **behavioristic segmentation.** Behavioral segments are determined by many variables, but the most important are *user status, usage rate, purchase occasion,* and *benefits sought.* These categories tell us who our customers are now, when and why they buy, and how much they consume.

Variables	Typical Breakdowns	Variables	Typical Breakdowns
Geographic		**Demographic**	
Region	Pacific; Mountain; West North Central; West South Central; East North Central; East South Central; South Atlantic; Middle Atlantic; New England	Age	Under 6, 6–11, 12–19, 20–34, 35–49, 50–64, 65+
		Sex	Male, female
County size	A, B, C, D	Family size	1–2, 3–4, 5+
Climate	Northern; southern	Family life cycle	Young, single; young, married, no children; young, married, youngest child under 6;
City or SMSA size	Under 5,000; 5,000–19,999; 20,000–49,999; 50,000–99,999; 100,000–249,000; 250,000–499,999; 500,000–999,999; 1,000,000–3,999,999; 4,000,000 or over		young, married, youngest child 6 or over; young, unmarried, with children; older, married, with children; older, unmarried, with children; older, married, no children under 18; older, single; other
Density	Urban, suburban, rural	Income	Under $10,000; $10,000–20,000; $20,000–30,000; $30,000–40,000; $40,000–60,000; $60,000–100,000; $100,000–150,000; $150,000 and over
Behavioristic			
Purchase occasion	Regular occasion, special occasion	Occupation	Professional and technical; managers, officials, and proprietors; clerical, sales; craftspeople, supervisors; operatives; farmers; retired; students; homemakers; unemployed
Benefits sought	Economy, convenience, prestige		
User status	Nonuser; ex-user; potential user; first-time user; regular user		
Usage rate	Light user, medium user, heavy user	Education	Grade school or less; some high school; high school graduates; some college; college graduates
Loyalty status	None, medium, strong, absolute		
Readiness stage	Unaware, aware, informed, interested, desirous, intending to buy	Religion	Catholic, Protestant, Jewish, Muslim, other
Marketing factor sensitivity	Quality, price, service, advertising, sales promotion	Race	White, Black, Asian, other
		Nationality	American, British, French, German, Scandinavian, Italian, Latin American, Middle Eastern, Japanese, other
Psychographic			
Societal divisions	Upper crust, movers and shakers, successful singles, social security, middle of the road, metro ethnic mix		
Lifestyle	Strivers, achievers, actualizers		
Personality	Compulsive, gregarious, authoritarian, ambitious		

Exhibit 6-1

Methods for segmenting consumer markets.

Old Spice is a mature brand. But with the use of clever, witty, and even somewhat absurd advertising, the brand rebounded strongly. Wieden+Kennedy's great work suggests that with the right message, brands can find their own Fountain of Youth, as exemplified in the ad above depicting a robot in a hot tub on a date with two attractive models.
Source: Procter & Gamble

User-Status Variables   Many markets can be segmented by the **user status** of prospective customers. Researchers Stephan and Tannenholz have identified six categories of consumers based on user status.

Sole users choose one brand exclusively. These consumers are the most brand loyal and require the least amount of promotion. *Semi-sole users* typically use Brand A but have an alternative selection if it is not available or if the alternative is promoted with a discount. *Discount users* are the semi-sole users of competing Brand B. They don't buy Brand A at full price but will consider buying it at a discount. *Aware nontriers* use competitive products in the category but haven't taken a liking to Brand A. A different advertising message could help, but these people rarely offer much potential. *Trial/rejectors* responded to Brand A's IMC messages but didn't like the product. More promoting won't help; only a reformulation of Brand A will bring them back. *Repertoire users* perceive two or more brands to have superior attributes and will buy at full price. They are the primary brand switchers and respond to persuasive information based on their fluctuating wants and desires. Therefore, they should be the primary target for brand messages.[7]

Usage-Rate Variables   It's usually easier to get a heavy user to use more than a light user. In **volume segmentation**, marketers measure people's **usage rates** to define consumers as light, medium, or heavy users of products (see Exhibit 6-2). One well-known rule of thumb suggests that 20 percent of all users consume 80 percent of the product. Marketers want to define that 20 percent and aim their advertising at them. Hardee's, a fast-food hamburger chain owned by CKE Restaurants, Inc., even has a pet name for its prized 17- to 34-year-old male market segment: the HFFU (pronounced who-foo). According to Andrew Pudzer, CKE's CEO, "That's the 'heavy fast-food user,' someone who eats there four or five times a week. . . . It is the sweet spot of the industry and what appeals to him is drippy, messy burgers. He is not interested in little 99-cent burgers or low-carb anything. He's not a big calorie counter."[8]

Repertoire users are concerned with quality. In this ad, by equating Rolex to gold, Rolex attracts consumers who are willing to pay a premium for a watch with added luxury.
Source: Rolex

PURE ROLEX.

ROLEX

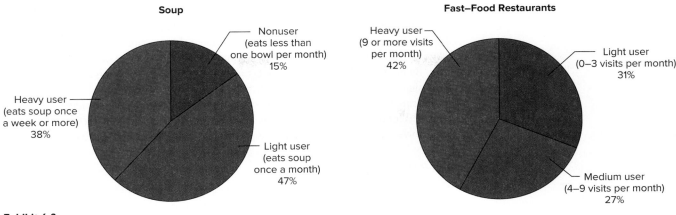

Exhibit 6-2
Usage rates vary for different products.

Source: Used by permission of Mediamark Research and Intelligence. *Journal of Advertising Research* (www.warc.com/jar). Reprinted with permission.

By finding similarities among heavy users of their products, marketers can define product differences and focus campaigns more effectively. For example, independent business-people who travel at their own expense, the group that Fallon Worldwide describes as "road warriors," are heavy users of budget hotel chains, with some spending over a hundred nights a year on the road. In creating a campaign that targeted this group for Holiday Inn Express, Fallon also discovered that road warriors make their travel plans at the beginning of the week and like to watch ESPN, CNN, and the Weather Channel. Such knowledge helped Fallon media people schedule messages when and where the target audience would be attentive.

Marketers of one product sometimes find their customers are also heavy users of other products and can define target markets in terms of the usage rates of the other products. Research indicates that heavy users of organic foods spend more on fruits and vegetables and less on prepared foods than do nonorganic food users.[9] Similarly, Claritas[10] suggests that the cluster they refer to as "Second City Elite" are much more likely than the typical American to enjoy cultural activities (books, attending theater and dance productions), are more likely to read magazines and to drive Lexus cars.

Purchase-Occasion Variables   Buyers can also be distinguished by when they buy or use a product or service—the **purchase occasion.** Air travelers, for example, may fly for business or vacation, so one airline might promote business travel while another promotes tourism. The purchase occasion might be affected by frequency of need (regular or occasional), a fad (candy, computer games), or seasons (water skis, raincoats). The Japan Weather Association tracked buying patterns on 20,000 items and correlated them to the outside temperature. Not surprisingly, when the temperature goes up, people buy more sunshades, air conditioners, watermelons, and swimwear. When there's a chill in the air, sales of suits, sweaters, and heaters take off.[11] A marketer who discovers common purchase occasions for a group has a potential target segment and can better determine when to run specials and how to promote certain product categories.

Benefits-Sought Variables   Marketers frequently segment according to the *benefits* being sought. Consumers seek various **benefits** in the products they buy—high quality, low price, status, sex appeal, good taste, health consciousness. A teenaged consumer getting lunch at McDonald's may be searching for an inexpensive, filling meal, while a parent with two young children might be looking for a place to enjoy a hot cup of coffee while the kids frolic in the restaurant playground. In addition to tangible benefits, customers are often motivated by *symbolism*—what the brand name means to them, to associates, or to some social reference group. **Benefit segmentation** is the prime objective of many consumer attitude studies and the basis for many successful ad campaigns.

Some product categories are characterized by substantial *brand switching* from one purchase occasion to the next. Researchers have determined that switching occurs in response to

Crest is a leader in identifying the benefits sought by consumers. This ad addresses one: whiter teeth. How many other dental-hygiene benefits can you think of? And how might these be addressed in a different ad?

Source: Procter & Gamble

different "need states" that consumers may experience from one occasion to another. Thus, a soft drink company competes not just for *drinkers* (users) but for *drinks* (occasions) based on the benefits the consumer is seeking at that moment. For example, a consumer who might not ordinarily buy ginger ale may do so during the holidays when he or she is having family visit. By measuring the importance of occasion-based motives, marketers can determine if a campaign needs to reposition the product.[12]

Using behavioristic segmentation, we can accomplish the first step of identifying likely prospects for our marketing efforts. The next step in developing rich profiles of these customers involves the use of geographic, demographic, and psychographic characteristics.

Geographic Segmentation

One simple way to define markets is by using **geographic segmentation.** People in one region of the country (or the world) have needs, wants, and purchasing habits that differ from those in other regions. People in Sunbelt states, for example, buy more sunscreen. Canadians buy special equipment for dealing with snow and ice—products many Floridians have never seen in stores.

When marketers analyze geographic data, they study sales by region, county size, city size, zip code, and types of stores. Many products sell well in urban areas but poorly in suburban or rural ones, and vice versa. As we'll see in Chapter 9, geographic information is critical in developing advertising media schedules because, with limited budgets, marketers want to advertise in areas where their sales potential is best.

Even in local markets, geographic segmentation is important. For example, a local progressive politician might send a mailer only to precincts where voters typically support liberal causes, and a retail store rarely draws customers from outside a fairly limited *trading area.*

One of the most respected geographic segmentation systems is Prizm, a product of Nielsen. Marketers have used the Prizm system for more than 30 years, and it is updated every 10 years with census results, most recently in 2010. Prizm analyzes urbanization measures, as well as household and neighborhood characteristics, in order to assign every U.S. zip code to one of 66 geographic segments with vivid descriptors that include "Young Digerati," "Money and Brains," "Bohemian Mix," and "American Dreams."

Demographic Segmentation

Demographic segmentation is a way to define population groups by their statistical characteristics: sex, age, ethnicity, education, occupation, income, and other quantifiable factors. Demographics are often combined with geographic segmentation to select target markets for advertising. This is called **geodemographic segmentation.** For example, research shows that people who identify themselves as "strongly Hispanic" tend to be very loyal to certain brands. And, as Exhibit 6-3 reveals, the numbers of Americans with Hispanic ancestry are expected to grow at a rate much faster than that of the overall population well into this century. This has meant a surge in advertising dollars allocated to Hispanic media. Many blue-chip advertisers, such as Procter & Gamble, AT&T, McDonald's, and General Motors, now aim a significant portion of their advertising specifically at this market, which reached nearly $1.2 trillion in 2010.[13] To do so efficiently, they measure the size of the "strongly Hispanic" community in each marketing area they plan to target, as well as its income, age distribution, and attitudes. JCPenney, for example, discovered that its Sandra Salcedo line of clothing for Hispanic women sold well in Texas and Northern California stores but not in heavily Mexican American Los Angeles, where urban influences hold greater sway. This is an excellent reminder that focusing on one consumer influence to the exclusion of others is usually overly simplistic.[14]

Best Buy discovered a large untapped market after data-mining technology revealed that women customers were being underserved in the company's stores. In an effort to boost sales to this demographic group, Best Buy opened 68 concept stores staffed with salespeople trained to provide information tailored to the needs of female shoppers. "We are enabling her transformation into a big-time electronics buyer by talking her language," noted Best Buy vice president, Nancy Brooks.[15]

Exhibit 6-3

Projected U.S. Hispanic population and Hispanic media ad spending growth rates.

Year	Hispanic	Total U.S.	Hisp. % Total
2000	35,621,721	282,124,631	12.6
2005	41,800,971	295,507,134	14.1
2010	47,755,585	308,935,581	15.5
2015	53,647,237	322,365,787	16.6
2020	59,755,555	335,804,546	17.8
2025	66,190,911	349,439,199	18.9
2030	73,055,166	363,584,435	20.1
2035	80,242,372	377,886,238	21.2
2040	87,584,907	391,945,658	22.3
2045	95,025,560	405,862,392	23.4
2050	102,559,846	419,853,587	24.4

Source: U.S. Census Bureau.

Hipsanic Media Spending Change vs. all U.S. Measured Media

Source: Hispanic Fact Pack, Supplement to *Advertising Age*, 2014 Edition.

As people mature and their incomes change, so do their interests in various product categories (see Exhibit 6-4). The biggest generational cohort as of 2015[16] is Millennials, whose numbers now just slightly exceed those of Baby Boomers. Millennials are consumers who in 2015 are between 18 and 34, and they number about 75 million.[17] Naturally, many businesses want to better understand how to successfully market to these new, increasingly affluent young consumers. Car seller AutoTrader interviewed a large group of Millennials and found similarities, and differences, between the cohort and those that came before it. For example, Millennials, like the other groups, are status-conscious and like luxury car brands. As a result, car makers such as BMW are creating lower priced, entry-level models. But unlike other generations, Millennials spend much more time shopping online, especially on their phones.

Exhibit 6-4

Heavy usage patterns of various age groups.

Age	Name of Age Group	Merchandise Purchased
0–5	Young children	Baby food, toys, nursery furniture, children's wear
6–19	Schoolchildren and teenagers	Clothing, sporting goods, CDs and DVDs, school supplies, fast food, soft drinks, candy, cosmetics, movies
20–34	Young adults	Cars, furniture, housing, food and beer, clothing, diamonds, home entertainment equipment, recreational equipment, purchases for younger age segments
35–49	Younger middle-aged	Larger homes, better cars, second cars, new furniture, computers, recreational equipment, jewelry, clothing, food and wine
50–64	Older middle-aged	Recreational items, purchases for young marrieds and infants, travel
65 and over	Senior adults	Medical services, travel, pharmaceuticals, purchases for younger age groups

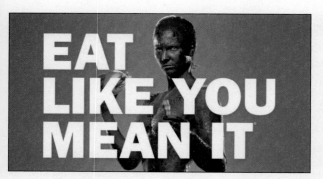

"Eat like you mean it" is a great tagline because it identifies the audience (individuals looking for a juicy, large hamburger) and the benefit (you can find those burgers at Hardee's).

Source: Carl's Jr. Restaurants LLC

Dealerships are finding that Millennials are well-educated about their options and car prices when they begin negotiations over a new car purchase. [18]

Demographic segmentation is vital in the fast-food industry, or QSR (quick-serve restaurant) industry, as it now prefers to be called. McDonald's, the industry's creator and perpetual frontrunner, runs the table. Once stigmatized as unsanitary meat fit only for poor people, chains like White Castle and McDonald's helped change the hamburger's image, fashioning it into the national cuisine by the 1950s.[19] Now, children are McDonald's primary target consumers. Decades of ads for Happy Meals and toys have made an impression. Among fictional characters, Ronald McDonald's cultural penetration is surpassed only by Santa Claus: 96 percent of schoolchildren in the United States can identify the yellow-jumpsuited clown.[20] Against this giant's brand value and advertising expenditures, competitors have returned to the hamburger's traditional consumer, the young male. In the segment where McDonald's is slightly weaker, Hardee's intends to be strong. Thickburger TV spots proclaim that consumers should "eat like you mean it."

In international markets, the demographics of many populations are changing rapidly. From India to Brazil to Poland, middle-class life is becoming available to more people. This emerging middle class has an insatiable appetite for consumer goods—everything from 3-D TVs and iPads to smartphones, cars, and refrigerators.[21] Currently, nearly 1.6 million Indian families spend an average of $9,000 annually on high-end goods.[22] China has emerged as one of the world's fastest-growing advertising markets as companies try to reach that country's increasingly wealthy consumers. According to CTR Market Research, China now ranks just behind the United States and Japan in the global advertising market.[23]

Geographic and demographic data provide information about markets but little about the psychology of individuals. In many instances, people in the same demographic or geographic segment have widely differing product preferences and TV viewing habits. Rarely can demographic criteria alone predict purchase behavior.[24] That's why marketers use *psychographics*.

Psychographic Segmentation

With **psychographics,** marketers group people by their values, attitudes, personality, and lifestyle. Psychographics enables marketers to view people as individuals with feelings and inclinations. Then they can classify people according to what they believe, the way they live, and the products, services, and media they use.[25]

Perhaps the best-known psychographic classification system is VALS ("Values, Attitudes And Lifestyles"), a product of SRI Consulting Business Intelligence (SRIC-BI). VALS assigns consumers to one of eight groups based on two dimensions: **primary motivation** and **resources.** According to SRIC-BI, individuals are primarily motivated by one of three things: ideals (or basic principles), achievement (tangible markers of success or accomplishment), or self-expression (a desire for experiences or to take risks). In addition, people possess varying levels of resources, which include money, education, or self-confidence. Those with the fewest resources are placed near the bottom of the VALS typology, while those with the most are at the top (see Exhibit 6-5).[26]

The purpose of VALS is to help marketers identify whom to target, uncover what the target group buys and does, locate where concentrations of the target group live, identify how best to communicate with them, and gain insight into why the target group behaves the way it does. The system has been applied to a variety of areas: new product development and design, target marketing, product positioning, advertising message development, and media planning, to name a few.[27]

In one case, for example, a foreign car manufacturer used VALS to reposition its sports utility vehicle after its award-winning but ineffective television campaign failed to result in higher sales. Using VALS, the company targeted a new "rebellious" consumer group with a new campaign using a "breaking the rules" theme. Nothing changed but the advertising. But sales increased 60 percent in six months.[28]

Later, SRIC-BI developed additional VALS products: Japan-VALS to determine the consumer effect of changing values and social behavior in Japan, and GeoVALS to determine where target customers live and show why they behave the way they do. This helps advertisers select the best site locations, target direct-mail campaigns effectively, and maximize advertising dollars.[29]

Exhibit 6-5

The VALS classification system places consumers with abundant resources—psychological, physical, and material means and capacities—near the top of the chart and those with minimal resources near the bottom. The chart segments consumers by their basis for decision making: ideals, achievement, or self-expression. The boxes intersect to indicate that some categories may be considered together. For instance, a marketer may categorize Thinkers and Believers together.

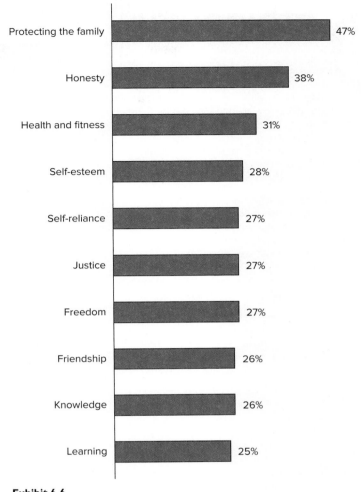

Exhibit 6-6

The world's top 10 values shared by people around the world.

In Europe and Asia, numerous lifestyle studies have produced a variety of other classification systems intended to help marketers understand the product use of different target groups across national boundaries. The research company RISC investigated how people react to social changes in 12 European countries. The basis of the research was the belief that when individuals share similar values, perceptions, and sensitivities, their purchasing behavior will also show consistent similarities. Roper Starch Worldwide has developed its ValueScope service to help marketers find "shared patterns of market space behavior" around the world in order to conduct global campaigns. The Roper model uses three drivers of consumer behavior—nationality, lifestage, and values—to define six consumer segments: creatives, fun seekers, intimates, strivers, devouts, and altruists.[30] An interesting aspect of Roper's research was the discovery of the top 10 values shared by people around the world (see Exhibit 6-6).

Another psychographic segmentation scheme is MindBase, (see Exhibit 6-7), which divides consumers into eight psychological categories, including "I am driven" (motto: nothing ventured, nothing gained) and "I measure twice" (motto: an ounce of prevention). Yankelovich developed the system after discovering that people with similar demographic backgrounds were very different in motives and feelings. The company's data also suggest that the groups differ in their receptivity to marketing messages and rely on different media.[31]

Simmons offers a psychographic tool called BehaviorGraphics. This classification scheme is based on attitudes and lifestyle measures, including information about the products that consumers like and the media they consume. The tool aggregates consumers into 31 different

Ethical Issues

The Youngest Target Market

Imagine you are a brand manager looking to uncover opportunities with a new target market. What is the youngest age group you would consider from the perspective of effectiveness? How about from the perspective of ethics?

Would you consider marketing to infants or children under 3? Seem too young? Not to Disney, or a growing number of other marketers. The following story was reported in *Adweek*:

Jenny Gill was in [the] hospital earlier this year for the birth of her son, Jack, when a photographer stopped by to take snapshots of the mother and newborn. The practice is common in hospitals, but what the photographer did next surprised Gill.

"In the middle of taking the pictures, she pulls out this cutely wrapped onesie and says, 'Oh, here's a free Disney onesie. We'll just need your e-mail address,'" Gill recalls. "It weirded me out. I just gave birth, please lay off with the Disney already!"

Disney wasn't marketing to Jenny, but to her baby. The idea is to make logos and brand characters visible to young children, even infants, to establish the brand as early as possible.

But why? What benefits come from imprinting brands on consumers who can't read, talk, or use a credit card? *Adweek* suggests several:

- Young children can recognize brands at an early age, and do form early brand preferences.
- Families are more attentive to product preferences of young children.
- Brand loyalty with very young kids can last a (very long) lifetime.

And Disney's efforts don't stop with onesies. The company has developed an extensive line of "baby apps" for phones and tablets. And if you think pretoddlers are too young to use apps, think again. One child advocacy organization estimates that 14 percent of kids under 2 spend at least a couple of hours a day with digital media. It seems Mom and Dad are increasingly likely to reach for a mobile phone instead of a pacifier when the little one gets cranky.

Companies have long been sensitive to criticisms about marketing to kids, even ones much older than infants, if, for no other reason, to prevent the FCC from strengthening its already stringent guidelines for television ads in children's programming. Some familiar complaints about kid-centered ads include kids are too young to evaluate product claims or understand an ad's purpose and ads encourage kids to influence family consumption decisions, often in unhealthy ways. Defenders of the practice say families should teach children about what ads are and about buying decisions. Dr. Susan Linn doesn't agree, "It's unfair and naïve to expect that parents, on their own, are going to be able to do a great job of coping with this . . . they need help from the government."

When dealing with the youngest consumers, those under 3, even many defenses of the practice of kid-focused marketing seem weak or irrelevant. For example, some point out that older children, say those aged 7 to 14, would have little media content directed to them without ad-sponsored shows. But should a 2-year-old ever find him- or herself in the target audience of a product?

Questions

1. Is it ever ethically justified to market to a child under 3? Why or why not?

2. Do you agree with Susan Linn that parents are not able to determine how best to respond to marketing efforts for their children?

3. From an ethical perspective, who are the stakeholders in this situation, and what values or conception of what is right is important to consider? Are the concerns about very young children more important than those of others?

Sources: Brian Braiker, "The Next Great American Consumer: Infants to 3-Year Olds, They're a New Demographic Marketers Are Hell-Bent on Reaching." *Adweek*, September 26, 2011, retrieved December 31, 2011, from www.adweek.com/news/advertising-branding/next-great-american-consumer-135207; Christine Lagorio, "The Hard Sell: Marketing to Kids," retrieved December 31, 2011, from www.cbsnews.com/8301-18563_162-2802643.html.

---

segments, with names such as Trendsetters (teens heavily attracted to media and to current styles, who make greater use of the Internet than any of the other 30 groups), Kid Focused (middle-class families whose activities and media use revolve around their children), and Sarcastics (predominantly young men who enjoy television programs on Comedy Central and are heavily into sports).[32]

An influential book, *The Tipping Point* by cultural observer Malcolm Gladwell, emphasizes another reason why advertisers may wish to psychologically segment consumers: small groups of people can have a great impact on the rest of us. Gladwell argues that certain types of people are involved in creating what he calls *social epidemics,* typified by the almost overnight increase in the popularity of a product, fashion, or idea. He offers the example of Hush Puppy shoes, which sold in low numbers for many years before suddenly surging in popularity again among young, cool consumers. This happened, Gladwell believes, because a small group of influential consumers began using the brand, thereby influencing others. Gladwell proposes that social epidemics are traceable to the actions of three types of people, which he labels *Connectors, Mavens,* and *Salesmen.* Connectors are

Who Are the MindBase Segments?

I am Expressive
my motto is *Carpe Diem.*

I live life to the fullest and I'm not afraid to express my personality. I'm active and engaged and I embody a true "live in the now" attitude with a firm belief that the future is limitless and that I can be or do anything I put my mind to.

I am Driven
my motto is *Nothing ventured, Nothing Gained*

I'm ambitious with a drive to succeed both personally and professionally. I think of myself as self-possessed and resourceful, and I'm determined to show the world I'm on top of my game in all I do, from career ambitions to family, home, and my social life.

I am At Capacity
my motto is *Time Is of the Essence*

My life is very busy and I'm looking for control and simplification. I am a demanding and vocal consumer, and I'm looking for convenience, respect, and a helping hand so I can devote more of my time to the important things in life.

I am Rock Steady
my motto is *Do the Right Thing*

I think of myself as a positive individual. I draw energy from my home and family. I'm dedicated to living an upstanding life and I listen to my own instincts in terms of making thoughtful decisions in my personal life and in the marketplace.

I am Down to Earth
my motto is *Ease on Down the Road*

I'm cruising down life's path at my own pace, seeking satisfaction where I can. I'm looking to enhance my life, stretch myself to try new things and treat myself through novel experiences and products along the way.

I am Sophisticated
my motto is *Sense and Sensibility*

I am intelligent and upstanding, and I have an affinity for the finer things in life. I also have high expectations both for myself and for the companies to which I give my business. I am dedicated to doing a stellar job at work but I balance my career dedication with a passion for enriching experiences.

I Measure Twice
my motto is *An Ounce of Prevention*

I'm a mature individual and I like to think of myself on a life path to actualization and fulfillment. I live a healthy, active life. I'm dedicated to ensuring that my future is both secure and highly rewarding and vitalized.

I am Devoted
my motto is *Home Is Where the Heart Is*

I'm traditional and rooted in the comforts of home. Some would say my beliefs are conventional, but they make sense to me. I'm spiritual and content with my life. I like things the way they have always been and I don't need novelty for novelty's sake or newfangled technology.

Exhibit 6-7
MindBase finds shared patterns of behavior among broad clusters of consumers.

people with very wide social circles. While ordinary people may have a few dozen acquaintances, Connectors often know and keep tabs on hundreds. With such a large social network, Connectors have the ability to bridge different social groups that would not ordinarily interact with each other. This increases the chances that an idea prevalent in one group will transfer to others. Mavens are people who spend the time and energy accumulating knowledge that most people can't be bothered to find out for themselves. A Maven will know where to get the best steak in town, where to find the best deal on a new TV, and what brand of phone provides the best options. Just as important, Mavens love sharing this information. Connectors and Mavens are sources of information about new products, trends, and ideas, but persuading people to embrace these things falls to Salesmen. Salesmen are people others find to be credible, trustworthy, and authoritative. Unlike the "hard sell" stereotype that the term may invoke, Gladwell's archetype is low-key, attractive, and, most of all, influential. Gladwell's analysis suggests that relatively small groups of people are very influential in affecting the consumption of much larger segments of society. The influence of his analysis is already incorporated in several segmentation tools, including BehaviorGraphics.[33]

Limitations of Consumer Segmentation Methods

Advocates of psychographic systems claim they help address the factors that motivate consumers. However, because the markets for many products comprise such a broad cross section of consumers, psychographics may in fact offer little real value—especially since it oversimplifies consumer personalities. Some typologies, such as VALS, are also criticized for being complicated and lacking proper theoretical underpinnings.[34]

AD Lab 6–A

Market Segmentation: A Dog of a Job

Market segmentation doesn't have to be boring. A Michael Reinemer article in *Advertising Age* described a market he could have fun with—dogs (or, at least, dog owners).

Reinemer shared what prompted his thinking. He saw a video for dogs in an upscale pet store. And an ad for dogs who can't brush after every meal. And an article about dog health insurance, puppy psychotherapy, and Prozac for canines. He suddenly realized that many dogs in the United States probably enjoy better nutrition and health care than millions of people in the world. His reaction: "How do I cash in on this thing?"

Reinemer thought of launching a new consulting firm called "Dog Trend\$" to sniff out every conceivable emerging dog-related trend or fad and sponsor a Dog Marketing Conference.

Then he created a few trends of his own for man's best friend:

Dog fitness centers. While the baby boomers pursue fitness, why not let the dog work out, too (SpaDog and DogAerobics)?

Dog video games. Interactive games that improve the dog's eye–paw coordination (Mortal Dogfight, Hydrant Finder, Car Chase).

Fashion magazines for dogs. When it's a cold winter day and you put that warm sweater on to keep you warm, why not put a fashionable sweater on your dog (*Dogmopolitan, smELLE, Dogue,* and *DQ*)?

Dog retirement communities (Sunset Leisure Kennels).

Cable networks (DoggieVision).

Upscale department stores (BloomingDog's).

Maybe Reinemer's ideas are more than fun. Could they really be the next phase in marketing?

Laboratory Applications

1. Come up with a market segment that you think would be fun to work with. What five products could you market?
2. Come up with your own trends for dogs (or cats if you prefer). Suggest five new business ideas that can capitalize on people's love for their animal companions.

Still, it's important for marketers to monitor and understand their customers. It helps them select target markets, create ads that match the attributes and images of their products with the types of consumers who use them, develop effective media plans, and budget their advertising dollars wisely. (For an amusing twist on satisfying market needs, see Ad Lab 6-A.)

Segmenting Business and Government Markets: Understanding Organizational Buying Behavior

Business (or *industrial*) **markets** include manufacturers, government agencies, wholesalers, retailers, banks, and institutions that buy goods and services to help them operate. These products may include raw materials, electronic components, mechanical parts, office equipment, vehicles, or services used in conducting business. Many business marketers sell to **resellers,** such as retail businesses. Some brands are produced, merchandised, and resold under their own names, like Levi's jeans. Other resellers offer both brand-name products and unbranded products. For example, much of Hardee's food is supplied by Siméus Foods International, a processing, production, and distribution conglomerate. Siméus's two plants produce and freeze menu items, such as hamburger and chicken patties, to the specifications of customers like Hardee's and Denny's. The end product is resold by Hardee's with no mention of Siméus. Hardee's reselling contract with Coca-Cola, however, is a much more visible "brand partnership"; Coke products are often featured in Hardee's advertising.

Identifying target markets of prospective business customers is just as challenging as identifying consumer markets. Many of the criteria used to identify consumer markets can also be used for business markets—for example, geography and behavior (purchase occasion, benefits sought, user status, and usage rate).

Business Purchasing Procedures

When businesspeople evaluate new products, they use a process far more complex than the consumer purchase process described in Chapter 5. Business marketers must design their promotional programs with this in mind.

Large firms have purchasing departments that act as professional buyers. They evaluate the need for products, analyze proposed purchases, weigh competitive bids, seek approvals

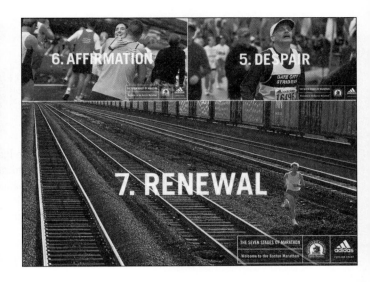

Ads for adidas (www.adidas.com) capture the attitude and lifestyle of its target market: athletic young people around the world who define themselves by their athletic achievements. This series of ads, placed at intervals throughout the Boston Marathon, was intended to simultaneously motivate runners as they hit certain points in their progress as well as reinforce key values shared by all athletes, which adidas hopes to embody.

Source: adidas

from managers, make requisitions, place orders, and supervise all product purchasing. This structured purchase decision process implies a rational approach. According to recent research, however, professional buyers often show a willingness to pay a substantial premium for their favorite brand. This suggests that advertising may play a larger role in business-to-business marketing than previously thought.[35]

Making a sale in business markets may take weeks, months, or even years, especially to government agencies. Purchase decisions often depend on factors besides price or quality, among them product demonstrations, delivery time, terms of sale, and dependability of supply. Marketers often emphasize these issues in promotional appeals.

Before choosing a target market, business marketers should consider how the purchase decision process works in various segments. New companies, for instance, may want to target smaller firms where the purchase decision can be made quickly. Or they may use commission-only reps to call on the larger prospects that require more time.

Industrial Classification System

Industrial customers need different products, depending on their business. For example, apparel manufacturers such as Levi's are customers for buttons and zippers. Marketing managers need to focus their sales and advertising efforts on firms that are in the right business for their products.[36] The U.S. Census Bureau classifies all U.S. businesses—and collects and publishes industry statistics on them—using the **North American Industry Classification System (NAICS) codes.** The NAICS (pronounced "nakes") system includes many new industries that are relevant to today's changing economy. The system was developed in cooperation with Canada and Mexico to ensure consistency throughout North America.

NAICS organizes all the industries into 20 broad sectors such as mining, manufacturing, wholesale trade, and information. These are then subdivided into four hierarchical levels of classification, including subsectors, industry groups, industries, and finally distinct

Business and government markets are also segmented. German office furniture retailer Bisley targets its business audiences with ads that feature a clever metaphor for reorganization.

Courtesy of Kolle Rebbe

Exhibit 6-8

NAICS hierarchy and codes. A business marketer selling goods or services to firms in the paging industry can use the NAICS codes to locate prospective companies in directories or in subscription databases.

Level	Code	Sector
Sector	51	Information
Subsector	513	Broadcasting and telecommunications
Industry group	5133	Telecommunications
Industry	51332	Wireless telecommunications carriers (except satellite)
U.S. industry	513321	Paging

U.S. industries. (See Exhibit 6-8 for a breakdown of NAICS codes in the information and wireless telecommunications industry.) The U.S. Census Bureau uses NAICS to offer marketers useful information, such as the number of firms, sales volumes, and number of employees by geographic area. Thus, the NAICS codes help companies segment markets and do research, and marketers can even obtain lists of companies in particular NAICS divisions for direct mailings.[37]

Market Concentration

Many countries' markets for industrial goods are concentrated in one region or several metropolitan areas. In the United States, for example, the industrial market is heavily concentrated in the Midwest, the South, and California (see Exhibit 6-9). Market concentration reduces the number of geographic targets for an advertiser.

Moreover, business marketers deal with fewer buyers than consumer marketers. Less than 7 percent of U.S. manufacturing firms account for almost 80 percent of all manufacturing dollars.[38] Customer size is important for market segmentation. A firm may concentrate its marketing and advertising efforts on a few large customers, many smaller ones, or both.

Levi Strauss markets through three channels: independent department stores; specialty stores (such as Urban Outfitters); and chain stores (such as JCPenney). Its top 100 accounts provide 80 percent of the company's annual sales and are made through 13,000 retail outlets. Its remaining accounts represent another 13,000 stores. Major accounts are served by sales reps from Levi's various divisions, smaller accounts by telemarketers and pandivisional sales reps. Bartle Bogle Hegarty creates and coordinates advertising for most Levi Strauss divisions in the United States.

Exhibit 6-9

The states in this map are represented in proportion to the value of their manufactured products.

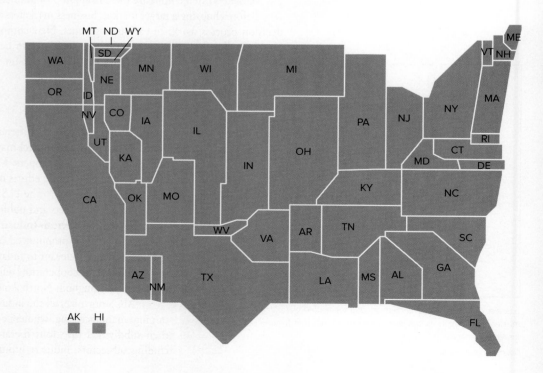

Business marketers can also segment by end users. For example, a firm may develop software for one industry, such as banking, or for general use in a variety of industries. That decision, of course, affects advertising media decisions.

Aggregating Market Segments

After marketers identify broad product-based markets with shared characteristics (behavioristic, geographic, demographic, or psychographic), they can proceed to the second segmentation step. This involves (1) selecting groups that have a mutual interest in the product's utility and (2) reorganizing and aggregating (combining) them into larger market segments based on their potential for sales and profit. Let's take a look at how this process might work for Levi Strauss.

First, management needs to know the market potential for jeans and casual pants in various market areas; that is, it needs to discover the **primary demand trend** of the total U.S. market for pants. To do this it uses a variety of *marketing research* techniques (discussed in Chapter 7).

Then management must identify the needs, wants, and shared characteristics of the various groups within the casual apparel marketplace who live near the company's retail outlets. It may use the services of a large marketing information company such as Nielsen, which collects data on people's purchasing behavior and creates profiles of geographic markets across the country.

The company finds a huge market of prospective customers throughout the United States: students, blue-collar workers, young singles, professional people, homemakers, and so on. It then measures and analyzes household groups in each major retail area by demographic, lifestyle, and purchasing characteristics; sorts them into 66 geodemographic segments; and refers to them with terms such as those in Exhibit 6-10: Upper Crust, Movers & Shakers, Bedrock America, Pools & Patios, and the like. All these people have apparel needs, and many may be interested in the style, cachet, and durability of the Levi's brand.

Selecting Groups Interested in Product Utility

Levi Strauss next selects groups that would like and be able to afford the utilities or benefits of Levi's apparel—suitability for work or play, comfort, style, reasonable cost, durability, and so on. Groups interested in all these features make up the total possible market for Levi's clothes.

Part of the challenge of market segmentation is estimating the profits the company might realize if it (1) aims at the whole market or (2) caters only to specific market segments. Apparel is a highly competitive market, but 10 percent of 1,000 is always larger than 90 percent of 100. So for a company such as Levi Strauss, the target market must be a large mass market or it won't be profitable.[39]

Combining Groups to Build Target Market Segments

The company needs to find groups that are relatively homogeneous (similar) and offer good potential for profit. Market data turn up a large number of demographic and lifestyle groups, including ethnically diverse families, young singles, and seniors with lower education and income who often live in rented homes or apartments: New Empty Nest (1.1 percent), Park Bench Seniors (1.1 percent), and Low Rise Living (1.3 percent). Because of their minimal retail or credit activity, these groups are not prime targets for premium-branded department store products.

Other segments offer greater potential—young to middle-aged households with medium to high incomes and average to high retail activity: Movers & Shakers (1.63 percent), Bohemian Mix (1.8 percent), and Home Sweet Home (1.8 percent). By combining these (and similar) groups with the young professionals in the Young Influentials (1.5 percent) and New Beginnings (1.5 percent) segments, Levi Strauss can target young to middle-aged people on their way up. Nationally, that amounts to 20 million U.S. households. That's not everybody, but it's a large and potentially very profitable mass-market segment. These people might like the style and comfort of Levi's 550s as well as the tradition of a brand they know

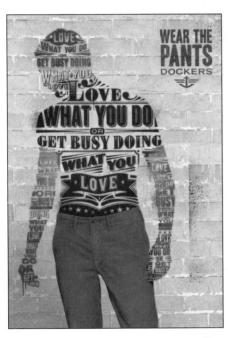

Levi's has introduced several product lines in an effort to satisfy needs and wants of different consumer segments. One of their successful lines is the Dockers brand of casual clothes. This beautiful ad cleverly expresses the image of the user and draws attention to the brand.

Source: Levi Strauss & Co.

Louisville, KY:
S. Hancock St. & E. Market St.

5 and 10 Mile Radii Showing Dominant PRIZM Cluster by ZIP Code

Dominant PRIZM NE Cluster
by ZIP Code

- 03 - Movers & Shakers
- 05 - Country Squires
- 09 - Big Fish, Small Pond
- 10 - Second City Elite
- 11 - God's Country
- 15 - Pools & Patios
- 19 - Home Sweet Home
- 20 - Fast-Track Families
- 23 - Greenbelt Sports
- 25 - Country Casuals
- 27 - Middleburg Manager
- 30 - Suburban Sprawl
- 33 - Big Sky Families
- 36 - Blue-Chip Blues
- 37 - Mayberry-ville
- 39 - Domestic Duos
- 44 - New Beginnings
- 46 - Old Glories
- 49 - American Classics
- 51 - Shotguns & Pickups
- 52 - Suburban Pioneers
- 53 - Mobility Blues
- 54 - Multi-Culti Mosaic
- 59 - Urban Elders
- 61 - City Roots
- 65 - Big City Blues

Exhibit 6-10

This exhibit shows how Claritas's Prizm NE system classifies prospective customers in the Louisville area by census tract and labels each area by the residents' shared characteristics.

Source: Claritas's Prizm NE System from Claritas.

 and trust, and the company could develop a campaign to appeal to their particular needs, wants, and self-images.

The Target Marketing Process

Once the market segmentation process is complete, a company can proceed to the **target marketing process.** This will determine the content, look, and feel of its advertising.

Target Market Selection

The first step in target marketing is to assess which of the newly created segments offer the greatest profit potential and which can be most successfully penetrated. The company designates one or more segments as a **target market**—that group of segments the company wishes to appeal to, design products for, and tailor its marketing activities toward.[40] It may designate another set of segments as a secondary target market and aim some of its resources at it.

Let's look at the most likely target market for loose-fitting jeans: customers between 30 and 50 years of age with moderate to high income and education who like the style, comfort, and fashion of Levi's apparel. This group represents a large percentage of the apparel market, and, if won, will generate substantial profits. Levi's offers what these prospects need and want: the style and fashion of the jeans they grew up with, updated to be more comfortable for the adult body.

AD Lab 6-B

Understanding the Product Element: Starbucks Coffee

America's java giant began as the seed of an idea by a man with a dream whose tender care and commitment eventually built the familiar coffee empire of today. While on a trip to Italy in 1983, Howard Schultz discovered and fell in love with the coffee bars of Milan and Verona. They were a combination of coffee and community. He was sure Americans would love this concept.

At the time, Starbucks was a little 11-store chain of roasted coffee stores in Seattle. Schultz was in charge of marketing. He pitched the coffee-bar concept to the company's management but received only a lukewarm response. They didn't want to be in the beverage business. Howard held on to his vision, though. Leaving Starbucks in 1987, he launched a handful of coffee bars on his own and named them Il Giornales. Two years later, with some investor backing, his demonstrated success enabled him to buy out Starbucks. Today, he is chair and chief global strategist of a publicly traded company that boasts more than 10,000 retail locations in North America, Latin America, Europe, the Middle East, and the Pacific Rim. Serving tens of millions of Americans each week, Starbucks has definitely become a household name.

To Schultz, the most important component for success is consistent product quality. "Our long-range goal is to be nothing less than the most recognized and respected brand of coffee in the world," Schultz says.

Thanks to management's demand for consistency, a double-tall latte tastes the same in New York as it does in Seattle; and your perfectly pulled espresso won't sit for more than 10 seconds before being poured into your cup. This attention to detail has earned Starbucks its place in the premium coffee category.

Of course a good product is best prepared and served by skilled, happy employees. And that also adds to an organization's profitability. Ranked as number 29 by the *Fortune* "100 Best Companies to Work for in 2006" poll, Starbucks' management believes that if it takes care of its workers, they in turn will take care of the public. Employees who work at least 20 hours a week receive full benefits, including dental, extended health care, and eyeglass and contact lens prescriptions—after only 90 days with the company. Starbucks even offers these benefits to the same-sex partners of employees. To further ensure consistent product quality, Starbucks implemented procedures for monitoring the working conditions of the overseas producers who supply materials to the company.

Today, the coffee market is quite competitive, but Starbucks retains its leading position by continually introducing new products. With PepsiCo, Starbucks formed a partnership to produce its Frappuccino beverage in 1995. In 1996, Starbucks entered into a joint venture with Dreyers Grand Ice Cream to market "Starbucks Coffee Ice Cream." In 1998 and 1999, Starbucks strengthened its presence within the tea segment by introducing a mixture of tea, fruit juice, and ice called Tiazzi, and it acquired Tazo, a Portland, Oregon–based tea company. In 2002, a bottled espresso drink dubbed the DoubleShot was added to the long line of creative products. In 2005, Starbucks teamed with Jim Beam Brands to introduce Starbucks Liqueurs, a line of premium coffee liqueurs. If you're drinking a cup of coffee these days, Starbucks may well have created it—even if it doesn't say so on the label.

Laboratory Application

A basic rule of advertising is that the most ingenious campaign in the world cannot save a bad product. Think of a product in the marketplace that you consider successful and analyze which elements make it profitable and unique. Are there any similarities to the product elements found in Starbucks? If so, what?

But the middle-class, comfort-oriented segment is not enough for Levi's to be profitable, so it also caters to at least two other important markets. Beginning in the early 2000s, in response to the enormous numbers of consumers shopping at giant, low-cost retailers like Walmart and Target, Levi's developed a new line, Levi's Signature, priced lower than its regular collection. These jeans appealed to budget-conscious families with children such as Family Thrifts and Big Sky Families. In addition, Levi's has found it profitable to cater to young, 20-something, image-conscious consumers who like premium designer jeans, which can cost upward of $200 or more. In 2005, the company introduced Warhol Factory X Levi's jeans, which retailed for $250. These premium jeans, like others in Levi's premium collection, are sold at high-end retailers such as Nordstrom.[41] For more about segmentation, look at Ad Lab 6-B and consider how Starbucks selected its new target market.

As consumers have sought greater variety and style in jeans, Levi's has continued to be successful by evolving its product lines, and its IMC. In this ad, Levi's appeals to the environmentally conscious consumer by creating a new approach in the finishing process of their jeans that uses less water.

Source: Levi Strauss & Co.

The Marketing Mix: A Strategy for Matching Products to Markets

Once a company defines its target market, it knows exactly where to focus its attention and resources. It can shape the product concept and even design special features for its target market (such as certain colors or special sizes). It can establish proper pricing. It can

My IMC Campaign 6

Segmenting the Audience

What is the target market for your product? The answer to this question is rarely simple; thus your choices again will require the application of strategic thinking. To make the decision you will need to gather as much information from your client and from secondary sources as you can, focusing on the product's market, users, and the competition. The information you gathered about the consumer in the My IMC Campaign from Chapter 5 will be important as well. And in some instances it may make sense to conduct primary research with current customers or with individuals who use competing products.

You may have the opportunity to offer counsel to your client about whether it is pursuing the right target market. Check to be sure before offering such advice; some clients may not wish to receive it. If the client is so interested, consider whether there are underserved segments that offer sales or profit potential. For example, if your client is a local pizzeria located near campus, it may be focusing on attracting students. This is to be expected since students normally represent a sizeable market in any college town. In addition, your client is doubtless using the timeworn strategy of attracting hungry, cash-strapped undergrads with messages that emphasize low prices, large servings, and coupons. But while students may represent a large market for pizza, there are probably dozens of other food businesses competing for this segment. If so, it might be smarter to refocus on a smaller but underserved segment, especially one that offers great profit potential. If your town lacks an upscale pizzeria that serves specialty pies, the client might be better served by improving its offerings and dining facility, raising prices, and promoting to nonstudents who would be willing to pay more for quality pizzas.

Of course, to evaluate opportunities in a market you will need to segment. Many advertisers find that it makes sense to segment on the basis of standard demographic characteristics such as age, gender, ethnicity, location, social class, or income level. Dividing your market according to product loyalty or product usage levels is also worth strongly considering. Understanding your market with respect to psychographics and lifestyles can be incredibly valuable, especially later when you begin to develop your creative brief. Such data can be more difficult to obtain, however.

Defining the Target Market

	Your Client's Customers	The Competition's Customers	Nonusers
Demographics			
Age			
Gender			
Ethnicity/race			
Location/region			
Social class			
Income			
Education			
Behaviors			
Product usage (light, medium, heavy)			
Brand loyalty (loyal, switchers)			
Psychographics			
Principle-oriented			
Status-oriented			
Action-oriented			
Benefits Sought			
Low price			
Quality			

Levi's understands that brands represent a bundle of values. How is the product concept depicted in the above ad an aggregation of all of the utilitarian and symbolic values embodied by a brand?

Source: Levi Strauss & Co.

determine the need for locating stores or dealers and prepare the most convincing advertising messages.

As we discussed in Chapter 5, a product offers a number of utilities, perceived by the consumer as a *bundle of values.* With this in mind, marketers and advertisers generally try to shape their basic product into a total **product concept:** the consumer's perception of a product as a bundle of utilitarian and symbolic values that satisfy functional, social, psychological, and other wants and needs.

Companies have many strategic options they can employ to enhance the product/service concept and effect marketing exchanges (make sales). Marketers categorize these options under four headings: (1) *product,* (2) *price,* (3) *distribution,* and (4) *communication.*[42] The way the marketer mixes and blends these different elements creates the company's marketing strategy—often called the **marketing mix.** For convenience, marketing educator E. Jerome McCarthy developed a mnemonic device to help recall these four functions: *product, price, place,* and *promotion*—or the **four Ps (4Ps).**[43]

The 4Ps are a simple way to remember the basic elements of the marketing mix. But within each element a company can employ numerous marketing activities to fine-tune its product concept and improve sales. Advertising, for example, is one instrument of the communication (promotion) element. The remainder of this chapter focuses on the relationship between advertising and the other elements of the marketing mix.

IMC and the Product Element

In developing a marketing mix, marketers generally start with the **product element.** Major activities typically include the way the product is designed and classified, positioned, branded, and packaged. Each of these affects the way the product is advertised.

Product Life Cycles

Marketers theorize that just as humans pass through stages in life from infancy to death, products (and especially product categories) also pass through a **product life cycle** (see Exhibit 6-11).[44] A product's position in the life cycle influences the target market selected and the kind of advertising used. The product life cycle has four major stages: *introduction, growth, maturity,* and *decline.*

Exhibit 6-11
A product's life cycle curve may vary, depending on the product category. Marketing objectives and strategies change as the product proceeds from one stage to the next.

The grooming habits of the American male have evolved over the years, creating an opportunity for established brands to develop new product uses. This funny ad from Gilette uses subtle imagery and a straight-forward tag line: take it all off.

Source: Procter & Gamble

When a company introduces a new product category, nobody knows about it. By using market segmentation, though, the company may try to identify those prospects who are known to be **early adopters**—willing to try new things—and begin promoting the new category directly to them. The idea is to stimulate **primary demand**—consumer demand for the whole product category, not just the company's own brand.

During the **introductory** (pioneering) **phase** of any new product category, the company incurs considerable costs for educating customers, building widespread dealer distribution, and encouraging demand. It must spend significant advertising sums at this stage to establish a position as a market leader and to gain a large share of market before the growth stage begins.

When mobile telephones were introduced in the late 1980s, advertisers had to first create enough consumer demand to pull the product through the channels of distribution (called a **pull strategy**). IMC educated consumers about the new product and its category, explaining what such phones are, how they work, and the rewards of owning one. **Sales promotion** efforts aimed at the retail trade (called a **push strategy**) encouraged distributors and dealers to stock, display, and advertise the new products (see Chapter 10).

When sales volume begins to rise rapidly, the product enters the **growth stage.** This period is characterized by rapid *market expansion* as more and more customers, stimulated by mass advertising and word of mouth, make their first, second, and third purchases. Competitors jump into the market, but the company that established the early leadership position reaps the biggest rewards. As a percentage of total sales, advertising expenditures should decrease, and individual firms will realize their first substantial profits.

During the early 1990s, the demand for phones exploded, and category sales quadrupled every year. Many competitors suddenly appeared. With increased production and competition, prices started to fall, which brought even more people into the market. By 2005, 70 percent of all U.S. families owned mobile phones.[45]

In the **maturity stage,** the marketplace becomes saturated with competing products and the number of new customers dwindles, so industry sales reach a plateau. Competition intensifies and profits diminish. Companies increase their promotional efforts but emphasize **selective demand** to impress customers with the subtle advantages of their particular brand. At this stage, companies increase sales only at the expense of competitors (conquest sales). The strategies of market segmentation, product positioning, and price promotion become more important during this shakeout period as weak companies fall by the wayside and those remaining fight for small increases in market share. By the mid-1990s, for example, phones that once sold for $1,500 were suddenly advertised regularly for $100 to $200. Ads emphasized features and low prices, and the product became a staple of discount merchandisers.[46]

Late in the maturity stage, companies may have to scramble to extend the product's life cycle. Without innovation or marketing support, name brands eventually see their sales erode. As of 2011, for example, BlackBerry devices, once market leaders, were struggling in their competition with Apple and Google phones. If the advertised brand has no perceived advantage, people will buy whatever is cheapest or most convenient. Professor Brian Wansink, who directs the Food and Brand Lab at Cornell University, suggests that the reason many old brands die is less for life cycle reasons and more for marketing neglect. He points out that aging brands often pack plenty of brand equity. The challenge for marketers is to determine which brands can be revitalized and then decide how to do it. But with today's high price tag on introducing new products (often $100 million or more), revitalization should be the strategy of choice whenever possible. Marketers may try to find new users for the brand, develop new uses for the product, change the size of packages, design new labels, improve quality, or use promotion to increase frequency of use.[47]

If they're not revitalized, products will finally enter the **decline stage** because of obsolescence, new technology, or changing consumer tastes. At this point, companies may cease all promotion and phase out the products quickly, as in the case of record turntables and LP albums, or let them fade slowly with minimal advertising, like most sheer hosiery brands.

By Market	By Rate of Consumption and Tangibility	By Purchasing Habits	By Physical Description

Consumer goods
   Products and services we use in our daily lives (food, clothing, furniture, cars).
 	
Industrial goods
   Products used by companies for the purpose of producing other products (raw materials, agricultural commodities, machinery, tools, equipment).
	Durable goods
	   Tangible products that are long-lasting and infrequently replaced (cars, trucks, refrigerators, furniture).
	Nondurable goods
	   Tangible products that may be consumed in one or a few uses and usually need to be replaced at regular intervals (food, soap, gasoline, oil).
	Services
	   Activities, benefits, or satisfaction offered for sale (travel, haircuts, legal and medical services, massages).
		Convenience goods
		   Purchases made frequently with a minimum of effort (soda, food, newspapers).
		Shopping goods
		   Infrequently purchased items for which greater time is spent comparing price, quality, style, warranty (furniture, cars, clothing, tires).
		Specialty goods
		   Products with such unique characteristics that consumers will make special efforts to purchase them even if they're more expensive (fancy electronic equipment, special women's fashions, computer components).
		Unsought goods
		   Products that potential customers don't yet want (insurance) or don't know they can buy (new products), so they don't search them out.
			Packaged goods
			   Cereals, hair tonics, and so forth.
			Hard goods
			   Furniture, appliances.
			Soft goods
			   Clothing, bedding.
			Services
			   Intangible products.

Exhibit 6-12
Product classifications.

Product Classifications

The way a company classifies its product is important in defining both the product concept and the marketing mix. As Exhibit 6-12 shows, there are many ways to classify tangible goods: by markets, by the purchasing habits of buyers, by the consumption rate or degree of tangibility, or by physical attributes.

Unlike tangible goods, a **service** is a bundle of *intangible* benefits that satisfy some need or want, are temporary in nature, and usually derive from completion of a task.[48] Thus we have *task utility,* as described in Chapter 5. Rail service, for example, is transitory, used and priced by time and distance. It offers the functional benefits of transporting people, livestock, and freight. But it can also offer psychological benefits. Just think of the romance and leisure of a train trip across Europe aboard the Orient Express. The railroad relies on the use of *specialized equipment*—vehicles able to pull huge loads over a unique track. This makes it an **equipment-based service.**

In contrast, an ad agency, like a law firm or a bank, is a **people-based service;** it relies on the creative talents and marketing skills of individuals. As one agency CEO said, "My inventory goes up and down the elevators twice a day."[49]

Product Positioning

Once an advertising person understands a product's stage in the life cycle, how it's classified, and how it's currently perceived by the marketplace, the first strategic decision can be made: how to **position** the product. The basic goal of positioning strategy is to own a word that ranks the product in the prospect's mind. Levi's owns "jeans." FedEx owns "overnight." And Volvo owns "safety." By developing a unique position for the brand in the consumer's mind, the marketer helps the consumer remember the brand and what it stands for.

Products may be positioned in many different ways. Generally, they are ranked by the way they are differentiated, the benefits they offer, the particular market segment to which they appeal, or the way they are classified. Xerox has repositioned itself as "The Document Company," moving from the narrow, glutted, copier market to the broader, growing, document-handling market. With one stroke, Xerox redefined the business it is in, differentiated itself from the competition, and created a new number one position for itself.[50]

Microsoft had a big hit with its Surface Pro 3. It used explicit comparisons with the Macbook Air to highlight its unique features, which include a detachable keyboard and interactive screen. This is product differentiation at its finest.

Source: Microsoft

Product Differentiation

Product differentiation creates the perception that a brand offers something unique and desirable to a market segment. In any campaign, nothing is more important than being able to tell prospects truthfully that your product is new and different. Unfortunately, in response to competitive pressures, innovation and technology, and constraints on distribution, new product development cycles have shortened. As a result, many brand managers find themselves launching new products that are "only 85 percent there."[51] So it's not surprising that most "new" products fail to impress consumers. (See Exhibit 6-13.) Simply adding new colors might differentiate a product enough to attract a new set of customers, but not all product differences need be that obvious. Differences between products may be *perceptible, hidden,* or *induced.*[52]

Perceptible differences are readily apparent to the consumer. Snapple, for example, received its initial impetus because of its unique taste, and to promote this difference to consumers nationwide, the company employed a variety of nontraditional marketing techniques, including sole sponsorship of a Boston radio station for 40 days.[53] **Hidden differences** are not so readily apparent. Trident gum may look and taste the same as other brands, but it is differentiated by the use of artificial sweeteners. While hidden differences can enhance a product's desirability, IMC is usually needed to let consumers know about them.

For many product classes, such as aspirin, salt, gasoline, packaged foods, liquor, and financial services, advertising can create **induced differences.** Banks, brokerage houses, and insurance companies, for example, which offer virtually identical financial products and services, use promotion to differentiate themselves. They also know the value of consistent

Product	New and Different	Purchase Probability	Price/ Value	Overall Grade
Airwick Botanicals	F	A	A	B
Mr. Clean Glass & Surface Cleaner	F	A	A	B
Spic & Span with Bleach	F	A	B	B
Aspirin-Free Bayer Select	F	B	B	C
Sugar Twin Plus low-calorie sweetener	F	B	A	C
Lady Power Clear Roll-On antiperspirant	F	B	A	C

advertising campaigns, favorable publicity, special event sponsorship, and good word of mouth.[54]

Product Branding

As discussed in Chapter 1, the fundamental differentiating device for products is the **brand**—that combination of name, words, symbols, or design that identifies the product and its source and distinguishes it from competing products. Without brands, consumers couldn't tell one product from another.

Branding decisions are difficult. A manufacturer may establish an **individual brand** for each product it produces. Unilever, for example, markets its toothpastes under the individual brand names Aim, Pepsodent, and Close-Up. Such companies designate a distinct target market for each product and develop a separate personality and image for each brand. However, this strategy is very costly.

On the other hand, a company might use a **family brand** and market different products under the same umbrella name. When Heinz promotes its ketchup, it hopes to help its relishes too.

Because it is so expensive for manufacturers to market **national brands** (also called *manufacturer's brands*), some companies use a *private-labeling strategy.* They manufacture the product and sell it to resellers (distributors or dealers), who put their own brand on the product. **Private labels,** typically sold at lower prices in large retail chain stores, include such familiar names as Kenmore, Craftsman, Cragmont, Kroger, and Party Pride. They now account for almost 20 percent of grocery purchases.[55] The responsibility for creating brand image and familiarity rests with the distributor or retailer, who is also the principal benefactor if the brand is successful. Recent trends have moved toward premium private labels, such as President's Choice, which has enjoyed immense success. These products feature better packaging, superior quality, and a higher price, comparable to national brands.

Branding decisions are critical because the brands a company owns may be its most important capital asset. Imagine the value of owning a brand name such as Coca-Cola, Nike, Porsche, or Levi's (see Exhibit 6-14).[56] Some companies pay a substantial fee for the right to use another company's brand name. Thus, we have **licensed brands** such as Sunkist vitamins, Coca-Cola clothing, Porsche sunglasses, and Mickey Mouse watches.

The Role of Branding

For consumers, brands offer instant recognition. They also promise consistent, reliable standards of quality, taste, size, or even psychological satisfaction, which adds value to the product for both the consumer and the manufacturer. In a survey conducted by TWICE/Campaigners, 44 percent of consumers ranked brand name as the most important factor when making a major electronics purchase. Price ranked second.[57]

Brands are built on differences in images, meanings, and associations. Marketers attempt to differentiate their products clearly and deliver value competitively. The product has to taste

Chanel is one of the top perfume brands in the world. To reinforce its image of luxury and glamor, Chanel ads feature stars such as Nicole Kidman and Keira Knightley.

Source: Chanel

Exhibit 6-14
World's most valuable brands.

Rank	Brand	2015 Brand Value (in billions)
1	Apple	$145.3
2	Microsoft	69.3
3	Google	65.6
4	Coca Cola	56.0
5	IBM	49.8
6	McDonald's	39.5
7	Samsung	37.9
8	Toyota	37.8
9	General Electric	37.5
10	Facebook	36.5

Source: "The Worlds's Most Valuable Brands," Forbes, retrieved at: http://www.forbes.com/powerful-brands/list/#tab:rank

Product packaging is important around the globe. Packaging and advertising converge as Amazon leverages the value of its global shipping materials to provide advertisers a new platform. These boxes help promote the release of the movie Minions.

Source: Amazon.com, Inc.

better, or get clothes cleaner, or be packaged in a more environmentally friendly container.[58] Advertising for an established brand, particularly a well-differentiated one, is much more effective if it exploits the brand's positioning.[59] Ideally, when consumers see a brand on the shelf, they instantly comprehend the brand's promise and have confidence in its quality. Of course, they must be familiar with and believe in the brand's promise (a function of IMC effectiveness). As we pointed out in Chapter 5, the goal is *brand loyalty*—because it serves both the consumer and the marketer. For the consumer, it reduces shopping time. For the marketer, it builds **brand equity,** the totality of what consumers, distributors, dealers—even competitors—feel and think about the brand over an extended period of time. In short, it's the value of the brand's capital.

High brand equity offers a host of blessings to the product marketer: customer loyalty, price inelasticity, long-term profits. A loyal customer can be nine times as profitable as a disloyal one.[60] But building brand equity requires time, effort, and money. Brand value and preference drive market share, but share points and brand loyalty are usually won by the advertisers who spend the most. And increasing brand loyalty may require a spending increase of 200 to 300 percent to affect loyalty dramatically.[61] Charlotte Beers, the former head of J. Walter Thompson, points out the importance of "brand stewardship." She believes companies must maintain consistency in their message by integrating all their marketing communications—from packaging and advertising to sales promotion and publicity—to maintain and reinforce the brand's personality in a real-life context and avoid doing something foolish such as changing the distinctive color of a Ryder rental truck.[62]

Product Packaging

The product's package is a component of the product element and is also an *exhibitive medium* that can determine the outcome of retail shelf competition. In fact, packaging may be a brand's one differential advantage—and it's the marketer's last chance to communicate at the point of sale. Package designers (who sometimes work in ad agencies) must make the package exciting, appealing, and functional. The four considerations in package design are *identification; containment, protection, and convenience; consumer appeal;* and *economy.* These functions may even become **copy points**—copywriting themes—in the product's advertising.

Identification

Why do some companies use the same package and label design for years? Because the unique combination of trade name, trademark, or trade character, reinforced by the package design, quickly identifies the brand and differentiates it from competitors. For example, the traditional contoured Coke bottle was so unusual and popular that in the 1990s Coca-Cola reintroduced it to U.S. markets. The company never stopped using it in many international markets because it differentiated Coke so well from other colas.

Packages should offer high visibility and legibility to penetrate shoppers' *physiological screens.* Product features must be easy to read, and color combinations must provide high contrast to differentiate the product. To penetrate consumers' *psychological screens,* the package design must reflect the tone, image, and personality of the product concept. In many product categories (wine, cosmetics), the package quality largely determines the consumer's perception of the product's quality.

Containment, Protection, and Convenience

The purpose of any package is to hold and protect the product and make it easy to use. Marketers also try to ensure it will keep the product fresh and protect its contents from damage, water vapor (for frozen goods), grease, infestation, and odors. And packages must adhere to legal protection requirements.

Placing the product label in an ad can help consumers quickly identify it in stores. By repeatedly placing the Tide label to create an image of a ship along with the message that by using Tide Coldwater, enough energy will be saved to power a cruise ship, the above ad reinforces the identity of a well-known brand and gives consumers another reason to choose it over the competitor.

Source: Procter & Gamble

Retailers want packages that are easy to stack and display; they also want a full range of sizes to fit their customers' needs. Consumers want packages that are easy to carry, open, and store, so these are important design considerations.

Consumer Appeal

Consumer appeal in packaging is the result of many factors: size, color, material, and shape. Certain colors have special meanings to consumers. Even a subtle change in color can result in as much as a 20 percent change in sales.[63]

In this age of environmental awareness, *green marketing* is an important issue for companies and consumers alike. New technology has made ecologically safe packaging available and affordable for many product categories. Many companies now advertise their packages as environmentally responsible.

A package's shape also offers an opportunity for consumer appeal based on whimsy, humor, or romance. Heart-shaped packages of Valentine's Day candy instantly tell what the product is. Some tins and bottles even become collectibles (Chivas Regal). These packages are really premiums that give buyers extra value.

Economy

LO 6-4

Investments in identification, protection, convenience, and consumer appeal add to basic production costs, but this increase may be more than offset by increased customer appeal. These benefits may make a considerable difference to the consumer and affect both the product concept and IMC messages.

IMC and the Price Element

Many companies, especially small ones, request input from their advertising people about pricing strategies. That's because the **price element** of the marketing mix influences consumer perceptions of the brand dramatically.

This print ad for Harvey Nichols in London was awarded a Silver Lion at Cannes. The stretched bathing suit is an apt metaphor for consumers who are interested in stretching their money. Of course, the ad could be read another way: This image might depict what happens when frantic shoppers fight for the same item.

Source: Harvey Nichols

Key Factors Influencing Price

Companies set their prices based on market demand for the product, costs of production and distribution, competition, and corporate objectives. As a practical matter, though, a company may have relatively few options for determining its price strategy, depending on the desired product concept.

Market Demand

If the supply of a product is stable but the desire (demand) for it increases, the price tends to rise. If demand drops below available supply, the price tends to fall. This may affect IMC messages in a major way (see Exhibit 6-15).

In the last recession, auto manufacturers faced a glut of unsold new cars and declining demand. Several companies offered substantial factory rebates—price cuts—to motivate prospective buyers. Dealers immediately sold more cars. No amount of image or awareness advertising would have had the same effect. But, of course, advertising was essential to communicate the price cut.

Some marketing researchers theorize that for new durable goods, advertising works with word-of-mouth and social media communication to generate awareness of and belief in the product's benefits. Once consumers perceive that the product's value warrants the purchase price, sales occur. As product experience and information spread, the risks associated with new products diminish, which increases consumers' willingness to purchase at a higher price.[64]

Production and Distribution Costs

The price of goods depends to some extent on the costs of production and distribution. As these costs increase, they must be passed on to the consumer, or the company will be unable to meet its overhead and will be forced out of business. One common IMC strategy is to tout the materials used in manufacturing a product. This can also help justify the prices manufacturers must charge to cover their production costs.

Competition

In many product categories, consumers are less concerned with a product's actual price than with its perceived price relative to competitors. For the marketer, maintaining the value perception during periods of intense price competition and fluctuation is challenging but important.[65]

Corporate Objectives and Strategies

A company's objectives also influence price. When introducing new products, companies often set a high price initially to recover development and start-up costs. In other cases, if the objective were to position the brand as an inexpensive convenience item aimed at a broad target market, ads would stress the product's economy.

Price also depends on the company's marketing strategy, and image advertising may be used to justify a higher price. Many premium-priced brands, such as L'Oréal, are touted for

Exhibit 6-15

This graph plots demand versus price and supply versus price. The demand curve shows the amounts purchased at various prices. The supply curve shows the amounts offered for sale at various prices. The point where the two curves cross is called the market clearing price, where demand and supply balance. It is the price that theoretically sells out the product.

the very fact that they do cost more. The important thing is that the price be consistent with the brand image; you can't charge a Rolex price for a Timex watch.

As products enter the maturity stages of their life cycles, corporate objectives tend to aim at increasing, or at least maintaining, market share. To accomplish this, competitive advertising and promotion heat up, and prices tend to drop.

Variable Influences

Economic conditions, consumer income and tastes, government regulations, marketing costs, and other factors also influence prices and thus advertising. Marketing management must consider all these to determine an appropriate pricing strategy and then create advertising that justifies the product's price.

IMC and the Distribution (Place) Element

LO 6-5

Before the first message can be created, the **distribution element,** or *place,* must be decided. It is important for marketers to understand that the method of distribution, like the price, must be consistent with the brand's image. To understand Starbucks' distribution strategy, see Ad Lab 6-C, "Starbucks and the Place Element." Companies use two basic methods of distribution: *direct* or *indirect.*

Direct Distribution

When companies sell directly to end users or consumers, they use **direct distribution.** Avon, for example, employs sales reps who work for the manufacturer rather than for a retailer and sell directly to consumers. Technology giants such as Dell and Apple sell a large percentage of their products directly to customers who order from their Websites. In these cases, the promotional burden is carried entirely by the manufacturer.

An interesting method of direct distribution is **network marketing** (also called *multilevel marketing*), in which individuals act as independent distributors for a manufacturer or private-label marketer. These people sign up friends and relatives to consume the company's products and recruit others to join. Through a gradual, word-of-mouth process, they form a "buying club" of independent distributors who buy the products wholesale directly from the company, use them, and tout them to more and more friends and acquaintances.

If successful, the rewards for the network marketing company (and many of the distributors) can be staggering. Amway International, the granddaddy of network marketing, now boasts international sales in excess of $6 billion, and many of its longtime distributors became multimillionaires in the process.[66] Other companies have broken the billion-dollar sales mark, too, among them Nikken (Japan), Herbalife, and Shaklee. These companies brag about the fact that they do *no media advertising.* Because they usually sell consumer products (which typically carry a heavy advertising and sales promotion burden), they save money. Most marketing communications are simply word of mouth. Of course, today word of mouth includes Facebook. So Avon lets its network marketers create their own groups for friends to follow.

Indirect Distribution

Manufacturers usually don't sell directly to consumers. Most companies market their products through a *distribution channel* that includes a network of *resellers.* A **reseller** (or *middleman*) is a business firm that operates between the producer and the consumer or industrial purchaser. It deals in trade rather than production.[67] Resellers include both wholesalers and retailers, as well as manufacturers' representatives, brokers, jobbers, and distributors. A **distribution channel** includes all the firms and individuals that take title, or assist in taking title, to the product as it moves from the producer to the consumer.

Indirect distribution channels make the flow of products available to customers conveniently and economically. Appliance companies, for example, contract with exclusive regional distributors that buy the products from the factory and resell them to local dealers, who then resell them to consumers. Many industrial companies market their products through reps or distributors to *original equipment manufacturers (OEMs).* These OEMs may use the product as a component in their own product, which is then sold to their customers.

AD Lab 6-C

Starbucks and the Place Element

The "place" (or distribution) element of marketing strategy is always integral to successful business. You may have the most wonderful product in the world—but potential customers won't buy it if they can't find it.

Starbucks (www.starbucks.com) is a phenomenon that changed the way people view coffee. This can be explained, in large part, by the creative use of the place element. You'll notice that Starbucks cafés are found in high-traffic, easily noticeable locations in each market area. In some markets a Starbucks seems to appear on virtually every street corner. Although the average consumer may find this excessive, Starbucks actually picks and plans each retail location with great care.

To a company like Starbucks, street space is the same as shelf space. In this sense, buying out existing coffeehouses is the same as Coca-Cola buying shelf space in a supermarket. Starbucks management believes that chain expansion is as much a part of the company's success as is its coffee bar and customer service concepts. Since its opening, stores have sprouted up in virtually every major city across the globe, and Starbucks has no intention of stopping. As of 2014 there are more than 21,000 Starbucks worldwide, including 12,000 in the U.S.

Aside from its store locations, Starbucks' unique coffee blends are now found in selected airlines, restaurants, hotels, and supermarkets. Additional venues include a mail-order business with catalog distribution, a coast-to-coast alliance with Barnes & Noble bookstores, a partnership with Star Markets in Boston, distribution to the Washington State Ferry system, Holland America Line–Westours cruises, Safeco Field in Seattle, and Chicago's Wrigley Field. Starbucks is also joining the Internet craze. Starting in 2001.

Obviously, Starbucks intends to fully saturate every coffee market. When consumers go shopping for groceries, they aren't likely to make a separate trip to Starbucks for coffee. So Starbucks now competes directly with other specialty coffees sold in supermarkets. In 1998 Kraft Foods signed on with Starbucks and agreed to distribute and market Starbucks coffee beans in more than 25,000 grocery stores in the United States. Kraft is the largest packaged-food company in North America. This collaboration is a major stepping stone in surpassing Folgers as the leading coffee brand in the United States. Another placement strategy is the incorporation of Starbucks' DoubleShot into supermarkets. By partnering with PepsiCo in developing and introducing the new drink, Starbucks can take advantage of PepsiCo's vast network of distribution channels and place its product almost anywhere, bringing the company one step closer to its original dream—"Planet Starbucks."

Laboratory Application

Take the product you used in Ad Lab 6-B and compare the distribution principles used by Starbucks with your product. In addition, think about the factors that should be considered when placing your product or service in other venues. How does it compare with Starbucks?

The advertising a company uses depends on the product's method of distribution. Much of the advertising we see is not prepared or paid for by the manufacturer, but by the distributor or retailer. Members of a distribution channel give enormous promotional support to the manufacturers they represent.

A part of marketing strategy is determining the amount of coverage necessary for a product. Procter & Gamble, for example, distributes Crest toothpaste to virtually every supermarket and discount, drug, and variety store. Other products might need only one dealer for every 50,000 people. Consumer goods manufacturers traditionally use one of three distribution strategies: *intensive, selective,* or *exclusive.*

Intensive Distribution

Soft drinks, candy, Timex watches, and other convenience goods are available at every possible location because of **intensive distribution.** In fact, consumers can buy them with a minimum of effort. The profit on each unit is usually very low, but the volume of sales is high. The sales burden is usually carried by the manufacturer's national advertising. Ads in trade magazines *push* the product into the retail "pipeline," and in mass media they stimulate consumers to *pull* the products through the pipeline. As a manufacturer modifies its strategy to more push or more pull, special promotions may be directed at the trade or at consumers to increase sales (see Chapter 10).

Selective Distribution

By limiting the number of outlets through **selective distribution,** manufacturers can cut their distribution and promotion costs. Many hardware tools are sold selectively through

Cooperative (co-op) advertising involves a manufacturer and a retailer sharing the costs of an ad that benefits both. A great example is this beautiful ad featuring Chanel and Neiman Marcus.

Source: Chanel

discount chains, home improvement centers, and hardware stores. Some pet foods are available at vet offices or pet stores, but not at grocery stores. Manufacturers may use national advertising, but the sales burden is normally carried by the retailer. The manufacturer may share part of the retailer's advertising costs through a **cooperative (co-op) advertising** program, as we discussed in Chapter 4. For example, a Levi's retailer may receive substantial allowances from the manufacturer for advertising Levi's clothing in its local area. In return, the retailer agrees to advertise and display the clothing prominently.

Exclusive Distribution

Under an **exclusive distribution** agreement, selected wholesalers or retailers are granted exclusive rights to distribute a particular product. For example, coffee retailer Starbucks was the exclusive seller of a CD of previously unreleased Bob Dylan songs. [68] The Rolling Stones released a concert video DVD that could be purchased only at Best Buy. This is also common in high fashion, major appliances, and furniture lines. What is lost in market coverage is often gained in the ability to maintain a prestige image and premium prices. Exclusive distribution agreements also force manufacturers and retailers to cooperate closely in advertising and promotion programs.

The vertical marketing system gave rise to a number of successful business plans, like franchising, in which franchisees pay a fee and operate under the guidelines of a parent company. For instance, the nearly 4,400 The UPS Store locations are franchised and provide greater access to UPS shipping services in addition to packing services and supplies, copying, digital printing, and more. In the ad above, The UPS Store cleverly compares their promises to their customers to those of wedding vows and depicts a UPS Store employee atop a wedding cake with a customer.

Source: The UPS Store

...dvertising is nonpersonal selling. However, like ...ersonal selling, it can be used to close the sale, ...specially in mail order. This humorous direct mail ...iece from Land Rover touts an "edible survival guide."

...ource: Land Rover

Vertical Marketing Systems: The Growth of Franchising

To be efficient, members of a distribution channel need to cooperate closely. This need gave rise to the **vertical marketing system (VMS),** a centrally managed distribution system that serves a group of stores or other businesses.

There are many types of vertical marketing systems. For the last quarter century, the greatest growth has been in **franchising**—such as McDonald's or Mailboxes, Etc.—in which retail dealers (or *franchisees*) pay a fee to operate under the guidelines and direction of the parent company or manufacturer (the *franchisor*).

Franchising and other vertical marketing systems offer both manufacturers and retailers numerous advantages, not the least of which are centralized coordination of marketing efforts and substantial savings and continuity in advertising. Perhaps most important is consumer recognition: The moment a new McDonald's opens, the franchisee has instant customers. Moreover, a single newspaper ad can promote all of a chain's retailers in a particular trading area.

Many marketers find that franchising is the best way to introduce their services into global markets. Subway sandwich shops, for example, is one of the fastest-growing franchise operations in the world with a total of more than 25,000 stores in 84 different countries.[69]

In the last decade, the European Union, a market of nearly 462 million people, has opened its doors to innovative marketers. As a result, franchising has grown rapidly, especially in the United Kingdom, France, Germany, Spain, Belgium, and the Netherlands. Some 6,500 franchised brands are now operating in 20 European countries.[70] Although franchising is less regulated in Europe, advertising is more regulated. This again points out the need for local experts to manage the advertising function in foreign markets.

IMC and the Communication (Promotion) Element

Once it determines product, price, and distribution, a company is ready to plan its marketing communications, of which advertising is just one component. (See Ad Lab 6–D.)

The **communication element** includes all marketing-related communications between the seller and the buyer. A variety of marketing communications tools comprise the **communications mix.** These tools can be grouped into *personal* and *nonpersonal communication* activities.

Personal communication includes all person-to-person contact with customers. **Nonpersonal communication** activities—which use some medium as an intermediary for communicating—include *advertising, direct marketing,* certain *public relations* activities, *collateral materials,* and *sales promotion.* Today, successful marketing managers blend all these elements into an *integrated marketing communications program.*

Personal Selling

Some consumer products are sold by clerks in retail stores, others by salespeople who call on customers directly. Personal selling is very important in business-to-business marketing. It establishes a face-to-face situation in which the marketer can learn firsthand about customer wants and needs, and customers find it harder to say no. We discuss personal selling further in Chapter 10.

Advertising

Advertising is sometimes called *mass* or *nonpersonal selling.* Its usual purpose is to inform, persuade, and remind customers about particular products and services. In some cases, like mail order, advertising even closes the sale.

AD Lab 6–D

Price and Promotion

Starbucks classifies its product as a "gourmet" coffee—in other words, it's positioned as a premium product. This suggests that it probably costs more than the typical coffee in the supermarket. However, since Starbucks targets a younger demographic of 20- to 49-year-olds, it must still be careful about how much it charges. Currently, regular brewed coffee at Starbucks costs $1.40 but the most expensive beverage runs approximately $5.00. Whole-bean coffee ranges from $9.95 to $43.90 per pound. Overall, Starbucks coffee may be a bit pricier, but it offers a higher quality product and tries to add value through superior employee service.

To promote awareness, many new companies dedicate enormous budgets to advertising. However, this is not always necessary. Starbucks certainly never dreamed it could establish the degree of brand loyalty that it did in such a short time. But it managed to do so—and with only a minimal amount of advertising. It wasn't that the company didn't believe in advertising; it just didn't think it could afford to advertise. So Starbucks focused on creating product value and giving better service.

Initially, the only promotional elements the company used were public relations and some small sales promotions. These were designed to create initial awareness and interest in its gourmet coffees. As interest and awareness have grown, so have promotional activities. Among these campaigns was the "Matches Made over Coffee" contest. To strengthen its brand and celebrate coffeehouse romances, Starbucks devised a competition in which the winner with the most "creative, romantic, and coffee-rich, true love story" received an all-expense-paid trip for two to Vienna, Austria.

To demonstrate its social concern, Starbucks also ventured into philanthropic activities. In fact, it is now the largest corporate sponsor of CARE, an international relief and development organization that aids the very communities from which the company buys its coffee.

With the coffee culture trend growing, increased competition was a given, forcing Starbucks to spend more on advertising to maintain its market share. Initially, Starbucks spent $17.8 million on a direct-response campaign.

It also sold merchandise, such as mugs, coffee grinders, espresso machines, and gourmet food bearing the Starbucks logo via catalog and the Internet. While Starbucks continues its public relations involvement with communities, it recognizes the growing need to invest in mass-media advertising. Its first major campaign began in 1997, under the creative design of Goodby, Silverstein & Partners, to promote its new Frappuccino beverage. Three television and three radio spots were created for the campaign, focusing on the jingle "Starbucks, purveyors of coffee, tea, and sanity." In the fall of 1997, though, Starbucks changed agencies and hired BBDO West, claiming that Goodby hadn't yet found the right "creative voice" for Starbucks. Since then, Starbucks has utilized the creative input of numerous top agencies, including Fallon McElligott as well as Saatchi & Saatchi.

The current focus of Starbucks' advertising is split between individual promotions for its wide array of products, such as the "What Stirs You?" tagline for its "Toffee Nut Latte," as well as more cause-related marketing programs that focus on philanthropic endeavors abroad. In an ad in *The New York Times*, Starbucks conveyed its charitable efforts in coffee-producing countries with copy that began "Every sip is born out of respect" and concluded with the tagline "We're always serving more than coffee." As more corporations such as Starbucks spread to a global level, many experts believe we are likely to see more such cause-related advertisements in the future, as these corporations attempt to maintain a positive image around the world.

Laboratory Application

When constructing the marketing mix for your chosen product or service (refer to Ad Labs 6–B and 6–C), consider these last two elements: price and promotion. What should your product's price be and why? Should you offer some kind of credit terms? Also, what media should you use to advertise your product or service, and why? Do you think that Starbucks should advertise in more traditional mass media or stick to public relations? What "creative voice" would you suggest for Starbucks?

Certain products lend themselves to advertising so much that it plays the dominant communications role. The following factors are particularly important for advertising success:

- A high primary demand trend.
- The chance for significant product differentiation.
- Hidden qualities that are important to consumers.
- The opportunity to use emotional appeals.
- The availability of substantial sums to support advertising.

Where these conditions exist, as in the cosmetics, auto, or wireless phone industries, companies spend large amounts on advertising, and the ratio of advertising to sales dollars is often quite high. For completely undifferentiated products, such as sugar, salt, and other raw materials or commodities, price is usually the primary influence, and advertising is minimally important. Sunkist is an interesting exception. This farmers' cooperative successfully brands an undifferentiated commodity (citrus fruit) and markets it internationally.

Direct Marketing **Direct marketing** is like taking the store to the customer. A mail-order house that communicates directly with consumers through ads and catalogs is one type of company engaged in direct marketing. It builds its own database of customers and uses a variety of media to communicate with them.

People **BEHIND** the Ads

Tere and Joe Zubi, Zubi Advertising

Courtesy of Zubi Advertising

The surging growth of Latino population numbers and economic power is one reason advertisers are shifting large portions of their promotional budgets to Hispanic media.

Coral Gables, near Miami, is home to one of the largest independent Hispanic agencies in America, Zubi Advertising. Zubi is short for Zubizarreta, and the agency was founded by Tere Zubi, after she and her husband fled Cuba for a better life in the United States. Of course, as with many immigrants, Tere did not find success easily or immediately. In fact, as she relayed to PBS in an interview, her own career was launched by necessity after her husband's small business failed in the early 1970s. Tere applied for jobs as a secretary to help make ends meet.

The second job (interview) I went to was an advertising agency. And I didn't know anything about advertising. I didn't even know how to use an electric typewriter because I had learned on a manual. And the person that interviewed me— everything he asked me—he would say, "Do you know anything about advertising?" And my answer would be, "I don't know, but I'll learn," and so forth. So that was a Friday. And Monday morning, I get the call that I got the job.

And then I asked later on—Mr. Gilmore, who was my boss, Al Gilmore, I said, "Why did you hire me?" He said, "Because I have never met a more honest answer in interviewing any person, because you did not try to fool me. You know, you were straightforward and said, 'I don't know, but I will learn.'"

And learn Tere did. Encouraged by friends, she went on to open her own small South Florida agency with little money or equipment and in office space loaned by friends. Within two decades, Zubi Advertising was handling $80 million in billings for clients like Ford and American Airlines.

A commitment to learning is still a part of Zubi Advertising today. Although Mama Zubi, as Tere was known to coworkers and clients alike, passed away in 2007, the business is still run by the Zubizarreta family, including son Joe and daughter Michelle.

As COO, Joe oversees Zubi's business development, strategic planning, and client relations. He joined Zubi after eight years with Beber, Silverstein and Partners, where within five years he became the youngest account supervisor.

As chief administrative officer, Michelle handles the agency's financial, budgetary, and operational matters, including personnel and management relations, as well as employee recruitment, retention, and benefits.

Current blue-chip accounts include Dunkin' Donuts, Ford Motor Company, Chase, Walgreens, and many others.

Joe Zubi shared some thoughts with us on the unique issues that confront a multicultural advertising agency.

CA: What is the role of a multicultural agency?

JZ: The role is twofold: First, we provide our clients with the cultural insights that can drive effective communication platforms. Second, we partner with general market advertising agencies to help them be more effective with campaigns that target all residents of the United States.

CA: How do you keep track of all the changes that are taking place in the demographic makeup of the United States?

JZ: It's a challenge. We regularly consult all of the important secondary sources of information, including the U.S. Census, Simmons Market Research Bureau reports, and research from pollsters such as Yankelovich and Nielsen. We also examine customized proprietary studies that are category specific. The adaptation to change is based on the category, its competitive set, and the brand's position in its life cycle.

CA: What are you looking for in the people that you will be hiring at Zubi Advertising over the next several years?

JZ: We want people who can grow beyond their potential. People who are confident, passionate, and eager to learn. We are looking for people who are willing to take chances.

CA: Is there anything else that you would like to share with students of advertising?

JZ: Yes. Don't hesitate to take on anything that is thrown your way. Take on any challenge, learn from your mistakes and celebrate your successes. Life is too short to take this too seriously, have fun! It's just advertising. If you want a serious career, be a doctor.

The field of direct marketing is growing rapidly because companies like the benefits of control, cost efficiency, and accountability. For example, many companies such as Levi Strauss use **telemarketing** (a direct marketing technique) to increase productivity through person-to-person phone contact. By using the phone to follow up direct-mail advertising, a company can increase the response rate substantially. Moreover, through telemarketing, it can develop a valuable database of customers and prospects to use in future mailings and promotions.[71] We discuss this topic more thoroughly in Chapter 10.

What better way to suggest that KLM Economy Comfort is like sitting on air, than to stage a publicity event at an airport suggesting a man is doing just that?

Source: KLM

Public Relations

Many firms supplement (or replace) their advertising with various public relations activities such as **publicity** (news releases, feature stories) and **special events** (open houses, factory tours, VIP parties, grand openings) to inform various audiences about the company and its products and to build corporate trustworthiness and image. As Al and Laura Ries point out, through decades of overuse and overpromising, advertising today has lost some of its effectiveness and credibility.[72] On the other hand, public relations activities, as we discuss in Chapter 11, are extremely credible brand-building tools that should always be integrated into a company's communication mix.

Collateral Materials

As mentioned in Chapter 4, **collateral materials** are the many accessory items companies produce to integrate and supplement their advertising or PR activities. These include booklets, catalogs, brochures, films, sales kits, promotional products, and annual reports. Collateral materials should always be designed to reinforce the company's image or the brand's position in the minds of customers.

Sales Promotion

As we discuss in Chapter 10, sales promotion is a special category of communication tools and activities. Designed to supplement the basic elements of the marketing mix for short periods of time, sales promotion is aimed at stimulating customers or members of the distribution channel to some immediate, overt behavior.[73] This broad category includes trade deals, free samples, displays, trading stamps, sweepstakes, cents-off coupons, and premiums, among others. *Reader's Digest,* for example, is famous for its annual sweepstakes designed to increase circulation. And the Promotion Marketing Association Coupon Council reports that 76 percent of U.S. shoppers use coupons, saving $3 billion annually.[74]

Some promotions are linked mainly to the communications function of the marketing mix (displays, events, trade shows), while others are linked more to the product element (free samples, premiums) or the price element (coupons, volume discounts, end-of-month sales). And some complement the distribution element (trade deals, sales contests). Sales promotion (often referred to simply as *promotion*) is used primarily as a tactical adaptation to some external situation such as competitive pressure, changing seasons, declining sales, or new product introductions.[75] Because advertising people are frequently called on to solve a variety of marketing problems, it is critical that they understand and know how to integrate the whole mix of communications techniques.

The Marketing Mix in Perspective

With the target market designated and the elements of the marketing mix determined, the company has a complete product concept and a strategic basis for marketing to that target. Now it can formalize its strategies and tactics in a written marketing and advertising plan. As part of the planning process, companies use marketing and advertising research. We discuss this in Chapter 7 before dealing with the formal planning process in Chapter 8.

Chapter Summary

Market segmentation is the process of identifying groups of people with certain shared characteristics within a broad product market and aggregating these groups into larger market segments according to their mutual interest in the product's utility. From these segments, companies then select a target market. Marketers use a number of methods to identify behavioral groups and segment markets. The most common are behavioristic, geographic, demographic, and psychographic.

Business markets are often segmented in the same way as consumer markets. They may also be grouped by business purchasing procedures, NAICS code, or market concentration.

In the target marketing process, companies designate specific segments to target and develop their mix of marketing activities. The product concept is the consumer's perception of the product as a bundle of utilitarian and symbolic need-satisfying values.

Every company can add, subtract, or modify four major elements in its marketing program to achieve a desired marketing mix. These elements are product, price, distribution (place), and communications (promotion)—the 4Ps.

The *product* element includes the way the product is designed and classified, positioned, branded, and packaged. Just as humans pass through a life cycle, so do products—and product categories. The stage of a product's life cycle may determine how it is promoted.

To satisfy the variety of consumer tastes and achieve competitive advantages, marketers build differences into their products. Even the product's package is part of the product concept. The concept may also be developed through unique positioning against competing products.

Price refers to what and how a customer pays for a product. Companies use many common pricing strategies. Some products compete on the basis of price, but many do not.

Distribution refers to how the product is placed at the disposal of the customer: where the product is distributed, how it is bought, and how it is sold. Companies may use direct or indirect methods of distribution. Consumer goods manufacturers use several types of distribution strategies.

Communications refers to all marketing-related communications between the seller and the buyer. Tools of the communications element include personal selling, advertising, direct marketing, public relations activities, collateral materials, and sales promotion. Marketers try to integrate all their marketing communications programs for greater effectiveness and consistency.

Important Terms

behavioristic segmentation, *175*

benefit segmentation, *177*

benefits, *177*

brand, *195*

brand equity, *196*

business markets, *184*

collateral materials, *205*

communication element, *202*

communications mix, *202*

cooperative (co-op) advertising, *201*

copy points, *196*

decline stage, *192*

demographic segmentation, *178*

direct distribution, *199*

direct marketing, *203*

distribution channel, *199*

distribution element, *199*

early adopters, *192*

equipment-based service, *193*

exclusive distribution, *201*

family brand, *195*

four Ps (4Ps), *191*

franchising, *202*

geodemographic segmentation, *178*

geographic segmentation, *178*

growth stage, *192*

hidden differences, *194*

individual brand, *195*

induced differences, *194*

intensive distribution, *200*

introductory phase, *192*

licensed brands, *195*

market segmentation, *174*

marketing mix, *191*

maturity stage, *192*

national brand, *195*

network marketing, *199*

nonpersonal communication, *202*

North American Industry Classification System (NAICS) codes, *185*

people-based service, *193*

perceptible differences, *194*

personal communication, *202*

position, *193*

price element, *197*

primary demand, *192*

primary demand trend, *187*

primary motivation, *180*

private labels, *195*

product concept, *191*

product element, *191*

product life cycle, *191*

psychographics, *180*

publicity, *205*

pull strategy, *192*

purchase occasion, *177*

push strategy, *192*

reseller, *184*

resources (axis), *180*

sales promotion, *192*

selective demand, *192*

selective distribution, *200*

service, *193*

special events, *205*

target market, *188*

target marketing process, *188*

telemarketing, *204*

usage rates, *176*

user status, *176*

vertical marketing system (VMS), *202*

volume segmentation, *176*

Review Questions

1. How does the concept of shared characteristics relate to the market segmentation process?

2. How could you use VALS to develop the marketing strategy for a product of your choice?

3. How does the segmentation of business markets differ from that of consumer markets?

4. What is the most important factor to consider when determining the elements of the marketing mix?

5. What is the difference between a product and a product concept?

6. What are some examples of product positioning not discussed in this chapter?

7. What effect does the product life cycle have on the advertising a company uses?

8. What factors influence the price of a product?

9. How do the basic methods of distribution affect advertising?

10. What product characteristics encourage heavy advertising? Little advertising? Why?

The Advertising Experience

1. **Product Life Cycles**

   Many well-established American brands may seem to be in the decline stage of the product life cycle, perhaps because changing tastes or new technologies have rendered the products obsolete. Choose one of these and describe a plan for revitalizing the product, especially in terms of the 4Ps.

2. **World of Marketing**

   Part I: Marketing. You have already learned the importance of marketing to the study and application of advertising. Visit the sites below to get a wider view of the scope of the marketing world and the importance of a good marketing strategy. Answer the questions below for each site:

   - American Marketing Association (AMA): www.marketingpower.com
   - Business Marketing Association (BMA): www.marketing.org
   - B to B: www.btobonline.com
   - Brand Republic: www.brandrepublic.com
   - Brandweek: www.brandweek.com
   - Marketing Magazine: www.marketingmag.ca
   - Dotfactor.com: www.dotfactor.com
   - Sales & Marketing Management: www.salesandmarketing.com

   a. What group sponsors the site? Who is the intended audience?

   b. What is the site's purpose? Does it succeed? Why?

   c. What are the size and scope of the organization? What is the organization's purpose?

   d. Who makes up the organization's membership? Its constituency?

   Part II: Marketing Mix. Visit Hardee's site (www.hardees.com) and then answer the following questions about one of its products:

   a. Identify the product, price, place, and promotion. (If there are multiple products, choose one.)

   b. Identify the product's stage in the product life cycle.

   c. What is the product's positioning?

   d. What are the key elements of the product's differentiation?

3. **Market Segmentation and Target Marketing**

   Segmenting markets and generating sound demographic, geographic, psychographic, and behavioristic profiles are critical to formulating advertising strategy. An abundance of market segmentation data is available on the Internet from both the government and the private sector. Peruse the following sample of online resources for target market information:

   - Claritas: www.claritas.com
   - Forrester Research: www.forrester.com
   - Market Segment Resource Locator: www.awool.com
   - Target Marketing: www.targetonline.com
   - U.S. Census Bureau American FactFinder: http://factfinder.census.gov
   - USA Data: www.usadata.com

   Now choose a company with a Website and use one of these online resources to answer the following questions. Be sure to cite any online resources you used in addition to the above.

   a. What type of segmentation approach did the company take (single-market, multiple-market, aggregate market)?

   b. Develop a demographic profile, including age, income, education, and gender for the target market.

   c. Describe the general geographic skew for the company's market.

   d. What consumption patterns are evident in the company's consumers?

4. The Old Spice campaign revitalized a brand whose image may have grown stale in the minds of consumers. Identify another brand whose image, in your opinion, needs revamping. Explain why the image is dated. Propose a new brand identity and suggest a way that an advertisement might help the brand acquire that identity.

5. Another important way that the Old Spice campaign succeeded was it identified an unusual target audience. The ads were directed at consumers who buy the product (women) rather than those who use it (men). Identify another brand whose buyers are different from its users. Which group does the brand target in its advertising and why?

Research: Gathering Information for IMC Planning

Learning Objectives

To examine how advertisers gather intelligence about the marketplace and how they apply their findings to marketing and advertising decision making.

After studying this chapter, you will be able to:

LO7-1   Elaborate on the purposes of IMC research.

LO7-2   Explain the basic steps in the research process.

LO7-3   Distinguish qualitative and quantitative research.

LO7-4   Describe the differences between pretesting and posttesting of campaign messages.

LO7-5   List the important considerations in effective IMC research.

Source: Anheuser Busch

"The Budweiser puppy has done what the Seattle Seahawks could not—it won back-to-back Super Bowls" glowed *USA Today* writer Bruce Horozvitz.[1] The commercial, "Lost Dog," focuses on a lost puppy aided by Budweiser's iconic Clydesdales. You can watch it here: https://www.youtube.com/watch?v=xAsjRRMMg_Q. ■ The ad is a heart warmer, to be sure. But it seems reasonable to ask whether the spot can be justified based on strategic considerations. First, a 30-second spot in the Super Bowl sold for $4 million in 2015, and this does not include the costs of production. Does Budweiser earn a return on its investment in the ads that justifies spending that much on just a single showing? ■ Some might question the focus of the ad as well. The commercial causes many viewers to feel a variety of emotions, ending with the warm glow of the puppy's reunion with its owner. Emotional response to advertising is generally good. But the emotions created

by this ad center on a cute puppy, some brave Clydesdales, and a pet owner's joy at the reunion. Since the true "star" of the campaign is supposed to be a brand of beer, did the ad miss the mark? ■ No advertiser would spend the kind of money ponied up (no pun intended) by Budweiser without answers to such questions. And based on careful, deliberate, and quantitative research, Anheuser Busch was reasonably certain their investment was justified. ■ To begin with, consumers loved the ad. Evidence for this comes from a variety of sources, including the popular *USA Today* AdMeter. The company obtains ratings from approximately 7000 consumer panelists, each of whom evaluated every one of the 61 ads that appeared in the game. "Lost Dog" finished first, beating every other slickly produced spot shown during the game. ■ But advertisers consider liking a means to an end, not an end in itself. A more relevant goal is using advertising to persuade consumers to like the brand. Can a cute puppy create positive feelings about a global brand of beer? The answer seems to be yes, based on research by a company named Bully Pulpit Interactive.[2] The company measured a sampled group of consumers' brand attitudes toward Super Bowl advertisers both before the game and immediately following. Budweiser saw a greater lift in brand favorability than any other game advertiser save one. Budweiser also topped all other brands save one in getting consumers interested in buying and was the most recalled ad of the game. ■ Still, a cynic might argue, liking, recall, brand favorability, these are surrogates for the real metric of interest, sales. What about sales? ■ To answer that question, it is important to recall that a purchase is the final step in a sequence of consumer responses. As you learned in Chapter 5, ads need to pass through perceptual and cognitive filters in order to affect consumers. The favorable reaction of viewers to the spot suggests the ad was successful. And as you will see in Chapter 8, a decision to take action, in this case a decision to purchase the brand, flows from a series of earlier steps that include brand awareness, message comprehension, conviction, and desire. Triggering these psychological responses is an important advertising goal, and research confirmed "Lost Dog" achieved these goals. ■ But back to sales. What evidence do we have that the ad's psychological effectiveness produced the desired increase in sales? Research was able to address this question as well. Wesley Hartmann, a marketing professor at Stanford University, analyzed data collected from 55 markets around the United States as well as sales figures provided by Nielsen. The analysis showed that Budweiser's ad spending on the big game produced sales increases of $96 million, or a return on investment (ROI) of 172 percent.[3] All-in-all, a pretty satisfactory return. ■ When agencies spend their clients' money, the stakes are high. Jon Wanamaker, an advertising professional from many years ago, famously said "I know 50 percent of my advertising is wasted. I just don't know which 50 percent." With modern research techniques, ignorance about advertising results is no longer inevitable. Or acceptable.

The Need for Research in Marketing and IMC

LO 7-1

Every year companies spend millions of dollars creating ads and promotions that they hope their customers and prospects will notice and relate to. Then they spend millions more placing their communications in media, hoping their customers will see and hear them and eventually respond.

Advertising is expensive. In the United States the cost of a single 30-second commercial on AMC's popular series "Walking Dead" is nearly $400,000.[4] Likewise, a single, full-page color ad in a national business magazine averages $100 to reach every thousand prospects.[5] That's too much money to risk unless companies have good information about who their customers are, what they want and like, and where they spend their media time. And that's why marketers need research. Research provides the information that drives marketing decision making. Without that information, firms are forced to use intuition or guesswork. In a fast-changing, highly competitive, global economy, that invites failure.

What Is Marketing Research?

To help managers make marketing decisions, companies develop systematic procedures for gathering, recording, and analyzing new information. This is called **marketing research** (it should not be confused with *market research,* which is information gathered about a *particular* market or market segment).[6] Marketing research does a number of things: It helps identify consumer needs and market segments; it provides the information for developing new products and marketing strategies; and it enables managers to assess the effectiveness of promotional activities. Marketing research is also useful in financial planning, economic forecasting, and quality control.

Research has become big business. Worldwide, the top 10 research companies had revenues of more than $5.5 billion for marketing, advertising, and public opinion research. Led by The Nielsen Company, with offices in more than 100 countries, the top 25 have corporate

Exhibit 7-1

Top 10 research companies by U.S. research revenues in 2012 ($ in millions).

US Rank 2012	US Rank 2011	Company	Headquarters	U.S. Revenue (millions)	Website
1	1	Nielsen Holdings	New York	$2,651	nielsen.com
2	2	Kantar	London	929	kantor.com
3	3	Ipsos	New York	590	ipsos-NA.com
4	4	Westat Inc	Rockville, MD	491	westat.com
5	5	IRI	Chicago	478	iriworldwide.com
6	6	Arbitron	Columbia, MD	444	arbitron.com
7	7	GfK USA	Nuremberg, Germany	331	gfk.com
8	8	IMS Health	Norwalk, CT	271	imshealth.com
9	9	NPD Group	Port Washington, NY	192	npd.com
10	10	ICF International	Fairfax, VA	191	icfi.com

Source: Honomichl Report, retrieved at: https://www.ama.org/Documents/Honomichl50Report_June2013.pdf

parents in the United Kingdom, Sweden, Brazil, France, Germany, Japan, the Netherlands, and the United States. But nearly one-half of their revenues come from operations outside their home countries.[7] Exhibit 7-1 lists the top 10 research companies by worldwide revenues.

Research is used to gather a lot of different types of information. It may be easiest to think of all these in terms of the *three Rs* of marketing: *recruiting* new customers, *retaining* current customers, and *regaining* lost customers.[8]

For example, to *recruit* new customers, researchers study different market segments and create *product attribute models* to match buyers with the right products and services. Marketers have many questions: What new products do consumers want? Which ideas should we work on? What product features are most important to our customers? What changes in the product's appearance and performance will increase sales? What price will maintain the brand's image, create profits, and still be attractive and affordable? Answers may lead to decisions that directly affect the product's nature, content, packaging, pricing—and IMC.[9]

On the other hand, to *retain* existing customers, a marketer may use *customer satisfaction studies*. Likewise, *databases* of customer transactions may identify reasons for customer satisfaction or dissatisfaction.[10] Today, companies realize that the best sales go to those who develop good relationships with individual customers.[11] As a result, customer satisfaction is now the fastest-growing field in marketing research.

Information gained for the first two Rs helps the third, *regaining* lost customers. For example, if an office equipment manufacturer discovers through research that an increase in service calls typically precedes cancellation of a service contract, it can watch for that pattern and take preventive action. Moreover, it can review service records of former customers and (if the pattern holds true) devise some marketing action or appeal to win them back.[12]

In short, good marketing research enables companies to devise a sophisticated, integrated mix of product, price, distribution, and communication elements. It gives them the information they need to decide which strategies will enhance the brand's image and lead to greater profits. Finally, it enables them to judge the effectiveness of past marketing programs and campaigns.

What Is IMC Research?

Before developing any campaign, a company needs to know how people perceive its products, how they view the competition, what brand or company image would be most credible, and what messages offer the greatest appeal. To get this information, companies use *IMC research*. While marketing research provides the information necessary to make marketing decisions, **IMC research** uncovers the information needed for making IMC decisions. By definition, it is the systematic gathering and analysis of information to help develop or evaluate message strategies, individual promotions, and whole campaigns.

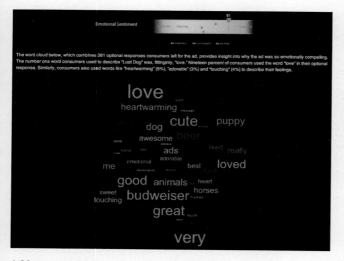

A 30-second spot in Super Bowl XLIX cost $4.5 million. At those prices advertisers are smart to do everything they can to make sure their ads resonate with consumers. Budweiser's "Lost Dog" spot topped the charts of many ad measures, including those employed by research company "Ace Metrix."

Source: Courtesy of Ace Metrix

In this chapter, we consider the importance of information gathering to the development of IMC plans and strategies; we look at how companies use research to test the effectiveness of ads before and after they run; and we explore a number of specific research techniques.

Applying Research to IMC Decision Making

IMC research serves various purposes, most of which can be grouped into four categories: *strategy research*, *creative concept research*, *pretesting*, and *posttesting*.

1. *IMC strategy research.* Used to help define the product concept or to assist in the selection of target markets, messages, or media vehicles.

2. *Creative concept research.* Measures the target audience's acceptance of different creative ideas at the concept stage.

3. *Message pretesting.* Used to diagnose possible communication problems before a campaign begins.

4. *Message posttesting.* Enables marketers to evaluate a campaign after it runs.

As Exhibit 7-2 shows, marketers use the different categories of research at different stages of campaign development. The techniques they use at each stage also vary considerably. We'll examine each of these categories briefly before moving on to discuss the research process.

Message Strategy Research

Companies develop a message strategy by blending elements of the *creative mix*. These include the *product concept*, the *target audience*, the *communication media*, and the *creative message*. To seek information about any or all of these various elements, companies use **IMC strategy research.**

Product Concept

As we saw at the beginning of this chapter, marketers need to know how consumers perceive their brands. They also want to know what qualities lead to initial purchases and, eventually, to brand loyalty.

	Advertising Strategy Research	Creative Concept Research	Pretesting	Posttesting
Timing	Before creative work begins	Before agency production begins	Before finished artwork and photography	After campaign has run
Research Problem	Product concept definition Target audience selection Media selection Message element selection	Concept testing Name testing Slogan testing	Print testing TV storyboard pretesting Radio commercial pretesting	Advertising effectiveness Consumer attitude change Sales increases
Techniques	Consumer attitude and usage studies Media studies	Free-association tests Qualitative interviews Statement comparison tests	Consumer juries Matched samples Portfolio tests Storyboard tests Mechanical devices Psychological rating scales	Aided recall Unaided recall Attitude tests Inquiry tests Sales tests

Exhibit 7-2
Categories of research in advertising development.

Using this information, they try to establish a unique *product concept* for their brand—that bundle of values we discussed in Chapter 6 that encompasses both utilitarian and symbolic benefits to the consumer.

The opening vignette of this chapter offers an illustration of how research informs the development of a product concept. Budweiser knew that its warm, emotional messages, created with a heavy emphasis on symbolism and storytelling, are effective in creating favorable attitudes toward the brand. It is one reason why Bud has had an exclusive Super Bowl ad buy in the beer category.[13]

It's this kind of information that can lead to an effective positioning strategy for the brand. IMC can shape and magnify a brand's position and image over time. But to use message strategies effectively, strategy research should inform a blueprint for creatives to follow.[14]

IMC works differently for different product categories and, often, even for different brands within a category. This means that each brand must develop a template for the creative based on an understanding of its particular consumers' wants, needs, and motivations. Only if this is done correctly over time (say, one to two years) can brand equity be built.[15]

To determine how brands are built and how they derive their strength, the Young & Rubicam agency developed a model called the BrandAsset Valuator. It measures brands in terms of differentiation, relevance, esteem, and familiarity, in that order. According to Y&R's theory, a brand must first develop differentiation—it must offer something unique and different—to survive. Second, it must be perceived by the target market as relevant to their needs and wants. Finally, it needs to build stature through esteem and knowledge. Once all these steps are accomplished, a brand achieves leadership status. Y&R performed a study in 19 countries and found that Disney scored high on all these dimensions.[16]

Following Y&R's lead, other agencies have developed their own brand equity studies. In 1998, WPP Group introduced a research tool titled "BRANDZ." Then, in 2000, DDB Worldwide introduced "Brand Capital," and Leo Burnett unveiled its brand of research dubbed "Brand Stock." All of these are designed to help agencies understand how consumers connect with brands before millions are spent on messages.[17]

Target Audience Selection

The second element of the creative mix is the target audience. We pointed out in Chapters 5 and 6 that no market includes everybody. Therefore, an important purpose of research is to develop a rich profile of the brand's target markets and audiences. The marketer will want to know which customers are the primary users of the product category and will study them carefully to understand their demographics, geographics, psychographics, and purchase behavior.

With any new product, there is never enough money to attack all geographic or demographic markets effectively at the same time. So the marketer will often decide to employ the *dominance concept*—researching which markets (geographic or otherwise) are most important to product sales and targeting those where it can focus its resources to achieve promotional dominance.

Fallon World Wide, a Minneapolis agency, worked closely with Holiday Inn Express to identify the target audience for the client's "Stay Smart" campaign. The agency believed it was important to find a target audience that would be heavy users of hotels but were being ignored by other hotel chains. Drive-ups, consisting of independent-minded male businessmen, typically working in small companies or for themselves, fit the bill perfectly. As heavy users of hotels, they represented a highly profitable market segment. And because drive-ups believed that no hotel brand was particularly interested in them, Fallon could design a campaign that targeted their needs and concerns.

Media Selection

To develop media strategies, select media vehicles, and evaluate their results, agencies use a subset of IMC research called **media research.** Agencies subscribe to syndicated research services (such as ACNielsen, Arbitron, Simmons, or @plan) that monitor and publish information on the reach and effectiveness of media vehicles—radio, TV, newspapers, Websites, and so on—in every major geographic market in the United States and Canada. (We'll discuss these further in Chapter 9).

Young & Rubicam's BrandAsset® Valuator is a model
used to quantitatively ascertain how brands are built
and the assets from which they derive their market
strength. BrandAsset® Valuator has to date surveyed
more than 1,100,000 consumers on over 50,000
brands. Data have been collected since 1993. The core
dimensions that determine where brands fall in the
matrix are differentiation (D), relevance (R), esteem (E),
and knowledge (K). D and R are measures of a brand's
strength while E and K tap its stature.

Source: Courtesy of Young & Rubicam New York

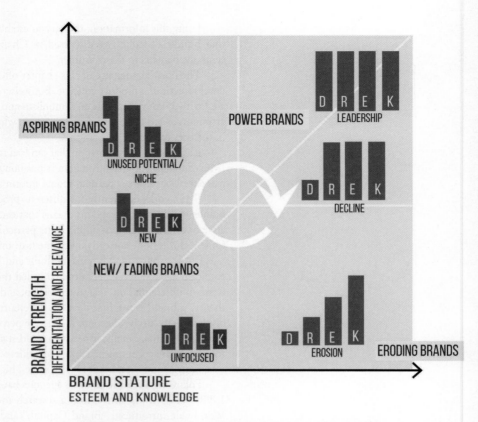

For Holiday Inn Express, Fallon researched the media habits of drive-ups and discovered that they tended to watch cable fare focused on news and sports, including programs on ESPN, CNN, and the Weather Channel. Research also suggested that the target audience formulated travel plans early in the week, so Fallon ran ads only on Sunday and Monday nights. While the overall ad budget was comparatively small, the concentration of ads on two evenings using a small number of networks gave the campaign a larger presence on those occasions when drive-ups would actually be watching TV and thinking about travel. In addition, because the campaign was so fresh and unusual, it got an additional boost from unpaid references to the "No, but I did stay at a Holiday Inn Express last night" slogan on ESPN, *Late Night with David Letterman*, NPR, and *The Washington Post*.

Message Element Selection

The final component of IMC strategy is the message element. Companies hope to find promising messages by studying consumers' likes and dislikes in relation to brands and products. Kraft Foods, for example, was looking for ways to dissuade parents from switching to less expensive brands of processed cheese. While its Kraft Singles brand dominated the processed cheese slices category, it was concerned that the brand wasn't keeping up with overall growth in the market.

Working with several research companies and its agency, J. Walter Thompson, the company conducted a series of qualitative consumer attitude studies to figure out how women, particularly mothers, felt about Kraft Singles with the hope of discovering possible message themes. The mothers said they felt good giving their kids Kraft Singles because of the brand's nutritional value. But there was a catch—they also said they'd switch to a competitive product if it were cheaper. Fortunately, a phone survey provided some clues for solving the problem. Among these polled, 78 percent considered the brand an extra source of calcium for their kids. And 84 percent of women with kids under 12 said they'd be motivated to buy the brand because of that added benefit.[18]

From this information, the agency used concept testing to determine which message element options might prove most successful. This was now category 2 research aimed at developing creative concepts.

Developing Creative Concepts

Once it develops an IMC strategy, the company (or its agency) will begin developing creative concepts. Here again, research is helpful in determining which concepts to use.

From all their studies, Kraft researchers came up with two concepts that might keep mothers from defecting to competitive brands. First, show how much kids like Kraft Singles, and second, emphasize the fact that the brand provides the calcium kids need. J. Walter Thompson prepared two tentative TV spots and then conducted focus groups of mothers to get their reactions. With a discussion leader moderating the conversation, each group viewed the commercials. The groups' reactions were measured, taped, and observed by JWT and Kraft staff behind a one-way mirror. Immediately, problems surfaced. The idea that kids love the taste of Kraft Singles just didn't come across strongly enough. And the statement that Kraft provides calcium wasn't persuasive. Parents said, "Of course it has calcium, it's cheese." The agency had to find a newsier way to communicate the information.

Tweaking the commercials, JWT came up with a new spot showing youngsters gobbling gooey grilled-cheese sandwiches while a voice-over announcer stated that two out of five kids don't get enough calcium. More focus groups ensued. Now the parents agreed that the shots of kids devouring sandwiches communicated the great taste theme, but some thought the two-out-of-five statement played too much on their guilt.

To soften the message, the agency switched to a female announcer and then brought in the Dairy Fairy, a character from an earlier campaign, to lighten the whole tone of the spot. This seemed to work better, so the agency proceeded to copy testing.

Pretesting and Posttesting

IMC is one of the largest costs in a company's marketing budget. Companies want to know what they are getting for their money—and whether their messages are working. And they'd like some assurance before their ads run.

Kraft was no exception. Millward Brown Research performed a number of copy tests to see how the agency's latest spot would perform. The tests showed that the spot performed significantly better than the norm on key measures such as branding and persuasion. Following the copy tests, the company aired "The Calcium They Need" commercial in five test markets to see how it would affect sales. Kraft quickly achieved a 10 percent increase in sales in those markets. Based on such a strong showing, Kraft rolled the campaign out nationally, and sales took off. Base volume soared 14.5 percent, and sales grew 11.8 percent.[19]

The campaign was so successful that the Advertising Research Foundation named Kraft and J. Walter Thompson finalists for its prestigious David Ogilvy Research Award, given to the most effective campaign guided by research.

The Purpose of Testing

Testing is used to ensure IMC dollars are spent wisely. Testing can prevent costly errors, especially in judging which strategy or medium is most effective. And it can give the marketer some measure of a campaign's value.

To increase the likelihood of preparing the most effective messages, companies use **pretesting.** Pretesting is somewhat controversial among creatives because it is believed it can lead to bland, safe copy. But large clients frequently insist on it, and the practice is now becoming common even in digital campaigns.[20] When companies don't pretest, they may encounter a surprising reaction from the marketplace. Schering Canada received a torrent of complaint letters from customers who said they didn't like its commercial introducing the antihistamine Claritin to the over-the-counter market in Canada. Most negative responses, though, are more insidious: Consumers simply turn the page or change the channel, and sales mysteriously suffer. This is why it's also important to evaluate the effectiveness of a campaign *after* it runs. **Posttesting** (also called *tracking*) provides the marketer with useful guidelines for future advertising.

Testing Helps Marketers Make Important Decisions

Companies use pretesting to help make decisions about a number of variables. It may be helpful to think of these as the five Ms: *merchandise, markets, motives, messages,* and *media.* Many of these can be posttested too. We'll discuss each of the five Ms briefly.

Merchandise   For purposes of alliteration, we refer to the product concept here as **merchandise.** Companies may pretest many things: the package design, how a message positions the brand, or how well it communicates the product's features.

Markets   Companies may pretest a strategy or particular commercials with different **markets.** The information they gain may cause them to alter their strategy and target the campaign to new segments. In posttesting, advertisers want to know if the campaign succeeded in reaching its target markets. Changes in awareness and increases in market share are two indicators of success.

Motives   Consumers' **motives** are outside a company's control, but the messages they create to appeal to those motives are not. Pretesting helps marketers identify and appeal to the most compelling needs and motives, and to evaluate whether consumers consider brand claims about meeting such needs as compelling and credible. Posttesting can indicate how effective they were.

Messages   Pretesting helps identify outstanding, as well as underperforming, messages. It helps determine what (from the customer's point of view) a **message** says and how well it says it. If the message is an ad, an agency might test the headline, the text, the illustration, the typography—or the message concept. Most important, pretesting guides the improvement of commercials.

However, pretesting is not foolproof. The only way to know for sure if a message is effective is through posttesting. Here the marketer determines to what extent the message was

Exhibit 7-3
Media categories.

Media Classes	Print	Electronic	Digital Interactive	Direct Mail	Out-of-Home
Media subclasses	Newspaper Magazines	Radio Television	Internet Kiosks, ATMs	Catalog Brochure	Outdoor Transit
Media vehicles	*The NY Times* *Elle*	KNX-AM Wheel of Fortune	Yahoo!, e-mail Facebook	Spiegel	Billboards Bus benches
Media units	Half page Full page	30-second spot Infomercial	Banner ATM video	16-page Letter size	30-sheet poster Inside card

seen, remembered, and believed. Virtually all testing assesses both cognitive change (e.g., increased awareness of a brand or the memorability of a slogan or benefit) and evaluative change (e.g., brand interest or more positive brand attitudes).

Media   The cost of media advertising is soaring, and marketers hold their agencies accountable for demonstrating the effectiveness of media buys. Information gained from pretesting can influence several types of media decisions: classes of media, media subclasses, specific media vehicles, media units of space and time, media budgets, and scheduling criteria.

The broad media categories of print, electronic, digital interactive, direct mail, and out-of-home are referred to as **media classes.** Conversely, **media subclasses** refer to newspapers or magazines, radio or TV, and so on. The specific **media vehicle** is the particular publication or program. **Media units** are the size or length of an ad: half-page or full-page ads, 15- or 30-second spots, 60-second commercials, and so forth (see Exhibit 7-3).

After a campaign runs, posttesting can determine how effectively the media mix reached the target audience and communicated the desired message. We discuss audience measurement further in Chapters 13 through 17.

A constant question facing all advertisers is how large the company's promotional budget should be. How much should be allocated to various markets and media? To specific products? Companies can use a number of pretesting techniques to determine optimum spending levels before introducing national campaigns. (Chapter 8 provides further information on budgeting.)

Media scheduling is another nagging question for many advertisers. Through pretesting, marketers can test consumer response during different seasons of the year or days of the week. They can test whether frequent advertising is more effective than occasional or one-time insertions, or whether year-round advertising is more effective than advertising concentrated during a gift-buying season. (Chapter 9 discusses the most common types of media schedules.)

Testing in digital media   A big appeal of digital media is the ease with which even small advertisers can test potential messages. Advertising with search engine Google can be prohibitively expensive unless a marketer knows which keywords are being used by potential customers. Google's *Keyword Planner* allows advertisers to view how many people are searching for a word or phrase at any given time.[21]

Similarly, Facebook encourages advertisers to test campaigns before committing large resources to running ads and provides valuable help on how to do so.[22] Effective online marketing is not just about attracting an audience, however, it is also about converting those who've been attracted into customers. Google Analytics is a well-known tool for tracking visits to a Website, but Twitter offers sophisticated tools for determining whether social media activity on the platform has resulted in a sale.[23]

Overall Results   Finally, marketers want to measure overall results to evaluate how well they accomplished their objectives. Posttesting is most helpful here to determine whether and how to continue, what to change, and how much to spend in the future. We'll discuss the methods used for pre- and posttesting in the next section on conducting primary research.

LO 7-2

Steps in the Research Process

Now that we understand the various types of decision-related information that marketers seek, let's explore how they gather this information by looking at the overall research process and some of the specific techniques they use.

Exhibit 7-4
The marketing research process begins with evaluation of the company's situation and definition of the problem.

There are five basic steps in the research process (see Exhibit 7-4):

1. Situation analysis and problem definition.
2. Informal (exploratory) research.
3. Construction of research objectives.
4. Primary research.
5. Interpretation and reporting of findings.

Step 1: Analyzing the Situation and Defining the Problem

The first step in the marketing research process is to *analyze the situation* and *define the problem.* Many large firms have in-house research departments. Often the marketing department also maintains a **marketing information system (MIS)**—a sophisticated set of procedures designed to generate a continuous, orderly flow of information for use in making marketing decisions. These systems ensure that managers get the information they need when they need it.[24]

Most smaller firms don't have dedicated research departments, and their methods for obtaining marketing information are frequently inadequate. These firms often find the problem definition step difficult and time-consuming. Yet good research on the wrong problem is a waste of effort.

Step 2: Conducting Informal (Exploratory) Research

The second step in the process is to use **informal** (or *exploratory*) **research** to learn more about the market, the competition, and the business environment, and to better define the problem. Researchers may discuss the problem with wholesalers, distributors, or retailers outside the firm; with informed sources inside the firm; with customers; or even with competitors. They look for whoever has the most information to offer. In creating the campaign for Holiday Inn Express, account planners at Fallon spoke with individuals from the target market, but also with company executives, franchise owners, and consumers of competing hotel chains.

There are two types of research data: *primary* and *secondary.* Information collected by the company or agency about a specific problem is called **primary data;** acquiring it is typically expensive and time-consuming. So during the exploratory stage, researchers frequently use **secondary data**—information previously collected or published, usually for some other purpose. This information is readily available, either internally or externally, and can be gathered more quickly and inexpensively than primary data. To give specific examples, when Fallon planners interviewed drive-ups, they were collecting primary data. When they searched the web for information on hotel chains, they were collecting secondary data.

Assembling Internal Secondary Data

Company records are often a valuable source of secondary information. Useful internal data include product shipment figures, billings, warranty card records, advertising expenditures, sales expenses, customer correspondence, and records of meetings with sales staff.

A well-developed marketing information system can help researchers analyze sales data, review past tracking studies, and examine previous marketing research data. This information might point the way toward an interesting headline or positioning statement such as Jiffy Lube's "The Well-Oiled Machine."

Gathering External Secondary Data

Much information is available, sometimes for little or no cost, from the government, market research companies, trade associations, various trade publications, or computerized databases. Most large companies subscribe to any of a number of syndicated research reports about their particular industry. For example, as the advertising manager for a large nutritional company introducing a new line of vitamins, you might need to know the current demand for vitamins and food supplements, the number of competitors in the marketplace, the amount of advertising each is doing, and the challenges and opportunities the industry faces.

In the United States, frequently used sources of secondary data include

- Library reference materials (*Business Periodicals Index* for business magazines, *Reader's Guide to Periodical Literature* for consumer magazines, *Public Information Service Bulletin, The New York Times Index,* and the *World Almanac and Book of Facts*).
- Government publications (*Statistical Abstract of the United States*).
- Trade association publications (annual fact books containing government data gathered by various industry groups listed in the *Directory of National Trade Associations*).
- Research organizations and their publications or syndicated information (literature from university bureaus of business research, Nielsen retail store audits, MRCA consumer purchase diaries, Simmons' Study of Media and Markets, Jupiter Research, IRI's InfoScan market tracking service, and Standard Rate & Data Service).
- Consumer/business publications (*Bloomberg Businessweek, Forbes, Fortune, American Demographics, Advertising Age, Prevention,* and thousands more).
- Computer database services (Dialog Information Service, ProQuest, Electric Library, Lexis-Nexis, and Dow Jones News Retrieval Service).
- Internet search engines (Google, Yahoo!, Bing, and others).

It's important to understand that secondary data carry some potential problems. Information may be out of date and therefore obsolete. Much of it is not relevant to the problem at hand. Some information from purported research is just wrong, so the findings are invalid. In other cases, the source may be unreliable. Finally, there is now so much information available (thanks to the Internet) that it's just overwhelming; it's extremely time-consuming to wade through it all.

Using Secondary Data for International Markets

In developing countries, the research profession is not as sophisticated or organized as in North America and Europe.[25] The available secondary research statistics may be outdated or invalid. When evaluating secondary data, managers should ask, Who collected the data and why? What research techniques did they use? Would the source have any reason to bias the data? When were the data collected? International advertising managers should exercise caution when dealing with "facts" about foreign markets.

Step 3: Establishing Research Objectives

Once the exploratory research phase is completed, the company may discover it needs additional information that it can get only from doing primary research. For example, it may want to identify exactly who its customers are and clarify their perceptions of the company and the competition. To do so, the company must first establish *specific research objectives*.

A concise written statement of the research problem and objectives should be formulated at the beginning of any research project. A company must be clear about what decisions it has to make that the research results will guide. Once it knows the application, it can set down clear, specific research objectives.[26] For example, a department store, noticing that it is losing market share, might write its problem statement and research objectives as follows:

Market Share

Our company's sales, while still increasing, seem to have lost momentum and are not producing the profit our shareholders expect. In the last year, our market share slipped 10 percent in the men's footwear department and 7 percent in the women's fine apparel department. Our studies indicate we are losing sales to other department stores in the same malls and that customers are confused about our position in the market. We need to make decisions about how we position ourselves for the future marketplace.

Research Objectives

We must answer the following questions: (1) Who are our customers? (2) Who are the customers of other department stores? (3) What do these customers like and dislike about us and about our competitors? (4) How are we currently perceived? (5) What do we have to do to clarify and improve that perception?

An extraordinary amount of secondary data can be found on the web. Services such as EDGAR Online (www.edgar-online.com) create databases of news articles published in a wide range of trade and business journals.

Source: EDGAR® Online

	Qualitative	Quantitative
Main techniques for gathering data	Focus groups and in-depth interviews.	Survey and experiments (copy or message testing).
Kinds of questions asked	Why? Through what thought process? In what way? In connection with what other behavior or thoughts?	How many? How much?
Role of interviewer	Critical: Interviewer must think on feet and frame questions and probes in response to whatever respondents say. A highly trained professional is advisable.	Important, but interviewers need only be able to read scripts. They should not improvise. Minimally trained, responsible employees are suitable.
Questions asked	Questions vary in order and phrasing from group to group and interview to interview. New questions are added, old ones dropped.	Should be exactly the same for each interview. Order and phrasing of questions carefully controlled.
Number of interviews	Fewer interviews tending to last a longer time.	Many interviews in order to give a projectable scientific sample.
Kinds of findings	Develop hypotheses, gain insights, explore language options, refine concepts, flesh out numerical data, provide diagnostics on advertising copy.	Test hypotheses, prioritize factors, provide data for mathematical modeling and projections.

Exhibit 7-5
Differences between qualitative and quantitative research.

This statement of the problem is specific and measurable, the decision point is clear, and the questions are related and relevant. The research results should provide the information management needs to decide on a new positioning strategy for the company. The positioning strategy facilitates the development of marketing and advertising plans that will set the company's course for years to come.

Step 4: Conducting Primary Research

When a company wants to collect its own data about a specific problem or issue, it uses **primary research.** There are two types of primary research: qualitative and quantitative.

To get a general impression of the market, the consumer, or the product, marketers typically start with **qualitative research.** This enables researchers to gain insight into both the population whose opinion will be sampled and the subject matter itself. Then, to get hard numbers about specific marketing situations, they may perform a survey or use some other form of **quantitative research.** Sophisticated agencies use a balance of both qualitative and quantitative methods, understanding the limits of each and how they work together.[27] (See Exhibit 7-5.)

Step 5: Interpreting and Reporting the Findings

The final step in the research process involves interpreting and reporting the data. Research is very costly (see Exhibit 7-6), and its main purpose is to help solve problems. The final report must be comprehensible to the company's managers and relevant to their needs.

Exhibit 7-6
The cost of professional research.

Type of Research	Features	Cost	Cost per Respondent	Factors That Can Affect Quality and Costs
Telephone and mail surveys	400 20-minute interviews, with report	$16,000 to $18,000	$40 to $45	Response rates Interview time Incidence of qualified respondents Level of analysis required in the report
E-mail surveys	400 surveys, with report	$3,000 to $5,000	$8 to $16	Extent population can be reached via e-mail Response rates Level of analysis required in the report
Focus group	2 groups with 10 respondents each, with report	$8,000 to $12,000	$400 to $600	Cost of focus group facilities Moderator costs Respondent costs

Sources: WestGroup Research, "Research Fundamentals: Estimating Telephone Survey Research Costs," www.westgroupresearch.com/research/phonecosts.html, accessed October 14, 2006; MC Squared Consulting, "Market Research," http://smallbusiness.yahoo.com/r-article-a-2188-m-6-sc-41 holding a focus group on a budget-i?aid=2188&mcid=6&scid=41&holding a focus group on a budget=i, accessed October 14, 2006; "Survey's Buyers Guide," http://Smallbusiness.yahoo.com/r-article-a-2040-m-6-sc-41-surveys buyers guide-i.

My IMC Campaign 7–A

Research

Research is a complicated aspect of preparing a campaign, and without at least one course in advertising research you may find it tough going. However, without research you will find it difficult to make some of the tough creative and strategic decisions that lie ahead. Even without an extensive research background, you can do some secondary and qualitative research that can result in better choices for your campaign.

Secondary Research

Secondary research involves obtaining information from existing sources, including your client. Be sure to obtain all that you can, with the understanding that information shared by your client is valuable and that most clients will insist on strict confidentiality. Breaking a confidentiality agreement is a very serious transgression and should not happen under any circumstances, whether deliberately or through neglect.

Qualitative Research

You can also plan some qualitative research studies. Two of the most common are focus groups and observational research. In a focus group, you bring together a collection of carefully chosen participants (users of your brand, users of competing brands, etc.) and lead a group discussion that has the potential to offer strategic insights.

Qualitative Research: Focus Groups

For a tutorial on using focus groups, see www.cse.lehigh.edu/~glennb/mm/FocusGroups.htm. Tips for using focus groups can be found at www.groupsplus.com/pages/mn091498.htm.

Observational Research

Observational research techniques involve monitoring the consumer in his or her native environment (the mall, a restaurant, a skateboard park, etc.). The goal is to see how the consumer behaves in a natural setting. Careful attention is ordinarily paid to language, dress, interactions, symbols, and style.

See the observational research tutorial at http:/writing. colostate.edu/guides/research/observe/index.cfm. Tips for observational research can be found at www.quirks.com/articles/a1997/19971208.aspx?searchID=625728.

Quantitative Research

Your project may also involve administering a survey. Google Forms, introduced in the My IMC Campaign from Chapter 2, may be useful for creating an online survey that is easy and inexpensive to administer. The hard part is writing a good survey instrument and then choosing data analysis techniques that will provide you and your client with useful information. Some web tutorials are listed below:

Surveys

Writing good questions: www.accesswave.ca/~infopoll/tips.htm
Response options: http:/dataguru.org/ref/survey/responseoptions.asp

Data Analysis Using Excel

www.ncsu.edu/labwrite/res/gt/gt-menu.html

Tables and graphs are helpful, but they must be explained in words management can understand. Technical jargon (such as "multivariate analysis of variance model") should be avoided, and descriptions of the methodology, statistical analysis, and raw data should be confined to an appendix. The report should state the problem and research objective, summarize the findings, and draw conclusions. The researcher should make recommendations for management action, and the report should be discussed in a formal presentation to allow for questions and to highlight important points.

Understanding Qualitative and Quantitative Research Approaches

LO 7-3

In this section we'll discuss the basic methods companies use for conducting qualitative and quantitative research, and then we'll look at how they apply these techniques to testing campaigns.

Methods of Qualitative Research

To get people to share their motives, beliefs, and perceptions, researchers use **qualitative research** that encourages consumers to openly discuss their thoughts and feelings in response to questions from an interviewer. Some marketers refer to this as *motivation research*. Unfortunately, no matter how skillfully posed, some questions are uncomfortable for consumers to answer. When asked why they bought a particular status car, for instance, consumers might reply that it handles well or is economical or dependable, but they rarely admit that it makes them feel important. The methods used in qualitative research are usually either *projective* or *intensive techniques*.

Projective Techniques   Advertisers use **projective techniques** to unearth people's underlying or subconscious feelings, attitudes, interests, opinions, needs, and motives. By asking indirect questions (such as "What kind of people do you think shop here?"), the researcher tries to involve consumers in a situation where they can express feelings about the problem or product. A technique used by one researcher includes asking individuals to find pictures that, for that individual, exemplify a brand, company, or person. These pictures are used as the starting point for a discussion of why the pictures were chosen and what they mean.

Projective techniques were adapted for marketing research after their use by psychologists in clinical diagnosis. But such techniques require the skill of highly experienced researchers.

Intensive Techniques   **Intensive techniques,** such as in-depth interviews, also require great care to administer properly. In the **in-depth interview,** carefully planned but loosely structured questions help the interviewer probe respondents' deeper feelings. The big pharmaceutical company Schering-Plough, for example, uses in-depth interviews with physicians to find out what attributes doctors consider most important in the drugs they prescribe and to identify which brands the doctors associate with different attributes.[28]

While in-depth interviews help reveal individual motivations, they are also expensive and time-consuming, and skilled interviewers are in short supply.

One of the most common intensive research techniques is the **focus group,** in which the company invites six or more people typical of the target market to a group session to discuss the product, the service, or the marketing situation. The session may last an hour or more. A trained moderator guides the often freewheeling discussion, and the group interaction reveals the participants' true feelings or behavior toward the product. Focus group meetings are usually recorded and often viewed from behind a one-way mirror.

Focus groups aren't a representative sample of the population, but the participants' responses are useful for several purposes. They can provide input about the viability of prospective spokespeople, determine the effectiveness of visuals and strategies, and identify elements in ads that are unclear or claims that don't seem plausible. Focus groups are best used in conjunction with surveys. In fact, focus group responses often help marketers design questions for a formal survey.[29] Following a survey, focus groups can put flesh on the skeleton of raw data.[30]

Focus groups are particularly useful to gain a deeper understanding of particular market segments. A *show-and-tell* focus group conducted by Grieco Research Group in Colorado

A focus group is an intensive research technique used to evaluate the effectiveness of the various elements of a sponsor's campaign. Focus groups are especially effective when used in conjunction with market surveys.

© Robert Churchill/Getty Images RF

provides a glimpse of the core values of baby boomers. Participants were asked to bring to the session three or four items that they felt represented their ideal environment. Items ranged from photographs to magazine pictures to mementos and souvenirs. One mother of two brought tickets to a retro rock concert; a conservative corporate executive brought in a pack of cigarettes to show he was still rebellious; a middle-aged father brought a lucky fishing lure his own father had given his kids.

The process uncovered five key themes regarding what matters most to urban boomers. Family love and support and a good home life are viewed as important achievements. Long-term friendships are also very important and provide continuity to boomers. City-dwelling boomers are driven to "get away from it all" and escape to the big outdoors. Spiritual fitness is as important as physical fitness, so they love to develop their intellectual potential. They also feel that they're never too old to improve themselves. Clearly, all these values can translate into interesting platforms for ads and commercials.[31]

Basic Methods of Quantitative Research

Companies use **quantitative research** to gain reliable, hard statistics about specific market conditions or situations. Three basic research methods can be used to collect quantitative data: *observation, experiment,* and *survey.*

Observation   In the **observation method,** researchers monitor consumer activities, typically in their native environments, such as a store, a park, or the workplace. They may count the traffic that passes by a billboard, count a TV audience through instruments hooked to TV sets, or study consumer reactions to products displayed in the supermarket. Most observation method research is performed by large, independent marketing research companies, such as ACNielsen and Information Resources, Inc. Healthtex, for example, subscribes to the services of NPD (National Panel Diary), which tracks the clothing purchases of 16,000 homes as a nationwide sample. From this, Healthtex can find out its market share and better understand statistical trends in the marketplace.

An important tool for assessing user experiences with new Websites and other digital content is called user experience testing, or more commonly **UX** for short. The testing is an important step in the development of an effective site given the need to ensure a straightforward, friction-free experience on the part of visitors.[31]

Technology has greatly improved the observation method. One example is the **Universal Product Code (UPC)** label. By reading the codes with optical scanners, researchers can tell which products are selling and how well. The UPC label not only increases speed and accuracy at the checkout counter; it also enables timely inventory control and gives stores and manufacturers accurate point-of-purchase data sensitive to the impact of price, in-store promotion, couponing, and advertising.

ACNielsen's ScanTrack provides data on packaged-goods sales, market shares, and retail prices from more than 4,800 stores representing 800 retailers in 52 markets. A companion service, Homescan, uses in-home bar-code scanners to collect data on consumer purchases and shopping patterns. As a result, marketers have reliable data on the effectiveness of IMC. With that information, they can develop models to evaluate alternative marketing plans, media vehicles, and promotional campaigns.[32] In one case, for instance, data might indicate that a 40-cent coupon for toothpaste would create $150,000 in profits, but a 50-cent coupon on the same item would create a $300,000 loss.

Companies used to assume that changes in market share and brand position happen slowly. But observation shows that the packaged-goods market is complex and volatile. At the local level, weekly sales figures may fluctuate considerably, making it difficult to measure advertising's short-term effectiveness.

Other technologies have also been effective in observation research. Envirosell, a New York–based research company, uses security-type cameras to capture consumer in-store shopping habits. To determine the effectiveness of packaging and displays, the company analyzes how much time people spend with an item and how they read the label.[33]

The Universal Product Code on packaging is scanned at checkout counters. It improves checkout time and inventory control, and it provides a wealth of accessible data for use in measuring advertising response.

© Kathy Willens/AP Images

Experiment   To measure cause-and-effect relationships, researchers use the **experimental method.** An experiment is a scientific investigation in which a researcher randomly assigns different consumers to two or more messages or stimuli. For example, a marketer might develop two print ads that feature different spokespeople, then randomly expose different consumers to each to determine who is more effective. This type of research is used often for new product and new campaign introductions. As we saw in the Kraft story, marketers go to a **test market,** and introduce the product in that area alone or test a new ad campaign or promotion before a *national rollout*. For example, a new campaign might run in one geographic area but not another. Sales in the two areas are then compared to determine the campaign's effectiveness. However, researchers must use strict controls so the variable that causes the effect can be accurately determined.

Survey   A common method of gathering primary research data is the **survey,** in which the researcher gains information on attitudes, opinions, or motivations by questioning current or prospective customers (political polls are a common type of survey). Surveys can be conducted by personal interview, telephone, mail, or on the Internet. Each has distinct advantages and disadvantages (see Exhibit 7-7). An important consideration in evaluating the validity of a survey is whether it has been administered to a randomly selected sample. If not, survey results cannot be treated as representative of the population of interest. We'll discuss some important issues regarding survey research in the last section of this chapter.

Message Testing before and after a Campaign

Pretesting Methods

Although there is no infallible way to predict a campaign's success or failure, pretesting and posttesting can give a marketer useful insights if properly applied. Pretesting refers to message testing that takes place before a campaign launches. Posttesting, on the other hand, describes testing activities that occur after a campaign has begun.

Companies pretest ads for likability and comprehension by using a variety of qualitative and quantitative techniques.

For example, when pretesting print ads, researchers often ask direct questions: What does the advertising say to you? Does the advertising tell you anything new or different about the company? If so, what? Does the advertising reflect activities you would like to participate in? Is the advertising believable? What effect does it have on your perception of the merchandise offered? Do you like the ads?

Exhibit 7-7
Comparison of data collection methods.

	Personal	Telephone	Mail	Internet
Data collection costs	High	Medium	Low	Low
Data collection time required	Medium	Low	High	Medium
Sample size for a given budget	Small	Medium	Large	Large
Data quantity per respondent	High	Medium	Low	Low
Reaches widely dispersed sample	No	Maybe	Yes	Yes
Reaches special locations	Yes	Maybe	No	Yes
Interaction with respondents	Yes	Yes	No	No
Degree of interviewer bias	High	Medium	None	None
Severity of nonresponse bias	Low	Low	High	Medium
Presentation of visual stimuli	Yes	No	Maybe	Yes
Field worker training required	Yes	Yes	No	No

My IMC Campaign 7–B

Methods for Pretesting

Companies rarely trust intuition alone when evaluating their creative work. There is simply too much on the line. Pretesting is what occurs when agencies or marketers test prototypes of their messages before they are run in the mass media. Below is a comprehensive list of ways that real agencies test their work. You don't have the resources to do many of them. But you can use some of these methods to test your creative ideas with a small sample drawn from your target audience. Doing so will give you added ammunition for persuading your client that you've developed a strong strategy for his or her brand.

Print Advertising

- **Direct questioning.** Asks specific questions about ads. Often used to test alternative ads in early stages of development.
- **Focus group.** A moderated but freewheeling discussion and interview conducted with six or more people.
- **Order-of-merit test.** Respondents see two or more ads and arrange them in rank order.
- **Paired comparison method.** Respondents compare each ad in a group.
- **Portfolio test.** One group sees a portfolio of test ads interspersed among other ads and editorial matter. Another group sees the portfolio without the test ads.
- **Mock magazine.** Test ads are "stripped into" a magazine, which is left with respondents for a specified time. (Also used as a post-testing technique.)
- **Perceptual meaning study.** Respondents see in timed exposures.
- **Direct-mail test.** Two or more alternative ads are mailed to different prospects on a mailing list to test which ad generates the largest volume of orders.

Broadcast Advertising

- **Central location projection test.** Respondents see test commercial films in a central location such as a shopping center.
- **Trailer test.** Respondents see TV commercials in trailers at shopping centers and receive coupons for the advertised products; a matched sample of consumers just gets the coupons. Researchers measure the difference in coupon redemption.
- **Theater test.** Electronic equipment enables respondents to indicate what they like and dislike as they view TV commercials in a theater setting.
- **Live telecast test.** Test commercials are shown on closed-circuit or cable TV. Respondents are interviewed by phone, or sales audits are conducted at stores in the viewing areas.
- **Sales experiment.** Alternative commercials run in two or more market areas.

Physiological Testing

- **Pupilometric device.** Dilation of the subject's pupils is measured, presumably to indicate the subject's level of interest.
- **Eye movement camera.** The route the subject's eyes traveled is superimposed over an ad to show the areas that attracted and held attention.
- **Galvanometer.** Measures subject's sweat gland activity with a mild electrical current; presumably, the more tension an ad creates, the more effective it is likely to be.
- **Voice pitch analysis.** A consumer's response is taped, and a computer is used to measure changes in voice pitch caused by emotional responses.
- **Brain pattern analysis.** A scanner monitors the reaction of the subject's brain.

Through **direct questioning,** researchers can elicit a full range of responses from people and thereby infer how well advertising messages convey key copy points. Direct questioning is especially effective for testing alternative messages in the early stages of development, when respondents' reactions and input can best be acted on. There are numerous techniques for pretesting print messages, including *focus groups, order-of-merit tests, paired comparisons, portfolio tests, mock magazines, perceptual meaning studies,* and *direct-mail tests.* (See My IMC Campaign 7–B, "Methods for Pretesting.")

Several methods are used specifically to pretest radio and TV commercials. In **central location tests,** respondents are shown test commercials, usually in shopping centers, and questions are asked before and after exposure. In **clutter tests,** test commercials are shown with noncompeting control commercials to determine their effectiveness, measure comprehension and attitude shifts, and detect weaknesses.

A company's own employees are an important constituency. Some companies, in fact, pretest new commercials by prescreening them on their in-house cable TV systems and soliciting feedback.

My IMC Campaign 7–B

Methods for Posttesting

Posttesting involves assessing the impact of a campaign after it has run. It is an important way that companies judge whether their messages have helped them to achieve their objectives (see Chapter 8). You will most likely not do posttesting for your client. However, it is good practice for you to propose HOW the client might posttest your campaigns. This is material that you can incorporate in your campaigns book. Be sure to reference your objectives when you propose a posttesting technique.

- **Aided recall (recognition–readership).** To jog their memories, respondents are shown certain messages and then asked whether their previous exposure was through reading, viewing, or listening.

- **Unaided recall.** Respondents are asked, without prompting, whether they saw or heard promotional messages.

- **Attitude tests.** Direct questions, semantic differential tests, or unstructured questions measure changes in respondents' attitudes after a campaign.

- **Inquiry tests.** Additional product information, product samples, or premiums are given to readers or viewers; messages generating the most responses are presumed to be the most effective.

- **Sales tests.** Measures of past sales compare campaign efforts with sales. Controlled experiments test different media in different markets. Consumer purchase tests measure retail sales from a given campaign. Store inventory audits measure retailers' stocks before and after a campaign.

The Challenge of Pretesting

There is no best way to pretest promotional messages. Different methods test different aspects, and each has its own advantages and disadvantages.

Pretesting helps distinguish strong messages from weak ones. But since the test occurs in an artificial setting, respondents may assume the role of expert or critic and give answers that don't reflect their real buying behavior. They may invent opinions to satisfy the interviewer, or be reluctant to admit they are influenced, or vote for the messages they think they *should* like.

Researchers encounter problems when asking people to rank messages. Respondents often rate the ones that make the best first impression as the highest in all categories (the **halo effect**). Also, questions about the respondent's buying behavior may be invalid; behavior *intent* may not become behavior *fact*. And some creative people mistrust testing because they believe it stifles creativity.

Despite these challenges, the issue comes down to dollars. Small marketers rarely pretest, but their risk isn't as great, either. When companies risk millions of dollars on a new campaign, they must pretest to be sure the message is interesting, believable, likable, and memorable—all while reinforcing the brand image.

Posttesting Methods

Posttesting can be more costly and time-consuming than pretesting, but it can test a campaign under actual market conditions. As we saw with Kraft, some marketers benefit from pretesting *and* posttesting by running ads in select test markets before launching a campaign nationwide.

As in pretesting, marketers use both quantitative and qualitative methods in posttesting. Most posttesting techniques fall into five broad categories: *aided recall, unaided recall, attitude tests, inquiry tests,* and *sales tests.* (See My IMC Campaign 7–B "Methods for Posttesting.")

Some use **attitude tests** to measure a campaign's effectiveness in creating a favorable image for a company, its brand, or its products. Presumably, favorable changes in attitude predispose consumers to buy the company's product.

IAG Research has developed a syndicated data service called IAG Ad that the company administers for such clients as American Express, General Motors, and Procter & Gamble.

Learning that the wash mitt usually given to customers with the purchase of a new Beetle convertible wasn't earning them particularly high marks, Volkswagen (www.vw.com) contacted Arnold Worldwide to come up with a better idea. Arnold decided to create a guidebook to the many things that new owners could see and do in a convertible and included a star chart and wild birdseed with the book.

Source: Volkswagen of America, Inc.

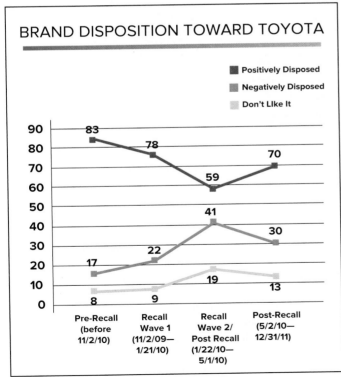

Source: GfK MRI Starch Advertising Research

GfK MRI Starch tracked consumer sentiments toward Toyota through two product recalls. The tracking showed the damage done by the recall, but also the rebound for Toyota after it addressed the issue.

© GfK MRI

Using more than 80,000 surveys, IAG Ad collects key data about the ads that viewers watched the night before and generates a detailed performance analysis that includes brand recall, message understanding, likability, and purchase intent. This tool helps companies understand the actual effectiveness of their campaigns.[34]

Similarly, Nissan interviews 1,000 consumers every month to track brand awareness, familiarity with vehicle models, recall of commercials, and shifts in attitude or image perception. If a commercial fails, it can be pulled quickly.[35]

Children's clothing manufacturer Healthtex conducted some print-ad posttesting and discovered that, while new mothers appreciated the information in the long copy format, more experienced mothers didn't. For them, the headline and one line of copy were sufficient to get the point across. They already understood the rest. As a result, the company used the shorter format and redesigned the ads aimed at experienced parents.

The Challenge of Posttesting

Each posttesting method has limitations. **Recall tests** reveal the effectiveness of message components, such as size, color, or themes. But they measure what respondents noticed, *not* whether they actually buy the product.

For measuring sales effectiveness, attitude tests are often better than recall tests. An attitude change relates more closely to product purchase, and a measured change in attitude gives management the confidence to make informed decisions about advertising plans. Unfortunately, many people find it difficult to determine and express their attitudes. For mature brands, brand interest may be a better sales indicator, and companies now measure that phenomenon.[36]

Ethical Issues

Research Statistics Can Be Friends or Foes

Marketing research gives the advertiser and its agency the data they need to identify consumer needs, develop new products and communication strategies, and assess the effectiveness of marketing programs. It also often provides the basis for advertising claims.

However, the way some advertisers use research data can lead to serious ethical lapses. Clever researchers can hide, shape, and manipulate statistics. Unfortunately, some researchers and marketers deliberately withhold information, falsify figures, alter results, misuse or ignore pertinent data, compromise the research design, or misinterpret the results to support their point of view.

Trying to spin the nutritional numbers to its advantage with consumers on the Atkins, South Beach, and other high-protein, low-carbohydrate diets, KFC created two television ads "aimed at educating the public that fried chicken can actually be part of a healthy diet." One ad showed a wife plopping down a bucket of fried chicken in front of her TV-engrossed husband, proudly explaining that they are starting to eat better ("healthier" is implied). A second ad showed a man sitting on the tailgate of a truck, again with a bucket of fried chicken; his friend compliments him on his "fantastic" appearance. Compared to a Burger King Whopper, the company claimed its fried chicken was veritable health food. Almost. According to the Federal Trade Commission (FTC), "although it is true that the two fried chicken breasts have slightly less total fat and saturated fat than a Whopper, they have more than three times the trans fat and cholesterol, more than twice the sodium, and more calories."

It didn't take a lawsuit or months of investigation for the public to know that KFC's statistics were skewed. Consumer protection groups were up in arms as soon as the ads aired, forcing the company to pull the ads within a month of their October 2003 launch. In response to the FTC's inquiry, KFC marketing executive Scott Bergen said, "We have always believed our ads to be truthful and factually accurate." In their settlement with the FTC, the company agreed to simply stop running the ads. Six months after the debacle, KFC tried the healthy tack again, this time offering *roasted* chicken.

Sometimes misleading health information in advertisements can be hazardous to more than just the waistline. Consider the fen-phen controversy in which Wyeth-Ayerst, a division of American Home Products, was accused of ignoring research findings. Wyeth manufactured Redux (dexfenfluramine) and Pondimin (fenfluramine), which become the "fen" portion of fen-phen. In 1996, fen-phen was approved for distribution in the United States, and by the end of 1996 thousands of people had reported health complications. In 1997, it was found that fen was linked to heart valve damage and an often-fatal lung disease called primary pulmonary hypertension. Subsequently, the manufacturer was pressured to pull the drug off the shelf.

By the end of 1997, American Home Products was the subject of thousands of civil lawsuits over fen-phen by people who claimed that the drug caused their health problems. In 1999, American Home Products went under fire for allegedly withholding important information from the FDA (Food and Drug Administration). Leo Lutwak, a physician and medical officer for the FDA, claimed in an interview with *CBS News,* "American Home Products twisted the meaning of my research to make it seem as if there was no way to predict fen-phen's hazards. What I had actually written was, that in view of the covering up of information by the drug company, the FDA had no way of predicting some of these side effects." He said, "I've asked to be allowed to set the record straight, but was told it was against FDA policy to testify in a civil suit." His testimony would have been crucial for the thousands of people who were involved in civil suits.

Then, the *Dallas Morning News* reported that American Home Products had received researcher reports of leaky heart valves in

By using **inquiry tests**—in which consumers respond to an offer for information or free samples—researchers can test a message's attention-getting value, readability, and understandability. These tests also permit fairly good control of the variables that motivate reader action, particularly if a *split-run* test is used (split runs are covered in Chapter 13). The inquiry test is also effective for testing small-space ads.

Unfortunately, inquiries may not reflect a sincere interest in the product, and responses may take months to receive. When advertising is the dominant element or the only variable in the company's marketing plan, sales tests are a useful measure of advertising effectiveness. However, many other variables usually affect sales (competitors' activities, the season of the year, and even the weather). Sales response may not be immediate, and **sales tests**, particularly field studies, are often costly and time-consuming.

For consumer packaged goods, though, the cost of sales tests has been greatly reduced thanks to grocery store scanners. Finally, sales tests are typically more suited for gauging the effectiveness of campaigns than of individual messages or promotions.

Important Issues in IMC Research

When marketers conduct primary research, there is always one legitimate concern—the accuracy of the findings. This is especially true when conducting formal quantitative research and when doing research in international markets.

fen-phen users in 1997. At the same time, though, it was lobbying members of Congress and the U.S. Drug Enforcement Administration to ease restrictions on the use of Pondimin and Redux. The lobbying campaign didn't work, and Pondimin and Redux were pulled from the market in September 1997.

In conjunction with lobbying legislators, American Home Products hired "ghostwriters" to write articles that promoted fen-phen. Then, according to lawsuit evidence cited in the Associated Press, the company used respected researchers to publish these articles under their own names. Because the drug was pulled off the shelves in 1997, only 2 of the 10 articles were actually published in medical journals; the other 8 were canceled. Doug Petkus, American Home Products spokesperson, defended the articles. "This is a common practice in the industry," he said. "The companies have some input, it seems, in the initial development of the piece ... but the proposed author has the last say." However, medical ethicists and editors of notable medical journals do not agree with this type of practice.

Dr. Jeffrey Drazen, editor-in-chief of the *New England Journal of Medicine*, believes "that line between the author's independent conclusions and the company's conclusions has been blurred." Critics allege that oftentimes drug companies influence authors to bury unfavorable results and that this undue influence leads the public to believe that these drugs are safer and more effective than they actually are. In response to these types of allegations, the medical journals are updating their policies and guidelines regarding journal submissions to ensure their own credibility, as well as the health and safety of the general public.

In November 1999, American Home Products agreed to settle the more than 11,000 fen-phen lawsuits for a whopping $4.83 billion. This was one of the biggest product liability settlements ever. Of course, as part of the settlement, the company admitted no wrongdoing.

There is a lot of money to be made in the pharmaceutical industry; companies go to great lengths and great expense to get their products approved. But ignoring, manipulating, or omitting pertinent research findings is not only unethical, it's potentially lethal.

Questions

1. Are there any circumstances that might justify portraying research findings in a biased or distorted fashion?

2. Why is it so important when discussing scientific research results with a client to report all results, not just those that put the client in a good light?

Sources: Rose Pike, "When Good Drugs Go Bad, ABC News, (http://more.abcnews.go.com/sections/newsuse/fenfollow/); Associated Press, "Fen-Phen Articles Questioned, ABC News, (http://abcnews.go.com/sections/living/DailyNews/fenphenghostwriters990523.html); Associated Press "Report Faults Drug Maker," ABC News, (http://abcnews.go.com/sections/living/DailyNews/fenphen990921.html); Associated Press, "Fen-Phen Settlement Clouded," ABC News, (http://moreabcnews.go.com/sections/living/DailyNews/fenphen991222.html); Associated Press, "Medical Journals Tighten Rules, CBS News, (www.cbsnews.com/stories/2001/09/10/national/main310621.shtml); "KFC Launches Campaign to Change High-Fat Image," *Advertising* Age online, October 28, 2003 (retrieved from www.adage.com, August 3, 2003); "KFC's Claims That Fried Chicken Is a Way to 'Eat Better,' Don't Fly," FTC For the Consumer online, June 3, 2004 (retrieved from www.ftc.gov/opa/2004/06/kfccorp.htm, August 4, 2004); Rob Walker, "Chicken-Fried Bull," MSN *Slate* online, November 10, 2003 (retrieved from http://slate.msn.com/id/2090861, August 4, 2004); Letter to the FTC, November 6, 2003, Center for Science in the Public Interest (retrieved from http://cspinet.org/new/pdf/letter_to_ftc.pdf, August 4, 2003); "KFC Responds to Resolution of Advertising Inquiry," KFC online press release, June 3, 2004 (retrieved from www.kfc.com/about/pr/060304.htm, August 4, 2004).

Considerations in Conducting Primary Quantitative Research

LO 7-5

Quantitative research requires formal design and rigorous standards for collecting and tabulating data to ensure their accuracy and usability. When conducting primary research, marketers must consider certain issues carefully, especially whether the research is *valid* and *reliable*. For more on the pros and cons of research statistics, see the Ethical Issues feature.

Validity and Reliability

Assume you want to determine whether a new toy will sell in a particular market. The market consists of 10 million individuals. You show a prototype of the toy to five people and four say they like it (an 80 percent favorable attitude). Is that test valid? Hardly. For a test to have **validity,** *results must be free of bias and reflect the true status of the market.*[37] Five people aren't enough for a minimum sample, and liking a toy is not necessarily a predictor of whether these people would buy it.

Moreover, if you repeated the test with five more people, you might get an entirely different response. So your test also lacks **reliability.** For a test to be reliable, it must be *repeatable*—it must produce approximately the same result each time it is administered (see Exhibit 7-8).

Validity and reliability depend on several key elements: the sampling methods, the survey questionnaire design, and the data tabulation and analysis methods.

Exhibit 7-8

The reliability–validity diagram. Using the analogy of a dartboard, the bull's-eye is the actual average of a value among a population (say, the average age in the community). The top row shows high reliability (repeatability) because the darts are closely clustered. When reliability drops, the darts land more randomly and spread across a wider area, as in both examples in the bottom row. The left column demonstrates high validity because in both examples the darts center around the bull's-eye. The right column represents low validity because bias in the testing process drew all the darts to one side. In the upper right quadrant, members of a fraternity are in the same age group (high reliability or repeatability), but their ages do not reflect the average of the community (low validity). The lower left quadrant suggests that the testing of our average age sample is highly valid, but it is not reliable because it includes people with a wide range of ages. The upper left quadrant reflects the truest picture of the data.

Sampling Methods

When a company wants to know what consumers think, it can't ask everybody. But its research must reflect the **universe** (the entire target population) of prospective customers. Researchers select from that population a **sample** that they expect will represent the population's characteristics. To accomplish this, they must decide whom to survey, how many to survey, and how to choose the respondents. Defining **sample units**—the individuals, families, or companies being surveyed—is very important.

A sample must be large enough to achieve precision and stability. The larger the sample, the more reliable the results. Statisticians note that the margin of error, an estimate of how likely sample statistics will diverge from numbers in the universe, is three times greater if a sample of 10 is chosen rather than a sample of 100. It is ten times greater for a sample of 10 compared to a sample of 1,000. Five hundred survey participants or more are generally recommended for accurate samples. There are two types of samples: random probability samples and nonprobability samples.

The greatest accuracy is gained from **random probability samples** because everyone in the universe has an equal chance of being selected.[38] For example, a researcher who wants to know a community's opinion on an issue starts with a complete list of all people in the community and selects members at random. But this method has difficulties. Every unit (person) must be known, listed, and numbered so each has an equal chance of being selected—an often prohibitively expensive and sometimes impossible task, especially with customers of nationally distributed products.

Instead, researchers use **nonprobability samples** extensively because they're easier than probability samples, as well as less expensive and time-consuming. Nonprobability samples don't give every unit in the universe an equal chance of being included, so there's no guarantee the sample is representative. As a result, researchers can't be confident in the accuracy of the responses.[39] Most marketing research needs only general measures of the data. For example, the nonprobability method of interviewing shoppers in malls may be sufficient to determine the shopping preferences, image perceptions, and attitudes of customers.

How Questionnaires Are Designed

Constructing a good questionnaire requires considerable expertise. Much bias in research is blamed on poorly designed questionnaires. Typical problems include asking the wrong types of questions, asking too many questions, using the wrong form for a question (which makes it too difficult to answer or tabulate), and using the wrong choice of words. Exhibit 7-9 shows some typical questions that might be used in a survey for a retail store.

Consider the simple question, "What kind of soap do you use?" The respondent may be confused. Does the question reference hand soap, shampoo, laundry detergent, or dishwashing soap? Does *kind* mean brand, size, or type? Finally, what constitutes use? What a person buys (perhaps for someone else) or uses personally—and for what purpose? In fact, one person probably uses several different kinds of soap, depending on the occasion. It's impossible to answer this question accurately. Worse, if the consumer does answer it, the researcher doesn't know what the answer means and will likely draw an incorrect conclusion. For these reasons, questionnaires must be pretested. (See My IMC Campaign 7–C on page 232, "Developing an Effective Questionnaire.")

Effective survey questions have three important attributes: focus, brevity, and clarity. They focus on the topic of the survey. They are as brief as possible. And they are expressed simply and clearly.[40] These qualities have a common purpose: to ensure respondents read and understand the questions in the same way.

The four most common types of questions are *open-ended, dichotomous, multiple-choice,* and *scale.* But there are many ways to ask questions within these four types. Exhibit 7-10, shows examples of each of these. Neutral responses can be removed from the scale question so the respondent must answer either positively or negatively.

Two goals for international research are flexibility and standardization, and both are necessary for the best results. Flexibility means using the best approach in each market. If you're studying the use of laundry products, it's just as irrelevant to ask Mexicans about soy sauce stains as it is to ask Thais how they get salsa out of their clothes.[47]

On the other hand, standardization is important so that information from different countries can be compared.[48] Otherwise the study will be meaningless. Balance is required to get the best of flexibility and standardization.

Thanks to a combination of computer-based interviewing, the Internet, e-mail, telephones, faxes, and courier services, the time required to conduct worldwide business-to-business research has been drastically reduced. Today, nearly three-quarters of market research firms use the Internet to conduct some form of market research.[49] With the global adoption of the Internet, experts anticipate further cuts in costs and time for getting valuable customer input for marketing and advertising decision making.

Chapter Summary

Marketing research is the systematic procedure used to gather, record, and analyze new information to help managers make decisions about marketing goods and services. Marketing research helps management identify consumer needs, develop new products and communication strategies, and assess the effectiveness of marketing programs and promotional activities. The many types of information gathered can help marketers recruit, retain, and regain customers.

IMC research, a subset of marketing research, is used to gather and analyze information for developing or evaluating advertising. It helps advertisers develop strategies and test concepts. The results of research help define the product concept, select the target market, and develop the primary message elements.

Businesses use testing to make sure their dollars are spent wisely. Pretesting helps detect and eliminate weaknesses before a campaign runs. Posttesting helps evaluate the effectiveness of an ad or campaign after it runs. Testing is used to evaluate several variables including merchandise, markets, motives, messages, media, and overall results.

The research process involves several steps: analyzing the situation and defining the problem, conducting informal (exploratory) research by analyzing internal data and collecting external secondary data, setting research objectives, conducting primary research using qualitative or quantitative methods, and, finally, interpreting and reporting the findings.

Marketers use qualitative research to get a general impression of the market. The methods used may be projective or intensive. Quantitative techniques include observation, experiment, and survey.

Techniques used in pretesting include central location tests, clutter tests, and direct questioning. Pretesting has numerous problems, including artificiality, consumer inaccuracy, and the halo effect of consumer responses. The most commonly used posttesting techniques are aided recall, unaided recall, attitude tests, inquiry tests, and sales tests.

The validity and reliability of quantitative surveys depend on the sampling methods used and the design of the survey questionnaire. The two sampling procedures are random probability and nonprobability. Survey questions require focus, brevity, and simplicity.

In international markets, research is often more expensive and less reliable than in the United States. But marketers must use research to understand cultural traits and habits in overseas markets.

Important Terms

attitude test, *226*

central location test, *225*

clutter test, *225*

direct questioning, *224*

experimental method, *224*

focus group, *222*

halo effect, *226*

IMC research, *211*

IMC strategy research, *212*

in-depth interview, *222*

Informal research, *218*

inquiry test, *228*

intensive techniques, *222*

marketing information system (MIS), *218*

marketing research, *210*

markets, *216*

media classes, *217*

media research, *214*

media subclasses, *217*

media units, *217*

media vehicles, *217*

merchandise, *216*

message, *216*

motives, *216*

nonprobability samples, *230*

observation method, *223*

posttesting, *215*

pretesting, *215*

primary data, *218*

primary research, *220*

projective techniques, *222*

qualitative research, *220, 221*

quantitative research, *220, 223*

random probability samples, *230*

recall test, *227*

reliability, *229*

sales test, *226*

sample, *230*

sample unit, *230*

secondary data, *218*

survey, *224*

test market, *224*

Universal Product Code (UPC), *223*

universe, *230*

validity, *229*

Review Questions

1. How does research help advertisers meet the challenge of the three Rs of marketing?

2. Give an example that demonstrates the difference between marketing research and market research.

3. Which kind of research data is more expensive to collect, primary or secondary? Why?

4. How have you personally used observational research?

5. motives

6. Which of the major surveying methods is most costly? Why?

7. How could the halo effect bias a pretest for a soft drink ad?

8. When might research offer reliability but not validity?

9. How would you design a controlled experiment to test the advertising for a chain of men's clothing stores?

10. When could research help in the development of an advertising strategy for an international advertiser? Give an example.

The Advertising Experience

1. **Marketing Research Organizations and Publications**

   Many advertisers choose to perform their own research. When collecting research data by themselves, they can use a number of advertising- and marketing-specific research sources available on the web. Visit the research organizations' and publications' Websites listed below and answer the questions that follow:

   - Advertising Research Foundation (ARF): www.thearf.org
   - American Marketing Association: www.marketingpower.com
   - Journal of Advertising Research: www.thearf.org/assets/pub-jar
   - Marketing Research Association (MRA): www.mra-net.org

   a. What research group sponsors the site? Who is/are the intended audience(s)?

   b. What is the site's purpose? Does it succeed? Why?

   c. What range of services is offered?

   d. What is the organization's purpose?

2. **Market Research Companies**

   Marketers and advertisers depend heavily on timely and accurate research in preparation for advertising planning. Many market research companies are available to serve nearly every marketing and advertising research need. Visit the following syndicated and independent research companies' Websites and answer the questions that follow:

   - ACNielsen: www.acnielsen.com
   - Burke: www.burke.com

   - Dun & Bradstreet: www.dnb.com
   - The Gallup Organization: www.gallup.com
   - GfK NOP: www.gfkamerica.com
   - International Data Corporation (IDC): www.idc.com
   - Ipsos Connect: www.ipsos.com/asi/
   - J. D. Power and Associates: www.jdpower.com
   - Research International: www.research-int.com
   - Qualtrics Online Sample: http://www.qualtrics.com/online-sample/

   a. What types of research does the company specialize in?

   b. What industries/companies would be best suited to utilize the company's resources?

   c. What specific services, products, or publications does the company offer?

   d. Are the information services offered by the company primary or secondary data?

   e. How useful is the company for conducting advertising and marketing research? Why?

3. **Market Research for Politics**

   Silver-maned Armand LeMouche, state senator for your district for 30 years, passed away recently, and his appointed replacement, Millard Frumpe, lacks a solid political base. Sally Daily, a self-made millionaire and the owner of a string of bakeries, would like to challenge Millard, but she wants to do some research first. She firmly believes that advertising research helped her get where she is. Find a site that could provide the research Sally needs in order to find out if her campaign is feasible or not, and, if it is, how she could win. Describe what the site could do for her. (One such site is www .rtnielson.com.)

4. What were the research challenges that Budweiser faced in creating a great Superbowl ad? What research techniques did the agency

use, and what kinds did it choose not to use? Why do you think that it made the decisions it did, and do you agree with them?

5. Do an "emotion" experiment with the Budweiser spot by identifying the emotions that you feel for each scene in the ad. Make an "emotion map" that can be tagged to each key scene. Compare the emotion map you generate with that of a classmate.

CHAPTER

8

Marketing and IMC Planning

Learning Objectives

To describe the process of marketing and IMC planning. Marketers need to understand the various ways plans are created. They must also know how to analyze situations; set realistic, attainable objectives; develop strategies to achieve them; and establish budgets for marketing communications.

(After) **studying this chapter, you will be able to:**

LO8-1 Explain strategic planning using a marketing plan.

LO8-2 Detail the tactical or "bottom-up" approach favored by smaller businesses.

LO8-3 Differentiate the IMC planning approach from the tactical.

LO8-4 Describe the important components of an IMC plan.

LO8-5 Explain how IMC budgets are determined.

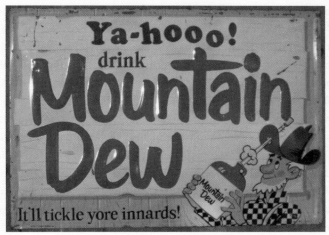

The changes in Mountain Dew advertising from inception to the present represent the evolution of the brand from a beverage popular in rural America to one that is more urban, youth-oriented, and high energy.

Source: Pepsi Cola Company

More than 60 years ago, Ally and Barney Hartman of Knoxville, Tennessee, decided to introduce their own lemon-lime soft drink. Family and friends liked the brew, so they started bottling and distributing it to the locals. In 1946, they designed a paper label featuring a gun-toting hillbilly and a signature that read "By Barnie and Olly." In honor of the mountain moonshine famous in Tennessee, they named their drink "Mountain Dew." The brothers were convinced they had a good thing going, but the general public did not agree. Mountain Dew was a sales failure. ■ Bill Jones, a salesman, needed some investors. He recruited a number of Pepsi bottlers, including Ally Hartman, who agreed to become an investor during a dinner meeting. In addition to his money, Ally offered the Mountain Dew brand under the condition that Bill Jones spring for dinner. ■ Over the course of time, the brand grew. The moonshine-drinking Willy the Hillbilly and the apt slogan, "Ya-hoo Mountain Dew," helped build it into a regional player. The Pepsi-Cola Company took notice and purchased Mountain Dew in 1964. For some years, Pepsi continued using the old advertising approach. But as sales failed to increase substantially, Pepsi decided a new direction was called for. ■ In 1973, it completely repositioned and relaunched Mountain Dew. The beverage would be cast as a high-energy, youth-oriented, flavored soft drink. New ads created by BBDO New York featured active young people enjoying outdoor activities to the theme "Hello Sunshine, Hello Mountain Dew." By 1978, the action-oriented approach sent Dew sales over the 100-million-case mark. In the 1980s Pepsi added high-octane sports and adventure to the advertising.[1] ■ Since that time, Mountain Dew has set a standard of how to remain true to its own definition of exuberance across a variety of marketing platforms. "We have a great unity of message and purpose that has been consistent over time about what we are and what we aren't," says Scott Moffitt, director of marketing for Mountain Dew.[2] "The brand is all about exhilaration and energy, and you see that in all that we do, from advertising and community to grassroots programs and our sports-minded focus. We have a very crystal clear, vivid positioning." ■ The positioning concept has allowed Mountain Dew great latitude: The brand's marketing extends from skateboarding parks and alternative events to mainstream extravaganzas such as the Super Bowl. Marketing across such a broad spectrum is known within PepsiCo as "mass intimacy."[3] ■ One Pepsi-Cola executive puts it this way: "It's our way of saying we haven't sold out. We have to make sure with programs like advertising on the Super Bowl that we are still letting customers see the brand in a way that is designed for them."[4] So whether Dew is talking advertising, events, endorsements, or simply premiums, a "Dew-x-perience" is paramount when talking to the brand's two key consumer groups: teenagers and 20- to 39-year-olds. ■ Mountain Dew's unique selling proposition remains the same—it is the "ultimate, indulgent, thirst-quenching soft drink." This positioning took it to the top of the "heavy citrus" soda category in the early 1990s. In 1999 it briefly passed Diet Coke to become the number three soft drink in the United States after Classic Coke and Pepsi. In the $62 billion carbonated soft drink industry, that is a huge success. ■ In the 2000s, the carbonated soft drink market flattened as people spent more on flavored drinks and bottled water. To stem the trend, PepsiCo introduced Code Red, a cherry-flavored Mountain Dew line extension. With a stealth launch, and using only limited radio ads aimed at trend-setting teenagers, Code Red was a smashing success. ■ Mountain Dew has continued to push the boundaries of IMC. For example, Pepsi financed a documentary on the history of snowboarding. The movie, called *First Descent*, included subtle rather than overt references to the

brand, primarily through Mountain Dew's sponsorship of two of the featured athletes. Although the brand appears on the gear of the two snowboarders, ads for the film make no mention of Mountain Dew. The decision to finance a film, which carried a cost close to that of a traditional 30-second TV spot, comes from the marketers' recognition that its target audience watches less TV than other groups.[5] ■ By understanding its consumers, defining its brand clearly and creatively, and ensuring that its messages are compelling, exciting, and on-strategy, Mountain Dew has proven that its growth is no flash in the pan. Can the Dew success story continue? Sales of carbonated soft drinks have been in decline for several years now, as newer competitors in other categories (sports drinks, vitamin water, energy drinks) nip at their heels. But Mountain Dew keeps growing and gaining market share within the category. The reason? One of the world's strongest brand images, bolstered by some of the world's best IMC.[6] ■

Strategic Planning: The Marketing Plan

LO 8-1

In spite of the brilliant creativity employed by BBDO in its ads for Mountain Dew, the Dew story actually demonstrates that business success often depends more on careful marketing and IMC planning than on creativity. Yet, every year, companies waste millions of dollars on ineffective messages due to a lack of planning.

A **marketing plan** is a document that serves as a guide for the present and future marketing activities of an organization. Marketing plans generally do a number of important things, such as to (1) state or restate the organization's mission; (2) assess a brand's current marketing situation and identify factors, both within the company and in the environment, that may help or hinder achieving marketing objectives; (3) present clear, measurable, time-delineated marketing objectives; (4) describe strategies that will be used to achieve marketing objectives with specific target markets; (5) describe tactics or action programs for implementing the marketing strategy; (6) explain how the effectiveness of the marketing efforts will be evaluated; and (7) propose a budget for marketing activities (see the Marketing Plan Outline in Appendix A).

The marketing plan has a profound effect on an organization's IMC. It dictates the role of promotional messages in the marketing mix. It enables better implementation, control, and continuity of campaigns, and it guides the allocation of promotional dollars. Successful organizations do not separate IMC plans from marketing. They view each as a vital building block for success.

The Mission Statement

A good marketing plan generally begins with the organization's mission statement. The **mission statement** is a short description of the organization's purpose and philosophy. Starting the plan with a mission statement helps remind planners and marketing partners about what the organization is and what it stands for. The Mountain Dew brand is owned by PepsiCo, whose mission is to be

the world's premier consumer products company, focused on convenient foods and beverages. We seek to produce healthy financial rewards to investors as we provide opportunities for growth and enrichment to our employees, our business partners and the communities in which we operate. And in everything we do, we strive to act with honesty, openness, fairness and integrity.

This mission statement nicely summarizes who Pepsi is, what it does, and how it does it.

The Situation Analysis

The second part of the marketing plan is the **situation analysis,** a detailed description of the brand's current marketing situation. You can see a sample outline for one in My IMC Campaign 8–A. The situation analysis presents all the facts that are relevant for planning a marketing strategy. Most situation analyses will, therefore, include a description of the brand's history, market share, growth, profitability, promotional expenditures, key competitors, and so on. A situation analysis is more than a presentation of facts, however. Good marketing plans provide the context for factual information. For example, Diet Mountain Dew's sales growth of 8 percent during the most recent year is put into a context when the marketing plan notes that overall sales of carbonated beverages declined. In that context, 8 percent growth is outstanding.

Planners draw attention to the most important aspects of a brand's situation through a **SWOT analysis.** The SWOT analysis uses the facts contained in the situation analysis to point out strengths, weaknesses, opportunities, and threats for the brand. *Strengths* and *weaknesses* represent company capabilities, while *opportunities* and *threats* represent environmental factors. One obvious strength for Mountain Dew is its well-defined, attractive brand image as a high-energy, full-flavored, carbonated beverage. A possible weakness could be the brand's age. An opportunity for Mountain Dew might be the increased interest in energy drinks. Since Mountain Dew is a highly caffeinated beverage, it stands to profit from such a trend. Threats to Mountain Dew might include rising prices for commodities used to make the product (sugar, flavorings) or distribute the product (fuel) that would force Mountain Dew to raise prices to remain profitable. Other threats might be changes in the consumption behaviors of its target markets (some of the fastest growing soft drinks today are vitamin-infused beverages such as Pepsi's Tava).

The Marketing Objectives

Marketing objectives, the third part of the marketing plan, are clear, quantifiable, realistic marketing goals that are to be accomplished within a defined time period. Marketing objectives generally fall into one of two broad categories: *sales-target objectives* and *communication* objectives.

Sales-target objectives include goals related to increasing or maintaining sales volume and market share. Such objectives, of course, must be realistic in light of the issues described in the situation analysis. In good economic times and in a new product category, a company might set very ambitious sales-target objectives. Since Mountain Dew is an established brand in a mature product category, it might propose a sales-target objective of 5 percent growth in overall sales over a period of one year. This overall sales objective might be a result of even more specific objectives by distribution point. For example, Mountain Dew might propose modest sales-target objectives at one distribution point (grocery stores) and higher objectives at another (restaurants).

Communication objectives are outcomes that can reasonably be associated with promotional activities, such as increases in brand recognition or awareness, increased comprehension of a brand's attributes or benefits, more positive attitudes about a brand or a more favorable image of the brand or its typical user, and stronger intentions to try or buy a brand. Mountain Dew's IMC is meant to help consumers view the brand as a flavorful, high-energy drink for youthful-thinking people looking for an alternative to colas.

Many experts believe that good marketing plans should place greater emphasis on communication objectives and less on sales-target objectives. This may seem counterintuitive. After all, isn't the purpose of IMC to drive sales? Isn't that really the bottom line? In one way, the answer is yes. Companies spend money on campaigns to generate an even greater return in

My IMC Campaign 8–A
Developing the Situation Analysis

In previous chapters you've honed your understanding of the consumer, segmented the audience, and conducted research. It is time to pull all of this information together and create an assessment of your client's current situation. Marketers call such an assessment a situation analysis. Use the list below to organize your analysis.

The Industry

- **Companies in industry:** Dollar sales, strengths.
- **Growth patterns within industry:** Primary demand curve, per capita consumption, growth potential.
- **History of industry:** Technological advances, trends.
- **Characteristics of industry:** Distribution patterns, industry control, promotional activity, geographic characteristics, profit patterns.

The Company

- **The company story:** History, size, growth, profitability, scope of business, competence, reputation, strengths, weaknesses.

The Product or Service

- **The product story:** Development, quality, design, description, packaging, price structure, uses, reputation, strengths, weaknesses.
- **Product sales features:** Exclusive, nonexclusive differentiating qualities, competitive position.
- **Product research:** Technological breakthroughs, improvements planned.

Sale History

- **Sales and sales costs:** By product, model, sales districts.
- **Profit history.**

Share of Market

- **Sales history industrywide:** Share of market in dollars and units.
- **Market potential:** Industry trends, company trends, demand trends.

The Market

- **Who and where is the market:** How was market segmented, how can it be segmented, what are consumer needs, attitudes, and characteristics? How, why, when, where do consumers buy?
- **Past IMC appeals:** Successful or unsuccessful.
- **Who are our customers:** Past and future? What characteristics do they have in common? What do they like about our product? What don't they like?

Distribution

- **History and evaluation:** How and where product is distributed, current trend.
- **Company's relationship:** With the distribution channel and its attitudes toward product/company.
- **Past policies:** Trade advertising, deals, co-op programs.
- **Status:** Trade literature, dealer promotions, point-of-purchase displays.

Pricing Policies

- **Price history:** Trends, relationship to needs of buyers, competitive price situation.
- **Past price objectives:** Management attitudes, buyer attitudes, channel attitudes.

Competition

- **Who is the competition:** Primary, secondary, share of market, products, services, goals, attitudes. What is competition's growth history and size?
- **Strengths and competition:** Sales features, product quality, size. Weaknesses of competition.
- **Marketing activities of competition:** Advertising, promotion, distribution, sales force. Estimated budget.

Promotion

- **Successes and failures:** Past promotion policy, sales force, advertising, publicity.
- **Promotion expenditures:** History, budget emphasis, relation to competition, trend.
- **IMC programs:** Review of strategies, themes, campaigns.
- **Sales force:** Size, scope, ability, cost/sale.

Exhibit 8-1
Traditional top-down marketing plan.

sales. But viewing IMC effectiveness only in terms of sales overlooks some key issues. For example, a campaign's impact on sales usually works through intermediate steps (see Exhibit 8-5 on page 251). In many instances consumers must travel through a sequence of awareness, comprehension, conviction, and desire before they are ready to take action and buy a product. These intermediate steps are best achieved by specifying communications objectives. In addition, the relationship between sales and IMC is a complex one. An effective campaign can make a consumer want to try a product, but a repeat sale is typically influenced by the consumer's product experiences. So even great campaigns can fail if consumers are dissatisfied with the product when they try it. Finally, many factors unrelated to IMC (a recession, new competitors, government regulation, and the like) can have a large impact on sales no matter how good or poor the advertising.

A Traditional Model for Setting Objectives: DAGMAR

Determining the objectives for a marketing program can be difficult, especially for planners without years of experience. The task was simplified considerably when Russell Colley introduced a system for defining advertising goals for measured advertising results (DAGMAR). The **DAGMAR** system emphasizes communication objectives because Colley believed that the proper way to evaluate a campaign is to determine how well it communicates information, within a given budget, to the target audience.

Planners who follow DAGMAR formulate objectives related to one of four outcomes: *awareness* (knowing the brand exists), *comprehension* (knowing about the brand's benefits or attributes), *conviction* (a favorable attitude toward the brand), and *action* (purchasing and using the brand). Like other hierarchical models, DAGMAR assumes that consumers travel through the stages in an ordered sequence. Thus a marketer knows that if there is little awareness of the brand in the target market, focusing on the other objectives may not be a good strategy. DAGMAR also specifies the qualities of a good objective. Good objectives specify an audience and define outcomes that are concrete and measurable. They are also clear about the current situation, the desired situation, and the time frame for moving from the former to the latter.

Let's consider a fictional example to see how a company might formulate objectives. Our fictional brand is a tax software program called EasyFile. The key difference between EasyFile and other tax software programs (or doing taxes without a software program) is that it dramatically simplifies tax preparation. The marketing planners at EasyFile know that simplifying tax preparation is a benefit that appeals to people who do their own taxes. The planners also believe that if they convince their target audience that EasyFile is much easier than other programs, sales will increase substantially. The sales-target objective for EasyFile could be stated this way: "EasyFile will increase unit sales to the target market of people who file their own taxes from 165,000 in 2012 to 355,000 in 2013." This optimistic assumption is based on the situation analysis, which shows that the product category of tax preparation software is growing rapidly and that people are frustrated with the difficulty of using existing programs.

Note that the sales-target objective described above offers little insight as to the strategy that could help EasyFile accomplish its sales increase. This is why communication objectives are so important in a marketing plan. Communication objectives help define what IMC should do in order to help a brand achieve its sales goals. The communication objective for EasyFile might be stated this way: "Currently 10 percent of our target market believes that EasyFile is the easiest way to prepare their own income taxes. In 2013 we plan to persuade 35 percent of the target market that EasyFile is the easiest way."

The Marketing Strategy

The **marketing strategy** describes how the company plans to meet its marketing objectives (see Ad Lab 8–A, "The Strategies of Marketing Warfare"). Marketing strategy typically involves three steps: (1) defining the particular target markets; (2) determining the strategic position; and (3) developing an appropriate marketing mix for each target market. A company's marketing strategy has a dramatic impact on its advertising. It determines the role and

Advertisers find it useful to frame their marketing strategies in terms of need-satisfying objectives. This ad for Peta contrasts our love of our pets to what the organization believes is callousness toward other animals.

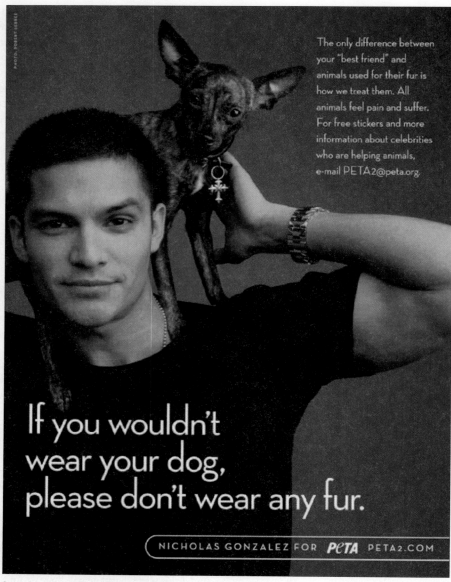

The only difference between your "best friend" and animals used for their fur is how we treat them. All animals feel pain and suffer. For free stickers and more information about celebrities who are helping animals, e-mail PETA2@peta.org.

If you wouldn't wear your dog, please don't wear any fur.

NICHOLAS GONZALEZ FOR PeTA PETA2.COM

Source: People for the Ethical Treatment of Animals

amount of advertising in the marketing mix, its creative thrust, and the media to be employed.

Selecting the Target Market   The first step in strategy development is to define and select the target market, using the processes of market segmentation and research discussed in Chapters 6 and 7.

When General Motors introduced its Saturn SC1 model, for instance, it defined its target market as "college-educated import owners and intenders"—highly educated young adults (18 to 34) considering their first or second car purchase. They were further defined as 60 percent female, living in one- or two-person households, and seeking a vehicle with sporty styling, fun performance, fuel economy, a good warranty, and sound quality/reliability/ dependability. They typically drive a Honda Civic, Toyota Corolla, or Nissan 240SX.[7]

Similarly, Mountain Dew defines its target market as active, young people in their teens as well as young adults 20 to 39 years old. In addition, the brand aims a significant portion of

AD Lab 8-A

The Strategies of Marketing Warfare

Jack Trout and Al Ries's *Marketing Warfare* is based on the classic book of military strategy, *On War*, written by Prussian general Carl von Clausewitz and published in 1832. The book outlines the principles behind all successful wars, and two simple ideas dominate: *force* and the *superiority of defense*.

The Strategic Square

How do the principles of warfare apply to marketing? It comes down to the "strategic square":

Out of every 100 companies:

One should play defense.

Two should play offense.

Three should flank.

And 94 should be guerrillas.

Defensive Warfare

Datril opened its war on Tylenol with a price attack. Johnson & Johnson immediately cut Tylenol's price, even before Datril started its price advertising. Result: It repelled the Datril attacks and inflicted heavy losses on the Bristol-Myers entry.

Here are the rules for defensive marketing warfare:

1. Participate only if you are a market leader.
2. Introduce new products and services before the competition does.
3. Block strong competitive moves by copying them rapidly.

Offensive Warfare

Colgate had a strong number one position in toothpaste. But rival Procter & Gamble knew a thing or two about von Clausewitz.

P&G launched Crest toothpaste with not only a massive $20 million advertising budget but also the American Dental Association "seal of approval." Crest went over the top to become the best-selling toothpaste in the country.

But overtaking the leader is not that common. Most companies are happy if they can establish a profitable number two position.

The rules for waging offensive marketing warfare are these:

1. Consider the strength of the leader's position.
2. Launch the attack on as narrow a front as possible, preferably with single products.
3. Launch the attack at the leader's weakest position.

Flanking Warfare

The third type of marketing warfare is where the action is for many companies. In practice, it means launching products where there is no competition. Unilever introduced Mentadent, the first baking soda/peroxide toothpaste, which became very successful.

Here are the principles of flanking marketing warfare:

1. Make flanking moves into uncontested areas.
2. Use surprise. Too much research often wastes precious time.
3. Keep up the pursuit; too many companies quit after they're ahead.

Guerrilla Warfare

Most of America's companies should be waging guerrilla warfare. The key to success in guerrilla wars is flexibility. A guerrilla should abandon any product or market if the tide of battle changes.

Here are the principles of guerrilla marketing warfare:

1. Find a market segment small enough to defend.
2. No matter how successful you become, never act like the leader.
3. Be prepared to "bug out" at a moment's notice.

Bottom Up

Trout and Ries's later book, *Bottom-Up Marketing* (discussed later in this chapter), continues the military analogy.

"Deep penetration on a narrow front is the key to winning a marketing war," they say. By this they mean that smaller companies should keep their products narrowly focused on single concepts. Too many companies spread their forces over a wide front. In fact, most large corporations today must fend off focused attacks by smaller companies.

Laboratory Applications

1. Think of a successful product and explain its success in terms of marketing warfare.
2. Select a product and explain how marketing warfare strategy might be used to gain greater success.

its marketing activities at urban youth, especially African Americans and Latinos.[8] To Mountain Dew, the prototypical consumer is an 18-year-old, street-smart, male teen.[9]

Positioning the Product   The famous ad executive David Ogilvy said one of the first decisions in marketing is also the most important: how to position the product. Positioning, which we introduced in Chapter 1, refers to the place a brand occupies competitively in the

Positioning is important for both the advertiser and the consumer because it helps differentiate products from the competition. Volkswagen focuses on its hands-free parking system to position itself against competing brands.

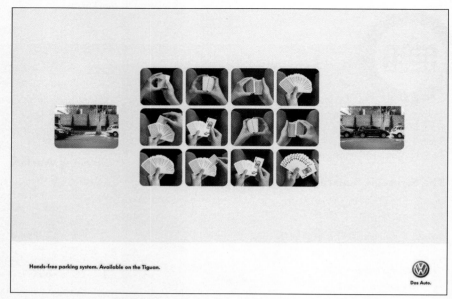

Hands-free parking system. Available on the Tiguan.

Source: Volkswagen Group

minds of consumers. Every product has some position—whether intended or not—even if the position is "nowhere." Positions are based on consumer beliefs, which may or may not reflect reality. Strong brands have a clear, often unique position in the target market. Ogilvy's agency (Ogilvy & Mather), for example, differentiated Dove soap in 1957 by positioning it as a complexion bar for women with dry skin. Now, over a half-century later, the company still uses the same cleansing cream demonstration, and Dove is consistently the number one brand, spending some $153.6 million in advertising annually to maintain its 24 percent share of the multibillion-dollar bar soap market.[10]

Many positions are available in a market. The big mistake many companies make is not staking out any position. They can't be everything; but they don't want to be nothing.[11] A company might pick a position similar to a competitor's and fight for the same customers. Or it might find a position not held by a competitor—a hole in the market—and fill it quickly, perhaps through product differentiation or market segmentation.

Professor Ernest Martin proposes seven distinct approaches to developing a positioning strategy:

1. *Product attribute*—setting the brand apart by stressing a particular product feature important to consumers.
2. *Price/quality*—positioning on the basis of price or quality.
3. *Use/application*—positioning on the basis of how a product is used (e.g., Arm & Hammer).
4. *Product class*—positioning the brand against other products that, while not the same, offer the same class of benefits.
5. *Product user*—positioning against the particular group that uses the product.
6. *Product competitor*—positioning against competitors (e.g., Avis/Hertz), using the strength of the competitor's position to help define the subject brand.
7. *Cultural symbol*—positioning apart from competitors through the creation or use of some recognized symbol or icon.[12]

We add an eighth approach: by category—positioning by defining or redefining the business category. A simple way for a company to get the number one position is to invent a new product category.

Apple was founded as a computer company. But its greatest successes came with innovations that defined new categories: tablets, an online music store, and smartphones. In turn, these successes bolstered sales of its laptops and desktops.[13]

With all its high energy and exhilaration, "youth" is not only the positioning of Mountain Dew, it's the heartbeat of the brand.[14] PepsiCo defines the Dew positioning this way:

> To 18-year-old males who embrace excitement, adventure, and fun, Mountain Dew is the great-tasting soft drink that exhilarates like no other because it is energizing, thirst-quenching, and has a unique citrus flavor.

Determining the Marketing Mix   The next step in developing the marketing strategy is to determine a cost-effective marketing mix for *each* target market the company pursues. As we discussed in Chapter 6, the mix blends the various marketing elements the company controls: *product, price, distribution,* and *communications.*

Mountain Dew was blessed with a broad marketing toolbox to draw upon. First, it offered consumers an energizing, thirst-quenching soft drink *product* with a unique citrus flavor and an image of youthful exuberance, exhilaration, and adventure. Then, to build *distribution,* it used a variety of promotions to the trade that would enable grocers and other resellers to increase both volume and profits. While its *price* was competitive with other soft drinks, Mountain Dew promoted itself aggressively with free samples, premiums, and prizes at various street and sporting events—which effectively lowered the price to consumers.

Finally, Mountain Dew initiated an integrated *communications* program that included extensive advertising on TV, radio, outdoor and print media, and the Internet; sports and event sponsorships; appearances at grass-roots geographical events; plus a host of public relations activities—all designed to develop and promote the distinct Mountain Dew personality.

Companies have a wide variety of marketing strategy options. They might increase distribution, initiate new uses for a product, change a product line, develop entirely new markets, or start discount pricing. Each option emphasizes one or more marketing mix elements. The choice depends on the product's target market, its position in the market, and its stage in the product life cycle.

Marketing Tactics

A company's objectives indicate where it wants to go; the strategy indicates the intended route; and the **tactics** determine the specific short-term actions to be taken, internally and externally, by whom, and when. Advertising campaigns live in the world of marketing tactics.

Tactical Planning: Small Company "Bottom-Up" Marketing

In a small company, everybody is both player and coach, and the day-to-day details seem to come first, leaving little or no time for formal planning. However, there is a solution to this dilemma: **bottom-up marketing** (see Exhibit 8-2).

Jack Trout and Al Ries think one of the best ways for a company to develop a competitive advantage is to focus on an ingenious tactic first and then develop that tactic into a strategy. By reversing the normal process, marketers sometimes make important discoveries.[15] Researchers at Vicks developed an effective liquid cold remedy but found it put people to sleep. Rather than throw out the research, Vicks positioned the formula as a nighttime cold remedy. NyQuil went on to become the number one cold remedy and the most successful new product in Vicks's history.

The *tactic* is a specific action for helping to accomplish a strategy. By planning from the bottom up, entrepreneurs can find unique tactics to exploit. But caution is required. Companies should find just *one* tactic, not two or three. The marketer can then focus all elements of the marketing mix on the tactic. The tactic becomes the nail, and the strategy is the hammer that drives it home.

Exhibit 8–2
Bottom-up marketing plan.

Ethical Issues

Subliminal Persuasion

Imagine you could inject an ad message directly into people's minds, bypassing ordinary perception. Consumers would be unable to challenge or ignore your communication, because they would never notice it in the first place.

Incredibly, in 1957 James Vicary claimed he had such a technique. The market researcher said that during a movie he had flashed the phrases "Drink Coca-Cola" and "Hungry? Eat popcorn" subliminally (shown the words so quickly people could not detect them). In response, he claimed, sales of popcorn and Coke shot up by 18 percent and 58 percent, respectively.

As psychologist Anthony Pratkanis notes, "people were outraged and frightened by a technique so devilish that it could bypass their conscious intellect and beam subliminal commands directly to their subconscious." Great Britain and Australia subsequently banned **subliminal advertising** and the FCC threatened to revoke the license of any TV station that showed subliminal ads.

Public concern abated when Vicary could not reproduce his effects under supervised tests. He later admitted making them up. But fascination with subliminal advertising reappeared in the early 70s when Wilson Bryan Key published books that claimed to find the word sex in hundreds of ads, seeing them in ice cubes from a gin ad and on the surface of a Ritz cracker! And while almost nobody else could see these "embeds," Key sold plenty of books.

Truth is, not one proven instance where an advertiser has used a subliminal message exists. In fact, doesn't the whole idea seem pretty ridiculous? How can you be influenced by a message that you can't detect? To act on a communication you must understand it, and to understand it you must see it. But the idea of a subliminal message is that you can't see it (otherwise it isn't subliminal). Case closed.

Well, not quite. It helps to separate subliminal advertising (demonstrating that a real advertiser has affected product sales with a hidden message embedded in a commercial) from subliminal influence (demonstrating that people can be affected by a hidden message). Current evidence is conclusive: *People can be influenced subliminally.*

Demonstrating subliminal influence requires a couple of things. First, you have to present the message (a picture, word, or phrase) so quickly that people can't tell it was there. Psychologists say that something shown for 120 milliseconds (0.12 of a second) or less is undetectable. Second, it has to be proven that the message influences people in some way. For example, a group shown a subliminal message must do something different from a control group that doesn't get the subliminal message.

Dozens of credible research studies have now reported such demonstrations. Consider just one example: A group of researchers wondered what would happen if people who are snake phobic are subliminally presented with a picture of a snake. Phobics typically begin sweating and become anxious when they see a snake photograph, whereas most people are fine. So what happens if snake photos are presented subliminally? The researchers found that even though subjects could not "see" the snake pictures, they responded as if they could: Phobics were anxious, nonphobics were not. So much for the idea that we are immune to messages we can't detect.

But snakes and phobias are far removed from the concerns of most advertisers. Advertisers want to influence buying behaviors, not fears. Which brings us to research done by three business professors, Yael Zemack-Rugar, James Bettman, and Gavan Fitzimons. In an ingenious experiment, they subliminally presented words related to either sadness or guilt to study participants. Both sadness words (i.e., *sad, miserable*) and guilt words (*guilty, blameworthy*) describe bad feelings. But people act differently when they feel sad as opposed to when they feel guilty. Sad people look for rewards to cheer themselves up, but guilty people deny themselves rewards. So the researchers predicted that in response to subliminal presentation of guilt words, guilt-prone people (as opposed to

The artful combination of tactic and strategy creates a position in the consumer's mind. When Tom Monaghan thought of the tactic of delivering pizza within 30 minutes to customers' homes, he focused his whole strategy on that singular idea. He ended up making a fortune and marketing history with Domino's Pizza.

Managers of small companies have an advantage here. Surrounded by the details of the business, they are more likely to discover a good tactic that can be developed into a powerful strategy. However, that's not to say that a large company cannot profit from bottom-up marketing. Many have, like 3M with its Post-it notes.

The IMC Approach to Marketing and Campaign Planning

Integrated marketing communications suggests a new approach to planning marketing and communications activities. It differs from the traditional processes by mixing marketing and communications planning together rather than separating them. Using the outside-in process, the IMC approach starts with the customer. Marketers learn about what media customers use, the relevance of their message to the customers, and when customers and non–guilt prone people) would be less likely to buy themselves an indulgence. Conversely, in response to sad words, guilt-prone people as compared with others would be just as likely to buy an indulgence. In fact, their experiments demonstrated these patterns of results. By subliminally influencing specific emotions, the researchers influenced purchase behaviors.

An even more direct demonstration that subliminal advertising can work comes from a study done by psychologists Johan Karremans, Wolfgang Stroebe, and Jaspar Claus. They argued that subliminal advertising influences brand preference only when someone is motivated to buy in the first place. In their experiment, people tracked strings of letters on a computer screen. Unbeknownst to the participants, subliminal messages were being flashed every so often. Half of the participants were exposed to the subliminal message "Lipton Ice," and half were exposed to a control word. Later, in a supposedly unrelated second study, participants were asked both how thirsty they were and whether they preferred Lipton or a competing brand. The results: When subjects were not thirsty the two groups showed the same preference for Lipton. But thirsty participants showed a different pattern: Those exposed to the Lipton subliminal message showed a strong preference for Lipton; those in the control group did not. The authors' explanation: Motivation plus subliminal prime equals increased preference for the primed brand.

Taken together, these studies and many others show conclusively that we can be affected by messages presented outside of awareness. Score one for Vicary. But it is a long way from saying this *can* be done to showing that it *is* done. In fact, as stated earlier, no one has ever shown that an ad campaign has used subliminal stimuli. And no research backs up Key's claims about "embeds" in print ads.

But can we be sure that no advertiser ever used subliminal advertising? Proving that something has never happened is pretty difficult (can you prove that Aunt Lois wasn't really abducted by aliens while she walked home from school back in 1975?). But the risks an advertiser would court by using a subliminal message far outweigh the likely rewards. What would consumers think of a company that was caught using subliminal ads? What would the legal repercussions be? Moreover, why would a company choose subliminal advertising when the nonsubliminal type can work so well?

People seem both repelled and attracted by the thought that they can be influenced below the threshold of awareness. It seems to imply a hidden power and dovetails nicely with a universal interest in the idea that not everything is what it seems. Interest in the phenomenon of subliminal advertising won't be going away soon. Especially now that we know it CAN work.

Questions

1. What are the ethical concerns that subliminal advertising would create? Who are the stakeholders (people or groups that would be affected by this practice)?
2. How does subliminal advertising relate to the free-market principle of complete information we discussed earlier?

Sources: Anthony R. Pratkanis, "The Cargo-Cult Science of Subliminal Persuasion," *Skeptical Inquirer* (1992) retrieved, March 4, 2007, from http://csicop.org/si/9204 /subliminal-persuasion.html; P. J. Lang, D. N. Levin, G. A. Miller, and M. J. Kozak, "Fear Behavior, Fear Imagery, and the Psychophysiology of Emotion: The Problem of Affective Response Integration," *Journal of Abnormal Psychology*, vol. 92, (1983), pp. 276–306; A. Ohman, A. Flykt, and D. Lundqvist, "Unconscious Emotion: Evolutionary Perspectives, Psychophysiological Data, and Neuropsychological Mechanisms," in R. D. Lane, L. Nade., and G. Ahern (Eds.), *Cognitive Neuroscience of Emotion.* (New York: Oxford University Press, 2000), pp. 296–327, and J. C. Karremans, W. Stroebe, and Claus, J. "Beyond Vicary's Fantasies: The Impact of Subliminal Priming and Brand Choice," *Journal of Experimental Social Psychology*, vol. 42 (2006), pp. 792–798.

prospects are most *receptive* to the message. As depicted in Exhibit 8-3 (starting at the bottom), IMC activities begin with the customer and work back to the brand.[16] In turn, all corporate marketing functions are dedicated to building and maintaining brand equity through a united focus on stakeholder loyalty.

Thanks to technology, marketers have a wealth of information at their fingertips. With supermarket scanner data, for instance, packaged-goods marketers can (1) identify specific users of products and services; (2) measure their actual purchase behavior and relate it to specific brand and product categories; (3) measure the impact of various advertising and marketing communications activities and determine their value in influencing the actual purchase; and (4) capture and evaluate this information over time.[17]

This ever-expanding database of customer behavior can be the basis for planning future marketing and communications activities, especially if the database contains information on customer demographics, psychographics, purchase data, and brand or product category attitudes (see Exhibit 8-4).

Exhibit 8-3

IMC macro model.

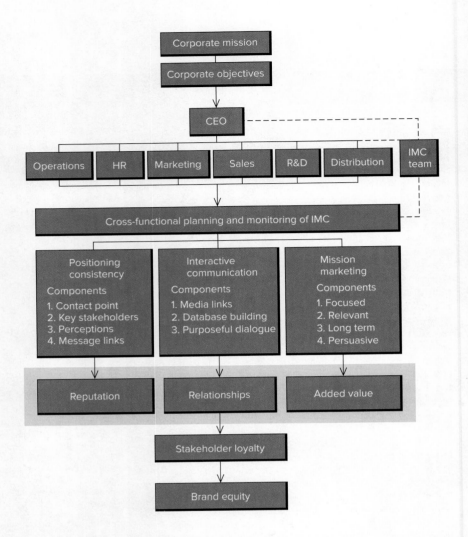

Starting the planning process with a database focuses the company on the consumer, or prospect, not the company's sales or profit goals. These marketing objectives are moved farther down in the planning process.[18]

So how does planning proceed under an integrated approach? Wang and Schultz developed a seven-step IMC planning model. The first step segments the customers and prospects in the database—either by brand loyalty, as illustrated, or by some other measurable purchase behavior (usage, for instance).

The second step analyzes information on customers to understand their attitudes, their history, and how they discover and interact with the brand or product. The goal is to find the best time, place, and situation to build and maintain relationships.

Next, the planner sets marketing objectives based on this analysis. In the illustrated example, these objectives relate to building and maintaining usage or nurturing brand loyalty.

The marketer then identifies what brand contacts and what changes in attitude are required to support the consumer's continuance or change of purchase behavior.

The fifth step sets communications objectives and strategies for reaching the consumer and influencing his or her attitudes, beliefs, and purchase behavior. The marketer can then decide what other elements of the marketing mix (product, price, distribution) will further encourage the desired behavior.

Finally, the planner determines what communications tactics to use—advertising, direct marketing, publicity, sales promotion, special events—to make further contact and influence the consumer's behavior.[19]

Exhibit 8-4

Wang–Schultz IMC planning model.

By following this model, the marketer sets objectives based on the needs of the customer or prospect. All forms of marketing are thus turned into communication, and all forms of communication into marketing.[20]

The Importance of IMC to the Study of Advertising

Because many customers see all sponsored communications as advertising, advertising people (account managers, creatives, media planners) must grow beyond their traditional specialty to become enlightened generalists, familiar with and able to integrate all types of marketing communications. Conversely, marketers traditionally viewed advertising as IMC. In other words, marketers failed to look beyond traditional advertising approaches when creating campaigns, and failed to acknowledge that effective communications can (and should) come from a variety of media, platforms, and sources. The IMC approach helps broaden the company's perspective, so that message tactics come from a consideration of broader marketing strategies, rather than the other way around.

Nestle To repeat: we welcome your comments, but please don't post using an altered version of any of our logos as your profile pic - they will be deleted.
3 hours ago · Comment · Like

👍 8 people like this.

 Paul Griffin Hmm, this comment is a bit "Big Brotherish" isn't it? I'll have whatever I like as my logo pic thanks! And if it's altered, it's no longer your logo is it!
2 hours ago · Report

 Nestle @Paul Griffin - that's a new understanding of intellectual property rights. We'll muse on that. You can have what you like as your profile picture. But if it's an altered version of any of our logos, we'll remove it form this page.
2 hours ago · Report

 Paul Griffin Not sure you're going to win friends in the social media space with this sort of dogmatic approach. I understand that you're on your back-foot due to various issues not excluding Palm Oil but Social Media is about embracing your market, engaging and having a conversation rather than preaching! Read www.cluetrain.com and rethink!
2 hours ago · Report

 Nestle Thanks for the lesson in manners. Consider yourself embraced. But it's our page, we set the rules, it was ever thus.
2 hours ago · Report

 Darren Smith Freedom of speech and expression
2 hours ago · Report

 Nestle you have freedom of speech and expression. Here, there are some rules we set. As in almost any other forum. It's to keep things clear.
2 hours ago · Report

 Paul Griffin Your page, your rules, true, and you just lost a customer, won the battle and lost the war! Happy?
2 hours ago · Report

 Nestle Oh please .. it's like we're censoring everything to allow only positive comments.
2 hours ago · Report

 Paul Griffin Don't beg, this debate for me is over, only boycotting your products will make you feel any pain I think, although your arrogance is quite extraordinary, it wasn't me that bought that palm oil!
2 hours ago · Report

 Nestle Was I begging? How odd you should think so.
2 hours ago · Report

Companies have control over their advertising but they must be careful about any unplanned messages they may inadvertently engender as the open exchange of opinions and beliefs promoted by social media can't be managed. The screenshot above shows an exchange between a Nestle employee and some consumers on Facebook over Nestle's request to not use an altered version of the company's logo as a profile picture. Do you think the above is an example of bad social networking? Could Nestle have handled this in a different manner?
Source: Nestlé

In a survey of 122 *Fortune* 500 marketing, advertising, and communications executives, most respondents indicated a general understanding of integrated marketing and agreed that synergy is the key benefit of IMC.[21] However, the study also showed that confusion remains concerning IMC use. Many practitioners today still lack the broad knowledge required to develop, supervise, and execute full IMC programs.[22]

The IMC Plan

The **IMC plan** is a natural outgrowth of the marketing plan and is prepared in much the same way. Appendix B at the end of the book outlines both a traditional advertising plan and an IMC plan.

Reviewing the Marketing Plan

The brand manager first reviews the marketing plan to understand where the company is going, how it intends to get there, and the role of IMC in the marketing mix. The first section of the plan should summarize briefly the situation analysis and SWOT analysis, review the target market segments, itemize the long- and short-term marketing objectives, and restate decisions regarding market positioning and the marketing mix.

Setting Objectives

LO 8-4

The brand manager then determines what tasks IMC must accomplish. What strengths and opportunities can be leveraged? What weaknesses and threats need to be addressed? Unfortunately, some corporate executives (and advertising managers) state vague goals, like "increasing sales and maximizing profits by creating a favorable impression of the product in the marketplace." When this happens, no one understands what the messages are intended to do, how much they will cost, or how to measure the results. Objectives should be specific, realistic, and measurable.

Understanding What Campaigns Can Do

Most IMC programs encourage prospects to take some action. However, it is usually unrealistic to assign IMC the whole responsibility for achieving sales. Sales goals are marketing objectives, not advertising objectives. Before a company can persuade customers to buy, it must inform, persuade, or remind its intended audience about the company, product, service, or issue. A simple adage to remember when setting objectives is "Marketing sells, IMC tells." In other words, IMC objectives should always be related to communication effects.

Earlier we suggested that communications objectives are important for the overall marketing plan too. Does the IMC plan merely restate these? In most cases, the communications objectives stated in the IMC plan will be those that message campaigns are best suited to accomplish. Objectives best achieved by other communication tools may be dealt with in separate plans.

The IMC Pyramid: A Guide to Setting Communications Objectives

Suppose you're advertising a new brand in a new product category, but you're not sure what kind of results to expect. The pyramid in Exhibit 8-5 shows some of the tasks IMC can perform. Obviously, before your product is introduced, prospective customers are completely unaware of it. Your first communication objective therefore is to create *awareness*—to acquaint people with the company, product, service, and brand.

The next task might be to develop *comprehension*—communicating enough information about the product so that some percentage of the aware group recognizes the product's purpose, image, or position, and perhaps some of its features.

Next, you need to communicate enough information to develop *conviction*—persuading a certain number of people to actually believe in the product's value. Once convinced, some people may be moved to *desire* the product. Finally, some percentage of those who desire the product will take *action*. They may request additional information, send in a coupon, visit a store, or actually buy the product.

The pyramid works in three dimensions: time, dollars, and people. Campaign results may take time, especially if the product is expensive or not purchased regularly. Over time, as a company continues communicating with prospects and customers, the number of people who become aware of the product increases. As more people comprehend the product, believe in it, and desire it, more take the final action of buying it.

Let's apply these principles to a hypothetical case. Suppose you are in charge of the new "Lightning Bug," a hybrid car built by Volkswagen. Your initial objectives for this fictional car might read as follows:

1. Within two years, communicate the existence of the Lightning Bug to half of the more than 500,000 people who annually buy foreign economy cars.

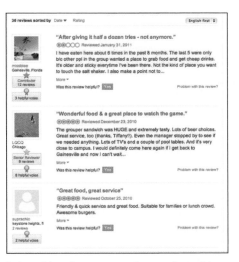

In the social media age, savvy marketers understand that audiences can receive negative brand information from a variety of sources. The above screenshot is a review for a restaurant from the popular Website, www.tripadvisor.com. The restaurant received both negative and positive reviews. Do you as a consumer place more value on the negative reviews over the positive reviews? Would these reviews influence your decision to eat at this establishment? How important are the comments and overall number of reviews to your decision?

Source: TripAdvisor LLC

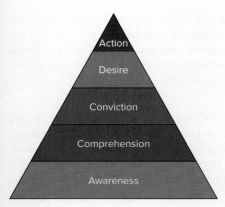

Exhibit 8-5

The IMC pyramid depicts the progression of communications effects on mass audiences—especially for new products. The initial message promotes awareness of the product to a large audience (the base of the pyramid). But only a percentage of this large group will comprehend the product's benefits. Of that group, even fewer will go on to feel conviction about, then desire for the product. In the end, compared with the number of people aware of the product, the number of people who take action is usually quite small.

2. Inform two-thirds of this "aware" group that the Lightning Bug is a superior economy car with many design, safety, and environmentally friendly features; that it is a brand new nameplate backed with unmatched service, quality, and value; and that it is sold only through dedicated Volkswagen dealers.
3. Convince two-thirds of the "informed" group that the Lightning Bug is a high-quality car, reliable, economical, and fun to drive.
4. Stimulate desire within two-thirds of the "convinced" group for a test drive.
5. Motivate two-thirds of the "desire" group to visit a retailer for a test drive.

These IMC objectives are specific as to time and degree and are quantified. Theoretically, at the end of the first year, research could determine how many people are aware of the Lightning Bug, how many people understand the car's primary features, and so on, thus measuring the program's effectiveness. See how IMC objectives can help a marketer succeed in Ad Lab 8–B.

Volkswagen's campaign may accomplish the objectives of creating awareness, comprehension, conviction, desire, and action. But once the customer is in the store, it's the retailer's responsibility to close the sale with effective selling and service.

With the advent of integrated marketing communications, we can look at the pyramid in another way. By using a variety of marketing communication tools and a wide menu of traditional and nontraditional media, we can accomplish the communication objectives suggested by the pyramid in a more efficient manner. For instance, for creating awareness of the new Lightning Bug as well as a brand image for the car and the company, public relations activities supported by mass media advertising might be the communication tools of choice. Comprehension, interest, and credibility can be augmented by media advertising, press publicity, direct mail brochures, and special events such as a sports car show. Desire can be enhanced by a combination of the buzz created by good reviews in car enthusiast magazines, plus media advertising, beautiful brochure photography, and the excitement generated by a sales promotion (such as a sweepstakes). Finally, action can be stimulated by direct mail solicitation, sales promotion, and the attentive service of a retail salesperson in an attractive new car showroom. Following the sale, direct mail could continue to reinforce the purchase decision. Calls from the retailer can be used to thank the customer, solicit feedback on that customer's experience, and offer assistance. This acknowledges that the sale was just the beginning of a valuable relationship. In fact, to maintain and deepen the relationship between marketer and customer, new buyers might be asked to like the Lightning Bug's Facebook page, encouraged to follow the brand on Twitter, and receive a Groupon discount for buying "Bug" accessories at the company's store. Whereas the traditional advertising approach often terminated with a sale, the IMC approach treats the sale as part of the broader relationship between the customer and the brand.

Different Ways Consumers Learn about Brands

The IMC pyramid represents the *learn–feel–do* model of effects. That is, it assumes that people rationally consider a prospective purchase, and once they feel good about it, they act. The theory is that IMC affects attitude, and attitude leads to behavior. That may be true for certain expensive, high-involvement products that require a lot of consideration (buying a home or car, or choosing a college). But other purchases may follow a different pattern. For example, impulse purchases at the checkout counter may involve a *do–feel–learn* model, in which behavior leads to attitude (picking up a pack of gum or a magazine after every visit to the supermarket). Other purchases may follow some other pattern. Thus, there are many marketing considerations when objectives are being set, and they must be thought out carefully.

The pyramid also reflects the traditional mass marketing monologue. The marketer talks and the customer listens.[23] That was appropriate before the advent of computers and databases, and it may still be appropriate in those categories where the marketer has little choice or does not expect a repeat purchase (as when a family has a garage sale or a shop at a vacation destination sells t-shirts).

Not every message follows the learn–feel–do approach. This ad for Dove invites readers to feel–learn–do with an attempt to challenge conventional standards of beauty.

Source: Unilever

My IMC Campaign 8–B

For the next big sets of decisions you will make, both media and creative, it will be essential that you specify what advertising and other promotions should *do*. Use the checklist below to focus your thinking on your objectives.

Does the message aim at immediate sales? If so, objectives might be

_____ Perform the complete selling function.

_____ Close sales to prospects already partly sold.

_____ Announce a special reason for buying now (price, premium, and so forth).

_____ Remind people to buy.

_____ Tie in with special buying event.

_____ Stimulate impulse sales.

Does the message aim at near-term sales? If so, objectives might be

_____ Create awareness.

_____ Enhance brand image.

_____ Implant information or attitude.

_____ Combat or offset competitive claims.

_____ Correct false impressions, misinformation.

_____ Build familiarity and easy recognition.

Does the message aim at building a "long-range consumer franchise"? If so, objectives might be

_____ Build confidence in company and brand.

_____ Build customer demand.

_____ Select preferred distributors and dealers.

_____ Secure universal distribution.

_____ Establish a "reputation platform" for launching new brands or product lines.

_____ Establish brand recognition and acceptance.

Does the message aim at helping to increase sales? If so, objectives would be

_____ Hold present customers.

_____ Convert other users to advertiser's brand.

_____ Cause people to specify advertiser's brand.

_____ Convert nonusers to users.

_____ Make steady customers out of occasional ones.

_____ Suggest new uses.

_____ Persuade customers to buy larger sizes or multiple units.

_____ Remind users to buy.

_____ Encourage greater frequency or quantity of use.

Does the message aim at some specific step that leads to a sale? If so, objectives might be

_____ Persuade prospect to write for descriptive literature, return a coupon, enter a contest.

_____ Persuade prospect to visit a showroom, ask for a demonstration.

_____ Induce sampling (trial offer).

How important are supplementary benefits of message? Objectives would be

_____ Help salespeople open new accounts.

_____ Help salespeople get larger orders from wholesalers and retailers.

_____ Help salespeople get preferred display space.

_____ Give salespeople an entrée.

_____ Build morale of sales force.

_____ Impress the trade.

Should the message impart information needed to consummate sales and build customer satisfaction? If so, objectives may be to use

_____ "Where to buy it" messages.

_____ "How to use it" messages.

_____ New models, features, package.

_____ New prices.

_____ Special terms, trade-in offers, and so forth.

_____ New policies (such as guarantees).

Should the message build confidence and goodwill for the corporation? Targets may include

_____ Customers and potential customers.

_____ The trade (distributors, dealers, retail people).

_____ Employees and potential employees.

_____ The financial community.

_____ The public at large.

What kind of images does the company wish to build?

_____ Product quality, dependability.

_____ Service.

_____ Family resemblance of diversified products.

_____ Corporate citizenship.

_____ Growth, progressiveness, technical leadership.

Exhibit 8-6

Messages go to the customer through advertising and other communication channels. Messages come back via direct response, surveys, and a purchase behavior database. The marketer's message can evolve based on this feedback.

But today, as the IMC model shows, many marketers have databases detailing where their customers live, what they buy, and what they like and dislike. When marketers can have a dialogue and establish a relationship, the model is no longer a pyramid but a circle (see Exhibit 8-6). Consumers and business customers can send messages back to the marketer in the form of coupons, phone calls, e-mail, social media posts, surveys, and database information on purchases. With interactive media, responses are in real time. This feedback can help the marketer's product, service, and messages evolve.[24] And reinforcement IMC, designed to build brand loyalty, will remind people of their successful experience with the product and suggest reuse.

By starting with the customer and then integrating all aspects of their marketing communications—package and store design, personal selling, advertising, public relations activities, special events, and sales promotions—companies hope to accelerate the communications process, make it more efficient, and achieve lasting loyalty from *good* prospects, not just prospects.[25]

IMC Strategy and the Creative Mix

The IMC *objective* declares what the marketer wants to achieve with respect to consumer awareness, attitude, and preference; the advertising (or creative) *strategy* describes how to get there.

IMC strategy blends the elements of the **creative mix:** *target audience, product concept, communications media,* and *advertising message.*

The Target Audience: Everyone Who Should Know

The **target audience,** the specific people the IMC will reach, is typically larger than the target market. Marketers need to know who the end user is, who makes the purchase, and who influences the purchasing decision. Children, for example, often exert a strong influence on where the family eats. So while McDonald's target market is adults, its target audience also includes children, and it spends much of its promotional budget on campaigns directed at kids.

Similarly, while companies may target heavy users of a product, many light users and nonusers are exposed to the campaign as well. That's good, because research shows that brand popularity (which IMC is uniquely good at creating) cuts across all levels of purchasing frequency.[26] The dominant brands are purchased most by both heavy and light users (see Exhibit 8-7). It's the accumulation of all these sales that makes a product dominant.

Exhibit 8-7

Brand popularity. Dominant brands are the most popular at each level of purchasing frequency.

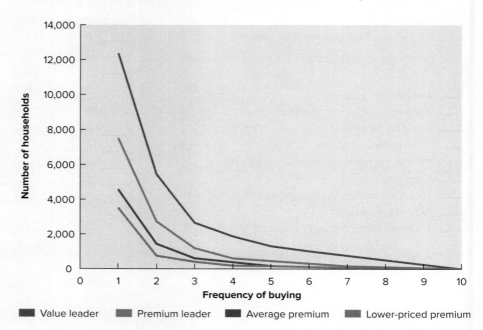

Affective involvement (feel)

	Low	High
High (Cognitive involvement (think))	College • • Video camera • Motor oil	• Car • Shampoo • Skin lotion
Low	• Laundry detergent • Paper towels	Greeting card • • Pizza • Bread

Exhibit 8-8

The Kim–Lord grid.

The Product Concept: A "Bundle of Values"

The "bundle of values" the marketer presents to the consumer is the **product concept.** General Motors markets essentially the same truck to two different audiences but presents two different product concepts. The Silverado is marketed to the vast middle class with campaigns that stress its rugged, macho durability. Promotions for the Sierra, on the other hand, are aimed at white-collar professionals and emphasize the vehicle's snob appeal.[27]

When writing the IMC plan, the brand manager must develop a simple statement to describe the product concept—that is, how IMC will present the product. To create this statement, the company first considers how consumers perceive the product and then weighs this against the company's marketing strategy.

Recall from Chapter 5 our discussion of the Elaboration Likelihood Model and the role of involvement with the product message. Some years ago, Richard Vaughn at Foote, Cone & Belding noted that different kinds of products typically evoke different levels of consumer involvement (either high or low) and different types of involvement, either *cognitive* (think) or *affective* (feel). This means different products call for different kinds of advertising. He created a two-dimensional model known as the FCB grid, which categorized consumer products into four quadrants based on "high involvement" or "low involvement" and "think" or "feel." By positioning brands in the grid based on the degree and type of involvement consumers brought to the purchase decision, the agency could determine which type of advertising would be most appropriate. Rossiter and Percy extended this research with the grid you saw in Exhibit 5-3, which also suggested different creative executions.

More recently, academics Kim and Lord recognized that people can be both cognitively and affectively involved at the same time. So they developed the Kim–Lord grid, shown in Exhibit 8-8. It too depicts the degree and the kind of involvement a consumer brings to the purchase decision for different products. Some purchases, like cars, require a high degree of personal involvement on both the cognitive and affective levels.[28] For others, like detergent, involvement is low on both axes. Sometimes a marketer uses an advertising strategy aimed at shifting the product to higher involvement on either axis. A product's location on the grid also indicates how the product is purchased (learn–feel–do or feel–learn–do) and how campaign copy should be written (more emotional or more rational).[29]

Pepsi marketers view Mountain Dew as a high-involvement purchase on the affective scale. "We continually need to give people a reason to pick us up," says one executive, "because we're not an obvious substitute [for cola]. People make a conscious choice to consume Mountain Dew, so we push to keep the positioning pure."[30]

The Communications Media: The Message Delivery System

As an element of creative strategy, the **communications media** are all the vehicles that might transmit the marketer's message. They include traditional media such as radio, TV, newspapers, magazines, and billboards, plus the Internet, direct marketing, public relations, special events, sales promotion, and personal selling.

Marketers at Mountain Dew use a variety of media to create a special environment for the product. This means not only promoting the product in mainstream media and sampling the product at sporting events but also creating the particular environment that the consumer wants for drinking the Dew. For example, Mountain Dew has used cars, radio stations, computer game demos, and extreme athletes as part of the experience. One summer, marketers decked out a subway car with "Do the Dew" memorabilia and hauled it around the country to major youth-oriented events where they passed out

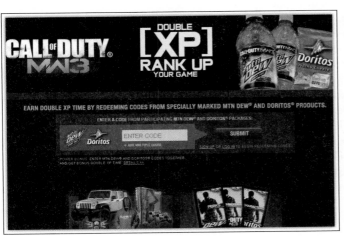

Mountain Dew excels at maintaining a relationship with its users. Understanding that video games and chips are popular with the soft drink's consumers helps Mountain Dew create effective campaigns. As illustrated in this screenshot, Mountain Dew and Doritos have done numerous promotions with the popular game Call of Duty, whereby Mountain Dew and Doritos purchasers are able to unlock exclusive perks on the video game.

Source: Pepsi Cola Company

Mountain Dew has a special relationship with consumers. Engaging them on Instagram is about more than exchanging messages. It is about sharing the brand with its most passionate users. Mountain Dew partnered with its fans in developing marketing messages and even a new flavor.

Source: Pepsi Cola Company

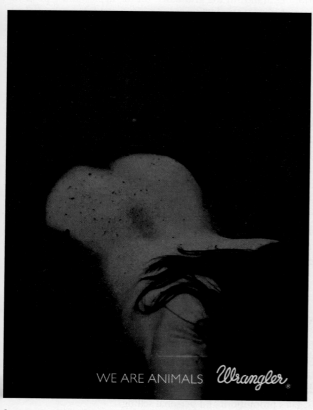

WE ARE ANIMALS *Wrangler*®

Setting a brand apart from its competitors requires a marriage of creative thinking and imaginative creative ideas. This ad for Wrangler is intended to appeal to our "animal instincts" and was meant to reposition the brand, which has long been associated with a Western lifestyle. What role does repositioning play in IMC budgeting? Is it a riskier move and do you think it would warrant a greater investment? Which of the budgeting strategies we've discussed seems most useful for developing a repositioning campaign?

Source: Wrangler

branded premiums such as snowboards, gear, and T-shirts—all relevant to the target market.

While balancing Dew on both ends of the grass-roots and mass-appeal spectrum, Pepsi marketers realize that not all teens are into alternative sports. The one-time hillbilly drink aggressively targets African American and Latino youth. Endorsement deals with hip-hop artists allow the Dew to appeal to the fast-growing ethnic market—which also coincides with the regional urban markets it targets.[31] "Mountain Dew is a brand whose core is inextricably linked to a pervasive human need for fun and exhilaration," says one executive. "That basic need has not changed over time, so we have to stick with that and be as current and leading edge as possible."[32]

The IMC Message: What the Campaigns Communicate

What the company plans to say and how it plans to say it, both verbally and nonverbally, make up the **IMC message.** As we discuss in Chapter 12, the combination of copy, art, and production elements forms the message, and there are infinite ways to combine these elements (see the Portfolio Review, "Strategic Use of the Creative Mix," on pages 258–260).

Dew personifies its product concept not only through events, but via a team of 10 extreme athletes, each representing a sport more daring than the next. That same attitude is passed on to Dew campaigns. With longtime agency BBDO helping the brand stay true to its youthful feel, its campaigns have an edginess and audacity that stand in stark contrast to the big cola brands. In one Super Bowl commercial, a Dew Dude on a bicycle chases down a cheetah and wrestles it to the ground. Reaching into the cat's mouth, he retrieves a stolen can of Dew.

"Bad cheetah," he says.

The ad was the second-highest rated commercial of the Super Bowl broadcast. In another highly rated spot, the Dew Dudes did a spoof version of the Queen classic "Bohemian Rhapsody." A third popular commercial, called "Showstoppers," featured choreographed mountain bikes in a spectacular extravaganza reminiscent of a 1930's MGM musical, with the Dew Dudes playing the role of directors. According to *USA Today,* teenagers loved the spot. "Retro is in with teens," said Dawn Hudson, senior vice president of marketing for Pepsi. "We try to see things through the eyes of a teenager, and that's full of energy and exhilaration. Besides, the brand can't keep relying on skateboarding high jinks. Mountain Dew should always have a fresh perspective on things. It can't be cookie cutter."[33]

Ted Sann, the chief creative director at BBDO, says, "The idea is to evolve the campaign—take it to the next plateau."[34]

The sales numbers point to the obvious—it's working. Moreover, the campaign has long legs—"Do the Dew" is the longest-running continuous campaign in the soft drink category.

The Secret to Successful Planning

Whether the marketer is a large corporation or a small company, the key to successful planning is information. But the genius of business is in interpreting what the information means. This leads to direction, which makes planning easier and more rewarding.

IMC Budgeting Approaches

In early 2008, the United States and Canada experienced the first throes of what would prove to be the longest recession in modern history. Consumer confidence declined, real estate sales dropped, construction of new homes slowed, and unemployment began to rise. To make matters worse, turmoil in the Middle East led to higher fuel prices.

When sales drop, many executives cut back their marketing communication budgets, some to zero. Later, when the recession is over, these executives will wonder why sales are still down and how their companies lost so much market share.

Money is the motor that drives every marketing and IMC plan. If you suddenly shut off the motor, the car may coast for a while, but before long it will stop running. The marketing department has the tough job of convincing top management that communication spending makes good business sense, even during adverse economic conditions.

IMC: An Investment in Future Sales

LO **8-5**

Accountants and the Internal Revenue Service consider many promotional expenditures to be a current business expense. Consequently, executives treat IMC as a budget item to be trimmed like other expense items when sales drop. This is understandable but frequently shortsighted.

The cost of a new plant or distribution warehouse is an investment in the company's future ability to produce and distribute products. Similarly, IMC—as one element of the marketing mix—is an investment in a product or brand. While IMC is often used to stimulate immediate sales, its greatest power is in its cumulative, long-range, reinforcement effect.[35]

Campaigns build consumer preference and promote goodwill. This, in turn, enhances the reputation and value of the company name and brand. And it encourages customers to make repeat purchases.

So while IMC is a current expense for accounting purposes, it is also a long-term capital investment. For management to see IMC as an investment, however, it must understand how message campaigns relate to sales and profits.

The Relationship of IMC to Sales and Profits

Economists have long studied the relationship between the amount a company spends on advertising, traditionally one of the most important IMC elements, and subsequent increases or decreases in sales or profitability. Such analyses are imperfect, as they occur in the real world rather than inside a laboratory, and most conclusions have followed from the study of advertising rather than IMC more broadly considered. However, substantial research does support the following principles:

- In consumer goods marketing, increases in market share are closely related to increases in the marketing budget. And market share is a prime indicator of profitability.[36]
- Sales normally increase with additional advertising. At some point, however, the rate of return plateaus and then declines. (See Ad Lab 8–B, "The Economic Effect of Advertising on Sales.")
- Sales response to advertising may build over time, but the durability of advertising is brief, so a consistent investment is important.
- Advertising expenditures below certain minimum levels have no effect on sales.
- Some sales will occur even if there is no advertising.
- Culture and competition impose saturation limits above which no amount of advertising can increase sales.

To management, these facts might say, spend more until it stops working. In reality, the issue isn't that simple. IMC isn't the only marketing activity that affects sales. A change in market share may occur because of quality perceptions, word of mouth, the introduction of

(continued on page 263)

Why are popular console games the perfect pairing for Dew? And, properly executed, how might this pairing convince consumers to buy more Dew, thereby increasing sales, and value the brand over its competitors, thereby increasing profits?
Source: Pepsi Cola Company

:: Strategic Use of the Creative Mix

During the marketing and advertising planning process, companies need to carefully consider who their target markets are and then who should be the targets of their advertising. They also need to consider the other elements of advertising strategy. This brings up a lot of questions: What product concept are we trying to communicate; what various media will be used to communicate the message; and what should the nature of our advertising message be? Once these things are decided, the creative team can begin its work.

• The ads in this portfolio demonstrate some good creative thinking, but more important, some outstanding strategic thinking. See if you can determine which element or elements of the creative mix are emphasized in each ad.

The Rich List is an annual feature of England's *Sunday Times*. The paper promotes itself by linking to wealthy (and famous) Brits. Every ad, including this one, finds a humorous way to communicate the relative wealth of different individuals.
Source: *The Sunday Times*

The web is more than a platform for beautifully designed messages as exemplified in this screenshot from Nike, www.nike.com. The Nike Website is a location for engagement and relationship building and provides consumers with a platform in which they can purchase products, find training tips, and connect with other Nike users.
Source: Nike, Inc.

The athletes Mountain Dew sponsors are different from those Nike supports. But that is a choice that makes perfect sense given the differences in the brands' marketing strategies.
Source: Pepsi Cola Company

Edding, a European brand of marker, shares an online "Wall of Fame" where visitors can create and share drawings with a digital marker. Try it yourself at http://wall-of-fame.com/.
By courtesy of edding International GmbH, Germany

New Zealand's Dulux brand challenges "do-it-yourselfer's" to answer the question "What's your Dulux Colour?"
Source: Dulux

The excitement of a visit to Universal's theme parks is conveyed powerfully through imagery from the popular films.
Source: Universal Studios

AD Lab 8–B

The Economic Effect of Advertising on Sales

As a rule, the level of sales of a product is proportional to the level of advertising expenditure—that is, within reasonable limits, the more you spend, the more you sell (assuming the advertising program is not too repugnant). Yet, even the most enthusiastic ad agency will admit, reluctantly, that it is possible to spend too much.

Ideally, managers would like to know how much more they will be able to sell per additional dollar of advertising and when additional advertising dollars cease being effective. They need to have not a fixed number representing potential demand, but a graph or a statistical equation describing the relationship between sales and advertising.

In our illustration, most of the curve goes uphill as we move to the right (it has a *positive* slope). This means that additional advertising will continue to bring in business until (at a budget of x million dollars) people become so saturated by the message that it begins to repel them and turn them away from the product.

Even if the saturation level cannot be reached within the range of outlays the firm can afford, the curve is likely to level off, becoming flatter and flatter as the amount spent on advertising gets larger and larger and saturation is approached. The point at which the curve begins to flatten is the point at which returns from advertising begin to diminish. When the total advertising budget is small, even a $1 addition to the campaign may bring in as much as $10 in new sales. But when the market approaches

saturation, each additional dollar may contribute only 30 cents in new sales, if anything at all.

Laboratory Application

1. When would an advertising expenditure curve have a negative slope?

2. Economists suggest that the quantity sold depends on the number of dollars the company spends on advertising. Is that a safe assumption? Discuss.

(continued from page 259)

new products, competitive trade promotion, the opening of more attractive outlets, better personal selling, seasonal changes in the business cycle, or shifts in consumer preferences.

As this edition was being revised, one of America's best-known companies, Kodak, was filing for bankruptcy. Simply increasing expenditures on IMC would not have prevented its decline. Kodak made profits for decades on film used in traditional cameras, a technology most consumers no longer use. Capitalism's ruthless edict requires that companies meet consumer needs and wants, or perish.

One thing remains clear. Because the response to promotional messages is spread out over time, IMC should be viewed as a long-term investment in future profits. Like all expenditures, campaigns should be evaluated for wastefulness. But historically, companies that make IMC the scapegoat during tough times end up losing substantial market share before the economy starts growing again.[37]

The corollary is also true. Sustained spending during difficult times protects, and in some cases even increases, market share and builds brands. During the last global recession, the leading European marketers recognized this fact, and fewer than 40 percent of the top spenders in Italy, Austria, Germany, France, and Spain cut their budgets.[38]

The Variable Environments of Business

Before attempting to determine IMC allocations, the brand manager must consider the company's economic, political, social, and legal situation. These factors affect total industry sales and corporate profits on sales. The manager must consider the institutional and competitive environments. What is the level of sales within the industry? How much are competitors spending, and what are they doing that might either help or hinder the company's marketing efforts?

My IMC Campaign 8–C

Ways to Set IMC Budgets

How much should you recommend that your client spend on promotions? Here is a list of ways companies set their marketing budgets.

- **Percentage of sales.** Budget is determined by allocating a percentage of last year's sales, anticipated sales for next year, or a combination of the two. The percentage is usually based on an industry average, company experience, or an arbitrary figure.

- **Percentage of profit.** Percentage is applied to profit, either past years' or anticipated.

- **Unit of sale.** Also called the *case-rate method.* A specific dollar amount is set for each box, case, barrel, or carton produced. Used primarily in assessing members of horizontal co-ops or trade associations.

- **Competitive parity.** Also called the *self-defense method.* Allocates dollars according to the amounts spent by major competitors.

- **Share of market/share of voice.** Allocates dollars by maintaining a percentage share of total industry spending comparable to or somewhat ahead of desired share of market. Often used for new product introductions.

- **Objective/task.** Also referred to as the *budget buildup method,* this method has three steps: defining objectives, determining strategy, and estimating the cost to execute that strategy.

- **Empirical research.** Companies determine the most efficient level by running experimental tests in different markets with different budgets.

- **Quantitative mathematical models.** Computer-based programs developed by major advertisers and agencies rely on input of sophisticated data, history, and assumptions.

- **All available funds.** Go-for-broke technique generally used by small firms with limited capital, trying to introduce new products or services.

Finally, the manager must consider the internal environment. Do the company's current policies and procedures allow it to fulfill the promises its campaign intends to make?

Developing an IMC Budget

Most business executives will spend more on IMC as long as they are assured it will mean more profit. However, the point of equilibrium is hard to predict when budgets are being developed.

Companies use a number of methods to determine how much to spend on IMC, including the *percentage of sales, percentage of profit, unit of sale, competitive parity, share of market,* and *objective/task methods* (see My Ad Campaign 8–C, "Ways to Set IMC Budgets").

No technique is adequate for all situations. The methods discussed here are used primarily for national advertising budgets. However, local retailers can use them too.

Percentage of Sales Method

The **percentage of sales method** is one of the most popular techniques for setting promotional budgets. It may be based on a percentage of last year's sales, anticipated sales for next year, or a combination of the two. Businesspeople like this method because it is simple, it doesn't cost them anything, it is related to revenue, and it is considered safe. The problem is knowing what percentage to use. As Exhibit 8-9 shows, even leaders in the same industry use different percentages. Across industries, promotional expenditures range from just 1.5 percent of sales to more than 22 percent.

Usually the percentage is based on an industry average or on company experience. Unfortunately, it is too often determined arbitrarily. An industry average assumes that every company in the industry has similar objectives and faces the same marketing problems. Company experience assumes that the market is highly static, which is rarely the case.

However, when applied against anticipated future sales, this method often works well. It assumes that a certain number of dollars will be needed to sell a certain number of units. If the company knows what the percentage is, the correlation between IMC spending and sales should remain constant, assuming the market is stable and competitors' spending remains

Exhibit 8-9

Advertising expenditures and sales by the top 15 advertisers (all dollars in billions). Looking over the exhibit, what factors do you think lead to a higher or lower amount for advertising as a percentage of sales?

Rank	Company	U.S. Advertising Expenditures	U.S. Sales	Advertising as a Percentage of Sales
1	Procter & Gamble	$4.9	$ 29.4	16.7%
2	AT&T	3.3	63.0	5.2
3	General Motors	3.3	129.0	2.6
4	Time Warner	3.1	35.6	8.7
5	Verizon	2.8	88.1	3.2
6	Ford	2.6	81.1	3.2
7	GlaxoSmithKline	2.4	18.9	12.7
8	Walt Disney Co.	2.3	26.6	8.6
9	Johnson & Johnson	2.3	29.8	7.7
10	Unilever	2.1	17.2	12.2
11	Toyota	2.0	77.7	2.6
12	Sony	2.0	19.2	10.4
13	DaimlerChrysler	1.9	79.9	2.4
14	General Electric	1.9	89.1	2.1
15	Sprint Nextel	1.8	41.0	4.4

unchanged. And because this method is common in the industry, it diminishes the likelihood of competitive warfare.

A big shortcoming of the percentage of sales method is that it violates a basic marketing principle. Marketing activities are supposed to *stimulate* demand and thus sales, not occur as a *result* of sales. If IMC automatically increases when sales increase and declines when sales decline, it ignores all other factors that might encourage an opposite move.

The percentage of sales method also ignores the strategic nature of marketing. Rather than encouraging planners to think carefully about the proper budget for accomplishing objectives, it forces them to develop objectives that fit the budget. This means planners often miss opportunities for building brand equity or long-term relationships with consumers.

Share of Market/Share of Voice Method

In markets with similar products, a strong relationship usually exists between a company's share of the market and its share of industry IMC.

The **share of market/share of voice method** is an attempt to link promotional dollars with sales objectives.[39] It holds that a company's best chance of maintaining its share of a market is to keep a share of IMC (voice) somewhat ahead of its market share. For example, a company with a 30 percent share of the market should spend 35 percent of the industry's promotional dollars.

The share of market/share of voice method is commonly used for new product introductions.[40] According to this formula, when a new brand is introduced, the budget for the first two years should be about one and a half times the brand's targeted share of the market in two years. This means that if the company's two-year sales goal is 10 percent of the market, it should spend about 15 percent of promotional spending during the first two years. The company's share of all promotional spending is what is meant by "share of voice."

To see how this method works, look at the three leading U.S. auto manufacturers in Exhibit 8-9, GM, Ford, and DaimlerChrysler. The domestic market, based on sales of the big three, was about $290 billion DaimlerChrysler, with almost $80 billion in sales, had roughly 27.6 percent of U.S. auto company sales. What was advertising share of voice? We can see that DaimlerChrysler spent nearly $1.9 billion on advertising, which was only about 24 percent of U.S. automaker expenditures. To grow its market share, a larger share of voice may have been required.

The ad above shows Lego as an iconic toy that is both fun and educational. It is targeted directly at parents and its goal is to inform them of the importance of creative play. Since Lego is a strong and established brand, would percentage of sales method be a good technique in determining the promotional budget for this campaign?
Source: The Lego Group

People BEHIND the Ads

Samantha Avivi, Marketing Director for Residential Business at ADT, former Global Marketing Director at Kimberly-Clark

Courtesy of Samantha Avivi

As the daughter of advertising giant Stan Harris, IMC was in Samantha Avivi's blood from the beginning. Launching her career after earning an advertising degree from the University of Florida, Sam spent two years learning her craft at her dad's agency before joining Young & Rubicam, where she provided account services for Advil and Fisher Price. Next came stints with DMB&B and BBDO before her biggest client, Procter & Gamble, convinced Sam to jump ship and become an assistant brand manager for Luvs. Today she is the Global Marketing Director at Kimberly-Clark, a job that takes her around the globe in support of some of the world's biggest brands. We had a chance to catch up with Samantha recently when she was honored as an alumna of distinction at UF.

CA: Describe your present job, including a description of a typical day (or days).

SA: During a typical day I synthesize category and consumer data from around the world to set a global brand vision, strategies and equity (including segmentation, positioning, and architecture), lead teams to set pathways for mid- and long-term innovation, establish frameworks for business fundamentals, and help Identify business and communication best practices to ensure global reapplication. As part of this process, I align regional and local company presidents, VPs, and directors. I also manage cross-functional teams and agencies to ensure they deliver on the category plan.

CA: What do you look for in students who would like to be you someday?

SA: I look for students who are smart, demonstrate leadership ability, and have the right attitude. A good GPA is important, but I know someone is a smart thinker when they prove they can gather and synthesize data to drive sound conclusions. Proven leadership ability is also important. Even at the beginning of someone's career he/she will need to lead projects and people. Finally, the right attitude sets someone apart from their peers. I look for someone with passion and commitment to their work.

CA: How does Kimberly-Clark think about its consumers, its brands, and its communications objectives?

SA: Kimberly-Clark places the consumer at the center of everything it does. We prioritize all work to meet the needs of our consumers around the world. This is clearly evident in our vision, "Leading the World in Essentials for a Better Life."

We view each of our brands such as Kleenex, Huggies, and Kotex as a promise to the consumer. The product lines offered under our brands are the delivery of that promise. Simply put, our consumers have an expectation on how our brands will meet their needs. Each of our products must deliver on that promise to maintain that level of trust and expectations from our consumer.

Communications is also critical at Kimberly-Clark. This function of marketing is to help us connect, engage, influence, and inspire our consumers. The right communications is at the heart of all our marketing activities.

CA: What have been the biggest changes you've seen over the past 10 years in brand promotions?

SA: The lines between brand promotions and "equity building" advertising have been blurred. It's all about building the business now and, as such, brands need to build their equity while driving immediate revenue.

An IMC focus helps to remind us that advertising is just one component of IMC, and for some marketers, not the most important one. The top national packaged-goods marketers spend 25 to 30 percent of their marketing budgets on consumer and trade promotion rather than consumer advertising.[41] That's how they get more shelf space in the store. And in certain packaged-goods categories, in-store trade promotions may generate 25 percent of a brand's short-term volume, while advertising may be responsible for only 5 percent.[42]

Strategic Budgeting: Objective/Task Method

The **objective/task method,** also known as the *budget buildup method,* is used by many large national marketers in the United States. It treats IMC as a marketing tool for generating sales.

The task method has three steps: defining objectives, determining strategy, and estimating cost. After setting specific, quantitative communication objectives, the company

CA: What value do you see in newer forms of media (social media, search, etc.) as compared to traditional forms?

SA: Social media has so much benefit. For one, it is a way to develop a two-way relationship with our consumers. Consumers now have the upper hand to tell manufacturers and their closest friends (the entire world on the Internet) what they think of our products. Companies that create great products and have strong brands will disproportionately win in those types of situations. Another benefit of social media is it provides a way to do low-cost research. Consumers want to give us their opinion. We need to find a way to productively use their input.

At Kimberly-Clark we leverage our Integrated Marketing Planning process which leads us to focus first on the overall business objective(s) of a brand and then determine the best ideas and channels for achieving those objectives. We don't believe in digital marketing. Instead, we believe today it is all about marketing in a digital world. That is a very different outlook than most have when it comes to new forms of media.

CA: How important are benchmarks for your brands, and what are some of your most important ones? Do you have different benchmarks for evaluating the performance of social as compared with traditional media?

SA: Benchmarks are critical to evaluate in-market potential. It helps in many aspects of my job including evaluation of product performance, commercial effectiveness, ROI, consumer attitudes, habits and practices, and most quantitative research. We haven't been able to use historical benchmarks on social media because it's so new. I have backed into the benchmarks for this medium by tying it back to our overall goals for an initiative.

CA: What does IMC mean to you and how does that affect KC's relationships with its agencies?

SA: Integrated Marketing Communications means that all agencies work with a common big creative idea that can drive business results. It does not mean that creative work is identical. Kimberly-Clark has a disciplined process called Integrated Marketing Planning that concentrates on identifying and understanding the business objectives of a specific brand first, creating the communications idea second, and then determining the best method for delivering that message and idea to our consumers in the right environment.

CA: You've been on both sides of the agency, client divide. What stands out about the differences and/or similarities of those experiences?

SA: Both sides are looking to build the business. Everyone feels ownership, love, and responsibility for the brand. Both have a deep understanding of the consumer. The difference is in the approach. The agency uses creative solutions while the client focuses more on analytics and data. The agency goes deep on one component, the communication. The client has a wider scope of responsibility that covers the entire brand experience.

CA: What excites you about your career over the next five years?

It's funny. The same thing excites me now as what excited me when I started my career. Over the next five years I'm excited to better understand and meet the needs of consumers. In the past, I've overheard people talking about work I've executed and how it's made a difference in their life. There's nothing more rewarding to know that you were part of that effort. I hope to have more experiences like that in the next five years.

CA: Anything else you'd like to comment on or that would be helpful to advertising and IMC students?

SA: My advice is to identify your passion and not give up. Careers have ups and downs. It takes twists and turns. What's most important is to learn from all experiences. Take chances that support your passion and work hard to make the most of each experience.

develops programs to attain them. If the objective is to increase awareness of Mountain Dew Code Red by 40 percent, PepsiCo determines which campaign approach will work best, how often messages must run, and which media to use. The estimated cost of the program becomes the basis for the budget. Of course, the company's financial position is always a consideration. If the cost is too high, objectives may have to be scaled back. If results are better or worse than anticipated after the campaign runs, the next budget may need revision.

The task method forces companies to think in terms of accomplishing goals. Its effectiveness is most apparent when campaign results can be readily measured. The task method is adaptable to changing market conditions and can be easily revised.

However, it is often difficult to determine in advance the amount of money needed to reach a specific goal. Techniques for measuring campaign effectiveness still have many weaknesses.

Additional Methods

Advertisers also use several other methods to allocate funds. In the **empirical research method,** a company runs a series of tests in different markets with different budgets to determine the best level of advertising expenditure.

Computers can generate quantitative mathematical models for budgeting and allocating promotional dollars. Many sophisticated techniques facilitate marketing planning, budget allocation, new product introductions, and media and promotion analysis. However, most are not easily understood by line executives, and all rely on data that may be unavailable or estimated. These methods require very sophisticated users and, for the most part, are still too expensive for the average small business.

The Bottom Line

Unfortunately, all these methods rely on one of two fallacies. The first is that IMC is a *result* of sales. Marketers know this is not true, yet they continue to use the percentage of sales method.

The second fallacy is that IMC *creates* sales. In certain circumstances (where direct-response messages are used), advertising closes the sale. But a campaign's real role is to reinforce current customers, locate new prospects, position the product competitively, build brand equity, and stimulate demand. It may even stimulate inquiries and product trial and, on the local level, build retail traffic.

But the principal job of IMC is to influence consumers by informing, persuading, and reminding. IMC *affects* sales, but it is just one of many influences on consumers. Brand managers must keep this in mind when preparing their plans and budgets.

Chapter Summary

The marketing plan may be the most important document a company possesses. It assembles all the pertinent and current facts about a company, the markets it serves, its products, and its competition. It sets specific goals and objectives and describes the precise strategies to use to achieve them. It musters the company's forces for the marketing battlefield and, in so doing, dictates the role of IMC in the marketing mix and provides focus for IMC creativity.

There are three types of marketing planning models: top-down, bottom-up, and integrated marketing communications planning.

The top-down marketing plan contains four principal sections: situation analysis, marketing objectives, marketing strategy, and tactics (action programs). A company's marketing objectives should be logical deductions from an analysis of its current situation, its prediction of future trends, and its understanding of corporate objectives. They should relate to the needs of specific target markets and specify sales objectives. Sales-target objectives should be specific, quantitative, and realistic.

The first step in developing a marketing strategy is to select the target market. The second step is to determine the product's positioning. The third step is to construct a cost-effective marketing mix for each target market the company pursues. The marketing mix is determined by how the company blends the elements it controls: product, price, distribution, and communications. IMC is a communications tool.

One way for small companies to construct the marketing and IMC plan is to work from the bottom up, taking an ingenious tactic and building a strategy around it.

Integrated marketing communications can help build long-term relationships with customers. IMC planning is driven by technology. Thanks to computers and databases, marketers can learn more about their customers' wants and needs, likes and dislikes.

IMC is a natural outgrowth of the marketing plan, and the IMC plan is prepared in much the same way as the top-down marketing plan. It includes a SWOT (strengths, weaknesses, opportunities, and threats) analysis, advertising objectives, and strategy.

IMC objectives may be expressed in terms of moving prospective customers up through the IMC pyramid (awareness, comprehension, conviction, desire, action). Or they may be expressed in terms of generating inquiries, coupon response, or attitude change.

The IMC (or creative) strategy is determined by the marketer's use of the creative mix. The creative mix is composed of the target audience, product concept, communications media, and the message. The target audience includes the specific groups of people IMC will address. The product concept refers to the bundle of product-related values the company presents to the customer. The communications media are the vehicles used to transmit the marketer's message. The message is what the company plans to say and how it plans to say it.

Several methods are used to allocate advertising funds. The most popular are the percentage of sales approach and the objective/task method. The share of market/share of voice method is often used in markets with similar products.

Important Terms

bottom-up marketing, *247*

communications media, *257*

communication objectives, *241*

creative mix, *256*

DAGMAR, *243*

empirical research method, *268*

IMC message, *258*

IMC plan, *252*

IMC strategy, *256*

marketing objectives, *241*

marketing plan, *240*

marketing strategy, *243*

mission statement, *240*

objective/task method, *266*

percentage of sales method, *264*

product concept, *257*

sales-target objectives, *241*

share of market/share of voice method, *265*

situation analysis, *241*

subliminal advertising, *248*

SWOT analysis, *241*

tactics, *247*

target audience, *256*

Review Questions

1. What is a marketing plan and why is it a company's most important document?
2. What examples illustrate the difference between need-satisfying objectives and sales-target objectives?
3. What are the three types of marketing plans? How do they differ?
4. What basic elements should be included in a top-down marketing plan?
5. How can small companies use bottom-up marketing to become big companies?
6. What are the elements of an advertising plan and an IMC strategy?
7. What types of involvement do consumers bring to the purchase decision?
8. What is the best method of allocating advertising funds for a real estate development? Why?
9. What types of companies tend to use the percentage of sales method? Why?
10. How could a packaged-foods manufacturer use the share of market/share of voice method to determine its advertising budget?

The Advertising Experience

1. **The importance of planning**

   Why is planning so important for the success of brand messages? How did planning help Mountain Dew to evolve not only its ads and other promotional activities, but its core identity?

2. **Strategic IMC Planning**

   You have explored various means of planning advertising strategy—top-down, bottom-up, and IMC. Browse through the Websites of the following marketers, and then answer the questions regarding the various means of planning IMC strategy:

   - American Automobile Association (AAA): www.aaa.com
   - Bristol Myers Squibb: www.bms.com
   - Proflowers.com: www.proflowers.com
   - Hudson Moving & Storage: www.moving-storage.com
   - Metro Goldwyn Mayer/UA: www.mgm.com
   - General Electric: www.ge.com
   - Hewlett-Packard: www.hp.com
   - Intel: www.intel.com
   - Kellogg's: www.kelloggs.com/us
   - Walt Disney: www.disney.com

   a. What are the size and scope of the company and its business? What is the company's purpose?

   b. Identify the target audience, product concept, communications media, and advertising message for each.

   c. What is the company's position within the industry? What is the type of communication used? Target market?

   d. Where does the company's product(s) fall within the Kim–Lord grid?

3. **WebSites and IMC**

   IMC can involve many different elements, and a Website can be an integral part of a company's marketing efforts. Discuss how the following three companies might make a Website part of an overall IMC effort:

   a. The Green Threads clothing retailer described in Chapter 1.

   b. A medium-sized candy maker with some brands that are nearly 100 years old.

   c. A small company that publishes books, CDs, and DVDs for a motivational speaker who has just had her first big break with an appearance on *The Dr. Phil Show*.

4. Mountain Dew has "owned" an association with extreme sports and youth since the early 1990s, and this strategy continues to be successful for the brand. What cultural or societal trends must the brand monitor in order to know how to communicate with its audience? Does its image also limit growth possibilities? If so, in what ways? How might it circumvent these limits?

5. Mountain Dew is an established brand in a mature product category. Which methods of allocating promotional funds—percentage of sales, share of market/share of voice, objective/task, or empirical research—would be wisest for Mountain Dew to utilize? Explain your preference

CHAPTER 9

Planning Media Strategy: Disseminating the Message

Learning Objectives

To show how communications media help advertisers achieve marketing and advertising objectives. To get their messages to the right people in the right place at the right time, media planners follow the same procedures as marketing and advertising planners: setting objectives, formulating strategies, and devising tactics. To make sound decisions, media planners must possess marketing savvy, analytical skill, and creativity.

 After studying this chapter, you will be able to:

LO9-1 Describe how a media plan helps accomplish a company's marketing and advertising objectives.

LO9-2 Explain the importance of creativity in media planning.

LO9-3 Define reach and frequency and debate the controversy surrounding the concept of effective frequency.

LO9-4 Discuss how reach, frequency, and continuity are related.

LO9-5 Calculate gross rating points and cost per thousand.

LO9-6 Describe different types of advertising schedules and the purpose for each.

LO9-7 Distinguish media planning in digital media from planning in traditional.

© vetkit/Getty Images RF

© John Shearer/Invision/AP Images

TV advertisers sometimes find it is better to weave their brands right into the shows rather than run traditional commercials. The Academy Awards and popular films like Wayne's World offer advertisers unique opportunities to draw attention to their brands.

© Ellen DeGeneres/Twitter/Getty Images

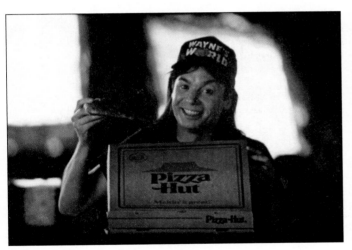

© Everett Collection

Television networks work with major sports associations and professional teams to develop integrated marketing "partnerships" for sports and event sponsors. General Motors and NBC, for example, raised the bar on Olympic sponsorships in 1997 with a 12-year, $600 million deal to make GM the official domestic car and truck of the U.S. Olympic Team. The NBC portion of the deal gave GM domestic category exclusivity and media placement for the network's coverage of the 2000, 2002, 2004, 2006, and 2008 Olympics. GM spent an estimated additional $300 million to leverage its Olympics involvement. As Phil Guarasco, GM's VP/general manager of marketing and advertising, said, "This isn't about dollars, it's about value. What we have here is a strong, cost-effective marketing initiative for the company."[14]

Value-added packages often employ communications vehicles outside traditional media planning, such as public relations activities, sales promotion, and direct marketing. The Food Network, for instance, host of *The Next Iron Chef International*, allowed product integration for the premier sponsor, Kikkoman, into the competition and also recorded one of the episodes on-site at Kikkoman headquarters in Japan. These type of integrations allow advertisers, in this case Kikkoman, to gain associative value that basic advertising cannot accomplish. But placing a value on these deals is difficult because the nonmedia elements are hard to quantify.

The trend toward integrated marketing communications and relationship marketing is creating a new breed of media planner: younger, computer literate, and schooled in marketing disciplines beyond traditional media. The good media specialist today is actually a real advertising generalist. And with many of the biggest client changes happening in *media-only* agency reviews, it's apparent that the media professionals have finally come into their own.

Increasing Competition

The final element making media planning more challenging today is the competitive environment, which in just a few years completely changed the structure of the advertising business. In the 1980s and early 1990s, as clients sought greater efficiency with their media dollars, independent media-buying services came to the fore, attracting some of the best and brightest talent in the business to compete with agencies for what was once their private domain. Initially, the independents bought advertising space and time at lower bulk rates and then sold it at a higher rate or for a handling commission to advertisers or ad agencies that didn't have a fully staffed media department. As the media specialists grew, though, clients came to realize the virtues of scale, and financial clout emerged as a potent weapon in negotiating media buys.[15] By 1994, the independents handled more than one-fourth of all national advertising media accounts.[16]

To respond to the competitive pressure, ad agencies started unbundling their own media departments, setting them up as separate media specialist subsidiaries. These companies could compete with the independents as well as with other agencies for media-only accounts. Over time, all these firms became quite expert at the media function. With the rapid increase in billings, they were able to pour a substantial amount of money into the development of new research tools, which was critical given the continued fragmentation of the mass media into smaller and smaller niches.

At this point, the big multinational advertisers realized that they could receive greater impact from their ad dollars by consolidating their media budgets within a single large shop. (For more on the agency–client relationship, see Ethical Issues: "The Ethical Dilemmas of Agency Compensation.")

Ethical Issues

The Ethical Dilemmas of Agency Compensation

The payment structure that defined the client–agency relationship for over a century has come under fire by both sides. Ad agency compensation was once a simple formula, but now it has become one of the foremost concerns for both advertisers and agencies in a world of high media costs, low budgets, and rising awareness of corporate fraud and scandal.

Founded in 1875, N.W. Ayer & Sons was the first ad agency to plan, create, and execute complete advertising campaigns in exchange for media-paid commissions—typically 15 percent of the client's media expenditures. Back then, 15 percent may have seemed a small amount as the avenues for advertising were limited to the low-cost advertising space of newspapers, magazines, posters, and other forms of print. However, by the late twentieth century, advances in technology had created many new avenues for reaching consumers. Today, advertisers can send their messages through a wide variety of print, electronic, and digital interactive media, all far more expensive—and profitable—than the newspapers and magazines of the nineteenth or early twentieth century. Take, for example, a 30-second TV spot on NBC's Sunday Night Football that averages over $500,000. Under the commission structure, the agency that placed this commercial would receive almost $113,000, considerable revenue considering the time directly spent placing that commercial. And that's for just one spot! When the client runs a schedule of ads, the ad agency's profits really balloon.

As a result of this high profitability, the standard 15 percent commission is under siege. Some observers regard an agency's so-called expert and impartial advice to the advertiser about commissionable media spending as suspect, if not outright biased. Commissions, they believe, negatively affect the ethics of the business by potentially causing the agency to be motivated by income rather than the client's best interests.

Consequently, advertising industry leaders sought change. In the early 1990s, clients began taking control of the process, establishing their own compensation systems. By 1995, only 14 percent of advertisers were still paying 15 percent commissions, as labor-based fees and incentive programs increased. Tying compensation directly to the time spent creating a campaign, as well as to the actual sales performance the campaign achieved, allowed advertisers to feel that their goals and needs were once again the primary focus.

However, by the turn of the twenty-first century, compensation concerns returned to the forefront of advertisers' agendas, as fraud and scandal created a need for greater agency accountability. SEC investigations have found that, by using complex billing statements and convoluted accounting methods, some agencies had once again started putting personal profit ahead of their clients' interests. Government probes found that some had even padded suppliers' bills in exchange for costly perks. These investigations have led to guilty pleas from 32 people and nine companies.

Fortunately, leaders on both the client and agency sides have been quick to find a proactive solution that would benefit both sides. In 2002, the Association of Advertising Agencies and the Association of National Advertisers, Inc., came together to create the first-ever set of guidelines covering compensation agreements between agencies and advertisers. In an effort to create the most effective compensation agreements possible, the joint document established dozens of guidelines. Among others, the guidelines state that the best compensation programs

- Align advertiser and agency interests and priorities.
- Match compensation with the resources required to do the work.
- Establish agreement on key compensation definitions and terms up front.
- Do not favor one solution or service over another.
- Finalize compensation before agency resources are committed.

While these guidelines do help provide a benchmark of best practices for compensation agreements, they are far from an end-all solution. In fact, some people within the ad agency community feel that the very search for an ultimate solution is aggravating the problem. Specifically, these members believe that there will always be certain aspects of the client–agency dynamic that cannot be standardized or measured. One example is the creative talent that differentiates one agency from the next. Surely a premium for creativity must be paid, but how do you standardize a price for such talents? Another question is how to tie compensation directly to results. Compensation should be tied to results, but how are results measured in such an inexact and intangible science?

The one thing both sides can agree on is that the debate on "fair" compensation is sure to last for many years to come.

Questions

1. Compare the advantages and disadvantages of the commission system with those of the fee or incentive system.

2. What problems, if any, does the commission system cause for small businesses that are less likely to use high-cost media?

Sources: Lisa Sanders, "Feds Probe Madison Ave. Bill-Padding Scams," *Advertising Age*, April 1, 2002; "AAAA and ANA Announce First Ever Guidelines for Compensation Agreements," December 12, 2002 (retrieved from www.aaaa.org); Jones Lundin Beals, "Trends in Agency Compensation," May 29, 2002 (retrieved from www.admworks.org/conference/2002/bealsagencypres.pdf).

The Role of Media in the Marketing Framework

 LO 9-2

As we've discussed in previous chapters, the key to successful advertising is proper planning. Thus, before media planning begins—indeed, before advertising is even considered—companies must first establish their overall marketing and advertising plans for their products.

Marketing Objectives and Strategy

In Chapter 8 you read how the top-down marketing plan defines the market need and the company's sales objectives and details strategies for attaining those objectives. Exhibit 9-2 shows how objectives and strategies result from the marketing situation (or SWOT) analysis, which defines the company's *strengths* and *weaknesses* and uncovers any marketplace *opportunities* and *threats*. Marketing objectives may focus on solving a problem ("regaining sales volume lost to major competitive introductions over the past year") or seizing an opportunity ("increasing share in the female buyer segment of the athletic-shoe market").

Marketing strategies lay out the steps for meeting these objectives by blending the four elements of the marketing mix. A company whose marketing objective is to increase sales of a particular brand in a certain part of the country has many options. For example, it can adapt the product to suit regional tastes *(product);* it can lower the price to compete with local brands *(price);* it can devise deals to gain additional shelf space in retail outlets *(distribution);* and it can reposition the product through intensive trade and consumer advertising *(communication).* Thus, advertising is just one of the many strategic tools a company may use to achieve its marketing objectives.

Advertising Objectives and Strategy

The objectives and strategies of an advertising plan unfold from the marketing plan. But advertising objectives focus on communication goals, such as

- Convincing 25 percent of the target market during the next year of the brand's need-satisfying abilities.
- Positioning the brand as a cost-effective alternative to the market leader in the minds of 30 percent of men ages 18 to 34 during the next two years.
- Increasing brand preference by 8 percent in the South during the next year.
- Improving the target stakeholder group's attitude toward the company's environmental efforts by at least 15 percent by campaign end.

To achieve these objectives, companies devise advertising strategies that employ the elements of the **creative mix:** the product concept, target audience, advertising message, and communications media.

The media department's job is to make sure the advertising message (developed by the creative department) gets to the correct target audience (established by the marketing managers and account executives) in an effective manner (as measured by the research department).

The Media-Planning Framework

In the age of integrated marketing communications, many agencies have moved the task of media planning earlier in the advertising management process, because people typically make contact with the brand through some medium. Before determining what creative approach to employ, it's important to know when, where, and under what conditions contact can best be made with the customer or other stakeholder and to plan for that. This sets the strategic direction for the creative department.

That's also why we present the topic of media planning now, in Part Two, "Planning the Campaign," because media planning is part of the strategic work done prior to developing

The situation analysis
Purpose: To understand the marketing problem. The company and its competitors are analyzed on
1. Internal strengths and weaknesses.
2. External opportunities and threats.

The marketing plan
Purpose: To plan activities that will solve one or more of the marketing problems.
Includes the determination of
1. Marketing objectives.
2. Product and spending strategy.
3. Distribution strategy.
4. Which marketing mix to use.
5. Identification of "best" market segments.

The advertising plan
Purpose: To determine what to communicate through ads.
Includes the determination of
1. How product can meet consumer needs.
2. How product will be positioned in ads.
3. Copy themes.
4. Specific objectives of each ad.
5. Number and sizes of ads.

Setting media objectives
Purpose: To translate marketing and advertising objectives and strategies into goals that media can accomplish.

Determining media strategy
Purpose: To translate media goals into general guidelines that will control the planner's selection and use of media. The best strategy alternatives should be selected.

Selecting broad media classes
Purpose: To determine which broad class of media best fulfills the criteria. Involves comparison and selection of broad media classes: newspapers, magazines, radio, television, and others. Audience size is a major factor used in comparing the various media classes.

Selecting media within classes
Purpose: To compare and select the best media within broad classes, again using predetermined criteria. Involves making decisions about the following:
1. If magazines were recommended, then which magazines?
2. If television was recommended, then
   a. Broadcast or cable TV?
   b. Network or spot TV?
   c. If network, which program(s)?
   d. If spot, which markets?
3. If radio or newspapers were recommended, then
   a. Which markets shall be used?
   b. What criteria shall buyers use in making purchases in local media?

Media use decisions—broadcast
1. What kind of sponsorship (sole, shared participating, or other)?
2. What levels of reach and frequency will be required?
3. Scheduling: On which days and months are commercials to appear?
4. Placement of spots: In programs or between programs?

Media use decisions—print
1. Numbers of ads to appear and on which days and months.
2. Placement of ads: Any preferred-position within media?
3. Special treatment: Gatefolds, bleeds, color, etc.
4. Desired reach or frequency levels.

Media use decisions—other media
1. Billboards:
   a. Location of markets and plan of distribution.
   b. Kinds of outdoor boards to be used.
2. Direct mail or other media: Decisions peculiar to those media.
3. Interactive media:
   a. Which kind of interactive media?
   b. How will responses be handled?

Exhibit 9-2
This diagram outlines the scope of media-planning activities.

creative concepts. Later, in Part 3, "Executing and Evaluating the Campaign," we'll discuss the tactical details of each medium, how it's used, and how it's bought—activities that typically occur after the creative process.

Development of a media plan involves the same process as marketing and advertising planning. First, review the marketing and advertising objectives and strategies and set relevant, measurable objectives that are both realistic and achievable by the media. Next, try to devise an ingenious strategy for achieving these objectives. Finally, develop the specific tactical details of media scheduling and selection.

Defining Media Objectives

Media objectives translate the advertising strategy into goals that media can accomplish. Exhibit 9-3 shows general media objectives for a hypothetical new food product. They explain who the target audience is and why, where messages will be delivered and when, and how much advertising weight needs to be delivered over what period of time.

Media objectives have two major components: *audience objectives* and *message-distribution objectives*.

Audience Objectives

Audience objectives define the specific types of people the advertiser wants to reach. Media planners typically use geodemographic classifications to define their target audiences. In Exhibit 9-3, for example, the target audience is food purchasers for large families who live in urban areas across the country.

The target audience may consist of people in a specific income, educational, occupational, or social group—any of the segments we discussed in Chapter 6. And the target audience is not necessarily the same as the product's target market. Often it is considerably larger. For example, in the case of a new product introduction, the target audience will often include members of the distribution channel, key opinion leaders, the financial community, and even the media itself—in addition to potential customers.

Many advertisers have to defend their media decisions with the retailers who stock and resell their products. Why? If these people construed a change in media strategy as a loss of advertising support, they might reduce the shelf space for the advertiser's products. Therefore, most consumer campaigns are supported by a concurrent campaign directed to the trade.

The consumer target audience may be determined from the marketer's research. However, planners rely largely on secondary research sources, such as Arbitron and Nielsen Media Research, which provide basic demographic characteristics of media audiences. Others, such as Simmons Market Research Bureau (SMRB) and Mediamark Research, Inc. (MRI), describe media audiences based on purchase tendencies (see Exhibit 9-4). These syndicated reports give demographic profiles of heavy and light users of various products and help planners define the target audience. The reports also specify which TV programs or magazines heavy and light users watch and read, which helps planners select media with large audiences of heavy users. Planners can then select **media vehicles**—particular magazines or shows—according to how well they "deliver" or expose the message to the media audience that most closely resembles the desired target consumer.

Advertisers using the IMC planning model start by segmenting their target audiences according to brand-purchasing behavior (e.g., loyal users, brand switchers, new prospects) and then ranking them by profit to the brand.[17] Communications objectives are then stated in terms of reinforcing or modifying customer purchasing behavior or creating a perceptual change about the brand over time.[18]

ACME Advertising

Client: Econo Foods
Product/Brand: Chirpee's Cheap Chips
Project: Media plan, first year introduction

Media Objectives

1. To target large families with emphasis on the family's food purchaser.
2. To concentrate the greatest weight of advertising in urban areas where prepared foods traditionally have greater sales and where new ideas normally gain quicker acceptance.
3. To provide extra weight during the announcement period and then continuity throughout the year with a fairly consistent level of advertising impressions.
4. To deliver advertising impressions to every region in relation to regional food store sales.
5. To use media that will reinforce the copy strategy's emphasis on convenience, ease of preparation, taste, and economy.
6. To attain the highest advertising frequency possible once the need for broad coverage and the demands of the copy platform have been met.

Exhibit 9-3
How media objectives are expressed.

Exhibit 9-4
A media planner's toolbox.

Secondary sources of information help media planners do their jobs.

- **GfK MRI** (http://www.mri.gfk.com/en/gfk-mri.html): report data on product, brand, and media usage by both demographic and lifestyle characteristics.
- **Broadcast Advertisers Reports (BAR), Leading National Advertisers (LNA), and Media Records:** report advertisers' expenditures by brand, media type, market, and time period.
- **Kantar Media / SRDS** (www.srds.com): provides information on media rates, format, production requirements, and audience.
- **Alliance for Audited Media** (www.accessabc.com): verifies circulation figures of publishers.
- **TNS Global** (http://www.tnsglobal.com): delivers strategic advertising intelligence to advertising agencies, advertisers, broadcasters, and publishers. The tracking technologies collect occurrence and expenditure data, as well as the creative executions of over 2.2 million brands across 21 media.
- **Nielsen** (http://www.nielsen.com/us/en.html): a privately held global information and media company, and is one of the world's leading suppliers of marketing information (ACNielsen), media information and TV ratings (Nielsen Media Research), online intelligence (Nielsen Online), mobile measurement (Nielsen Mobile), trade shows, and business publications (*Billboard, The Hollywood Reporter, Adweek, R&R*).
- **eMarketer** (http://www.emarketer.com/): is the go-to source for information on digital and mobile advertising.
- **comScore** (www.comscore.com): delivers innovative and comprehensive Internet measurement, analysis, intelligence, and events to provide businesses with global resources for understanding and profiting from the Internet.

Unfortunately, due to cost restraints, much media research does not provide the specificity that marketers would really like. Most radio, TV, newspaper, and outdoor audience reports, for example, are limited to age and gender. So media planners often have to rely on their judgment and experience to select the right media vehicles.[19]

Message-Distribution Objectives

LO 9-3

Distribution objectives define where, when, and how often advertising should appear. To answer these questions, a media planner must understand a number of terms, including *message weight, reach, frequency,* and *continuity.*

Audience Size and Message Weight

Marketers are naturally interested in having their messages exposed to as many customers and prospects as they can afford. So they are also logically most interested in those media opportunities that offer the largest audiences.[20] The basic way to express audience size is simply to count the number of people in a medium's audience. This is what media research firms like Nielsen and Arbitron do for the broadcast media, typically using a statistical sample to project the total audience size. For print media, firms like the Audit Bureau of Circulations actually count and verify the number of subscribers (the **circulation**) and then multiply by the estimated number of **readers per copy (RPC)** to determine the total audience.

Media planners often define media objectives by the schedule's **message weight,** the total size of the audience for a set of ads or an entire campaign, because it gives some indication of the scope of the campaign in a given market. There are two ways to express message weight: *gross impressions* and *gross rating points.*

If planners know the audience size, they can easily calculate the number of advertising impressions in a media schedule. An **advertising impression** is a possible exposure of the advertising message to one audience member. It is sometimes referred to as an **opportunity to see (OTS).** By multiplying a medium's total audience size by the number of times an advertising message is used during the period, planners arrive at the **gross impressions,** or potential exposures, possible in that medium. Then, by summing the gross impressions for each medium used, they know the total gross impressions for the schedule (see Exhibit 9-5).

Exhibit 9-5

Gross impressions analysis for Brand X in the second quarter, 2006.

Media Vehicle	Target Audience*	Messages Used	Gross Impressions
"TV Ch. 6 News"	140,000	15	2,100,000
Daily newspaper	250,000	7	1,750,000
Spot radio	10,000	55	550,000
Total gross impressions			4,400,000

*Average.

With large media schedules, though, gross impressions can run into the millions and become very awkward to handle, so that's where the concept of *ratings* came from. The **rating** is simply the percentage of homes (or individuals) exposed to an advertising medium. Percentages are not only simpler numbers to deal with, they are also more useful in making comparisons. Thus, one rating point is equal to 1 percent of a given population group. When we hear that a particular TV show garnered a 20 rating, it means 20 percent of the households with TV sets (expressed as **television households** or **TVHH**) were tuned in to that show. The higher a program's rating, the more people are watching.[21] This definition applies to many media forms, but it is most commonly used for radio and TV.

By adding the ratings of several media vehicles (as we did for gross impressions), we can determine the message weight of a given advertising schedule, only now it's expressed as **gross rating points (GRPs)** (see Exhibit 9-6). When we say a schedule delivered 180 GRPs, that means the gross impressions generated by our schedule equaled 180 percent of the target market population. For broadcast media, GRPs are often calculated for a week or a month. In print media, they're calculated for the number of ads in a campaign. For outdoor advertising, they're calculated on the basis of daily exposure.

Media planners may use GRPs to determine the optimal level of spending for a campaign. The more GRPs they buy, the more it costs. However, because of discounting, the unit cost per GRP decreases as more GRPs are bought. Beyond a certain point, the effectiveness of additional GRPs diminishes.

Through the use of computer models and certain assumptions based on experience, sophisticated planners can detect the relative impact of ad-related variables on sales and determine the *return on investment (ROI)* from each. This can potentially save clients substantial sums of money.[22]

In the calculation of message weight, advertisers disregard any overlap or duplication. As a result, certain individuals within the audience may see the message several times while others don't see it at all. While message weight gives an indication of size, it does not reveal much about who is in the audience or how often they are reached. This fact necessitated the development of other media objectives, namely *reach, frequency,* and *continuity.*

Reach

The term **reach** refers to the total number of unique (or different) people or households exposed, at least once, to a medium during a given period of time, usually four weeks.[23] For example, if 40 percent of 100,000 people in a target market tune in to radio station WKKO at least once during a four-week period, the reach is 40,000 people. Reach may be expressed as a percentage of the total market (40 percent) or as a raw number (40,000). Reach should not be confused with the number of people who will actually be exposed to and consume the advertising, though. It is just the number of people who are exposed to the medium and therefore have an *opportunity to see* the ad or commercial.

While traditional media buys are still made by a buyer contacting a seller and negotiating a price for placing an ad, digial media space is often purchased by computer programs efficiently matching sellers (content providers such as news Websites) with buyers (firms looking to place ads that match specific audience characteristics). A key player in this type of programmatic advertising is DoubleClick, which is owned by Google.

Source: Google

Exhibit 9-6

Gross rating points analysis for Alpha brand in the second quarter, 2016.

Media Vehicle	Adult Rating*	Messages Used	Gross Rating Points
TV *Channel 6 News*	14	15	210
Daily newspaper	25	7	175
Spot radio	1	55	55
Total gross rating points			440

*Assumes market size of 1 million people.

An advertiser may accumulate reach in two ways: by using the same media vehicle continuously or by combining two or more media vehicles.[24] Naturally, as more media are used, some duplication occurs. Exhibit 9-7 is a statistical table that shows how unduplicated reach builds as additional media are added.

Frequency

To express the number of times the same person or household is exposed to a message—a radio spot, for example—in a specified time span, media people use the term *frequency*. **Frequency** measures the *intensity* of a media schedule, based on repeated exposures to the medium or the program. Frequency is important because repetition is the key to memory.

Frequency is calculated as the *average* number of times individuals or homes are exposed to the medium. For instance, suppose in our hypothetical 100,000-person market that 20,000 people tune in to WKKO and have three OTSs during a four-week period, and another 20,000 have five OTSs. To calculate the average frequency, divide the total number of exposures by the total reach:

$$\text{Average frequency} = \text{Total exposures} \div \text{Audience reach}$$
$$= [(20{,}000 \times 3)\,(20{,}000 \times 5)] \div 40{,}000$$
$$= 160{,}000 \div 40{,}000$$
$$= 4.0$$

	Reach of First Medium														
	25	30	35	40	45	50	55	60	65	70	75	80	85	90	95
25	46	47	51	55	59	62	66	70	74	77	81	85	89	92	95
30	—	51	54	58	61	65	68	72	75	79	82	86	90	93	95
35	—	—	58	61	64	67	71	74	77	80	84	87	90	93	95
40	—	—	—	64	67	70	73	76	79	82	85	88	91	94	95
45	—	—	—	—	70	72	75	78	81	83	86	89	92	94	95
50	—	—	—	—	—	75	77	80	82	85	87	90	92	95	95
55	—	—	—	—	—	—	80	82	84	86	89	91	93	95	95
60	—	—	—	—	—	—	—	84	86	88	90	92	94	95	95
65	—	—	—	—	—	—	—	—	88	89	91	93	95	95	95
70	—	—	—	—	—	—	—	—	—	91	92	94	95	95	95
75	—	—	—	—	—	—	—	—	—	—	94	95	95	95	95
80	—	—	—	—	—	—	—	—	—	—	—	95	95	95	95
85	—	—	—	—	—	—	—	—	—	—	—	—	95	95	95
90	—	—	—	—	—	—	—	—	—	—	—	—	—	95	95
95	—	—	—	—	—	—	—	—	—	—	—	—	—	—	95

(Row labels at left: Reach of Second Medium)

Exhibit 9-7

Random combination table. Find the reach of the first medium on the horizontal axis. Find the reach of the second medium on the vertical axis. The point of intersection shows the combined reach of the two media. If three or more media forms are combined, use the same procedure, finding the combined reach of the first two media on the horizontal axis and reading down to the intersection with the reach of the third medium.

For the 40,000 listeners reached, the average frequency, or number of exposures, was four.

Once we understand reach and frequency, we have another simple way to determine the message weight. To calculate gross rating points, just multiply a show's reach (expressed as a rating percentage) by the average frequency. In our radio example, 40 percent of the radio households (a 40 rating) had the opportunity to hear the commercial an average of four times during the four-week period:

$$\text{Reach} \times \text{Frequency} = \text{GRPs}$$

$$40 \times 4 = 160 \text{ GRPs}$$

Thus, the message weight of this radio campaign would be equal to 160 percent of the total market—or 160,000 gross impressions.

Continuity

Media planners refer to the duration of an advertising message or campaign over a given period of time as **continuity.** Few companies spread their marketing efforts evenly throughout the year. They typically *heavy up* before prime selling seasons and slow down during the off-season. Likewise, to save money, a media planner for a new product might decide that after a heavy introduction period of, say, four weeks, a radio campaign needs to maintain *continuity* for an additional 16 weeks but on fewer stations. We'll discuss some common scheduling patterns in the section on media tactics.

While frequency is important to create memory, continuity is important to *sustain* it. Moreover, as people come into and out of the market for goods and services every day, continuity provides a means of having the message there when it's most needed. Ads that hit targets during purchase cycles are more effective and require less frequency.[25]

LO 9-4

Optimizing Reach, Frequency, and Continuity: The Art of Media Planning

Good media planning is both an art and a science. The media planner must get the most effective exposure on a limited budget. As Exhibit 9–8 shows, the objectives of reach, frequency, and continuity have inverse relationships to each other. To achieve greater reach, some frequency and/or continuity has to be sacrificed, and so on. Research shows that all three are critical. But since all budgets are limited, which is most critical? This is currently the subject of hot debate in advertising circles.

Effective Reach

One of the problems with reach is that, by themselves, the numbers don't take into account the *quality* of the exposure. Some people exposed to the medium still won't be aware of the message. So, on the surface, reach doesn't seem to be the best measure of media success. Media people use the term **effective reach** to describe the quality of exposure. It measures the number or percentage of the audience who receive enough exposures to truly receive the message. Some researchers maintain that three OTSs over a four-week period are usually enough to reach an audience.[26]

Effective Frequency

Similar to the concept of effective reach is **effective frequency,** defined as the average number of times a person must see or hear a message before it becomes effective. In theory, effective frequency falls somewhere between a minimum level that achieves message awareness and a maximum level that becomes overexposure, which leads to "wearout" (starts to irritate consumers).

Exhibit 9-8

Reach, frequency, and continuity have an inverse relationship to one another. For instance, in the example, an advertiser can reach 6,000 people once, 3,000 people 5.5 times, or 1,000 people 9 times for the same budget. However, to gain continuity over time, the advertiser would have to sacrifice some reach and some frequency.

Following the publication of Michael Naples's classic book *Effective Frequency* in 1979, most of the industry fell in love with his claim that, in most cases, effective frequency could be achieved by an average frequency of three over a four-week period. Here was a nice, simple conclusion that all the low-level media planners could use. Naples's conclusion seemed to be intuitively correct, and it was supported by some researchers who viewed advertising effects as a learning situation. While this might be true for some new products, most of the time advertising is for established products and therefore is not about "learning" but rather about "reminding." Syracuse University professor John Philip Jones writes that "a massive, multitiered edifice" of belief was built on the evidence in Naples's book—evidence that he believes led the industry down the wrong path.[27]

While the concepts of effective reach and frequency are now hotly debated, virtually all agencies still use them. Cannon and Riordan point out that conventional media planning is based on *media vehicle exposure* (the number of people in a medium's audience), but effectiveness should relate to *advertising message exposure*. For example, only 20 percent of viewers may pay attention when a commercial runs. It may take 10 opportunities-to-see to reach an average frequency of one!

Cannon and Riordan would replace effective frequency with *optimal frequency*. Most studies of the **advertising response curve** indicate that incremental response to advertising actually diminishes, rather than builds, with repeated exposures (see Exhibit 9-9). The optimal frequency concept moves the focus of media planning from exposure effectiveness to *effective exposures per dollar*.

> With a response curve that is characterized by continually diminishing returns, the first ad will be the most profitable. But subsequent exposures—advertising frequency—are still important. How important depends on the slope of the response curve and the cost of advertising. Obviously, the less money it costs per exposure to advertise, the more the firm can afford to advertise. The profit-maximizing firm will continue to spend until the revenue resulting from an additional advertisement placed is offset by its cost[28]

The implications of Cannon and Riordan's theory are immense. Historically, media planning has emphasized frequency as the most important media objective. This assumes an S-shaped advertising response curve in which the first two or three exposures don't count. But Cannon and Riordan's analysis indicates that response curves are convex. The first exposure is the most effective, followed by diminishing returns. If that's the case, then the basic emphasis in advertising should switch from maximizing frequency to maximizing target market reach, adding less profitable second exposures only as the budget permits.[29]

This approach is now supported by numerous researchers who believe effective frequency planning is seriously flawed and who make a strong case for the primacy of reach and continuity as the most important media objectives.[30] In fact, for fast-moving consumer products, researcher Erwin Ephron suggests the concept of **recency planning**, based on "the sensible idea that most advertising works by influencing the brand choice of consumers who are ready to buy." Therefore, the important thing for advertising is to be there when the consumer is ready to buy, and that suggests continuity.[31] His theories have gained the attention of many of the nation's largest advertisers, among them Procter & Gamble, Kraft Foods, and Coca-Cola.[32]

One problem with all these theories is that they assume all exposures are equal. If that's the case, then where does advertising creativity come in? And what about the programs where the advertising appears? Doesn't that have some effect on the quality of exposure?

For most media planners, the only solution to this debate is to establish first which type of response curve is most likely to apply to the particular situation and then to develop the campaign's media objectives accordingly.

Once the media objectives have been determined—that is, the optimum levels of message weight, reach, frequency, and continuity—the media planner can develop the strategy for achieving them.

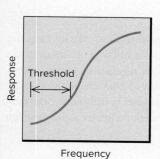

a. **S-shaped response curve**   b. **Convex response curve**

Exhibit 9-9

Two advertising response curves. The S-shaped curve would be applicable for products that require a frequency of more than one to reach a threshold of greatest response. After that threshold is reached, the response diminishes for each subsequent exposure. The convex curve applies to products for which the first exposure produces the best return and all subsequent exposures produce a slightly lower response.

Developing a Media Strategy: The Media Mix

Elements of the Media Mix: The Five Ms

The media strategy describes how the advertiser will achieve the stated media objectives: which media will be used, where, how often, and when. Just as marketers determine marketing strategy by blending elements of the marketing mix, media planners can develop media strategies by blending the elements of the *media mix.*

Many factors go into developing an effective media strategy. For simplicity and ease of memory, we have sorted them into five categories and given them the alliterative moniker of the **five Ms (5Ms):** *markets, money, media, mechanics,* and *methodology.*

Markets refers to the various targets of a media plan: trade and consumer audiences; global, national, or regional audiences; ethnic and socioeconomic groups; or other stakeholders. In an integrated marketing communications plan, the IMC planner wants to find the reasons and motivations for the prospect's purchase and usage patterns and then create a media plan based on those findings.[33]

Using intuition, marketing savvy, and analytical skill, the media planner determines the second element, **money**—how much to budget and where to allocate it. How much for print media, how much in TV, how much to nontraditional or supplemental media, how much to each geographic area? We discuss this issue in depth in the chapters on using and buying media (Chapters 15 through 18).

From the IMC perspective, **media** include *all* communications vehicles available to a marketer. This includes radio, TV, newspapers, magazines, outdoor, online and direct mail, plus sales promotion, direct marketing, public relations activities and publicity, special events, brochures, and even shopping bags.

Good media planners champion the integration of all marketing communications to help achieve their companies' marketing and advertising objectives. They look at the media element both analytically and creatively.

The media planner also has to deal with the complex **mechanics** of advertising media and messages. Radio and TV commercials come in a variety of time units, and print ads are created in a variety of sizes and styles. IMC planners may also deal with the mechanics of nontraditional media, everything from shopping bags to multimedia kiosks to the Internet. The myriad media options now available offer exciting, creative ways to enhance consumer acceptance of the advertiser's message and offer the consumer a relevant purchase incentive.

The **methodology** element refers to the overall strategy of selecting and scheduling media vehicles to achieve the desired message weight, reach, frequency, and continuity objectives. It offers the opportunity for creativity in planning, negotiating, and buying.

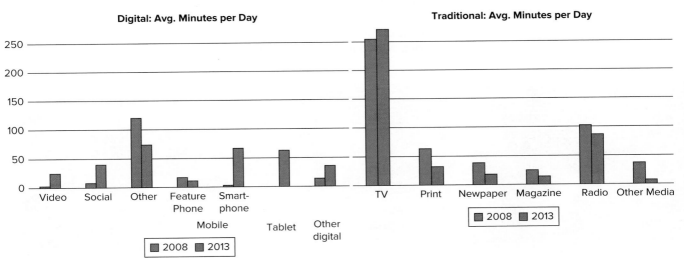

Exhibit 9-10

Average Time Spent with Media: 2008-2013

Source: Ad Age Datacenter. Original source: eMarketer, July 2013. More info: emarketer.com. Time spent with each medium includes all time including multitasking.

Factors That Influence Media Strategy Decisions

Media decisions are greatly influenced by factors over which the media planner has little or no control. These include the scope of the media plan, sales potential of different markets, competitive strategies and budget considerations, availability of different media vehicles, nature of the medium, mood of the message, message size and length, and buyer purchase patterns.

Scope of the Media Plan

The location and makeup of the target audience strongly influence the breadth of the media plan, thereby affecting decisions regarding the *market,* the *money,* and the *media* elements.

Domestic Markets   A media planner normally limits advertising to areas where the product is available. If a store serves only one town, or if a city has been chosen to test market a new product, then the advertiser will use a *local* plan.

A *regional* plan may cover several adjoining metropolitan areas, an entire state or province, or several neighboring states. Regional plans typically employ a combination of local media, regional editions of national magazines, TV spots and radio, and the Internet.

Advertisers who want to reach several regions or an entire country use a *national* plan. This may call for network TV and radio, full-circulation national magazines and newspapers, nationally syndicated Sunday newspaper supplements, and the Internet.

International Markets   Foreign media can be a challenge for U.S. advertisers. While many broadcast stations are being privatized in countries as diverse as Israel and Russia, governments around the world still control many broadcast media, and some still do not permit commercials. Others limit advertising to a certain number of minutes per hour or per day.

In countries that do allow TV advertising, advertisers face other problems: how many people own TV sets, who they are, and what channels they receive. While this is not an issue in Europe and is becoming less so in Latin America, it is still a problem in many of the less-developed nations of Africa and Asia. There, TV ownership may be limited to upper-income consumers, or the availability of commercial channels may be severely limited. In those markets, advertisers must use a different media mix. Likewise, Internet access may be severely limited—or too expensive for consumers to afford. So that option may not even be available for some markets.

In many countries of Europe, about 48 percent of total advertising expenditures are still spent in print media versus about 35 percent on television.[34] However, like the United States, Europe and Asia are experiencing a virtual explosion of new media and technology. Advertisers and agencies alike are realizing the importance of developing integrated marketing communications plans to build their brands and establish long-term relationships with their customers.

Most marketers develop an international media plan by formulating individual national plans first. But it's not as simple as it sounds. Depending on the country, precise media information may not be available, circulation figures may not be audited, audience demographics may be sketchy, and even ad rates may be unreliable. Finally, the methodology used in media research may be considerably different from one market to another, making comparisons

Reaching international markets presents unique challenges, especially in some Asian and African markets. This trilingual ad combines wordplay in two alphabets.

Source: Weibo

virtually impossible. At the same time, in some European countries, media research and planning may be more sophisticated than in the United States, which creates another problem for U.S. advertisers who are unfamiliar with European terms, concepts, and methodologies.[35]

Because of the media variations from country to country, most international and global advertisers entrust national media plans to in-country foreign media specialists or the local foreign branches of global media agencies such as MindShare, OMD Worldwide, Mediaedge:cia, or Carat, rather than risk faulty centralized media planning.[36]

Sales Potential of Different Markets

The *market* and *money* elements of the media mix also depend on the sales potential of each area. National advertisers use this factor to determine where to allocate their advertising dollars. Planners can determine an area's sales potential in several ways.

The Brand Development Index   The **brand development index (BDI)** indicates the sales potential of a particular brand in a specific market area. It compares the percentage of the brand's total U.S. sales in an area to the percentage of the total U.S. population in that area. The larger the brand's sales relative to the area's percentage of U.S. population, the higher the BDI and the greater the brand's sales potential. BDI is calculated as

$$\text{BDI} = \frac{\text{Percent of the brand's total U.S. sales in the area}}{\text{Percent of total U.S. population in the area}} \times 100$$

Suppose sales of a brand in Los Angeles are 1.58 percent of the brand's total U.S. sales, and the population of Los Angeles is 2 percent of the U.S. total. The BDI for Los Angeles is

$$\text{BDI} = \frac{1.58}{2} \times 100 = 79$$

An index number of 100 means the brand's performance balances with the size of the area's population. A BDI index number below 100 indicates poor potential for the brand.

The Category Development Index   To determine the potential of the whole product category, media planners use the **category development index (CDI),** which works on the same concept as the BDI and is calculated in much the same way:

$$\text{CDI} = \frac{\text{Percent of the category's total U.S. sales in the area}}{\text{Percent of total U.S. population in the area}} \times 100$$

If category sales in Los Angeles are 4.92 percent of total U.S. category sales, the CDI in Los Angeles is

$$\text{CDI} = \frac{4.92}{2} \times 100 = 246$$

The combination of BDI and CDI can help the planner determine a media strategy for the market (see Exhibit 9-11). In our example, low BDI (under 100) and high CDI (over 100) in Los Angeles indicate that the product category has high potential but the brand is not selling well. This may represent a problem or an opportunity. If the brand has been on the market for some time, the low BDI raises a red flag; some problem is standing in the way of brand sales. But if the brand is new, the low BDI may not be alarming. In fact, the high CDI may indicate the brand can grow substantially, given more time and greater media and

Exhibit 9-11

Media buyers compare the brand development index with the category development index for their products to better understand which markets will respond best to advertising. Advertising can be expected to work well when BDI and CDI are both high, but probably not when both are low.

	Low BDI	High BDI
High CDI	Low market share *but* Good market potential	High market share *and* Good market potential
Low CDI	Low market share *and* Poor market potential	High market share *but* Monitor for sales decline

marketing support. At this point, the media planner should assess the company's share of voice (discussed in Chapter 8) and budget accordingly.

Competitive Strategies and Budget Considerations

Advertisers always consider what competitors are doing, particularly those that have larger advertising budgets. This affects the *media, mechanics,* and *methodology* elements of the media mix. Several services, like TNS Media Intelligence, detail competitive advertising expenditures in the different media. By knowing the size of competitors' budgets, what media they're using, the regionality or seasonality of their sales, and any new-product tests and introductions, advertisers can better plan a counterstrategy.

Again, the media planner should analyze the company's share of voice in the marketplace. If an advertiser's budget is much smaller than the competition's, the brand could get lost in the shuffle. Advertisers should bypass media that competitors dominate and choose other media that offer a strong position.

When Anne Myers, media director of Palmer Jarvis DDB, Toronto, had to develop a media plan for Panasonic Canada's Power Activator batteries, she didn't have the budget of Energizer or Duracell to work with. So she didn't want to place her ads where theirs were. Myers and her team creatively fashioned a guerrilla media plan that targeted a cynical, hard-to-reach audience, 15- to 22-year-olds, right where they lived—in the clubs, on the street, and on the Internet. The campaign included posters in the dance clubs; sponsorship of popular DJs and VJs; free PA T-shirts, hats, posters, and stickers; an eight-week run of television spots on popular music shows tied to a month-long cross-promotion with a new CD release; and a special contest run on a microsite that linked back to Panasonic Canada's main site. The response was excellent: Sales were up 136 percent over the previous year, and the contest promotion generated more than 16,300 entries on the site with a click-through rate of 35 percent.[37]

It sometimes makes sense to use media similar to the competition's if the target audiences are the same or if the competitors are not using their media effectively.

Media Availability and Economics: The Global Marketer's Headache

North American advertisers are blessed—or cursed—with an incredible array of media choices, locally and nationally. Such is not always the case in other areas of the world, which is one reason their per capita advertising expenditures are so much lower than in the United States.

A global media strategy requires understanding options available around the world. China restricts or denies access to social media sites popular in the United States and Europe, but has functional "equivalents" that advertisers can use to reach consumers in this enormous market, as shown in this beautiful exhibit from China Business Review.

Source: Thomas Crampton, "Social Media in China: The Same, but Different," China Business Review, January 1, 2011 (retrieved from http://www.chinabusinessreview.com/social-media-in-china -the-same-but-different/).

Every country has communications media, but they are not always available for commercial use (especially radio and television) and coverage may be limited. Lower literacy rates and education levels in some countries restrict the coverage of print media. Where income levels are low, TV ownership is also low. These factors tend to segment markets by media coverage.

To reach lower-income markets, radio is the medium of choice, as both Coke and Pepsi have demonstrated successfully for years. Auto manufacturers make good use of TV and magazine advertising to reach the upper class. And movie advertising can reach whole urban populations where TV ownership is low because motion picture attendance in such countries is very high.

Some companies are attempting to become true global marketers of their brands with centralized control of media and standardized creative. As a group, global media are growing, which is good news for global marketers.[38] However, there are still few true global media. So these major advertisers must continue to use local foreign media in the countries where they do business and localize their campaigns for language and cultural differences.

Finally, there's the problem of **spillover media,** local media that many consumers in a neighboring country inadvertently receive. For example, media from Luxembourg regularly spill over into France, Belgium, and the Netherlands. Media often spill over into countries lacking indigenous-language publications, particularly specialty publications. English and German business media enjoy a large circulation in Scandinavian countries, for example, where there are relatively few specialized trade publications written in Swedish, Danish, or Norwegian.

Spillover media pose a threat for the multinational advertiser because they expose readers to multiple ad campaigns. If the advertiser runs both international and local campaigns for the same products, discrepancies in product positioning, pricing, or advertising messages could confuse potential buyers. Advertisers' local subsidiaries or distributors need to coordinate local and international ad campaigns to avoid such confusion. On the positive side, spillover media offer potential cost savings through regional campaigns.

Nature of the Medium and Mood of the Message

An important influence on the *media* element of the mix is how well a medium works with the style or mood of the particular message.

Advertising messages differ in many ways. Some are simple messages: "Just do it" (Nike). Others make emotional or sensual appeals to people's needs and wants: "The great taste of fruit squared" (Jolly Rancher candies). Many advertisers use a reason-why approach to explain their product's advantages: "Twice the room. Twice the comfort. Twice the value. Embassy Suites. Twice the hotel."

Complex messages, such as ads announcing a new product or concept, require more space or time for explanation. Each circumstance affects the media selection as well as the *methodology* of the media mix.

A new or highly complex message may require greater frequency and exposure to be understood and remembered. A dogmatic message like Nike's may require a surge at the beginning, then low frequency and greater reach.

Once consumers understand reason-why messages, pulsing advertising exposures at irregular intervals is often sufficient. Emotionally oriented messages are usually more effective when spaced at regular intervals to create enduring feelings about the product. We discuss these scheduling methods further in the next section on media tactics.

And sometimes, as educator, philosopher, and scholar Marshall McLuhan famously claimed, "the medium is the message." The very medium that an advertiser chooses can have as much or more of an impact on an audience as the communication. For instance, a local jeweler who chooses to advertise on TV may present the perception of being a successful business, which will appeal to some consumer groups, regardless of the message being conveyed in the 30-second spot.

Message Size, Length, and Position Considerations

The particular characteristics of different media, over which the media planner has no control, affect the *mechanics* element of the media mix. For example, in print, a full-page ad attracts

Fractional ads — 24%
One-page ads — 41%
Two-page spread ads — 56%

a. Size—as size increases so does readership.

Fractional — 24%
One-page black-and-white — 33%
One-page 2-color — 35%
One-page 3- and 4-color — 44%
Black-and-white spreads — 43%
4-color spread ads — 57%
Inserts — 63%

b. Size and color—advertising readership increases with size and the use of color.

Exhibit 9-12

Effect of size and color on ad readership (total ads studied = 107,506).

Source: From Alan Flekker and Paul Winn "An Intermagazine Analysis of Factors in Advertisement Readership," *Journalism Quarterly*, Vol.51, Issue 3, Autumn 1974.

more attention than a quarter-page ad and a full-color ad more than a black-and-white one. Color and larger units of space or time cost dearly in terms of reach and frequency.

Should a small advertiser run a full-page ad once a month or a quarter-page ad once a week? Is it better to use a few 60-second commercials or many 15- and 30-second ones? The planner has to consider the nature of the advertising message; some simply require more time and space to explain. Competitive activity often dictates more message units. The product itself may demand the prestige of a full page or full color. However, it's often better to run small ads consistently rather than one large ad occasionally. Unfortunately, space and time units may be determined by someone other than the media planner—creative or account service, for example—in which case the planner's options are limited.

The position of an ad is another consideration. Preferred-positions for magazine ads are front and back covers; for TV, sponsorship of prime-time shows. Special positions and

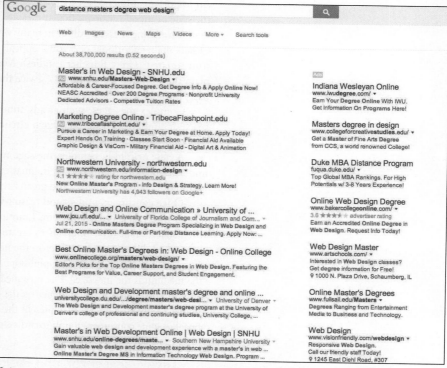

Online advertising plays by different rules than does conventional. Advertisers pay for behavior (clicks) rather than for exposure.

Source: Google

My IMC Campaign 9

Developing Media Objectives and Strategies

Over the past 20 years the media landscape has changed dramatically, becoming much more fragmented and full of choice. This has elevated the complexity of the media planning role. In this part of your assignment you are nonetheless considering all types of media to help distribute your message. You will most likely be given a media budget and asked to formulate a plan of attack. To better support your choices it is imperative that you develop sound objectives and strategies.

In some cases, your professor may have given you a set of marketing objectives, or your research on clients may have indicated their main goals for advertising. It is important to note here that marketing objectives do not equal media objectives. They do, however, help us shape our media objectives, which in turn help us develop sound media strategy.

Developing Media Objectives

The first place to start in developing media objectives is with the marketing objectives themselves. You should view media objectives as the goals that become the building blocks of the media plan and that ultimately help clients meet their marketing goals.

Here are some examples of marketing objectives, translated into media objectives:

Marketing Objectives	Media Objectives
■ Increase awareness among target audience by 23 percent. ■ Steal 2 percent share of sales from competitors. ■ Build customer database of 5,000 individuals.	■ Generate mass awareness among target audience. ■ Differentiate brand from competitors. ■ Generate leads/requests for more information.

While the media objectives seem very similar to marketing objectives, they are actually quite different. Media objectives should focus on only what the media can achieve. Remember that the media plan is one of many components that go into building a successful promotional or communications plan and it has a distinct role, which is what you are trying to highlight in the objectives.

Developing Media Strategies

Media strategies are born out of the media objectives and describe a specific plan of action for achieving stated objectives. The strategy seeks to accomplish two things: setting the foundation for media ideas that help you meet the objective or goal and providing a position of advantage over your client's competitors.

The media strategy itself is built on key plan parameters on which the entire communications team has had input:

■ Target audience
■ Seasonality
■ Geography
■ Overall communication goals
■ Budget
■ Creative
■ Competitive analysis

So how do media objectives translate into strategies? Let's look at the three we detailed earlier:

Media Objectives	Media Strategies
■ Generate mass awareness among target audience. ■ Differentiate brand from competitors. ■ Generate leads/requests for more information.	■ Use mass media (broadcast) to build reach against M18–34. ■ Secure high-profile sponsorship with category exclusivity. ■ Use interactive media to elicit registration.

In the subsequent media chapters (Chapters 13–15), we'll discuss the different ways to better evaluate the opportunities within each of the media.

---

sponsorships cost more, so the media planner must decide whether the increased reach and frequency are worth the higher costs.

As we can see, the nature of the creative work has the potential to greatly affect the media strategy. This means that media planners have to be flexible, since the initial media plan may well have been determined prior to beginning the creative work.

Buyer Purchase Patterns

Finally, the customer's product purchasing behavior affects every element of the media mix. The media planner must consider how, when, and where the product is typically purchased and repurchased. Products with short purchase cycles (convenience foods and paper towels) require more constant levels of advertising than products purchased infrequently (refrigerators and furniture).

Stating the Media Strategy

A written rationale for the media strategy is an integral part of any media plan. Without one, it's difficult for client and agency management to analyze the logic and consistency of the recommended media schedule.

Generally, the strategy statement begins with a brief definition of target audiences (the *market* element) and the priorities for weighting them. It explains the nature of the message and indicates which media types will be used and why (the *media* element). It outlines specific reach, frequency, and continuity goals and how they are to be achieved (the *methodology* element). It provides a budget for each medium (the *money* element) including the cost of production and any collateral materials. Finally, it states the intended size of message units, any position or timing considerations (the *mechanics* element), and the effect of budget restrictions.

Once the strategy is delineated, the plan details the tactics to be employed, the subject of the next section.

LO 9-5

Media Tactics: Selecting and Scheduling Media Vehicles

Once the general media strategy is determined, the media planner can select and schedule particular media vehicles. The planner usually considers each medium's value on a set of specific criteria (see Ad Lab 9–B).

Criteria for Selecting Individual Media Vehicles

In evaluating specific media vehicles, the planner considers several factors: overall campaign objectives and strategy; size and characteristics of each medium's audience; attention, exposure, and motivational value of each medium; and cost efficiency.

Overall Campaign Objectives and Strategy

The media planner's first job is to review the nature of the product or service, the intended objectives and strategies, and the primary and secondary target markets and audiences. The characteristics of the product often suggest a suitable choice. A product with a distinct personality or image, such as a fine perfume, might be advertised in media that reinforce this image. The media planner considers how consumers regard various magazines and TV programs—feminine or masculine, highbrow or lowbrow, serious or frivolous—and determines whether they're appropriate for the brand.

The content and editorial policy of the media vehicle and its compatibility with the product are important considerations. *Tennis* magazine is a poor vehicle for alcohol ads even though its demographic profile and image might match the desired target audience.

Consumers choose a particular media vehicle because they gain some "reward": self-improvement, financial advice, career guidance, or simply news and entertainment. Advertising is most effective when it positions a product as part of the solution that consumers seek. Otherwise, they may see it as an intrusion.[39]

If the marketing objective is to gain greater product distribution, the planner should select media that influence potential dealers. If the goal is to stimulate sales of a nationally distributed product in isolated markets, ads should be placed in local and regional media that penetrate those markets. Pricing strategy influences media choices too. A premium-priced product should use prestigious or classy media to support its market image.

Advertising in digital media changes the planning process substantially when it is accomplished through **programmatic advertising.** Programmatic advertising buys are done largely via computer programs that match content sites (such as CNN.com or MTV.com) to advertisers via an advertising exchange.

Sellers
- Website A
- Website B
- Website C

Ad Exchange

Buyers
- Network A
- Network B
- Network C

Exhibit 9-13
Ad Exchange

AD Lab 9–B

Media Selection: A Quicklist of Advantages

Medium	Advantages
Newspapers	Many ad sizes available. Quick placement, local targeting. Audience interest.
Magazines	High-quality graphics/reproduction. Prestige factor. Color. Selective targeting.
TV	Combines sight, sound, movement. A single message. Demonstration. Social dominance.
Radio	Intimacy. Loyal following. Ability to change message quickly. Repetition and frequency.
Internet	Immediate response. Interactive. Highly selective targeting. Global.
Direct mail	Measurable. Graphics, color. 3-D. Highly personal. Adaptable message length.
Outdoor/Transit	Local targeting. Graphics, color. Simple message. Larger than life. Repetition.
Mobile	Immediate Response. Interactive. Personal. Fastest-growing medium.

Laboratory Applications

1. If you wanted a set of complementary media to cover all the creative advantages, which mix would you select?
2. What creative advantages can you add to the list?

Characteristics of Media Audiences

An **audience** is the total number of people or households exposed to a medium. The planner needs to know how closely the medium's audience matches the profile of the target market and how interested prospective customers are in the publication or program. A product intended for a Latino audience, for example, would likely appear in specific media directed toward Hispanics. Simmons Market Research Bureau provides research data on age, income, occupational status, and other characteristics of magazine readers. Simmons also publishes demographic and psychographic data on product usage of consumers. Likewise, Nielsen provides audience statistics for television programs and Arbitron for radio stations.

The *content* of the medium usually determines the type of people in the audience. Some radio stations emphasize in-depth news or sports; others feature jazz, rock, or classical music. Each type of programming attracts a different audience.

Exposure, Attention, and Motivation Value of Media Vehicles

The media planner has to select media that will not only achieve the desired exposure to the target audience, but also attract *attention* and *motivate* people to act.

Exposure   To understand the concept of **exposure value,** think of how many people an ad "sees" rather than the other way around. How many of a magazine's 3 million readers will an ad actually see? How many of a TV program's 10 million viewers will a commercial actually see?

As we discussed earlier, just because someone reads a particular magazine or watches a certain program doesn't mean he or she sees the ads. Some people read only one article, set the magazine aside, and never pick it up again. Many people change channels during commercial breaks or leave to get a snack. Comparing the exposure value of different media vehicles, therefore, is very difficult. Without statistics, media planners have to use their best judgment based on experience.

Five main factors affect the probability of ad exposure:

1. The senses used to perceive messages from the medium (e.g., scratch-and-sniff ads really improve the exposure value of magazines).
2. How much and what kind of attention the medium requires (higher involvement suggests greater ad exposure).
3. Whether the medium is an information source or a diversion (e.g., radio news programs offer greater ad exposure than elevator music).
4. Whether the medium or program aims at a general or a specialized audience (exposure value will be higher with specialized audiences).
5. The placement of the ad in the vehicle (placement within broadcast programs gives greater exposure than placement between programs; ads placed next to editorial material get greater exposure than ads placed next to other print ads).

Attention   Degree of attention is another consideration. As we discussed in Chapter 5, consumers with no interest in motorcycles or cosmetics won't typically remember ads for those products. For a variety of reasons, they fail to penetrate the viewer's perceptual screens. But someone in the market for a new car tends to notice every car ad.

Exposure value relates only to the medium; **attention value** concerns the advertising message and copy, as well as the medium. Special-interest media, such as boating magazines, offer good attention value to a marine product because the reader is in the boating mindset. But what kind of attention value does the daily newspaper offer such a product? Do sailors think about boats while reading the newspaper? Much research still needs to be done, but six factors are known to increase attention value:[40]

1. Audience involvement with editorial content or program material.
2. Specialization of audience interest or identification.
3. Number of competitive advertisers (the fewer, the better).
4. Audience familiarity with the advertiser's campaign.
5. Quality of advertising reproduction.
6. Timeliness of advertising exposure.

Motivation   These same factors affect a medium's **motivation value,** but in different ways. Familiarity with the advertiser's campaign may affect attention significantly but motivation very little. The attention factors of quality reproduction and timeliness can motivate someone, however.

Media planners analyze these values by assigning numerical ratings to their judgments of a medium's strengths and weaknesses. Then, using a weighting formula, they add them up. Planners use similar weighting methods to evaluate other factors, such as the relative importance of age versus income.

Cost Efficiency of Media Vehicles

Finally, media planners analyze the cost efficiency of each medium. A common term used in media planning and buying is **cost per thousand,** or **CPM** (M is the Roman numeral for 1,000). If a daily newspaper has 300,000 subscribers and charges $5,000 for a full-page ad, the cost per thousand is the cost divided by the number of thousands of people in the audience. Since there are 300 thousand subscribers, you divide $5,000 by 300:

$$\text{CPM} = \frac{\$5,000}{300,000 \div 1,000} = \frac{\$5,000}{300} = \$16.67 \text{ per thousand}$$

However, media planners are more interested in **cost efficiency**—the cost of exposing the message to the target audience rather than to the total circulation. Let's say the target audience is males ages 18 to 49, and 40 percent of a weekly newspaper's subscriber base of 250,000 fits this category. If the paper charges $3,000 for a full-page ad, the CPM is computed as follows:

$$\text{Total audience} = 0.40 \times 250,000 = 100,000$$

$$\text{CPM} = \frac{\$3,000}{100,000 \div 1,000} = \$30 \text{ per thousand}$$

The daily paper, on the other hand, might turn out to be more cost efficient if 60 percent of its readers (180,000) belong to the target audience:

$$\text{CPM} = \frac{\$5,000}{180,000 \div 1,000} = \$27.78 \text{ per thousand}$$

Comparing different media by CPMs is important but does not take into account each medium's other advantages and disadvantages. The media planner must evaluate all the criteria to determine

1. How much of each medium's audience matches the target audience, also described as *composition*.
2. How each medium satisfies the campaign's objectives and strategy.
3. How well each medium offers attention, exposure, and motivation.

To evaluate some of these issues in broadcast, the media planner may want to calculate the **cost per point (CPP)** of different programs. This is done the same way as cost per thousand, except you divide the cost by the rating points instead of the gross impressions.

Economics of Foreign Media

The main purpose of media advertising is to communicate with customers more efficiently than through personal selling. In some developing countries, though, it's actually cheaper to send people out with baskets of samples. For mass marketers in the United States, this kind of personal contact is virtually impossible.

In many foreign markets, outdoor advertising enjoys far greater coverage than in the United States because it costs less to have people paint the signs and there is also less government restriction.

Cost inhibits the growth of broadcast media in some foreign markets, but most countries now sell advertising time to help foot the bills. China and Vietnam, for example, have recently become booming markets for advertising.[41] As more countries allow commercial broadcasts and international satellite channels gain a greater foothold, TV advertising will continue to grow.

 LO 9-7

The Synergy of Mixed Media

A combination of media is called a **mixed-media approach.** There are numerous reasons for using mixed media:

- To reach people who are unavailable through only one medium.
- To provide repeat exposure in a less expensive secondary medium after attaining optimum reach in the first.
- To use the intrinsic value of an additional medium to extend the creative effectiveness of the ad campaign (such as music on radio along with long copy in print media).
- To deliver coupons in print media when the primary vehicle is broadcast.
- To produce **synergy,** where the total effect is greater than the sum of its parts.

Exhibit 9-14

Three ways to schedule the same number of total gross rating points: continuous, flighting, and pulsing.

Newspapers, for example, can be used to introduce a new product and give immediacy to the message. Magazine ads can then follow up for greater detail, image enhancement, longevity, and memory improvement.

A mixed-media campaign was effective for General Electric's lighting products. The promotion used a combination of network TV spots, print advertising, Sunday supplement inserts, in-store displays in more than 150,000 stores, and a highly creative publicity program. By using an integrated, mixed-media approach, the campaign produced "unprecedented" consumer awareness and dealer support. It achieved synergy.[42]

Methods for Scheduling Media

After selecting the appropriate media vehicles, the media planner decides how many space or time units to buy of each vehicle and schedules them for release over a period of time when consumers are most apt to buy the product.

Continuous, Flighting, and Pulsing Schedules

To build continuity in a campaign, planners use three principal scheduling tactics: *continuous, flighting,* and *pulsing* (see Exhibit 9-14).

In a **continuous schedule,** advertising runs steadily and varies little over the campaign period. It's the best way to build continuity. Advertisers use this scheduling pattern for products consumers purchase regularly. For example, a commercial is scheduled on radio stations WTKO and WRBI for an initial four-week period. Then, to maintain continuity in the campaign, additional spots run continuously every week throughout the year on station WRBI.

Flighting alternates periods of advertising with periods of no advertising. This intermittent schedule makes sense for products and services that experience large fluctuations in demand throughout the year (tax services, lawn-care products, cold remedies). The advertiser might introduce the product with a four-week flight and then schedule three additional four-week flights to run during seasonal periods later in the year.

The third alternative, **pulsing,** mixes continuous and flighting strategies. As the consumer's purchasing cycle gets longer, pulsing becomes more appropriate. The advertiser maintains a low level of advertising all year but uses periodic pulses to heavy up during peak selling periods. This strategy is appropriate for products like soft drinks, which are consumed all year but more heavily in the summer.

Additional Scheduling Patterns

For high-ticket items that require careful consideration, **bursting**—running the same commercial every half hour on the same network during prime time—can be effective. A variation is **roadblocking,** buying air time on all three networks simultaneously. Chrysler used this technique to give viewers the impression that the advertiser was everywhere, even if the ad showed for only a few nights. Digital Equipment used a scheduling tactic called **blinking** to stretch its slim ad budget. To reach business executives, it flooded the airwaves on Sundays (on both cable and network TV channels) to make it virtually impossible to miss the ads.[43]

Once the scheduling criteria are determined, the media planner creates a flowchart of the plan. The flowchart is a graphic presentation of the total campaign to let the creative department, media department, account services, and the client see the pattern of media events that will occur throughout the campaign, usually over one year (see Exhibit 9-15).

200MS: The Life of a Programmatic RTB Ad Impression

"Jane Doe" clicks on a URL, and the publisher's content begins to load in browser. **(0)**

(10) Publisher may find information it has stored on Jane Doe, possibly in its Data Management Platform (DMP).

Winning bidder's ad server receives ad tag data on Jane Doe's initial interaction experience. **(200)**

(30) Publisher sends available information to its ad server asking ad server whether an ad campaign is available that would target Jane Doe. If there is a campaign matching Jane Doe's profile, an ad is served.

Jane Doe's browser pulls ad from winning bidder's ad server and sends matching ad to browser. Browser displays web page including matching ad. **(175)**

(40) If no campaign targets Jane Doe, the server seeks to match the impression programmatically requesting response from selected traders, ad networks and supply-side platforms (SSPs).

Ad exchange sends winning ad URL and price from winning bid to Publisher's ad server. Publisher's ad server tells Jane Doe's browser which ad to display. **(150)**

200 MILLISECONDS
The Life of a Programmatic RTB Ad Impression

(65) If the impression is not cleared, the server may seek to clear the impression in a programmatic direct way via private exchanges. If the impression is not cleared, the request is sent to an open ad exchange in hopes of achieving liquidity.

Ad exchange selects winning bid from bidder responses through second-price auction. **(125)**

Each bidder processes bid request, overlays it with additional user data and marketers' targeting and budget rules. Each bidder's algorithm evaluates the request, selects the creative, and sends it along with optimal bid price to ad exchange. **(100)**

(75) Open ad exchange sends a bid request containing information on Jane Doe's browser, Website URL, and ad type to multiple bidders including traders, ad networks and demand-side platforms (DSPs).

Exhibit 9-15

MediaCrossing, a leading independent digital media trading company, created this graphic that sequences the 200 millisecond birth of a programmatic ad. You can watch a video of the process here: https://www.youtube.com/watch?v=rTg9I4d8MU4.

© Media Crossing

Computers in Media Selection and Scheduling

As suggested earlier in the chapter, programmatic advertising relies on computers to match messages and audiences in real-time based on complex algorithms of what advertisers are willing to pay and content providers are willing to sell. While programmatic advertising is largely found in digital media buys, some believe it will become a bigger part of the way traditional media are bought and sold as well. Exhibit 9-15 shows how quickly a variety of complicated processes take place during programmatic advertising.

Even when not relying on programmatic, most planners use software to determine optimized buys of traditional media. Telmar was the first company to provide media planning systems on a syndicated basis. Today, it is the world's leading supplier of media planning software and support services. More than 3,500 users in 85 countries, including the majority of the world's top agencies, use Telmar systems for media and marketing decision making.[44]

Telmar's software suite is designed to help media planners, buyers, research analysts, and sellers work more efficiently and make better judgments in the evaluation or sales process. The software allows advertising executives to estimate the effectiveness of multifaceted marketing plans that use various combinations of media including print, broadcast, in-store, special promotions, special events, PR, and other "new media." Its flexibility permits the user to analyze the potential effectiveness of any and every marketing tool used to reach the consumer.

Similarly, Interactive Market Systems (IMS) provides a wide range of information systems for the advertising industry. The company produces easy-to-use, sophisticated media planning and analysis software that planners use to analyze both industry and proprietary research.

People BEHIND the Ads

Ken Cervantes, Senior Partner at Moroch Brothers

Courtesy of Ken Cervantes

As Senior Partner at Moroch Brothers, Ken Cervantes leads multicultural strategy and investment for McDonald's.

Most recently a strategist at MediaVest, and before that a member of the Coca-Cola team for Starcom MediaVest Group, Ken was instrumental in negotiating high-profit properties including the 2006 World Cup and Coca-Cola's Mexican National team marketing sponsorship, which aired on networks including NBC/Universal, Telemundo, UCI, and Univision.com. He was also recognized by *Media* magazine's "Creative Media Awards" in 2005.

Ken earned a bachelor's degree in business, with a concentration in marketing and a minor in Spanish from the University of Notre Dame.

We asked Ken to comment on the dramatic changes taking place in media and on the skills and qualities that make for a top media planner.

CA: Ken, what are the biggest changes right now in the world of media planning?

Ken: The biggest change in media planning is incorporating the new ways that consumers are using media. Today, consumers control the media they consume. They decide what, when, where, and how, so it's necessary to look at media planning differently, and to look at new ways to engage them in order to deliver our client's business goals.

CA: What do you do to stay current and abreast of these changes?

Ken: We're living most of these changes every day. First and foremost, we are consumers of media and are part of the digital revolution. We are all consuming content on different video screens (TVs, IPods, cell phones, broadband). It seems so long ago that there was only one screen . . . your television. In addition to living this reality, it's important to develop and maintain relationships with the media community.

CA: What qualities do you consider important in a budding media planner?

Ken: Beyond a typical college education, the qualities that I want a media planner on my team to possess are creativity, passion, and the desire to learn. I believe that these three qualities are very important in today's media landscape. You need to be creative in order to be able to identify the new "cool" thing or to make the new cool thing if it doesn't exist. Passion is essential. You need to love what you do because then you will put 100 percent behind it. Finally, we live in a time when change occurs on a daily basis, so you need to always want to learn. We need to be smarter for our clients' success.

CA: What was your own path to your present career?

Ken: After graduating from the University of Notre Dame and majoring in marketing, I pursued a job at Leo Burnett Media. After starting there in June 1995, I was part of the evolution of Starcom Worldwide as I worked on a variety of accounts, like Reebok, McDonald's, Comcast, and ComEd. Then I moved to our New York-based sister agency, Mediavest, to lead the multicultural media team for Coca-Cola. After three years on Coca-Cola, I moved to Forty-Two Degrees at Mediavest (MV42°) to lead investment for all our multicultural clients, including Avon, Heineken USA, Kraft, and Mars.

CA: Part of your job title is activation director and investment director. What do those positions entail?

Ken: The activation/investment director is the lead negotiator of media. This person works with planning, clients, and media partners in order to bring media plans to life. They also are on the pulse of what is new in the industry and look out for new ideas to bring to clients.

CA: Are there any insights about your work for Heineken you can share? What do your multicultural strategies involve for that brand?

Ken: It's all about making an emotional connection between the consumer and the brand. This is true for all our clients. We look for consumer insights that we can build a platform around and separate our brand from the competition. We then provide consumers with a brand experience that allows them to touch and feel the brand in a way that truly captivates them.

CA: Is there anything else you would like to share with students of advertising?

Ken: Never lose your creativity no matter what aspect of advertising you are in. In media, we believe that it's part science and part art. The art is what keeps you going because you get to pursue the new, fun "thing" each and every day.

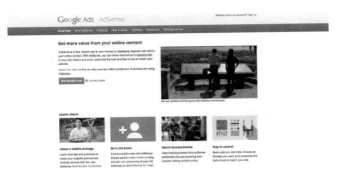

AdSense by Google is an invaluable tool for media planning especially for small Websites as it allows them to generate revenue from visitors. And it offers ad buyers access to tens of thousands niche markets.

Source: Google

IMS has developed Agency RollUp, a web-based system that consolidates and summarizes planning data in a single relational database. The Brandfx flowcharting system, which is an integral part of RollUp, enables media planners to track planned spending and other crucial information by brand, campaign, market, and region.[45]

Even with all the technological timesavers and shortcuts, though, it's still up to the media planner to know the product, the market, and the media, and to then make the call. Computers can't decide which medium or environment is best for the message. They can't evaluate the content of a magazine or the image of a TV program. They can't judge whether the numbers they're fed are valid or reliable, and they can't interpret the meaning of the numbers. What they can do is help the process along.

Chapter Summary

Media planning directs the advertising message to the right people at the right time. It involves many decisions: where to advertise and when, which media to use, and how often to use them. Media planners need both financial skills and creativity. Like good art and copy ideas, media decisions should be based on sound marketing principles and research.

The task of media planners has become more complicated and competitive in recent years due to the dramatic increase in media options, the continuing fragmentation of audiences, the rising cost of space and time, and the increasing complexity in the way media buys are made. But this has also given the professionals who work in media departments new prominence.

The media function involves two basic processes: planning media strategy and selecting media vehicles. Media planning begins with defining audience objectives—the specific types of people the advertising message will be directed to—and then setting the goals for communicating with those audiences. The target audience is often determined from the marketer's past experience, through special research studies, or through secondary research sources such as Simmons Market Research Bureau and Mediamark Research. Planners who follow an IMC model start by segmenting their audiences according to brand purchasing behavior and then ranking these segments by profit to the brand. Once the target audience is determined, the planner sets the message-distribution objectives. These specify where, when, and how often the advertising should appear. They may be expressed in terms of message weight, reach, frequency, and continuity. In this process, the planner considers the amount of advertising needed to achieve effectiveness.

To create the appropriate media strategy, the planner develops the best blend of the five Ms: markets, money, media, mechanics, and methodology. The planner must also consider many uncontrollable variables: the scope of the media plan, which is determined by the location and makeup of the target audience; the sales potential of different markets for both the brand and the product category; competitive strategies and budget considerations; media availability and economics; the nature of the medium and the mood of the message; the size, length, and position of the message in the selected media; and buyer purchase patterns. IMC planners try to discover the reasons and motivations for people's purchase and usage patterns and then create media plans based on those findings.

For international markets, media planners have to consider the availability and cost structure of foreign media and the differing cultural markets they serve. Some advertisers attempt to standardize their messages through the use of global media, but these media are still quite limited.

After the media strategy is developed, the planner selects specific media vehicles. Both the quantitative and qualitative criteria used to make this decision are important in the evaluation process. Factors that influence the selection process include campaign objectives and strategy; the size and characteristics of each medium's audience; geographic coverage; the exposure, attention, and motivation value of each medium; cost efficiency; and the advisability of a mixed-media approach.

Once media vehicles are selected, the media planner decides on scheduling—how many of each medium's space or time units to buy over what period of time. A media campaign can run continuously or in erratic pulses. These decisions are affected by consumer purchase patterns, the product's seasonality, and the balance of reach, frequency, and continuity that meets the planner's media objectives and budget.

The media planner must spend money wisely to maximize the campaign's effectiveness. To that end, many computer models have been developed, both in the United States and overseas, to help planners determine optimum levels of expenditure or compare alternative media schedules.

Important Terms

advertising impression, *282*

advertising response curve, *286*

attention value, *296*

audience, *281*

audience objectives, *281*

blinking, *298*

brand development index (BDI), *289*
bursting, *298*
category development index (CDI), *289*
circulation, *282*
continuity, *285*
continuous schedule, *298*
cost efficiency, *297*
cost per point (CPP), *297*
cost per thousand (CPM), *296*
creative mix, *279*
distribution objectives, *282*
effective frequency, *285*
effective reach, *285*
exposure value, *295*

five Ms (5Ms), *287*
flighting, *298*
frequency, *284*
gross impressions, *282*
gross rating points (GRPs), *283*
markets, *287*
mechanics, *287*
media, *272*
media planning, *272*
media vehicles, *281*
message weight, *282*
methodology, *287*
mixed-media approach, *297*
money, *287*

motivation value, *296*
opportunity to see (OTS), *282*
pulsing, *298*
programmatic advertising, *294*
rating, *283*
reach, *283*
readers per copy (RPC), *282*
recency planning, *286*
roadblocking, *298*
spillover media, *291*
synergy, *297*
television households (TVHH), *283*

Review Questions

1. What major factors contribute to the increased complexity of media planning?
2. What must media planners consider before they begin?
3. What secondary research sources are available to planners?
4. How does the IMC approach differ from the top-down media planning approach?
5. What are the "right" reach and frequency for a given message?
6. How are GRPs and CPMs calculated?
7. What are the 5Ms of the media mix, and how are they determined?
8. What major factors influence the choice of individual media vehicles?
9. Why might an advertiser use a mixed-media approach?
10. What are the principal methods used to schedule media?

The Advertising Experience

1. **Media-Buying Decisions**
   As a media buyer working on behalf of a large toy company, it is your job to buy media space for the launch of the Kitchi Kiss doll, which all advertising research shows will be a tremendous profit maker for the company. Using Exhibit 9–13 as an example, create a flowchart for a year's advertising for Kitchi Kiss. Explain your decisions about the types of media involved, when to use which types, and for how long each type should run.

2. **Media-Buying Service**
   There are three sides to the media business: planning, buying, and selling. Media planning and media buying are often in-house functions at an advertising agency, while sellers are those who represent the various media to clients, agencies, and media-buying services.
   Visit the Websites for the media companies listed below, consider the impact and importance of each to advertisers and their agencies, and answer the questions that follow.

   ■ The Davis Group: www.thedavisgrouptx.com
   ■ Initiative Media: www.initiative.com
   ■ Mediaedge:cia: www.mecglobal.com
   ■ Media Solutions: www.mediasol.com
   ■ Worldata: www.worldata.com
   ■ Zenith Optimedia: www.zenithoptimedia.com
   a. Who is the intended audience(s) of the site?
   b. What is the site's purpose? Does it succeed? Why or why not?
   c. What is the company's purpose?
   d. Does the company specialize in any particular segment (consumer, business-to-business, agriculture, automotive)?

3. **Media Organizations**
   The world of media is vast and constantly changing. Many media giants own properties in several media categories and are major forces in the world of advertising. Visit the Websites for the following media companies and answer the questions below.

   ■ Advo Inc.: www.advo.com
   ■ Cox Enterprises: www.coxenterprises.com
   ■ Gannett: www.gannett.com

- Hearst Corporation: www.hearst.com
- McGraw-Hill: www.mcgraw-hill.com
- Time Warner: www.timewarner.com
- Tribune Company: www.tribune.com
- Viacom: www.viacom.com

a. Who is the intended audience of the site?

b. What is the size and scope of the organization?

c. What is the organization's purpose? The site's purpose?

d. How important is this organization to the advertising industry? Why?

4. Reread the AIDS.gov chapter opening vignette. Next, answer the following questions:

1. What media options are not being used that perhaps should be?
2. What target audiences that are not being targeted should be?

Be sure to justify your answers to both questions.

5. Imagine you were a media planner and a client suggested that to help provide information about preventing the spread of AIDS to teens it would be useful to use Snapchat. How would you evaluate that request? What are the pros and cons of using Snapchat as an advertising medium for this target audience? Do some research to justify your recommendations.

Creative Strategy and the Creative Process

Learning Objectives

To show how IMC strategies are translated into creative briefs and message strategies that guide the creative process. The chapter examines the characteristics of great campaigns, styles of thinking, the nature of creativity and its importance in advertising, and the role of the agency creative team. We discuss how research serves as the foundation for creative development and planning, and we review common problems and pitfalls faced by members of the creative team.

 studying this chapter, you will be able to:

LO10-1 Discuss the attributes of great creative.

LO10-2 Describe how creative strategy is developed and used.

LO10-3 Elaborate on ways that creativity enhances advertising.

LO10-4 Explain the role that agency talent plays in the creative process.

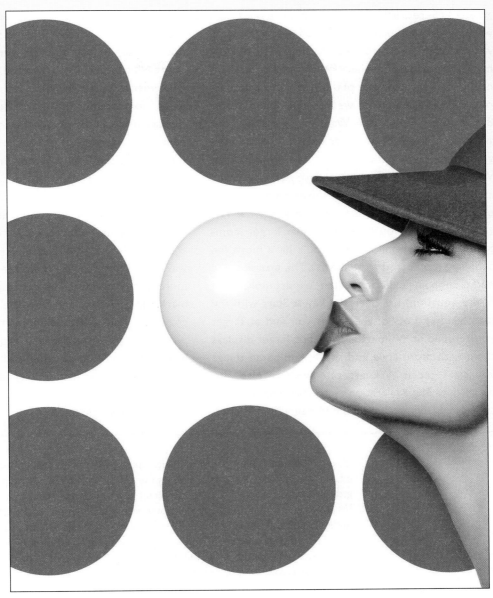

Source: Target Brands, Inc.

Walmart fundamentally changed the retail world, a result of its relentless focus on offering a broad selection of goods at low prices. This approach has made it the largest public company by annual revenue in the world. ■ For stores that compete with Walmart (and in this day and age, that is most stores), finding the right strategy for success is an ongoing challenge. ■ Some focus on a single product category, like clothes, electronics, pet supplies, or toys, and presenting a broader selection within that category. Sometimes that strategy pays off (American Eagle); sometimes it doesn't (Circuit City, Sharper Image, Linens 'n Things). ■ An even riskier strategy is going head-to-head, as Kmart, Sears, Montgomery Ward, and others have learned the hard way. But standing tall among the scattered ruins of Walmart's direct competitors is one company that has found a way to prosper. And that is Target. ■ Target's origins date to 1962 when the Dayton Company opened the first store in a Minneapolis suburb. The company grew through a strategy of both store openings and competitor acquisitions.[1] ■ With nearly 1,700 stores throughout the United States, Target ranked 31 in the 2008 *Fortune* 500, and is fifth in overall revenue among U.S. retailers. Not bad for an organization whose greatest expansion occurred during the same years that Walmart conquered the world. ■ How has Target succeeded where other retail giants have not? In part by being one of the greatest practioners of positioning, a concept we introduced in Chapter 8. Everyone knows that Walmart is synonymous with the concept of a "big box store." To the individual who is looking to save money but finds Walmart's offerings just a bit ordinary or who wants a more attractive shopping environment, Target proudly proclaims "Expect more, pay less." ■ The slogan says it all. You'll save money at Target (compared to many retailers) and you'll have more fun shopping (compared to Walmart). The promise of a better shopping experience (the "expect more" part of the equation) has been the key. ■ Start with the merchandise. Lots of the things you find at Target you can find at Walmart as well, but Target displays them with more style and space. And some things you can't get at Walmart, or anywhere else—in-house lines like Xhilaration[2] and Cherokee, and specially produced products from Mossimo and Michael Graves.[3] ■ Then, there is the red. Lots of red. As Michael Francis, senior VP of marketing at the retailer notes, "Trust us, red does go with everything." The strategy at Target is to "own red," that is, have the consumer associate the color with the brand. ■ One means for communicating that Target owns red is through its retail stores. But the color plays a prominent role in Target advertising as well and helps tie the many executions together in a seamless campaign. ■ Target spends nearly four times as much on its advertising as a percentage of sales than does Walmart.[4] Its ads are fun and quirky, in direct contrast to Walmart's more conservative, "hard-sell," approach. Target uses lifestyle themes to suggest ways that their products help the shopper become more of an individual. The campaigns have been remarkably effective, and have helped fuel Target's growth. "Value" means different things to different people. Target's creative and captivating ads have helped the company position itself as a more enjoyable place to shop than its biggest competitor. The strategy has helped Target thrive even in the midst of Walmart's successes. ■

Creativity is vitally important for all elements of IMC. This chapter focuses on advertising creation, as advertising is the component of IMC over which creative people typically have greatest control. Many of the more general creative processes are equally important for other IMC elements as well. In the next chapter we'll explain several of the unique considerations in developing copy and art for public relations, social media, and other elements of IMC.

The creative spark begins with a team made up of an art director and a copywriter. The **copywriter** develops the *verbal* message, the copy (words) spoken by the imaginary persona. The **art director** is responsible for the *nonverbal* aspect of the message, the design, which determines the visual look and intuitive feel. Together, they work under the supervision of a **creative director** (typically, a former copywriter or art director), who is ultimately responsible for the creative product—the form the final message takes. As a group, these people are generally referred to as **creatives.**

This chapter focuses on the creative process: where it comes from, how it's developed, and how it relates to marketing and advertising strategy. We then examine production: the events between the creative ideas and the ultimate execution.

What Makes for Great Creative?

Pause for a moment and before reading on, think of some ads you've seen that you would describe as great. The ones you'll always remember. As you think of these different ads, what is the common characteristic? And what, in the end, makes an ad great?

If we look at some of the classic ads in history, we may get a clue: Volkswagen's famous "Think small" ad; DeBeers' "A diamond is forever" line; Clairol's "Does she or doesn't she?"; Burger King's "Have it your way"; the Army's "Be all you can be"; and Coca-Cola's "The real thing." What makes these campaigns great?

This is a very important question, since research indicates that "ad liking" helps predict "ad success." No wonder, then, that agencies want to create ads that people like. But is liking all that is required for an ad to be great?

Bright colorful images, geometric shapes, and strong contrasts in both copy and graphics are qualities for great creative ads. Not only do they successfully draw the reader's attention, they help brand Target as an "upscale" discount store.

Source: Target Brands, Inc.

Whether it's a billboard, print ad, a TV or radio spot, or a Website, great ads do have certain commonalities. We can group most of these characteristics into two dimensions: *audience impact* and *strategic relevance.*

The Impact Dimension

A great ad makes an impact on its intended audience. It *resonates.*

Why? Because of the boom factor.

When a cannon goes "boom," it gets your attention—right now. So it is with an ad. It's the surprise element—the "aha." It not only gets your attention, it catches your imagination. In this sense it's like great art. It invites you to stop and think about the message.

One way Target communicates that it offers an extraordinary shopping experience is through the use of extraordinary ads that successfully capture the attention of its consumers. This ad showcases the effective use of color to hook audiences.

Source: Target Brands, Inc.

Microsoft emphasizes a transformational motive by showing the rewards achievable by using Office 2010.

Source: Microsoft

Other ads have an impact for different reasons. Look at the Target ad on the bottom of page 305, juxtaposing colors, the expressions of the models, and copy (i.e., "all about warm" versus "all about sparkle.") The ad is unusual, even for Target, so we stop to examine it more closely. And as we do so, the colors and the familiar logo convey so much about Target. Ads like this help the retailer convincingly claim you should "expect more." The ad resonates.

Recall from Chapter 5 our discussion of consumer motives. *Negatively originated motives,* such as problem avoidance or problem removal, provide the foundation for many great ads. These resonate by being highly **informational,** by offering relief from some problem (e.g., one gym's advertising headline reads, "Need to lose 30 pounds?"). Other motives are *positively originated* as consumers seek sensory gratification, intellectual stimulation, or social approval. Here, ads achieve greatness by being **transformational,** using positive reinforcement to offer a reward (Microsoft's headlines for Office 2010 read "I want to make it great" followed by reasons, such as "for a VIP presentation at work," or "so I can get an A at school.").

Unfortunately, most ads, whether they're informational or transformational, have little impact. Why? Because they lack a "big idea" or they fall down in the *execution.* The copy may be uninspiring, the visual may be less than attractive, or the production techniques may be of low quality. From the consumer's point of view, these ads are just a waste of time. From the client's, they are a waste of money.

The Relevance Dimension

The second dimension of great advertising is strategic relevance. An ad may get you to think, but what does it get you to think about? A classic example is the old Taco Bell "Yo Quiero Taco Bell" campaign featuring a speaking chihuahua. It captured everyone's imagination, but it reinforced the wrong feeling—people took delight in the cute dog, not the menu items.

Behind every creative team's choice of tone, words, and ideas lies an advertising strategy. When the ad is completed, it must be relevant to the strategy, or it will fail—even if it resonates with the audience. In other words, it may be great *entertainment,* but not great *advertising.* Great advertising always has a strategic mission to fulfill.

Developing and Implementing the Creative Strategy

Let's look at the advertising strategy that Target and its agencies developed. Then we'll see how they translated that into a message strategy and a big idea and, finally, into effective ads.

Recall from Chapter 8 that creative strategy consists of four elements: the *target audience,* the *product concept,* the *communications media,* and the *message.*

What is Target's **target audience?** Target focuses on value-conscious shoppers, usually adults ages 25 to 49 with families, who seek products that are nicer than those typically found at deep-discount stores. These shoppers are not poor, but they do look to save money (Target reports that the median household income of its shoppers, or "guests," as the company calls them, is $60,000). This group is Target's *primary market*—that's who the company sells to. So Target definitely wants them to see its advertising. Because Target offers both value and a sense of style, 18- to 25-year-olds are another important market. While this group as a whole may not spend as much as the primary market, they act as *centers of influence* (or *key influentials*). This group is a *secondary target audience.*

What is Target's **product concept?** Target has been described by some as "cheap chic." In other words, it is a mass merchandiser that appeals to those with a sense of style.

With respect to **communications media,** Target spends nearly three out of four ad dollars on ads that run on television and in newspapers. Some money is also spent on outdoor and radio as a means for reaching consumers while they drive. And like many companies, Target is increasing its spending on digital media, including e-mail, viral ads, and Facebook.

What is Target's **IMC message?** In its simplest terms, message strategy is determined by *what* a company wants to say and *how* it wants to say it. Target's ads stress the dual benefit proposition, "Expect more, pay less." While Walmart ads are product focused, Target's campaigns emphasize the consumer and her lifestyle. This reinforces the "expect more" benefit. To do this effectively, the messages have to exude an aura of quality. So the agency creative team chose a message strategy that is simple yet thoughtful, entertaining, credible, and most of all, distinctive.

The agency and client team must understand and agree to these four elements of the IMC strategy—target, product, media, and message—before any creative work begins. In most agencies, the account management group is responsible for developing the campaign strategy. In some large agencies, account planners spend a great deal of time researching the market. Then they prepare the campaign strategy with input from, and the approval of, account management. When the strategy-development task is completed, the account people prepare a *creative brief* to communicate the strategy to the creative department.

Writing the Creative Brief (Copy Platform)

After message objectives and strategy are determined, the account managers write a brief statement of the intended strategy. The **creative brief** is the creative team's guide for writing and producing the campaign. In some agencies it may be referred to as a *copy platform,* a *work plan,* or a *copy (or creative) strategy document.* Regardless of the name, it is a simple written statement of the most important issues to consider in the development of the campaign: the who, why, what, where, and when.

- *Who?* Who is the prospect in terms of behavioristic, geographic, demographic, and/or psychographic qualities? What is the typical prospect's personality?
- *Why?* Does the consumer have specific wants or needs the ad should appeal to? Marketers use two broad categories of appeals. **Rational appeals** are directed at the consumer's practical, functional need for the product or service; **emotional appeals** target the consumer's psychological, social, or symbolic needs. For a sampling of specific appeals within these categories, see Exhibit 10-1.
- *What?* What features of the product will satisfy the consumer's needs? What is the "proof" the company offers to support the product claim? How is the product positioned? What personality or image (of the product or the company) can be or has been created?
- *Where* and *when* will these messages be communicated? Through what medium? What time of year? What area of the country?
- Finally, *what style, approach,* or *tone* will the campaign use? And, generally, what will the copy say?

Exhibit 10-1
Selected IMC appeals.

Approach	Selected IMC appeals		
Needs	Rational	Emotional	
Self-actualization	Opportunity for more leisure / Efficiency in operation or use	Ambition / Avoidance of laborious task / Curiosity / Entertainment	Pleasure of reaction / Simplicity / Sport/play/physical activity
Esteem	Dependability in quality / Dependability in use / Enhancement of earnings / Variety of selection	Pride of personal appearance / Pride of possession	Style/beauty / Taste
Social	Cleanliness / Economy in purchase	Cooperation / Devotion to others / Guilt / Humor / Home comfort	Romance / Sexual attraction / Social achievement / Social approval / Sympathy for others
Safety	Durability / Protection of others / Safety	Fear / Health	Security
Physiological	Rest or sleep	Appetite	Personal comfort

Procter & Gamble and Leo Burnett use a simple creative brief with three parts:

1. *An objective statement.* A specific, concise description of what the campaign is supposed to accomplish or what problem it is supposed to solve. The objective statement also includes the name of the brand and a brief, specific description of the target consumer. For example,

   The campaign will convince value-conscious consumers that Target stores offer them a way to save money on their everyday purchases. In addition, Target offers a vast selection of products that make life better.

2. *A support statement.* A brief description of the evidence that backs up the product promise. For example,

   Support is found in two types of ads that Target regularly runs. Newspaper ads, including weekly inserts, demonstrate to consumers the low prices of the products sold at Target. Television ads emphasize the quality and value of the everyday products found at Target. Both TV and newspaper ads should do more than focus on the product alone; rather, they should help demonstrate that the products sold at Target make life easier and better. Social media efforts will also reinforce value and a better life by focusing on ways Target products brighten up the household even for families on tight budgets.

3. *A tone or brand character statement.* A brief statement of either the advertising's tone or the long-term character of the brand. Tone statements are short-term emotional descriptions of the advertising strategy. Brand character statements are long-term descriptions of the enduring values of the brand—things that give the product brand equity. A tone statement might be phrased

   The tone of Target ads should convey a spirit of optimism and energy. The ads should suggest that Target understands the consumer and the challenges she faces in her life. They should suggest that shopping at Target is fun.

   On the other hand, a brand character statement might be phrased

   Target offers consumers the selection and value typical of a mass merchandizer in stores that have elegance and flair.

The delivery of the creative brief to the creative department concludes the process of developing an IMC strategy. It also marks the beginning of the next step: the *campaign creative process,* in which the creative team develops a *message strategy* and begins the search for the *big idea.* After writing the first message, the copywriter should again check the brief to see if the message measures up on the resonance and impact dimensions. If it doesn't, the team must start again.

Elements of Message Strategy

Armed with the brief, the creative team is ready to develop creative ideas. The first step is to create a message strategy.

The **message strategy** (or **rationale**) is a simple description and explanation of a campaign's overall creative approach—what the campaign says, how it says it, and why. The message strategy has three components:

- **Verbal.** Guidelines for what the messages should say, considerations that affect the choice of words, and the relationship of the copy approach to the medium (or media) that will carry the message.

- **Nonverbal.** Overall nature of the campaign's graphics, any visuals that must be used, and the relationship of the graphics to the media in which the message will appear.

- **Technical.** Preferred execution approach and mechanical outcome, including budget and scheduling limitations (often governed by the media involved); also any **mandatories**—specific requirements such as addresses, logos, and slogans.

Target ads are quirky and creative. But the nonverbal elements of the red and white colors and repetition of the Target logo make them instantly recognizable.

Source: Target Brands, Inc.

Because all these elements of the message strategy intertwine, they typically evolve simultaneously. Language affects imagery, and vice versa. However, the verbal elements are the starting point for many campaigns.

The message strategy helps the creative team sell the campaign concept to the account managers and helps the managers explain and defend the creative work to the client. Of course, the message strategy must conform to the strategy outlined in the creative brief or it will probably be rejected.

In the development of message strategy, certain basic questions need to be answered: How is the market segmented? How will the product be positioned? Who are the best prospects for the product? What is the key consumer benefit? What is the product's (or company's) current image? What is the product's unique advantage?[5] At this point, research data are important. Research helps the creative team answer these questions.

How Creativity Enhances IMC

The powerful use of imagery, copy, and even humor in the Target campaign demonstrates how creativity enhances IMC. But what exactly is creativity or the creative process? What is the role of creativity? And where does creativity come from?

What Is Creativity?

To create means to originate, to conceive a thing or idea that did not exist before. Typically, though, **creativity** involves combining two or more previously unconnected objects or ideas into something new.

Many people think creativity springs directly from human intuition. But the creative process can also follow from a very disciplined approach. We'll discuss such an approach in this chapter.

The Role of Creativity in IMC Campaigns

Companies often select an agency specifically for its creative style and its reputation for coming up with original concepts. While creativity is important to a campaign's basic mission of informing, persuading, and reminding, it is vital to achieving the boom factor.

Creativity Helps Messages Inform

A campaign's ability to inform is greatly enhanced by creativity. Good creative work makes a campaign more vivid, and many researchers believe vividness attracts attention, maintains interest, and stimulates thinking.[6] A common technique is to use word plays and verbal or visual metaphors, such as "Like a rock," "Fly the friendly skies," or "You're in good hands." The metaphor describes one concept in terms of another, more familiar one, helping the audience member learn about the product.[7]

Other creative techniques can also improve a message's ability to inform. Writers and artists must arrange visual and verbal message components according to a genre of social meaning so that readers or viewers can easily interpret the message using commonly accepted symbols. For example, aesthetic cues such as lighting, the pose of the model, setting, and clothing style can instantly signal viewers nonverbally whether a fashion ad reflects a romantic adventure or a sporting event.[8]

Creativity Helps Messages Persuade

The ancients created legends and myths about gods and heroes—symbols for humankind's instinctive, primordial longings and fears—to affect human behavior and thought. To motivate people to some action or attitude, copywriters have created new myths and heroes, like the Marlboro man and the Energizer Bunny. A creative story or persona can establish a unique identity for the product in the collective mindset, a key factor in helping a product beat the competition.[9]

Creativity also helps position a product on the top rung of consumers' mental ladders. The Target ads featured in this chapter, for example, metaphorically suggest that ordinary products can be combined creatively to make life better. The higher form of expression creates a grander impression. And when such an impression spreads through the market, the product's perceived value also rises.

To be persuasive, the verbal message must be reinforced by the creative use of nonverbal message elements. Artists govern the use of these elements (color, layout, and illustration, for example) to increase vividness. Research suggests that, in print and digital media, *info graphics* (colorful explanatory charts, tables, and the like) can raise the perception of quality.[10] Artwork can also stimulate emotions. Color, for example, can often motivate consumers, depending on their cultural background and personal experiences (see Ad Lab 10–A, "The Psychological Impact of Color"). So it should be no surprise that Michael Francis, brand czar at Target, wants the retailer to "own red." Translation? When you see red in a campaign, you should anticipate that it is a Target message, even before the brand is identified.[11]

Creativity Helps IMC Remind

Imagine using the same invitation, without any innovation, to ask people to try your product again and again, year after year. Your invitation would become stale very quickly. Only creativity can transform boring reminders into interesting, entertaining messages. Nike is proof. Many of Nike's campaigns never mentioned the company name or even spelled it on the screen. Instead they told stories. And the only on-screen cue identifying the sponsor was

AD Lab 10-A

The Psychological Impact of Color

National origin or culture can play a role in color preferences. For example, warm colors—red, yellow, and orange—tend to stimulate, excite, and create an active response. People from warmer climes, apparently, are most responsive to these colors. Certain color combinations stimulate ethnic connotations. Metallic golds with reds, for example, are associated with China. Turquoise and beige are associated with the Indian tribes of the American Southwest.

Colors can impart lifestyle preferences. Vivid primary colors (red, blue, yellow) juxtaposed with white stripes exude decisiveness and are often used in sporting events as team colors. Thus, they are associated with a sporting lifestyle.

The colors we experience during the four seasons often serve as guides for combining colors and for guessing the temperaments of individuals who dress themselves or decorate their house in specific seasonal colors. Spring colors such as yellows, greens, and light blues, for example, suggest a fresh, exuberant character. Winter colors such as dark blues, deep violets, and black are associated with cool, chilly attitudes.

Because we usually feel refreshed after sleeping, we associate the colors of the morning—emerald green, raspberry, and pale yellow—with energy. And because the mellow colors of sunset predominate when we're usually home relaxing after work, we may associate sunset colors—peach, turquoise, and red-orange—with relaxation and reflective moods.

Some colors are ambiguous. Violet and leaf-green fall on the line between warm and cool. They can be either, depending on the shade. Here are some more observations:

Red

Symbol of blood and fire. Second to blue as people's favorite color but more versatile, the hottest color with highest "action quotient." Appropriate for soups, frozen foods, and meats.

Brown

A masculine color, associated with earth, woods, mellowness, age, warmth, comfort. Used to sell anything, even cosmetics.

Yellow

High impact to catch consumer's eye, particularly when used with black. Good for corn, lemon, or suntan products.

Green

Symbol of health and freshness; popular for environmentally friendly products.

Blue

Coldest color with most appeal; effective for frozen foods (ice impression); if used with a lighter tint it becomes "sweet" (Lowenbrau beer, Wondra flour).

Black

Conveys sophistication and high-end merchandise, and is used to stimulate purchase of expensive products. Good as background and foil for other colors.

Orange

Most "edible" color, especially in brown-tinged shades; evokes autumn and good things to eat.

Laboratory Application

Explain the moods or feelings that are stimulated by two-color ads or packages illustrated in this text.

---

the single, elongated "swoosh" logo inscribed on the final scene. A Nike spokesperson said this approach wasn't risky "given the context that the Nike logo is so well known."[12] We are entertained daily by creative campaigns—for soft drinks, snacks, and cereals—whose primary mission is simply to remind us to indulge again.

Creativity Puts the "Boom" in Campaigns

Successful comedy also has a boom factor—the punchline. It's that precise moment when the joke culminates in a clever play on words or turn of meaning, when the audience suddenly gets it and shows its approval.

Good punchlines are the result of taking an everyday situation, looking at it creatively, adding a bit of exaggeration, and then delivering it as a surprise. Great campaigns often do the same thing. Apple's famous "I'm a Mac, I'm a PC" ads used gentle humor to make a powerful point: Macs are better.

The boom doesn't always have to be funny. It may come from the sudden understanding of an unexpected double-meaning, as in the case of Target ads. Or from a funny or charming response from a Dell social media rep. Or the breathtaking beauty of a magnificent nature

The simplicity, vibrant colors, and cleverness of Target's ads do more than share a message. They help to create a brand personality and give consumers a reason to shop at the store. The "boom" factor in this ad is Target encouraging and celebrating diversity.

Source: Target Brands, Inc.

photograph for Timberland shoes. In a business-to-business situation, it may come from the sudden recognition that a new high-tech product can improve workplace productivity. In short, the boom factor may come from many sources. But it always requires the application of creativity.

Understanding Creative Thinking

Some people may exhibit more of it than others, but creativity lives within all of us. Human creativity, developed over millions of years, enabled our ancestors to survive. As individuals, we use our natural creativity every time we select an outfit to wear, style our hair, contrive an excuse, decorate our home, or cook a meal.

Styles of Thinking

The German sociologist Max Weber proposed that people think in two ways: an objective, rational, fact-based manner and a qualitative, intuitive, value-based manner. For example, while studying for a test, we use our rational, fact-based style of thinking. But when we buy a car, we call on taste, intuition, and knowledge to make a qualitative value judgment of the car's features, styling, and performance weighed against its price.

Roger von Oech defined this dichotomy as hard and soft thinking. *Hard thinking* refers to concepts like logic, reason, precision, consistency, work, reality, analysis, and specificity. *Soft thinking* refers to less tangible concepts: metaphor, dream, humor, ambiguity, play, fantasy, hunch. On the hard side, things are right or wrong, black or white. On the soft side, there may be many right answers and many shades of gray.[13]

Fact-Based versus Value-Based Thinking

Most theories of thinking fit into two general categories: value-based or fact-based. Let's examine these styles of thinking more closely.

Elegance and Value. Ads like this make credible the Target promise that their customers can expect both and appeal to both the hard and soft sides of thinking.

Source: Target Brands, Inc.

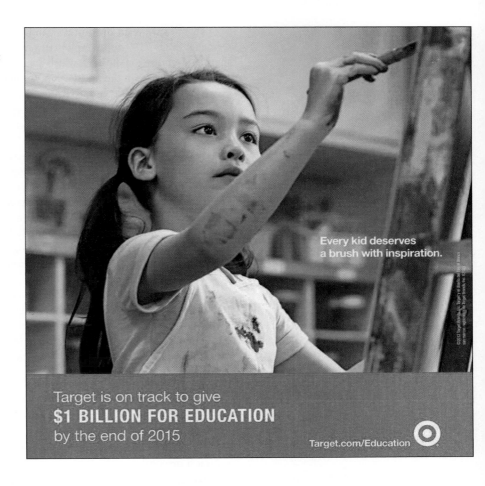

People whose preferred style of thinking is **fact-based** tend to fragment concepts into components and to analyze situations to discover the one best solution. Although fact-based people can be creative, they tend to be linear thinkers and prefer to have facts and figures—hard data—they can analyze and control. They are not comfortable with ambiguous situations. They like logic, structure, and efficiency.

In contrast, **value-based** thinkers make decisions based on intuition, values, and ethical judgments. They are better able to embrace change, conflict, and paradox. This style fundamentally relies on blending concepts together. Value-based thinkers, for example, attempt to integrate the divergent ideas of a group into an arrangement that lets everyone win. They are good at using their imagination to produce a flow of new ideas and synthesizing existing concepts to create something new.

How Styles of Thinking Affect Creativity

If the creative team prefers a value-based thinking style, it tends to produce ads such as those in the Target and Nike campaigns—emotional and metaphorical. That's fine if the client also prefers that style of thinking.

On the other hand, clients who prefer a fact-based style often seek agencies that produce practical, hard-edged work characterized by simple, straightforward layouts, rational appeals, and lots of data. A fact-based client may even find a value-based campaign to be unsettling.

The Saatchi & Saatchi ad campaign for Hewlett-Packard's laser printers, for example, created a stir internally. The ads simulated interviews. The actors portrayed harried customers talking about how they didn't have time to think about their printers. "Some people within Hewlett-Packard are somewhat uncomfortable with the direction of the campaign," reported Arlene King, a marketing communications manager for HP, "because we are a high-tech company and the ads don't focus on any aspect of the technology."[14]

The creative team must understand the campaign's target audience. In some market segments (high-tech, for example) customers may tend toward one style of thinking over another. And that could dictate which approach to use.

As we shall see in the next section, the best art directors and copywriters use both styles to accomplish their task. In the creative process, they need to use their imagination (value-based thinking) to develop a variety of concepts. But to select the best alternative and get the job done, they have to use the fact-based style.

The Creative Process

The **creative process** is the step-by-step procedure used to discover original ideas and reorganize existing concepts in new ways. By following it, people can improve their ability to unearth possibilities, cross-associate concepts, and select winning ideas.

The new generation of creatives will face a world of ever-growing complexity. They must handle the many challenges of integrated marketing communications (IMC) as they help their clients build relationships with highly fragmented target markets. They will need to understand the wide range of new technologies affecting advertising. And they will have to learn how to advertise to emerging international markets. To do this, they need a model that handles many situations simply.

Over the years, many notions of the creative process have been proposed. Although most are similar, each format has unique merits. Roger von Oech published a four-step creative model that many *Fortune* 100 companies use today. It offers flexibility for fact-based and value-based thinkers alike. Von Oech describes four distinct, imaginary roles (Explorer, Artist, Judge, and Warrior) that every art director and copywriter has to adopt at some point in the creative process:[15]

1. *The Explorer* searches for new information, paying attention to unusual patterns.
2. *The Artist* experiments and plays with a variety of approaches, looking for an original idea.
3. *The Judge* evaluates the results of experimentation and decides which approach is most practical.
4. *The Warrior* overcomes excuses, idea killers, setbacks, and obstacles to bring a creative concept to realization.

The Explorer Role: Gathering Information

Copywriters and art directors thrive on the challenge of creating advertising messages—the encoding process. But first they need the raw materials for ideas: facts, experiences, history, knowledge, feelings.

Taking on the role of the **Explorer,** the creatives examine the information they have. They review the creative brief and the marketing and advertising plan; they study the market, the product, and the competition. They may seek additional input from the agency's account managers and from people on the client side (sales, marketing, product, or research managers).

When the creative team developed ads for Target, they first assumed the Explorer role. They spoke with people about the nature of the company, its products, its marketing history, its competitors, and the competitors' styles of advertising.

Develop an Insight Outlook

It's important that when creatives play the Explorer role, they get off the beaten path to look in new and uncommon places for information—to discover new ideas and to identify unusual patterns. One reviewer of Target campaigns asked whether its campaigns or store designs would have been possible without the influence of Andy Warhol. In all likelihood, the answer is no. Creative inspiration in this case came from the world of art.

Von Oech suggests adopting an "insight outlook" (a positive belief that good information is available and that you have the skills to find and use it). This means opening up to the outside world to receive new knowledge. Ideas are everywhere: in museums, art galleries, hardware stores, and history books. The more diverse the sources, the greater your chance of uncovering an original concept.

When Target started opening in stores in Canada, it used clever ads like the one shown above. This is a great example of the development of a big idea unique to a specific region while still maintaining the strong Target brand.

Source: Target Brands, Inc.

Know the Objective

Philosopher John Dewey said, "A problem well-stated is a problem half-solved." This is why the creative brief is so important. It helps define what the creatives are looking for. The creatives typically start working on the message strategy during the Explorer stage because it helps them define what they're looking for.

To get their creative juices flowing, most copywriters and art directors maintain an extensive library of award books and trade magazines. Many also keep a *tickler* (or *swipe*) *file* of ads they like that might give them direction.

Brainstorm

As Explorers, the creative team looks first for lots of ideas. One technique is **brainstorming,** a process in which two or more people get together to generate new ideas. A brainstorming session is often a source of sudden inspirations. To succeed, it must follow a couple of rules: all ideas are above criticism (no idea is "wrong"), and all ideas are written down for later review. The goal is to record any inspiration that comes to mind, a process that psychologists call *free association,* allowing each new idea an opportunity to stimulate another.

Von Oech suggests other techniques for Explorers: leave your own turf (look in outside fields and industries for ideas); shift your focus (pay attention to a variety of information); look at the big picture (stand back and see what it all means); don't overlook the obvious (the best ideas are right in front of your nose); don't be afraid to stray (you might find something you weren't looking for); and stake your claim to new territory (write down any new ideas or they will be lost).

The Explorers' job is to find new information. To be effective Explorers, they must exercise flexibility, courage, and openness.[16]

The Artist Role: Developing and Implementing the Big Idea

The Artist's role is both the toughest and the longest. But it's also the most rewarding. The **Artist** must actually accomplish two major tasks: searching for the big idea and then implementing it.

Task 1: Develop the Big Idea

The first task for Artists is the long, tedious process of reviewing all the pertinent information gathered during the Explorer role, analyzing the problem, and searching for a key verbal or visual concept.

Creating a mental picture of the message, also called **visualization** or **conceptualization,** is important. It's where the search for the **big idea**—that flash of insight—takes place. The big idea is a bold, creative initiative that builds on the strategy, joins the product benefit with consumer desire in a fresh, involving way, brings the subject to life, and makes the audience stop, look, and listen.[17]

What's the difference between a strategy and a big idea? A strategy describes the direction the message should take. A big idea gives it life. For example, the creative brief discussed earlier for Target contains a strategic brand character statement:

> Target offers consumers the selection and value typical of a mass merchandiser in stores that have the elegance and flair of a department store.

Target could have used that strategy statement as a headline. But it would have been dreadfully dull. It lacks what a big idea headline delivers: a set of multiple meanings that create interest, memorability, and, in some cases, drama. Note the short, punchy headline that Target chose to convey the same strategic concept:

> Expect more. Pay less.

John O'Toole said, "While strategy requires deduction, a big idea requires inspiration."[18] The big idea is almost invariably expressed through a combination of art and copy. Target's approach is to use short but witty copy, beautiful photography, and the immediately recognizable red "target" logo to visually communicate the essence of the brand.

My **IMC** Campaign 10

The Creative Brief

Every agency has a slightly different twist on a creative brief. In this chapter we outline the components of most briefs this way:

- Who (the prospect).
- Why (specific wants or needs the ad should appeal to).
- What (are the product features that can satisfy consumer needs?).
- Where and when (will the messages be transmitted?).
- Style, approach, tone.

We also describe the creative brief that Leo Burnett uses for P&G. It is even simpler:

- An objective statement (what are you trying to do?).
- A support statement (the evidence that backs up the promised benefit).
- A tone or brand character statement (emotional descriptions of the advertising strategy).

Are you interested in creativity? Visit one of the best agency resources on the web, Ogilvy.com, for lots of information about effective creative, including the agency's take on creative briefs, summarized here:

1. What are the communications objectives?
2. What should consumers do differently? Why?
3. How will messages affect consumer beliefs and actions?
4. How are our competitors advertising? How can we make our ads different?
5. Who is the target audience and what is their shared need that the brand can fulfill?
6. Demographics of the audience, but even more importantly, shared attitudes.
7. The brand

- How does the brand address the shared need?
- How should the brand experience (as defined by both planned and unplanned messages) be defined?
- What is the proposition (or benefit)?
- What evidence gives people a reason to believe the proposition?
- What is the personality of the brand?
- How can the mood or tone of the ads be matched to the personality of the brand?

The Ogilvy site is filled with a lot more useful information, including suggestions for maximizing the likelihood that the brief will spark a big idea. Check it out.

Transforming a Concept: Do Something to It Von Oech points out that when we take on the Artist role, we have to do something to the information we collected as Explorers to give it value. That means asking lots of questions: What if I added this? Or took that away? Or looked at it backward? Or compared it with something else? The Artist changes patterns and experiments with various approaches.

For example, one Target ad for cosmetics uses a traditional, high-fashion layout. The twist is found in the multiple headlines in which the suffix "less" is highlighted. This simple yet powerful change transforms the ad from a somewhat snobbish appeal to a value proposition. It suggests the Target consumer can buy a great product for a low price.

At this point in the creative process, a good Artist may employ a variety of strategies for transforming things. Von Oech suggests several techniques for manipulating ideas:[19]

1. *Adapt.* Change contexts. Think what else the product might be besides the obvious. A Campbell's Soup ad showed a steaming bowl of tomato soup with a headline: "HEALTH INSURANCE."

2. *Imagine.* Ask what if. Let your imagination fly. What if people could do their chores in their sleep? What if there was one place where people could leave all disagreements behind? Clyde's Bar in Georgetown actually used that idea. The ad showed a beautifully illustrated elephant and donkey dressed in business suits and seated at a table toasting one another. The headline: "Clyde's. The People's Choice."

3. *Reverse.* Look at it backward. Sometimes the opposite of what is expected has great impact and memorability. A cosmetics company ran an ad for its moisturizing cream under the line: "Introduce your husband to a younger woman." A vintage Volkswagen ad used "Ugly is only skin deep."

4. *Connect.* Join two unrelated ideas together. Ask yourself: What ideas can I connect to my concept? A Target ad showed the rear view of a high-fashion-type model clad only

Metaphor is a powerful creative tool. Consider the metaphor of the artwork in this ad and the way the artist transformed the balloons in this image to make it more effective.

Source: Smith & Milton, London

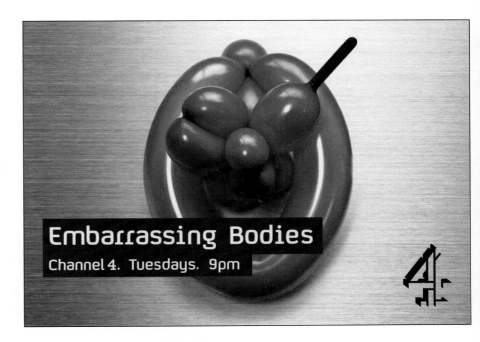

with a backpack and a lampshade—the latter wrapped around her middle like a miniskirt. Next to the Target logo the ad said simply "fashion and housewares."

5. *Compare.* Take one idea and use it to describe another. Ever notice how bankers talk like plumbers? "Flood the market, laundered money, liquid assets, cash flow, take a bath, float a loan." The English language is awash in metaphors. Jack in the Box advertised its onion rings by picturing them on a billboard and inviting motorists to "Drive thru for a ring job." An elegant magazine ad for the Parker Premier fountain pen used this sterling metaphor: "It's wrought from pure silver and writes like pure silk."

6. *Eliminate.* Subtract something. Or break the rules. In IMC there's little virtue in doing things the way they've always been done. Seven-Up became famous by advertising

what it wasn't ("the Uncola") and thereby positioned itself as a refreshing alternative. To introduce its new models one year, Volkswagen used a series of humorous teaser ads that didn't show any cars. In one, a shaggy dog sat patiently in front of a fan. He was presumably replicating what dogs do in cars, sticking their heads out the window to catch the breeze. The only difference was he was doing it indoors.

7. *Parody.* Fool around. Have some fun. Tell some jokes—especially when you're under pressure. There is a close relationship between the *ha-ha* experience of humor and the *aha!* experience of creative discovery. Humor stretches our thinking and, used in good taste, makes for some great advertising. A classical radio station ran a newspaper ad: "Handel with care." William Shatner parodies the public's image of himself in Priceline.com ads. In one, he was even "fired" and replaced by fellow Star Trek castmember Leonard Nimoy.

Blocks to Creativity   Everybody experiences times when the creative juices just won't flow. There are many causes: information overload, mental or physical fatigue, stress, fear, insecurity. Often, though, the problem is simply the style of thinking being used.

Many of Roger Von Oech's suggestions for transforming a concept are embodied in Target's ads. How many can you spot in this execution?

Source: Target Brands, Inc.

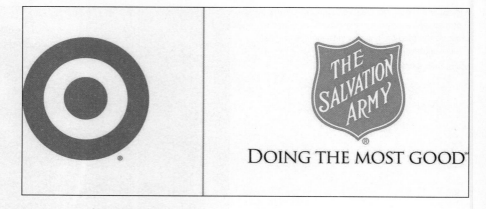

In the Explorer stage, when creatives study reams of marketing data, the facts and figures on sales and market share may put them in a fact-based frame of mind. But to create effectively, they need to shift gears to a value-based style of thinking.

As von Oech says, "Creative thinking requires an attitude that allows you to search for ideas and manipulate your knowledge and experience." Unfortunately, it is sometimes difficult for creatives to make that mental switch instantly. Von Oech recommends some techniques to stimulate integrative thinking. For example: look for the second right answer (there is usually more than one answer to any problem, and the second may be more creative); seek cross-fertilization (TV people could learn a lot from teachers, and vice versa); slay a sacred cow (sacred cows make great steaks); imagine how others would do it (stretch the imagination by role playing); laugh at it (make up jokes about what you're doing); and reverse your viewpoint (open up your thinking and discover things you typically overlook).[20]

George Gier, cofounder of the Leap Partnership, says, "The only thing agencies have left to sell to clients that they can't get anywhere else is creative ideas."[21] Perhaps this is why Derek Walker, owner of a small agency in South Carolina, writes that in advertising, "the client is not always right."[22]

Creative blocking may occur when people in the agency start "thinking like the client," especially if the client is a fact-based thinker. This can also be hazardous to the agency's creative reputation and is one reason agencies sometimes resign accounts over "creative differences." An agency can eliminate a lot of frustration and wasted time and money by evaluating the client's corporate culture, its collective style of thinking, and its creative comfort level in advance.

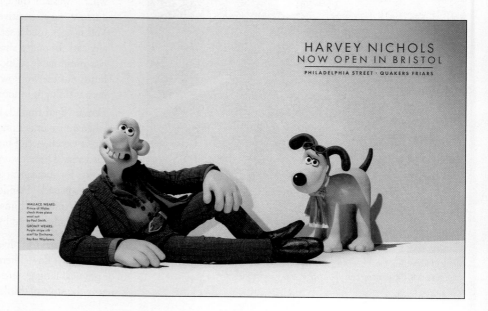

Creative fatigue sometimes happens when an agency has served an account for a long time and all the fresh ideas have been worked and reworked. It can also happen when a client has rejected a series of concepts; the inspiration is lost and the creatives start trying to force ideas. They suddenly find it hard to shift their style of thinking or to crank up the creative process again. If this becomes chronic, the only solutions may be to appoint an entirely new creative team or resign the account.

Incubating a Concept: Do Nothing to It   When the brain is overloaded with information about a problem, creatives sometimes find it's best to just walk away from it for a while, do something else, and let the unconscious mind mull it over. This approach yields several benefits. First, it puts the problem back into perspective. It also rests the brain, lets the problem incubate in the subconscious, and enables better ideas to percolate to the top. When they return to the task, creatives frequently discover a whole new set of assumptions.

Task 2: Implement the Big Idea

Once creatives latch onto the big idea, they have to implement it. This is where the real art of advertising comes in—writing the exact words, designing the precise layout. To have a sense of how advertising creatives do that, it helps to understand what *art* is in advertising, how artistic elements and tools are selected and used, and the difference between good art and bad art.

Art shapes the message into a complete communication that appeals to the senses as well as the mind. So while **art direction** refers to the act or process of managing the visual presentation of the message, the term **art** actually refers to the whole presentation—visual, verbal, and aural. For example, the artful selection of words not only communicates information but also stimulates positive feelings for the product. An artfully designed typeface not only makes reading easier, it also evokes a mood. By creatively arranging format elements—surrounding the text with lines, boxes, and colors, and relating them to one another in proportion—the art director can further enhance the appeal. Art also shapes the style of photography and illustration. An intimate style uses soft focus and close views, a documentary style portrays the scene without pictorial enhancements, and a dramatic style features unusual angles or blurred action images.

In short, if *copy* is the verbal language of a message, *art* is the body language. TV uses both sight and sound to involve viewers. Radio commercials use sound to create *word pictures* in the minds of listeners. The particular blend of writing, visuals, and sounds makes up an ad's expressive character. So while the quality may vary, every ad uses art.

In advertising, balance, proportion, and movement are guides for uniting words, images, type, sounds, and colors into a single communication so they relate to and enhance each other. We'll discuss more of these concepts in Chapter 11.

The Creative Pyramid: A Guide to Formulating Copy and Art

The **creative pyramid** is a model that can help the creative team convert the advertising strategy and the big idea into the actual physical ad or commercial. It uses a simple five-step structure (see Exhibit 10-2).

Exhibit 10-2

The creative pyramid offers a simple guide for establishing copywriting objectives.

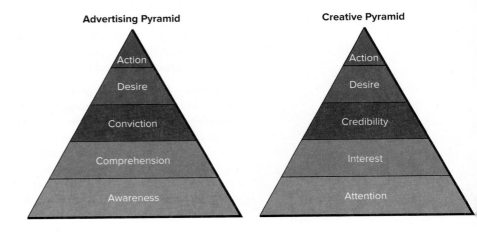

Advertising Pyramid

Action
Desire
Conviction
Comprehension
Awareness

Creative Pyramid

Action
Desire
Credibility
Interest
Attention

Ethical Issues

It's one of the more blatant uses of sex in advertising in recent memory: a billboard features a young woman, holding a grease gun cartridge in each hand, and leaning over to exhibit an ample amount of cleavage. The headline reads "This is Debbie. She wants you to have this pair in your car." The ad is for auto parts, but the implication seems to be that if you buy *this manufacturer's* auto parts, you'll get Debbie or someone like Debbie in the bargain. Nothing in the ad says so explicitly, but the innuendo is all that's required to capture the viewer's attention.

Advertisers frequently use the power of suggestion to imply sex, encouraging viewers to come to their own conclusions. However, advertisers who run such risqué ads must contend with the critics and with the often-tricky legal distinction between obscenity and indecency. Obscenity is illegal and carries criminal charges, whereas indecency does not. To be considered obscene, an ad must meet three conditions: it appeals to prurient interests, it is patently offensive, and it lacks any redeeming social value.

In general, most ads with sexual appeals don't meet the criteria for obscenity, but they may still be considered indecent, since indecency is in the eyes of the beholder. If enough people believe sexually oriented material is indecent, then "community standards" reflect this belief. In such cases, citizen pressure groups, along with media organizations and local courts, enforce community standards by disallowing advertising that offends those standards.

Consider Abercrombie & Fitch. The clothing retailer recently sparked controversy at a mall in Omaha when its window posters featured a topless model covering her breasts with her hands. A Christian group, Family First, quickly objected, claiming that Abercrombie's posters created a "sexualized walkway." Commenting on the objections, a spokesperson for A&F said the displays might have been "sexy" but were not the "sexually charged monstrosities" that Family First asserted. Nevertheless, the community standards had been revealed. Family First began pressuring shoppers and other retailers in the mall to object to the photographs, and within nine days the window displays were changed.

Were the posters obscene or indecent? Advertisers like A&F, who continue to strive for the "sexy" appeal, are beginning to find it increasingly difficulty to draw the line between simple sex appeal and unethical exploitation.

There is no easy solution to this dilemma, especially since research shows that sexual appeals can be effective when sexuality relates to the product. However, when it doesn't, it can distract audiences from the main message and severely demean the advertiser in the consumer's eyes. This brings up an important and rather common paradox about sexually oriented advertising. How is a naked model in a window poster an advertisement for clothing? Many argue that it is not, making such ads not only a distraction, but also a source of negative *externalities*—the social costs to consumers outside the target market, such as children who might be indirectly affected.

Advertisers must examine, on a case-by-case basis, at what point sexual appeals become counterproductive. In one case, an executive on the Valvoline advertising account justified using "girlie calendars" for mechanics by noting that "the calendar may offend some groups—but they aren't our customers."

Miller Lite's "Catfight" campaign raised a few eyebrows. The campaign appeared to signal the company's return to "beer and babes" ads, depicting women as sexual objects. In the commercial, two women in a restaurant begin the classic "tastes great/less-filling" debate over Miller

The purpose of much copy and design is either to persuade prospective customers to take some action to satisfy a need or want, or to remind them to take the action again. In a new-product situation, people may first need to be made aware of the problem or, if the problem is obvious, that a solution exists. For a frequently purchased product, the marketer simply has to remind people of the solution close to the purchase occasion. In either case, the company must first get the prospect's *attention*. The second step is to stimulate *interest*—in either the message or the product itself. Next, it's important, especially for new products, to build *credibility* for the product claims. Then the campaign can focus on generating *desire* and finally on stimulating *action*. These five elements should be addressed in just about every marketing appeal. We'll deal with each step briefly.

Attention A product message is a *stimulus*. It must break through consumers' physiological screens to create the kind of attention that leads to perception. *Attention*, therefore, is the first objective of any campaign and the fundamental building block in the creative pyramid. The Artist may spend as much time and energy figuring out how to express the big idea in an interesting, attention-getting way as searching for the big idea itself.

Print ads often use the headline as the major attention-getting device. The copywriter's goal is to write a headline that expresses the big idea with verve. Usually designed to appear in the largest and boldest type in the ad, the headline is often the strongest focal point conceptually as well as visually. Many other devices also help gain attention. In print media, they

Lite. The debate quickly turns into a full-fledged catfight, with the two women stripped down to their bras and panties, splashing around in an adjacent fountain. Moments later, we see the two buxom brawlers going at it in a soggy cement pit. The ad cuts to a bar. It turns out the fight was only the fantasy of two guys in a bar who were dreaming of the perfect beer commercial, much to the shock and disgust of their girlfriends, who were with them at the time. The cable TV version then takes things a little further as it cuts back to the near-naked women with one saying to the other, "Do you want to make out?"

So what does any of this have to do with selling beer? Hillary Chura, who covers the beer industry for *Advertising Age,* explains that ads such as the "Catfight" commercial are "aspirational." After watching these two beautiful women wrestle around for 30 seconds, Miller wants guys to say, "Hey, if I drink Miller Genuine Draft, I'll get those hot women." And Miller wants women to think "If I drink this beer, I'll look like those women."

But what is the social cost of these unrealistic "aspirations"? In a society rife with confidence-related disorders, should advertisers exploit consumer insecurities in an effort to sell more of their product? At what point do advertisers need to accept some ethical responsibility for the interests of the society to which they owe their existence?

Unfortunately, this debate over sex in advertising may actually be fueling advertisers' desire to continue using blatant sex appeals. The "Catfight" campaign sparked nationwide attention on talk radio, CNN's Crossfire, in *USA Today,* and in other media outlets. Similarly, Abercrombie & Fitch continues to spark controversy with its provocative ads featuring scantily clad models. Controversy equals publicity. Publicity stimulates interest. And interest spawns sales.

In short, sex, and the controversy surrounding it, sells. Until this changes, industry or government policymakers will certainly continue to encounter difficulties in treating advertising sex in a way satisfactory to everyone—or perhaps anyone.

Questions

1. How would you explain the "redeeming value" of sexual appeals in advertising?

2. If sexual appeals are considered OK by the audiences that are directly targeted, what responsibility does the advertiser have for any effect on indirect targets, such as children? How can advertisers protect themselves from this problem?

Sources: Erin Cooksley, "Sex Sells, Ethics Absent from Advertising Industry," *The Daily Skiff,* February 11, 2004 (retrieved from www.skiff.tcu.edu/2004 /spring/issues/02/11/sex.html); Florence Kennel, "Burgundy Ads Banned for Sexual Innuendo," January 23, 2004 (retrieved from www.decanter.com); "Does Sex Really Sell?" *Adweek,* October 17, 2005; Robynn Tysver, "Family Group Protests 'Sexualized' Ads at Stores in Lincoln Mall," *Omaha World-Herald,* February 12, 2003; Deborah Alexander, "Family Group Ends Protest after Shop Changes Displays," *Omaha World-Herald,* February 21, 2003 (both retrieved from www.nexis.com); Rance Crain, "Relevance Is Operative Word in 'Catfight' or Chip-Dip Ads," *Advertising Age,* January 27, 2003; Basem Boshra, "Uh, Can You Say Appallingly Sexist?" *Montreal Gazette,* February 1, 2003 (retrieved from www.nexis.com); Julie Dunn, "The Light Stuff. Coors Loves the Young Male Demographic—and Twins!" *Denver Westword,* January 23, 2003 (retrieved from www.nexis.com); Tom Daykin, "Miller Gets Down and Dirty with Lite Ad; Reaction Mixed, but Commercial Is Being Noticed," *Milwaukee Journal Sentinel,* January 26, 2003 (retrieved from www.nexis.com).

may include dynamic visuals, unusual layout, vibrant color, or dominant ad size. In electronic media, they may include special sound effects, music, animation, or unusual visual techniques.

Some factors are beyond the creatives' control. The budget may determine the size of a sponsorship or length of the viral video. And that may influence how well or quickly it breaks through consumers' screens. Similarly, a TV spot's position in a cluster of commercials between shows or an ad's position in a publication may determine who sees it.

The attention-getting device should be dramatic, powerful, and intense. It must also be appropriate, relating to the product, the tone of the campaign, and the needs or interests of the intended audience. This is especially true in business-to-business campaigns where rational appeals and fact-based thinking dominate. The natural attention-drawing value of sexual themes is often exploited by marketers. See our "Ethical Issues" box on page 320 and above to find out more about the pros and cons of using sex as an attention-getting device.

Headlines that make a promise lacking in credibility won't make a sale; in fact, they may alienate a potential customer. Messages that use racy headlines or nude figures unrelated to the product often lose sales because prospects can't purchase the item that first attracted their attention.

Interest   The second step in the creative pyramid, *interest,* carries the prospective customer—now paying attention—to the heart of the message. The message must keep the prospect excited or involved as the information becomes more detailed. To do this, the copywriter may answer a question asked in the attention step or add facts that relate to the headline. To maintain audience interest, the tone and language should be compatible with the target market's attitude. As we discussed earlier, the successful message has impact.

The writer and designer must lead prospects from one step to the next. Research shows that people read what interests them and ignore what doesn't, so the writer must maintain prospects' interest at all times.[23] One way to do so is to credibly demonstrate that the sponsor understands the prospect and knows about his or her problems, needs, and how the product or service will answer them. Copywriters use the word *you* a lot.

There are many effective ways to stimulate interest: a dramatic situation, a story, cartoons, charts. In radio, copywriters use sound effects or catchy dialogue. Television frequently uses quick cuts to maintain interest. We discuss some of these techniques in the chapter on advertising production.

Credibility The third step in the creative pyramid is to establish *credibility* for claims about the product or service. Customers are skeptical. They want proof. Comparison ads can build credibility, but they must be relevant to customers' needs—and fair.

Well-known presenters may lend credibility to a campaign. For example, actress Keira Knightley effectively represents Chanel with her glamorous and elegant style, just as snowboarder Shaun White represents Mountain Dew with a personality that is athletic and free-spirited.

Marketers often show independent test results to substantiate product claims. To work, such "proofs" must be valid, not just statistical manipulation. Many consumers have extensive product knowledge, even in specialized areas.

Desire In the *desire step,* the writer encourages prospects to picture themselves enjoying the benefits of the product or service. Essentially, they are invited to visualize.

In print, copywriters initiate visualization by using phrases like "picture yourself" or "imagine." In film or video, Jenny Craig shows before and after images of customers who've lost weight, while e-Harmony shows happily married couples who met through the service. The not-so-subtle message: "This could be you!"

The desire step hints at the possibilities and lets the consumer's mind take over. If prospects feel they're being led by the nose, they may feel insulted, resent the ad, and lose interest. In some cases, writers maintain this delicate balance by having a secondary character agree

AD Lab 10-B

Applying the Creative Pyramid

Notice how the five objectives of advertising copy apply to the ad shown here for the Salvation Army.

Attention The photograph of a man in what appears to be a superhero outfit draws the reader's attention quickly. What's happened to Superman?

Interest The reader quickly realizes that something is amiss. This is no superhero, but a destitute man living in squalid conditions. In a flash the reader has moved from one set of assumptions about the ad to ones that are completely different. Because his situation looks so bleak, the reader might start losing interest, thinking he or she can do little to help. That's when the headline maintains interest by suggesting that helping is easy.

Credibility Is helping easy? Sure it Is. Take the old clothes you'd just throw away, and bring them to a nearby Salvation Army location. What could be easier?

Desire The man's plight is contrasted with the ease of giving away unwanted clothing. The ad is respectful in tone, asking the reader to "Please donate your unwanted clothes to the homeless this winter." By phrasing the request this way, the ad makes clear that the reader's actions will have a direct impact on the population in need.

Action If the previous steps have been accomplished, then the key to success is to get people to act now, while the plight of the homeless is fresh in their minds. The ad makes it easy to help by asking the reader to "Call the Salvation Army" and giving the phone number to call.

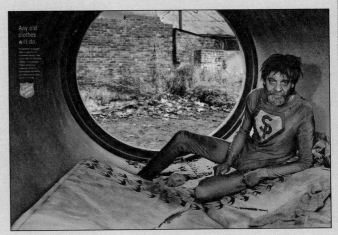

Source: The Salvation Army

Laboratory Applications

1. Find an ad that exhibits the five elements of the creative pyramid. *(A print ad will be the easiest to find and talk about, but radio and TV commercials also feature the five elements. Beware: The desire step may be hard to find.)*

2. Why do so many good ads lack one or more of the five elements listed here? How do they overcome the omission?

---

with the main character and prattle off a few more product benefits. The secondary character allows the main character, the one audiences relate to best, to retain integrity.

Action The final step up the creative pyramid is *action.* The purpose is to motivate people to do something—send in a coupon, visit a Website, visit the store—or at least to agree with the advertiser.

This block of the pyramid reaches the smallest audience but those with the most to gain from the product's utility. So the last step is often the easiest. If the copy is clear about what readers need to do and asks or even nudges them to act, chances are they will (see Ad Lab 10–B "Applying the Creative Pyramid").

The call to action may be explicit—"Call for more information"—or implicit—"Fly the friendly skies." Designers cue customers to take action by placing dotted lines around coupons to suggest cutting and by highlighting the company's telephone number with large type or a bright color.

Marketers use technology to make it easy for people to act, sometimes through either a toll-free phone number or an attractive Website. In relationship marketing, the campaign enables people to select themselves as being interested in a relationship. Then the marketer can use more efficient one-on-one media to develop the relationship.

The Judge Role: Decision Time

The next role in the creative process is the **Judge.** This is when the creatives evaluate the value of their big ideas and decide whether to implement, modify, or discard them.[24]

The Judge's role is delicate. On the one hand, the creatives must be self-critical enough to ensure that when it's time to play the Warrior they will have an idea worth fighting for. On the other hand, they need to avoid stifling the imagination of their internal Artist. It's easier to be critical than to explore, conceptualize, or defend. But the Judge's purpose is to produce good ideas, not to revel in criticism. Von Oech suggests focusing first on the positive, interesting aspects of a new idea. The negatives will come soon enough.

When playing the Judge, the creatives ask certain questions: Is this idea an aha! or an uh-oh? (What was my initial reaction?) What's wrong with this idea? (And what's right with it?) What if it fails? (Is it worth the risk?) What is my cultural bias? (Does the audience have the same bias?) What's clouding my thinking? (Am I wearing blinders?)

In an effort to create world-class campaigns Michael Conrad, formerly the worldwide chief creative officer for Leo Burnett and currently the dean of the new Cannes Lions Academy, developed the rating scale shown in Exhibit 10-3. The agency's Global Product Committee now uses this scale to evaluate every message before presenting it to a client. Ones that score 4 or below don't get presented. The objective is to develop campaigns that score 8 and above, and those receive full agency support. The top rating, world-class, means "best in the world, bar-none."

Risk is an important consideration. When the campaign is a hit, everybody's happy, sales go up, people get raises, and occasionally there's even positive publicity. But when a campaign flops, sales may flatten or even decline, competitors gain a couple of points in market share, distributors and dealers complain, and the phone rings incessantly with calls from disgruntled client executives. Perhaps worst of all is the ridicule in the trade. Advertising pundits say nasty things about the campaign in TV interviews; reviewers write articles in *Ad Age* and *Adweek;* and even the big daily papers get in their licks. This is not good for either the agency's stock or the client's. And it's how agencies get replaced. So the Judge's role is vital.

If the Artist-as-Judge does a good job, the next role in the creative process, the Warrior, is easier to perform.

The Warrior Role: Overcoming Setbacks and Obstacles

In the final step of the creative process, the **Warrior** wins territory for big new ideas in a world resistant to change. The Warrior carries the concept into action. This means getting the big idea approved, produced, and placed in the media. Von Oech says Warriors must be bold, sharpen their sword (skills), strengthen their shield (examine criticism in advance), follow through (overcome obstacles), use their energy wisely, be persistent, savor their victories, and learn from defeat.

To get the big idea approved, the Warrior has to battle people within the agency and often the client, too. So part of the Warrior's role is turning the agency account team into co-warriors for the presentation to the client. At this point, it's imperative that the creatives finish their message strategy document to give their rationale for the copy, art, and production elements in the concept they're trying to sell. And the message strategy had better mesh with the creative brief, or the valiant Warrior will likely face a wide moat with no drawbridge (see Ad Lab 10–C, "The Creative Gymnasium").

Part of the Warrior's task may be to help the account managers present the campaign to the client. Bruce Bendinger says, "How well you *sell* ideas is as important as how *good* those ideas are." To give a presentation maximum selling power, he suggests five key components:[25]

1. *Strategic precision.* The selling idea must be on strategy. The presenting team must be able to prove it, and the strategy should be discussed first, before the big selling idea is presented.

2. *Savvy psychology.* The presentation should be receiver-driven. The idea has to meet the client's needs.

10	World-class
9	New standard in advertising
8	New standard in product category
7	Excellence in craft
6	Fresh idea(s)
5	Innovative strategy
4	Cliché
3	Not competitive
2	Destructive
1	Appalling

Exhibit 10-3
Leo Burnett Global Product Committee's rating scale.

AD Lab 10-C

The Creative Gymnasium

The Explorer

The explorer looks for fresh, new ways to see things. To become an explorer, be conscious of how you see the world, and try to discover the new and unusual patterns that exist right below the surface.

© Shutterstock RF

The Judge and the Warrior

As a creative person, what verdict would your Judge give to ads that feature creative gymnastics? How would your Warrior present ads like this to a client for approval?

The Artist

The Artist uses humor and absurd what-if questions to mentally loosen up. Try these warm-up techniques:

1. Think up a new set of conversion factors:

    10^{12} microphones = 1 megaphone

10^{12} pins = 1 terrapin

3⅓ tridents = 1 decadent

4 seminaries = 1 binary

10^{21} piccolos = 1 gigolo

1 milli-Helen = the amount of beauty required to launch 1 ship

2. Another mental muscle stretcher is to change the context of an idea. You can turn the Roman numeral for 9 into a 6 by adding only a single line:

IX

Some people put a horizontal line through the center, turn it upside down, and then cover the bottom. This gives you a Roman numeral VI. A more artistic solution might be to put "S" in front of the IX to create "SIX." What we've done here is take the IX out of the context of Roman numerals and put it into the context of "Arabic numerals spelled out in English."

Another right answer might be to add the line "6" after the IX. Then you get IX6, or one times six.

Laboratory Applications

1. Attempt to solve the exercises above. Explain your choices.

2. Create a metaphor for each of these paired concepts:
   a. Boxing + Water.
   b. Magnet + Library.
   c. Rainbow + Clock.

---

3. *Polished presentation.* The presentation must be prepared and rehearsed; it should use great visuals and emotional appeals. A good presentation makes people want to do the campaign.

4. *Structural persuasion.* The presentation should be well structured, since most clients relate well to organized thinking. The opening is all-important because it sets the tone for the entire presentation.

5. *Solve the problem.* Clients have needs, and they frequently report to big shots who ask tough questions about the campaign. Solve the client's problem and you'll sell the big idea—and do it with style.

For clients, recognizing a big idea and evaluating it are almost as difficult as coming with one. (For some examples of big ideas, see the Portfolio Review, "The Creative Directo Greatest Ads.") When the agency presents the concepts, the client is suddenly in the role the Judge, without having gone through the other roles first. David Ogilvy recommend

(continued on page 33

Portfolio Review

:: The Creative Director's Greatest Ads

The creative director always wants to produce the most effective advertising possible in order to give the client the greatest bang for the buck. That means first conceiving a brilliant idea that will both resonate with the particular target audience and relate to the client's marketing and advertising strategy. Then the idea must be executed in a masterful way.

• Study all the striking ads in this portfolio and consider how well they measure up to this definition of greatness. To do this, start by analyzing whether the ad is informational or transformational. Then evaluate and describe the "boom" factor each one uses. Next, see if you can determine from the ad what the company's advertising strategy was and discuss how relevant the ad is to that strategy. Finally, evaluate how well the creative director's staff executed the concept.

As a general merchandise store, Target has many products to feature in its ads. As these two examples make clear, creativity and beauty are not sacrificed when the store focuses attention on its pharmaceuticals.

Source: Target Brands, Inc.

The typeface of an ad doesn't usually do as much of the heavy lifting in attracting attention and persuading as it does in this ad for Billboard.

Source: Billboard Magazine

The somewhat unusual photograph raises a question (why does this woman dress in such an old-fashioned way) that is answered in the headline.

Source: Eurostar

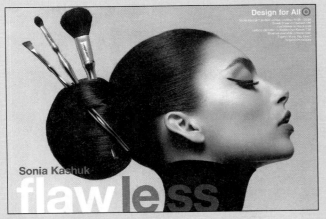

How does Target's use of space, color, font, and design help the ads draw attention and achieve instant recognition (and admiration)?

Source: Target Brands, Inc.

Source: Target Brands, Inc.

This ad for Febreze fabric freshener easily tells us that it can get any odor out of any fabric, including fish and French fries. How does the power of the images in these ads translate into perceptions of the brand benefit for Febreze?

Source: Procter & Gamble

Great ads capitalize on the shared understanding of members of a culture. The power of these images comes from the familiarity that many in the audience have with an iconic Beatles record cover. For those unfamiliar with the cover or the band, the ads hold little meaning.

Sources: Rolling Stone Magazine; Spuk Pictures

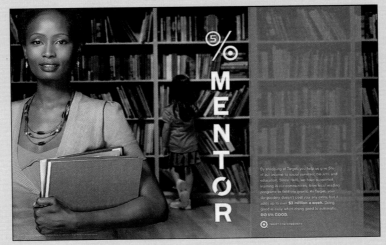

Target aims for a stronger emotional bond with its customers with these beautiful ads.

Source: Target Brands, Inc.

People **BEHIND** the Ads

Tim Piper, Writer/Director for PiRo, former Associate Creative Director, Ogilvy & Mather, Toronto

Courtesy of Tim Piper

After all is said and done, creativity is the fuel that makes the ad agency business run.

So it must please Ogilvy & Mather, Toronto, that it can count among its employees an individual named one of the top 100 creative people in the world by *Time* magazine in 2008, a person named the top art director in the world by *Strategy* magazine, AND someone named the second-best copywriter in the world by *The Big Won,* a database that tracks industry recognition.

And what's really remarkable is that all of this recognition is for the same guy.

Tim Piper, 36, former associate creative director for Ogilvy & Mather, Toronto is currently at work at Piro, an agency that he co-founded. The native-born Australian helped O&M, Toronto, draw rave reviews for creative for several years. And 2007 was an exceptionally good year. Piper served as copywriter and art director for *Evolution,* winner of the 2007 Cannes Grand Prix, the industry's most prestigious award.

Evolution is the commercial for Dove that helped drive home the "Real Beauty" campaign big idea. A pretty but ordinary looking young woman sits in a studio. Using time lapse photography, makeup crews transform the woman into a model-quality beauty. But, since that is still not beautiful enough, her image is then digitally altered to lengthen her neck and sharpen her face lines. The new photo, which hardly resembles the original woman at all anymore, is shown in a final shot as a billboard on the street near a place where young girls walk by. The message is clear: sometimes even the models can't live up to the beauty industry's standards. So why should girls try to?

The campaign resonated with women in a powerful way and started thousands of discussions about beauty and the expectations foisted on girls. It remains an example of how advertising has the potential to surprise and move us.

Of course with success, the big question becomes what next? Piper did not disappoint, as he helped create *Evolution's* successor, *Onslaught. Onslaught* begins with a close-up on the freckled face of a young girl, looking innocently at the camera. We are then treated to a blitz of images of women modeling, dieting, exercising, using beauty products. These early images suggest the power of the beauty industry to compel women to focus on their looks as a standard for happiness. But then the images get worse, and we are treated to brief but emotionally powerful flashes of women enduring plastic surgery, going through drastic weight fluctuations, and finally, demonstrating eating disorder behaviors. The commercial ends with an admonition to "talk to your daughter before the beauty industry does."

That's how you follow up the best ad in the world. With a better one.

Like everyone else, Piper admits he runs into creative blocks. He told *Strategy* that his solution is to "watch a movie, read a book, send an abusive e-mail that could get me fired, that sort of thing."

Piper's career began as a graphic designer, working freelance, in the small town of Adelaide, Australia. When *Strategy* asked him what his first job taught him, he said wryly, "I didn't want to be a freelance graphic designer." He admits that the Grand Prix was his most coveted award, but said that the best feeling he'd ever had about his work was "when my family back in Australia told me they saw it on the news there."

Based on the quality of his work so far, we just have one piece of advice for Tim Piper. Get used to that feeling.

(continued from page 327)

that clients ask themselves five questions: Did it make me gasp when I first saw it? Do I wish I had thought of it myself? Is it unique? Does it fit the strategy to perfection? Could it be used for 30 years?[26]

As Ogilvy pointed out, campaigns that run five years or more are the superstars: Dove soap (33 percent cleansing cream), BMW ("the ultimate driving machine"), the U.S. Army

("Be all you can be"). Some of these campaigns are still running today, and some have run for as long as 30 years. Those are big ideas!

When the client approves the campaign, the creative's role as a Warrior is only half over. Now the campaign has to be executed. That means the Warriors shepherd it through the intricate details of design and production to see that it is completed on time, under budget, and with the highest quality possible. At the same time, the creatives revert to their Artist roles to design, write, and produce the ads.

The next step in the process, therefore, is to implement the big idea, to produce the ads for print and electronic media—the subject of our next two chapters.

Chapter Summary

In the marketing communications process, the creative team is responsible for encoding advertising messages. It is the author of the communications. The creative team typically comprises an art director and a copywriter who report to a creative director.

Their job is to create great advertising for their clients. Great campaigns are characterized by two dimensions: audience impact and strategic relevance. To truly resonate, messages need the boom factor—that element of surprise that instantly attracts the audience's attention, gets them involved, and stirs their imagination. Some campaigns are informational and resonate with the audience by offering relief from some real or perceived problem. Others are transformational and achieve resonance through positive reinforcement by offering some reward.

The second dimension of great campaigns, strategic relevance, is behind the visuals and the text of every message. In fact, strategy is the key to great creative work.

Typically written by the account management team, the creative strategy includes four elements: the target audience, the product concept, the communications media, and the message. Once the general parameters of the plan are developed, the account managers prepare a creative brief that outlines the key strategic decisions. The creative brief should contain at least three elements: an objective statement, a support statement, and either a tone statement or a brand character statement. The brief gives strategic guidance to the art director and copywriter, but it is their responsibility to develop a message strategy that lays out the specifics of how the message will be executed. The three elements of message strategy are copy, art, and production.

Copy is the verbal and art is the nonverbal (visual) presentation of the message strategy. Production refers to the mechanical details of how the promotional messages will be produced.

To create means to originate, and creativity involves combining two or more previously unconnected elements, objects, or ideas to make something

new. Creativity helps to inform, persuade, and remind customers and prospects by making the campaign more vivid. All people have creativity; they just differ in degree.

Scholars believe certain styles of thinking are more conducive to creativity than others. The two basic thinking styles are fact-based and value-based. People who prefer the fact-based style tend to be linear thinkers, analytical, and rational. Value-based thinkers tend to be less structured, more intuitive, and more willing to use their imagination. They are good at synthesizing diverse viewpoints to arrive at a new one. And, with their ability to think metaphorically, they tend to be more creative.

In one model of the creative process, the creative person must play four roles along the way to acceptance of a new idea: the Explorer, Artist, Judge, and Warrior. The Explorer searches for new information, paying attention to unusual patterns. The Artist experiments with a variety of approaches looking for the big idea. The Artist also determines how to implement it. For this, the creative pyramid may help. The pyramid models the formation of an ad after the way people learn new information, using five steps: attention, interest, credibility, desire, and action.

The Judge evaluates the results of experimentation and decides which approach is most practical. The Warrior overcomes excuses, idea killers, setbacks, and obstacles to bring a creative concept to realization. Each role has unique characteristics, and there are many techniques for improving performance in each role. During the creative process, it's better to use a value-based style of thinking. During the Judge and Warrior phases, a fact-based style is more effective.

One of the worst blocks to creativity is getting stuck in the wrong mindset, the wrong style of thinking, for the task at hand. However, there are numerous techniques for escaping these mental blocks.

Important Terms

art, *321*

art direction, *321*

art director, *306*

Artist, *317*

big idea, *317*

brainstorming, *317*

communications media, *308*

conceptualization, *317*

copywriter, *306*

creative brief, *309*

creative director, *306*

creative process, *316*

creative pyramid, *321*

creatives, *306*

creativity, *311*

emotional appeal, *309*

Explorer, *316*

fact-based thinking, *315*

IMC message, *309*

informational, *308*

Judge, *326*

mandatories, *310*

message strategy (rationale), *310*

nonverbal, *310*

product concept, *308*

rational appeal, *309*

target audience, *308*

technical, *310*

transformational, *308*

value-based thinking, *315*

verbal, *310*

visualization, *317*

Warrior, *326*

Review Questions

1. Select an ad from an earlier chapter in the book. What do you believe is the sponsor's advertising and message strategy? What is the ad's boom factor?

2. What are the most important elements of a creative brief?

3. What are the elements of message strategy and how does it differ from advertising (or creative) strategy?

4. In what ways have you exercised your personal creativity in the last week?

5. What qualities characterize the two main styles of thinking? Which style do you usually prefer? Why?

6. What are the four roles of the creative process? Have you played those roles in preparing a term paper? How?

7. What is the difference between a strategy statement and a big idea?

8. Select five creative ads from a magazine. What techniques of the Artist can you recognize in those ads?

9. In those same ads, can you identify each step of the creative pyramid?

10. What are the important things to remember about making a presentation?

The Advertising Experience

1. **Impact of Color**

   Different colors create subtle differences in the impression an image makes. Find a black-and-white print advertisement. Recreate it in color three times, each time using different color combinations. Ask different audiences (such as your classmates, your friends, or your family) for their impressions of each color scheme. Write an analysis of the results for each, explaining how the colors enhance or diminish the ad's message.

2. **Effective Creative Strategy and Execution**

   Apply the creative process and the various means of deriving and judging "good" advertising to the following Websites, noting the quality of the creative and the strategic intent behind the work. Be sure to answer the questions below.

   ■ adidas: www.adidas.com

   ■ Energizer: www.energizer.com

   ■ Xbox: www.xbox.com

   ■ Nissan: www.nissan-usa.com

   ■ AT&T: www.att.com

   ■ Sea World: www.seaworld.com

   ■ Taco Bell: www.tacobell.com

   a. Who is the intended audience of the site?

   b. What is it that makes the site's creativity good or bad? Why?

   c. Identify the "who, why, what, when, where, style, approach, and tone" of the communication.

   d. Write an objective statement, support statement, and brand character statement for each.

3. **Account Planning**

   Account planners help ensure that the research process has reaped the proper information for the creatives. The importance of account planning—namely the gathering of research and the formulation of strategy for the creative team—cannot be understated. The Account Planning Group (APG) is an organization that brings together 700 account planners and communications strategists. Browse through the documents held on the APG Website (www.apg.org.uk) and answer the questions that follow.

a. Who is the intended audience of the site?

b. What is account planning? Why is it important?

c. What is the primary document that the account planning function generates? What are the main elements in the document?

d. Choose an essay or article on any of the APG sites and discuss at length, explaining the relevance of the topic to account planning and the advertising business.

4. **How Strategy dictates execution**
Target's value-based advertising tends to take a humorous and unexpected approach to communicating its message to the reader. But Target also uses "hard-sell" ads in newspaper inserts. Why?

CHAPTER

Creative Execution: Art and Copy

Learning Objectives

To present the role of art and copy—the nonverbal and verbal elements of message strategy—in print, radio, television, and on the web. Artists and copywriters include a variety of specialists who follow specific procedures for conceptualizing, designing, writing, and producing IMC messages. To be successful, creatives must be conversant with the copywriting and commercial art terms and formats used in the business. They must also develop an aesthetic sensitivity so they can recognize, create, evaluate, or recommend quality work.

 After studying this chapter, you will be able to:

LO11-1 Describe the key principles involved in designing print layouts.

LO11-2 Explain how to create great copy in print.

LO11-3 Identify the important aspects of writing for radio and TV.

LO11-4 Review ways to develop great spots in radio and TV.

LO11-5 Suggest ways to write effectively for Websites and social media.

LO11-6 List the challenges involved in creating messages for international markets.

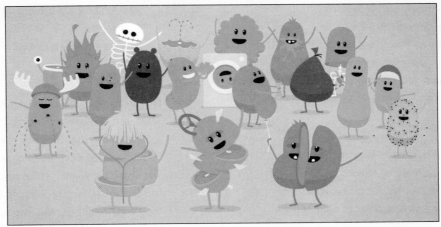

Source: Metro Trains Melbourne

What seems like the easiest persuasion goals are actually the hardest. For example, how hard should it be to persuade people to not do things that may injure them, ruin their health, or even get them killed? ■ Nothing has been more frustrating in the history of PSAs than the failure of message campaigns to get people to quit smoking, not use drugs, not drink too much, not have unprotected sex, etc. ■ There are a host of reasons why campaigns to stop risky behaviors fail. For one, many focus on convincing people they are taking risks, even though their target audience already knows that. Smokers, for example, know perfectly well that smoking is dangerous. They do it anyway. Second, people don't like to be preached at or told what to do. ■ These realities were understood by McCann's Melbourne, Australia office when the Metro Trains network asked them to develop a campaign that would reduce fatal accidents around trains. What behaviors, you may ask, can result in a fatal accident around a train? Running across the tracks to an opposite platform. Walking along tracks. Standing too close to the edge of a platform. Even racing around a lowered gate at a crossing. ■ Why would people do these things? One reason could be ignorance, but it's also possible that certain individuals see risky behaviors around trains as heroic or as showing a devil may care attitude. For example, one news article reported on a gang of teens engaging in an initiation rite by standing on subway tracks until the last possible moment.[1] ■ Given all of that, what would you advise an agency to do to reduce accidents around trains? Messages that scare or frighten people could actually incentivize those who take risks around trains. And messages that preach tend to turn everyone off. ■ This is exactly the kind of creative challenge that a great agency embraces. And McCann's proved it was up for the challenge. The agency concluded a reframing was in order. They decided to show that dying by crossing rails when a train is coming isn't heroic. It's just dumb. To make their point, they developed a campaign named by *Advertising Age* one of the best campaigns of the 21st century, "Dumb Ways to Die." ■ The hook is simple: show cartoon characters taking risks that others would not judge as just foolhardy, but as absurdly stupid. Use soft, almost child-like music and amusing, funny colors and movements to keep viewers watching. You can watch the video here:

https://www.youtube.com/watch?v=IJNR2EpS0jw.
"Dumb Ways To Die"
(from public service announcement campaign by Metro Trains)
Set fire to your hair
Poke a stick at a grizzly bear
Eat medicine that's out of date
Use your private parts as piranha bait

[Refrain:]

Dumb ways to die
So many dumb ways to die

Dumb ways to di-ie-ie
So many dumb ways to die
Get your toast out with a fork
Do your own electrical work
Teach yourself how to fly
Eat a two-week-old un-refrigerated pie

[Refrain]

Invite a psycho-killer inside
Scratch a drug dealer's brand new ride
Take your helmet off in outer space
Use a clothes dryer as a hiding place

[Refrain]

Keep a rattlesnake as a pet
Sell both your kidneys on the Internet
Eat a tube of superglue
I wonder, what's this red button do?

[Refrain]

Dress up like a moose during hunting season
Disturb a nest of wasps for no good reason
Stand on the edge of a train station platform
Drive around the boom gates at a level crossing
Run across the tracks between the platforms

They may not rhyme but they're quite possibly
The dumbest ways to die
The dumbest ways to die

The dumbest ways to di-ie-ie-ie
So many dumb
So many dumb ways to die

Be safe around trains . . . a message from Metro

■ The campaign has been enormously successful as measured by views and attracting attention. Intended as a viral spot, the three-minute video had attracted 50 million views on YouTube by the end of 2013.[2] ■ It was also a big winner at Cannes, perhaps the advertising top festival. In fact, by winning five awards, Dumb Ways to Die (DWTD) became the most successful campaign in Cannes history.[3] ■ Whether the campaign has reduced preventable accidents and deaths is a matter of some dispute. The client, Metro Trains, claimed a 21 percent decrease.[4] But that claim has been challenged, including by judges at Australia's Effie Awards.[5] The Effies, unlike awards at Cannes, require evidence of advertising effectiveness. The debate over the final impact of the campaign on train deaths may not be resolved anytime soon. But there is no debate about the reach, influence, or success of the spots to raise awareness about dangerous behaviors around trains. ■ McCann's success calls to mind the words of Bill Bernbach, perhaps the greatest creative mind in the history of advertising, once said, "You can say the right thing about a product and nobody will listen. You've got to say it in such a way that people will feel it in their gut. Because if they don't feel it, nothing will happen."

As "Dumb Ways to Die" shows, what's shown is just as important as what's said. The nonverbal aspect of a message carries at least half the burden of communication. It helps position the product and create personality for the brand. It creates a mood, determining the way a campaign *feels* to the audience. That mood flavors the verbal message, embodied in the *copy*.

In this chapter, we discuss how creative concepts are executed from the standpoints of both art and copy. We examine the visual and the verbal details, first of print and then of electronic and digital media. Campaigns must inform (see My IMC Campaign 11-A), but they should do so in a clear, attractive, and engaging way. Design is about making that happen. More so than others, this chapter focuses on planned messages, like advertising, since marketers and agencies have the greatest control over their look and content. Design is a less important consideration in sites that compel certain layouts (such as Facebook or other social media), and it is least important in many kinds of public relations activities, especially publicity.

Designing Print Layouts

LO 11-1

The term **design** refers to how the art director and graphic artist (or graphic designer) choose and structure the artistic elements of an ad. A designer sets a *style*—the manner in which a thought or image is expressed—by choosing particular artistic elements and blending them in a unique way.

In general, clean lines, formally composed photographs, and sparse copy give an ad the breathing room it needs to draw the reader's eye from one element to the next.

A number of designers, working under the art director, may produce initial layouts of the ad concept. In collaboration with copywriters, these artists draw on their expertise in graphic design (including photography, typography, and illustration) to create the most effective ad, brochure, or Website.

The Use of Layouts

A **layout** is an overall orderly arrangement of all the format elements of an ad: visual(s), headline, subheads, body copy, slogan, seal, logo, and signature. The layout serves several purposes. First, it helps both the agency and the client develop and evaluate, in advance, how the ad will look and feel. It gives the client (usually not an artist) a tangible item to correct, change, comment on, and approve.

Second, the layout helps the creative team develop the message's psychological elements: the nonverbal and symbolic components. Sophisticated marketers want their messages to create personality for the product—image, if you will—and to build the brand's (and the company's) equity with the consumer. To do this, the "look" of the message needs to elicit an image or mood that reflects and enhances both the marketer and the product.

Therefore, when designing the initial layout, the creative team must be very sensitive to the desired image of the product or business. In the ads shown above and below for "Dumb Ways to Die," the layouts reiforce the campaign's big idea., which is that there is nothing heroic about taking risks around trains. In addition, the childish figures, colors, and spacing, soften a message about a serious thing and add humor to what might otherwise might be distressing. As you look over the ads, how do you think this was accomplished?

Third, once the best design is chosen, the layout serves as a blueprint. It shows the size and placement of each element in the ad. Once the production manager knows the dimensions of the ad, the number of photos, the amount of typesetting, and the use of art elements such as color and illustrations, he or she can determine the cost of producing the ad (see Ad Lab 11–A, "The Role of the Artist").

Design and Production: The Creative and Approval Process

The design process is both a creative and an approval process. In the creative phase, the designer uses thumbnails, roughs, dummies, and comprehensives—in other words, *nonfinal art*—to establish the message's look and feel. Then in the *prepress* (or *production art*) phase, the artist prepares a mechanical: the final artwork with the actual type in place along with all the visuals the printer or the media will need to reproduce the ad. In Chapter 12 we'll see how this design process works to produce a finished ad.

These two ads from McCann's campaign Dumb Ways to Die use the nonverbal element and symbolic components successfully. The campaign also included lots of social media, a YouTube video that attracted tens of millions of visits, and even a game available at the Google Play and iTunes app stores.

Source: Metro Trains Melbourne

My IMC Campaign 11–A

Product Facts for Creatives

Art directors and copywriters must have a thorough understanding of the brand to create advertising that resonates. Make sure your creatives have the information that will help them write copy that sizzles and create layouts that stop consumers dead in their tracks.

- **Proprietary information**
  Product's trade name
  Trademark
  Product symbol
  Other copyrighted or patented information

- **History**
  When was the product created or invented?
  Who introduced it?
  Has it had other names?
  Have there been product changes?
  Is there any "romance" to it?

- **Research**
  Are research results available?
  What research about the product does the supplier have?
  Which research will be most useful for each medium?

- **Life cycle**
  What is the product's life or use span?
  What stage is it in now and what style of copy should be used for that stage?
  What stages are competitors in?

- **Market position**
  What is the product's share of the total market?
  Does its market share suggest a positioning strategy?
  What position does the company wish to occupy?

- **Competitive information**
  Who are the product's competitors?
  Does the product have any advantages over them?
  Does it have any disadvantages?
  Are they all about the same?
  Do rival products present problems that this one solves?

- **Product image**
  How do people view the product?
  What do they like about it?
  What do they dislike about it?
  Is it a luxury?
  Is it a necessity?
  Is it a habit?
  Is it self-indulgent?
  Do people have to have it but wish they didn't?

- **Customer use**
  How is the product used?
  Are there other possible uses?
  How frequently is it bought?
  What type of person uses the product?
  Why is the product bought?
  Personal use

The approval process takes place at each step along the way. At any point in the design and production process, the ad—or the ad concept—may be altered or even canceled.

Thumbnail Sketches

The thumbnail sketch, or **thumbnail,** is a small rough, rapidly produced drawing that the artist uses to visualize layout approaches without wasting time on details. Thumbnails are very basic. Blocks of straight or squiggly lines indicate text placement, and boxes show placement of visuals. The best sketches are then developed further.

Rough Layout

In a rough, the artist draws to the actual size of the ad or Website. Headlines and subheads suggest the final type style, illustrations and photos are sketched in, and body copy is simulated with lines. The agency may present roughs to clients, particularly cost-conscious ones, for approval.

Gift

Work

What type of person uses the product most (heavy user)?

How much does the heavy user buy?

Where do the best customers live?

- **Performance**

What does the product do?

What might it be expected to do that it does not?

How does it work?

How is it made or produced?

What's in it?

Raw materials

Special ingredients

Preservatives

Chemicals

Nutrients

- **What are its physical characteristics?**

Smell

Appearance

Color

Texture

Taste

Others

- **Effectiveness**

Is there proof the product has been tested and works well?

Do any government or other regulations need to be mentioned or observed?

How does it work compared to its competitors?

- **Manufacturing**

How is the product made?

How long does it take?

How many steps are in the process?

How many people are involved in making it?

Are any special machines used?

Where is it made?

- **Distribution**

How widely is the product distributed?

Are there exclusive sellers?

Is there a ready supply or a limited amount?

Is it available for a short season?

What channels of distribution must be reached?

- **Packaging**

Unit size or sizes offered.

Package shape

Package design

Styling

Color

Special protection for product

A carrier for product

Package label

Comprehensive

The **comprehensive layout,** or **comp,** is a highly refined facsimile of the finished ad. A comp is generally quite elaborate, with colored photos, the final type styles and sizes, subvisuals, and a glossy spray coat. Copy for the comp is typeset on a computer and positioned with the visuals, and then printed as a full-color proof. At this stage, all visuals should be final.

Dummy

A dummy presents the handheld look and feel of brochures, multipage materials, or point-of-purchase displays. The artist assembles the dummy by hand, using color markers and computer proofs, mounting them on sturdy paper, and then cutting and folding them to size. A dummy for a brochure, for example, is put together, page by page, to look exactly like the finished product.

AD Lab 11-A

The Role of the Artist

All the people employed in commercial art are called artists, but they may perform entirely different tasks. Some can't even draw well; instead, they're trained for different artistic specialties.

Art Directors

Art directors are responsible for the visual presentation of the ad. Along with a copywriter, they develop the initial concept. They may do initial sketches or layouts, but after that they may not touch the ad again. Their primary responsibility is to supervise the ad's progress to completion.

The best art directors are good at presenting ideas in both words and pictures. They are usually experienced graphic designers with a good understanding of consumers. They may have a large or small staff, depending on the organization. Or they may be freelancers (independent contractors) and do more of the work themselves.

Web Designers

Website designers help plan and compose the layouts and content for Websites. Web designers are able to compose pages using HTML, CSS, and other languages that can be read by web browsers. Designers also use software, such as Adobe Dreamweaver, to create sites.

Compared to other creatives, web designers have two unique challenges. First, their messages must be effective across a variety of different viewing platforms. While a print ad will appear in only one execution, a Website will be seen in a variety of browsers, each of which may handle code differently. In addition, many people view web pages on mobile devices such as phones and tablets. The second challenge for designers is that sites are not a single page, but a collection of different, linked pages. Conceptualizing the structure of this collection is an important design consideration.

Graphic Designers

Graphic designers are precision specialists preoccupied with shape and form. In advertising they arrange the various graphic elements (type, illustrations, photos, white space) in the most attractive and effective way possible. While they may work on ads, they usually design and produce collateral materials, such as posters, brochures, and annual reports.

In an agency, the art director often acts as the designer. Sometimes, however, a separate designer is used to offer a unique touch to a particular ad.

Illustrators

Illustrators paint or draw the visuals in an ad. They frequently specialize in creating visuals for products such as automotive, fashion, or furniture. Very few agencies or advertisers retain full-time illustrators; most advertising illustrators freelance. Typically, agencies hire different illustrators for different jobs, depending on an ad's particular needs, look, and feel.

Photographers

Like the illustrator, the advertising photographer creates a nonverbal expression that reinforces the verbal message. Photographers use the tools of photography—cameras, lenses, and lights—to create images. They select interesting angles, arrange subjects in new ways, carefully control the lighting, and use many other techniques to enhance the subject's image quality. A studio photographer uses high-powered lights to photograph products in front of a background or as part of an arranged setting. A location photographer generally shoots in real-life settings such as those in the Timberland ads. Many photographers specialize—in cars, celebrities, fashion, food, equipment, or architecture. Agencies and advertisers rarely employ staff photographers. They generally hire freelancers by the hour or pay a fee for the assignment. Photographers also sell stock photography, which are photos on file from prior shootings.

Production Artists

Production artists assemble the various elements of an ad and mechanically put them together the way the art director or designer indicates. Good production artists are fast, precise, and knowledgeable about the whole production process. Production artists use a variety of software programs for pagemaking, drawing, painting, and photo scanning. Most designers and art directors start their careers as production artists and work their way up. It's very difficult work, but it is also very important, for this is where an ad actually comes together in its finished form.

Laboratory Applications

1. Select an ad in the Chapter 10 Portfolio Review (pp. 326–329). Explain which advertising artists were probably involved in its creation and what the responsibility of each artist was.

2. Which ad in the Chapter 10 Portfolio Review do you think needed the fewest artists? How many?

Mechanical (Pasteup)

The type and visuals must be placed in their exact position for reproduction by a printer. Most designers do this work on the computer, completely bypassing the need for a mechanical. Some advertisers, however, still make traditional **mechanicals,** where black type and line art are pasted in place on a piece of white artboard (called a **pasteup**) with overlay sheets indicating the hue and positioning of color. Printers refer to the mechanical or pasteup as **camera-ready art** because they photograph it using a large production camera before starting the reproduction process—creating color keys, prints, and films of the finished ad.

At any time during the design process—until the printing press lays ink on paper—changes can be made on the art. However, the expense may grow ten-fold with each step from roughs to mechanicals to printing.

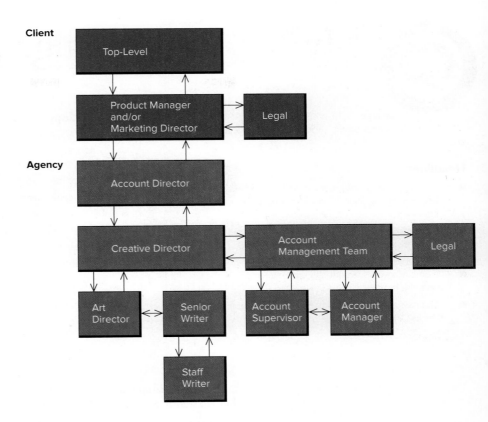

Approval

The work of the copywriter and art director is always subject to approval. The larger the agency and the larger the client, the more formidable this process becomes (see Exhibit 11-1). A new ad concept is first approved by the agency's creative director. Then the account management team reviews it. Next, the client's product managers and marketing staff review it, often changing a word or two or sometimes rejecting the whole approach. Both the agency's and client's legal departments scrutinize the copy and art for potential problems. Finally, the company's top executives review the final concept and text.

The biggest challenge in approval is keeping approvers from corrupting the style of the ad. The creative team works hard to achieve a cohesive style. Then a group of nonwriters and nonartists has the opportunity to change it all. Maintaining artistic purity is extremely difficult and requires patience, flexibility, maturity, and the ability to articulate an important point of view and explain why artistic choices were made. Bringing decision makers great copy right from the start is a good way to build credibility and smooth the approval process. For tips on writing great copy and headlines, see some suggestions from one of the best, George Felton, in My IMC Campaign 11-B.

Creating Effective Layouts: Tools and Formats

By using graphics or imaging software, today's graphic artist or designer can do much of the work previously performed by staff artists. On the screen, the artist can see an entire page layout, complete with illustrations and photos, and easily alter any of them in a few minutes. Before computers, designing layouts could take days, and final art was not so detailed or complete as designs created on the computer.

Small Windows- and Mac-based systems are ideal for computer design, and sophisticated graphics software is now available for page layouts *(InDesign),* painting and drawing *(Adobe Illustrator),* image manipulation *(Adobe Photoshop),* and web design *(Adobe Dreamweaver and Flash).*[6] Their moderate cost makes such software accessible to freelancers, small businesses, and agency creative departments. Today's graphic artist, illustrator, and retoucher, in addition to having a thorough knowledge of aesthetics, must be skilled in the use of design software.

My IMC Campaign 11–B

Creating Great Headlines and Copy

George Felton, in his book *Advertising Concept and Copy*, offers the following suggestions for aspiring copywriters:

Headlines

- "Achieve synergy, not redundancy." The headlines and artwork should work together to create an idea, but not be completely redundant.

- "Let the consumer do some of the work." Avoid ads that insult the audience's intelligence (a philosophy articulated by Bill Bernbach. (See "People behind the Ads" in Chapter 2.)

- "Combine overstatement and understatement." If the visual is BIG, make the headline small. And vice versa.

- "Emphasize one idea per ad." If you have several ideas, show how they are linked to make them one.

Art and Copy

Freelance copywriter John Kuraoka offers some excellent advice for new copywriters at www.kuraoka.com/.
Here are summaries of his recommendations for art and copy:

- Capture the reader's attention.
- Clarify copy claims.
- Let the reader know the ad is directed at him or her.
- Show the product in use.
- Offer evidence for copy claims.
- Emphasize the product's unique features or benefits.
- Unify the different ads in the campaign.

Promotional appeals are designed to attract consumers, but they have a lot of competition. Indeed, studies show that the average American sees 3,000 ads each day. At the same time, a majority of consumers, about 53 percent, believe that "most marketing is a bunch of B.S."[7] Studies also show virtually no relationship between how much the marketer spends and how well the ad is recalled. But the quality of the message's appearance is important. Good design not only commands attention but holds it. Good design also communicates as much information as possible in the shortest amount of time and makes the message easier to understand.[8]

Creatives use many different types of layouts (see Portfolio Review, "The Art Director's Guide to Layout Styles," later in this chapter). Traditionally, the ads that score the highest recall employ a standard, **poster-style format** (also called a **picture-window layout** and **Ayer No. 1** in the trade) with a single, dominant visual that occupies 60 to 70 percent of the ad's total area.[9] Next in ranking are ads that have one large picture and two smaller ones. The visuals are intended to stop the reader and arouse interest, so their content must be interesting.

As we discuss in the next section, headlines should stop the reader and contribute to the memorability of the ad's key points.[10] As a design element, the total headline area should normally fill only 10 to 15 percent of the ad, so the type need not be particularly large. Headlines may appear above or below the visual, depending on the situation. As Altstiel and Grow note, the effectiveness of a headline ultimately relates to how well it works within its context.[11]

Research also shows that readership drops considerably if ads have more than 50 words. So to attract a large number of readers, copy blocks should be kept to less than 20 percent of the ad. However, with many high-involvement products, the more you tell, the more you sell. If selling is the objective, then informative body copy becomes important. And long copy works when it's appropriate—when the advertiser is more interested in *quality* of readership than *quantity*.[12]

Finally, most people who read ads want to know who placed the ad. Company signatures or logos need not be large or occupy more than 5 to 10 percent of the area. For best results, they should be placed in the lower right-hand corner or across the bottom of the ad.

Advertising author Roy Paul Nelson points out that the principles of design are to the layout artist what the rules of grammar are to the writer. The basic rules include the following:

- The design must be in *balance*.
- The space within the ad should be broken up into pleasing *proportions*.
- A directional pattern should be evident so the reader knows in what *sequence* to read.

My IMC Campaign 11–C

Design Principles

Make sure your layout follows these rules of thumb for creating attractive, informative ads.

Balance

The optical center is the reference point that determines the layout's balance. The optical center is about one-eighth of a page above the physical center of the page. Balance is achieved through the arrangement of elements on the page—the left side of the optical center versus the right, above the optical center versus below.

_____ **Formal balance.** Perfect symmetry is the key to formal balance: matched elements on either side of a line dissecting the ad have equal optical weight. This technique strikes a dignified, stable, conservative image.

_____ **Informal balance.** A visually balanced ad has elements of different size, shape, color intensity, or darkness at different distances from the optical center. Like a teeter-totter, an object of greater optical weight near the center can be balanced by an object of less weight farther from the center. Many ads use informal balance to make the ad more interesting, imaginative, and exciting.

Movement

Movement is the principle of design that causes the audience to read the material in the desired sequence. It can be achieved through a variety of techniques.

_____ People or animals can be positioned so that their eyes direct the reader's eyes to the next important element.

_____ Devices such as pointing fingers, boxes, lines, or arrows (or moving the actors or the camera or changing scenes) direct attention from element to element.

_____ Design can take advantage of readers' natural tendency to start at the top left corner of the page and proceed in a Z motion to the lower right.

_____ Comic-strip sequence and pictures with captions force the reader to start at the beginning and follow the sequence in order to grasp the message.

_____ Use of white space and color emphasizes a body of type or an illustration. Eyes will go from a dark element to a light one, or from color to noncolor.

_____ Size itself attracts attention because readers are drawn to the biggest and most dominant element on the page, then to smaller elements.

Proportion

_____ Elements should be accorded space based on their importance to the entire ad. Attention-getting elements are usually given more space. Avoid the monotony of giving equal amounts of space to each element.

White Space (Isolation)

_____ White space is the part of the ad not occupied by other elements (note that white space may be some color other than white). White space helps focus attention on an isolated element—it makes the copy appear to be in a spotlight. White space is an important contributor to the ad's overall image.

Contrast

_____ An effective way of drawing attention to a particular element is to use contrast in color, size, or style; for example, a reverse ad (white letters against a dark background) or a black-and-white ad with a red border.

Clarity and Simplicity

_____ Any elements that can be eliminated without damaging the overall effect should be cut. Too many type styles; type that is too small; too many reverses, illustrations, or boxed items; and unnecessary copy make for an overly complex layout and an ad that is hard to read.

Unity

_____ Unity means that an ad's many different elements must relate to one another in such a way that the ad gives a singular, harmonious impression. Balance, movement, proportion, contrast, and color may all contribute to unity of design. Many other techniques can be used: type styles from the same family, borders around ads to hold elements together, overlapping one picture or element on another, judicious use of white space, graphic tools such as boxes, arrows, or tints.

Continuity

_____ Continuity is the relationship of one ad to the rest of the campaign. This is achieved by using the same design format, style, and tone; the same spokesperson; or the same graphic element, logo, cartoon character, or catchy slogan.

- Some force should hold the ad together and give it _unity_.
- One element, or one part of the ad, should have enough _emphasis_ to dominate all others.[13]

For more on the basic principles of advertising design (balance, proportion, sequence, unity, and emphasis), see My IMC Campaign 11-C, "Design Principles."

The Use of Visuals in Print

The artists who paint, sketch, and draw in advertising are called **illustrators.** The artists who produce pictures with a camera are **photographers.** Together they are responsible for the **visuals,** or pictures, we see in IMC.

Purpose of the Visual

When confronted with a print ad, most prospects spot the picture first, then read the headline, and then peruse the body copy, in that order. Since the visual carries so much responsibility for an ad's success, it should be designed with several goals in mind. Some of the most obvious follow:

- Capture the reader's attention.
- Clarify claims made by the copy.
- Identify the subject.
- Show the product actually being used.
- Qualify readers by stopping those who are legitimate prospects.
- Help convince the reader of the truth of copy claims.
- Arouse the reader's interest in the headline.
- Emphasize the product's unique features.
- Create a favorable impression of the product or advertiser.
- Provide continuity for the campaign by using a unified visual technique.

Determining the Chief Focus for Visuals

The visuals capture a mood and create a feeling, a context for the consumer's perception of the product.

Selecting the focus for visuals is a major step in the creative process. It often determines how well the big idea is executed. Print promotions use many standard subjects for ad visuals, including

1. *The package containing the product.* Especially important for packaged goods, it helps the consumer identify the product on the grocery shelf.
2. *The product alone.* This usually does not work well for nonpackaged goods.
3. *The product in use.* Cosmetic ads usually show the product in use with a close-up photo of a beautiful woman or a virile man.
4. *How to use the product.* Recipe ads featuring a new way to use food products have historically pulled very high readership scores.
5. *Product features.* Automobile ads frequently show the technologies used in the car that help distinguish it from competitors.
6. *Comparison of products.* The marketer shows its product next to a competitor's and compares important features.
7. *User benefit.* It's often difficult to illustrate intangible user benefits. However, marketers know that the best way to get customers' attention is to show how the product will benefit them, so it's worth the extra creative effort.
8. *Humor.* If used well, a humorous visual can make an entertaining and lasting impression. But it can also destroy credibility if used inappropriately.
9. *Testimonial.* Before-and-after endorsements are very effective for weight-loss products, skin-care lotions, and bodybuilding courses.
10. *Negative appeal.* Sometimes visuals point out what happens if you don't use the product. If done well, that can spark interest.

Selecting the Visual

The kind of picture used is often determined during the conceptualization process. But frequently the visual is not determined until the art director or designer actually lays out the ad.

Strong visuals coupled with really big ideas can often break out of the confines of a campaign and enter the broader culture. The Dumb Ways To Die effort achieved that recognition when parodies began appearing. In this example, a Russian programmer created a "Dumb Ways to Die: Game of Thrones Edition." The strong visuals in the campaign have also led to a line of toys featuring the Dumb Ways to Die characters.

Source: Metro Trains Melbourne

Selecting an appropriate photo or visual is a difficult creative task. Art directors deal with several basic issues. For example, not every ad needs a visual to communicate effectively. Some all-type ads are quite compelling. If the art director determines that a visual is required, how many should there be: one, two, or more? Should the visual be black-and-white or color? These may be budgetary decisions.

The art director must then decide the subject of the picture. Should it be one of the standard subjects listed earlier? Or something else altogether? And how relevant is that subject to the advertiser's creative strategy? The art director also has to decide how the visual should be created. Should it be a hand-rendered illustration? A photograph? What about a computer-generated illustration?

Finally, the art director has to know what technical and/or budgetary issues must be considered. With so many options, selecting visuals is obviously no simple task. In Chapter 14, we'll see how all these decisions come together in the process of producing the final ad.

This ad for Wonderbra swimwear appeals to its audience both visually and with the headline. By using the visual of a fish and a turtle with "ogling" eyes, it doesn't take itself too seriously—ads that use humor are more likely to be remembered.

Source: Wonderbra

(continued on page 351)

:: The Art Director's Guide to Layout Styles

Art directors use many different types of layouts. Creating an ad for the fictitious Imperial Cruise Lines, Tom Michael, the president and creative director of Market Design (Encinitas, CA), first prepared several thumbnail sketches using a variety of different layout styles and headlines to see which ideas would work best.

Note how the copy in each ad is indicated by lines of recurring gibberish. The computer programs art directors use frequently offer an option to represent layout text with such incoherent ramblings, referred to in the business as "greek."

• Study the different layouts and discuss the advantages and disadvantages of each. Which approach would you recommend for Imperial Cruise Lines? Why? What additional layout or copy ideas can you come up with?

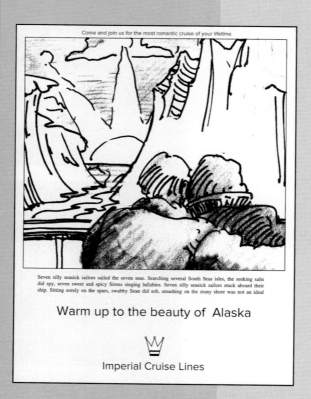

Picture-window layout—"Warm up to the beauty of Alaska." Also called a *poster-style layout*, note how the single, large visual occupies about two-thirds of the ad. The headline and copy may appear above or below the "window."

Source: Tom Michael, Market Design, Encinitas, CA

Mondrian grid layout—"Alaska: The last frontier for family fun." Named after Dutch painter Piet Mondrian, the Mondrian layout uses a series of vertical and horizontal lines, rectangles, and squares within a predetermined grid to give geometric proportion to the ad.

Source: Tom Michael, Market Design, Encinitas, CA

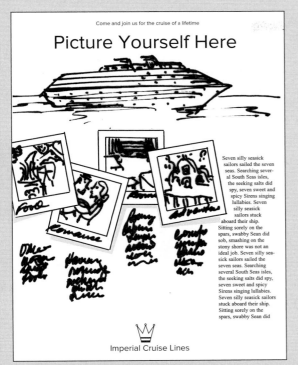

Circus layout—"Picture Yourself Here." Filled with multiple illustrations, oversize type, reverse blocks, tilts, or other gimmicks to bring the ad alive and make it interesting.

Source: Tom Michael, Market Design, Encinitas, CA

Frame layout—"Guaranteed to disrupt your biological clock." The copy is surrounded by the visual. Or, in some cases, the visual may be surrounded by the copy.

Source: Tom Michael, Market Design, Encinitas, CA

Copy-heavy layout—"Get rocked to sleep on our waterbed." When you have a lot to say and visuals won't say it, use text. But be sure the headlines and subheads make it interesting. In this case, the heavy copy actually frames the headline and visual to add visual interest. However, the headline might just as well have run above or below the copy.

Source: Tom Michael, Market Design, Encinitas, CA

Open all night. Loitering encouraged.

Seven silly seasick sailors sailed the seven seas. Searching several South Seas isles, the seeking salts did spy, seven sweet and spicy Sirens singing lullabies. Seven silly seasick sailors stuck aboard their ship. Sitting sorely on the spars, swabby Sean did sob, smashing on the stony shore was not an ideal job. Seven silly

seasick sailors sailed the seven seas. Searching several South Seas isles, the seeking salts did spy, seven sweet and spicy Sirens singing lullabies. Seven silly seasick sailors stuck aboard their ship. Sitting sorely on the spars, swabby Sean did sob, smashing on the stony shore was not an ideal job. Seven silly seasick sailors sailed the

♛ Imperial Cruise Lines

Montage layout—"Open all night. Loitering encouraged." Similar to the circus layout, the montage brings multiple illustrations together and arranges them by superimposing or overlapping to make a single composition.

Source: Tom Michael, Market Design, Encinitas, CA

Combo layout—"Warm up to Alaska." Creativity often involves combining two or more unrelated elements to make a new element. The same is true in design. To make an ad more interesting or contemporary, the art director may combine two or more layout types to make a combo layout. This ad, for instance, starts out with a grid layout, but in the center of the grid note how the copy surrounds the headline and logo as in a frame layout.

Source: Tom Michael, Market Design, Encinitas, CA

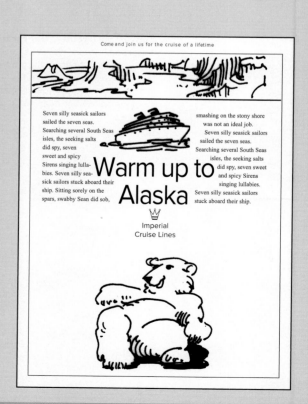

Come and join us for the cruise of a lifetime

Seven silly seasick sailors sailed the seven seas. Searching several South Seas isles, the seeking salts did spy, seven sweet and spicy Sirens singing lullabies. Seven silly seasick sailors stuck aboard their ship. Sitting sorely on the spars, swabby Sean did sob,

smashing on the stony shore was not an ideal job. Seven silly seasick sailors sailed the seven seas. Searching several South Seas isles, the seeking salts did spy, seven sweet and spicy Sirens singing lullabies. Seven silly seasick sailors stuck aboard their ship.

Warm up to Alaska

♛ Imperial Cruise Lines

Creating Great Copy in Print

LO 11-2

Headlines

(continued from page 347)

Now that you understand the objectives and format elements of good design, let's examine some basic copywriting formats to see how art and copy are linked.

In print, the key layout elements are the *visual(s), headlines, subheads, body copy, slogans, seals, logos,* and *signatures.* As Exhibit 11-2 shows, copywriters can correlate the visual, headline, and subhead to the *attention* step of the creative pyramid (discussed in Chapter 12). The *interest* step typically corresponds to the subhead and the first paragraph of body copy. Body copy handles *credibility* and *desire,* and the *action* step takes place with the logo, slogan, and signature block. We'll discuss these elements first and then look at the formats for radio and television commercials.

If your interests lie in copywriting, pay careful attention to the messages you are exposed to every day. Try not to read them only as a consumer, but also as a student of creative work. Think carefully about the choices the writer has made in the words and structure of the message. And remember that while good copy may come from imitating others (see the Ethical Issues box on page 351), great copy comes from true originality.

The **headline** contains the largest type on the page—the words that will be read first and are situated to draw the most attention.

Role of Headlines

Effective headlines attract attention, engage the audience, explain the visual, lead the audience into the body of the ad, introduce the brand, and present the selling message.

One popular way to attract attention is to occupy the entire top half of the ad with a headline written in large letters. This technique can be just as eye-catching as a dramatic photo or illustration.

Another goal of a headline is to engage the reader—fast—and give a reason to read the rest of the ad. If the headline lacks immediacy, prospects turn their attention to another subject and pass the ad's message by.[14]

An ad for Esser's wine store is a good example of a headline leading the reader into the body copy.

Headline: "Esser's Knows."
Body copy: "Manfred Esser's nose knows a good wine . . ."

The headline is the most important thing a company says to the prospect. It explains or gives greater meaning to the visual and then immediately dictates the marketer's position in that person's mind, whether or not the prospect chooses to read on.

Exhibit 11-2

An ad's success depends on the viewer's ability to absorb and learn its message. The creative pyramid helps the copywriter present the conceptual elements of the message. The format elements (headlines, subheads, body copy, slogan) segment the copy to help audiences decode the message.

Creative Pyramid

The creativity embodied by this headline for IFAW comes from more than its meaning. It is also present in the artistic typography. The headline also does a great job of driving home the product's benefit, which is protecting wildlife.

Source: International Fund for Animal Welfare

Ideally, headlines present the complete selling idea. Research shows that, on average, three to five times as many people read the headline as read the body copy. So if the message doesn't sell in the headline, the advertiser is wasting money.[15] Nike uses beautiful magazine and outdoor ads featuring only an athlete, the logo, and the memorable headline: "Just do it." Working off the visual, the headline creates the mood and tells the reader, through implication, to take action—buy Nikes. Headlines help trigger a recognition response, which reinforces brand recognition and brand preference.

The traditional notion is that short headlines with one line are best but a second line is acceptable. Many experts believe that headlines with 10 words or more gain greater readership. But one researcher's effort to confirm this failed to find an impact of headline length, at least for ad recall. He concluded "For the time being, we must assume that for magazine advertising, what you have to say in a headline is more important than how many words you use to say it."[16] David Ogilvy said the best headline he ever wrote contained 18 words—and became a classic: "At 60 miles an hour, the loudest noise in the new Rolls-Royce comes from the electric clock."[17]

Headlines should offer a benefit that is compelling and easy to grasp. For example: "Please do not drive faster than your GPS satellite can fly" (Lamborghini), or "Not all mind expanding substances are illegal" (*The Economist*). A simple print ad honored at Cannes was little more than a headline that read "Cancer cures smoking." Alstiel and Grow cite a classic example of this from a 1934 newspaper ad: "It pays to buy at Brooks Brothers."[18]

Finally, headlines should present *product news.* Consumers look for new products, new uses for old products, or improvements on old products. If they haven't been overused in a category, "power" words that suggest newness can increase readership and improve the boom factor of an ad. They should be employed whenever *honestly* applicable.[19] Examples include *free, now, amazing, suddenly, announcing, introducing, it's here, improved, at last, revolutionary, just arrived, new,* and *important development.*

Types of Headlines

Copywriters use many variations of headlines depending on the strategy. Typically, they use the headline that presents the big idea most successfully. Headlines may be classified by the type of information they carry: *benefit, news/information, provocative, question,* and *command.*

Benefit headlines promise the audience that experiencing the utility of the product or service will be rewarding. Benefit headlines shouldn't be too cute or clever, just simple statements of the product's most important benefit. Two good examples are

America runs on Dunkin   and   Speak a foreign language in
                                                      30 days or your money back.

Note that both of these headlines focus on the benefit of using the product, not the features of the product itself.[20]

The **news/information headline** announces news or promises information. Sea World began its TV announcement of a new baby whale with the headline "It's a girl." The information must be believable, though. A claim that a razor "shaves 200% smoother" probably isn't.[21]

Copywriters use **provocative headlines** to provoke the reader's curiosity—to stimulate questions and thoughts. "Betcha can't eat just one" (Lay's Potato Chips) is an example. Another example is William Bernbach's famous headline for Volkswagen, "Lemon." To learn more, the reader must read the body copy. The danger, of course, is that the reader won't read on. To avoid this, the creative team designs visuals to clarify the message or provide some story appeal.

A **question headline** asks a question, encouraging readers to search for the answer in the body of the ad. An ad for 4day Tire Stores asked: "What makes our tire customers smarter & richer than others?" A good question headline piques the reader's curiosity and imagination. But if a headline asks a question the reader can answer quickly (or even worse, negatively), the rest of the ad may not get read. Imagine a headline that reads: "Do you want to buy insurance?" The reader answers, "No," and turns the page.

Ethical Issues

Imitation, Plagiarism, or Flattery?

When two companies run strikingly similar ads, is it imitation, plagiarism, or coincidence? In December 1999, two beverage companies began running television commercials that closely resembled each other. The commercials, for Michelob Light beer and Colombian coffee, were set in supermarkets and shared the same plot: store employees manhandled groceries until the product being advertised came down the conveyer belt. For both Michelob Light and Colombian, the bagger wraps the package in bubble wrap and carefully gives it to the buyers.

Advertisers and media commonly point to "coincidence." Bob Garfield, ad critic for *Advertising Age*, said, "It's seldom plagiarism, especially if the ads are appearing simultaneously." Both of the agencies representing Michelob Light beer and Colombian coffee agree. Peter le Comte, president of DDB Worldwide Marketing, said, "We have written it off as an incident of coincidence. Besides, I don't think we share the same consumers. They will run their commercial and we will run ours."

Stephen Bergerson, an attorney specializing in advertising and promotion law at Fredrikson & Byron, Minneapolis, is skeptical. "When you get four or five words that are so specific, simultaneously used by people in the same category, the nose starts to quiver." But Ron Redfern, senior vice president of sales and marketing for the *Orange County Register*, calls it "coincidental invention. It's like the automobile being invented in France and in the U.S. within weeks of each other."

Some advertisers try to ignore the problem by convincing themselves that being copied is actually good. Hugh Thrasher, executive VP of marketing for Motel 6, says of his often-imitated Tom Bodett commercials: "We think these copycat ads just remind people of the originality of our concept." Nancy Shalek, president of L.A.'s Shalek Agency, maintains, "If you haven't been ripped off, you're really in trouble."

But Ellen Kozak, a Milwaukee copyright and publishing lawyer, warns against this form of flattery. "There's a fine line between the kind of borrowing that constitutes an admiring bow to a classic work and the kind that's really the theft of another writer's efforts."

Unfortunately, plagiarism is almost impossible to prove, as long as you make a few changes. It's also hard to define, making it tough for advertisers to know just when they cross the line. There is no set number of words that make up a plagiarized effort. And plagiarism covers not only words but ideas, plots, and characters. In 1996, Kendall-Jackson Winery filed a suit against E&J Gallo Winery, charging that Gallo's Turning Leaf Vineyards brand infringed on K-J's Colored Leaf brand trademark. The suit said that Gallo intentionally designed the bottle, labeling, and packaging to imitate that of Kendall-Jackson's Colored Leaf mark. More recently, overseas, manufacturers of two brands of potato chips have become embroiled in a similar battle.

Tesco, a supermarket giant in England, recently launched a brand of chips called Temptations that are very reminiscent of competitor Walker's Sensations. The two brands have been placed side by side on the shelves, and the Tesco brand is being sold for 23 pence, approximately $0.40, cheaper than Walker's. Both chips are packaged in white bags that feature black and white pictures, and both are offered in strikingly similar flavors. Although Martin Glenn, a chief executive at Walker, has hinted at legal action, lawyers are divided over the success of such litigation. Nick Johnson, an attorney with Osborne Clark, agrees that "Tesco may have been inspired [by Walker's], but just because you are inspired by another brand

doesn't mean you are trying to pass off as it." The fact that the legal criteria to prove "passing off" are so strict in Great Britain, combined with the fact that Walker's itself has been guilty of brand motif plagiarism in the past, diminishes the likelihood of this lawsuit's success.

The crux of the problem is that imitation is an accepted part of the business, at least unofficially. Clients tend to avoid the debate, perhaps because they're more comfortable with well-worn ideas than with bold, original concepts. Many art directors and writers collect competitive ads for inspiration. And advertising is such a highly collaborative process that it's often difficult to determine each individual's creative contribution. With personal responsibility so unclear, ignoring professional ethics is relatively easy.

But every so often, someone creates an ad that moves beyond the gray zone of imitation into outright plagiarism. In July 2000, Anheuser-Busch asked Heiser Automotive Group to drop its TV spots with animated frogs croaking, "Buy . . . Hei . . . ser." Heiser had manipulated its "Be Wiser . . . Buy Heiser" slogan to imitate the Budweiser frogs without permission from Anheuser-Busch. Anheuser-Busch lawyer Valerie Benkert Paci wrote Heiser: "We consider Heiser's imitation of the BUDWEISER Frogs commercials to be a violation of our federal and common law rights. Consequently, we must ask that you refrain from all future use of those commercials."

Even flagrant infringement cases are very hard to win because copyright laws don't protect ideas, and creative advertising is an idea business. "There are very few original ideas," according to Philip Circus, an advertising law consultant to the Newspaper Society in London. "Plagiarism is the name of the game in advertising. It's about recycling ideas in a useful way."

That's why some industry leaders are passionate about the need for personal ethics. Jim Golden, executive producer of DMH MacGuffin, says, "All we have in this business are creativity and ideas. The moment someone infringes on that, they're reaching into the very core of the business and ripping it out." Ultimately, advertisers must stop "borrowing" ideas from each other and demand greater creativity from themselves.

Questions

1. Some art directors claim that "independent invention" explains why many ads look the same. Is that possible? If so, does it excuse running imitative advertising—or should the originator of an idea be the only one allowed to use it?

2. Should clients be more concerned about the ethics of copycat advertising? What would you do if a client asked you to copy an ad that was already running?

Sources: Richard A. Posner, "On Plagiarism," *Atlantic Monthly,* April 2002, Copyright and Plagiarism," *Copyright—CopySense,* August 1, 2003 (retrieved from http://stellar-one.com/copyrightcopysense/plagiarism.htm); "Grey Rejects Plagiarism Claims," *B&T,* June 19, 2003; "Plagiarism," *Screen & Media Studies,* May 20, 2004 (retrieved from www.waikato.ac.nz/film/handbook/plagiarism.html); David Greer, "Imitation: The Smartest Form of Flattery" (retrieved from www.businesstoolchest.com/articles/data/20041208051428.shtml); "What Is Plagiarism?" December 5, 2003 (retrieved from www.abc.net.au/mediawatch/transcripts/s852818.htm); Hans Kullin, "More Plagiarism in Scandinavian Media," *Media Culpa,* August 2, 2004 (retrieved from www.kullin.net); David Benady, "Crunch Time for Copycats," *Marketing Week,* February 13, 2002, p. 24.

A **command headline** orders the reader to do something, so it might seem negative. But readers pay attention to such headlines. Sprite soft drink ads target youth with the hip headline: "Obey your thirst." Some command headlines make a request: "Please don't squeeze the Charmin" (bathroom tissue).

Many headline types are easily combined. But the type of headline used is less important than the way it's used. Copywriters must always write with style—for the audience's pleasure, not their own.

Headlines in Search ads

When headlines are used in search-related ads, such as the sponsored ads that appear next to Google's search results, several additional considerations come into play, largely driven by the clarity of the goal for such a headline: a click. WordStream, an online advertising company, offers a number of suggestions for effective PPC headlines (pay-per-click). These are a sampling: (1) Include keywords specific to the advertiser's offering, (2) Solve the prospect's problem, (3) Limit characters to 25. The limit relates to restrictions in characters shown in sponsored search headlines.[22]

Subheads

The **subhead** is an additional smaller headline that can appear above the headline or below it. A subhead above the headline is called a **kicker** (or *overline*) and may be underlined. Subheads may also appear in body copy.

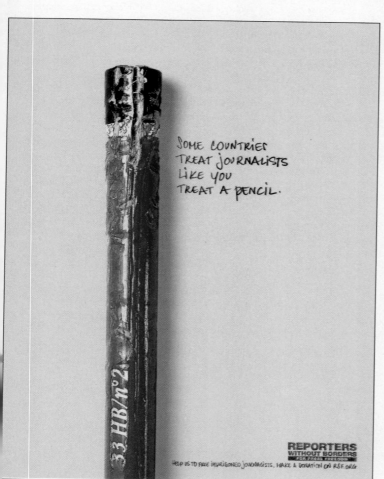

Some topics are so frightening that a direct representation could overwhelm the reader. In this ad, Reporters Without Borders uses metaphor to communicate the dangers its members face in bringing news to the world and the headline helps clarify the significant issue that the pencil metaphor is illustrating.

Source: Reporters Without Borders

Subheads are usually set smaller than the headline but larger than the body copy or text. Subheads generally appear in **boldface** (heavier) or *italic* (slanted) type or a different color. Like a headline, the subhead transmits key sales points fast. But it usually carries less important information than the headline. Subheads are important for two reasons: Most people read only the headline and subheads, and subheads usually support the interest step best.

Subheads are longer and more like sentences than headlines. They serve as stepping stones from the headline to the body copy, telegraphing what's to come.

Body Copy

The advertiser tells the complete sales story in the **body copy,** or **text.** The body copy comprises the interest, credibility, desire, and often even the action steps. It is a logical continuation of the headline and subheads, set in smaller type. Body copy covers the features, benefits, and utility of the product or service.

The body copy is typically read by only a fraction of readers, so the writer must speak to the reader's self-interest, explaining how the product or service satisfies the customer's need. The best ads focus on one big idea or one clear benefit. Copywriters often read their copy aloud to hear how it sounds, even if it's intended for print media. The ear is a powerful copywriting tool.[23]

Some of the best copywriting techniques of leading experts are highlighted in My IMC Campaign 11-D, "Writing Effective Copy."

Body Copy Styles

Experienced copywriters look for the technique and style with the greatest sales appeal for the idea being presented. Common copy styles include *straight sell, institutional, narrative, dialogue/monologue, picture caption,* and *device.*

My IMC Campaign 11–D

Writing Effective Copy

- **Get to the main point—fast.**
- **Emphasize one major idea simply and clearly.**
- **Be single-minded.** Don't try to do too much. If you chase more than one rabbit at a time, you'll catch none.
- **Position the product clearly.**
- **Keep the brand name up front and reinforce it.**
- **Write with the consumer's ultimate benefit in mind.**
- **Write short sentences.** Use easy, familiar words and themes people understand.
- **Don't waste words.** Say what you have to say—nothing more, nothing less. Don't pad, but don't skimp.
- **Avoid bragging and boasting.** Write from the reader's point of view, not your own. Avoid "we," "us," and "our."
- **Avoid clichés.** They're crutches; learn to get along without them. Bright, surprising words and phrases perk up readers and keep them reading.
- **Write with flair.** Drum up excitement. Make sure your own enthusiasm comes through in the copy.

- **Use vivid language.** Use lots of verbs and adverbs.
- **Stick to the present tense, active voice.** It's crisper. Avoid the past tense and passive voice. Exceptions should be deliberate, for special effect.
- **Use personal pronouns.** Remember, you're talking to just one person, so talk as you would to a friend. Use "you" and "your" whenever appropriate.
- **Use contractions.** They're fast, personal, natural. People talk in contractions (listen to yourself).
- **Don't overpunctuate.** It kills copy flow. Excessive commas are the chief culprits. Don't give readers any excuse to jump ship.
- **Read the copy aloud.** Hear how it sounds; catch errors. The written word is considerably different from the spoken word so listen to it.
- **Rewrite and write tight.** Edit mercilessly. Tell the whole story and no more. When you're finished, stop.

In **straight-sell copy,** writers immediately explain or develop the headline and visual in a straightforward, factual presentation. The straight-sell approach appeals to the prospect's reason. Because it ticks off the product's sales points in order of importance, straight-sell copy is particularly good for high think-involvement products or products that are difficult to use. It's very effective for direct response advertising, search advertising, and for industrial or high-tech products.

Breaking through the clutter requires fresh approaches. How many ways, in both the visual and the copy, does this Dove ad challenge your expectations?

Source: Unilever

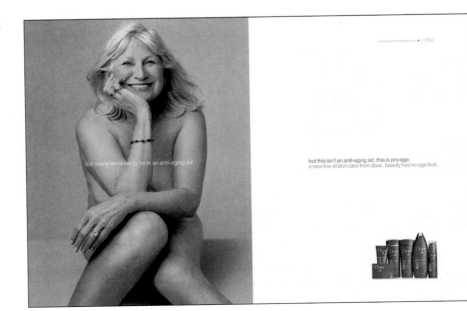

Advertisers use **institutional copy** to promote a philosophy or extol the merits of an organization rather than product features. Institutional copy is intended to lend warmth and credibility to the organization's image. Banks, insurance companies, public corporations, and large manufacturing firms use institutional copy in both print and electronic media. However, David Ogilvy warned against the "self-serving, flatulent pomposity" that characterizes the copy in many corporate ads.[24]

Copywriters use **narrative copy** to tell a story. Ideal for the creative writer, narrative copy sets up a situation and then resolves it at the last minute by having the product or service come to the rescue. Narrative copy offers good opportunities for emotional appeals. An insurance company, for example, might tell the poignant story of the man who died unexpectedly but, fortunately, had just renewed his policy.[25]

By using **dialogue/monologue copy,** the copywriter can add the believability that narrative copy sometimes lacks. The characters portrayed in a print ad do the selling in their own words. A caution: Poorly written dialogue copy can come off as dull or, even worse, hokey and unreal.

Sometimes it's easier to tell a story with illustrations and captions. A photo with **picture-caption copy** is especially useful for products that have a number of different uses or come in a variety of styles or designs.

With any copy style, the copywriter may use some device copy to enhance attention, interest, and memorability. **Device copy** uses figures of speech (such as puns, alliteration, assonance, and rhymes) as well as humor and exaggeration. Copywriter Paul Suggett offers an example: "Dead batteries, now free of charge." Some believe that verbal devices help people remember the brand and affect attitude favorably. But Suggett argues that device copy should be avoided.

Humor can be effective when the advertiser needs high memorability in a short time, wants to dispel preconceived negative images, or needs to create a distinct personality for an undifferentiated product. However, humor should always be used carefully and never be in questionable taste.

Formatting Body Copy

The keys to good body copy are simplicity, order, credibility, and clarity. Or, as John O'Toole says, prose should be "written clearly, informatively, interestingly, powerfully, persuasively, dramatically, memorably, and with effortless grace. That's all."[26]

Four basic format elements are used to construct long copy ads: *the lead-in paragraph, interior paragraphs, trial close,* and *close.*

Lead-in paragraph   The **lead-in paragraph** is a bridge between the headline and the sales ideas presented in the text. Like a subhead, the lead-in paragraph is part of the *interest* step. It must be engaging and able to convert a prospect's reading interest to product interest.

Interior paragraphs   The **interior paragraphs** of the body copy should develop *credibility* by providing proof for claims and promises and they should build *desire* by using language that stirs the imagination. Advertisers should support their product promises with research data, testimonials, and warranties. Such proofs help avoid costly lawsuits, convince customers of the validity of the product, improve goodwill toward the advertiser, and stimulate sales.

Trial close   Interspersed in the interior paragraphs should be suggestions to *act* now. Good copy asks for the order more than once; mail-order ads ask several times. Consumers often make the buying decision without reading all the body copy. The **trial close** gives them the opportunity to make the buying decision early.

A great headline and a well-chosen illustration are the key elements in this print ad.
Source: Discovery Communications, Inc.

Ad agency Saatchi & Saatchi was honored at Cannes for this simple "problem–solution" ad. It was produced for out-of-home locations in Romania.

Ad developed by Saatchi & Saatchi Romania for PSI Romania. Brand: Love Plus. Creative Directors: Nick Hine, Jorg Riommi; Art directors: Daniela Nedelschi, Florin Roman; Copywriter: Sorana Caracudovici; Photography: Octav Ionita

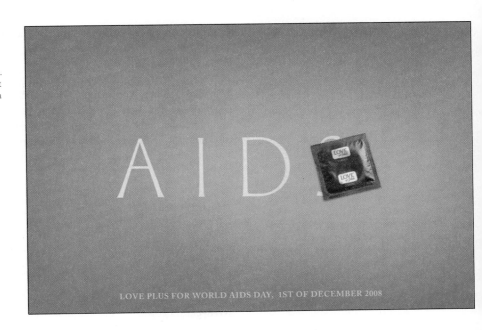

Close   The **close** is the real *action* step. A good close asks consumers to do something and tells them how. The close can be indirect or direct (a subtle suggestion or a direct command). A *direct close* seeks immediate response in the form of a purchase, a store or Website visit, or a request for further information.

The close should simplify the audience's response, making it easy for them to order the merchandise, send for information, or visit a showroom or a Website. A business reply card or a toll-free phone number may be included.

Of course, not all ads sell products or services. Advertisers may want to change attitudes, explain their viewpoints, or ask for someone's vote. By giving a Website address, the advertiser can offer additional information to those readers who are interested in learning more at their leisure.

Slogans

Many **slogans** (also called **themelines** or **taglines**) begin as successful headlines, like AT&T's "Reach out and touch someone." Through continuous use, they become standard statements, not just in advertising but for salespeople and company employees.

Slogans have two basic purposes: to provide continuity to a series of ads in a campaign and to reduce an advertising message strategy to a brief, repeatable, and memorable positioning statement. Wheaties cereal, for example, positions itself as the "Breakfast of Champions." And ads for DeBeers still use the famous "Diamonds are forever" slogan. But Miller Lite's corny "It's it and that's that" was "major league pathetic," according to one *Wall Street Journal* article. Lacking the creativity, freshness, and power to become a full-fledged slogan, it was short-lived.[27]

Seals, Logos, and Signatures

A **seal** is awarded only when a product meets standards established by a particular organization, such as the Organic Crop Improvement Association, the Good Housekeeping Institute, Underwriters Laboratories, or Parents Institute. Because these organizations are recognized authorities, their seals provide an independent, valued endorsement for the advertiser's product.

Logotypes (*logos*) and **signature cuts** (*sig cuts*) are special designs of the advertiser's company or product name. They appear in all company ads and, like trademarks, give the product individuality and provide quick recognition at the point of purchase.

Writing for Radio and TV

For electronic media, the fundamental elements—the five steps of the creative pyramid—remain the primary guides, but the copywriting formats differ. Radio and television writers prepare *scripts* and *storyboards*.

Writing Radio Copy

LO 11-3

A radio script format resembles a two-column list, with speakers' names and sound effects on the left and the dialogue in a wider column on the right. This national public service announcement (PSA) was created by McCann-Erickson and is one of many in a campaign designed to inspire Americans to take small steps toward a healthier lifestyle.

A **script** resembles a two-column list. On the left side, speakers' names are arranged vertically, along with descriptions of any sound effects and music. The right column contains the dialogue, called the **audio.**

Copywriters first need to understand radio as a medium. Radio provides entertainment or news to listeners who are busy doing something else—driving, washing dishes, reading the paper, or even studying. To be heard, an advertising message must be catchy, interesting, and unforgettable. Radio listeners usually decide within five to eight seconds if they're going to pay attention. To attract and hold the attention of listeners, particularly those not attracted to a product category, radio copy must be intrusive.

Healthier America
Lost Campaign
Radio: 60
"Neighbor"
Expiration date: 2/23/05

SFX: Phone ringing

Bill:	Hello . . . ?
George:	Hi, Bill? This is George Dewey from up the street.
Bill:	Hey, George. How ya doin?
George:	Good, good. Say, I noticed you've been walking to work these days instead of driving . . . and I, uh, don't quite know how to say this, but . . . but . . .
Bill:	But what?
George: *(stammering)*	But . . . But . . . Your butt, your buttocks, your butt—I think I found your butt on my front lawn. Have you recently lost it?
Bill:	As a matter of fact, I have, George *(pleased)* It's about time someone noticed.
George: *(playful)*	Well, it was kinda hard to miss if you know what I mean . . . . . . Anyways, would you like it back?
Bill:	Would I like it back? No, not really.
George:	So, it's okay if I throw it out?
Bill:	Sure, that's fine. Take it easy, George.

SFX: Phone ringing

| **Announcer:** | Small step #8—Walk instead of driving whenever you can. It's just one of the many small steps you can take to help you become a healthier, well, you. Get started at www.smallstep.gov and take a small step to get healthy. |
| **Legal:** | A public service announcement brought to you by the U.S. Department of Health and Human Services and the Ad Council. |

Intrusive, yes; offensive, no. An insensitive choice of words, overzealous effort to attract listeners with irritating everyday sounds (car horn, alarm clock, screeching tires), or characters that sound too exotic, odd, or irritating can cause listener resentment and ultimately lose sales. Other guidelines are given in My IMC Campaign 11-E, "Creating Effective Radio Commercials."

One of the most challenging aspects is making the script fit the time slot. The delivery changes for different types of commercials, so writers read the script out loud for timing. With electronic compression, recorded radio ads can now include 10 to 30 percent more copy than text read live. Still, the following are good rules of thumb:

10 seconds: 20–25 words   30 seconds: 60–70 words

20 seconds: 40–45 words   60 seconds: 130–150 words[28]

Radio writing has to be clearer than any other kind of copywriting. For example, the listener can't refer back, as in print, to find an antecedent for a pronoun. Likewise, the English language is so full of homonyms (words that sound like other words) that one can easily confuse the meaning of a sentence ("who's who is whose").

My IMC Campaign 11–E

Creating Effective Radio Commercials

Writing for radio takes a sharp ear, empathy for the listener, and the ability to create pictures inside the consumer's head. These tips will help you create great radio spots.

- **Make the big idea crystal clear.** Concentrate on one main selling point. Radio is a good medium for building brand awareness, but not for making long lists of copy points or complex arguments.

- **Mention the advertiser's name early and often.** If the product or company name is tricky, consider spelling it out.

- **Take time to set the scene and establish the premise.** A 30-second commercial that nobody remembers is a waste of money. Fight for 60-second spots.

- **Use familiar sound effects.** Ice tinkling in a glass, birds chirping, or a door shutting can create a visual image. Music also works if its meaning is clear.

- **Paint pictures with your words.** Use descriptive language to make the ad more memorable.

- **Make every word count.** Use active voice and more verbs than adjectives. Be conversational. Use pronounceable words and short sentences.

- **Be outrageous.** The best comic commercials begin with a totally absurd premise from which all developments follow logically. But remember, if you can't write humor really well, go for drama.

- **Ask for the order.** Try to get listeners to take action.

- **Remember that radio is a local medium.** Adjust your commercials to the language of your listeners and the time of day they'll run.

- **Presentation counts a lot.** Even the best scripts look boring on paper. Acting, timing, vocal quirks, and sound effects bring them to life.

Writing Television Copy

Radio's basic two-column script format also works for television. But in a TV script, the left side is titled "Video" and the right side "Audio." The video column describes the visuals and production: camera angles, action, scenery, and stage directions. The audio column lists the spoken copy, sound effects, and music.

Broadcast commercials must be believable and relevant. And even outlandish or humorous commercials must exude quality in their creation and production to imply the product's quality. While the art director's work is very important, the copywriter sets the tone of the commercial, establishes the language that determines which visuals to use, and pinpoints when the visuals should appear. Research and the experience of professionals suggest the techniques given in My IMC Campaign 11-F, "Creating Effective TV Commercials" work best.

An effective campaign for Lubriderm skin lotion illustrates these principles nicely. Many people want smooth, soft skin and consider a patch of rough, flaky skin anywhere on their body a disappointment. If you were the copywriter for Lubriderm, how would you approach this somewhat touchy, negative subject?

The creative staff of J. Walter Thompson crafted an artistic solution for Lubriderm. An alligator was the big idea. The gator's scaly sheath was a metaphor for rough, flaky skin. Its appearance ignited people's survival instincts; they paid attention, fast. A beautiful, sophisticated woman with smooth, feminine skin was seated in a lounge chair, completely unruffled by the passing gator. The swing of the animal's back and tail echoed the graceful curves of the two simple pieces of furniture on the set, and its slow stride kept the beat of a light jazz tune.

This commercial opened with an attention-getting big idea that was visually surprising, compelling, dramatic, and interesting. It was also a quasi-demonstration: we saw the alligator's scaly, prickly skin and the woman's confidence and willingness to touch the alligator as it passed by, which symbolized the confidence Lubriderm can bring.

This ad follows the creative pyramid. The alligator captures attention visually while the announcer's first words serve as an attention-getting headline: "A quick reminder." The ad commands us to listen and sets up the interest step that offers this claim: "Lubriderm restores lost moisture to heal your dry skin and protect it." Now for the credibility step: "Remember the one created for dermatologists is the one that heals and protects." Then a quick trial close

My IMC Campaign 11–F

Creating Effective TV Commercials

- **Begin at the finish.** Concentrate on the final impression the commercial will make.
- **Create an attention-getting opening.** An opening that is visually surprising or full of action, drama, humor, or human interest sets the context and allows a smooth transition to the rest of the commercial.
- **Use a situation that grows naturally out of the sales story.** Avoid distracting gimmicks. Make it easy for viewers to identify with the characters.
- **Characters are the living symbol of the product.** They should be appealing, believable, nondistracting, and most of all, relevant.
- **Keep it simple.** The sequence of ideas should be easy to follow. Keep the number of elements in the commercial to a bare minimum.

- **Write concise audio copy.** The video should carry most of the weight. Fewer than two words per second is effective for demonstrations. For a 60-second commercial, 101 to 110 words is most effective; more than 170 words is too talky.
- **Make demonstrations dramatic but believable.** They should always be true to life and avoid the appearance of camera tricks.
- **Let the words interpret the picture and prepare viewers for the next scene.** Use conversational language; avoid "ad talk," hype, and puffery.
- **Run scenes five or six seconds on average.** Rarely should a scene run less than three seconds. Offer a variety of movement-filled scenes without "jumping."
- **Keep the look of the video fresh and new.**

(action): "Lubriderm." And then the desire step recaps the primary product benefit and adds a touch of humor: "See you later, alligator."

Developing Great Spots in Radio and TV

Developing the Artistic Concept for Commercials

Advertising Age columnist Bob Garfield, asked to name the year's best ad, described one created by Delvico Bates, Barcelona, for Esencial hand cream. The spot opens with a woman riding her bicycle to the persistent squeak of its unlubricated chain. She dismounts, opens a jar of Esencial, and rubs some of the cream onto the chain. Then she rides away—but the squeak is still there. Why? Because, as the voice-over points out, "Esencial moisturizes, but it has no grease."

No big production. No digital effects. No jingle. No celebrity. No big comedy payoff. Just a pure creative idea: a problem–resolution spot where the brand pointedly cannot solve the problem. It's a vivid demonstration of brand nonattributes. Inspired. Cunning. Brilliant. And a demonstration of what creatives mean by "the big idea."[29]

Creating the concept for a radio or TV commercial is similar to creating the concept for print ads. The first step is to determine the big idea. Then the art director and copywriter must decide what commercial format to use. Should a celebrity present the message? Or should the ad dramatize the product's benefits (or deficiencies) with a semifictional story? The next step is to write a script containing the necessary copy or dialogue plus a basic description of any music, sound effects, and/or camera views.

In both radio and TV, the art director assists the copywriter in script development. But in television, artistic development is much more extensive. Using the TV script, the art director creates a series of **storyboard roughs** to present the artistic approach, the action sequences, and the style of the commercial. When the storyboard is approved, it serves as a guide for the final production phase.

Good casting is critical. The most important consideration is relevance to the product; agencies don't use a comic to sell financial products—or cremation services. And in spite of Michael Jordan's success for Nike, Gatorade, and McDonald's, some experts don't believe in using celebrities. David Ogilvy, for example, thought viewers remember the celebrity more than the product.[30] As the concept evolves, the creative team defines the characters' personalities in a detailed, written **casting brief.** These descriptions serve as guides in casting sessions when actors audition for the roles. Sometimes agencies discover new, unknown stars who

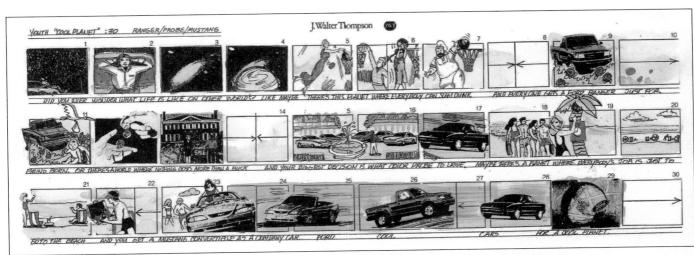

After the initial concepts for a television ad are finalized, creatives develop a storyboard rough composed of small sketches that depict the various scenes of the ad. The storyboard rough, including camera angles and script, is used to provide a visual guideline for shooting the various scenes during the final production phase.

Source: J. Walter Thompson and Ford Motor Company

evolve into solid, memorable characters and who go beyond the simple role by actually creating a personality or image for the product.

Formats for Radio and TV Commercials

Similar to print advertising, the format for a broadcast ad serves as a template for arranging message elements into a pattern. Once the art director and copywriter establish the big idea, they must determine the commercial's format.

Many radio and TV commercial styles have been successful. Some of these are listed in Ad Lab 11–B, "Creative Ways to Sell on Radio." Hank Seiden, the former chair of Ketchum Advertising, developed the Execution Spectrum: 24 basic formats that range from frivolous to serious (see Exhibit 11-3). Here we consider eight common commercial formats that can be used in either radio or television: *straight announcement, presenter, testimonial, demonstration, musical, slice of life, lifestyle,* and *animation*.

Straight Announcement

The oldest and simplest type of radio or TV commercial is the **straight announcement.** One person, usually a radio or TV announcer, delivers the sales message. Music may play in the background. Straight announcements are popular because they are adaptable to almost any product or situation. In radio, a straight announcement can also be designed as an **integrated commercial**—that is, it can be woven into a show or tailored to the style of a given program.

For TV, an announcer may deliver the sales message **on camera** or off screen, as a **voice-over,** while a demonstration, slide, or film shows on screen. If the script is well written and the announcer convincing, straight announcements can be very effective. Since they don't require elaborate production facilities, they save money, too.

Straight announcements are commonly used on late-night TV programs, by local advertisers, and by nonprofit or political organizations.

Presenter

The **presenter commercial** uses one person or character to present the product and carry the sales message. Som

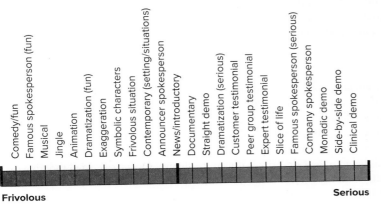

Exhibit 11-3

The Execution Spectrum, developed by Hank Seiden, shows 24 execution formats ranging in style from frivolous to serious, for both print and electronic advertising.

Source: The Execution Spectrum from spectrum analysis developer Hank Seiden, 1928–2008. Reprinted with permission.

AD Lab 11–B

Creative Ways to Sell on Radio

Product demo The commercial tells how a product is used or the purposes it serves.

Voice power A unique voice gives the ad power.

Electronic sound Synthetic sound-making machines create a memorable product-sound association.

Customer interview A spokesperson and customer discuss the product advantages spontaneously.

Humorous fake interview The customer interview is done in a lighter vein.

Hyperbole (exaggeration) statement Overstatement arouses interest in legitimate product claims that might otherwise pass unnoticed; often a spoof.

Fourth dimension Time and events are compressed into a brief spot involving the listener in future projections.

Hot property Commercial adapts a current sensation: a hit show, performer, or song.

Comedian power Established comedians do commercials in their own unique style, implying celebrity endorsement.

Historical fantasy Situation with revived historical characters is used to convey product message.

Sound picture Recognizable sounds involve the listener by stimulating imagination.

Demographics Music or references appeal to a particular segment of the population, such as an age or interest group.

Imagery transfer Musical logo or other sound reinforces the memory of a TV campaign.

Celebrity interview Famous person endorses the product in an informal manner.

Product song Music and words combine to create a musical logo, selling the product in the style of popular music.

Editing genius Many different situations, voices, types of music, and sounds are combined in a series of quick cuts.

Improvisation Performers work out the dialogue extemporaneously for an assigned situation; may be postedited.

Laboratory Applications

1. Select three familiar radio commercials and discuss which creative techniques they use.

2. Select a familiar radio commercial and discuss how a different creative technique would increase its effectiveness.

---

presenters are celebrities, such as William Shatner for Priceline.com. Others may be corporate officers of the sponsor, such as Pete Coors, who speaks for his company, or they may be actors playing a role (the lonely Maytag repairman).

A **radio personality,** such as Rush Limbaugh or Howard Stern, may *ad lib* an ad message live in his or her own style. Done well, such commercials can be very successful. However, the advertiser surrenders control to the personality. The main risk, outside of occasional blunders, is that the personality may criticize the product. Even so, this sometimes lends an appealing realism. The personality gets a highlight sheet listing the product's features, the main points to stress, and the phrases or company slogans to repeat. But he or she can choose the specific wording and mode of delivery.

Testimonial

The true **testimonial**—where a satisfied user tells how effective the product is—can be highly credible in both TV and radio advertising. Celebrities may gain attention, but they must be believable and not distract from the product. Actually, people from all walks of life endorse products, from known personalities to unknowns and nonprofessionals. Which type of person to use depends on the product and the strategy. Satisfied customers are the best sources for testimonials because their sincerity is usually persuasive. Ogilvy suggested shooting candid testimonials when the subjects don't know they're being filmed.[31] Of course, marketers must be sure to get their permission before using the piece.

Demonstration

Television is well suited for visual demonstration. And a **demonstration** convinces an audience better and faster than a spoken message. So don't say it, show it. Naturally, it's easier to

"More Cat Chow" :30
(Open on Sue sitting on her living room floor giving one of her cats a pedicure)
Super: Sue Collister's "Cat Chat"

Sue: Yes, I like the dusty rose on you too ... Oh ... Hello, welcome back to "Cat Chat." Today we're having a spa day, so let's all be extra quiet.
(Reveal the room filled with cats. Cats are resting on their backs, cucumber slices over their eyes. This continues for about 10 seconds. It is silent and peaceful. Cut to Jack, sitting in his office. He means business.)

Jack: You thought I was bluffing? Try my new smokehouse bacon cheddar burger with grilled onions, barbecue sauce and melting cheese or it's gonna be a "Cat Chat" summer.
Super: Limited time only

(Cut back to all the cats sleeping)
Sue: Shhh. Evanka is in her happy place.
Who's next for a mini-pedi?

(Bag drops)
Bag 1: Stop Cat Chat
Bag 2: New Smokehouse Bacon Cheddar Burger.
Super: Jack in the Box logo.

Advertisers often use presenter commercials to carry out their sales message. In this humorous example, Jack in the Box's spokesperson, Jack, threatens to air the awful show "Cat Chat" if people don't buy the featured sandwich.

Source: Jack In The Box, Inc.

demonstrate the product on TV than on radio, but some advertisers have used the imagina tive nature of radio to create humorous, tongue-in-cheek demonstrations.

Products may be demonstrated in use, in competition, or before and after. These tech niques help viewers visualize how the product will perform for them.

Musical

The **musical commercials,** or **jingles,** we hear on radio and TV are among the best—and worst—ad messages produced. Done well, they can bring enormous success, well beyond the average nonmusical commercial. Done poorly, they can waste the advertising budget and an noy audiences beyond belief.

Musical commercials have several variations. The entire message may be sung; jingles may be written with a **donut** in the middle (a hole for spoken copy); or orchestras may play symphonic or popular arrangements. Many producers use consistent musical themes for back ground color or to close the commercial. An example is Intel's brief musical snippet at the end of each of its ads. This is called a **musical logo.** After many repetitions of the advertiser theme, the listener begins to associate the musical logo with the product. To achieve this, the jingle should have a **hook**—that part of the song that sticks in your memory.[32]

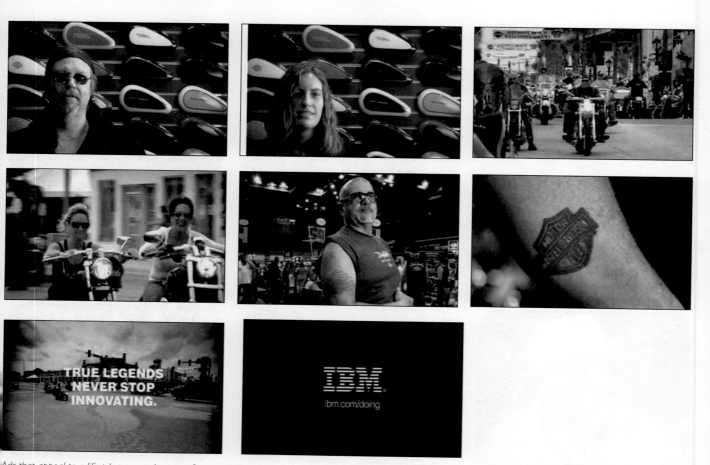

Ads that appeal to a lifestyle present the type of user associated with the product, rather than the product itself. This ad for IBM uses Harley-Davidson employees to illustrate how IBM can help every business—large and small.
Source: IBM

Advertisers have three sources of music. They can buy the right to use a tune from the copyright owner, which is usually expensive. They can use a melody in the public domain, which is free. Or they can hire a composer to write an original song. Some original tunes, including Coke's famous "I'd like to teach the world to sing," or the "Dumb Ways to Die" song featured in the chapter opener, have become hits.

Slice of Life (Problem–Solution)

Commercials that dramatize real-life situations are called **slice of life.** This approach usually starts with just plain folks, played by professional actors, discussing some problem or issue. Often the situation deals with a problem of a personal nature: bad breath, loose dentures, dandruff, body odor, or yellow laundry. A relative or a co-worker drops the hint, the product is tried, and the next scene shows the result—a happier, cleaner, more fragrant person off with a new date. The drama always concludes with a successful trial. Such commercials can get attention and create interest, even though they are often irritating to viewers and hated by copywriters.

The key to effective slice-of-life commercials is simplicity. The ad should concentrate on one product benefit and make it memorable. Often a **mnemonic device** can dramatize the product benefit and trigger instant recall. Users of Imperial margarine, for example, suddenly discover crowns on their heads.

Believability in slice-of-life commercials is difficult to achieve. People don't really talk about "the sophisticated taste of Taster's Choice," so the actors must be highly credible to put the fantasy across. That's why most *local* advertisers don't use the slice-of-life technique. Creating that believability takes very professional talent and money. In all cases, the story should be relevant to the product and simply told.

Lifestyle

To present the user rather than the product, advertisers may use the **lifestyle technique.** For example, Diesel pitches its denim to urbanites by showing characters working and playing while wearing its latest line. Likewise, beer and soft drink advertisers frequently target their messages to active, outdoorsy young people, focusing on who drinks the brand rather than on specific product advantages.

Animation

Cartoons, puppet characters, and demonstrations with computer-generated graphics are very effective **animation** techniques for communicating difficult messages and reaching specialized markets, such as children. The way aspirin or other medications affect the human system is difficult to explain. Animated pictures of headaches and stomachs can simplify the subject and make a demonstration clear and understandable.

Computer animation requires a great deal of faith on the part of advertisers. Since most of this very expensive work is done on the computer, there's nothing to see until the animation is well developed and a good bit of money has been spent (this is more fully discussed in Chapter 12).

Basic Mechanics of Storyboard Development

After the creative team selects the big idea and the format for a TV commercial, the art director and the writer develop the script. Television is so visually powerful and expressive that the art director's role is particularly important. Art directors must be able to work with a variety of professionals—producers, directors, lighting technicians, and set designers—to develop and produce a commercial successfully.

Storyboard Design

Once the basic script is completed, the art director must turn the video portion of the script into real images. This is done with a **storyboard,** a sheet preprinted with a series of 8 to 20 blank windows (frames) in the shape of TV screens. Below each frame is room to place the text of the commercial, including the sound effects and camera views as abbreviated in Exhibit 11-4. The storyboard works much like a cartoon strip.

Through a process similar to laying out a print ad (thumbnail, rough, comp), the artist carefully designs how each scene should appear, arranging actors, scenery, props, lighting, and camera angles to maximize impact, beauty, and mood. The storyboard helps the creatives visualize the commercial's tone and sequence of action, discover any conceptual weaknesses, and make presentations for management approval. It also serves as a guide for filming.

Even when designed to the level of a comp, though, the storyboard is only an approximation of the final commercial. Actual production often results in many changes in

Exhibit 11-4
Common abbreviations used in TV scripts.

CU: Close-up. Very close shot of person or object.
ECU: Extreme close-up. A more extreme version of the above. Sometimes designated BCU (big close-up) or TCU (tight close-up).
MCU: Medium close-up. Emphasizes the subject but includes other objects nearby.
MS: Medium shot. Wide-angle shot of subject but not whole set.
FS: Full shot. Entire set or object.
LS: Long shot. Full view of scene to give effect of distance.
DOLLY: Move camera toward or away from subject. Dolly in (DI), dolly out (DO), or dolly back (DB).
PAN: Scan from one side to the other.
ZOOM: Move in or out from the subject without blurring.
SUPER: Superimpose one image on another (as showing lettering over a scene).
DISS: Dissolve (also DSS). Fade out one scene while fading in another.
CUT: Instantly change one picture to another.
WIPE: Gradually erase picture from screen. (Many varied effects are possible.)
VO: Voice-over. An off-screen voice, usually the announcer's.
SFX: Sound effects.
DAU: Down and under. Sound effects fade as voice comes on.
UAO: Up and over. Voice fades as sound effects come on.

lighting, camera angle, focal point, and emphasis. The camera sees many things that the artist couldn't visualize, and vice versa (see Chapter 12 for more details on working with storyboards).

Animatic: The Video Comp

To supplement the storyboard or pretest a concept, a commercial may be taped in rough form using the writers and artists as actors. Or an **animatic** may be shot—a film strip of the sketches in the storyboard accompanied by the audio portion of the commercial synchronized on tape. Computers have cut the costs involved in producing a standard animatic. Avid Technologies, for example, developed an editing system that lets the agency process and edit moving pictures on the screen, lay sound behind them, and transfer the entire package to the client. Apple produces a similar high-performance digital nonlinear editing system called Final Cut Studio. This kind of technology has enabled agencies to serve clients' needs better for less money.

Upon approval of the storyboard and/or the animatic, the commercial is ready for production, a subject we cover in detail in Chapter 12.

Writing Effectively for Websites and Social Media

A generation has grown up never remembering a time without the Internet. Internet use within these younger cohorts (teens 12 to 17 and young adults 18 to 29) was 93 percent in 2010. And majorities of all age groups, save adults over 65, use the medium. But within these millions of users are an especially important group.

According to research by Burson-Marsteller, a large New York public relations firm, there are 11 million heavy online users in the United States, and their opinions affect the buying decisions of 155 million consumers both online and off. Burson-Marsteller refers to these opinion leaders as *e-fluentials.*

"An e-fluential is the rock that starts the ripple," said Chet Burchett, president and chief executive officer, Burson-Marsteller USA. "Each one communicates with an average of 14 people." E-fluentials can be reputation builders or busters.[33]

Interestingly, Burson-Marsteller's research found that, across a wide variety of sectors—technology, retail, finance, pharmaceutical, and automotive—90 percent of e-fluentials use company Websites to verify advertising information, but only 20 percent report that they find the corporate Websites credible.

So writing effectively for the Internet, especially for the e-influential audience, is critical. Company Websites that provide e-fluentials with straightforward, easy-to-use information are crucial to building and enhancing brand value.

Reid Goldsborough, a widely syndicated technology columnist and former copywriter, maintains that although image is everything in traditional advertising, on the Internet content is king. He points to research showing that, unlike readers of newspapers and magazines, people using the Internet typically focus on the text first, looking at photos and graphics later. In other words, the words are most important. The words connote substance, and substance triumphs over style.

Second, people don't really read a Website, they scan it, so the information presented must be at once concise and comprehensive. Numbered lists and bulleted items thus can be used more than in print media. Rather than scanning down the page like newspaper readers, Internet users just read the first text screen of any site and then move on. But if they like what they see, then they will want more, and they will stay on the site to search for more information. Having fewer space limitations than any other medium, the Internet is ideal for in-depth elaboration. But dumping screen after screen of text on a site is, according to Goldsborough, reader abuse.

Finally, Websites should always offer interactivity—a way for the reader to respond, either through e-mail or Internet response forms. The Internet is about interactivity. Companies that forget that feature are wasting their money.

Of course, digital media involve more than Websites. They include social media like Facebook, YouTube, and Twitter, a popular platform that allows people to interact with many others using "tweets". Twitter allows companies like Dell, Apple, Starbucks, and others to stay in regular, instant contact with loyal customers. Part of Twitter's appeal is its 140-character limit. Users know that messages have to be focused and to the point. Other suggestions for ways companies can communicate effectively with customers come from Joel Comm, author of "Twitter Power." His suggestions for companies that want to practice "the art of the tweet" include (1) don't spam, (2) follow Twitter style rules (e.g., texting abbreviations are a no-no on Twitter), (3) give credit for retweets, (4) stick to 140 characters, and (5) follow people who follow you. We have more to say about social media in Chapter 16.[34]

Effective copywriting in social media also presents creative challenges, according to former agency copywriter Jason Falls. He recommends that copywriters get to "know SEO" (search engine optimization) since copy has to attract web searchers. Creatives should also emphasize short, exciting messages that will get the audience to "click, share, and respond." Falls suggests that copywriters keep in mind that while "messages are two-way now" it is also more than a dialogue because "you can also watch them talking to each other. That's powerful."[35]

Falls notes that "your message needs to be more human. . . . 'We're here to hang out with you. If you want to talk about your car repairs, we know a thing or two about that.'" In fact, it's best if the message doesn't appear to be "copywritten" at all. Put the brand "in a natural environment" that allows someone to "show off the product and show how cool, smart or helpful the company is." The less staged, the better.[36]

Creating Ads for International Markets

In international markets, the most important consideration for copywriters and creative directors is language. In western Europe, people speak at least 15 different languages and more than twice as many dialects. A similar problem exists in Asia, Africa, and, to a lesser extent, South America.

International advertisers have debated the transferability of campaigns for years. One side believes it's too expensive to create a unique campaign for each national group. They simply translate one overall campaign into each language. Another method is to think globally but act locally, creating ads in various languages and reflecting the needs of different groups, but maintaining a consistent theme worldwide. Other advertisers believe the only way to ensure success is to create a special campaign for each market. Citigroup uses a variation of this approach. With branches in more than 100 countries, the financial service giant adapts its ads and products to the needs of each market. For example, the large Indian population working abroad can open checking accounts in rupees instead of the local currency; family members back home can access the accounts via Citibank ATMs in 34 cities in India, avoiding the steep fees usually associated with transferring money. Some advertisers find such solutions expensive and unnecessary. They run their ads in English worldwide, promoting their products generically rather than specifically.

Marketers must address their unique situations. Moreover, they have to weigh the economics of various promotional strategies.

Translating Copy

Regardless of strategy, translation remains a basic issue. Classic examples of mistranslations and faulty word choices abound in international advertising. A faulty Spanish translation for Perdue chickens reads "It takes a sexually excited man to make a chick affectionate" instead of "It takes a tough man to make a tender chicken."[37]

A poorly chosen or badly translated product name can undercut advertising credibility in foreign markets. A classic case was when Coke's product name was widely translated into Chinese characters that sounded like "Coca-Cola" but meant "bite the wax tadpole."[38]

People in the United States, Canada, England, Australia, and South Africa all speak English, but with wide variations in vocabulary, word usage, and syntax. Similarly, the French spoken in France, Canada, Vietnam, and Belgium may differ as much as the English spoken by a British aristocrat and a Tennessee mountaineer. Language variations exist even within countries. The Japanese use five lingual "gears," ranging from haughty to servile, depending on the speaker's and the listener's respective stations in life. Japanese translators must know when to change gears.

People BEHIND the Ads

Alex Bogusky, Former Cochair, Crispin Porter + Bogusky

Courtesy of Alex Bogusky, photo by Jason Leiva

Certain people in advertising become recognized as the best talents of their times. Claude Hopkins was the preeminent creative of the time before broadcast media. In the 1950s, David Ogilvy defined creative genius. During the birth of the television era, Bill Bernbach was widely acknowledged as the greatest creative mind in the business. Who today will be remembered by future generations as the greatest creative working in U.S. advertising?

Trade journal *Adweek*'s choice is Alex Bogusky, former creative director and cochair at Crispin Porter + Bogusky. You've seen the ads: the Burger King spots where customers react with outrage that their favorite burger, the Whopper, has been "discontinued." The "subservient chicken" Website that defines viral marketing effectiveness. The hysterical "Square Butts" spots that promote Sponge Bob Kids Meals. The powerful "Truth" ads that shine a harsh light on the tobacco industry. The early MINI ads and, more recently, the great campaigns for Volkswagen. Unique, even quirky? Undeniably. But they also demonstrate a special flair for slashing through the clutter and for building brands. And that has helped make CP+B one of America's best-known and most respected ad agencies.

How does Alex Bogusky describe himself? Here's how:

Things You May Know about Alex Bogusky

He started at what was then called Crispin and Porter Advertising in 1989 as an art director. He was employee number 16. He became creative director of the agency five years later, was named a partner in 1997, and became cochair in January 2008. Under his direction, the agency has grown to over 700 employees and has become the world's most awarded advertising agency over the last few years. Alex has been profiled in *Communication Arts, Adweek, Ad Age, Fast Company,* and *Business-Week.* His work has been featured in *The New York Times, The Wall Street Journal, USA Today, Newsweek,* and *Time,* as well as on national television

and radio. And in 2002, Alex was inducted into the American Advertising Federation's Hall of Achievement.

Things You May Not Know about Alex Bogusky

Alex Bogusky loses his wallet way more often than most people. He would be perfectly content eating Tex-Mex food every day for the rest of his life. Most Mondays, he will come to work with at least one bloody, puss-oozing injury. He rarely drinks anymore, but when he does he goes straight for the tequila. He has the attention span of a mating fruit fly. In grade school, his teacher recommended he be put in a special class. He owns eleven bicycles, four dirt bikes, and one crotch rocket. He has a photographic memory, but only for ads. He has an irrational dislike of St. Louis. Yet many of his favorite people are from St. Louis. At one time, he was a good enough motocross racer to turn pro. His mom and dad are both designers and more talented than he is. And he cuts his own hair. With a Flowbee.

Alex spoke with *Contemporary Advertising* about his influences, the things he finds rewarding, his philosophy of managing a creative department, and his advice for students finding their career paths. Not long after speaking with us, Bogusky left his position with CP+B and started his own consulting firm.

CA: You've often acknowledged the role your parents played in your creative development. How did they do that?

AB: Both my parents are more creative people than I am. My mom taught art at an elementary school and our house always had books on art and design. When my parents threw parties they'd play a game where people had to come up with the best logo for a product in three minutes.

CA: So did they encourage you to go in a creative direction?

AB: Not directly. They were so good I actually found it a bit discouraging. But my mom taught me some practical creative skills, like doing paste-ups and mechanicals. It helped me to get my first agency job.

CA: Did you respond to feeling less creative than your parents as a challenge?

AB: Not really. I just came to terms with it and accepted it. Ultimately, I think it gave me a very healthy work ethic. I realized that there is no shortcut for putting in the time. Being smart can take the place of talent and because of that some people don't put the rigor they should into their work.

CA: So humility is an important asset for a creative person?

AB: Humility is an asset for any person, but certainly for a creative. It helps you realize that your ideas are not good just because you've thought of them. In an ad agency ideas get built up and torn down all the time. You can't see that happen to your ideas if you have a big ego. I like to think that I have millions of ideas, so I don't worry too much about any one of them. If others think an idea is a bad one I'm always confident I can come up with another.

CA: Over the years you've talked a lot about the collaborative nature of the creative department at CP+B. The phrase you've used is that your creatives are willing to "jump on hand grenades" for each other. What do you mean by that?

AB: At CP+B we trust the process. You can spend too much time wondering and worrying about what you will come up with. At the agency we believe that you have a role, others have a role, and we try to help each other out when we need to. It gives you some comfort, and it helps you enjoy the work.

CA: How important is that sense of enjoyment?

AB: If you've done it for a while you realize that the job never changes, it never gets easier. The creative process can be torture, so you have to love it. Each time you achieve something or win some award, you realize that you go back to work on Monday and the job is exactly the same. The work is the benefit.

CA: As a creative director, your job is a lot less about creating the ad and a lot more about overseeing and working with creative people. How do you do that?

AB: The job is different from being a copywriter or art director; it is more about helping people to find their own process, about mentoring.

CA: What is your philosophy about mentoring and getting great work from people?

AB: Realizing that everyone wants to contribute. Sometimes there is just not that much for a creative director to do. We have great people at CP+B and they know how to do their job. I think some creative directors have a hard time standing back from the work, but I don't. Of course, sometimes there are days where you are just praying for someone to come in with a good idea. But even when I have to give a lot of feedback, I'll write my comments in the margins of a draft. I don't ever get on someone's computer and start writing. After I scratch up a piece of paper I give it back to them and let them do it themselves. It's important that a creative person is allowed to have that sense of contribution.

CA: What else is important?

AB: One of the hardest parts of my job is keeping the bar high. What level of work do we need to keep our aim high? It can be

easy to lower the bar and wherever you put it, that's where people aim. Having the energy to keep the bar high is critical. I think it can be easy for a creative director to say "I'm really good but the people around me are not." I believe that is death; you have to expect as much from the people around you as you expect from yourself.

CA: What advice do you have for students looking for a career at an agency like CP+B?

AB: Well, I've gotten lots of advice over the years, and I've learned to be cautious about giving it. When I talk to interns I like to say that I've never made a tough decision. When I've made decisions, even about tough matters, I've always sensed what feels right to me. In making decisions about my own career I've always tried to move closer to a place that feels like the sweet spot, that lets me do what I enjoy. So many people get into advertising with a preconceived idea about what the business is like. Maybe they've seen it on TV or read about it. They often don't allow themselves to slide and move. But there are so many places to go in this business, literally millions of niches. To me, so much success depends on simply finding the right niche. I always felt that I didn't have to find it right away, so I've done a lot of jobs in advertising, but inevitably I try to gravitate toward the jobs that give me satisfaction and pleasure. I like to call it the feeling of "running downhill." I've had jobs where I felt like I was pushing uphill, and there is no point in staying in a job like that. I think you should go with the momentum, with your energies. Don't fight those things; go with what makes you happy. I think a lot of students are too worried about money. My favorite example is Michael Jordan. He found his exact right thing. M J is a very talented guy, a good baseball player, a good marketer. But he found his thing in basketball.

CA: Does that carry over to what you look for in the people you hire?

AB: Yes. I interviewed one person, actually a very talented person who is one of our top creative people now. I asked him what he would like to do if he didn't get the job. He began describing a career as a musician, playing small clubs, maybe making a few small recordings. He had really thought this through and I could see his passion for it. Midway through the story, he knew he had blown the interview.

CA: But the story has a happy ending?

AB: A few years later he was interviewing with us again. He knew how to answer that question the second time! What we are really looking for is somebody who wants to do advertising more than anything else. That's how we feel and that's who we want to work with.

Companies should follow some basic rules in using translators:

- *The translator must be an effective copywriter.* In the United States and Canada, most people speak English, yet relatively few are good writers and even fewer are good copywriters. Too often marketers simply let a translation service rewrite their ads in a foreign language. That's not good enough.

- *The translator must understand the product.* The translator must also know the product's features and its market. It is always better to use a translator who is a product or market specialist rather than a generalist.

- *Translators should translate into their native tongue.* Ideally, they should live in the country where the ad will appear. This way the company can be sure the translator has a current understanding of the country's social attitudes, culture, and idioms.

- *Give the translator easily translatable English copy.* The double meanings and idiomatic expressions that make English such a rich language for an advertiser rarely translate well. They only make the translator's job more difficult.

There is no greater insult to a national market than to misuse its language. The translation must be accurate and punctuated properly, and it must also be good copy.

When preparing an ad for the international market, the art director must be sure that the imagery and concepts will not be too foreign to the intended audience. This South African ad for Lego (www.lego.com) doesn't need long copy or a striking headline to make its point; the imagery of a Lego periscope peering up from a Lego ocean is enough to inspire building enthusiasts everywhere.

Source: The Lego Group

English is rapidly becoming the universal language for corporate campaigns directed to international businesspeople, and some firms print their instructional literature and brochures in English as well. But this approach can incite nationalistic feelings against the company. Worse yet, it automatically limits a product's use to people who understand technical English.

Art Direction for International Markets

Philosophers often refer to the arts as a kind of international language whose nonverbal elements translate freely regardless of culture. A nice idea but, in advertising, a very costly one. People ascribe different meanings to color depending on their culture. When designing ads for use in other countries, the art director must be familiar with each country's artistic preferences and peculiarities.

Some consider color to indicate emotion: Someone "has the blues" or is "green with envy" (refer back to Ad Lab 10–A, "The Psychological Impact of Color"). National flags—the Canadian maple leaf, the red, white, and blue of the United States, the tricolor of France—are nonverbal signals that stir patriotic emotions, thoughts, and actions. However, these same symbols could hurt sales. For example, a promotion using the colors in the U.S. and French flags could easily fail in Southeast Asia, where some people still have painful memories of wars fought against the two countries.

An **icon,** a visual image representing some idea or thing, can have a meaning that cuts across national boundaries and reflects the tastes and attitudes of a group of cultures. An ad with a snake (an icon for the devil and eroticism in many Western cultures) could easily lose sales in North American markets. But in the Far East, where the snake represents renewal (by shedding its skin), the same visual might work as a dynamic expression of a product's staying power.

On a more personal level, a culture's icons can express social roles. When an agency calls a casting company or talent agent in search of a model, the agency, in essence, seeks an icon. It hopes the model will effectively symbolize the product's benefits or help the target market relate better to the ad. A model considered attractive in one culture is not necessarily seen that way in another, however.

Catchy phrases popular in a local culture are often used for advertising. But even if the idea translates verbally into another language, which is rarely the case, the art director may still have difficulty using the same imagery. Advertisers working in global markets must pretest art and design concepts with natives of each country.

Legal Restraints on International Marketers

Finally, all advertising creativity, including what the ads say, show, or do, is at the mercy of foreign governments and cultures. As we discussed in Chapter 3, many countries strongly regulate advertising claims and the use of particular media.

Chapter Summary

The nonverbal aspect of a message carries half the burden of communicating the big idea. In fact, the nonverbal message is inseparable from the verbal. Either can enhance the other or destroy it.

Design refers to how the art director and graphic artist conceptually choose and structure the artistic elements that make up a message's appearance or set its tone. For print, the first work from the art department is a simple, undeveloped design of the layout. The layout has several purposes: It shows where the parts are to be placed; it is an inexpensive way to explore creative ideas; it helps the creative team check the message's psychological or symbolic function; and it serves as a blueprint for the production process.

As copy goes through the editing process, copywriters must be prepared for an inevitable (and sometimes lengthy) succession of edits and re-edits from agency and client managers and legal departments. Copywriters must be more than creative; they must be patient, flexible, mature, and able to exercise great self-control.

Several steps are used to develop a design: thumbnail sketch, rough layout, and comprehensive layout. The mechanical is the final art ready for reproduction. Brochures and other multipage materials use a three-dimensional rough called a dummy.

The computer has dramatically affected graphic design. Software programs allow artists to paint and draw, make up pages, and manipulate images in ways that would not be possible manually. Every graphic designer must now be computer literate.

In print, the visual has a great deal of responsibility for a message's success. The picture may be used to capture the reader's attention, identify the subject, create a favorable impression, or serve a host of other functions.

The two basic devices for illustrating a message are photos and drawings. Photography can contribute realism; a feeling of immediacy; a feeling of live action; the special enhancement of mood, beauty, and sensitivity; and speed, flexibility, and economy. Drawn illustrations do many of these things, too, and may be used if the artist feels they can achieve greater impact than photos. The chief focus for visuals may be the product in a variety of settings, a user benefit, a humorous situation, a testimonial, or even some negative appeal.

The key format elements for writing print are headlines, subheads, body copy, slogans, seals, logos, and signatures. Many headline types and copy styles are used in print. There are five basic types of headlines: benefit, provocative, news/information, question, and command. Copy styles also fall into several categories: straight sell, institutional, narrative, dialogue/monologue, picture caption, and device.

The creative pyramid and the format elements come together in creating effective print messages. The headline carries the attention step, the subhead and lead-in paragraph hold the interest step, and the interior paragraphs, trial close, and close of body copy contain the credibility and desire steps. The action step takes place with the last line of copy or with the logo, slogan, and signature block.

In electronic media, copy is normally spoken dialogue that is prepared using a script; it is referred to as the audio portion of the commercial. The copy may be delivered as a voice-over by an unseen announcer or on camera by an announcer, spokesperson, or actor.

Radio commercials must be intrusive to catch and hold the attention of people who are usually doing something else. Radio copy must be more conversational than print copy and should paint word pictures for listeners to see in their mind's eye.

Television copywriters use scripts and storyboards to communicate the verbal and nonverbal ideas of a commercial. When writing TV ads, the creative team must strive for credibility, relevance, and consistency in tone. While TV commercials should be entertaining, the entertainment should not interfere with the selling message.

In radio and TV, art plays an important role. Art includes concept development, character definition, set and scene design, costuming, lighting, scripting, camera angles—everything having to do with the visual value of the commercial.

Common formats for radio and TV commercials include straight announcement, presenter, testimonial, demonstration, musical, slice of life, lifestyle, and animation. The art director works with a writer to develop the artistic qualities of the big idea, the format, and the storyboard. The storyboard, the basic rough design of a TV commercial, contains sketches of the scenes along with the script. To supplement the storyboard and pretest a commercial, an animatic may be used.

Writing for Websites and social media requires understanding how consumers find and respond to information online. Content is king on the web and most audiences scan rather than read. Social media is about audiences sharing content and addressing one another, so copywriters should use styles of writing that encourage such behaviors.

When creating campaigns for international markets, advertisers must consider the variations in language and the legal restrictions imposed by foreign governments or cultures. Art direction for international markets requires an in-depth knowledge of the foreign culture. Even if the verbal message translates well, the icons and images may not.

Important Terms

animatic, *366*

animation, *365*

audio, *358*

Ayer No. 1, *344*

benefit headline, *352*

body copy, *354*

boldface, *354*

camera-ready art, *342*

casting brief, *360*

close, *357*

command headline, *354*

comprehensive layout (comp), *340*

demonstration, *362*

design, *339*

device copy, *356*

dialogue/monologue copy, *356*

donut, *363*

headline, *351*

hook, *363*

icon, *371*

illustrator, *346*

institutional copy, *356*

integrated commercial, *361*

interior paragraph, *356*

italic, *354*

jingle, *363*

kicker, *354*

layout, *339*

lead-in paragraph, *356*

lifestyle technique, *365*

logotype, *357*

mechanical, *341*

mnemonic device, *364*

musical commercial, *363*

musical logo, *363*

narrative copy, *356*

news/information headline, *352*

on camera, *361*

pasteup, *341*

photographer, *346*

picture-caption copy, *356*

picture-window layout, *344*

poster-style format, *344*

presenter commercial, *361*

provocative headline, *352*

question headline, *352*

radio personality, *362*

script, *358*

seal, *357*

signature cut, *357*

slice of life, *364*

slogan, *357*

storyboard, *365*

storyboard rough, *360*

straight announcement, *361*

straight-sell copy, *355*

subhead, *354*

tagline, *357*

testimonial, *362*

text, *354*

themeline, *357*

thumbnail, *340*

trial close, *356*

visuals, *346*

voice-over, *361*

Review Questions

1. What is a layout? What is its purpose?
2. What are the steps in the design process for a print ad?
3. What color is white space?
4. From any chapter in the book, select an ad that contains a visual. What is the visual's purpose? How would you improve the visual if you were the art director?
5. What kind of headline does the ad from question 4 have? How well has the creative team followed the steps up the creative pyramid? Explain.
6. Choose an ad you don't like. Rewrite the headline using three different styles.
7. What is a storyboard, and what is its role?
8. Give examples of television spots that typify the eight major types of TV commercials.
9. Find an international ad or commercial you like. What is its message strategy? Can you discern the copy style? Do you think the copy and headline reflect the strategy? What do you like about the ad? Why?
10. What guidelines can you cite for preparing an ad in a foreign language?

The Advertising Experience

1. Big Stan's Tri-State Mattress Outlet usually advertises by sponsoring monster truck shows or demolition derbies. However, Big Stan wants to expand his business and has decided to try radio advertising. Using the script format found on page 356 create the kind of radio ad that would please Big Stan and his potential customers.

2. **Creative Boutiques**
   One of the growing trends in advertising is the increased use of creative boutiques. Many of these smaller shops have won clients previously handled by larger, full-service advertising agencies. Peruse the small sampling of creative boutiques below and answer the questions that follow.
   - AdWorks: www.adworks.com
   - B Creative: www.bcreative.com
   - Brolik: http://brolik.com/
   - Crispin Porter + Bogusky: www.cpbgroup.com
   - The Idea Boutique: http://www.theideaboutique.com/index/agency/
   - JDG Designs: www.jdgdesign.com
   - Love and War: www.thisisloveandwar.com
   a. What is the focus of the company's work (consumer, business-to-business, ethnic, general market)?
   b. What are the scope and size of the company's business?
   c. What services does the company offer?
   d. What is your overall impression of the company and its work? Why?

3. **Creative Resources**
   As you saw when reading this chapter, a lot goes into writing good copy or scripts and developing effective visuals. Because of the Internet, many new resources are available to the creative team that is developing a concept.

   Copywriters often rely on different sources to aid them in developing their copy. Visit the following Websites and explain how each relates to copywriters and their task of developing effective copy.
   - Copy Chef: www.copychef.com
   - The Slot: www.theslot.com
   - Writers Guild of America: www.wga.org

   Like copywriters, art directors require many resources while developing their art. Familiarize yourself further with art direction by browsing the following Websites. Be sure to discuss the importance of each site to art directors.
   - American Institute of Graphic Arts: www.aiga.org
   - Art Directors Club: www.adcglobal.org
   - Creative Cafe: www.creativity.net
   - Design & Publishing Center: www.graphic-design.com
   - Digital Directory: www.digitaldirectory.com
   - Gnomon Online: www.gnomononline.com
   - PhotoDisc: www.photodisc.com
   - Photographer's Index: www.photographersindex.com
   - Portfolios Online: www.portfolios.com
   - Right Brain Works: www.gocreate.com

4. How does the "Dumb Ways to Die" campaign use metaphor to change behaviors around trains? How does the campaign suggest that there is something even worse than death for those who might be tempted to take risks around trains?

12

Print, Electronic, and Digital Media Production

Learning Objectives

To present an overview of how marketing messages are produced for print, electronic, and digital media. With their dynamic effect on the production process, computers now give companies many more options for saving money and time and enhancing production quality. But to control cost and quality, marketers still need a basic knowledge of the processes and methods used in printing, broadcasting, and digital media.

After studying this chapter, you will be able to:

LO12-1 Discuss the challenges of managing the production process.

LO12-2 Explain the stages of the print production process.

LO12-3 Review procedures for quality control in print production.

LO12-4 List the key steps and events in the radio commercial production process.

LO12-5 Describe the key events in the TV commercial production process.

LO12-6 Explain how producing advertising for social media and the web differs from traditional production.

Source: Sony Corporation

The Sony name stands for quality technology, so when the company introduced its BRAVIA line (BRAVIA stands for Best Resolution Audio Visual Integrated Architecture) of HDTVs, it wanted a campaign that would distinguish the brand from other sets. To do so, Sony retained the London office of Fallon Worldwide (you may remember Fallon from its American office's work for Holiday Inn Express, recounted in Chapter 7). ■ In the mid-2000's, high-definition TV was still very new. For most consumers, just replacing an old console with an HDTV would bring a huge jump in viewing quality. But because the technology was quite expensive at the time, many consumers looked for brands offering the lowest price. ■ Sony's challenge was to convince shoppers that spending a bit more on their new HDTV was well worth the viewing experience a BRAVIA could provide. Chris Willingham, a Fallon account executive, told Sony that research showed people wanted vibrant colors in an HDTV. Sony and Fallon agreed on a strategic focus summarized by the campaign's slogan, "Color like no other?" ■ The creative team was led by long-time Fallon star Richard Flintham. His idea: a dreamlike ad in which two San Francisco streets (Filbert and Leavenworth) burst forth in an array of brilliant colors. He would do so without any special effects. Instead, the agency would release hundreds of thousands of bouncing colored balls. Careening down the steep inclines of the two roads, each ball would follow its own idiosyncratic path, bouncing past cars, homes, street lamps, and sidewalks. The ad would have no dialog, just haunting, simple music and superimposed text highlighting the brand. ■ Of course, no one had ever produced such an ad. The logistics of creating the spot began with a very simple question: what kind of balls should they use? After testing a variety (tennis, ping pong, etc.), the agency chose a staple of every kid's toy chest, the super ball. These high-bouncing spheres made from synthetic rubber compressed under high pressure seem, when dropped, to almost have minds of their own. ■ On the day of the shoot, the agency set up several mechanisms for launching the balls. For massive ball drops, it used three large skips capable of dropping tens of thousands of balls from 50 feet in the air (creating very big bounces!). These were supplemented with 12 air mortars for firing balls at different angles. ■ The agency did six takes over a four-day period. To protect the neighborhood, large nets were placed strategically on the streets and over drains. Large rubber hoses helped gather up the balls for reuse at the end of each take. Despite the precautions, a couple of neighborhood cars sustained some damage. ■ Over a dozen cameras were set up to capture the flight of the balls, many requiring shields to ensure camera men were not picked off by the ricocheting orbs. Balls were released from everywhere, the top of the street, side streets, even from gutters. ■ Agency interns (naturally) helped with the rather unglamorous task of collecting each of the balls. Not the most exciting work, but Assistant Director Chris

Williams pointed out the advantages of working with high-bouncing, but low-maintenance, spheres. "They don't talk back to you," noted Williams, "and they never sit in makeup, they never make you wait on the set, and they throw no tantrums." ■ The shoot went well, and the crew sent film off for processing at a major London studio, The Mill. Flintham considered several musical scores before settling on a haunting song "Heartbeats," originally written by a Swedish group, The Knife. For the ad, a version recorded by José González, another Swedish artist, was used. The spot proved to be stunning, impressing the judges at Cannes enough to win a Gold Lion. You can see the ad, and how it was made, here: http://www.youtube.com/watch?v=9NymcQJjPCs. Like all great ads, this one started with an inspired idea. But spectacular production made it a spot like no other.

Managing the Production Process

LO 12-1

Marketers know that ad production is hardly an afterthought. In fact, careful management of the production process is an important component of a successful campaign.

Every ad or commercial represents the completion of a highly complex process that includes many steps, such as reproducing visuals in full color, shooting and editing scenes, the precise specifying and placing of type, and checking, approving, duplicating, and shipping final art, negatives, tape, or film to various communications media (newspapers, magazines, radio and TV stations, and even web publishers).

These tasks are usually the responsibility of a **print production manager** or, for electronic media, a **producer.** The overall responsibility of the producer is to keep the project moving smoothly and under budget, while maintaining the required level of quality through every step of the production process.

Producers perform the four classic functions of management: *planning, organizing, directing,* and *controlling.*

Planning and Organizing

An important facet of management is the *allocation of time.* Each phase of a project comprises many tasks, so the production manager must anticipate where irregularities may occur within each phase. For example, five phases are needed to complete one animated commercial, but the amount of time required for each may vary greatly from spot to spot, as shown in Exhibit 12-1.[1]

Directing and Controlling

Supervising the production staff and suppliers is another challenge. If artists fail to follow the art director's design correctly, they can kill an ad's power, beauty, and effectiveness. Improper printing processes, papers, or inks can also weaken the impact of the image, increase costs, and even lead to time-consuming reprinting. Print production managers can squander their client's or agency's dollars (and sometimes their jobs) by forgetting to double-check the details of print production and the work of the production staff.

The producer also has to keep up with all the technological changes occurring in print and electronic production, including *digital media* (multimedia, interactive media, and online networks).[2]

Making a great ad within the budget established by the client involves avoiding common "budget busters." Sony's campaign came in under budget because of expert planning.

Source: Sony Corporation

Managing Production Costs

When an agency begins a campaign it submits an estimate for anticipated production costs, including computer artwork and subcontracted work such as photography, reproduction services, and delivery. It is understood that the agency will make every effort to keep the actual costs below the estimate.

A good production manager continually monitors the time spent on a job and the charges submitted by outside suppliers so as not to exceed the budget. The big effort is to control *unplanned costs.*

Common Budget Busters

Five problems commonly break budgets. The most frequent cause of cost overruns is *inadequate planning* and lack of preparation. Another culprit is *production luxuries.* When the creative director wants to reward the staff by taking everyone to lunch at the company's expense, the first question should be: Was money budgeted for this? The third budget buster is *overtime:* night and weekend work. Whenever possible, managers should develop alternative plans to avoid overtime hours. *Special equipment* for unusual production effects can also wreak havoc on budgets. It's often far more expensive to use an exotic computer gizmo than standard equipment. Finally, a complex *hierarchy* of decision makers, approvers, and lawyers can stall decision making, cause negative debate, and stop progress.

International advertisers should also be aware that foreign taxation on production costs varies widely from country to country. Argentina, for instance, charges a blanket 21 percent VAT (value-added tax) on all production costs as well as on media-buying commissions.[3]

Some other budget issues are peculiar to each medium.

Managing the Cost of Print Production

Print production refers to the systematic process an approved design goes through from concept to final publication.

For print media, production managers can choose from more than 60 techniques to execute the creative team's design and get it printed on any of a variety of materials (usually paper). They must translate the rough or comprehensive design into a final assembly of black-and-white artwork called a *mechanical* or *pasteup.* Then, working with an engraver or printer, they make sure the mechanical is converted into a correct set of negatives for the printer to use to make printing plates.

A big cost factor in the production of many print ads is the *engraver* that provides all the color separations, retouching, press proofs, and digital files. Many production managers prefer using their printer to provide all the *prepress graphic services* (such as processing negatives from artwork or disk). Most printers today offer digital graphic services in-house, and they know exactly which processing specifications yield the most suitable negatives for their

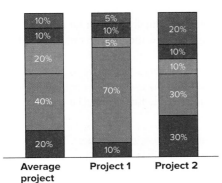

	Average project	Project 1	Project 2
	10%	5%	20%
	10%	10%	
	20%	5%	10%
	40%	70%	10%
	20%		30%
		10%	30%

■ Conceptual design/planning phase
■ Production
■ Editing
■ Rendering and final output
■ Review process

Exhibit 12-1

Time allocation comparison. All projects are different, and thus the amount of time needed for each phase of a project may vary widely. Although about 40 percent of the time spent on an average project may be production hours, other projects might involve more production time (Project 1) or less production time (Project 2).

platemaking equipment and printing presses. They also often charge less than outside service bureaus. Other production managers feel safer ordering the negatives from a high-quality engraver because it typically offers highly specialized service, personnel skilled at color reproduction, and the expertise to deliver the right materials correctly and on time to media across the country.

Paper costs affect budgets, too. When agencies place ads in print media, the cost of paper is included in the charge for the ad. But when an agency prints collateral materials such as brochures or packaging for a client, the cost of paper is noticeable. For example, on a full-color job, a short run of 2,000 units would require only a few thousand sheets of paper (a variable cost), while the prepress and press setup charges (fixed costs) would comprise the bulk of the final selling price. But if the same job had a long run of 100,000 or more units, the prepress and press setup charges would remain the same, while the cost for paper would rise according to the volume used—a cost increase of 700 to 1,000 percent.

A big cost saver comes from the near universal use of digital print production processes.[4] The savings come, in part, from the need for fewer individuals with specialized skills. Jobs that would have required typesetters, designers, trade shop personnel, and printers, now often require only a designer and a printer.

Managing the Cost of Electronic Production

The term **electronic production** refers to the process of converting a script or storyboard to a finished commercial for use on radio, TV, or digital media. **Digital production** refers to the same process when the finished product is digital rather than tape. While the overall process is similar to print production, the technical details and the costs of electronic production are quite different. And the end result, rather than print film or negatives, may be audio or video, motion picture film, or some digital format.

Radio   Radio is the least expensive electronic medium to produce. Equipment and labor costs are less than for, say, TV production. There's no need for hairstylists, makeup artists, or cue-card holders.

The primary control factors in producing radio spots, therefore, are the costs of talent and music. Celebrity talent, especially, can be very expensive. But even the cost of standard union talent, paid at **scale** (the regular charge agreed to in the union contract), can mount rapidly if there are multiple voices or if the commercial is aired in many markets or for an extended period of time. The advertiser, for example, may initially contract for a 4-week or a 13-week run. If the commercial is extended beyond that time, the advertiser owes a **residual fee** to the talent.

Likewise, the cost of original music can range from very inexpensive to frightful, depending on the talent and scope of use. For this reason, many clients—especially small local and regional advertisers—prefer prerecorded music available for commercial use from the studio or radio station.

Television   Many companies desire the sight, sound, and motion TV offers. However, the television industry is susceptible to prohibitive costs of equipment and labor. In 2011, the average cost of producing a 30-second national television spot was over $300,000.[5] With costs like that, clients become very picky very quickly (see Exhibit 12-2).

Numerous factors can torture TV production budgets. They include the use of children and animals, superstar talent and directors, large casts, animation, involved opticals, special effects, stop-motion photography, use of both location and studio shooting for one commercial, expensive set decoration or construction, additional shooting days, and major script changes during a shoot.[6] Commercial producers have to be aware of all these factors and plan for them very carefully.

Digital Media   The computer has engendered a whole new class of digital media. This has dramatically increased the importance of the tasks performed by the agency producer and creative staff and made it critical for them to stay current with new recording and duplicating processes as well as special-effects technology.

Commercial Type	Approximate Cost
Special effects	$447,000
Large-scale product	437,000
Single situation—voice-over	362,000
Monologue	368,000
Song and dance	241,000
Single situation—dialogue	363,000
Multistory line/vignettes	313,000
Animation	248,000
Interview/testimonial	180,000
Table top/ECU	301,000

Exhibit 12-2

Average cost to produce a TV commercial.

Production is important in a traditional TV commercial, but even more so in a viral spot like this one featuring martial artist Bruce Lee. If the production values fail to impress, users won't share the viral.

Source: Nokia Corporation

The production manager can construct ads using off-the-shelf image and text development software. But to go onto the Internet, the completed files have to be combined with computer programming. For this service, most production managers subcontract the work—but they have to know the suppliers, and charges can range from $50 to $150 per hour.[7] Saatchi & Saatchi, for instance, has a special design and interactive media group that creates advertising for Toyota and other clients.[8]

The overall production process for creating images, graphic design, texts, and interactive digital programs for various electronic media is similar to working in print. Final output, though, is to a medium suitable for storage and transmission of data such as a DVD, Website, or mass storage USB device.

Finally, with the penetration of broadband connections increasing to nearly 90 percent of active Internet users, consumers are more apt to engage with video content. As user adoption grows, so too do advertisers embrace the tactic. Savvy online marketers incorporate video in their online efforts, even by simply repurposing their TV spot(s). This, however, can be a sure budget breaker if online distribution rights were not negotiated ahead of time with the "talent." Savvy producers will seek complete distribution rights at the beginning to ensure that the firm can act on any last minute media opportunities.[9]

The Print Production Process

The **print production process** consists of four major phases: *preproduction, production, prepress,* and *printing and distribution.* For a simple model of this process, see Exhibit 12-3.

The Preproduction Phase: Planning the Project

The first step, **preproduction,** begins when the creative department submits the approved creative concepts—rough or comprehensive layout and copy—to the production department. The production manager's first task is to communicate with the agency's traffic manager and log the project into the department's *traffic system.* Together they examine the general nature of the job and consider several questions pertinent to managing it efficiently. For example,

- What equipment will be needed?
- How will we get it? (Will we have to lease another machine?)
- What materials are necessary? (If this is a packaging job, what material will we be printing on: tin, paper, cardboard?)
- What human resources are needed? (Do we need to hire any freelancers?)
- Will there be any special expenses associated with the job? (Do we need to do location photography, for example?)
- How many production artists will be needed? (Is the deadline so near that we'll have to call up the reserves?)

Classic manual print production process

- Rough or comprehensive layout
- Type specification and typesetting
- Pasteup and mechanical

Printer

- Prepress
  - Color separations
  - Negatives
  - Stripping
  - Platemaking
- Presswork
  - Printing
  - Cutting
  - Binding

Computerized print production process

- Design
- Type
- Mechanicals
- Color separations
- Negatives
- Stripping

- Platemaking

Printer

- Presswork
  - Printing
  - Cutting
  - Binding

Exhibit 12-3
The print production process.

Once these general questions are answered, the production manager can look more closely at the specific needs of the project.

Working backward from publication **closing dates** (deadlines), the traffic and production managers decide when each step of the work must be completed. Deadlines can vary from months to hours. The manager tries to build extra time into each step because every word, art element, and aesthetic choice may need some last-minute change. The traffic manager's job is to make sure deadlines are not missed and that all the proper approvals are obtained in a timely fashion.

Typography and Copy Casting

Art directors select type styles to enhance the desired personality of the product and complement the tone of the ad. Typefaces affect an ad's appearance, design, and readability. Good type selection can't compensate for a weak headline, poor body copy, or an inappropriate illustration, but it can create interest and attract readers.

It's imperative that production managers as well as graphic artists understand **typography,** the art of selecting and setting type. Advertising artists have to know the five major type groups, the artistic variations within a type family, and the structure of type. They should consider four important concepts when selecting type: *readability, appropriateness, harmony or appearance,* and *emphasis.* Ad Lab 12–A, "The Characteristics of Type," describes these and other type-related topics.

Artists who plan to buy type outside must **copy cast** (or *copyfit*) to calculate the total block of space the type will occupy in relation to the typeface's letter size and proportions.

Twenty years ago, copyfitting ability was essential for all artists, but now type is manipulated in minutes on computers. However, copyfitting is still useful in the preproduction phase for avoiding typesetting problems later.

Planning the Job

The overall purpose of the preproduction phase is to plan the job thoroughly, which usually entails making a number of strategic choices before launching into full production. For example, since the art director's conceptual rough layouts are often made with marker colors that do not match printing inks, the production manager should consult with the art director to formally select a color palette in advance, using a color guide such as the PANTONE system.

For brochures, there is also the question of which printing process and which type of printing press to use for the job. This will affect the budget and dictate how art is prepared in the production and prepress phases.

Similarly, the art director and production manager usually consult on the paper to be used. Three categories of paper are used for advertising purposes: *writing, text,* and *cover stock.* Letters and fliers, for example, commonly use **writing paper.** Bond writing paper is the most durable and most frequently used. For brochures, there are many types of **text papers,** such as news stock, antique finish, machine finish, English finish, and coated. These range from the inexpensive to the smooth, expensive, coated stocks used in upscale magazines. **Cover papers,** available in many finishes and textures, are used on soft book covers, direct-mail pieces, and brochure covers, so they're thicker, tougher, and more durable.

Finally, the production manager must decide early which is most important for a particular project: *speed, quality,* or *economy.* Typically, the manager must sacrifice one in favor of the other two. The answer determines the production methods used and the personnel employed. Once all these decisions are made, the manager can begin the production phase.

The Production Phase: Creating the Artwork

The **production phase** involves completing ancillary functions such as illustrations or photography, setting up the artwork and typesetting, and then melding all these components into a final form for the printer.

In a multicolor piece of art, the printer needs layers that can be reproduced individually. This is done by computer or assembled by hand with plastic overlays. The total image is then reconstructed as each layer is printed over the other.

© Didier Maillac/REA/Redux

© Zigy Kaluzny-Charles Thatcher/Getty Images

Creating the Visual

Almost every ad has some kind of a visual besides typography, and many ads have several pictures. The visual may be an illustration or a photograph. But where do these pictures come from?

When reviewing the layout with the art director, the decision will be made whether to use illustration or photography and how to get just the pictures the creatives envision. In many cases, to save money, the art director or producer will choose to use stock photography for a reasonable licensing fee. The fee will typically be based on the intended usage and the length of time the usage will continue.

Most expensive is commissioning an illustrator to draw an original picture or hiring a photographer to go on location to shoot a specific visual. Producers must plan for hiring the right photographer. Some are well versed in photojournalistic techniques. Others are especially good at shooting interiors. And some specialize in food or fashion photography.

Preparing Mechanicals

To create the art for an ad, brochure, or package, the production artist normally begins by marking out a grid on which to lay the type and art. Art directors use computers to do this with commands for setting up columns and guides. The grid provides an underlying consistency to the spacing and design of the piece.

The production artist then specifies the style and size of the typefaces for the text and inputs this information, along with the copy, into the computer.

The art elements must be properly positioned in the artwork (whether mechanical or computer generated) because the printer needs to have layers of art that can be reproduced individually. The total image is then constructed as each layer is printed over the previous one. Because the printer must photograph each layer to make separate plates, this kind of artwork is called **camera-ready art.**

This procedure is easily performed in the computer. The various elements of art are assigned to a layer the operator names and can be run out as separate film negatives or paper positive images as needed.

Camera-Ready Art and Halftones

Production art for the printing process is like an on/off switch: Where the art is black, ink will stick; where the art is white, ink won't stick. The production artist adheres to this printing principle by using black-and-white artwork that is called *line art* and by converting gray images to a form of line art called *halftones*.

A halftone screen breaks up continuous-tone artwork into tiny dots. The combination of printed dots produces an optical illusion of shading, as in a photograph. The color dots show the separation for the color photo above. The other set of dots show the range that would appear in a black-and-white photo.

© McGraw-Hill Companies, Inc.

Line Art   Normal photographic paper (such as snapshots made with a camera) produces images in **continuous tones**—black and white with shades of gray in between. But printing presses cannot print gray. So printers use special **orthographic film,** a high-contrast film yielding only black-and-white images with no gray tones. The artwork is simply

AD Lab 12–A

The Characteristics of Type

Readability

The most important consideration in selecting a typeface is readability. As David Ogilvy said, good typography helps people read; bad typography prevents them from doing so. General factors that contribute to readability include the type's style, boldness, and size; the length of the line; and the spacing between words, lines, and paragraphs. An ad is meant to be read, and reduced readability kills interest. Difficult-to-read typefaces should be used infrequently and only to create special effects.

Large, bold, simply designed typefaces are the easiest to read. However, the amount of space in the ad and the amount of copy that must be written limit the use of these type forms. The length of the line of copy can also affect the readability. Newspaper columns are usually less than 2 inches wide; magazine columns slightly wider. For ads, columns of copy should be less than 3 inches (18 picas) wide.

Spacing between lines also influences an ad's readability. Space between lines of type allows for descenders (the part of the letter that extends downward, as in the letters j, g, p) and ascenders (the part of the letter that extends upward, as in the letters b, d, k). When this is the only space between lines, type is said to be "set solid." Sometimes an art director adds extra space between lines (called **leading,** pronounced "ledding") to give a more "airy" feeling to the copy. The name comes from the thin lead strips that used to be inserted between lines of metal type.

Kerning (spreading or narrowing the spaces between letters) also improves an ad's appearance and readability. The narrower the kerning, the more type can fit into the available space. Narrow kerning is effective in headlines because people read large type faster when the letters are close together. But narrow kerning is hard to read if overdone or in smaller type sizes.

Appropriateness

A typeface must be appropriate to the product being advertised. Each typeface and size convey a mood and feeling quite apart from the meanings of the words themselves. One typeface whispers "luxury," another screams "bargain!" A typeface that looks old-fashioned is probably inappropriate for an electronic watch.

Harmony/Appearance

Advertising novices often mix too many typefaces, creating disharmony and clutter. Type should harmonize with the other elements of an ad, including the illustration and layout. Skilled artists choose typefaces in the same family or faces that are closely related in appearance.

Emphasis

Contrast creates emphasis. Artists often use more than one type style or mix italic and roman, small and large type, lowercase and uppercase. But they must be careful not to emphasize all elements or they won't emphasize any.

Classes of Type

Two classes of type are used in advertising.

Display type is larger and heavier than text type; useful in headlines, subheads, logos, and addresses, and for emphasis.

Text type is smaller and finer, used in body copy.

Type Groups

Serif *(roman)* type is the most popular type group due to its readability and warm personality. It is distinguished by small lines or tails called serifs that finish the ends of the main strokes and by variations in the thickness of the strokes. It comes in a wide variety of designs and sizes.

Sans serif *(gothic)* type is the second most popular type group; it is also referred to as block or contemporary. Characterized by lack of serifs (hence the name *sans serif*) and relatively uniform thickness of the strokes, it is not as readable as roman but is widely used because the simple, clean lines give a slick, modern appearance (see **a**).

Roman type	Square serif type
Typography	Typography
Typography	
Typography	Script type
Typography	*Typography*
	Typography
Sans serif type	Ornamental type
Typography	Typography
Typography	Typography
TYPOGRAPHY	Typography

a.

photographed as is, and the result is called a **line film.** From that a **line plate** is produced for printing.

A *continuous-tone photograph* or other illustration requiring gradations in tone cannot be reproduced on orthographic film or a plate without an additional process, the *halftone screen.*

Halftone Screens   While line plates print lines and solid areas (like type), **halftone plates** print dots. The key element is the **halftone screen,** which breaks up continuous-tone artwork

Square serif type combines sans serif and serif typefaces. It has serifs, but letter strokes have uniform thickness.

Cursive or *script type* resembles handwriting; letters often connect and may convey a feeling of femininity, formality, classicism, or beauty. It is difficult to read and is used primarily in headlines, formal announcements, and cosmetic and fashion ads.

Ornamental type uses novel designs with a high level of embellishment and decorativeness. It adds a "special effects" quality but is often difficult to read.

Type Families

A **type family** is made up of related typefaces. The serif typeface used for the text of this book is called Garamond Book. Within a family, the basic design remains the same but varies in the proportion, weight, and slant of the characters. The type may be light, medium, bold, extra bold, condensed, extended, or italic. Variations enable the typographer to provide contrast and emphasis without changing the family (see **b**).

A **font** is a complete assortment of capitals, small capitals, lowercase letters, numerals, and punctuation marks for a particular typeface and size.

Measuring Type

Type characters have height, width, weight, and, for some ornamental typefaces, depth. They also come in shapes called a case. And with the advent of computers, type comes in a variety of resolutions.

Size is the height of a character (or letter) measured in **points** (72 points to the inch) from the bottom of the descenders to the top of the ascenders (see **c**).

The set width of a letter, known as an *em space,* is usually based on the maximum width and proportions of the capital letter M for that particular typeface. The set width of the letter N is called an *en space.*

Capital letters are uppercase, small letters lowercase (in the hot-type era, compositors stacked the case containing the capital letters above the one with the small letters). It's easiest to read a combination of uppercase and lowercase. Type may be set in all caps (for emphasis) or in commoncase (caps and small caps).

Resolution refers to the fineness of the type. The goals of fine typesetting are readability, clarity, and smoothness of appearance. Type on a computer screen is usually 72 to 78 dots per inch (dpi). A dot-matrix printer outputs type at 360 dpi, a laser printer at up to 1,200 dpi. The preferred level of quality for magazines and brochures begins at 1,000 dpi; advertisers often use resolutions of 2,400 to 3,750 dpi.

Laboratory Applications

Use the various figures and terms in this Ad Lab to answer the following:

1. Describe the class, group, family, and size of the type used in the title "Print, Electronic, and Digital Media Production," which appears on the first page of this chapter.

2. Do the same for the captions that appear with the exhibits in this book.

Garamond Book	Garamond Condensed Book
Garamond Book Italic	*Garamond Condensed Book Italic*
Garamond Bold	**Garamond Condensed Bold**
Garamond Bold Italic	***Garamond Condensed Bold Italic***
Garamond Light	Garamond Condensed Light
Garamond Light Italic	*Garamond Condensed Light Italic*
Garamond Ultra	**Garamond Condensed Ultra**
Garamond Ultra Italic	***Garamond Condensed Ultra Italic***

b.

Text type	Display type
6 pt. Type size	16 pt. Type size
8 pt. Type size	18 pt. Type size
9 pt. Type size	20 pt. Type size
10 pt. Type size	24 pt. Type size
12 pt. Type size	30 pt. Type size
14 pt. Type size	36 pt. Type size

c.

into tiny dots. The combination of dots, when printed, produces an optical illusion of shading, as in a photo. In the dark areas of the image, the dots bump into each other and make the paper appear nearly black. In the gray areas, the size of the black dots equals the amount of white paper showing through; in the white areas, the black dots are surrounded by a lot of white or are almost completely missing. The human eye perceives the dots as gradations of tone.

The artist's final step is to mark any halftones and line art for size and indicate where they should be placed. The artist simply sticks a photocopy of the visual to the artboard in its

65-line screen

100-line screen

150-line screen

Halftone screens help the printer control ink flow when trying to emulate the continuous-tone quality of photos. On newsprint, where the ink soaks in and spreads, a coarse 65-line screen gives the ink some room between dots. The finer, 150-line screen gives a better appearance, but it works best with magazine-quality paper that has a compressed chalk coating to keep ink from spreading.

© M. Hruby

exact location with the letters FPO (for position only) written across the image. That way the printer doesn't think the copy is the actual final art.

The Prepress Phase: Stripping, Negs, and Plates

In the **prepress phase,** the printer makes a plate from the base art and one from each overlay. Each pasteup (mechanical) has to be photographed separately.

The various layers of line art and halftones are converted to film negatives, which are carefully mounted together in perfect registration—through a process known as **stripping**—onto opaque plastic sheets called **flats.** A completed flat is a mask that allows light to pass through only where lines and dots are to appear on the plate. The flat is pressed against the printing plate, and ultraviolet light exposes the plate's photosensitive emulsion. Once exposed, the emulsion is developed, etching the plate in the process. This leaves some areas of the plate capable of holding ink and others unable to do so. Once dry, the plates are "hung" on the press, ready for printing.

Printing in Color

A printing plate can print only one color at a time. An advertiser who wants to print an ad or a brochure in blue, green, and black needs three different plates (one for each color), and the job is referred to as a three-color job. To print in full color, though, the **four-color process** is used. This process can simulate nearly all colors by combining the four primary colors: *process blue* (cyan), *process yellow, process magenta,* and *black* (which provides greater detail and density as well as shades of gray). In the parlance of the trade, this is also called **CYMK printing,**

Special screens lend an artistic look to photos. Whether the screens use lines, scratches, or some other technique, they work on the same principle as the halftone dot screen.

© Corbis RF, Special screen by McGraw-Hill Companies, Inc.

the K standing for black. To print in full color, therefore, the printer prepares four different printing plates—one for each process color plus black.

Designs that don't need full color are printed in blended inks rather than process colors. For example, it would take two process colors (magenta and yellow) to make red or three process colors (magenta, yellow, and cyan) to make burgundy. To print a brochure in black and burgundy, it's cheaper to use only two ink colors rather than black plus three process colors.

A PANTONE color, one of a spectrum of colors that makes up the **PANTONE Matching System (PMS),** is a single ink premixed according to a formula and given a specific color number. The PANTONE swatch book features more than 100 colors in solid and screened blocks printed on different paper finishes.[10]

Four-Color Separations

Four separate halftone negatives are needed to make a set of four-color plates: one each for cyan, yellow, magenta, and black. Each of the resulting negatives appears in black and white, and the set is called the **color separation.** In printing, the process color inks are translucent, so two or three colors can overlap to create another color. For example, green is reproduced by overlapping yellow and cyan dots.

Today, sophisticated electronic scanning systems—such as the workstations from Silicon Graphics, Hell ScriptMaster, Scitex, and Crosfield—can produce four-color separations and screens in one process, along with enlargements or reductions.

The outcome is tiny clusters of halftone dots in various colors, sizes, and shapes that give the eye the illusion of seeing the colors of the original photograph or painting.

The Duplication and Distribution Phase: Printing, Binding, and Shipping

The last phase of the traditional print production process involves the actual printing, proofing, and finishing steps of drying, cutting, binding, and shipping.

The Press Run

Once the paper, plates, and ink are readied, the press is started and stopped a few times to adjust the image's alignment on the paper. In multicolored printing, proper alignment of all the colors is critical. When the initial proofs show good alignment, the presses are sped up to maximum output.

Finishing

Once all the pieces are printed, the ink must dry (unless heat-set or cold-set inks were used). Then the excess paper (or other material) is cut away using huge cutting machines. Depending on the nature of the job, the pieces may be delivered to special subcontractors who emboss or die-cut or perform other special techniques to enhance the final printed piece. The final stop may be the bindery for two- and three-hole drilling, wire stapling, and folding.

LO 12-3

Quality Control in Print Production

At various stages of the print production process, the production manager needs to verify the quality. Artwork for a newspaper or magazine ad, for example, must be camera-ready. Many agencies now just send a disk, and the publisher converts the computer image to negatives. Magazines provide specific instructions and measurements for each ad size they offer. If there is any question, the production manager should call the publication and ask how current the data are.

Finally, the production manager must check all proofs for errors and obtain approvals from agency and client executives before releasing ads to publications or artwork to printers. Proofing is a time-consuming task made more so by the fact that not everyone is available when the work is ready for approval.

For the production process to run smoothly, everyone concerned must understand the procedure. The later in the process errors are discovered, the more expensive they are to fix.

My **IMC** Campaign 12

Producing Ads

You probably think it is unrealistic to plan on producing a real ad for your client. After all, advertisers spend millions of dollars getting their ads produced for television. Even print and radio are expensive.

But you might think differently if you knew the costs were low. Even free. Which is not to say it will be easy. But if you want to take a stab at producing an attractive and effective ad, here are some tools that are low cost or free.

If you want to:

Do desktop publishing. Try Indesign alternative Scribus (www.scribus.net/). Price: free.

Work with and manipulate images. Try Photoshop alternative GIMP (www.gimp.org/). Price: free.

Create logos and simple designs. Try Raven (http://aviary.com/home). Price: free.

Create more complicated illustrations. Try Inkscape (www.inkscape.org/). Price: free.

Edit a video (and you're new at it). Try Windows MovieMaker (http://windows.microsoft.com/en-us/windows/movie-maker) Price: free.

Post videos online where the world can see them: Try YouTube (www.youtube.com). Price: free.

Build a Website for your client (and you're new at it). Try Google Sites (http://sites.google.com/). Price: free.

Build a Website for your client (and you really know what you're doing). Try Aptana (http://aptana.com/). Price: free.

Edit sound files: Try Audacity (www.audacity.sourceforge.net). Price: free.

Spice up your ads with royalty-free photos: Try Creative Commons (http://creativecommons.org/) or Flickr (https://www.flickr.com/).

Production Phase Quality Issues

The task of quality control really begins in the production phase. Proofs of the production art, with all its type and images, must be carefully inspected for misspellings, mismeasured lines, improperly sized images, misplaced cropmarks, or a myriad of other minutiae that could lead to a problem later.

Prepress Quality Issues

The slightest flaw in the final printed piece can have serious repercussions. The production manager must check and double-check, even triple-check, the film negatives before they're sent off to a magazine. An analog or digital proof (described below) of the negatives should be carefully checked and sent with the negatives.

Ways to Proof Print Production

When printing collateral materials or projects like brochures, the production manager will typically see a *blueline, color key, analog* or *digital proof,* and *press proof* from the printer.

A **blueline** is a proof that is created by shining light through the negatives and exposing a light-sensitive paper that turns from white to blue. The blueline helps reveal scratches and flaws in the negatives as well as any assembly errors, such as a reversed illustration.

The **analog proof** (also called a **Chromalin**) uses a series of four very thin sheets of plastic pressed together. Each layer's light-sensitive emulsion turns one of the process colors when exposed to certain wavelengths of light. Together they form a full, four-color image proof. The **color key** is a less expensive form of the Chromalin with relatively thick plastic sheets that can be lifted up.

When the presses begin printing, the press operator "pulls" a few proofs to align the press and check ink densities. At this time the production manager should sign one of these actual press proofs as a guide for the operator to follow and for the agency's protection if something goes wrong later during the printing process.

What to Look for in a Proof

When checking proofs, production managers look for any scratches, minute holes or dots, blemishes, or unevenness of ink coverage. Using a *loupe* (magnifying glass), they inspect the dot pattern in halftones to make sure the registration of color is perfectly tight. Then they check *traps* and *bleeds*.

Computer animation is becoming an increasingly sophisticated means of communicating with and persuading an audience. Disney studios has been a pioneer in the development of high-quality animation in films and on the web.

Source: Disney

enthrall viewers that they pay more attention to it than to the product—or the strategic message. Further, more than one fantasy or **mnemonic device** (such as the GEICO Gecko) might confuse audiences. David Ogilvy suggested that, to make the strongest impression on the viewer, fantasies should relate to the product's claims and be repeated heavily.[13]

Planning Production

The commercial is a group effort; the team includes a writer, art director, producer, director, and sometimes a musical composer and choreographer. The agency producer, who is responsible for completing the job on schedule and within budget, usually sends copies of the storyboard to three studios for competitive bids.

When the studio is chosen, the producer and casting director select the cast and hire the announcer. Next the set is built, and the crew and cast rehearse under the director's supervision.

During the preproduction period, meetings are necessary between the director, the agency producer, the account representative, the writer, the art director, the commercial director, possibly the advertiser, and anyone else important to the production. This is where they iron out any last-minute problems and make final decisions about the scenes, the actors, and the announcer. They should review everything—music, sets, action, lighting, camera angles. A finished 60-second film commercial takes only 90 feet of film, but the shooting often requires several days and 3,000 to 5,000 feet of film. And unlike video, film can't be used again (see Ad Lab 12–B, "The Film versus Digital Video Decision").

The soundtrack may be recorded before, during, or after actual production. Recording sound in advance ensures that the commercial will be neither too long nor too short; it also helps when the subject has to move or dance to a specific music theme or rhythm.

Production: The Shoot

The actual shooting day can be very long and tedious. It may take several hours just to light the set to the director's liking.

Quiet on the Set: Sound

Procedures for recording and controlling music and sound effects are similar to those used in radio. Microphones capture sound; recorders transfer the sound and store it on a medium. Then, with the use of a multichannel control board, a sound engineer manipulates sounds for effect and records them onto film, video, or a playback system synchronized with film.

But the original recording is important for two reasons. First, the original sound recording is synchronized with the original visual recording and with the action and the emotion expressed by the actors. A re-creation never quite matches the timing or feel of the original.

Second, before it reaches its final form, the original recording undergoes rerecording many times, with some loss of fidelity each time. So high-quality sound-recording equipment is mandatory.

Lights

Cinematographers and directors collaborate on creating proper lighting. Experienced **cinematographers** (motion picture photographers) can guess the range and intensity of light

AD Lab 12-B

The Film versus Digital Video Decision

Today, live TV commercials are rare. Even those that look live are usually videotaped, and most national commercials are shot on color film. Film projects a soft texture that live broadcasts and video do not have. Because film is the oldest method, producers have a large pool of skilled talent to choose from. Also, film is extremely versatile. It works for numerous optical effects, slow motion, distance shots, mood shots, fast action, and various animation techniques.

However, digital video offers a more brilliant picture and better fidelity. It looks more realistic and more "live." Digital is also more consistent in quality than film stock. The chief advantage of digital video is that it provides immediate playback, so scenes can be checked and redone while the props and actors are still together on the set. Moreover, computerization has cut editing time up to 90 percent. Digital video can be replayed forever, but a film commercial can be run only about 25 times.

Today, many directors shoot their commercials on film for texture and sensitive mood lighting, but then transfer the processed film to digital media for editing. This process is more costly, but it gives them faster finishing and lets them see optical effects instantly. Some directors, however, still prefer to edit on film because they get the wider range of effects and thus achieve a higher level of creative storytelling.

Laboratory Application

Some products and some types of commercials are more effective shot on film, while others are better on video. Make a list of three product categories (or three brands) and three types of commercials. Describe which medium (film or video) you think would be more effective in each case and why.

---

by briefly studying its source. However, they use light meters to determine how to set the camera's lens **aperture,** the opening that controls the amount of light that reaches the film or digital media. To record the correct color and brightness, all light sources must be in balance.

Lighting helps establish a visual mood. Intense light from a single source gives a harsh appearance and may be used to create anxiety in the viewer. By using filters, warmer lights, diffusion screens, and reflectors, the cinematographer can create a reddish, more consistent, softer illumination—and a more romantic mood.

Camera

Professional film cameras used for making TV commercials shoot 16 millimeter (mm; the diagonal measure of one frame), 35 mm, 75 mm film and digital.

Producers of local TV commercials used to shoot with the grainier but less expensive 16 mm film; national spots were shot on 35 mm for extra quality and precision; and 75 mm film provided the highest quality image. While film is still widely used for national spots because of the atmosphere it brings to an image, most local spots are now shot in digital video.

Heavy-duty studio video cameras mounted on a stand with wheels can carry a number of accessories. One of the most important is the lens-mounted **teleprompter,** which allows the camera to see a spokesperson through the back of a two-way mirror while he or she reads moving text reflected off the front.

Action: Staging and Talent

Staging for a commercial may be done in the isolation of a studio, outside on a studio lot, or on location. The studio offers the most control.

Most film and video studios have heavy soundproofing to eliminate outside noises such as sirens and low-flying aircraft. The studios are lightproof, which allows for complete lighting control. Special equipment is easier to use in the controlled environment of a studio. But studio lighting can make a scene appear artificial.

For scenes requiring large amounts of space, scenery, and the full effect of outdoor lighting, the studio lot offers the best control. The **lot** is outside acreage shielded from stray, off-site sounds. The lot is

Digital equipment provides advertisers the option to create an illusion of almost any background. Green elements on the set are replaced with digital elements in postproduction.

© Ultimatte Corporation

In any commercial production, it's typical to have many more people behind the camera than in front of it. In addition to the director and assistant director, other important players behind the scenes may include a sound editor, lighting technicians, electricians, and grips.

© Nick Morris/SCG/ZUMAPRESS.com/Newscom

convenient to the studio's carpentry shop, and sets can be left standing until all shootings and retakes are completed.

Although it adds realism, **location** shooting is often a technical and logistical nightmare. Every location has natural and manufactured features that create obstacles. Natural lighting creates bright highlights that contrast with harsh shadows. Large reflective screens and high-intensity lights are required to brighten up shadows for a more even-toned exposure. Energy sources for lighting and equipment may be insufficient, requiring long cables and mobile generators.

Whether at the studio or on location, most scenes require several takes for the **talent** (actors) to get them right. Lighting may need readjusting as unexpected shadows pop up. Each scene is shot from two or three different angles: one to establish the characters, one to show only the speaker, and one to show the listener's reaction.

A long time may be needed between scenes to move the camera, reset the lights, reposition the talent, and pick up the action, sound, and look to match the other scenes. Each action must match what comes before and after. Commercials with disconcerting jumps destroy credibility. The adoption of digital technology allows for green studios. In these studios, elements that are colored green are replaced in postproduction using computer technologies. The backgrounds that can then be substituted are almost limitless.

Once all the scenes are "in the can," the commercial enters the postproduction, or finishing, phase.

Postproduction

In the **postproduction phase,** the film editor, sound mixer, and director actually put the commercial together.

With digital technology, editors can add effects such as wipes and dissolves electronically. Although a director will spend many hours editing a commercial shot on video, it will still be considerably less than what is needed for film editing and lab work.

Many professionals still prefer film. The visual portion of the commercial appears on one piece of celluloid without the effects of dissolves, titles, or **supers** (words superimposed on the picture). The sound portion is assembled on another piece of celluloid. This is the **work print** stage (also called the *rough cut* or *interlock*).

External sound is recorded next. The sound engineer records the musicians and singers, as well as the announcer's voice-over narrative. Prerecorded stock music may be bought and integrated into the commercial. The mixing also includes any sound effects, such as doorbells ringing or doors slamming.

Once sound editing is complete, the finished sound is put on one piece of celluloid. That, combined with the almost-completed visual celluloid, yields the **mixed interlock.** The addition of optical effects and titles results in the **answer print.** This is the final commercial. If it is approved, **dupes** (duplicate copies) are made for delivery to the networks or TV stations.[14]

LO 12-6

In the postproduction phase, the director and editor can save a lot of time and money by using computerized video and sound editing equipment for the assembly of the final product. At this stage, the director and editor will select and splice scenes into their respective order, removing all the unneeded footage. Next, they add off-camera special effects, like supers, and incorporate any necessary music or voice-overs.

© Alex Wong/Getty Images

Producing Advertising for Social Media and the Web

An important trend in digital media is **viral video.** A viral video involves creating a digital video with a subtle promotional message. The video is designed to tempt viewers to share it with their friends. While many of these videos are professionally produced and are the result of expensive

People **BEHIND** the Ads

John Posey Actor, Director, Producer and Scriptwriter

© JC Olivera/Getty Images

Our feature individual in this chapter, John Posey, may look familiar. Fans of the hit series *24* may remember him taking a bullet intended for Jack Bauer. Or perhaps you caught John guest starring on other popular shows, like *E.R., Boston Legal,* or *Crossing Jordan.*

It's also possible you've seen or heard him in any of over 300 commercials, on both TV and radio. And if that were not enough to keep John busy, this multitalented actor is also a screen writer and a playwright who regularly tours the United States in an acclaimed one-man play (to see all of the activities that John is involved with, visit his Website: www.johnposey.com).

John's path to an acting career has taken several turns. He graduated from college with an advertising degree and actually started out on the agency side—working for several years as a copywriter, especially for radio. Dismayed at the poor quality of some commercial actors his agency worked with, he decided to switch careers and take a shot at making a living in front of the camera (or microphone). He wrote a play that won rave reviews, and he soon caught the attention of TV producers anxious to take advantage of his gift for comedy. John headed for Hollywood with an offer to play the dad in the then-new show, *Full House* only to find that the producers changed their mind shortly after he arrived.

Armed with a better sense of how uncertain the Hollywood scene is, John headed east and began doing commercials and corporate videos, first in Atlanta, and eventually in New York. He remembers his time in Atlanta especially fondly. "The commercial budgets were smaller, so we did more freelancing," he explained. "Those shoots were a lot of fun to work on."

Atlanta was a good place to start as an actor because working in L.A. requires getting a union card. In Atlanta, John could hone his craft in theater, commercials, and industrial training films. Life in Atlanta was simpler too. "In Atlanta, I'd have one agent who would handle all my bookings—commercials, voice-overs, corporate videos, whatever," he

explained. "Here in Los Angeles, different agents specialize in different projects. So I currently work with five different agents."

We asked John what agencies and studios look for when casting a commercial. "Different actors have different skills, and the ones that you really need in commercials are unlike those needed for the stage or TV work," he observed. "The reason I work in so many commercials is I'm dependable, and I find a way to bring my lines to life. I know from studying advertising and working as a copywriter that the star of a commercial is not the actor, it's the brand. Commercials really require someone who can have a conversation with viewers, who is natural and credible. Viewers want to see someone who is a real person."

We asked John if he had a favorite commercial that he had worked on. "Yes," he confided. I was hired to do a national spot for American Express. This was back in 93 or 94. The idea was that your purchases made with American Express were insured. In the commercial, I am showing the actor who plays my son how to "feed" VHS tape into a video recorder. Later, the son feeds the recorder oatmeal, which, of course, ruins the equipment. The idea is that because it was purchased with American Express you don't have to worry about getting it replaced."

We asked why this one stuck out in his mind. "Well, we knew it would run a lot, it was a big campaign. It was also a really well-done spot and lots of people remember it."

It is hard to think of everything in advance, as John's experience on the American Express commercial showed. "The big scene was supposed to be when the recorder spits out oatmeal after I hit a button," John recalls. "But they couldn't quite figure out how to make that happen. In one attempt, they set up a fan to blow the oatmeal out, but it came flying out of the machine like it was blown by a propeller. I'm pretty sure it would have injured someone if they had been standing in front of it." The solution? "The director just put a guy behind the machine and he pushed the oatmeal out with his hands" Sometimes low technology really is the way to go!

Listening to John describe his life now, one can't help but be impressed with the variety of creative projects that take up his time. "I almost never turn down a commercial or voice-over opportunity," he said, "but I'm involved in a lot of things. I work on a series on ABC called HOW TO GET AWAY WITH MURDER. My film, Legendary, was produced in 2010, starring Patricia Clarkson and Danny Glover. I have two other scripts in development and my play, Father, Son, and Holy Coach, was produced again this year in LA to rave reviews. We are considering a run again in the fall."

John is actually a dad to three sons, one of whom is following in his footsteps. "My son Tyler is the real actor in the house," he proudly says. If you've seen the Jennifer Lopez film *Maid in Manhattan,* you know Tyler Posey. He played JLo's son. Now grown up, Tyler is the star of MTV's Teen Wolf.

After talking with this friendly and remarkable man for a while, we could not fail to be impressed with the incredible range of creative activities that he has been involved with. John laughed and said, "There are always new challenges and every day is different. It can even lead to just a tiny bit of trouble." Curious, we asked him to explain. "Well, I was watching TV once and I was a guest star on Perry Mason. In the big courtroom scene Raymond Burr is arguing my case before a jury. Then, when they cut to a commercial, I show up in a Budweiser ad. Probably not what the advertiser had in mind!"

budgets, some very popular efforts have originated with ordinary consumers working on shoestring budgets (see My IMC Campaign in this chapter for ideas about helping your client go viral).

The People Who Produce Digital Media

The ranks of production managers and producers are already swelling as media vehicles multiply beyond anybody's recent imagination. New titles increasingly found on agency rosters include multimedia producers, directors, and engineers; interactive planners and writers; computer programmers and system designers; and so on. At Saatchi & Saatchi, Nathan Hackstock holds the title of creative director for integrated marketing. Working with him is a staff of art directors, copywriters, and producers who specialize in creating interactive ads for Saatchi's clients. Outside the agencies are a host of new suppliers: interactive software developers, DVD manufacturers, digital media-buying services, and so on.

Producing a WebSite

Web designer Chris McConnell offers a systematic process for Website production that includes six steps: learn, plan, design, code, launch, and maintain. Throughout the six steps, designers should engage in continuous testing and solicit regular feedback.[15]

The *learning* phase involves seeking information from clients about what they want in a Website. Of course, in some instances clients may not be sure what they want, but regular communications can help develop a mutual understanding of what the designer should accomplish. The designer may wish to ask the client a series of questions such as, Who is the target audience? What are the goals of the site? What is the client's budget? What are his or her deadlines? From the client's answers, the designer can develop a creative brief.

The *planning* phase begins with a design strategy. The strategy orients the designer to consider how audiences will use the site and where they will access it. Knowing the audience is vital, since some audiences may access the site on a computer while others may be more reliant on tablets or smart phones. Planning typically also includes looking for related sites to get a sense of typical design characteristics.

The planning phase is also where the designer creates a blueprint of the site. Some artists begin with sketches on paper, while others use sketching tools such as OmniGraffle, Photoshop, or Illustrator to lay out the basic look. This Website blueprint is known as a **wireframe,** a visual guide that specifies the arrangement of the elements on the page.

Because business sites are typically far more complex than amateur sites, many employ a **web content management system (WCMS)** that best fits the site's purpose. WCMSs

*Production of a Website begins with a **wireframe** in which the designer maps out the layout of the page or pages, either by sketching or using software.*

Source: smartdraw

provide authoring and administration tools that make it easier for designers and producers to collaborate. Popular systems include Joomla and LightCMS.

In the *design* phase, the designer begins bringing the site to life. At this point, the wireframe is developed to look like the final product, often in Photoshop or some other graphics program. The designer employs the colors, patterns, and layouts that he or she hopes to execute in the final site. It is crucial for the designer to get feedback from the client at this step before proceeding to create code.

The *coding* phase is where the attractive template is transformed into a working Website. Almost all sites rely on HTML (hypertext markup language) and CSS (cascading style sheets). HTML is used to create site content, while CSS provides elements of design such as typography, color, and layout.

The *launch* phase is where the completed (and approved) site is birthed to the world. Finally, the *maintain* phase, which lasts until the site is removed or undergoes another overhaul, involves specifying the updates and tasks necessary to keep the site fresh, functioning, and useable. Designers may offer suggestions to their clients about how to keep the site running smoothly.

Macromedia, a subsidiary of Adobe, offers a similar production process that includes several phases including discovery (analyzing the industry and understanding the audience); definition (establishing goals, creating a plan, and establishing requirements); structure (determining content and layout); design and prototype; build and test; launch; and maintain. For more details on Macromedia's approach, visit www.adobe.com/resources/techniques/discover/.

Another popular tool employed on the web is the viral ad. Viral ads are posted at a Website or in Facebook, with the goal of attracting an initial small but influential audience that shares the ad with dozens or even hundreds of others. Because sharing is the critical factor in whether a viral campaign succeeds, production of viral videos differs from ordinary video production in several key ways.

Lauren Drell, writing for AOL Small Business, makes several recommendations. First, spots should create strong emotional reactions, particularly humor. She quotes Scott Lamb, a Buzzfeed managing editor, who suggests that virals play to "some sort of social imperative, some reason that the average person is moved to share it." He points to Blendtec's "Will It Blend" virals as an example. If seeing an iPhone blended seems appealing to you, check it out at www.youtube.com/watch?v=qg1ckCkm8YI.

Drell also argues that virals should be short, perhaps 30 to 90 seconds, and involve minimal production values. The ideal viral is almost the antithesis of a Super Bowl ad. It's produced quickly in a variety of formats. Virals are often filmed using relatively primitive technology, such as a mobile phone or a simple video camera. Editing is often accomplished with free or inexpensive consumer editing software. Of course, what this means is that producing a viral spot emphasizes the creative component of message planning, and minimizes the production challenges that can be costly. It also means that viral videos can be used by anyone, whether large marketing firms or small businesses.[16]

Chapter Summary

Careful management is the key to success in producing advertising. If the production process is not handled correctly, an otherwise beautiful ad or commercial can be destroyed. The task of managing this process is the responsibility of a print production manager or an electronic media producer. The manager's job is to keep the project moving smoothly and under budget, while maintaining the required level of quality through every step of the production process.

Production managers perform the classic functions of management: planning, organizing, directing, and controlling. They also have to keep up with changing technology, monitor costs, and meet budgets.

Many factors can destroy budgets. The five most common are inadequate planning and preparation, production luxuries, overtime, special equipment, and too many decision makers. Factors specific to each medium can also affect budgets drastically.

The print production process consists of four phases: preproduction, production, prepress, and printing and distribution. In the preproduction phase, the manager plans the overall job carefully and then starts to deal with the specific needs of the job, such as typography.

Typography affects an ad's appearance, design, and legibility. There are four important concepts when selecting type: readability, appropriateness, harmony or appearance, and emphasis. A key skill is copy casting, knowing how to fit type into a particular space in a layout. The production manager also considers what kind of paper will be used, since it affects the way the art is prepared.

In the production phase, artists prepare mechanicals (or pasteups) of the art to be printed. Most agencies use sophisticated desktop publishing. The artists prepare the mechanicals as line art and use a photographic process to turn continuous-tone artwork into halftones. Halftone images (illustrations and photos) simulate gradations of tone with different sizes of black dots.

In the prepress stage, the printer makes a plate from the base art and one from each overlay. Each mechanical must be photographed separately. For full color, four halftone plates are used (one for each color process color plus black). The set of negatives used to make the four plates is called a color separation. This work is now mostly done on large computerized scanner systems.

The final phase of the production process includes the actual printing of the job, as well as cutting, embossing, binding, and shipping. Quality control is critical throughout the process. The production manager has to make sure computer disks are compatible with the reprographics service bureau and contain all the elements needed to produce the negatives. Along the way, the manager must check several printer's proofs for scratches or blemishes and to make sure traps and bleeds are handled correctly.

Radio spots are among the quickest, simplest, and least expensive ads to produce. A producer manages the production process through the preproduction, production, and postproduction stages. The producer contracts with a recording studio, selects talent, and collects music and sound effects for the recording session. At the session, the talent works in a studio, while the director and sound engineer work in the control room at an audio console, monitoring and modulating the sound as it's recorded.

In the postproduction phase, the director and sound engineer select the best takes, splice them together, mix in sound effects and music, and then edit the sound until the master tape is completed. Dubs are made from this and sent to radio stations for airing.

Television production involves the same three stages. In preproduction, the producer determines which production technique is most suitable for the script: live action, animation, special effects, or a combination. The studio is chosen, the cast selected, and rehearsals held. As much work as possible is done during preproduction to reduce the shooting time required.

The production phase is when the commercial is actually shot, in a studio, on a lot, or on location. Specialized technicians are responsible for the sound, lights, and cameras, all of which can diminish the commercial if not handled correctly. Scenes are shot and reshot until the director and producer feel they have a good take. For cost reasons, scenes are frequently not shot in order. The sound track may be recorded before or after the shoot.

In the postproduction stage, the commercial is actually put together on either film or digital. External sound and music are added to the video and the sound track until the master (or answer print for film) is completed. Then dupes are made and shipped to TV stations.

A multimedia presentation provides information or entertainment using several communications media simultaneously, typically slides, digital, and audio. The electronic capabilities of computer technology were added to the multimedia presentation to create digital media.

Digital media are a whole new industry. The overall production process is similar to those of print and electronic media, but the details involve new technologies, terminologies, and costs that advertisers and agencies are not yet familiar with. This means opportunities for new people coming into the field. Creatives in web design have unique questions to answer in helping clients develop usable, elegant, and effective Websites.

Important Terms

analog proof (Chromalin), *386*

animation, *390*

answer print, *393*

aperture, *392*

audio console (board), *388*

bleeds, *387*

blueline, *386*

camera-ready art, *381*

cinematographer, *391*

closing date, *380*

color key, *386*

color separation, *385*

continuous tones, *381*

control room, *388*

copy cast, *380*

cover paper, *380*

CYMK printing, *384*

digital video effects (DVE) units, *390*

director, *388*

display type, *382*

dubs, *389*

dupes, *393*

electronic production, *378*

flats, *384*

font, *383*

four-color process, *384*

halftone plate, *382*

halftone screen, *382*

kerning, *382*

leading, *382*

line film, *382*

line plate, *382*

live action, *390*

location, *393*

lot, *392*

master tape, *389*

mixed interlock, *393*

mnemonic device, *391*

orthographic film, *381*

PANTONE Matching System (PMS), *385*

points, *383*

postproduction phase, *393*

prepress phase, *384*

preproduction phase, *387, 390*

print production manager, *376*

print production process, *379*

producer, *376*

production phase, *380*

residual fee, *378*

sans serif, *382*

scale, *378*

serif, *382*

session, *388*

special effects, *390*

spots, *387*

stripping, *384*

supers, *393*

talent, *393*

teleprompter, *392*

text paper, *380*

text type, *382*

trap, *387*

type family, *383*

typography, *380*

viral video, *393*

web content management system (WCMS), *395*

wireframe, *395*

work print, *393*

writing paper, *380*

Review Questions

1. What are the five common budget busters every production manager should be aware of?

2. What is the primary role of the print production manager?

3. What does copy casting mean? Explain how it is done.

4. What is a halftone? Why is it important, and how is it produced?

5. How are color photographs printed? What are the potential problems with printing in color?

6. What are the advantages and disadvantages of animation?

7. What leads to the greatest waste of money in TV commercial production? Explain.

8. When is it better to use film and when is it better to use digital media? Why?

9. What are the most common forms of digital media? How do they differ from media in the past?

10. What are some ways an advertiser such as McDonald's could use digital media to enhance its IMC program? Explain.

The Advertising Experience

1. **The Importance of Type**

   The selection of a particular typeface makes a strong contribution to the overall effect of an advertisement. Create ads with appropriate typefaces for three of the following media products. (Typefaces are not restricted to those discussed in Ad Lab 14–A.)

   a. The Gettysburg Address

   b. The King James Bible

   c. Stephen King's (or Stanley Kubrick's, your choice) *The Shining*

   d. A DVD collection of *Lost* episodes

   e. A boxed set of "Barney's Greatest Hits" CDs

   f. An astronomy textbook

   g. A collection of *Lord of the Rings* fan fiction

2. **Print Production**

   Take a moment to go online and learn more about print production. Numerous organizations and companies that specialize in some aspect of print production are on the web. Visit the sites listed below and answer the questions that follow.

   ■ Acme Printing: www.acmeiowa.com

   ■ Advertising Production Association of Los Angeles: www.apala.org

   ■ AlphaGraphics: www.alphagraphics.com

   ■ Graphic Connections: www.grconnections.com

   ■ Graphic Arts Information Network (GAIN): www.gain.org

   ■ Hart Graphics: www.hartgraphics.com

   ■ International Digital Enterprise Alliance: www.idealliance.org

   ■ National Association for Printing Leadership (NAPL): www.napl.org

   ■ PANTONE: www.pantone.com

   ■ Specialty Graphic Imaging Association (SGIA): www.sgia.org

   a. Who is the intended audience of the site?

   b. What type of company or organization is it? What are the scope and size of its operations?

   c. What print-related activities does the company or organization specialize in?

   d. What is your overall impression of the company and its work? Why?

3. **Broadcast Production**

   Producing broadcast commercials is even more complex than creating a print ad. Peruse the Websites below of some broadcast production-related organizations. Then answer the questions that follow.

   ■ Aardman Animation: www.aardman.com

   ■ @radical.media: www.radicalmedia.com

   ■ Digital Hollywood: www.digitalhollywood.com

   ■ Directors Guild of America: www.dga.org

   ■ Duck Studios: www.duckstudios.com

   ■ Johnson Burnett: www.johnsonburnett.com

   ■ Jones Film & Video: www.jonesinc.com

   ■ Screen Actors Guild (SAG): www.sag.org

   a. What type of production-related company or organization is it? What are the scope and size of its operations?

   b. What kind of broadcast production activities does the company specialize in? Are these typically preproduction, production, or postproduction activities?

   c. What benefit does the company or organization provide the advertising community?

   d. What impresses you most about this organization and its work? Least? Why?

4. For decades, Apple has relied on a consistent font family—Garamond—for its print advertising. Find a sample of this font and explain which of its qualities help communicate Apple's message. Can you find another font you might use instead?

5. Given that Apple no longer produces colorful computers—only models in white, black, or aluminum—why should it bother to use color in its print ads? Make the case for or against color ink in Apple's print advertising.

6. Considering recent advances in computer animation technology, many clients and viewers expect to be wowed with the latest technology in commercials, especially those representing technical innovations. For the BRAVIA launch, do you think Fallon and Sony made the right choice to shoot the TV ad with a minimum of special effects? Why or why not?

7. Search typography collections to find any new fonts appropriate for both the headline and copy of a print ad for your college or university. Why do you believe they are more effective than what your school uses now?

Using Print Media

Learning Objectives

To examine how print advertising enhances the advertiser's media mix. Newspapers and magazines, with their unique qualities, can complement broadcast, direct mail, and other media. By using print wisely, advertisers can significantly increase the reach and impact of their campaigns and still stay within their budget.

 After studying this chapter, you will be able to:

LO13-1 Explain the advantages and disadvantages of magazine advertising.

LO13-2 Discuss the various ways to analyze a magazine's circulation.

LO13-3 Analyze how rates are determined for print media.

LO13-4 List the advantages and disadvantages of newspaper advertising.

LO13-5 Describe how newspapers are categorized.

LO13-6 Define the major types of newspaper advertising.

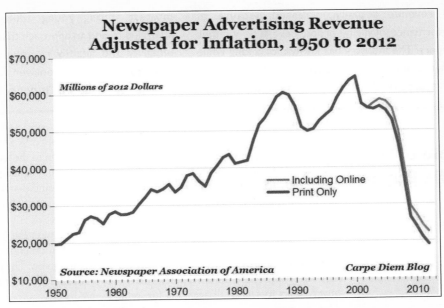

Newspaper Advertising Revenue Adjusted for Inflation, 1950 to 2012

Millions of 2012 Dollars

— Including Online
— Print Only

Source: Newspaper Association of America

Carpe Diem Blog

Source: Newspaper Association of America

Whither newspapers? ■ The word "whither," with an "h," refers to place and in the first sentence means "what will happen to print media?" Drop the "h," as in "wither," and the term refers to shriveling. Sadly, both words are appropriate in discussing the oldest advertising medium. ■ The digital revolution has challenged all media, but especially newspapers. To see why it is helpful to consider several trends that started years ago and are, to a lesser degree, continuing today. The statistics presented below are from the Pew Research Center's Project for Excellence in Journalism entitled "The State of the News Media 2013." You can read the original report here: http://www.stateofthemedia.org /2013/newspapers-stabilizing-but-still-threatened /newspapers-by-the-numbers/, ■ To start, the percentage of adults who report that they read a newspaper "yesterday" is down and this trend is especially pronounced among the group most attractive to advertisers, 18- to 24-year-olds. So while just under 60 percent of people 65 and older read a newspaper in 2012, only about 22 percent of 18- to 24-year-olds did so. And this percentage is about the same for 25- to 34-year-olds.[1] ■ Newspapers are more likely to be read by the better educated, so it should be a positive development that U.S. citizens, on average, have more education today than they did in times past. For example, in 1947 just 5 percent of Americans held a four-year degree but by 1998 nearly 25 percent did. And in 2012, 30 percent of Americans held a four-year degree, a historic high. However, college-educated adults are less likely to read a newspaper than at any time in history.[2] ■ While the declines in newspaper readership are consistent and significant, they pale in comparison to the decline in advertising revenue. In 2006 revenues from print and online ads peaked at about $49 billion.[3] By 2012 that number had shrunk to $22 billion and *Advertising Age* predicts in 2015 the number will shrink to $19 billion. ■ Where has the money gone? If you guessed the Internet, you would be right. Advertisers have shifted major portions of their spending to online and social media. In fact, in 2015 online spending will approach $52 billion, an increase of 18 percent over 2014.[4] ■ What about online newspapers? Have they helped stop revenue bleed? Unfortunately, no. Newspapers still only receive a small fraction of advertising and circulation revenues from their online products. Pew reports that for every $1 newspapers gain in digital advertising income they are losing $7 from print ads.[5] ■ The pain has been felt by most papers, including top brands. Advertising revenue at the *Wall Street Journal* declined 11 percent from 2014 to 2015, leading to staff layoffs.[6] *The New York Times* saw ad revenues slip just under 1 percent in 2014, which it celebrated as the slowest decline in a decade.[7] Print revenues at Gannett, parent company of *USA Today*, declined almost 9 percent in the first quarter of 2015. But overall revenue actually increased because of the performance of digital properties.[8] ■ So whither newspapers? The industry has known for a long while now that a new model is needed. Buffeted by the perfect storm of digital challengers and a lack of interest among young adults, newspapers have struggled to find an approach that promises both news integrity and healthy revenue growth. Clearly, the industry must find an answer soon if the answer to "whither newspapers?" is not continued "withering."

The Role of the Print Media Buyer

Once the media planning is complete, the advertiser can turn to the tactical details of actually scheduling and buying media time on radio and television and media space in magazines and newspapers. This is where the big money is spent in advertising—on the actual placement of ads in the media. So the competent performance of the media-buying task is critical to getting the most bang for the advertiser's buck.

The person in charge of negotiating and contracting with the media is called a **media buyer.** Media buyers often specialize in one medium or another, so there are print media buyers, spot TV media buyers, network media buyers, and so on. The degree of specialization depends on the size of the advertiser or the agency or the independent media-buying firm the buyer works for. In small agencies, for example, media buyers frequently don't specialize. They do it all.

Success as a *print media buyer* requires a range of knowledge and abilities. First, media buyers must have a broad understanding of all available print media and the terminology used in the field. They need to know, for example, how magazines and newspapers are categorized, the advertising possibilities each form offers, and the pros and cons of using various types of vehicles. They should also have an understanding of the impact of new technologies on the print media.

Second, buyers need to know how to buy magazine and newspaper space. They must understand how to analyze circulation, read rate cards, get reliable information, and calculate and negotiate the most efficient media buys.

Finally, media buyers require creativity for developing ingenious, sophisticated ways to integrate the advertiser's print media efforts into the whole creative mix.

This is no small task. But for the student of advertising beginning his or her career in a media department, these issues are quite important. The purpose of this chapter is to bring clarity to these subjects.

Using Magazines in the Creative Mix

Advertisers use magazines in their creative mix for many reasons. First and foremost, magazines allow an advertiser to reach a particular target audience with a high-quality presentation. The American Legacy Foundation is just one of the many leading advertisers that uses magazines as an important element of its creative mix. After reading this section, see the Ethical Issues box on page 419 to understand how creativity can lead to some scrupulous practices.

The Pros and Cons of Magazine Advertising

LO 13-1

Magazines offer a host of features: flexible design options, prestige, authority, believability, and long shelf life. They may sit on a coffee table or shelf for months and be reread many times. People can read a magazine ad at their leisure; they can pore over the details of a photograph; and they can carefully study the information presented in the copy. This makes magazines an ideal medium for high-involvement think and feel products.

Magazines also have a number of drawbacks (see My IMC Campaign 13–A, "The Pros and Cons of Magazine Advertising"). They are expensive (on a cost-per-thousand basis), especially for color ads. And since they typically come out only monthly, or weekly at best, it's difficult to build up reach and frequency quickly. For these reasons, many advertisers use magazines in combination with other media—such as newspapers, which we'll discuss later in this chapter (see Ad Lab 13–A, "Magazines and the Creative Mix").

Special Possibilities with Magazines

Media buyers need to be aware of the many creative possibilities magazines offer advertisers through various technical or mechanical features. These include bleed pages, cover positions, inserts and gatefolds, and special sizes, such as junior pages and island halves.

My IMC Campaign 13–A
The Pros and Cons of Magazine Advertising

The Pros

- **Flexibility** in readership and advertising. Magazines cover the full range of prospects; they have a wide choice of regional and national coverage and a variety of lengths, approaches, and editorial tones.

- **Color** gives readers visual pleasure, and color reproduction is best in slick magazines. Color enhances image and identifies the package. In short, it sells.

- **Authority and believability** enhance the commercial message. TV, radio, and newspapers offer lots of information but lack the depth needed for readers to gain knowledge or meaning; magazines often offer all three.

- **Permanence,** or long shelf life, gives the reader time to appraise ads in detail, allowing a more complete education/sales message and the opportunity to communicate the total corporate personality.

- **Prestige** for products advertised in upscale or specialty magazines such as *Architectural Digest, Connoisseur,* and *Town and Country.*

- **Audience selectivity** is more efficient in magazines than any other medium except direct mail. The predictable, specialized editorial environment selects the audience and enables advertisers to pinpoint their sales campaigns. Examples: golfers (*Golf Digest*), businesspeople (*Bloomberg Businessweek*), 20-something males (*Details*), or teenage girls (*Seventeen*).

- **Cost efficiency** because wasted circulation is minimized. Print networks give advertisers reduced prices for advertising in two or more network publications.

- **Selling power** of magazines is proven, and results are usually measurable.

- **Reader loyalty** that sometimes borders on fanaticism.

- **Extensive pass-along readership.** Many people may read the magazine after the initial purchaser.

- **Merchandising assistance.** Advertisers can generate reprints and merchandising materials that help them get more mileage out of their ad campaigns.

The Cons

- **Lack of immediacy** that advertisers can get with newspapers or radio.

- **Shallow geographic coverage.** They don't offer the national reach of broadcast media.

- **Inability to deliver mass audiences at a low price.** Magazines are very costly for reaching broad masses of people.

- **Inability to deliver high frequency.** Since most magazines come out only monthly or weekly, the advertiser can build frequency faster than reach by adding numerous small-audience magazines to the schedule.

- **Long lead time** for ad insertion, sometimes two to three months.

- **Heavy advertising competition.** The largest-circulation magazines have 52 percent advertising to 48 percent editorial content.

- **High cost per thousand.** Average black-and-white cost per thousand (CPM) in national consumer magazines is high; some trade publications with highly selective audiences have a CPM over $50 for a black-and-white page.

- **Declining circulations,** especially in single-copy sales, is an industrywide trend that limits an advertiser's reach.

When the dark or colored background of the ad extends to the edge of the page, it is said to **bleed** off the page. Most magazines offer bleed pages, but they charge 10 to 15 percent more for them. The advantages of bleeds include greater flexibility in expressing the advertising idea, a slightly larger printing area, and more dramatic impact.

If a company plans to advertise in a particular magazine consistently, it may seek a highly desirable **cover position.** Few publishers sell ads on the front cover, commonly called the *first cover.* They do sell the inside front, inside back, and outside back covers (the *second, third,* and *fourth covers,* respectively), usually through multiple-insertion contracts at a substantial premium.

A less expensive way to use magazine space is to place the ad in an unusual place on the page or dramatically across spreads. A **junior unit** is a large ad (60% of the page) placed in the middle of a page and surrounded with editorial matter. Similar to junior units are **island halves,** surrounded by even more editorial matter. The island sometimes costs more than a regular half-page, but because it dominates the page, many advertisers consider it worth the extra charge. Exhibit 13-1 shows other space combinations that create impact.

Sometimes, rather than buying a standard page, an advertiser uses an **insert.** The advertiser prints the ad on high-quality paper stock to add weight and drama to the message, and then ships the finished ads to the publisher for insertion into the magazine at a special price. Another

AD Lab 13–A

Magazines and the Creative Mix

Read My IMC Campaign 13–B, "The Pros and Cons of Magazine Advertising," and see if you can apply that information to the following situation:

You manage an elegant French restaurant in Los Angeles that is known for its intimate setting, excellent service, and lovely outdoor garden patio. You decide to build the business by promoting the special ambience your restaurant offers. To enhance the sense of romance, you plan to give away a long-stemmed rose and a glass of champagne with each entrée. Your clientele consists primarily of wealthy, educated business leaders and celebrities. However, a growing segment of your customers includes tourists and middle-class couples out for a special evening.

Laboratory Applications

1. Is a magazine the best way to advertise this special? If not, explain why. If so, explain why and include which type of magazine would be best.

2. How can magazine advertising help you build the restaurant's image?

option is multiple-page inserts. Calvin Klein once promoted its jeans in a 116-page insert in *Vanity Fair*. The insert reportedly cost more than $1 million, but the news reports about it in major daily newspapers gave the campaign enormous publicity value. Advertising inserts may be devoted exclusively to one company's product, or they may be sponsored by the magazine and have a combination of ads and special editorial content consistent with the magazine's focus.

A **gatefold** is an insert whose paper is so wide that the extreme left and right sides have to be folded into the center to match the size of the other pages. When the reader opens the magazine, the folded page swings out like a gate to present the ad. Not all magazines provide gatefolds, and they are always sold at a substantial premium.

Some advertisers create their own **custom magazines.** These look like regular magazines and are often produced by the same companies that publish traditional magazines. However, they are essentially magazine-length ads, which readers are expected to purchase at newsstands. Custom magazines have been published for Sony, General Motors, General

Exhibit 13-1

An ad's position on the page influences its effectiveness. The size and shape of the ad often determine where it will fall on the page. These eight two-page spreads show most of the positions an ad can take.

Facing horizontal half-pages to dominate a spread

Vertical halves across the gutter with the same objective

Checkerboard facing a half-page ad

Staggered horizontal half-pages

Outside halves of a spread

Checkerboard (multiple small space units on a single page)

Staircase units and double staircases on facing pages

Island spread

Source: From "Magazine Newsletter of Research," Magazine Publishers Asssociation, Vol. 8, No. I. Reprinted with permission of Magazine Publishers of America.

AD Lab 13–B

Innovations in Magazine Advertising

Magazines work closely with advertisers to develop new technologies for presenting ideas and products. From these efforts have come such innovations as fragrance strips, color strips, pop-up ads, and 3-D ads.

Fragrance strips are a great favorite with perfume advertisers. With the Scentstrip, readers sample a scent by opening a sealed insert tucked into a magazine. Despite some consumer complaints, Scentstrips have proved incredibly popular. Fragrances are useful for other products as well. For example, a Rolls-Royce ad in *Architectural Digest* carried a Scentstrip bearing the essence of leather. For a St. Mungo's (London's largest homeless charity) ad, Saatchi & Saatchi played on consumers' expectations that Scentstrips accompany only ads for luxury goods. The urine-scented ad drove shocked readers to St. Mungo's Website, where they could make a donation. The campaign won a Bronze Lion at Cannes.

Cosmetics manufacturers insert **color strip** samples of eye shadow, blush, lipstick, and other makeup that readers can try immediately. Color strips are expensive to produce, but many advertisers think they're worth it.

Another costly innovation is the **pop-up ad.** Corporate advertisers such as Honeywell and TransAmerica were among the first to try this eye-catching approach. Product ads, such as a pop-up for the Dodge Dakota, followed.

Other intriguing approaches include **3-D ads** (complete with 3-D glasses), product samples (facial tissues and paper towels), and unusual shapes and sizes for preprinted inserts. An ad for Sara Lee cheesecake used a single heavy-stock page with what appeared to be a bite taken out of a life-size cheesecake slice. A half-page insert for Gleem toothpaste featured a metallic graphic of a mirror with the slogan "Check your mirror."

Researchers are probing the possibilities of holograms and ads that talk when readers pass a device across the page. Already ads can sing—liquor companies included microchips that played Christmas carols in their December magazine ads, and ads for a cigarette brand played "Happy Birthday" on the brand's 75th anniversary.

Recently, Global Commerce Group invented the Web Decoder, a transparent device made of clear polyester Mylar. The recipient is invited to interact with an image on a Website. When the piece is positioned over the designated image, a hidden word, icon, or phrase is revealed.

Advertisers can tailor the Web Decoder to their specific promotional needs, from cents-off coupons to instant-winner prizes.

And in early 2008 the final "sense" barrier was broken when Welch's sponsored a "Peel 'n Taste" flavor strip that appeared in *People* magazine. Now homemakers, the target of the ad, could actually taste the concord grape flavor of Welch's Grape Juice.

The ad below for the MINI uses a technology called Augmented Reality to show a 3-D image using a webcam and the information on the printed page.

Such innovative approaches not only attract readers' attention but also involve them in the experience by appealing to more than just the visual sense.

Laboratory Application

What products besides cars could Augmented Reality be used to advertise?

Source: BMW

Electric, Jenny Craig, and Ray-Ban sunglasses. Kraft Foods decided to expand its free, custom-published magazine *Food & Family,* which offers recipes and cooking tips, to 1 million U.S. households. This came after Kraft's successful test in Canada of another custom magazine, *What's Cooking.* The popularity of that publication even inspired a TV spin-off of the same name.[9] Ad Lab 13–B discusses other innovations in magazine advertising.

How Magazines Are Categorized

In the jargon of the trade, magazines are called books, and media buyers commonly categorize them by content, geography, and size.

Content

One of the most dramatic developments in publishing is the emergence of magazines with special content, which has given many books good prospects for long-term growth. The

(continued on page 409)

:: **Outstanding Magazine Ads**

Magazines provide creatives with an unlimited palette of colorful opportunities for their imagination. Offering permanence, color, unmatched reproduction quality, and excellent credibility, magazines are a powerful weapon in the advertiser's arsenal. In this portfolio, we've selected some outstanding examples of magazine advertising.

• See if you can look past the beauty of these ads and determine the underlying strategy that guided the artists' thinking. Who is the target audience? Is that different from the target market? What are they trying to say about the advertiser? How is the advertiser positioned? Once you've determined the strategy, which magazines would you place these ads in?

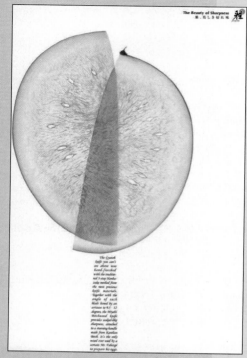

Where is the product? You can't see the knife being advertised here, but you can see the benefit it provides the consumer.

Source: ZWILLING J.A. Henckels AG

Pets are family to their owners, so a campaign that humorously mimics human weight-loss ads is both attention-getting and effective.

Source: Jardiland

This ad has an implicit comparison, the 15 minutes of drudgery most people feel on their daily subway ride.

Source: Livraria Da Vila

WWF ads have a big challenge: calling attention to the challenge of protecting endangered species, educating people about trade practices that create the problem, and helping people learn how they can help. This beautiful ad accomplishes all of this with few words.

Source: World Wildlife Fund

Fiat mixes passion, humor, and a bold claim about the brand's performance in this award-winning ad.

Source: Fiat Chrysler Automobiles

Many visitors to Paris may never think to visit the city's zoo, but that doesn't diminish the power of this campaign which associates iconic images of the city with the attraction.

Source: Parc Zoologique de Paris

Perfetti van Melle is a worldwide manufacturer and distributor of candy products. These bright ads convey the sweet bold flavors of the candy through great color and design.

Source: Perfetti Van Melle

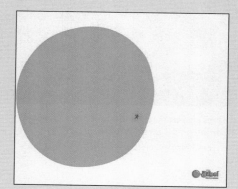

(continued from page 405)

broadest classifications of content are *consumer magazines, farm magazines,* and *business magazines.* Each may be broken down into hundreds of categories.

- **Consumer magazines,** purchased for entertainment, information, or both, are edited for consumers who buy products for their own personal consumption: *Time, Maxim, Glamour, Good Housekeeping.* The Portfolio Review, "Outstanding Magazine Ads," shows the range of creativity in consumer magazine advertising.
- **Farm publications** are directed to farmers and their families or to companies that manufacture or sell agricultural equipment, supplies, and services: *Farm Journal, Progressive Farmer, Prairie Farmer, Successful Farming.*
- **Business magazines,** by far the largest category, target business readers. They include *trade publications* for retailers, wholesalers, and other distributors *(Progressive Grocer, Packaging World); business* and *industrial magazines* for businesspeople involved in manufacturing and services *(Electronic Design, American Banker);* and *professional journals* for lawyers, physicians, architects, and other professionals *(Archives of Ophthalmology).*

Geography

A magazine may also be classified as *local, regional,* or *national.* Today, most major U.S. cities have a **local city magazine:** *San Diego Magazine, New York, Los Angeles, Chicago, Palm Springs Life.* Their readership is usually upscale business and professional people interested in local arts, fashion, and business.

Regional publications are targeted to a specific area of the country, such as the West or the South: *Sunset, Southern Living.* National magazines sometimes provide special market runs for specific geographic regions. *Time, Newsweek, Woman's Day,* and *Sports Illustrated* allow advertisers to buy a single major market. Exhibit 13-2 shows the nine

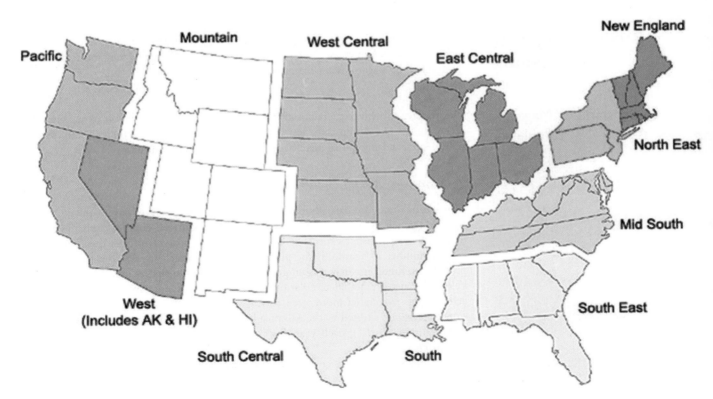

Exhibit 13-2

Advertisers benefit from selecting regional print editions similar to the nine geographic regions shown on the map. With regional binding and mailing, advertisers can buy ad space for only the amount of distribution they need.

Source: U.S. News & World Report, L.P., 2007.

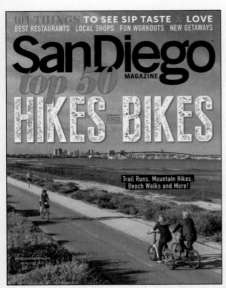

Magazines that cater to specific geographic areas are regional publications. Most metropolitan areas publish magazines specific to their city. San Diego Magazine gives its readers information on everything they need to know about San Diego from the best places to dine, shop and even hike and bike.

Source: SDM, LLC

major geographic breakdowns of regional editions of *U.S. News.* This is important for local or regional advertisers who want the benefit of advertising in larger more well-known publications while staying geographically relevant to the audience that may be reading the magazine.

National magazines range from those with enormous circulations, such as *TV Guide,* to small, lesser-known national magazines, such as *Nature* and *Volleyball.* The largest circulation magazine in the United States today is *AARP The Magazine,* distributed to the 22.4 million members of the AARP.[10]

Size

It doesn't take a genius to figure out that magazines come in different shapes and sizes, but it might take one to figure out how to get one ad to run in different-size magazines and still look the same. Magazine sizes run the gamut, which can make production standardization a nightmare. The most common magazine sizes follow:

Size Classification	Magazine	Approximate Size of Full-Page Ad
Large	*Spin, Interview*	4 col. × 170 lines (9½ × 11 1/3 inches)
Flat	*Time, Newsweek*	3 col. × 140 lines (7 × 10 inches)
Standard	*National Geographic*	2 col. × 119 lines (6 × 8½ inches)
Small or pocket	*Reader's Digest, Jet*	2 col. × 91 lines (4½ × 6½ inches)

Buying Magazine Space

When analyzing a magazine vehicle, media buyers consider readership, cost, mechanical requirements, and ad closing dates (deadlines). To buy effectively, they must thoroughly understand the magazine's circulation and rate-card information.

Understanding Magazine Circulation

The first step in analyzing a publication's potential effectiveness is to assess its audience. The buyer studies circulation statistics, primary and secondary readership, subscription and vendor sales, and any special merchandising services the magazine offers.

Guaranteed versus Delivered Circulation

A magazine's rates are partially based on its circulation. The **rate base** is the circulation figure on which the publisher bases its rates; the **guaranteed circulation** is the number of copies the publisher expects to circulate. This assures advertisers they will reach a certain number of people. If the publisher does not reach its *delivered figure,* it must provide a refund. For that reason, guaranteed circulation figures are often stated safely below the average actual circulation. However, this is not always true. Circulation actually gets overstated more often than people think. As many as 30 percent of consumer magazines audited by the **Alliance for Audited Media**, formerly the Audit Bureau of Circulation (ABC), each year don't meet the circulation levels they guarantee to advertisers.[11]

So media buyers expect publications to verify their circulation figures. Publishers pay thousands of dollars each year for a **circulation audit**—a thorough analysis of the circulation procedures, outlets of distribution, readers, and other factors—by companies such as ABC. Directories such as those published by Standard Rate & Data Service (SRDS) feature the logo of the auditing company in each listing for an audited magazine.

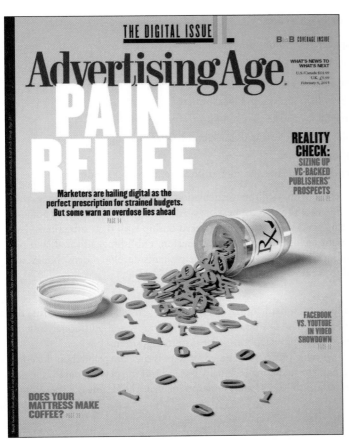

Advertising Age *is a good example of a vertical publication. The magazine is geared toward a variety of issues specific to the advertising industry. Unlike horizontal publications, which focus on a single job function across various industries,* Ad Age *is read by a wide range of people throughout the industry.*

Source: Crain Communications

Primary and Secondary Readership

Data from the ABC or other verified reports tell the media buyer the magazine's total circulation. This **primary circulation** represents the number of people who buy the publication, either by subscription or at the newsstand. **Secondary** (or **pass-along**) **readership,** which is an estimate determined by market research of how many people read a single issue of a publication, is very important to magazines. Some have more than six readers per copy. Multiplying the average pass-along readership by, say, a million subscribers can give a magazine a substantial audience beyond its primary readers.

Vertical and Horizontal Publications

Business publications are classified in two ways based on readership: *vertical* and *horizontal.* A **vertical publication** covers a specific industry in all its aspects. For example, Cahners Publishing produces *Restaurants & Institutions* strictly for restaurateurs and food-service operators. The magazine's editorial content includes everything from news of the restaurant industry to institutional-size recipes.

Horizontal publications, in contrast, deal with a particular job function across a variety of industries. Readers of *Purchasing* work in purchasing management in many different industries. Horizontal trade publications are very effective advertising vehicles because they usually offer excellent reach and they tend to be well read.[12]

Subscription and Vendor Sales

Media buyers also want to know a magazine's ratio of subscriptions to newsstand sales. Today, subscriptions account for the majority of magazine sales. Newsstands (which include bookstore chains) are still a major outlet for single-copy sales, but no outlet can handle more than a fraction of the many magazines available.

From the advertiser's point of view, newsstand sales are impressive because they indicate that the purchaser really wants the magazine and is not merely subscribing out of habit. According to the Magazine Publishers Association, single-copy sales account for 34 percent of total revenues for a representative sampling of leading magazines.

Paid and Controlled Circulation

Business publications may be distributed on either a *paid circulation* or *controlled circulation* basis. A paid basis means the recipient must pay the subscription price to receive the magazine. *Bloomberg Businessweek* is a **paid-circulation** business magazine.

In **controlled circulation,** the publisher mails the magazine free to individuals who the publisher thinks can influence the purchase of advertised products. Executives at *Fortune* 1000 corporations receive a *strategy + business* magazine. To qualify for the free subscription, people must specify that they want to receive the magazine and must give their professional title and information about the size of their company. Dues-paying members of organizations often get free subscriptions. For example, members of the National Association for Female Executives receive free copies of *Executive Female.*

Publishers of paid-circulation magazines say subscribers who pay are more likely to read a publication than those who receive it free. But controlled-circulation magazines can reach good prospects for the goods and services they advertise.

Merchandising Services: Added Value

Magazines, and newspapers too, often provide liberal *added-value services* to their regular advertisers, such as:

- Special free promotions to stores.
- Marketing services to help readers find local outlets.
- Response cards that allow readers to request brochures and catalogs.
- Help handling sales force, broker, wholesaler, and retailer meetings.
- Advance editions for the trade.
- Research into brand preferences, consumer attitudes, and market conditions.

If a publication's basic factors—editorial, circulation, and readership—are strong, these additional services can increase the effectiveness of its ads.[13] Magazines offer great potential for relationship marketing since they already have a relationship with their subscribers. New added-value options might include using magazines' custom publishing, editorial, and production knowledge, along with their databases, to help clients develop videos, books, and Websites that create added value for the brand.[14]

Reading Rate Cards

LO 13-3

Magazine rate cards follow a standard format. This helps advertisers determine costs, discounts, mechanical requirements, closing dates, special editions, and additional costs for features like color, inserts, bleed pages, split runs, or preferred positions.

Three dates affect magazine purchases. The **cover date** is the date printed on the cover. The **on-sale date** is the date the magazine is actually issued. And the **closing date** is the date all ad material must be in the publisher's hands for a specific issue. Lead time may be as much as three months.

Rates

As we discussed in Chapter 9, one way to compare magazines is to look at how much it costs to reach a thousand people based on the magazine's rates for a one-time, full-page ad. You compute the **cost per thousand (CPM)** by dividing the full-page rate by the number of *thousands* of subscribers:

$$\frac{\text{Page rate}}{(\text{Circulation} \div 1,000)} = \text{CPM}$$

If the magazine's black-and-white page rate is $10,000, and the publication has a circulation of 500,000, then:

$$\frac{\$10,000}{500,000 \div 1,000} = \frac{10,000}{500} = \$20 \text{ CPM}$$

Consider this comparison. In January 2012, the page rate for a full-color, one-page ad in *Car & Driver* was $196,632 on total paid circulation of 1,200,000. *Road & Track* offered the same ad for $105,309 on total paid circulation of 600,000. Which was the better buy on a CPM basis?[15]

Discounts

Magazines and newspapers often give discounts. **Frequency discounts** are based on the number of ad insertions, usually within a year; **volume discounts** are based on the total amount of space bought during a specific period. Most magazines also offer *cash discounts* (usually 2 percent) to advertisers who pay right away, and some offer discounts on the purchase of four or more consecutive pages in a single issue. In fact, many magazine publishers now negotiate their rates. According to Harold Shain, executive VP/publisher of *Newsweek,* "Every piece of business is negotiated."[16]

Premium Rates

Magazines charge extra for special features. Color normally costs 25 to 60 percent more than black and white. Some publications, such as *Money,* even offer metallic inks and special colors. Bleed pages can add as much as 20 percent to regular rates, although the typical increase is about 15 percent.

Second and third cover rates (the inside covers) typically cost less than the fourth (back) cover. According to SRDS, however, in 2008, *ESPN the Magazine* charged $208,000 for a normal color page, $457,600 for the second cover, and $270,400 for the fourth cover.[17]

Magazines charge different rates for ads in geographic or demographic issues. **Geographic editions** target geographic markets; **demographic editions** reach readers who share a demographic trait, such as age, income level, or professional status. *Time* offers one-page, four-color ads (one-time insertion) in its Boston edition for $21,495 (135,000 circulation) and in its New York edition for $34,708. For full-page, four-color ads, advertisers in the top management edition pay $90,000 (circulation 805,489). To run the same ad in *Time Gold,* which is targeted to baby boomers and has a circulation of more than 1 million, advertisers pay $69,000.

Software for Buying Print Media

One of the most important tasks in advertising is the placement of ads in various media. So the role of the media buyer is critical to the overall success of the campaign.

Placing an ad in a magazine or newspaper is not as easy as it may seem, especially when there are hundreds of newspapers and magazines around the country with different deadlines, different mechanical requirements, and different rates. To say the least, the job can be very tedious and time-consuming.

Fortunately, thanks to technology, print media buyers now have a variety of software programs available to assist them.

STRATA Marketing, Inc., for example, has developed media-buying software for each form of media. Its print software programs offer media buyers various ways to keep track of orders, clients, and rate information, while providing a large variety of formats for insertion order reports. This program also allows media buyers to copy insertion orders to numerous publications, all with a single keystroke.

These programs, and others similar in function, save media buyers a lot of time, thereby increasing productivity and efficiency. More time can be spent analyzing information, evaluating various print vehicles, and exercising creativity. By using software like this, media buyers gain flexibility and control over the placement of ads in print media.

Using Newspapers in the Creative Mix

When a small, alternative newspaper in Manhattan asked one of the newest and hottest creative shops in the city for help in promoting subscriptions, it had no idea what the little agency with the funny name, Mad Dogs & Englishmen, would do for it.

The *Village Voice* newspaper had always knocked the Establishment with its radical coverage of social issues, politics, media, and culture. So perhaps it shouldn't have come as a surprise when the Mad Dogs took the newspaper's own prose style and turned it around in a series of impertinent, self-mocking ads.

"Hell, I wouldn't have my home contaminated with a subscription to your elitist rag if you were giving away five-speed blenders," rants one ad in the series. "You people think New York is the friggin' center of the world." But then a second paragraph offers a dramatic alternative: "YES, I want to buy a year's subscription to the *Village Voice,*" along with a coupon.

The paper's readers aren't spared either. One ad skewers New Age tree-huggers: "Murderers! Trees are being systematically swallowed up by the jaws of industry and still you insist I take part in this horror by subscribing?"

Mad Dogs principal Nick Cohen said he thought the *Voice* would like the campaign because the newspaper is honest. "It really stands behind the freedom of the writers, even when they criticize the management itself," he said.

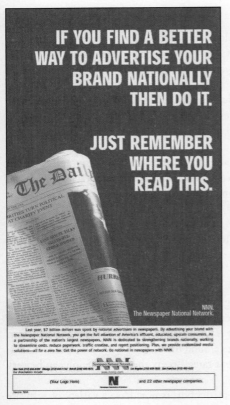

IF YOU FIND A BETTER
WAY TO ADVERTISE YOUR
BRAND NATIONALLY
THEN DO IT.

JUST REMEMBER
WHERE YOU
READ THIS.

Newspapers are an important medium in the creative mix, when used strategically.

Selecting the medium was easy. Because most people who would be interested in a subscription are *Village Voice* readers, the campaign ran in the paper itself. It proved to be a wise choice. In the first year of the campaign, the *Voice* saw a 30 percent increase in its subscriber base, surpassing all expectations.[18]

Who Uses Newspapers?

Newspapers are now the third-largest medium (after television and magazines) in terms of advertising volume, receiving 13.7 percent of the dollars spent by advertisers in the United States.[19]

Consider these important facts:

- Less than half of all adults (44%) read a daily newspaper.[20]
- Each section is read by about two-thirds of all adult readers; even more (80%) read the main news sections.[21]
- More than 46 million newspapers are sold daily, and every copy has an average of 2.3 readers.
- In 2009, there were 1,397 daily newspapers in the United States, with a total circulation of 40.8 million. The same year, the nation's 919 Sunday newspapers had a circulation of 46.9 million.[22]
- Newspaper advertising expenditures in 2011 totaled $21 billion.[23]
- Spending on print newspaper advertising has been declining for the past five years, but spending on Internet newspaper advertising has been growing at double-digit rates over the same time period until 2008, when it was flat.
- Spending on newspaper Websites accounts for 13.6 percent of all newspaper ad expenditures.

Although the newspaper is the major community-serving medium for both news and advertising, more and more national advertisers are shifting to radio and television. As a result, radio and TV carry most of the national advertising in the United States, while 84 percent of newspaper advertising revenue comes from local advertising. As Exhibit 13-3 shows, retailers and phone services are the primary national advertisers in newspapers.

The Pros and Cons of Newspaper Advertising

The *Village Voice* promotion shows how small businesses with even smaller budgets can benefit from creative newspaper advertising. Print ads in general and newspapers in particular provide a unique, flexible medium for advertisers to express their creativity—especially with businesses that rely on local customers.

Newspapers offer advertisers many advantages. One of the most important is *timeliness;* an ad can appear very quickly, sometimes in just one day. Newspapers also offer geographic targeting, a broad range of markets, reasonable cost, and more. But newspapers suffer from lack of selectivity, poor production quality, and clutter. And readers criticize them for lack of depth and follow-up on important issues.[24]

Use My IMC Campaign 13–B, "The Pros and Cons of Newspaper Advertising," to answer the questions in Ad Lab 13–C, "Newspapers and the Creative Mix."

How Newspapers Are Categorized

Newspapers can be classified by *frequency of delivery, physical size,* or *type of audience.*

Frequency of Delivery

A **daily newspaper** is published as either a morning or evening edition at least five times a week, Monday through Friday. Of the 1,397 dailies in the United States, 528 are evening papers and 869 are morning papers.[25] Morning editions tend to have broader geographic circulation and a larger male readership; evening editions are read more by women.

Exhibit 13-3

Top 10 newspaper advertisers in the United States.

Rank	Advertiser	Newspaper Ad Spending in 2008 ($ in Millions)
1	Verizon Communications	$686.7
2	Macy's	609.7
3	Sprint Nextel Corp	460.6
4	AT&T	328.3
5	Time Warner	311.6
6	Fry's Electronics	229.3
7	Procter & Gamble	213.7
8	Sears Holding Co	200.7
9	General Electric	200.7
10	Walt Disney	185.2

Newspapers create special sections. In turn, these are attractive to advertisers interested in their unique readership. The Sunday Times is Britain's largest selling Sunday newspaper. The Sunday Times also publishes several supplement magazines including The Sunday Times Rich List, The Sunday Times Magazine and The Sunday Times Travel Magazine.

Source: The Sunday Times

With their emphasis on local news and advertising, **weekly newspapers** characteristically serve small urban or suburban residential areas and farm communities. They are now the fastest-growing class of newspapers. A weekly newspaper's cost per thousand is usually higher than a daily paper's, but a weekly has a longer life and often has more readers per copy.

Physical Size

There are two basic newspaper formats, standard size and tabloid. The **standard-size newspaper** is about 22 inches deep and 13 inches wide and is divided into six columns. The **tabloid newspaper** is generally about 14 inches deep and 11 inches wide. National tabloid newspapers such as the *National Enquirer* and the *Star* use sensational stories to fight for single-copy sales. Other tabloids, such as the *New York Daily News,* emphasize straight news and features.

Newspapers used to offer about 400 different ad sizes. But in 1984, the industry introduced the **standard advertising unit (SAU)** system, which standardized the newspaper column width, page sizes, and ad sizes. An SAU **column inch** is $2^1/_{16}$ inches wide by 1 inch deep. There are now 56 standard ad sizes for standard papers and 32 for tabloids. Virtually all dailies converted to the SAU system (some at great expense) and so did most weeklies.

Type of Audience

Some dailies and weeklies serve special-interest audiences, a fact not lost on advertisers. They generally contain advertising oriented to their special audiences and they may have unique advertising regulations.

Some serve specific ethnic markets. Today, more than 200 dailies and weeklies are oriented to the African American community. Others serve foreign-language groups. In the United States, newspapers are printed in 43 languages other than English.

Specialized newspapers also serve business and financial audiences. *The Wall Street Journal,* the leading national business and financial daily, enjoys a circulation of 1.8 million. Other papers cater to fraternal, labor union, or professional organizations, religious groups, or hobbyists.

Other Types of Newspapers

The United States has 919 Sunday newspapers, mostly Sunday editions of daily papers, with a combined circulation of more than 46.9 million.[26] Sunday newspapers generally combine standard news coverage with special functions like these:

- Increased volume of classified ads.
- Greater advertising and news volume.
- In-depth coverage of business, sports, real estate, literature and the arts, entertainment, and travel.
- Review and analysis of the past week's events.
- Expanded editorial and opinion sections.

Most Sunday newspapers also feature a **Sunday supplement** magazine. Some publish their own supplement, such as *Los Angeles Magazine* of the *Los Angeles Times.* Other papers subscribe to syndicated supplements; *Parade* magazine has a readership of more than 67 million each week.[27]

Printed by rotogravure on heavier, coated paper stock, Sunday supplements are more conducive to color printing than newsprint, making them attractive to national advertisers who want better reproduction quality.

Another type of newspaper, the **independent shopping guide** or free community newspaper, offers advertisers local saturation. Sometimes called *pennysavers,* these

My IMC Campaign 13–B

The Pros and Cons of Newspaper Advertising

The Pros

- **Mass medium** penetrating every segment of society. Most consumers read the newspaper.
- **Local medium** with broad reach. Covers a specific geographic area that comprises both a market and a community of people sharing common concerns and interest.
- **Comprehensive in scope,** covering an extraordinary variety of topics and interests.
- **Geographic selectivity** is possible with zoned editions for specific neighborhoods or communities.
- **Timeliness.** Papers primarily cover today's news and are read in one day.
- **Credibility.** Studies show that newspaper ads rank highest in believability. TV commercials are a distant second.
- **Selective attention** from the relatively small number of active prospects who, on any given day, are interested in what the advertiser is trying to tell them or sell them.
- **Creative flexibility.** An ad's physical size and shape can be varied to give the degree of dominance or repetition that suits the advertiser's purpose. The advertiser can use black and white, color, Sunday magazines, or custom inserts.

- **An active medium** rather than a passive one. Readers turn the pages, clip and save, write in the margins, and sort through the contents.
- **A permanent record,** in contrast to the ephemeral nature of radio and TV.
- **Reasonable cost.**

The Cons

- **Lack of selectivity** of specific socioeconomic groups. Most newspapers reach broad, diverse groups of readers, which may not match the advertiser's objectives.
- **Short life span.** Unless readers clip and save the ad or coupon, it may be lost forever.
- **Low production quality.** Coarse newsprint generally produces a less impressive image than the slick, smooth paper stock of magazines, and some newspapers can't print color.
- **Clutter.** Each ad competes with editorial content and with all the other ads on the same page or spread.
- **Lack of control** over where the ad will appear unless the advertiser pays extra for a preferred position.
- **Overlapping circulation.** Some people read more than one newspaper. Advertisers may be paying for readers they already reached in a different paper.

Ads that provoke an emotional reaction are often developed for video. But as this ad for McDonald's shows, print can be creatively exploited to do the same thing. This ad, with the headline "Leave your Morning Mood Behind," playfully illustrates the power of print advertising. Do you think this style of print advertising would be effective in newspapers? What type of newspaper would you run this advertisement in?

Source: McDonald's

shoppers offer free distribution and extensive advertising pages targeted at essentially the same audience as weekly newspapers—urban and suburban community readers. Readership is often high, and the publishers use hand delivery or direct mail to achieve maximum saturation.

North Americans also read national newspapers, including the *Globe and Mail* in Canada, *USA Today,* and the *Christian Science Monitor.* With a circulation of 2.1 million *The Wall Street Journal* is the largest national newspaper, followed by *USA Today* (1.8 million) and *The New York Times* (0.95 million).[28]

Types of Newspaper Advertising

The major classifications of newspaper advertising are *display, classified, public notices,* and *preprinted inserts.*

Display Advertising

Display advertising includes copy, illustrations or photos, headlines, coupons, and other visual components—such as the ads for the *Village Voice* discussed earlier. Display ads vary in size and appear in all sections of the newspaper except the first page of major sections, the editorial page, the obituary page, and the classified advertising section.

One common variation of the display ad, the **reading notice,** looks like editorial matter and sometimes costs more than normal display advertising. To prevent readers from mistaking it for editorial matter, the word *advertisement* appears at the top.

AD Lab 13-C

Newspapers and the Creative Mix

Study My IMC Campaign 13–B, "The Pros and Cons of Newspaper Advertising," and see if you can apply that information to the following situation:

You're the product manager for a major brand of bar soap and you wish to go nationwide with an ad featuring a coupon.

Laboratory Applications

1. Which newspaper would be best?
   a. A weekly.   b. A daily.

2. If you use a daily, in what section of the paper do you want your ad to appear?

3. If you decided on the Sunday supplement, which of the following would you choose and why?
   a. *Parade* magazine.   b. Color coupon supplement.

As we discussed in Chapters 4 and 6, retailers often run newspaper ads through **cooperative** (or **co-op**) **programs** sponsored by the manufacturers whose products they sell. The manufacturer pays fully or partially to create and run the ad, which features the manufacturer's product and logo along with the local retailer's name and address.

Classified Advertising

Classified ads provide a community marketplace for goods, services, and opportunities of every type, from real estate and new-car sales to employment and business opportunities. A newspaper's profitability often depends on a large and healthy classified section.

Classified ads usually appear under subheads that describe the class of goods or the need the ads seek to satisfy. Most employment, housing, and car advertising is classified. To promote the use of classified ads in the *Village Voice,* Mad Dogs & Englishmen created a series of display ads that used humorous "Situation Wanted" ads as the main visuals.

Classified rates are typically based on how many lines the ad occupies and how many times the ad runs. Some newspapers accept **classified display ads,** which run in the classified section of the newspaper but feature larger type and/or photos, art borders, abundant white space, and sometimes even color.

Public Notices

For a nominal fee, newspapers carry legal **public notices** of changes in business and personal relationships, public governmental reports, notices by private citizens and organizations, and financial reports. These ads follow a preset format.

Preprinted Inserts

Like magazines, newspapers carry **preprinted inserts.** The advertiser prints the inserts and delivers them to the newspaper plant for insertion into a specific edition. Insert sizes range from a typical newspaper page to a double postcard; formats include catalogs, brochures, mail-back devices, and perforated coupons.

Some large metropolitan dailies allow advertisers to limit their inserts to specific circulation zones. A retail advertiser that wants to reach only those shoppers in its immediate trading area can place an insert in the local-zone editions. Retail stores, car dealers, and large national advertisers are among those who find it less costly to distribute their circulars this way compared to mailing them or delivering them door to door.

How Advertisers Buy Newspaper Space

To get the most from the advertising budget, the media buyer must know the characteristics of a newspaper's readership: the median age, sex, occupation, income, educational level, and buying habits of the typical reader.

Understanding Readership and Circulation

Readership information is available from various sources, such as Simmons Market Research Bureau and Scarborough Research Corp. Most large papers also provide extensive data on their readers.

In single-newspaper cities, reader demographics typically reflect a cross section of the general population. In cities with two or more newspapers, however, these characteristics may vary widely. The *Los Angeles Times* is directed to a broad cross section of the community while *La Opinion* targets L.A.'s large Hispanic population.

Advertisers must understand the full extent of the newspaper's circulation. The paper's total circulation includes subscribers and single-copy newsstand buyers, as well as secondary readers.

Rate Cards

Like the magazine rate card, the newspaper **rate card** lists advertising rates, mechanical and copy requirements, deadlines, and other information. Because rates vary greatly, advertisers should calculate which papers deliver the most readers and the best demographics for their money.

Local versus National Rates

Most newspapers charge local and national advertisers at different rates. The **national rate** averages 75 percent higher, but some papers charge as much as 254 percent more.[29] Newspapers attribute higher rates to the added costs of serving national advertisers. For instance, an ad agency usually places national advertising and receives a 15 percent commission from the paper.

But many national advertisers reject the high rates and take their business elsewhere. Only 6.1 percent of national ad money now goes to newspapers.[30] In response to declining national advertising revenue, newspapers are experimenting with simplified billing systems and discount rates for their national clients.

Flat Rates and Discount Rates

Many national papers charge **flat rates,** which means they allow no discounts; a few newspapers offer a single flat rate to both national and local advertisers.

Newspapers that offer volume discounts have an **open rate** (their highest rate for a one-time insertion) and **contract rates,** whereby local advertisers can obtain discounts of up to 70 percent by signing a contract for frequent or bulk space purchases. **Bulk discounts** offer advertisers decreasing rates (calculated by multiplying the number of inches by the cost per inch) as they use more inches. Advertisers earn **frequency discounts** by running a given ad repeatedly in a specific time period. Similarly, advertisers can sometimes get **earned rates,** a discount applied retroactively as the volume of advertising increases through the year. Many newspapers also participate in Newsplan, a program that gives national and regional advertisers discounts for purchasing six or more pages per year.

Short Rate

An advertiser who contracts to buy a specific amount of space during a one-year period at a discount and then fails to fulfill the promise is charged a **short rate,** which is the difference between the contracted rate and the earned rate for the actual inches run. Conversely, an advertiser who buys more inches than contracted may be entitled to a rebate or credit because of the discounted earned rate for the additional advertising space.

Combination Rates

Combination rates are often available for placing a given ad in (1) morning and evening editions of the same newspaper; (2) two or more newspapers owned by the same

The newspaper rate report for the Seattle Times is similar to that for magazines. It shows a variety of ad units available and lists their costs.
Source: The Seattle Times Company

PACIFIC NW

MECHANICAL SPECS
FOR THE SEATTLE TIMES SUNDAY MAGAZINE

AD SIZES

Standard ads (no bleed)

1/20 vertical	1.95" x 2.6"
1/10 horizontal	4.025" x 2.6"
1/10 vertical	1.95" x 5.175"
3/20 vertical	1.95" x 7.837"
1/5 horizontal	4.025" x 5.175"
3/10 vertical	4.025" x 7.837"

Ads with bleed

1/5 vertical	2.137" x 10.875"
3/10 horizontal	6.712" x 5.362"
1/2 horizontal	9" x 5.37"
1/2 vertical	4.4375" x 10.875"
3/5 horizontal	9" x 6.724"
3/5 vertical	5.6" x 10.875"
7/10 horizontal	9" x 7.862"
7/10 vertical	6.719" x 10.875"
Full page	9" x 10.875"
Double truck	18" x 10.875"

MECHANICAL SPECIFICATIONS

Images placed in the document need to be in bitmap, grayscale or CMYK, saved as TIFF or composite EPS format and flattened with no masking channels.

• When converting RGB to CMYK images, customize the Photoshop color settings to SWOP inks, 15% dot gain, GCR, medium black generation and 300% total ink limit. This color setting file can be provided on request. Avoid using RGB, LAB or indexed color images in your document. Do not use PICT, GIF or JPEG for placed images.

• Grayscale and color images should be provided at 300 dpi resolution.

• When scaling images up in size, make sure to maintain sufficient resolution.

Screen-tint builds should have a value of a minimum of 5% for any color.

For large areas with heavy black-ink coverage, create a **rich black**. The preferred build is 60% cyan, 40% magenta and 100% black. Do not use rich black for text, except for bold type larger than 72 points in size.

Specify **rule weight** value at a minimum of .5 points, and avoid hairline rules in your document. Any rules that are screened or built from process colors must be a minimum value of 2 points in weight. For borders or frames, specify a custom minimum size of no less than .3 points.

ADDITIONAL INFORMATION

Contact your sales support staff if you have any questions.

1/20 vertical	1/10 horizontal	1/10 vertical	3/20 vertical	1/5 horizontal	3/10 vertical
1.95" x 2.6"	4.025" x 2.6"	1.95" x 5.175"	1.95" x 7.837"	4.025" x 5.175"	4.025" x 7.837"

Bleed specifications

Material intended to bleed must be furnished with a minimum of .25" image area beyond the trim.

1/5 vertical	3/10 horizontal	1/2 horizontal	1/2 vertical
2.137" x 10.875"	6.712" x 5.362"	9" x 5.37"	4.4375" x 10.875"

Live area

All type or graphics not intended to trim should be positioned .1875" from trim.

3/5 horizontal	3/5 vertical	7/10 horizontal	7/10 vertical	Full Page
9" x 6.724"	5.6" x 10.875"	9" x 7.862"	6.719" x 10.875"	9" x 10.875"

All ads must use these dimensions. If they do not, the ad will be resized to fit the designated space.

13

RATE CARD

PACIFIC NW

2012 AD RATES

SIZES	FREQUENCY LEVEL				
	1x	6x	13x	26x	40x
1/20	$540	$510	$480	$450	$425
1/10	1,085	1,020	960	900	845
3/20	1,625	1,530	1,435	1,350	1,270
1/5	2,170	2,040	1,915	1,800	1,695
3/10	3,255	3,060	2,875	2,700	2,540
1/2	5,205	4,895	4,600	4,325	4,065
3/5	6,245	5,870	5,520	5,190	4,875
7/10	7,285	6,850	6,440	6,050	5,690
Full Page	8,675	8,675	8,675	8,155	7,665
Double Truck	17,350	17,350	17,350	16,310	15,330

Cancellation policy

Pacific Northwest magazine ads canceled fewer than 20 days before publication or power position ads canceled fewer than 30 days before publication will be charged 10% of the total cost of the ad.

Readers say:

"It is what I want my backyard to look like."

publisher; and (3) in some cases, two or more newspapers affiliated in a syndicate or newspaper group.

Run of Paper versus Preferred Position

Run-of-paper (ROP) advertising rates entitle a newspaper to place a given ad on any newspaper page or in any position it desires. Although the advertiser has no control over where the ad appears in the paper, most newspapers try to place an ad in the position the advertiser requests.

An advertiser can ensure a choice position for an ad by paying a higher **preferred-position rate.** A tire manufacturer, for example, may pay the preferred rate to ensure a position in the sports section.

There are also preferred positions on a given page. The preferred position near the top of a page or at the top of a column next to reading matter is called **full position.** It's usually surrounded by reading matter and may cost the advertiser 25 to 50 percent more than ROP rates. Slightly less desirable is placement *next to reading matter (NR),* which generally costs 10 to 20 percent more than ROP rates.

Color Advertising

Color advertising is available in many newspapers on an ROP basis. Because of their high-speed presses and porous paper stock, newspapers are not noted for high-quality color printing. So advertisers frequently preprint ads using processes known as HiFi color and Spectracolor. The cost of a color ad is usually based on the black-and-white rate plus an extra charge for each additional color.

Split Runs

Many newspapers (and magazines) offer **split runs** so that advertisers can test the *pulling power* of different ads. The advertiser runs two ads of identical size, but different content, for the same product on the same day in the same or different press runs. The idea is to eliminate as many variables as possible. By measuring responses to the two ads, the advertiser is able to compare and contrast the effectiveness of each. For this service, newspapers typically charge extra and set a minimum space requirement.

Co-ops and Networks

As an aid to national advertisers, the NAB created the Newspaper Co-op Network (NCN). Salespeople from participating newspapers helped national advertisers line up retailers for dealer-listing ads. The advertiser would produce the ad and include a blank space for each paper to insert local retailers' names. The system also helped manufacturers manage local advertising tie-ins to national campaigns and themes. Before the development of NCN, national advertisers had to place ads and recruit local dealers individually.

In 1992, the Newspaper Advertising Bureau merged with the American Newspaper Publishers Association and five other marketing associations to form the **Newspaper Association of America (NAA),** which continued to simplify national newspaper ad buys. In 1994, the NAA launched a *one-order, one-bill system* for national advertising, called the Newspaper National Network. Advertisers can make multimarket newspaper buys by placing one order and paying one bill, instead of having to contact—and pay—each paper individually.[31]

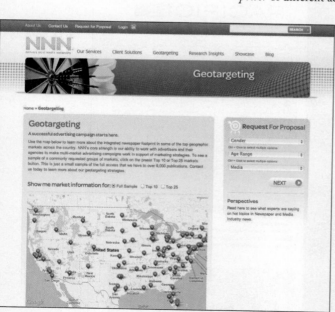

Co-ops and networks help simplify the ad-buying process for advertisers by consolidating the purchasing paperwork and requirements for publications in a single location. The geomarketing page shows advertisers where they can buy ads to better target their markets. Important information such as run date, size, and identifying captions is included.

Ethical Issues

What's at Stake with Sweepstakes?

Many of us have probably received an envelope in the mail with the phrase "You Are a Winner!" or something similar, plastered in large, bold type behind the front window. And perhaps, for a split second you believed that you had won the $100,000 prize. Then you discovered the disclosure, in such small print that you overlooked it at first glance, telling you otherwise. Believe it or not, there have been some who didn't notice the disclosure and traveled to the sweepstakes' headquarters believing that they had won the jackpot. Similarly, others were misled into believing that purchasing advertised products would increase their chances of winning, so they spent thousands of dollars each in magazine subscriptions. Were these people deceived?

Until recently, this is how many sweepstakes were pitched to consumers. According to the Direct Marketing Association, sweepstakes are, by definition, "an advertising or promotional device by which items of value (prizes) are awarded to participating consumers by chance, with no purchase or 'entry fee' required in order to win." However, by entering a sweepstakes you are volunteering your name, address, and possible tastes in the advertised product to be put on lists for other direct marketers to acquire. In turn you are offered a chance to win what seems like easy money. For years it was difficult for recipients to tell whether or not they had a winning entry. With statements claiming "You are a winner," simulated checks, and material resembling communications from the government, the line separating promotion and deception became very thin.

All of this changed in 2000. Following investigations of sweepstakes firms in more than 40 states, numerous state regulators brought three of the biggest sweeps marketers—Publisher's Clearing House (PCH), Time Inc., and U.S. Sales Corp.—to court, alleging that the marketing giants conducted deceptive sweepstakes promotions. In California alone, state officials claimed that 5,000 consumers spent more than $2,500 each a year in unnecessary magazine subscriptions through PCH because they believed that it improved their odds of winning. Accusations were similar for all three companies, and each defended their marketing practices claiming they always believed their mailings were clear. One PCH spokesperson stated that 98 percent of the consumers who purchased magazines through their promotions were spending less than $300 a year. However, because litigation in so many states—47 in Time Inc.'s case—would have been too costly, each company decided to settle and agreed to reform its practices. Combined, the three marketers refunded more than $50 million in fines and restitution to state regulators and consumers who excessively purchased unnecessary magazines.

The reforms these companies agreed to were in accord with the Deceptive Mail Prevention and Enforcement Act that became effective in April 2000. The act changed how direct-mail sweepstakes are presented and packaged. Some of the most significant changes included abandoning any "winner" proclamations unless the recipient had truly won a prize, and displaying a "fact box" that "clearly and conspicuously" explained all the terms and rules of the sweepstakes, including the odds of winning. Each mailing was also required to include the statements "No purchase is necessary to enter" and "A purchase does not improve your chances of winning" in boldfaced capital letters in the mailing, in the rules, and on the order/entry form itself. In addition, each company is required to include a statement providing an address or toll-free number where recipients can either write or call to have their name and addresses removed from their mailing lists.

Does this mean the end to sweepstakes? Probably not, since many people seem to jump at the chance to strike it rich for the cost of a stamp.

How much harm, if any, are sweepstakes really causing? Isn't part of promotion getting consumers to believe that they want what is being advertised? Without question, the ethical issues involved are complicated, but at least now you won't have to read the fine print to get the whole story.

Questions

1. Are sweepstakes companies really at fault for misleading their consumers? Why or why not?

2. Do you believe it is ethical for sweepstakes to "disguise" their promotions for the purpose of advertising?

Sources: www.crimes-of-persuasion.com/Crimes/Telemarketing/Outbound/Major/Sweepstakes/sweepstakes.htm; "Sweepstakes Advertising: A Consumer's Guide," *Consumers: A Helpful Guide* (www.dmaconsumers.org/sweepstakeshelp.html); "Be Smart Buy Smart," State of California Department of Consumer Affairs (www.dca.ca.gov/r_r/sweep.pdf); "Sweepstakes Assistance: A Caregiver's Guide," *Consumers: A Helpful Guide* (www.dmaconsumers.org/olderconsumers.html); "Stop Calling Me!" National Consumers League (www.nclnet.org/privacy/stopcalling2.htm); "How to Opt Out," *Consumer Privacy Guide* (www.consumerprivacyguide.org/howto/optout.shtml)

Chrysler was the first marketer to use the new network, placing ads for its national minivan sale in 75 newspapers in March 1994.[32] The Newspaper National Network offers advertisers competitive CPM pricing and guaranteed positioning, in addition to its one-order, one-bill appeal.[33] It also allows smaller papers to participate in national advertising.[34]

Insertion Orders and Tearsheets

When advertisers place an ad, they submit an **insertion order** to the newspaper stating the date(s) on which the ad is to run, its size, the desired position, the rate, and the type of artwork accompanying the order.

An insertion order serves as a contract between the advertiser (or its agency) and the publication. If an advertiser fails to pay the agency, the agency still must pay the publication. To avoid this liability, many agencies now place a disclaimer on their insertion orders stating that they are acting solely as an *agent for a disclosed principal* (legal terminology meaning the agency is just a representative for the advertiser and is therefore not liable for the payment). Some publications refuse to accept insertion orders with disclaimers unless payment accompanies the order. In 1991, the American Association of Advertising Agencies recommended to its agency members that they no longer accept sole liability for their clients' bills.[35] However, many agencies do still accept liability, perhaps out of some insecurity about possibly losing their agency commission—or their client.

When a newspaper creates ad copy and art, it gives the advertiser a **proof copy** to check. In contrast, most national advertising arrives at the newspaper *camera ready,* either in the form of a photo print or an electronic file via e-mail. To verify that the ad ran, the newspaper tears out the page on which the ad appeared and sends it to the agency or advertiser. Today, most **tearsheets** for national advertisers are handled through a private central office, the Advertising Checking Bureau.

When a tearsheet arrives, the advertiser examines it to make sure the ad ran according to instructions: in the right section and page position, and with the correct reproduction. If the ad did not run per instructions, the agency or advertiser is usually due an adjustment, a discount, or even a free rerun.

Print: A Worldwide Medium

Every country has newspapers and magazines to serve its population (see Exhibit 13-4). U.S. advertisers in foreign markets generally use either international or local media, depending on their campaign objectives and intended audience. Whether at home or abroad, advertisers must study the audience and remember the basics of print advertising. Study the My IMC Campaign 13–C on page 426 to better understand how advertisers evaluate print as a medium.

Several large U.S. publishers, including Time Warner and *Scientific American,* circulate international editions of their magazines abroad. The *International Herald Tribune, The Wall Street Journal,* and London's *Financial Times* are widely read in Asia, Europe, and the Middle East. In China, numerous publications such as *Elle, Esquire,* and *Forbes* are now available to the country's increasingly wealthy residents.[36]

United Kingdom		Canada	
Title	**Circulation (000)**	**Title**	**Circulation (000)**
TV Choice	1,369	Reader's Digest	851
What's on TV	1,318	Chatelaine	570
Radio Times	1,023	Canadian Living	520
Take a Break	943	Movie Entertainment	419
Reader's Digest	602	Maclean's	352

Australia		United States	
Title	**Circulation (000)**	**Title**	**Circulation (000)**
Australian Women's Weekly	491	AARP The Magazine	24,349
Woman's Day	405	Reader's Digest	8,168
Better Homes and Gardens	380	Better Homes and Gardens	7,659
Reader's Digest	344	National Geographic	5,060
New Idea	330	Good Housekeeping	4,684

Exhibit 13-4

International consumer magazine paid circulation.

Source: Data from Standard Rate and Data Service, The Lifestyle Market Analyst.

My IMC Campaign 13–C

Planning and Evaluating Print Media

At this point in your project you should have decided whether or not to use print (magazine and newspaper) as a communication vehicle. The next step is deciding which of the thousands of options makes the most sense for your client's brand.

The beauty of media planning and buying is that you have a blank slate from which to build your plan. As you start to build your plan, however, you need to consider what you are working toward. By answering a set of simple questions you can build the foundation of your recommendation. You should approach planning print media in the same way you would approach planning the brand strategy:

- Whom do you want to reach?
- Why use print?
- What are the brand objectives?
- Where do you want to place your advertising to best achieve your objectives?
- How should you execute your plan?

When you have answered these questions, it is time to analyze and evaluate your opportunities and develop your plan.

Selecting publications requires both critical thinking and hard and fast numbers. For instance monthly magazines can take up to 12 weeks to gain full readership (called "to cume" their audience). This can obviously be an issue if your communication objectives are centered on building reach quickly. On the other hand, weekly magazines cume their audience in approximately one to two weeks, making them great to generate reach around key events. Finally, the number of insertions by title also depends on your strategy. If you are telling a sequenced story through three ads, then you need to plan for three insertions in each publication (pub). This will obviously be expensive and likely will reduce the number of pubs on the plan, ultimately limiting your reach.

The great thing about print advertising is that it offers a large number of opportunities for brands to engage consumers in niche environments, thereby limiting brand wastage. However, not all brands want or need such niche vehicles, and lucky for those brands there are more mass-oriented publications too:

Targeted	Mass Books
Golf	*People*
Field and Stream	*TV Guide*
Baby Talk	*Parade*
Ski	*National Enquirer*
Martha Stewart Living	*Reader's Digest*

Some of you will be focusing on large national advertisers and can utilize nearly all types of print options. But what opportunities exist for the local advertiser? First, newspapers are typically a staple of any large local advertiser. Second, most of the print publications that we have discussed thus far will allow you to layer in demogeographical targeting to help fine-tune your plan. Take this into account as you build your plan. It doesn't make sense to advertise in a national pub if your client is only located in the southeastern United States.

See My IMC Campaigns 13–A and 13–B for checklists of the pros and cons of magazine and newspaper advertising.

As you can see, common sense plays a major role in planning print campaigns, especially for large advertisers. But for other brands, advertising in print is a bit more difficult because the names of the targeted publications don't just roll off the tongue like *Sports Illustrated or People*. To plan for those campaigns, most advertisers use syndicated research such as Media Mark's MRI product. This is a piece of planning software that indexes, through surveys, people's readership of tens of thousands of different publications. So when Microsoft wants to reach IT decision makers in the enterprise (in companies with over 100 employees), MRI tells the media planner that she can find a high composition (concentration of overall readership) of that target in publications like *eWeek, InformationWeek,* and *Baseline* magazine.

While we detail a number of tools in this chapter, for the large majority of projects, access to these tools will be limited. Therefore, think about the medium in terms of the mindset of the readers when you place an ad in front of them. The closer you can get that mindset to match the category, industry, or association of your brand's product, the better off you are.

Well-educated, upper-income consumers read these newspapers and magazines, even though they are typically printed in English. So these publications are the closest things to global print media for reaching this audience. *Reader's Digest*—the oldest international mass-audience medium—reaches more than 60 foreign countries. However, the publisher prints the magazine in local languages and tailors it to each country, so advertisers often view it as a local medium.

The number of international business, trade, or specialty publications is growing. CNBC's *European Business* and *Brewing & Distilling International,* both English-language magazines, are distributed throughout Europe.

Political changes in the former Soviet Union and Eastern bloc countries spurred many new trade publications. Most are published locally in association with foreign publishers. In 1990, for example, McGraw-Hill launched Russian-language editions of *Aviation Week & Space Technology* and *Bloomberg Businessweek.* And International Data Group launched several trade publications, including *Mir PK Russia* (formerly *PC World USSR*) and *ComputerWorld Poland.*

Posters are another print medium. This powerful ad for
UNICEF highlights the plight of childern by taking
advantage of the protective barrier surrounding a tree.

© Outdoor Advertising Association of America

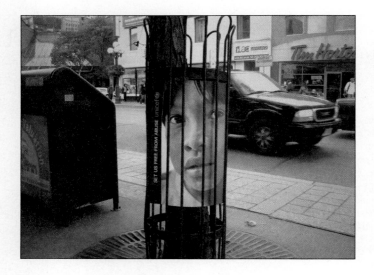

In the past, international advertising media consisted mainly of newspapers and magazines. Today, satellite-to-cable broadcast options, such as Superchannel and Sky Channel in Europe and Star TV in Asia, supplement print media.

Print Media and New Technologies

With computers came revolutionary media options, such as the Internet, challenging both traditional print media and advertisers to adapt. Newspapers and magazines are rushing to make alliances with cable, regional telephone, and online companies to get a toehold in the interactive information market.

Over the last five years, for example, virtually all metropolitan news organizations and national magazines have incorporated electronic services. News organizations are information-rich, and much of the specialized information they don't run in the paper or the magazine fits perfectly with the online world's narrower interests. They are still, however, trying to figure out how to incorporate advertising into their new ventures. Most ads are still simply banners, but customers who are interested can click on the banners and scroll down to more in-depth information. This becomes a value-added service for the print medium's advertising customers. George Gilder, media expert and author, believes that the newspaper industry is in a particularly advantageous position because "the convergence of text and video will cause a revolution in advertising, with targeted messages leading consumers step-by-step to a transaction."[37]

We'll deal with these issues in greater depth in Chapter 15.

Many resources for advertisers and media buyers are
now available, on demand, through the Internet. Today,
most large organizations, like The Wall Street
Journal, provide such information online, giving media
personnel instant access to critical information. Some
organizations even offer direct online transactions to
purchase information or media space.

© NetPhotos/Alamy Stock Photo

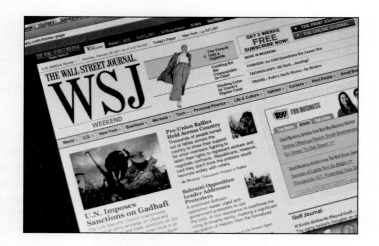

People BEHIND the Ads

Nancy Cardone Berger, VP/Publisher and CRO at Marie Claire

Courtesy of Nancy Berger Cardone

When Advertising Age wrote that "Marie Claire keeps on outdoing itself," it gave much of the credit to VP, Publisher, and Chief Revenue Officer Nancy Berger Cardone and her team. In fact, it named her Publisher of the Year and placed her on the Magazine A-List. When CA spoke with Nancy, we knew she would have energy, passion for her job, and excitement about the future. But Nancy's real secret is a talent for great ideas every bit as developed and sophisticated as that of a top agency creative director. Evidence? Marie Claire has little trouble attracting conventional "women's" brands. But Nancy drove ad growth by showing the value of Marie Claire to brands that often don't target the magazine's readers, such as Ruth's Chris Steak Houses. We asked Nancy to tell us a bit about her job and to offer advice to those who will follow in her footsteps.

CA: Describe the culture of your group at Marie Claire

NBC: MC is a media brand in the print, digital, social, broadcast and event space. We have a total audience of 16 million educated, stylish and influential women across all channels. The magazine is the largest piece of our revenue, but other platforms are growing quickly. Marie Claire is a global brand, published in 33 additional countries around the world. We are an organization of passionate media executives who are committed to innovation, relevance and story telling.

CA: Describe a "typical" day that highlights your career responsibilities

NBC: We publish the magazine on a monthly basis, and close each issue two month ahead of the month published on the cover. Our digital and social closing dates are more timed to the actual delivery of the communications, so in effect, we are constantly closing business. My day consists of a lot of meetings, internal and external. I typically have a business breakfast and lunch appointment every day. I travel about 25% of the time around the country (bigger advertising markets like Chicago, Dallas, San Francisco, Los Angeles), as well as internationally (mostly London, Paris and Milan). I consume a lot of media, to stay on top of what is happening in the industries that affect my business.

CA: What are the most important changes taking place in media selling today? How will things be different in the future?

NBC: When I started in this business, my job was to sell advertising pages and that was it. And my competition was other magazines. Today, we are selling content on all delivery channels and competing for marketing dollars within every media category. A typical sale today encompasses multiple engagement points to bring an advertiser closer to our audience. We host events, create advertising, do custom research, connect and create marketing partnerships, create ideas, create ownership opportunities for clients. And the sale is ongoing all year long. The future will continue to evolve and change as new products and measurement tools are being developed.

CA: How important is approaching selling from an IMC perspective? From a global perspective? Would you say it is increasing in importance? How can students become more globally aware?

NBC: Marie Claire is a global brand and a majority of our advertisers are also global brands. In the past, each country has operated independently, but we have all realized the benefits of communicating with a common position and DNA around the world. As clients begin to do this more as well, we have been able to spearhead some exciting global initiatives. We have had great successes over the past few years, and look forward to continuing this momentum on the global stage.

CA: What do you look for in new talent?

NBC: I look for ambition. I look for creativity and pro-activeness. I look for a strong work ethic. I want to see a passion for the work. I want someone who always wants to learn and improve. I respect someone who wants my job one day.

CA: What is the most enjoyable part of your job?

NBC: I love mentoring people. I love creating things/ideas that have never been done before. I love finding a white-space opportunity and filling it. I love interacting with other informed and passionate people.

CA: What should a university student be doing to prepare to follow in your footsteps someday?

NBC: A university student should always bring a strong sense of curiosity, ambition and knowledge that they have honed throughout their years at university into the workforce.

CA: What do you do in your spare time?

NBC: I do a lot of charity work. My youngest son, Jakob, was diagnosed with Type 1 Diabetes 5 years ago, and I am committed to raising funds and awareness. I am addicted to Soul Cycle. I love to cook, spend time with my family, travel and learn new things.

CA: What is your favorite place in the world?

NBC: My favorite place in the world is home.
My second favorite place in the world is Italy… for the people, for the food, and for the shoes!

Chapter Summary

The printed page—in magazines and newspapers—provides a unique, flexible medium for advertising creativity.

In selecting magazines for advertising, the media buyer must consider a publication's circulation, its readership, its cost, and its mechanical requirements. A magazine's rates may be determined by several factors: its primary and secondary readership, the number of subscription and vendor sales, and the number of copies guaranteed versus those actually delivered.

Magazine rate cards follow a standard format so advertisers can readily compare advertising costs. They list black-and-white and color rates, discounts, issue and closing dates, and mechanical requirements.

Magazines offer distinct advantages. They are the most selective of all mass media and are flexible in both readership and advertising. They offer unsurpassed color, excellent reproduction quality, authority and believability, long shelf life, and prestige at an efficient cost. However, they often require long lead times, have problems offering reach and frequency, and are subject to heavy advertising competition. The cost of advertising in some magazines is also very high.

The newspaper is a mass medium that almost everybody reads. It offers great flexibility, which assists creativity, and its printed message lasts longer than ads in electronic media. However, newspapers also have disadvantages: lack of audience selectivity, short life span, poor production quality, heavy advertising competition, potentially poor ad placement, and overlapping circulation. Still, the newspaper is the major community-serving medium today for both news and advertising.

The newspaper's rate card lists prices, deadlines, mechanical requirements, and other pertinent information. Rates vary for local and national advertisers. Also listed are the newspaper's short-rate policy, combination rates, frequency discounts, run-of-paper rates, and other data.

Print is a worldwide medium; every country has newspapers and magazines. The international advertiser may have to choose between local and international media. The most educated consumers in many countries often read English-language publications. Political changes in eastern Europe spurred the introduction of many trade and business publications in the local language. Advertisers must study the audience they wish to reach before buying any media, whether at home or abroad.

Newspapers and magazines are making alliances with cable, regional telephone, and online computer companies to enter the interactive information market. They are still experimenting with ways to sell advertising on their electronic publications. Some experts believe that the convergence of text, video, and graphics will cause a creative revolution in advertising, with targeted, information-rich messages able to lead consumers step by step to a transaction without ever leaving home.

Important Terms

Alliance for Audited Media, *407*

bleed, *403*

bulk discount, *418*

business magazines, *406*

circulation audit, *407*

classified ad, *417*

classified display ad, *417*

closing date, *412*

color strip, *405*

column inch, *415*

combination rate, *418*

consumer magazines, *406*

contract rate, *418*

controlled circulation, *411*

cooperative (co-op) program, *417*

cost per thousand (CPM), *412*

cover date, *412*

cover position, *403*

custom magazines, *404*

daily newspaper, *414*

demographic editions, *413*

display advertising, *416*

earned rate, *418*

farm publications, *406*

flat rate, *418*

fragrance strip, *405*

frequency discount, *412, 418*

full position, *420*

gatefold, *404*

geographic editions, *413*

guaranteed circulation, *407*

horizontal publication, *411*

independent shopping guide, *415*

insert, *403*

insertion order, *421*

island half, *403*

junior unit, *403*

local city magazine, *406*

media buyer, *402*

national magazines, *407*

national rate, *418*

Newspaper Association of America (NAA), *420*

on-sale date, *412*

open rate, *418*

paid circulation, *411*

pop-up ad, *405*

preferred-position rate, *420*

preprinted insert, *417*

primary circulation, *411*

proof copy, *422*

public notice, *417*

rate base, *407*

rate card, *418*

reading notice, *416*

regional publications, *406*

run-of-paper (ROP) advertising rate, *420*

secondary (pass-along) readership, *411*

short rate, *418*

split run, *420*

standard advertising unit (SAU), *415*

standard-size newspaper, *415*

Sunday supplement, *415*

tabloid newspaper, *415*

tearsheet, *422*

3-D ad, *405*

vertical publication, *411*

volume discount, *412*

weekly newspaper, *415*

Review Questions

1. If you worked in the advertising department of a premium-priced furniture manufacturer, would you recommend magazine advertising? Why or why not?

2. If you were the advertising manager for a magazine aimed at senior citizens, what advantages would you cite to potential advertisers?

3. What is the advantage of magazine advertising to businesses that sell to other businesses?

4. What is the importance of the Audit Bureau of Circulations?

5. Why do retailers advertise so heavily in local newspapers?

6. How can advertisers improve the selectivity of their newspaper ads?

7. What factors should advertisers consider in deciding among several local papers (including dailies and weeklies)?

8. Should national advertisers be charged a higher rate than local advertisers? Support your position.

9. Should agencies be liable for their clients' advertising bills? Why or why not?

10. How could a local newspaper use an online database service or the Internet to help itself or its advertisers?

The Advertising Experience

1. **Using Print Advertising**
   As a maker of soy-based products, you are very excited about your new chocolate soy-milk drink. As long as they don't know it contains soy, children actually prefer its taste to that of milk. The product, now named Swoosh and represented by a toothy cartoon surfer, is all set for a print campaign. Choose a geographic area similar to the ones shown on page 409, examine the leading regional magazines and newspapers, and decide how to allocate funds for advertising. Explain why you chose newspapers, magazines, or both.

2. **Print Media Organizations**
   Visit the following print industry Websites and familiarize yourself further with the size and scope of the print media world. Be sure to answer the questions for each site.
   - American Society of Newspaper Editors (ASNE): www.asne.org
   - International Newspaper Marketing Association (INMA): www.inma.org
   - National Newspaper Association (NNA): www.nna.org
   - National Newspaper Publishers Association (NNPA): www.nnpa.org
   - Newspaper Association of America (NAA): www.naa.org
   a. What is the purpose of the organization that sponsors this site?
   b. Who is the intended audience(s) of this site?
   c. Who makes up the organization's membership? Its constituency?
   d. How important do you feel this organization is to the advertising industry? Why?

3. **Print Media Tools**
   Were it not for the products and services offered by the following companies, planning and buying print vehicles could be an overwhelming task for media professionals. From audit reports to media kits, agencies and media houses are aided every day by companies that specialize in easing the lives of media planners and buyers. Visit the following syndicated and independent media companies' Websites and answer the questions that follow:
   - Advertising Checking Bureau: www.acbcoop.com
   - Advertising Media Internet Center (AMIC): www.amic.com
   - Audit Bureau of Circulations: www.accessabc.com
   - BPA International (BPA): www.bpai.com
   - Certified Audit of Circulations: www.certifiedaudit.com
   - MediaCentral: www.mediacentral.net
   - MediaFinder: www.mediafinder.com
   - Print Measurement Bureau (PMB): www.pmb.ca
   - Scarborough: www.scarborough.com
   - Standard Rate & Data Service (SRDS): www.srds.com
   a. Who is the intended audience of the site?
   b. What is the size and scope of the company?
   c. What type(s) of print media information does the company specialize in?
   d. How useful do you believe the company or organization is for obtaining print media information? Why?

Using Electronic Media: Television and Radio

Learning Objectives

To present the important factors advertisers need to evaluate when considering the use of radio and television in the creative mix. Each medium has its own characteristics, advantages, and drawbacks. Advertisers must be able to compare their merits and understand the most cost-effective ways to buy advertising time.

After studying this chapter, you will be able to:

LO14-1 Describe the advantages and drawbacks of broadcast television as an advertising medium.

LO14-2 Discuss the advantages and drawbacks of cable television as an advertising medium, and explain how it differs from broadcast television.

LO14-3 Explain the process of buying cable and broadcast TV time.

LO14-4 Evaluate the different types of television advertising available.

LO14-5 Describe the process of TV audience measurement.

LO14-6 Discuss the main factors to consider when buying television time.

LO14-7 Analyze the pros and cons of using radio in the creative mix.

LO14-8 Explain the major factors to consider when buying radio time.

Source: Hyundai Motor Co.

Source: Hyundai Motor Co.

In early 2009 the economy had been depressed for nearly four months and consumer confidence was at an all-time low. Most car companies were pulling back their ad funding in hopes the saved dollars could afford them a longer runway during the unsettling times. However, a few companies saw this as an opportunity, a chance to take down the historically aggressive spending U.S. automakers and the highly popular Japanese automakers. One of these companies was Hyundai Motor America, the same company that just 10 years prior was the afterthought of the auto industry. Because of durability and reliability issues, sales plummeted in the United States in the mid- to late-nineties. Rather than abandoning the American market, Hyundai invested heavily in new product designs and overall quality and reliability. However, just making the product better wasn't going to win over a now-jaded consumer. In fact studies done at the time suggested that although quality had improved, public perceptions had changed very little. ■ The automaker had to take action, and it did by shocking the automotive world with an unprecedented,

10-year, 100,000-mile warranty. Rightly dubbed "America's Best," the Hyundai Advantage, covered all major components for the entire fleet, going far beyond any other car company's offerings. "We thought an improved warranty would make a statement about our quality and get us on more people's shopping lists," Finbarr O'Neill, chief executive of Hyundai Motor America, said in an interview.[1] ■ The next challenge was convincing American consumers. Their launch pad was Super Bowl XLIII. Luckily for Hyundai, that night the Super Bowl was highest-rated game of all time with 98.7 million viewers.[2] With agency partner Goodby, Silverstein, they planned a three-tier onslaught. First they unveiled the brand-new 2010 Hyundai Genesis Coupe. Next up was a brilliant ad showing fictitious executives from the major luxury automotive brands around the world yelling angrily in their native tongues, with the only understandable word being "HYUNDAI," in response to the Genesis winning North American Car of the Year by J.D. Powers and Associates. Actor Jeff Bridges intones: "Win one little award and suddenly everybody gets your name right. Hyundai, like Sun(day)." ■ They could have stopped there and most people would have thought, great advertisement, but was it worth the estimated $3 million price tag? They didn't stop, and the last of the ads sent shockwaves through the industry. Hyundai realized that in troubling times the last thing that anyone wants, after losing a job, is facing creditors. As a result most consumers were not buying cars. Hyundai's idea was simple—take away the risk. So the Hyundai Assurance program was born. If you lose your job after you buy a Hyundai, the company will allow you to return the car with no fee or penalty and be exempt from all final payments. ■ That the ad was unprecedented is probably an understatement, and it worked. Year-over-year sales for February 2009 were actually down 1.5 percent; however, when the industry as a whole was down 37 percent to start the year, that number looked pretty good, especially when it represented a 25 percent increase in sales volume from January 2009.[3] ■ The Super Bowl is a big, and expensive, stage. Many companies produce over-the-top, elaborate spots designed to entertain. Hyundai took a different approach, use television's biggest ad buy to announce something important. The results, literally, were a game changer for the brand.

The Medium of Television

LO 14-1

Back in 1950, U.S. advertisers spent $171 million, or only 3 percent of total U.S. advertising volume, on the new medium of television. It didn't take long, though, for the nation's advertisers to discover the power of this new medium to reach mass audiences quickly and frequently. TV offered advertisers unique creative opportunities to imbue their brands with personality and image like never before. In 2015, advertisers spent nearly $68 billion on cable and broadcast TV, ensuring it remains the largest category of spending in the industry.[4] Exhibit 14-1 lists the top network television advertisers in the United States and their annual expenditures.

Today, television is available to advertisers in two principal forms: broadcast and cable TV. **Broadcast TV** reaches its audience by transmitting electromagnetic waves through the air across some geographic territory. **Cable TV** reaches its audience through wires, which may be strung from telephone poles or laid underground.

Broadcast TV

Until the advent of the Internet, broadcast television grew faster than any other advertising medium in history. As both a news and entertainment medium, it caught people's fancy very quickly. From its beginnings after World War II, broadcast TV rapidly emerged as the only medium that offered sight, sound, and motion. People could stay home and still go to the movies. As TV's legions of viewers grew, the big national-brand advertisers quickly discovered they could use the medium efficiently to expand distribution across the country and sell products like never before. Not only that, the medium was ideal for building an image for their brands—even better than magazines, which had previously been the image-building medium of choice. It didn't take long for marketers to switch their budgets from radio, newspapers, and magazines. Today, broadcast TV still attracts the largest volume of *national* advertising, over $26 billion in 2013.[5]

The United States now has 1,390 commercial TV stations. About 35 percent of the U.S. stations are **VHF** (very high frequency, channels 2 through 13); the rest are **UHF** (ultrahigh frequency, channels 14 and above).[6] Stations in the United States operate as independents unless they are affiliated with one of the national networks (ABC, NBC, CBS, Fox, CW). Both network affiliates and independent stations may subscribe to nationally syndicated programs as well as originate their own programming. However, increasing competition from cable TV is taking viewers from the national network programs. To compensate, some networks invest in cable TV systems or starting their own. NBC,

Rank	Advertiser	($ in Millions) 2013
1	Procter & Gamble	$1,852
2	General Motors	1,267
3	AT&T	1,239
4	Toyota	959
5	Comcast	901
6	Fiat Chrysler	900
7	Berkshire Hathaway	833
8	Verizon	811
9	Ford	797
10	General Mills	775

Exhibit 14-1
Top 10 network TV advertisers in the United States (2013).

for example, started CNBC and MSNBC, and ABC (owned by Disney) has an 80 percent interest in ESPN.

Cable TV

LO 14-2

For more than 30 years, broadcast TV, especially network TV, was the dominant entertainment medium for most Americans. Today, other electronic media have dramatically changed that dominance. Chief among the challengers is cable television.

Cable TV first appeared in the late 1940s. Initially, it carried television signals by wire to areas with poor reception such as mountainous regions. But in the 1970s, the advent of satellite TV signals, the proliferation of channels, and the introduction of uncut first-run movies via pay-cable channels such as Home Box Office and Showtime made cable TV more attractive to all viewers, even people in urban areas.

At first, subscribers valued cable simply for the full array of regional channels and access to premium services such as HBO. But once this novelty wore off, subscribers wanted more. A variety of advertiser-supported cable networks soon appeared with specialized programming in arts, history, sports, news, and comedy, along with diversified pay services and many more local shows. As the number of cable customers grew, viewers began abandoning program on the big broadcast networks.

In the last three decades, cable's growth has been extraordinary. In 1975, only 13 percent of TV households in the United States had cable. By 2010, cable reached almost 90 percent of all homes.[7] Although cable subscribers may receive more than 100 channels, most households watch only 15 to 20.[8] The My IMC Campaign 14–A guides you through the planning process for all of these choices for TV.

Most channels are privately owned and commercially operated. These include local network affiliates and independents, cable networks, superstations, local cable system channels, and community access channels. The cable fees represent about one-third of cable TV revenues; advertising makes up the remainder. Networks such as CNN, USA, the Discovery Channel, Arts & Entertainment, Lifetime, Comedy Central, and Spike TV now compete for advertisers' dollars, each selling its own niche audience.[9] For an additional price, subscribers can receive premium services such as HBO, Showtime, and Cinemax and see special events such as first-run films, championship boxing matches, and sports (through pay-per-view service).

There are now more than 900 cable networks in the United States. Exhibit 14-2 lists the most widely carried ones.[10] There are also a handful of *superstations,* local over-the-air TV stations whose signals are delivered via satellite to cable systems across the country and that carry some national advertising.

DTV

On June 12, 2009, as mandated by Congress, the United States made the switch to digital television (DTV). DTV sends and receives moving images and sound by digital signals rather than the analog signals of terrestrial (broadcast) TV. Congress authorized the distribution of an additional broadcast channel to each broadcast TV station in 1996 so the station could begin to broadcast in digital format. It was later decided that June 12, 2009, would be the last day of the simultaneous broadcast and that all full-power stations would broadcast in digital format only.

Digital TV has many benefits. As stated on the Website www.dtv.gov, consumer will benefit because digital broadcasting allows stations to offer improved picture and sound quality, and digital is much more efficient than analog. For example, rather than being limited to providing one analog program, a broadcaster is able to offer a super sharp "high definition" (HD) digital program or multiple "standard definition" (SD) digital programs simultaneously through a process called "multicasting." Multicasting allows broadcast stations to offer several channels of digital programming at the same time, using the same amount of spectrum required for one analog program. So, for example, while a station broadcasting in analog on channel 7 is able to offer viewers only one program, a station broadcasting in digital on channel 7 can offer viewers one digital program on channel 7-1, a second digital program on channel 7-2, a third digital program on channel 7-3, and so on. This means more programming choices for viewer

Exhibit 14-2
Most Viewed Cable Networks in 2014.

ESPN	2.28 million
USA	2.18 million
TNT	2.04 million
Disney	1.94 million
TBS	1.87 million
History	1.86 million
Fox News	1.73 million
FX	1.45 million
Discovery	1.41 million
AMC	1.36 million

Source: Rick Kissell, "ESPN No. 1 in Cable Ratings for 2014," *Variety,* January 2, 2015 (retrieved at: http://variety .com/2015/tv/news/ratings-espn-tops-cable-for-year-own -hallmarkwe- tv-among-few-gainers-1201391036/).

My IMC Campaign 14–A

Planning and Buying TV and Radio

Media planners use a variety of syndicated and proprietary research tools to plan and buy both TV and radio ads. Primarily, these tools help identify the larger concentrations (composition) of a target audience in specific programming, and the cost associated with those audiences. The complexity of TV and radio arises from the need to build plans that cost efficiently reach a target audience with an effective frequency. The currency for these two media is a rating point, which represents 1 percent of the target audience a media buyer is trying to reach. Both TV and radio, therefore, are bought based on demographics. So when certain prime-time shows have a rating of 14 for A25–49, it means that a particular program reaches 14 percent of all adults between the ages of 25 and 49. A buyer's cost per point (CPP) is her way of determining a vehicle's (program's) efficiency in delivering her target audience. As this chapter will explain, ratings points are additive. Therefore, two spots on shows with 14 targeted rating points means that advertiser has purchased 28 gross rating points or GRPs.

Most of you will not have access to the types of tools that help you plan and optimize broadcast media plans, so your focus should be on the merits of each of these media in achieving your marketing and advertising objectives and how they match your overall media strategies. (Refer back to My IMC Campaign 9 for a refresher on building media strategies.) First we will discuss the advantages and nonmonetary value of TV and then of radio.

Television

TV is still the largest mass medium; 115 million homes in America have at least one TV set. However, it is becoming a fragmented marketplace. In fact, the average home receives 117 different channels. While the average viewer watches only 15 channels on a regular basis, those channels may not be the same 15 channels as the ones his neighbor watches, making the media planner's job that much more difficult in building mass audiences.

Besides the large audiences, the other core benefit of TV is that it builds awareness relatively quickly. If you are launching a new product or trying to gain a high level of awareness in a relatively short period of time, TV is your medium. While TV will take up a large portion of your budget, its dynamic nature and its ability to include sight, sound, and motion in the advertisement, make it a great story-telling medium.

Last, TV is still the best medium to generate excitement around a brand, whether that is with internal constituents (employees) or external audiences. As stated in Chapter 9, the medium is the message, and no medium, to date, gives people the same perception of legitimacy as a well-produced TV advertisement.

Radio

Like TV, radio is a broadcast medium, but its ability to generate mass awareness immediately is different. The radio formats appeal to more specific targets, giving it less spillover than TV, which can be both good and bad—good in that your audience is the only one that hears the message, bad in that an advertiser may not extend out of its target market and hit markets it wasn't aware would be receptive to its message.

So why do advertisers use radio? One reason is that radio is much more efficient than TV; CPPs are sometimes one-tenth those of TV. Radio also is much less expensive to produce; in fact, typically all you need is copy and talent, making the lead time to go live with radio as short as one to two weeks. It also happens to be more promotional in nature—stations typically have a loyal audience following, and advertisers can usually be a part of any local station events and get the station personalities to endorse the brand. Testimonials, and especially personality testimonials, can be very valuable to advertisers that are looking to build legitimacy in themselves or their product.

So while you think about what your TV and radio ads will do for your brand(s), it is important to reflect on what part of the objectives and strategies each will fulfill and how they might work in concert with each other. Think of starting a new advertising campaign with TV messages and the support of radio. The TV will generate awareness and legitimacy immediately, and the radio will allow you to get out of the higher cost media quickly while allowing for long-term continuity of messaging at a more efficient rate.

Further, DTV can provide interactive video and data services that are not possible with analog technology.

TV Audience Trends

LO 14-3

As a way to reach a mass audience, no other medium today has the unique creative abilities of television: the combination of sight, sound, and motion; the opportunity to demonstrate the product; the potential to use special effects; the chance to develop the empathy of the viewer; and the believability of seeing it happen right before your eyes (see My IMC Campaign 14–B, "The Pros and Cons of Broadcast TV Advertising"). As Exhibit 14-3 shows, over half of viewers believe TV is the most authoritative advertising source, compared to only 15.4 percent for newspapers, 10.8 percent for magazines, 8.6 percent for radio, and 4.4 percent for the Internet. Television was also rated as the most influential, persuasive, and exciting medium.[11]

The heaviest viewers of broadcast TV are middle-income, high school–educated individuals and their families, so most programming is directed at this group. People with

My **IMC** Campaign 14–B
The Pros and Cons of Broadcast TV Advertising

The Pros

Contemporary broadcast television offers advertisers many advantages over competing media.

- **Mass coverage.** A full 98 percent of all U.S. homes have a TV (most have more than one), and viewing time for the average household increased from about five hours a day in 1960 to more than eight hours in 2004.

- **Relatively low cost.** Despite the often huge initial outlays for commercial production and advertising time, TV's equally huge audiences bring the cost per exposure down to $2 to $10 per thousand viewers.

- **Some selectivity.** Television audiences vary a great deal depending on the time of day, day of the week, and nature of the programming. Advertising messages can be presented when potential customers are watching, and advertisers can reach select geographic audiences by buying local and regional markets.

- **Impact.** Television offers a kind of immediacy that other forms of advertising cannot achieve, displaying and demonstrating the product with sound, motion, and full color right before the customer's eyes.

- **Creativity.** The various facets of the TV commercial—sight, sound, motion, and color—permit infinite original and imaginative appeals.

- **Prestige.** Because the public considers TV the most authoritative and influential medium, it offers advertisers a prestigious image. Hallmark, Xerox, Coca-Cola, and IBM increase their prestige by regularly sponsoring cultural programs on network TV.

- **Social dominance.** In North America, most people under age 35 grew up with TV as a window to their social environment. They continue to be stirred by TV screenings of the Olympics, space travel, assassinations, wars, and political scandals around the world.

The Cons

Sometimes broadcast TV just doesn't "fit" the creative mix because of cost, lack of audience selectivity, inherent brevity, or the clutter of competitive messages.

- **High production cost.** One of broadcast TV's greatest handicaps is the high cost of producing quality commercials. Depending on the creative approach, the cost of filming a national commercial today may run from $200,000 to more than $1 million.

- **High airtime cost.** The average cost of a prime-time network commercial ranges from $200,000 to $400,000. A single 30-second commercial for a top-rated show in prime time may cost more than $500,000, and in special attractions like the Super Bowl more than $2 million. The cost of wide coverage, even at low rates, prices small and medium-size advertisers out of the market.

- **Limited selectivity.** Broadcast TV is not cost-effective for advertisers seeking a very specific, small audience. And it is losing some of its selectivity because of changing audience trends. More women are working outside the home or watching cable TV, hurting advertisers on network soap operas.

- **Brevity.** Studies show that most TV viewers can't remember the product or company in the most recent TV ad they watched—even if it was within the last five minutes. Recall improves with the length of the commercial; people remember 60-second spots better than 30-second spots.

- **Clutter.** TV advertising is usually surrounded by station breaks, credits, and public service announcements, as well as six or seven other spots. All these messages compete for attention, so viewers become annoyed and confused and often misidentify the product.

- **Zipping and zapping.** DVR users who skip through commercials when replaying recorded programs are zipping; remote-control users who change channels at the beginning of a commercial break are zapping.

---

considerably higher incomes and more education typically have a more diverse range of interests and entertainment options.

The number of TV viewing hours continues to increase. The U.S. Census Bureau estimates that the average American watches over four hours of TV each day. That is about 25 percent of all waking hours.[12]

Around the world, older women watch TV the most (36 hours per week in both the United States and Canada). This makes the medium very popular with advertisers like Weight Watchers, whose primary target is middle-aged and older women who are concerned with how they look.

Cable in North American homes has significantly altered TV viewing patterns and the use of other media. Households with cable spend less time watching broadcast TV

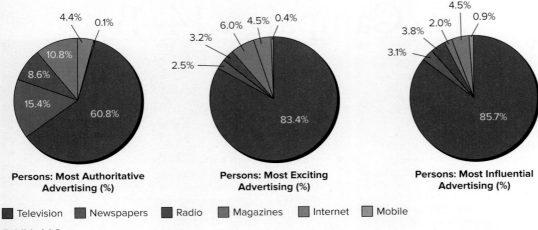

Exhibit 14-3

In 2010, adult viewers rated television as the most authoritative, exciting, and influential advertising medium.

Source: 2010 Report www.tvb.org/media/file/TVB_PB_Media_Comparisons_2010_PERSONS.pdf.

They also spend less time listening to the radio, reading, or going to the movies. Cable seems to reach an audience that is difficult to get to in any other way.[13] As a result of this *audience fragmentation,* advertising on broadcast networks has become less cost effective. DVD rentals have also increased dramatically, drawing more viewers away from advertiser-supported TV, both broadcast and cable (which is why ads have now started appearing on DVDs).

National advertisers have been using cable since the late 1970s, and cable advertising revenues have grown steadily, reaching more than $21 billion in 2010.[14] One reason is that cable's upscale audience buys proportionately more goods and services than noncable subscribers (see Exhibit 14-4). Procter & Gamble traditionally spends the most on network cable. However, local retailers also find local cable a good place to advertise.

Nielsen studies indicate that the average U.S. household receives 118.6 TV channels. A larger number of channels, however, doesn't translate into more TV viewing.

Exhibit 14-4

Cable households provide advertisers with attractive demographics (Index of 100 = U.S. average).

Cable versus Noncable Household Characteristics			
Upscale Profiles	**Cable HH vs. U.S. Average (Index)**	**Noncable HH vs. U.S. Average (Index)**	**% Advantage Cable HH**
Occupation: Professional	108	88	+23%
Education: Graduated college+	110	85	+29%
Occupation: Management/financial	105	93	+13%
Household Income: $75,000+	112	80	+40%
Value of Home: $500,000+	109	87	+25%
Downscale Profiles	**Cable HH vs. U.S. Average (Index)**	**Noncable HH vs. U.S. Average (Index)**	**% Advantage Cable HH**
Education: Did not graduate HS	86	122	−30%
Employment: Not working	99	101	−2%
Occupation: Construction/maintenance	87	120	−17%
Household Income: <$20,000	87	121	−28%
Value of Home: <$60,000	83	127	−35%

Source: Cable TV Advertising Bureau.

Rank	Advertiser	Cable TV Spending (in Millions)
1	Procter & Gamble	$886.2
2	Time Warner	276.3
3	Johnson & Johnson	215.9
4	General Motors Corp.	210.6
5	General Mills	208.3
6	Walt Disney Co.	201.0
7	Sprint Nextel	195.4
8	AT&T	185.3
9	Kraft Foods	183.5
10	Berkshire Hathaway	182.8

Exhibit 14-5
Top 10 cable network advertisers (2008).

The Nielsen data indicate that the more channels a household has, the lower the percentage of channels watched. Households with the most channels (more than 150) tuned in to only 16 channels.[15]

While there is no doubt that the media play an ever-expanding role in our daily lives, there is a finite limit to the number of advertising exposures people can absorb. When that limit is reached, any new media will simply be fighting for market share. This is the reason for the increasing fragmentation of the audience and the precipitous decline in the huge share of audience once held by the broadcast networks. This is also why media buyers and planners are growing in importance as advertisers search for the elusive audience and fight for their share of that audience in an overcrowded media environment.

The Use of Television in IMC

Television today is very versatile. For many years it was strictly a mass medium, used to great advantage by the manufacturers of mass consumption goods: toiletries and cosmetics, food, appliances, and cars (see Exhibit 14-5). But today, thanks to the narrowcasting ability of cable TV, television can also be a highly selective niche medium. It's not unusual, for instance, to see ads for special feed for thoroughbreds and show horses on ESPN's *Grand Prix of Jumping*. And thanks to local cable, TV is now affordable for even small local advertisers. This makes it a very viable option for use in an IMC program.

While single programs don't deliver the mass audience they once did, television is still the most cost-effective way to deliver certain kinds of messages to large, well-defined audiences. When it comes to awareness and image advertising, for instance, television has no rival. The same is true for brand reinforcement messages.[16]

Since marketing integrators are looking to establish, nourish, and reinforce relationships with many groups of stakeholders, television serves another role quite efficiently. It can speak to many different kinds of stakeholders—not just customers—at the same time. Moreover, through its unique ability to deliver a creative big idea, television can impart *brand meaning* (the symbolism or personality of the brand) to either attract people to the brand or reinforce their current relationship with it.

Television is also a good leverage tool. That is, an advertiser might take advantage of the relatively low CPM of television to reach out to many prospects. Prospects can identify themselves by responding to the commercial, and then the advertiser can follow up with less expensive, one-to-one or addressable media.[17]

What's important to remember in all this is that the high visibility of TV forces the sponsor to create ads that people find interesting and that consistently reinforce the brand's strategic position (remember our definition of great advertising). The brands that succeed are the ones that are the most popular. And "ad liking" has a lot to do with brand popularity.

Types of TV Advertising

LO 14-4

Advertisers use different strategies to buy time on broadcast and cable television. The major broadcast networks offer a variety of programs that appeal to different audiences. So the advertiser buys ads based on the viewing audience of each program. A national advertiser that wants to reach a broad cross section of women ages 25 to 45, for example, might find *Grey's Anatomy* an efficient buy at a cost of $203,078 for a 30-second commercial.[18] Advertising isn't always a cut-and-dried process. See the Ethical Issues box on page 444 for the guidelines on advertising to children.

When buying cable TV, an advertiser can buy ads over the full schedule of a channel because cable networks typically aim their overall programming to relatively specific *audiences.* The Lifetime and Family channels heavily weigh programs toward women; MTV targets viewers 16 to 25. Cable companies sell their network channels in bundles at a discount and offer discounts for *run-of-schedule* positioning—multiple ad purchases they can

My IMC Campaign 14–C
The Pros and Cons of Cable TV Advertising

The Pros

- **Selectivity.** Cable offers specialized programming aimed at particular types of viewers. Narrowcasting allows advertisers to choose programming with the viewer demographics that best match their target customers.

- **Audience demographics.** Cable subscribers are younger, better educated, and more affluent; have higher-level jobs; live in larger households; and are more likely to try new products and buy more high-ticket items, such as cars, appliances, and high-tech equipment.

- **Low cost.** Many small companies get TV's immediacy and impact without the enormous expenditures of broadcast TV. Cable advertising can sometimes cost as little as radio. Many national advertisers find sponsorship attractive, since an entire cable series can cost less to produce than a single broadcast TV commercial.

- **Flexibility.** Broadcast TV commercials need to be short because of the high costs of production and airtime, but cable ads can run up to two minutes and, in the case of infomercials, much longer. They can also be tailored to fit the programming environment.

- **Testability.** Cable is a good place to experiment, testing both new products and various advertising approaches: ad frequency, copy impact, and different media mixes.

The Cons
Like every medium, cable TV has its drawbacks.

- **Limited reach.** About 23 percent of households don't have cable. This was cable's main weakness in the past, but it is less so today.

- **Fragmentation.** With more than 50 channels at their disposal, cable viewers do not watch any one channel in enormous numbers. To reach the majority of the cable audience in a particular market, ads must run on many stations.

- **Quality.** Cable, particularly local cable, sometimes has poorer production quality and less desirable programming than broadcast TV.

- **Zipping and zapping.** Cable TV has some of the same drawbacks as broadcast TV, such as zipping and zapping.

---

place throughout a channel's daily schedule (see My IMC Campaign 14–C, "The Pros and Cons of Cable TV Advertising").

Advertisers can buy time on TV in several ways. They include sponsoring an entire program, participating in a program, purchasing spot announcements between programs, and purchasing spots from syndicators. Exhibit 14-6 shows how much money is spent nationally on the various types of television advertising. The exhibit suggests that cable continues to be attractive to advertisers.

Network Advertising

Historically, major U.S. advertisers purchased airtime from one of the national broadcast **networks:** ABC, CBS, NBC, or Fox. In 1995, relaxed FCC rules enabled two of the biggest producers of prime-time shows, Warner Bros. and Paramount, to launch their own broadcast networks—WB and UPN—giving them captive distribution outlets for programs they produce and buy.[19] With 31 affiliated stations, UPN immediately covered 80 percent of the country, even though it initially programmed only a couple of nights a week. In 2006, UPN and WB merged to become CW.[20]

Cable has slowly eroded the audience of the broadcast networks. At one time the big three (ABC, CBS, and NBC) had more than 90 percent of the prime-time audience. Today their total share is about 38.3 percent, with ad-supported cable networks comprising 60 percent.[21]

Networks offer large advertisers convenience and efficiency because they broadcast messages simultaneously across many affiliate stations throughout the country. Broadcast networks tend to reach masses of American consumers representing a cross section of the population, while cable networks tend to reach more selective niches.

Exhibit 14-6
Where does all the money go? Measured TV spending in billions of dollars.

	2013	2012	
Network TV	$26.9	$27.4	−1.9%
Syndicated TV	5.2	5.1	0.5%
Spot TV	15.8	17.1	−7.9%
Cable TV	26.1	24.4	7.1%

Source: Ad Spending Totals from Kantar Media, Advertising Age Marketing Fact Pack,2015, retrieved at http://www.slideshare.net/aidelisagutierrez/ad-age-marketingfact-pack2015

Television plays an important role in its ability to impart brand personality. Television communicates with many stakeholders simultaneously and can deliver a "big idea" in a uniquely creative manner. This commercial for the Kia Soul shows that anyone can be "cool" if they drive a Soul, even hip-hop hamsters.

Source: Kia Motors Corporation

An advertiser who underwrites the cost of a program is engaging in **sponsorship.** In a sole sponsorship, the advertiser is responsible for both the program content and the total cost of production. Sponsorship is so costly that single sponsorships are usually limited to specials. Companies that sponsor programs (e.g., AT&T, Xerox, and Hallmark) gain two important advantages. First, the public more readily identifies with the product(s) due to the prestige of sponsoring first-rate entertainment. Second, the sponsor controls the placement and content of its commercials. The commercials can be fit to the program and run any length the sponsor desires so long as they remain within network or station regulations. Further, because networks are centralized, the advertiser gets only one bill.

Sponsorship offers many opportunities. When the popular drama series *24* started its second season, the first episode was presented commercial-free, thanks to a full sponsorship by Ford Motor Company. The episode also featured numerous Ford vehicles in the show. To save money and reduce risks, many advertisers cosponsor programs, sponsoring on alternate weeks or dividing the program into segments. NFL games, for instance, are always sold as multiple sponsorships.

Most network TV advertising is sold on a **participation basis,** with several advertisers buying 30- or 60-second segments within a program. This enables them to spread their budgets and avoid long-term commitments to any one program. It also lets smaller advertisers buy a limited amount of time and still get the nationwide coverage they need.

Network advertising also has several disadvantages: lack of flexibility, long lead times, inconvenient restrictions, and forced adherence to network standards and practices, not to mention high prices. Costs range from a low of $29,374 (for "Nikita", which appears Friday nights on *The CW*) to a high of over $502,900 for "American Idol" (see Exhibit 14-7). For this reason, most advertisers decide to buy *spot announcements.*

© Photo by Eric McCandless/ABC via Getty Images

Spot Announcements

National **spot announcements** run in clusters between programs. They are less expensive than participations and more flexible than network advertising because they can be concentrated in specific regions of the country. An advertiser with a small budget or limited distribution may use spots to introduce a new product into one area at a time. Or an advertiser can vary its message for different markets to suit promotional needs.[22]

Spots may run 10, 15, 30, or 60 seconds and be sold nationally or locally. Spot advertising is more difficult to buy than network advertising because it involves contacting each station directly. This is a headache with cable channels, since one city may be served by 10 or more cable companies. For the broadcast stations, the *national rep system,* in which individuals act as sales and service representatives for a number of stations, alleviates this problem through the use of *electronic data interchange (EDI).*[23] This technology enables agency buyers to electronically process orders, makegoods (free advertising time to compensate for problems), and revisions, and to maintain an electronic audit trail through the life of a schedule. Likewise, reps can transmit orders directly to their stations via satellite while keeping in day-to-day contact with agency buyers.[24]

Meanwhile, a number of large cable rep firms are also working to make the purchase of spot cable more convenient for national advertisers through satellite technology and digital systems that interconnect various cable companies in a region.[25]

Spot advertising is available only at network station breaks and when network advertisers purchase less than a full lineup, so spot ads may get lost in the clutter—which is why they tend to have fewer viewers and a smaller piece of the ad spending pie.

Movie product placements also benefit the advertiser when the films are later shown on TV. Apple and Pepsi have found this to be a useful strategy for promoting products.

© Warner Bros. Pictures/Courtesy Everett Collection

Exhibit 14-7

Advertising cost per 30-second spot on the 10 most expensive prime-time shows 2015.

Source: Variety, retrieved at http://variety.com/2015/tv/news/tv-advertising-prices-football-empire-walking-dead-big-bang-theory-1201603800/

Rank	Show and Network	Price (000)
1	Sunday Night Football (NBC)	$637
2	Empire (Fox)	521
3	The Walking Dead (AMC)	502
4	Thursday Night Football (CBS)	463
5	Fear the Walking Dead (AMC)	395
6	Monday Night Football (ESPN)	388
7	The Big Bang Theory (CBS)	289
8	Modern Family (ABC)	236
9	The Voice (NBC)	234
10	How to Get Away With Murder (ABC)	230

Syndication

As audiences fragment, syndicated programs become an increasingly popular adjunct or alternative to network advertising. Over the years, the syndication industry has grown from almost nothing into a $4.1 billion advertising medium.[26]

Syndication is the sale of programs on a station-by-station, market-by-market basis. In other words, the producer (e.g., Warner Bros. or Disney) deals directly with the stations, often through a distribution company, rather than going through the networks. This efficient "direct-from-the-factory" approach gives local TV stations more programming control and greater profits. It also gives advertisers access to **inventory** (commercial time) for their spots that they might not get on network programs—often at better prices.[27] Syndication has become the largest source of programming in the United States (see Exhibit 14-8).

Television syndication comes in three forms: off-network, first-run, and barter. In **off-network syndication,** former popular network programs (reruns) are sold to individual stations for rebroadcast. Examples include *Seinfeld* and *Friends*. **First-run syndication** involves original shows, like *Oprah, Inside Edition,* and *Extra,* which are produced specifically for the syndication market. One of the fastest-growing trends in television is **barter syndication** (also called *advertiser-supported syndication*). These are first-run programs offered free or for a reduced rate, but with some of the ad space (usually 50%) presold to national advertisers. *Wheel of Fortune, Jeopardy,* and *Oprah,* all distributed by King World Productions, are some of the most popular examples.[28]

Exhibit 14-8

TV network and syndication distribution.

a. The networks are essentially middlemen.

b. Syndication is often a more efficient way of financing and distributing programs.

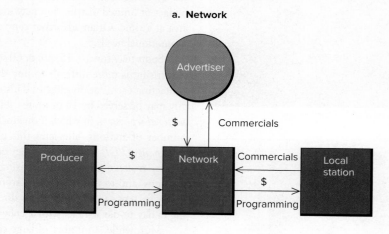

a. Network

b. Syndication

Exhibit 14-10

This map of the area surrounding Columbus, Georgia, shows media planners which counties are included in the designated market area (DMA) and will be reached by advertising placed on the local television stations. Columbus, Georgia, is the 125th largest DMA in the United States and contains over 200,000 TV households.

Source: From Billboard/Howard Appelbaum Publisher.

Columbus, GA Audience Figures

- DMA Market Size: #125
- Total DMA TV Households: 207,820
- Total DMA Persons 18+: 388,000
- Total DMA Adults 25-54: 214,000
- Total DMA Working Women: 92,000
- % of Cable in DMA Households: 76%

Local TV Stations

WTVM ABC - Columbus (Muscogee) Georgia
WRBL CBS - Columbus (Muscogee) Georgia
WCGT Ind. - Columbus (Muscogee) Georgia
WMCF TBN - Opelika (Lee) Alabama
WJSP/WGTV PBS - Columbus (Muscogee) Georgia
WLGA UPN - Opelika (Lee) Alabama
WCAG UATV - Lagrange (Troupe) Georgia
WLTZ NBC - Columbus (Muscogee) Georgia
WGIQ/WBIQ PBS - Louisville (Barbour) Alabama
WXTX FOX - Columbus (Muscogee) Georgia
WLGA UPN - Opelika (Lee) Alabama

Viewing is highest during **prime time** (8 to 11 p.m. Eastern Standard Time; 7 to 10 p.m. Central Standard Time). Late fringe ranks fairly high in most markets among adults, and daytime and early fringe tend to be viewed most heavily by women. To reach the greatest percentage of the advertiser's target audience with optimal frequency, the media planner determines a **daypart mix** based on TV usage levels reported by the rating services.

Audience Measures

Rating services and media planners use many terms to define a station's audience, penetration, and efficiency. **TV households (TVHH)** refers to the number of households that own television sets. The number of TVHH in a particular market gives an advertiser a sense of the market's size. Likewise, the number of TVHH tuned in to a particular program helps the advertiser estimate the program's popularity and how many people a commercial is likely to reach.

The percentage of homes in a given area that have one or more TV sets turned on at any particular time is expressed as **households using TV (HUT).** If there are 1,000 TV sets in the survey area and 500 are turned on, HUT is 50 percent.

The **program rating** refers to the percentage of TV households in an area that are tuned in to a specific program. The rating is computed as follows:

$$\text{Rating} = \frac{\text{TVHH tuned to specific program}}{\text{Total TVHH in area}}$$

Networks want high ratings because they measure a show's popularity. More popular shows can command higher advertising rates. Local stations often change their programming (e.g., buy different syndicated shows) to increase their popularity and thereby their ratings (and their revenues).

The percentage of homes with sets in use (HUT) tuned to a specific program is called the audience **share.** A program with only 500 viewers can have a 50 *share* if only 1,000 sets are turned on. *Ratings,* in contrast, measure the audience as a percentage of all TVHH in the area, whether the TV sets are on or off.

The total number of homes reached by some portion of a program is called **total audience.** This figure is normally broken down to determine **audience composition** (the distribution of the audience into demographic categories).

Gross Rating Points

In television, **gross rating points (GRPs)** are the total rating points a particular media schedule achieves over a specific period. As we discussed in Chapter 9, a weekly schedule of five commercials on programs with an average household rating of 20 would yield 100 GRPs. Recall that GRPs are computed as follows:

$$\text{Reach (average rating)} \times \text{Frequency} = \text{Gross rating points}$$

GRPs allow advertisers to draw conclusions about the different markets available for a client's ads by providing a comparable measure of advertising weight. However, GRPs do not reflect a market's size. For example, while campaigns in Knoxville and Charlotte might have the same GRPs, they would differ significantly in their reach:

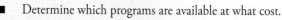

	TV Homes (000s)	Average Cost per Spot	Average Rating	No. of Spots	GRPs
Knoxville	1,002	$1,500	15	5	75
Charlotte	638	1,250	15	5	75

To better determine the relative value of television advertising markets, other measures are used, such as *cost per rating point (CPP)* and *cost per thousand (CPM),* which were described in Chapter 9.

Buying Television Time

The process of buying TV time can be lengthy and, depending on the number of stations in the buy, quite involved. Advertisers or media buyers must

- Determine which programs are available at what cost.
- Analyze the various programs for efficiency.
- Negotiate price with station reps.
- Determine what reach and frequency they are achieving.
- Sign broadcast contracts.
- Review affidavits of performance to be sure the commercials ran as agreed.

These procedures are so complex that most large advertisers use ad agencies or media-buying services. Buying services have gained in popularity because they charge less and can save advertisers money by negotiating for desirable time slots at reduced rates. Local advertisers typically rely on station reps to determine the best buys for the money.

Requesting Avails

To find out which programs are available, media buyers contact stations' sales reps—local station salespeople, national media rep organizations that sell for one station in each market, or network reps. The media buyer gives the rep information about the advertiser's media objectives and target audiences and asks the rep to supply a list of **avails** (available time slots) along with prices and estimated ratings. Many media buyers ask for the information based on the last few Nielsen books to see whether a show's ratings are consistent, rising, or falling.

AD Lab 14-B

Getting "You're Out" on TV

"You're Out" baseball mitts have expanded to television. As the marketing director, you choose to examine the gross rating points (GRPs) for placing your advertising. You have an idea of the days and times you want the ads to be placed. Chart 1 indicates the best programs for Memphis, Tennessee, and relevant planning data your assistant has gathered according to your preferences. Due to time constraints the chart is incomplete, but enough data are available for you to finish the chart.

Chart 1 shows the marketing figures for a single city, but now you decide to determine which of the three major cities in Tennessee will serve "You're Out" baseball mitts the best. Your assistant didn't quite finish Chart 2, but with the help of Chart 1 you can complete the needed calculations.

Laboratory Applications

1. Using the formulas in the text as a guide, complete Chart 1.

2. Assuming your budget is $68,000, use Chart 1 to decide which programs would be most effective for reaching children. Explain your selection.

3. Using Chart 1, complete the "per spot" and "rating" figures in Chart 2. Next, calculate how many GRPs each city will deliver if you buy five spots of advertising.

4. Using the completed Chart 2, calculate for each city the number of household impressions.

5. Knowing that you are running five spots, find the CPP and CPM for all three cities.

6. Based on the completed Chart 2, what city is ideal for "You're Out" baseball mitts?

Chart 1: Best Programs for Memphis, TN				
Program	**Rating**	**Cost**	**Spots**	**GRP**
KC Undercover (*early evening daily, rerun, 30/70 adults to kids*)	15	$34,000	32	——
Saturday morning cartoons (kids ages 2–12)	——	34,000	30	300.0
Major League Baseball game (weekends, mostly adults)	7.8	34,000	29	——
After-school special (kids ages 7–13, afternoon, daily)	——	34,000	27	205.0

Chart 2				
City	**TV Homes (000s)**	**Average Cost per Spot**	**Average % of Rating**	**GRP**
Memphis	1,002	$1,500	15%	——
Charlotte	638	1,250	15	——
Knoxville	847	——	——	——
		Frequency: 5 spots		

Selecting Programs for Buys

The media buyer selects the most efficient programs in relation to the target audience using the **CPP** and the **CPM** for each program:

$$CPP = \frac{Cost}{Rating} \qquad CPM = \frac{Cost}{Thousands\ of\ people}$$

For example, assume *CSI* has a rating of 25, reaches 200,000 people in the primary target audience, and costs $2,000 for a 30-second spot with a fixed guarantee on station WALB-TV in Albany, Georgia. Then,

$$CPP = \frac{\$2,000}{25} = \$80 \qquad CPM = \frac{\$2,000}{(200,000 \div 1,000)} = \$10$$

By calculating CPP, the media buyer can compare the cost of a rating point from one program or network to another. That's good information for beginning negotiations. But rating points relate to the whole market. The real important figure is the cost of reaching 1,000 prospects in the *target* market. That's why the CPM must be calculated against the size of the target audience, not the whole market. The lower the cost per 1,000/target audience (CPM-TA), the more efficient the show is at reaching real prospects.

To get the best buys within the available budget, then, the media buyer substitutes stronger programs for less efficient ones (see Ad Lab 14–B, "Getting 'You're Out' on TV").

Negotiating Prices and Contracts

TV stations and cable companies publish rate cards to sell their airtime. However, since TV audiences are estimated at best, television reps will always negotiate prices.

The media buyer contacts the rep and explains what efficiency the advertiser needs in terms of delivery and CPM to make the buy. The buyer has numerous ways to negotiate lower rates: work out a package deal, accept *run-of-schedule positioning* (the station chooses when to run the commercials), or take advantage of preemption rates. A **preemption rate** is lower because the advertiser agrees to be "bumped" (preempted) if another advertiser pays the higher, nonpreemption rate.

The media buyer must read the advertising contract carefully before signing it. The contract indicates the dates, times, and programs on which the advertiser's commercials will run, the length of each spot, the rate per spot, and the total amount. The reverse side of the contract defines payment terms and responsibilities of the advertiser, agency, and station. After the spots run, the station returns a signed and notarized **affidavit of performance** to the advertiser or agency, specifying when the spots aired and what makegoods are available. **Makegoods** refer to free advertising time an advertiser receives to compensate for spots the station missed or ran incorrectly or because the program's ratings were substantially lower than guaranteed.[38]

Electronic Media Buying Software

With the Internet, today's broadcast media buyers don't ever have to leave the office but can, right from their desktops, pore over SRDS and Simmons research data to create and even buy media schedules with electronic avails.

With software like Arbitron's SmartPlus media-buying suite, media planners and buyers can analyze, plan, and report from one application. Most spot broadcases are revised many times, and SmartPlus allows for revisions and transfers seamlessly in the planning process. Nowadays software can integrate with almost everything through a simple XML/API feed. SmartPlus integrates with Outlook, increasing the efficiency of communications between buyers and sellers.

Nielsen's PAL software is a national media planning system. It takes into account market-by-market differences in media delivery for network TV, syndicated TV, cable TV, and magazines. PAL can be used in different ways. First, it evaluates market-by-market performance of a national media schedule in terms of GRPs and/or budgets. Also, PAL can define your marketing objectives by using BDI or sales data, along with selected spot weight.

Alternatively, Nielsen's Clear Decisions and Reach and Frequency help media planners generate schedule results with minimal effort, identify insights from a suite of reports, and even create presentation-ready charts and graphs from one screen. The planner can perform R&F analyses using Clear Decisions to get to the answers faster.

Other Forms of Television

Cable isn't the only electronic challenger to traditional broadcast TV. Cable providers have their own competitors: DBS, MDS, STV, and SMATV.

- DBS (direct broadcast satellite) beams programs from space via satellites to satellite dishes mounted in the home or yard. For a monthly fee, consumers can subscribe to one of the DBS program distributors, such as Dish or DirecTV, to receive from 20 to 150 channels.[39]

- MDS (multipoint distribution system), a microwave delivery system that can carry a dozen channels, is occasionally offered in rural areas where cable has not been installed.

- STV (subscription television) is over-the-air pay TV. Subscribers buy a descrambler that allows them to watch programs carried over a regular TV channel.

- SMATV (satellite master antenna television) uses a satellite dish to capture signals for TV sets in apartment buildings and other complexes, acting as a sort of minicable system.

- IPTV (Internet Protocol Television) uses a broadband connection to deliver a digital TV service.

And with the increase in connected TVs (TVs or other electronic devices such as DVD players or game systems like the Xbox 360), Internet apps that deliver Netflix and Hulu Plus are also slowly eating away at market share.

The Medium of Radio

Radio is a personal, one-on-one medium; people listen alone. And radio is mobile. It can entertain people who are driving, walking, at home, or away from home. This makes it a particularly strong way to reach people who commute by car.

Radio is also adaptable to moods. In the morning, people may want to hear the news, upbeat music, or interesting chatter; in the afternoon, they may want to unwind with classical or easy-listening music.

Who Uses Radio?

In an average week, 93 percent of the U.S. population listens to radio; in an average day, about 72 percent. The average American listens to the radio more than two and a half hours each day. In fact, during the prime shopping hours of 6 a.m. to 6 p.m., the average U.S. adult spends more time with radio than with broadcast and cable TV combined.[40] As Exhibit 14-11 shows, radio is also cost-effective. In the last decade, the CPM for radio advertising has risen less than for any other major medium and substantially less than the consumer price index.[41] As a result, radio's advertising revenues have grown steadily.

More national advertisers are discovering radio's reach and frequency potential. Certainly it has worked well for brands like Lindsay Olives. Similarly, Snapple profited greatly from radio. Back when it was still a little company in Queens, New York, and strapped for money, Snapple Natural Beverages decided to use radio. It put its entire ad budget into a year-long schedule with a young, relatively unknown radio show host named Howard Stern. Snapple liked the way he delivered its spots as a live reader.

A few years later, Snapple began receiving letters and phone calls from people in the Midwest and West, where it didn't even have distribution. It seems that nationally syndicated talk show host Rush Limbaugh, on a restricted-calorie diet, had been giving enthusiastic on-air endorsements for Snapple Diet Iced Tea. The firm moved quickly to sign him as a paid endorser. What it learned was the power of radio, especially when combined with a popular radio personality. This combination doubled Snapple's sales every year for five years, propelled it into national distribution, and turned it into a major national advertiser.[42] The company continues to use radio to promote its products. In 2006, Snapple paid $2 million to sponsor a Boston radio station for 40 days.[43]

The Use of Radio in IMC

While television tends to be a passive medium that people simply watch, radio actively involves people. They listen intently to their favorite personalities; they call in to make requests, participate in a contest, or contribute to a discussion; they use their ears and imaginations to fill in what they cannot see. Most people listen faithfully to two or three different radio stations with different types of programming. This means that smart advertisers can use the medium to establish an immediate, intimate relationship with consumers and other stakeholders. That makes radio an ideal medium for integrated marketing communications.

With radio, national companies can tie in to a local market and target the specific demographic group they want to reach. Most important, radio enables advertisers to maintain strategic consistency and stretch their media dollars through **imagery transfer.** Research shows that when advertisers run a schedule on TV and then convert the audio portion to radio commercials, fully 75 percent of consumers replay the video in their minds when they hear the radio spot.[44] That extends the life and builds the impact of a TV campaign at greatly reduced cost.[45] In an IMC campaign, where message consistency is a primary objective, this is a very important feature of radio.

Exhibit 14-11

Daily and weekly reach of radio for people 18 and older exceeds other media.

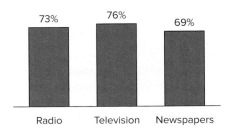

Daily reach: Adults 18+

Radio 73%   Television 76%   Newspapers 69%

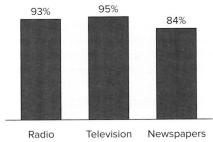

Weekly reach: Adults 18+

Radio 93%   Television 95%   Newspapers 84%

Source: the Radio Advertising Bureau.

Local retailers like the medium for the same reasons. Also, they can tailor it to their needs. It offers defined audiences; its recall characteristics are similar to TV's; and retailers can create an identity by doing their own ads. Finally, since radio is so mobile, retailers can reach prospects just before they purchase. Hence, recent years have seen major spending increases by local grocery stores, car dealers, banks, and home-improvement, furniture, and apparel stores.[46]

Radio Programming and Audiences

Radio stations plan their programming carefully to reach specific markets and to capture as many listeners as possible. The larger the audience, the more a station can charge for commercial time. Therefore, extensive planning and research go into radio programming and program changes.

Stations can use tried-and-true formats, subscribe to network or syndicated programming, or devise unique approaches. Programming choices are greatly influenced by whether a station is on the AM or FM band. FM has much better sound fidelity, fewer commercial interruptions, and more varied programming.

Depending on a company's advertising needs, radio has many uses within the IMC model. This ad for Lindsay Olives (www.lindsayolives.com) personifies the quality and selectivity that define the brand in a humorous and memorable way.

MUSIC UP AND UNDER THROUGHOUT.

MALE VOICEOVER: I was a homely looking olive when I was born. Not ugly ... but homeliness is next to nothingness if you're trying to be a handsome Lindsay Olive.

So I tried to change ... to become one of the beautiful olives. I wore contact lenses ... I had my pimento styled by Mr. Joe ... Nothing helped.

So, I turned to olive surgery. I mean, I was desperate to become a quality Lindsay Olive! Now, some surgeons wouldn't touch an olive that looked like me, they said it was too risky. But you can always find someone who'll take out a wrinkle here, or inject an imitation of that great Lindsay flavor there.

The Lindsay people gave me a second look, and I almost got in! ... But one inspector saw a scar and I was through. I guess the Lindsay people were right after all: Beauty is only skin deep, but ugliness goes all the way to the pit ...

FEMALE VOICEOVER ANNOUNCER: An olive is just an olive, unless it's a Lindsay.

MALE VOICEOVER ANNOUNCER: Well, maybe another olive company will give me a break.

MUSIC UP AND OUT.

To counteract FM's inroads, many AM stations switched to programs that don't rely on sound quality, such as news, talk, and sports. Some stations are experimenting with all comedy, midday game shows with audience participation, or formats geared to specific regions, such as KHJ's "car radio" in Los Angeles. AM stations are also trying to win back music listeners by improving their sound quality and offering stereo broadcasting.

When buying radio time, advertisers usually buy the station's *format,* not its programs. Most stations adopt one of the dozen or so standard **programming formats:** contemporary hit radio (CHR-TOP 40), adult contemporary, country, rock, easy listening, news/talk, adult standards, classical, religious, and so on, as shown in Exhibit 14-12. Each format tends to appeal to specific demographic groups. The most popular format is country music, which is programmed by 18.9 percent of the stations in the United States (both AM and FM) and appeals to a broad cross section of Americans from 25 to 54 years old.

Contemporary hit radio (CHR), always found on FM stations, appeals to teenagers and women under 30. It provides a constant flow of top 40 hits, usually with minimal intrusion by disk jockeys. Another popular format, adult contemporary (or "easy oldies"), is often advertised as "light rock, less talk." This format aims at the desirable target group of working women between 25 and 54. The news/talk, easy-listening, and nostalgia formats tend to have high listenership among men and women over 35.[47]

A major trend in radio today is the resurgence of radio networks, which offer services and programs that complement a station's local programming. A station might subscribe to Premiere Radio Network's "Delilah," Cumulus Media Network's "The Sean Hannity Show," or the self-syndicated "Dave Ramsey Show."

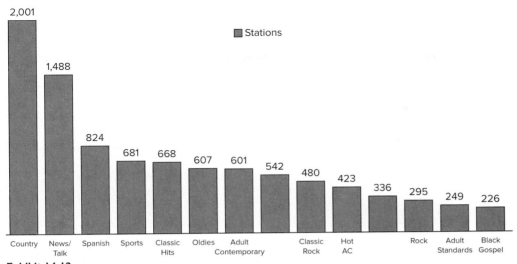

Exhibit 14-12

Radio's most popular formats. Graph shows number of radio stations for each format.

Source: Data provided with permission from the M Street Database. Copyright © 2008.

There are now more than 20 national radio networks, including the multiple "mininetworks" of ABC, CBS, Westwood One, and Unistar (see Exhibit 14-13), and numerous syndicators offer programs from live rock concerts to public-affairs discussions. To stand out, 80 percent of licensed radio stations are opting for syndicated and network offerings.[48] As more stations carry these programs and more listeners tune in, national advertisers find them increasingly attractive.

Although spending on radio advertising accounts for only about 4 percent of all ad spending, consumers spend about 44 percent of their total time with media listening to the radio.[49] Clearly, although it is much cheaper to produce than television advertising, radio ad spending has room to grow. In 2010, however, revenue for radio measured $8.2 billion, down slightly

Exhibit 14-13

The radio mininetworks provide various types of programming including news, talk, and sports. Each network targets a specific demographic group such as Adults 25–54 (CBS) or Men 18 years and older (ESPN).

ABC Radio Networks			Westwood One Radio Networks		
Network	**Target Demo**	**Affiliates**	**Network**	**Target Demo**	**Affiliates**
Prime	A 25–54	2,566	Westwood One Mutual	A 25–54	1,385
Platinum	A 25–54	2,566	Westwood One NBC	A 25–54	1,338
Galaxy	A 12+	1,030	Westwood One Source	A 12–34	115
Genesis	A 12–34	317	Westwood One Programming	A 12–54	3,600
Excel	A 18–49	111	Westwood One Play by Play Sports	A 18+	1,192
ESPN	M 18+	231	Westwood One Talk	A 25–54	1,236
ABC Special Programming	A 12+	3,829			

CBS Radio Networks			Unistar Radio Networks		
Network	**Target Demo**	**Affiliates**	**Network**	**Target Demo**	**Affiliates**
CBS Radio Network	A 25–54	470	Super	A 25–54	1,256
CBS Spectrum	A 25–54	570	Power	A 18–49	218
CBS Radio Sports	A 25–54	300	CNN+	A 25–54	1,248
CBS Radio Programs	A 18–54	126	CNBC Business Radio	A 25–54	72
CBS Hispanic Radio Network	A 25–54	39	Unistar Weekly Music/ Personality Programs	A 12–49	1,700

Source: Data from the M Street Database.

My IMC Campaign 14–D
The Pros and Cons of Radio Advertising

The Pros

The principal advantages of radio are high reach and frequency, selectivity, and cost efficiency.

- **Reach and frequency.** Radio offers an excellent combination of reach and frequency. The average adult listens more than three hours a day, radio builds a large audience quickly, and a normal advertising schedule easily allows repeated impact on the listener.

- **Selectivity.** Specialized radio formats, with prescribed audiences and coverage areas, enable advertisers to select the market they want to reach: a specific sex, age group, ethnic or religious background, income group, employment category, educational level, or special interest.

- **Cost efficiency.** Radio offers its reach, frequency, and selectivity at one of the lowest costs per thousand, and radio production is inexpensive. National spots can be produced for about one-tenth the cost of a TV commercial. And local stations often produce local spots for free.

- **Other advantages.** Radio also offers timeliness, immediacy, local relevance, and creative flexibility.

The Cons

In spite of these advantages, radio has limitations: It's an aural medium only, its audience is highly segmented, the advertiser's commercials are short-lived and often only half-heard, and each ad must compete with the clutter of other advertising.

- **Limitations of sound.** Radio is heard but not seen, a drawback if the product must be seen to be understood. Some agencies think radio restricts their creative options.

- **Segmented audiences.** If a large number of radio stations compete for the same audience, advertisers that want to blanket the market have to buy at multiple stations, which may not be cost-effective.

- **Short-lived and half-heard commercials.** Radio commercials are fleeting. They can't be kept like a newspaper or a magazine ad. Radio must compete with other activities for attention, and it doesn't always succeed.

- **Clutter.** Stations with the greatest appeal for advertisers have more commercials. Advertisers must produce a commercial that stands out from the rest.

Rank	Advertiser	National Spot Radio Spending ($ in Millions)
1	Home Depot	$72.5
2	T-Mobile Wireless	65
3	GEICO	63.5
4	Comcast	58.8
5	Verizon Wireless	41.3
6	AT&T Wireless	40.3
7	O'Reilly Auto Parts	35.4
8	Macy's Department Store	34.2
9	Walgreens Drug Store	29.1
10	Sprint Wireless	28.2

Exhibit 14-14

Top 10 national spot radio advertisers 2014.

from the previous year.[50] The largest national radio advertisers are major retailers and telecommunications companies (see Exhibit 14-14).

Buying Radio Time

Advertisers need a basic knowledge of the medium to buy radio time effectively: the types of radio advertising available for commercial use, a basic understanding of radio terminology, and the steps involved in preparing a radio schedule.

Types of Radio Advertising

An advertiser may purchase network, spot, or local radio time. Advertisers like the reach and frequency, selectivity, and cost efficiency of radio (see My IMC Campaign 14–D, "The Pros and Cons of Radio Advertising").

Networks

Advertisers may use one of the national radio networks to carry their messages to the entire national market simultaneously via stations that subscribe to the network's programs. In addition, more than 100 regional radio networks in the United States operate with information oriented toward specific geographic markets.

Networks provide national and regional advertisers with simple administration and low effective net cost per station. Disadvantages include lack of flexibility in choosing affiliated stations, the limited number of stations on a network's roster, and the long lead times required to book time.

Spot Radio

Spot radio affords national advertisers great flexibility in their choice of markets, stations, airtime, and copy. They can put commercials on the air quickly—some stations require as

AD Lab 14–C

The Reports That Make or Break Radio Stations

Media buyers use the data from three major audience rating services to determine which programs and stations will deliver the greatest number of target listeners.

Arbitron

The Arbitron rating service chooses a group of representative listeners in each of 257 cities and gives them a diary for tracking the time they spend listening to radio. Listeners return the diaries to Arbitron at the end of each week for tabulation, and Arbitron compiles the results into a quarterly report.

The Arbitron Book, available on Arbitron's Website (www.arbitron.com), reports the number of listeners to particular stations and shows their ages, sexes, and preferred listening times. Radio stations are major clients, but some ad agencies and radio sales reps also subscribe.

Arbitron is also developing the Portable People Meter (see Ad Lab 16–A), which will enable the electronic measurement of radio audiences.

Birch Research

Birch Research uses phone surveys rather than diaries to obtain listener data. Interviewers talk to representative listeners in 130 major radio markets. Results are published monthly and summarized quarterly. Birch also offers Birchscan, a monthly computerized report.

RADAR

RADAR (Radio's All-Dimension Audience Research) also rates network radio programs based on phone interviews with listeners. Each listener is called daily for a week and asked about listening habits from the day before until that moment. RADAR conducts research year-round and publishes results annually in *Radio Usage* and *Network Radio Audiences*. A number of specialized reports are also available.

Laboratory Application

1. What are the advantages and disadvantages of these radio audience measurement methods?

2. Which audience measurement method, diary or phone interview, is best? Why?

---

little as 20 minutes' lead time, and advertisers can build local acceptance by using local personalities. Radio rep firms, like Katz Radio, represent a list of stations and sell spot time to national advertisers and agencies.

Local Radio

Local time denotes radio spots purchased by a local advertiser or agency. It involves the same procedure as national spots.

Radio advertising can be either live or taped. Most radio stations use recorded shows with live news in between. Likewise, nearly all radio commercials are prerecorded to reduce costs and maintain broadcast quality.

Radio Terminology

For the most part, the terminology used for radio is the same as for other media, but some terms are particular to radio. The most common of these are the concepts of *dayparts, average quarter-hour audiences,* and *cumes* (cumulative audiences).

Dayparts

The radio day is divided into five dayparts:

6 a.m.–10 a.m.	Morning drive
10 a.m.–3 p.m.	Daytime
3 p.m.–7 p.m.	Afternoon (or evening) drive
7 p.m.–midnight	Nighttime
Midnight–6 a.m.	All night

Rating services measure audiences for only the first four dayparts because all-night listening is very limited and not highly competitive. Ad Lab 14–C describes the major radio audience

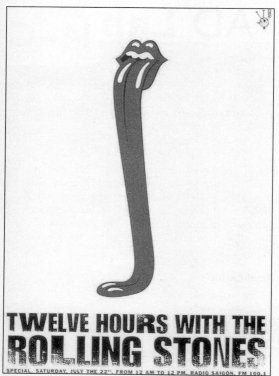

Radio stations that choose to accept programming from external sources, like the Westwood One Radio Network (www.westwoodone.com), can increase their market share during instances of special programming. Westwood One is well known for bringing high-quality recordings of top-name concerts, such as The Rolling Stones, to radio stations that might not otherwise be able to acquire such programming.

Source: Westwood One, Inc.

rating services. Heaviest radio use occurs during **drive times** (6–10 a.m. and 3–7 p.m.) during the week (Monday through Friday), when many listeners are commuting to or from work or school.

Radio stations base their rates on the time of day the advertiser wants commercials aired, but the rates are negotiable according to supply and demand at any given time. For the lowest rate, an advertiser orders spots on a **run-of-station (ROS)** basis, similar to ROP in newspaper advertising. However, this leaves total control of spot placement up to the station. So most stations offer a **total audience plan (TAP)** package rate, which guarantees a certain percentage of spots in the better dayparts if the advertiser buys a total package of time.

Average Quarter-Hour Audience

Average quarter-hour audience (AQH persons) identifies the average number of people listening to a specific station for at least five minutes during a 16-minute period of any given daypart. For example, station KKDA in Dallas–Fort Worth, Texas, has an average quarter-hour listenership of 33,800, meaning that any day, during any 16-minute period between 3 and 7 p.m., about 33,800 people ages 12 and older are tuned in.

The **average quarter-hour rating** expresses the AQH persons as a percentage of the population. Since KKDA is located in an area of 3,072,727 people, its average quarter-hour persons could be expressed as an average quarter-hour *rating* of 1.1:

$$\frac{\text{AQH persons}}{\text{Population}} \times 100 = \text{AQH rating}$$

$$\frac{33,800}{3,072,727} \times 100 = 1.1\%$$

The same idea can be expressed in terms of **average quarter-hour share:** the station's audience (AQH persons) expressed as a percentage of the total radio listening audience in the area. For example, if the total average quarter-hour persons for all stations is 676,000, then radio station KKDA's average quarter-hour *share* is 5:

$$\frac{\text{AQH persons of a station}}{\text{AQH persons of all stations}} \times 100 = \text{AQH share}$$

$$\frac{33,800}{676,000} \times 100 = 5\%$$

The **gross rating points** of a radio schedule are the sum of all ratings points delivered by that schedule, or the *gross impressions* (see Chapter 9) expressed as a percentage of the population being measured:

$$\text{AQH rating} \times \text{Number of spots} = \text{GRPs}$$

$$1.1 \times 24 = 26.4$$

or

$$\frac{\text{Gross impressions}}{\text{Population}} \times 100 = \text{GRPs}$$

$$\frac{33,800 \times 24}{3,072,727} \times 100 = 26.4$$

Cume Estimates

The **cume persons** is the total number of *different* people who listen to a radio station for at least five minutes in a quarter-hour within a reported daypart (also called *unduplicated audience*).

In the example, our schedule on station KKDA generated 811,200 gross impressions, but that does not mean that 811,200 different people heard our commercials. Many people heard the commercials three, four, or five times. By measuring the cumulative number of different people who listened to KKDA, rating services provide the *reach potential* of our radio schedule, which in this case is 167,800.

The **cume rating** is the cume persons expressed as a percentage of the population being measured. For example,

$$\frac{167,800 \times 100}{3,072,727} = 5.5\%$$

Satellite Radio

A challenge to "terrestrial" radio has been mounted by networks that transmit signals nationwide via satellite. As of 2008, **satellite radio** has been a two-player system between first-out-of-the-block XM and Sirius, now the owner of both services. Within a short period of time the networks have succeeded in signing a sizable number of subscribers, about 7.7 million for Sirius and nearly 8.6 million for XM.

In order to receive satellite radio, an audience member must pay a monthly subscription fee and invest in a receiver capable of receiving one of the two networks' signals. XM and Sirius have attempted to convince people that radio is worth paying for by offering two important benefits not available to terrestrial radio listeners: a large number of program choices (each network offers dozens of stations and features a variety of music and nonmusic formats) and exclusive programming, such as Howard Stern on Sirius and Oprah Winfrey on XM.

How significant is satellite radio as an alternative to terrestrial radio? It is difficult at present to be sure. XM and Sirius have successfully leveraged exclusive talent (Stern, Winfrey), and programming (NBA and NFL games on Sirius, MLB games on XM) to attract subscribers.[51] Internet giant Google has partnered with XM to extend its AdWords program to bidding on radio ads.[52] And XM's addition of programming associated with Oprah Winfrey has attracted big advertisers, including Acuvue, Dove, General Electric, Iams, JCPenney, SlimFast, Splenda, Target, and Warners TrueFit.[53] In addition, in 2007 the two rivals announced intention to merge, and in 2008 the FCC gave its approval.

The Seven Steps in Preparing a Radio Schedule

The procedure advertisers use to prepare radio schedules is similar to that used for TV schedules.

1. Identify stations with the greatest concentration (cume) of the advertiser's target audience by demographics (say, men and women ages 35 to 49).
2. Identify stations whose format typically offers the highest concentration of potential buyers.
3. Determine which time periods (dayparts) on those stations offer the most (average quarter-hour) potential buyers.
4. Using the stations' rate cards for guidance, construct a schedule with a strong mix of the best time periods. At this point, it is often wise to give the advertiser's media objectives to the station reps, suggest a possible budget for their station, and ask what they can provide for that budget. This gives the media buyer a starting point for analyzing costs and negotiating the buy.

People BEHIND the Ads

Randy Falco, CEO, Univision

© Desiree Navarro/WireImage/Getty Images

"You're fired."

As the star of the reality entertainment show "The Apprentice," Donald Trump has fired a lot of people (including celebrities on his "Celebrity Apprentice" variation). But in June of 2015, it was Trump himself who was shown the door.

Launching his bid for the Republican nomination for president, Trump chose language describing undocumented immigrants from Mexico that many considered incendiary. That, in turn, created a crisis for Randy Falco, head of the largest Spanish-language network in the United States, Univision. Falco announced that his network would no longer air the Miss USA beauty pageant, a program owned by Trump, a response made to what Falco called Trump's "insulting remarks about Mexican immigrants."

Falco explained his decision this way:

At Univision, a U.S. based Company that proudly serves as the voice of Hispanics, we had to act according to our values as a mission-driven company dedicated to serving our community. We cannot be associated with insulting and intolerant speech that brands an entire community of Mexican immigrants in the U.S. as people who bring drugs, crime and rape into our country. To the contrary, as I said in our statement, we see first-hand the work ethic, love for family, strong religious values and the important role Mexican immigrants and Mexican-Americans have had and will continue to have in building the future of our country. We took this action because it preserves the dignity of our community and our employees and our relationship with them.

With humble origins as a Spanish-language TV station in San Antonio, Univision is now present on nearly every big cable system in the United States. Like any network, Univision needs content. Some is produced by local affiliates, including news and programming. Many popular shows come from Grupo Televisa, a Mexican production company. But Univision also looks for quality shows throughout Central and South America. To celebrate its 50th anniversary, the network introduced a new logo and tagline, positioning Univision as the "Hispanic Heartbeat of America."

Falco's tenure has been marked by many aggressive moves to increase the value of the Univision brand and continue viewership growth. These include creating channels such as Univision tlNovelas (limited-run serial dramas more popular globally than in the United States), Univision Noticias (a news service), and Univision Deportes. Deportes focuses on sports programming, especially Mexican soccer league coverage. Falco also collaborated with ABC to create an English-language cable news channel called "Fusion."

The results have been nothing short of impressive. In February of 2013 the network ranked fourth, beating NBC for the first time ever. And during July sweeps in both 2013 and 2014, Univision finished first, beating all English-language networks. Falco acknowledged the significance of his network's accomplishment by writing, "Wrapping up July—during a time when other networks are investing more than ever in summer programming—as the No. 1 network among both Adults 18–49 and 18–34 for the first time, is making history."

In 2014 Falco notched another win when he reached an agreement with cable giant Comcast. Some had speculated Comcast's disinterest in offering Univision was related to its ownership of rival Spanish-language network Telemundo. With the deal, Univision gained access to over 90 percent of U.S. Hispanic households.

Given the growth of Hispanic audiences in the United States and the attractiveness of the demographic to leading advertisers, no one would blame Falco for playing it safe. But safe is not his style, and it is not the reason the company put him in charge. Falco is playing to win.

And Donald Trump shouldn't take things too personally. He's not the first NBC target Falco has publicly challenged. After watching an NBC News interview in which journalist Chuck Todd served up softball questions to President Obama, Falco tweeted that Todd could learn a thing or two from Univsion's own news star: "Chuck Todd should watch Jorge Ramos and learn how to interview the President and ask tough questions."

(DAD READING TO DAUGHTER)

DAD: OK, honey. One story, then it's bedtime . . .

LITTLE GIRL: OK, Daddy!

DAD: Once upon a time, there was the Letter A. But A couldn't find any other letters to play with . . .

LITTLE GIRL: Ohhh . . . that's so sad!

DAD: Wait, it gets better . . .

So A called a meeting. There, he met Letter B, who thought they should merge . . .

LITTLE GIRL (LAUGHING): Daddy, you're silly!

DAD: I know. Then, they did a leveraged buyout for letters C through L . . .

LITTLE GIRL: Really? . . .

DAD: And offered stock options for M through Z . . .

LITTLE GIRL: What's that? . . .

DAD: And they all lived happily ever after! . . .

LITTLE GIRL: Yayyyy!

SEGUE TO ANNOUNCER VOICEOVER OVER DISTINCTIVE NEEDLEDROP MUSIC. If you're a parent, you don't have to invent stories to get your kids to love reading. Just go to the best place in cyberspace for help . . . the Hooked on Phonics Website. Visit us today at A-B-C-D-E-F-G dot-com. Take the FREE personalized reading assessment to find out how to help your child become a more confident reader.

So for all this—and much, much more—log onto Hooked on Phonics at the most memorable web address anywhere: A-B-C-D-E-F-G dot-com. (Musical logo played under VO.)

NEEDLEDROP MUSIC OUT.

---

5. Assess the proposed buy in terms of reach and frequency.

6. Determine the cost for each 1,000 target people each station delivers. The key word is *target;* the media buyer isn't interested in the station's total audience.

7. Negotiate and place the buy.

Chapter Summary

As a means of reaching the masses, no other medium today has the unique creative ability of television. Broadcast TV grew faster than any previous advertising medium because of the unique advantages it offered advertisers: mass coverage at efficient cost, impact, prestige, and social dominance.

Television is a powerful creative tool, but the medium still has many drawbacks, including high actual cost, limited selectivity, brevity, clutter, and susceptibility to zipping and zapping.

Broadcast TV dominance is being challenged by new electronic media, particularly cable. Cable offers the visual and aural appeal of TV at much lower cost and with greater flexibility. Cable audiences are highly fragmented, which helps advertisers target specific markets but is a drawback for those wanting to reach a mass audience.

TV advertising can be done at the national, regional, or local level and can take the form of program sponsorships, segment sponsorships, and spots of varying lengths, including program-length infomercials.

To determine which shows to buy, media buyers select the most efficient ones for their target audience. They compare the packages of each station, substitute stronger programs for less efficient ones, and negotiate prices to get the best buy. Media buyers must have a firm grasp of certain important terms: *designated market areas (DMAs), TV households (TVHH), households using TV (HUT), program rating, share of audience, gross rating points,* and *cost per thousand.*

Like television, radio is a highly creative medium. Its greatest attribute is its ability to offer excellent reach and frequency to selective audiences at a very efficient price. Its drawbacks are the limitations of sound, segmented audiences, and its short-lived and half-heard commercials.

Radio stations are normally classified by the programming they offer and the audiences they serve. Radio stations may be AM or FM. They may use network or syndicated programs and follow any of a dozen or more popular formats. Advertisers purchase radio time in one of three forms: local, spot, or network. Buying radio time requires a basic understanding of radio terminology. The most common terms are *dayparts, average quarter hour,* and *cumulative audiences.*

Important Terms

affidavit of performance, *446*

audience composition, *444*

avails, *444*

average quarter-hour audience
(AQH persons), *452*

average quarter-hour rating, *452*

average quarter-hour share, *452*

barter syndication, *438*

broadcast TV, *430*

cable TV, *430*

cost per rating point (CPP), *444*

cost per thousand (CPM), *444*

cume persons, *453*

cume rating, *453*

daypart mix, *442*

designated market areas (DMAs), *441*

drive time, *452*

first-run syndication, *438*

gross rating points (GRPs), *444, 452*

households using TV (HUT), *443*

imagery transfer, *447*

infomercial, *439*

inventory, *438*

local time, *451*

makegoods, *446*

networks, *436*

off-network syndication, *438*

participation basis, *437*

preemption rate, *446*

prime time, *442*

program-length advertisement (PLA), *439*

program rating, *443*

programming format, *448*

rating service, *441*

run of station (ROS), *452*

satellite radio, *453*

share, *443*

sponsorship, *437*

spot announcement, *437*

spot radio, *450*

total audience, *444*

total audience plan (TAP), *452*

TV households (TVHH), *442*

UHF, *430*

VHF, *430*

Review Questions

1. What are the advantages of broadcast TV advertising for a product like milk?

2. What steps can advertisers take to overcome zipping and zapping?

3. Why has advertising on network TV become less desirable in recent years?

4. In what ways is cable TV's selectivity a strength? A drawback?

5. What are the various ways to buy broadcast television time?

6. How can TV be best used in an integrated marketing communications program?

7. How can radio be best used in an IMC program?

8. What is the format of the radio station you listen to most? How would you describe the demographics of its target audience?

9. What is the difference between average quarter-hour and cume audiences? Which is better?

10. What is the significance of dayparts in radio and TV advertising? What are the best dayparts for each?

The Advertising Experience

1. **Radio Advertising**

   Valentine's Day is approaching, and as the owner of Dream Flower Florists, you want to increase your share of local business by advertising on the radio. After researching local stations, choose one whose format suits your target audience. Decide what kind of buys you will make and when they will be aired.

2. **TV Organizations**

   The size of the television industry and the advertising dollars that are spent within it are extraordinary. Many TV-related organizations were formed to help serve the industry. Discover a little more about the nature and scope of the television industry as you peruse the following Websites. Be sure to answer the questions that follow.

   - Broadcast Education Association (BEA): www.beaweb.org
   - Cable/Telecommunications Association for Marketing (CTAM): www.ctam.com

   - Cable World: www.cableworld.com
   - National Association of Broadcasters (NAB): www.nab.org
   - a. Who is the intended audience(s) of the site?
   - b. What is the site's purpose? Does it succeed? Why?
   - c. What is the organization's purpose?
   - d. What benefit does the organization provide individual members/subscribers? The overall advertising and television and cable communities?

3. **Broadcast Media Tools**

   Broadcast advertising reports and audience studies are critical to the development and implementation of effective media strategy. As with print media, advertisers have a set of "staple" companies and reports they regularly use to help plan and implement their broadcast media buys. Visit the following syndicated and independent broadcast media companies' Websites and answer the questions that follow:

- Arbitron: www.arbitron.com
- Bureau of Broadcast Measurement (BBM): www.bbm.ca
- Cabletelevision Advertising Bureau (CAB): www.onetvworld.org
- Nielsen Media Research: www.nielsenmedia.com
- Radio Advertising Bureau: www.rab.com
- Radio Marketing Bureau (RMB): www.rmb.ca
- Television Bureau of Advertising: www.tvb.org
- Television Bureau of Canada (TVB): www.tvb.ca
- TV RunDown: www.tvrundown.com

a.   What type(s) of broadcast media information does the company specialize in and what specific services, products, or publications does the company offer?

b.   What industries/companies would be best suited to utilize the company's media resources?

c.   Does the company represent syndicated or independent research?

d.   How useful do you feel the company is for gathering broadcast media information? Why?

4.   If Hyundai asked its agency to come up with a corresponding radio complement to its Assurance TV campaign, what would its agency want to keep in mind when converting this concept to an audio-only format?

5.   Given the audience for Hyundai's Assurance campaign—middle-class America—in what daypart do you think its TV commercial would be most effectively broadcast?

Using Digital Interactive Media

Learning Objectives

To explore the important factors advertisers weigh when considering digital interactive media. This medium has its own distinct characteristics, unique advantages, and drawbacks. Advertisers must be able to compare the merits of this medium and understand the most cost-effective ways to use them in their media mix.

 studying this chapter, you will be able to:

LO15-1 Discuss the various opportunities and challenges presented by digital interactive media.

LO15-2 Explain the evolution of interactive media.

LO15-3 Discuss the digital audience and the challenges involved in measuring it.

LO15-4 Explain how programmatic advertising works.

LO15-5 Define the various kinds of digital advertising.

LO15-6 Debate the pros and cons of the Internet as an advertising medium.

CSP_Mazirama/age fotostock RF

Source: Voyages-sncf.com

How many banner ads have you clicked in the past couple of hours? Days? Weeks? Can you even remember the last time you scrolled over to a blinking banner ad and clicked to leave your intended destination? If you are like a lot of people, the answer is probably no. ■ The Internet marketer Hubspot recently posted some pretty gruesome stats about banner ads, including that the average click through rate (CTR) is 0.1 percent (i.e., 1 in 1000 people) and that about 50 percent of clicks on mobile banner ads are accidental.[1] ■ These numbers offer a clue why banner ads suffer a poor reputation as a marketing tool. In fact, Bob Hoffman, a partner at Type A Group, recently wrote that banners are "the worst advertising."[2] ■ Not everyone agrees with these dim assessments. As with all forms of advertising, careful planning and smart strategy make a big difference. Do the ads appear on sites with related content? Does the ad feature a specific product or does it link to a general Website? Is the banner message simple and easy to digest or complicated? Finally, is the creative execution inspired or trite? ■ The last point brings us to one of the best banner ads of 2014. The intriguingly named "Banner Contest for Psychopaths" was created by TBWA\Paris for the client Voyages-SNCF, a rail travel company. ■ A set of three different banners pitched a contest which could be won in one of two ways. The "easy way" was to go to Voyages' Website and answer a small number of easy questions. The "other way" varied according to which of the three banner ads the audience member encountered. In one, the "24 hours banner," the web user had to grab a moving ticket in the banner and hold it. For 24 hours straight. In another, the user had to click the banner 1,000,000 times. And in the final one, the user had to scroll the banner. Ambitious players had to scroll 708 miles, or the distance from London to Barcelona. Less ambitious players needed only scroll for 587 miles, the distance from London to Geneva. ■ The agency estimated that for those choosing "the other" ways, it would take just under 48 hours of non-stop mouse behavior to win the tickets. Hence the campaign's name. And, in fact, hundreds of people did try the "other way," and six people somehow managed to complete the task. More importantly for Voyages, the click-through rate soared to nearly six times the average for web display ads.[3] ■ The campaign's success originated in TBWA's awareness that without a creative spark, banners are not terribly effective. In this case, the banners worked well, not only because of a unique idea, but because the idea would have special appeal with the younger target audience interested in rail travel. ■ The campaign was also aided by publicity. The irresistible title and silly challenge attracted media attention, which ensured many people would learn about Voyages even if they were not exposed to the ad. ■ The "Psychopaths" campaign shows that proper strategy, well-designed creative, and a deep understanding of the audience, can turn the lowly banner ad into a powerful marketing asset.[4]

Digital Interactive Media

LO 15-1

Today, we are all participating in a media revolution, brought on by incredible achievements in communications technology. We're talking, of course, about the Internet, the fastest-growing medium in history.

To understand the dramatic effect this is having on marketing and advertising, imagine for a moment what life was like before radio and TV. Back then, if you had a product to sell, you made your appeal to the consumer directly, often on her front doorstep. If she didn't like what you were peddling, she slammed the door in your face. She was in complete control of the selling environment.[5] Then along came radio and, 30 years later, TV. Now mass marketers had a captive audience, people who would willingly pay for an evening's entertainment at home by simply sitting through the commercials. Advertisers prospered—and so did consumers, as they enjoyed a rapidly growing standard of living.

But now the sands are shifting across the advertising landscape. The remote control was the first step toward convenient interactivity, and it had a major impact on commercial viewership. Instead of watching commercials, people could now use the station breaks to channel surf, effectively slamming the door once again in the salesperson's face.

Right on the heels of the remote came the widespread distribution of cable TV. In little more than a decade, the network TV audience plunged from 90 to 50 percent. SLAM!

Then, of course, came the VCR. People could now record shows and watch them later at their convenience, zipping through the commercials. Or they could just rent a movie and

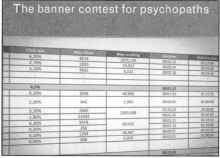

The Banner Contest for Psychopaths is an example of a successful digital interactive media campaign. Over 300,000 people clicked on the banners and one tenacious customer completed the 24 hour challenge by holding the moving ticket in the banner for 24 hours straight.

Source:Voyages-sncf.com

The Internet has ventured out from the computer to the millions of mobile "smartphones" that can access Websites. Soon many more people will access web content from mobile devices than from computers.

Source: © Stanca Sanda/Alamy Stock Photo

skip the commercials altogether. TiVo brought ad-avoidance into the digital age, allowing viewers to customize their entertainment schedules. SLAM!

Meanwhile, technology keeps on going and going and going. It's already given us the 3D TV, tablets, the mobile phone, the Internet, digital media players, IPTV, and VOIP—and the software to make it all simple enough for virtually anybody to use. With growing consumer acceptance of all this wizardry, prices have plummeted, making most of it affordable for almost everyone.

These are not just advertising media. In many cases, they represent completely new ways of living and doing business. The fastest-growing advertising medium in history has also opened the door to electronic commerce.

From the convenience of your own personal computer, you can bank online, buy a car or a beautiful piece of art, trade stocks, book your airline reservations, purchase concert tickets, buy a complete new wardrobe from your favorite department store, or even order your week's groceries and have them delivered to your door.

The Internet has also changed the way we send mail, eliminating the need for an overseas airmail stamp if you want to communicate with your brother in Berlin. You can do library research in the comfort of your den, or you can start your own home-based business and market your products worldwide.

The Internet is truly revolutionary in its effect on our daily lives, and it's a revolution for marketers, too. As the nation's biggest traditional advertisers realized that Internet media offered wonderful opportunities for achieving real, bottom-line results, they started increasing their online spending dramatically. In light of this change, the Internet research company eMarketer projected that online advertising spending would reach $51 billion by 2012, and make up 15 percent of total U.S. media spending.[6] Similarly, the U.S. Census Bureau has estimated that e-commerce revenues for 2011 were $194.3 billion.

In addition to this phenomenal growth, by offering true interactivity, online media enable businesses and other organizations to develop and nurture relationships with their customers and other stakeholders, in a way never before available, on a global scale at very efficient cost.

In just 15 years as a commercial medium, the Internet has become a mass forum for advertising as well as other communications (see Exhibit 15-1). In recognition of this explosive growth, we need to understand how advertisers buy Internet advertising and use it in their marketing plans.

The Internet as a Medium

The Internet has come a long way from its simple roots. While some people assume it is very new, in fact the technological infrastructure of the Internet has been around for over 50 years.

The **Internet** is a global network of computers that communicate with one another through **protocols,** which are common rules for linking and sharing information. Although it still seems quite new, the Internet began in the early 1960s as a result of the Defense Department's Advanced Research Projects Agency (ARPA) plan to create a network that could survive a cold war attack. ARPAnet had little commercial value; its primary users were governmental organizations and research universities, and the Internet of today is a far different medium. However, ARPAnet was important because its structure, a **distributed network,** was a revolutionary system. Traditionally,

Exhibit 15-1

U.S. online advertising spending, 2011 to 2016 ($ in billions).

Source: Data provided from eMarketer.com.

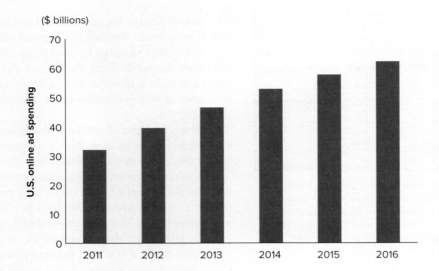

($ billions)

media content has been delivered through **centralized networks,** in which a hub, such as a TV station, a newspaper publisher, or a cable company, distributes content to many receivers (see Exhibit 15-2). In a centralized system, if the hub is knocked out, receivers are left without information. But a distributed network is characterized by many different hubs and links, which allows continuous communication even if some connections stop working.

There are at least three other important distinctions between the Internet and traditional media. The first is the cost of time and/or space. In traditional media, time (on TV or radio) and space (in print) are precious and limited resources. Network TV commercials average 30 seconds, which is a very small window, and that window is expensive, averaging in the hundreds of thousands of dollars. In contrast, space on the Internet is vast and relatively inexpensive. Websites generally can store as much information as a company wishes to share. For consumers who require lots of facts before they make a decision to buy, this is a real plus.

The second distinction between traditional media and online media is the consumption of content. In traditional space, audiences consume content in an appointment-viewing mode. For instance, NBC develops and schedules a show and, if you enjoy it, you sit down on a certain night and time each week to watch. With the Internet and the ability to deliver content to multiple places at simultaneous and various times, consumers can now initiate the viewing or consumption of content when they "demand" to watch. As audience viewership numbers decrease and online interactivity increases, more content owners will incorporate a digital strategy that allows them to both appease the consumer's need for on-demand viewing and deliver the audience to advertisers that help support the content. Hulu.com, which is a

Exhibit 15-2

In a centralized network, a hub distributes content to many receivers. A distributed network has many different hubs and links.

Centralized Network   Distributed Network

joint venture of NBC Universal and News Corp., provides content from over 50 providers, such as FOX, NBC, MGM, Sony Pictures Television, and others, allows users to watch full-length episodes of their favorite TV shows, old and new; and gives users the ability to cut out and create "clips" of their favorite scenes for reposting onto their own social networking pages such as myspace.com. While obviously appealing to the consumer, Hulu also gives advertisers the opportunity to connect their brands with premium content online, to interact with highly engaged consumers, and to extend their reach via Hulu's broad distribution network.

A third distinction is the relationship between those who create content and those who consume it. Traditional media historically were content creators while audiences were content consumers. In our previous NBC example, NBC is the creator and you are the consumer. But the Internet, from its beginnings, has been *interactive,* blurring the line between content providers and consumers. The Internet audience doesn't just consume online content, it interacts with it and creates it. As an example, imagine a teenager who uploads a video to YouTube. The teen is both a content creator (of her video or Website) and a consumer (when she watches other videos). In addition, the Internet makes it easy and cheap for the teen to promote her video. She can e-mail friends and ask them to watch it or she can create links to the video on her Facebook page. If her friends like it, they may recommend the video to others on their own social platforms. Eventually, a huge audience might watch the teen's video, even though it was produced very inexpensively. Something like this actually happened in 2006

Marks and Spencer uses the Internet and Instagram to stay connected to their shoppers. Take a look at their beautiful site here: https://instagram.com/marksandspencer
Source: Marks and Spencer

with video diary entries posted by a young woman, identified only as Lonelygirl15, on You-Tube. The videos showed the musings of a typical but expressive teen about her parents, boyfriend, and life in general. After the first audience for the videos shared them with friends, Lonelygirl15's videos received more than 15 million cumulative views, equivalent to the number of people who watch a top 20 network TV show. Major media outlets such as *Ad Age* and *The New York Times* picked up on the phenomenon, eventually raising questions as to whether Lonelygirl15 was real or a clever fake. She was eventually revealed as the latter (the videos were created by two young filmmakers), but the fact that people were unable to tell for a long time makes one thing clear: there has never been a medium quite like this one.

A Brief History of the Internet and the World Wide Web

How did the Internet become such a pervasive and interactive medium? To understand that, we have to know how it came to be. In the early 1980s, the National Science Foundation expanded what had been ARPAnet by supporting a fast data network that linked information centers across the United States. At the same time, online content providers such as AOL and CompuServe were building an Internet audience by providing news, information, and e-mail services to subscribers. These services anticipated the World Wide Web by encouraging people to use their computers to find information and communicate with others. But AOL and CompuServe still retained the structure of a centralized network because most content either originated with or flowed through a centralized hub. If you were an AOL subscriber, you couldn't get access to content on CompuServe or Prodigy unless you subscribed to them as well.

Throughout the 1990s, the numbers of people using the Internet were doubling each year. Fueling the medium's growth were the increasing popularity and affordability of personal computers and the growing use of modems, which allowed computers to tap into the Internet via an ordinary phone line. The 1990s was also the decade in which people began going online to access a particular part of the Internet known as the **World Wide Web (WWW).** The web, as its name implies, was a distributed network of content providers and users, communicating through a protocol known as **HTML,** or HyperText Markup Language. HTML allowed for the relatively easy creation of displays, called **web pages**, that can be easily linked to all kinds of content, including other web pages or sites (and, later, photographs, movies, databases, sound files, and such). Viewing web pages was made easy by the development of **web browsers,** software that interpreted HTML (and later other code that permitted greater interactivity, such as Sun's JAVA and Adobe's Flash). Although Microsoft was not the first to develop a web browser, chair Bill Gates recognized the potential of the web for his company relatively early, and Microsoft developed the most popular browser in use today, Internet Explorer.

In the 2000s, the Internet is a global medium. People around the world use the Internet to read news, research products, stay in touch with friends, and find out what is new. They are increasingly doing this using high-speed *broadband* access rather than slower telephone lines, which makes it easy to watch videos, listen to audio programming, and download large files.

In a centralized system such as television it is relatively easy to find content: Sit down, turn the set on, and watch. If the show on one channel is boring, switch to another. Even with a couple of hundred channels, a viewer can quickly find out what is on. But the web is the home of millions of destinations, available at all times of the day and on every day of the week. The experience of the web is only partially determined by content creators. Just as important, it is created by its users, who are free to follow their own inclinations in finding entertainment and information.

This new medium has proven highly popular. The web exploded from about 50 sites in 1993 to more than 30 million active sites and 70 million registered sites worldwide in 2005.

The Internet Audience

In the past several years we have seen a steady migration of people who used to spend time in front of the TV moving over to the computer. A 2006 study by Nielsen//NetRatings suggested that some Internet users are watching as much as 25 percent less TV. According to Mainak Mazumdar, Nielsen vice president of product marketing and measurement science, "It's not that people are abandoning TV for the Internet. Sometimes they do both. We only have 24 hours a day. . . . (That's) a finite amount of time to consume media."[7] Of course,

Rank	Site	Country
1	Google.com	USA
2	Facebook.com	USA
3	Youtube.com	USA
4	Baidu.com	China
5	Yahoo.com	USA
6	Amazon.com	USA
7	Wikipedia.com	USA
8	Qq.com	China
9	Twitter.com	USA
10	Taobao.com	China

some TV networks also maintain popular Websites, and this strategy is paying dividends in the digital age. For example, although overall TV use is down among Internet users, this same group watches more programming on cable networks such as Bravo and Comedy Central than do non-Internet users. This is doubtless due, at least in part, to the strong, feature-rich Website that each channel maintains (see www.comedycentral.com and www.bravotv.com). Exhibit 15-3 indicates which Websites were most popular in 2015. Google, the top site, serves more than a billion search requests each month, more than half of which arrive from mobile devices.

Who Uses the Internet

The percentage of the U.S. population able to access the Internet on a regular basis continues to climb. In 1997, only 50 million people were wired. This number had doubled by 2000 and has since doubled again. In 2011, more than 273 million people in the United States accessed the Internet each month.[8] Worldwide, the active Internet audience is estimated at 2.3 billion, with many more occasional users (see Exhibit 15-4). According to Internet World Stats (www.internetworldstats.com), Internet penetration is currently growing fastest in Africa, where the percentage of users is more than 30 times greater than in 2000. Iceland (98%) and Norway (97%) top the list of the most wired nations.

Media budgets tend to be very pragmatic. As audiences migrate, so do the media dollars. As a result, media spending on Internet advertising has grown substantially. One of the great draws of the Internet from the marketer's point of view is its demographics.

Historically, the majority of people who surfed the Internet were well educated, upscale, white males who used the Internet for business or scientific purposes. Yet, recent surveys of Internet demographics suggest the reach of the medium is much more diverse and in some ways closely resembles the U.S. population (see Exhibit 15-5). Women and men use the Internet in roughly the same proportion (women 79%, men 81%). Internet reach is still greatest among non-Hispanic whites (83%).

Internet usage is growing steadily, but still lags, for users over 65 (48%). There is now no area where Internet usage has decreased.

And what is this audience doing? Of the 273 million monthly Internet users, the Pew Internet & American Project Life Study suggests that more than 250 million use e-mail and search

Region	Population (000,000) 2011 est.	Internet Users (000,000)	Penetration (%)
Africa	1,037	139	13.5%
Asia	3,879	1,016	26.2
Europe	816	500	61.3
Middle East	216	77	35.6
North America	347	273	78.6
Latin America/Caribbean	597	236	39.5
Oceania/Australia	35	24	67.5
World Total	6,930	2,267	32.7

engines to find information. Almost 230 million use maps. Use of the Internet for weather and travel also ranks very high, 231 million and 177 million people, respectively. As would be anticipated from a growth medium, all of these numbers are still increasing.

Measuring the Internet Audience

How People Access the Internet

LO 15-3

Exhibit 15-5

Percentage of demographic groups that use the Internet, according to a 2008 Pew Internet & American Life Project survey.

% Who Use the Internet	
All Adults	**80**
Men	81
Women	79
Race/Ethnicity	
White, Non-Hispanic	83
Black, Non-Hispanic	71
Hispanic (English- and Spanish-speaking)	71
Age	
18–29	94
30–49	88
50–64	79
65+	48
Household Income	
Less than $30,000/yr	65
$30,000–$49,999	85
$50,000–$74,999	94
$75,000 +	98
Educational Attainment	
No High School diploma	45
High School grad	73
Some College	91
College +	97

The Pew Research Center's Internet & American Life Project's February Tracking Survey conducted January 20–February 10, 2012. N = 2,253 adults age 18 and older, including 901 interviews conducted by cell phone. Interviews were conducted in both English and Spanish.

When marketers and the media first began trumpeting the marvels of the Internet, they quickly noted the potentially vast size of its user population. As noted, internet users comprise most people in industrialized nations and a fast growing portion of the rest of the globe.

While traditionally people think of accessing the Internet through a computer, the reality is that most people are accessing the Internet these days in a variety of ways with a variety of devices. The introduction of the smart phone, for instance, has also increased consumer awareness and demand for access to the Internet via a mobile device. One of the more popular Internet uses is meeting others online for gaming on devices from Microsoft, Sony, or Nintendo.

This is all made possible through high-speed connections, both wired and wireless. According to a summer 2009 study by @plan (a Nielsen-Online tool), 91 percent of the 18-and-over online population has broadband Internet access, making it the main connection type to the Internet. **Broadband** connections are really just a description of the ability to transmit multiple signals simultaneously on one data line. What it means for consumers is faster Internet surfing and faster data uploads and downloads. Broadband connections have helped revolutionize industries such as photography and personal home videos and launched popular sharing sites such as Flickr and Youtube. Equally important is the increased speed of cellular networks, allowing people to quickly upload pictures or videos from their phones to sharing sites such as Instagram and Snapchat.

Why is this important to advertisers? There are many reasons, but primarily because as consumers get more comfortable interacting with and seeking out rich content such as videos, they will become more likely to supplement their other media usage with the Internet.

How People Use the Internet

Some people believe that the first era of the World Wide Web has already passed, and that a new philosophy drives the activities of some companies. This philosophy has been dubbed Web 2.0 and represents the idea that the future of the web is in companies that encourage user sharing and collaboration (see Exhibit 15-6). Wikipedia, the popular online encyclopedia, is often cited as a prime example of this new philosophy.[9] Unlike most other encyclopedias, Wikipedia is not constructed from articles penned by authorities or experts. Instead, anyone can create an entry, which in turn can be edited by someone else. In this sense, the site represents the efforts of thousands of users, rather than hundreds of authorities. Other examples of this type of collaboration include Twitter, Digg, and Craigslist.

One of the unique features of the Internet is the relative ease of finding and accumulating data based on advertising efforts. In this section we will discuss how the technology allows us to better understand users and refine our advertising efforts not only from campaign to campaign, but also while a campaign is in market. We will reflect on the two phases of online advertising that utilize and generate the most data: planning and tracking. Last, we will look at the issues surrounding all these data and how the industry approaches standardization.

Media Planning Tools

As with all other media, there are companies that specialize in delivering audited measurement of potential reach to help media planners choose the right vehicles based on their target audience. Two main companies help in the media planning process on the Internet:

Exhibit 15-6

Contenders for Web 2.0 activities, according to a Pew Internet & American Life Project surveys. Some of these activities have been around for a long time, but might qualify as Web 2.0 because they provide opportunities for content creation and interaction. Since the time this survey appeared, social web activities have exploded.

% of Internet Users Who Do This	Internet Activities (all)
71	Watch a video on a video-sharing site like YouTube or Vimeo.
64	Use an online social networking site like MySpace, Facebook, or LinkedIn.com.
53	Look for information on Wikipedia.
46	Upload photos to a Website so you can share them with others online.
37	Rate a product, service, or person using an online rating system.
32	Post a comment or review online about a product you bought or a service you received.
32	Post comments to an online news group, Website, blog, or photo site.
30	Share something online that you created yourself.
22	Participate in an online discussion, a listserv, or other online group forum that helps people with personal issues or health problems.
15	Create or work on Web pages or blogs for others, including friends, groups you belong to, or for work.
15	Download or share files using peer-to-peer file-sharing networks, such as BitTorrent or LimeWire.
14	Create or work on your own Web page.
14	Create or work on your own online journal or blog.
12	Use Twitter.

Source: Pew Internet and American Life Project, www.pewinternet.org.

Nielsen-Online and comScore. Both companies have a suite of tools that help define target market size, behavior, and composition relative to each major Website on the Internet. They also provide views into how other advertisers are using the Internet, thereby giving competitive insights into industry and category best practices.

These companies measure the activities of a set number of people or a panel of people and provide reports on their usage patterns across Websites and Internet applications, such as iTunes. Nielsen randomly recruits individuals to download and utilize a *desktop meter* so all Internet activity on that computer is then tabulated, measured, and recorded. This process is very similar to one of the methods Nielsen utilizes to measure TV audiences. Using a limited sample size, Nielsen then projects these numbers to the rest of the Internet audience as averages. For instance, if a panel identifies that 50 percent of all men aged 18–34 go to ESPN.com daily, whereas on average most sites garner only 25 percent of the male panel audience, Nielsen will project those numbers to the rest of the Internet to arrive at an index of 200 for ESPN.com relative to the entire Internet traffic for men between the ages of 18 and 34. Media planners utilize these numbers to identify the highest concentration, or **composition,** of the target they are trying to reach. However, because of lack of standardization, many companies report many different numbers, and it is a media planner's job to make heads or tails of the data. (See Ad Lab 15–A for a deeper explanation.)

The Promise of Enhanced Tracking

Today's software now provides some of the most precise tracking and targeting tools ever. In fact, every time you step into the Internet, some computer may be watching to see just where you go. Software using HTTP interacts with what are known as **cookies,** small pieces of information that get stored in your web browser when you load certain Websites. Cookies track whether a certain user has ever visited a specific site. This allows the site to give users different information depending

Samsung uses Facebook display advertising and short, benefit-focused copy to attract social media users.

Source: Samsung Electronics Co., Ltd.

AD Lab 15-A

Internet Ratings: A Call for Standards

With the increased popularity of the Internet as an advertising medium comes increased reliance on measurement. However, because of a lack of standards, many measurement methods are available and it can be challenging to make heads or tails of the various solutions.

Each measurement company has its own way of "counting" and measuring, but for the most part there are two main buckets of measurement. There are planning tools such as comScore and Nielsen//NetRatings and tracking tools such as Doubleclick, Omniture, and WebTrends. All of these companies help quantify Internet usage, but the main difference between the sets is that one is based on projected activity from samples of consumers and the others are census-based, where census means complete records of activity at a site or ad campaign level.

The panel-based, or sample, approach has to date been widely accepted in the planning community for the main reason that it offers demographic and targeting-based information that is still considered unreliable from the census companies. However, both comScore and Nielsen have come under tremendous pressure to come up with a better solution as they have been highly scrutinized for undercounting by up to two to three times what most publishers count from their own server logs. In fact, in April 2007, the CEO of the Interactive Advertising Bureau (IAB) sent a scathing open letter to both companies complaining that they better get their acts together. The IAB is a standards body committee, made up of over 375 leading interactive companies, that actively engages in and supports the sale of online advertising. An excerpt from the letter:

Imagine my surprise when I came to the IAB and discovered that the main audience measurement companies are still relying on panels—a media-measurement technique invented for the radio industry exactly seven decades ago—to quantify the Internet. . . . To persist in using panels that undercount or ignore the diverse populations that are the future of consumer marketing is to deny marketers the insights they need to build their businesses. And it certainly appears to us as if they are being undercounted or

disregarded, for our members' server logs continue to diverge starkly from your companies' sample-based assessments, by [two times to three times] magnitudes in some cases—far beyond any legitimate margin of sampling error.

However, everything isn't all peaches and cream on the census side either. In fact anyone can perform a basic search for Internet measurement information and find a number of blogs, articles, and press releases about the monumental discrepancies between all of the various census-based reporting tools, and there are many. The discrepancies stem from a multitude of reasons: different data collection methods, unique data models, untagged pages, blocking software, cookie issues, and many more reasons. In fact Google Analytics, Google's free-to-use Website tracking tool, has pages on its help site about why Google AdWords' clicks don't match Google Analytics' page visits. So is there hope? Yes, and it comes in two forms: Media Rating Council (MRC) and start-ups.

The MRC's number one objective is **To secure for the media industry and related users audience measurement services that are valid, reliable, and effective.** Hallelujah . . . right? It is definitely a step in the right direction; however, since the MRC is an organization that can tell you only what you "should do," not what you "must do," it is up to the advertisers and publishers to come to resolution if the industry really wants to see a change happen.

Or, you rely on the start-ups to make a better black box. Companies like Alexa, Quantcast, and even Google AdPlanner are coming up with different, possibly more acceptable, ways to measure Internet usage. But as with all start-ups, they have yet to truly prove themselves. Their task is to engage with advertisers and publishers and reliably deliver numbers that both sides feel comfortable with.

Laboratory Applications

1. What are some of the problems of Internet audience measurement?

2. Do you think these problems can be fixed? How?

---

on whether they are repeat visitors. Cookies also indicate the users' frequency of visits, the time of last visit, and the domain from which they are surfing. Additionally, cookies give marketers great insights into their campaigns on a daily basis, such as the number of times users call for an ad, time of day, type of browsers they use, whether or not they click, and so on.

Typical online marketers employ the services of **third-party ad servers.** Third-party ad servers deliver ads from one central source, or server, across multiple web domains, allowing advertisers the ability to manage the rotation and distribution of their advertisements. The best-known companies are DoubleClick, now owned by Google, and Atlas DMT, now owned by Microsoft. These companies allow advertisers to monitor the performance of their buys on a daily basis all the way down to conversion to sales or any other action advertisers desire. By placing a line of javascript code on the last page of the sales process (in this case the confirmation page), DoubleClick and/or Atlas can match the user back to the last advertisement they saw or clicked on, via the cookies they place on the user's browser, and

One reason media budgets are shifting to the Internet is that the medium offers a variety of ways to track interactions of consumers with ads. One company that helps provide such metrics is comScore (www.comscore.com).

Source: comScore, Inc.

credit that advertisement with the sale. This allows the agency to understand direct metrics from advertising to sales in near real time. This hyperaccountability is what ultimately brought the online ad industry out of the dot-com crash of the early 2000s—marketers could easily justify their advertising spending's direct effect on the company's bottom line.

More sophisticated technology provides marketers with additional details about the consumer. The computer first assigns each user an anonymous and encrypted identification number for tracking purposes. A user profile is then created with data on the content of the pages read, what keywords may have been used in a search, the time and day that a web page was viewed, the frequency with which an ad is seen, the sequence of ads that are seen, the computer operating system of the user, the browser type, and the IP address. From these data, marketers' computers can again guess the user's ISP, telephone area code, and NAIC code. Marketers may then match these data with demographic information gathered offline to create a clearer picture of consumer behavior than has ever been available.

However, **behavioral targeting,** this new ability to track people's behavior on the Internet, has stirred considerable debate. Although software developers claim that the users are tracked anonymously with encrypted identification numbers, privacy advocates believe the marketing method is too invasive into consumers' lives (see Ethical Issues on pages 472–473).

Seeking Standardization

As much as Madison Avenue may want web measurements to resemble traditional media measurements, the Internet cannot provide them. As we'll describe shortly, simply counting advertising impressions from a web page is an impractical method of tabulation. However, the basic questions remain the same: Do people see our ads? Are they effective? Until fairly recently, when a task force of the Internet Advertising Bureau (IAB) provided some practical definitions, Internet audience measurement information lacked the standardization needed to be able to compare its advertising effectiveness to other media.

The most simple measurement, yet an area of great controversy, is the **advertising impression.** The IAB defines an ad impression as "an opportunity to deliver an advertising element to a Website visitor."[10] When a user loads a web page with ads on it, the browser will pull the advertisement from its host ad server and bring it up as a banner, button, or interstitial. The number of ad requests received can then be translated into the familiar cost form. The problem with this definition, from the point of view of advertisers and agencies, is that the advertiser is not guaranteed that a user will ever see an ad. People often click away to some other site before the requested ad ever comes up. Under the IAB definition, an advertiser would be charged for an ad that never had the opportunity to be seen. The AAAA prefers to define an ad request as an ad that is actually delivered to users' screens. Only then do they truly have an opportunity to see the ad. This controversy over definitions has a huge impact on the business because it also creates reporting differences between what web publishers count and what the agencies count and are willing to pay for. These considerations prevent marketers from obtaining the foolproof numbers they want. But as technology improves the speed and methods of online advertising, we can anticipate increased accuracy in measurement. For more on Internet ratings, see Ad Lab 15–A.

A second measurement, unique to the Internet, is the **click rate** or *click-through rate.* A click occurs when a visitor moves the mouse's pointer to a web link and clicks on the mouse button to get to another page. The click rate is the number of clicks on an ad divided by the number of ad impressions. In essence, marketers are measuring the frequency with which users try to obtain additional information about a product by clicking on an advertisement.

Buying Time and Space on the Internet

LO 15-4

Media planners cannot think of the Internet in mass media terms. Interactive media are *personal audience venues,* as we discussed in Chapter 12. That means one on one. So cost per thousand, rating points, and share of audience don't really mean the same things in the interactive world. With interactive media, we're not always building sales volume. We're building relationships, one customer at a time. And the care companies exercise in buying and developing their interactive programs and integrating them with their mass media programs will determine their overall success.

Currently, the leading national advertisers spend a small piece of their marketing communications pie on interactive media—less than 15 percent of their budgets. However, it still is the fastest-growing segment. Online advertising spending grew to a record 23.4 billion in 2008.[11] Exhibit 15-7 lists the top 10 Internet advertisers ranked by spending. The best marketers are testing extensively. That means being willing to lose money for a while, which is, of course, not exciting to most advertisers or agencies. Many direct marketers are investing heavily in online catalogs. Some places like Dell Computers (www.dell.com) generate several million dollars from online sales each *day*.

Pricing Methods

Advertising space on the Internet can be purchased in several different ways, as we will discuss later in the chapter. The most common means is the banner ad, typically billed on a cost-per-thousand basis determined by the number of ads displayed. On most web pages, the base banner rate pays for exposure on a rotating display that randomly selects which ads to show.

The real marketing power of the Internet, however, is the ability to specifically target an audience in a way that is virtually impossible in traditional media. In addition to general banners, media buyers may opt to purchase more selective space. For example, ads may be purchased in a portal's information categories and subcategories, such as finance, news, travel, or games. Prices vary according to category and increase as the buyer targets a more selective audience. Costs are tiered according to thousands, hundreds of thousands, or even millions of page requests per month.

Another augmentation to the general banner purchase is the **keyword** purchase, available on major search engines. Advertisers may buy specific keywords that bring up their ads when a user's search request contains these words. Keywords may be purchased individually or in packages that factor in the information categories and subcategories of a search engine site. In the early days of the Internet, some "keyword entrepreneurs" purchased large numbers of keywords from the search engines. They were later able to license these words to third parties at a substantial profit. This model has since changed to a bidding model, effectively

Exhibit 15-7

Top 10 U.S. Internet advertisers.

Rank	Company	Estimated Spending (Millions)
1	TD Ameritrade Holding Corp.	$262.9
2	Experian Group	250.4
3	FMR Corp. (Fidelity Investments)	242.6
4	Sprint Nextel Corp.	241.1
5	General Motors Co.	240
6	E-Trade Financial Corp.	191.2
7	Walt Disney Co.	186.9
8	Scottrade	181.8
9	Netflix	177.6
10	Verizon Communications	169.2

Source: AdAge www.adage.com/datacenter.

killing keyword "entrepreneurs." We will go into more depth on these issues later in this chapter.

Some publishers will charge their clients according to **click-throughs**—that is, when a user actually clicks on a banner ad to visit the advertiser's landing page. Although the CPM for simple impressions is considerably lower, this method is still unpopular with publishers. When an advertiser buys on a per-click basis, the publisher may expose many users to an advertiser's banner message without being able to charge for the service.

For advertisers involved in e-commerce, some publishers offer an **affiliate marketing program** whereby they charge a percentage of the transaction cost. For example, a site devoted to music reviews may have a banner link to an online music retailer. When consumers buy music from the retailer, the site publisher receives a percentage of the sale for showing the banner.

The Cost of Targeting

The very selective nature of the Internet can, for additional cost, be combined with tracking technology to be discussed later. This makes for a very focused campaign. Companies such as Tacoda work behind the scenes to meet the advertiser's CPM guarantees by using software that directs specific ads to a highly selective audience. Because Tacoda technology "tags" users, it can build a consumer profile and show those ads that are likely to be of the greatest interest to that specific web user.

But contrary to popular belief, consumer targeting on the Internet is very cost intensive. While it is true that millions of people do indeed scour the Net each day, it is still difficult to find and reach the specific consumers that you want. Thus, prices for precise Internet business-to-business targeting can eclipse even those of direct mail.

Stretching Out the Dollars

One of the problems facing most Internet marketers is how to get enough reach from their advertising. The enormous numbers of users who utilize the major search engines make these sites attractive for advertisers. However, web browsers surf millions of other web pages each day, many of which are potential sites for effective ads. Contacting all these sites and negotiating advertising contracts on each is a nearly impossible task.

For this reason, most advertisers work through **ad networks,** which act as brokers for advertisers and Websites. Ad networks pool hundreds or even thousands of web pages together and facilitate advertising across these pages. The advantage is that this allows advertisers to gain maximum exposure by covering even the smaller sites. The drawback is that such advertising is more difficult to monitor. Each site must be watched for traffic and content, which creates problems when trying to calculate costs. A few web masters have been known to try to cheat the system by artificially increasing the number of page requests. So, as with any medium, caution is always the watchword.

Types of Internet Advertising

The nature of the Internet is a constant state of evolution. Therefore advertisers have new and interesting ways to reach target audiences that extend beyond the more standard ad placements (see Exhibit 15-8). We will discuss the less fluid advertising elements first and then look at the ways in which the medium is continuing to grow. In approaching this topic we will work our way back up the generic online "sales funnel." The Internet is truly unique as a medium in its ability to lead directly to sales so we will approach the section in that way, but beware of pigeonholing the Internet as a direct marketing medium. It has often been said that the accountability factor is not only the Internet's saving grace, it is also the bane of its existence. (See the Portfolio Review on page 480 for different online creative executions discussed in this section.)

WebSites, Microsites, and Landing Pages

The technical definition of a **Website** is a collection of web pages, images, videos, or data assets that is hosted on one or more web servers, usually accessible via the Internet. Wikipedia.com lists 22 different types of Websites. We will be primarily referencing two:

Ethical Issues

Who's watching you?

It is safe to assume that a large percentage of the readership of this book, by virtue of the fact that it is a college-level textbook, fall within the adult 18–24 demographic. This isn't hard to extrapolate, nor is it all that intrusive to the reader that someone somewhere has this information. However, if the knowledge were much deeper, and that someone knew where you were from, what your marital status is, what college you are attending, if you are female or male, and what type of cologne or perfume you like, that might be a bit scary. If the information could go even deeper, well that would perhaps be unsettling.

It is just these types of feelings that drive the consumer privacy issues online. Throughout this chapter we've highlighted the various ways in which consumers can be targeted and messaged online. This is all possible due to a few lines of code called cookies that track, categorize, and filter your every click.

Companies like BlueKai, an online behavioral data company, supply marketers with access to consumers online who have exhibited behavior that match their intended target audience. For instance, if Audi wanted to be within the consideration set of a potential new car buyer, they would pay BlueKai a fee to identify and target all of those people that have exhibited such behavior—recently went to an auto Website, spent a lot of time on that site, and has frequently returned over a specific duration. Companies like BlueKai can even suggest what type of car the person is interested in, so Audi could potentially buy all of the BMW "Auto Intenders," as classified by BlueKai.

Companies like BlueKai partner with large Websites, like Expedia.com, which allows them to (a) capture this data, (b) mine it for insights, (c) organize and categorize the information, and (d) sell it to advertisers. In exchange, BlueKai shares the information and the revenue it creates with their partners. This allows their partners to have multiple revenue streams and do a better job of classifying their monthly Internet traffic that they too sell to advertisers.

While trying to understand consumer purchase behavior by tracking activity is not new—credit card companies have engaged in these practices selling their data to direct mail fulfillment houses—the amount of personal data and the ability to predict from that data is what has some people leery about the process. The insight into people's traffic patterns has sparked much debate over what is and what isn't intrusive to the consumer. When polled, 62 percent of consumers say they do not want their activities to be tracked online. However, behaviorally targeted advertising is some of the highest performing online ads. So how does a marketer make heads or tails of this, as consumers are clearly more interested in the targeted advertising, but don't trust the way in which that information is gathered, and perhaps used.

To further complicate the issue, when an advertiser also has a web property that has high monthly visitation, like Amazon.com, then the question of who owns the data arises. While most argue that the data of any individual is owned by that individual, there are no clear directions to the consumer, nor are there any industry-wide practices, that allow customers to turn off access to this data by advertisers. The savviest of online consumers turn off their cookies, however by doing so they limit the ability of the Internet to truly personalize their experience. Amazon.com's recommendation engine is a very good example of this. If you subscribe to the Amazon.com newsletter and spend a few minutes and a few pages looking for a particular type of item, say barbeques, but don't purchase. Then within a few days Amazon.com's

corporate and commerce sites. A corporate site is used to give background information about an organization, product, or service. A commerce site is used primarily to sell a product or service. Of course there is a fine line between these definitions; for companies like Amazon.com the corporate site is the commerce site and vice versa. Good marketers look at their Website as more than the above definitions. They understand that the Website is an extension of the brand and that the Website experience is synonymous with a brand experience. Knowing that not all corporate sites are quite up to snuff to deliver on this brand extension, many marketers use microsites and landing pages to circumvent this issue and deliver the desired experience.

A **microsite** is used as a supplement to a Website. For advertisers it is typically singular in focus and delivers on the current advertising message. For instance, when Electronic Arts (EA) launched the *Return of the King* video game after the very popular movie trilogy *The Lord of the Rings*, it had Freestyle Interactive build a robust microsite that gave users cheats, codes, game screens, and exclusive videos and also gave users a chance to win a replica sword from the movie. The kicker was that to unlock the content, users actually had

Exhibit 15-8
U.S. Online ad spending share, by format, 2011–2016

% of Total and billions						
Rank	**2011**	**2012**	**2013**	**2014**	**2015**	**2016**
Search	48.0	49.4	49.2	48.1	47.6	46.9
Banners	24.1	23.4	22.6	21.8	21.1	20.5
Video	6.3	7.9	9.8	12.1	13.6	15.0
Classifieds and directories	7.8	6.4	5.7	5.3	5.2	5.2
Lead generation	5.1	4.9	4.9	4.8	4.7	4.6
Rich media	4.9	4.2	3.8	3.6	3.4	3.3
Sponsorships	3.4	3.5	3.7	4.0	4.1	4.2
E-mail	0.4	0.4	0.3	0.3	0.3	0.3
Total	$32.03	$39.50	$46.50	$ 52.80	$57.50	$62.00

Source: Data from eMarketer.com

e-mail communications will miraculously be filled with barbeques, some of which you looked at, some of which are recommended to you. It must be known that Amazon.com works from a registered user base, thereby not utilizing cookies to track behavior but uses user sessions instead. However, the example still applies for the thousands of Websites who practice something similar without ever registering for the site. Like.com (now owned by Google) was one such site. If you looked for a watch on their site but did not purchase, incredibly a banner ad displaying the last item you looked at would appear on your Yahoo! Mail login screen within minutes.

The Federal Trade Commission (FTC) has been investigating the issue, much like they did in the early 2000s when they ultimately passed the CAN-SPAM act, making it illegal to spam—send e-mail without permission. In late 2011, the FTC issued a privacy report that called for a "do not track" system to be put in place. Since that announcement all major browser software companies have supported the issue. What it means is that the default setting on browsers will have a header call (DNT:1) identifying that this individual wishes to not be tracked when they arrive at a Website. However, the directive of this header call can only be acted upon by the server of the Website, which makes the system as a whole honor-based. This means that Websites, as of this writing, are not legally bound to take action on the browser header call, and since very few consumers even understand this, most Websites do not comply.

Evidon, a privacy technology company, was founded to help consumers and business see, understand, and control data online. Their technology makes it easier for companies to comply with the "do not track" system, and insure that companies are maintaining a healthy consumer-focused set of privacy policies. As the debate and awareness continues to build, companies like Evidon will be important for brands and publishers to align with. Jon Leibowitz, the Chairman of the FTC, thinks that more privacy will actually be more lucrative for the online industry. However, not everyone agrees, especially those that can't see a better technology than cookie-based tracking. However, almost everyone would agree that consumer trust is paramount in the long-view of revenue generation. What do you think?

Questions:

1. Why would companies want to track everyone's online behavior?

2. Think of the last five Websites you were on, what did you look at? How do you think advertisers could use that information to better target you?

3. Has the online media industry taken tracking too far? Do you think it is okay, or not okay to watch people's behavior online?

Sources: Abbey Klassen, "Behavioral Targeting Might Scare Consumers Less if we Did a Better Job Explaining it," *Ad Age Blogs*, October 17, 2011 http://adage.com /article/abbey-klaassen/behavioral-targeting-scare-consumers-job-explaining /230431/ Do Not Track, Wikipedia.org, http://en.wikipedia.org/wiki/Do_Not_Track Colleen Taylor, "FTC Chairman Leibowitz: More Privacy Could Actually Bring Bigger Revenue for Web Giants, *TechCrunch.com* May 31, 2012 http://techcrunch .com/2012/05/31/ftc-chairman-leibowitz-do-not-track-effects-on-advertising / About Evidon, May 31, 2012 http://www.evidon.com/about/index

to go on an Internet-based scavenger hunt to find four pieces, or shards, of the sword. Each piece unlocked more content until the sword was "reforged" and the user could open the cheats and enter to win the replica sword. The microsite was able to identify how many pieces each user had found due to the ability to store and read data on cookies placed on the user's browser.

Any web page can be a **landing page**—the term used to describe direct links to deeper areas of the Website that advertising drives consumers to beyond the homepage. Typically advertisers use landing pages to give consumers a more relevant experience as it relates to the message from the advertising. For instance, if someone searches for "men's dress pants" on Google, Dockers wants to send them directly to the *men's apparel* section, and more specifically all the way to the pants page, rather than making the user click two or three more times just to find the relevant products. Advertisers use landing pages to streamline the selling or information-gathering process, as studies have found that people's attention spans are limited online. If they cannot find what they are looking for right away, they may be lost forever. Consumers are fickle and anything to help them on their online journey is typically a smart approach.

Search Engine Marketing

Most people looking to find information on the web now use a **search engine.** Search engines are Websites that allow people to type a word or phrase into a text box and then quickly receive a listing of information on a **search-results page.**

Exhibit 15-9

Percentage of online searches by search engine used, December 2011, as reported by comScore Search.

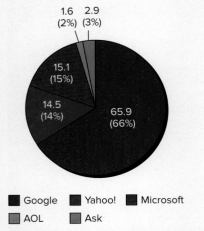

- ■ Google
- ■ Yahoo!
- ■ Microsoft
- ■ AOL
- ■ Ask

Source: ComScore Release April 2009, U.S. Search Engine Rankings, retrieved from www.comscore.com/Press_Events/Press_Releases/2009/5/comScore_Releases_April_2008_U.S._Search_Engine_Rankings.

In the late 1990s, several companies competed to be the leading brand for searches. For now, there is a clear winner: Google (see Exhibit 15-9). Moreover, the story of how Google used a superior search capability to become one of the fastest-growing and most profitable companies in the world offers important lessons for advertising on the Internet.

Like most other people, when Google's creators, Sergey Brin and Larry Page, first met at Stanford, they did not know how search could be profitable either. But at the time, profits were not their main interest. Brin and Page were interested in helping users find information and believed they had a better system for doing so.

The two created an algorithm, eventually named *Pagerank,* that analyzed the links and relationships of Internet sites to come up with rankings. When a keyword is entered in a search, Google looks for Websites that mention the word. This is no different from what many of their early competitors did. But in addition, Google analyzes Website links in order to determine what sites are considered useful. Consider two sites that each use the term *marketing* five times. If a web user used *marketing* as a search term, Google's search engine would locate both sites on its servers. But which site should be listed relatively high, where it will be viewed quickly, and which should be listed much lower? This is where Pagerank comes in. Sites that many other sites link to are assigned higher Pageranks and end up relatively high in search results. For example, if 20 Websites link to one of the two marketing sites and just one links to the other, the first site will get a more prominent listing. The algorithm also analyzes the quality of the links. Specifically, sites with especially popular or authoritative Websites linking to them get very high Pageranks. The net result of this is a fast search engine that returns remarkably relevant search results.

Because the company created a better search engine, Google was able to attract growing numbers of web users. However, throughout the 1990s it lacked a clear way to make money from the search mechanism. Like many companies at the time, Google sustained itself on venture capital. After the dot-com bust of the early 2000s, Google investors strongly encouraged Brin and Page to develop a revenue model. Their response was two advertising programs, AdWords and AdSense. It is difficult to overstate how successful these programs have been, because in a few short years Google has used them to create an annual revenue stream approaching nearly $80 billion.

AdWords

Do a search on Google and you will notice that search results are not the first thing you encounter on the results page. The first listings are in a light-blue shaded area that is described as "Sponsored Links." The two sponsored links at the top and all of the sponsored links on the right are not search results, but rather paid listings. For advertisers there is really no better place to put a message. There is no other environment that allows advertisers to gain such insight into what consumers are thinking while at the same time placing a targeted advertisement in front of that consumer. For instance, if you are working for Dockers and you are targeting men seeking business attire, where do you spend your money? On a magazine ad that may or may not get in the hands of someone thinking about clothes or on an AdWords placement for the word *dress pants?*

Google's search results page is thus composed of two distinct areas: search results, which are organic (unaffected by sponsorship), and **sponsored links.** Google's sponsored links have three important characteristics. First, advertisers do not pay just for being seen, a common practice with banner ads. Instead, advertisers pay Google only when a search engine user clicks on the link and visits the sponsor's site. This performance-based pay-per-click model has proven very attractive to advertisers. Second, the amount that an advertiser owes for each click-through is not actually set by Google. Instead, it is determined in an auction, where companies can bid for keywords used in search, such as the term *marketing.* Higher bids generally lead to better listings, such as those located on the first search results page and located near the top of the page. These are locations where the search engine user is most likely to see them. Holding true to their relevancy algorithm for organic searches, Google adds one additional twist to their AdWords: the ranking of sponsored listings is not completely

Source: Yahoo! Inc.

Apps are another digital advertising platform. These are some of the most honored apps of 2014.

Source: Hidden Variable Studios

DEVICE 6

· CHAPTER 1 ·

Awakening

There was

ɐuu∀ glanced at the paintings as she wal

12

Anna was facing a huge steel door, that looked decidedly out of place and more fitting to some kind of bomb shelter. In front of it was a screen apparently displaying the output of a security camera. With no handle, she pushed herself against the door, even though she knew it would not budge.

She took a few steps back and turned around.

Source: Simogo

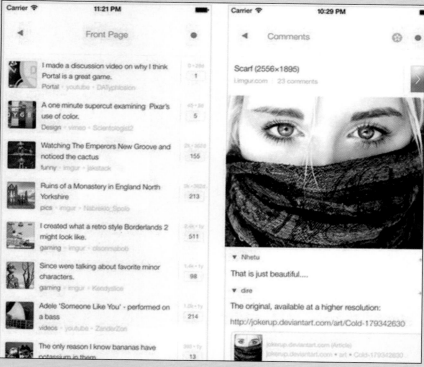

Here are two more award winning apps, from Simogo and reddit.

Source: reddit inc.

The highly interactive nature of AirBnB's site ensures that customers come back often.

Source: Airbnb, Inc.

Southwest's award-winning heart campaign has its own microsite.

Source: Southwest Airlines Co.

Vogue's challenge is clear: as a brand known for fashion it must have a Website that reinforces the magazine's reputation for taste, beauty, and design.

Source: Vogue

Coca Cola encourages recycling at its Ekocycle site.

Source: The Coca-Cola Company

Google's famously sparse search site may not garner artistic awards. But it is the starting point for over a trillion searches each year and digital commerce is hard to imagine without it.

Source: Google

(continued from page 475)

Universal Ad Package, a suite of 16 standard ad sizes (including skyscrapers, rectangles, pop-ups, banners, and buttons) designed to improve the efficiency and ease of planning, buying, and creating online media.

Similar to banners are **buttons,** small versions of the banner that often look like an icon and usually provide a link to an advertiser's landing page, a marketing tool that leads people into the purchasing or relationship-building process. Because buttons take up less space than banners, they also cost less.

The advancements in Adobe's Flash have greatly enhanced the once-static banner and button ads. Full motion, animation, and user interaction, for example, are now commonplace. In fact, one of the greatest areas of recent growth has been **rich-media advertising,** which includes graphical animations and ads with audio and video elements that overlay the page or even float over the page. Many of the rich-media ads complement the standard banners endorsed by the IAB, as each of these can display 15-second animations.[13]

Some of the more common types of rich-media ads include animated banners, interstitials, Superstitials, and preroll. The **interstitial** is a catchall term for a variety of ads that play between pages on a Website, popping up on the screen while the computer downloads a Website that the user has clicked on. All of their various formats tend to perform well in terms of click-through rates and brand recall—which is what the advertisers care about. The Superstitial is actually a trademark of Unicast, now owned by Viewpoint. The Superstitial makes use of a "polite download" technology to push ads into a web browser's cache only when the computer's bandwidth is idle; the ads then play from the cache when the user requests a new web page. With polite download technology, the ad avoids tying up bandwidth when the user needs it. The standard Superstitial ad is quite large and plays for a long period of time (up to 20 seconds). The size and playing time of this type of ad are similar to television ads, making them as rich as any experience available online.

Rich mail, on the other hand, allows graphics, video, and audio to be included in the e-mail message. When you open up a rich e-mail, your e-mail client automatically calls up your Internet connection and launches an HTML page in your e-mail window. E-mail clients

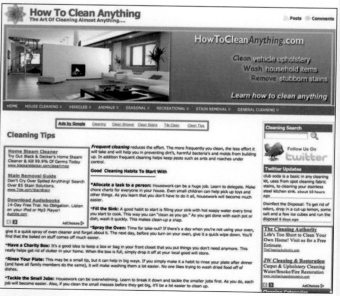

Google's advertising revenue comes primarily from two sources: AdWords (left above) and AdSense (right above). AdWords generates revenue when web users click sponsored links during search. AdSense does the same when users visit Websites that are part of Google's program.
Source: Google

Nothing demonstrates the web's power better than sites that offer the helping professions ways to improve their efforts. The site teAchnology is one such web destination. Teachers can find thousands of lesson plans and worksheets, as well as teaching tips and themes. Revenue from advertising helps keep the site fresh and easy to use.

Source: 2015 Teachnology, Inc.

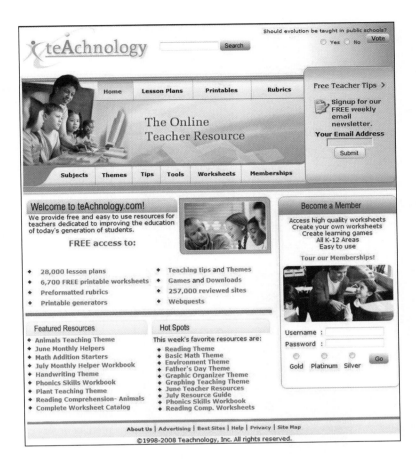

that are offline will invite you to click on the link when you have your Internet connection open again. If your e-mail client does not support graphics, you will receive the e-mail in text only. We can anticipate seeing more audio and animation integrated into these ads as improving technology accommodates them.

Preroll is now a fast-growing advertising segment. With more bandwidth comes the consumption of more video entertainment online, and companies such as Broadband Enterprises and YuMe Networks are trying to capitalize on this by aggregating much of this content and placing 5-second to 30-second video advertisements as a **third-party ad server.** How is this different from TV? As we discussed previously, the Internet's ability to hypertarget is one of the many ways it sets itself apart. So, imagine if you could get the great qualities of TV advertising—sight, sound, and motion—to a highly targeted audience, at prices lower than those of TV.

Sponsorships and Added-Value Packages

A form of advertising on the Internet that is growing in popularity is the **sponsorship** of web pages. Corporations sponsor entire sections of a publisher's web page or sponsor single event for a limited period of time, usually calculated in months. In exchange for sponsorship support, companies are given extensive recognition on the site. Sometimes an added-value package is created by integrating the sponsor's brand with the publisher's content, as a sort of advertorial, or with banners and buttons on the page.

IBM has exclusively sponsored the Super Bowl web page, at an estimated cost of $1 million for each event. Other forms of sponsorships have included web serials, site devoted to women's issues, contests, and giveaways.

IKEA garnered worldwide praise for its banner campaign "Smallest Store in the World," which featured a tiny banner that connects users to the enormous IKEA shopping site.

Source: Ikea

Crispin Porter + Bogusky struck gold with its web campaign for Virgin Atlantic Airways (www.virgin-atlantic.com), which won a Pencil (a prestigious ad award) at the One Show Awards. The lighthearted banners deliver the benefits of Virgin's services and keep to the brand's playful, cheeky tone.

Source: Virgin Atlantic Airways

Classified Ads

Another growing area for Internet advertisers, and an excellent opportunity for local advertisers, is the plethora of **classified ad Websites,** like Craigslist. Many of these offer *free* classified advertising opportunities because they are typically supported by ad banners of other advertisers. In style, the classifieds are very similar to what we are all familiar with from newspapers. You can search for homes, cars, jobs, computer equipment, business opportunities, and so on. Moreover, the search can be narrowed to your city or expanded nationwide. Many of these sites are sponsored by the search engines themselves or by local newspapers around the country.

E-Mail Advertising

According to *Forbes's* "2009 Ad Effectivness Study," 74 percent of marketers send **e-mail advertising** to customers who have asked for it. Marketers have always known that direct-mail advertising (discussed in Chapter 18) is the most effective medium for generating inquiries and leads and for closing a sale. It's also been the most expensive medium on a cost-per-exposure basis. Now, thanks to the Internet, the power of direct mail is increased even more, and the cost is reduced dramatically.

A word of caution, though: It's important to differentiate responsible e-mail advertising from **spam,** which is really just electronic junk mail. Spam generally refers to unsolicited, mass e-mail advertising for a product or service that is sent by an unknown entity to a purchased mailing list or newsgroup. Spammers face the wrath of frustrated customers, tired of having their inboxes filled with unwanted e-mails. Since January 2004, spammers also face litigation under the CAN-SPAM Act (Controlling the Assault of Non-Solicited Pornography and Marketing). Legitimate e-mail advertisers are required to (1) clearly mark the e-mail as advertising, (2) provide a valid reply-to e-mail address, and (3) allow recipients to opt out of future mailings. The first lawsuits under the act were filed in April 2004 against two companies that had sent nearly a million e-mails advertising bogus diet patches and growth hormones.[14] With this in mind, wary marketers are focusing their e-mail efforts on **customer retention and relationship management (CRM)** rather than on prospecting.

One of the hottest trends on the Internet today actually started as an application of e-mail, but has been enhanced by social media. Thanks to *viral marketing,* Amazon.com, Napster, eBay, Blue Mountain Arts, and Hotmail all made it big on the web, reaching unexpected heights in short time spans, most with surprisingly low marketing budgets.[15] **Viral marketing** is the Internet version of word-of-mouth advertising. The term was coined in 1997 by Steven Jurvetson and his partners at the venture capital firm Draper Fisher Jurvetson. They were describing free e-mail provider Hotmail's incredible growth to 12 million users in just 18 months through the use of a little message at the bottom of every e-mail.[16] The message invited recipients to sign up for their own free Hotmail account.

Since that time, many other marketers have come up with ways to induce their satisfied customers to recommend their product or service to friends and family members. One of the keys to viral marketing success is to present an offer with real perceived value—one that people will want to share with one another. Audible, a Website featuring digital audiobooks, for example, uses a referral program whereby members are rewarded with free books each time someone they refer to the site signs up and becomes a member. Since members enjoy the

My IMC Campaign 15–A

Using Interactive Media

Every medium offers unique creative options that media planners can incorporate into each campaign to help break through the clutter. However, no other medium has the same degree of flexibility as the Internet does. While the IAB has done a good job of setting banner ad standards, the development of new technologies continually pushes the boundaries of what advertisers can do online. In concert with technological advancements, now-standard technologies are also decreasing in cost.

For every new campaign, advertisers need to think about how each element of their online presence communicates the company's message. From the Website, to the banner advertisements, to social media, a brand appears on multiple online sites, and coordinating its image across all of them is time consuming. It can also be very creative and rewarding. Here is a list of avenues you should explore, but not limit yourself to, as you think about building your online campaigns:

- Website, microsites, and landing pages

- Search engine marketing

- Banner ads

- Rich media

- Social media

As you embark on the online portion of your campaign, think of the online platform as a blank canvas for you to meet your objectives. Start by determining the Website's purpose and move out into the online world. Think about what users will do after seeing your print or TV ads and how you will capture the interest and demand generated by that promotion. The Internet, while extremely important in your communication strategies, may not be the first place your audience notices your ads. However, remember that most online sessions start with a web search, whether that occurs on sites like Google or Yahoo!, or on the intended Website itself. So it is imperative that you have a good search strategy in place for all online activity.

To understand what sites your audience regularly uses, look to free services like Quantcast and/or Google AdPlanner as a means of identifying sites where you will want to advertise. When you plug in some information about your target at these sites, you will get a list of sites your intended audience frequently uses. This is a helpful guide in determining the appropriate venues to capture your target's mindshare. While the Internet is in a constant state of evolution, savvy marketers commonly use some technologies associated with it, such as rich media. *Rich media* is the term for web ads that have a high degree of interactivity or motion or that pull info directly from the advertiser's Website into the banner ad. Today rich media is so widely accepted that almost any site where you are thinking about advertising will be able to handle its creative demands. That wasn't always so, but companies with a long-standing history of producing great rich media executions, such as PointRoll, Eyeblaster, DART Motif, and Atlas Rich Media, have paved the way for turnkey solutions.

Last, think about ways to connect with loyalists of your brand in ways outside of push communications. How do you create a conversation with them and empower that audience to help you in your marketing efforts? We are speaking, of course, of social media. Does your brand warrant a Facebook page or a Twitter feed? If so, how will you use these arenas creatively and how will you incite participation and pass-along?

Online media can be fun, but they can also be daunting because the virtual sky is the limit. Remember to make sound judgments and to put yourself in the consumers' shoes. Are you asking too much of them with your online strategies, or will your approach resonate?

---

site so much, it's natural that they would want to share the pleasure with their friends and families. Another example is Blendtec's "Will It blend" series, which was started on Youtube .com (it can now be found at www.willitblend.com) and has brought a new consumer market to a blender company that formerly served industry. See the My IMC Campaign above to better understand interactive media and how to effectively choose the different types of online media.

Problems with the Internet as an Advertising Medium

 LO 15-6

The Internet, like any medium, has its drawbacks. It is not a mass medium in the traditional sense, and it may never offer mass media efficiency. Some marketers may decide it's too complex, too cumbersome, too cluttered, or not worth the time and effort.

Moreover, the Internet is not controlled by any single entity, so there may be no one to hold accountable. Security (e.g., for credit card purchases online) has improved, but it's still a problem for some. The technology for running television-quality video is still not in place, and the long-term cost of full participation in the Internet is anybody's guess. The final drawback is also one of the Net's greatest appeals: It is the most democratic of media—anybody can get on it and do or say just about anything. That's both good and bad.[17]

Using the Internet in IMC

As we discussed in Chapter 8, one of the keys to successfully developing an integrated marketing communications program is to promote purposeful dialogue between the company and its stakeholders. That is what interactivity really means. And that is where the Internet offers its greatest potential.

For the first time, customers and other stakeholders can truly respond to a company's media communications in real time, using the same channel for feedback that the company used for promotion. This means that even if a customer finds herself accidentally at the company's Website, she can commence a dialogue (relationship) with the company immediately if something there strikes her fancy. Of course, this also means that, if the Website triggers her memory of a less-than-satisfactory experience with the company, she can use the same mechanism for complaining. But that's actually good, because a customer who complains usually cares. And a complaint gives the company the opportunity to correct the situation and set things right. It also gives the company information on how to improve. Sophisticated marketers cherish complaints.

While all of this is well and good, it also brings up a new problem for marketers today. In the good-old days of simple mass media advertising, manufacturers placed their ads on network TV and went on about their business. The retailers took care of customers, so the manufacturers didn't really have to be concerned about them. In the new age of integrated marketing communications, that is no longer the case. Yes, the retailer is still there, but Ms. Consumer doesn't want to talk to the retailer. She's a pretty sophisticated person. She knows who makes the product and if she's got a complaint that's who she wants to talk to. So it's not good enough for companies to put up a pretty Website on the Internet and then walk away from it. It has to be staffed—daily—and it must be kept up to date—daily. If you go online on Sunday morning and check your local newspaper's Website for yesterday's baseball scores, you don't want to read about how your team got whipped Friday night. You already read about that yesterday. While this may seem obvious, the fact is that these problems still occur regularly, and they defeat the whole purpose of having an interactive location for your customers to visit. Realizing this, companies are now finally beginning to staff up. But this is very expensive—often requiring companies to double or triple their Internet budget with no increase in advertising exposure. So the decision to use the Internet for integration is a big one and cannot be taken lightly.

The Global Impact of the Internet

The United States overwhelmingly outspends the rest of the world in Internet advertising. However, in only three countries—Norway, Sweden, and the United Kingdom—is the share of online ad spending 10 percent or greater. By 2009, ZenithOptimedia predicts that Australia, Canada, Israel, Japan, South Korea, Taiwan, and the United States will join that club.[18] Online marketing and advertising budgets will soon rival the amounts spent on radio and outdoor spending, at about 8 percent of all advertising expenditures.

Currently, the United States enjoys fairly heavy international web traffic, caused mostly by a lack of telephone and Internet infrastructure and Websites overseas. International Websites also tend to remain primitive in design and function compared to U.S. competitors, which are strongly consumer oriented. Furthermore, the international appeal of U.S. brands, especially companies such as Coca-Cola and Disney, is strong.[19]

But as the Internet has increasingly become a household word, the content of Websites for local businesses overseas will also grow. Already Yahoo! has staked claim by servicing Japan, Germany, France, Norway, Sweden, Denmark, and Korea in their native languages. And while today most international web surfers are proficient in English, this can be expected to change. As local online markets grow, so will the number of non-English-speaking users.

With the growth of an overseas online market, we can anticipate that American companies will try harder to cater to the native population.[20] Expanding their horizons to encompass the whole world will be the key to businesses' success in the 21st century.

Other Interactive Media

In addition to the Internet, advertisers now also use other new media vehicles, such as interactive TV and mobile advertising. While they are not major media forms, they do warrant some brief discussion.

Craigslist provides Internet users a free marketplace to buy and sell products. The rapid growth and dramatic success of such sites have come at the expense of newspaper classified sections.

Source: Craigslist Inc.

Interactive TV

Imagine you're watching Empire and a spot for State Farm Insurance appears. You remember you're not happy with your current insurance carrier. You pick up your remote control and click it on a box in the corner of the screen: "For more information." A menu appears. You click on "Auto insurance," and a multimedia presentation begins. At various prompts, you click your remote to get more information. At the end you request the location of a State Farm agent. The directions print out on a PC printer attached to your TV. Then it's back to Empire.[21]

Although this rosy scenario fills the dreams of many advertisers, the reality is not nearly so encouraging. **Interactive TV** is powered by digital video recorders (DVRs, sometimes also called *personal video recorders*). In 2003, interactive TV, provided by companies such as TiVo and DirecTV, reached 3.2 million U.S. households.[22] TiVo subscribers take full advantage of their commercial-skipping powers, zooming past three-quarters of advertisements in programs they have recorded.[23]

Experts predict that within a decade, interactive TV will be as common as cable is today. Accordingly, advertisers like Coca-Cola, Pfizer, and Chrysler are scrambling to innovate and adapt to the new medium, which compels them to reach consumers with advertising vehicles other than the traditional 30-second commercial. In particular, television advertisers are working to increase program sponsorship and product placement. Forrester Research asked television advertising executives how they might cope in a DVR-saturated environment. Exhibit 15-10 indicates that advertisers will respond by investing more money in TV to make their spots and sponsorships DVR-resistant. Other forms of advertising, like TiVo's "Showcase" feature, allow subscribers to access entertaining, long-format ads. For example, Best Buy sponsored a Rolling Stones concert segment in order to advertise the group's latest live DVD boxed set.[24] For the moment, however, because the percentage of interactive TV households remains so low, most advertisers are simply repackaging existing TV or Internet spots for the interactive TV format rather than investing in developing unique content.

The stand-alone digital kiosk provides businesses and municipal organizations with a new technology for communication and advertising. Kiosks today are used for a variety of purposes, ranging from the sale of train tickets to distribution of coupons, to renting DVDs.

© McGraw-Hill Companies, Inc./Mark Dierker, photographer

Exhibit 15-10

Responses of 133 national advertisers when asked "If large numbers of consumers could skip commercials while watching television, how would your advertising spending change, if at all, in each of the following types of programming?"

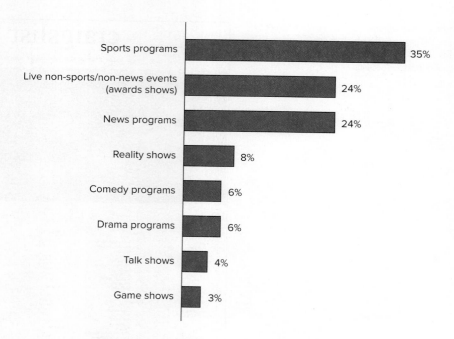

Sports programs	35%
Live non-sports/non-news events (awards shows)	24%
News programs	24%
Reality shows	8%
Comedy programs	6%
Drama programs	6%
Talk shows	4%
Game shows	3%

Mobile Advertising

When mobile advertising was first introduced, the carriers controlled a lot of the inventory as they limited the amount of traffic that went outside their **deck.** The deck refers to the content and experience that the carrier made available to their users when they loaded a web browser on their phones. This was due in large part to the carriers' desire to boost revenues from their own data services and not bog down their networks with massive data downloads from off-deck web surfing. However, iPhone has revolutionized the mobile phone business and the way consumers interact with their phones.

The iPhone has increased data plan usage, or non–voice-related consumption over the carriers' networks. iPhone users are 12 times more likely to use their phones for video and mobile TV.[25] Because of this increase, people are using their phones to download applications and games, surf the web, and send multimedia messages. All of this presents opportunities to advertisers. Typically these applications, which are now available for most smartphones and some feature phones, connect periodically to the network to check for updates, identify a person's location, or for games to connect one user with another. The appeal to advertisers is that unlike any other medium, the phone is the only real portable and personally identifiable medium.

While it still constitutes a relatively small share of all advertising globally, mobile ad spending continued its track record of double-digit growth in 2015.[26] The most common form of mobile advertising, banner advertising (also called WAP, Wireless Access Protocol, Banner), is very similar to online banner advertising. Banner advertising is standardized by the Mobile Marketing Association (MMA) which, much like the Interactive Advertising Bureau (IAB) for online banner advertising, has issued guidelines and standards for mobile web advertising (they can be found here: http://mmaglobal.com/policies/global-mobile-advertising-guidelines). Banner ads can also be placed into applications that have been downloaded to a user's phone, and can be swapped as those applications reconnect with the network.

The other form of advertising and the one that represents the largest inventory is sponsored SMS (Short Message System). Companies like 4INFO, in the United States, offer news, horoscopes, and sports scores, among other things, for free to users via SMS, and advertisers sponsor these messages. The carriers have set up very strict guidelines in the use of SMS and act as a gatekeeper for all messages that go over their networks in an effort to reduce SMS spam. A person can reply back to the SMS message to opt-in to the marketing message that has been displayed, or can go directly from that SMS, via a link, to a mobile web page.

People **BEHIND** the Ads

Courtesy of Brian Green

For just under 20 years now, Yahoo! has been a staple in the lives of numerous online surfers. So much so that it still has one of the largest daily reach vehicles on the Internet. On any given day well over 100 million unique users traffic Yahoo!'s pages, according to Yahoo!'s Advertising Solutions page. Name a TV program with that type of reach that doesn't involve helmeted players throwing a pigskin.

On nearly all Yahoo! pages you'll find an advertisement, and with all of those users turning multiple pages, the resulting amount of ad inventory is staggering. So staggering in fact that Yahoo! has a group dedicated to monetizing all that traffic. The group is called the Marketing Solutions Group and it's their responsibility to package, price, and present the opportunity to advertisers, working in conjunction with the client-facing sales team.

One of the men leading this group of skilled negotiators—and by that we mean internal negotiation, as they have to work with multiple groups to do their jobs, such as product, sales and yield management—is Brian Green, Senior Director, Property and Advertiser Solutions. Brian has been in the digital advertising industry since early 2000. His resume includes big brand agencies like Foote, Cone and Belding (now a part of Draftfcb), and publishers such as Fox Interactive Group and IGN. He's worked as a media planner, a digital sales representative, and a performance marketing specialist. Truly a well-rounded set of skills that make him just right for this group within Yahoo!.

Contemporary Advertising sat down with Brian Green to learn more about his role and how he faces the challenges of the fast-moving digital advertising industry.

CA: How does Yahoo! set their prices for advertising?

Brian: In most cases we act like most large Internet companies—we use a variety of tools that help price our products. From third-party research tools like ComScore and Nielsen, to proprietary programs and databases that give us a robust history on our prices and their respective fill rates. We use these tools to give us a healthy picture on our competition, supply and demand, and industry trends that may affect our rates.

In other cases, we are given objectives from our clients and our work is less analytical and more creative in how we package our various offerings together to truly achieve that objective. This is where knowledge, experience, and a little marketing know-how are actually more effective than the most efficient of CPMs (cost per thousand).

CA: What types of advertisers seem most interested in buying on Yahoo!?

Brian: Most advertisers are actually not classified by their industry categorization, for example auto, but rather by the tactics they are trying to achieve. Because of Yahoo!'s broad reach we are big enough to reach all advertisers' objectives and therefore have a healthy cross section of advertisers that include those trying to achieve branded metrics, direct marketing measures, and those that seek a hybrid approach—building brand through direct marketing methods.

This ability to work with advertisers of any ilk is what makes Yahoo! still, after all these years, a very relevant vehicle for brands. And because Yahoo! continues to innovate and push the envelope, we have been able to maintain a healthy audience at a time where audiences migrate to the next big thing, seemingly daily.

CA: Your homepage is one of the most expensive one-day advertising placements on the web, why can you continue to sell it at such a high out-of-pocket cost?

Brian: Yahoo!'s stable and massive one-day reach makes it unique to the Internet. Most web properties accrue their reach over a 30-day period. Very few properties can actually give an advertiser tens of millions of eyeballs with one advertising placement. Because of that, the out-of-pocket is definitely high, but what we have found is that our rate is actually extremely competitive.

CA: How do you feel you help advertisers meet their objectives better than your competition?

Brian: Because of Yahoo!'s size it's difficult to point to just one thing as the reason we are so unique. Saying that we have invested a lot of time and money in ensuring that we have a unique mix of ad products such as search, targeted content, and ad exchanges, along with a unique programing and content strategy that gives ample opportunity for advertisers of all objectives.

CA: Lastly, with so many people using phones and tablets to access Yahoo!, how does Yahoo! handle cross channel engagement?

Brian: Like any other brand, it's important for Yahoo! to think of their users and their customers in an integrated way, therefore we provide an integrated sales process that is solution-oriented to meet the needs of the advertisers. We also have been very bullish on our distribution strategies ensuring that our users can access all of the Yahoo! content in a variety of ways within a robust set of Internet-enabled devices such as mobile phones, tablets, and even on Internet-connected TVs.

QR codes, mobile coupons, and video present other opportunities, but are still not readily available to the masses as each phone needs to have functionality or a software/application that will allow it to interact and use these emerging technologies.

Chapter Summary

Digital interactive media, which include online database services, the World Wide Web, interactive television, and mobile advertising represent a revolution in the making. From an advertising standpoint, these media offer an opportunity to develop customer relationships rather than volume. These media are still in flux, but they're growing at an exponential rate and offer an array of challenges and opportunities for advertising creativity.

The commercialization of the Internet really began with the commercial online services that offered a large subscriber base to potential advertisers. However, the Internet itself dwarfed the online services in potential since it reached so many people around the globe. Once web browser software became available, it made the Internet user-friendly to noncomputer specialists.

Similarly, search engines made sites on the World Wide Web available to PC users with just the click of a mouse. When people began

migrating to the web, so did advertisers. The first banner ad was sold by *Wired* magazine.

Web users tend to be upscale, college-educated men and women. This is an ideal target, especially for business-to-business advertisers. This group is rapidly broadening, which will make the web even more attractive to many mainline advertisers.

The most common types of online advertising are search, banners, buttons, sponsorships, interstitials, and classifieds. Like all media, the Internet has many advantages and disadvantages.

Most Internet advertising is sold by CPM. Some, though, is sold by click-through or results. Today the biggest advancements are in social media which present a relationship opportunity to brands never before realized. Mobile advertising is a burgeoning medium that presents advertisers the opportunity to reach on-the-go consumers.

Important Terms

ad networks, *471*

advertising impression, *469*

affiliate marketing
    program, *471*

banner, *475*

behavioral targeting, *469*

broadband, *466*

button, *482*

centralized networks, *462*

classified ad Website, *484*

click rate, *469*

click-throughs, *471*

composition, *467*

cookies, *467*

customer retention and relationship
    management (CRM), *484*

deck, *488*

distributed network, *461*

e-mail advertising, *484*

HTML, *464*

interactive TV, *487*

Internet, *461*

interstitial, *482*

keyword, *470*

landing page, *473*

microsite, *472*

preroll, *483*

protocols, *461*

rich mail, *482*

rich-media advertising, *482*

search engine, *473*

search-results page, *473*

spam, *484*

sponsored links, *474*

sponsorship, *483*

third-party ad servers, *468, 483*

viral marketing, *484*

web browser, *464*

web page, *464*

Website, *471*

World Wide Web (WWW), *464*

Review Questions

1. How did the Internet evolve to its present status as an advertising medium?

2. Which companies on the Internet receive the greatest amount of advertising revenue? Why?

3. What are the different ways of advertising online?

4. What are cookies, and what are they used for?

5. What are the different ways web publishers charge for advertising?

6. How would you describe the advantages the Internet offers advertisers over traditional media?

7. How does audience measurement on the web differ from that for traditional media?

8. What is the importance of interactive media to small advertisers?

9. What do best practices suggest that advertisers first do before engaging in social media?

The Advertising Experience

1. **Internet Advertising**

   Advertising banners on the Internet are akin to outdoor billboards and fill the information superhighway with advertising messages, corporate signage, and hyperlinks. Companies like DoubleClick (www.doubleclick.com) are flourishing as they introduce new and better ways of managing web advertising—helping advertisers feel more confident about the ad programs they place.

   Visit the following advertising-related sites on the Internet and discover more about this fast-changing segment of the advertising industry. Then answer the questions that follow.

   - DoubleClick: www.doubleclick.com
   - Clickz: www.clickz.com
   - iMedia Connection: www.imediaconnection.com
   - Interactive Advertising Bureau (IAB): www.iab.net
   - Internet Advertising Resource Guide: www.bannerreport.com
   - Jupiter Research: www.jup.com
   - mediapost: www.mediapost.com

   a. What group sponsors the site and what is the organization's purpose?

   b. What are the size and scope of the organization?

   c. Who is the intended audience(s) of the Website?

   d. What services does the organization offer Web advertisers?

2. **Designing a Banner Ad**

   X-Scream magazine, which is dedicated to extreme sports of all kinds, would like to dedicate some of its advertising budget to banner ads. Taking into account the target market this magazine would have, find three Websites its consumers might visit, and design a banner ad that would motivate them to learn more about (and subscribe to) the magazine.

3. Visit Dove's special Website, www.campaignforrealbeauty.com, and watch the ad featured there titled "Evolution." What do you think of the ad? What do you think are the advantages of placing the ad on the web? Where else on the Internet might you expect to find the ad?

4. In 2006 Dove asked visitors to its Website to open a free account and create a Dove ad. The company provided tools that allowed visitors to construct the ad easily at the site. The best ad was then featured in the 2007 Academy Awards program. What communications objectives do you think were behind this effort? What metrics do you think Dove used to gauge the success of this web initiative?

5. IKEA's Kitchen View Website is an innovative way to increase brand exposure. But do you think it ultimately sold more kitchen solutions? Make a case for why or why not.

6. Assume that you are an interactive media designer working on the Kitchen View project, and you have been assigned the task of developing a banner ad to promote the Website. What information would be essential to present? How might this be accomplished given the inherent limitations of banner ads?

Social Media

Learning Objectives

To explore how social media are changing the way that advertisers think about engaging with their audiences. Advertisers must understand how to effectively employ social strategies that enhance the relationships they have with their current and potential customers.

 studying this chapter, you will be able to:

LO16-1 Discuss how social media differs from traditional media.

LO16-2 Explain the various ways that social media can be used.

LO16-3 Discuss how social media have changed consumer's behavior.

LO16-4 Explain how to manage social media on behalf of a brand.

LO16-5 Define the different applications of social media.

#IceBucketChallenge

Mark Zuckerberg
Yesterday, Governor Chris Christie **challenged me to do the ALS Ice Bucket Challenge.**

I accepted his challenge, and now I'm challenging Bill Gates, Sheryl Sandberg **and** Reed Hastings **next.**

Shared with: 🌐 **Public**

Embed Video

Embed Post

Source: Facebook

This is the story of how the face of charitable giving evolved from Jerry Lewis to Mark Zuckerberg. And Bill Gates. Not to mention Justin Bieber, Dave Grohl, Patrick Stewart, Katie Perry, Tom Cruise, and over two million other individuals. ■ Americans are generous people. According to the National Philanthropic Trust, more than 95 percent of households give to charity and the average household donation is nearly $3,000. The total donated by Americans in 2014 was more than $358 billion, a record amount and a 7 percent increase over the previous year. ■ That said, many charitable organizations struggle to raise funds for a variety of notable causes and there is never enough. The Foundation Center estimates that there are more than 1.5 million charities and nonprofits in the United States alone. Standing out in such a large group is challenging, to say the least. ■ For many years the charitable organization with the most famous media presence was the Muscular Dystrophy Association (MDA). It's Labor Day Telethon, hosted for 55 years by Jerry Lewis, raised more than $2 billion in the fight against muscular dystrophy. ■ Far less well known than the MDA, the ALS Association also fights motor neuron disease. The Association specifically provides research funding and support to causes in the fight against amyotrophic lateral sclerosis (ALS), better known as Lou Gehrig 's Disease. The debilitating and ultimately fatal illness was named after the famous New York Yankee whose career and life was cut short by its devastation. Compared with MDA's $65 million haul from its 2008 telethon, the ALS Association managed to attract only $5 million in 2013. ■ The year 2014 looked as though it would be another fairly ordinary one for the ALS Association. Then something happened that seems, in retrospect, so unusual and unexpected that it resembles a Hollywood movie. The unusual happening was the "Ice Bucket Challenge."

■ How it started is a matter of some dispute. *Sports Illustrated* suggested that a former college baseball star Peter Frates got the whole thing going. Frates posted a video on Facebook in which he challenged friends to either donate to the ALS Association or pour a bucket of freezing ice water over their heads. They were then to challenge their friends to do the same within 24 hours. ■ For several months nothing big happened. But soon, some sports stars, including professional golfers and pro hockey players, issued their own Facebook challenges. In June, 2014, the morning program of the Golf Channel broadcast a live challenge, and in mid-July Matt Lauer did his own on NBC's "Today Show" at the request of former golfer Greg Norman. Still through the first week of August, 2014, Facebook posts about the challenge barely registered a blip. Then, toward the middle of the month, a tsunami of postings appeared. From just a few thousand videos, postings grew through the third week of August to easily exceed a half million in just one day. ■ The results were staggering. It was estimated that more than 2.4 million videos were posted to Facebook. As the campaign went on, many of the videos incorporated entertaining dimensions, as when Bill Gates created his own ice bucket challenge bucket-pouring machine. The viral nature of the video was aided by public callouts to others to join in.[1] ■ Since the original challenge was to either donate or pour ice water, you may be wondering what good this all did for ALS. Most people, it was clear, did both. They posted the icy videos and donated. In fact, donations to the ALS Association went from $5 million to $115 million in the United States alone, and the organization estimates that global contributions surged to more than $200 million. ■ Of course, the campaign was not without critics. Some argued that it distracted attention from other causes. Others wondered what pouring ice water had to do with educating the public about ALS. As for the association, excited about its success, it proactively posted information for donors about where the money would go and promised to revisit the campaign in 2015. ■ Is this a testament to the power of new media? The MDA must have thought so. In response to the success of the ALS Association challenge, the MDA announced it was retiring its long-running telethon and would be looking for new ways to engage with donors in the future.

Introducing Social Media

Throughout Chapter 15 we alluded to social media platforms such as Facebook, YouTube, MySpace, and Twitter. But what are social media? No doubt any of you reading this textbook have used some of them. In fact, most mainstream Websites have incorporated social media elements to gain more stickiness, an industry term that refers to the ability of a site to keep audience. More likely than not, each of you has either a Spotify profile or a Facebook profile, or both. These sites have been dubbed "social" for their ability to connect like individuals in a manner that has never been seen before. Social media replicate the real world without its geographic barriers.

Until recently, if you wanted to socialize with individuals who had similar likes and dislikes you would form clubs, such as a book club. However, you were limited to people who resided in your general vicinity, which would typically limit the size of the club. Social media allow people to "meet" virtually to discuss and share their interests with each other. You might ask why this is considered new if the Internet has been around for more than 15 years? That's a good question, and in fact some forms of social media have been utilized since the beginning of the commercial web.

But Facebook, Yik Yak, Instagram, and Snapchat have revolutionized the way we communicate with each other, allowing one person to broadcast, for lack of a better term, to his or her entire friends list—an accumulation of the people he or she knows who share some interest, whether

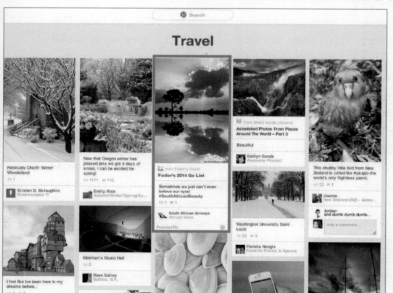

The visual beauty of Pinterest is reminiscent of the importance of design in traditional print media.
Source: Pinterest

it's related to work, politics, leisure, family, or other. Unfortunately for marketers, harnessing social media is not as cut-and-dried as it is for other forms of media, both digital and analog. In fact, most best practices suggest that a brand first listen to what is being said, rather than jump right into the social conversation. This can be easy enough to do because when someone writes a blog or microblog post, comments on another's blog, or bookmarks a page using Digg, that information is open for anyone to see. A host of tools collect all of this information using key words. Companies like Nielsen's BuzzMetrics or J.D.Power's Umbria Communications help marketers aggregate all the information being posted about their brands or products to understand the general consensus, negative or positive, about them. In turn, large advertisers like Electronic Arts, Coca-Cola, Virgin America, and Procter & Gamble all have a social media component to each brand or product they market. For marketers, then, social media go beyond promotion or advertising. In social media, people will interact with each product or brand differently, and the brand promise must really shine through.

Our Social Media Peronas

We noted in Chapter 15 how the web gave rise to the consumer as content creator. Social media platforms are the catalyst for this behavior change. Their value proposition is primarily centered on ease of use. Social media make it easier to maintain more friendships, to find people with similar interests, and to share information with friends. Used in conjunction with search engines, social media also make it easier to find content.

In a well-publicized research piece, Forrester Research described the many different ways in which consumers engage with social media. Exhibit 16-1 illustrates the seven user types

Exhibit 16-1

Seven user types identified by Forrester Research.

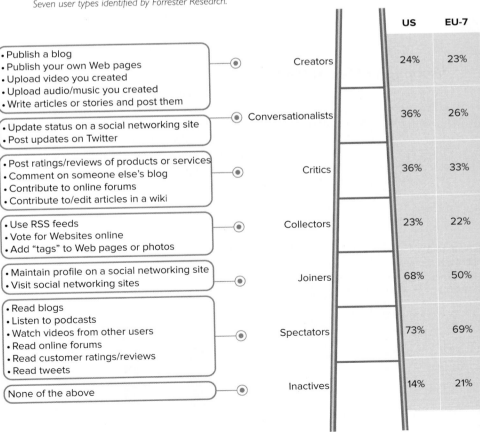

	US	EU-7
Creators	24%	23%
Conversationalists	36%	26%
Critics	36%	33%
Collectors	23%	22%
Joiners	68%	50%
Spectators	73%	69%
Inactives	14%	21%

Creators
- Publish a blog
- Publish your own Web pages
- Upload video you created
- Upload audio/music you created
- Write articles or stories and post them

Conversationalists
- Update status on a social networking site
- Post updates on Twitter

Critics
- Post ratings/reviews of products or services
- Comment on someone else's blog
- Contribute to online forums
- Contribute to/edit articles in a wiki

Collectors
- Use RSS feeds
- Vote for Websites online
- Add "tags" to Web pages or photos

Joiners
- Maintain profile on a social networking site
- Visit social networking sites

Spectators
- Read blogs
- Listen to podcasts
- Watch videos from other users
- Read online forums
- Read customer ratings/reviews
- Read tweets

Inactives
- None of the above

Source: Retrieved from www.mindjumpers.com/blog/2012/01/global-social-media-adoption-2011/.

identified by Forrester. From creators to inactives, each of us falls into a bucket that broadly defines how we use social media. Unlike traditional media, where consumption is inherently passive, social media consumption can be both passive and active.

Social Is More Than Media

Social media resist easy classification because they are as much technology as they are media and can take on many different forms, including magazines, forums, weblogs, social blogs, microblogs, wikis, podcasts, photographs or pictures, videos, ratings, and social bookmarking. As one author suggests,

> there are six different types of social media: collaborative projects (e.g., Wikipedia), blogs and microblogs (e.g., Twitter), content communities (e.g., YouTube), social networking sites (e.g., Facebook), virtual game worlds (e.g., World of Warcraft), and virtual social worlds (e.g., Second Life). Technologies include: blogs, picture-sharing, vlogs, wall-postings, e-mail, instant messaging, music-sharing, crowdsourcing and voice over IP, to name a few. Many of these social media services can be integrated via social network aggregation platforms. Social media sites are sites like Facebook, Twitter, Bebo and MySpace.[2]

The Rise of Social Media

Our need to feel connected to others is what drives the now mass adopted social media. While some advertisers are still struggling to figure out how to play in the social arena, most companies agree that success in social media is necessary for their brands. In some radical instances, companies have used social media as their main web presence, and have all but forgotten an actual Website. This is counterintuitive to how the Internet grew as a medium, however it makes sense given the characteristics of social media. Since all social media require a profile to engage, one could argue that the profile of a company is essentially the job of a corporate Website. If that were the case, then why would a company need multiple profiles? As you will learn in this chapter, social media is an open environment and for some companies that is a scary proposition. The lack of control defies how marketers were taught to protect the brand. Conservative or risk-averse brands find engaging in social media difficult and cumbersome, and young brands, like Zynga and Zappos.com (now owned by Amazon.com), are reaping the benefits.

Adoption of Social Media

The inherent nature of social media—the fact that they are social—thereby connecting and relating people to one another, helps explain their monumental rise in popularity. The media carry attributes that allow a single point, in any part of a system of connected points, to broadcast to the entirety of the system or network. The promise of social media has not been missed by advertisers. In 2013 it was estimated that social ad revenue was about $6.1 billion in the United States. That number is expected to hit nearly $10 billion in 2016 (see Exhibit 16-2). And a big reason for that growth is the power of social media in the technology that more and more people use to access the Internet: the smartphone.

Exhibit 16-2
Social Media Ad revenues.
Source: Douglas Karr, *Brief History of Social Media Advertising*, June 24, 2014, retrieved at: https://www.marketingtechblog.com/brief-history-social-media-advertising/.

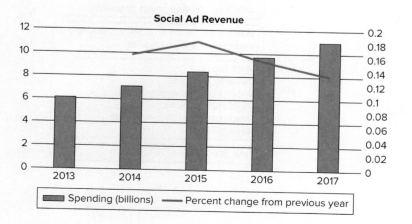

Exhibit 16-3

Demographics of Popular Social Media Platforms.

Source: Maeve Duggan, Nicole B. Ellison, Cliff Lampe, Amanda Lenhart and Mary Madden, "Demographics of Key Social Networking Platforms," Pew Research Center, January 9, 2015, retrieved at: http://www.pewinternet. org/2015/01/09/demographics-of-key-social-networking-platforms-2/.

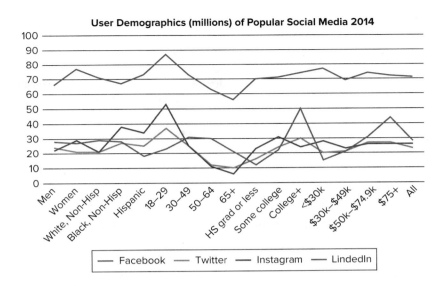

Another attraction of social media for advertisers is the ability to target. As can be seen in Exhibit 16-3, Facebook is popular among virtually all key demographics. Conversely, Instagram and LinkedIn have particular appeal to specific groups, the young and the well educated, respectively.

Despite its appeal, social media still poses risks for brands that don't "get" how to relate to their customers. In fact, one story of an advertiser's misfortune involved what seemed to be an innocent video advertisement. However, the Johnson & Johnson brand Motrin took a major hit with a very influential audience: "mommy bloggers." These women took offense to a small portion of the video that suggested that women "wear their babies" as if they were fashion statements. While the company was only trying to identify the physical effects of having to tote your baby in a wearable baby carrier, the mommy bloggers didn't appreciate the brand's tongue-in-cheek humor. Motrin felt forced to write an apology on its Website, pulling it off the air and losing millions in valuable media space.[3] Despite these misfortunes, brands are still actively engaged in social media and we will discuss later how advertisers are harnessing the power of social media platforms.

While Facebook is the king of the mountain (Exhibit 16-4 shows that Facebook owns a whopping 55% market share), it was by no means the first social site; most people are

Exhibit 16-4

Visit market share 2012–2015.

Source: 2015 data from Experian Marketing Services as reproduced at Marketingcharts.com, retrieved at http:// www.marketingcharts.com/updates/top-10-multi-platform-social-networking-websites-forumsjanuary-2015-50943/. The 2012 data from Experian Marketing Services as reproduced at Marketingcharts.com, retrieved at: www. marketingcharts.com/interactive/top-10-social-networkingwebsites-forumsmarch-2012-21698/.

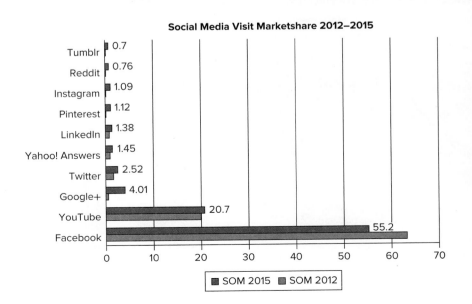

hard-pressed to identify the first social media Website that reached 50 million users, and are astonished to find that it came long before the time that is affectionately called **Web 2.0**. Where Web 1.0 was considered the static Internet full of pages and links, Web 2.0 is the social web, where everything is open and sharable. Have you thought of the answer yet? Alumni-focused social site Classmates.com reached 50 million users in the late 1990s. And it wasn't until 2002–2004 that social media really took off and companies like Friendster, LinkedIn, MySpace, and a small college-oriented social network named Facebook experienced their monumental growth. Another trend visible in Exhibit 16-4 is the new players in the social media space. Instagram, Tumblr, and Reddit were no-shows on the 2012 list while they are top-ten and growing in 2015. And while Facebook is the undisputed champ, its share of visits is shrinking.

Social Trends

In spite of Facebook's popularity, some still think the site, and even social media generally, is a fad. One poll by the Associated Press and CNBC stated that 51 percent of American adults believe that Facebook's appeal is just a fad.[4] These results came mere days before what was anticipated to be another historic initial public offering (IPO) from a web-based company. While many will debate for years the impact of the Facebook IPO, one thing is for certain: the IPO generated the most trading in history, causing havoc on the technology that performs the actual trades. So much so that Facebook had to pay back millions of dollars to some brokerages as a settlement for not being able to manage the volume of trading. Regardless of what may become of social media networks like Facebook, the reality is that social media technologies have infiltrated our lives and are a technological interpretation of our own natural behavior. That said, there are still flaws in social technology that limit its ability to imitate more complex human behavior, but the simple act of sharing, connecting, and keeping up with friends, family, and acquaintances thus far has made social networking the king of social media. Perhaps social media reign over traditional media, too, if you add up the sheer mass of global users that Facebook has attracted. At the end of March 2015, Facebook claimed 1.44 billion monthly users, 83 percent of whom are outside North America.[5]

Trending is a term used by tweeters to describe what people are talking, or tweeting about on Twitter. And as we mentioned earlier, because social media platforms are open, in some cases what's being tweeted isn't actually happening on Twitter but in a third-party tool, application, or Website. Facebook Connect and Twitter's open **application protocol interface (API)** means that any site, tool, or application can feed and extract information from the social network sites in accordance with how the user has granted permissions. For instance, if a person wants to find friends in her local area and see what they are doing, she might load up Foursquare on her iPhone and see where her friends have "checked-in." She might check-in too, and that information is then fed to Twitter or Facebook or both as a tweet or status update. But how did Foursquare know who her friends were? Easy, when our subject signed up for the service she used Facebook Connect. This allows her not to have to input any information on yet another site. It also allows Foursquare to see all the people she is connected with on Facebook, cross-referencing those friends with active Foursquare users and instantly attaching them to her account.

Twitter offers advertisers several programs to engage users, from modest efforts like Promoted Posts to expensive, cross-platform campaigns such as Promoted Trends. In the middle, and useful for gaining followers, is the Promoted Account campaign, illustrated here.

Source: McDonald's

Exhibit 16-5

Teen use of social media platforms.

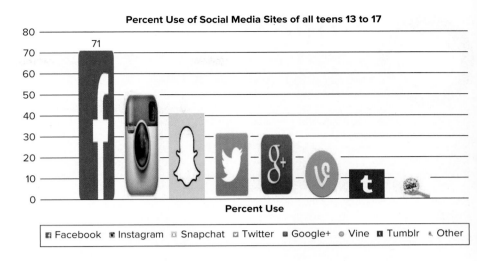

Who Uses Social Media

We've already established that social media are the fastest growing media in history, but that doesn't mean that every demographic is on board, Earlier, in Exhibit 16-3, we showed a broader demographic breakdown of social media sites. In Exhibit 16-5 above, we present usage rates for a group of increasing interest to advertisers: teens. As can be seen in the exhibit, Instagram and Snapchat have far more appeal with this group than with older age groups. This is important as brands begin to wonder if they should be actively participating in the media. Naturally, brands that cater to the older demographic are not so quick to adopt social practices. As the penetration continues to grow for the 65 and older segment, however, those same brands will quickly move to participate in social media.

Types of Social Media

Social media include any web- or mobile-based technology that is used for interactive communication between groups, communities, companies, and individuals. This broad definition helps explain why there are so many different types of technologies that fall under the social media umbrella. Worldwide there are over 2.8 billion social media profiles, which represents about half of all Internet users.[6] Here are some of the most common types of social media:

Forums

Forums are typically sections of sites that connect individuals around a specific topic. For instance, a Mustang forum will have users conversing about the iconic automobile. Some technology companies like Disqus and Livefyre actually connect people horizontally on different forums, meaning a user can manage one Disqus login for several forums on many sites about different topics. In 2011, monthly forum contribution declined significantly from the previous year, from 38 to 32 percent of total Internet users.[7]

Weblogs (Blogs)

A **blog** is a reverse chronological journaling site. Typically blogs are personal in nature; however, they have become so pervasive that some Websites use a blog format as their main page. Word-Press and Blogger (owned by Google) are two of the more common blog content management systems (CMSs). These CMSs are web-publishing tools that allow for nontechnical users to **post** content easily. Twenty-seven percent of global Internet users actively engage in blog-writing on a monthly basis.[8]

Ethical Issues

It's Not Always Nice to Share

If you are using this text for a college course, the popular social networking application Facebook needs little introduction. You already know all about it. Facebook has many users, over 900 million worldwide.

But it is especially popular on college campuses. This is due partially to its origins—while Facebook is now available to anyone over age 13, it was started with a focus on college students. In fact, when founder Mark Zuckerberg (see People behind the Ads, Mark Zuckerberg, in this chapter) launched the site in 2004, it was open only to members of his school, Harvard College.

What makes Facebook so irresistible? Certainly, highly addictive features like the "Wall," where friends can post messages, "pokes," and "status," and where there's lots of space for posting pictures, are part of the appeal. Users of Facebook can stay in touch with lots of people, almost in real time. The site is so addictive, in fact, that universities have begun trying to find ways to limit access during class hours.

So Facebook is a Website that is visited by young, influential, highly educated users who spend inordinate amounts of time at the site and are passionate about what they do there. Can you think of anyone who might be interested in that group?

Of course the answer is advertisers, and in fact, advertising has, from the beginning, been a part of Facebook. The costs of running and maintaining the site are defrayed by ads, which is why it is free for users.

Software giant Microsoft has an exclusive contract with Facebook to serve display ads. Microsoft sells space to advertisers, then pays Facebook for the opportunity to show ads on the site's pages. The particular ads that appear on a given page are determined by data collected by Microsoft. The goal is to place the right banner ad on the right page. As you know from Chapter 15, this is typical practice on the Internet, not only for Microsoft but for other large companies like Google and Yahoo!

But in November of 2007, Facebook launched a program that was anything but typical. "Beacon" was designed to let users share information about offsite activities, including purchases, with their friends. Here's how it worked, at least in theory. You join Facebook. Later you visit a different Website, like that of movie ticket vendor Fandango, and you buy a movie ticket. Just a short while later, your Facebook profile updates and tells your friends about the tickets you bought.

It was almost inevitable that Facebook would develop something like Beacon. That is because what excites advertisers about social networks like Facebook, even more than the desirable demographics, is the fact that people are busy influencing one another at the site. This is the real power of social networks, and the real draw for advertisers.

Recall our earlier discussion of Gladwell's The *Tipping Point*. Gladwell describes the power of a few influential people in starting social epidemics. Advertisers see Facebook as a place where influentials can share information about what they buy with many other people, potentially starting many such epidemics. This is why Zuckerberg has long claimed that Facebook would start an advertising "revolution." And not coincidentally, it is why some valued Facebook's worth to be in excess of $100 billion.

But from the start, Beacon was flawed. For one thing, even though third-party sites were supposed to inform Facebook users about what would happen when they bought at the site, it appears that some did not. So a Facebook user who bought something at Overstock.com was supposedly never told that Overstock was a member of the Facebook advertising network and that his or her purchase would be shared with friends.

Second, users did not "opt in" to the program (sign up for it), they had to "opt out" (cancel it). That virtually guaranteed that a lot of people would be unaware of how much information they were sharing with others. Eventually this was changed so that users had to opt in, but not before significant damage to Facebook's credibility had occurred.

Even worse, a software engineer discovered that even if Facebook users explicitly indicated that they did not want to share information

---

Blogs can also be multimedia in nature whereby the post is a photo or a video, like Flickr and YouTube. While some of the nomenclature describing the activities on these sites differs, in essence they feature the same easy-to-use web publishing format. However, in Flickr and YouTube the user creates channels rather than pages and uploads content rather than posting content. Uploading video has increased from 21 to 27 percent among global Internet users.[9]

Microblogs

A microblog, according to *PC Magazine,* is a blog that contains brief entries about the daily activities of an individual or company. The most popular microblog on the web today is Twitter. Much like blogs, **microblog postings** are organized in reverse chronological order, but users are allowed only 140 characters of text in their posts (or tweets). This allows for the transfer of small bits of information or content with many people at the same time, giving it a broadcast characteristic. The activity of updating a microblog has increased from 13 to 24 percent among global Internet users.[10]

about purchases, Facebook collected the information anyway. This turned out to be a practice that directly contradicted Facebook's publicly stated policies.

In the end, Zuckerberg decided that Beacon had to be changed. This was prompted by the bad press the program had received, the cancellation of several large advertisers, including Vodafone, Virgin Media, and Prudential, and several user-based petitions, including one organized by Moveon.org.

The founder posted an apology to users at the Facebook blog on December 52007. It read in part (go to http://blog.facebook.com/blog. php?post57584397130 to read the entire apology):

> About a month ago, we released a new feature called Beacon to try to help people share information with their friends about things they do on the web. We've made a lot of mistakes building this feature, but we've made even more with how we've handled them.... When we first thought of Beacon, our goal was to build a simple product to let people share information across sites with their friends.... But we missed the right balance. At first we tried to make it very lightweight so people wouldn't have to touch it for it to work. The problem with our initial approach of making it an opt-out system instead of opt-in was that if someone forgot to decline to share something, Beacon still went ahead and shared it with their friends. It took us too long after people started contacting us to change the product so that users had to explicitly approve what they wanted to share.... I'm not proud of the way we've handled this situation and I know we can do better. Thanks for taking the time to read this.

Zuckerberg was good to his word, and the program was changed. The modern incarnation of Beacon is far different from the version introduced in late 2007. For example, according to the Facebook site, "When [an advertiser sends information about a purchase] to Facebook, the user is immediately alerted . . . and will be alerted again when they sign into Facebook. The user must proactively consent to have [the information] from your Website published." This, of course, is a far cry from how things started.

So, for Zuckerberg and many Facebook users, the Beacon experience was a hard lesson learned. To Zuckerberg's credit, he acted fast and apologized for his mistakes when it became clear that users would not tolerate Beacon's privacy settings. Facebook continues to be one of the most popular (and valuable) locations on the web. And there is little doubt that advertisers will continue to search for ways to leverage the unique attributes of social networks for promoting their brands.

Questions

1. Why was Beacon created? Was it ethical to ask users to "opt out" rather than "opt in" to the program?

2. Think of a purchase you have recently made that you would not want shared with your friends. How would you feel about a site that did so without your explicit permission?

3. Did Facebook's missteps with Beacon amount to a poor business decision, or do you think that it rose to the level of being unethical?

Sources: Brad Stone, "Facebook Executive Discusses Beacon Brouhaha, New York Times Bits," http://hits.blogs.nytinles.cod2007/11/29/facebook-responds-to-beacon-brouha11a/; CA Security Advisor Research Blog, "Facebook's Misrepresentation of Beacon's Threat to Privacy; Tracking Users Who Opt Out or Are Not Logged In," http://community.ca.com/blogs/securityadvisor/archive/2007/l1/29/facebook-s-misrepresentation-of-beacon-s-theat-to-privacy-acking-users-who-opt-out-or-are-not-logged-in.aspx; Juan Carlos Perez, "Facebook's Beacon More Intrusive Than Previously Thought," *PCWorld*, www.pcworld.codarticle/id.140182-c.onlineprivacy/article.html; "Facebook Beacon," www.facebook.com/business/?beacon; "Leading Websites Offer Facebook Beacon for Social Distribution," www.facebook.conm./press/releases.php?p59166.

Wikis

A **wiki** is a user-collaborated content site, typically text in nature. Wikis allow the community to create, edit, or delete content. They are typically used to share knowledge across diverse groups of individuals. Wikipedia is the most well-known wiki.

RSS

Really Simple Syndication (RSS) is an old technology, by web standards, but can be used in many different forms to distribute content. It is the backbone for things like podcasts, vodcasts, or vlogs, and text-based headlines. RSS feeds benefit publishers by automatically syndicating content.

Social Bookmarking

A once-popular form of sharing content on the web, **social bookmarking** has recently declined in popularity. However, out of this form of social media came a very important

Exhibit 16-6

The top social networks based on unique visitors.

Site	Estimated Unique Monthly Visitors
Facebook	900,000,000
Twitter	310,000,000
LinkedIn	255,000,000
Pinterest	250,000,000
Google+	120,000,000
Tumblr	110,000,000
Instagram	100,000,000
VK	80,000,000
Flickr	65,000,000
Vine	40,000,000
Chinese Sites	
WeChat	350,000,000
Douban	80,000,000
RenRen	54,000,000

Source: ComScore, November 2011, http://en.wikipedia.org /social_networking.

categorization tool—tagging. Tagging is the act of self-classification with key words that make content easier to search for and therefore find. Tags are now used in every form of social media as a way to organize the information. Popular social bookmarking sites are Reddit.com, Stumbleupon.com, and Tumblr.com.

Social Networking

Social networking is the term used to describe Websites where people congregate based on some shared interest. In the case of Facebook, that interest is information on people; on LinkedIn, the shared interest is business; and so on. Exhibit 16-6 shows the top social network sites based on unique visitors. Social networking is still the fastest-growing active social media behavior online, increasing from 36 percent of global Internet users to 59 percent managing their profile on a monthly basis by the end of 2011.[11] The fastest-growing social network as of mid-2012 is Pinterest. com, where people can "pin" pictures of the things they are interested in and write a short caption.

The Data Explosion

In Chapter 15 we wrote of the tracking mechanisms that allow marketers to measure usage and patterns of behavior. Couple that information with the data flowing into and out of these social platforms and you have more data being produced in two days than that from the beginning of recorded history through 2003.[12] All of this information gives marketers a greater understanding of how their audience interacts with, shares, likes, dislikes, and feels about their brand. This unprecedented feedback mechanism is the advertiser's holy grail; however, most advertisers haven't had the wherewithal to truly take advantage of this opportunity. There might be a number of explanations as to why, but most likely the reasons stem from a lack of resources and not enough understanding about how some indirect measures, like brand likability, ultimately affect the companies' bottom line.

This is starting to change; as advertisers ask these tough questions, handfuls of entrepreneurs seek to answer them. Companies like Turn, a media technology company, are building **software as a service (SaaS)** for marketers to truly harness the power of these data. Their technology, and others like it, is so powerful that it will take data from the marketers' existing databases (CRM, Transactions/Sales, Newsletters, etc.) along with data from third-party data providers (BlueKai and Targus Info) and Website traffic to give a view of the makeup of the brand's customers. Then the marketers are able to use those data to target them and people like them on the Internet, all in real time while optimizing the campaign based on the actions people take on the ads and the effect on the sales or transactional data. This technology allows marketers to make split-second decisions on whom to send a message to, on what site, and with what execution to increase the probability of a desired action, such as a sale. Sounds a lot like what we discussed in Chapter 9 about the role of a media planner. No wonder the advertising agencies are scrambling to figure out how they play in this world of new social media and technology.

Managing Social Media

With all these different types of social media comes the task of managing the various outposts that a brand may accumulate. One of the biggest differences between social media and traditional media is that social media consist of 20 percent planning and 80 percent execution and management, whereas traditional media is the exact opposite: 80 percent planning and 20 percent execution and management. This means that social media are more labor- and resource-intensive. The plus side to that equation is that social does not bring with it large media costs, unlike traditional media. This runs counter to the way that most companies think of purchasing media, where the majority of the budget goes to working media—placed advertisements—not actual resources.

Owned Media and Fragmentation

LO 16-3

One of the things that we have yet to mention about social media is that unlike traditional media, in the past social media sites were not paid for. Rather, most brands spent time and effort in *owned properties*. The distinction here is that an owned property, like a Website, is not a place where you have to pay a media company to gain a presence to distribute your message. Like the brand Website, social media worked the same way: The various pages or groups that a brand deploys are free in that no money changed hands from Disney to Facebook, for example, despite Disney having multiple pages for its parks, movies, TV channels, cruises, and more. But be careful what you wish for, because the worst thing that a brand can do is let these pages languish. This means that each brand has to employ or outsource to an agency the management of these pages. Page management is more than likely the easy part; the hard part is to continually create and update these presences with enough engaging content not to bore or overwhelm the audience. The biggest reason "unfollowing" happens on Twitter is overtweeting. Finally, social media sites like Facebook are beginning to monetize brand pages, so the days of a free ride are ending.

Going back to our Disney example, with so many brands and so many avenues to deploy their owned presence, managing the fragmentation is resource-intensive and requires several policies and procedures to ensure accurate portrayal of the brand in these arenas. But like everything else in our new technology era, where there's a headache, aspirin is being made. Buddy Media and Hoot Suite are two young companies that help brands and agencies take control of all their social presences from one dashboard. They provide analytics and measurement tools that help define success from every promotion, tweet, poll, or other content mechanism that is deployed. Trend analysis will help brands explain the effects of every action they take on social media sites.

Listening tools, which we will discuss later in the chapter, also are very beneficial in understanding what's going on in the *blogosphere* (the aggregation of all blogs online). For example, how is a company's brand being talked about, and is it negative or positive? Text analytics—the measurement and analysis of text-based **user-generated content (UGC)**—is a burgeoning field in the social space, giving rise to unprecedented insights from the mere words and syntax we use when expressing our opinion about a product, brand, or service on the Internet.

These tools help make the fragmentation of social media a bit easier to manage; however, the tools are only as good as the people using them. Therefore, it is still a very labor-intensive way of connecting with an audience.

Google, which dominates search and digital display advertising, has set its sights on social media with Google+. The company has a variety of ways of linking audiences with platforms, and while the Google's reach in social cannot match Facebook, it is clearly determined to be successful.

Source: Google

Building Social Authority

LO 16-4

Social media bring a new element into advertising and marketing—the human element. When a company or a brand engages in social media, it must use people to administer their profiles in different communities. This means that the consumers know they can connect with actual people from a company in real time, not an anonymous Website. The effect is that a relationship is started between consumers and brand that, hopefully, elevates the perception of the company as an authority in the area where they are selling their products or services. The subsequent increase in brand favorability increases the likelihood of a sales increase too. This is what most companies strive for when planning

In social media the only thing needed to build a following is creativity, passion, and a sense of what audiences find interesting. Red Bull was one of the first brands to take advantage of Instagram's advertising platform. Their campaign involved posting both their own images and that of their many followers.

Source: Red Bull

social media into the media mix. However, building authority is not as easy to accomplish as it is to describe. As we discussed earlier with the mommy bloggers, and Motrin, it is sometimes hard to predict the outcomes of the human interactions, just like in the physical world.

Transparency and Authenticity

The tenets that social media have encouraged such as openness, transparency, and authenticity have caused marketers to rethink their traditional promotional messages. As Brian Stolis, principal at Altimeter Group, wrote in a 2011 *Forbes* article, "I actually see businesses changing how they approach social media to deliver value to the customer."[13] What Stolis is saying here is that historically, value was an expression of the relative cost of a product or service being advertised. Nowadays value goes beyond just the pricing or product and extends into the customer's life, perhaps in many different ways, such as Nike creating a jogging social network to connect more joggers together under the umbrella of the Nike brand. This service doesn't directly sell shoes, but it begins to connect the brand with the heart of the customer in such a way that the brand has now become part of his or her passion. This is a very powerful and emotional attachment that is unmatched by the more in-your-face promotional messages of other media.

However, many companies aren't built to be as open and connected as social media platforms demand. These companies need to figure out whether, if they do not make efforts to maintain a level of openness, it's worth their participation in the media: Do they walk away from social media as a viable marketing tactic? Or do they fundamentally change their business structure to be more open to the two-way dialogue of social media?

Two-Way Brand Communication

Market research is nothing new to brands. Understanding the perspective of the target audience has helped brands create better products, services, and communications. However, the instantaneous feedback mechanism that social media provide is new and is so immediate that most companies, until recently, haven't been able to handle the demands of social media. Consider that just 10 years ago, getting information about how a brand's audience felt about its product required weeks to recruit, administer, compile, and report the findings. Now it can happen within seconds by just typing a few key words into a **social listening** tool and poof, you have information not only about the brand, but about the competition, the category, and the industry. Best of all, you can assess sentiment based on the syntax of the text.

It has also been known that **word of mouth (WOM)**—for example, a friend's recommendation—is the most effective form of communication in persuading a future sale (see Exhibit 16-7). In social media, WOM is replicated on sites that post user reviews. Here audiences can find detailed and helpful perspectives on businesses of all kinds. This kind of social intelligence rewards businesses that provide value. It also punishes businesses that fail to serve customers well.

Social media platforms are tools that amplify WOM and make it measurable. A brand can now know how often an asset (link, photo, video, promotion) has been shared and how many people it has reached. This makes social media very powerful in their ability to move the proverbial needle on WOM recommendations. Most brands want to figure out how to encourage that behavior and social media provide that platform. Through branded pages,

Driving traffic to a brand's Website is not the sole purview of Google. Facebook's "Click to website" posts can accomplish the same objective.

Source: Facebook

Exhibit 16-7

Source: Myles Anderson, "88% of Consumers Trust Online Reviews as Much as Personal Recommendations," *Search Engine Land*, July 7, 2014, retrieved at: http://searchengineland .com/88-consumers-trust-online-reviews-much -personal-recommendations-195803.

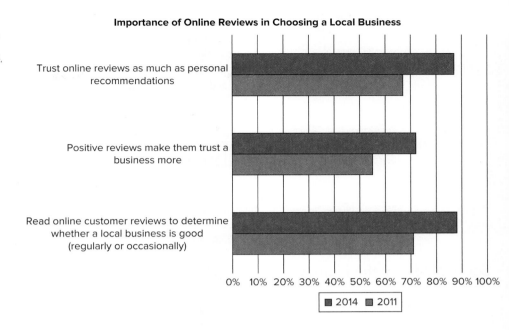

Importance of Online Reviews in Choosing a Local Business

Facebook, Pinterest, Twitter, and others can engage in the conversation and hopefully move the conversation in the right direction.

This is why authenticity and transparency are important. If a consumer is engaged in a give-and-take conversation, the less authentic it feels, the more impatient he or she will grow with the brand. But brands need to be very clear on what it means to be truly authentic and truly transparent. Clearly it would make bad business sense for a company to be 100 percent transparent or authentic because chances are, its competition is listening. Besides that, we are dealing with humans and humans have a tendency to say one thing and mean another. Consider the word *convenience* as an explanation for banking services. For different people that word means different things; it might mean that the bank makes it easy by offering mobile services, or that the bank is located nearby for easy walk-in service, or that the bank has customized the experience especially for the individual customer. All of those elements are convenient, so it isn't enough to just suggest that authenticity and transparency are the tent poles of the business's social strategy. The brand needs to define how authentic and transparent it is going to be, and typically what this two-way communication really offers is an opportunity for the brand to be helpful in its own way (authentic) and not just push promotional offers, but rather give the customer greater opportunity to explore behind the scenes with the product or service (transparency).

Customer Service in Social Media

As we suggested in the last section, being helpful is a very powerful mechanism for a company to engender trust and loyalty within a customer base. This was evidenced by Zappos .com, Comcast, and many other brands that utilize social media as an extension to their customer service efforts.

Log in to Twitter and search @comcastcares, and you'll find a stream of questions, comments, and statements from customers to @comcastcares with near-immediate responses. There are even updates from the Comcast Twitter feed when they are stepping away from the computer for a few minutes so no one gets angry if Comcast doesn't reply right away. What started out as a project quickly became an initiative for reducing support costs at the company.

Other companies like DirecTV provide forums for their customers to self-support. They will even bring in top volunteer commenters to be "beta customers" on new products and services, asking for their valued feedback. This keeps the customers happy, and the beta customer now feels obligated to help others and to maintain goodwill within the forum of frustrated and irate customers. By playing to the ego of some of these top influential customers DirecTV customer service reps, who are usually not as knowledgeable on technical issues, deal with a lot fewer customer issues, saving millions of dollars a year.

Consider the implications of this story. A man arrives late to the Four Seasons hotel in Palo Alto and gets bumped to a room that doesn't meet his standards. Not happy about this, he tweets his displeasure. The Four Seasons sees the tweet immediately and rectifies the situation. As it turns out, the guest visits Palo Alto nearly 60 times a year. He then tweets his pleasure and the Four Seasons has just created a loyal customer.[14] Prior to the advent of social media, the guest would have channeled his frustration in ways that the hotel could never have known about, and could possibly have lost him as a guest forever. As the best-selling author and creator of @comcastcares, Frank Eliason, says, social media mark the end of business as usual.

Social Media by the Numbers

Social media have changed our behavior. It's safe to say that the world has drastically changed in the past 20 years. Consider these numbers:

- There are over 4 billion e-mail accounts in the world, with an average of 1.7 per user. The number of e-mails sent each day is over 205 billion, a number that will grow by 3 percent over the next few years.
- 1.83 million images a day are uploaded to Flickr alone.
- Over 500 million tweets are posted each day.
- About 300 hours of video are uploaded to YouTube every minute.[15]
- More than 700 million "snaps" and 500 million stories are sent on Snapchat every day.[16]

These are mindboggling statistics that depict the massive scale of social media and the onslaught of information that everyone receives on a daily basis, not to mention the sea of change in our day-to-day lives, since none of these activities were even possible before the advent of the commercial Internet.

Kleenex attracted 27 million views and nearly as many comments with its viral "unlikely best friends." Chance needed a break when he lost the use of his hind legs after being struck by a car. Michael, who lives with a disability himself, found him at a shelter and created a way to give the dog mobility. While the sharing statistics are important, it was the heartfelt stories that people posted that made this viral so powerful.
Source: Kimberly-Clark Worldwide, Inc.

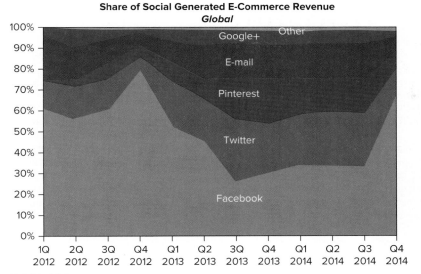

Share of Social Generated E-Commerce Revenue
Global

Exhibit 16-8

Source: Cooper Smith, "It's Time for Retailers to Start Paying Close Attention to Social Media," *Business Insider,* June 30, 2015, retrieved at: http://www.businessinsider.com/social-commerce-2015-report-2015-6.

How Social Media Have Transformed Business

There are countless ways to describe how social media are changing the business environment. As Exhibit 16-8 shows, the flurry of engagement created by social media is not useful for branding alone. It has real consequences for revenues from e-commerce. Here are some demonstrations of how social media platforms continue to push the boundaries of what is standard practice:

- In 2010, Pepsi dropped TV advertising for the Super Bowl and invested $20 million in social media instead.
- Comcast has at least 11 full-time employees dedicated to customer service via social media sites.
- Dell has attributed well over $6.5 million in revenue directly from Twitter.
- JetBlue Website visitors who also visited Twitter were 35 percent more likely to complete a booking than visitors who did not visit Twitter.[17]

- 36 percent of social media users post brand-related content.
- Two out of three social media users believe Twitter influences purchases.
- 50 percent of people follow brands on social media sites.
- 75 percent of companies now use Twitter as a marketing channel.
- 41 percent of the class of 2011 used social media sites in their job search.
- 89 percent of agencies said they would use Facebook to advertise for their clients in 2012—either by purchasing ads, creating pages, or using other methods of engagement.
- 39 percent of agencies said they would focus on Twitter, 36 percent on YouTube, 21 percent on LinkedIn, and 18 percent on Google+.[18]
- Twitter advertising options include promoted tweets that cost up to $2 an engagement and promoted trends that run to $200,000 a day. Snapchat charges $750,000 a day for advertising on the platform.[19]

Application of Social Media

Social media are not one-size-fits-all marketing tools. So much is predicated on the type of company, the audience, and objectives for using the medium. We'll cover some of the more common uses of social media in the following sections.

Common Uses of Social Media

Although not all brands are active in social media— and not all brands have to be—there are some common ways in which advertisers are starting to harness the power of social media.

Blogs

One of the easiest and best ways to get started in social media is to be a practitioner. Blogs are simple, reverse chronological order web pages that are typically opinionated in nature. Many brands deploy blogs as a way for customers to hear the voice of the brand and get to know the brand on a deeper, more personal level. Zappos.com has an extensive site that lists blogs by category of shopping items: outdoor, running, or housewares, to name a few. We'll revisit Zappos.com later in the chapter.

My IMC Campaign

Using Social Media

Unlike any other media choice, social media platforms aren't necessarily about placing ads in the areas that have the highest concentration of a company's target audience. In fact, that traditional process simply doesn't apply.

Social media are about engagement. However, *engagement* is a tricky word because it is typically defined differently for each brand. But defining what engagement means for your brand is what will help you determine how you will approach social media appropriately. Take a moment to think about how your target audience uses social media and where there might be entry points for you to engage the users. This is the first step in figuring out how to use social media for IMC.

As you have read throughout this chapter, the use of social media is now a very important part of integrated marketing communications. Basically, social media's function is to make brands remember that their target audiences are actually just people, and that they need to treat them like that.

The great thing about social media is that they allow you to be very creative. But don't go overboard on one creative idea because social media are as much about sustained and consistent presence as they are about having a one-off creative execution. Also remember that social media are inherently open, which means that seemingly disparate technologies can actually work together to create something new, rather than having to invent a new "thing."

Approach the use of social media for your campaign as a way to connect with your loyalists, and perhaps provide them with the tools to share your brand. Remember that word of mouth is the king of communications, and who better than your loyalists to sing your praises? There are many different ways in which people interact with social media, and you need to understand how the loyalists for your particular brand use them to achieve their goals. If you can identify that, and come up with some creative ideas that deliver on those goals, then you will have a winning strategy.

Brand Monitoring and Social Listening

We've talked briefly in this chapter about listening tools such as Nielsen's BuzzMetrics. These tools allow brands to aggregate all of the commentary, positive, negative or otherwise, into a user-friendly dashboard with robust analytics and trend analysis of how conversations are growing and sentiment is changing over time. These tools are great for learning how people are actively talking about your brand. There are many different ways you can use these data. A very common way is to track new product launches and gauge the receptiveness from the customer base.

Remarketing

It used to be standard for brands to give their web audience the ability to sign up for newsletters right from their Website. They would then take those names and remarket to them on an ongoing basis until they opted out of the communications. In some cases, the brands became so sophisticated they could tell you the exact number of sales from each newsletter drop based on the day, time, and offer. Nowadays these customer databases have moved to the social web, where likes and followers dominate the way in which most brands remarket to their customers. There are efficiencies to this replacing e-mail as the main form of remarketing, mostly around scale—it is much easier to follow or friend a brand than to fill in a lead form. Also, the message is distributed in multimedia formats where a customer *wants* to interact with the brand or company, and not necessarily in his or her inbox. A brand can create a channel on YouTube.com or Vimeo.com, have a Twitter page and Facebook page, and even have a LinkedIn group or Slideshare.net or Flickr channel—all of which allow the brand to distribute communications to its *own* **network**.

Marketing Research Online Communities (MROCs)

Communispace and Passenger are the largest suppliers of online communities for marketing research purposes. Imagine that you were a brand and you had what you thought was the next big idea. Well, if you had a marketing research online community (MROC), you could ask your loyal customer advocates what they thought of the idea or the

Leo Burnett Company Canada

Pity the billboard. For all of the excitement advertisers have about the digital and social media platforms you read about in the last two chapters, who gets worked up about billboards? ■ And yet a moment's reflection on some of the great advertising creative that appears on boards suggests that used properly, billboards and other out-of-home opportunities, can be important assets in an IMC campaign. ■ But using billboards effectively is a challenge. And using them to drive brand engagement is a big challenge. To put it starkly, how can an advertiser use billboards to get people talking about a brand? Enter James Ready Brewing Company and Leo Burnett Toronto. ■ For those who don't know the James Ready Brewing Company, here is a quick introduction. Based in Ontario, Canada, it prides itself on being a discount lager and features jokes on the underside of the bottle cap. Most notably it sells for "a buck" ($1), and that is real value. So when Ontario decided to raise taxes on alcoholic beverages, James Ready and Leo Burnett Toronto devised the "Share Our Billboard" campaign to help keep James Ready at a buck.[1] ■ James Ready fans were already

accustomed to helping the brand maintain its low price by sending back bottle caps and labels for reuse. Taking that idea a step further only helped reinforce the cultlike status the beer was achieving with its loyal audience. The idea was simple, but truly effective. The message was to "Help Keep James Ready a Buck" by sharing its billboard space. To enlist the community, Burnett used a multimedia approach centered on showcasing the space to be shared on the billboards. The agency used out-of-home, classifieds, e-mails, banner ads, and newsletters. All of the ads directed consumers to a simple sign-up sheet where they could upload photos and "make their offer." ■ Within a week, the Website was flooded with requests to share the billboard, from posting band posters; to wedding announcements, to photos demonstrating love for the brand. And as is true with any social endeavor, there was content that could never be put on a billboard. But most importantly the billboards showcased hundreds of people in their hometowns, making them instant celebrities and spokespeople for the beer. Under each highlighted customer the copy read: "THANKS – – – FOR KEEPING J. R. A BUCK."[2] ■

The unspoken goal of advertising is to get people to talk about your brand. Pick up any study about what influences people to purchase and by and large word of mouth is always the first answer. So advertising's main goal is to involve people in such a manner that they "pass it on." Many brands try to do this, so why did James Ready succeed where others do not? The best answer is that what the company asked its consumers to do stayed true to the brand. There was no high-gloss photography, or expensive TV and magazine gatefolds. But what is even more remarkable is the amount of consumer participation that came from a "low tech" social media campaign. Which just goes to show that good campaigns leverage the medium of choice, and great campaigns have no media barriers. ■ The James Ready case study is an excellent example of how brands can engage with their consumers and establish lifelong loyalists, enable WOM, and generally build a buzz around the brand from a single campaign taking home a few awards—a Gold Lion from Cannes, a Gold ANDY, and a Gold CLIO. ■

Out-of-Home Media

LO 17-1

Ads that reach prospects outside their homes—like outdoor advertising, bus and taxicab advertising, subway posters, and terminal advertising—are part of the broad category of **out-of-home advertising (OOH)** (see Exhibit 17-1). Today, there are more than 100 different types of out-of-home media, generating $7 billion in revenues in 2014.[3] While not considered OOH (because they are not measured or bought), the most common are *on-premise signs,* which promote goods and services, or identify a place of business, on the property where the sign is located.[4] The golden arches at McDonald's franchises are a good example. On-premise signs are important for helping us find a place of business, but they don't provide any kind of market coverage, and they aren't an organized medium like, for instance, the standardized outdoor advertising business.

In the past three chapters, we've looked at the traditional mass media forms as well as some of the interesting new media vehicles that have burst upon the advertising scene. Now, to round out our discussion of advertising media, we'll present in this last media chapter some of the other vehicles that advertisers use today.

Exhibit 17-1
Breakdown of out-of-home media.

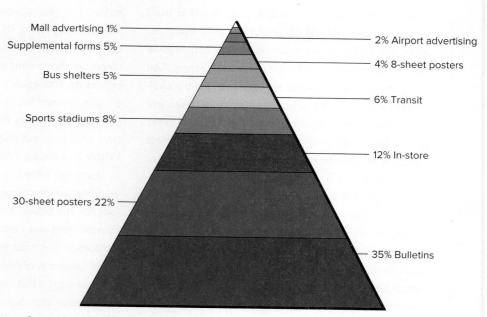

Mall advertising 1%
Supplemental forms 5%
Bus shelters 5%
Sports stadiums 8%
30-sheet posters 22%

2% Airport advertising
4% 8-sheet posters
6% Transit
12% In-store
35% Bulletins

Source: Adapted from The Outdoor Advertising Association of America, Inc.

Engagement can be important in outdoor advertising, especially in urban settings. This clever Mountain Dew ad not only gets people to interact with a billboard that is 40 feet off the ground, but it actually gets people to take pictures, ensuring a longevity beyond the time the ad will run.

Source: Pepsi Cola Company

We'll start with the last major media category: the organized out-of-home media. These include standardized outdoor advertising and transit advertising. We'll also briefly discuss some other out-of-home vehicles that are gaining in popularity: mobile billboards, electronic signs and displays, and even the ads that are now cropping up on phone booths and parking meters.

Next we'll discuss a category we call *exhibitive media,* which includes product packaging and trade shows and exhibits. Finally, we'll examine some of the media that advertisers typically consider supplementary to their other advertising activities—things like promotional products (specialty advertising) and **directories**—as well as some of the emerging media that are beginning to gain advertiser interest.

Out of Home (OOH) Advertising

As a national and global medium, outdoor advertising has achieved great success. It was the first advertising medium ever used, dating back more than 5,000 years to when hieroglyphics on obelisks directed travelers. In the Middle Ages, bill posting was an accepted form of advertising in Europe. And in the nineteenth century, it evolved into a serious art form, thanks to the poster paintings of both Manet and Toulouse-Lautrec.[5]

Today, around the globe, marketers use OOH for the same reasons as James Ready; to communicate a succinct message or image in the local language to a mass audience quickly and frequently at the lowest cost per thousand of any major medium.

Growth in OOH is slow compared to newer media. Expenditures increased just 1 percent from 2013 to 2014.[6] However, growth is expected to continue to increase as advertisers seek alternatives to the declining audiences and ad clutter of other mass media forms. Now that TV viewers can choose from hundreds of channels, it has become increasingly difficult for national advertisers to tell their story to mass audiences. But there's still one medium that can carry their message 24 hours a day, seven days a week, without interruption. It's never turned off, zipped, zapped, put aside, or left unopened. And it's big. That's OOH. For that reason, some experts refer to billboards as the *last* mass medium.[7]

Out-of-home advertising may be used for a variety of purposes. For example, nothing beats outdoor as a directional medium for motorists. But in an IMC program, OOH also greatly enhances awareness of or reinforces the advertiser's core message with high frequency at a very reasonable cost.

Standardization of the Outdoor Advertising Business

Standardized outdoor advertising uses scientifically located structures to deliver an advertiser's message to markets around the world.

In the United States, more than 400,000 outdoor ad structures are owned and maintained by some 3,000 outdoor advertising companies, known as *plants*.[8] Plant operators find suitable locations (usually concentrated in commercial and business areas), lease or buy the property, acquire the necessary legal permits, erect the structures in conformance with local building codes, contract with advertisers for poster rentals, and post the panels or paint the bulletins. Plant operators also maintain the outdoor structures and keep surrounding areas clean and attractive.

The plant operator may have its own art staff to supply creative services for local advertisers; ad agencies usually do the creative work for national advertisers. The biggest outdoor advertisers are traditionally in the entertainment and amusement category. The next largest category is local retail. Typically, the smaller the market, the larger the percentage of local advertisers.

Exhibit 17-2

Number of vehicles within OOH categories.

Source: Number of out-of-home Displays (2015), Outdoor Advertising Association of America, retrieved at: https://www.oaaa.org/ OutofHomeAdvertising/OOHMediaFormats/ OOHMediaFormats.aspx.

This ad for Lego blends in with the street it has been placed on. Using existing surroundings to accent an ad is a creative and memorable strategy.

Source: The Lego Group

Types of Outdoor Advertising

Outdoor advertising options are plentiful. According to the Outdoor Advertising Association of American (OAAA), there are five major kinds of out of home media: billboards, street furniture (bus shelters, store displays, urban furniture, kiosks), transit (buses, subway and rail, airports, truckside, taxi display, and wrapped vehicles), broadcast using place based TVs (stores, schools, bars), radio (drive time, in-office, in-store) and alternative (elevators, stadiums, airborne, shopping malls). We begin our discussion with a focus on the category that is probably most familiar to you, billboards. Standardized structures come in three basic forms: *bulletins, poster panels,* and *junior posters.* For extra impact, some companies may use the nonstandard *spectacular.*

Bulletins

Where traffic is heavy and visibility is good, advertisers find that large **bulletin structures** work best, especially for long-term use. Bulletins measure 14 by 48 feet, plus any extensions, and may carry either painted or printed messages. They are created in sections in the plant's shop and then brought to the site, where they are assembled and hung on the billboard structure.

Painted displays are normally lighted and are repainted several times each year (color is very important for readability; see Ad Lab 17–A). Some bulletins are three-dimensional or embellished by extensions (or cutouts) that stretch beyond the frames of the structure. Variations include cutout letters, backlighting, moving messages, and electronic time and temperature units called jump clocks.

Painted bulletins are very costly, but some advertisers overcome this expense by rotating them to different choice locations in the market every 60 or 90 days. Over time, this gives the impression of wider coverage than the advertiser is actually paying for. As James Ready found out, the dominating effect of bulletins frequently makes them well worth the extra cost—especially in small markets.

Poster Panels

The **poster panel** (*standard billboard*) is less costly per unit and is the basic outdoor advertising structure. A poster consists of blank panels with a standardized size and border. Its message is first printed at a lithography or screen plant on large sheets of paper, then mounted by hand on the panel.

Poster sizes are referred to in terms of *sheets.* The poster sheets are mounted on a board with a total surface of 12 by 25 feet and usually change every 30 days.

Some local advertisers get high-quality outdoor advertising at reduced cost by using **stock posters.** These ready-made posters are available in any quantity and often feature the work of first-class artists and lithographers. Local florists, dairies, banks, or bakeries simply place their name in the appropriate spot.

Junior Posters

Manufacturers of grocery products, as well as many local advertisers, use smaller poster sizes. Called **junior posters** (or *junior panels*), these offer a 5- by 11-foot printing area on a panel surface (feet high by 12 feet wide. They are typically concentrated in urban areas, where they can reach pedestrian as well as vehicular traffic In an integrated marketing communications campaign, they are also an excellent medium for coverage close to the point of purchase.

Spectaculars are expensive, elaborate animated signs found primarily in the hearts of large cities. They incorporate movement, color, and flashy graphics to grab attention in high-traffic areas.

© TongRom Image Stock/Alamy RF

AD Lab 17–A

How to Use Color and Type in Out of Home Advertising

These 14 color combinations represent the best use of color contrast for advertising readability. The chart evaluates primary and secondary color combinations taking into account hue and value. Example 1 is the most legible color combination with example 14 is the least legible.

Hue is the identity of color, such as red, yellow, or blue.

Value is the measure of lightness or darkness and can be separated into shades and tints.

Shades are the relative darkness of colors. Tints are the relative lightness of colors.

A standard color wheel illustrates the importance of contrast in hue and value. Like sound waves, light rays have varying wave lengths or frequencies. Some pigments absorb light while others reflect it. Reflected frequencies are perceived as color.

Opposite colors on a wheel are complementary. An example is red and green. They represent a good contrast in hue, but their values are similar. It is difficult for the cones and rods of the human eye to process the wavelength variations associated with complementary colors. Consequently, a quivering or optical distortion is sometimes detected when two complementary colors are used in tandem.

Adjacent colors, such as blue and green, make especially poor combinations since their contrast is similar in both hue and value. As a result, adjacent colors create contrast that is hard to discern.

Alternating colors, such as blue and yellow, produce the best combinations since they have good contrast in both hue and value. Black contrasts well with any color of light value and white is a good contrast with colors of dark value. For example, yellow and black are dissimilar in the contrast of both hue and value. White and blue are also a good color combination.

CONTRAST   VIBRATION

LOW VISIBILITY   **HIGH VISIBILITY**

Typestyles

Fonts selected for OOH designs must be easy to read from variable distances. Use large and legible typefaces. Choose fonts that are easily read

Source: Victors & Spoils

Spectaculars

Times Square in New York is well known for its **spectaculars**—giant electronic signs that incorporate movement, color, and flashy graphics to grab attention in high-traffic areas. Spectaculars are very expensive to produce and are found primarily in the world's largest cities, such as Tokyo, London, Atlanta, Los Angeles, and, of course, Las Vegas (see the Portfolio Review, "Out-of-Home Advertising").

Buying OOH Advertising

Advertisers use OOH advertising for a variety of purposes. For example, to introduce a new product or announce a change in package design, an advertiser might want to saturate the market. Altoids created "Curiously Strong" brand awareness after implementing a campaign using alternative newspapers and a variety of OOH advertising formats. OOH advertising generated an awareness of 76 percent, market share grew by a 5-to-1 margin vs. markets without advertising, and the brand's business grew by 31 percent to $18.7 million.[9]

Bolthouse Farms ■ Without mentioning a single health benefit, Bolthouse used bold messaging to establish a persona for broccoli that was bold and refused to be ignored.

Source: Victors & Spoils

at long distances. Fonts with thin strokes or ornate script will be difficult to read.

Adequate spacing between letters, words, and lines will enhance visibility. The relative size of letter characters is also an important consideration. When designing for roadside displays, a one foot letter height is unreadable, while a two-foot letter height is marginal. A letter height greater than three feet is clearly readable. Words comprised of both upper and lower characters are generally easier to read than words constructed solely of capital letters.

Laboratory Applications

1. Which billboard ads in this chapter use color most effectively? Explain.

2. What billboard ads have you seen that don't use color effectively? How can they be improved?

Text Legibility Guide

Distance in Feet	Print Resolution	Resolution for LED	Examples	Minimal Readable Text Height in Inches
5'-50'	High	3mm-8mm	Malls, Airports, Retail, Lobbies, Offices, etc.	1"-2"
50'-100'	High	6mm-12mm	Window, Street Display, Drive Through	2"-4"
100'-200'	Normal	12mm-25mm	Posters, Surface Streets	4"-8"
200'-300'	Normal	25mm-34mm	Posters, Surface Streets and Highway Bulletins	8"-10"
300'-350'	Normal	34mm-66mm	Highway Bulletins, Highway Posters	10"-15"
350'-500'	Normal	34mm-66mm	Highways, Spectaculars	15"-20"
500'-600'	Low - Normal	66mm-76mm	Highways, Spectaculars, Stadiums	20"-24"
600' +	Low	76mm-90mm	Skyscrapers, Spectaculars, Set back from road	24"-40"

Source: Reprinted with permission of The Outdoor Advertising Association of America.

The basic unit of sale for billboards, or posters, is *100 gross rating points daily*, or a **100 showing.** One rating point equals 1 percent of a particular market's population. Buying 100 gross rating points does *not* mean the message will appear on 100 posters; it means the message will appear on as many panels as needed to provide a daily exposure theoretically equal to the market's total population. Actually, a showing of 100 gross rating points achieves a *daily* reach of about 88.1 percent of the adults in a market over a 30-day period.[10]

For less saturation, units of sale can be expressed as fractions of the basic unit, such as 75, 50, or 25 gross rating points. If a showing provides 750,000 total impression opportunities daily in a market with a population of 1 million, it delivers 75 GRPs daily. Over a period of 30 days, the showing would earn 2,250 GRPs (30 × 75).

A showing, as indicated above, has historically been measured by a rudimentary equation that takes the number of people who pass by an out-of-home display as its main sort

(continued on page 527)

Portfolio Review

:: Out-of-Home Advertising

As the oldest medium on earth, outdoor advertising benefits from its inherent nature as a "sign" as well as the modern features of graphic design and technology. In fact, thanks to technology, advertisers can do things in outdoor today they couldn't have dreamed of just a few years ago. Plus, no other medium is this big—commanding attention from motorists and pedestrians 24 hours a day, seven days a week, at a fraction of the cost of other media. However, outdoor is limited in what it can say. For normal outdoor structures on the highway, seven words is the rule of thumb. That places an additional burden on the nonverbal (artistic) aspects of the ad, and this definitely challenges the creative muscle of every advertising ad agency.

• Study the ads in this portfolio to see how big, strategic ideas get translated into outstanding outdoor or transit advertising. Then consider why the advertiser chose this particular medium. Was outdoor or transit the right choice for this advertiser? Why? Or why not? Could the same concept be used in other media? How?

reporter
phonebooth
cape
blue tights
red underpants
x-ray vision
superhuman strength

two all-beef patties
special sauce
lettuce
cheese
pickles
onion
sesame seed bun

know the ingredients, know the legend.

One rule of thumb in outdoor is focus on graphics and minimize copy. However this McDonald's poster, "Big Mac Legends—Superman" flips common wisdom on its head. How does copy in this ad convey the superiority of the brand?
Source: McDonald's

THIS IMAGE HAS NOT BEEN MODIFIED. IT'S TIME TO CHANGE THAT.
ERASE THE DIFFERENCE AT WWW.ROBERTOHERNANDEZ.COM

In this ad the art is everything, creating the contrast of luxury and poverty that the sponsor wishes to highlight. The sparse copy makes the message credible by indicating that the photo has not been altered.
Source: Banamex/CDC

Consider the importance of color, space, and repetition in the effectiveness of these brand messages on escalators and stairs.

Source: The Coca-Cola Company

How does proximity, speed, and the power of the subway car amplify this ad for the TBS sports?

Source: TBS

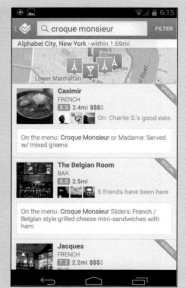

Another branch of OOH advertising is location-based advertising, a popular method of delivering ads to a consumer based on his or or her location. Location-based advertising is growing quickly because of the ubiquity of mobile phones. A major player in this space is Foursquare.

Source: Foursquare

The ubiquity of mobile phones has also made QR codes and Near Field Communication (NFC) more prevalent and common in outdoor advertising. Consumers have the ability to quickly access sales information and even purchase products while walking down the street.

Source: Victoria Secret's

Absolut Vodka went above and beyond with this billboard, which displays a typical Manhattan apartment.
© Jorge Vasconcelos/Flickr/Getty Images

Creativity is as the heart of every great media placement. Here the World Wildlife Foundation uses the depletion of paper towels to convey their conservation message.
Source: World Wildlife Foundation

Going beyond the boundaries of the ad placement
has a dramatic effect, however
it is sometimes not scalable.
Source: Perfetti Van Melle

Art and media combine in this execution to make
sure it stands out, despite the fact the ad is merely a
two dimensional image.
© Rex Features/AP Images

(continued from page 521)

of reach. This measurement is called Daily Estimated Circulation, or DEC. However, in 2009, the Outdoor Advertising Association of America (OAAA) and the Traffic Audit Bureau developed a new method of measuring out-of-home's true reach and frequency. Their new rating system is called Eyes On Impressions (EOI). EOI actually takes into account many other factors other than the number of people who pass a display, such as size of the display, angle to the road, format, street type, distance from the road, and roadside position. This new rating system then calculates those factors into a formula that estimates the number of people who *actually* see the ad in a week. The main factor that differentiates DECs from EOIs is estimation of traffic on a daily basis versus estimation of *seers* of the ad on a weekly basis. The net effect is twofold: (1) that out-of-home is now the only ad medium that tracks viewers of ads, rather than just the potential to see ads and (2) that the frequency of out-of-home has been drastically reduced over a monthly period where the reach difference is negligible.[11]

Location, Location, Location

As in real estate, location is everything in outdoor advertising. Advertisers that want more saturation can increase the number of posters or purchase better locations to achieve 200 or 300 GRPs per day. The map in Exhibit 17-3 shows billboard locations in Los Angeles, California. Rates vary considerably from market to market due to variations in property rentals, labor costs, and market size. As a rule of thumb, a standard billboard offers the lowest cost per thousand of any major mass medium.[12]

Technology in Outdoor Advertising

In the past it was always a problem for a media buyer in New York to adequately supervise the posting of outdoor boards in Peoria, Illinois. A buyer can't just jump on a plane and travel to all the cities where the client's boards are posted to verify the value of the locations. Fortunately, though, new technology has helped solve this dilemma and has thus made outdoor an even more attractive medium to national advertisers. OOH companies use **global positioning systems (GPSs)** to give the exact location of particular boards using satellite technology. Media buyers, equipped with sophisticated software, can then integrate this information with demographic market characteristics and traffic counts to determine the best locations for their boards.[13]

Some outdoor companies even provide digitized video of their locations so the buyer can see the actual board and the environment in which it is located. Bar coding technology allows materials to be tracked, posted, and authenticated, all by computer. Computerized painting on flexible vinyl guarantees a high-quality, high-resolution, faithful reproduction of the advertiser's message regardless of the market. Additional advances include the use of LED technology on billboards. Because LED screens can change instantly, advertisers can connect better with consumers by displaying up-to-the-minute messages that can be fine-tuned or updated depending on the time of day.[14]

Exciting new technologies may change the future of how we "see" outdoor and other out-of-home ads. TeamOne recently launched a revolutionary campaign for Lexus that included a full-size hologram of the new IS sedan. Using interactive kiosks located in Times Square and other prime U.S. locations, the display featured a hologram of the Lexus in motion and touch pads that allowed visitors to change the car's color and other features.[15] This opens up many thrilling possibilities for advertisers: Imagine a bulletin-size structure on the highway promoting the latest Batman film, with a larger-than-life superhero coming at you in 3-D.

The newest entry into OOH advertising is **location-based advertising**. Location-based advertising integrates advertising messages and prospect location by taking advantage of technologies such as smartphones that can

Exhibit 17-3

Billboard and other OOH Locations in Los Angeles.

Source: Reprinted with permission of Lamar Advertising.

be reached via bluetooth or other localized transmitting devices. Social media companies Foursquare and Gowalla are major players in this growing area. The idea is simple: since people are on their phones throughout the day, why not capture their attention with an offer or service that is close by? So, for example, a person walking near a Starbucks might find a coupon for a latte in their News Feed or other social feed. Facebook, not to be outdone, is already distributing technologies to companies that will make it easy to do.

Regulation of Outdoor Advertising

The Highway Beautification Act of 1965 controls outdoor advertising on U.S. interstate highways and other federally subsidized highways. It was enacted partly in response to consumer complaints that outdoor advertising was spoiling the environment. Over 700,000 billboards were removed by 1991, the year Congress banned the construction of new billboards on all scenic portions of interstate highways.[16] Since that time, the image of outdoor advertising has improved dramatically, and most people polled say they like billboards, believe they promote business, and find them useful travel information for drivers.[17]

Each state also regulates, administers, and enforces outdoor advertising permit programs through its department of transportation. Some states (Maine, Vermont, Hawaii, and Alaska) prohibit billboards altogether. Ironically, though, some of these states use outdoor advertising themselves in other states to promote tourism (see Ethical Issues, "Does Spillover Need Mopping Up?").

Transit Advertising

LO 17-4

When Campbell Soup started advertising in 1910, the company spent its first $5,000 placing ads on one-third of the buses in New York City for one year. The ads were so successful that after only six months, Campbell enlarged the contract to include all surface vehicles in the city. People started trying more Campbell's and soon sales were up 100 percent. For the next 12 years, transit advertising was the only medium Campbell employed. Today, Campbell is still a major user of transit advertising.

Transit advertising is a category of out-of-home media that includes bus and taxicab advertising as well as posters on transit shelters, terminals, and subways. Although transit is not considered a major medium by most advertising practitioners, standardization, better research, more statistical data, and measured circulation have made transit advertising more attractive to national advertisers. National marketers of designer apparel and movies, for example, are two of the many categories of advertisers spending dramatically more in this medium, replacing the traditional transit advertising leaders such as petroleum products, financial services, and proprietary medicines.[18]

Transit advertising is a cost-effective way for marketers to reach a large audience of people. Buses and taxis provide high ad exposure by traversing the busiest streets of a city many times a day. A recent 1-800-Flowers.com campaign promoting the company's specialty bouquets featured ads on buses, on subway stations, and in other urban locations. The company's sales were seven times higher in markets where the outdoor campaign ran.[19]

Transit advertising is equally popular with local advertisers. Retailers can expand their reach inexpensively and often receive co-op support from national marketers, which thrive on the local exposure.[20]

Outdoor advertising doesn't consist of billboards only. Customers entering the parking lot to fetch their cars are met with this inventive ad for Matchbox, which employs photographic adhesives to create a lifelike image.
Source: Mattel, Inc.

Types of Transit Advertising

Transit advertising targets the millions of people who use commercial transportation (buses, subways, elevated

Ethical Issues

Does Spillover Need Mopping Up?

While numerous laws and self-regulatory efforts have banished products like tobacco and hard liquor from the airwaves, it is virtually impossible to keep minors from being exposed to such advertising due to the *spillover* nature of some media. The ethical issues involved with spillover media are complex, including the kind of advertising appeals used to target audiences.

Take outdoor advertising, for example. It is the most public mass medium. It cannot be turned off like television, radio, or the Internet, and it's displayed 24 hours a day for all to see—even children.

The trend in outdoor advertising today is toward eye-catching, sexually explicit ads, seen especially in dense urban areas. Most outdoor advertising regulations have focused on the *location* of billboards, not the *content*. The Outdoor Advertising Association of America's (OAAA) Code of Principles says that they "support the right to reject advertising that is misleading, offensive, or otherwise incompatible with community standards." But it is unknown how often this clause is invoked. Communities, therefore, have taken it upon themselves to regulate the placement and content of outdoor advertising, rather than relying on self-regulation by the advertising industry. In 1998, for example, the Los Angeles City Council passed an ordinance that prohibited alcoholic beverage advertising on virtually all publicly visible sites, even store windows. In response, the OAAA and other local Los Angeles trade association members filed a federal civil rights action, claiming that the ordinance violates the right to free speech.

As technology advances, so do the venues for advertising. And advertisers have found ways to work around billboard restrictions. Taxicabs and buses have carried ads for years; however, now appearing on Boston cabs are electronic billboards that have the ability to change their message minute by minute—depending on a few desired variables. Using a satellite feed and wireless Internet links, color messages change depending on time of day and location. Different neighborhoods see different ads and, if appropriate, even different languages. The taxi's location is monitored by an Internet link to a satellite tracking system. This new technology is inexpensive for advertisers and may become a common feature on taxicabs across America. However, it raises legal and ethical questions. Should mobile billboards be subjected to the same restrictions as stationary billboards? Neighborhoods and schools may theoretically be protected from unwanted advertising, but can concerned parents protect their children from viewing advertising that travels on taxis?

Spillover also reaches children in other media vehicles besides out-of-home. The movies, for example, consistently show people smoking. And if the smoker is a celebrity, an impressionable child might interpret that as an endorsement. In a study conducted by Dartmouth Medical School, researchers found that actor endorsements of tobacco brands jumped tenfold in the 1990s. The study also found that 87 percent of popular movies contain tobacco use and about one-third display identifiable brand-name logos. Minors make up a large percentage of moviegoers and through movies they may be getting more exposure to smoking endorsements than in real life. Young people who look up to sport stars and movie celebrities may be vulnerable to intentional and unintentional endorsements. Benedict Carey of the *Los Angeles Times* calls today's movies "almost as smoke-laden as the stock car racing circuit."

Many people think that ads are not to blame for the rise of teen sexual activity and tobacco and alcohol use. Others believe that advertisers have a greater responsibility to separate youth from the adult world of unhealthy and explicit activity. Regardless of who is right, advertisers, agencies, and media companies must be sensitive to public opinion and seek creative solutions to protect impressionable children. Otherwise, the industry will risk severe restriction and regulation for having failed to responsibly and conscientiously assert firm ethical standards itself.

Questions

1. Do you believe the goal of protecting children justifies banning advertising for legal products? Which products specifically?

2. Should ads in spillover media be censored for sexually explicit content? If so, who should the censors be and what specifically should they prohibit?

3. What alternatives might be available to fight teenage smoking, drinking, and sexual promiscuity besides banning advertising for legal adult products?

Sources: "Los Angeles Alcoholic Beverage Ban Statement," Outdoor Advertising Association of America, September 30, 1999 (retrieved from www.oaaa.org, April 2001); Benedict Carey, "Cigarettes Are Doing Big Box Office," *Los Angeles Times*, January 8, 2001; OAAA Code of Principles (retrieved from www.oaaa.org/government); Jon P. Nelson, "Advertising Bans in the United States," May 21, 2004 (retrieved from http://econ.la.psu .edu/papers/adbans_critical.pdf); "Tobacco Menace," Consumer-Voice.org (retrieved from www.consumer-voice.org/tobacco/tobacco3.htm); "Beer Advertising Facts," Beer Institute (retrieved from www.beerinstitute.org/pdfs /beeradfacts.pdf); David Goetz, "Liquor Industry Gets Stricter on Advertising," *Courier-Journal*, September 10, 2003 (retrieved from www.courier-journal .com/business); "Framework Convention on Tobacco Control," Health Canada, October 2002 (retrieved from www.hc-sc.gc.ca/english/media /releases/2002/2002_66bk.htm).

trains, commuter trains, trolleys, and airlines), plus pedestrians and car passengers, with a variety of formats: transit shelters; station, platform, and terminal posters; inside cards and outside posters on buses; and taxi exteriors.

Transit Shelters

In cities with mass-transit systems, advertisers can buy space on bus shelters and on the backs of bus-stop seats. **Transit shelter advertising** is a relatively new out-of-home form enjoying

A Hong Kong insurance company offering a competitively priced plan uses a clever subway poster to advertise that it "Doesn't hurt at all."

Source: J. Walter Thompson, Hong Kong

great success. It reaches virtually everyone who is outdoors: auto passengers, pedestrians, bus riders, motorcyclists, bicyclists, and more. It is extremely inexpensive and available in many communities that restrict billboard advertising in business or residential areas. In fact, shelter advertising is sometimes the only form of outdoor advertising permitted. It's also an excellent complement to outdoor posters and bulletins, enabling total market coverage in a comprehensive outdoor program.

Terminal Posters

In many bus, subway, and commuter train stations, space is sold for one-, two-, and three-sheet **terminal posters.** Major train and airline terminals offer such special advertising forms as floor displays, island showcases, illuminated cards, dioramas (3-D scenes), and clocks with special lighting and moving messages.

In Paris, Nike made a splash at the French Open tennis tournament even though a competitor had locked up advertising rights within the stadium. Nike covered the city by buying space on some 2,500 buses during the tournament. As the coup de grace, it bought up every bit of signage space at the Porte d'Auteuil metro (subway) station close to the stadium and turned it into a Nike gallery of terminal posters featuring famous tennis players from around the world.[21]

Inside and Outside Cards and Posters

The **inside card** is placed above the seats and luggage area in a wall rack. Cost-conscious advertisers print both sides of the card so it can be reversed to change the message, saving on paper and shipping charges. Inside **car-end posters** (in bulkhead positions) are usually larger than inside cards, but sizes vary. The end and side positions carry premium rates.

Outside posters are printed on high-grade cardboard and often varnished for weather resistance. The most widely used outside posters are on the side, rear, and front of a bus.

Advertisers may also buy space on **taxicab exteriors,** generally for periods of 30 days, to display internally illuminated, two-sided posters positioned on the roofs. Some advertising also appears on the doors or rear of taxicabs. In some major areas, sponsors can buy cards mounted on the trunks. In Southern California, advertisers can rent cards mounted on the tops of cabs that travel throughout Los Angeles, Orange, and San Diego counties, serving major airports and traveling the busiest freeways in the country. Costing from $110 to $130 per month per cab, this is a very cost-effective way to reach the mobile public.

Buying Transit Advertising

LO 17-5

The unit of purchase is a **showing,** also known as a *run* or *service.* A **full showing** (or *No. 100 showing*) means that one card will appear in each vehicle in the system. Space may also be purchased as a *half* (No. 50) or *quarter* (No. 25) *showing.*

Rates are usually quoted for 30-day showings, with discounts for 3-, 6-, 9-, and 12-month contracts. Advertisers supply the cards at their own expense, but the transit company can help with design and production.

Cost depends on the length and saturation of the showing and the size of the space. Rates vary extensively, depending primarily on the size of the transit system. Advertisers get rates for specific markets from local transit companies.

Special Inside Buys

In some cities, advertisers gain complete domination by buying the **basic bus**—all the inside space on a group of buses. For an extra charge, pads of business reply cards or coupons (called **take-ones**) can be affixed to interior ads for passengers to request more detailed information, send in application blanks, or receive some other benefit.

Congress removed a long-standing ban on advertisements appearing on stamps, opening the doors to yet another subtle form of media to influence and persuade consumers.

Courtesy of stamps.com

Special Outside Buys

Some transit companies offer **bus-o-rama signs,** jumbo full-color transparencies backlighted by fluorescent tubes and running the length of the bus. A bus has two bus-o-rama positions, one on each side. A single advertiser may also buy a **total bus**—all the exterior space, including the front, rear, sides, and top.

For years, New York subways have been running **brand trains,** which include all the subway cars in a particular corridor. However, with the July 2004 opening of its monorail system, the city of Las Vegas has taken the concept further. The glitz of the city's strip extends to its public transportation: Each of the nine monorail trains and seven stations has a corporate sponsor, and many feature elaborate **immersive advertising** themes. City officials banked on the monorail system, which is entirely funded by passenger fares instead of tax dollars, to generate at least $6.5 million annually in advertising revenue. Consider the deal that the city struck with Nextel (now owned by Sprint), estimated at $50 million. The company has signed on for a 12-year sponsorship of one train and the system's "crown jewel," the main station at the Las Vegas Convention Center, which more than 1 million annual visitors are expected to pass through each year.[22] Nextel is even paying construction costs for the station, which is adjacent to the company's largest retail venture yet, the full-service, interactive Nextel Pavilion and Theater. Sprint, General Motors, and Monster energy drink have also signed train and station sponsorship deals. See My IMC Campaign to better understand how to choose from all the various forms of transit and other outdoor advertising.

Other Out-of-Home Media

As mentioned earlier, there are many forms of out-of-home media. Some are so new that they are still unproven. However, several seem to be gaining in popularity, and they demonstrate how far advertisers will go to get their messages seen by the consuming public.

Mobile Billboards

The **mobile billboard,** a cross between traditional billboards and transit advertising, was conceived as advertising on the sides of tractor-trailer trucks. Today in some large cities, specially designed flatbed trucks carry long billboards up and down busy thoroughfares. Local routes for mobile ads are also available on delivery trucks in San Francisco, Los Angeles, and Seattle.

Electronic Signs and Display Panels

Electronic signs display text and graphic messages much like the big screens in sports stadiums. The signs transmit commercial messages to retail stores, where shoppers see them. The stores pay nothing for the signs and receive 25 percent of the advertising revenue. In Montreal, Telecite used its new visual communication network (VCN) technology to install electronic display panels on subway cars. Advertisers got a powerful, inexpensive, and flexible medium with a large, captive audience; the transit authority got a modern, self-financed emergency and public information system; and passengers got something to watch while they rode.[23] Telecite is negotiating with numerous U.S. and European cities to install the systems in their subway and metro cars.

Parking Meters and Public Phones

Thanks to a couple of enterprising companies, American Parking Meter Advertising and American Telephone Advertising (ATA), marketers can now advertise on parking meters and public phones. ATA offers 20 market segments, such as hotels, restaurants, airports, college campuses, and convenience stores.

LO 17-6

Exhibitive Media

Some media are designed specifically to help bring customers eyeball-to-eyeball with the product—often at the point of sale or close to it. These **exhibitive media** include *product packaging* and *trade-show booths and exhibits.* When successful, the synergy of combining exhibitive media with other media can improve product or brand awareness by as much a 500 percent.[24]

My IMC Campaign 17–A

Using Out-of-Home, Exhibitive, and Supplementary Media

Go to Google.com and do an image search for the keyword phrase "creative outdoor advertising" and you will most likely see some of the most outrageous and ingenious advertisements in the world. Because most other media are set to standards that deal with time and space delivered in a linear programming mechanism (think TV, radio, and print), rather than just space, creativity is restricted to what can be construed in that limited window. Out-of-home (OOH) on the other hand is typically constrained only by space, and even then most creative OOH placements end up breaking out of their dimensional boxes.

Planning for OOH can be challenging and fun. Marshall McLuhan, the author of *Understanding Media: The Extensions of Man*, coined the phrase "the medium is the message," meaning that the medium embeds itself in the message, creating a relationship by which the medium influences how the message is interpreted. In no other medium is this truer than OOH; in fact a high percentage of the more creative ads have little to no copy relying solely on the media to do the heavy-lifting of communicating.

The major limitations to OOH center on the fact that because you are dealing with physical real estate, your exposure is limited to the geographical location of that real estate. If people do not pass by your billboard or ride public transportation, they likely will not be exposed to your message. Unfortunately for national advertisers, the cost to produce OOH advertisements in all markets is extremely expensive and 99 percent of advertisers cannot achieve it. So most advertisers take this into consideration when planning and typically weigh the reach restrictions with the impact of the people exposed. Most likely they will turn their OOH efforts to a handful of important markets for their business. For instance, there is no reason a surfboard company should be advertising in Kansas City, Missouri, but it would be appropriate to choose San Diego, Los Angeles, Miami, and the like. Sometimes the decision to use OOH actually comes down to a strategic decision in which an advertiser would rather focus on quality impressions rather than volume or quantity of impressions.

As you come up with your IMC campaigns, think of how you might be able to represent the message in a clever way in OOH. But also remember that to build your plan you will have to consider these factors:

- What types of OOH make the most sense for my brand? If the medium is the message, what does it say to my consumer if I am advertising on billboards versus bus shelters versus inside bars?
- In which cities will I be advertising?
- How does this fit with the other media that I am choosing?
- Am I getting enough reach, or is OOH going to be my main reach driver?

Another thing to think about is how the digital revolution is affecting OOH advertising. Today, through companies like Captivate Networks, NBC Outdoor, Danoo, Wall Street Journal Office Displays, and eCast, an advertiser can run a national OOH campaign on video displays that exist in coffee shops, gas stations, doctors' offices, office buildings, restaurant juke boxes, elevators, and even airports, all from the comfort of their PC. By delivering a digitized version of a video advertisement, they can deliver the ads to their thousands of displays reaching people in a variety of different ways. This is a great way for advertisers to extend their TV campaigns and possibly gain a bit more reach at a much lower cost.

If you are planning to have a TV spot for your campaign, don't forget to leverage all the different ways that you can syndicate that spot. The 30-second spot has been set free from the lonely confines of the TV set.

Last, don't limit yourself to traditional ways of thinking. Media can be derived from a number of things. In one case study from Initiative Media, tune-in messages for a new fall show on CBS were stamped onto eggs so that people received an ad impression when they opened the cartons at the store. You have probably heard of the phrase "location, location, location" and in no other medium is that more of a mantra.

Product Packaging

In 2012, global companies spent close to $485 billion on packaging.[25] Since upward of 70 percent of all buying decisions are made at the point of purchase, packages play a major role in both advertising and selling. And in the world of integrated marketing communications, the package is not only the last "ad" a consumer sees before purchasing the product, it is the only "ad" the consumer sees when using the product. So it is more than just another *planned message*. Packaging influences the *product message* as well, since (as we discussed in Chapter 6) it is often an intrinsic aspect of the basic product concept.

Packaging encompasses the physical appearance of the container and includes design, color, shape, labeling, and materials. Packaging serves marketers in four major ways: protection, preservation, information, and promotion.[26] Although the protection and preservation aspects reduce the costly effects of damage, pilferage, and spoilage, the importance of packaging as an informational and promotional tool cannot be underestimated. An attractive package can create an immediate relationship with the customer, influence in-store shopping decisions, help set the product apart from competitors, and inform customers of the product's features and benefits.

Designers consider three factors: the package's stand-out appeal, how it communicates verbally and nonverbally, and the prestige or image desired.

Consumers respond to packaging intuitively, so packaging design can be as important as advertising in building a product's brand image. Packaging establishes or reinforces the brand's personality at the point of sale. So if status is the goal, the package designer must consider what consumers regard as prestigious. This is especially important for so-called nonrational products—cosmetics and perfumes, sports accessories, confection gifts, and certain luxury products—in which fantasy, impulsiveness, or mystique may overrule rational choice.

To sell products off the shelf, packages may use shape, color, size, interesting visuals, or even texture to deliver a marketing message, give product information, and indicate application. After they are purchased, packages continue promoting the product in the home, reinforcing the brand's image, so they should open and close with minimal effort and be easy to handle.

Buying packaging includes two major phases: *concept* and *production.* The *conceptual process* involves input from five major groups: consumers, manufacturers, marketing intermediaries, consumer advocacy groups, and government agencies.[27] The conflicting concerns of these groups strongly influence the nature and the cost of packaging (see Exhibit 17-5).

Environmental Issues in Packaging

As manufacturers continue to produce environmentally safe packaging, the marketer's cost of materials rises. And what some consumers expect from *green packaging* is not necessarily what manufacturers traditionally offer or what marketing intermediaries prefer to use.[28]

With the public's growing concern for the environment, especially in international markets, recyclable tin-coated steel and aluminum packages are enjoying a resurgence in popularity. Because European countries are so densely populated, their regulations requiring environmentally friendly packaging are far more stringent than in North America. Marketers need to take this into consideration since such regulations add to the cost of doing business overseas.

Exhibit 17-4

Expectations and concerns in packaging development.

Consumers	Manufacturers	Marketing Intermediaries (Retailers/ Wholesalers)	(Consumer Advocacy Groups	Government Agencies
Ease (to handle and store)	Sturdiness	Sturdiness (of case and packages)	Package safe to	Free of deception
Convenience	Suppleness	Convenience (of removal)	– handle	Free of harmful effects to ecology
List of ingredients	Attractiveness	Tamperproof	– use	Biodegradable
Instructions	Safety (to users and for the product)	Identifiable	Environmentally safe (biodegradability, etc.)	Free of health hazards
Life of product	Cost of	Safety (to users and for the product)	Package free of health hazards	All-around safety
Disposal method	– materials	Ease of	Self-informative	– Safe to handle
Toll-free phone number for emergencies	– fabrication	– storage	– List of ingredients	– Safe to use
Performance guarantees	– labor	– shelving stocking	– Instructions	Labeled properly
Safety guarantees	– inventory	– package stacking	– Disposal method	– List of ingredients
Environmental safety (biodegradability)	– shipping	– inventory (by computer)	– Toll-free phone number for emergencies	– Nutritional facts with guidelines
Reusable	– storage	Room for price	– Warranties	Expiration date for certain products
Recyclable	Need to change	Stickers	– Expiration date	Recyclable
	Lighter weight (with safety)		Recyclable	Adherence to federal and local regulations
	Tamperproof		Adherence to federal and local regulations	
	Package size (promotion space versus materials cost and environmental safety)			
	Availability of materials			

Source: From "Balancing Traditional Packaging Functions with the New "Green Packaging Concerns," by W. Wossen Kassage and Dharmendra Verma, *SAM Advanced Management Journal*, pp. 15–23, 29, Volume 57, Number 4, Autumn 1992. Reprinted with permission.

Government Impact on Packaging

Government agencies also affect package design. The Food and Drug Administration (FDA), for example, and the Nutrition Labeling and Education Act of 1990 (which went into effect in 1994) imposed stricter labeling requirements for nutrition and health products. And sometimes a state's packaging requirements differ from the federal government's, adding even more complexity for manufacturers.

Package Manufacturing

Packages may come in many forms: wrappers, cartons, boxes, crates, cans, bottles, jars, tubes, barrels, drums, and pallets. And they may be constructed of many materials, from paper and steel ("tin" cans) to wood, glass, and burlap. Newer packaging materials include plastic-coated papers, ceramics, metal foils, and even straw. The plastic film pouch for food products has become a substitute for tin cans and is more flexible, light, and compact. For pharmaceutical products, consumers prefer plastic containers.[29]

The second phase of packaging, the *production process,* may require the use of many packaging specialists: experts in package engineering (box designers, packaging materials consultants, and specialists in equipment configuration); graphic artists (designers, production/computer artists, illustrators, and photographers); label producers (printers and label manufacturers); die-cutters for custom packages; and package warehousing companies (wholesalers of prefabricated packages and package manufacturers).

Ad agencies are not usually involved in packaging decisions. This is typically the realm of specialists. However, it's not uncommon for an agency to be consulted on the design of labels and packages, and some may even prepare the copy that goes on them. In an IMC program, the agency can be very helpful in coordinating this work with the overall theme of the ad campaign.

Generally, the package's design should be kept simple for three reasons: Typical packaging materials (such as corrugated cardboard) cannot support high-resolution printing, intricate folding and die-cutting can be very expensive, and packaging that requires exact folding and fitting often creates excessive assembly costs and leads to structural challenges that most cost-effective packaging materials cannot support.[30]

Knowing When a Package Should Change

There are many reasons to change a package: product alteration or improvement, substitution in packaging materials, competitive pressure, environmental concerns, changes in legislation, or the need to increase brand recognition.[31]

Advertisers spend millions researching and promoting new images. And packages have to reflect a contemporary brand image consistent with constantly changing consumer perceptions and desires. However, marketers should always exercise caution. Designers often change packaging very gradually to avoid confusing consumers.

Trade-Show Booths and Exhibits

Every major industry sponsors annual **trade shows**—exhibitions where manufacturers, dealers, and buyers get together for demonstrations and discussion. More than 14,000 industrial, scientific, and medical shows are held in the United States and Canada each year, and many companies exhibit at more than one show. Trade shows are also very important for global marketers, because they may be the only place where an advertiser can meet the company's major international prospects at one time. Moreover, some of the world's largest trade shows (e.g., the Paris Air Show) are held overseas.

The construction of trade-show **booths** and **exhibits** has become a major factor in sales promotion plans. To stop traffic, a booth must be simple and attractive and have good lighting and a large visual. It should also provide a comfortable atmosphere to promote conversation between salespeople and prospects. Many regular trade-show exhibitors use state-of-the-art technology, such as holograms, fiber optics, and interactive computer systems to communicate product features quickly and dramatically.

When establishing an exhibit booth program, managers should consider planning, budgeting, promotion, people, and productivity.[32]

Want to stand out from the rest of the booths at a trade show? Pacific Domes (www.pacificdomes.com) made a unique geodesic dome for this Lord of the Rings trade-show promotion.

Courtesy of Pacific Domes

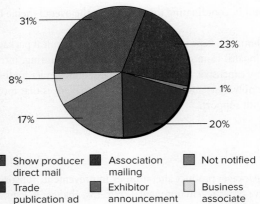

31% 23%

8% 1%

17% 20%

- ■ Show producer direct mail
- ■ Association mailing
- ■ Not notified
- ■ Trade publication ad
- ■ Exhibitor announcement
- □ Business associate

Exhibit 17-5
How do customers learn about trade shows?

Planning

Planning pivots on four major areas: the budget, the image of the company or brand, the frequency of the shows, and the flexibility of booth configuration.[33] In planning the actual exhibits or trade-show booths, advertisers need to consider numerous factors: size and location of space; desired image or impression of the exhibit; complexities of shipping, installation, and dismantling; number of products to be displayed; need for storage and distribution of literature; use of preshow advertising and promotion; and the cost of all these factors.

Budgeting

Trade shows are expensive, and costs have increased substantially in the last decade. A large company may spend $1 million or more on a booth for one trade show. With staffers' travel, living, and salary expenses added to booth costs and preshow promotion, the cost per visitor reached rises to more than $195.[34] Despite the expense, trade shows can still be a cost-effective way to reach sales prospects.

Budgeting for trade shows and a booth may require an extensive review of more than 60 factors.

Promotion

To build traffic for a trade-show booth or exhibit, marketers send out personal invitations, conduct direct-mail campaigns, place ads in trade publications, issue news releases, and perform telemarketing. The pie chart in Exhibit 17-6 portrays how customers typically learn about the trade shows they attend.[35]

At the show itself, activities at the booth and promotional materials (handouts, brochures, giveaway specialty items, raffles) can stimulate customer interest and improve product exposure. 3M's Telcomm Products Division mailed 6,000 potential show attendees a Pony Express theme folder that invited them to pick up a trail map at the booth. The map guided the visitors (Pony Express riders) through a series of stations shared by seven product groups within the huge booth. Once the visitors' maps had been stamped at each station, they were given a "pay envelope" containing replicas of 1850 coins and vouchers redeemable for merchandise awards.[36]

People

The company representatives staffing the booth personify the kind of service the customer can expect to receive. They should be articulate, people-oriented, enthusiastic, knowledgeable about the product, and empathetic listeners.[37]

The primary goal of a trade-show booth is to meet with qualified prospects face-to-face. However, research shows that 58 percent of the people visiting a booth will not wait more than one minute to meet a representative (see Exhibit 17-7). Ideally, 80 percent of the salesperson's time should be spent listening and 20 percent talking.[38]

Productivity

A company's trade-show effort may be wasted if prospects' names are not collected and organized properly. Each lead should be evaluated as to the prospect's readiness to receive another contact (A = now; B = 2 weeks; C = 6 months; D = never).[39] The resulting lead list is the link to future sales and augments the company's prospect database.

Exhibit 17-6
How long a visitor will wait for a sales rep at a trade-show booth.

41%

28%

14%

11%

6%

Will not wait | 30 sec. | 1 min. | 3 min. | 5 min.

Source: Data From INCOMM Research.

Supplementary Media

Many promotional media are difficult to classify because they are tailored to individual needs. Such supplementary media include specialty advertising, directories and Yellow Pages, and a variety of emerging alternative media vehicles.

Specialty Advertising

The Promotional Products Association International (PPAI) defines an **advertising specialty** as a promotional product, usually imprinted with an advertiser's name, message, or logo, that is distributed free as part of a marketing communications program.[40] Today, nearly every business uses advertising specialties of some sort. As many as 15,000 different specialty items, ranging from coffee mugs to ballpoint pens, key chains, and T-shirts, represent an annual volume of more than $18.1 billion.[41]

An advertising specialty is different from a premium. **Premiums** are also promotional products; they are typically more valuable and usually bear no advertising message. However, to get a premium, recipients must buy a product, send in a coupon, witness a demonstration, or perform some other action advantageous to the advertiser. An advertising specialty, on the other hand, is always given *free* as a goodwill item. Some specialty items may be kept for years and serve as continuous, friendly reminders of the advertiser's business. Companies often spend substantial sums for goodwill items to promote their businesses, and studies indicate that this investment pays off: an extensive survey conducted by L. J. Market Research found that promotional items produced higher product recall than print ads. More than 75 percent of respondents could recall the name of the advertiser on a promotional item from the past year, but only 53 percent could name an advertiser in a print publication from the last week.[42]

Business-to-Business Specialties

In the business-to-business arena, companies use more structured specialty promotions to improve their goodwill standing over competitors. Over half of those surveyed in the L. J. Market Research study claimed their impression of the promotional-product advertiser was "somewhat" or "significantly" more favorable after they had received the item.[43]

The dollar amount spent on each promotional item may be less important than the sponsorship itself. In one test, a group of realtors received a $1.49 ballpoint pen imprinted with a mortgage company's name, a second group received a $10 sports bag (also imprinted), and a third group got nothing. In a follow-up questionnaire, realtors who received nothing were least inclined to recommend the product, but both the sports bag and ballpoint pen groups responded equally positively. Evidently, gift recipients felt obliged to reciprocate, but the value of the gift was not crucial. So the $1.49 pen was the better return on investment.[44]

Inappropriate specialty items can backfire no matter what the cost. A recipient may perceive an overly expensive gift as a form of bribery, yet a cheap trinket could make a quality-conscious business look cheap. Finally, marketers should realize that the value and nature of gifts may raise ethical issues.

Fossil Watches (www.fossil.com) used this specialty packaging as a gift to consumers. The container is modeled after automotive oil cans and is reusable. This novelty gift is more useful and appealing than the typical key chain or pencil. The text proclaims the quality and style of the watch that can be found inside and serves as both a reminder to the customer and an ad for others who see it.

© Fossil, Inc

Emerging Media

As traditional advertising media become more expensive and audiences become more fragmented, many advertisers seek new ways to reach their customers. Several types of alternative media are potentially viable options.

People BEHIND the Ads

Cliff Marks, CineMedia

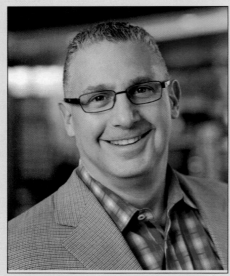

Courtesy of Cliff Marks

For the past few years, if you've arrived at a movie theater a bit early, instead of staring at a blank screen or a curtain, you've been able to watch branded entertainment while waiting for the show to start.

The man behind the "premovie" showings is Clifford ("Cliff") Marks, president of sales and marketing at National CineMedia (NCM).

The idea that consumers waiting to see a film might actually enjoy polished, entertaining advertising content seems so sensible that you might wonder why it hasn't been tried before, especially when you consider the power of the movie theater: big screens, high-definition content, Dolby sound systems, and zero distractions. But the truth is, the logistics of making the thousands of screens in U.S. theaters available to advertisers are more difficult than they might seem at first blush.

Marks and NCM found a way to make it happen. Using agreements with large theater chains such as the Regal Entertainment Group, Marks and his company introduced *The 2wenty*, a digitally transmitted entertainment and advertising pre-feature program. *The 2wenty* featured both traditional (30-second) and longer-format ads that placed a premium on entertainment value. Audiences were happy to have something to watch while waiting for the film to begin. Advertisers were thrilled to be getting an audience that could not be reached as efficiently in any other medium. Making it a win-win situation.

The successor to the *2wenty* is *FirstLook. FirstLook* takes pre-movie advertising to an even higher level, providing advertisers with bundled offerings of on-screen and lobby marketing products that provide multiple ways to interact with theater goers. Using digital transmission, NCM can target advertising and content to specific auditoriums and lobby areas within a network of more than 1,600 network affiliate movie theatres, including over 20,150 digital screens nationally. In 2015, NCM estimates that its programming reached approximately 700 million movie patrons.

Before creating these innovative cinema programs, Marks served as president of sales and marketing with Regal Entertainment Group's media subsidiary, Regal CineMedia Corporation. Before joining NCM Marks was a 14-year veteran of ESPN/ABC Sports, where as senior vice president he versaw its $2 billion sales organization. Working with top national advertisers such as Anheuser Busch, Circuit City, MCI, Toyota, AT&T, Pizza Hut, Taco Bell, and KFC, Marks was instrumental in developing vertically integrated advertising packages for clients across multiple platforms including ABC Sports programming, ESPN, ESPN2, ESPN Classic, ESPNews, ESPN.com, *ESPN Magazine*, ESPN radio, and ESPNZone restaurants.

Cliff Marks shared some of his thoughts about cinema advertising with *Contemporary Advertising*.

CA: How was the idea for nationwide cinema advertising born?

Cliff: It was born in Europe many years ago, primarily as a result of the lack of advertising in European TV. While North America has always had a very mature commercial television industry and Americans have grown up with commercials being a staple of their television experience, the same is not true in Europe, where government-owned broadcast stations were created to be noncommercial "public service" programmers. The cinema became the place where marketers could communicate with consumers using the big screen to market to captive audiences who are entertainment focused and receptive to messaging portrayed in an entertaining and respectful way.

CA: When you speak with advertisers, how do you distinguish the opportunities they can get from cinema advertising from other channels, especially other out-of-home?

Cliff: We explain that cinema has the best elements of out-of-home and broadcast television, a unique combination of sight, sound, and motion. Unlike most out-of-home, advertisers can reach a national audience—it has scale. Plus, there is NO MIGA (Make It Go Away) device for consumers to avoid the commercials. Cinema has much in common with television; for example, it is a scalable national medium with touch points in every major market in America and can be bought nationally, regionally, or locally. Cinema has also invested in digital satellite delivery technology allowing marketers to target specific messages in any way they desire. A brand may target by market, by region, by film rating (PG/PG 13/R), film genre—comedy, suspense, horror, romance or chick flicks, guy films, kid films, etc. . . . The investment in digitizing America's movie theaters has changed the advertising landscape forever as marketers are now empowered to hyper-target their audiences with no additional cost to the marketer. This makes cinema in many ways more valuable than broadcast.

Cinema is primarily sold to national marketers as a complement to national broadcast. We tell advertisers that cinema is itself just another network. Of course, cinema's affiliates are not TV stations, but movie theaters. But that's really where the network model difference ends. We also stress the unique aspects of cinema, which include a 40-foot screen, complete attention captivity, digital targeting ability, lobby and other sampling and consumer-centric assets, and a reasonable barrier to entry making new competitors unlikely.

CA: How do you do market research on cinema advertising? What does it tell you about your audience?

Cliff: Our research is generally comparable to other media, allowing for some direct apples-to-apples comparisons. Of course, cinema has the luxury of knowing exactly how many people attend a film as they share the revenue with their studio partners and must account for every single ticket sold. There is a lot of syndicated research on the movies and the kinds of people that attend different genres. The research shows that cinema casts a pretty wide net—we reach everybody from 4-year-olds to 84-year-olds, depending on the kind and rating genre. Cinema's sweet spot is 12–34 year olds, as this audience is more likely to see a film several times, and most likely to go over six times per year. They are the "heavy users."

CA: What is the future of cinema advertising? How will it evolve?

Cliff: Cinema advertising has grown by strong double digits every year since 2002 and the future is very bright. Cinema will evolve to compete with both network TV and spot TV for both national and local funds. We've invested heavily in digital technologies, which allow advertisers to carve up the network and target specific kinds of audiences or specific markets. These technologies make cinema a highly targetable medium with mass scale.

Advertisers will view cinema the same way they view TV networks. If you look at NCM *FirstLook* program prior to the movies, it fits this definition because it plays on over 17,000 screens throughout the United States.

One other interesting development in the evolution of cinema advertising is alternative content, which is played over the digital screens when movies are not the predominant product. We have seen various events like music concerts, opera, sports, and other specialty events make their big screen debut with varying degrees of success. This model will be perfected and the cinema will become a common venue to view alternative content over an HD satellite network.

CA: Which advertisers seem most interested in cinema? My impression is that many of the advertisers are TV networks. What do they like about cinema?

Cliff: Most brands that take advantage of cinema make highly entertaining, brand-image advertising. Cinema is less strong with very retail-centric ads, ads which have an immediate call to action. One thing all advertisers know is that there are no refrigerators, computers, phones, changing the baby, using the men's room and of course, no remote controls or TiVo machines and other common distractions that affect advertising on television.

CA: Any other thoughts about the future of this exciting new advertising medium?

Cliff: The world is changing a lot and I would suspect that many more companies are going to reevaluate their media options in the coming years. I do not think that networks will go away. They are still a reasonably good deal for marketers as they still sell their time at a reasonable price (especially cable nets). But cinema stands to be one of the big winners (certainly not the only big winner!) as other digital networks which offer scale, sight, sound, motion, and measurability will help marketers reach their designated target audiences.

Product placement is an increasingly popular way to advertise consumer products. For product placement to work, the brand must be prominent, identifiable, and credible in the context. The Omega Seamaster seems natural but is clearly identifiable in this screen shot from the film "50 Shades of Grey."

© Focus Features/Everett Collection

Cinema Advertising

Advertising in movie theaters (**cinema advertising**) is a growing but controversial practice. Although some movie-going audiences resent watching ads, cinema advertising is becoming more and more attractive to marketers. "Unlike traditional media, we don't have to fight for our audience's attention; they don't flip channels," says Bob Martin, president and chair of the Cinema Advertising Council.[45] Cinema advertising grew to a $456 million industry in 2006, up 15 percent from 2005. Nonetheless, some movie theater chains prohibit filmed advertising for fear of offending their audience.

Product Placement

Another way to reach movie and television audiences is to pay a fee to have the product written into the movie or program. Such **product placement** is becoming more common. Notice the number of identifiable products in the next movie you see.

Increasingly, product placement in the multibillion-dollar movie industry has become an important advertising medium. By getting their brands appearances, and sometimes roles, in movies, companies benefit from the association with top films and big-name actors. Nokia has had great success with this technique: Its phones were so prominent in the 1999 film *The Matrix* that 31 percent of moviegoers thought that characters in 2003's *The Matrix Reloaded* sequel were still using Nokia phones, when in fact they had switched to Samsung.[46]

Constantly fretting about viewers' newfound ability to avoid commercials by using TiVo, advertisers are also embedding their products more frequently in television programs. Ford and Coca-Cola both had high-profile presences on "American Idol"—judges drank from red cups with the Coca-Cola logo and contestants performed in Ford vehicles—just one example of the emerging "brand casting" trend, worth an estimated $1.5 billion in the United States in 2005. Product placement growth is expected to significantly outpace that of traditional advertising. According to promomagazine.com, global paid product placement reached $7.6 by 2010.[47]

However, controversy surrounds some product placement categories. In response to severe new laws prohibiting most forms of tobacco advertising, the Canadian Tobacco Manufacturers' Council withdrew all product placements in films, TV programs, and computer games.

ATMs

With so many thousands of money devices in service, it's only natural that the captive audience of ATMs are targeted for creative promotional tactics. Fleet Financial Group has capitalized on ATM technology by printing retailer coupons on the back of receipts, the other piece of paper that customers receive from the machines. The coupons, which were initially redeemable at Bruegger's Bagels, Firestone, Great Cuts, Oil Doctor, and Pizza Hut, originated in Massachusetts and provided advertising that customers were likely to carry around in their wallets or cars.

One ATM innovation, developed by Electronic Data Systems Corp., puts full-motion video ads on the machine's screen as customers wait for their transaction to be processed. The 15-second ads, which debuted in 7-Eleven stores in San Diego, replace the "Transaction being processed" or "Please wait" messages that appeared on the screen. The original ads promoted Fox Searchlight Pictures' films *The Ice Storm* and *The Full Monty.*

Digital technologies are revolutionizing many media forms, including jukebox screens. The vast number of such machines guarantees advertiser interest.

Source: TouchTunes

This ad, which rests on the bottom shelf of shopping carts, encourages shoppers to have their cars serviced while they shop.

© Outdoor Advertising Association of America

Other promotions run through ATMs include a MasterCard International and Coca-Cola USA collaboration on the "Coca-Cola incredible summer," in which customers could win cash instantly by using a special disposable ATM card.

Chapter Summary

Media that reach prospects outside their homes are called out-of-home media. They include outdoor advertising, transit advertising, and exotica like electronic signs and parking meters. Of the major advertising media, outdoor advertising is the least expensive per message delivered. It also offers other attractive features: instant broad coverage (reach), very high frequency, great flexibility, and high impact. Drawbacks include the limits of brief messages, long lead times, high initial preparation costs, and the difficulty of physically inspecting each billboard.

The standardized outdoor advertising industry consists of about 3,000 local and regional plant operators. National advertising makes up the bulk of outdoor business. The three most common forms of outdoor advertising structures are the 30-sheet poster, the junior poster, and the bulletin. A form of outdoor available in some cities is the spectacular, an expensive electronic display. The basic unit of sale for outdoor advertising is the 100 showing, or 100 GRPs, which means the message will appear on enough panels to provide a daily exposure equal to the market's total population.

Transit advertising includes transit shelters; station, platform, and terminal posters; inside cards and outside posters on buses; and taxi exteriors. This medium offers high reach, frequency, exposure, and attention values at very low cost. It gives long exposure to the advertiser's message and offers repetitive value and geographic flexibility. In addition, advertisers have a wide choice in the size of space used.

But transit advertising does not cover some segments of society. Also, it reaches a nonselective audience, it lacks prestige, and copy is still somewhat limited.

Other out-of-home media include mobile billboards, electronic signs and display panels, parking meters, and public phones.

Exhibitive media include product packaging and trade-show booths and exhibits. These media are designed to help bring consumers or business customers eyeball-to-eyeball with the product, often at the point of sale or close to it.

Supplementary media include specialty advertising, Yellow Pages directories, and emerging media like DVDs, movie theaters, product placements, and ATMs. Product placement includes films, videos, computer games, and the Internet. The advantage of film is that it creates brand association with top movies and actors.

ATMs provide several means of exposure, from printed ads on receipts to full-motion video to promotionals like ATM-card cash giveaways. Because most Americans today use ATMs, they offer a high frequency of exposure.

Important Terms

advertising specialty, *537*

basic bus, *530*

booth, *535*

brand trains, *531*

bulletin structure, *519*

bus-o-rama sign, *531*

car-end poster, *530*

cinema advertising, *540*

directories, *517*

electronic sign, *531*

exhibit, *531*

exhibitive media, *531*

full showing, *530*

global positioning system (GPS), *527*

immersive advertising, *531*

inside card, *530*

junior poster, *519*

mobile billboard, *531*

100 showing, *521*

out-of-home media, *516*

outside poster, *530*

packaging, *532*

premium, *537*

product placement, *540*

showing, *521*

spectaculars, *520*

standardized outdoor advertising, *518*

stock poster, *519*

take-ones, *530*

taxicab exterior, *530*

terminal poster, *530*

30-sheet poster panel, *519*

total bus, *531*

trade show, *535*

transit advertising, *528*

transit shelter advertising, *529*

Review Questions

1. What is the difference between out-of-home media and outdoor advertising?
2. Why is outdoor advertising sometimes referred to as the last mass medium?
3. Which advertising objectives are the outdoor media most suitable for?
4. Is outdoor an effective advertising medium for a local political candidate? Why?
5. How do gross rating points for outdoor media differ from GRPs for electronic media?
6. What are the principal categories of transit advertising?
7. What is a brand train and what advantages does it offer over less expensive forms of transit advertising?
8. Which are the exhibitive media and why are they called that?
9. What is the principal benefit of trade shows and exhibitions?
10. How does specialty advertising differ from premiums? How could a local computer store use these media, and which would be better for the store to use?

The Advertising Experience

1. **Using Billboard Advertising**

   Upshaw Books, the largest independent bookstore in the area, wants to advertise on billboards along the main commuter route. Create a series of three standard billboards that would grab commuters' attention and motivate them to visit the store.

2. **Outdoor Advertising**

   As you have learned in this chapter, out-of-home advertising and communication have been a mainstay in consumers' lives for quite some time. The outdoor advertising industry certainly makes up the largest portion of such advertising.

   Although often overlooked in advertising and media decision making, outdoor advertising can have a powerful effect as a supplemental medium to broader print or broadcast campaigns. To find out more about this side of the advertising business, visit five of the Websites for the outdoor advertising organizations listed below and answer the questions that follow.

   - Burkhart Advertising: www.burkhartadv.com
   - Outfront Media: www.cbsoutdoor.com
   - Clear Channel Outdoor: www.clearchanneloutdoor.com
   - Gallop & Gallop Advertising: www.gallop.ca
   - Kinetic: www.kineticww.com
   - Lamar Outdoor Advertising: www.lamar.com
   - Outdoor Advertising Association of America, Inc. (OAAA): www.oaaa.org
   - SignCraft magazine: www.signcraft.com
   - SignIndustry.com: www.signindustry.com
   - Steen Outdoor Systems: www.steen.com
   - Wilkins Media Company: www.wilkins-media.com

   a. What organization sponsors the site? Who is the intended audience(s)?
   b. What is the purpose of the site? Does it succeed? Why?
   c. What services (if any) does the organization provide advertisers?
   d. How important do you believe this organization is to outdoor advertising today and in the future? Why?

3. **Specialty Advertising**

   Promotional specialty items are, perhaps, one of the oldest forms of media. Though consumers do not always think of these items as "advertising," they most certainly are—being clearly composed, nonpersonal communications by an identified sponsor. Many organizations and firms are involved in specialty advertising and the industry is still growing today. Peruse some of the Websites below and learn more about the products, processes, and promotional power of specialty ad items. Then answer the questions that follow.

   - AD
   - BCG Creations: www.bcgcreations.com
   - Bells Advertising: www.bells.com
   - Corporate Graphics, Inc.: www.wearables.com

- Cowan Imaging Group: www.cowan.ca
- Image Pointe: www.imagepointe.com
- LogoZ: www.logoz.com
- PromoMart: www.promomart.com
- PROMO'S: www.coolgifts.com
- Promotional Product Association International (PPAI): www.ppa.org
- Promotions Online: www.promosonline.com
- S-N-T Graphics: www.sntgraphics.com

a. What is the focus of the organization sponsoring this site?

b. Who is the intended audience of the site?

c. What services (if any) does the organization offer?

d. What is your overall impression of the organization and its work? Explain?

4. Some companies are known for their beautiful packaging. Apple comes to mind. Identify three other brands that enhance the value of their brands by using exceptionally designed packages.

5. If, at the time of the launch of the James Ready campaign featured at the start of the chapter, it had decided that a transit medium would have better suited the campaign, would the campaign have been adjusted to meet the needs of this new format? If so, how?

6. If you were responsible for media placement of the James Ready campaign, do you think the spots would be better suited by running on the same billboard every week, or by appearing on different billboards around Ontario?

CHAPTER

18

Relationship Building: Direct Marketing, Personal Selling, and Sales Promotion

Learning Objectives

To emphasize the importance of relationships in today's high-tech, overcommunicated world and to demonstrate how marketing communications can be integrated with advertising to manage an organization's relations with its stakeholders. Relationship marketing and IMC are two of the most important trends in marketing today. Direct marketing, personal selling, and sales promotion play different but often overlapping roles in IMC programs. Each offers many opportunities but also has limitations.

 After studying this chapter, you will be able to:

LO18-1   Define direct marketing and explain its role in IMC.

LO18-2   Distinguish personal selling from other forms of IMC.

LO18-3   List the activities that constitute sales promotion, including push and pull tactics, and explain their roles in IMC.

Source: GEICO

The rules of using direct response advertising are straightforward. Use a simple pitch. Keep the campaign unified. Don't worry too much about the creative, since it's the offer that closes the sale. For several years now, insurer GEICO has done pretty well ignoring two out of three of those rules. ■ The pitch is certainly simple—contact GEICO and save money on insurance. Ads encourage consumers to make a toll-free call or visit a Website to get a quote. ■ But GEICO's campaigns are anything but unified. One, accompanied by the tagline "So easy a caveman could do it," humorously portrays the disgust of cavemen, modern in every way but their appearance, at the slogan's insensitivity. In another, a gentle, computer-generated gecko whimsically proclaims the benefits of GEICO to anyone who'll listen. Still another parodies advertising itself by using spots that appear to be commercials for other products. The humor comes when the viewer recognizes the ads are actually from GEICO. ■ So, despite a clear direct-response purpose, GEICO's ads show plenty of creativity. But why so many different executions? Doesn't that just confuse consumers? And how successful have the campaigns been? ■ GEICO's approach is guided by a clear "share of voice" strategy (see Chapter 8). The company, which has a relatively small share of the insurance market—behind giants like State Farm and Allstate—spends more on advertising than any of its competitors, nearly $2 billion since 2001. The investment has paid off—91 percent of shoppers recall being exposed to a GEICO message over the past year versus 80 and 78 percent for competitors. Advertising has helped with the bottom line, too. GEICO is the top insurer in new-customer acquisition and the only top-four brand to grow at a double-digit pace.[1] ■ So consumers are clearly not confused by all of the executions. In fact, the reason GEICO runs so many different campaigns simultaneously is that each is intended for a different audience.[2] As a large insurance company, GEICO sells policies to customers from many demographic and psychographic backgrounds. Knowing that one campaign will not be equally effective with everyone, the company uses some of the spots, like the Cavemen, to appeal to younger audiences. Others, like the gecko, resonate more with older audiences.[3] ■ Committing a relatively large amount to advertising is also part of the company's overall IMC strategy since GEICO relies on a much smaller sales force than its competitors. As we will see later in this chapter, personal selling is an effective but expensive way to market a product. Using a smaller sales force means lower

Source: GEICO

costs, which GEICO passes along to customers. But it also means advertising does much of the heavy lifting for reaching new customers. That can be a smart move, but only if the ads are effective. ■ Ted Ward, VP of marketing at GEICO, notes that "We have essentially a direct-to-consumer business model. We try to strip out costs to deliver the lowest price—it includes having very few agents in a process by having a superior technology model, which back in the '70s was direct mail; in the '80s and '90s, a telephone; and in the last 10 years, the online delivery of rates."[4] ■ Creating the ads is the Martin Agency, headquartered in Richmond, Virginia. The agency and advertiser have an unusually long working relationship, almost 15 years. The value of a close and comfortable fit between advertiser and agency is reinforced in Ward's recall of how the gecko was born. "I was sitting around with … [an] art director at Martin, shooting the breeze after some focus groups and literally it was on a napkin and the rest just played out."[5] ■ Not that Ward was completely sold. "It was not my favorite campaign, personally" he recalls, "I quickly became much more fond of him as we sold more policies. I'm a big fan of anything that makes our phone ring or Website click. He really has helped us brandwise."[6] ■ GEICO's success reveals that an advertiser does not have to choose between generating an immediate response versus building brand equity. Great ads can do both. ■ The GEICO story also says something important about the value of a healthy, trusting relationship between a company and its agency. "It's partnership. It was very purposeful hiring them. … We share a lot of information," Ward says. "We get all our partners together, and we are all focused. … I'd like to say one of the strengths I've added is a sense of consistency. We [don't] diverge from the central plot."[7] ■

Throughout the text, we've suggested that the key to building brand equity in the 21st century is the development of interdependent, mutually satisfying relationships with customers and other stakeholders. Further, to benefit from these relationships, companies should consciously (and *conscientiously*) integrate their marketing communications activities with all their other functions so that the messages the marketplace receives about the company are consistent.

However, this is a lot easier said than done, since everything a company does (and doesn't do) sends a message. Seamless, consistent communication—from every corner of the company—is how a firm earns a good reputation. And that is the principal objective of IMC.

GEICO is a good example of how IMC works. To attract prospects and initiate the relationship-building process, GEICO integrates its advertising efforts with a host of other marketing communication tools—direct marketing, sales promotion, personal selling, and public relations activities. While the forms and styles of these messages may vary, all reinforce a consistent proposal—that GEICO can save you money on insurance.

It is important for communications specialists to understand how to integrate the various tools of marketing communications. As they plan a campaign, practitioners need a basic understanding of what other communications tools are available to them and how they can best be used in the overall marketing communications mix. In this chapter, we will discuss the interactive, one-to-one communication tools of direct marketing and personal selling. We'll also look at sales promotion, which might be called the "value-added" tool. In the next chapter, we'll address the "credibility" tools companies use to enhance their reputations. These include various public relations activities, sponsorships, and corporate advertising.

Understanding Direct Marketing

LO 18-1

There is a lot of confusion surrounding the term *direct marketing*, even among the experts.

The Direct Marketing Association (DMA) defines **direct marketing** as "an interactive process of addressable communication that uses one or more advertising media to effect, at any location, a measurable sale, lead, retail purchase or charitable donation, with this activity analyzed on a database for the development of ongoing mutually beneficial relationships between marketers and customers, prospects or donors."[8]

Direct Marketing magazine goes even further: "Direct marketing is a measurable system of marketing that uses one or more advertising media to effect a measurable response and/or transaction at any location, with this activity stored in a database." From this definition a virtually synonymous term has emerged: **database marketing.** Database marketers build and maintain a pool of data on current and prospective customers (and other stakeholders) and communicate with them using a variety of media (from personal contact to direct mail to mass media). Database marketing is a widely adopted marketing method because it has proven to be a cost-efficient way to increase sales. A good **database** enables marketers to target, segment, and grade customers. It helps them to know who their customers and prospects are, what and when they buy, and how to contact them. That, of course, leads to the possibility of a relationship.

The various definitions of direct marketing share much in common. First and foremost, direct marketing is a *system of marketing* and it is *interactive,* meaning buyers and sellers exchange information with each other directly.

A second shared part of the definition is the concept of *one or more advertising media.* Part of the confusion with the name is its similarity to *direct mail.* But direct mail is just one of the many media that direct marketers use.

In the GEICO story, for instance, we saw how the company used a mass media form—television—to elicit responses from people who might be interested in saving on insurance. GEICO uses other media as well, including radio and direct mail, to reach its target audience. In fact, experienced direct marketers have known for years that using more than one medium tends to be far more productive than using a single medium.[9]

The third key point of the direct marketing definition is a *measurable response.* In fact, the kind of advertising direct marketers use is called **direct-response** (or **action**) **advertising.** This is because direct marketing efforts are always aimed at stimulating action or response on the part of the customer or prospect. While it can be argued that all advertising is ultimately directed at getting consumers to take action, the response intended by a direct-response ad is meant to happen relatively quickly after the receiver encounters the message. It may be in the

Direct marketing is intended to stimulate a response in the form of a request for information, an actual purchase, or a visit. In the case of a social organization like Britain's NSPCC, direct marketing can have a powerful impact on a wide constituency beyond the primary target market. This poster, which won a Gold Lion at Cannes, prompted calls from abused teenagers to jump 124 percent in just six weeks.

Source: National Society for the Prevention of Cruelty to Children form of a request for information, a store visit, or an actual purchase. Because these responses can be tallied and analyzed, direct marketing becomes accountable. And that, more than any other reason, accounts for the tremendous growth of direct marketing in recent years. Managers like it because they can see what they got for their money.

The final point most of the definitions make is that the response can be at *any location.* In other words, direct marketing is *not* restricted to mail order or catalog sales. Customers may respond by telephone, via mail-in coupons, social media, at a retail store or other place of business, or even at a kiosk. GEICO processes the vast majority of its quote requests by phone and via the web.

The Role of Direct Marketing in IMC

Today, sophisticated companies use the skills developed by direct marketers to establish, nourish, and maintain relationships, not just with customers, but with all stakeholders.

GEICO, for instance, uses TV advertising as one of its **linkage media**—media that help prospects and customers link up with a company—to inform prospects how to inquire about its products. Next, it uses these responses to build its database of names, addresses, and e-mail addresses. Then it uses the database to communicate with prospects, open a dialogue, and establish a relationship. It may send a mail piece with ordering information or direct people to its Website to enable prospects to connect with GEICO directly.

The Evolution of Direct Marketing

Direct marketing is the oldest marketing method, and today it is growing incredibly fast, propelled by the major social and technological changes. About 57 percent of American women work outside the home.[10] So while families have more income, they have less time to spend shopping, thus making the convenience of telephones, the Internet, and credit cards important factors in direct marketing.

Likewise, the expanding use of credit cards has revolutionized the way consumers buy goods and services. Electronic, cashless transactions make products (especially large, costly items) easier and faster to purchase. And now, with advances in credit card security technology, more and more people are shopping right from their computers.

In 2014, sales driven by direct marketing grew by 5.5 percent, a pace that is faster than overall U.S. sales. In fact, nearly 9 percent of the U.S. GDP originates in direct marketing.[11]

An integrated campaign through a variety of media for the American Red Cross including direct response TV, print ads and web banners ensures their messages will work together and help attract donations ensuring the organization can serve those in need.

Source: American Red Cross

Exhibit 18-1

Largest direct-response agencies in the United States.

2014	2013	AGENCY [COMPANY]	U.S. Revenue (Million) 2014	% CHG from 2013
1	1	Epsilon	$1,298	7.2%
2	2	Wunderman*	1,175	3.8
3	3	Experian Marketing Services	881	0.8
4	4	DigitasLBi*	871	7.8
5	5	Acxiom Corp.*	810	0.6
6	6	Rapp*	760	5.9
7	7	OgilvyOne Worldwide*	631	10.8
8	8	Proximity*	586	9.5
9	9	Harte Hanks*	499	−0.9
10	11	Merkle	448	15.1

Source: Ad Age Datacenter.

Working with direct-response specialists, marketers are fueling this growth by pouring money into direct marketing campaigns. Exhibit 18-1 shows the largest direct-response agencies in the United States. The greatest overall spending increases in 2015 are expected in search (11%), Display and Mobile advertising (21%), and e-mail (9.7%).[12]

The boom in telecommunications and computer technology is spurring the growth of direct marketing worldwide. Today, Germany is by far the largest national market in Europe, spending more than $41 billion on direct marketing efforts annually. Britain comes in second at more than $26 billion, followed closely by France. Interestingly, outside the United States, Japan is by far the number-one market for direct marketing, with estimated annual spending close to $97 billion.[13]

Telephone companies worldwide provide toll-free numbers for customers to place orders or request information. Toll-free numbers give companies immediate, direct responses and help them collect information to create and refine their databases. GEICO relies heavily on a toll-free number to sell insurance.

However, certain challenges in foreign markets have limited the growth of direct market-ing efforts. Foreign markets have a wide variety of laws and regulations to contend with. Likewise, payment and postal systems vary considerably, as do conventions for addressing mail. And finally, cultural nuances and language can get in the way. For example, the same name can indicate different genders in different countries. In England Abigail is a woman's name, but in Portugal it's a man's name. Again, though, technology comes to the rescue. "Ad dress hygiene" software, which improves the deliverability of mail by cleaning and formatting address databases, is widely available, but one French company has taken the idea a step fur-ther. Addressing Technology has developed a solution to these problems with its universal mailing software. It makes sure the correct salutation and gender code are used for some 125,000 given names in various countries and also enables marketers to satisfy the differing postal regulations of more than 208 countries.[14]

The Impact of Databases on Direct Marketing

Modern computer technology enables marketers to compile and analyze important cus-tomer information in unprecedented ways. Pitney Bowes, for instance, is the dominant company in the postal meter business. However, its growth rate and profitability were flat-tening. So the company used its database to identify its best customers, their value to the organization, and their needs and buying behavior. From this information, Pitney Bowes created a **customer lifetime value (LTV)** model based on historical and potential share of business. Computing and ranking the *lifetime value* of all of its 1.2 million customers showed that more than two-thirds of the customer base value resided in fewer than 10 per-cent of the customers. The company also found it had a major retention problem within its low-volume, low-cost accounts. Cancellation rates were running as high as 40 percent per year in some segments. This analysis enabled Pitney Bowes to develop a distinct direc-

Direct-response ads allow Geico to save marketing dollars. The effective ads help save money on a personal sales force.

Source: GEICO

marketing strategy for both its best and its worst customers. It began a sophisticated *loyalty program* for its best customers and a *retention program* for its problem accounts. By the end of the first year, the program had reduced attrition by 20 percent, and the reduction in cost of sales alone paid back the entire direct marketing investment.[15] In another situation, a company might determine from its LTV analysis that its best course of action is simply to drop the most unprofitable customers.

The database is the key to direct marketing success, especially in an IMC program. It enables marketers to target, segment, and grade customers. It is the corporate memory of all important customer information: name and address, telephone number, e-mail address, NAIC code (if a business firm), source of inquiry, cost of inquiry, history of purchases, and so on. It should record every transaction across all points of contact with both channel members and customers. The company that understands its customers' needs and wants better than any of its competitors, and retains more of its best customers, will create a sustainable competitive advantage. Strategically, therefore, companies have to determine if they focus on share of market or on retention and loyalty (share of customer).[16] More often than not, this is a short-term versus long-term trade-off.

The database also lets the company measure the efficiency of its direct-response advertising efforts to see, for instance, which radio or TV commercials, or which mailing lists, perform the best.

Working with a marketing database requires two processes: data management and data access. **Data management** is the process of gathering, consolidating, updating, and enhancing the information about customers and prospects that resides in the database.

Most important, the database gives marketers **data access,** enabling them to manipulate, analyze, and rank all the information to make better marketing decisions. Thanks to new software, this can now usually be accomplished on PCs connected to client–server computers.

Rob Jackson, coauthor of *Strategic Database Marketing,* suggests that database marketing should start with *customer profiling.* Profiling allows marketers to get a snapshot of what their customers look like at any given time by identifying common characteristics and ranking their relative importance in different segments.[17]

In the same vein, direct marketing experts Stone and Jacobs use an **RFM formula** (recency, frequency, monetary) to identify the best customers—the ones most likely to buy again (see Exhibit 18-2). The best customers have bought recently, buy frequently, and spend the most money. Customers may be further ranked by the type of merchandise or services they buy, information that becomes very useful in the effort to cross-sell other merchandise.[18]

Some companies may simply purchase a mailing list as its initial database. Three types of data are typically available for purchase: demographics, lifestyle (leisure interests), and behavioristics (purchase habits).[19]

Perhaps the greatest reason for direct marketing's current growth is that marketers and agencies realize they can't do the job with just one medium anymore. As the mass audience fragmented and companies began to integrate their marketing communications, customer databases became key to retaining and growing customers.

Direct marketing is the best way to develop a good database. The database enables the marketer to build a relationship by learning about customers in depth: what and where they buy, what they're interested in, and what they need. With a database, companies can choose the prospects they can serve most effectively and *profitably*—the purpose of all marketing. "You don't want a relationship with every customer," says Philip Kotler. "In fact, there are some bad customers out there."[20] Retailer Best Buy uses direct mail to send sales promotions materials, but only to its best customers.[21]

People like to see themselves as unique, not part of some 100-million-member mass market. Through direct marketing, especially addressable electronic media, companies can send discrete messages to individual customers and prospects. With different types of sales promotion (discussed in the last part of this chapter), a company can encourage individuals, not masses, to respond and can develop a relationship with each person. By responding, the prospect *self-selects,* giving the marketer permission to begin a relationship.[22] The direct

My IMC Campaign 18–A

Developing a Plans Book

A plans book, quite simply, is the representation of all the hard work you have put in to develop the ideas for your project. For some of you this is an actual deliverable for the project; for the rest of you, it is good practice and good process management to develop a plans book to ensure that all of your thinking exists in one place.

Don't let the word *book* fool you—what we are talking about here is a binder or a set of binders that house information relevant to your client's problem. Whether it is competitive news and information, industry news, research on target audiences, and/or SWOT analysis, this binder should comprise all of that organized information. The plans book is the foundation you will use to build the final presentation (we talk about the final presentation in Chapter 19), a concise explanation of how you will utilize the information in the plans book to put your campaign ideas into action.

Here is the information that should be represented in your plans book:

- Objectives
- Challenges
- SWOT analysis
- Target audience analysis
- Communications strategy
- Creative and media brief(s)
- Creative concepts
- Media strategy and plan
- Evaluation or success metrics

Objectives

This is a statement or a set of statements that describe what you hope to achieve from advertising for your client's product. Some common goals are lifting awareness within a new audience, stealing share from competitors, or changing perceptions of consumers. It is better to stay focused and not try to do too much.

Challenges

Think about what you are trying to achieve and what barriers exist that make your work that much harder. If you are trying to lift sales for your client's products, one challenge may be that there is little to no awareness.

SWOT or Situation Analysis

Understanding the strengths, weaknesses, opportunities, and threats for your client's product(s) helps you focus on the appropriate strategy to market the brand. Along with target analysis, the SWOT analysis should lead right into your strategy for marketing the product/brand.

Target Audience Analysis

Hopefully you have done a combination of primary research (interviews) and secondary research (syndicated or already done by a third party) to help understand what motivates your consumers to take action. Once you understand this, advertising becomes much easier; this section should highlight the research done and the insights from that work.

Communications Strategy

Your communications strategy is an overarching guide to how you will approach reaching your target with your client's message. All of your tactics should easily fall out of your strategy statements.

Creative and Media Brief(s)

This can be a single document or a set of documents, but either way it should present the parameters for all of your creative and media work. Look back to Chapter 10 for how to develop a brief.

Creative Concepts

The creative concept is a visual representation of your idea or set of ideas, complete with messaging and layouts.

Media Strategy and Plan

Like the communication strategy, the media strategy should act as a framework for all of your tactical media ideas. The media plan itself is just a representation of the tactical ideas with timing included. (See Exhibit 9–13 in Chapter 9 for an example of a media plan.)

Evaluation or Success Metrics

Of course all of your ideas will work, because you have done all of your homework, but what if one of them didn't . . . how would you know? This is where you detail how you plan to track and measure your campaign's effectiveness. This could be as simple as sales growth or more complex, like a pre/post attitudinal study.

is clear: Of all media, direct-mail advertising offers the straightest line to the desired cus tomer. Decades of mailboxes stuffed with catalogs, credit card offers, and music club pack ets have made today's advertising-weary consumers harder to reach, though.

Types of Direct Mail   Direct mail comes in a variety of formats, from handwritten postcard to dimensional mailings like ShipShapes. The message can be one sentence or dozens of page And within each format—from tiny coupon to thick catalog or box—the creative options a infinite. In addition to the dimensional direct-mail category are the following:

Sales letters, the most common direct-mail format, are often mailed with brochure price lists, or reply cards and envelopes. **Postcards** are used to announce sales, off discounts, or generate customer traffic. National postal services regulate formats and dimensions. Some advertisers use a double postcard, enabling them to send both an advertising message and a perforated reply card. A recipient who wants the product or service tears off the reply card and mails it back to the advertiser. To encourage response, some advertisers use **business reply mail** so the recipient can respond without paying postage. The advertiser needs a special first-class postal permit and must print the number on the face of the return card or envelope. On receiving a response, the advertiser pays postage plus a handling fee of a few cents. "Postage-free" incentives usually increase response rates.

Folders and **brochures** are usually printed in multiple colors with photos or other illustrations on good paper stock that reproduces printed images well. **Broadsides** are larger than folders and are sometimes used as window displays or wall posters in stores. They fold to a compact size to fit in a mailbag.

Self-mailers are any form of direct mail that can travel without an envelope. Usually folded and secured by a staple or seal, they have special blank spaces for the prospect's name and address to be written, stenciled, or labeled.

Statement stuffers are ads enclosed in monthly customer statements from department stores, banks, oil companies, and the like. To order, customers write in their credit card number and sign the reply card.

House organs are publications produced by associations or business organizations—for example, stockholder reports, newsletters, consumer magazines, and dealer publications.

Using Direct Mail in the Media Mix   Direct mail is an efficient, effective, and economical medium for sales and business promotion. That's why a wide variety of companies, charity and service organizations, and individuals use it. Direct mail can increase the effectiveness of ads in other media. Publishers Clearinghouse uses TV spots to alert viewers to the impending arrival of its direct-mail sweepstakes promotions.

Direct mail has two main drawbacks: cost and the "junk mail" image, both of which are almost inescapable. No other medium (except personal selling and consumer targeting on the Internet) has such a high cost per thousand. For this reason, many small marketers participate in cooperative mailings with companies such as ADVO, which serves most major U.S. cities. ADVO mails an envelope containing a coupon for each participating company to targeted zip codes.

Some large companies don't send unsolicited mail. To locate prospects, they use other direct-response media. Then they use direct mail to respond to inquiries. They save money by mailing only to qualified prospects, and by sending higher-quality materials, they build their image and improve their chances of establishing a worthwhile relationship.

Buying Direct Mail   Direct mail has three basic costs: list acquisition, creative production, and distribution.

The heart of any direct-mail program is the mailing list. Each list actually defines a market segment. Direct-mail advertisers use three types of lists: *house, mail-response,* and *compiled.*

The company's relational database of current, recent, and long-past customers as well as future prospects comprises the **house list** for direct-mail programs. Because customers are its most important asset, every company should focus sufficient resources on developing a rich database of customer and prospect information and profiles. There are several ways a company can build its own house list, from offering credit plans to sending useful information to exchanging names with other businesses with similar customer profiles.

Consumer product companies like General Electric gather customer data by enclosing an owner registration form with their products. On the mail-in form, purchasers give their name, address, phone number, birth date, occupation, income range, credit card preferences, home ownership status, and number of children. They also indicate their hobbies and interests (such as golf, foreign travel, photography, or bowling).

Exhibit 18-3

Typical listing from Direct-Mail List Rates and Data, published by Standard Rate & Data Service.

Source: SRDS Media Solutions

Becoming president requires large amounts of cash. So while some ads try to convince voters to support a candidate with their vote, direct-response ads are used to raise money.

© Mike Segar/Reuters/Landov Images

Companies use this information for their own mailings and sell it to other direct-mail advertisers.

The marketer's second most important prospects are people who respond to direct-mail pieces from other companies—especially those with complementary products or services. **Mail-response lists** are the house lists of other direct-mail advertisers, and they can be rented with a wide variety of demographic breakdowns.

The most readily available lists are those that some entity compiles for a different reason and then rents or sells—for example, lists of car owners, new-home purchasers, business owners, and so on. **Compiled lists**, which are lists purchased from list vendors, typically offer the lowest response rate, so experts suggest using numerous sources, merging them on the computer with mail-response and house lists, and then purging them of duplicate names.[30]

Direct-mail lists can be bought or rented. Purchased lists can be used without limit; rented lists may be used for a single mailing only. List owners plant decoy names in the list to be sure renters don't use it more than once.

Some list owners pay a **list broker** a commission (usually 20%) to handle the rental details. The company, in turn, benefits from the broker's knowledge of list quality without having to pay more than the rental cost.

Lists can be brokered or exchanged with list houses or other noncompetitive companies. And they can be tailored to reflect customer location (zip code); demographics such as age, income, and credit card ownership; or psychographic characteristics such as personality and lifestyle. The SRDS *Direct Mail List Rates and Data* comes in two volumes, *Consumer Lists* and *Business Lists,* and contains more than 48,000 list selections in hundreds of classifications (see Exhibit 18-3).

The quality of mailing lists varies enormously. The wrong list can have out-of-date addresses and names of people who live too far away, don't use the product advertised, and can't afford it anyway. Mailing list prices vary according to quality. The more stringent the advertiser's selection criteria, the more expensive the list. An extra $10 per thousand is often well worth the savings in mailers and postage that would otherwise be wasted.

The average mailing list changes more than 40 percent a year as people relocate, change jobs, get married, or die. So mailing lists must be continually updated (*cleaned*) to be sure they're current and correct. Marketers can also test the validity and accuracy of a given list. They rent or buy every *n*th name and send a mailer to that person. If the results are favorable, they purchase additional names, usually in lots of 1,000.

To create a direct-mail package, the marketer may use in-house staff, an ad agency, or a freelance designer and writer. Some agencies specialize in direct mail.[31]

The direct-mail piece normally goes through the same production process as any other print piece. The size and shape of the mailing package, as well as the type, illustrations, and colors, all affect printing costs. Special features such as simulated blue-ink signatures, cardboard pop-ups, and die-cutting (the cutting of paper stock into an unusual shape) add to the cost. But the larger the printing volume, or *run,* the lower the printing cost per unit (see Ad Lab 18–A, "Developing Effective Direct-Mail Packages").

Remaining production and handling tasks can be done by a local **letter shop** (or *mailing house*), or the company can do them internally.[32] On a cost-per-thousand basis, letter shops stuff and seal envelopes, affix labels, calculate postage, and sort, tie, and stack the mailers. Some shops also offer creative services. If the marketer is using third-class bulk mail, the letter shop separates mailers by zip code and ties them into bundles to qualify for low bulk rates. Then the letter shop delivers the mailers to the post office.

Distribution costs are based chiefly on the weight of the mailer and the delivery method. U.S. advertisers can use the U.S. Postal Service, air freight, or private delivery services like UPS and FedEx. The most common, the U.S. Postal Service, offers several types of delivery. Direct-mail advertising is most effective when it arrives on Tuesdays, Wednesdays, or Thursdays.[34]

Catalogs The largest direct marketers are the catalog companies. **Catalogs** are reference books that list, describe, and picture the products sold by a manufacturer, wholesaler,

AD Lab 18-A

Developing Effective Direct-Mail Packages

Good direct-mail campaigns help build relationships between advertisers and customers. As with an ad, the effectiveness of a direct-mail campaign relies strongly on both its message and its overall appearance.

Shaping the Message

When the AICPA (American Institute of Certified Public Accountants) wanted to present the cooler side of accounting to high school and college students, it contacted Wunderman. The AICPA had created a recruiting Website called "Start Here. Go Places." which featured a trivia game. Wunderman's task was to get the students to the Website where they would play the game and learn more about the accounting profession as a result. Lucky players of the game could win prizes like cash, iPods, and gift cards. Wunderman created the highly graphic, attention-getting postcard shown here, which was sent to targeted high school and college students.

To develop the message element in direct mail, experts suggest several techniques: stress the benefits; repeat your offer more than once; offer an incentive; offer a guarantee; don't be afraid of long copy; don't write copy that is over the reader's head; and give the customer more than one option for responding.

Integrating the Message with the Direct-Mail Pieces

Creating direct mail involves fitting the message with the key physical components of the direct-mail package. As discussed in Chapter 10, the five steps of the creative pyramid (attention, interest, credibility, desire, and action) may be guidelines for forming the message. Next, this information must be incorporated into all the components of the direct-mail package.

The AICPA postcard attracts *attention* with its colorful and humorous graphics. The mismatched fonts and image of the Contador beckon the recipient to look further. The specifics within the postcard build *credibility* by providing data that the offer is real and important. The prizes offered further attract the target's *desire* to visit the site. What student could turn down a chance at winning cash or an iPod? The desired *action* (playing the game), is made easy by providing the web address of the game on both the front and the back of the postcard.

Some Secrets of Direct Mail

Research has revealed countless direct-mail techniques that improve response rates: indent type and set it flush left with a ragged right edge; avoid printing in reverse type; list dollars saved in your offer rather than percentages; use the word *you* in the text; provide a reason for sale pricing (almost any will do); and do not paste labels over old addresses—print new materials.

Laboratory Applications

1. Locate a direct-mail package that has the four components common to most mailings and list how the elements of the creative pyramid are integrated throughout the components.

2. Review the copywriting in your direct-mail package and identify how many of the techniques mentioned in this Ad Lab are used or could be improved.

This colorful, attention-grabbing mail piece is meant to attract high school and college students who might be interested in accounting.

Source: AICPA and Wunderman

Exhibit 18-4
Who watches (and buys from) infomercials.

	Total Viewers	**Total Nonviewers**	**Total Buyers**
Primary gender	Female, 53.2%	Male, 55.4%	Female, 51.7%
Mean age	41.2	45.2	45.9
Primary ethnicity	Caucasian	Caucasian, 76.4%	Caucasian
Primary employment	Full-time	Not employed	Full-time
Marital status	Married, 49.3%	Married, 52.8%	Married, 60.3%
Children present	Yes, 40.1%	Yes, 38.5%	Yes, 43.1%
Residence	Suburban	Small town, 31.5%	Suburban
Mean household income	$56,000	$49,000	$55,000

retailer. With more high-income families shopping at home, specialized catalogs are becoming very popular. Some catalog retailers prosper with specialized approaches like lifestyle clothing (L.L.Bean, Anthropologie, Lands' End), electronic gadgets (Sharper Image), and gourmet foods (Dean & Deluca).

Catalogs are big business. Close to 10 billion catalogs are mailed each year, and an estimated 167 million people have purchased something from a catalog during the last 12 months.[35] The top 10 catalog companies did over $92.2 billion in business in 2005. The industry experienced a significant decline after the recession of 2007, but unlike some other traditional media, has staged a comeback as of 2015.[36]

To increase readership and stand out from the glut of other catalogs, some marketers have added editorial and slick photography, all designed to sell a certain image. Abercrombie & Fitch, for instance, publishes its *A&F Magazine,* which supplements the clothing line with advice on how to attain a "cool" lifestyle beyond what you wear. The magazine suggests acquiring the right mode of transportation (a Vespa scooter), drinking the right beer (Belgian Chimay), and using the right accessories (a Nokia phone). By selling the Abercrombie lifestyle, A&F hopes to bring more people into the stores.[37] At the same time, though, A&F has stirred up a lot of controversy by featuring nude and seminude models, often in suggestive poses.

Direct-Response Print Advertising   Newspaper ads and inserts featuring coupons or listing toll-free phone numbers can be very effective at stimulating customer responses. Today, the same is true with magazines. Moreover, in magazines, advertisers can devote most of the space to image-building, thus maximizing the medium's power. We discussed the use of print media in Chapter 13.

Direct-Response Broadcast Advertising   Direct marketers' use of TV and radio has increased dramatically in recent years. Total Gym, whose products are normally sold through health care and physical fitness professionals, worked with American Telecast to develop a 30-minute infomercial featuring TV star Chuck Norris and supermodel Christie Brinkley. The campaign exceeded their wildest expectations, producing more than $100 million in the first year and continuing to generate similar returns for the next four years.[38] As Exhibit 18- shows, more people are watching infomercials and buying the advertised products. In fact, one survey found that 60 percent of infomercial purchasers preferred this type of shopping to buying items in a store.[39]

Because millions of consumers are comfortable shopping on the web, direct-response messages only need to provide a compelling benefit and a memorable web address. Priceline.com is successful at both of these objectives.

Source: The Priceline Group

For many years, radio commentator Paul Harvey was very successful pitching a wide variety of products to his loyal audience. Likewise, talk jocks Howard Stern and Rush Limbaugh made Snapple an overnight success by drinking the product and touting its good taste on the air. Still, until fairly recently, radio has rarely been the medium of choice for direct-response advertising. But that has made the medium all the more intriguing to some marketers.

Direct response can occur in a variety of media. The Home Shopping Network is a great example of how to use television to sell directly to consumers.

Source: HSN, Inc.

Radio industry executives now expect to see a dramatic increase in the number of direct-response ads on radio. Radio, TV, and infomercials are discussed in depth in Chapter 14.

Direct-Response Digital Advertising   Direct-response advertising represents the vast majority of online advertising efforts. These are discussed more thoroughly in Chapters 15 and 16. Using e-mail to distribute marketing messages remains popular because of its low cost and effectiveness. Online direct response includes display, or banner, ads and search ads. Social media sites are increasingly featuring ads that allow an immediate response. Mobile is another popular direct-response medium. Mobile includes SMS (short message service or text ads), MMS (multimedia message service, or text plus images, audio, or video), mobile applications (better known as apps), QR (or quick-response) bar codes, and mobile banner ads.

Understanding Personal Selling

LO 18-2

"If it is to be, it is up to me."

Ten little words, two letters each. That was Sid Friedman's philosophy for success. Typical sales rep, right?

Well, not exactly. Sid Friedman sold insurance. He'd been doing it for some time. He was the president and chair of the Philadelphia-based insurance, financial planning, and consulting firm, Corporate Financial Services. Friedman managed his 200-plus employees, ran three other companies, and directed the Philadelphia chapter of the children's Make-a-Wish Foundation. *Forbes* magazine's article "People at the Top, What Do They Earn?" included Sid, along with the likes of Arnold Schwarzenegger, Tom Clancy, and Ralph Lauren.

Sid made the *Forbes* article because his selling techniques, augmented by the use of direct marketing, resulted in personal commissions of $2.6 million—in one year. Sid liked telephone marketing. It worked for him. Every week he called 100 people, got 15 appointments, sold three, and earned lots of money.

"Sometimes," he said, "you earn even more money, but only when you do three things: See the people, see the people, and see the people."[41]

That's what personal selling is all about: seeing the people. And that's also why personal selling is the best marketing communication tool for relationship building—because the sales rep and the customer are face-to-face. It's the ultimate one-to-one medium. It's also the most expensive medium. For most companies, personal selling expenditures far exceed expenditures for advertising. And in many companies, the primary role of advertising is to lend support to the sales force either directly by producing leads or indirectly by creating a positive atmosphere for the sales call. That is certainly true for all of the GEICO ads that direct audiences to the company's toll-free number.

Personal selling can be defined in a number of ways, depending on the orientation of the company using it. In an integrated marketing communications program, though, the sales effort of the reps must be consistent with the mission, vision, and strategies of the firm and with all the firm's other communications.

Therefore, for our purposes we define **personal selling** as the *interpersonal communication process* by which a seller ascertains and then satisfies the needs of a buyer, to the mutual, long-term benefit of both parties.[42]

Thus, the task of personal selling is a lot more than just making a sale. In an IMC program, the objective of personal selling is to build a relationship, a partnership, that will provide long-term benefits to both buyer and seller (a win–win situation). The salesperson discovers the buyer's needs by helping the customer identify problems, offers information about potential solutions, assists the buyer in making decisions, and provides after-sale service to ensure long-term satisfaction. Influence and persuasion are only one part of selling. The major part is problem solving.

Apple's creation of retail stores that allow the company to engage in personal selling was a bold move by the late Steve Jobs. The result has been nothing short of spectacular, as Apple generates higher sales per square foot of floor space than any other retailer.

Xaume Olleros/Bloomberg/Getty Images

Types of Personal Selling

Everyone sells, at one time or another. Children sell lemonade, magazine subscriptions, and Girl Scout cookies. Students sell prom tickets, yearbook ads, and term papers. Doctors sell diets to unwilling patients. Lawyers sell briefs to skeptical juries. And cops sell traffic safety to nervous motorists.

As a business process and a profession, though, personal selling is something else. It's just one of a company's mix of communications tools, and its relative importance depends on the type of business or industry, the nature of the product or service, and the strategy of the business.

The fact is that everything has to be sold, by someone to somebody. A retail clerk may sell you a cell phone. Behind that clerk is a virtual army of other salespeople who sold processed materials to the manufacturer, capital equipment for use in the manufacturing process, business services such as human resources and accounting, plant and office furniture, vehicles, advertising services, media space and time, and insurance. Then the manufacturer's salespeople sold the phone (and a few others) to a wholesaler who, of course, had to buy transportation services and warehousing from other salespeople. And then the wholesaler's sales reps sold the phone to the retail outlet where you bought it.

As this scenario shows, people in sales work for a wide variety of organizations and call on an equally wide variety of customers. They may call on other businesses to sell products or services used in the manufacture of other products. They may call on resellers or sell to consumers, either in a retail store or, as we discussed earlier, in a direct selling situation away from a retail location.

Because marketing messages are designed to support and reinforce a company's sales efforts, marketers (whether in the company or at an agency) have to understand the selling environment in which their companies or clients deal. Many companies have their marketing people make calls with the sales force for this very reason. They can experience firsthand what questions prospects ask, how customers view the company (and its competitors), how people use the company's product, and what information (in either an ad or a piece of sales material) might help the salesperson communicate better with the prospect.

Advantages of Personal Selling

The greatest strength of personal selling is its personal nature. Nothing is as persuasive as personal communication. A skilled salesperson can observe a prospect's body language and read between the lines to detect what's troubling the customer. The rep can ask questions and provide answers. And the rep has the flexibility to adjust the presentation, tailoring it specifically to the needs and interests of the particular prospect. Not only that, the salesperson can demonstrate the product live. And the rep can negotiate, finding those terms that best suit the buyer's needs.

Time is on the rep's side, too. The sale doesn't have to be made today. The relationship has to be established, though, and a human being is better at doing that than any nonpersonal medium.

One of the major jobs of personal selling is to gain distribution for new products—a task no other communication tool can do as well. In fact, in many trade and industrial situations, personal contact may be vital to closing the sale. This is also true for certain high-ticket or technical consumer products such as camcorders, health care, and estate planning. In these cases, personal selling is well worth its high cost—because it gets the job done.

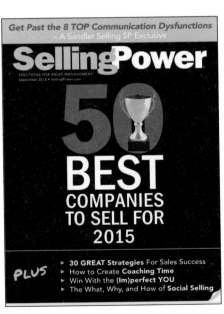

Because of the potential of personal selling, an entire industry is devoted to educating and informing salespeople about the skills needed for success. Selling Power Magazine is an excellent tool for the salesforce.

Source: Selling Power Magazine

Drawbacks of Personal Selling

Personal selling is labor intensive, making it the most costly way to communicate with prospects. This is its single biggest weakness. A business-to-business sales call costs well in excess of $300. Not only that, it's very time-consuming. Because it is a one-on-one medium, there are few economies of scale. In fact, two or three salespeople will sometimes go to an important customer's office to make a presentation. In personal selling we don't talk about cost per thousand.

This is why one important role of IMC is to *reduce the cost of sales* by communicating as much relevant information as possible about the company and its products to prospects and customers before the salesperson even calls. That information may be functional (specifically about the product) or symbolic (building image and credibility for the company).

Another drawback is the poor reputation of personal selling with many people. Decades of "suede shoe" salesmen employing high-pressure tactics, usually in retail venues, have sullied the profession. Thus the common jibe: "Would you buy a used car from that man?" In health care services, for example, selling activities have limited philosophical acceptance. Salespeople are frequently given fancier titles such as marketing associate, marketing representative, admissions coordinator, clinical liaison, professional services representative, or program manager in an attempt to avoid the tarnished image associated with personal selling.[43] Of course, the advertising profession doesn't fare much better when it comes to image and reputation—or fancy titles.

There's an old saying about one bad apple ruining a barrel. Imagine spending millions of dollars on a nationwide advertising campaign to communicate your expertise and good customer service, and then sending an unprofessional sales force out that is ignorant of product features and benefits and lacks empathy for customer needs. Unfortunately, it happens all the time. The salesperson has the power to either make or break a delicate relationship. As a result, sophisticated firms go to great lengths to screen sales applicants to find the right personality attributes and then invest heavily in training. Of course, this goes both ways. A tasteless advertising campaign can hurt a company's national reputation more than one bad salesperson. As always, it's the responsibility of marketing management to ensure consistency between what the advertising presents, what the sales force promises, and what the company actually delivers.

The Role of Personal Selling in IMC

Salespeople are the company's communicators. They are the human medium. In fact, to the customer who doesn't know anybody else at the company, the salesperson doesn't just represent the firm; he or she *is* the firm. The customer's impression of the salesperson, therefore, will frequently govern his or her perception of the company. Again, this makes the sales rep a very important person.

In an integrated marketing communications program, personal selling can play a very important role. Salespeople provide four distinct communications functions: information gathering, information providing, order fulfillment, and relationship building. We'll discuss each of these briefly.

Gathering Information

Sales reps often serve as the eyes and ears of the company. Because they are out in the field talking to customers or attending trade shows, they have access to information and they can see trends. For example, salespeople provide information on who's new in the business, how customers are reacting to new products or styles, what the competition is doing, and where new sales might be made. Generally, information gathering by the sales force relates to three areas: prospecting; determining customer wants, needs, and abilities; and monitoring the competition.

Providing Information

Salespeople also impart information. In fact, the stereotype (both negative and positive) of a good salesperson is someone who is a good talker, articulate and persuasive. In truth, a superior salesperson is a good listener first and a good talker second. Salespeople impart information both upstream and downstream within their organization. They deliver information to customers about the company and its products, they recommend solutions to problems, and they use information to communicate value and to build relationships and trust.

Personal selling incorporates all three legs of the IMC triangle, the "say → do → confirm," because what the rep says and does will either confirm or contradict the company's other

Amazon's success can be directly traced to the sophisticated fulfillment centers it uses to ship products quickly to customers. This photo of the center near Phoenix shows both the complexity and organization that makes the company so effective.

© Joshua Lott/Bloomberg/Getty Images

Nordstrom strives to provide exceptional service to its customers. An engaging and helpful Website is part of that effort. So is the company's lenient returns policy and justifiably famous focus on consumer satisfaction.

Source: Nordstrom

messages. The rep's skill, therefore, will definitely color the relationship between the company and the customer. It's critically important that the salesperson's performance be consistent with the firm's positioning and reinforce its other marketing communications.

Fulfilling Orders

There comes a time in every relationship when someone has to make a commitment. Asking for that commitment can be difficult if the preceding steps have not been handled well. The tasks of personal selling are to motivate the customer to action, close the sale, and then make sure the goods and services are delivered correctly.

An important part of personal selling is following up after the sale, making sure the goods or services are delivered in a timely fashion, and seeing to it that the customer is completely satisfied. This is a combination of the "do" and "confirm" steps, and it's critical to continued relationship building.

This is also where cross-functional management and open communication come back into play. If there is any kind of manufacturing glitch or delay in shipping, the salesperson needs to notify the customer immediately. But to do that, the salesperson must be

Snapple's clever promotion of its Mango Madness flavor demonstrates an ingenious integration of sales promotion and product positioning. By placing a sticker ad on actual mangoes in the fresh-fruit section, Snapple reinforced its slogan of "100% natural" and grabbed the attention of customers not necessarily looking to buy the beverage. The marketing strategy was supported by placing bottles of Mango Madness in close proximity to the fruit.

Source: Snapple Beverage Corp.

Understanding Sales Promotion

LO 18-3

informed. Similarly, goods need to be protected and shipped with care. Salespeople hate to receive calls from new customers saying their first shipment arrived with damaged goods. Every employee, including those in the warehouse, needs to understand the impact of *unplanned* product messages.

Likewise, if the company is advertising a certain model of a product and the salesperson closes the sale on the product, that model had better be in stock. Again, good internal communication is a key to good external relationships.

Building Relationships

A company's sales staff should be the ultimate relationship marketers. When all things are equal, people naturally want to buy from the salesperson they like and trust. Salespeople build relationships by paying attention to three simple things: keeping commitments, servicing their accounts, and solving problems.

Here again, marketers can help. When a company communicates, it is making a commitment to its customers and prospects. It is very difficult for a salesperson to keep those commitments if the IMC has overpromised.

Likewise, it's difficult for customer service reps to adequately service their accounts if every time people call they get a busy signal. This happened to the giant telephone utility U.S. West when it downsized and reengineered the company. It continued running ads touting its great service, but nobody could get through to them. Not smart. Marketers have to know what's going on in the company, and sometimes they need to recommend that advertising be stopped.

Finally, advertising as well as salespeople should be concerned with solving problems. If the sales staff uncovers a problem that customers frequently encounter, and the company's product can help solve that problem, then that should become the focus of some planned communications—advertising, publicity, or company-sponsored events.

Imagine walking into the fresh-fruit section of your local grocery store, picking up a big, juicy mango, and discovering a sticker on it stating: "Now available in Snapple. Mango Madness." You turn around and suddenly notice that there, right next to the fresh-fruit bin, stands a big Snapple display of, you guessed it, Mango Madness.

It actually happened. New York agency Kirshenbaum, Bond & Partners launched Snapple's new Mango Madness drink nationally with stickers on the back of 30 million pieces of fruit. Talk about out-of-the-box thinking and creative media planning! Moreover, it was an outstanding example of how sales promotion can be perfectly integrated with a company's positioning, in this case Snapple's overall "100% natural" message strategy.

The term *sales promotion* is often misunderstood or confused with advertising or publicity. This may be because sales promotion activities often occur simultaneously and use both advertising and publicity as part of the process. In truth, though, it is a very specific marketing communications activity.

Sales promotion is a direct inducement that offers extra incentives anywhere along the marketing route to enhance or accelerate the product's movement from producer to consumer. Within this definition, there are three important elements to consider. Sales promotion:

- May be used anywhere in the marketing channel: from manufacturer to wholesaler, wholesaler to dealer, dealer to customer, or manufacturer to customer.
- Normally involves a direct inducement (such as money, prizes, extra products, gifts, or specialized information) that provides an incentive to buy now or buy more, visit a store, request literature, display a product, or take some other action.
- Is designed to change the timing of a purchase or to shift inventory to others in the channel.

Let's see how this definition applies to Snapple. In an interesting combination of both consumer advertising and *trade promotion* (sales promotion aimed at members of the distribution channel), Snapple used the fresh mangoes as an unusual new advertising medium to introduce its Mango Madness to consumers and to stimulate initial demand for the drink. The magnitude of that media effort (30 million pieces of fruit) served as a huge incentive to retailers to grant Snapple extra floor space (very expensive real estate, by the way) to display Mango Madness right next to the fresh-fruit stand. The result: Snapple, and the retailers, sold a lot more Mango Madness a lot faster, and for a lot less money, than they would have if they had run ads in consumer magazines or on TV. Moreover, by creatively integrating different forms of marketing communications, Snapple simultaneously bolstered its positioning strategy and enhanced its relationship with the retail trade—its primary customer.

Sales promotion is expensive. But it's also effective. Unfortunately, it has serious drawbacks, which lead to furious battles in marketing circles between proponents of sales promotion and proponents of advertising. Each approach has an important role to play, but advertisers must consider the positives and negatives and get the balance right.

The Role of Sales Promotion in IMC

Effective sales promotion accomplishes a number of things. First of all, it adds tangible, immediate added value to the brand. Snapple's creative media buy suddenly made Mango Madness more valuable to the retail trade. This induced retailers to stock up on the new product and display it prominently. Similarly, when McDonald's runs its Monopoly game, it's adding instant value to the products it sells. This is why we refer to sales promotion as the *value-added tool.*

Second, by adding immediate value, sales promotion *maximizes* sales volume. A short-term price cut or rebate, for instance, may be very effective at boosting sales. While advertising helps develop and reinforce a quality, differentiated brand reputation, and build long-term *market value,* sales promotion helps build *market volume.* To become a market leader, therefore, a brand needs both advertising and sales promotion.

Finally, when all brands appear to be equal, sales promotion can be more effective than advertising in motivating customers to try a new brand or to select one brand over another. It can also motivate some customers who might be unmoved by advertising efforts. And certain sales promotions generate a more immediate, measurable payoff than traditional advertising campaigns. This is why we might also refer to sales promotion as the "sales accelerator."

To succeed, sales promotions should be creative and hard to imitate. Kirshenbaum, Bond & Partners certainly demonstrated that with its Snapple labels.

Advertisers need to understand the negative effects of sales promotion, too. For instance, excessive sales promotion at the expense of advertising hurts profits. Some marketers believe a proper expenditure balance for consumer packaged-good products is approximately 60 percent for trade and consumer promotion and 40 percent for advertising.

A high level of trade sales promotion relative to advertising and consumer sales promotion has a positive effect on short-term market share but may have a negative effect on brand attitudes and long-term market share. Without an effective advertising effort to emphasize brand image and quality, customers become deal-prone rather than brand loyal. And overemphasis on price (whether in advertising or sales promotion) eventually destroys brand equity.[44]

Another drawback of sales promotion is its high cost. One analysis showed that only 16 percent of sales promotions were profitable. In other words, the manufacturer spent more than $1 to generate an extra $1 of profits.[45]

Finally, overly aggressive sales promotion or advertising can draw competitors into a price war, which leads to reduced sales and profits for everyone.

Thus, if too much of the marketing mix is allocated to advertising, the brand may gain a high-quality, differentiated image but not enough volume to be a market leader. On the other hand, as Larry Light, McDonald's chief global marketing officer says, "Too much [sales] promotion, and the brand will have high volume but low profitability. Market leadership can be bought through bribes, but enduring profitable market leadership must be earned through building both brand value as well as volume."[46]

Sales Promotion Strategies and Tactics

To move their products through the distribution channel from the point of manufacture to the point of consumption, marketers employ two types of strategies: push and pull. **Push strategies** are primarily designed to secure the cooperation of retailers, gain shelf space, and protect the product against competitors. **Trade promotions**—sales promotions aimed a

Exhibit 18-5
Two marketing communications approaches.

members of the distribution channel—are one of the principal tactics marketers use to *push* products through the distribution pipeline and gain shelf space. We'll discuss some of these tactics in the next section. Marketers may also use **trade advertising** (advertising in publications read by members of the trade) as a push tactic.

Pull strategies, on the other hand, are designed to attract customers and increase demand for the product (see Exhibit 18-5). Consumer advertising and **consumer sales promotions** are examples of pull strategies because they are designed to induce consumers to seek out or ask for the product, in effect pulling the product through the pipeline. Today, some national advertisers spend more dollars on trade sales promotions than on either consumer sales promotions or media advertising. But that is often the price they have to pay to gain distribution, without which they cannot make any sales.

Giving Brands a Push with Trade Promotions

In supermarkets today, shelf space and floor space are hard to come by. To maintain their own images, department stores set standards for manufacturers' displays. This means that retailers often can't use the special racks, sales aids, and promotional literature manufacturers supply.

These are minor problems; major ones have to do with control of the marketplace. **Trade concentration**—more products going through fewer retailers—gives greater control to the retailers and less to the manufacturers. Increased competition for shelf space gives retailers even more power, enabling them to exact hefty deals and allowances. As a result, manufacturers of national brands often don't have enough money left to integrate consumer advertising or sales promotion.[47]

Despite these problems, many manufacturers still implement effective push strategies. And the smart ones safeguard enough money for consumer advertising. Trade tactics include slotting allowances, trade deals, display allowances, buyback allowances, advertising allowances, cooperative advertising and advertising materials, dealer premiums and contests, push money, and company conventions and dealer meetings.

Allowances and Trade Deals In response to the glut of new products, some retailers charge manufacturers **slotting allowances**—fees ranging from $15,000 to $40,000 for the privilege of obtaining shelf or floor space for a new product. The practice is controversial because some manufacturers think they're being forced to subsidize the retailer's cost of doing business. On

Trade promotions are business-to-business programs that are strategically aimed at increasing distribution. This ad for Payne Heating and Cooling (www.payne.com) aims to persuade buyers for HVAC companies to purchase and install Payne units for their customers.

Source: Payne Heating & Cooling

Manufacturers like Under Armor often pay a display allowance for their in-store exhibits. These fees benefit retailers by compensating them for the space occupied by the displays. And the manufacturer benefits from the increased exposure.

© Rick Maiman/AP Images

the other side of the coin, small-scale sellers, such as family farms trying to market their produce, complain that the allowances shut out all but the largest suppliers. Although a 1994 ruling by the Federal Trade Commission and the Bureau of Alcohol, Tobacco and Firearms determined that they were acceptable as long as the same promotional allowances were offered to all retailers on "proportionally equal terms," the allowances remain controversial, and the FTC has recommended further research.[48]

In an effort to avoid slotting allowances, some marketers have made major shifts in strategy. Following a four-year investigation, the FTC signaled its willingness to fight egregious slotting allowance abuses by taking legal action against spice giant McCormick. Through agreements with "favored purchasers," the company had managed to command 90 percent of shelf space set aside for spices and offered a range of prices for its customers. The FTC ordered McCormick to refrain from selling its products to a purchaser at a net price that was higher than that charged to the purchaser's competitors. The order's narrow scope dismayed some critics, but overall the action was hailed as "a thoughtful beginning to the evolution of a sound and measured antitrust response to slotting fee abuses."[49]

Manufacturers make **trade deals** with retailers by offering short-term discounts or other dollar inducements. To comply with the Robinson-Patman Act, trade deals must be offered proportionally to all dealers. Dealers usually pass the savings on to customers through sale prices, or "specials."

Excessive trade deals threaten brand loyalty because they encourage customers to buy whatever brand is on sale. Furthermore, marketers who use trade discounts extensively find themselves in a vicious circle: If they cut back on the promotions, they may lose shelf space and then market share.

Some retailers capitalize on trade discounts by engaging in forward buying and diverting. With **forward buying,** a retailer stocks up on a product when it is on discount and buys smaller amounts when it sells at list price. **Diverting** means using the promotional discount to purchase large quantities of an item in one region, then shipping portions of the buy to areas where the discount isn't offered. These tactics enable both the manufacturer and the dealer to shift inventory when they need to.

Retailers often charge manufacturers **display allowances**—fees assessed in exchange for featuring an item prominently on end caps or displays. In-store displays include counter stands, floor stands, shelf signs, and special racks that give the retailer ready-made, professionally designed vehicles for selling more of the featured products.

When introducing a new product, manufacturers sometimes offer retailers a **buyback allowance** for the old product that hasn't sold. To persuade retailers to take on their product line, some manufacturers even offer a buyback allowance for a competitor's leftover stock.

Manufacturers often offer **advertising allowances** as either a percentage of gross purchases or a flat fee. Advertising allowances are more common for consumer than industrial products. They are offered primarily by large companies, but some smaller firms give them to high-volume customers.

Co-op Advertising and Advertising Materials   With **cooperative (co-op) advertising,** national manufacturers reimburse dealers for advertising the manufacturer's products or logo. The manufacturer usually pays 50 to 100 percent of the dealer's advertising costs based on a percentage of the dealer's sales. Special co-op deals are used to introduce new products, promote profitable lines, or combat aggressive competitors.

Unlike advertising allowances, co-op programs typically require the dealer to submit invoices and proof of the advertising (tearsheets from the newspaper or affidavits of performance from radio or TV stations). Many manufacturers also give their dealers prepared advertising materials: ads, glossy photos, sample radio commercials, and so on. To control the image of their products, some advertisers insist that dealers use these materials to qualify for the co-op advertising money.

Other Push Strategies   To encourage retail dealers and salespeople to reach specific sales goals or stock a certain product, manufacturers may offer special prizes and gifts. Ethics can be a thorny issue when companies award prizes and gifts to dealers and salespeople.

Retail salespeople are often encouraged to push the sale of particular products. One inducement is called **push money (PM),** or **spiffs.** For example, a shoe salesperson may suggest shoe polish or some other high-profit extra; for each item sold, the salesperson receives a 25- to 50-cent spiff.

Most major manufacturers hold **company conventions and dealer meetings** to introduce new products, announce sales promotion programs, or show new advertising campaigns. They may also conduct sales and service training sessions. Meetings can be a dynamic sales promotion tool for the manufacturer.

Push strategies are virtually invisible to consumers. Yet successful inducements mean the product gets more shelf space, a special display, or extra interest and enthusiasm from salespeople. And extra interest can spell the difference between failure and success.

Using Consumer Promotions to Pull Brands Through

One reason for today's increased focus on consumer sales promotions is the change in TV viewing habits. With cable TV, DVRs, and DVDs, fewer people watch any one program. Advertising audiences are more fragmented, and major manufacturers must turn to new methods to reach these moving targets.

Common consumer sales promotions include point-of-purchase materials, coupons, electronic coupons and convenience cards, cents-off promotions, refunds, rebates, premiums, sampling, combination offers, contests, and sweepstakes. A successful IMC campaign may integrate several of these techniques along with media advertising, product publicity, and direct marketing. Ad Lab 18–B offers the opportunity to apply what you've learned about push and pull strategies to the marketing of textbooks.

Point-of-Purchase (P-O-P) Materials   Walk into any store and notice the number of display materials and advertising-like devices that are designed to build traffic, exhibit and advertise the product, and promote impulse buying. Collectively, these are all referred to as **point-of-purchase (P-O-P) materials.**

P-O-P works best when used with other forms of IMC. For example, by advertising its gum and candy, one marketer increased sales by about 150 percent. But when P-O-P was added to the same program, the purchase rate jumped 550 percent.[50]

Pull campaigns rely on the power of consumers to pull brands through the distribution chain. A product called Full Core makes it easy for consumers to demand its product by supplying them with this ad.
Source: Full Core, LLC

AD Lab 18-B

Applying Push–Pull Strategies to Sales Promotion

Moving a product from the manufacturer to the consumer is not a simple task. Goods often have to go through four or five separate steps: from the manufacturer to an agent or broker, then to the wholesaler, to the retailer, and finally to the consumer. Communicating messages along this same path can also be tortuous. Something's bound to get lost in the middle. This is why push and pull promotions are so important.

By offering incentives in the form of money, prizes, trips, and promotional materials to "push" products into the distribution pipeline, the marketer can also obtain invaluable intermediary assistance. Pushing is when a company uses any form of marketing communication (personal selling, advertising, or sales promotion) to the trade with the purpose of gaining shelf space and cooperation. Reversing the process, the company can also use consumer advertising or offer rebates, coupons, two-for-one deals, or some other incentive directly to the customer. By stimulating demand, that form of communication helps "pull" products through the pipeline.

Laboratory Application

If you were working for McGraw-Hill/Irwin (the publisher of this textbook), how would you suggest using push–pull strategies to increase the sales of the company's textbooks? Which strategy do you think would be more effective?

In one poll, 56 percent of mass-merchandise shoppers and 62 percent of grocery shoppers said they noticed point-of-purchase materials. More than half reported noticing signs and displays, 18 percent remembered coupon dispensers, and 14 percent could recall samplings and demonstrations.[51]

Today's consumers make their decisions in the store 66 percent of the time and make unplanned (impulse) purchases 53 percent of the time, so P-O-P can often be the major factor in stimulating purchases.[52]

P-O-P materials may also include window displays, counter displays, floor and wall racks to hold the merchandise, streamers, and posters. Often, the product's shipping cartons are designed to double as display units. A complete information center may even provide literature, samples, product photos, or an interactive computer in a kiosk.

The trend toward self-service retailing has increased the importance of P-O-P materials. With fewer and less knowledgeable salespeople available to help them, customers are forced to make purchasing decisions on their own. Eye-catching, informative displays can give them the nudge they need. Even in well-staffed stores, display materials can offer extra selling information and make the product stand out from the competition.

The proliferation of P-O-P displays has led retailers to be more discriminating in what they actually use. Most are beginning to insist on well-designed, attractive materials that will blend harmoniously with their store atmosphere.

The emphasis on P-O-P has led to a variety of new approaches, including ads on shopping carts, "talking" antacid boxes, beverage jingles activated when in-store refrigerator doors are opened, and interactive computers for selecting everything from shoe styles to floor coverings. Digital technology has led to Hallmark Cards' Touch-Screen Greetings interactive kiosks, which print a customer's personal message onto any card. To send it, look for one of the new Automated Postal Centers rolled out by the U.S. Postal Service. The kiosks allow customers to weigh materials to be mailed, buy postage, and even look up zip codes.

Most coupons reach consumers through newspaper freestanding inserts (FSIs), which have a higher redemption rate than regular newspaper or magazine coupons.

Source: Campbell Soup Company

Coupons   A **coupon** is a certificate with a stated value presented to the retail store for a price reduction on a specified item. More than 278 billion coupons were distributed by consumer packaged goods companies in the United States in 2005, but only about 3 billion were ever redeemed.[53]

Coupons may be distributed in newspapers or magazines, door to door, on packages, in stores, and by direct mail. Most reach consumers through colorful preprinted newspaper ads

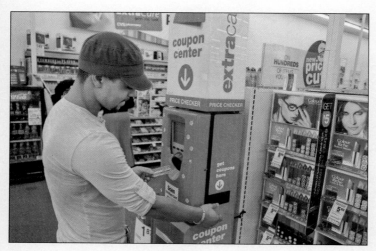

Kiosks like this coupon center at CVS Pharmacy use a consumer's membership card to allow customers to print in-store coupons and view weekly specials.

© Art Directors & TRIP/Alamy

called **freestanding inserts (FSIs).** FSIs have a higher redemption rate than regular newspaper and magazine coupons; coupons in or on packages have the highest redemption levels of all.[54]

Manufacturers lose hundreds of millions of dollars annually on fraudulent coupon submissions. Some coupons are counterfeited; others are submitted for products that were never purchased. To fight this problem, some companies have developed computerized systems to detect fraudulent submissions and charge them back to the retailers who made them.

Electronic Coupons and Convenience Cards   High-tech **electronic coupons** work like paper coupons in that they entitle the shopper to a discount, but their method of distribution is entirely different. Interactive touch-screen videos at the point of purchase generate instant-print discounts, rebates, and offers to try new brands. Electronic coupons are spreading quickly in the nation's supermarkets, though they still represent only a small percentage of the total coupons distributed annually.

Nonetheless, all the nation's top brand marketers are currently involved in tests being conducted by the two leaders in the field, Catalina Marketing and Advanced Promotion Technologies. Catalina's system is installed in more than 21,000 supermarkets across the country and reaches some 250 million shoppers per week.[55]

Electronic couponing gives the retailer access to information about consumers that would not be available with paper coupons. Many supermarket chains now issue customers convenience cards entitling them to instant discounts at the checkout counter. When customers use the card, a record of their purchases is sent to a database and sorted into various lifestyle groups. The card saves customers the hassle of clipping paper coupons, and it allows retailers to better understand its customers' purchasing behaviors.

Similar systems are used in Europe. Multipoints is an interactive system that lets customers collect points for visiting stores or watching commercials on TV. The points can be redeemed for prizes and discounts on various products at participating stores. Quick Burger, France's second-largest restaurant chain, noticed a significant increase in traffic after joining Multipoints, even when the system was less than a year old.[56]

Cents-Off Promotions, Refunds, and Rebates   **Cents-off promotions** are short-term reductions in the price of a product in the form of cents-off packages, one-cent sales, free offers, and boxtop refunds. Some packages bear a special cents-off sticker, which the clerk removes and credits at the checkout counter.

Some companies offer *refunds* in the form of cash or coupons that can be applied to future purchases of the product. To obtain the refund, the consumer must supply proof of purchase, such as three boxtops.

Rebates are larger cash refunds on items from cars to household appliances. Large rebates (like those given on cars) are handled by the seller. For small rebates (like those given for coffeemakers), the consumer sends in a certificate.

Research indicates that many people purchase a product because of an advertised rebate but never collect the rebate because of the inconvenience.[57] More than $500 million worth of rebates goes unclaimed every year.

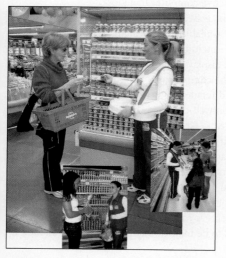

In-store sampling displays allow consumers to test products in an environment where they may be readily purchased. Dannon successfully promoted new yogurt flavors in stores by offering free samples and taste testing to shoppers.

Source: The Dannon Company, Inc.

Premiums   A **premium** is an item offered free or at a bargain price to encourage the consumer to buy an advertised product. Premiums affect purchase behavior the same way as rebates but tend to be more effective at getting consumers to buy a product they don't really need (see Exhibit 18-6). Premiums are intended to improve the product's image, gain goodwill, broaden the customer base, and produce quick sales.

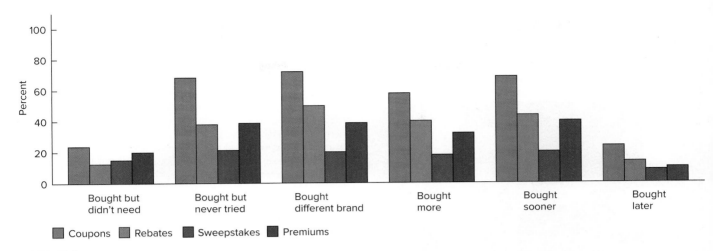

Exhibit 18-6

Next to coupons, premiums are one of the most effective sales promotion techniques for changing consumer behavior.

Source: Adapted from the American Marketing Association.

A premium should have strong appeal and value and should be useful or unusual. It may be included in the product's package *(in-pack premium)*, on the package *(on-pack premium)*, mailed free or for a nominal sum on receipt of proof of purchase (boxtop or label), or given with the product at the time of purchase. Cosmetics companies often hold department store promotions in which scarves, purses, and cosmetic samplers are given free or for a low price with a purchase.

The purchased cosmetics sampler is an example of a *self-liquidating premium:* The consumer pays enough that the seller breaks even but doesn't make a profit. A variation is the *continuity premium,* given weekly to customers who frequent the same store. With a minimum dollar purchase of other items, the customer receives a dish or book each week to complete a set.

Sampling **Sampling** is the most costly of all sales promotions. It is also one of the most effective for new products because it offers consumers a free trial in hopes of converting them to habitual use. Sampling should be supported by advertising and must involve a product available in small sizes and purchased frequently. Successful sampling depends heavily on the product's merits. It offers the greatest credibility and can turn a nonuser into a loyal customer instantly—if the product lives up to its promise.

Samples may be distributed by mail, door to door, via coupon advertising, or by a person in the store. They may be given free or for a small charge. Sometimes samples are distributed with related items, but this limits their distribution to those who buy the other product. In **polybagging,** samples are delivered in plastic bags with the daily newspaper or a monthly magazine. This enables distribution to targeted readers and lets publications give their subscribers added value at no cost.[58]

In-store sampling is very popular. Most in-store sampling programs are tied to a coupon campaign. Depending on the nature of the product, samples can be used as either a push strategy or a pull strategy.

Combination Offers Food and drug marketers use **combination offers,** such as a razor and a package of blades or a toothbrush with a tube of toothpaste, at a reduced price for the two. For best results, the items should be related. Sometimes a combination offer introduces a new product by tying its purchase to an established product at a special price.

People **BEHIND** the Ads

Flint McGlaughlin Founder and CEO, MecLabs

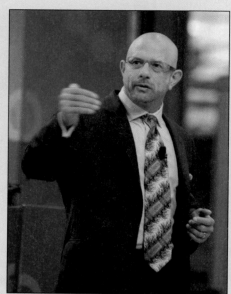

Courtesy of Flint McGlaughlin

CA: Flint, your research institute, MECLabs, does a variety of things, all centered on expertise at communicating value. How did the institute develop?

Flint: When I first began, I was interested in a single question: why do people say yes? In the earliest days of the net, I talked to many leaders, and could find no one who knew what the Internet was. No one was interested in doing research around it or with it and I came to the conclusion that if anything was going to happen I was going to have to fund it myself. I thought transactions could occur online, banking could occur online, media could occur online. But in those days no one was talking like that.

CA: There is a tremendous amount of data on what people are doing and how they're relating to one another on the internet. MECLabs offers clients a deep understanding of relationships through the use of data.

Flint: We knew that the implication of the findings was greater than its commercial application. I mean, why people choose impacts everything

from relationships to faith to careers. We thought this very discreet transaction that occurs online between one organization and one customer was important. They are choosing each other and there is an exchange of value. We could see this unfold, we could pattern it, and start building a meta-theory and test the aspects of that theory. Data made all that possible.

CA: Many people are concerned about behavioral traces that they are leaving or the data that they're creating that are being observed by others.

Flint: Oh yes.

CA: On the other hand, I'm impressed at how companies that I engage with online seem to understand my tastes and preferences even better than I do myself. Good companies quickly learn how to serve me better because they understand the things that I'm interested in.

Flint: The violation of our privacy and unethical use, we'll call that "bad". And "good" might be giving you a better experience online, or even enabling you to diagnose a medical condition faster. Things like this are happening all the time.

But in the end I think it all comes back to the marketer's motive and objective. This is what makes marketing so interesting to me because with a proper understanding of the value proposition, marketing becomes a service. You're not just serving the company but you're serving the customer.

CA: You've written about the importance of clarity. I agree with you that when practiced ethically and properly, marketing is a noble calling. Correctly done it's about bringing clarity to a puzzling and often confusing world where choices are not easily made.

Flint: We've analyzed thousands of campaigns—20,000 plus pages and paths we've tested over the years, over a billion emails, and a lot of other things. We've recorded five million phone conversations. We've interviewed 500,000 decision makers and the one thing we have discovered over and over again is simply this: for most of us, the true enemy is confusion. The focus on value proposition causes not just the marketer to rethink but the manager to rethink, because the company must deliver a product that is of genuine value. It's hard to be the best choice for everyone. When you try to do that, often you have to resort to fancy words and confusion.

CA: *You focus on understanding the audience and acknowledging that it makes the judgement about value and about whether a company is communicating well.*

Flint: No matter how logical you are, if you start with the wrong suppositions, you're still going to come up to the wrong answer. This is happening every day in board rooms.

At MECLabs, we've focused on moving away from company-centric logic to customer-centric logic. Customer-centric logic really enables you to see differently. Sometimes when I'm teaching, I'll begin by saying it's not that I want to help you see better; it's that I want to give you new eyes to see with. You can watch the jaded look from seasoned advertising executives and marketers and leaders because it's the sort of thing you might hear at a motivational speech. But soon, that evaporates because they start to realize that, no, what we are trying to do is help you to see with the eyes of the customer.

CA: *Speaking of saying "yes", you've written that the big yes often results from a series of micro-yeses.*

Flint: I think it began with my conception of the sales and marketing funnel. I imagine in my mind traffic is moving through this funnel. The problem is it distorts the task of the marketer because gravity is not working for us, gravity is working against us. People are not falling into the funnel. They're falling out.

The true task of the marketer is to move someone up one micro step at a time against all the forces of gravity. This helped me understand that the central draw, the central attractant, is the value proposition. That's what people are moving up and towards. You must control the experience at each of these junctures. It might take 100 micro-yeses to get to yes, but it only takes one no to end the entire process.

CA: *So you anticipate what an individual is thinking about at each micro step. People are predisposed to answer "no" in many instances to such questions, so it's really respecting that people make judgments.*

Flint: Well, people don't buy from websites, people don't buy from television commercials or even from companies. People buy from people,

and you don't optimize websites, web pages or radio spots. You optimize the thought sequence that exists as the decision maker processes a message.

CA: *And that's empathy.*

Flint: The key here is that there's a difference between actuality and perception. The business leader who doesn't understand this is satisfied that they have achieved some level of value to offer a customer, but value that is not perceived is value that's not going to be accepted. So you must learn to communicate this and work through these micro-yeses in a way that helps customers perceive value. That's where empathy comes in because I have to think through their perspective. I can't do it from this side of the equation. I've actually got to get over on the other side of the equation and experience the offer the way that they experience it.

CA: *Flint, what kinds of people are you looking for to work here at MECLabs? I ask that from the perspective of the many students reading this interview today who want to know how to join a fantastic company like this.*

Flint: You've been defining that person, First, someone with high empathy. We don't mind if your background is marketing or it's food services. One of the best optimizers I ever had went to the University of Florida and studied nutrition. But Jimmy—that was his first name—had remarkable instinct and empathy that helped him see.

Also, a curious mind, someone who's interested in why. It's not enough to ask how. "How" doesn't get you deep enough in the sort of intellectual work necessary to learning.

Third is someone who wants to grow because every day here is about growing. It's not growing our revenue, it's growing our people. We want to have an impact on people. We want to transform thinking.

I think those are three of the highest qualities. If you have those three, there's probably a place for you here.

CA: *Flint, thank you so much. This has been, as always, an opportunity for me to learn a great deal from someone who is performing at the very highest level and transforming our understanding about human relationships, so thank you.*

Flint: It is a pleasure to spend time with you today.

Contests and Sweepstakes   A **contest** offers prizes based on entrants' skill. A **sweepstakes** offers prizes based on a chance drawing of entrants' names. A **game** has the chance element of a sweepstakes but is conducted over a longer time (like local bingo-type games designed to build store traffic). A game's big marketing advantage is that customers must make repeat visits to the dealer to continue playing.

Both contests and sweepstakes encourage consumption of the product by creating consumer involvement. These devices pull millions of entries. Usually contest entrants must send in some proof of purchase, such as a boxtop or label. For more expensive products, consumers may only have to visit the dealer to pick up an entry blank.

To encourage entries, sponsors try to keep their contests as simple as possible. The prize structure must be clearly stated and all the rules listed. National contests and sweepstakes are handled and judged by independent professional contest firms.

Sweepstakes and games are now more popular than contests because they are much easier to enter and take less time. Sweepstakes require careful planning by the advertiser. Companies cannot require a purchase as a condition for entry or the sweepstakes becomes a lottery and therefore illegal. Marketers must obey all postal laws. If they run the sweepstakes in Canada, they may have to pay a percentage of the prizes to the Quebec government.

Contests and sweepstakes must be promoted and advertised to be successful, and this can be expensive. And sales promotions need dealer support. To ensure dealer cooperation, many contests and sweepstakes require the entrant to name the product's local dealer. They may also award prizes to the dealer who made the sale.

Chapter Summary

The key to building brand equity in the 21st century is to develop interdependent, mutually satisfying relationships with customers and other stakeholders. To manage these relationships, companies consciously integrate their marketing communications activities with their other company functions so that all the messages the marketplace receives about the company are consistent.

As part of this process, it is important to understand how to integrate the various tools of marketing communications. Advertising practitioners need to have a basic understanding of what other tools are available to them and how they can best be used in the overall communications mix.

In direct marketing, the marketer builds and maintains a database of customers and prospects and uses anything from personal contact to mass media to communicate with them directly in the effort to generate a response, a transaction, or a visit to a retail location.

The database is the key to direct marketing success, especially in an IMC program. Databases let marketers target, segment, and grade customers. This allows them to identify their best customers, their value to the organization, and their needs and buying behavior. They can then calculate the customer's lifetime value. The database is the corporate memory of all important customer information. It should record every transaction across all points of contact with both channel members and customers. The database also enables the company to measure the efficiency of its direct-response advertising efforts.

Direct marketing is a rapidly growing industry, but it still suffers from problems of cost, clutter, and image.

Direct marketers use a variety of activities, from direct sales (personal selling and telemarketing) to direct-response advertising. Telemarketing, followed by direct mail, is the medium of choice for most direct marketers, but more are beginning to use other media, especially TV infomercials. Interactive TV may be the direct-marketing medium of the future.

Direct mail attracts nearly 20 percent of all ad dollars. While it has historically been the most expensive major medium on a cost-per-exposure basis, it has also been effective in terms of tangible results. Marketers like direct mail for its accountability. There are many types of direct-mail advertising, from catalogs and brochures to statement stuffers.

One of the great features of direct mail is that it can increase the effectiveness of ads in other media. However, direct mail has many drawbacks too—primarily its cost and the junk-mail image.

The two most important things that affect direct-mail success are the mailing list and the creativity used. The direct-mail piece normally goes through the same production process as any other print piece. The size and shape of the mailing package, as well as the type, illustrations, and colors, all affect printing costs.

Personal selling is actually the ultimate interactive medium. It is the interpersonal communication process by which a seller ascertains and then satisfies the needs of a buyer, to the mutual, long-term benefit of both parties.

There are many types of personal selling: retail, business-to-business, and direct selling. Since advertising is a support service for a company's sales efforts, advertising people have to understand the selling environment their companies deal in.

The greatest strength of personal selling is its personal nature. Nothing is as persuasive as personal communication. The one-to-one situation facilitates instant feedback. And the rep has the flexibility to adjust the presentation, tailoring it specifically to the needs and interests of the particular prospect.

Like all communications tools, personal selling also has some drawbacks. It is very expensive. Additionally, the salesperson has the power to make or break a delicate relationship. So one of the risks is that one bad apple can ruin a previously unblemished association.

Salespeople provide four communications functions: information gathering, information providing, order fulfillment, and relationship building.

Sales promotion complements advertising and personal selling by stimulating sales. It includes direct inducements (such as money, prizes, or gifts) aimed at salespeople, distributors, retailers, consumers, and industrial buyers.

Marketers must balance sales promotion with advertising. Advertising creates market value for a brand; promotion creates market volume. Advertising has a positive effect on profits; promotion can have a negative effect. Sales promotion techniques are used in the trade to push products through the distribution channels and with consumers to pull them through.

Manufacturers use many sales promotion techniques with dealers: slotting allowances, trade deals, display allowances, buyback allowances, advertising allowances, co-op advertising and advertising materials, dealer premiums and contests, push money, and company conventions and dealer meetings. Sales promotions aimed at the ultimate purchaser include point-of-purchase materials, coupons, electronic coupons and convenience cards, cents-off promotions, refunds, rebates, premiums, sampling, combination offers, contests, and sweepstakes.

Important Terms

advertising allowance, *568*

broadsides, *556*

brochures, *556*

business reply mail, *556*

buyback allowance, *568*

catalog, *557*

cents-off promotion, *570*

combination offer, *571*

company conventions and dealer meetings, *568*

compiled lists, *557*

consumer sales promotion, *566*

contest, *574*

cooperative (co-op) advertising, *568*

coupon, *569*

customer lifetime value (LTV), *549*

data access, *550*

data management, *550*

database, *547*

database marketing, *547*

direct-mail (action) advertising, *554*

direct marketing, *546*

direct-response (action) advertising, *547*

direct-sales strategy, *553*

direct selling, *553*

display allowance, *567*

diverting, *567*

electronic coupon, *570*

folders, *556*

forward buying, *567*

freestanding insert (FSI), *570*

game, *574*

house lists, *556*

house organs, *556*

in-store sampling, *571*

letter shop, *557*

linkage media, *548*

list broker, *557*

mail-response lists, *557*

personal selling, *560*

point-of-purchase (P-O-P) materials, *568*

polybagging, *571*

postcards, *555*

premium, *570*

pull strategies, *566*

push money (PM), *568*

push strategies, *565*

rebate, *570*

RFM formula, *550*

sales letters, *555*

sales promotion, *564*

sampling, *571*

self-mailers, *556*

slotting allowance, *566*

spiffs, *568*

statement stuffers, *556*

sweepstakes, *574*

telemarketing, *553*

trade advertising, *566*

trade concentration, *566*

trade deal, *567*

trade promotion, *565*

Review Questions

1. Who are a company's best prospects for additional sales and profits? Why?

2. How should a large insurance company view integrated marketing communications?

3. What are the basic strategic and tactical decisions direct marketers face?

4. How can an advertiser use a newspaper for direct-response advertising?

5. What distinct communications functions do salespeople provide?

6. What are the three things salespeople must do to build relationships?

7. What are the main purposes of sales promotion?

8. Why is trade promotion controversial?

9. What are the most common pull strategies? Which would you use to launch a new soft drink?

10. Why is there a trend away from push strategies and toward pull strategies?

11. How could you use direct mail in an integrated marketing communications program? Give an example.

12. What factors have the greatest influence on the success of a direct-mail campaign?

The Advertising Experience

1. **Push and Pull Techniques**

   Advertisers commonly use both push and pull techniques. Explore the situation of a company of your choice, identifying its pull techniques and also tracking down its push techniques. (Push techniques might be more difficult to find.) Trade publications are a good place to look. Create a report detailing the overall strategy of the company and discuss why you think one area might be emphasized over another.

2. **Direct Marketing and Direct Response**

   Direct marketing is not only vast, it's ever changing in all its facets—direct sales, direct mail, direct response. Likewise, direct marketing agencies tend to differ from traditional advertising agencies in strategy, organization, and clientele. Take a look at some of the Websites below and answer the questions that follow for each site.

   Direct Marketing Organizations

   - Canadian Marketing Association (CMA): www.the-cma.org
   - Direct Marketing Association (DMA): www.the-dma.org
   - Direct Marketing News: www.dmnews.com
   - Give to Get Marketing: www.givetogetmarketing.com
   - Direct Response Forum, Inc.: www.directresponse.org
   - Direct Marketing Association of Southern California: www.ladma.org
   - Federation of http://www.dmanc.org/ European Direct Marketing: www.fedma.org

   a. What group sponsors the site? Who is the intended audience(s)?

   b. What are the size, scope, and purpose of the organization?

   c. What benefits does the organization provide to individual members or subscribers? To the overall advertising and direct marketing communities?

   d. How important do you believe this organization is to the direct marketing industry? Why?

   Direct Marketing Firms

   - Select five of the following direct marketing firms, visit their Websites, and answer the questions that follow.
   - Acxiom Digital: www.acxiomdigital.com
   - Exposed Brick: www.exposedbrick.com
   - GEICO: www.geico.com
   - Harte-Hanks: www.harte-hanks.com

   - DDB Seattle: www.hunt.DDBdirect.com
   - Wunderman: www.wunderman.com

   a. Who is the intended audience of the site?

   b. How does the agency position itself (i.e., creative-driven, strategy- (account) driven, media-driven, etc.)?

   c. What is your overall impression of the agency and its work? Why?

3. **Direct Mail**

   Despite its junk-mail image, direct mail requires a great deal of creativity. Jones Educational Services, which provides GMAT, GRE, and MCAT preparation, has agreed that a direct-mail campaign may be the best way to increase its market share. Create a campaign for your college or university designed to attract top high school recruits. Browse the direct-mail–related Websites below for ideas.

   - Direct Mail Express: www.dmecorporate.com
   - Direct Marketing Association: www.the-dma.org
   - L.I.S.T. Incorporated: www.l-i-s-t.com
   - Association (MFSA): www.mfsanet.org
   - PostMaster Direct Response: www.postmasterdirect.com
   - www.responsemail.com
   - United States Postal Service: www.usps.com

4. **Sales Promotion**

   Sales promotion vehicles are often key elements in integrated marketing communication campaigns. Browse the Websites of the following support organizations for the sales promotion field and answer the questions for each site.

   Sales Promotion Organizations

   - Promotional Product Association International (PPAI): www.ppai.org/
   - Creative Magazine: www.creativemag.com

   a. What group sponsors the site? Who is the intended audience(s)?

   b. What is the organization's purpose?

   c. Who makes up the organization's membership? Its constituency?

   d. What benefit does the organization provide individual members/subscribers? The overall advertising and sales promotion communities?

Sales Promotion Agencies

Promotional companies, like their direct marketing counterparts, differ somewhat from traditional advertising firms. Visit five of the Websites for the following sales promotion companies, and answer the questions below for each.

■ AdSolution: www.adsolution.com

■ BIC Graphic: www.bicgraphic.com

■ InterPromo, Inc.: www.interpromo.com

■ Val-Pak Coupons: www.valpak.com

a. What is the focus of the company's work (i.e., consumer or trade)?

b. What are the scope and size of the company's business?

c. What promotional services does the company offer?

d. What is your overall impression of the company and its work? Why?

5. Other insurance companies rely more heavily on a sales force to gain customers than does GEICO. Given what you know about direct-response advertising and personal selling, what are the pros and cons of each approach?

6. How does GEICO use advertising to both get an immediate response from prospects *and* build brand equity? Who else do you think does this well?

19

Relationship Building: Public Relations, Sponsorship, and Corporate Advertising

Learning Objectives

To explain the role of public relations, sponsorships, and corporate advertising in relationship marketing and integrated marketing communications. By integrating public relations, event sponsorships, and institutional advertising with its general advertising activities, a company can improve the overall effectiveness of its marketing efforts.

 After **studying this chapter, you will be able to:**

LO19-1 Define public relations and distinguish it from advertising.

LO19-2 List the functions performed by public relations professionals.

LO19-3 Identify the tools public relations practioners use.

LO19-4 Explain the growing interest in sponsorships and describe when sponsorships should be included in an IMC plan.

LO19-5 Define corporate advertising and list the activities that are included under this concept.

© Varley/SIPA/Newscom Images

This vignette might be subtitled: how to squander a decade's worth of goodwill and then compound the damage with poor public relations. ■ The story begins with one of today's successful companies, Netflix. Most people know of Netflix as a company that streams movies and TV shows. But in its original incarnation, the firm challenged an earlier model of content distribution: DVD rentals. Legend has it that founder and CEO Reed Hastings launched his company after balking at fees he owed for a late DVD rental. His great idea was to deliver DVD rentals without three annoyances: late fees, return dates, and driving to the store. ■ Launched in 1998, Netflix allowed consumers to get their movie in the mail, keep it as long as they wanted, and drop it in the mailbox to return when they were done. All for one low monthly fee. ■ The company grew from one million subscribers in 2002 to nearly 14 million just eight years later. And while it was not profitable until 2003, once Netflix's model took hold, the writing was on the wall for brick-and-mortar companies like Blockbuster. ■ Netflix benefited from a number of technologies in its surge to the top, not least of which was the Internet. Customers could go to the company's Website and order or plan for their next selection. But by 2010, the Internet also ensured that Netflix would face a new, nimbler, faster-growing, and more convenient challenger: itself. Netflix began competing with itself when it allowed a small portion of its catalog to be streamed to computers or TVs. The streaming service was offered for no additional charge to individuals on the mail plan. ■ While most customers, at first, still ordered their DVDs by mail, streaming was clearly the future. But now Netflix had two delivery models, and the company was therefore, in a sense, competing with itself. Supporting both models was expensive. Netflix saw its profit margins eroding as the streaming service grew. ■ So Hastings made a decision: Customers who wanted to continue receiving DVDs by mail and enjoy unlimited streaming would see their monthly rate jump from $9.99 to $15.98. When the company introduced the price increase, it called the change "a terrific value." True or not, customers did not respond to this public relations message favorably. In fact many, shocked at the price jump, were outraged. Austin Carr, writing for

Fastcompany.com, wrote "Subscribers saw right through this corporate boilerplate, leaving nearly 13,000 comments on Netflix's blog, creating a social media nightmare for the company on Twitter and Facebook, and overwhelming Netflix's call center with complaints." ■ But there was more to come. Hastings decided to split mail delivery and streaming into two different companies. Netflix would focus on streaming delivery, and a new independent subsidiary, Qwikster, would deliver DVDs by mail. The companies would be completely separate and require subscriptions. The public response? More outrage. ■ Hastings understood that he had done a poor job explaining his decisions. He blogged,

> When Netflix is evolving rapidly . . . I need to be extra-communicative. This is the key thing I got wrong . . . In hindsight, I slid into arrogance based upon past success. We have done very well for a long time by steadily improving our service, without doing much CEO communication. Inside Netflix I say, 'Actions speak louder than words,' and we should just keep improving our service. But now I see that given the huge changes we have been recently making, I should have personally given a full justification to our members of why we are separating DVD and streaming, and charging for both.

The CEO also dove into the comments section of his blog to deal with consumers directly. Fastcompany.com recounts the following exchange between Hastings and a customer:

> Seriously, you thought a good idea to make up for miscommunications was to separate the websites and make it more complicated for us to manage our queues? Really?
>
> Responds Hastings, "We think the separate websites (a link away from each other) will enable us to improve both faster than if they were single websites." (Only 54 Likes, at last count.)

Consumers were unhappy, and Netflix estimated that it lost nearly a million subscribers in the third quarter of 2011. But while it was easy for consumers to dislike the company's decisions, in truth Hastings had little choice. Offering both services for under $10 was unsustainable. Netflix needed to alter its pricing model, or face the harsh realities dictated by the marketplace. Could they have done so in a better way, one that would have allowed its customers to clearly understand the need for the company's actions? ■ Perhaps. But Netflix has survived this bump in the road. By the fourth quarter of 2011, it was adding subscribers again, finishing the year with over 20 million subscribers. And by 2015, the company had an amazing 60 million subscribers. Hastings may have stumbled early in his explanations to the loyal customers of Netflix. But by showing a willingness to engage, listen to complaints, and respond proactively, he was able to quickly right the ship.

Public Relations: IMC and More

LO 19-1

The primary role of public relations is to manage a company's reputation and help build public consent for its enterprises. Today's business environment has become so competitive that public consent can no longer be assumed; it must be earned.[1]

The term *public relations* is widely misused. Part of the confusion is because public relations covers a broad range of activities. Depending on the context and one's point of view, it can be a concept, a profession, a management function, or a practice. For our purposes, we define **public relations (PR)** as the strategic management of the relationships and communications that individuals and organizations have with other groups for the purpose of creating mutual goodwill.

Every company, organization, or government body has relationships with groups of people who are affected by what it does or says. They may be employees, customers, stockholders, competitors, suppliers, legislators, or the community in which the organization

Reed Hastings, pictured above, has always understood the need to consider public relations activities with loyal customers. His diligence paid off when Netflix received criticism for changing its business model and pricing.

© Kyodo/Landov

resides. Marketing professionals refer to these people as *stakeholders* because they have some vested interest in the company's actions. In PR terminology, each of these groups is considered one of the organization's **publics,** and the goal of PR is to develop and maintain goodwill with most, if not all, of its publics. Failure to do so may mean loss of customers and revenues, time lost dealing with complaints or lawsuits, unwanted regulation or legislation that negatively impacts the firm, and loss of esteem (which weakens the organization's brand equity as well as its ability to secure financing, make sales, and grow).

A company's publics change constantly. When acquired by Unilever, Ben & Jerry's faced previously silent, content publics. It still generally projects a sunny, caring image even though it is now part of Unilever, but criticism of the company increased after the acquisition. The Center for Science in the Public Interest (CSPI) accused Ben & Jerry's of misleading the public by claiming that some of its products were "all-natural" when they in fact contained hydrogenated oils and artificial flavors. CSPI called on the FDA to take action against the company.[2] Ben & Jerry's hedged response was that the term "all-natural" had various definitions in the food industry, but that it would work with natural food organizations on the issue.[3] Subsequently, the company voluntarily recalled pints of its Karamel Sutra ice cream that contained peanuts not mentioned on the label. After receiving one illness complaint about this common food allergen, the recall went forward, with CEO Yves Couette stating that "Our primary concern is always for the health and safety of our consumers."[4]

Because of the powerful effect of public opinion, companies must consider the breadth of impact of their actions. This is especially true in times of crisis. But it also holds true for major policy decisions: changes in management or pricing, labor negotiations, introduction of new products, or changes in distribution methods. Each decision affects stakeholders in different ways. Effective public relations can channel groups' opinions toward mutual understanding and positive outcomes.

In short, the goals of public relations are to improve public opinion, build goodwill, and establish and maintain a satisfactory reputation for the organization. PR efforts may rally public support, obtain public understanding or neutrality, or simply respond to inquiries. Well-executed public relations is an ongoing process that molds good long-term relationships and plays an important role in relationship marketing and IMC.[5]

The Difference between Advertising and Public Relations

Advertising and public relations are similar—but they're not the same. Advertising reaches its audience through paid media. It appears just as the advertiser designed it, with the advertiser's bias built in. Knowing this, the public views ads with some skepticism. So in an IMC program, advertising is rarely the best vehicle for building credibility.

Many public relations messages, like publicity, are not openly sponsored (see the ethical issues this raises in the Ethical Issues box on the next page). People receive these communications in the form of reviews, news articles, corporate blogs, or feature stories. Such messages are reviewed and edited—filtered—by the media. Since the public thinks they come from a news organization rather than a company, it trusts public relations messages more readily. For building credibility, therefore, public relations is usually the better approach. Netflix, for example, benefitted heavily from favorable press reviews during its heady growth years.

However, while advertising is carefully placed to gain particular reach and frequency objectives, PR is less precise. Public relations objectives are not as easy to quantify. In fact, the results gained from public relations activities depend greatly on the experience and skill of the people executing them and the relationship they have with the press. But PR can go only so far. Editors won't run the same story over and over. An ad's memorability, however, comes from repetition. While PR activities may offer greater credibility, advertising offers precision and control. This is why some companies relay their public relations messages through *corporate advertising,* which we discuss later in this chapter.

Ellen DeGeneres has enormous influence with millions of consumers who enjoy her shows. So when Ellen suggests she has a strong brand preference, the impact on sales can be substantial.

© Neil Rasmus/BFA/Sipa/Newscom

Ethical Issues
Public Relations—Meet Social Media and the Web

What happens when unregulated meets anonymous? Welcome to public relations in the Internet age.

PR practitioner Todd Defren raises several real-world digital public relations ethical issues in his blog "PRsquared." In one, Defren asked "What would you do if a client contact—who had a pretty solid Twitter following—asked you to tweet from his account as if you were him? Crazy? Wrong? Unethical?"

Defren raises the same issue about a corporate blog. He refers to the practice of a PR agency writing unattributed posts for a client as "ghost-blogging." "You can rail against it as a black mark against authenticity," notes Defren, "but it is happening and it is a trend that will only grow. Not enough people see this as a bright line separating 'good' from 'bad'..."

And speaking of blogs, how ethical is it to pay people to give a brand or company favorable coverage? The site "payperpost.com" encourages visitors to "Make money blogging! PayPerPost lets you pick your advertisers, name your own price and negotiate your own deals. You can get paid to blog on virtually any subject. Sign up below!" How credible would you find such posts if you knew they were sponsored?

Even big brands are getting in on the game. Coach collaborates with bloggers, even asking them to appear in its ad campaigns. WWD.com quotes David Duplantis, executive VP of global and digital media, as saying "We see bloggers as editors, influencers and entrepreneurs who reach a very specific and unique audience. We find great value in working with those who are relevant to our brand, and are willing to pay fairly for projects." Duplantis believes that while Coach benefits from bloggers, the bloggers in turn benefit from working with a brand as important as Coach. But how do consumers benefit if they are unaware of a brand-blogger relationship?

The analyst firm Forrester thinks it's smart for companies to pay bloggers to engage in "sponsored conversations." Marshall Kirkpatrick at ReadWriteWeb.com disagrees, noting "We respectfully disagree with Forrester's recommendations on this topic. In fact, we think that paying bloggers to write about your company is a dangerous and unsavory path for new media and advertisers to go down."

Maybe all of this has convinced you that if you are looking for advice, you might want to skip blogs. Better to use a search engine, like Google, that can deliver search results that reflect the wisdom of millions of consumers. But what if a company tried to take advantage of Google's search engine? JC Penney decided it would try. Thousands of fake pages were created featuring key words valuable to the store. The initiative was designed to take advantage of Google's PageRank system and send shoppers to Penney's Website. Not illegal, certainly. But ethical? Google eventually intervened and made it less likely Penney's results would show up in "organic" search.

But if Google polices Penney's, who polices Google? The company admitted that it paid bloggers to promote its Chrome browser. Dailytech.com reported that Google indicated it had "investigated" and that it would be "taking manual action to demote www.google.com/chrome and lower the site's PageRank for a period of at least 60 days." Maybe all of this seems so frustrating to you that you've resolved to stick to Twitter, where at least you can judge a source's credibility by observing the number of followers that the individual or group has. After all, millions of followers can't be wrong. Unfortunately, the number of "followers" of a Twitter source may be very misleading, because sources can actually buy followers. The New York Times and USA Today reported recently that up to 70 percent of Barack Obama's followers, and 71 percent of Lady Gaga's, are "fake" or "inactive."

The web is an evolving medium, and companies are searching for ways to profit from it. The history of advertising suggests that consumers will reject companies that try to take advantage of them unfairly, unethically, or dishonestly. That is something every brand manager might want to keep in mind.

Questions

1. Do any of the activities described above strike you as unethical? Why?
2. Do you agree that consumers will not long stand for deceptive or underhanded practices? What actions, both corporate and governmental, will evolve if consumers lose faith in social media and the web as sources of marketing information?

Source: "For more information visit Todd Defren's blog at: http://www.pr-squared.com/index.php/2010/02/guess-whos-talking-social-media-ethical-dilemmas, and Marshall Kirkpatrick at http://www.readwriteweb.com/archives/forrester_is_wrong_about_payin.php. Austin Considine, "Buying their way to Twitter fame," http://www.nytimes.com/2012/08/23/fashion/twitter-followers-for-sale.html.

Advertising and PR in the Eyes of Practitioners

Another major difference between public relations and advertising is the orientation of professional practitioners. Advertising professionals see *marketing* as the umbrella process companies use to determine what products and services the market needs and how to distribute and sell them. To advertising professionals, advertising and public relations are marketing tools used to promote sales.

Public relations professionals take a different view. With their background typically in journalism rather than marketing, they believe *public relations* should be the umbrella process. They think companies should use PR to maintain relationships with all publics, including consumers. As *Inside PR* magazine says, "Public relations is a management discipline that encompasses a wide range of activities, from *marketing and advertising* to investor relations and government affairs."[6] To PR professionals, public relations should be integrated "corporate" or strategic communications, which is broader than integrated "marketing"

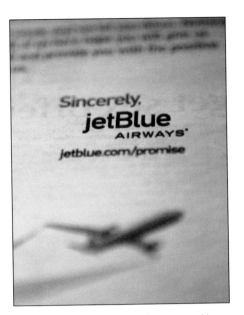

Every company makes mistakes. Smart ones address them head on and renew their commitment to great products and service. This apology from David Neeleman, founder and CEO of JetBlue, shows why JetBlue customers are so loyal to the company.

© Andrew Harrer/Bloomberg/Getty Images

communications. Public relations people, for example, are also concerned with employee relations and investor relations. Marketing and advertising people rarely are.

Apple is one of the world's most popular brands, but it too discovered the value of good public relations. Like many companies, Apple uses Chinese factories to produce iPads and other technologies at relatively low costs. This in turn helps Apple market iPads for a price that makes it difficult for competitors to beat in the marketplace. Offering a strong value proposition is, of course, an important marketing goal. But when rumors of terrible factory conditions at its Chinese plant began circulating, Apple faced a problem that went beyond marketing. Acting on the basis of its public relations counsel, Apple invited ABC news to tour its Chinese partner's factory. ABC found that the rumors were false and that employees were well treated. Crisis averted.

To date, though, few companies are structured with a public relations orientation; most are still marketing oriented, perhaps due to marketing's bottom-line orientation. But in a world of downsizing, reengineering, and total quality management (TQM), marketing people would be well advised to adopt the multiple-stakeholder approach and relationship consciousness that PR people bring to the table.

Moreover, in times of crisis, the candid, open-information orientation of PR is invariably the better perspective to adopt. Fortunately, with the growing interest in relationship marketing, two-way interactivity, and IMC, companies are finally beginning to embrace a public relations philosophy. Exhibit 19-1 shows some indicators of the PR industry's health and growth.

When PR activities are used for marketing purposes, the term **marketing public relations (MPR)** is often used. In support of marketing, public relations activities can raise awareness, inform and educate, improve understanding, build trust, make friends, give people reasons or permission to buy, and create a climate of consumer acceptance.[7] Marketing strategists Al and Laura Ries believe the best way to build a brand is through publicity—a PR activity. They cite numerous examples of leading companies that achieved their cachet with relatively little advertising but extensive publicity: Starbucks, The Body Shop, and Walmart, to name a few.[8]

In an integrated marketing communications program, advertising and MPR need to be closely coordinated. Many ad agencies now have PR departments for this very purpose. And many companies now have communications departments that manage both advertising and PR

Exhibit 19-1
Top U.S. Public Relations Agencies 2014.

	Firm, City, State	Net Fees	Number of Employees	% Fee Change from 2013
1.	Edelman, New York, NY APCO Worldwide,	$797,328,238	5,308	8.6
2.	Washington, DC Waggener Edstrom Communications, Bellevue,	118,112,600	635	−1.9
3.	WA W2O Group, San Francisco,	106,676,000	705	−9.3
4	CA	82,625,000	402	10.1
5.	Ruder Finn, New York, NY	73,891,000	522	16.8
6.	Finn Partners, New York, NY	52,796,000	339	19
7.	MWWPR, New York, NY	51,775,000	248	7.8
8.	ICR, New York, NY	50,687,714	144	19.4
9.	DKC Public Relations, New York, NY	41,500,000	199	26.2
10.	Zeno Group, New York, NY	39,921,576	276	11.2

Source: "Wordwide Fees of Top PR Firms with Major U.S. Operations," O'Dwyer's, March 2015, retrieved at http://www.odwyerpr.com/pr_firm_rankings/independents.htm.

This Adidas press release is a good example of a company notifying both current shareholders and prospective shareholders of a win for their company that may increase business. A company's public relations department will notify the press when new products are introduced, a business is bought or sold, or a crisis is afoot. The idea is to disseminate important information while maintaining the company's public reputation. To maintain credibility with the press, news releases should be distributed only for newsworthy events—those that affect some significant segment of the company's various publics.

The Public Relations Job

Public relations involves a variety of activities, from crisis communications to fundraising. And PR practitioners use many tools besides press conferences and news releases.

PR Planning and Research

The first function of a PR practitioner is to plan and execute the public relations program. Part of this task may be integrated with the company's marketing efforts (for instance, product publicity), but the PR person typically takes a broader view. He or she must prepare a public relations program for the whole organization.

Effective planning requires that public relations professionals constantly monitor, measure, and analyze changes in attitudes and behaviors among a variety of publics. When some Belgian consumers became ill after drinking Coca-Cola, the investment firm of Goldman, Sachs & Co. monitored Coke's standing with the general consuming public so that it could make better investment recommendations to its clientele. Analysts realized that rebuilding consumer confidence would probably require substantial marketing investment. And invest Coke did. Coke sponsored a "Coca-Cola Beach Party" featuring Beach Boys songs and dancing over tons of imported sand. Summer tours and thousands of premiums were also supported. Within three months of lifting a ban on the sale of Coke products, Coke's primary consumers had purchase intentions that matched those of the pre-crisis period.[9] Some 19 percent of consumers polled in Belgium, France, and Germany expressed at least some reservations about drinking Coke products in the future—even after Coke had begun airing a new campaign. However, 77 percent of Belgians, 70 percent of French, and 61 percent of the Germans said they had complete faith in the company's products.[10]

A common form of public relations research is **opinion sampling** using techniques discussed in Chapter 7: shopping center or phone interviews, focus groups, analysis of incoming mail, and field reports. Some companies set up toll-free phone lines and invite consumer feedback.

The practitioner analyzes the organization's relationships with its publics; evaluates people's attitudes and opinions toward the organization; assesses how company policies and actions relate to different publics; determines PR objectives and strategies; develops and implements a mix of PR activities, integrating them whenever possible with the firm's other communications; and solicits feedback to evaluate effectiveness.

Social media provide PR experts a window into the minds of consumers, especially "influentials," the individuals whose opinions matter a great deal to others (we referred to these individuals as "centers of influence" in earlier chapters). Influentials are easy to spot online—they have large numbers monitoring their tweets, blog postings, or comments (although see the Ethical Issues box on page 584 for a different take on "followers"). It is no surprise then that the arrival of social media has transformed public relations so dramatically that some now refer to it as "public relations 2.0."[11]

Reputation Management

One of the principal tasks of public relations is managing the standing of the firm with various publics. **Reputation management** is the name of this long-term strategic process. PR practitioners employ a number of strategies and tactics to help them manage theirs' clients' reputation, including publicity and press agentry, crisis communications management, and community involvement.

Publicity and Press Agentry

Many public relations professionals focus primarily on generating news and placing it in the media for their companies or clients. **Publicity** is the generation of news about a person, product, or service that appears in print or electronic media. Companies employ this activity either for marketing purposes or to enhance the firm's reputation.

Some people think of publicity as "free" because the media don't charge firms to run it (they also don't guarantee they'll use it). This is a misnomer, though. Someone still gets paid to write the release and coordinate with the press. However, as a marketing communications vehicle, publicity often offers a considerably greater return on money invested than other communications activities. A large ad campaign might require an investment of 5 to 20 percent of sales; a major publicity program, only 1 to 2 percent.

To attract media attention, publicity must be *newsworthy.* Typical publicity opportunities include new-product introductions, awards, company sales and earnings, major new contracts, mergers, retirements, parades, and speeches by company executives. Sometimes publicity accrues unintentionally, such as when Netflix instituted its price increases. And since publicity can originate from any source, it may be difficult—or impossible—to control. In IMC terms, unintentional publicity is an *unplanned message.*

The planning and staging of events to generate publicity is called **press agentry.** Press agentry helps bring attention to new products or services or to portray their organization favorably. For print media, the publicity person deals with editors and feature writers. For broadcast media, he or she deals with program directors, assignment editors, or news editors. Successful PR practitioners maintain close, cordial relations with their editorial contacts. An MPR professional practicing IMC sees the press as an important *public,* and writers and editors as important *stakeholders.* PR people pay attention to the phenomenon of stakeholder overlap: A company's customer might also work for the press. An employee might also be a stockholder and a customer. Awareness of these potentially multifaceted relationships helps create consistent communications, the hallmark of IMC. To learn about an intriguing example of press agentry, listen to the father of American Public Relations (and Freud's nephew) Edward Bernays describe his early campaign to get Americans to eat eggs and bacon for breakfast. You can see it at http://www.youtube.com/watch?v=KLudEZpMjKU.

Crisis Communications Management

One of the most important public relations tasks for any corporation is **crisis management.** Brand value can be quickly destroyed if "damage control" is not swift and thorough. For example, Martha Stewart's formerly profitable marketing persona quickly became a liability in 2002 when her involvement in an insider-trading scheme surfaced (She was later tried and sentenced to a prison term). Even though her company, Martha Stewart Living Omnimedia, immediately began efforts to distance itself from its founder's legal troubles by removing her name from some products and publications, its stock value and revenues both dropped by more than 30 percent.[12]

The classic case of exemplary crisis communication management was Johnson & Johnson's handling of a product-tampering episode in 1982. Several people died when a criminal laced bottles of J&J's Extra-Strength Tylenol with cyanide on retail shelves. The moment they received the

VERY FEW CRIME REPORTS START WITH "THE SUSPECT, A FORMER CUB SCOUT, WAS LAST SEEN..."

CUB SCOUT ENROLLMENT IS HERE. WWW.JOINCUBS.COM

Nonprofits and service organizations also rely on publicity to educate others about the good that they do. This clever message for the Cub Scouts creates goodwill, even among people who are not parents of Scouts, by speaking to a broader social benefit provided by the organization.

Source: Northern Star Council, BSA

news, management strategists at J&J and McNeil Products (the J&J subsidiary that markets Tylenol) formulated three stages of action:

1. Identify the problem and take immediate corrective action. J&J strategists got information from the police, FBI, FDA, and press; identified the geographic area affected; corrected rumors; and immediately withdrew the product from the marketplace.

2. Actively cooperate with authorities in the investigation. Johnson & Johnson was proactive. It helped the FBI and other law enforcement agencies generate leads and investigate security at the plants, and it offered a $100,000 reward.

3. Quickly rebuild the Tylenol name and capsule line, including Regular Strength capsules, which were recalled too. Although J&J believed the poisoning had taken place at the retail end of the chain, it first made sure that the tampering hadn't occurred at McNeil. The company's two capsule production lines were shut down, and dog teams were brought in to search for cyanide.

The insatiable appetite of the news media plus a flood of inquiries from anxious consumers put J&J's PR people under enormous pressure. All communications between the media and the company were channeled through the corporate communications department. All customer, trade, and government communications were coordinated within the company. This way, J&J maintained open, clear, consistent, legal, and credible communications and avoided rumors, political backbiting, and corporate defensiveness.

In the first 48 hours after the news broke, phone calls to Johnson & Johnson and McNeil were incessant. In the basement at McNeil, a bank of phones usually used for sales was staffed by employees who were briefed on what to say, what not to say, and where to refer tough questions.

At the same time, management and employees had to be informed, authorities contacted, and many others notified. J&J and McNeil public relations managers and staff had to plan, coordinate, and supervise this enormous task.

As infrequent as disasters are, there is no more important activity for PR professionals and public information officers than crisis communications management—especially those in highly sensitive fields such as airlines, government agencies, the military, law enforcement, chemical and oil companies, health and public utilities.

Since the Tylenol incident, many companies in normally nonsensitive industries have prepared crisis management plans. The manner in which a company handles communications during emergencies or catastrophes will determine to a great extent how the public responds to the news. When corporations have no plans for coping with crisis, the resulting press coverage can be disastrous. Experts on crisis management encourage all companies to follow J&J's example by being open and candid. Withholding information or evading questions inevitably backfires, as many politicians have learned.

Attitudes toward a former crisis can soften over time. Netflix, after losing subscribers over its botched growth plans, eventually resumed growth. And Martha Stewart, Michael Vick, Tiger Woods, and many others have had "second chances" after bad publicity.

Community Involvement

The goal of **community involvement** is to develop a dialogue between the company and the community.[13] This is best done by having company officers, management, and employees contribute to the community's social and economic development. Every community offers opportunities for corporate involvement: civic and youth groups, charitable fundraising drives, cultural or recreational activities, and so on. As we discussed in Chapter 8, a company should ideally adopt one program relevant to its expertise and focus its *mission marketing* activities. The PR department may help set up such programs and publicize them to the community (see Ad Lab 19–A).

AD Lab 19–A

"Green" Advertising

Since its introduction in the mid-1980s, environmental advertising has become a significant aspect of marketing. Advertisers saw the consumer desire for environmentally safe products and tried to meet the demand as quickly as possible. Many advertisers embraced genuine concern for the environment. But it didn't take long for consumers to catch on to the fact that some companies were making false claims, using such vague terms as *environmentally friendly* and *green*.

In a short time, consumers grew wary of the environmental appeal, and advertisers reacted by reducing its emphasis. To avoid future trouble, many companies waited for state and federal governments to define terms and provide legal guidelines. Over the past decade, the Federal Trade Commission (FTC) has established rules and guidelines, while several states adopted a set of laws setting definitions for terms like *ozone friendly, biodegradable,* and *recycled.* In 1995, California's Truth in Environmental Advertising law was enacted. It was shortly repealed and introduced again in 1997 without success.

Presently, there are no federal laws governing what a seller can say about a product. The FTC, in cooperation with the Environmental Protection Agency (EPA), has developed new guidelines for advertisers to ensure that their environmental marketing claims do not mislead consumers. These Guidelines for the Use of Environmental Advertising Claims carry no force of law, and compliance is voluntary.

Several companies and organizations act as intermediaries between advertisers and consumers regarding environmental claims. Scientific Certification Systems (SCS) (http://www.planetinc.com/certification.htm), for instance, verifies claims of recycled content in products. It uses an environmental report card, which measures a product's total environmental impact.

Green Seal (www.greenseal.org), an independent, nonprofit organization, promotes the manufacture and sale of environmentally responsible consumer products. It awards a Green Seal of Approval to products that cause less harm to the environment than other similar products. Founded in 1994, Green Seal "focuses on the measure of environmental damage that scientists have found to be most important in certain product categories," says Norman Dean, president.

Today's new marketing sensitivity toward the environment and social consciousness focuses on consumer purchasing behavior.

Seventy-nine percent of Americans consider themselves environmentalists, 83 percent say they have changed their shopping habits to help protect the environment, and 67 percent say they would be willing to pay 5 to 10 percent more for environmentally friendly products. The data, however, are contradicted by more recent studies that reveal that people in America do not actually buy the products they claim to prefer. Even though studies show a high concern for the environment, the public lacks a behavior consistent with such concerns. Researchers believe that this attitude–behavior gap exists when the competitive advantage of green products is overcome by factors of price, quality, and convenience.

But in an increasingly competitive marketplace, firms must ultimately benefit from their green actions. A new environmental management tool called SPINE was developed to help industries achieve environmental recognition. SPINE makes it possible for customers to verify marketers' environmental claims by following a product's manufacturing process through every step.

Even with organizations such as Scientific Certification Systems and Green Seal, and reference tools such as SPINE, it is still a major challenge to get businesses and consumers to understand the value of green advertising, especially when no stringent regulations are in effect. Today, the consumer can only speculate how "environmentally friendly" a company actually is. Thinking about the future, either through regulation or voluntary action, companies will have to provide consumers with more information about the environmental friendliness of their products so customers may decide for themselves how well a product suits their needs.

Laboratory Applications

1. Imagine you are marketing a new product that sells for $1.25 and is environmentally safe. Would you spend thousands of dollars for a green seal on your impulse product if consumers are ambivalent toward such environmentally safe goods as observed in the first wave? Explain.

2. Imagine that you just made manufacturing changes to your product so that it is now easily recyclable. Would you advertise these changes, knowing the restrictions on the term *recycle?*

Other Public Relations Activities

In addition to planning and reputation management, public relations professionals are often involved in activities such as public affairs and lobbying, speechwriting, fundraising and membership drives, creation of publications, and special-events management.

Public Affairs and Lobbying

Organizations often need to deal with elected officials, regulatory and legislative bodies, and various community groups—the realm of **public affairs.** Public affairs usually requires a specialist. Many experts think PR and public affairs should become more integrated, combine the skills and policy expertise of the specialist with the PR person's media and community relations savvy.

The Internet has created new methods of public relations activities. Corporate blogs, such as this example from Netflix, are an important way for companies to stay in touch with the press, customers and other publics.

Source: Netflix

Lobbying refers to informing government officials and persuading them to support or thwart administrative action or legislation in the interests of some client. Every organization is affected by the government, so lobbying is big business.

Speechwriting

Because company officials often have to speak at stockholder meetings, conferences, or conventions, PR practitioners often engage in **speechwriting.** They are also frequently responsible for making all the arrangements for speaking opportunities and developing answers for questions company representatives are likely to be asked. Since public relations people may sometimes represent their employers at special events, press conferences, and interviews, they too should be articulate public speakers.

Fundraising and Membership Drives

A public relations person may be responsible for soliciting money for a nonprofit organization or for a cause the company deems worthwhile, such as the United Way or a political action committee (PAC).

Charitable organizations, labor unions, professional societies, trade associations, and other groups rely on membership fees or contributions. The PR specialist must communicate to potential contributors or members the goals of the organization and may integrate promotional tie-ins to publicize the drive or encourage participation. In the process, the company PR people may work closely with the advertising department or agency to create ads promoting the particular cause or to publicize the company's involvement with the cause in product ads.

Publications

Public relations people prepare many of a company's communications materials: news releases and media kits; booklets, leaflets, pamphlets, brochures, manuals, and books; letters, inserts, and enclosures; annual reports; posters, bulletin boards, and exhibits; audiovisual materials; and speeches and position papers. Here again, they may work with the advertising department or agency to produce these materials. The advertising people need to keep the company's overall positioning strategy in mind while trying to help accomplish the particular PR objectives.

Social Media

With the advent of social media and the rise in popularity of blogging and microblogging, staying on top of who is writing about what is a full-time job. It used to be that a PR professional would have to know a score of people for each industry; nowadays that score is exponentially bigger. However, with the bad comes the good, and the clarity that comes from social media allows PR professionals to stay on top of any trends and deal with them before they become brand epidemics. With a good social media strategy PR professionals can help get influential people to showcase their client's products as they launch, keeping the early adopters and/or loyalists abreast of new developments before the advertising hits.

Corporate Blogs

Maintaining and managing a **corporate blog** can help address important concerns, introduce new products or services, and maintain a dialogue between a company and its publics. My IMC Campaign 19–A, "Corporate Blogging," provides some guidelines for using this public relations activity.

Special-Events Management

The sponsorship and management of special events is a rapidly growing field. In fact, it has become such an important topic that we devote the next major section of this chapter to it, following our discussion of PR tools.

My IMC Campaign 19–A

Corporate Blogging

Most corporations have guidelines for blogging. Here is a set of marketing-related guidelines that every corporation should think about if they intend to use blogging for a marketing tool.

- **Know the environment.** What are people saying about you and your products? Venture out into the web and see what happens when you type your company name into Google or visit popular blogs that deal with your company's product category.

- **Determine what you hope to accomplish.** What is your purpose? Why have you started the blog? To address rumors? Share company news? Inform customers about new products? Develop a corporate personality? Having clear objectives will make decisions about what and when to blog much easier.

- **Practice, practice, practice.** Do a trial run. Blogging is time-consuming, sometimes difficult, and a different kind of activity for many organizations. Smart companies generate initial blog posts internally until it is clear that the tactic will be useful and rewarding.

- **Remember that it's a two-way street.** Learn to share control. Blogs without comments have minimal value, but with comments comes criticism. Smart companies value input from critics at their blogs because it offers them an opportunity to respond and educate.

- **Live up to the commitment.** Attention to blogs withers if postings aren't regular.

- **Offer value.** Providing information that publics can't find elsewhere gives people a reason to visit your blog or subscribe to feeds.

- **Ask if you have readers.** Is your public suitable for blogging? Not every market contains people who read blogs. If yours doesn't, you're wasting time and resources. Search for other blogs related to your industry or product and locate secondary information on your target market's use of the web to find out whether your blog might make a difference.

- **Avoid hype and puffery.** The online community has a different personality than that of people who rely on traditional media. Web users are suspicious of hype and can be critical when they sense they are being preached to or misled.

- **Monitor the one place everyone visits**—its name is Wikipedia. If your company or product is mentioned there it is important to monitor, and occasionally correct, what is posted.

- **Use blogging as one piece of the puzzle.** Blogging can be an effective way to reach and respond to your publics. But it is rarely a stand-alone tactic. Smart companies make it a part of their overall IMC and public relations plans.

Public Relations Tools

The communications tools at the PR person's disposal vary widely, from news releases and photos to audiovisual materials and even advertising. We'll discuss some of the more common ones briefly.

News Releases and Press Kits

A **news release** (or **press release**), the most widely used PR tool, consists of one or more typed sheets of information (usually 8½ by 11 inches) issued to generate publicity or shed light on a subject of interest. News releases cover time-sensitive hard news. Topics may include the announcement of a new product, promotion of an executive, an unusual contest, landing of a major contract, or establishment of a scholarship fund.

A **press kit** (or **media kit**) supports the publicity gained at staged events such as press conferences or open houses. It includes a basic fact sheet of information about the event, a program or schedule of activities, and a list of the participants and their biographical data. The kit also contains a news story about the event for the broadcast media, news and feature stories for the print media, and any pertinent photos and brochures.

Photos

Photos of events, products in use, new equipment, or newly promoted executives can lend credence or interest to a dull news story. In fact, a photo tells the story faster. Photos should be high quality and need little or no explanation. Typed captions should describe the photo and accurately identify the people shown.

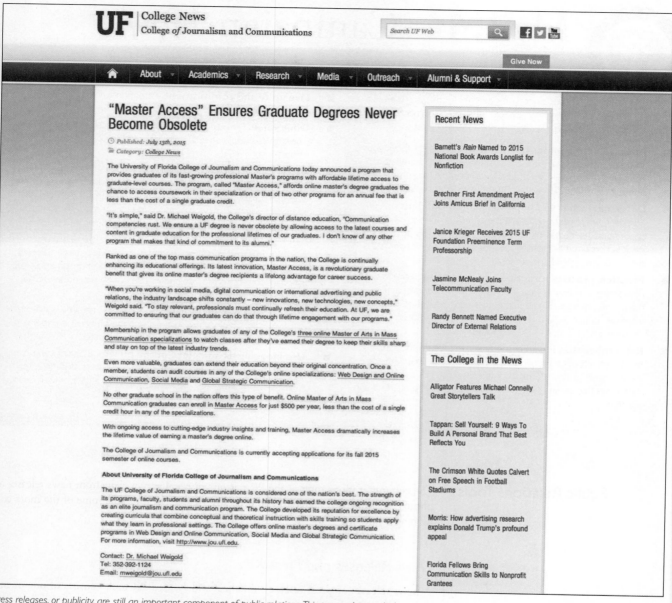

Press releases, or publicity, are still an important component of public relations. This press release, which quotes one of your text's authors, is intended to announce a new educational offering.

Courtesy of Dr. Michael Weigold

Feature Articles

Many publications, especially trade journals, run **feature articles** (soft news) about companies, products, or services. They may be written by a PR person, the publication's staff, or a third party (such as a freelance business writer). As an MPR tool, feature articles can give the company or product great credibility. Editors like them because they have no immediate deadline and can be published at the editor's convenience.

Features may be case histories, how-to's (such as how to use the company's product), problem-solving scenarios (how one customer uses the company's product to increase production), or state-of-the-art technology updates. Other formats include roundups of what's happening in a specific industry and editorials (such as a speech or essay by a company executive on a current issue).

My IMC Campaign 19–B

The Client Presentation

For most of you, the culmination of your project will be a presentation to the class or client that will be judged by the teacher, a group of peers, or local marketing and advertising executives. This presentation is by far the most important aspect of selling your ideas to the "client." It is not always the best idea that wins, and a great presentation can make a bad idea look great.

By now you have spent hours belaboring the who, what, when, and where of your campaign, and now you need to explain why. You should think of your presentation as a Cliff Notes version of your thinking. While going through the process of developing a campaign, it is likely that you did not work sequentially—in fact most IMC processes are done in parallel—but your presentation should illustrate the linear path of thinking that netted your results.

Most presentations utilize PowerPoint, but if you have the resources and the gumption, think about different ways to illustrate your thinking and your ideas. Remember that the more creative your approach, the more (virtual) points you'll receive, assuming of course that the creativity doesn't get in the way of coherent thoughts. Prezi, an online software program, is more difficult than PowerPoint to master, but can help you create a dazzling presentation that goes far beyond that of your competition.

Follow this basic outline and focus on how each section transitions from one to the other:

- Goals and/or objectives of the campaign—What is the campaign trying to achieve?
- Target audience analysis—Who are we planning on speaking to and why?
- SWOT analysis—What are the strengths of the brand, the weaknesses, the opportunities, and the impending threats that factor into our decision-making process?

- Strategic insight(s)—Based on everything mentioned earlier, how are you going to solve the business challenge at hand?
- Creative presentation—Ideas, ideas, ideas. And don't forget to explain why these ideas will help achieve the goals/objectives.
- Media presentation—Where will these ads be placed, and what target and strategy insights led you to choose those vehicles?

The main objective of the presentation is to communicate, in a concise and succinct manner, your ideas, both strategic and tactical. One of the biggest misconceptions is that the strategy should be an ah-ha moment. In truth, the strategy should feel more like a statement of the obvious because all of your research has led you down a certain path. If you explain the path appropriately you will receive the proverbial head-nods on the strategy slides. Where the whiz-bang should come in is how you tactically execute the strategy in its creative and placement (media) form.

Be sure to include everyone on your team in the presentation. This will be difficult, as some people are better presenters than others, but that's okay because if the ideas and thinking are good they will break through.

Last, if you are doing a PowerPoint, hand out copies of the presentation (in color) so the "clients" can follow along and take notes. Props and gadgets are great to use too, as long as they don't distract from the presentation. When Foote, Cone and Belding was pitching kibu.com (a teen girl site) in 2000, it turned one of its conference rooms into a girl's bedroom, setting the mood and ambience for the presentation. It helped the agency win the pitch because elements of the room were used to highlight the insights into the mindset of the site's main user, a teen girl.

Printed Materials

Printed materials are the most popular tools used by public relations professionals.[14] The may be brochures or pamphlets about the company or its products, letters to customers, in serts or enclosures that accompany monthly statements, the *annual report* to stockholder other reports, or house organs.

A **house organ** is a publication about happenings and policies at the company. An inte nal house organ is for employees only. External house publications go to company-connecte people (customers, stockholders, suppliers, and dealers) or to the public. They may take th form of a newsletter, tabloid-size newspaper, magazine, or even a periodic e-zine. Their pu pose is to promote goodwill, increase sales, or mold public opinion. A well-produced hou organ can do a great deal to motivate employees and appeal to customers. However, writin printing, and distributing can be expensive—and very time-consuming.

Posters, Exhibits, and Bulletin Boards

Posters can be used internally to stress safety, security, reduction of waste, and courte Externally, they can impart product information, corporate philosophy, or other news interest to consumers.

Companies use **exhibits** to describe the organization's history, present new products, show how products are made, or explain future plans. Exhibits are often prepared for local fairs, colleges and universities, and trade shows.

Internally, the public relations staff often uses **bulletin boards** to announce new equipment, new products, meetings, promotions, construction plans, and recreation news to employees. Many companies now maintain an *intranet* site where they can post their internal messages.

Audiovisual Materials

Slides, films, filmstrips, and DVDs are all forms of **audiovisual materials** and may be used for training, sales, or public relations. Considered a form of *corporate advertising,* nontheatrical or sponsored films (developed for public relations reasons) are often furnished without charge to movie theaters, organizations, and special groups, particularly schools and colleges. Classic examples include *Why Man Creates,* produced for Kaiser Aluminum, and Mobil Oil's *A Fable,* starring the famous French mime Marcel Marceau.

Many PR departments provide **video news releases (VNRs)**—news or feature stories prepared by a company and offered free to TV stations, which may use the whole video or just segments. Video news releases are somewhat controversial. Critics see them as subtle commercials or even propaganda and object when stations run the stories without disclosing that they came from a public relations firm, not the station's news staff.

Sponsorships and Events

In 1984, the owner of a large bicycle shop in the upper Midwest sent some of his mechanics to a local bicycle race sponsored by a national charity. At the time, his store was doing about $200,000 per year in retail sales, and the owner wanted to help out the charity while finding out what the racers thought of his and his competitors' businesses.

An unexpected benefit of the company's presence at the race was that participants started showing up in his store. Encouraged by these results, the company now supports more than a hundred bicycle events each year and sends staff members to dozens of them. It has hired a full-time representative to coordinate company involvement in special bicycle events that have the potential of increasing its exposure and business revenue.

In 20 years the company went from a low-key presence at bicycling events, donating a few water bottles embossed with the company's name, to large-scale sponsorship, participating in event registration, providing event participants with workshops on bicycle maintenance, and offering in-store discounts to event participants. Within a week of one event, 30 participants had visited the store. Even better news for the company was that nearly half of the more than 5,000 riders reported purchasing goods from it. The owner attributes much of his success to his sponsorship of bicycle events. In his words, "Support them, and they support us."[15]

The Growth of Sponsorship

Marketers are involved in sponsoring many kinds of special events. Sponsorship actually embraces two disciplines: sales promotion and public relations. Some sponsorships are designed to create publicity, others to improve public relations through personal contact and affiliation with a worthy cause, and others to immediately improve the bottom line.

A **sponsorship** is a cash or in-kind fee paid to a property (which may be a sports, entertainment, or nonprofit event or organization) in return for access to the exploitable commercial potential associated with that property.[16] In other words, just as advertisers pay a fee to sponsor a program on radio or TV, they may also sign on to sponsor a bike race, an art show or chamber music festival, a fair or exhibition, or the Olympics. The sponsorship fee may be paid in cash or **in kind** (i.e., through a donation of goods and services). For instance, if a local TV station signs on as a sponsor of a 10K run, it will typically pay for some part of its sponsorship with advertising time for the event.

The continued popularity of sports makes them attractive targets for corporate sponsorship dollars. DuPont and the National Guard help sponsor Jeff Gordon.

© Joe Stevens /Retna Ltd./Corbis

While the sponsored event or organization may be nonprofit, sponsorship is not the same as philanthropy. **Philanthropy** is support of a cause without any commercial incentive. Sponsorship (and a related strategy, *cause marketing*) is used to achieve commercial objectives.[17] In 2007, U.S. companies spent nearly $15 billion on sponsorships. That figure rose to almost $17 billion in 2008. Part of the surge is doubtless due to the cost of global sponsorship at the Beijing Olympic games, estimated at $78 million for each of the 12 companies taking part.[18]

The reasons for this phenomenal growth relate to the economics of marketing we discussed earlier: the escalating costs of traditional advertising media, the fragmentation of media audiences, the growing diversity in leisure activities, and the ability to reach targeted groups of people efficiently. Initial growth probably came from the tobacco and alcohol companies, which many governments banned from broadcast advertising. Recent legislation in the United Kingdom, Canada, and the United States threatens to end tobacco sponsorships altogether, but their success at sponsoring sports and events has shown the way for mainstream advertisers.

Today, there is greater media coverage of sponsored events—everything from beach volleyball to grand prix horse shows to Xtreme games to cultural events. This provides a highly desirable venue for advertisers seeking young, upwardly mobile, educated consumers. Likewise, for transnational marketers, there is growing interest in global events such as World Cup soccer, the Olympics, and the America's Cup yacht race. Even traditional business-to-business marketers, such as Sweden's Ericsson Corp., are making a play for greater brand awareness in the United States by sponsoring the World Championships of Beach Volleyball, which is staged and marketed by Nike.[19]

Benefits of Sponsorship

Today, the many benefits of sponsorship are well documented. Certainly one benefit is that the public approves of it. One study by Roper Starch Worldwide reported that 80 percent of Americans believe corporate sponsorship is an important source of money for professional sports and 74 percent believe sponsorships provide benefits to the cities where events occur.[20] Supporting this view, an economic analysis by the American Coalition for Entertainment and Sports Sponsorship showed that the 100 events it studied pumped more than $1.8 billion into local economies.[21] In the Roper Starch study, 74 percent of the people also said government should have little or no influence on which types of companies sponsor professional sports events. This is a far higher approval rating than most companies would get for their advertising programs.

More than almost any other marketing communications tool, sponsorships and events have the ability to involve customers, prospects, and other stakeholders. Naturally, events vary in degree of participation. A person attending a seminar or workshop will have greater involvement with the sponsor than someone attending a sponsored stock-car race.[22] However, events are also highly self-selective of their target audience. Someone who actually attends a stock-car race will most likely have a higher degree of interest than the average person. So marketers that define their audiences tightly can select just those sponsorships that offer the closest fit. Of course, marketers that sponsor an event simply because it has a large audience are misusing this tool.[23]

Unlike advertising, sponsorships and events can provide face-to-face access to current and potential customers. Depending on the venue, this access can be relatively clean and uncluttered by competition. Sponsoring a seminar, for instance, creates an opportunity for both customer education and brand involvement. In some cases, it even enables product demonstrations and the opportunity to give a personal sales pitch to multiple prospects at a time when they are open to new information.[24] This is especially good for business-to-business marketers.

A significant benefit is the opportunity to enhance the company's public image or merchandise its positioning through affiliation with an appropriate event.

Also important, but often overlooked, is the effect sponsorship can have on employees. Affiliating with a dynamic event can really boost the morale and pride of the troops in the trenches. And many companies offer attendance at the event (Super Bowl, Olympics, etc.) as an incentive to their sales staff.[25]

Some marketers have discovered that sponsorships can rapidly convert fan loyalty into sales. For example, 74 percent of stock-car racing fans report that they often buy products they see promoted at the racetrack. This is also true for other sports: 58 percent for baseball, 52 percent for tennis, 47 percent for golf. One fan told Greg Penske, president/CEO of Penske Motorsports, how upset he was that NASCAR driver Rusty Wallace had switched from Pontiac to Ford: "I'm only one year into my Pontiac lease and it's costing me $3,000 to get out of it and into a Ford."[26]

Finally, sponsorships can be very cost-efficient. Volvo International believes the media exposure it gets from its $3 million sponsorship of local tennis tournaments is equivalent to $25 million worth of advertising time and space.[27]

Drawbacks of Sponsorship

Like all marketing communications tools, sponsorship has some drawbacks. First, it can be very costly, especially when the event is solely sponsored. For this reason, most companies participate in cosponsored events, which spreads the cost among several participants.

The problem with cosponsored events is clutter. Some events have so many sponsors that getting one marketer's message through is extremely difficult. Look again at stock-car racing. How many logos do those cars sport?

Finally, evaluating the effectiveness of a particular sponsorship can be tricky at best—especially since it rarely happens in a vacuum. The problem is in separating the effects of a sponsorship from the effects of other concurrent marketing activities. We'll deal with these issues shortly.

Types of Sponsorship

While there are many, many avenues and events available for sponsorship, IEG Inc. groups most of them into six categories: sports; entertainment; causes; the arts; festivals, fairs, and annual events; and associations, organizations, and members (see Exhibit 19-2).[28]

Sports Marketing

North American corporations spent approximately $11.6 billion in 2008 on sports marketing sponsorships. The most popular of these are motorsports and golf.[29] In fact, the vast majority of all sponsorship budgets, more than 65 percent, is spent on sports events. This includes everything from the Olympics to NASCAR racing to professional athletic leagues. As we saw from the bicycle shop story, companies don't have to be big multinationals to reap rich rewards from sponsorships—if they do it properly.

By buying the rights to serve Gatorade on the sidelines of professional basketball and football games, that brand has received more credibility than any television ad could provide, at a fraction of the cost. During every game, TV cameras show pros drinking the product in big Gatorade cups. And it's clear they're doing it because they want to, not because their agent told them to.[30]

In hotly contested markets, the giants in their fields fight over sponsorship rights. Nike battles adidas, Coke spars with Pepsi, and Visa struggles against American Express. This has certainly contributed to the rising cost of sponsorships. General Motors, for instance, signed an unprecedented $1 billion, eight-year sponsorship deal to ensure its exclusivity as the automotive sponsor for the U.S. Olympic Committee.[31]

In addition to spending more than $1 million for each 30-second television spot during the 2012 London Olympics, Nike and adidas outfitted a combined 6,000 Olympic athletes. Although adidas's

Global marketers look for global sponsorship opportunities. The Qatar Foundation made headlines when it became the premiere sponsor of one of the world's great soccer teams: FCBarcelona.

© Albert GEA/Reuters/Landov Images

Exhibit 19-2

Sponsorship Spending in the United States.

North American Sponsorship Spending by Property Type (000,000)

	2013 Spending	2014 Spending	Increase from 2013	2015 Spending (Projected)	Increase from 2014 (Projected)
Sports	$13,680	$14,350	4.9%	$14,350	4.4%
Entertainment	1,970	2,050	4.1%	$2,130	3.8%
Causes	1,780	1,850	3.9%	1,920	3.7%
Arts	914	923	1.0%	938	1.6%
Festivals, Fairs, and Annual Events	839	847	1.0%	859	1.5%
Associations and Membership Organizations	568	574	1.1%	590	2.8%

Projected 2015 Shares of North American Sponsorship

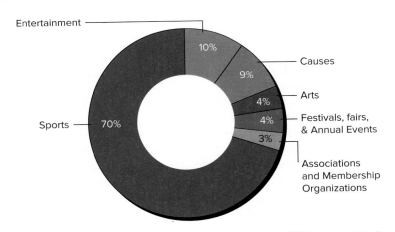

Source: "New Year to be One of Growth and Challenges for Sponsorship Industry, IEGSR, January 6, 2015, retrieved at http://www.sponsorship.com /IEGSR/2015/01/06/New-Year-To-Be-One-Of-Growth-And-Challenges-for-Sp.aspx.

traditional stronghold is in soccer gear, it still supplied an estimated 1.5 million pieces of clothing, equipment, and other logo-emblazoned articles for the two-week event. Nike is not an official Olympic sponsor, but it traditionally attempts to blanket the host city with its Swoosh anyway (see ambush marketing later). Since adidas is estimated to have paid in excess of $61 million to be an official sponsor of the games, it is not surprising that event hosts do everything they can to stop unauthorized associations.[32]

Many sports events are strictly local and therefore cost much less while giving the sponsor closer access to attendees and participants. Firms with modest event-marketing budgets, for example, use options ranging from local golf tournaments and tennis matches to surfing contests.

An increasingly popular promotion is the company-sponsored sports event. The event can serve as an effective focal point for an IMC campaign if it ties the company to the local community hosting the event as well as to the event's regional or national audience. But without a concerted effort to tie an event to other marketing communications activities like a currently running ad campaign, the money spent on sponsorships is generally wasted.[33]

Some companies associate their names with existing events. Mountain Dew, Taco Bell, Sony, and T-Mobile, for instance, are the "gold" sponsors of ESPN's Winter X Games and regularly renew their sponsorships.[34]

But controversy often swirls around big sports sponsorships. The most controversial practice is **ambush marketing,** a promotional strategy nonsponsors use to capitalize on the popularity or prestige of an event or property by giving the false impression that they are sponsors. The competitors of the property's official sponsor often employ ambush marketing techniques, like buying up all the billboard space around an athletic stadium. Fuji did this to Kodak in the Winter Olympics held in Nagano. One of the reasons this works is because people are often confused about who the official sponsors actually are—again, the problem is clutter. Just because a company advertises on the Olympic broadcast, for instance, does not mean it is an official sponsor. Ambush marketers take advantage of this confusion.[35] In fact Nike executive Mark Parker reported that his company, a notorious ambush marketer, routinely posts stock-market performances 20 percent higher than market average during Olympic years.

Sports marketing is now a worldwide phenomenon and growing at a faster rate than other marketing channels. And while spending in North America increased approximately 14.8 percent in 2008, it grew at a 16.1 percent clip elsewhere in the world.[36] The greatest spending outside North America is found in Europe ($11.7 billion), Asia ($9.5 billion), and Central/South America ($3.5 billion).[37]

Indeed, sports sponsorship is such a driving force in some countries that, for example, in Spain, football (soccer) sponsorship alone accounts for approximately 8 million euros a year, which is equivalent to 1.17 percent of that country's GDP.[38] It seems clear that companies view sponsorship as an important IMC tool. Recent trends suggest the growth of sponsorship is faster than that of either sales promotion or advertising.

Entertainment

After sports marketing, the largest area of sponsorship is **entertainment,** which includes things like concert tours, attractions, and theme parks. For instance, numerous attractions at Disneyland and Disney World are sponsored by major corporations such as GE, AT&T, ARCO, and Carnation.

Brands even sponsor entire tours. The Vans Warped Tour (subtitled "Presented by Cingular Wireless and Samsung Mobile") has a rotating lineup of 50 bands, with multiple stages and compounds sponsored by other companies, like Eastpak. Booths and tents at the festival provide ample targeted-marketing opportunities for cosponsors like Wells Fargo, MySpace.com, and Vagrant Records: The "Girlz Garage" offers fashion and makeup, and the PlayStation tent offers the latest games for the PSP.[39]

Festivals, Fairs, and Annual Events

When the IEG Network surveyed 1,000 members of the International Association of Fairs and Expositions the findings revealed a very healthy, growing environment. The average yearly sponsorship increased a whopping 20 percent over the previous four years, with the biggest growth (30%) occurring between 1996 and 1997. By 2004, sponsorship revenue increased to an estimated $792 million. The year 2005 marked a decline in sponsorship revenue. But in 2011 North American–based companies spent approximately $820 million on festivals, fairs, and annual events.[40]

One of the largest annual events in the state of Michigan is the National Cherry Festival in Traverse City. Held every year around the Fourth of July, it boasts an impressive lineup of events and promotional activities that drives both attendance and sponsor visibility. Events include band parades, races, concerts, tournaments, an antiques show, an air show, Native American exhibits, and much more. Among the official sponsors are Pepsi, Ford, Toyota, Intel, BankOne, and Sony.

Similarly, annual events such as business-to-business trade shows attract large numbers of sponsors as well as exhibitors because of the economics of being able to talk to prospects and customers in the same place at the same time (see Exhibit 19-2).

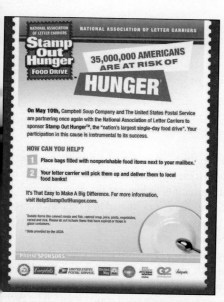

n addition to enormous and expensive sports sponsorships like the Olympics, many smaller, charity-focused events also attract corporate support. In this ad, sponsors link to an annual food drive.
Source: Campbell Soup Company

Sometimes the competition to sponsor an event even comes from within the same company. The Florida Renaissance Festival, for instance, received calls from three AT&T entities inquiring about sponsorship availabilities. Two calls were from different departments and the third was from one of AT&T's agencies. The festival ultimately signed with the phone company's Hispanic marketing department.[41]

Causes

Sponsorship of charity events and educational institutions is a tried-and-true PR activity that often fits with the IMC strategy of mission marketing. A number of large corporations (including Chevrolet, AT&T, American Airlines, Pepsi, and Kodak) cosponsored the Live Aid concerts, for instance. In 2011, marketers spent an estimated $1.8 billion in cause-related sponsorships.

A vice president for corporate relations at one large event sponsor referred to mission marketing activities as "enlightened self-interest." People appreciate the fact that the business does not really get anything tangible out of them to put in the bank.[42]

Health care marketers such as hospitals, HMOs, and managed-care companies are increasing their sponsorship activities. Oxford Health Plans, for example, signed up with the Franklin Institute Science Museum to host Cyber Seniors, a free seminar at the Philadelphia museum that teaches older people how to use the Internet.[43]

Arts and Culture

Symphony orchestras, chamber music groups, art museums, and theater companies are always in desperate need of funding. In 2011, sponsors spent an estimated $885 million to support the arts—one of the least funded of the major sponsorship categories. What this means is that this is still a relatively untapped area, and it provides outstanding sponsorship and underwriting opportunities for both national and local firms interested in audiences on the highest end of the income scale.

Unfortunately, this group is likely to be hardest hit by any legislation aimed at ending tobacco sponsorships. For instance, The Gallaher Group, Northern Ireland's largest cigarette manufacturer, regularly donates about a million pounds (U.S. $1.5M) to the Ulster Orchestra, the flagship of the arts in Northern Ireland. In the face of government plans to curtail tobacco advertising and sponsorships, the Association for Business Sponsorship for the Arts gave Gallaher its highest award for outstanding corporate citizenship, citing it for investing in the cultural life of the community in which it operates.[44]

Venue Marketing

Finally, an area not covered by IEG's report is **venue marketing,** a form of sponsorship that links a sponsor to a physical site such as a stadium, arena, auditorium, or racetrack. In 2000, for instance, the Great American Insurance Company made a good name for itself by offering

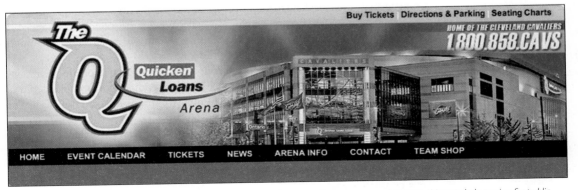

Venue marketing has surged in popularity. By selling the naming rights to stadiums, arenas, and centers, cities get help paying for public venues. Advertisers get a high-profile way to see their brands mentioned thousands of times each year in sports stories.

Source: Quicken Loans Arena

the city of Cincinnati about $75 million over 30 years for the naming rights to the soon-to-be-built baseball stadium on the Ohio River. The city accepted the offer, and since 2003 the Cincinnati Reds have played at the Great American Ballpark.[45]

Likewise, Denver has Coors Field, and Charlotte, North Carolina, has Bank of America Stadium. And AT&T has put its name on San Francisco's baseball park. But what happens when sponsors with naming rights become a liability? When Enron filed for bankruptcy in 2001, the Houston Astros shelled out $2.1 million to buy back the naming rights to Enron Field. The story had a happy ending, however, when the Minute Maid Company, a locally based subsidiary of the Coca-Cola Company since 1960, paid an estimated $170 million for a 28-year naming rights deal.

Venue marketing is changing the economics of professional sports. Sponsorships help pay for stadium renovations and upgrades and may assist the home team in defraying the high cost of leasing. Many teams keep the money from their stadium luxury suites, stadium advertising, naming rights, and food and beverage concessions. Under the new economic rules, big stadium revenues are essential to signing big-name players and staying competitive.[46]

Methods of Sponsorship

Companies interested in sponsorship have two choices: buy into an existing event or create their own. Event marketing specialist Paul Stanley predicts that corporate event sponsorships will likely become "sponsownerships," where the sponsor owns and controls the entire event. This would allow more control and would likely be more cost-effective. It would also help the company achieve its marketing objectives.[47]

For most companies, though, it's easier to buy into an existing event, either as the sole sponsor (the Buick Invitational) or as one of many cosponsors. What's most important is to get a good fit between the sponsor and the event. Nabisco's Cornnuts brand, for instance, teamed up with the Aggressive Skaters Association (ASA) to sponsor the ASA Pro Tour and Amateur Circuits and to use the ASA World Champion female skater Fabiola da Silva as the product's spokesperson. According to Rich Bratman, president of the ASA, he chose Cornnuts because "the brand management and promotions team at Cornnuts really understands how important it is to reach teens in a credible way and is committed to supporting the skating lifestyle."[48]

In his book *Aftermarketing,* Terry Vavra suggests several guidelines for selecting the right sponsorship opportunity or event.

Measuring Sponsorship Results

One of the problems with event sponsorship (as with public relations activities in general) has historically been how to evaluate results. Experts suggest there are really only three ways to do this:

1. Measure changes in awareness or image through pre- and postsponsorship research surveys.
2. Measure spending equivalencies between free media exposure and comparable advertising space or time.
3. Measure changes in sales revenue with a tracking device such as coupons.

Unfortunately, none of these methods covers all the reasons for sponsoring. For example, how do you measure the effect on employee morale? What if the sponsorship is aimed at rewarding current customers or enhancing relationships within the trade? These are important possible objectives, but they are very difficult to measure.

Still, most companies are very concerned about the bottom line and look for a substantial return on investment for their sponsorship dollars. Delta Airlines, for example, is said to require $12 in new revenue for every dollar it spends on sponsorship—a ratio the airline claims to have achieved during its Olympic sponsorship.[49]

IEGSR, the sponsorship industry's leading association, suggests the following pointers for measuring the value of event sponsorships:[50]

- Have clear goals and narrowly defined objectives.
- Set a measurable goal.
- Measure against a benchmark.
- Do not change other marketing variables during the sponsorship.

- Incorporate an evaluation program into the overall sponsorship and associated marketing program.
- At the outset establish a budget for measuring results.

Corporate Advertising

When a company wants to communicate a PR message and control its content, it may use a form of *corporate advertising.* In an integrated marketing communications program, corporate advertising can set the tone for all of a company's public communications. **Corporate advertising** covers the broad area of nonproduct advertising, including public relations advertising, institutional advertising, corporate identity advertising, and recruitment advertising.

Public Relations Advertising

To direct a controlled public relations message to one of its important publics, a company uses **public relations advertising.** PR ads may be used to improve the company's relations with labor, government, customers, suppliers, and even voters.

When companies sponsor art events, programs on public television, or charitable activities, they frequently place public relations ads in other media to promote the programs and their sponsorship, enhance their community citizenship, and create public goodwill. If the public relations people don't have advertising experience, they will typically turn to the firm's advertising department or agency for help.

Corporate/Institutional Advertising

In recent years, the term *corporate advertising* has come to denote a particular type of nonproduct advertising aimed at increasing awareness of the company and enhancing its image. The traditional term for this is **institutional advertising.** These ad campaigns may serve a variety of purposes: to report company accomplishments, position the company competitively in the market, reflect a change in corporate personality, shore up stock prices, improve employee morale, or avoid communications problems with agents, dealers, suppliers, or customers (for some excellent examples, see the Portfolio Review on pages 602–606).

Historically, companies and even professional ad people have questioned, or misunderstood, the effectiveness of corporate advertising. Retailers in particular cling to the idea that institutional advertising, although attractive and nice, "doesn't make the cash register ring." A series of marketing research studies, however, offered dramatic evidence to the contrary. Companies using corporate advertising registered significantly better awareness, familiarity, and overall impression than those using only product advertising. Five corporate advertisers in the study drew higher ratings in every one of 16 characteristics measured, including being known for quality products, having competent management, and paying higher dividends.[51]

(continued on page 607)

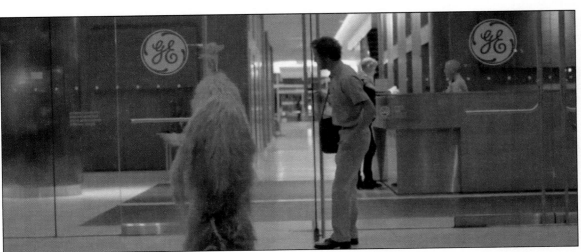

GE's "Ideas are scary" ads are meant to support the company's reputation for having a daring, creative culture. The ads use the metaphor of an unloved creature whose value is recognized. Using tangible things as metaphors for ideas and abstract concepts is important in corporate advertising.

Source: General Electric

People BEHIND the Ads

Bill Imada Chair and Chief Connectivity Officer, the IW Group

Courtesy of Bill Imada

Bill Imada is Chairman and Chief Connectivity Officer at the IW Group, Inc. His company describes itself as Culture Purveyors & Content Creators. They note that "Our workplace is the world around us. We uncover the most captivating stories and let the gems inspire the content we create." Their clients include Lexus, Walmart, and McDonalds.

CA: What is your current title, and set of responsibilities?

BI: Chair and Chief Connectivity Officer. I am responsible for new business development, client relations, civic engagement and partnership marketing. I also serve as the chairman of the board of directors (which meets annually).

CA: Describe the IW Group and its culture

BI: We are a participatory company. In other words, we believe that every associate has a stake in how our agency is organized, managed and operated. We are changing the dynamics of our company to make it more engaging, fun and avant garde. This includes a new organizational structure that allows for greater creativity, innovation and bottom-up engagement.

CA: Describe a "typical" day, or if none of them are typical, describe a recent day that highlights your career responsibilities

BI: A typical day for me begins at 7:30 a.m.—the best time to reflect on the day prior and the day ahead. It is also a great time to catch-up on emails, social media, and the latest news online.

- Coffee or tea. Heaps of coffee and tea.
- Early morning calls and conversations with clients on the East Coast and in Midwest. Checking in to see how things are going.

Conversations are usually personal and not always business related. Offering thoughts, ideas and suggestions on "connecting the dots" for different clients. (This occasionally includes career and professional advice.)

- About two-to-three hours of pro bono work. IW Group associates and I serve on more than thirty not-for-profit boards and advisory councils. Several conversations with nonprofit and civic leaders about fundraising, sustainability, succession planning, board development, events and activities, program development, etc.
- A review of regional and national speaking opportunities. I'm on the speakers' circuit and have a problem saying no. A review of the week's speaking engagements finds me traveling to different cities in less than two week. Next week: Houston, New York and Chicago. The following week I'm in Honolulu.
- A walk around the agency several times per day to see how things are going, department by department.
- Inquiries to different people in the office about lunch options. Usually eat lunch at my desk; someone always offers to fetch lunch for me. Rarely, if ever, make lunch. Prefer salads.
- An update to the voicemail each day. I change my voicemail daily.
- A review of different presentation materials for new business opportunities. This week, there are three different new business opportunities. One meeting in the office; two outside of the office.
- End the day with a rough game of foosball with a few colleagues. The interns usually jump in.
- Usually leave the office at around 6:30 p.m. Continue working at home.

CA: What are the most important changes taking place in IMC today?

BI: Workspace environments continue to change; more communal, less-structured. Office walls are coming down in favor of more communal work spaces. Cubicles are becoming a thing of the past. Office spaces look more like game rooms, playgrounds or living spaces. Furniture is more modular (often with wheels) and can be moved quickly and efficiently. PlayStation and other video games are commonplace. Food and snacks are everywhere. Who uses traditional coffee makers these days? We have a massive machine that makes lattes and other coffee and chocolate drinks. Titles are shifting. I was once chairman and CEO. Last year, chairman and Chief Collaboration Officer. Now, Chief Connectivity Officer. My job is to connect the dots or to create the dots. Silos are now blurred. Advertising, planning, public relations, media, etc. are no longer divided strictly by function but by teams. All of the teams are fluid. Team members shift from team to team, as needed. Digital and social technologies now dominate the psyche of the agency; traditional public relations and advertising are no longer the norm or the expectation. It is getting harder and harder to find digital talent; salaries are sky high and the talent can now pick and choose where they wish to work. Talented individuals aren't always hung-up on salaries, however. They are also concerned about work environment and perks;

a creative space; fun; and active engagement (in causes and issues they believe in). The democratization of content has changed the way we work with content creators. Anyone can create content these days using their mobile devices; clients understand this but are uncertain about how to deal with user-generated content. There is lots of pressure on agencies to work with less funding. Budgets are down; however, the clients will always find money and resources for fresh ideas (regardless of what they say about their budgets). IMC agencies are also shifting their focus to teams that specialize in lifestyle and social movements (e.g., foodies and chefs; music, writers and composers; social media evangelists; experience creators; social inventors, et al.).

CA: How important is approaching IMC from a global perspective for you? Would you say it is increasing in importance? How can students acquire a start on becoming more globally aware?

There are no borders. Everything seems porous. People are freely traveling across the country and across continents. The world, no longer revolves around the U.S. There is a stronger and greater focus on what is happening in developing countries such as Brazil, India, South Africa, Russia, China. People are also finding inspiration in other places such as Iceland and other small countries.

Students today need to be more intellectually curious. American students as a whole lack the intellectual curiosity that is needed for them to play in a more globalized world. The U.S. is one of the most diverse countries in the world, but we often fail to see the value of our diversity. Students often graduate saying they'd like to be a change-agent in the world. However, when they start their careers, their global views change. The reality of school debt sets in and they aren't quite sure where their lives will take them. Integrated marketing requires a level of open-mindedness in all aspects of our lives. The academy doesn't always teach or expose students and faculty to this need for greater open-mindedness (e.g., consumption of different foods, lifestyles, values, interests, mindsets, perspectives, etc.).

CA: What does the IW Group look for in new hires?

BI: IW Group looks for people who have the capacity and the spirit to live more worldly. We need people with a global perspective; however, they must also be able and willing to apply what they have learned at home. They need demonstrated level of creativity. How do they present themselves in their written documents (e.g., résumés, cover letters, writing samples)? How do they use typeface, quotes and paper to accent their knowledge, experience and ambitions? How do they present themselves in an interview? Do they know how to act and speak beyond their elevator speech? What happens after they reach their floor?

Do they have soft skills? Can they talk about themselves in a story-telling fashion? Do they even have a story to tell? Can they relate their knowledge and experience to the needs, interests and aspirations of the agency and our clients? Are they unafraid to offer ideas and suggestions, even in a first interview? Have they interned? Have they traveled or lived abroad? Do they speak a language other than English? Do they have questions for you during the interview? Or ask follow-up questions? Do they have great follow-up skills? And, have they sent a hand-written thank-you note?

CA: What is the most enjoyable part of your job?

Connecting the dots; creating new dots; finding new ways to reach consumers. Helping people connect with others. Building new organizations. (So far, I've started two new national organizations.) Bringing clients together for conversations over drinks or dinner. Finding the opportunities that exist in every intersection you traverse. Hanging out with the interns and new staff. Discovering an ah-ha moment. New business development. Finding solutions to every challenge.

CA: What should a university student be doing to prepare to follow in your footsteps someday?

They should learn how to network properly. Furthermore, they should recognize that every challenge they face often has multiple solutions. If they take on an internship (or two), they should ask if they can shadow the executives of the company or organization for a day or two. They should get to know their employer, and the people who make things happen. They should never be afraid to say, "I need help" or "I'd like to know more." They should get involved in extracurricular activities and take an active role in leading an organization. They should take time to help others. And they should always remember to give back as they advance outside of the academy.

CA: What are your pastimes, hobbies, things you enjoy doing?

Mountain biking and buying old homes. (I have a fixer-upper in historic Napa, Calif.). I am also addicted to Kickstarter and Indiegogo. I have supported more than fifty Kickstarter and Indiegogo campaigns. If I do support a crowdfunding campaign on Kickstarter, I ask the folks who are promoting the campaign to allow me to be a part of their journeys. I have met more than a dozen people I've supported on Kickstarter, and have introduced several of them to clients and staff. For instance, I invited five Kickstarter folks to Oak Brook, Ill. to meet with leaders of McDonald's. I have also agreed to serve on the board of trustees for another organization I supported via Kickstarter: MOFAD (Museum of Food and Drink).

CA: What is your favorite place in the world?

New Zealand. Clean. Mostly unspoiled. And, less than five million people.

CA: Please feel free to add anything else I've not asked about

My favorite quotes:

"Make a customer, not a sale"
—Katherine Barchetti

"If you want to lift yourself up, lift up someone else."
—Booker T. Washington

"There is no finish line."
—Phil Knight

Portfolio Review

:: Corporate Advertising

Companies use public relations activities and various forms of public relations advertising to communicate with a wide constituency. PR people refer to these groups of people as *publics*. Marketing people call them *stakeholders*.

- As you study the ads in this portfolio, see if you can determine what stakeholders the company was targeting. Then analyze the ad to determine what objective the company was trying to achieve and if it succeeded.

Corporate advertising is employed by all kinds of companies and organizations. In this example, the Army Special Forces (www.sf.goarmy.com) dares potential applicants to scale a cable car to take a brochure—the very kind of daring feat that actual Special Forces soldiers might find themselves executing.

Source: US Army

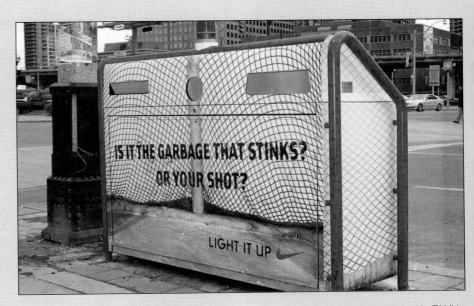

Outdoor advertising in unusual places is becoming increasingly popular. This ad for Nike, created by TAXI in Toronto, encourages people to keep the streets clean by making a game of it: The goal light goes off when trash enters the bin.

Source: Nike, Inc.

Alex Morgan, one of the stars of the World Cup champion U.S. women's soccer team, has attracted corporate sponsorship from Coke and Nike, among others.

Source: The Coca-Cola Company

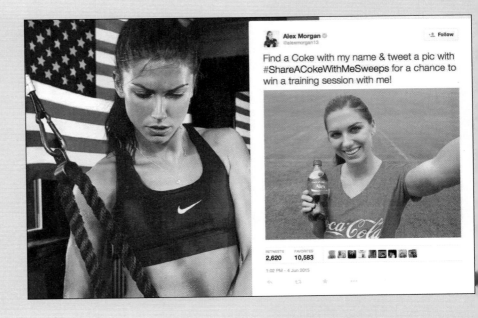

The Internet is a powerful tool for corporations to keep in touch with their consumers and other key stakeholders. Even small businesses can participate in e-commerce or communicate their services to consumers or other businesses worldwide. Africa Propaganda (www.africa.com.br), an advertising agency in São Paulo, Brazil, won a Bronze Lion at the International Advertising Festival in Cannes for the beautiful and exotic design of the agency's corporate Website.

Source: Grupo ABC

Organizations sponsor advocacy advertising to support important social or political causes. This German ad for the World Wildlife Fund (www.wwf.org) was part of a brilliant campaign that won a Silver Lion at Cannes. The concept of superimposing the sewing pattern for a leopard-skin coat over the image of a live leopard communicates the WWF's conservation message to international audiences regardless of language.

Source: World Wildlife Fund

Corporate logos can reinforce the company name through a clever demonstration of qualities identified with the corporate culture or those of its consumers. Unilever's beautiful logo focuses on the brands the company manages.

Source: Unilever

In this ad that won a Bronze Lion at Cannes, the German Foundation for the Preservation of Historic Monuments (www.denkmalschutz.de) showed how its stakeholders' euros could support its mission to preserve buildings like Dresden's Katholische Hofkirche (Catholic Cathedral).

Source: German Foundation For The Preservation Of Historic Monuments

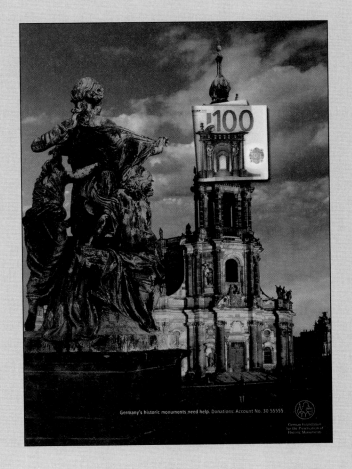

The Buenos Aires Zoo celebrated its 115th birthday with the metaphor of wrinkles. In a campaign that won a Gold Lion at Cannes, the zoo demonstrated its age with images of an orangutan's weathered hands and an elephant's crinkled eyes.

Source: The Buenos Aires Zoo

AD Lab 19–B

David Ogilvy on Corporate Advertising

David Ogilvy, the late founder and former creative director of Ogilvy & Mather, worked with Shell, Sears, IBM, International Paper, Merrill Lynch, General Dynamics, Standard Oil of New Jersey, and other successful corporations.

According to Ogilvy, big corporations are increasingly under attack from consumer groups, environmentalists, governments, and antitrust prosecutors who try their cases in the newspapers. If a corporation does not take the time to cultivate its reputation, it loses by default.

"If it were possible, it would be better for corporations to rely on public relations (that is, favorable news stories and editorials) rather than paid advertising. But the media are too niggardly about disseminating favorable information about corporations. That is why an increasing number of public relations directors have come to use paid advertising as their main channel of communication. It is the only one they can control with respect to content, with respect to timing, and with respect to noise level. And it is the only one which enables them to select their own battleground," he said.

"So I guess that corporate advertising is here to stay. Why is most of it a flop?"

First, because corporations don't define the purpose of their corporate campaigns.

Second, because they don't measure the results. In a survey conducted by *The Gallagher Report*, only one in four U.S. corporate advertisers said it measured changes in attitude brought about by its corporate campaigns. "The majority fly blind," said Ogilvy.

Third, because so little is known about what works and what doesn't work. The marketing departments and their agencies know what works in brand advertising, but when it comes to corporate advertising they are amateurs.

Fourth, very few advertising agencies know much about corporate advertising. It is only a small part of their business. "Their creative people know how to write chewing-gum jingles for kids and how to sell beer to blue-collar workers. But corporate advertising requires copywriters who are at home in the world of big business. There aren't many of them," believed Ogilvy.

"I am appalled by the humbug in corporate advertising. The pomposity. The vague generalities and the fatuous platitudes. Corporate advertising should not insult the intelligence of the public," he said.

Unlike product advertising, Ogilvy said, a corporate campaign is the voice of the chief executive and his or her board of directors. It should not be delegated.

What can good corporate advertising hope to achieve? Ogilvy thought at least one of four objectives:

1. It can build awareness of the company. Opinion Research Corp. states, "The invisibility and remoteness of most companies is the main handicap. People who feel they know a company well are five times more likely to have a highly favorable opinion of the company than those who have little familiarity."

2. Corporate advertising can make a good impression on the financial community, enabling you to raise capital at lower cost—and make more acquisitions.

3. It can motivate your present employees and attract better recruits. "Good public relations begins at home," Ogilvy said. "If your employees understand your policies and feel proud of your company, they will be your best ambassadors."

4. Corporate advertising can influence public opinion on specific issues. Abraham Lincoln said, "With public opinion against it, nothing can succeed. With public opinion on its side, nothing can fail."

"Stop and go is the typical pattern of corporate advertising. What a waste of money. It takes years for corporate advertising to do a job. It doesn't work overnight. Only a few companies have kept it going long enough to achieve measurable results," Ogilvy concluded.

Laboratory Application

Find and discuss a corporate ad that demonstrates what Ogilvy referred to as the humbug in corporate advertising, the pomposity, vague generalities, and fatuous platitudes.

(continued from page 599)

Ironically, the companies in the study that did no corporate advertising spent far more in total advertising for their products than the corporate advertisers did. Yet, despite the higher expenditures, they scored significantly lower across the board.

David Ogilvy, the late founder and creative head of Ogilvy& Mather, was an outspoken advocate of corporate advertising, but he was appalled by some corporate ads. For more on Ogilvy's views, see Ad Lab 19–B.

Responding to such criticisms and to marketplace forces, corporations now design their corporate advertising to achieve specific objectives: develop awareness of the company and its activities, attract investors, improve a tarnished image, attract quality employees, tie together a diverse product line, and take a stand on important public issues. The primary media companies used for corporate advertising are consumer business magazines and network TV.

A variation on corporate advertising is **advocacy advertising.** Companies use it to communicate their views on issues that affect their business (to protect their position in the marketplace), to promote their philosophy, or to make a political or social statement. Such ads are frequently referred to as **advertorials** since they are basically editorials paid for by an advertiser.

Corporate advertising can also build a foundation for future sales, traditionally the realm of product advertising. Many advertisers use umbrella campaigns, called **market prep corporate advertising,** to simultaneously communicate messages about the products and the company.

While corporate advertising is an excellent vehicle for promoting the company's desired image, it cannot succeed if the image doesn't fit. If a big high-tech corporation like GE, for example, tried to project a homey, small-town image, it would not be very credible.

Corporate Identity Advertising

Companies take pride in their logos and corporate signatures. The graphic designs that identify corporate names and products are valuable assets, and companies take great pains to protect their individuality and ownership. What does a company do when it changes its name, logos, trademarks, or corporate signatures, as when it merges with another company? This is the job of **corporate identity advertising.**

When software publisher Productivity Products International changed its name to Stepstone, Inc., it faced an interesting dilemma. It needed to advertise the change. But in Europe, one of its key markets, a corporate name change implies that a bankrupt business is starting over with a new identity. So rather than announcing its new name in the print media, Stepstone used direct mail targeted at customers, prospects, investors, and the press. The campaign was a success.

More familiar corporate name changes include the switch from American Harvester to Navistar International, the change from Consolidated Foods to Sara Lee Corp., and the creation of Unisys to replace the premerger identities of Burroughs and Sperry.

Recruitment Advertising

Companies use **recruitment advertising** to attract new employees. Most recruitment advertising appears in the classified help-wanted sections of daily newspapers and is placed by the human resources department rather than the advertising department. But many ad agencies now employ recruitment specialists, and some agencies even specialize in recruitment advertising.

Chapter Summary

Public relations is a process used to manage an organization's relationships with its various publics, including employees, customers, stockholders, competitors, and the general populace. The term *public relations* can describe a concept, a profession, a management function, and a practice. Many PR activities involve media communications. However, unlike product advertising, these communications are not normally sponsored or paid for.

Public relations activities include planning and research, reputation management (publicity and press agentry, crisis management, and community involvement), public affairs and lobbying, speechwriting, fundraising and membership drives, publication preparation, and special-events management.

The tools used in public relations include news releases and press kits, photos, feature articles, all sorts of printed materials, posters and exhibits, and audiovisual materials.

Sponsorship is one of the fastest-growing forms of marketing today. It actually embraces two disciplines: sales promotion and public relations. A sponsorship is a cash or in-kind fee paid to a property (which may be a sports, entertainment, or nonprofit event or organization) in return for access to the exploitable commercial potential of that property. It should not be confused with philanthropy.

Sponsorship offers many benefits. It meets with public approval. It has the ability to involve customers, prospects, and other stakeholders. Most events are highly self-selective of their target audience. Sponsorships and events can provide face-to-face access to current and potential customers. They can enhance the company's public image or reinforce its positioning through affiliation with an appropriate event. And they can boost employee morale.

However, sponsorships can be very costly, and they are also subject to clutter, which reduces their effectiveness.

Types of sponsorships include sports marketing; entertainment; festivals, fairs, and annual events; causes; the arts; and venue marketing. Sports marketing is by far the largest category, consuming over two-thirds of all sponsorship dollars.

Companies may either buy into an existing event or start their own. One problem with sponsorship is evaluating the results. Three methods include measuring changes in awareness, measuring spending equivalencies with advertising, and measuring changes in sales revenue.

To help create a favorable reputation in the marketplace, companies use various types of corporate advertising, including public relations advertising, institutional advertising, corporate identity advertising, and recruitment advertising.

Important Terms

advertorials, *607*

advocacy advertising, *607*

ambush marketing, *596*

audiovisual materials, *592*

bulletin board, *592*

community involvement, *586*

corporate advertising, *599*

corporate blog, *588*

corporate identity advertising, *607*

crisis management, 585

entertainment, 596

exhibit, 592

feature article, 590

house organ, 591

in kind, 593

institutional advertising, 599

lobbying, 588

market prep corporate advertising, 607

marketing public relations (MPR), 583

news (press) release, 589

opinion sampling, 584

philanthropy, 593

poster, 592

press agentry, 585

press (media) kit, 589

public affairs, 587

public relations (PR), 580

public relations advertising, 599

publicity, 585

publics, 581

recruitment advertising, 607

reputation management, 585

speechwriting, 588

sponsorship, 592

venue marketing, 597

video news release (VNR), 592

Review Questions

1. How does public relations differ from advertising?

2. How is the perspective of advertising practitioners different from that of PR professionals? How is marketing public relations used?

3. What is the role of public relations in relationship marketing and integrated marketing communications?

4. What are some activities used in reputation management?

5. Why is it important to establish a crisis management plan? What types of companies are most likely to need one?

6. What types of sponsorship activities are available to marketers today?

7. Which sponsorships are likely to offer the best return on investment, and how can that be measured?

8. What are the various types of corporate advertising? Describe them.

9. What is the purpose of corporate identity advertising?

10. What is the purpose of recruitment advertising? Why is it under the domain of corporate advertising and public relations?

The Advertising Experience

1. **Advertising for Future Stakeholders**

   Every company wants the best and brightest employees. Look at five recruitment advertisements and evaluate them. Which one seems to be the most effective? What makes it superior? Then look at the one you think is the least effective. Consider what could be done to improve it: then redesign the ad to make it more attractive to the most qualified candidates possible.

2. **Public Relations Firms and Corporate Advertising**

   Chapter 18 discussed the difference between traditional advertising agencies and direct marketing or sales promotion firms. Public relations firms, too, differ substantially from ad agencies. And, in some cases, they are stealing corporate advertising duties away from traditional advertising shops. It is important to explore the function of public relations firms. Visit the Websites for five of the following PR companies and answer the questions that follow.

   ■ Burson-Marsteller: www.bm.com
   ■ Hill & Knowlton: www.hillandknowlton.com
   ■ Ketchum Public Relations: www.ketchum.com
   ■ Edelman: http://www.edelman.com
   ■ Euro RSCG Magnet: www.magnet.com
   ■ Porter Novelli: www.porternovelli.com
   ■ Rowan & Blewitt: www.rowanblewitt.com
   ■ S&S Public Relations, Inc.: www.sspr.com
   ■ Stanton Communication: www.stantoncomm.com

   a. Who is the intended audience of the site?
   b. What are the scope and size of the firm's business?
   c. What is the focus of the firm's work (i.e., consumer, business-to-business, nonprofit)?
   d. What is your overall impression of the firm and its work? Why?

3. **PR Organizations**

   As you learned in this chapter, perhaps no other marketing communications function plays a more integrated role with advertising than public relations. Now take a moment to explore the world of PR a bit further by visiting the Websites for the following public relations-related organizations and answering the following questions for each site.

   ■ American Association for Public Opinion Research (AAPOR): www.aapor.org
   ■ PR Newswire: www.prnewswire.com
   ■ Public Relations Society of America (PRSA): www.prsa.org
   ■ Public Relations Student Society of America (PRSSA): www.prssa.org

   a. What is the organization's purpose?
   b. Who makes up the organization's membership? Its constituency?
   c. What benefit does the organization provide individual members/subscribers? The overall advertising and PR communities?
   d. How important is this organization to the public relations community? Why?

4. Reid Hastings had some missteps in his efforts to change the business model of Netflix. How might he have handled it differently? Create a press release announcing the change to the Netflix subscriptions that might have been better received by subscribers.

epilogue

Repositioning a Brand
MasterCard's "Priceless" Campaign

One of the riskiest endeavors in marketing is to relaunch a product from scratch. It takes a long time—and lots of money—to develop a clear position for a brand, and major changes to the brand concept may confuse consumers and weaken brand equity. This is especially true when the brand in question is a global giant, universally recognized and used almost everywhere that people spend money.

So why, in 1997, did MasterCard issue a call to dozens of top agencies to help overhaul the venerable MasterCard brand? And what made the eventual winner, the "Priceless" campaign developed by McCann Worldwide, such a dramatic success?

In the pages that follow, you'll see how everything you've studied—from the basic truths about consumers to the most complex media strategies—can come together to make a runaway hit, in which a big idea, based on consumer insights, electrifies a brand and provides a boost for all its constituencies. You'll also see how such a campaign can be executed around the world and take the idea to the next level through IMC. In short, you'll see how to translate theory into practice: from ideas to the bottom line.

A Universal Emotional Chord

The scene is immediately familiar—a father and son arriving at the ballpark for an afternoon baseball game—but the narrative device is not. As the crew-cut, all-American boy hands his ticket to the usher, a voice-over accompanied by white lettering superimposed on the screen announces, "Two tickets: $28." Next we see the boy holding two large boxes of popcorn and the voice-over and lettering (super) continue: "Two hot dogs, two popcorns, and two sodas: $18."

The male voice-over (anonymously executed by film star Billy Crudup) is warm and comforting; the soft musical soundtrack of piano and classical guitar equally so; the production values are top quality, giving this scene as much emotional force as an Oscar-winning movie. But why the "shopping list" of costs? Within 10 seconds, the viewer is hooked, needing to know where this is going. But the mystery continues as the father and son make their way toward their seats: "One autographed baseball: $45."

Finally, the pair takes their seats, and we see the father gesturing at the field, to explain some aspect of the game that is getting under way. The voice-over and super continue: "Real conversation with 11-year old son: Priceless."

Boom!

The emotional connection—dangled temptingly throughout the commercial—is finally made with the viewer. But a subtle message has also gotten across: All of those everyday purchases—the tickets, the concessions, and the autographed ball—have somehow added up to this memorable and traditional bonding experience between a father and son. And then, the new tagline puts it all together: "There are some things money can't buy—for everything else there's MasterCard."

A Marriage of Analytic Research and Creative Execution

With the launch of this new campaign, and its subsequent global rollout, McCann started the process of rebuilding a gold standard brand in the minds of consumers everywhere.

The remarkable "Priceless" MasterCard campaign has been an enormous success because it resonates with consumers, and it's strategically dead on target. It is consistent with contemporary values and provides a positive message—something truly refreshing for a credit card company—in a format that's familiar. Every spot expresses an underlying concept that is

Since McCann Worldwide can safely assume that consumers have seen many of the "Priceless" television commercials, this print ad requires very little text to communicate the benefits of owning a MasterCard.

Source: MasterCard

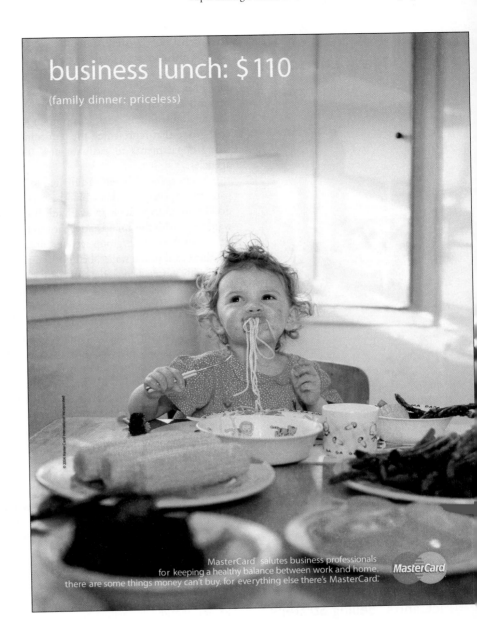

immediately recognizable to everybody. It is eminently executable. And it translates into an culture around the world, for every nation has its own local "Priceless" stories. If you don look too closely it might seem easy, like a stroke of astounding good luck—one of those rar moments when a whole campaign is born from a single moment of insight that is legendar to advertising executives. But it took more than luck. A lot more.

This is the story of how McCann Worldwide and MasterCard used sophisticated propr etary techniques to reposition MasterCard within the credit card category, giving the brand completely new face and a meaningful, likeable point of difference in a competitive enviror ment. It started with McCann conducting painstaking research, performing meticulous ana ysis, and then developing some big creative ideas, all aimed at helping MasterCard reclaim i position as the world's leading credit card. Its work shows how the commitment to researc which we discussed in Part Two, combined with the high standard in creative developmer and production values we presented in Part Three, helped MasterCard launch a histori award-winning global campaign.

A Search for New Direction

In March 1997, MasterCard put its advertising account into review. The one thing everybody in the company could agree on was that MasterCard—one of the most recognized brands in the world—needed a makeover. While successful past marketing efforts had made MasterCard a ubiquitous presence in the United States and around the world, the brand now needed a new identity and one that could endure, guiding the company into the next millennium. Nick Utton, then MasterCard's chief marketing officer, assembled a core group that represented the best minds in the global research, marketing, and advertising departments to evaluate new ideas from a variety of world-class advertising agencies.

Every agency MasterCard invited to join the pitch relished the opportunity to participate. It's not every day that a brand as well known and universally recognized as MasterCard decides to undergo such an overhaul. But what sort of overhaul? Where did the company want to go with this brand and what was the problem with where it was already?

Matt Weiss, SVP/group account director at McCann, put it this way at the time, "It was the third card in the wallet, behind Visa and American Express. Visa, the main competitor, was firmly entrenched as the top credit card with its worldly, 'Everywhere You Want to Be' campaign. Our challenge was to find a way to bring emotional aspiration back to the MasterCard brand." The current campaign, "Smart Money," developed by another agency, simply wasn't resonating with customers.

"The problem wasn't just with consumers," explained Elisa Romm, VP of U.S. advertising at MasterCard. MasterCard is an association that supports more than 30,000 member banks across the country, and these banks needed to become excited again about the brand. "The members looked to MasterCard to support them and they were very concerned about finding a consistent direction that could have a lasting impact with consumers. We needed a new, enduring campaign to energize consumers and member banks. We needed to demonstrate consistency, along with superior strategy and execution."

The company needed a big idea to bring the member banks together and lift their spirits. It was no small challenge—and the image of a major worldwide company hung in the balance.

McCann believed it could meet this challenge. "We considered it a travesty that Visa was *it* and MasterCard was just another card, even though you could use your MasterCard wherever you could use your Visa—and actually in more places around the world," explained Eric Einhorn, EVP and marketing director of McCann World Group. To discover why this situation existed, McCann turned to its proprietary brand planning process, a comprehensive arsenal of services and tools developed over many years of experience implementing campaigns for companies like Coca-Cola, Microsoft, and L'Oréal.

McCann's "Selling Strategy"

McCann Worldwide's Selling Strategy would provide the roadmap for developing the MasterCard campaign. The Selling Strategy is a service that is single-mindedly focused on generating brand-building ideas—ideas that attract customers, develop corporate and brand franchises, and create market dominance for McCann's clients. The McCann Selling Strategy uncovers the motivations of conceptual target audiences and results in a strategic concept that pinpoints a unique "selling idea."

According to Matt Weiss, "the Selling Strategy is a discipline to be pursued with passion—it's a way of thinking and a way of working meant to encourage greater strategic focus, consumer insight, and creative depth, resulting in advertising that sells." In the fast-paced and diversified global marketplace, a comprehensive brand campaign needs to be both consistent enough to be readily identified with the brand and flexible enough to appeal to

he strength, longevity, and popularity of the
MasterCard campaign help ensure that banner ads
uch as the one shown here are immediately
cognized and understood.

urce: MasterCard

different target consumer groups and fit into different media formats, whether they be print, electronic, or interactive.

The Selling Strategy begins with the Brand Footprint, which discovers where the brand is in the marketplace and in consumers' minds, why it is there, where it should be, and how it will get there. This process of mapping the brand footprint of MasterCard and its competitors would allow McCann to discover areas that MasterCard's brand could grow into and inhabit naturally, without a forced appearance that might alienate consumers or be confused with the brand footprints of its competitors.

Once it had identified MasterCard's current Brand Footprint and those of its competitors, McCann moved to the task of developing a new brand positioning, "the most basic of all strategic statements about the brand." This internal statement grows out of the Brand Footprint and, in turn, inspires the creative brief. The creative brief addresses several issues: what the advertising is going to do; what insights about the target consumer the advertising will connect with; and what the target consumers will think and feel about the brand. The creative brief serves as the stimulus for the selling idea—the bridge between the communications strategy and the campaign's creative execution.

The first thing the Selling Strategy calls for is information—lots of it.

Researching the Industry and a Lot More

McCann's management understood the challenge. "We knew we had to come up with a campaign that had breakthrough ability—a campaign that could endure," explains Matt Weiss. They began by teaming up with MasterCard for a comprehensive research and information-gathering program that would give them as much data as possible to help discover MasterCard's Brand Footprint.

"We started with a review of where MasterCard was," explains Weiss. They reviewed annual reports, payment industry overview/situation analyses, strategic marketing overviews, market research highlights, global issues, and Nielsen reports, the comprehensive positioning for the current advertising concept. They did content audits of MasterCard's business and consumer advertising, and they reviewed the competitive landscape in great detail.

Next, they conducted secondary data analysis: credit card usage data, and the Yankelovich Monitor and Roper Reports of credit card and financial services attitudes and behavior.

Many agencies might stop there. But McCann always relies on primary research where it talks directly to consumers. The agency conducted 28 focus groups, 24 one-on-one personal interviews, and 250 telephone interviews among credit card users. And while it learned a lot about attitudes toward MasterCard and its competitors and some preliminary campaign ideas, the agency went much further. To fully understand the

McCann-Erickson's research discovered that important changes had taken place in consumer attitudes during the previous decade.

Source: MasterCard

psychological space that MasterCard did—and could—inhabit, McCann conducted wide-ranging sociological surveys that helped it understand the feelings and emotions behind the brand category.

Finding the Sweet Spot

This process of mapping the brand against its available "brand-scape" was a crucial step in the journey toward an executable and winning campaign. Studying consumer perceptions of MasterCard's principal competitors, McCann determined the Brand Footprint for American Express included the three personality characteristics of "Membership," "The Business Life," and "The Charge Card." Its three descriptors were "Professional," "Worldly," and "Responsible." Visa's Brand Footprint was not so different. The personality characteristics were "Everywhere," "The High Life," and "The Credit Card," and its descriptors were "Sociable," "Stylish," and "On-the-Go." MasterCard's Brand Footprint, on the other hand, was very different. Its personality characteristics were "Everyday," "Ordinary Life," and "Generic"; its descriptors were "Unassuming," "Unpretentious," and "Practical."

MasterCard's existing Brand Footprint was, in McCann's estimation, neutral. As a rule, this is not a good place for a brand to be. But there was an upside. MasterCard had an opportunity to use that neutrality to create a new, more powerful and relevant brand positioning that reflected contemporary attitudes not only about credit cards and spending, but about much more far-reaching and important themes, like success. In short, the agency felt it had an opportunity to turn a neutral brand footprint into a powerful and meaningful space.

"We found that consumers had some feelings about MasterCard as the card for regular people, while Visa and American Express had a more exclusive, worldly appeal," says Joyce King Thomas, EVP deputy creative director at McCann. In an industry based on spending money, that might seem like a negative, but McCann saw it as a potential positive. With American Express and Visa inhabiting dated brand spaces, MasterCard's current brand image gave the company an opportunity to claim a fresh, new, and more contemporary brand territory, closer to today's consumption ideals than its main competitors. "We decided to give value to those everyday situations and emotions, the little things that add up to the big things in life," explains Thomas.

McCann also learned that along with these new attitudes about spending, consumers were feeling more responsible about themselves as users of credit cards. In one study,

The "Priceless" campaign is ultimately about of every consumer's unique dreams. In this ad, one of Justin Timberlake's biggest fans is surprised to meet her idol.

Source: MasterCard

82 percent felt their unpaid credit card balance was "necessary and justified." McCann identified a MasterCard "sweet spot" that melded the new consumer values with the emerging credit card mind-set and dubbed it "Good Spenders."

McCann had found the Brand Footprint for MasterCard, the truth of what the brand stood for in the minds of consumers. More important, it had found insight into where the brand could grow: McCann could use this "sweet spot," the overlap of new values combined with an adjustment in attitudes toward credit cards, to define a reenergized, repositioned, prescribed Brand Footprint for MasterCard. "Good spenders use credit cards to acquire the things that are important to them—the things that enrich their everyday lives," explains Nat Puccio, McCann's strategic planning director. This new mind-set was in sharp contrast to that of MasterCard's competitors. With this realization—that MasterCard's core brand values were closer to credit card consumption ideals than Visa or American Express—what had been a liability was suddenly a strength. Now McCann had to figure out how to demonstrate this to MasterCard and then to leverage it with the public.

Moving from the Brand Footprint to an Executable Campaign

As the day for the pitch presentation grew closer, Puccio and his team came up with a brilliant way of differentiating MasterCard's footprint from the competitors. Alongside two identical photographs of a large-screen TV, they put an image of a Visa card under one and a MasterCard under another. Under the Visa symbol, they put the words, "The Super Bowl is going to look great on that large-screen TV"; under the MasterCard, "We really need a family entertainment center." With a single, deft touch, McCann found a way to demonstrate how different values and spending attitudes could add up to the *same* purchase.

To further the point, Puccio and his team added another page to the presentation, with two identical images of a skier and the two credit cards. Under the Visa card were the words, "I haven't been to that hot new ski resort yet"; under the MasterCard, "I should really take a moment to relax and recharge from all this stress." The message was clear: These new spending attitudes provided a new justification for the same purchases previously associated with consumption-oriented lifestyles. Consequently, that opened up a whole new space for the MasterCard brand.

Next, McCann developed the Selling Idea, "The Best Way to Pay for Everything That Matters." This wasn't the tagline, but a strategic articulation of what the agency wanted brand messages to express. With "The Best Way to Pay for Everything That Matters," McCann's planners had synthesized their painstaking research into an idea so simple that it would make what followed look effortless.

Next came the moment of inspiration. Jonathan Cranin, McCann's chief creative officer for North America, Europe, Africa, and the Middle East, was actually in the shower one morning, mulling over the fruits of the agency's research, when the line popped into his head, "There are some things money can't buy. For everything else there's Master Card." From there, everything fell into place with amazing speed. Joyce King Thomas and creative director partner Jeroen Bours quickly came up with the shopping list approach that was expressed in the baseball spot. This would become the hallmark of the whole campaign.

McCann wasn't pitching a campaign: It was pitching an idea. And it was such a powerful idea that the agency needed to come up with a special way to present it. Bours came up with the inspiration of making giant blue velvet storybooks and a large wooden box to house them all. "We put a big cover over the box, and when we pulled the cover off, the client actually gasped," reports Thomas. MasterCard's Debra Coughlin, SVP, global brand building remembers the moment—and the gasp—well. "One of my colleagues literally did gasp. They'd caught lightning in a bottle."

Matt Weiss remembers overhearing MasterCard officials in the halls immediately after the pitch. "They were ecstatic, talking about how we'd 'struck gold.' It was amazing."

Implementing the Campaign

The first spot, shot by Tony Kaye, a world-renowned director, was the father–son baseball story described earlier. It first aired in Game Three of the 1997 World Series. Other spots were quick to follow. Each story was different and unique, but the structure was consistent: a family prepares to pose for a photo; the voice-over (always supplied by Billy Crudup) supplies the costs of the camera and new clothes, arriving at "Five Generations in One Photograph: Priceless." In another, a young woman prepares herself meticulously for an evening out, until we're told, "Look on Old Boyfriend's Face at High School Reunion: Priceless." In still another, two golfers have a day at the course, ending with, "A Hole in One, with a Witness: Priceless."

The results of the campaign were instant and dramatic. Consumers responded immediately, with higher levels of advertising empathy and likeability toward the brand. Member banks commented on the insights embodied in the campaign and how it would improve perceptions of the brand. Importantly, neither MasterCard nor McCann lost sight of the "rational" side of the brand positioning—that MasterCard is accepted everywhere.

In 2002, MasterCard won the inaugural Gold Effie for Sustained Success—given to the most effective campaign over the course of three years. By 2004, the campaign won a total of three Effies and eight AMEs (which stands for Advertising Marketing Effectiveness).

And in what may be the surest sign of the campaign's success, it thoroughly entered the popular consciousness. People looked forward to the new spots and talked about them around the water cooler in the office. It soon became a part of the cultural vernacular. Another sign of success was when the format and line were spoofed and lampooned by top comedians, including Jay Leno (on a remarkable five separate occasions), David Letterman, *Saturday Night Live, Talk Soup,* Gannett Newspapers, NBC's *Will and Grace,*

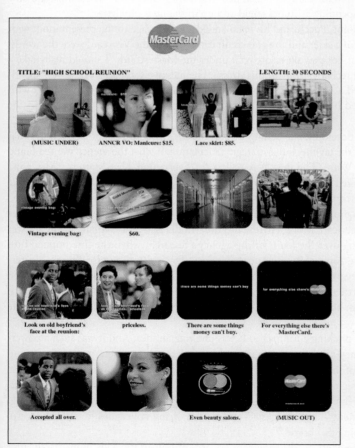

All the little purchases paid for with a MasterCard add up to one memorable moment that's so big, so important, it's priceless—in this case, the look on the old boyfriend's face.

Source: MasterCard

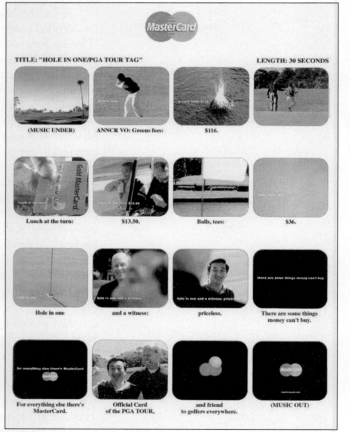

Every golfer knows the emotional value of a hole-in-one—priceless. The same is true for advertising people. A campaign like "Priceless" is so good and has such long legs that it can run for years. It is the advertising equivalent of a hole-in-one—with lots of witnesses.

Source: MasterCard

Consumers loved the "Priceless" campaign, and that translated into greater likeability for the brand. The advertising industry loved it, too, showering the campaign with a slew of awards.

Source: MasterCard

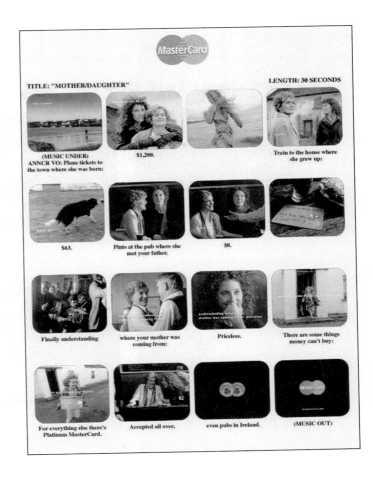

MTV, VH1, *The Simpsons,* and many popular Internet sites. Ralph Nader even used the "priceless" idea in his 2008 campaign for president. The millions of dollars' worth of free exposure that the campaign received on television and in print resulted primarily from the real appeal of the campaign. But also at work here was a parallel and deft public relations campaign by MasterCard that used publicity to build up anticipation before every major new spot. The company understood the value of high-profile spoofs and encouraged them.

The Next Step: Integrated Marketing

Now that the campaign was such a hit, there were new challenges. The first was integrating the positioning idea across all of MasterCard's different communications channels. Larry Flanagan developed an integration model that had the "Priceless" concept at the center, with all positioning and marketing activities supporting the center. While MasterCard developed sponsorships with Major League Baseball, the PGA, and the National Hockey League, McCann created new spots to promote them—and the concept applied easily to every new venture.

The MasterCard All-Century Team

In numerous ways, MasterCard integrated "Priceless" across the whole marketing mix. For example, in 1999, the company wanted to increase the efficiency and impact of its number one sponsorship property, Major League Baseball. With McCann's help, MasterCard created a fully integrated program—the MasterCard All-Century Team—that used the "Priceless" campaign to add dimension to the brand and appeal to those consumers who follow baseball.

Consumer research indicated MasterCard cardholders loved Major League Baseball. This "love of the game" ran deep and often found its way into family life. Fathers, for example, clearly remembered taking their sons to their first "big league" game—the ba

Many of the ad concepts were adapted to fit international markets. In less than a decade, MasterCard has completely redeveloped and rejuvenated its image, and the "Priceless" campaign has become part of our popular culture. For the 2004 Oscars telecast, McCann developed the epic "Dog Trilogy" in grand Hollywood style.

Part One: "Lost Dog"

VO: film and dog food for Badger in the Redwoods: $10
Super: film and dog food: $10

VO: bandana for lost dog in Napa Valley: $3
Super: bandana: $3

VO: dog bone in Fresno: $7
Super: dog bone: $7
VO/Super: forgetting you're far from home: priceless

VO: there are some things money can't buy.
VO: for your journey there's MasterCard.

Part Two: "On the Road"

VO: water for a lost dog in the Mojave: $2
Super: water: $2

VO: rhinestone collar in Vegas: $40
Super: rhinestone collar: $40

VO: meatloaf special in Arizona: $8
Super: meatloaf special: $8

VO/Super: Feeling at home when you're only halfway there: priceless

VO: there are some things money can't buy.
VO: for your journey there's MasterCard.

Source: MasterCard

Part Three: "Home"

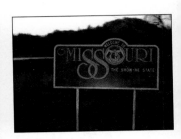

VO: chew toy for lost dog in
Colorado: $5
Super: chew toy: $5

VO: silk doggy bed for trip across
Kansas: $200
Super: silk doggy bed: $200

VO: bubble bath in Jefferson City: $15
(dog at pet groomer)
Super: bubble bath: $15

VO: coming home after a long trip:
priceless
Super: coming home: priceless

Source: MasterCard

VO: there are some things money
can't buy.
VO: for your journey there's
MasterCard.

premise of the very first "Priceless" spot. Moms often talked of the "good quality" times shared at the ballpark. McCann found that consumers wanted to experience the game frequently and were positively predisposed to brands that had a strong association with Major League Baseball.

For MasterCard, this presented a huge opportunity. The positioning, as demonstrated by the "Priceless" campaign, was founded on the premise of "what matters" in everyday life. To this target, Major League Baseball mattered greatly. Thus, the positioning—The Best Way to Pay for Everything That Matters—was ultimately used to form the link between the brand (MasterCard), the sponsorship partner (Major League Baseball), and the consumer (the MasterCard/Major League Baseball fan). The strategic positioning became: "MasterCard: The card at the heart of Major League Baseball," and the implementation was the wildly popular MasterCard All-Century Team, something that truly mattered to baseball fans. Without such a strong and flexible positioning to work from, it wouldn't have been such a runaway success.

By 2003, "Priceless" had gone from being an advertising campaign that lived primarily within the traditional realm of TV and print to a truly integrated global platform encompassing event sponsorship, sales promotion, and public relations activities and spanning a myriad of communication vehicles including radio, the Internet, point-of-sale (POS), and direct mail.

Fastfoward nearly 20 years from 1997. New Mastcard CMO Raja Rajamannar faces a big decision: keep the campaign going or chart a new course. "Dealing with an iconic campaign is both a blessing and a challenge," said Rajamannar. "How do you take it to the next level when it's doing so well? And how do you convince the system, and convince yourself, that change is indeed needed?"

The evolution first started in 2010 when a campaign labeled "Priceless Cities" aimed at specific audiences defined by demographics and geographics. Next came "Priceless Surprises," which moved advertising heavily into digital and social media. An example is the Justin TImberlake viral shown below.

The brand's core areas, which for now include Priceless "cities," "surprises," "causes," and "perks," will expand to nine in 2016. Rajamannar, it seems, will keep nudging the brand to embrace 21st century strategies while retaining a 20th century big idea.

A Textbook Case

Why has the campaign been so successful, not only in the United States but around the world? Larry Flanagan told *Advertising Age*, "People ask, 'How do you develop and execute a global campaign like that?' But we didn't set out with a global campaign mandate. We came up with a strong idea for the United States and, because its insights were so global and its strategic foundation so nonbiased toward any culture, we found it could resonate around the world. The core values of 'Priceless' translate well everywhere and have driven results for us globally."

As one of the most recognizable campaigns in the world, "'Priceless' has become an icon in a very short time," says former MasterCard marketer Jim Accomando. "As an ad campaign, it's as good as any I've seen."

The strategic and creative brilliance of "Priceless" has garnered lots of recognition for its creators, including over 100 creative awards worldwide. *Fortune* magazine even named the campaign's creative team as one of "Six Teams That Changed the World."

More importantly, "Priceless" has helped MasterCard achieve its marketing objectives. In 1991, a few years before the campaign began, the card was accepted at fewer than 2 million locations in the United States. Today it is accepted at more than 7 million. And since the campaign's debut, MasterCard has issued twice as many new U.S. credit cards as Visa.

It seems reasonable to wonder whether a campaign that's run nearly 20 years, involving more than 350 commercials, viewed in 108 countries and 50 languages, can keep on going. As our update shows, Mastercard's new CMO and ad agency McCann plan to ensure that "Priceless" stays fresh and relevant.

One of Mastercard's new spots is "Priceless Causes," in which antagonists (like the Mets and Phillies mascots) work together to fight cancer.
Source: MasterCard

As of 2015, the campaign continues with this execution, titled "Priceless Surprises." David Ogilvy once claimed that an indicator of a Big Idea is that it could last a long time. The "Priceless" campaign has met that standard.

Source: MasterCard

After all of that success, you have to wonder if the folks at MasterCard ever think,

- Creative spots that consistently win awards—pretty good.
- A campaign that effectively conveys the essence of the MasterCard brand to the target audience—sensational.
- Almost twenty years of compelling spots that continue to resonate with viewers—outstanding.
- IMC that meets and then exceeds every marketing and communications objective—Priceless!

Marketing Plan Outline

Date:

Company Name:

Brand or Service:

Encapsulation, for executive review, of entire marketing plan in no more than two or three pages.

I. Executive Summary

    A.   Summary of situation analysis

    B.   Summary of marketing objectives

    C.   Summary of marketing strategies

    D.   Budget summary

Complete statement of where the organization is today and how it got there.

II. Situation Analysis

    A.   The industry

        1. Definition of industry and company business

        2. History of industry

           a. Technological advances

           b. Trends

What business the organization is in and characteristics of the industry as a whole. Information available from industry trade publications, trade association newsletters, consumer business press, Department of Commerce publications.

        3. Growth patterns within industry

           a. Demand curve

           b. Per capita consumption

           c. Growth potential

        4. Characteristics of industry

           a. Distribution patterns and traditional channels

           b. Regulation and control within industry

           c. Typical promotional activity

           d. Geographic characteristics

           e. Profit patterns

All relevant information on the company and its capabilities, opportunities, and/or problems. Information may be found in annual reports, sales records, warranty card records, customer correspondence, sales staff reports.

    B.   The company

        1. Brief history

        2. Scope of business

        3. Current size, growth, profitability

        4. Reputation

        5. Competence in various areas

           a. Strengths

           b. Weaknesses

Complete description and all relevant information on the product/service mix, sales, and the strengths and weaknesses therein. See sales literature, sales reports, dealer correspondence, and so on.

    C.   The product/service

        1. The product story

           a. Development and history

           b. Stage of product life cycle

              (1) Introduction

          (2)   Growth

          (3)   Maturity

          (4)   Decline

    c. Quality factors

    d. Design considerations

    e. Goods classification

          (1)   Consumer or industrial good

          (2)   Durable or nondurable good or service

          (3)   Convenience, shopping, or specialty good

          (4)   Package good, hard good, soft good, service

    f. Packaging

    g. Price structure

    h. Uses

          (1)   Primary

          (2)   Secondary

          (3)   Potential

    i. Image and reputation

    j. Product/service strengths

    k. Product/service weaknesses

  2. Product sales features

    a. Differentiating factors

          (1)   Perceptible, imperceptible, or induced

          (2)   Exclusive or nonexclusive

    b. Position in mind of customer

    c. Advantages and disadvantages (customer perception)

  3. Product research and development

    a. Technological breakthroughs

    b. Improvements planned

    c. Technical or service problems

  4. Sales history

    a. Sales and cost of sales

          (1)   By product/service

          (2)   By model

          (3)   By territory

          (4)   By market

    b. Profit history for same factors

  5. Share of market

    a. Industry sales by market

    b. Market share in dollars and units

    c. Market potential and trends

D. The market

  1. Definition and location of market

    a. Identified market segments

          (1)   Past

          (2)   Potential

    b. Market needs, desires

All relevant information about the people or organizations that comprise the current and prospective market for the firm's offerings. See market research reports, consumer/business press, trade publications, Census of Manufacturers, trade association reports.

       c. Characteristics of market
- (1) Geographic
- (2) Demographic
- (3) Psychographic
- (4) Behavioral

       d. Typical buying patterns
- (1) Purchase patterns
- (2) Heavy users/light users
- (3) Frequency of purchase

       e. Buying influences on market

2. Definition of our customers
   - *a.* Present, past, and future
   - *b.* Characteristics
     - (1) Shared characteristics with rest of market
     - (2) Characteristics unique to our customers
   - *c.* What they like about us or our product
   - *d.* What they don't like

3. Consumer appeals
   - *a.* Past advertising appeals
     - (1) What has worked
     - (2) What has not worked and why
   - *b.* Possible future appeals

4. Results of research studies about market and customers

E. The competition

Complete information about the competition, the competitive environment, and the opportunities or challenges presented by current or prospective competitors. See SEC Form 10-Ks, consumer/business press articles, Moody's Industrial Manual, Standard & Poor's reports, Dun & Bradstreet report, Thomas Register of American Corporations.

1. Identification of competitors
   - *a.* Primary competitors
   - *b.* Secondary competitors
   - *c.* Product/service descriptions
   - *d.* Growth and size of competitors
   - *e.* Share of market held by competitors

2. Strengths of competition
   - *a.* Product quality
   - *b.* Sales features
   - *c.* Price, distribution, promotion

3. Weaknesses of competition
   - *a.* Product features
   - *b.* Consumer attitude
   - *c.* Price, distribution, promotion

4. Marketing activities of competition
   - *a.* Product positioning
   - *b.* Pricing strategies
   - *c.* Distribution
   - *d.* Sales force
   - *e.* Advertising, publicity
   - *f.* Estimated budgets

Complete discussion of how the firm's products/ services are distributed and sold, what channels are available, and characteristics of channel members. See dealer and distributor correspondence, sales staff reports, advertising reports, trade publication articles.

F. Distribution strategies

1. Type of distribution network used

    a. History of development

    b. Trends

2. Evaluation of how distribution is accomplished

3. Relationships with channel members

4. Promotional relationship with channel members

    a. Trade advertising and allowances

    b. Co-op advertising

    c. Use of promotion by dealer or middlemen

    d. Point-of-purchase displays, literature

    e. Dealer incentive programs

5. Strengths/weaknesses of distribution systems

6. Opportunities/threats related to distribution

Background and rationale for firm's pricing policies and strategies, discussion of alternative options. Study sales reports, channel-member correspondence, customer correspondence, competitive information.

G. Pricing policies

1. Price history

    a. Trends

    b. Affordability

    c. Competition

2. Price objectives and strategies in past

    a. Management attitudes

    b. Buyer attitudes

    c. Channel attitudes

3. Opportunities/threats related to pricing

H. Communication strategies

1. Past promotion policy

    a. Personal versus nonpersonal selling

    (1) Use of sales force

    (2) Use of traditional advertising, public relations, sales promotion, sponsorship

    (3) Use of digital communications media, social media, e-mail, mobile

    b. Successes and failures of past policy

All relevant data concerning the firm's personal sales efforts and effectiveness as well as complete discussion of the firm's use of advertising, public relations, and sales promotion programs. Examine sales reports, advertising reports, articles in Advertising Age, Marketing Communications, and so on, in-house data on advertising, sales, and training.

2. Sales force

    a. Size

    b. Scope

    c. Ability/training

    d. Cost per sale

3. Traditional advertising programs

    a. Successes and failures

    b. Strategies, themes, campaigns, media employed

    c. Appeals, positionings, and so on

    d. Expenditures

    (1) Past budgets

    (2) Method of allocation

    (3) Competitor budgets

    (4) Trends

4. Digital advertising programs
   a. Successes and failures
   b. Strategies, themes, campaigns, digital media employed
   c. Appeals, positioning
   d. Expenditures
5. Opportunities/threats related to communications

I. Environmental factors

Enumeration of environmental factors that may be beyond the firm's immediate control but affect the firm's business efforts. See government reports and announcements, consumer/business press, trade association articles.

1. Economy
   a. Current economic status
   b. Business outlook and economic forecasts
2. Political situation
3. Societal concerns
4. Technological influences

J. Corporate objectives and strategies

Recitation of relevant attitudes and directives of management as they pertain to the firm's marketing and advertising efforts. Information available from corporate business plan, management interviews, internal memos and directives.

1. Profitability
   a. Sales revenue
   b. Cost reductions
2. Return on investment
3. Stock price
4. Shareholder equity
5. Community image
6. New product development
7. Technological leadership
8. Mergers and/or acquisitions
9. Overall corporate mission

K. Potential marketing problems

Enumeration or summary of problems considered most serious to the firm's marketing success.

L. Potential marketing opportunities

Summary of those opportunities that offer the greatest potential for the firm's success. What general and specific needs the firm seeks to satisfy. Determine through study of situation analysis factors and management discussions and interviews.

III. Marketing Objectives

A. Market need objectives
   1. Market need-satisfying objectives
   2. Community need-satisfying objectives
   3. Corporate need-satisfying objectives

B. Sales target objectives

Organization sales goals defined for whole company or for individual products by target market, by geographic territory, by department, or by some other category. Must be specific and realistic based on study of company capabilities, funding, and objectives.

   1. Sales volume
      a. Dollars
      b. Units
      c. Territories
      d. Markets
   2. Share of market
   3. Distribution expansion
   4. Other

IV. Marketing Strategy

The method(s) by which the organization plans to achieve the objectives enumerated above.

A. General marketing strategy

A general description of the type of marketing strategy the organization intends to employ.

   1. Positioning strategy
   2. Product differentiation strategy

3. Price/quality differentiation strategy
4. Mission marketing strategy

A detailed description of the marketing mix(es) the firm intends to use to achieve its objectives.

B. Specific market strategies
1. Target market A
   a. Product
   b. Price
   c. Distribution
   d. Communication
      (1) Personal selling
      (2) Advertising
      (3) Direct marketing
      (4) Sales promotion
      (5) Public relations
      (6) Digital and social media
2. Target market B
   a. Product
   b. Price
   c. Distribution
   d. Communication
      (1) Personal selling
      (2) Advertising
      (3) Direct marketing
      (4) Sales promotion
      (5) Public relations
      (6) Digital and social media

The detailed tactical plans for implementing each of the elements of the firm's marketing mix.

V. Action Programs (Tactics)
A. Product plans
B. Pricing plans
C. Distribution plans
D. Communication plans
   1. Sales plan
   2. Advertising plan
   3. Direct marketing plan
   4. Sales promotion plan
   5. Public relations plan
   6. Digital and social media plan
E. Mission marketing plan

Description of the methods the firm will use to review, evaluate, and control its progress toward the achievement of its marketing objectives.

VI. Measurement, Review, and Control
A. Organizational structure
B. Methodology for review and evaluation
C. Interactivity monitoring

Determination of the amount of money needed to conduct the marketing effort, the rationale for that budget, and the allocation to various functions.

VII. Marketing Budget
A. Method of allocation
B. Enumeration of marketing costs by division
   1. New product research
   2. Marketing research

3. Sales expenses
4. Advertising, direct marketing, sales promotion, public relations, digital and social media

Details of information, secondary data, or research conducted to develop information discussed in the marketing plan.

VIII. Appendixes
A.   Sales reports
B.   Reports of market research studies
C.   Reprints of journal or magazine articles
D.   Other supporting documents

appendix B

Advertising Plan Outline

Date:
Company (Brand/Service) Name:

Brief encapsulation, for executive review, of entire advertising plan in no more than two or three pages.

I. Executive Summary
   A. Premises—summary of information presented in marketing plan
   B. Summary of advertising objectives
   C. Summary of advertising strategy
   D. Budget summary

Condensed review of pertinent elements presented in the marketing plan.

II. Situation Analysis
   A. Company's (or product's) current marketing situation
      1. Business or industry information
      2. Description of company, product, or service
         a. Stage of product life cycle
         b. Goods classification
         c. Competitive or market positioning
      3. General description of market(s) served
      4. Sales history and share of market
      5. Description of consumer purchase process
      6. Methods of distribution
      7. Pricing strategies employed
      8. Implications of any marketing research
      9. Communications history
   B. Target market description
      1. Market segments identified
      2. Primary market
      3. Secondary markets
      4. Market characteristics
         a. Geographic
         b. Demographic
         c. Psychographic
         d. Behavioral
   C. Marketing objectives
      1. Need-satisfying objectives
      2. Long- and short-term sales target objectives
   D. Marketing mix for each target market—summarized from marketing plan
      1. Product
      2. Price
      3. Distribution
      4. Communication

E. Intended role of advertising in the communications mix

F. Miscellaneous information not included before

III. Advertising Objectives

Analysis and statement of what the advertising is expected to accomplish—see My IMC Campaign: Developing Advertising Objectives.

A. Primary or selective demand

B. Direct action or indirect action

C. Objectives stated in terms of:
1. Advertising pyramid
2. Direct response, including purchases
3. Other

D. Quantified expression of objectives
1. Specific quantities or percentages
2. Length of time for achievement of objectives
3. Other possible measurements
   a. Inquiries
   b. Increased order size
   c. Morale building
   d. Social media activity
   e. Other

Intended blend of the creative mix for the company as a whole, for each product, or for each target market.

IV. Advertising (Creative) Strategy

A. Product concept—how the advertising will present the product in terms of:
1. Product or market positioning
2. Product differentiation
3. Life cycle
4. Classification, packaging, branding
5. FCB grid purchase-decision position
   a. High/low think involvement
   b. High/low feel involvement

B. Target audience—the specific people the advertising will address
1. Detailed description of target audiences
   a. Relationship of target audience to target market
   b. Prospective buying influences
   c. Benefits sought/advertising appeals
   d. Demographics
   e. Psychographics
   f. Behavioristics
2. Prioritization of target audiences
   a. Primary
   b. Secondary
   c. Supplementary

The strategy for selecting the various media vehicles that will communicate the advertising message to the target audience—see Chapters 8, 12–14.

C. Communications media
1. Definition of media objectives
   a. Reach
   b. Frequency
   c. Gross rating points
   d. Continuity/flighting/pulsing
2. Determination of which media reach the target audience best
   a. Traditional mass media
      (1) Radio

           (2)   Television

           (3)   Newspapers

           (4)   Magazines

           (5)   Outdoor

      b. Interactive media

           (1)   Direct response

           (2)   Digital media, including search

           (3)   Social media

      c. Support media

           (1)   Trade shows

           (2)   Sales promotion devices

           (3)   Publicity/public relations

           (4)   Off-the-wall media

           (5)   Sponsorship

  3. Availability of media relative to purchase patterns

  4. Potential for communication effectiveness

  5. Cost considerations

      a. Size/mechanical considerations of message units

      b. Cost efficiency of media plan against target audiences

      c. Production costs

  6. Relevance to other elements of creative mix

  7. Scope of media plan

  8. Exposure/attention/motivation values of intended media vehicles

What the company wants to say and how it wants to say it, verbally and nonverbally—see Chapters 10–11.

D. Advertising message

  1. Copy elements

      a. Advertising appeals

      b. Copy platform

      c. Key consumer benefits

      d. Benefit supports or reinforcements

      e. Product personality or image

  2. Art elements

      a. Visual appeals

           (1)   In ads and commercials

           (2)   In packaging

           (3)   In point-of-purchase and sales materials

      b. Art platform

           (1)   Layout

           (2)   Design

           (3)   Illustration style

  3. Production elements

      a. Mechanical considerations in producing ads

           (1)   Color

           (2)   Size

           (3)   Style

      b. Production values sought

           (1)   Typography

           (2)   Printing

　　　　　　　　　　　　　　　　　　　　(3)　Color reproduction
　　　　　　　　　　　　　　　　　　　　(4)　Photography/illustrations
　　　　　　　　　　　　　　　　　　　　(5)　Paper
　　　　　　　　　　　　　　　　　　　　(6)　Electronic effects
　　　　　　　　　　　　　　　　　　　　(7)　Animation
　　　　　　　　　　　　　　　　　　　　(8)　Film or video
　　　　　　　　　　　　　　　　　　　　(9)　Sound effects
　　　　　　　　　　　　　　　　　　　(10)　Music

The amount of money to be allocated to advertising and the intended method of allocation—Chapters 7, 18.

V. The Advertising Budget
- A. Impact of marketing situation on method of allocation
  1. New or old product
  2. Primary demand curve for product class
  3. Competitive situation
  4. Marketing objectives and strategy
  5. Profit or growth considerations
  6. Relationship of advertising to sales and profits
  7. Empirical experience
- B. Method of allocation
  1. Percentage of sales or profit
  2. Share of market
  3. Objective/task method
  4. Unit of sale
  5. Competitive parity

The research techniques that will be used to create the advertising and evaluate its effectiveness—see Chapter 7.

VI. Testing and Evaluation
- A. Advertising research conducted
  1. Strategy determination
  2. Concept development
- B. Pretesting and posttesting
  1. Elements tested
     - *a.* Markets
     - *b.* Motives
     - *c.* Messages
     - *d.* Media
     - *e.* Budgeting
     - *f.* Scheduling
  2. Methodology
     - *a.* Central location tests
     - *b.* Sales experiments
     - *c.* Physiological testing
     - *d.* Aided recall tests
     - *e.* Unaided recall tests
     - *f.* Attitude tests
     - *g.* Inquiry tests
     - *h.* Sales tests
     - *i.* Other
  3. Cost of testing

important terms

AAAA   See *American Association of Advertising Agencies*.

AAF   See *American Advertising Federation*.

ABC   See *Audit Bureau of Circulations*.

account executive (AE)   The liaison between the agency and the client. The account executive is responsible for both managing all the agency's services for the benefit of the client and representing the agency's point of view to the client.

account planning   A hybrid discipline that bridges the gap between traditional research, account management, and creative direction. Planners represent the view of the consumer in order to better define and plan the client's advertising program.

action advertising   Advertising intended to bring about immediate action on the part of the reader or viewer; see also *direct-response advertising*.

action programs   See *tactics*.

actual consumers   The people in the real world who comprise an ad's target audience. They are the people to whom the sponsor's message is ultimately directed.

ad networks   The Internet equivalent of a media rep firm, *ad networks* act as brokers for advertisers and Websites. Ad networks pool hundreds or even thousands of Web pages together and facilitate advertising across these pages, thereby allowing advertisers to gain maximum exposure by covering even the small sites.

advertising   The structured and composed nonpersonal communication of information, usually paid for and usually persuasive in nature, about products (goods and services) or ideas by identified sponsors through various media.

advertising agency   An independent organization of creative people and businesspeople who specialize in developing and preparing advertising plans, advertisements, and other promotional tools for advertisers. The agency also arranges for or contracts for purchase of space and time in various media.

advertising allowance   A fee paid to the retailer for advertising the manufacturer's product.

advertising impression   A possible exposure of the advertising message to one audience member; see also *opportunity to see (OTS)*.

advertising research   The systematic gathering and analysis of information specifically to facilitate the development or evaluation of advertising strategies, ads and commercials, and media campaigns.

advertising response curve   Studies of this indicate that incremental response to advertising actually diminishes—rather than builds—with repeated exposure.

advertising specialty   A promotional product, usually imprinted with an advertiser's name, message, or logo, that is distributed free to the target audience.

advertorial   An ad aimed at swaying public opinion rather than selling products.

advocacy advertising   Advertising used to communicate an organization's views on issues that affect society or business.

affidavit of performance   A signed and notarized form sent by a television station to an advertiser or agency indicating what spots ran and when. It is the station's legal proof that the advertiser got what was paid for.

affiliate marketing program   An advertising program, often used in e-commerce, in which a seller pays a manufacturer, marketer, or other business a percentage of the sale price of an item sold. This payment is compensation for services or cooperation in making the sale. Ordinary consumers are often affiliates for online retailers like Amazon. By posting links to products at their blogs or Websites, consumers can earn a percentage of Amazon's sale.

affirmative disclosure   Advertisers must make known their product's limitations or deficiencies.

ambush marketing   A promotional strategy used by nonsponsors to capitalize on the popularity or prestige of an event or property by giving the false impression that they are sponsors, such as by buying up all the billboard space around an athletic stadium. Often employed by the competitors of the property's official sponsor.

American Advertising Federation (AAF)   A nationwide association of advertising people. The AAF helped establish the Federal Trade Commission, and its early "vigilance" committees were the forerunners of the Better Business Bureaus.

American Association of Advertising Agencies (AAAA)   The national organization of the advertising business. It has members throughout the United States and controls agency practices by denying membership to any agency judged unethical.

ANA   See *Association of National Advertisers*.

animatic   A rough television commercial produced by photographing storyboard sketches on a film strip or video with the audio portion synchronized on tape. It is used primarily for testing purposes.

animation   The use of cartoons, digital actions, or demonstrations of inanimate characters come to life in television commercials; often used for communicating difficult messages or for reaching specialized markets, such as children.

answer print   The final print of a filmed commercial, along with all the required optical effects and titles, used for review and approval before duplicating.

aperture   The opening in a camera that determines the amount of light that reaches the film or videotape. To a media planner it refers to the place and time that a target audience is ready to attend to an ad message.

API   Refers to Application Programming Interface, which is a specification intended to be used as an interface to communicate between two disparate software components.

art The whole visual presentation of a commercial or advertisement—the body language of an ad. Art also refers to the style of photography or illustration employed, the way color is used, and the arrangement of elements in an ad so that they relate to one another in size and proportion.

art direction The act or process of managing the visual presentation of an ad or commercial.

art director Along with graphic designers and production artists, determines how the ad's verbal and visual symbols will fit together.

artist role A role in the creative process that experiments and plays with a variety of approaches, looking for an original idea.

art studio Company that designs and produces artwork and illustrations for advertisements, brochures, and other communication devices.

Association of National Advertisers (ANA) An organization composed of 400 major manufacturing and service companies that are clients of member agencies of the AAAA. These companies, which are pledged to uphold the ANA code of advertising ethics, work with the ANA through a joint Committee for Improvement of Advertising Content.

attention value A consideration in selecting media based on the degree of attention paid to ads in particular media by those exposed to them. Attention value relates to the advertising message and copy just as much as to the medium.

attitude An evaluative response—positive or negative—regarding some idea or object.

attitude test A type of posttest that usually seeks to measure the effectiveness of an advertising campaign in creating a favorable attitude or evaluation for a company, its brand, or its products.

audience The group of people exposed to a particular medium.

audience composition The distribution of an audience into demographic or other categories.

audience objectives Definitions of the specific types of people the advertiser wants to reach.

audio The sound portion of a commercial. Also, the right side of a script for a television commercial, indicating spoken copy, sound effects, and music.

audio console In a sound studio control room, the board that channels sound to the appropriate recording devices and that blends both live and prerecorded sounds for immediate or delayed broadcast.

audiovisual materials Slides, films, CDs, and DVDs that may be used for training, sales, or public relations activities.

Audit Bureau of Circulations (ABC) An organization supported by advertising agencies, advertisers, and publishers that verifies circulation and other marketing data on newspapers and magazines for the benefit of its members.

author In Stern's communication model, a copywriter, an art director, or a creative group at the agency that is commissioned by the sponsor to create advertising messages.

autobiographical messages A style of advertising that utilizes the first person "I" to tell a story to the audience, "You."

avails An abbreviated term referring to the TV time slots that are *available* to an advertiser.

average quarter-hour audience (AQH persons) A radio term referring to the average number of people who are listening to a specific station for at least 5 minutes during a 15-minute period of any given daypart.

average quarter-hour rating The average quarter-hour persons estimate expressed as a percentage of the estimated population.

average quarter-hour share The radio station's audience (AQH persons) expressed as a percentage of the total radio listening audience in the area.

awareness advertising Advertising that attempts to build the image of a product or familiarity with the name and package.

Ayer No. 1 See *poster-style format*.

banner Part of a Website reserved for an advertising message. Clicking a banner normally redirects an Internet user to the advertiser's Website.

barter syndication Marketing of first-run television programs to local stations free or for a reduced rate because some of the ad space has been presold to national advertisers.

basic bus In transit advertising, all the inside space on a group of buses, which thereby gives the advertiser complete domination.

behavioral targeting The ability for an advertiser to send an ad to someone based on their online activity.

behavioristic segmentation Method of determining market segments by grouping consumers based on their purchase behavior.

benefit headline Type of headline that makes a direct promise to the reader.

benefits The gratifications or relief from problems offered by a particular brand, product, or service.

benefit segmentation Method of segmenting consumers based on the benefits being sought.

Better Business Bureau (BBB) A business-monitoring organization funded by dues from more than 100,000 member companies. It operates primarily at the local level to protect consumers against fraudulent and deceptive advertising.

big idea The flash of creative insight—the bold advertising initiative—that captures the essence of the strategy in an imaginative, involving way and brings the subject to life to make the reader stop, look, and listen.

billboards The basic outdoor advertising structure; it consists of blank panels with a standardized size and border.

bleeds Colors, type, or visuals that run all the way to the edge of the page.

blinking A scheduling technique in which the advertiser floods the airwaves for one day on both cable and network channels to make it virtually impossible to miss the ads.

blog A personal journal published on the Internet consisting of posts displayed in reverse chronological order.

blogs (weblogs) Online sites where companies and individuals place regular posts and readers place comments.

blueline A proof created by shining light through the negatives and exposing a light-sensitive paper that turns from white to blue; it helps reveal scratches and flaws in negatives.

board See *audio console*.

body copy The text of an advertisement. It is a logical continuation of the headline and subheads and is usually set in a smaller type size than headlines or subheads.

boldface Heavier type.

boosted post Facebook social advertising tool for making a post more prominent in users News Feeds.

booths Trade show display areas. To stop traffic, they must be simple and attractive and have good lighting and a large visual.

bottom-up marketing The opposite of standard, top-down marketing planning, bottom-up marketing focuses on one specific tactic and develops it into an overall strategy.

brainstorming A process in which two or more people get together to generate new ideas; often a source of sudden inspiration.

brand That combination of name, words, symbols, or design that identifies the product and its source and distinguishes it from competing products—the fundamental differentiating device for all products.

brand development index (BDI) The percentage of a brand's total sales in an area divided by the total population in the area; it indicates the sales potential of a particular brand in a specific market area.

brand equity The totality of what consumers, distributors, dealers, and competitors feel and think about a brand over an extended period of time; in short, it is the value of the brand's capital.

branding A marketing function that identifies products and their source and differentiates them from all other products.

brand interest An individual's openness or curiosity about a brand.

brand loyalty The consumer's conscious or unconscious decision—expressed through intention or behavior—to repurchase a brand continually. This occurs because the consumer perceives that the brand has the right product features, image, quality, or relationship at the right price.

brand manager The individual within the advertiser's company who is assigned the authority and responsibility for the successful marketing of a particular brand.

brand trains An advertising program in which all the advertising in and on a train is from a single advertiser. This advertising concept was first used in subway trains in New York City and is being used on the Las Vegas monorail.

broadband A type of digital data transmission that enables a single wire to carry multiple signals simultaneously.

broadcast TV Television sent over airwaves as opposed to over cables.

broadside A form of direct-mail advertisement, larger than a folder and sometimes used as a window display or wall poster in stores. It can be folded to a compact size and fitted into a mailer.

brochures Sales materials printed on heavier paper and featuring color photographs, illustrations, typography. See also *folders*.

bulk discounts Newspapers offer advertisers decreasing rates (calculated by multiplying the number of inches by the cost per inch) as they use more inches.

bulletin structure Typically the largest outdoor advertising formats, also known as billboards.

bursting A media scheduling method for promoting high-ticket items that require careful consideration, such as running the same commercial every half-hour on the same network in prime time.

business advertising Advertising directed at people who buy or specify goods and services for business use. Also called *business-to-business advertising*.

business magazines The largest category of magazines, they target business readers and include: *trade publications* for retailers, wholesalers, and other distributors; *industrial magazines* for businesspeople involved in manufacturing and services; and *professional journals* for lawyers, physicians, architects, and other professionals.

business markets Organizations that buy natural resources, component products, and services that they resell, use to conduct their business, or use to manufacture another product.

business reply mail A type of mail that enables the recipient of direct-mail advertising to respond without paying postage.

business-to-business (B2B) advertising See *business advertising*.

business-to-business agency Represents clients that market products to other businesses; also called *high-tech* agency.

bus-o-rama sign In transit advertising, a jumbo roof sign, which is actually a full-color transparency backlighted by fluorescent tubes, running the length of the bus.

button In Internet advertising, buttons are small versions of a banner and sometimes look like an icon, and they usually provide a link to an advertiser's home page. Because buttons take up less space than banners, they also cost less.

buyback allowance A manufacturer's offer to pay for an old product so that it will be taken off the shelf to make room for a new product.

cable TV Television signals carried to households by cable and paid by subscription.

camera-ready art A finished ad that is ready for the printer's camera to shoot—to make negatives or plates—according to the publication's specifications.

car-end posters Transit advertisements of varying sizes, positioned in the bulkhead.

CARU See *Children's Advertising Review Unit*.

casting brief A detailed, written description of the characters' personalities to serve as guides in casting sessions when actors audition for the roles.

catalogs Reference books mailed to prospective customers that list, describe, and often picture the products sold by a manufacturer, wholesaler, jobber, or retailer.

category development index (CDI) The percentage of a product category's total U.S. sales in an area divided by the percentage of total U.S. population in the area.

cease-and-desist order   May be issued by the FTC if an advertiser won't sign a consent decree; prohibits further use of an ad.

centers of influence   Customers, prospective customers, or opinion leaders whose opinions and actions are respected by others.

centralized advertising department   A staff of employees, usually located at corporate headquarters, responsible for all the organization's advertising. The department is often structured by product, advertising subfunction, end user, media, or geography.

centralized network   A network of connections that form from a single point, considered the center of the system.

central location test   A type of pretest in which videotapes of test commercials are shown to respondents on a one-to-one basis, usually in shopping center locations.

central route to persuasion   One of two ways researchers Petty, Cacioppo, and Schumann theorize that marketers can persuade consumers. When consumers have a high level of involvement with the product or the message, they are motivated to pay attention to the central, product-related information in an ad, such as product attributes and benefits, or demonstrations of positive functional or psychological consequences; see also *Elaboration Likelihood Model*.

cents-off promotion   A short-term reduction in the price of a product designed to induce trial and usage. Cents-off promotions take various forms, including basic cents-off packages, one-cent sales, free offers, and box-top refunds.

channel   Any medium through which an encoded message is sent to a receiver, including oral communication, print media, television, and the Internet.

channels of distribution   See *distribution channels*.

Children's Advertising Review Unit (CARU)   This entity, created by the Council of Better Business Bureaus, provides a general advisory service for advertisers, agencies, children, parents, and educators.

cinema advertising   Advertising in movie theaters.

cinematographer   A motion picture photographer.

circulation   A statistical measure of a print medium's audience; includes subscription and vendor sales and primary and secondary readership.

circulation audit   Thorough analysis of circulation procedures, distribution outlets, and other distribution factors by a company such as the Audit Bureau of Circulations (ABC).

classified ads   Newspaper, magazine, and now Internet advertisements usually arranged under subheads that describe the class of goods or the need the ads seek to satisfy. Rates are based on the number of lines the ad occupies. Most employment, housing, and automotive advertising is in the form of classified advertising.

classified ad Websites   Websites, such as Craigslist, that specialize in providing classified advertisements, often provided for free. Many classified ad Websites are supported by ad banners of other advertisers.

classified display ads   Ads that run in the classified section of the newspaper but have larger-size type, photos, art borders, abundant white space, and sometimes color.

clearance advertising   A type of local advertising designed to make room for new product lines or new models or to get rid of slow-moving product lines, floor samples, broken or distressed merchandise, or items that are no longer in season.

click-through   A term used in reference to when a World Wide Web user clicks on an ad banner to visit the advertiser's site. Some Web publishers charge advertisers according to the number of click-throughs on a given ad banner.

click-through rate (CTR)   The percentage of site visitors who click a display or search ad.

click to Website   Social advertising program designed to attract Facebook users to a Website.

close   That part of an advertisement or commercial that asks customers to do something and tells them how to do it—the action step in the ad's copy.

closing date   A publication's final deadline for supplying printing material for an advertisement.

clutter tests   Method of pretesting in which commercials are grouped with noncompetitive control commercials and shown to prospective customers to measure their effectiveness in gaining attention, increasing brand awareness and comprehension, and causing attitude shifts.

cognition   The mental processes involved in perception, thinking, recognition, memory, and decision making.

cognitive dissonance   See *theory of cognitive dissonance*.

collateral material   All the accessory nonmedia advertising materials prepared by manufacturers to help dealers sell a product—booklets, catalogs, brochures, films, trade show exhibits, sales kits, and so on.

color key   A color proof that is a less-expensive form of the Chromalin, with thicker plastic sheets that can be lifted up.

color separations   Four separate continuous-tone negatives produced by photographing artwork through color filters that eliminate all the colors but one. The negatives are used to make four printing plates—one each for yellow, magenta, cyan, and black—for reproducing the color artwork.

color strip   Samples of eye shadow, blush, lipstick, and other makeup inserted into magazines.

column inch   The basic unit by which publishers bill for advertising. It is one vertical inch of a column. Until 1984, the column width in newspapers varied greatly. In 1984, the industry introduced the standard advertising unit (SAU) system, which standardized newspaper column width, page sizes, and ad sizes. Today, most newspapers—and virtually all dailies—have converted to the SAU system. A SAU column inch is 21/16 inches wide by 1 inch deep.

combination offers   A sales promotion device in which two related products are packaged together at a special price, such as a razor and a package of blades. Sometimes a combination offer may be used to introduce a new product by tying its purchase to an established product at a special price.

combination rates   Special newspaper advertising rates offered for placing a given ad in (1) morning and evening editions of the same newspaper; (2) two or more newspapers owned by the same publisher; or (3) two or more newspapers affiliated in a syndicate or newspaper group.

command headline   A type of headline that orders the reader to do something.

communication element   Includes all marketing-related communications between the seller and the buyer.

communications media   An element of the creative mix, comprising the various methods or vehicles that will be used to transmit the advertiser's message.

communications mix   A variety of marketing communications tools, grouped into personal and nonpersonal selling activities.

community involvement   A local public relations activity in which companies sponsor or participate in a local activity or supply a location for an event.

company conventions and dealer meetings   Events held by manufacturers to introduce new products, sales promotion programs, or advertising campaigns.

comparative advertising   Advertising that claims superiority to competitors in one or more aspects.

compiled list   A type of direct-mail list that has been compiled by another source, such as lists of automobile owners, new home purchasers, business owners, union members, and so forth. It is the most readily available type of list but offers the lowest response expectation.

composition   The amount of a target audience that exists on a Website or a TV program.

comprehensive layout   A facsimile of a finished ad with copy set in type and pasted into position along with proposed illustrations. The "comp" is prepared so the advertiser can gauge the effect of the final ad.

conceptualization   See *visualization.*

consent decree   A document advertisers sign, without admitting any wrongdoing, in which they agree to stop objectionable advertising.

consumer advertising   Advertising directed at the ultimate consumer of the product, or at the person who will buy the product for someone else's personal use.

consumer advocates   Individuals and groups who actively work to protect consumer rights, often by investigating advertising complaints received from the public and those that grow out of their own research.

consumer behavior   The activities, actions, and influences of people who purchase and use goods and services to satisfy their personal or household needs and wants.

consumer decision process   The series of steps a consumer goes through in deciding to make a purchase.

consumer information networks   Organizations that help develop state, regional, and local consumer organizations and work with national, regional, county, and municipal consumer groups. Examples include the Consumer Federation of America (CFA), the National Council of Senior Citizens, and the National Consumer League.

consumerism   Social action designed to dramatize the rights of the buying public.

consumer magazines   Information- or entertainment-oriented periodicals directed toward people who buy products for their own consumption.

consumer package goods (CPGs)   A product consumed daily by the average person. Consumers must continuously replace CPGs (such as soft drinks or paper towels), in contrast to durable goods, which can be used for long periods of time (such as dishwashers). CPG brands often advertise heavily to ensure brand loyalty.

consumer sales promotions   Marketing, advertising, and sales promotion activities aimed at inducing trial, purchase, and repurchase by the consumer. Also called *pull strategy.*

consumers, consumer market   People who buy products and services for their own, or someone else's, personal use.

contest   A sales promotion device for creating consumer involvement in which prizes are offered based on the skill of the entrants.

continuity   The duration of an advertising message or campaign over a given period of time.

continuous schedule   A method of scheduling media in which advertising runs steadily with little variation.

continuous tone   Normal photographic paper produces images in black and white with shades of gray in between.

contract rate   A special rate for newspaper advertising usually offered to local advertisers who sign an annual contract for frequent or bulk-space purchases.

controlled circulation   A free publication mailed to a select list of individuals the publisher feels are in a unique position to influence the purchase of advertised products.

control room   In a recording studio, the place where the producer, director, and sound engineer sit, monitoring and controlling all the sounds generated in the sound studio.

cookies   Small pieces of information that get stored in a Web user's hard drive when visiting certain Websites. Cookies track whether the user has ever visited a specific site and allow the site to give users different information according to whether or not they are repeat visitors.

cooperative (co-op) advertising   The sharing of advertising costs by the manufacturer and the distributor or retailer. The manufacturer may repay 50 or 100 percent of the dealer's advertising costs or some other amount based on sales. See also *horizontal cooperative advertising, vertical cooperative advertising.*

copy   The words that make up the headline and message of an advertisement or commercial.

copy cast   To forecast the total block of space the type in an ad will occupy in relation to the typeface's letter size and proportions.

copy points   Copywriting themes in a product's advertising.

copyright   An exclusive right granted by the Copyright Act to authors and artists to protect their original work from being plagiarized, sold, or used by another without their express consent.

copywriters   People who create the words and concepts for ads and commercials.

corporate advertising   The broad area of nonproduct advertising aimed specifically at enhancing a company's image and increasing lagging awareness.

corporate blog   A Web-based source of information about a company, its policies, products, or activities. Corporate blogs are one way companies can facilitate relationships with their consumers or other publics.

corporate identity advertising Advertising a corporation creates to familiarize the public with its name, logos, trademarks, or corporate signatures, especially after any of these elements are changed.

corrective advertising May be required by the FTC for a period of time to explain and correct offending ads.

cost efficiency The cost of reaching the target audience through a particular medium as opposed to the cost of reaching the medium's total circulation.

cost per point (CPP) A simple computation used by media buyers to determine which broadcast programs are the most efficient in relation to the target audience. The CPP is determined by dividing the cost of the show by the show's expected rating against the target audience.

cost per thousand (CPM) A common term describing the cost of reaching 1,000 people in a medium's audience. It is used by media planners to compare the cost of various media vehicles.

coupon A certificate with a stated value that is presented to a retail store for a price reduction on a specified item.

cover date The date printed on the cover of a publication.

cover paper Paper used on soft book covers, direct-mail pieces, and brochure covers that is thicker, tougher, and more durable than text paper.

cover position Advertising space on the front inside, back inside, and back cover pages of a publication which is usually sold at a premium price.

CPM See *cost per thousand.*

CPP See *cost per point.*

creative boutique An organization of creative specialists (such as art directors, designers, and copywriters) who work for advertisers and occasionally advertising agencies to develop creative concepts, advertising messages, and specialized art. A boutique performs only the creative work.

creative brief A written statement that serves as the creative team's guide for writing and producing an ad. It describes the most important issues that should be considered in the development of the ad (the who, why, what, where, and when), including a definition and description of the target audience; the rational and emotional appeals to be used; the product features that will satisfy the customer's needs; the style, approach, or tone that will be used in the copy; and, generally, what the copy will say.

creative director Heads a creative team of agency copywriters and artists that is assigned to a client's business; is ultimately responsible for the creative product—the form the final ad takes.

creative mix Those advertising elements the company controls to achieve its advertising objectives, including the target audience, the product concept, the communications media, and the advertising message. See also *advertising strategy.*

creative process The step-by-step procedure used to discover original ideas and reorganize existing concepts in new ways.

creative pyramid A five-step model to help the creative team convert advertising strategy and the big idea into the actual physical ad or commercial. The five elements are: attention, interest, credibility, desire, and action.

creatives The people who work in the creative department, regardless of their specialty.

creativity Involves combining two or more previously unconnected objects or ideas into something new.

crisis management A company's plan for handling news and public relations during crises.

culture A homogeneous group's whole set of beliefs, attitudes, and ways of doing things, typically handed down from generation to generation.

cume persons The total number of different people listening to a radio station for at least one 15-minute segment over the course of a given week, day, or daypart.

cume rating The estimated number of cume persons expressed as a percentage of the total market population.

current customers People who have already bought something from a business and who may buy it regularly.

customer lifetime value (LTV) The total sales or profit value of a customer to a marketer over the course of that customer's lifetime.

customer retention and relationship management (CRM) A promotional program that focuses on existing clients rather than prospecting for new clients. Due to negative reaction to spam (unsolicited e-mail), e-mail programs are often focused on CRM rather than prospecting.

custom magazines Magazine-length ads that look like regular magazines but are created by advertisers. They are sold at newsstands and produced by the same companies that publish traditional magazines.

CYMK printing See *four-color process.*

DAGMAR The acronym stands for defining advertising goals for measured advertising results. DAGMAR is a planning tool for setting communications abjectives for a compaign.

daily newspapers Often called *dailies*, these newspapers are published at least five times a week, in either morning or evening editions.

data access Characteristic of a database that enables marketers to manipulate, analyze, and rank all the information they possess in order to make better marketing decisions.

database The corporate memory of all important customer information: name and address, telephone number, NAIC code (if a business firm), source of inquiry, cost of inquiry, history of purchases, and so on. It should record every transaction across all points of contact with both channel members and customers.

database marketing Tracking and analyzing the purchasing patterns of specific customers in a computer database and then targeting advertising to their needs.

data management The process of gathering, consolidating, updating, and enhancing the information about customers and prospects that resides in a company's database.

daypart mix A media scheduling strategy based on the TV usage levels reported by the rating services.

decentralized system The establishment of advertising departments by products or brands or in various divisions, subsidiaries, countries, regions, or other categories that suit the firm's needs, which operate with a major degree of independence.

deceptive advertising   According to the FTC, any ad in which there is a misrepresentation, omission, or other practice that can mislead a significant number of reasonable consumers to their detriment.

decline stage   The stage in the product life cycle when sales begin to decline due to obsolescence, new technology, or changing consumer tastes.

decoding   The interpretation of a message by the receiver.

deck   The online experience provided to its customers by a mobile carrier, typically curated by the wireless carrier.

demarketing   Term coined during the energy shortage of the 1970s and 1980s. It refers to advertising that is used to slow the demand for products.

demographic editions   Magazines that reach readers who share a demographic trait, such as age, income level, or professional status.

demographics   The statistical characteristics of the population.

demographic segmentation   Based on a population's statistical characteristics such as sex, age, ethnicity, education, occupation, income, or other quantifiable factors.

demonstration   A type of TV commercial in which the product is shown in use.

departmental system   The organization of an ad agency into departments based on function: account services, creative services, marketing services, and administration.

design   Visual pattern or composition of artistic elements chosen and structured by the graphic artist.

designated market areas (DMAs)   The geographic areas in which TV stations attract most of their viewers.

development stage   In the agency–client relationship, the honeymoon period when both agency and client are at the peak of their optimism and are most eager to quickly develop a mutually profitable mechanism for working together.

device copy   Advertising copy that relies on wordplay, humor, poetry, rhymes, great exaggeration, gags, and other tricks or gimmicks.

dialogue/monologue copy   A type of body copy in which the characters illustrated in the advertisement do the selling in their own words either through a quasi-testimonial technique or through a comic strip panel.

digital interactive media   Electronic channels of communication—including online databases, the Internet, CD-ROMs, and stand-alone kiosks—with which the audience can participate actively and immediately.

digital video effects (DVE) units   In video, special-effects equipment for manipulating graphics on the screen to produce fades, wipes, zooms, rotations, and so on.

direct distribution   The method of marketing in which the manufacturer sells directly to customers without the use of retailers.

direct-mail advertising   All forms of advertising sent directly to prospective customers without using one of the commercial media forms.

direct marketing   An interactive process of addressable communication that uses one or more media to effect, at any location,

a measurable sale, lead, retail purchase, or charitable donation, with this activity analyzed on a database for the development of ongoing mutually beneficial relationships between marketers and customers, prospects or donors.

director   The director supervises preproduction, production, and postproduction of radio and television commercials.

directories   Listings, often in booklet form, that serve as locators, buying guides, and mailing lists.

direct questioning   A method of pretesting designed to elicit a full range of responses to the advertising. It is especially effective for testing alternative advertisements in the early stages of development.

direct-response advertising   An advertising message that asks the reader, listener, or viewer to respond to the sender. Direct-response advertising can take the form of direct mail, or it can use a wide range of other media, from matchbook covers or magazines to radio, TV, or billboards.

direct-sales strategy   Strategy where representatives sell to customers directly at home or work rather than through a retail establishment or other intermediary.

direct selling   Face-to-face selling away from a fixed retail location. Usually refers to a method of marketing consumer goods—everything from encyclopedias and insurance to cosmetics and nutritional products.

display advertising   Type of newspaper advertising that includes copy, illustrations or photographs, headlines, coupons, and other visual components.

display allowances   Fees paid to retailers to make room for and set up manufacturers' displays.

display type   A style of typeface used in advertising that is larger and heavier than normal text type. Display type is often used in headlines, subheads, logos, and addresses, and for emphasis.

distributed network   A system of connections that does not contain a main hub or central point.

distribution channel   The network of all the firms and individuals that take title, or assist in taking title, to the product as it moves from the producer to the consumer.

distribution element   How and where customers will buy a company's product; either direct or indirect distribution.

distribution objectives   Where, when, and how advertising should appear.

diverting   Purchasing large quantities of an item at a regional promotional discount and shipping portions to areas of the country where the discount isn't being offered.

DMAs   See *designated market areas.*

donut   When writing a jingle, a hole left for spoken copy.

drama message   One of the three literary forms of advertising messages in which the characters act out events directly in front of an imagined empathetic audience.

drive times   Radio use Monday through Friday at 6–10 a.m. and 3–7 p.m.

dubs   Duplicates of radio commercials made from the master tape and sent to stations for broadcast.

dupes   Copies of a finished television commercial that are delivered to the networks or TV stations for airing.

earned rate   A discount applied retroactively as the volume of advertising increases through the year.

effective frequency   The average number of times a person must see or hear a message before it becomes effective.

effective reach   Term used to describe the quality of exposure. It measures the number or percentage of the audience who receive enough exposures for the message to truly be received.

Elaboration Likelihood Model   A theory of persuasion. Psychologists Petty, Cacioppo, and Schumann theorize that the route of persuasion depends on the consumer's level of involvement with the product and the message. When consumers have high involvement with the product or the message, they will attend to product-related information, such as product attributes and benefits or demonstrations, at deeper, more elaborate levels. This can lead to product beliefs, positive brand attitudes, and purchase intention. On the other hand, people who have low involvement with the product or the message have little or no reason to pay attention to it or to comprehend the central message of the ad. As a result, direct persuasion is also low, and consumers form few if any brand beliefs, attitudes, or purchase intentions. However, these consumers might attend to some peripheral aspects of the ad or commercial—say, the pictures in the ad or the actors in a commercial—for their entertainment value. And whatever they feel or think about these peripheral, nonproduct aspects might integrate into a positive attitude toward the ad. See also *central route to persuasion* and *peripheral route to persuasion*.

electronic couponing   In supermarkets, the use of frequent-shopper cards that automatically credit cardholders with coupon discounts when they check out. Also using touch-screen videos at the point of purchase, instant-print discounts, rebates, and offers to try new brands.

electronic media   Radio and television, which may be transmitted electronically through wires or broadcast through the air.

electronic production   The process of converting a script or storyboard into a finished commercial for use on radio, TV, or digital media.

electronic signs   Large displays that provide text and graphic messages, similar to those found in sports stadiums.

e-mail advertising   Has become one of the fastest growing and most effective ways to provide direct mail.

emotional appeals   Marketing appeals that are directed at the consumer's psychological, social, or symbolic needs.

empirical research method   A method of allocating funds for advertising that uses experimentation to determine the best level of advertising expenditure. By running a series of tests in different markets with different budgets, companies determine the most efficient level of expenditure.

encoding   Translating an idea or message into words, symbols, and illustrations.

endorsement   See *testimonials*.

entertainment   The second largest area of sponsorship, which includes things like concert tours, attractions, and theme parks.

environments   Surroundings that can affect the purchase decision.

equipment-based service   A service business that relies mainly on the use of specialized equipment.

ethical advertising   Doing what the advertiser and the advertiser's peers believe is morally right in a given situation.

evaluation of alternatives   Choosing among brands, sizes, styles, and colors.

evaluative criteria   The standards a consumer uses for judging the features and benefits of alternative products.

evoked set   The particular group of alternative goods or services a consumer considers when making a buying decision.

exchange   The trading of one thing of value for another thing of value.

exclusive distribution   The strategy of limiting the number of wholesalers or retailers who can sell a product in order to gain a prestige image, maintain premium prices, or protect other dealers in a geographic region.

exhibitive media   Media designed specifically to help bring customers eyeball-to-eyeball with the product. These media include product packaging and trade show booths and exhibits.

exhibits   A marketing or public relations approach that involves preparing displays that tell about an organization or its products; exhibits may be used at fairs, colleges and universities, or trade shows.

experimental method   A method of scientific investigation in which a researcher alters the stimulus received by a test group or groups and compares the results with those of a control group that did not receive the altered stimulus.

exploratory research   See *informal research*.

Explorer role   A role in the creative process that searches for new information, paying attention to unusual patterns.

exposure value   The value of a medium determined by how well it exposes an ad to the target audience. In other words, how many people an ad "sees" rather than the other way around.

fact-based thinking   A style of thinking that tends to fragment concepts into components and to analyze situations to discover the one best solution.

family brand   The marketing of various products under the same umbrella name.

farm advertising   Advertising directed to farmers as businesspeople and to others in the agricultural business. Also called *agricultural advertising*.

farm publications   Magazines directed to farmers and their families or to companies that manufacture or sell agricultural equipment, supplies, and services.

FCC   See *Federal Communications Commission*.

FDA   See *Food and Drug Administration*.

feature article   Soft news about companies, products, or services that may be written by a PR person, the publication's staff, or a third party.

Federal Communications Commission (FCC)   Federal regulatory body with jurisdiction over radio, television, telephone, and telegraph industries. Through its licensing authority, the FCC has indirect control over broadcast advertising.

Federal Trade Commission (FTC)   The major federal regulator of advertising used to promote products sold in interstate commerce.

fee–commission combination A pricing system in which an advertising agency charges the client a basic monthly fee for its services and also retains any media commissions earned.

feedback A message that acknowledges or responds to an initial message.

first-run syndication Programs produced specifically for the syndication market.

five Ms (5Ms) The elements of the media mix that include markets, money, media, mechanics, and methodology.

flat rate A standard newspaper advertising rate with no discount allowance for large or repeated space buys.

flats Opaque plastic sheets that film negatives are mounted on in perfect registration; light passes through only where lines and dots are to appear on the printing plate.

flighting An intermittent media scheduling pattern in which periods of advertising are alternated with periods of no advertising at all.

focus group A qualitative method of research in which four or more people, typical of the target market, are invited to a group session to discuss the product, the service, or the marketing situation for an hour or more.

folders Large, heavy-stock fliers, often folded and sent out as self-mailers.

font A uniquely designed set of capital, small capital, and lower-case letters, usually including numerals and punctuation marks.

Food and Drug Administration (FDA) Federal agency that has authority over the labeling, packaging, and branding of packaged foods and therapeutic devices.

foreign media The local media of each country used by advertisers for campaigns targeted to consumers or businesses within a single country.

Forum Sections of Websites that connect individuals around a specific topic.

forward buying A retailer's stocking up on a product when it is discounted and buying smaller amounts when it is at list price.

four-color process The method for printing color advertisements with tonal values, such as photographs and paintings. This process is based on the principle that all colors can be printed by combining the three primary colors—yellow, magenta (red), and cyan (blue)—plus black (which provides greater detail and density as well as shades of gray).

four Ps (4Ps) See *marketing mix*.

forum An online discussion board.

fragrance strips Perfume samples included in sealed inserts in magazines.

franchising A type of vertical marketing system in which dealers pay a fee to operate under the guidelines and direction of the parent company or manufacturer.

freestanding inserts (FSIs) Coupons distributed through inserts in newspapers.

frequency The number of times the same person or household is exposed to a vehicle in a specified time span. Across a total audience, frequency is calculated as the average number of times individuals or homes are exposed to the vehicle.

frequency discounts In newspapers, advertisers earn this discount by running an ad repeatedly in a specific time period.

FTC See *Federal Trade Commission*.

full position In newspaper advertising, the preferred-position near the top of a page or on the top of a column next to reading matter. It is usually surrounded by editorial text and may cost the advertiser 25 to 50 percent more than ROP rates.

full-service advertising agency An agency equipped to serve its clients in all areas of communication and promotion. Its advertising services include planning, creating, and producing advertisements as well as performing research and media selection services. Nonadvertising functions include producing sales promotion materials, publicity articles, annual reports, trade show exhibits, and sales training materials.

full showing A unit of purchase in transit advertising where one card will appear in each vehicle in the system.

game A sales promotion activity in which prizes are offered based on chance. The big marketing advantage of games is that customers must make repeat visits to the dealer to continue playing.

gatefold A magazine cover or page extended and folded over to fit into the magazine. The gatefold may be a fraction of a page or two or more pages, and it is always sold at a premium.

general consumer agency An agency that represents the widest variety of accounts, but it concentrates on companies that make goods purchased chiefly by consumers.

geodemographic segmentation Combining demographics with geographic segmentation to select target markets in advertising.

geographic editions Magazines that target geographic markets and have different rates for ads.

geographic segmentation A method of segmenting markets by geographic regions based on the shared characteristics, needs, or wants of people within the region.

global advertising Advertising used by companies that market their products, goods, or services throughout various countries around the world with messages that remain consistent.

global marketers Multinationals that use a standardized approach to marketing and advertising in all countries.

global positioning system (GPS) New satellite-based system whereby outdoor advertising companies give their customers the exact latitude and longitude of particular boards. Media buyers, equipped with sophisticated new software on their desktop computers, can then integrate this information with demographic market characteristics and traffic counts to determine the best locations for their boards without ever leaving the office.

goods Tangible products such as suits, soap, and soft drinks.

government markets Governmental bodies that buy products for the successful coordination of municipal, state, federal, or other government activities.

gross impressions The total of all the audiences delivered by a media plan.

gross rating points (GRPs) The total audience delivery or weight of a specific media schedule. It is computed by dividing the total number of impressions by the size of the target population and multiplying by 100, or by multiplying the reach, expressed as a percentage of the population, by the average frequency. In television, gross rating points are the total rating points achieved by a particular media schedule over a specific period. For example, a weekly schedule of five commercials with an average household rating of 20 would yield 100 GRPs. In outdoor advertising, a 100 gross rating point showing (also called a number 100 showing) covers a market fully by reaching 9 out of 10 adults daily over a 30-day period.

group system   System in which an ad agency is divided into a number of little agencies or groups, each composed of an account supervisor, account executives, copywriters, art directors, a media director, and any other specialists required to meet the needs of the particular clients being served by the group.

growth stage   The period in a product life cycle that is marked by market expansion as more and more customers make their first purchases while others are already making their second and third purchases.

GRPs   See *gross rating points*.

guaranteed circulation   The number of copies of a magazine that the publisher expects to sell. If this figure is not reached, the publisher must give a refund to advertisers.

habit   An acquired or developed behavior pattern that has become nearly or completely involuntary.

halftone plate   Plate that prints dots, the combination of which, when printed, produces an optical illusion of shading as in a photograph.

halftone screen   A glass or plastic screen, crisscrossed with fine black lines at right angles like a window screen, which breaks continuous-tone artwork into dots so that it can be reproduced.

halo effect   In ad pretesting, the fact that consumers are likely to rate the one or two ads that make the best first impression as the highest in all categories.

headline   The words in the leading position of an advertisement—the words that will be read first or that are positioned to draw the most attention.

hidden differences   Imperceptible but existing differences that may greatly affect the desirability of a product.

hierarchy of needs   Maslow's theory that the lower biological or survival needs are dominant in human behavior and must be satisfied before higher, socially acquired needs become meaningful.

hook   The part of a jingle that sticks in your memory.

horizontal cooperative advertising   Joint advertising effort of related businesses (car dealers, realtors, etc.) to create traffic for their type of business.

horizontal publications   Business publications targeted at people with particular job functions that cut across industry lines, such as *Purchasing* magazine.

households using TV (HUT)   The percentage of homes in a given area that have one or more TV sets turned on at any particular time. If 1,000 TV sets are in the survey area and 500 are turned on, the HUT figure is 50 percent.

house list   A company's most important and valuable direct-mail list, which may contain current, recent, and long-past customers or future prospects.

house organs   Internal and external publications produced by business organizations, including stockholder reports, newsletters, consumer magazines, and dealer publications. Most are produced by a company's advertising or public relations department or by its agency.

HTML   Refers to Hyper Text Markup Language used primarily to build Websites on the Internet.

icon   A pictorial image that represents an idea or thing.

ideas   Economic, political, religious, or social viewpoints that advertising may attempt to sell.

illustrators   The artists who paint, sketch, or draw the pictures we see in advertising.

image advertising   Type of advertising intended to create a particular perception of the company or personality for the brand.

imagery transfer   When advertisers run a schedule on TV and then convert the audio portion to radio commercials, fully 75 percent of consumers replay the video in their minds when they hear the radio spot.

IMC message   An element of the creative mix comprising what the company plans to say in its advertisements and how it plans to say it—verbally or nonverbally.

IMC plan   The written document that directs the company's advertising effort. A natural outgrowth of the marketing plan, it analyzes the situation, sets advertising objectives, and lays out a specific strategy from which ads and campaigns are created.

IMC strategy   The methodology advertisers use to achieve their advertising objectives. The strategy is determined by the particular creative mix of advertising elements the advertiser selects, namely: target audience; product concept; communications media; and advertising message. Also called the *creative mix*.

IMC strategy research   Used to help define the product concept or to assist in the selection of target markets, advertising messages, or media vehicles.

immersive advertising   Proprietary technique developed by Neopets.com for integrating an advertiser's products or services into the Website experience.

implied consumers   The consumers who are addressed by the ad's persona. They are not real, but rather imagined by the ad's creators to be ideal consumers—acquiescing in whatever beliefs the text requires. They are, in effect, part of the drama of the ad.

incentive system   A form of compensation in which the agency shares in the client's success when a campaign attains specific, agreed-upon goals.

independent production house   Supplier company that specializes in film or video production or both.

independent research companies   Research firms that work outside an agency. They may come in all sizes and specialties, and they employ staff statisticians, field interviewers, and computer programmers, as well as analysts with degrees in psychology, sociology, and marketing.

independent shopping guide   Weekly local ad vehicles that may or may not contain editorial matter. They can be segmented into highly select market areas.

in-depth interview   An intensive interview technique that uses carefully planned but loosely structured questions to probe respondents' deeper feelings.

individual brand   Assigning a unique name to each product a manufacturer produces.

induced differences   Distinguishing characteristics of products effected through unique branding, packaging, distribution, merchandising, and advertising.

industrial age   A historical period covering approximately the first 70 years of the 20th century. This period was marked by tremendous growth and maturation of the U.S. industrial base. It saw the development of new, often inexpensive brands of the luxury and convenience goods we now classify as consumer packaged goods.

industrial markets   Individuals or companies that buy products needed for the production of other goods or services such as plant equipment and telephone systems.

infomercial   A long TV commercial that gives consumers detailed information about a product or service; see also *program-length advertisement.*

informal research   The second step in the research process, designed to explore a problem by reviewing secondary data and interviewing a few key people with the most information to share. Also called *exploratory research.*

informational motives   The negatively originated motives, such as problem removal or problem avoidance, that are the most common energizers of consumer behavior.

in-house agency   Agency wholly owned by an advertiser and set up and staffed to do all the work of an independent full-service agency.

in kind   The donation of goods and services as payment for some service such as a sponsorship.

inquiry test   A form of test in which consumer responses to an ad for information or free samples are tabulated.

insert   An ad or brochure that the advertiser prints and ships to the publisher for insertion into a magazine or newspaper.

insertion order   A form submitted to a newspaper or magazine when an advertiser wants to run an advertisement. This form states the date(s) on which the ad is to run, its size, the requested position, and the rate.

inside card   A transit advertisement, normally 11 by 28 inches, placed in a wall rack above the windows of a bus.

institutional advertising   A type of advertising that attempts to obtain favorable attention for the business as a whole, not for a specific product or service the store or business sells. The effects of institutional advertising are intended to be long term rather than short range.

institutional copy   A type of body copy in which the advertiser tries to sell an idea or the merits of the organization or service rather than the sales features of a particular product.

in-store sampling   The handing out of free product samples to passing shoppers.

integrated commercial   A straight radio announcement, usually delivered by one person, woven into a show or tailored to a given program to avoid any perceptible interruption.

integrated marketing communications (IMC)   The process of building and reinforcing mutually profitable relationships with employees, customers, other stakeholders, and the general public by developing and coordinating a strategic communications program that enables them to make constructive contact with the company/brand through a variety of media.

intellectual property   Something produced by the mind, such as original works of authorship including literary, dramatic, musical, artistic, and certain other "intellectual" works, which may be legally protected by copyright, patent, or trademark.

intensive distribution   A distribution strategy based on making the product available to consumers at every possible location so that consumers can buy with a minimum of effort.

intensive techniques   Qualitative research aimed at probing the deepest feelings, attitudes, and beliefs of respondents through direct questioning. Typical methods include in-depth interviews and focus groups.

interactive agency   An advertising agency that specializes in the creation of ads for a digital interactive medium such as Web pages, CD-ROMs, or electronic kiosks.

interactive TV   A personal audience venue where people can personally guide TV programming through a remote control box while watching TV.

interior paragraphs   Text within the body copy of an ad where the credibility and desire steps of the message are presented.

international advertising   Advertising aimed at foreign markets.

international agency   An advertising agency that has offices or affiliates in major communication centers around the world and can help its clients market internationally or globally.

international media   Media serving several countries, usually without change, available to an international audience.

international structure   Organization of companies with foreign marketing divisions, typically decentralized and responsible for their own product lines, marketing operations, and profits.

Internet   A worldwide network of computer systems that facilitates global electronic communications via e-mail, the World Wide Web, ftp, and other data protocols. Currently the fastest growing medium for advertising.

interpersonal influences   Social influences on the consumer decision-making process, including family, society, and cultural environment.

interstitial   Animated screens, often advertisements, that pop up momentarily as the computer searches for and downloads information for a requested Web page. Also known as *splash pages.*

interview   See *in-depth interview.*

introductory phase   The initial phase of the product life cycle (also called the *pioneering phase*) when a new product is introduced, costs are highest, and profits are lowest.

inventory   Commercial time for advertisers.

island half   A half-page of magazine space that is surrounded on two or more sides by editorial matter. This type of ad is designed to dominate a page and is therefore sold at a premium price.

italic   A style of printing type with letters that generally slant to the right.

jingle   A musical commercial, usually sung with the sales message in the verse.

Judge role   A role in the creative process that evaluates the results of experimentation and decides which approach is more practical.

junior posters   A type of outdoor advertising offering a 5-foot by 11-foot printing area on a panel surface 6 feet tall by 12 feet wide.

junior unit   A large magazine advertisement (60% of the page) placed in the middle of a page and surrounded by editorial matter.

kerning   The measurement of the space between individual letters of text.

keyword   A single word that a user inputs into an Internet search engine to request information that is similar in subject matter to that word. Advertisers may buy keywords from search engines so that their advertisements appear when a user inputs the purchased word.

kicker   A subhead that appears above the headline. Also known as *overline*.

landing page   A specially designed destination for those that click on online advertising.

layout   An orderly formation of all the parts of an advertisement. In print, it refers to the arrangement of the headline, subheads, visuals, copy, picture captions, trademarks, slogans, and signature. In television, it refers to the placement of characters, props, scenery, and product elements, the location and angle of the camera, and the use of lighting. See also *design*.

leading   The measurement of the space between separate lines of text (pronounced *ledding*).

lead-in paragraph   In print ads, a bridge between the headlines, the subheads, and the sales ideas presented in the text. It transfers reader interest to product interest.

learning   A relatively permanent change in thought processes or behavior that occurs as a result of reinforced experience.

letter shop   A firm that stuffs envelopes, affixes labels, calculates postage, sorts pieces into stacks or bundles, and otherwise prepares items for mailing.

licensed brands   Brand names that other companies can buy the right to use.

lifestyle technique   Type of commercial in which the user is presented rather than the product. Typically used by clothing and soft drink advertisers to affiliate their brands with the trendy lifestyles of their consumers.

lifetime customer value (LTCV)   A measurement of a consumer's economic value to a company over the course of his or her entire lifetime which comes from developing lasting relationships.

line film   The product of a photograph shot with orthographic film which yields a high-contrast black-and-white image with no gray tones.

line plate   A printing plate used to produce black-and-white artwork from line film.

linkage media   In direct marketing, media that help prospects and customers link up with a company.

list broker   An intermediary who handles rental of mailing lists for list owners on a commission basis.

live action   The basic production technique in television that portrays real people and settings, as opposed to animation.

lobbying   Informing government officials and persuading them to support or thwart administrative action or legislation in the interests of some client.

local advertising   Advertising by businesses within a city or county directed toward customers within the same geographic area. Also called *retail advertising*.

local agency   Advertising agency that specializes in creating advertising for local businesses.

local city magazine   Most major U.S. cities have one of these publications. Typical readership is upscale, professional people interested in local arts, fashion, and business.

local time   Radio spots purchased by a local advertiser.

location   Shooting away from the studio. Location shooting adds realism but can also be a technical and logistical nightmare, often adding cost and many other potential problems.

logotype   Special design of the advertiser's name (or product name) that appears in all advertisements. Also called a signature cut, it is like a trademark because it gives the advertiser individuality and provides quick recognition at the point of purchase.

long-term macro arguments   Criticisms of advertising that focus on the social or environmental impact of marketing.

lot   Acreage outside a studio that is shielded from stray, off-site sounds.

mail-response list   A type of direct-mail list, composed of people who have responded to the direct-mail solicitations of other companies, especially those whose efforts are complementary to the advertiser's.

maintenance stage   In the client–agency relationship, the day-to-day interaction that, when successful, may go on for years.

makegoods   TV spots that are aired to compensate for spots that were missed or run incorrectly.

management (account) supervisors   Managers who supervise account executives and who report to the agency's director of account services.

mandatories   The address, phone number, Web address, and so on that the advertiser usually insists be included within an ad to give the consumer adequate information.

market   A group of potential customers who share a common interest, need, or desire; who can use the offered good or service to some advantage; and who can afford or are willing to pay the purchase price. Also, an element of the media mix referring to the various targets of a media plan.

marketer   Any person or organization that has products, services, or ideas to sell.

marketing   The process of planning and executing the conception, pricing, promotion, and distribution of ideas, goods, and services to create exchanges that satisfy the perceived needs, wants, and objectives of individuals and organizations.

marketing communications   The various efforts and tools companies use to initiate and maintain communication with customers and prospects, including solicitation letters, newspaper ads, event sponsorships, publicity, telemarketing, statement stuffers, and coupons, to mention just a few.

marketing information system (MIS) A set of procedures for generating an orderly flow of pertinent information for use in making market decisions.

marketing mix Four elements, called the 4Ps (product, price, place, and promotion), that every company has the option of adding, subtracting, or modifying in order to create a desired marketing strategy.

marketing objectives Goals of the marketing effort that may be expressed in terms of the needs of specific target markets and specific sales objectives.

marketing plan The plan that directs the company's marketing effort. First, it assembles all the pertinent facts about the organization, the markets it serves, and its products, services, customers, and competition. Second, it forces the functional managers within the company to work together—product development, production, selling, advertising, credit, transportation—to focus efficiently on the customer. Third, it sets goals and objectives to be attained within specified periods of time and lays out the precise strategies that will be used to achieve them.

marketing public relations (MPR) The use of public relations activities as a marketing tool.

marketing research The systematic gathering, recording, and analysis of information to help managers make marketing decisions.

Marketing Research Online Communities (MROC) Suppliers of online communities for marketing research purposes.

marketing strategy The statement of how the company is going to accomplish its marketing objectives. The strategy is the total directional thrust of the company, that is, the how-to of the marketing plan, and is determined by the particular blend of the marketing mix elements (the 4 Ps), which the company can control.

market prep corporate advertising Corporate advertising that is used to set up the company for future sales; it simultaneously communicates messages about the products and the company.

market segmentation Strategy of identifying groups of people or organizations with certain shared needs and characteristics within the broad markets for consumer or business products and aggregating these groups into larger market segments according to their mutual interest in the product's utility.

markup A source of agency income gained by adding some amount to a supplier's bill, usually 17.65 percent.

mass media Print or broadcast media that reach very large audiences. Mass media include radio, television, newspapers, magazines, and billboards.

master tape The final recording of a radio commercial, with all the music, sound, and vocals mixed, from which dubs (duplicates) are recorded and sent to radio stations for broadcast.

maturity stage That point in the product life cycle when the market has become saturated with products, the number of new customers has dwindled, and competition is most intense.

mechanical The set type and illustrations or photographs pasted into the exact position in which they will appear in the final ad. Also called a *pasteup,* this is then used as the basis for the next step in the reproduction process.

mechanics One of the five Ms of the media mix; dealing creatively with the available advertising media options.

media A plural form of *medium,* referring to communications vehicles paid to present an advertisement to its target audience. Most often used to refer to radio and television networks, stations that have news reporters, and publications that carry news and advertising.

media buyer Person responsible for negotiating and contracting the purchase of advertisement space and time in various media.

media-buying service An organization that specializes in purchasing and packaging radio and television time.

media classes Broad media categories of electronic, print, outdoor, and direct mail.

media commission Compensation paid by a medium to recognized advertising agencies, usually 15 percent (16⅔% for outdoor), for advertising placed with it.

media planning The process that directs advertising messages to the right people in the right place at the right time.

media research The systematic gathering and analysis of information on the reach and effectiveness of media vehicles.

media subclasses Smaller divisions of media classes, such as radio, TV, magazines, newspapers, and so on.

media units Specific units of advertising in each type of medium, such as half-page magazine ads, 30-second spots, and so on.

media vehicles Particular media programs or publications.

medium An instrument or communications vehicle that carries or helps transfer a message from the sender to the receiver. Plural is *media.* See also *media.*

mental files Stored memories in the consumer's mind.

merchandise Synonymous with *product concept* when used in reference to the 5Ms of advertising testing.

message In oral communication, the idea formulated and encoded by the source and sent to the receiver.

message strategy The specific determination of what a company wants to say and how it wants to say it. The elements of the message strategy include verbal, nonverbal, and technical components; also called *rationale.*

message weight The total size of the audience for a set of ads or an entire campaign.

methodology The overall strategy of selecting and scheduling media vehicles to achieve the desired reach, frequency, and continuity objectives.

microblog A broadcast medium in the form of blogging.

microsite Refers to a specially designed portion of a larger domain (Website) typically constructed to drive a specific action.

mixed interlock The edited version of a filmed television commercial mixed with the finished sound track. Used for initial review and approval prior to being duplicated for airing.

mixed-media approach Using a combination of advertising media vehicles in a single advertising campaign.

mnemonic device A gimmick used to dramatize the product benefit and make it memorable, such as the Imperial Margarine crown or the Avon doorbell.

mobile app installs Facebook social advertising encouraging users to install Facebook apps.

mobile billboard A cross between traditional billboards and transit advertising; some specially designed flatbed trucks carry long billboards up and down busy thoroughfares.

money In media planning, one of the five elements in the media mix.

motivation The underlying drives that stem from the conscious or unconscious needs of the consumer and contribute to the individual consumer's purchasing actions.

motivation value A consideration in selecting media based on the medium's ability to motivate people to act. Positive factors include prestige, good quality reproduction, timeliness, and editorial relevance.

motives Emotions, desires, physiological needs, or similar impulses that may incite consumers to action.

multinational corporations Corporations operating and investing throughout many countries and making decisions based on availabilities worldwide.

musical commercial See *jingle*.

musical logo A jingle that becomes associated with a product or company through consistent use.

NAD See *National Advertising Division*.

NAICS See *North American Industry Classification System*.

NARB See *National Advertising Review Board*.

NARC See *National Advertising Review Council*.

narrative copy A type of body copy that tells a story. It sets up a problem and then creates a solution using the particular sales features of the product or service as the key to the solution.

narrative message Advertising in which a third person tells a story about others to an imagined audience.

national advertisers Companies that advertise in several geographic regions or throughout the country.

national advertising Advertising used by companies that market their products, goods, or services in several geographic regions or throughout the country.

National Advertising Division (NAD) The National Advertising Division of the Council of Better Business Bureaus. It investigates and monitors advertising industry practices.

National Advertising Review Board (NARB) A five-member panel, composed of three advertisers, one agency representative, and one layperson, selected to review decisions of the NAD.

National Advertising Review Council (NARC) An organization founded by the Council of Better Business Bureaus and various advertising industry groups to promote and enforce standards of truth, accuracy, taste, morality, and social responsibility in advertising.

national agency Advertising agency that produces and places the quality of advertising suitable for national campaigns.

national brands Product brands that are marketed in several regions of the country.

national magazines Magazines that are distributed throughout a country.

national rate A newspaper advertising rate that is higher, attributed to the added costs of serving national advertisers.

needs The basic, often instinctive, human forces that motivate us to do something.

negatively originated motives Consumer purchase and usage based on problem removal or problem avoidance. To relieve such feelings, consumers actively seek a new or replacement product.

network marketing A method of direct distribution in which individuals act as independent distributors for a manufacturer or private-label marketer.

network The amount of connections that are made by one individual.

networks Any of the national television or radio broadcasting chains or companies such as ABC, CBS, NBC, or Fox. Networks offer the large advertiser convenience and efficiency because the message can be broadcast simultaneously throughout the country.

news/information headline A type of headline that includes many of the "how-to" headlines as well as headlines that seek to gain identification for their sponsors by announcing some news or providing some promise of information.

Newspaper Association of America (NAA) The promotional arm of the American Newspaper Publishers Association and the nation's newspaper industry.

news release A typewritten sheet of information (usually 8½ by 11 inches) issued to print and broadcast outlets to generate publicity or shed light on a subject of interest. Also called *press release*.

NLEA See *Nutritional Labeling and Education Act*.

noise The sender's advertising message competing daily with hundreds of other commercial and noncommercial messages.

noncommercial advertising Advertising sponsored by or for a charitable institution, civic group, religious order, political organization, or some other nonprofit group to stimulate donations, persuade people to vote one way or another, or bring attention to social causes.

nonpersonal communication Marketing activities that use some medium as an intermediary for communication, including advertising, direct marketing, public relations, collateral materials, and sales promotion.

nonpersonal influences Factors influencing the consumer decision-making process that are often out of the consumer's control, such as time, place, and environment.

nonprobability samples Research samples that do not provide every unit in the population with an equal chance of being included. As a result, there is no guarantee that the sample will be representative.

nonproduct advertising Advertising designed to sell ideas or a philosophy rather than products or services.

nonproduct facts Product claims not about the brand but about the consumer or the social context in which the consumer uses the brand.

nonverbal Communication other than through the use of words, normally visual.

North American Industry Classification System (NAICS) codes Method used by the U.S. Department of Commerce to classify all businesses. The NAICS codes are based on broad industry groups, subgroups, and detailed groups of firms in similar lines of business.

Nutritional Labeling and Education Act (NLEA)   A 1994 congressional law setting stringent legal definitions for terms such as *fresh, light, low fat,* and *reduced calorie;* setting standard serving sizes; and requiring labels to show food value for one serving alongside the total recommended daily value as established by the National Research Council.

objectives   See *marketing objectives.*

objective/task method   A method of determining advertising allocations, also referred to as the *budget-buildup method,* that defines objectives and how advertising is to be used to accomplish them. It has three steps: defining the objectives, determining strategy, and estimating the cost.

observation method   A method of research used when researchers actually monitor people's actions.

off-network syndication   The availability of programs that originally appeared on networks to individual stations for rebroadcast.

on camera   Actually seen by the camera, as an announcer, a spokesperson, or actor playing out a scene.

100 showing   The basic unit of sale for billboards or posters is 100 gross rating points daily. One rating point equals 1 percent of a particular market's population.

on-sale date   The date a magazine is actually issued.

open rate   The highest rate for a one-time insertion in a newspaper.

opinion leader   Someone whose beliefs or attitudes are respected by people who share an interest in some specific activity.

opinion sampling   A form of public relations research in which consumers provide feedback via interviews, toll-free phone lines, focus groups, and similar methods.

opportunity to see (OTS)   A possible exposure of an advertising message to one audience member. Also called an *advertising impression.* Effective frequency is considered to be three or more opportunities to see over a four-week period; but no magic number works for every commercial and every product.

organizational buyers   People who purchase products and services for use in business and government.

orthographic film   A high-contrast photographic film yielding only black-and-white images, no gray tones.

outdoor advertising   An out-of-home medium in the form of billboards.

out-of-home media   Media such as outdoor advertising (billboards) and transit advertising (bus and car cards) that reach prospects outside their homes.

outside posters   The variety of transit advertisements appearing on the outside of buses, including king size, queen size, traveling display, rear of bus, and front of bus.

overline   See *kicker.*

packaging   The container for a product—encompassing the physical appearance of the container and including the design, color, shape, labeling, and materials used.

page likes   Facebook tool allowing brands to cultivate followers.

paid circulation   The total number of copies of an average issue of a newspaper or magazine that is distributed through subscriptions and newsstand sales.

PANTONE Matching System (PMS)   A collection of colors that are premixed according to a formula and given a specific color number. PANTONE swatch books feature over 100 colors in solid and screened blocks printed on different paper finishes.

participation basis   The basis on which most network television advertising is sold, with advertisers buying 30- or 60-second segments within the program. This allows the advertiser to spread out the budget and makes it easier to get in and out of a program without a long-term commitment.

pasteup   See *mechanical.*

patent   A grant made by the government that confers upon the creator of an invention the sole right to make, use, and sell that invention for a set period of time.

people-based service   A service that relies on the talents and skills of individuals rather than on highly technical or specialized equipment.

percentage of sales method   A method of advertising budget allocation based on a percentage of the previous year's sales, the anticipated sales for the next year, or a combination of the two.

perceptible differences   Differences between products that are visibly apparent to the consumer.

perception   Our personalized way of sensing and comprehending stimuli.

peripheral route to persuasion   One of two ways researchers Petty, Cacioppo, and Schumann theorize that marketers can persuade consumers. People who have low involvement with the product or message have little or no reason to pay attention to it or to comprehend the central message of the ad. However, these consumers might attend to some peripheral aspects of an ad or commercial for their entertainment value. Whatever they feel or think about these peripheral, nonproduct aspects might integrate into a positive attitude toward the ad. At some later date, these ad-related meanings could be activated to form some brand attitude or purchase intention. Typical of advertising for many everyday low-involvement purchases such as many consumer packaged goods: soap, cereal, toothpaste, and chewing gum. See also *Elaboration Likelihood Model.*

persona   A real or imaginary spokesperson who lends some voice or tone to an advertisement or commercial.

personal communication   Marketing activities that include all person-to-person contact with customers.

personal processes   The three internal, human operations—perception, learning, and motivation—that govern the way consumers discern raw data (stimuli) and translate them into feelings thoughts, beliefs, and actions.

personal selling   A sales method based on person-to-person contact, such as by a salesperson at a retail establishment or by a telephone solicitor.

persuasion   A change in belief, attitude, or behavioral intention caused by a message (such as advertising or personal selling).

philanthropy Support for a cause without any commercial incentive.

photographers The artists who use cameras to create visuals for advertisements.

physiological screens The perceptual screens that use the five senses—sight, hearing, touch, taste, and smell—to detect incoming data and measure the dimension and intensity of the physical stimulus.

picture-caption copy A type of body copy in which the story is told through a series of illustrations and captions rather than through the use of a copy block alone.

picture-window layout Layout that employs a single, dominant visual that occupies between 60 and 70 percent of an advertisement's total area. Also known as *poster-style format* or *Ayer No. 1.*

point In retailing, the place of business. In typography, the measurement of the size and height of a text character. There are 72 points to an inch.

point-of-purchase (P-O-P) materials Materials set up at a retail location to build traffic, advertise the product, and promote impulse buying. Materials may include window displays, counter displays, floor and wall displays, streamers, and posters.

polybagging Samples are delivered in plastic bags with the daily newspaper or a monthly magazine.

pop-up ad A three-dimensional magazine ad.

position The way in which a product is ranked in the consumer's mind by the benefits it offers, by the way it is classified or differentiated from the competition, or by its relationship to certain target markets.

positioning strategy An effective way to separate a particular brand from its competitors by associating that brand with a particular set of customer needs.

positively originated motives Consumer's motivation to purchase and use a product based on a positive bonus that the product promises, such as sensory gratification, intellectual stimulation, or social approval.

post An entry in a blog or Internet forum.

postcards Cards sent by advertisers to announce sales, offer discounts, or otherwise generate consumer traffic.

posters For public relations purposes, signs that impart product information or other news of interest to consumers, or that are aimed at employee behavior, such as safety, courtesy, or waste reduction.

poster-style format Layout that employs a single, dominant visual that occupies between 60 and 70 percent of an advertisement's total area. Also known as *picture-window layout* and *Ayer No. 1.*

postindustrial age Period of cataclysmic change, starting in about 1980, when people first became truly aware of the sensitivity of the environment in which we live.

postproduction phase The finishing phase in commercial production—the period after recording and shooting when a radio or TV commercial is edited and sweetened with music and sound effects.

postpurchase dissonance See *theory of cognitive dissonance.*

postpurchase evaluation Determining whether a purchase has been a satisfactory or unsatisfactory one.

posttesting Testing the effectiveness of an advertisement after it has been run.

preemption rates Lower TV advertising rate that stations charge when the advertiser agrees to allow the station to sell its time to another advertiser willing to pay a higher rate.

preferred-position rate A choice position for a newspaper or magazine ad for which a higher rate is charged.

preindustrial age Period of time between the beginning of written history and roughly the start of the 19th century, during which the invention of paper and the printing press and increased literacy gave rise to the first forms of written advertising.

premium An item offered free or at a bargain price to encourage the consumer to buy an advertised product.

prepress phase The process of converting page art and visuals into materials (generally film negatives and color separation) needed for printing.

preprinted inserts Newspaper advertisements printed in advance by the advertiser and then delivered to the newspaper plant to be inserted into a specific edition. Preprints are inserted into the fold of the newspaper and look like a separate, smaller section of the paper.

preproduction phase The period of time before the actual recording or shooting of a commercial—the planning phase in commercial production.

prerelationship stage The initial stage in the client–agency relationship before they officially do business.

preroll Refers to the placement of a video advertisement in front of a piece of online video content.

presenter commercial A commercial format in which one person or character presents the product and sales message.

press agentry The planning of activities and the staging of events to attract attention to new products or services and to generate publicity about the company or organization that will be of interest to the media.

press kit A package of publicity materials used to give information to the press at staged events such as press conferences or open houses. Also, a package of sales material promoting a specific media vehicle. Also called a *media kit.*

press release See *news release.*

pretesting Testing the effectiveness of an advertisement for gaps or flaws in message content before recommending it to clients, often conducted through focus groups.

price element In the marketing mix, the amount charged for the good or service—including deals, discounts, terms, warranties, and so on. The factors affecting price are market demand, cost of production and distribution, competition, and corporate objectives.

primary circulation The number of people who receive a publication, whether through direct purchase or subscription.

primary data Research information gained directly from the marketplace.

primary demand Consumer demand for a whole product category.

primary demand trend The projection of future consumer demand for a whole product category based on past demand and other market influences.

primary motivation   The pattern of attitudes and activities that help people reinforce, sustain, or modify their social and self-image. An understanding of the primary motivation of individuals helps advertisers promote and sell goods and services.

primary research   Collecting primary data directly from the marketplace using qualitative or quantitative methods.

prime time   Highest level of TV viewing (8 p.m. to 11 p.m. EST).

printer   Business that employs or contracts with highly trained specialists who prepare artwork for reproduction, operate digital scanning machines to make color separations and plates, operate presses and collating machines, and run binderies.

print media   Any commercially published, printed medium, such as newspapers and magazines, that sells advertising space to a variety of advertisers.

print production manager   Manager who oversees the entire production process, including reproduction of visuals in full color, shooting and editing of scenes, precise specification and placement of type, and the checking, approving, duplicating, and shipping of final art, negatives, tape, or film to the communication media.

print production process   The systematic process a layout for an ad or a brochure goes through from concept to final printing. The four major phases are preproduction, production, prepress, and printing and distribution.

privacy rights   Of or pertaining to an individual's right to prohibit personal information from being divulged to the public.

private labels   Personalized brands applied by distributors or dealers to products supplied by manufacturers. Private brands are typically sold at lower prices in large retail chain stores.

process   A planned series of actions or methods that take place sequentially, such as developing products, pricing them strategically, making them available to customers through a distribution network, and promoting them through sales and advertising activities.

producer   For electronic media, the person responsible for keeping the project moving smoothly and under budget, while maintaining the required level of quality through every step of the production process.

product   The particular good or service a company sells. See also *product concept*.

product advertising   Advertising intended to promote goods and services; also a functional classification of advertising.

product concept   The consumer's perception of a product as a "bundle" of utilitarian and symbolic values that satisfy functional, social, psychological, and other wants and needs. Also, as an element of the creative mix used by advertisers to develop advertising strategy, it is the bundle of product values the advertiser presents to the consumer.

product element   The most important element of the marketing mix: the good or service being offered and the values associated with it—including the way the product is designed and classified, positioned, branded, and packaged.

production phase   An element of creative strategy. The whole physical process of producing ads and commercials; also the particular phase in the process when the recording and shooting of commercials is done.

product life cycle   Progressive stages in the life of a product—including introduction, growth, maturity, and decline—that affect the way a product is marketed and advertised.

product placement   Paying a fee to have a product included in a movie.

professional advertising   Advertising directed at individuals who are normally licensed to operate under a code of ethics or set of professional standards.

program-length advertisement (PLA)   A long-form television commercial that may run as long as an hour; also called an *infomercial*.

programmatic advertising   Advertising in which computers make decisions about what ads are inserted in what content providers. Advertisers bid for audiences and based on their willingness to pay and the demographic match of audiences on content sites.

programming format   The genre of music or other programming style that characterizes and differentiates radio stations from each other (i.e., contemporary hit radio, country rock, etc.).

program rating   The percentage of TV households in an area that are tuned in to a specific program.

projective techniques   In marketing research, asking indirect questions or otherwise involving consumers in a situation where they can express feelings about the problem or product. The purpose is to get an understanding of people's underlying or subconscious feelings, attitudes, opinions, needs, and motives.

promoted account   Twitter social advertising that appears in a user's "Who to Follow" tab. They are used to increase followers as the primary audience is not current followers of the brand.

promoted trend   Twitter social advertising allowing companies get their hashtag near the list of trending topics on Twitter which can be seen by all users.

promoted tweet   Social advertising on Twitter that helps to raise the prominence of a tweet to the top of follower's feeds.

proof copy   A copy of the completed advertisement that is used to check for final errors and corrections.

prospective customers   People who are about to make an exchange or are considering it.

protocols   Refers to the digital message sent between Web browser and Website server in an effort to communicate with each other.

provocative headline   A type of headline written to provoke the reader's curiosity so that, to learn more, the reader will read the body copy.

psychographics   The grouping of consumers into market segments on the basis of psychological makeup—values, attitudes, personality, and lifestyle.

psychological screens   The perceptual screens consumers use to evaluate, filter, and personalize information according to subjective standards, primarily emotions and personality.

public affairs   All activities related to the community citizenship of an organization, including dealing with community officials and working with regulatory bodies and legislative groups.

publicity   The generation of news about a person, product, or service that appears in broadcast or print media.

public notices   For a nominal fee, newspapers carry these legal changes in business, personal relationships, public governmental reports, notices by private citizens and organizations, and financial reports.

public relations (PR)   The strategic management of the relationships and communications that individuals and organizations have with other groups (called *publics*) for the purpose of creating mutual goodwill. The primary role of public relations is to manage a company's reputation and help build public consent for its enterprises.

public relations activities   Publicity, press agentry, sponsorships, special events, and public relations advertising used to create public awareness and credibility—at low cost—for the firm.

public relations advertising   Advertising that attempts to improve a company's relationship with its publics (labor, government, customers, suppliers, etc.).

publics   In PR terminology, employees, customers, stockholders, competitors, suppliers, or general population of customers are all considered one of the organization's publics.

puffery   Exaggerated, subjective claims that can't be proven true or false such as "the best," "premier," or "the only way to fly."

pull strategy   Marketing, advertising, and sales promotion activities aimed at inducing trial purchase and repurchase by consumers.

pulsing   Mixing continuity and flighting strategies in media scheduling.

purchase occasion   A method of segmenting markets on the basis of *when* consumers buy and use a good or service.

push money (PM)   A monetary inducement for retail salespeople to push the sale of particular products. Also called *piffs*.

push strategy   Marketing, advertising, and sales promotion activities aimed at getting products into the dealer pipeline and accelerating sales by offering inducements to dealers, retailers, and salespeople. Inducements might include introductory price allowances, distribution allowances, and advertising dollar allowances to stock the product and set up displays.

qualitative research   Research that tries to determine market variables according to unquantifiable criteria such as attitudes, beliefs, and lifestyle.

quantitative research   Research that tries to determine market variables according to reliable, hard statistics about specific market conditions or situations.

question headline   A type of headline that asks the reader a question.

RSS   Refers to really simple syndication, a family of Web feeds used to publish updated works.

radio personality   A disk jockey or talk show host.

random probability samples   A sampling method in which every unit in the population universe is given an equal chance of being selected for the research.

rate base   With magazines, the circulation figure on which the publisher bases its rates.

rate card   A printed information form listing a publication's advertising rates, mechanical and copy requirements, advertising deadlines, and other information the advertiser needs to know before placing an order.

rating   The percentage of homes or individuals exposed to an advertising medium.

rating services   These services measure the program audiences of TV and radio stations for advertisers and broadcasters by picking a representative sample of the market and furnishing data on the size and characteristics of the viewers or listeners.

rational appeals   Marketing appeals that are directed at the consumer's practical, functional need for the product or service.

rationale   See *message strategy*.

reach   The total number of *different* people or households exposed to an advertising schedule during a given time, usually four weeks. Reach measures the *unduplicated* extent of audience exposure to a media vehicle and may be expressed either as a percentage of the total market or as a raw number.

readers per copy (RPC)   Variable used to determine the total reach of a given print medium. RPC is multiplied by the number of vendor and subscription sales to determine the total audience size.

reading notice   A variation of a display ad designed to look like editorial matter. It is sometimes charged at a higher space rate than normal display advertising, and the law requires that the word *advertisement* appear at the top.

rebates   Cash refunds on items from cars to household appliances.

recall tests   Posttesting methods used to determine the extent to which an advertisement and its message have been noticed, read, or watched.

receiver   In oral communication, this party decodes the message to understand it and responds by formulating a new idea, encodes it, and sends it back.

recency planning   Erwin Ephron's theory that most advertising works by influencing the brand choice of consumers who are ready to buy, suggesting that continuity of advertising is most important.

recruitment advertising   A special type of advertising, most frequently found in the classified sections of daily newspapers and typically the responsibility of a personnel department aimed at attracting employment applications.

reference groups   People we try to emulate or whose approval concerns us.

regional advertiser   Company that operates in one part of the country and markets exclusively to that region.

regional advertising   Advertising used by companies that market their products, goods, or services in a limited geographic region.

regional agency   Advertising agency that focuses on the production and placement of advertising suitable for regional campaigns.

regional publications   Magazines targeted to a specific area of the country, such as the West or the South.

regular price-line advertising   A type of retail advertising designed to inform consumers about the services available or the wide selection and quality of merchandise offered at regular prices.

relationship marketing Creating, maintaining, and enhancing long-term relationships with customers and other stakeholders that result in exchanges of information and other things of mutual value.

reliability An important characteristic of research test results. For a test to be reliable, it must be repeatable, producing the same result each time it is administered.

reputation management In public relations, the name of the long-term strategic process to manage the standing of the firm with various publics.

reseller markets Individuals or companies that buy products for the purpose of reselling them.

resellers Businesses that buy products from manufacturers or wholesalers and then resell the merchandise to consumers or other buyers; also called *middlemen*. These businesses do not change or modify the goods before they resell them. Resellers make their profits by selling the goods they buy for more than they paid. The most common examples of resellers are retail stores and catalog retailers. Internet retailers comprise a growing portion of the reseller business segment.

residual fee Payment to the talent if the commercial is extended beyond its initially contracted run.

resources axis A term in the Values and Lifestyles (VALS) typology relating to the range of psychological, physical, demographic, and material capacities that consumers can draw upon. The resources axis includes education, income, self-confidence, health, eagerness to buy, and energy level.

retail advertising Advertising sponsored by retail stores and businesses.

retainer method See *straight-fee method.*

RFM formula The RFM formula is a mathematical model that provides marketers with a method to determine the most reliable customers in a company's database, according to Recency, Frequency, and Monetary variables.

rich mail Technology that allows graphics, video, and audio to be included in an e-mail message.

rich-media advertising The graphical animations and ads with audio and video elements that overlay the Web page or even float over the page. Most common types include animated banners, interstitials, superstitials, and rich mail.

roadblocking Buying simultaneous airtime on all four television networks.

ROP advertising rates Run of paper. A term referring to a newspaper's normal discretionary right to place a given ad on any page or in any position it desires—in other words, where space permits. Most newspapers make an effort to place an ad in the position requested by the advertiser.

run of paper See *ROP advertising rates.*

run of station (ROS) Leaving placement of radio spots up to the station in order to achieve a lower ad rate.

sale advertising A type of retail advertising designed to stimulate the movement of particular merchandise or generally increase store traffic by placing the emphasis on special reduced prices.

sales letters The most common form of direct mail. Sales letters may be typewritten, typeset and printed, printed with a computer insert (such as your name), or fully computer typed.

sales promotion A direct inducement offering extra incentives all along the marketing route—from manufacturers through distribution channels to customers—to accelerate the movement of the product from the producer to the consumer.

sales promotion department In larger agencies, a staff to produce dealer ads, window posters, point-of-purchase displays, and dealer sales material.

sales-target objectives Marketing objectives that relate to a company's sales. They should be specific as to product and market, quantified as to time and amount, and realistic. They may be expressed in terms of total sales volume; sales by product, market segment, or customer type; market share; growth rate of sales volume; or gross profit.

sales test A useful measure of advertising effectiveness when advertising is the dominant element, or the only variable, in the company's marketing plan. Sales tests are more suited for gauging the effectiveness of campaigns than of individual ads or components of ads.

sample A portion of the population selected by market researchers to represent the appropriate targeted population. Also, a free trial of a product.

sample unit The actual individuals chosen to be surveyed or studied.

sampling Offering consumers a free trial of the product, hoping to convert them to habitual use.

sans serif A type group that is characterized by a lack of serifs.

satellite radio An analogue or digital radio signal that is relayed through one or more satellites.

SAU See *standard advertising unit.*

scale The regular charge for talent and music agreed to in the union contract.

script Format for radio and television copywriting resembling a two-column list showing dialog and/or visuals.

seal A type of certification mark offered by such organizations as the Good Housekeeping Institute and Underwriters' Laboratories when a product meets standards established by these institutions. Seals provide an independent, valued endorsement for the advertised product.

search engines Websites that are devoted to finding and retrieving requested information from the World Wide Web. Because search engines are the gatekeepers to information on the Internet they are extremely popular with advertisers.

search results page The list of potential links that are returned after a query on a search tool bar or Website.

secondary data Information that has previously been collected or published.

secondary (pass-along) readership The number of people who read a publication in addition to the primary purchasers.

selective demand Consumer demand for the particular advantages of one brand over another.

selective distribution Strategy of limiting the distribution of a product to select outlets in order to reduce distribution and promotion costs.

self-mailer Any type of direct-mail piece that can travel by mail without an envelope. Usually folded and secured by a staple or a seal, self-mailers have a special blank space for the prospect's name and address.

serif   The most popular type group that is distinguished by smaller lines or tails called serifs that finish the ends of the main character strokes and by variations in the thickness of the strokes.

services   A bundle of benefits that may or may not be physical, that are temporary in nature, and that come from the completion of a task.

session   The time when the recording and mixing of a radio commercial take place.

share   The percentage of homes with TV sets in use (HUT) tuned to a specific program.

share of market/share of voice method   A method of allocating advertising funds based on determining the firm's goals for a certain share of the market and then applying a slightly higher percentage of industry advertising dollars to the firm's budget.

short rate   The rate charged to advertisers that, during the year, fail to fulfill the amount of space for which they have contracted. This is computed by determining the difference between the standard rate for the lines run and the discount rate contracted.

short-term manipulative arguments   Criticisms of advertising that focus on the style of advertising (e.g., that it is manipulative or deceptive).

showing   A traditional term referring to the relative number of outdoor posters used during a contract period, indicating the intensity of market coverage. For example, a 100 showing provides an even and thorough coverage of the entire market.

signature cut   See *logotype*.

situation analysis   A factual statement of the organization's current situation and how it got there. It includes relevant facts about the company's history, growth, products and services, sales volume, share of market, competitive status, market served, distribution system, past advertising programs, results of market research studies, company capabilities, and strengths and weaknesses.

slice of life   A type of commercial consisting of a dramatization of a real-life situation in which the product is tried and becomes the solution to a problem.

slogan   A standard company statement (also called a *tagline* or a *themeline*) for advertisements, salespeople, and company employees. Slogans have two basic purposes: to provide continuity for a campaign and to reduce a key theme or idea to a brief, memorable positioning statement.

slotting allowances   Fees that manufacturers pay to retailers for the privilege of obtaining shelf or floor space for a new product.

social bookmarking   A method for Internet users to organize, store, manage, and search for online resources.

social classes   Traditional divisions in societies by sociologists—upper, upper-middle, lower-middle, and so on—who believed that people in the same social class tended toward similar attitudes, status symbols, and spending patterns.

social listening   A way for companies to aggregate and analyze online posts about a specific key term.

social network   A Website that exists solely to connect like individuals.

social responsibility   Acting in accordance with what society views as best for the welfare of people in general or for a specific community of people.

software as a service   A software delivery model in which software and associated data are centrally hosted on the cloud or the Internet.

source   In oral communication, this party formulates the idea, encodes it as a message, and sends it via some channel to the receiver.

spam   Unsolicited, mass e-mail advertising for a product or service that is sent by an unknown entity to a purchased mailing list or newsgroup.

special effects   Unusual visual effects created for commercials.

special events   Scheduled meetings, parties, and demonstrations aimed at creating awareness and understanding for a product or company.

spectaculars   Giant electronic signs that usually incorporate movement, color, and flashy graphics to grab the attention of viewers in high-traffic areas.

speculative presentation   An agency's presentation of the advertisement it proposes using in the event it is hired. It is usually made at the request of a prospective client and is often not paid for by the client.

speechwriting   Function of a public relations practitioner to write speeches for stockholder meetings, conferences, conventions, etc.

spiff   See *push money*.

spillover media   Foreign media aimed at a national population that are inadvertently received by a substantial number of the consumers in a neighboring country.

split runs   A feature of many newspapers (and magazines) that allows advertisers to test the comparative effectiveness of two different advertising approaches by running two different ads of identical size, but different content, in the same or different press runs on the same day.

sponsor   The company or organization ultimately responsible for the message and distribution of an advertisement. Although the sponsor is often not the author, the sponsor typically pays for the creation of the ad and its distribution.

sponsorial consumers   A group of decision makers at the sponsor's company or organization who decide if an ad will run or not, typically composed of executives and managers who have the responsibility for approving and funding a campaign.

sponsorship   The presentation of a radio or TV program, or an event, or even a Website by a sole advertiser. The advertiser is often responsible for the program content and the cost of production as well as the advertising. This is generally so costly that single sponsorships are usually limited to TV specials.

spot announcements   An individual commercial message run between programs but having no relationship to either. Spots may be sold nationally or locally. They must be purchased by contacting individual stations directly.

spot radio   National advertisers' purchase of airtime on individual stations. Buying spot radio affords advertisers great flexibility in their choice of markets, stations, airtime, and copy.

stakeholders In relationship marketing, customers, employees, centers of influence, stockholders, the financial community, and the press. Different stakeholders require different types of relationships.

standard advertising unit (SAU) A system of standardized newspaper advertisement sizes that can be accepted by all standard-sized newspapers without consideration of their precise format or page size. This system allows advertisers to prepare one advertisement in a particular size or SAU and place it in various newspapers regardless of the format.

standardized outdoor advertising Specialized system of outdoor advertising structures located scientifically to deliver an advertiser's message to an entire market.

standard-size newspaper The standard newspaper size, measuring approximately 22 inches deep and 13 inches wide and divided into six columns.

statement stuffers Advertisements enclosed in the monthly customer statements mailed by department stores, banks, utilities, or oil companies.

stimulus Physical data that can be received through the senses.

stock posters A type of outdoor advertising consisting of ready-made 30-sheet posters, available in any quantity and often featuring the work of first-class artists and lithographers.

storyboard A sheet preprinted with a series of 8 to 20 blank frames in the shape of TV screens, which includes text of the commercial, sound effects, and camera views.

storyboard rough A rough layout of a television commercial in storyboard form.

straight announcement The oldest type of radio or television commercial, in which an announcer delivers a sales message directly into the microphone or on-camera or does so off-screen while a slide or film is shown on-screen.

straight-fee (retainer) method A method of compensation for ad agency services in which a straight fee, or *retainer,* is based on a cost-plus-fixed-fees formula. Under this system, the agency estimates the amount of personnel time required by the client, determines the cost of that personnel, and multiplies by some factor.

straight-sell copy A type of body copy in which the text immediately explains or develops the headline and visual in a straightforward attempt to sell the product.

stripping Assembling line and halftone negatives into one single negative, which is then used to produce a combination plate.

subculture A segment within a culture that shares a set of meanings, values, or activities that differ in certain respects from those of the overall culture.

subhead Secondary headline in advertisements that may appear above or below the headline or in the text of the ad. Subheads are usually set in a type size smaller than the headline but larger than the body copy or text type size. They may also appear in boldface type or in a different ink color.

subliminal advertising Advertisements with messages (often sexual) supposedly embedded in illustrations just below the threshold of perception.

substantiation Evidence that backs up cited survey findings or scientific studies that the FTC may request from a suspected advertising violator.

Sunday supplement A newspaper-distributed Sunday magazine. Sunday supplements are distinct from other sections of the newspaper since they are printed by rotogravure on smoother paper stock.

supers Words superimposed on the picture in a television commercial.

suppliers People and organizations that assist both advertisers and agencies in the preparation of advertising materials, such as photography, illustration, printing, and production.

survey A basic method of quantitative research. To get people's opinions, surveys may be conducted in person, by mail, on the telephone, or via the Internet.

sweepstakes A sales promotion activity in which prizes are offered based on a chance drawing of entrants' names. The purpose is to encourage consumption of the product by creating consumer involvement.

SWOT analysis An acronym for internal *strengths* and *weaknesses* and external *opportunities* and *threats,* which represent the four categories used by advertising managers when reviewing a marketing plan. The SWOT analysis briefly restates the company's current situation, reviews the target market segments, itemizes the long- and short-term marketing objectives, and cites decisions regarding market positioning and the marketing mix.

synergy An effect achieved when the sum of the parts is greater than that expected from simply adding together the individual components.

tabloid newspaper A newspaper sized generally about half as deep as a standard-sized newspaper; it is usually about 14 inches deep and 11 inches wide.

tactics The precise details of a company's marketing strategy that determine the specific short-term actions that will be used to achieve its marketing objectives.

tagline See *slogan.*

take-ones In transit advertising, pads of business reply cards or coupons, affixed to interior advertisements for an extra charge that allow passengers to request more detailed information, send in application blanks, or receive some other product benefit.

talent The actors in commercials.

target audience The specific group of individuals to whom the advertising message is directed.

target market The market segment or group within the market segment toward which all marketing activities will be directed.

target marketing process The sequence of activities aimed at assessing various market segments, designating certain ones as the focus of marketing activities, and designing marketing mixes to communicate with and make sales to these targets.

taxicab exteriors In transit advertising, internally illuminated two-sided posters positioned on the roofs of taxis. Some advertising also appears on the doors or rear.

tearsheet The printed ad cut out and sent by the publisher to the advertiser as a proof of the ad's print quality and that it was published.

technical   One of the three components of message strategy, it refers to the preferred-execution approach and mechanical outcome including budget and scheduling limitations.

telemarketing   Selling products and services by using the telephone to contact prospective customers.

telephone sales   See *telemarketing*.

teleprompter   A two-way mirror mounted on the front of a studio video camera that reflects moving text to be read by the speaker being taped.

television households (TVHH)   Households with TV sets.

terminal posters   One-sheet, two-sheet, and three-sheet posters in many bus, subway, and commuter train stations as well as in major train and airline terminals. They are usually custom designed and include such attention getters as floor displays, island showcases, illuminated signs, dioramas (three-dimensional scenes), and clocks with special lighting and moving messages.

termination stage   The ending of a client–agency relationship.

testimonials   The use of satisfied customers and celebrities to endorse a product in advertising.

test market   An isolated geographic area used to introduce and test the effectiveness of a product, ad campaign, or promotional campaign, prior to a national rollout.

text   See *body copy*.

text paper   Range of less expensive papers that are lightweight. More porous versions are used in printing newspapers, and finer, glossier versions are used for quality printed materials like magazines and brochures.

text type   The smaller type used in the body copy of an advertisement.

themeline   See *slogan*.

theory of cognitive dissonance   The theory that people try to justify their behavior by reducing the degree to which their impressions or beliefs are inconsistent with reality.

30-sheet poster panel   See *billboards*.

3-D ads   Magazine ads requiring the use of 3-D glasses.

third-party ad server   Refers to the companies that help manage online advertising for the entire online ecosystem.

thumbnail   A rough, rapidly produced pencil sketch that is used for trying out ideas.

total audience   The total number of homes reached by some portion of a TV program. This figure is normally broken down to determine the distribution of the audience into demographic categories.

total audience plan (TAP)   A radio advertising package rate that guarantees a certain percentage of spots in the better dayparts.

total bus   A special transit advertising buy that covers the entire exterior of a bus, including the front, rear, sides, and top.

trade advertising   The advertising of goods and services to middlemen to stimulate wholesalers and retailers to buy goods for resale to their customers or for use in their own businesses.

trade concentration   More products being sold by fewer retailers.

trade deals   Short-term dealer discounts on the cost of a product or other dollar inducements to sell a product.

trademark   Any word, name, symbol, device, or any combination thereof adopted and used by manufacturers or merchants to identify their goods and distinguish them from those manufactured or sold by others.

trade promotions   See *push strategy*.

trade shows   Exhibitions where manufacturers, dealers, and buyers of an industry's products can get together for demonstrations and discussion; expose new products, literature, and samples to customers; and meet potential new dealers for their products.

transformational motives   Positively originated motives that promise to "transform" the consumer through sensory gratification, intellectual stimulation, and social approval. Also called *reward motives*.

transit advertising   An out-of-home medium that actually includes three separate media forms: inside cards; outside posters; and station, platform, and terminal posters.

transit shelter advertising   A newer form of out-of-home media, where advertisers can buy space on bus shelters and on the backs of bus-stop seats.

transnational (global) markets   Consumer, business, and government markets located in foreign countries.

trap   Where, in the printing process, one color overlays the edge of another to keep the paper from showing through.

trending   Refers to the topics that are currently being talked about online.

trial close   In ad copy, requests for the order that are made before the close in the ad.

TV households (TVHH)   The number of households in a market area that own television sets.

type families   Related typefaces in which the basic design remains the same but in which variations occur in the proportion, weight, and slant of the characters. Variations commonly include light, medium, bold, extra bold, condensed, extended, and italic.

typography   The art of selecting, setting, and arranging type.

UHF (ultrahigh frequency)   Television channels 14 through 83; about half of the U.S. commercial TV stations are UHF.

unfair advertising   According to the FTC, advertising that causes a consumer to be "unjustifiably injured" or that violates public policy.

Universal Product Code (UPC)   An identifying series of vertical bars with a 12-digit number that adorns every consumer packaged good.

universe   An entire target population.

usage rates   The extent to which consumers use a product: light, medium, or heavy.

User Generated Content (UGC)   Media content that is produced by consumers, not by companies.

user status   Six categories into which consumers can be placed, which reflect varying degrees of loyalties to certain brands and products. The categories are *sole users, semisole users, discount users, aware nontriers, trial/rejectors,* and *repertoire users*.

U.S. Patent and Trademark Office   Bureau within the U.S. Department of Commerce that registers and protects patents and trademarks.

utility A product's ability to provide both symbolic or psychological want satisfaction and functional satisfaction. A product's problem-solving potential may include form, time, place, or possession utility.

validity An important characteristic of a research test. For a test to be valid, it must reflect the true status of the market.

value The ratio of perceived benefits to the price of the product.

value-based thinking A style of thinking where decisions are based on intuition, values, and ethical judgments.

venue marketing A form of sponsorship that links a sponsor to a physical site such as a stadium, arena, auditorium, or racetrack.

verbal Words, written or spoken.

vertical cooperative advertising Co-op advertising in which the manufacturer provides the ad and pays a percentage of the cost of placement.

vertical marketing system (VMS) A centrally programmed and managed system that supplies or otherwise serves a group of stores or other businesses.

vertical publications Business publications aimed at people within a specific industry; for example, Restaurants & Institutions.

VHF (very high frequency) Television channels 2 through 13; about half of the U.S. commercial TV stations are VHF.

video news release (VNR) A news or feature story prepared in video form and offered free to TV stations.

viral marketing The Internet version of word-of-mouth advertising e-mail.

visualization The creative point in advertising where the search for the "big idea" takes place. It includes the task of analyzing the problem, assembling any and all pertinent information, and developing some verbal or visual concept of how to communicate what needs to be said.

visuals All of the picture elements that are placed into an advertisement.

voice-over In television advertising, the spoken copy or dialogue delivered by an announcer who is not seen but whose voice is heard.

volume discount Discount given to advertisers for purchasing print space or broadcast time in bulk quantities.

volume segmentation Defining consumers as light, medium, or heavy users of products.

wants Desires learned during a person's lifetime.

Warrior role A role in the creative process that overcomes excuses, idea killers, setbacks, and obstacles to bring a creative concept to realization.

Web 2.0 The intersection of Web application features the facilitate participatory sharing.

Web browser Computer program that provides computer users with a graphical interface to the World Wide Web.

Web design houses Art/computer studios that employ specialists who understand the intricacies of HTML and Java programming languages and can design ads and Internet Web pages that are both effective and cost efficient.

Web page A single page out of an online publication of the World Wide Web, known as a Website. Websites are made up of one or more Web pages and allow individuals or companies to provide information and services with the public through the Internet.

Website An Internet destination designed to be read in a Web browser.

weekly newspapers Newspapers that are published once a week and characteristically serve readers in small urban or suburban areas or farm communities with exclusive emphasis on local news and advertising.

wiki A Website whose users can add, modify, or delete its content via a browser using a rich text editor.

word of mouth (WOM) The passing of information from one individual to another individual.

work print The first visual portion of a filmed commercial assembled without the extra effects or dissolves, titles, or supers. At this time, scenes may be substituted, music and sound effects added, or other changes made.

World Wide Web (WWW) A hypertext-based, distributed information system designed to be interpreted by Web browser such as Internet Explorer or Mozilla Firefox.

writing paper Form of plain, lightweight paper commonly used for printing fliers and for letterhead.

endnotes

Chapter One

1. La Rubia, "Shakira's Activia Ad is Confusing Everyone," *LasGringasBlog*, March 30, 2014, http://lasgringasblog.com/2014/03/shakiras-activia-ad-confusing/.

2. Avi Dan, "11 Marketing Trends to Watch for in 2015," *Forbes*, November 9, 2014, http://www.forbes.com/sites/avidan/2014/11/09/11-marketing-trends-to-watch-for-in-2015/.

3. MDG Advertising, "The Five Most Important Digital Marketing Trends to Watch 2015," Advertising and Marketing Blog, January 5, 2015, http://www.mdgadvertising.com/blog/the-5-most-important-digital-marketing-trends-to-watch-in-2015/.

4. Mark Hoelzel, "The Social-Media Advertising Report: Growth Forecasts, Market Trends, and the Rise of Mobile," *Business Insider*, December 2, 2014, http://www.businessinsider.com/socialmedia-advertising-spending-growth-2014-9.

5. Grace Chung, "Shakira's Activia-Sponsored Music Video Vanquishes 'The Force' as Most-Shared Ad," *Advertising Age*, July 30, 2014, http://adage.com/article/digital/activia-s-video-shakirashared/294398/.

6. Corrine Gretler, "Danone First-Quarter Sales beat Estimates on Dairy Rebound," *Bloomberg Business*, April 15, 2015, http://www.bloomberg.com/news/articles/2015-04-15/danone-firstquarter-sales-beat-estimates-on-baby-food-boost.

7. Stephen R. Fox, *The Mirror Makers: A History of American Advertising and Its Creators* (University of Chicago Illinois Press, 1997).

8. Jef I. Richards and Catharine M. Curran, "Oracles on 'Advertising': Searching for a Definition," *Journal of Advertising* 31 (2002), pp. 63–77.

9. Steve Olenski, "This is the Most Important Word When it Comes to Relationship Marketing," *Forbes*, May 09, 2013, http://www.forbes.com/sites/marketshare/2013/05/09/this-is-the-mostimportant-word-when-it-comes-to-relationship-marketing/.

10. Lisa Nirell, *The Mindful Marketer* (London: Palgrave Macmillan, 2014); Larry Weber and Lisa L. Henderson, *The Digital Marketer* (Wiley, 2014).

11. Philip Kotler and Kevin Lane Keller, *Marketing Management* (New York, NY: Pearson, 2011).

12. Rolph Anderson, Sriinvasan Swaminathan, and Rajiv Mehta, "Prospering in Tough Economic Times Through Loyal Customers," *International Journal of Management and Economics* 41 (2014), pp. 76–91.

13. Ibid.

14. D. Van den Poel and B. Larivière, "Customer Attrition Analysis for Financial Services Using Proportional Hazard Models," *European Journal of Operational Research* 157 (2004), pp. 196–217

14. Kotler and Keller, Marketing Management.

15. Philip Kotler and Gary Armstrong, *Principles of Marketing* (Englewood Cliffs, NJ: Prentice Hall, 2014).

16. Jessica Tsai, "Are You Smarter Than a Neuromarketer?" *Customer Relationship Management*, January 2010, pp. 19–20.

17. E. J. Shultz, "Mtn Dew Plans Big Spending Boost behind Kickstart, Diet Dew," *Advertising Age*, 2014, http://adage.com/article/news/mtn-dew-plans-big-spending-boost-kickstart-dietdew/291192/.

18. Kotler and Armstrong, Principles of Marketing.

19. Sandra Luxton, Mike Reid and Felix Mavondo, "Integrated Marketing Communication Capability and Brand Performance," *Journal of Advertising* 44 (2015), pp. 37–46.

20. Glen Nowak and Joseph Phelps, "Conceptualizing the Integrated Marketing Communications Phenomenon: An Examination of Its Impact on Advertising Practices and Its Implications for Advertising Research," *Journal of Current Issues and Research in Advertising*, Spring (1994), pp. 49–66.

21. ibid.

22. Jerry G. Kiatchko, "Revisiting the IMC Construct: A Revised Definition and Four Pillars," *International Journal of Advertising* 27 (2008), pp. 133–160.

23. Charles R. Taylor, "Integrated Marketing Communications in 2010 and Beyond," *International Journal of Advertising* 29 (2010), p. 161.

24. Thomas R. Duncan and Sandra E. Moriarty, *Driving Brand Value: Using Integrated Marketing to Manage Stakeholder Relationships* (New York: McGraw-Hill, 1997).

25. ibid.

26. Jerry G. Kliatchko and Don E. Shultz, "Twenty years of IMC: A study of CEO and CMO Perspectives in the Asia-Pacific Region," *International Journal of Advertising* 33 (2014), pp. 373–390, http://www.academia.edu/7295960/Twenty_Years_of_IMC.

27. Luxton, Sandra, Mike Reid, and Felix Mavondo, "Integrated Marketing Communication Capability and Brand Performance," *Journal of Advertising* 44 (2014): pp. 37–46.

28. Claude Elwood Shannon and Warren Weaver, *The Mathematical Theory of Communication* (University of Chicago Illinois Press, 1971).

29. Barbara B. Stern, "A Revised Communication Model for Advertising: Multiple Dimensions of the Source, the Message, and the Recipient," *Journal of Advertising*, June 1994, pp. 5–15.

30. Definition of Marketing, American Marketing Association, www.marketingpower.com/AboutAMA/Pages/DefinitionofMarketing.aspx.

Chapter Two

1. "The Story of Coca-Cola," http://heritage.coca-cola.com/The_Story_of_Coca-Cola.pdf; Barbara Mikkelson, "Cocaine-Cola," *Urban Legends Reference Pages: Coca-Cola,* May 2, 1999, www.snopes.com/cokelore/cocaine.asp.

2. Quoted in Frederick Allen, *Secret Formula: How Brilliant Marketing and Relentless Salesmanship Made Coca-Cola the Best-Known Product in the World* (New York: HarperCollins, 1994), p. 76; U.S. Library of Congress American Memory Collection, "Highlights in the History of Coca-Cola Television Advertising," updated November 29, 2000, http://memory.loc.gov/ammem/ccmphtml/colahist.html#darcy.

3. Donald Keough, quoted in Blair Matthews, "Coca-Cola's Big Mistake: New Coke 20 Years Later," *Soda Pop Dreams Magazine*, Spring 2005, www.pww.on.ca/36_newcoke.htm; Barbara Mikkelson, "Knew Coke," *Urban Legends Reference Pages: Coca-Cola,* May 2, 1999, www.snopes.com/cokelore/snewcoke.asp.

4. Marc Inboden, quoted in "Ads Aim to Put Fizz Back in Coke," *Tulsa World*, April 2, 2006, p. E3.

5. Super Bowl Commercials, "Coca Cola #Make It Happy," http://www.superbowl-commercials.org/35151.html.

6. N. Gregory Mankiw, *Principles of Economics* (Cengage, 2014), p. 10.

7. Quoted in "The Chronicle of Coca-Cola: Birth of a Refreshing Idea," www2.coca-cola.com/heritage/chronicle_birthrefreshing_idea.html; Coca-Cola Heritage Timeline, http://heritage.coca-cola.com; Barbara Mikkelson, "Design Err Shape," *Urban Legends Reference Pages: Coca-Cola,* May 2, 1999, www.snopes.com/cokelore/bottle.asp.

8. "The Chronicle of Coca-Cola," op. cit.; Jack Hayes, "Dr. John S. Pemberton (inventor of Coca-Cola)," *Nation's Restaurant News*,

February 1996, pp. 120–21, Library of Congress American Memory Project, *http://rs6.loc.gov/ammem/ccmphtml/colainvnt.html.*

9. Frederick Allen, *Secret Formula: How Brilliant Marketing and Relentless Salesmanship Made Coca-Cola the Best-Known Product in the World* (New York: HarperCollins, 1994), cited in Eleanor Jones and Florian Ritzmann, "Coca-Cola Goes to War: Coca-Cola at Home," *http://xroads.virginia.edu/~class/coke/coke.html*; Pat Watters, *Coca-Cola: An Illustrated History* (New York: Doubleday, 1978), cited in Eleanor Jones and Florian Ritzmann, "Coca-Cola Goes to War: Coca-Cola at Home," *http://xroads.virginia.edu/~class/coke/coke.html.*

10. "Sales Call Costs," *The Controller's Report,* January 2001, p. 9; Claire Atkinson, "Cost of 'American Idol' Finale Spot Hits $1.3 Million," *Advertising Age* (online) April 17, 2006.

11. Scott M. Davis and Michael Dunn, *Building the Brand-Driven Business* (San Francisco: Wiley, 2002), p. 15.

12. Ibid., pp. 17–18.

13. William O'Barr, address to the Council on Advertising History, Duke University, March 12, 1993, reported in *Advertising in America: Using Its Past, Enriching Its Future* (Washington, DC: Center for Advertising History of the National Museum of American History, 1994), p. 6.

14. Leonard L. Bartlett, "Three Giants—Leo Burnett, David Ogilvy, William Bernbach: An Exploration of the Impact of the Founders' Written Communications on the Destinies of Their Advertising Agencies," paper presented to the annual meeting of the Association for Education in Journalism and Mass Communication, Kansas City, August 13, 1993.

15. Marcel Bleustein-Blanchet, *La Rage de Convaincre* (Paris: Editions Robert Laffont, 1970), pp. 307–10, 375; Jean-Marc Schwarz, "A Brief History of Ad Time," *Adweek,* February 14, 1994, p. 46.

16. Schwarz, "A Brief History of Ad Time."

17. Ibid.

18. Ibid.

19. Cannon, *Course Packet for Advertising Management.*

20. William F. Arens and Jack J. Whidden, "La Publicité aux Etats-Unis: Les Symptômes et les Stratégies d'une Industrie Surpeuplée," *L'Industrie de la Publicité au Québec* (Montreal: Le Publicité Club de Montréal, 1992), pp. 383–84.

21. Warren Berger, "Chaos on Madison Avenue," *Los Angeles Times Magazine,* June 5, 1994, pp. 12, 14.

22. Bob Coen, "Bob Coen's Insider's Report," December 2002, McCann-Erickson WorldGroup, *www.universalmccann.com/ourview.html.*

23. Judann Pollock, "Marketing Put on Hold," *Advertising Age,* September 17, 2001, pp. 1, 25.

24. Coen, "Bob Coen's Insider's Report."

25. R. Craig Endicott, "Interactive Marketing & Media Fact Pack 2006," *Advertising Age,* April 17, 2006, p. 10.

26. Tom Cuniff, "The Second Creative Revolution," *Advertising Age,* December 6, 1993, p. 22.

27. "US, China, Japan, Germany and the UK Lead as the Top Five Ad Markets," eMarketer, December 10, 2014, *http://www.emarketer.com/Article/Advertisers-Will-Spend-Nearly-600-Billion-Worldwide-2015/1011691.*

28 Matt Schiavenza, "China Economy Surpasses US in Purchasing Power, But Americans Don't Need to Worry," *International Business Times,* October 8, 2014, *http://www.ibtimes.com/china-economy-surpasses-us-purchasing-power-americans-dont-need-worry-1701804.*

29. Jason Abbruzzese, "Showtime Planning Standalone Internet Offering," Mashable, November 5, 2014, *http://mashable.com/2014/11/05/showtime-internet-offering/.*

30. Newspaper Association of America, "Trends and Numbers," updated May 25, 2012, *www.naa.org/Trends-and-Numbers/Advertising-Expenditures/Quarterly-All-Categories.aspx.*

Chapter Three

1. Jagdish Agrawal and Wagner A. Kamakura, "The Economic Worth of Celebrity Endorsers," *Journal of Marketing* 59 (2005), pp. 56–63.

2. Jeremy Mullen, "Reducing the Risk of Vick-timization," *Advertising Age,* July 23, 2007, *http://web.ebscohost.com.lp.hscl.ufl.edu/ehost/detail?vid=4&hid=109&sid=4dc8792c-c1b3-4c6d-9798-4d64035c4755%40sessionmgr108.*

3. John O'Toole, *The Trouble with Advertising* (New York: Times Books, 1985), pp. 7–14.

4. Eric Chemi, "Advertising's Century of Flat-Line Growth," *Bloomberg Business,* March 3, 2014, *http://www.bloomberg.com/bw/articles/2014-03-03/advertisings-century-of-flat-line-growth.*

5. "Average Ad Spending per Capita," Marketing Charts, June 12, 2015, *http://www.marketingcharts.com/traditional/average-ad-spending-per-capita-us-tops-list-51916/attachment/strategyanalytics-average-ad-spend-per-capita-in-2014-mar2015/.*

6. Ernest Dichter, *Handbook of Consumer Motivations* (New York: McGraw-Hill, 1964), pp. 6, 422–31.

7. Richard E. Kihlstrom and Michael H. Riordan, "Advertising as a Signal," *Journal of Political Economy,* June 1984, pp. 427–50.

8. Steve McKee, "What Should You Spend on Advertising?," *Bloomberg Businessweek,* February 10, 2009, *www.businessweek.com/smallbiz/content/feb2009/sb20090210_165498.htm.*

9. John Kenneth Galbraith, "Economics and Advertising: Exercise in Denial," *Advertising Age,* November 9, 1988, pp. 80–84.

10. Fabiana Giacomotti, "European Marketers Keep Up Ad Budgets," *Adweek,* January 24, 1994, pp. 16–17.

11. Michael Schudson, *Advertising, The Uneasy Persuasion: Its Dubious Impact on American Society* (New York: Basic Books, 1984).

12. Ivan Preston, "A New Conception of Deceptiveness," paper presented to the Advertising Division of the Association for Education in Journalism and Mass Communication, August 12, 1993.

13. Ibid.

14. "Pizza Hut Files Suit against Pizza Rival," *Advertising Age,* August 13, 1998; "Papa John's Ordered to Move 'Better' Slogan," *Advertising Age,* January 5, 2000, *http://adage.com.*

15. Barry Newman, "An Ad Professor Huffs against Puffs, but It's a Quixotic Enterprise," *The Wall Street Journal,* January 24, 2003, pp. A1, A9.

16. Ivan Preston, *The Tangled Web They Weave* (Madison: University of Wisconsin Press, 1994), pp. 185–98.

17. Andrew Jaffe, "Advertiser, Regulate Thyself," *Adweek,* August 2, 1993, p. 38.

18. Ibid.

19. Preston, *The Tangled Web They Weave,* p. 164.

20. Kevin Downey, "TV Ad Clutter Worsens, and Buyers Grouse," *Media Life,* February 15, 2002, *www.medialifemagazine.com.*

21. Brian Steinberg, "Spike's Supersized Ad Breaks Buck TV's Clutter-Busting Trend," *Ad Age Media News,* September 13, 2010.

22. Sean Leahy, "Encouraging Words for Less Is More," *Media Life,* July 20, 2005, *www.medialifemagazine.com/News2005/jul05/jul18/3_wed/news2wednesday.html.*

23. FCC Guide, "Commercial Time Limitations," *www.fcc.gov/guides/childrens-educational-television.*

24. Europa, "TV without Frontiers: Commission Proposes Modernised Rules for Digital Era TV and TV-Like Services," press release, December 13, 2005, *http://europa.eu.int/rapid/pressReleasesAction.do?reference=IP/05/1573.*

25. Cliff Peale and Gregory Korte, "Drowning in TV Political Ads?" *Cincinnati Enquirer,* October 30, 2004, *www.enquirer.com/editions/2004/10/30/loc_elexads.html.*

26. Steve Mcclellan, "Political Ad Spend to Soar," *Adweek,* August 23, 2010.

27. Shelly Garcia, "What's Wrong with Being Politically Correct?" *Adweek,* November 15, 1993, p. 62.

28. Adrienne Ward, "What Role Do Ads Play in Racial Tension?" *Advertising Age,* August 10, 1992, pp. 1, 35.

29. Joy Dietrich, "Women Reach High," *Advertising Age International,* January 1, 2000; quoted in Genaro C. Armas, "Women Gaining in Workplace," *Advocate,* Baton Rouge, LA, April 24, 2000 (retrieved from Lexis-Nexis Academic Universe).

30. U.S. Census Bureau, *Statistical Abstract of the United States,* 2007, www.census.gov.

31. John B. Ford and Michael S. LaTour, "Differing Reactions to Female Role Portrayals in Advertising," *Journal of Advertising Research,* September/October 1993, pp. 43–52.

32. Gavin O'Malley, "Marketers Advised to Target Ethnic Preferences," *Online Media Daily,* November 29, 2011.

33. "Revealing Abercrombie Catalog Sparks a Boycott," *Cincinnati Enquirer,* June 26, 2001, www.enquirer.com/editions/2001/06/26/tem_revealing.htm.

34. "Intimacy Ads Gain Prime-Time Permission," *Drug Store News,* September 26, 2005, p. 70.

35. Laurel Wentz and Geoffrey Lee Martin, "Cheaply Made Gore Scores," *Advertising Age,* July 4, 1994, p. 38.

36. William M. O'Barr, "Sex and Advertising," *Advertising & Society Review* 12, no. 2 (2011), http://muse.jhu.edu/journals/advertising_and_society_review/v012/12.2.o-barr.html.

37. John E. Calfee, "Fear of Persuasion: A New Perspective on Advertising and Regulation," 96 (Agora Association, 1997).

38. Robert W. McChesney, *The Political Economy of Media: Enduring Issues, Emerging Dilemmas* (New York: Monthly Review Press, 2008).

39. Ivan Preston, *The Tangled Web They Weave* (Madison: University of Wisconsin Press, 1994), pp. 94, 127–31.

40. James Maxeiner and Peter Schotthoffer, eds., *Advertising Law in Europe and North America* (Deventer, the Netherlands: Kluwer Law and Taxation Publishers, 1992), p. v; Rein Rijkens, *European Advertising Strategies* (London: Cassell, 1992), pp. 201–2.

41. Bob Sullivan, "'La difference' is Stark in EU, U.S. Privacy Laws," *NBCNews,com,* October 19, 2006, http://www.nbcnews.com/id/15221111/ns/technology_and_science-privacy_lost/t/ladifference-stark-eu-us-privacy-laws/#.VYFJfs9VhBc.

42. Jo Best, "Google has to Apply 'Right to Be Forgotten' Everywhere, Says France," *ZDNet,* June 15, 2015, http://www.zdnet.com/article_google-has-to-apply-right-to-be-forgotteneverywhere-says-france/.

43. Karly Preslmayer, "Austria," in Maxeiner and Schotthoffer, eds., *Advertising Law in Europe and North America.*

44. Peter Schotthoffer, "European Community," in Maxeiner and Schotthoffer, eds., *Advertising Law in Europe and North America,* p. 89.

45. "Last Minute News: Singapore Condemns Ads with Harmful Values," *Advertising Age,* August 29, 1994, p. 42.

46. Steven Elsinga, "New Advertising Law Expected in China," *China Briefing,* March 4, 2015, http://www.china-briefing.com/news/2015/03/04/new-advertising-lawexpected.html.

47. Ad Age Staff, "The Golden Rules of Operating in China," *Advertising Age,* April 23, 2012, http://adage.com/china/article/china-news/the-golden-rules-ofoperating-in-china/234257/.

48. Supreme Court of the United States, "Valentine, Police Commissioner of the City of New York v. Chrestensen," www.bc.edu/bc_org/avp/cas/comm/free_speech/valentine.html.

49. James R. Maxeiner, "United States," in Maxeiner and Schotthoffer, eds., *Advertising Law in Europe and North America,* p. 321; see also *Virginia State Board of Pharmacy v. Virginia Citizens Consumer Council,* 425 U.S. 748 (1976).

50. See *Central Hudson Gas & Electric Corp. v. Public Service Commission of New York,* 447 U.S. 557 (1980).

51. Steven W. Colford, "Big Win for Commercial Speech," *Advertising Age,* March 29, 1993, pp. 1, 47.

52. "Tobacco Settlement Agreement at a Glance," National Association of Attorneys General Website, www.naag.org.

53. Joy Johnson Wilson, "Summary of the Attorneys General Master Tobacco Settlement Agreement," March 1999, http://academic.udayton.edu/health/syllabi/tobacco/summary.htm.

54. John Malmo, "Restricting Commercial Speech Isn't Justifiable," *The Commercial Appeal,* Memphis, TN, July 5, 1999, p. B3; John Malmo, "Banning Tobacco Ads Spells Monopoly," *The Commercial Appeal,* Memphis, TN, August 9, 1999, p. B4 (retrieved from ProQuest).

55. U.S. Food and Drug Administration, "Electronic Cigarettes (e-Cigarettes), http://www.fda.gov/NewsEvents/PublicHealthFocus/ucm172906.htm.

56. Monte Morin, "Jury is out on health effects of e-cigarettes," *Los Angeles Times,* January 16, 2014, http://articles.latimes.com/2014/jan/16/science/la-sci-e-cigarettes-science-20140117.

57. Children's Advertising Review Unit, "Self-Regulatory Program for Children's Advertising," Council of Better Business Bureau, Inc., 2008, www.caru.org/guidelines.

58. "A Spoonful of Sugar: Television Food Advertising Aimed at Children: An International Comparative Survey," Consumers International.

59. Richard Qiu, "Beyond the Cookie: Digital Advertising and Privacy in the Cross-Screen Age," *The Guardian,* September 25, 2013, http://www.theguardian.com/media-network/media-network-blog/2013/sep/25/cookiedigital-advertising-privacy-screens.

60. Simon Hill, "Google Photos: Should you be Worried about Privacy?" *Android Authority,* June 16, 2015, http://www.androidauthority.com/google-photosworried-privacy-616339/.

61. Mark Sakalosky, "DoubleClick's Double Edge," ClickZ, September 3, 2002.

62. Mary Madden, "Privacy and Cybersecurity: Key fidings from Pew Research," Pew Research Center, January 16, 2015, http://www.pewresearch.org/key-datapoints/privacy/.

63. www.ftc.gov/os/2000/07/onlineprofiling.htm.

64. Eric Gross and Susan Vogt, "Canada," in Maxeiner and Schotthoffer, eds., *Advertising Law in Europe and North America,* pp. 39, 41.

65. Federal Trade Commission, "Vision, Mission, and Goals," 1997.

66. Minette E. Drumwright, "Ethical Issues in Advertising and Sales Promotion," in N. Craig Smith and John A. Quelch, eds., *Ethics in Marketing* (Burr Ridge, IL: Irwin, 1993), p. 610.

67. Ann Carrns, "FTC Settles with Office Depot, Buy.com, Value America over 'Low Cost' PC Ads," *The Wall Street Journal,* June 30, 2000, p. B4.

68. Dean Keith Fueroghne, *But the People in Legal Said . . .* (Burr Ridge, IL: Professional, 1989), p. 14.

69. Christy Fisher, "How Congress Broke Unfair Ad Impasse," *Advertising Age,* August 22, 1994, p. 34.

70. "Editorial: A Fair FTC Pact?" *Advertising Age,* March 21, 1994, p. 22.

71. "Arizona Trade Association Agrees to Settle FTC Charges It Urged Members to Restrain Competitive Advertising," FTC News Release, February 25, 1994, www.ftc.gov/opa/predawn/F95/azautodealers.htm.

72. "Comparative Advertising," ADLAW, copyright 2000 Hall Dickler Kent Goldstein & Wood, www.adlaw.com/rc/handbk/rf_comparative.html.

73. "Crackdown on Testimonials," *The Wall Street Journal,* July 13, 1993, p. B7.

74. Drumwright, "Ethical Issues in Advertising and Sales Promotion," pp. 615–16.

75. Ira Teinowitz, "Doan's Decision Sets Precedent for Corrective Ads," *Advertising Age,* September 4, 2000, p. 57.

76. Gross and Vogt, "Canada," pp. 50, 67.

77. www.census.gov and www.fda.gov.

78. www.fda.gov.

79. "The Growing Brouhaha over Drug Advertisements," *The New York Times,* May 14, 1989, p. F8.

80. "FDA to Review Standards for All Direct-to-Consumer Rx Drug Promotion," FDA news release, August 8, 1997.

81. Jean Grow, "'Your Life Is Waiting!': Symbolic Meanings in Direct-to-Consumer Antidepressant Advertising," *Journal of Communication Inquiry,* April 2006, pp. 163–88.

82. "FDA Seeks Rx for Drug Ads; New Policy Delays Process," *Newsday* (Nassau and Suffolk edition), December 5, 2002.

83. Steven W. Colford, "Labels Lose the Fat," *Advertising Age,* June 10, 1991, pp. 3, 54; Steven W. Colford and Julie Liesse, "FDA Label Plans under Attack," *Advertising Age,* February 24, 1992, pp. 1, 50; John E. Calfee, "FDA's Ugly Package: Proposed Label Rules Call for Vast Changes," *Advertising Age,* March 16, 1992, p. 25; Pauline M. Ippolito and Alan D. Mathios, "New Food Labeling Regulations and the Flow of Nutrition Information to Consumers," *Journal of Public Policy & Marketing,* Fall 1993, pp. 188–205.

84. John Carey, "The FDA Is Swinging a Sufficiently Large Two-by-Four," *BusinessWeek,* May 27, 1991, p. 44; Steven W. Colford, "FDA Getting Tougher: Seizure of Citrus Hill Is Signal to Marketers," *Advertising Age,* April 29, 1991, pp. 1, 53.

85. Joe Mandese, "Regulation," *Advertising Age,* November 30, 1992, p. 23.

86. Todd Shields, "Viacom Battles FCC Kids' Ad Rules," *Media-Week,* October 10, 2005, www.mediaweek.com/mw/news/recent_display.jsp?vnu_content_id=1001263021.

87. U.S. Constitution, Article 1, Section 8.

88. U.S. Copyright Office, Library of Congress, 1997.

89. Wayne E. Green, "Lawyers Give Deceptive Trade-Statutes New Day in Court, Wider Interpretations," *The Wall Street Journal,* January 24, 1990, p. B1.

90. Howard Schlossberg, "Marketers Say State Laws Hurt Their 'Green' Efforts," *Marketing News,* November 11, 1991, pp. 8–9.

91. Frank Phillips, "Mass. in Court to Defend Curbs on Tobacco Ads," *Boston Globe,* April 7, 2000, p. A1; Gaylord Shaw, "Smoking Ads a Smoldering Issue: High Court May Review City's Ban on Tobacco Displays," *Newsday,* Long Island, NY, March 18, 2000, p. A31.

92. E. J. Gong, "Fraud Complaints on the Rise, Reports D.A.," *Los Angeles Times,* February 13, 1994, p. B1.

93. "Closet Factory to Pay Penalty for Misleading Advertising," Orange County District Attorney press release, June 24, 2002.

94. Maxeiner, "United States," p. 321.

95. Ibid.

96. Felix H. Kent, "Control of Ads by Private Sector," *New York Law Journal,* December 27, 1985; reprinted in Kent and Stone, eds., *Legal and Business Aspects of the Advertising Industry,* 1986, pp. 20–79.

97. www.narbreview.org.

98. "NAD Pilots Successful Resolution between Neil Cooper and Avirex," Better Business Bureau news release, August 11, 2000, www.nadreview.org/casereports.asp.

99. "Self-Regulatory Principles for Online Behavioral Advertising," http://www.iab.net/media/file/ven-principles-07-01-09.pdf.

100. Public Relations Department, KLBJ, Austin, TX, 1991.

101. Public Relations Department, KDWB, Minneapolis/St. Paul, MN, 1991.

102. Public Relations Department, KSDO, San Diego, CA, 1991.

103. Kevin Goldman, "From Witches to Anorexics, Critical Eyes Scrutinize Ads for Political Correctness," *The Wall Street Journal,* May 19, 1994, p. B1.

104. Garcia, "What's Wrong with Being Politically Correct?" p. 62.

105. Ibid.

106. Jaffe, "Advertiser, Regulate Thyself," p. 38.

107. Federal Trade Commission, 1991.

Chapter Four

1. United States Census, "Business & Industry," www.census.gov/econ.

2. www.bajagrill.com.

3. Jim Rowe, "Integrated Marketing Tips? Study Retail Trade," *Advertising Age,* April 4, 1994, p. 32.

4. Henry A. Laskey, J. A. F. Nicholls, and Sydney Roslow, "The Enigma of Cooperative Advertising," *Journal of Business and Industrial Marketing* 8, no. 2 (1993), pp. 70–79.

5. Kathy Crosett, "Best of 2012: CPG Trade Promotion, Co-op Ads Shifting to Digital in 2012," *Audience Scan,* December 19, 2012, http://www.audiencescan.com/best-of-2012-cpg-trade-promotion-co-op-ads-shifting-to-digital-in-2012/.

6. David Barkholz, "Ford Co-op Program Pushes More Digital Ads," *Automotive News,* June 19, 2015, http://www.autonews.com/article/20140113/RETAIL/301139986/ford-co-op-program-pushes-more-digital-ads.

7. "Helping Dealers Sell More Tires," *Printing Impressions* 48, no. 4 (2005), p. 96.

8. "100 Leading National Advertisers, 2014," *Ad Age DataCenter,* http://adage.com/article/datacenter-advertising-spending/100-leading-national-advertisers/293054/.

9. Ibid.

10. "Brands," General Mills, http://www.generalmills.com/en/Brands/Overview.

11. William O. Bearden, Thomas N. Ingram, and Raymond W. LaForge, *Marketing Principles & Perspectives* (Burr Ridge, IL: Irwin, 1995), p. 96.

12. http://www.pginvestor.com/.

13. "100 Leading National Advertisers."

14. Alan Mitchell, "P&G Drops Old Job Tags in Rejig," *Marketing* (UK), October 14, 1993, p. 4.

15. Aelita G. B. Martinsons and Maris G. Martinsons, "In Search of Structural Excellence," *Leadership & Organization Development Journal* 15, no. 2 (1994), pp. 24–28.

16. Ellen Byron, "P&G's Internal Memo on Management Shakeup," *Wall Street Journal,* October 22, 2014, http://blogs.wsj.com/corporate-intelligence/2014/10/22/pgs-internal-memo-on-management-shakeup/.

17. E. Jerome McCarthy and William D. Perreault Jr., *Basic Marketing,* 11th ed. (Burr Ridge, IL: Irwin, 1993), p. 593.

18. "Global Marketer's Index," *Ad Age DataCenter,* December 7, 2014, http://adage.com/article/datacenter-advertising-spending/global-marketers-index/106350/.

19. Eric N. Berkowitz, Roger A. Kerin, Steven W. Hartley, and William Rudelius, *Marketing,* 3rd ed. (Burr Ridge, IL: Irwin, 1992), p. 609.

20. Strategiy.com, www.strategiy.com/consumerproductsnew.asp?id=20050526141229.

21. James E. Ellis, "Why Overseas? 'Cause That's Where the Sales Are," *BusinessWeek,* January 10, 1994, p. 63; "How CAA Bottled Coca-Cola," *Fortune,* November 15, 1993, p. 156; Deborah Hauss, "Global Communications Come of Age," *Public Relations Journal,* August 1993, pp. 22–23; Sally Solo, "How to Listen to Consumers," *Fortune,* January 11, 1993, pp. 77–78; Jennifer Lawrence, "Delta Gears Up for Global Fight," *Advertising Age,* August 19, 1991, pp. 3, 44; Charles Hennessy, "Globaldegook," *BusinessLondon,* March 1990, p. 131; Raymond Serafin, "W. B. Doner Hits a Gusher," *Advertising Age,* June 6, 1988, p. 43.

22. Jim Patterson, "Viewpoint: Global Communication Requires a Global Understanding," *Adweek,* October 31, 1994, p. 46; "Efficacy of Global Ad Prospects Is Questioned in Firm's Survey," *The Wall Street Journal,* September 13, 1984, p. 29.

23. Patterson, "Viewpoint: Global Communication Requires a Global Understanding."

24. Martinsons and Martinsons, "In Search of Structural Excellence."

25. Frederick R. Gamble, *What Advertising Agencies Are—What They Do and How They Do It,* 7th ed. (New York: American Association of Advertising Agencies, 1970), p. 4.

26. "Brands on Trial," *Adweek,* May 24, 1993, pp. 24–31.

27. Melanie Wells, "The Interactive Edge—Part II: Desperately Seeking the Super Highway," *Advertising Age,* August 22, 1994, pp. 14–19.

28. Jennifer Gilbert, "Gotham Gathers Interactive under Hinkaty," *Advertising Age,* July 31, 2000, p. 42, http://webgate.sdsu.edu.

29. Andrew McMains, "Debunking the Consolidation Myth," *Adweek*, February 20, 2006, *www.adweek.com/aw/national/article_display.jsp?vnu_content_id=1002035233*.

30. *Advertising Age* Data Center, "World's 10 Largest Media Agencies," 2014.

31. Beth Snyder, "True North Unites Modem, Poppe into Digital Force," *Advertising Age*, May 1998, (Articles & Opinions, *http://adage.com*; Kate Maddox, "Agency Pitch Heats Up Camp Interactive Show," *Advertising Age*, August 1998, (Articles & Opinions, *http://adage.com*; "Think New Ideas Takes AnswerThink Moniker," *Advertising Age*, April 3, 2000, (Interactive Daily, *http://adage.com*.

32. "Inside the AAAA," *Fact Sheet*, American Association of Advertising Agencies, August 15, 2000, *www.aaaa.org/inside/about_us.html*.

33. Kevin Goldman, "IBM—Account Fight Lifts Planner Profile," *The Wall Street Journal*, October 26, 1993, p. B8.

34. Nancy D. Holt, "Workspaces/A Look at Where People Work," *The Wall Street Journal*, January 22, 2003, p. B6.

35. Sally Goll Beatty, "Leo Burnett Group to Decentralize U.S. Operations," *The Wall Street Journal*, September 17, 1997, p. B10; Sally Goll Beatty, "Leo Burnett to Offer Small-Agency Style," *The Wall Street Journal*, September 18, 1997, p. B4; Dottie Enrico, "Ad Agency Ready for a New Day," *USA Today*, September 19, 1997, p. 5B.

36. Alison Fahey, "Agencies Look to Shape Up, Slim Down," *Adweek*, August 16, 1993, p. 4.

37. William F. Arens and Jack J. Whidden, "La Publicité aux Etats-Unis: Les Symptómes et les Stratégies d'une Industrie Surpleuplée," *L'Industrie de la Publicité au Québec* (Montreal: Le Publicité-Club de Montréal, 1992), pp. 383–84.

38. Jon Lafayette and Cleveland Horton, "Shops to Clients: Pay Up—4A's Members Call for an End to Free Services," *Advertising Age*, March 19, 1990, pp. 1, 66.

39. Andrew Jaffe, "Has Leo Burnett Come to the End of the 'Free Overservice' Era?" *Adweek*, December 6, 1993, p. 46; Melanie Wells and Laurel Wentz, "Coke Trims Commissions," *Advertising Age*, January 31, 1994, p. 2.

40. John Micklethwait, "Cut the Ribbon," *The Economist*, June 9, 1990, pp. S16–S17; Tom Eisenhart, "Guaranteed Results' Plan May Suit Business Marketers," *Business Marketing*, July 1990, p. 32; Jim Kirk, "Miller Sets Free Rates," *Adweek*, January 24, 1994, p. 4.

41. James R. Willis Jr., "Winning New Business: An Analysis of Advertising Agency Activities," *Journal of Advertising Research*, September/October 1992, pp. 10–16.

42. Andrew Jaffe, "The Fine Art of Keeping Clients Happy While Chasing New Business," *Adweek*, May 9, 1994, p. 38.

43. Melanie Wells, "Courtship by Consultant," *Advertising Age*, January 31, 1994, pp. 10–11; "Accounts on the Move," *Advertising Age*, June 2, 1997, *http://adage.com*; "H&R Block Review Down to 3," *Advertising Age*, May 17, 2000, (Daily Deadline, *http://adage.com*; "Monster, L.L. Bean Open Account Review," *Advertising Age*, July 12, 2000, (Daily Deadline, *http://adage.com*; "Deutsch Tunes in $70 Mil DirecTV Account," *Advertising Age*, August 18, 2000, (Daily Deadline, *http://adage.com*.

44. Thorolf Helgesen, "Advertising Awards and Advertising Agency Performance," *Journal of Advertising Research*, July/August 1994, pp. 43–53.

45. Daniel B. Wackman, Charles T. Salmon, and Caryn C. Salmon, "Developing an Advertising Agency–Client Relationship," *Journal of Advertising Research*, December 1986/January 1987, pp. 21–28.

46. Kevin Goldman, "FCB Bumps Ayer as AT&T's Top Agency," *The Wall Street Journal*, November 22, 1994, p. B8.

47. Kevin Goldman, "Ties That Bind Agency, Client Unravel," *The Wall Street Journal*, November 16, 1994, p. B6.

48. Yumiko Ono, "Apple Picks TBWA," *The Wall Street Journal*, August 11, 1997, p. B3.

49. Burt Helm and David Kiley, "Wal-Mart Leaves Draft Out in the Cold," *Bloomberg Businessweek*, December 7, 2006.

50. Steven Raye, "Agencies, Clients: It's Mutual Contribution for Mutual Gain," *Brandweek*, September 12, 1994, p. 20; Ed Moser, "Inside Information," *Adweek*, January 24, 1994, p. 22; Mat Toor, "Fear and Favour in Adland," *Marketing* (UK), November 15, 1990, pp. 30–32.

51. Paul C. N. Mitchell, Harold Cataquet, and Stephen Hague, "Establishing the Causes of Disaffection in Agency–Client Relations," *Journal of Advertising Research*, March/April 1992, pp. 41–48.

52. Isabelle T. D. Szmigin, "Managing Quality in Business-to-Business Services," *European Journal of Marketing* 27, no. 1 (1993), pp. 5–21.

53. Ron Jackson, "If You Hire a Vendor, You Get a Vendor Mindset," *Marketing News*, April 25, 1991, pp. 13–14.

54. Steven A. Meyerowitz, "Ad Agency Conflicts: The Law and Common Sense," *Business Marketing*, June 1987, p. 16.

55. Andrew Jaffe, "For Agencies, Conflict Taboo Seems Strong as Ever," *Adweek*, January 24, 1994, p. 46.

56. Betsy Sharkey, "New Suit," *Adweek*, June 20, 1994, p. 20.

57. Newspaper Association of America, "Total Paid Circulation," *www.naa.org/TrendsandNumbers/Total-Paid-Circulation.aspx*.

58. "Circulation Data," The New York Times Company online, *www.nytco.com/inverstors-nyt-circulation.html*.

59. Magazine Publishers of America, *Magazines: A Comprehensive Guide and Handbook 2008/2009*, *www.magazine.org/research/index.aspx*.

60. U.S. Census Bureau, *Statistical Abstract of the United States*, "Information and Communications," *www.census.gov*.

61. Sean Savage, "For Firms on Network, Net Gains Can Be Great," *ComputerLink*, Knight Ridder News Service, November 29, 1994, pp. 3–4.

62. Amy Dockser Markus, "Advertising Breezes along the Nile River with Signs for Sale," *The Wall Street Journal*, July 18, 1997, p. A1.

Chapter Five

1. Walter Isaacson, *Steve Jobs* (New York: Simon & Schuster, 2011).

2. Ted Friedman, "Apple's 1984: The Introduction of the Macintosh in the Cultural History of Personal Computers." Revised version of a paper presented at the Society for the History of Technology Convention, Pasadena, CA, 1997, *www.duke.edu/~tlove/mac.htm*.

3. Caroline McCarthy, "Remembering the '1984' Super Bowl Mac Ad," cnet, January 23, 2009, *http://news.cnet.com/8301-13577_3-10148380-36.html*.

4. Tom Hormby, "The Story behind Apple's 1984 Ad," *http://lowendmac.com/orchard/06/1984-apple-superbowl-ad.html*.

5. 1984 Apple's Macintosh Commercial, *www.youtube.com/watch?v=OYecfV3ubP8*.

6. E. Jerome McCarthy and William D. Perreault Jr., *Basic Marketing: A Global-Managerial Approach*, 11th ed. (Burr Ridge, IL: Irwin, 1993), pp. 5–6; Eric N. Berkowitz, Roger A. Kerin, Steven W. Hartley, and William Rudelius, *Marketing*, 3rd ed. (Burr Ridge, IL: Irwin, 1992), p. 27.

7. Kathryn Kranhold, "Ford Woos 'Echo Boomers' with Live TV," *The Wall Street Journal*, August 13, 1999, p. B8.

8. James J. Kellaris, Anthony D. Cox, and Dena Cox, "The Effect of Background Music on Ad Processing: A Contingency Explanation," *Journal of Marketing*, October 1993, pp. 114–25.

9. William O. Bearden, Thomas N. Ingram, and Raymond W. LaForge, *Marketing Principles and Perspectives*, 2nd ed. (Burr Ridge, IL: Irwin/McGraw-Hill 1997), p. 49.

10. U.S. Census Bureau, *The 2012 Statistical Abstract*, January 3, 2012, *www.census.gov/compendia/statab/*.

11. Ibid.

12. Ibid.

13. Bearden, Ingram, and Laforge, *Marketing Principles and Perspectives*, p. 99.

14. S. Kent Stephan and Barry L. Tannenholz, "The Real Reason for Brand Switching," *Advertising Age*, June 13, 1994, p. 31.

15. "Ad Nauseum," *Advertising Age,* July 10, 2000.

16. Kellaris, Cox, and Cox, "The Effect of Background Music on Ad Processing," p. 123.

17. Alice Z. Cuneo, "Dockers Takes a Sexier Approach in New Ad Push," *Advertising Age,* January 19, 1999, p. 8.

18. Daniel Kahneman, *Thinking Fast and Slow* (New York: Farrar, Straus and Giroux, 2011).

19. Elnora W. Stuart, T. A. Shimp, and R. W. Engle, "Classical Conditioning of Consumer Attitudes: Four Experiments in an Advertising Context," *Journal of Consumer Research* 14 (1987), pp. 334–49.

20. Albert Bandura, "Social Cognitive Theory," in P. A. M. van Lange, A. W. Kruglanski, and E. T. Higgins, eds., *Handbook of Social Psychological Theories* (London: Sage, 2011), pp. 349–73.

21. J. Paul Peter and Jerry C. Olson, *Consumer Behavior and Marketing Strategy,* 4th ed. (Burr Ridge, IL: Irwin, 1996), p. 554.

22. R. E. Petty, J. T. Cacioppo, and D. Schumann, "Central and Peripheral Routes to Advertising Effectiveness: The Moderating Role of Involvement," *Journal of Consumer Research* 10, 1983, pp. 135–46.

23. This section and the model are adapted from Peter and Olson, *Consumer Behavior and Marketing Strategy,* pp. 554–55.

24. Ibid., pp. 556–57.

25. Yumiko Ono, "Overcoming the Stigma of Dishwashers in Japan," *The Wall Street Journal,* May 19, 2000, p. B2.

26. Karen A. Machleit, Chris T. Allen, and Thomas J. Madden, "The Mature Brand and Brand Interest: An Alternative Consequence of Ad-Evoked Affect," *Journal of Marketing,* October 1993, pp. 72–82.

27. Ibid.

28. Peter and Olson, *Consumer Behavior and Marketing Strategy,* p. 513.

29. Ken Dychtwald and Greg Gable, "Portrait of a Changing Consumer," *Business Horizons,* January/February 1990, pp. 62–74; Larry Light, "Trust Marketing: The Brand Relationship Marketing Mandate for the 90s," address to the American Association of Advertising Agencies annual meeting, Laguna Niguel, CA, April 23, 1993.

30. Colin McDonald, "Point of View: The Key Is to Understand Consumer Response," *Journal of Advertising Research,* September/October 1993, pp. 63–69.

31. McCarthy and Perreault, *Basic Marketing,* p. 204.

32. Vanessa O'Connell, "Nabisco Portrays Cookies as Boost to Women's Self-Esteem," *The Wall Street Journal,* July 10, 1998, p. B7.

33. John R. Rossiter and Larry Percy, *Advertising Communications and Promotion Management,* 2nd ed. (New York: McGraw-Hill, 1997), pp. 120–22.

34. Ibid., p. 121.

35. Ken Bryson and Lynne M. Casper, "Current Population Reports, Household and Family Characteristics: March 1997 and March 1998," U.S. Bureau of the Census; Laura Zinn, "Move Over, Boomers, the Busters Are Here—And They're Angry," *BusinessWeek,* December 14, 1992, pp. 74–82; Jeffrey Zaslow, "Children's Search for Values Leading to Shopping Malls," *The Wall Street Journal,* March 13, 1987; U.S. Census Bureau, *Statistical Abstract of the United States: 2006,* Table 53, *www.census.gov.*

36. "The Worth of the Cool: Asking Teenagers to Identify the Coolest Brands," *Adweek,* May 9, 1994, p. 18.

37. Greg Farrell, "Star Search," *Adweek,* December 6, 1993, p. 26.

38. Ashley Bergner, "Have Product Placements in Films Become a Necessary Evil?", morningsun.net, April 23, 2012, *www.morningsun.net/news/entertainment/x1780488795/Have-product-placements-in-films-become-a-necessary-evil.*

39. McCarthy and Perreault, *Basic Marketing,* p. 131; Peter and Olson, *Consumer Behavior and Marketing Strategy,* p. 368.

40. Carolyn A. Lin, "Cultural Differences in Message Strategies: A Comparison between American and Japanese TV Commercials," *Journal of Advertising Research,* July/August 1993, pp. 40–48.

41. Ibid.

42. Ibid.

43. Peter and Olson, *Consumer Behavior and Marketing Strategy,* p. 413.

44. U.S. Census Bureau, *Statistical Abstract of the United States: 2010, www.census.gov.*

45. "Hispanic Fact Pact 2005," *Advertising Age, http://adage.com/article?article_id=46168.*

46. Rebecca Purto, "Global Psychographics," *American Demographics,* December 1990, p. 8.

47. The classic studies on cognitive dissonance were initiated by Leon Festinger, *A Theory of Cognitive Dissonance* (Evanston, IL: Row, Peterson, 1957), p. 83; for more recent views, see Hugh Murray, "Advertising's Effect on Sales—Proven or Just Assumed?" *International Journal of Advertising* (UK) 5, no. 1 (1986), pp. 15–36; Delbert Hawkins, Roger Best, and Kenneth Coney, *Consumer Behavior,* 7th ed. (Burr Ridge, IL: McGraw-Hill/Irwin, 1998), pp. 609–10; Ronald E. Milliman and Phillip J. Decker, "The Use of Post-Purchase Communication to Reduce Dissonance and Improve Direct Marketing Effectiveness," *Journal of Business Communication,* Spring 1990, pp. 159–70.

48. Larry Light, "Advertising's Role in Building Brand Equity," speech to annual meeting of the American Association of Advertising Agencies, April 21, 1993.

Chapter Six

1. Axe Ads: Website, *http://axeads.blogspot.com/.*

2. Jeff Hirsch, "Reinvigorating the 'Solid Citizen' Brand," July 11, 2011, *www.therightbrainstudio.com/reinvigorating-the-%E2%80%9Csolid-citizen%E2%80%9D brand/.*

3. "Old Spice: The Man Your Man Could Smell Like," *www.youtube.com/watch?v=owGykVbfgUE.*

4. Todd Wasserman, "How Old Spice Revived a Campaign that No One Wanted to Touch," Mashable.com, *http://mashable.com/2011/11/01/old-spice-campaign/.*

5. Ibid.

6. Noreen O'Leary, Todd Wasserman, "Old Spice Campaign Smells Like a Sales Success, Too," *AdWeek,* July 25, 2010, *http://www.adweek.com/news/advertising-branding/old-spice-campaign-smells-sales-success-too-107588?page=2.*

7. S. Kent Stephan and Barry L. Tannenholz, "The Real Reason for Brand Switching," *Advertising Age,* June 13, 1994, p. 31, and "Six Categories That Hold Elusive Consumers," *Advertising Age,* June 20, 1994, p. 32.

8. Quoted in Al Stewart, "Edgy Ads, Burgers Drive CKE," *Orange County Business Journal* 27, no. 30 (July 26, 2004), p. 5.

9. "Descriptive Materials for the VALS2 Segmentation System," *Value and Lifestyles Program* (Menlo Park, CA: SRI International, 1989).

10. "Second City Elite," Nielsen: My Best Segments, 2014 PRIZM Segmentation Systems, *http://www.claritas.com/MyBestSegments/Default.jsp?ID=37&id1=1027&id2=10.*

11. "Weather or Not to Sell," *Personal Selling Power,* September 1994, p. 79.

12. Joel S. Dubow, "Occasion-Based vs. User-Based Benefit Segmentation: A Case Study," *Journal of Advertising Research,* March/April 1992, pp. 11–18.

13. "Hispanic Media and Marketing Factoids," Association of Hispanic Advertising Agencies Media Room, *www.ahaa.org/media/FinalFacts04.htm.*

14. Leon E. Wynter, "Business and Race: JCPenney Launches Diahann Carroll Line," *The Wall Street Journal,* July 2, 1997, p. B1.

15. Pallavi Gogoi, "Retailing, the High-Tech Way," *BusinessWeek Online,* July 6, 2005, *www.businessweek.com/technology/content/jul2005/tc2005076_5703.htm?campaign_id=search.*

16. Richard Fry, "This Year, Millennials Will Overtake Baby Boomers," Pew Research Center, January 16, 2015, *http://www.pewresearch.org/fact-tank/2015/01/16/this-year-millennials-willovertake-baby-boomers/.*

17. Ibid.

18. Mark Huffman, "Millennials Buy Cars Differently Than Their Parents," *Consumer Affairs*, September 15, 2014, http://www.consumeraffairs.com/news/millennials-buy-cars-differently-thantheir-parents-091514.html.

19. Eric Schlosser, "Meat & Potatoes," *Rolling Stone* 800, November 26, 1998 (retrieved via EBSCO).

20. Eric Schlosser, "The True Cost of America's Diet," *Rolling Stone* 794, September 3, 1998 (retrieved via EBSCO).

21. Peter D. Kiernan, "The World's Middle Class Is Growing—and America is Getting Left Behind," *Business Insider*, June 18, 2015, http://www.businessinsider.com/world-is-more-middleclass-2015-6.

22. Shoba Narayan, "India's Lust for Luxe," *Time.com*, April 3, 2006, www.time.com/time/nation/article/0,8599,1179415,00.html.

23. "Global Ad Spending Growth to Double This Year," *eMarketer*, July 9, 2014, http://www.emarketer.com/Article/Global-Ad-Spending-Growth-Double-This-Year/1010997.

24. Henry Assael and David F. Poltrack, "Can Demographic Profiles of Heavy Users Serve as a Surrogate for Purchase Behavior in Selecting TV Programs?" *Journal of Advertising Reserach*, January/February 1994, p. 11.

25. Sulekha Goyat, "The Basis of Market Segmentation: A Critical Review of the Literature," *European Journal of Business and Management*, 2011, Vol. 3.

26. SRI Consulting Business Intelligence, "Welcome to VALS," www.sric-bi.com/vals.

27. Ibid.

28. Ibid.

29. SRI Consulting Business Intelligence, "VALS Links Global Strategies to Local Efforts through GeoVALS," www.sric-bi.com/vals/geovals.shtml; SRI Consulting Business Intelligence, "Japan-Vals," www.sric-bi.com/vals/jvals.shtml.

30. "Re-Mapping the World of Consumers," special advertising section by Roper Starch Worldwide, *American Demographics*, October 2000.

31. "MindBase," http://thefuturescompany.com/what-we-do/mindbase/.

32. www.tvbehaviorgraphics.com/about.html.

33. Malcolm Gladwell, *The Tipping Point: How Little Things Can Make a Big Difference* (New York: Little, Brown, 2002).

34. Lewis C. Winters, "International Psychographics," *Marketing Research: A Magazine of Management & Application*, September 1992, pp. 48–49.

35. James Hutton, "A Theoretical Framework for the Study of Brand Equity and a Test of Brand Sensitivity in an Organizational Buying Context," dissertation, University of Texas, Austin, 1993.

36. William D. Perreault Jr. and E. Jerome Mccarthy, *Basic Marketing*, 12th ed. (Burr Ridge, IL: Irwin, 1996), p. 261.

37. *New Data for a New Economy*, U.S. Bureau of the Census, Economic Classification Policy Committee (Washington, DC: U.S. Department of Commerce, 1998).

38. U.S. Bureau of the Census, *Statistical Abstract of the United States: 1999*, 119th ed. (Washington, DC: U.S. Department of Commerce, 1999), pp. 741–42, 744.

39. Michael Schrage, "Think Big," *Adweek*, October 11, 1993, p. 25.

40. Perreault and McCarthy, *Basic Marketing*, pp. 48–49, 91–112.

41. Theresa Howard, "Levi's Charms Buyers Back," *USA Today*, October 10, 2004, www.usatoday.com/money/advertising/adtrack/2004-10-24-levis_x.htm.

42. Walter van Waterschoot and Christophe Van den Bulte, "The 4P Classification of the Marketing Mix Revisited," *Journal of Marketing*, October 1992, pp. 83–93.

43. The now widely popularized conceptual model of the 4Ps was developed by E. J. McCarthy, *Basic Marketing* (Homewood, IL: Irwin, 1960); the usage of the marketing mix derived from Neil H. Borden, "The Concept of the Marketing Mix," *Journal of Advertising Research*, June 1964, p. 27.

44. Perreault and McCarthy, *Basic Marketing*, pp. 310–21.

45. Gene Koprowski, "Cell Phone Services Vendors Banking on Mobile Gaming Apps," *TechNewsWorld*, April 8, 2006, www.technewsworld.com/story/49707.html.

46. "Use of Cellular Phones Trends Upward, Survey Shows," press release, Decision Analyst, Inc., July 24, 1998; Matthew Klein, "More Callers Unleashed," *Forecast*, September 1998, www.demographics.com.

47. Brian Wansink, "Making Old Brands New," *American Demographics*, December 1997, www.demographics.com.

48. Adapted from William O. Bearden, Thomas N. Ingram, and Raymond W. LaForge, *Marketing: Principles & Perspectives* (Burr Ridge, IL: Irwin, 1995), pp. 211–13; and from Philip Kotler and Gary Armstrong, *Principles of Marketing* (Englewood Cliffs, NJ: Prentice Hall, 1994), pp. 640–43.

49. Hank Seiden, *Advertising Pure and Simple, The New Edition* (New York: AMACOM, 1990), p. 11.

50. Pat Sabena, "Tough Market for New Products Requires Partnership," *Marketing Review*, June 1996, pp. 12–13.

51. Adrienne Ward Fawcett, "In Glut of New Products, 'Different' Becomes Key," *Advertising Age*, December 13, 1993, p. 28.

52. Seiden, *Advertising Pure and Simple*, pp. 23–30; Robert Pritikin, *Pritikin's Testament* (Englewood Cliffs, NJ: Prentice Hall, 1991), pp. 25–33.

53. "Snapple Promotional Campaign Pays for 40 Ad-Free Days on WFNX-FM," *Boston Business Journal*, May 26, 2006, http://boston.bizjournals.com/boston/stories/2006/05/22/daily64.html.

54. Haim Oren, "Branding Financial Services Helps Consumers Find Order in Chaos," *Marketing News*, March 29, 1993, p. 6.

55. Frank Bilorsky, "Grocers Labels Offer a New Kind of Branding," *Rochester Democrat and Chronicle*, July 11, 2004, www.rochesterdandc.com.

56. "The Best Global Brands; *BusinessWeek* and Interbrand Tell You What They're Worth," *BusinessWeek* Special Report, August 5, 2007, www.businessweek.com.

57. Alan Wolf, "TWICE/Campaigners Poll Shows Shoppers Choose Brand Over Price," *Twice: This Week in Consumer Electronics*, December 5, 2005, p. 18.

58. C. Manly Molpus, "Brands Follow New Shopping Patterns," *Advertising Age*, February 14, 1994, p. 22.

59. Stephan and Tannenholz, "The Real Reason for Brand Switching," p. 31.

60. Annetta Miller, "The Millennial Mind-Set," *American Demographics*, January 1999, www.demographics.com/publications/AD/99_ad/9901_ad/ad990102a.htm.

61. Larry Light, "Brand Loyalty Marketing Key to Enduring Growth," *Advertising Age*, October 3, 1994, p. 20.

62. Andrew Jaffe, "A Compass Point Out of Dead Calm: 'Brand Stewardship,'" *Adweek*, February 7, 1994, p. 38.

63. Linda Trent, "Color Can Affect Success of Products," *Marketing News*, July 5, 1993, p. 4.

64. Shlomo Kalish, "A New Product Adoption Model with Price, Advertising, and Uncertainty," *Management Science*, December 1985, pp. 1569–85.

65. Raymond Serafin, "Brands in Demand—BMW: From Yuppie-Mobile to Smart Car of the '90s," *Advertising Age*, October 3, 1994, p. S2.

66. "Case Study: Amway," *Business 2000*, www.business2000.ie/amway/index.htm.

67. Perreault and McCarthy, *Basic Marketing*, p. 16.

68. Mya Frazier, "Retailers Scramble for Exclusive Music Rights," *Advertising Age*, September 19, 2005, http://adage.com/article.php?article_id=46812.

69. www.subway.com/subwayroot/index.aspx.

70. Carol Chopra, "Perspectives for the Franchising Sector in Europe—2006," *Franchising World*, March 2006, www.allbusiness.com/periodicals/article/874710-1.html.

71. Jim Emerson, "Levi Strauss in the Early Stages of Shift to Database Marketing," *DM News,* December 7, 1992, pp. 1–2; Lisa Benenson, "Bull's-Eye Marketing," *Success,* January/February 1993, pp. 43–48.

72. Al Ries and Laura Ries, *The Fall of Advertising and the Rise of PR* (New York: HarperBusiness, 2002), pp. 8–12.

73. van Waterschoot and Van den Bulte, "The 4P Classification of the Marketing Mix Revisited," p. 89.

74. Promotion Marketing Association, "For the Love of the Deal: Consumers Rave about Deal Enjoyment of Using Coupons, as Well as Cost Savings," press release, September 1, 2005, *www.couponmonth.com/pages/news.htm*.

75. van Waterschoot and Van den Bulte, "The 4P Classification of the Marketing Mix Revisited," pp. 89–90.

Chapter Seven

1. Bruce Horovitz, "Budweiser 'Lost Dog' Finds Way to Top of Super Bowl Ad Meter," *USA Today,* February 2, 2015, *http://www.usatoday.com/story/money/business/2015/02/01/usa-today-ad-meter-2015-super-bowl-money/22378605/*.

2. "Here Are the Super Bowl Advertisers That Got the Biggest Brand Lifts," *AdWeek,* February 5, 2015, *http://www.adweek.com/news/advertising-branding/here-are-super-bowladvertisers-got-biggest-brand-lifts-162805*.

3. Clifton B. Parker, "Super Bowl Ads Not Profitable for Competing Brands, Stanford Scholar Says," *Stanford News,* January 26, 2015, *http://news.stanford.edu/news/2015/january/super-bowl-ads-012615.html*.

4. Jeanine Poggi, "Football and 'Big Bang' are Broadcast TV's Most Expensive Ad Buys," *Advertising Age,* September 25, 2014, *http://adage.com/article/media/football-big-bang-tv-s-expensive-adbuys/295130/*.

5. Media kits: *www.businessweek.com* and *www.forbes.com,* October 2000; Chad Rubel, "Some Cute Super Spots Now Just a Memory," *Marketing News,* March 13, 1995, p. 15.

6. William Perreault Jr., Joseph Cannon, and E. Jerome McCarthy, *Basic Marketing: A Marketing Strategy Planning Approach* (Burr Ridge, IL: McGraw-Hill Education, 2013).

7. "Top 50 Research Organizations," American Marketing Association online, *www.data.marketingpower.com*.

8. Edward F. McQuarrie, *The Market Research Toolbox* (Thousand Oaks, CA: Sage, 2016).

9. Livia Marian, Polymeros Chrysochou, Athanasios Krystallis, and John Thorgersen, "The Role of Price as a Product Attribute in the Organic Food Context: An Exploration Based on Actual Purchase Data," Food Quality and Preference, October, 2014, pp. 52–60.

10. Ibid.

11. Dennis B. Arnett and C. Michael Wittman, "Improving Marketing Success: The Role of Tacit Knowledge Exchange Between Sales and Marketing," *Journal of Business Research,* March, 2014, pp. 324–331.

12. V. Kumar, Yashoda Bhagwat, and Zi (Alan) Zhang, "Regaining 'Lost' Customers: The Predictive Power of First-Time Behavior, the Reason for Defection, and the Nature of the Win-Back Offer," *Journal of Marketing,* 2015.

13. Parker, "Super Bowl Ads Not Profitable for Competing Brands, Stanford Scholar Says."

14. Tom Alstiel and Jean Grow, *Creative Strategy, Copy, Design* (Menlo Park, CA: Sage, 2013).

15. Ibid.

16. "BrandAsset Valuator," *Landor,* retrieved at: *http://young-rubicam.de/tools-wissen/tools/brandasset-valuator/?lang=en*.

17. Kathryn Kranhold, "Agencies Boost Research to Spot Consumer Views," *The Asian Wall Street Journal,* March 10, 2000, p. 6.

18. Story adapted from "Cheese, Please!" *American Demographics,* March 2000, pp. S6–S8. (Copyright Primedia Intertec March 2000.)

19. Ibid.

20. Jack Neff, "Copy Testing Coming to Digital Marketing," *Advertising Age,* February 27, 2011, *http://adage.com/article/digital/copy-testing-coming-digital-marketing/149100/*.

21. Perry Marshall, Mike Rhodes, and Bryan Todd, *Entrepreneur Ultimate Guide to Google AdWords,* 4th ed. Irvine, CA: (Entrepreneur Press, 2014).

22. "How Can I A/B Split Test My Facebook Ads?" Facebook Help Center, *https://www.facebook.com/help/community/question/?id=10152988283170078*.

23. "Conversion Tracking for Websites," Twitter Help Center, *https://support.twitter.com/articles/20170807-conversion-tracking-for-websites*.

24. Perreault and McCarthy, *Basic Marketing,* p. 153.

25. Jack Honomichl, "Research Cultures Are Different in Mexico, Canada," *Marketing News,* May 10, 1993, pp. 12, 13.

26. Paul Conner, "Defining the 'Decision Purpose' of Research," *Marketing News,* September 23, 1996, p. 18.

27. Michael L. Garee and Thomas R. Schori, "Focus Groups Illuminate Quantitative Research," *Marketing News,* September 23, 1996, p. 41.

28. Robert West, Schering Canada, personal interview, May 17, 1993.

29. William Weylock, "Focus: Hocus Pocus?" *Marketing Tools,* July/August 1994, pp. 12–16; Thomas L. Greenbaum, "Focus Groups Can Play a Part in Evaluating Ad Copy," *Marketing News,* September 13, 1993, pp. 24–25.

30. Pat Sloan and Julie Liesse, "New Agency Weapon to Win Clients: Research," *Advertising Age,* August 30, 1993, p. 37.

31. Rex Hartson and Partha S. Pyla, *The UX Book: Process and Guidelines for Ensuring a Quality User Experience* (Elsevier, 2012).

32. Jack Honomichl, "The Honomichl 50," *Marketing News,* June 10, 2002, p. H2; Don E. Schultz, Stanley I. Tannenbaum, and Robert F. Lauterborn, *Integrated Marketing Communications: Putting It Together and Making It Work* (Lincolnwood, IL: NTC Business Books, 1993), pp. 149–50; ACNielsen, *http://us.acnielsen.com/products*.

33. Leah Rickard, "Helping Put Data in Focus," *Advertising Age,* July 11, 1994, p. 18.

34. IAG Research, *www.iagr.net*.

35. Richard Gibson, "Marketers' Mantra: Reap More with Less," *The Wall Street Journal,* March 22, 1991, p. B1.

36. Karen A. Machleit, Chris T. Allen, and Thomas J. Madden, "The Mature Brand and Brand Interest: An Alternative Consequence of Ad-Evoked Affect," *Journal of Marketing,* October 1993, pp. 72–82.

37. Pamela L. Alreck and Robert B. Settle, *The Survey Research Handbook,* 2nd ed. (Burr Ridge, IL: Irwin, 1995), pp. 56–59.

38. Ibid., p. 40.

39. Perreault and McCarthy, *Basic Marketing,* p. 173.

40. Alreck and Settle, *The Survey Research Handbook,* pp. 88–90.

41. George S. Fabian, panelist, "Globalization: Challenges for Marketing and Research," *Marketing Review,* February 1993, p. 23.

42. Maureen R. Marston, panelist, "Globalization: Challenges for Marketing and Research," pp. 20–21.

43. Suzanne Bidlake, "Nestlé Builds Database in Asia with Direct Mail," *Advertising Age International,* January 1998, p. 34.

44. Michael Brizz, "How to Learn What Japanese Buyers Really Want," *Business Marketing,* January 1987, p. 72.

45. Simon Chadwick, panelist, "Globalization: Challenges for Marketing and Research," p. 18.

46. Thomas L. Greenbaum, "Understanding Focus Group Research Abroad," *Marketing News,* June 3, 1996, pp. H14, H36.

47. Marston, "Globalization," p. 24.

48. Ibid.

49. Deborah Szynal, "Big Bytes," *Marketing News,* March 18, 2002, p. 3.

Chapter Eight

1. Updated promo sheet and letter from BBDO-NY (1995).

2. Theresa Howard, "Brand Builders: Being True to Dew," *Brandweek* April 24, 2000, p. 28.

3. Ibid., p. 30.

4. Ibid.

5.   Christopher Lawton, "PepsiCo's Mountain Dew Backs Film," *The Wall Street Journal,* September 12, 2005, p. B4.

6.   Jillian Berman, "Here's Why Mountain Dew Will Survive the Death of Soda," *Huffington Post,* January 26, 2015, *http://www.huffingtonpost.com/2015/01/26/mountain-dew-regions_n_6524382.html.*

7.   "Saturn SC1 and the Young, College-Educated Import Intenders," 1993 Case Study, NSAC: AAF College World Series of Advertising, pp. 2, 11, 23.

8.   Kate MacArthur and Hillary Chura, "Urban Youth," *Advertising Age,* September 4, 2000, pp. 16–17.

9.   Duane Stanford, "Mountain Dew Wants Some Street Cred," *Bloomberg Business,* April 26, 2012, *http://www.bloomberg.com/bw/articles/2012-04-26/mountain-dew-wants-some-street-cred.*

10.   R. Craig Endicott, "100 Leading National Advertisers," *Advertising Age,* June 26, 2006, *http://adage.com/images/random/lna2006.pdf.*

11.   Automation Marketing Strategies, "The Art of Market Positioning," *Strategic Advantage Newsletter,* January 2000.

12.   Ernest Martin, "Target Marketing: Summary and Unit Learning Outcomes," Course Syllabus CADV 213.

13.   Carmine Gallo, "The 7 Innovation Secrets of Steve Jobs, Forbes, May 2, 2014, retrieved at: *http://www.forbes.com/sites/carminegallo/2014/05/02/the-7-innovation-secrets-of-steve-jobs/.*

14.   Farrell, "Dew Poses Real Pepsi Challenge to Coke," p. B2.

15.   Adapted from Al Ries and Jack Trout, *Bottom-Up Marketing* (New York: McGraw-Hill, 1989), p. 8.

16.   Don E. Schultz, "Integration Helps You Plan Communications from Outside-In," *Marketing News,* March 15, 1993, p. 12.

17.   Regis McKenna, "Marketing Is Everything," *Harvard Business Review,* January/February 1991, p. 65.

18.   Don E. Schultz, Stanley I. Tannenbaum, and Robert F. Lauterborn, *Integrated Marketing Communications: Putting It Together & Making It Work* (Lincolnwood, IL: NTC Business Books, 1993), pp. 55–6.

19.   Paul Wang and Don E. Schultz, "Measuring the Return on Investment for Advertising and Other Forms of Marketing Communication, Using an Integrated Marketing Communications Planning Approach," paper presented at the annual conference of the Association for Education in Journalism and Mass Communication, Kansas City, August 13, 1993.

20.   Schultz, Tannenbaum, and Lauterborn, *Integrated Marketing Communications,* p. 58.

21.   Wayne Henderson, "The IMC Scale: A Tool for Evaluating IMC Usage," *Integrated Marketing Communications Research Journal* 3, no. 1 (Spring 1997), pp. 11–17.

22.   Ibid.; Cyndee Miller, "Everyone Loves 'IMC,' but . . . ," *Marketing News,* August 16, 1993, pp. 1, 6.

23.   Don E. Schultz and Paul Wang, "Real World Results," *Marketing Tools,* premier issue, May 1994, pp. 40–47.

24.   Ibid.

25.   Don E. Schultz, "Integrated Marketing Communications: A Competitive Weapon in Today's Marketplace," *Marketing Review,* July 1993, pp. 10–11, 29.

26.   Ned Anschuetz, "Point of View: Building Brand Popularity: The Myth of Segmenting to Brand Success," *Journal of Advertising Research,* January/February 1997, pp. 63–66.

27.   Sally Beatty, "Two GM Divisions Try to Create Different Images for Their Trucks," *The Wall Street Journal,* October 14, 1998, p. B8.

28.   Chung K. Kim and Kenneth R. Lord, "A New FCB Grid and Its Strategic Implications for Advertising," in *Proceedings of the Annual Conference of the Administrative Sciences Association of Canada* (Marketing), Tony Schellinck, ed. (Niagara Falls, Ontario: Administrative Sciences Association of Canada, 1991), pp. 51–60.

29.   Johan C. Yssel and Mark W. Walchle, "Using the FCB Grid to Write Advertising Strategy," paper presented at the annual conference of the Association for Education in Journalism and Mass Communication, 1992.

30.   Howard, "Brand Builders," p. 30.

31.   Ibid., p. 31; Kate MacArthur, "Mountain Dew: Dawn Hudson," *Advertising Age,* June 26, 2000, p. 27.

32.   Howard, "Brand Builders," p. 31.

33.   Farrell, "Dew Poses Real Pepsi Challenge to Coke."

34.   Ibid.

35.   Gregg Ambach and Mike Hess, "Measuring Long-Term Effects in Marketing," *Marketing Research: A Magazine of Management and Applications,* American Marketing Association, Summer 2000, pp. 23–30.

36.   Robert D. Buzzell and Frederick D. Wiersema, "Successful Share-Building Strategies," *Harvard Business Review,* January/February 1981, p. 135; Siva K. Balasubramanian and V. Kumar, "Analyzing Variations in Advertising and Promotional Expenditures: Key Correlated in Consumer, Industrial, and Service Markets," *Journal of Marketing,* April 1990, pp. 57–68.

37.   Bernard Ryan Jr., *Advertising in a Recession: The Best Defense Is a Good Offense* (New York: American Association of Advertising Agencies, 1991), pp. 13–29; Priscilla C. Brown, "Surviving with a Splash," *Business Marketing,* January 1991, p. 14; Edmund O. Lawler, "A Window of Opportunity," *Business Marketing,* January 1991, p. 16; Rebecca Colwell Quarles, "Marketing Research Turns Recession into Business Opportunity," *Marketing News,* January 7, 1991, pp. 27, 29.

38.   Fabiana Giacomotti, "European Marketers Keep Up Ad Budgets," *Adweek,* January 24, 1994, pp. 16–17.

39.   Leo Bogart, *Strategy in Advertising,* 2nd ed. (Chicago: Crain Books, 1984), pp. 45–47.

40.   John Philip Jones, "Ad Spending: Maintaining Market Share," *Harvard Business Review,* January/February 1990, pp. 38–42; James C. Schroer, "Ad Spending: Growing Market Share," *Harvard Business Review,* January/February 1990, pp. 44–49.

41.   Peter Breen, "Seeds of Change," *Promo Sourcebook Supplement,* Copyright 2000, INTERTEC, p. 18, *www.global.lexisnexis.com/us.*

42.   Ambach and Hess, "Measuring Long-Term Effects in Marketing."

Chapter Nine

1.   "Campaigns," AIDS.gov, *https://www.aids.gov/federal-resources/campaigns/.*

2.   "Prevention is Care," Centers for Disease Control and Prevention, March 26, 2009, *http://www.cdc.gov/actagainstaids/campaigns/pic/index.html.*

3.   Ana Swanson, "Video: What Happens When a Man with HIV Asks Strangers to Touch Him?" *The Washington Post,* June 27, 2015, *http://www.washingtonpost.com/blogs/wonkblog/wp/2015/06/27/video-what-happens-when-a-manwith-hiv-asks-strangers-to-touch-him/.*

4.   AIDS.gov, "Communication Strategy: Internal working plan," January, 2013, *https://www.aids.gov/pdf/communication-plan.pdf.*

5.   Laurie Freeman, "Experience Worth More than Byte," *Advertising Age,* July 23, 1996, p. S15.

6.   Yumiko Ono, "Cordiant Puts Hamilton in Key U.S. Post," *Advertising Age,* July 18, 1997, p. B2.

7.   Stephanie Thompson, "Universal McCann Gets $150 Million Nestlé Account," April 12, 2002, *http://adage.com.* Richard Linnett and Jack Neff, "Mindshare Wins $600 Million Gillette Media Account," September 26, 2002, *http://adage.com.*

8.   Alexandra Bruell, "GM Parks $3 Billion Media Account at Carat," January 24, 2012, *http://adage.com;* Alexandra Bruell, "Media Vest Emerges Winner in Cox Communications Review," December 07, 2011, *http://adage.com.*

9.   Lisa E. Phillips, "Trends in Consumers' Time Spent with Media," *eMarketer,* December 28, 2010, *www.emarketer.com.*

10.   Jasper Jackson, "Know Your Audience: How the Digital Native Generation Consumer Media," The Media Briefing, August 30, 2013, *http://www.themediabriefing.com/article/know-your-audience-how-digital-native-millennial-generation-consume-media.*

11.   "Business: Hi Ho, Hi Ho, Down the Data Mine We Go," *The Economist,* August 23, 1997, pp. 47–48.

12. Larry Allen, "The Traditional Media Buying Agency is Dead," *Business Insider,* January 17, 2012, *http://www.businessinsider.com/the-traditional-media-buying-agency-is-dead-2012-1.*

13. Callum Borchers, "In Ad Wars, Clients want Proof of Success," *Boston Globe,* May 8, 2015, *https://www.bostonglobe.com/business/2015/05/07/firms-face-new-pressure-deliverly9gLXbmWHwBkMEgoonlcPM/story.html.*

14. Rick Klein and Jeff Jensen, "GM's Huge Pact Raises Olympics Bar," *Advertising Age,* August 4, 1997, p. 6.

15. Christina Merrill, "Media Rising," *Adweek,* November 9, 1998.

16. Joe Mandese, "Boost for Media Buyers," *Advertising Age,* March 7, 1994, p. 47.

17. Liesse, "Inside Burnett's Vaunted Buying Machine," p. S6.

18. Don E. Schultz, Stanley I. Tannenbaum, and Robert F. Lauterborn, *Integrated Marketing Communications: Putting It Together & Making It Work* (Lincolnwood, IL: NTC Business Books, 1993), pp. 81–82, 108.

19. Adapted from Donald W. Jugenheimer, Arnold M. Barban, and Peter B. Turk, *Advertising Media: Strategy and Tactics* (Dubuque, IA: Brown & Benchmark, 1992), p. 131.

20. Ibid., pp. 131–33.

21. Jim Surmanek, *Introduction to Advertising Media: Research, Planning, and Buying* (Chicago: NTC Business Books, 1993), p. 54.

22. Shula Bigman, "First, Let's Find Out How Media Works: Making Media Accountable Means Creating New Tools," *Advertising Age,* October 5, 1998, p. 40.

23. Adapted from Surmanek, *Introduction to Advertising Media,* p. 106.

24. Jugenheimer, Barban, and Turk, *Advertising Media: Strategy and Tactics,* p. 135.

25. Joe Mandese, "Revisiting Ad Reach, Frequency," *Advertising Age,* November 27, 1995, p. 46.

26. George B. Murray and John G. Jenkins, "The Concept of 'Effective Reach' in Advertising," *Journal of Advertising Research* 32, no. 3, 1992, pp. 34–44.

27. John Philip Jones, *When Ads Work: New Proof That Advertising Triggers Sales* (New York: Simon & Schuster/Lexington Books, 1995); Colin McDonald, "From 'Frequency' to 'Continuity'—Is It a New Dawn?" *Journal of Advertising Research,* July/August 1997, p. 21.

28. Hugh M. Cannon and Edward A. Riordan, "Effective Reach and Frequency: Does It Really Make Sense?" *Journal of Advertising Research,* March/April 1994, pp. 19–28.

29. Ibid., pp. 27–28; John Philip Jones, "What Does Effective Frequency Mean in 1997?" *Journal of Advertising Research,* July/August 1997, pp. 14–20.

30. Kenneth A. Longman, "If Not Effective Frequency, Then What?" *Journal of Advertising Research,* July/August 1997, pp. 44–50; Hugh M. Cannon, John D. Leckenby, and Avery Abernethy, "Overcoming the Media Planning Paradox: From (In)Effective to Optimal Reach and Frequency," *Proceedings of the 1996 Conference of the American Academy of Advertising,* pp. 34–39.

31. Erwin Ephron, "Recency Planning," *Journal of Advertising Research,* July/August 1997, pp. 61–64.

32. Laurie Freeman, "Added Theories Drive Need for Client Solutions," *Advertising Age,* August 4, 1997, p. S18.

33. Schultz, Tannenbaum, and Lauterborn, *Integrated Marketing Communications: Putting It Together & Making It Work,* pp. 116–22, 132–33; Julie Liesse, "Buying by the Numbers? Hardly," *Advertising Age,* July 25, 1994, p. S16.

34. "The European Advertising & Media Forecast," *European Advertising & Media Forecast,* April 2006.

35. Joe Mandese, "Cultures Clash as 'Optimizers' Sort Out U.S. Media," *Advertising Age,* August 4, 1997, p. S2.

36. Rein Rijkens, *European Advertising Strategies* (London: Cassell, 1992), pp. 86–87.

37. Special Report: Best Media Plan Competition, "Guerrilla Tactics Get Panasonic Noticed," *Strategy* (Canada), March 27, 2000, p. BMP10.

38. Todd Pruzan, "Global Media: Distribution Slows, but Rates Climb," *Advertising Age International,* January 16, 1995, p. 119.

39. Neil Kelliher, "Magazine Media Planning for 'Effectiveness': Getting the People Back into the Process," *Journal of Consumer Marketing,* Summer 1990, pp. 47–55.

40. Kenneth Longman, *Advertising* (New York: Harcourt Brace Jovanovich, 1971), pp. 211–12.

41. Kevin Goldman, "With Vietnam Embargo Lifted, Agencies Gear Up for Business," *The Wall Street Journal,* February 7, 1994, p. B8.

42. "The Power of Partnership," NBC Marketing Supplement, *Advertising Age,* November 16, 1992, p. 13.

43. Kevin Goldman, "Digital Warms Couch Potatoes with Only-on-Sunday TV Ads," *The Wall Street Journal,* November 22, 1994, p. B8.

44. Telmar Website, July 2006, *www.telmar.com.*

45. Interactive Market Systems Website, *www.imsms.com.*

Chapter Ten

1. "Target Through the Years," Target Corporate Website, *https://corporate.target.com/about/history/Target-through-the-years.*

2. "xhiliaration," Target.com, *http://www.target.com/bp/xhilaration.*

3. Catherine Anderson, "Michael Graves Set Himself Apart Through His Joyful, Colourful Designs," City Metric, April 10, 2015, *http://www.citymetric.com/skylines/michael-gravesset-himself-apart-through-his-joyful-colourful-designs-897.*

4. Steve McKee, "What Should You Spend on Advertising?" *Bloomberg Business,* February 1, 2009, *http://www.businessweek.com/smallbiz/content/feb2009/sb20090210_165498.htm.*

5. Pat Fallon and Fred Senn, *Juicing the Orange: How to Turn Creativity into a Powerful Business Advantage* (Cambridge, MA: Harvard Business School Press, 2006).

6. J. Scott Armstrong, *Persuasive Advertising Evidence Based Principles* (New York: Palgrave Macmillan, 2006).

7. Nancy A. Mitchell, Diane M. Badzinski, and Donna R. Pawlowski, "The Use of Metaphors as Vivid Stimuli to Enhance Comprehension and Recall of Print Advertisements," in Karen Whitehill King, ed., *Proceedings of the 1994 Conference of the American Academy of Advertising* (Athens, GA: Henry W. Grady College of Journalism and Mass Communication, the University of Georgia, 1994).

8. Charles Forceville, "The Strategic Use of the Visual Mode in Advertising Metaphors," in Emilia Djonov and Sumin Zhao, eds., Critical Multimodal Studies of Popular Discourse (Routledge, 2013).

9. Matt Britton, *Youthnation: Building Remarkable Brands in a Youth-Driven Culture* (Hoboken, NJ: John Wiley & Sons, Inc., 2015).

10. Andrea Ovans, "What Makes the Best Infographics so Convincing," *Harvard Business Review,* April 22, 2014, *https://hbr.org/2014/04/what-makes-the-best-infographics-soconvincing.*

11. ALeksi Tzatzev, "10 Colors that Might Get You Sued," *Business Insider,* September 29, 2012, *http://www.businessinsider.com/colors-that-are-trademarked-2012-9.*

12. Kevin Goldman, "Nike, H-P Gamble on New Sales Pitches," *The Wall Street Journal,* April 8, 1994, p. B8.

13. Roger von Oech, *A Whack on the Side of the Head* (New York: Warner Books, 1990).

14. Godlman, "Nike, H-P Gamble on New Sales Pitches."

15. Roger von Oech, *A Kick in the Seat of the Pants* (New York: HarperPerennial, 1986).

16. Adapted with permission from von Oech, *A Kick in the Seat of the Pants.*

17. Eleftheria Parpis, "What's the 'Big Idea'"? *Adweek,* September 13, 2010, *http://www.adweek.com/news/advertising-branding/whats-big-idea-103274.*

18. John O'Toole, *The Trouble with Advertising,* 2nd ed. (New York: Random House, 1985), p. 132; Fred Danzig, "The Big Idea," *Advertising Age,* November 9, 1988, pp. 16, 138–140.

19. von Oech, *A Whack on the Side of the Head.*

20. Ibid.

21. Kevin Goldman, "Leap Partnership Touts All-Creative Shop," *The Wall Street Journal*, December 23, 1993.
22. Derek Walker, "If the Client Was Always Right, It Wouldn't Need an Ad Agency," *Advertising Age*, July 29, 2011, *http://adage.com/article/small-agency-diary/client-adagency/228932/*.
23. Joseph Sugarman, *The Adweek Copywriting Handbook* (New York: John Wiley & Sons, 2012).
24. Adapted with permission from von Oech, *A Kick in the Seat of the Pants*.
25. Ibid.
26. David Ogilvy, *Ogilvy on Advertising* (New York: Random House, 1985).

Chapter Eleven
1. Hannah Rand, "Horrifying Video Shows Gang of Youths Risking Death by Playing Game of Chicken on New York Subway Tracks," *Daily Mail*, April 18, 2012, *http://www.dailymail.co.uk/news/article-2131549/Horrifying-video-shows-gang-youths-riskingdeath-playing-game-chicken-New-York-subway-tracks.html*.
2. "What's So Good about 'Dumb Ways to Die'? *Adweek*, June 17, 2013, *http://www.adweek.com/news/advertising-branding/whats-so-good-about-dumb-ways-die-150314*.
3. Mark Sweney, "Cannes Lions: Dumb Ways to Die scoops Top Award," *The Guardian*, June 22, 2013, *http://www.theguardian.com/media/2013/jun/22/cannes-lions-advertisingawards*.
4. "Metro Trains: Dumb Ways to Die," Top Ad Campaigns of the 21st Century, *Advertising Age*, *http://adage.com/lp/top15/#tapproject*.
5. Miranda Ward, "Has Dumb Ways to Die been Effective?" *mUmBRELLA*, January 30, 2015.
6. Adobe Agency Partner Program, Adobe.com, *http://www.adobe.com/solutions/advertising.html*.
7. "The State of Online Advertising," *Adobe*, *http://www.adobe.com/aboutadobe/pressroom/pdfs/Adobe_State_of_Online_Advertising.pdf*.
8. Roy Paul Nelson, *The Design of Advertising* (Dubuque, IA: Brown & Benchmark, 1994), p. 107; J. Douglas Johnson, *Advertising Today* (Chicago: Science Research Associates, 1978).
9. Robyn Blakeman, *Advertising Campaign Design: Just the Essentials* (Armonk, NY: M. E. Sharpe, 2015).
10. Nathan Collins, "Poorly Chosen Headlines Can Hurt Your Memory," *Pacific Standard*, November 6, 2014, *http://www.psmag.com/politics-and-law/headlines-hurt-memory-94053*.
11. Tom Altstiel and Jean Grow, *Advertising Creative: Strategy, Copy, Design*, (Thousand Oaks, CA: Sage, 2013).
12. Ibid.
13. Roy Paul Nelson, *The Design of Advertising* (Dubuque, IA: Brown & Benchmark, 1994).
14. Altstiel and Grow, *Advertising Creative: Strategy, Copy, Design*; Neil Raphel and Murray Raphel, "Rules to Advertise By," Progressive Grocer, December 1993, pp. 13–14; Murray Raphel, "How to Get Ahead in Direct Mail," *Direct Marketing*, January 1990, pp. 30–32, 52.
15. Nathan Safran, "5 Data Insights into the Headlines Readers Click," Moz Blog, July 17, 2013, retrieved at: *https://moz.com/blog/5-data-insights-into-the-headlines-readers-click*.
16. David A. Wesson, "Headline Length as a Factor in Magazine Ad Readership," *Journalism Quarterly, Summer*, 1889, p. 468.
17. David Ogilvy, *Ogilvy on Advertising* (New York: Random House, 1985).
18. Altstiel and Grow, *Advertising Creative: Strategy, Copy, Design*.
19. Burton, *Advertising Copywriting*, p. 54; Arthur J. Kover and William J. James, "When Do Advertising 'Power Words' Work? An Examination of Congruence and Satiation," *Journal of Advertising Research*, July/August 1993, pp. 32–38.
20. MCNG Marketing, "Market the Benefits, Not the Features of Your Product," From the Blog, May 16, 2013, *http://www.mcngmarketing.com/market-the-benefits-not-the-featuresof-your-product/#.VZgsdflVhBc*.
21. Altstiel and Grow, *Advertising Creative: Strategy, Copy, Design*.
22. Dan Shewan, "21 Tips for Writing Great Ad Headlines," *WordStream*, February 2, 2015, *http://www.wordstream.com/blog/ws/2015/02/02/ppc-ad-headlines*.
23. Margo Berman, *The Copywriter's Toolkit* (Malden, MA: Wiley-Blackwell, 2012).
24. David Ogilvy, *Ogilvy on Advertising*.
25. Philip Ward Burton, *Advertising Copywriting*, 6th ed. (Lincolnwood, IL: NTC Business Books, 1991); Marjorie Zieff-Finn, "It's No Laughing Matter," *Direct Marketing*, September 1992.
26. John O'Toole, *The Trouble with Advertising*, 2nd ed. (New York: Random House, 1985).
27. Joanne Lipman, "It's It and That's a Shame: Why Are Some Slogans Losers?" *The Wall Street Journal*, July 16, 1993.
28. Herschell Gordon Lewis, "Radio Copywriting—Not as Easy as You May Think," *Direct Marketing*, July 1992.
29. Adapted with permission from Bob Garfield, "The Best Ad Missed the Boat to Cannes," *Advertising Age*, June 23, 1997.
30. David Ogilvy, *Ogilvy on Advertising*.
31. Ibid.
32. Fast Company Staff, "The 10 Most Addictive Sounds in the World," *Fast Company*, February 22, 2010, *http://www.fastcompany.com/1555211/10-most-addictive-sounds-world*.
33. "Corporate Advertising Study," *Burson-Marsteller*, October 13, 2003, *www.efluentials.com/documents/pr_101303.pdf*.
34. Joel Comm and Dave Taylor, *Twitter Power 3.0* (Hoboken, NJ: John Wiley & Sons, 2015).
35. Jason Falls, "Why you Shouldn't Trust Social Media to an SEO Consultant," *Social Media Explorer*, March 9, 2009, *https://www.socialmediaexplorer.com/search-enginemarketing/why-you-shouldnt-trust-social-media-to-an-seo-consultant/*.
36. Jason Falls, "Copywriting for Social Media," *Social Media Explorer*, June 9, 2010, *https://www.socialmediaexplorer.com/digital-marketing/copywriting-for-social-media/*.
37. John Freiralds, "Navigating the Minefields of Multilingual Marketing," *Pharmaceutical Executive*, September 1994.

Chapter Twelve
1. Ivan Cury, *TV Commercials: How to Make Them or How Big Is the Boat?* (Amsterdam: Elsevier, 2005).
2. Personal interview, Lorraine Alper Kramer, Saatchi & Saatchi Los Angeles, January 2001.
3. "Argentinian Ad Industry Rocked by New 10.5% Tax," *Advertising Age*, August 1996 *http://adage.com*.
4. Claudia McCue, *Real World Print Production with Adobe Creative Cloud* (Peachpit, 2014).
5. 2011 AAAA Television Production Cost Survey, accessed at *www.aaaa.org/pubs/essentials/pages/production.aspx*.
6. Gerald Millerson and Jim Owens, *Television Production*, 14th ed. (Burlington, MA: Focal Press, 2009).
7. Personal interview, Dean Van Eimeren, Saatchi & Saatchi Los Angeles, April 2001, p. 51.
8. Ibid., January 2001.
9. @ plan 2008 winter Study.
10. PANTONE® is a registered trademark of PANTONE, Inc.
11. Bonnie L. Drewniany and A. Jerome Jeweler, *Creative Strategy in Advertising*, 10th ed. (Boston: Wadsworth, 2011).
12. 2011 AAAA Television Production Cost Survey.
13. David Ogilvy, *Ogilvy on Advertising* (New York: Random House, 1985).
14. Robert B. Musburger and Gorham Kindem, *Introduction to Media Production* (Burlington, MA: Focal Press, 2009).
15. Chris McConnell, "A 6-Step General Process for Producing a Website," *http://sixrevisions.com/web-development/a-6-step-general-process-for-producing-a-website*; Rex Hartson and Pardha Pyla, The UX Book (Amsterdam: Elsevier, 2012).
16. Lauren Drell, "Making a Viral Video: 5 Things You Need to Know," *http://smallbusiness.aol.com/2011/01/30/making-a-viral-video-5-things-you-need-to-know/*.

Chapter Thirteen

1. Rick Edmonds, "Newspapers: By the Numbers," State of the News Media 2013, May 7, 2013, *http://www.stateofthemedia.org/2013 /newspapers-stabilizing-but-stillthreatened/newspapers-by-the-numbers/*.

2. Daniel de Vise, "Number of U.S. Adults with College Degrees Hits Historic High," *The Washington Post*, February 23, 2012, *http://www .washingtonpost.com/national/highereducation/number-of-us-adults-with- college-degrees-hits-historichigh/2012/02/23/glQAi80bWR_story.html*.

3. Edmonds, "Newspapers: By the Numbers," State of the News Media 2013.

4. "Marketing Fact Pack 2015 Edition," *Advertising Age*, *adage.com/ annual2015*.

5. Tom Rosenstiel, Mark Jurkowitz and Hon Ji, "The Search for a New Business Model," Pew Research Center, March 5, 2012, *http://www .journalism.org/2012/03/05/searchnew-business-model*.

6. "Wall Street Journal Hit with Layoffs that Could Top 100," *CNN Money*, June 18, 2015, retrieved at: *http://money.cnn.com/2015/06/18/ media/wall-street-journal-layoffs/*.

7. Lukas I. Alpert, "New York Times Slows Decline of Advertising Revenue in 2014," *The Wall Street Journal*, February 3, 2015, *http://www .wsj.com/articles/new-york-times-slowsdecline-of-advertising-revenue-in- 2014-1422998864*.

8. Roger Yu, "Gannett Q1 Earnings Rise 4% Due to Digital Unit Revenue Gain," *USA Today*, April 23, 2015, *http://www.usatoday.com/story /money/2015/04/21/gannett-q1-earningsrise/26115571/*.

9. Audit Bureau of Circulation, December 31, 2008, *http://abcas3 .accessabc.com/ecirc/magtitlesearch.asp*.

10. Audit Bureau of Circulation, June 30, 2011, *http://adage.com/datacenter /datapopup.php?article_id=229488*.

11. Patrick M. Reilly and Ernest Beck, "Publishers Often Pad Circulation Figures," *The Wall Street Journal*, September 30, 1997, p. B12.

12. Shu-Fen Li, John C. Schweitzer, and Benjamin J. Bates, "Effectiveness of Trade Magazine Advertising," paper presented to the annual conference of the Association for Education in Journalism and Mass Communication, Montreal, Quebec, August 1992.

13. Gene Willhoft, "Is 'Added Value' Valuable?" *Advertising Age*, March 1, 1993, p. 18.

14. Stephen M. Blacker, "Magazines' Role in Promotion," *Advertising Age*, June 30, 1994, p. 32.

15. *Car and Driver* Website, *www.caranddrivermediakit.com/hotdata/publishers /cardrivermk/cardrivermk/materials/Car_and_Driver_General_Rates.pdf*; *Road and Track* Website, *www.roadandtrackmediakit.com/r5/showkiosk.asp? listing_id=4182649*.

16. Lisa I. Fried, "New Rules Liven Up the Rate-Card Game," *Advertising Age*, October 24, 1994, p. S8.

17. SRDS Media Solutions, "Sample SRDS Listing," *www.srds.com /frontMatter/ips/consumer/sample.html*.

18. Joyce Rutter Kaye, *Print Casebooks 10/The Best in Advertising, 1994–95* ed. (Rockville, MD: RC Publications, 1994), pp. 63–65; Tony Case, "Getting Personal," *Editor & Publisher*, February 1, 1992, pp. 16, 31; Ann Cooper, "Creatives: Magazines—Believers in the Power of Print," *Adweek* (Eastern ed.), April 12, 1993, pp. 34–39.

19. "ZenithOptimedia: U.S. Ad Spending Forecasts through 2012," *http://adage.com/datacenter/datapopup.php?article_id=228231*.

20. Scarborough USA+ 2011 Release 2 Total, August 2010–September 2011, *www.naa.org/Trends-and-Numbers/Readership/Age-and-Gender.aspx*.

21. Scarborough USA+ 2011 Release 1 Total, February 2010–March 2011, *www.naa.org/Trends-and-Numbers/Readership/~/media/NAACorp /Public%20Files/TrendsAndNumbers/Readership/Daily_Sections_2011.ashx*.

22. U.S. Census Bureau, Statistical Abstract of the United States, "Information and Communications," *www.census.gov*, 2009.

23. *www.naa.org/trendsand numbers/Advertising-Expenditeves.aspx*.

24. Ronald Redfern, "What Readers Want from Newspapers," *Advertising Age*, January 23, 1995, p. 25.

25. U.S. Census Bureau, *Statistical Abstract of the United States*, "Information and Communications," *www.census.gov*, 2009.

26. "Newspaper Circulation Volume," Newspaper Association of America, *www.naa.org*.

27. "Parade Media Solutions," Parade Website, *http://mediakit.parade.com /parade/audience_demo.html*.

28. Audit Bureau of Circulations, March 31, 2010, *http://en.wikipedia.org /wiki/Newspaper_circulation*.

29. Newspaper Rate Differentials (New York: American Association of Advertising Agencies, 1990); Christy Fisher, "NAA Readies National Ad-Buy Plan," *Advertising Age*, March 1, 1993, p. 12.

30. *The Source: Newspapers by the Numbers,* Newspaper Association of America, *www.naa.org/thesource*.

31. John Flinn, "State of the National Buy," *Adweek*, June 26, 1995, p. 56.

32. Christy Fisher, "Chrysler's One-Stop Ad Buys Boost Ailing Newspapers," *Advertising Age*, March 7, 1994, p. 49.

33. Dorothy Giobbe, "One Order/One Bill System Gets a Dress Rehearsal," *Editor & Publisher*, March 12, 1994, pp. 26, 46.

34. Fisher, "Chrysler's One-Stop Ad Buys Boost Ailing Newspapers," p. 49; Ibid.

35. Joe Mandese and Scott Donaton, "Wells Rich Tests 4A's Liability Clause," *Advertising Age*, April 22, 1991, pp. 1, 40; Willie Vogt, "Defining Payment Liability," *AgriMarketing*, May 1992, pp. 42–43.

36. Dexter Roberts, "*Rolling Stone*: A Hit in China?" *BusinessWeek*, March 20, 2006, *www.businessweek.com/globalbiz/content/mar2006/ gb20060320_117894.htm?chan=search*.

37. Stephen Barr, "Moving Ahead," *Adweek*, January 31, 1994, p. 26.

Chapter Fourteen

1. Michelle Krebs, "To Counter Stigma, Hyundai Bolsters Warranty," *The New York Times*, November 8, 1998, *www.nytimes.com /1998/11/08/automobiles/to-counter-stigma-hyundai-bolsters-warranty.html*.

2. Associated Press, "Updated Ratings Make Super Bowl XLIII the Most-Watched Ever," *USA Today*," February 4, 2009, *www.usatoday.com /sports/football/nfl/2009-02-04-ratings_N.htm*.

3. Hyundai Motor America Reports February 2009 Sales, press release, March 3, 2009, *www.marketwatch.com/story/hyundai-motor- america-reports-february-2009?dist=msr_2*.

4. Publicis Groupe's ZenithOptimedia (Advertising Expenditure Forecasts, December 2014). Numbers rounded. More info: zenithoptimedia.com. Reported in *Advertising Age's* Marketing Fact Pack, 2015.

5. Ad Age DataCenter. Measured-media spending by medium from WPP's Kantar Media.

6. Broadcast Station Totals, FCC.gov, July 7, 2015, *https://www.fcc.gov /encyclopedia/broadcast-radio-am-and-fm-application-status-lists*.

7. Ibid.

8. Ibid.

9. "TV Basics: Channels—Receivable versus Tuned," Television Bureau of Advertising, Inc., *www.tvb.org*.

10. "Number of Cable Channels in the United States, 2014," National Cable & Telecommunications Association, *https://www.ncta.com /industry-data*.

11. "2008 Media Comparisons Study," Television Bureau of Advertising, Inc., *www.tvb.org*.

12. "Statistical Abstract of the United States," *www.census.gov/prod/www /statistical-abstract.html*.

13. "Cable Viewership Summary," Cable Advertising Bureau, *www .onetvworld.org*.

14. Ad Age DataCenter, "Measured Spending by Medium."

15. "Average U.S. Home Now Receives a Record 118.6 TV Channels According to Nielsen," *http://en-us.nielsen.com/main/news /newsreleases/2008/june/averageushome*.

16. Thomas R. Duncan and Sandra E. Moriarty, *Driving Brand Value: Using Integrated Marketing to Manage Stakeholder Relationships* (New York: McGraw-Hill, 1997), pp. 101–2.

17. Ibid.

18. "What a Spot Costs 2011," *Advertising Age* Annual 2011, *http://adage.c*

19. Eric Schmuckler, "Betting on a Sure Thing," *MediaWeek*, January 23, 1995, pp. 18–20; Steve Coe, "UPN Beats . . . Everybody," *Broadcasting & Cable*, January 23, 1995, pp. 4, 10; T. L. Stanley, "Network Branding," *Brandweek*, January 9, 1995, pp. 30–32; Ronald Grover, "Are Paramount and Warner Looney Tunes?" *BusinessWeek*, January 9, 1995, p. 46; David Tobenkin, "New Players Get Ready to Roll," *Broadcasting & Cable*, January 2, 1995, pp. 30–33.

20. Michael Freeman, "Lucie Salhany," *MediaWeek*, January 23, 1995, pp. 34–35; Eric Schmuckler, "New Network Ready to Roll," *MediaWeek*, October 10, 1994, p. 3; Eric Schmuckler, "Media Outlook '95: Network TV," *Adweek*, September 19, 1994, pp. S8–S12.

21. "Why Ad-Supported Cable?," Cabletelevision Advertising Bureau, *www.thecab.tv/main/bm~doc/why-cable_2012-p.pdf* April 19, 2012.

22. Kathy Haley, "Spot TV Is Power Tool," *The Power of Spot TV*, supplement to *Advertising Age*, September 29, 1993, p. T3.

23. "National Sales Reps Are Key to the Spot TV Mix," *The Power of Spot TV*, supplement to *Advertising Age*, September 23, 1992, pp. T10, T12.

24. Haley, "Spot TV Is Power Tool," p. T3; Kathy Haley, "Reps Zero In on Advertiser Goals," *The Power of Spot TV*, supplement to *Advertising Age*, September 29, 1993, p. T6.

25. Michael Burgi, "Welcome to the 500 Club," p. 45; Christopher Stern, "Advertisers Hear Promise of Smooth Spot Cable Buys," *Broadcasting & Cable*, April 26, 1993, pp. 56, 58.

26. "100 Leading National Advertisers," *Advertising Age*, June 26, 2006.

27. "What Is Syndication?" *1994 Guide to Advertiser-Supported Syndication*, supplement to *Advertising Age* (New York: Advertiser Syndicated Television Association, 1994), p. A6; David Tobenkin, "Action Escalates for Syndicators," *Broadcasting & Cable*, August 29, 1994, pp. 29–35.

28. "Syndication Showcase," *Broadcasting & Cable*, January 24, 1994, pp. 82–86.

29. Kathy Haley, "The Infomercial Begins a New Era as a Marketing Tool for Top Brands," *Advertising Age*, January 25, 1993, p. M3.

30. James B. Arndorfer, "Guthy-Renker Gives the Infomercial Street Cred," *Advertising Age*, May 2, 2005.

31. Jim Cooper, "Long-Form Ad Used in Contract Dispute," *Broadcasting & Cable*, May 24, 1993, p. 71.

32. Kevin Goldman, "CBS to Push Videotaping of Infomercials," *The Wall Street Journal*, November 15, 1993, p. B7.

33. Ibid.; Tom Burke, "Program-Length Commercials Can Bring These Six Benefits to a Major Brand Campaign," *Advertising Age*, January 25, 1993, p. M5.

34. Media Billings Long-Form DRTV and Short-Form DRTV, *www.responsemagazine.com*.

35. "100 Leading National Advertisers," *Advertising Age*, June 26, 2007.

36. Jack Honomichl, "Top 25 Global Firms Earn $6.1 Billion in Revenue," *Marketing News*, August 18, 1997, p. H2; Nielsen Media Research, *www.nielsenmedia.com*; "Media Measured," *www.nielsenmedia.com/monitor-plus*.

37. Nielsen, "C3 TV Ratings Show Impact of DVR Ad Viewing," Nielsen Media and Entertainment, October 14, 2009, retrieved at: *http://www.nielsen.com/us/en/insights/news/2009/c3-tv-ratings-show-impact-of-dvr-ad-viewing.html*.

38. Kevin Goldman, "CBS Pays Price for Losing Bet on Ratings," *The Wall Street Journal*, November 30, 1993, p. B4; Kevin Goldman, "CBS Again Must Offer Make-Good Ads," *The Wall Street Journal*, October 27, 1994, p. B6; Kevin Goldman, "'Scarlett' Make-Goods," *The Wall Street Journal*, November 21, 1994, p. B8.

39. Kevin Goldman, "Cable-TV Ads Fight Satellite Dish Threat," *The Wall Street Journal*, February 6, 1995, p. B8.

40. *Radio Marketing Guide and Fact Book*, 2007–2008, Radio Advertising Bureau *www.rab.com*.

41. "Radio Is Cost-Effective," *1997 Radio Marketing Guide and Fact Book for Advertisers*.

42. "Radio's Personalities Help Find Snapple's Sales Targets," *The Power of Radio*, special advertising supplement to *Advertising Age*, October 18, 1993, p. R3.

43. "Snapple Promotional Campaign Pays for 40 Ad-Free Days on WFNX-FM," *Boston Business Journal*, May 26, 2006, *http://boston.bizjournals.com/boston/stories/2006/05/22/daily64.html*.

44. "Media Comparisons," *1997 Radio Marketing Guide and Fact Book for Advertisers; Imagery Transfer Study* (New York: Network Radio Association, 1993).

45. Ibid.; Media Facts: *The Complete Guide to Maximizing Your Advertising* (New York: Radio Advertising Bureau, 1994), pp. 8–9.

46. "Maximize Your Marketing Message with Radio," *1997 Radio Marketing Guide and Fact Book for Advertisers; Radio Marketing Guide and Factbook for Advertisers: 1993–1994*, pp. 29–33.

47. "There's a Radio Format for Everybody," *1997 Radio Marketing Guide and Fact Book for Advertisers*.

48. *Network Radio: Targeting the National Consumer*, supplement to *Advertising Age*, September 6, 1993, pp. R2, R4; *Marketer's Guide to Media*, Fall/Winter 1992–93, pp. 69–70.

49. *2006 Marketing Guide and Fact Book*, Radio Advertising Bureau, *www.rab.com*.

50. "100 Leading National Advertisers," *Advertising Age*, June 26, 2009.

51. Abbey Klaassen, "XM and Sirius Satellite Radio Report Continuing Losses," *Advertising Age*, August 1, 2006.

52. Abbey Klaassen, "Google Inks First Satellite Radio Ad Sales Deal," *Advertising Age*, August 2, 2006.

53. Meredith Deliso, "Oprah Delivers for XM Satellite," *Advertising Age*, September 25, 2006.

Chapter Fifteen

1. Mike Volpe, "10 Horrifying Display Advertising Stats," Hubspot, April 29, 2013, retrieved at: *http://blog.hubspot.com/marketing/horrifying-display-advertising-stats*.

2. Bob Hoffman, "Banners are the Worst Advertising: Invisible," Digiday, May 16, 2013, retrieved at: *http://digiday.com/publishers/banners-are-the-worst-advertising/*.

3. "Voyages-SNFC.Com's Psycho Banner Campaign from France Wins the Best of Global Digital Monthly Awards in January," The Best of Global Digital Marketing, January, 2015, retrieved at: *http://www.best-marketing.eu/january-2015/*.

4. Ibid.

5. Thom Forbes, "Ads in Cyberspace: Light Your Beacon, but Don't Get Flamed," *Agency*, Winter 1995, p. 32.

6. "Marketing Fact Pack," *Advertising Age*, 2015 Edition.

7. Frank Barnako, "Bravo, Comedy Central Get Boost from Net Homes," MarketWatch, October 11, 2006, *www.marketwatch.com/news/story/story.aspx?guid=%7BBB3EE203-B6DE-4371-8D2F-9A1D7279DE5F%7D*.

8. "United States: Average Web Usage, March 31, 2009," Nielsen//NetRatings, *www.nielsen-netratings.com/news.jsp?section=dat_to&country=us*.

9. Tim O'Reilly, "What Is Web 2.0: Design Patterns and Business Models for the Next Generation of Software," O'Reilly Media, September 30, 2005, *www.oreillynet.com/pub/a/oreilly/tim/news/2005/09/30what-is-web-20.html*.

10. "Metrics and Methodology," The Media Measurement Task Force, Internet Advertising Bureau, September 15, 1997.

11. Internet Advertising Revenues at $5.5 Billion in Q1 '09, New Media Group of PriceWaterhouseCoopers LLP June 1, 2009, *www.iab.net/about_the_iab/recent_press_releases/press_release_archive/press_release/pr-060509*.

12. Samantha Yaffe, "Are Marketers Undervaluing the Internet?" *Strategy*, March 8, 2004, p. 1, *www.global.lexisnexis.com/us*.

13. Claudia Kuehl, "Spam's Good Twin. If E-mail Is Done Just Right, People Will Want to Receive It. Really," The DMA Interactive, Library White Papers, May 2000, *www.the-dma.org/library/whitepapers/spamsgoodtwin.shtml*.

14. "FTC Announces First Can-Spam Act Cases," FTC, April 29, 2004, retrieved at: *https://www.ftc.gov/news-events/press-releases/2004/04/ftc-announces-first-can-spam-act-cases*

15. Amanda Beeler, "Word-of-Mouth Pitches Mutate into New Forms on the Internet," *Advertising Age,* April 2000, *http://adage.com.*

16. Steve Jurvetson and Tim Draper, "Viral Marketing: Viral Marketing Phenomenon Explained, DFJ.com, January 1, 1997, retrieved at: *http://dfj.com/news/article_26.shtml.*

17. Tom Risen, "Is the Internet Bad for Society and Relationships?" U.S. News, Feb. 27, 2014, retrieved at: *http://www.usnews.com/news/blogs/data-mine/2014/02/27/is-the-internet-bad-for-society-and-relationships*

18. "United States," Ad Age Dataplace, *http://adage.*

19. Ibid.

20. Craig Reed, The Growing Importance of International eCommerce," Pitney Bowes Website, Janjary 1, 2015, retrieved at: *http://www.pitneybowes.com/us/global-ecommerce/case-studies/the-growing-importance-of-international-ecommerce.html*

21. Dinesh C. Sharma, "Study: DVR Adoption on the Rise," CNET News.com, March 30, 2004, *http://news.com.com/Study+DVR+adoption+on+the+rise/2100-1041_3-5182035.html?tag=nl.*

22. Ann M. Mack, "Ad-justment," *Adweek* 45, no. 35 (September 20, 2004), pp. 28–31, *www.proguest.com.*

23. Ibid.

24. Alice Z. Cuneo, "Wireless Giants Leap into Third-Screen Marketing," *Advertising Age,* September 11, 2006, *http://adage.com/digital/article?articleid=111748.*

25. Steve Miller and Mike Beirne, "The iPhone Effect," *Brandweek,* April 28, 2008, *www.adweek.com/aw/content_display/news/agency/e3ibef1ad200773laba65le6216ba3b6267.*

26. Buzzcity, "Mobile Advertising Continues Strong Growth," *Buzzcity,* July 22, 2009, *www.mobile-tech-today.com/story.xhtml?story_id=67945&full_skip=1.*

Chapter Sixteen

1. "Ice Bucket Challenge," Wikipedia, *https://en.wikipedia.org/wiki/Ice_Bucket_Challenge.*

2. "Classification of Social Media," Wikipedia.org, May 2012, *http://en.wikipedia.org/wiki/social_media.*

3. "National Face Your Fears Day: Content Marketing & Social Media," Idealaunch.com, October 13, 2009, *www.idealaunch.com/blog/content/face-your-fears-content-marketing-social-media/.*

4. "Half of Americans Call Facebook a 'Fad,'" Associated Press/CNBC, May 15, 2012, *www.psfk.com/2012/05/americans-call-facebook-fad-headlines.html.*

5. "Stats," Facebook Newsroom, July 14, 2015, *http://newsroom.fb.com/company-info/.*

6. Cara Pring, "100 Social Media Statistics for 2012," Thesocialskinny. com, posted January 11, 2012, *http://thesocialskinny.com/100-social-media-statistics-for-2012/.*

7. Ibid.

8. Ibid.

9. Ibid.

10. Ibid.

11. Ibid.

12. M. G. Siegler, "Eric Schmidt: Every 2 Days We Create as Much Information as We Did up to 2003," Techcrunch.com, August 4, 2010, *http://techcrunch.com/2010/08/04/schmidt-data/.*

13. Jennifer Leggio, "The Battle for Social Media Authenticity," Forbes.com, October, 13, 2011, *www.forbes.com/sites/jenniferleggio/2011/10/13/the-battle-for-social-media-authenticity/2/.*

14. Rohit Bhargava, "9 Ways Top Brands Use Social Media for Better Customer Service," Mashable.com, October 28, 2011, *http://mashable.com/2011/10/28/social-customer-service-brands/.*

15. Radicati Group, Inc., "Email Statistics Report, 2015-2019," *http://www.radicati.com/wp/wp-content/uploads/2015/02/Email-Statistics-Report-2015-2019-Executive-Summary.pdf;* Franck Michel, "How Many Public Photos Are Uploaded to Flickr Every Day, Month, Year?" Flickr, *https://www.flickr.com/photos/franckmichel/6855169886;* Twitter Usage Statistics," Internet Live Stats, July 15, 2015, *http://www.internetlivestats.com/twitter-statistics/;* "Statistics," YouTube Pressroom, July 15, 2015, *https://www.youtube.com/yt/press/statistics.html.*

16. Pring, "100 Social Media Statistics for 2012."

17. Bodnar, "The Ultimate List."

18. Pring, "100 Social Media Statistics for 2012."

19. Brandon Bailey, Peter Delevett, and Steve Johnson, "Facebook IPO Huge, but No 'Pop,'" *Mercury News,* May 18, 2012, *www.mercurynews.com/business/ci_20656753/facebook-ipo-huge-but=no-pop.*

20. David DiSalvo, *What Makes Your Brain Happy and Why You Should Do the Opposite* (Amherst, NY: Prometheus Books, 2011), pp. 225–26.

Chapter Seventeen

1. James Ready (Beer), Wikipedia.org, *http://en.wikipedia.org/wiki/James_Ready_(beer).*

2. "James Ready—Share Our Billboard Campaign," Case Study, Adforum.com, *www.adforum.com/adfolio/reel_detail.asp?page=1&ID=34444670&TDI=Vdnpg80Qj8.*

3. Nicole Hayes, "Out of Home Advertising Up 1.1% to $7.0 billion in 2014," Outdoor Advertising Association of America, March 4, 2015, *https://www.oaaa.org/NewsEvents/News/IndustryRevenue/tabid/322/id/4159/Default.aspx.*

4. "Introduce Yourself to Outdoor Advertising," Outdoor Advertising Association of America, Inc., *www.oaaa.org.*

5. *Billboard Basics* (New York: Outdoor Advertising Association of America, 1994), p. 5.

6. "Facts and Figures," Outdoor Advertising Association of America, Inc., *http://www.oaaa.org/marketingresources/factsandfigures.aspx.*

7. Mary Jo Haskey, "The Last Mass Medium," *MediaWeek,* December 6, 1993, p. 17.

8. Ibid., pp. 11, 21; Kevin Goldman, "Billboards Gain Respect as Spending Increases," *The Wall Street Journal,* June 27, 1994, p. B5.

9. Monique Reece-Myron ."The Advantages of Outdoor Advertising," *Denver Business Journal,* August 30, 1998 (Taken from *http://www.bizjournals.com/denver/stories/1998/08/31/smallb4.html?page=all*).

10. Institute of Outdoor Advertising, press release, 1991.

11. TAB Eyes On—Out-Of-Home Media Measurement The Basics 2009, *www.eyesonrating.com.*

12. "Facts and Figures," OAAA about Outdoor, *www.oaaa.org/outdoor/facts/cpmcomparison.asp.*

13. "Technology Standards," Outdoor Advertising Association of America, *www.oaaa.org/presscenter/technology.asp.*

14. Ibid.

15. Karl Greenberg, "Lexus Accelerates into All Venues in Push for Revamped IS Sedan," *Brandweek,* August 31, 2005, *www.brandweek.com/bw/news/autos/article_display.jsp?vnu_content_id=1001052022.*

16. Cyndee Miller, "Outdoor Advertising Weathers Repeated Attempts to Kill It," *Marketing News,* March 16, 1992, pp. 1, 9; *Billboard Basics,* pp. 15–16.

17. "Surveys Show Americans Like Their Billboards," Outdoor Advertising Association of America, 1997, *www.oaaa.org.*

18. Davis, "Apparel, Movies Orchestrate an Outdoor Rebirth," p. S1.

19. Melissa Korn, "Bricks Rivaling Clicks in Ad Spending," *Financial Times,* July 21, 2006, *http://search.ft.com/searchArticle?queryText=1-800-flowers&y=4&javascriptEnabled=true&id=060721008312&x=8;* "Outdoor Grows Online Sales: 1-800-Flowers.com Sales 7 Times Greater in Outdoor Markets," CBS Outdoor, *www.cbsoutdoor.com/news.php.*

20. Riccardo A. Davis, "Retailers Open Doors Wide for Co-op," *Advertising Age,* August 1, 1994, p. 30.

21. "Advertising That Imitates Art," *Adweek,* June 20, 1994, p. 18.

22. Fara Warner, "DKNY Takes Upscale Ads Underground," *The Wall Street Journal,* October 6, 1994, p. B4; "Nextel, Las Vegas Link Brand in Monorail Deal," *Los Angeles Times,* November 17, 2003.

23. James Ferrier, "Spotlight on Technology—Telecite," *Advertising Age,* November 22, 1993, p. SS10.

24. *The Point of Purchase Advertising Industry Fact Book* (Englewood, NJ: Point of Purchase Advertising Institute, 1992), p. 51.

25. "Market Statistics—America," Packaging-Gateway.com, *www.packaging-gateway.com/market_statistics_americas.asp#3*.

26. W. Wossen Kassaye and Dharmendra Verma, "Balancing Traditional Packaging Functions with the New 'Green' Packaging Concerns," *SAM Advanced Management Journal*, Autumn 1992, pp. 15–23.

27. Ibid.

28. Ibid.

29. Chris Baum, "10th Annual Packaging Consumer Survey 1994: Consumers Want It All—And Now," *Packaging*, August 1994, pp. 40–43.

30. Wayne Robinson, *How'd They Design and Print That?* (Cincinnati, OH: North Light Books, 1991), pp. 74–75.

31. Kassaye and Verma, "Balancing Traditional Packaging Functions with the New 'Green' Packaging Concerns."

32. Susan A. Friedmann, *Exhibiting at Trade Shows* (Menlo Park, CA: Crisp, 1992), p. V.

33. Ibid., p. 16.

34. Carla Waldemar, "Show Selection—The Five-Step Shuffle," *Exhibitor Online*, *www.exhibitoronline.com/exhibitormagazine/article.asp?ID=932*.

35. Friedmann, *Exhibiting at Trade Shows*, p. 24.

36. Ibid., pp. 34–39.

37. Ibid., p. 44.

38. Ibid., pp. 70–71.

39. Ibid., p. 90.

40. "Promotional Products Fact Sheet," Promotional Products Association International, Irving, TX, 1995.

41. "2008 Estimate of Promotional Products Distributor Sales," Promotional Products Association International, *www.ppa.org/NR/rdonlyres/F3282468-5F3D-4E86-B398-B710E207DD25/0/2008SalesVolume.pdf*.

42. Leslie Joseph and Rick Ebel, "Promotional Strategies: Research That Can Put Money In Your Pocket," *www.epromos.com/educationCenter/research.jsp*.

43. Ibid.

44. Avraham Shama and Jack K. Thompson, "Promotion Gifts: Help or Hindrance?" *Mortgage Banking*, February 1989, pp. 49–51.

45. Shahna Mahmud, "Cinema Ad Revenue up 15 Percent," *Adweek*, October 15, 2007.

46. Emma Hall, "Young Consumers Receptive to Movie Product Placement," *Advertising Age*, March 29, 2004, *www.global.lexisnexis.com/us*.

47. Amy Johannes, "Global Paid Product Placement to Reach $7.6 Billion by 2010: Report," Promomagazine.com, August 2006, *http://chiefmarketer.com/research/global-paid-product-placement-reach-76-billion-2010-report*.

Chapter Eighteen

1. Maya Frazier, "GEICO's $500 M Outlay Pays Off," *Advertising Age*, July 9, 2007.

2. Ibid.

3. Little Lizard Says "Ello to a New Inflection," *Hartford Courant*, February 22, 2006.

4. Maya Frazier, "GEICO Ad Chief Builds Insurer into Master of Marketing," *Advertising Age*, June 19, 2006.

5. Ibid.

6. Theresa Howard, "Gecko Wasn't First Choice for GEICO," *USA Today*, July 16, 2006, *www.usatoday.com/money/advertising/adtrack2006-07-16-geico_x.htm*.

7. Maya Frazier, "GEICO," *Advertising Age*, October 15, 2007, p. 50.

8. Direct Marketing Association, "What Is the Direct Marketing Association?" *www.the-dma.org/aboutdma/whatisthedma.shtml*.

9. Bob Stone and Rob Jacobs, *Successful Direct Marketing Methods*, 8th ed. (New York: McGraw-Hill, 2007).

10. "Women in the Labor Force," United States Department of Labor, *http://www.dol.gov/wb/stats/stats_data.htm*.

11. Ginger Conlon, "Outlook 2014: Marketing to Rise," *Direct Marketing*, January 10, 2014, *http://www.dmnews.com/marketing-strategy/outlook-2014-marketing-spending-to-rise/article/328925/g News*.

12. Ginger Conlon, "Marketing Spending in 2015," Direct Marketing News, January 27, 2015, retrieved at: *http://www.dmnews.com/marketing-strategy/marketing-spending-in-2015-infographic/article/400487/*

13. DHL, "Facts & Figures about International Direct Marketing," *www.dhl.com/en/mail/mail_essentials/dm_guide/international_direct_marketing/facts_and_figures.html#facts_figures2*.

14. Addressing Technology Website, 2003, *www.addressing.fr*.

15. Peppers and Rogers Group, *Marketing 1 to 1*, *www.m1to1.com/success_stories*.

16. Nicholas G. Poulos, "Customer Loyalty and the Marketing Database," *Direct Marketing*, July 1996, pp. 33–34.

17. Rob Jackson, "Database Doctor," *Direct*, January 9, 1996.

18. Stone and Jacobs, *Successful Direct Marketing Methods*.

19. Jackson, "Database Doctor."

20. Thomas E. Caruso, "Kotler: Future Marketers Will Focus on Customer Data Base to Compete Globally," *Marketing News*, June 8, 1992, pp. 21–22.

21. Tom Van Riper, "The Why of Best Buy," *www.forbes.com/business/2008/04/02/retail-best-buy-biz-commerce-cx_tvr_0402_retail.html*.

22. Seth Godin, "GUEST COLUMNIST: Permission Key to Successful Marketing," *Advertising Age*, November 1997, *http://adage.com*.

23. Poulos, "Customer Loyalty and the Marketing Database," pp. 32–35.

24. Meghan Kelly, "Google Defends Its New Privacy Policy in Letter to Congress," February 1, 2012, *www.washingtonpost.com/business/technology/google-defends-its-new-privacy-policy-in-letter-to-congress/2012/01/31/gIQAV7nuhQ_story.html*.

25. Robert A. Peterson and Thomas R. Wotruba, "What Is Direct Selling?—Definition, Perspectives, and Research Agenda," *Journal of Personal Selling and Sales Management* 16, no. 4 (Fall 1996), pp. 1–16.

26. Conlon, "Marketing Spending in 2015."

27. Cyndee Miller, "Telemarketing Cited as Chief Form of Direct Marketing," *Marketing News*, p. 6.

28. "Brief History of Toll-Free Numbers," *www.tollfreenumbers.com*.

29. Conlon, "Marketing Spending in 2015."

30. Robert H. Hallowell III, "The Selling Points of Direct Mail," *Trusts & Estates*, December 1994, 99, 39–41.

31. Ami Miyazaki, *New Absolute Appeal: Direct Mail Design* (Tokyo: PIE International, 2010).

32. Ken Boone, Terry Woods, and John Leonard, "Direct Mail Pal: A Direct Mail Production Handbook, Sewickley, PA: GATF Press, 2002.

33. *www.usps.com*.

34. Gwen Moran, "Postal Power—Direct Mail Tips for Small Business," 2002, *www.bnet.com*.

35. Jim Emerson, "Catalogs and the Web: A Beautiful Friendship," *www.directmag.com/exclusive/specialreports/2005_05_20_especial_report/*.

36. Sherry Chiger, "Top of the Industry, Ma," *Multichannel Merchant*, August 2005, *http://mutlichannelmerchant.com/mag/top_industry_ma_0801/index.html*.

37. Laura Bird, "Beyond Mail Order: Catalogs Now Sell Image, Advice," *The Wall Street Journal*, July 29, 1997, pp. B1, 2.

38. Personal Interview with Tom Campanaro, President, Total Gym Inc., December 2000.

39. "Consumer Spending Shows Electronic Retailing Shopper as Loyal, Satisfied, and Likely to Return for More Purchases," Electronic Retailing Association press release, June 9, 2004, *www.retailing.org*.

40. Nancy Colton Webster, "Radio Tuning in to Direct Response," *Advertising Age*, October 10, 1994, pp. S14, S15.

41. Murray Raphel, "Meet One of America's Top Salespeople," *Direct Marketing*, March 1994, p. 31.

42. Adapted from Barton A. Weitz, Stephen B. Castleberry, and John F. Tanner Jr., *Selling: Building Partnerships* (Burr Ridge, IL: Irwin, 1992), p. 5.

43. Edwin Klewer, Robert Shaffer, and Bonnie Binnig, "Sales Is an Investment, Attrition an Expense," *Journal of Health Care Marketing*, September 1995, p. 12.

44. Larry Light, "Trustmarketing: The Brand Relationship Marketing Mandate for the 90s," address to American Association of Advertising Agencies annual meeting, Laguna Niguel, CA, April 23, 1993.

45. Magid M. Abraham and Leonard M. Lodish, "Getting the Most Out of Advertising and Promotion," *Harvard Business Review*, May/June 1990, p. 51.

46. Light, "Trustmarketing."

47. Larry Light, "At the Center of It All Is the Brand," *Advertising Age*, March 29, 1993, p. 22.

48. Federal Trade Commission, *Report of the Federal Trade Commission Workshop on Slotting Allowances and Other Marketing Practices in the Grocery Industry*, February 2001, p. 69.

49. Robert A. Skitol, "FTC Spices Up Debate over Slotting Fees and the Robinson-Patman Act with Its McCormick Action," March 13 2000, American Antitrust Institute FTC: Watch #540, www.antitrustinstitute.org.

50. *The Point of Purchase Advertising Industry Fact Book* (Washington, DC: POPAI, 1997), p. 51.

51. Kelly Shermach, "Study: Most Shoppers Notice P-O-P Material," *Marketing News*, January 1995, pp. 27.

52. *The Point of Purchase Advertising Industry Fact Book*, p. 39. Kelly Shermach, "Great Strides Made in P-O-P Technology," *Marketing News*, January 2, 1995, pp. 8–9.

53. Angela Lawson, "The End of the Line," June 18, 2004, www.kioskmarketplace.com/article.php?id=13673.

54. Carol Angrisani, "Coupon Competition," *SN: Supermarket News*, March 3, 2006, pp. 23–25.

55. "About Us," Catalina Marketing, www.catalinamarketing.com/our_advantage/index.html.

56. Bruce Crumley, "Multipoints Adds Up for Quick Burger," *Advertising Age*, November 29, 1993, p. 14.

57. Stephanie Moore, "Rebate Madness: How to Defend Yourself against Ruthless Rebate Scams," www.consumeraffairs.com.

58. Lorraine Calvacca, "Polybagging Products to Pick Up Customers," *Folio: The Magazine for Magazine Management*, January 1993, p. 26.

Chapter Nineteen

1. "What is Public Relations?" Public Relations Society of America, http://www.prsa.org/aboutprsa/publicrelationsdefined/#.VcnR9flVhBc.

2. CSPI Newsroom, "Ben & Jerry's Fudging the Truth, Says CSPI: Nothing 'All-Natural' about Ingredients," July 30, 2002, www.cspinet.org/new/200207301.html.

3. Ben & Jerry's Homemade, Inc., press release, "Ben & Jerry's Response to CSPI Concerns," July 31, 2002, www.benjerry.com.

4. Ben & Jerry's Homemade, Inc., press release, "Ben & Jerry's Voluntarily Initiates the Recall of Pints of Karamel Sutra Ice Cream with Code 02/14/04," March 28, 2003, www.benjerry.com.

5. Mitchell Friedman, "Public Relations, Integrated Marketing Communications, and Professional Development in PR," October, 2012, presented to PRSSA, http://prssa.prsa.org/events/Conference/Program/12Program/12Presentations/IMC_MitchellFriedman.pdf.

6. Publisher's Statement, *Inside PR*, March 1993, p. 3.

7. Thomas L. Harris, "PR Gets Personal," *Direct Marketing*, April 1994, pp. 29–32.

8. Al Ries and Laura Ries, *The 22 Immutable Laws of Branding* (New York: HarperCollins, 1998), pp. 25–31.

9. "Coke Faces Struggle in Europe Recovery, Goldman Report Says," *The Wall Street Journal*, July 28, 1999, p. B5.

10. Ibid.

11. Bill Patterson, "Crisis Impact on Reputation Management," *Public Relations Journal*, November 1993, p. 48.

12. Ben White, "Stewart's Legal Problems Hurt Firm," *Washington Post*, August 4, 2004, p. E01, www.washingtonpost.com/wp-dyn/articles/A38202-2004Aug3.html.

13. Dennis L. Wilcox, *Public Relations Strategies and Tactics* (New York: HarperCollins, 1994), p. 381.

14. "What's Your Best Marketing Tool?" *Public Relations Journal*, February 1994, p. 12.

15. Adapted from Stephanie Gruner, "Event Marketing: Making the Most of Sponsorship Dollars," *Inc.*, August 1996, p. 88.

16. IEG FAQ: "What Is Sponsorship?" IEG Network 1998, www.sponsorship.com.

17. Ibid.

18. "Sponsorship Spending to Total $16.18 Billion in 2008, www.sponsorship.com/About-IEG/PressRoom/Sponsorship-SpendingTo-Total-$16.78-Billion-in-20.@asp; "Lenovo Ducks out of Olympic Sponsorship, Cost a Factor, www.marketingvex.com.

19. "Telco Ericsson Calls on James Bond, Volleyball," *Advertising Age*, June 1997, http://adage.com.

20. "Let Sponsors Do Their Thing," *Advertising Age*, May 23, 1996, http://adage.com.

21. "Impact of Sponsored Events Cited," *Advertising Age*, December 9, 1997, http://adage.com.

22. Thomas R. Duncan and Sandra E. Moriarty, *Driving Brand Value: Using Integrated Marketing to Manage Stakeholder Relationships* (New York: McGraw-Hill, 1997), p. 203.

23. Ibid.

24. Ibid.; Terry G. Vavra, *Aftermarketing: How to Keep Customers for Life through Relationship Marketing* (Burr Ridge, IL: Irwin, 1992), p. 190.

25. Vavra, *Aftermarketing*, p. 192.

26. "Assertions," *IEG Sponsorship Report*, www.sponsorship.com; Ron Lemasters Jr., "Sponsorship in NASCAR Breeds Fan Loyalty," Turner Sports Interactive, July 7, 2004, www.nascar.com/2004/news/business/07/07/sponsor_nascar.

27. Vavra, *Aftermarketing*, p. 192.

28. *IEG 2005 Sponsorship Report*, www.sponsorship.com.

29. David Sweet, "Everything Is for Sale in the World of Sports," January 24, 2008, www.msnbc.com.

30. Jonathan Bond and Richard Kirshenbaum, *Under the Radar: Talking to Today's Cynical Consumers* (New York: Wiley, 1998), p. 63.

31. Melanie Wells, "Going for Nagano Gold; Nagano's Remoteness Challenges Marketers," *USA Today*, February 6, 1998, p. 1B.

32. Boaz Herzog, "Let the Ads Begin," *The Oregonian*, August 13, 2004, p. B01.

33. Junu Bryan Kim, "Most Sponsorships Waste Money: Exec," *Advertising Age*, June 21, 1993, pp. S2, S4.

34. "California, L.A. a Contender to Host Next Summer's X Games," *Los Angeles Times*, October 11, 2002, www.proquest.com.

35. Lesa Ukman, "Assertions," *IEG Sponsorship Report*, February 23, 1998, www.sponsorship.com.

36. Ben Klayman, "North America Sponsorship Spending Seen Up in 108," January 22, 2008, reuters.com.

37. Ibid.

38. "Soccer and the Winning Mentality," Banco Solidario, www.banco-solidario.com/fondo_futbol.php.

39. Vans Warped Tour '06, www.warpedtour.com/.

40. "Spending to Rise 2.2 Percent in 2009," IEG, LLC February 2009, www.sponsorship.com/About-IEG/Press-Room/Sponsorship-Spending-To-Rise-2.2-Percent-in-2009.aspx.

41. Lesa Ukman, "Assertions," *IEG Sponsorship Report*, November 3, 1997, www.sponsorship.com.

42. Wilcox, *Public Relations Strategies and Tactics*, p. 384.

43. Lesa Ukman, "Assertions," *IEG Sponsorship Report,* November 3, 1997, *www.sponsorship.com.*

44. David Lister and Colin Brown, "Arts World Takes Sides with Tobacco Kings," *Independent* (UK), June 30, 1997, p. 3.

45. Cliff Peale, "Great American to Name Ballpark," *Cincinnati Enquirer,* July 1, 2000.

46. John Karolefski, "The Sport of Naming," Brand Channel.com, May 13, 2002, *www.brandchannel.com.*

47. Paul Stanley, "Sponsownership: Sponsorships Will Become Standard for Events," *Potentials in Marketing,* June 1990, p. 64.

48. "Nabisco's Cornnuts Sponsors Skaters Association Pro Tour," e-sports! *PR Sportswire,* December 1, 2000, *www.e-sports.com.*

49. Lesa Ukman, "Assertions," *IEG Sponsorship Report,* January 26, 1998, *www.sponsorship.com.*

50. Vavra, *Aftermarketing,* p. 191.

51. "Corporate Advertising/Phase II, An Expanded Study of Corporate Advertising Effectiveness," conducted for *Time* magazine by Yankelovich, Skelly & White, undated.

name index

Note: page numbers with "n" indicate note

A

Abbruzzese, Jason, 657n
Abernethy, Avery, 665n
Abraham, Magid M., 671n
Agrawal, Jagdish, 61, 657n
Ahern, G., 249
Alexander, Deborah, 323
Allen, Chris T., 661n, 663n
Allen, Frederick, 656n, 657n
Allen, Larry, 665n
Alpert, Lukas I., 667n
Alreck, Pamela L., 663n
Altstiel, Tom, 663n, 666n
Ambach, Gregg, 664n
Anderson, Catherine, 665n
Anderson, Rolph, 656n
Angrisani, Carol, 671n
Anschuetz, Ned, 664n
Arens, William F., 657n, 660n
Ariely, Dan, 146
Armstrong, Gary, 656n, 662n
Armstrong, J. Scott, 665n
Armstrong, Lance, 61, 62
Arndorfer, James B., 668n
Arnett, Dennis B., 663n
Assael, Henry, 662n
Atkinson, Claire, 657n
Avivi, Samantha, 266–267
Ayer, Francis, 46

B

Badzinski, Diane M., 665n
Bagley, Jason, 174
Bailey, Brandon, 669n
Balasubramanian, Siva K., 664n
Bandura, Albert, 155, 661n
Barban, Arnold M., 665n
Barchetti, Katherine, 601
Barkholz, David, 659n
Barnako, Frank, 668n
Barr, Stephen, 667n
Bartlett, Leonard L., 657n
Bates, Benjamin J., 667n
Baum, Chris, 670n
Beals, Jones Lundin, 278
Bearden, William O., 659n, 660n, 662n
Beatty, Sally, 664n

Beatty, Sally Goll, 660n
Beck, Ernest, 667n
Beeler, Amanda, 669n
Beers, Charlotte, 196
Beirne, Mike, 669n
Benady, David, 353
Bendinger, Bruce, 326
Benenson, Lisa, 663n
Bergen, Scott, 228
Berger, Warren, 657n
Bergerson, Stephen, 353
Bergner, Ashley, 661n
Berkowitz, Eric N., 659n, 660n
Berlin, Andy, 169
Berman, Jillian, 664n
Berman, Margo, 666n
Bernays, Edward, 585
Bernbach, Doyle Dane, 56
Bernbach, William (Bill), 29, 47, 48, 56, 168, 169, 552
Best, Jo, 658n
Best, Roger, 661n
Bettman, James, 248
Bhagwat, Yashoda, 663n
Bhargava, Rohit, 669n
Bidlake, Suzanne, 663n
Bieber, Justin, 493
Bigman, Shula, 665n
Bilorsky, Frank, 662n
Binnig, Bonnie, 671n
Bird, Laura, 670n
Blacker, Stephen M., 667n
Blakeman, Robyn, 666n
Bleustein-Blanchet, Marcel, 49, 657n
Bodett, Tom, 353
Bogart, Leo, 664n
Bogusky, Alex, 368
Bond, Jonathan, 671n
Boone, Ken, 670n
Borchers, Callum, 665n
Borden, Neil H., 662n
Boshra, Basem, 323
Boyd, Edward, 96–97
Bratman,Rich, 598
Breen, Peter, 664n
Bridges, Jeff, 429
Brin, Sergey, 51, 474
Brinkley, Christie, 559
Britton, Matt, 665n

Brizz, Michael, 663n
Brooks, Nancy, 178
Brown, Colin, 672n
Brown, Priscilla C., 664n
Bruell, Alexandra, 664n
Bryant, Kobe, 61, 62
Bryson, Ken, 661n
Bunche, Ralph, 96
Burgi, Michael, 668n
Burke, Tom, 668n
Burnett, Leo, 47
Burton, Philip Ward, 666n
Buzzell, Robert D., 664n
Byron, Ellen, 659n

C

Cacioppo, J. T., 661n
Calfee, John E., 658n, 659n
Calvacca, Lorraine, 671n
Campanaro, Tom, 670n
Candler, Asa, 33
Cannon, Hugh M., 665n
Cannon, Joseph, 663n
Canseco, Jose, 61
Capparell, Stephanie, 97
Cardone, Nancy Berger, 425
Carey, Benedict, 529
Carey, John, 659n
Carr, Austin, 579–580
Carrns, Ann, 658n
Caruso, Thomas E., 670n
Case, Tony, 667n
Casper, Lynne M., 661n
Castleberry, Stephen B., 671n
Cataquet, Harold, 660n
cCarthy, E. Jerome, 662n
Cervantes, Ken, 300
Chadwick, Simon, 663n
Chemi, Eric, 657n
Chiat, Jay, 169
Chiger, Sherry, 670n
Chopra, Carol, 662n
Chrysochou, Polymeros, 663n
Chung, Grace, 656n
Chura, Hillary, 664n
Cimino, Bill, 122
Circus, Philip, 353
Clancy, Tom, 560

Clark, Osborne, 353
Claus, Jaspar, 249
Clow, Lee, 168
Coe, Steve, 668n
Coen, Bob, 657n
Cohen, Emily, 79
Colford, Steven W., 658n, 659n
Collins, Nathan, 666n
Comm, Joel, 666n
Comte, Peter le, 353
Coney, Kenneth, 661n
Conlon, Ginger, 670n
Conner, Paul, 663n
Conrad, Michael, 326
Considine, Austin, 582
Cooksley, Erin, 323
Cooper, Ann, 667n
Cooper, Jim, 668n
Cooray, Mark, 77
Couette, Yves, 581
Covey, Stephen, 50
Cox, Anthony D., 660n
Cox, Dena, 660n
Crain, Rance, 323
Crosett, Kathy, 659n
Cruise, Tom, 493
Crumley, Bruce, 671n
Cuneo, Alice Z., 127, 661n, 669n
Cuniff, Tom, 52, 657n
Curran, Catharine, 8
Curran, Catharine M., 656n
Curtis, Helene, 130
Curtis, Jamie Lee, 3, 4
Cury, Ivan, 666n

D

Danzig, Fred, 665n
D'Arcy, William, 33
Davis, Gray, 552
Davis, Riccardo A., 669n
Davis, Scott M., 657n
Daykin, Tom, 323
Dean, Norman, 587
Decker, Phillip J., 661n
Defren, Todd, 582
DeGeneres, Ellen, 174, 581
Delevett, Peter, 669n
Deliso, Meredith, 668n
de Vise, Daniel, 667n
Dewey, John, 317
DiCaprio, Leonardo, 61
Dichter, Ernest, 657n
Dietrich, Joy, 658n
DiSalvo, David, 669n
Djonov, Emilia, 665n
Donaton, Scott, 667n
Douglas, Norman, 40

Downey, Kevin, 657n
Drake, O. Burtch, 136
Drakoulias, Peter, 127
Draper, Don, 72
Draper, Tim, 669n
Drazen, Jeffrey, Dr., 229
Drell, Lauren, 666n
Drewniany, Bonnie L., 666n
Drumwright, Minette E., 658n
Dubow, Joel S., 661n
Duncan, Thomas R., 656n, 667n, 671n
Duncan, Tom, 12
Dunn, Julie, 323
Dunn, Michael, 657n
Duplantis, David, 582
Dychtwald, Ken, 661n
Dylan, Bob, 201

E

Ebel, Rick, 670n
Edmonds, Rick, 667n
Eisenhart, Tom, 660n
Ellis, James E., 659n
Elsinga, Steven, 658n
Emerson, Jim, 663n, 670n
Eminem, 61
Endicott, R. Craig, 657n, 664n
Engle, R. W., 661n
Enrico, Dottie, 660n
Ephron, Erwin, 665n

F

Fabian, George S., 663n
Fabio, 174
Fahey, Alison, 660n
Fallon, Pat, 665n
Falls, Jason, 666n
Farid, Hany, 45
Farrell, Greg, 661n
Fawcett, Adrienne Ward, 662n
Ferrier, James, 669n
Fisher, Christy, 658n, 667n
Fitzimons, Gavan, 248
Flinn, John, 667n
Flintham, Richard, 375
Flykt, A., 249
Forbes, Thom, 668n
Forceville, Charles, 665n
Ford, John B., 658n
Fox, Stephen R., 656n
Francis, Michael, 306, 312
Frank, Thomas, 56
Franklin, Ben, 44
Franklin, Benjamin, 44
Frazier, Maya, 670n
Frazier, Mya, 662n

Freeman, Laurie, 664n, 665n
Freeman, Matt, 128
Freeman, Michael, 668n
Freiralds, John, 666n
Freud, Sigmund, 585
Fried, Lisa I., 667n
Friedman, Mitchell, 671n
Friedman, Sid, 560
Friedman, Ted, 660n
Friedman, Thomas, 103
Friedmann, Susan A., 670n
Fry, Richard, 661n
Fudge, Ann, 72
Fueroghne, Dean Keith, 658n

G

Gable, Greg, 661n
Gabor, Harvey, 42
Galbraith, John Kenneth, 67, 657n
Gallo, Carmine, 664n
Gallup, George, 46, 234
Gamble, Frederick R., 659n
Garcia, Shelly, 95, 657n
Garee, Michael L., 663n
Garfield, Bob, 353, 666n
Gates, Bill, 464, 493, 494
Giacomotti, Fabiana, 657n, 664n
Gibson, Richard, 663n
Gier, George, 320
Gilbert, Jennifer, 659n
Giobbe, Dorothy, 667n
Gladwell, Malcolm, 182–183, 500, 662n
Gleason, Mark, 127
Glenn, Martin, 353
Godin, Seth, 670n
Goetz, David, 529
Gogoi, Pallavi, 661n
Golden, Jim, 353
Goldman, Kevin, 94, 659n, 660n, 665n, 666n, 668n, 669n
Goldwater, Barry, 552
Gong, E. J., 659n
González, José, 376
Goodby, Jeff, 169
Gordon, Jeff, 61, 593
Gossage, Howard, 169
Goyat, Sulekha, 662n
Graves, Michael, 306
Green, Brian, 489
Green, Wayne E., 659n
Greenbaum, Thomas L., 663n
Greenberg, Karl, 669n
Greer, David, 353
Gretler, Corrine, 656n
Grohl, Dave, 493
Gross, Eric, 658n
Grover, Ronald, 668n

Grow, Jean, 659n, 663n, 666n
Gruner, Stephanie, 671n
Gurwitch, Annabelle, 145
Gutenberg, Johannes, 44

H

Hague, Stephen, 660n
Hainer, Herbert, 584
Haley, Kathy, 668n
Hall, Emma, 670n
Hallowell, Robert H., III, 670n
Harper, Jennifer, 552
Harris, Thomas L., 671n
Hartley, Steven W., 659n, 660n
Hartman, Ally, 239
Hartman, Barney, 239
Hartson, Rex, 663n
Harvey, Paul, 559
Haskey, Mary Jo, 669n
Hastings, Reed, 579–580, 581
Hauss, Deborah, 659n
Hawkins, Delbert, 661n
Hayden, Steve, 95
Hayes, Jack, 656n
Hayes, Nicole, 669n
Heathfield, Susan, 50
Helgesen, Thorolf, 660n
Helm, Burt, 660n
Henderson, Lisa L., 656n
Henderson, Wayne, 664n
Hennessy, Charles, 659n
Herzog, Boaz, 671n
Hess, Mike, 664n
Hill, Nancy, 72, 120, 136–137, 163
Hill, Simon, 658n
Hirsch, Jeff, 661n
Hoelzel, Mark, 656n
Hoffman, Bob, 460, 668n
Holt, Nancy D., 660n
Honomichl, Jack, 663n, 668n
Hopkins, Claude, 28–29, 46, 56
Hormby, Tom, 660n
Horovitz, Bruce, 663n
Horozvitz, Bruce, 209
Horton, Cleveland, 660n
Howard, Theresa, 662n, 663n, 670n
Huffman, Mark, 662n
Hutton, James, 662n

I

Imada, Bill, 600–601
Inboden, Marc, 656n
Ingram, Thomas N., 659n, 660n, 662n
Ippolito, Pauline M., 659n
Isaacson, Walter, 660n

J

Jackson, Jasper, 664n
Jackson, Rob, 550, 670n
Jackson, Ron, 660n
Jacobs, Rob, 550, 670n
Jaffe, Andrew, 657n, 660n, 662n
James, LeBron, 158
James, William J., 666n
Jenkins, John G., 665n
Jensen, Jeff, 665n
Jeweler, A. Jerome, 666n
Ji, Hon, 667n
Jobs, Steve, 143–144, 164, 560
Johannes, Amy, 670n
Johnson, Douglas, 666n
Johnson, Lyndon, 552
Johnson, Nick, 353
Johnson, Steve, 669n
Jones, Bill, 239
Jones, Eleanor, 657n
Jones, John Philip, 664n, 665n
Jordan, Michael, 61
Joseph, Leslie, 670n
Jugenheimer, Donald W., 665n
Jurkowitz, Mark, 667n
Jurvetson, Steve, 669n
Jurvetson, Steven, 484

K

Kahneman, Daniel, 661n
Kalish, Shlomo, 662n
Kamakura, Wagner, 61, 657n
Karolefski, John, 672n
Karremans, J.C., 249
Karremans, Johan, 249
Kassage, W. Wossen, 534
Kassaye, W. Wossen, 670n
Kaye, Joyce Rutter, 667n
Kellaris, James J., 660n
Keller, Kevin Lane, 656n
Kelliher, Neil, 665n
Kelly, Meghan, 670n
Kendall, Donald, 96
Kennedy, John E., 29
Kennel, Florence, 323
Kent, Felix H., 659n
Keough, Donald, 656n
Kerin, Roger A., 659n, 660n
Kern-Foxworth, Marilyn, 71
Key, Wilson Bryan, 248
Kiatchko, Jerry G., 656n
Kidman, Nicole, 195
Kiernan, Peter D., 662n
Kihlstrom, Richard E., 657n
Kiley, David, 660n
Kim, Chung K., 664n

Kim, Junu Bryan, 671n
Kindem, Gorham, 666n
King, Arlene, 315
King, Karen Whitehill, 665n
Kirk, Jim, 660n
Kirkpatrick, Marshall, 582
Kirshenbaum, Richard, 671n
Klaassen, Abbey, 473, 668n
Klayman, Ben, 671n
Klein, Matthew, 662n
Klein, Rick, 665n
Klewer, Edwin, 671n
Kliatchko, Jerry G., 656n
Knight, Phil, 601
Knightley, Keira, 195, 324
Knightley, Kiera, 163
Koprowski, Gene, 662n
Korn, Melissa, 669n
Korte, Gregory, 657n
Kotler, Philip, 550, 656n, 662n
Kover, Arthur J., 666n
Kozak, Ellen, 353
Kozak, M. J., 249
Kramer, Lorraine Alper, 666n
Kranhold, Kathryn, 660n, 663n
Krebs, Michelle, 667n
Krystallis, Athanasios, 663n
Kuehl, Claudia, 668n
Kullin, Hans, 353
Kumar, V., 663n, 664n

L

LaBahn, Douglas, 127
Lady Gaga, 582
Lafayette, Jon, 660n
LaForge, Raymond W., 659n, 660n, 662n
Lane, R. D., 249
Lang, P. J., 249
Larivière, B., 656n
Lasker, Albert, 8, 28–29, 46
Laskey, Henry A., 659n
LaTour, Michael S., 658n
Lauer, Matt, 494
Lauren, Ralph, 560
Lauterborn, Robert F., 663n, 664n, 665n
Lawler, Edmund O., 664n
Lawrence, Jennifer, 659n
Lawrence, Mary Wells, 163
Lawson, Angela, 671n
Lawton, Christopher, 664n
Leahy, Sean, 657n
Leckenby, John D., 665n
Leggio, Jennifer, 669n
Leibowitz, Jon, 473
Lemasters, Ron, Jr., 671n
Leonard, John, 670n

Levin, D. N., 249
Lewis, Herschell Gordon, 666n
Lewis, Roger, 126
Li, Shu-Fen, 667n
Liesse, Julie, 659n, 663n, 665n
Light, Larry, 565, 661n, 671n
Limbaugh, Rush, 559
Lin, Carolyn A., 661n
Lin, Carolyn A., 164
Linnett, Richard, 664n
Lipman, Joanne, 666n
Lister, David, 672n
Lodish, Leonard M., 671n
Lohr, Steve, 45
Longman, Kenneth, 665n
Longman, Kenneth A., 665n
Lord, Kenneth R., 664n
Ludacris, 61
Lundqvist, D., 249
Lutwak, Leo, 228
Luxton, Sandra, 656n

M

MacArthur, Kate, 664n
Machleit, Karen A., 661n, 663n
Mack, Ann M., 669n
Mack, Walter S., 96, 97
MacNeal, James, 439
Madden, Mary, 658n
Madden, Thomas J., 661n, 663n
Maddox, Kate, 660n
Madison, James, 76, 77
Madonna, 61
Mahmud, Shahna, 670n
Malmo, John, 658n
Mandese, Joe, 659n, 665n, 667n
Mankiw, N. Gregory, 656n
Marceau, Marcel, 592
Marian, Livia, 663n
Marks, Cliff, 538–539
Markus, Amy Dockser, 660n
Marsak, Michael, 127
Marshall, Perry, 663n
Marston, Maureen R., 663n
Martin, Bob, 540
Martin, Ernest, 664n
Martin, Geoffrey Lee, 658n
Martinsons, Aelita G. B., 659n
Martinsons, Maris G., 659n
Maslow, Abraham, 158, 159, 160
Mathios, Alan D., 659n
Mavondo, Felix, 656n
Maxeiner, James, 658n
Maxeiner, James R., 658n
Mazumdar, Mainak, 464
McAlear, Henry, 47

McCarthy, Caroline, 660n
McCarthy, E. Jerome, 191, 659n, 660n,
    662n, 663n
McCartney, Geoff, 122
McChesney, Robert W., 658n
Mcclellan, Steve, 657n
McConnell, Chris, 666n
McCue, Claudia, 666n
McDonald, Colin, 661n, 665n
McGlaughlin, Flint, 572–573
McKee, Steve, 657n, 665n
McKenna, Regis, 664n
McLuhan, Marshall, 17, 532
McMains, Andrew, 660n
McQuarrie, Edward F., 663n
Mehta, Rajiv, 656n
Merrill, Christina, 665n
Messina, Phil, 42
Meyerowitz, Steven A., 660n
Meyerson, Debra, 71
Micklethwait, John, 660n
Mikkelson, Barbara, 656n
Milentha, Rick, 163
Miller, Annetta, 662n
Miller, Cyndee, 669n, 670n
Miller, G. A., 249
Miller, Steve, 669n
Milliman, Ronald E., 661n
Mitchell, Alan, 659n
Mitchell, Nancy A., 665n
Mitchell, Paul C. N., 660n
Miyazaki, Ami, 670n
Moffitt, Scott, 239
Molpus, C. Manly, 662n
Monkhouse, Bob, 75
Moore, Stephanie, 671n
Moran, Gwen, 670n
Morgan, Alex, 603
Moriarty, Sandra E., 656n, 667n, 671n
Morin, Monte, 658n
Moser, Ed, 660n
Moss, Kate, 61
Mullen, Jeremy, 657n
Mullman, Jeremy, 62
Murray, George B., 665n
Musburger, Robert B., 666n
Mustafa, Isaiah, 174

N

Nade, L., 249
Narayan, Shoba, 662n
Neeleman, David, 583
Neff, Jack, 663n, 664n
Nelson, Jon P., 529
Nelson, Roy Paul, 666n
Newman, Barry, 657n

Newman, Jane, 169
Nicholls, J. A. F., 659n
Nielsen, A. C., 46
Nimoy, Leonard, 319
Nirell, Lisa, 656n
Norman, Greg, 494
Norris, Chuck, 559
Nowack, Glen, 12
Nowak, Glen, 656n

O

Obama, Barack, 8, 67, 552, 582
O'Barr, William, 657n
O'Barr, William M., 658n
O'Connell, Vanessa, 661n
Ogilvy, David, 29, 47, 327, 332, 607, 666n
Ohman, A., 249
O'Leary, Noreen, 661n
Olenski, Steve, 656n
Olsen, Mary Kate, 61
Olson, Jerry C., 661n
O'Malley, Gavin, 658n
O'Neill, Finbarr, 429
Ono, Yumiko, 660n, 661n, 664n
O'Reilly, Tim, 668n
Oren, Haim, 662n
Orwell, George, 143
O'Toole, John, 62, 63, 317n, 657n, 665n, 666n
Ovans, Andrea, 665n

P

Page, Larry, 51, 474
Palmer, Volney B., 46
Paltrow, Gwyneth, 115
Parker, Clifton B., 663n
Parker, Mark, 596
Parpis, Eleftheria, 665n
Patterson, Bill, 671n
Patterson, Jim, 659n
Paul, Chris, 61
Pavlov, Ivan, 154
Pawlowski, Donna R., 665n
Peale, Cliff, 657n, 672n
Pemberton, John, 33, 40
Penske, Greg, 594
Percy, Larry, 160, 661n
Perez, Juan Carlos, 501
Perreault, William, Jr., 663n
Perreault, William D., Jr., 659n, 660n, 662n
Perry, Katie, 493
Perry, Katy, 153
Peter, J. Paul, 661n
Peterson, Robert, 553
Peterson, Robert A., 670n
Petkus, Doug, 229

Petty, R. E., 661n
Phelps, Joe, 12
Phelps, Joseph, 656n
Phillips, Frank, 659n
Phillips, Lisa E., 664n
Pike, Rose, 229
Piper, Tim, 332
Poggi, Jeanine, 663n
Pollitt, Stanley, 168
Pollock, Judann, 657n
Poltrack, David F., 662n
Posey, John, 394
Posner, Richard A., 353
Poulos, Nicholas G., 670n
Pratkanis, Anthony, 248, 249
Preslmayer, Karly, 658n
Preston, Ivan, 45, 68, 73, 657n, 658n
Preston, Ivan L., 45
Pring, Cara, 669n
Pritikin, Robert, 662n
Pruzan, Todd, 665n
Pudzer, Andrew, 176
Purto, Rebecca, 661n
Pyla, Partha S., 663n
Pytka, Joe, 122

Q

Qiu, Richard, 658n
Quelch, John A., 658n

R

Rainey, M.T., 169
Rand, Hannah, 666n
Raphel, Murray, 666n, 670n
Raphel, Neil, 666n
Raye, Steven, 660n
Redfern, Ron, 353
Redfern, Ronald, 667n
Reece-Myron, Monique, 669n
Reed, Craig, 669n
Reeves, Rosser, 29, 48
Reid, Mike, 656n
Reilly, Patrick M., 667n
Reinemer, Michael, 184
Rhodes, Mike, 663n
Richards, Jeff, 8
Richards, Jef I., 656n
Rickard, Leah, 663n
Ries, Al, 48, 205, 583, 663n, 664n, 671n
Ries, Laura, 205, 583, 663n, 671n
Rijkens, Rein, 658n, 665n
Riordan, Edward A., 665n
Riordan, Michael H., 657n
Risen, Tom, 669n
Ritzmann, Florian, 657n

Roberts, Dexter, 667n
Robinson, Jackie, 96
Robinson, Phyllis, 56
Robinson, Wayne, 670n
Romney, Mitt, 552
Rosenstiel, Tom, 667n
Roslow, Sydney, 659n
Rossiter, John R, 160
Rossiter, John R., 661n
Rowe, Jim, 659n
Rubel, Chad, 663n
Rubio, Ralph, 105, 108
Rudelius, William, 659n, 660n
Russell, Jack, 80
Ryan, Bernard, Jr., 664n

S

Saatchi, Charles, 49
Saatchi, Maurice, 49
Sabena, Pat, 662n
Safran, Nathan, 666n
Sakalosky, Mark, 658n
Sanders, Lisa, 278
Savage, Sean, 660n
Schellinck, Tony, 664n
Schiavenza, Matt, 657n
Schlossberg, Howard, 659n
Schlosser, Eric, 662n
Schmuckler, Eric, 668n
Schori, Thomas R., 663n
Schotthoffer, Peter, 658n
Schrage, Michael, 662n
Schroer, James C., 664n
Schudson, Michael, 657n
Schultz, Don E., 663n, 664n, 665n
Schultz, Howard, 189
Schumann, D., 661n
Schwarz, Jean-Marc, 657n
Schwarzenegger, Arnold, 552, 560
Schweitzer, John C., 667n
Scott, Ridley, 143–144
Seiden, Hank, 662n
Senn, Fred, 665n
Serafin, Raymond, 659n, 662n
Settle, Robert B., 663n
Shaffer, Robert, 671n
Shakira, 3–4, 23
Shalek, Nancy, 353
Shama, Avraham, 670n
Shanahan, Steven, 439
Shannon, Claude Elwood, 656n
Sharapova, Maria, 61
Sharkey, Betsy, 660n
Sharma, Dinesh C., 669n
Shatner, William, 319
Shaw, Gaylord, 659n

Shermach, Kelly, 671n
Shewan, Dan, 666n
Shields, Todd, 659n
Shimp, T. A., 661n
Shultz, Don E., 656n
Shultz, E. J., 656n
Siegler, M. G., 669n
Silva, Fabiola da, 598
Silverstein, Rich, 169
Skinner, B. F., 154–155
Skitol, Robert A., 671n
Sloan, Pat, 663n
Smith, Herman T., 96
Smith, N. Craig, 658n
Smith, Reed, 80
Snyder, Beth, 660n
Socrates, 75
Solo, Sally, 659n
Stanford, Duane, 664n
Stanley, Paul, 598, 672n
Stanley, T. L., 668n
Starch, Daniel, 46
Steel, Jon, 168–169
Steinberg, Brian, 657n
Stephan, S. Kent, 660n, 661n
Stern, Barbara, 15, 656n
Stern, Howard, 559
Stewart, Al, 661n
Stewart, Martha, 585, 586
Stewart, Patrick, 493
Stone, Bob, 550, 670n
Stone, Brad, 501
Stroebe, W., 249
Stroebe, Wolfgang, 249
Stuart, Elnora W., 661n
Sugarman, Joseph, 666n
Sullivan, Bob, 658n
Surmanek, Jim, 665n
Swaminathan, Sriinvasan, 656n
Swanson, Ana, 664n
Sweet, David, 671n
Sweney, Mark, 666n
Szmigin, Isabelle T. D., 660n
Szynal, Deborah, 663n

T

Tannenbaum, Schultz, 665n
Tannenbaum, Stanley I., 663n, 664n, 665n
Tannenholz, Barry L., 660n, 661n
Tanner, John F., Jr., 671n
Taylor, Charles R., 656n
Taylor, Colleen, 473
Taylor, Dave, 666n
Teinowitz, Ira, 658n
Thompson, Jack K., 670n

Thompson, J. Walter, 115
Thompson, Stephanie, 664n
Thorgersen, John, 663n
Thrasher, Hugh, 353
Tobenkin, David, 668n
Todd, Bryan, 663n
Toor, Mat, 660n
Treise, Debbie, Dr., 106
Trent, Linda, 662n
Trout, Jack, 48, 664n
Tsai, Jessica, 656n
Turk, Peter B., 665n
Tysver, Robynn, 323
Tzatzev, ALeksi, 665n

U

Ukman, Lesa, 671n, 672n
Uva, Joe, 454

V

Van den Bulte, Christophe, 662n, 663n
Van den Poel, D., 656n
Van Riper, Tom, 670n
van Waterschoot, Walter, 662n, 663n
Vavra, Terry, 598
Vavra, Terry G., 671n
Verma, Dharmendra, 534, 670n
Vicary, James, 248, 249
Vick, Michael, 61–62, 586
Vogt, Susan, 658n
Vogt, Willie, 667n
Volpe, Mike, 668n
Von Oech, Roger, 316, 317, 318, 319, 320, 326, 665n

W

Wackman, Daniel B., 660n
Walchle, Mark W., 664n
Waldemar, Carla, 670n
Walker, Derek, 320, 666n
Walker, Rob, 229
Walker, Scott, 552
Wallace, Rusty, 594
Wang, Paul, 664n
Wansink, Brian, 192, 662n
Ward, Adrienne, 657n
Ward, Miranda, 666n
Ward, Ted, 546
Warden, Sharon P., 94
Warner, Fara, 669n
Washington, Booker T., 601
Wasserman, Todd, 661n
Waterschoot, Walter van, 662n, 663n
Watters, Pat, 657n
Weaver, Warren, 656n
Weber, Larry, 656n
Weber, Max, 314
Webster, Nancy Colton, 670n
Weiner, Mathew, 34
Weitz, Barton A., 671n
Welch, Jack, 50
Wells, Melanie, 659n, 660n, 671n
Wentz, Laurel, 658n, 660n
Wesson, David A., 666n
West, Gordon, 122
West, Robert, 663n
Weylock, William, 663n
Whidden, Jack J., 657n, 660n
White, Ben, 671n
White, Rob, 169
Wiersema, Frederick D., 664n

Wilcox, Dennis L., 671n
Willhoft, Gene, 667n
Williams, Raymond, 34
Williams, Serena, 61
Willingham, Chris, 375
Willis, James R., Jr., 660n
Wilson, Joy Johnson, 658n
Winters, Lewis C., 662n
Wittman, C. Michael, 663n
Wolf, Alan, 662n
Wood, Douglas J., 80
Woods, Terry, 670n
Woods, Tiger, 61, 62, 586
Wotruba, Thomas, 553
Wotruba, Thomas R., 670n
Wozniak, Steve, 143
Wynter, Leon E., 661n

Y

Yaffe, Samantha, 668n
Young, John Orr, 29
Yssel, Johan C., 664n
Yu, Roger, 667n

Z

Zaslow, Jeffrey, 661n
Zemack-Rugar, Yael, 248
Zhang, Zi (Alan), 663n
Zhao, Sumin, 665n
Zieff-Finn, Marjorie, 666n
Zinn, Laura, 661n
Zubi, Joe, 204
Zubi, Tere (Mama), 204
Zuckerberg, Mark, 51, 493, 500–501, 511

company index

A

AAAA (American Association of Advertising Agencies), 45, 62, 72, 74, 91, 93, 98, 116, 120, 126, 136, 163, 422, 469

AADA (Arizona Automobile Dealers Association), 86

AAF (American Advertising Federation), 45, 57, 74, 98

AARP The Magazine, 410, 422

Abacus Direct, 84

ABC (Audit Bureau of Circulation), 135, 410, 430, 431, 436, 449

ABC News, 583

ABC Sports, 538

Abercrombie & Fitch, 72, 322, 559

Absolut Vodka, 525

ACNielsen and Information Resources, Inc., 223

ACNielsen's ScanTrack, 223

Activia, 3–4, 11, 23–25

Acura, 10

Acuvue, 453

Acxiom Corp., 549

Ad Age (magazine), *see Advertising Age* (magazine)

Ad Council, 55, 74, 128

Adidas, 584, 595–595

Adlaw by Request, 80

Adobe, 396

Adobe Dreamweaver, 342, 343

Adobe Flash, 343

Adobe Illustrator, 343

Adobe InDesign, 343

Adobe Photoshop, 343

Adoptuskids.org, 55

AdSense, Google, 301, 474, 475, 482

Advance Publications, 134

Advertising, Technology, and Media Group, 80

Advertising Age (magazine), 56, 62, 117, 136, 163, 184, 219, 326, 337, 353, 360, 401, 411, 439, 464

Advertising Checking Bureau, 422

Advertising Concept and Copy (Felton), 343

Advertising Division of the Better Business Bureau, 552

Advertising Federation Hall of Achievement, 168

Advertising Week, 163

Advil, 266

Adweek (magazine), 95, 98, 126, 326

AdWords, Google, 51, 474–475, 482

A&F Magazine, 559

Africa Propaganda, 604

Aftermarketing (book), 598

AGB Research, 442

Aggressive Skaters Association (ASA), 598

AICPA (American Institute of Certified Public Accountants), 558

AIDS.gov, 271–272

Aim, 195

AirBnB, 479

Albert and Mary Lasker Foundation, 29

Alexa, 468

Alien (film), 143–144

ALS Association, 493–494

Altimeter Group, 504

Amazon Prime, 52

Amazon.com, 196, 471, 473, 475, 496, 563

American Advertising Federation (AAF), 45, 57, 74, 98

American Airlines, 110, 204, 597

American Association of Advertising Agencies (AAAA), 45, 62, 72, 74, 91, 93, 98, 116, 120, 126, 136, 163, 422, 469

American Banker (magazine), 409

American Cancer Society, 8, 20

American Coalition for Entertainment and Sports Sponsorship, 593

American Demographics, 219

American Eagle, 305

American Express, 226, 594

American Harvester, 608

American Home Products, 228, 229

American Indian College Fund, 128

American Institute of Certified Public Accountants (AICPA), 558

American Legacy Foundation, 402

American Newspaper Publishers Association, 420

American Parking Meter Advertising, 531

American Public Relations, 585

American Red Cross, 8, 548

American Society of Magazine Editors, 94

American Society of Magazine Editors (ASME), 94

American Telecast, 559

American Telephone Advertising (ATA), 531

America's Cup, 593

Amundsen, 52

Amway, 553

Amway International, 199

ANA (Association of National Advertisers), 57, 98, 110

Anheuser-Busch, 130, 209–210, 353, 538

ANPAA (National Association for Prevention of Alcoholism and Addiction), 49

Anthropologie, 559

AOL, 136, 464

AOL Small Business, 396

APCO Worldwide, 583

Apple, 21, 38, 56, 65, 84, 110, 130, 143–144, 146, 147, 149, 152, 153, 158, 164, 199, 313, 367, 437, 560, 583

Apple, iPad, 144, 149, 150, 180

Apple I, 143

Apple II, 143

Apple iPad, 583

Apple iPhone, 21, 65, 144, 153, 488, 498

Apple iPod, 558

Apple iPods, 65

Apple iTunes, 157

Apple Macintosh computer, 21, 143–144, 156

Arbitron, 442

Arbitron Book, 451

Architectural Digest (magazine), 405

Archives of Ophthalmology (magazine), 21, 409

ARCO, 596

Arizona Automobile Dealers Association, 86

Arizona Automobile Dealers Association (AADA), 86

Army, U.S., 160, 161, 332

Army Special Forces, 602

ARPA (Defense Department's Advanced Research Projects Agency), 461

ARPAnet, 461

Arts & Entertainment, 431

ASA Amateur Circuits, 598

ASA Pro Tour, 598

ASA World Champion, 598

ASME (American Society of Magazine Editors), 94

Associated Press, 498

Association for Business Sponsorship for the Arts, 597

Association of National Advertisers (ANA), 57, 98, 110

ATA (American Telephone Advertising), 531

Atkins diet, 228

Atlanta Journal, 33, 40

Atlas DMT, 468

Atlas Rich Media, 485

AT&T, 65, 75, 89, 111, 130, 143, 165, 178, 357, 415, 437, 538, 596, 597, 598

Audi, 472

Audit Bureau of Circulation (ABC), 135, 410, 430, 431, 436, 449

Audubon Society, 165

Australian Women's Weekly (magazine), 422
Automated Postal Centers, 569
Avenue A/Razorfish, 120
Aviation Week & Space Technology (magazine), 423
Avis, 48, 56
Avon, 553
Axe, 173

B

Baby Talk (magazine), 423
Bank of America, 110
Bank of America Stadium, 598
BankOne, 596
Barbie doll, 233
Barnes & Noble, 200
Barron's, 134
Bartle Bogle Hegarty, 186
Baseline (magazine), 423
Batman (film), 527
Bayer, 161
BBB (Better Business Bureau), 57, 75, 91–92
BBDO New York, 239
BBDO West, 203
BBDO Worldwide, 117, 126
Beacon, 500, 501
Beber, Silverstein and Partners, 204
BehaviorGraphics, 181–182, 183
Belgian Chimay, 559
Ben & Jerry's, 581
Best Buy, 178, 201, 550
BET, 72
Better Business Bureau (BBB), 57, 75, 91–92
Better Homes and Gardens (magazine), 422
The Big Won, 332
Bing, 134, 219
BlackBerry, 192
Blade Runner (film), 143–144
Blendtec, 485, 512
Blogger, 499
Bloomberg Businessweek (magazine), 219, 411, 423
BlueKai, 471, 502
BMP (Boase Massimi Pollitt), 168, 169
BMW, 21, 179, 332, 370, 405
Boase Massimi Pollitt (BMP), 168, 169
The Body Shop, 583
Bolthouse Farms, 521
Bonux, 233
The Book (Nielsen), 441
Boomers, 149
Boston, 194
Boston Legal (TV program), 394
Boston Marathon, 185
Boston Newsletter, 44
Bounty Paper Towels, 72
Boycott Anorexic Marketing group, 95
Bravia, Sony, 375

Bravo channel, 465
Brewing & Distilling International (magazine), 423
Brisk Iced Tea, 17
British Airways, 115
British Petroleum, 115
Bruegger's Bagels, 540
Buddy Media, 503
Budweiser, 209, 210, 213, 439
Buenos Aires Zoo, 606
Buick Invitational, 598
Bully Pulpit Interactive, 210
Bureau of Alcohol, Tobacco and Firearms, 567
Burger King, 512
Burrell Communications, 104, 119
Burroughs, 608
Burson-Marsteller, 366
Business Lists, 557
Business Periodicals Index, 219
Buy.com, 85

C

CA, 583
Cadillac, 48
Cahners Publishing, 411
California Department of Health Services, 49
California Egg Commission, 61
California Farmer (magazine), 21, 135
California Fluid Milk Processors Advisory
          Board, 169
California Grocer (magazine), 21
California Milk Processor Board, 67
Calvin Klein, 45, 72, 95, 404
Campbell's Soup Company, 46, 153, 528,
          569, 596
Canadian Tobacco Manufacturers' Council, 540
Cannes Grand Prix, 174
Cannes International Advertising Festival, 49,
          51, 72
Cannes Lions Academy, 326
Captivate Networks, 532
Car & Driver (magazine), 412
CARE, 203
Carnation, 596
CARU (Children's Advertising Review Unit), 83
Catalina Marketing and Advanced Promotion
          Technologies, 570
Catholic Channel, 93
CBS, 135, 430, 436, 449, 532
Census Bureau, 105, 165
Center for Science in the Public Interest
          (CSPI), 581
CFA (Consumer Federation of America), 95
Chambers of Commerce, 75
Chanel, 61, 162, 195, 201, 324
Charles Schwab, 150
Chase, 204

Cherokee, 306
Chevrolet, 111, 597
Chiat/Day, 143, 144, 169
Chicago (magazine), 135, 409
Chicago's Wrigley Field, 200
Children's Advertising Review Unit (CARU), 83
Chili's, 161
Chivas Regal, 130, 197
Christian Science Monitor (newspaper), 416
Chrysler, 94, 421, 487
Cincinnati Reds, 598
Cinema Advertising Council, 540
Cinemax, 431
Cingular Wireless, 596
Circuit City, 305, 538
Cisco Systems, 136
Citibank ATMs, 367
Citrus Hill Fresh Choice, 89
CKE Restaurants, Inc., 176
Clairol, 306
Claritas, 162, 177, 188
Classic Coke, 239
Clear Channel, 70
Cliff Notes, 591
Closet Factory, Inc., 91
Close-Up, 195
Clyde's Bar, 318
CNBC, 431, 498
CNet.com, 512
CNN, 72, 138, 177, 215, 431
CNN.com, 294
Coca-Cola, 26, 28, 32–33, 40–43, 46, 51, 65, 79,
          89, 90, 104, 115, 119, 138, 184, 195,
          200, 306, 367, 433, 480, 486, 487,
          495, 540, 584
Coca-Cola Beach Party, 584
Coca-Cola Company, 33, 34, 42, 43, 53, 523, 598
Coca-Cola USA, 541
Coke, 38, 41, 43, 119, 196, 364, 367, 510, 584,
          594, 603
Colgate-Palmolive, 49, 126
Colored Leaf, 353
Comcast, 450, 505, 507, 509
@comcastcares, 506
Comedy Central, 72, 431, 465
Communispace, 509
CompuServe, 464
ComputerWorld Poland (magazine), 423
ComScore, 467, 489
Consolidated Foods, 608
Consumer Federation of America (CFA), 95
Consumer Lists, 557
Consumers' Research, 95
Consumers Union, 95
Contemporary Advertising (magazine), 136,
          169, 532
Coors Field, 598

Coral Gables, 204
Cornnuts, 598
Corporate Financial Services, 560
Cossette Communications-Marketing, 118
Council of Better Business Bureaus, 92, 93
CP+B (Crispin Porter+Bogusky), 118, 368–369, 484
Craftsman, 195
Cragmont, 195
Craigslist, 466, 484, 487
Creative Artists Agency, 119
Creative Edge, 34
Crest, 115, 177, 200
Crispin Porter+Bogusky (CP+B), 118, 368–369, 484
Crosfield, 385
Crossing Jordan (TV program), 394
Crowdspring, 510
CSS, 342
CTR Market Research, 180
Cub Scouts, 586
Cumulus Media Network, 448
CW television network, 430, 437
Cyber Seniors, 597

D

Dailytech. com, 582
Dallas Morning News, 228
Dancer, 49
Dannon, 4, 570
Danoo, 532
D'Arcy Masius Benton & Bowles (DMB&B), 130
DART Motif, 485
Darty, 66
Dayton Company, 305
DDB Asia Pacific, 128
DDB Chicago, 122
DDB Group Sydney, 128
DDB Needham, 49, 126, 130
DDB Worldwide, 117, 118
De Beers Diamonds, 71, 306, 357
Dean & Deluca, 559
DeBeers Diamonds, 71, 306, 357
Deceptive Mail Prevention and Enforcement Act, 421
Defense Department's Advanced Research Projects Agency (ARPA), 461
Del Rivero Messiano DDB, 121
Dell Computers, 199, 313, 367, 470, 507
Delta Airlines, 110, 126, 598
Denny's, 184
Dentsu, 49, 117
Detroit Free Press, 94
Dialog Information Service, 219
Diet Coke, 38, 240
Digg, 466, 495

Digital Equipment, 298
Digitas, 120
DigitasLBi, 549
Direct Mail List Rates and Data, 557
Direct Marketing Association, 421
Direct Marketing Association (DMA), 93
Directory of National Trade Associations, 219
DirecTV, 487, 505
Discovery Channel, 431
Disney, 89, 110, 213, 391, 438, 486, 503, 510
Disney World, 596
Disneyland, 596
Disqus, 499
DKC Public Relations, 583
DMA (Direct Marketing Association), 93
DMB&B (D'Arcy Masius Benton & Bowles), 130
DMH MacGuffin, 353
Doan's Pills, 87
Dockers, 154, 187, 473
Document Company, 193
Dodge Dakota, 405
Doner, 136
DoubleClick, 84, 468
Dove, 332, 355, 453
Dow Jones News Retrieval Service, 219
Doyle Dane Bernbach, 163, 169
Draft FCB, 118, 130, 272
Draper Fisher Jurvetson, 484
Dreamweaver, Adobe, 343
Dreyers Grand Ice Cream, 189
Duncan and Moriarty, 13, 14
Dunkin' Donuts, 204
DuPont, 593

E

EA (Electronic Arts), 472, 495
Eastpak, 596
EasyFile, 243
eCast, 532
The Economist (magazine), 146
EDGAR Online, 219
Edsel, 69
Effie Award, 338
eGrocery, 570
E&J Gallo Winery, 353
Electric Library, 219
Electronic Arts (EA), 472, 495
Electronic Data Systems Corp., 540
Electronic Design (magazine), 409
Electronic News, 134
Elle (magazine), 134, 422
Ellen (TV program), 94
Energizer Bunny, 306
Enron, 598
Enron Field, 598

Environmental Protection Agency (EPA), 85
Envirosell, 223
EPA (Environmental Protection Agency), 85
Epsilon, 549
Equifax, 162
E.R. (TV program), 394
Ericsson Corp., 593
ESPN Classic, 532
ESPN Magazine, 532
ESPN radio, 532
ESPN television network, 135, 177, 215, 435, 449, 532
ESPN the Magazine, 413
ESPN2, 532
ESPN.com, 467, 532
ESPNews, 532
ESPN's Winter X Games, 596
ESPN's X Games, 11
ESPNZone restaurants, 532
Esquire (magazine), 422
Esser's wine store, 351
Estée Lauder, 115
E*Trade, 475
E-Trade Financial Corp., 470
European Business (magazine), 423
European Common Market, 49
Evidon, 473
Evolution (advertising campaign), 332
EWeek (magazine), 423
Executive Female (magazine), 411
Expedia.com, 471
Experian Group, 470
Experian Marketing Services, 549
Extra (TV program), 438
Extra-Strength Tylenol, 585, 586
Exxon, 85, 115
ExxonMobil, 26
Eyeblaster, 485

F

A Fable, 592
Facebook, 4, 5, 51, 55, 84, 135, 148, 174, 199, 252, 310, 338, 366, 396, 463, 467, 485, 493–494, 497, 498, 500–501, 502, 503, 505, 509–510, 511, 528, 580
Facebook Connect, 498
Fallon Worldwide, 177, 213, 375
Family First, 322
Fandango, 500
Farm Journal (magazine), 409
Fastcompany.com, 580
FBI (Federal Bureau of Investigation), 586
FCA, 49
FCB (Foote, Cone & Belding), 49, 62, 126, 130, 132, 159, 160, 257, 489, 591

FCBarcelona, 594
FCC (Federal Communications Commission), 70–71, 84, 89, 248, 433, 453
FDA (Food and Drug Administration), 84, 87–89, 228, 534
Febreze, 330
Federal Bureau of Investigation (FBI), 586
Federal Communications Commission (FCC), 70–71, 84, 89, 248, 436, 453
Federal Trade Commission (FTC), 45, 57, 65, 70, 84–87, 228, 473
FedEx, 20, 115, 193, 557
Field and Stream (magazine), 423
50 Shades of Grey (film), 540
Final Cut Studio, 366
Financial Times (newspaper), 422
Finn Partners, 583
Firestone, 540
First Descent (film), 240
FirstLook (theater advertising program), 538, 539
Fisher Price, 266
Fitzgerald, 49
Fixodent, 17
Flash, Adobe, 343
Fleet Financial Group, 540
Flickr, 466, 500, 506, 508
Florida Renaissance Festival, 597
FMC Corp., 21
FMR Corp., 470
Focus, 145
Folgers, 115, 200
Food & Family (magazine), 405
Food and Brand Lab, 192
Food and Drug Administration (FDA), 84, 87–89, 228, 534, 581, 586, 658n
Foote, Cone & Belding (FCB), 29, 62, 126, 130, 132, 159, 160, 257, 489, 591
Forbes (magazine), 72, 219, 484, 504, 560
Ford Motor Company, 21, 61, 109, 115, 145, 149, 165, 204, 437, 594, 596
Forrester Research, 487, 495, 496, 582
Fortune, 189, 219, 305, 316, 511
Fossil Watches, 537
4INFO, 488
Four Seasons, 506
4day Tire Stores, 352
Foursquare, 498, 512, 528
Fox, 72, 94, 135, 430, 436, 463
Fox Interactive Group, 489
Fox Sports, 509
Franklin Institute Science Museum, 597
Frappuccino, Starbucks, 189
Freestyle Interactive, 472
Friends (TV program), 438
Friendster, 498
Fruit and Maple Oatmeal, 121

Fry's Electronics, 415
FTC (Federal Trade Commission), 45, 57, 65, 70, 84–87, 228, 473
Fuel Industries, 120
Fuji, 596
Full Core, 568
Full House (TV program), 394
The Full Monty (film), 540

G

Galaxy G92 FM, 69
Gallagher Report, 607
Gallaher Group, 597
Gannett, 134
Garnier, 17
Gatorade, 360, 594
GE (General Electric), 8, 161, 298, 404–405, 415, 453, 556, 596, 599, 608
GEICO, 450, 545–546, 547, 548, 550, 553–554, 560
Geico, 111
General Dynamics, 607
General Electric (GE), 8, 161, 298, 404–405, 415, 453, 556, 596, 599, 608
General Mills, 113
General Motors (GM), 70, 178, 226, 244, 257, 404, 470, 531, 594
GeoVALS, 180
German Foundation for the Preservation of Historic Monuments, 605
Gilette, 192
Girl Scout cookies, 561
Girlz Garage, 596
Gladiator (film), 143–144
Glamour (magazine), 409
Gleem, 405
Global Commerce Group, 405
Global Product Committee, 326
GlobalGiving, 128
Globe and Mail (newspaper), 416
GM (General Motors), 70, 178, 226, 244, 257, 404, 470, 531
Goldman, Sachs & Co., 584
Golf (magazine), 423
Golf Channel, 494
Golf Plus, 94
Good Housekeeping (magazine), 92, 93, 409
Good Housekeeping Institute, 357
Goodby Silverstein & Partners, 67, 168–169, 429
Google, 14, 50, 51, 79, 83, 84, 115, 134, 217, 219, 292, 301, 468, 473, 474–475, 481, 482, 485, 500, 503, 509, 553, 582, 589
Google+, 503, 507, 509
Google AdPlanner, 468, 485

Google AdSense, 301, 474, 475, 482
Google AdWords, 468, 474–475, 482
Google Analytics, 217, 468
Google Maps, 83
Google PageRank, 474
Gotham, Inc., 118
Gowalla, 528
Grand Prix of Jumping (TV program), 435
Gravity Games, 11
Great American Ballpark, 598
Great American Insurance Company, 597
Great Cuts, 540
Green Seal, 587
Green Threads, 4–5, 12, 14
Grey Worldwide, 118
Grieco Research Group, 222
Groupon, 109
Guidelines (CARU), 83

H

Hallmark, 433, 437
Hallmark Cards, 569
Hanes, 47
Happy Meals, 120, 180
Hardee's, 176, 184
Harley-Davidson, 364
Harper's Magazine, 56
Harte Hanks, 549
Harvey Nichols, 197, 320
HBO (Home Box Office), 52, 431
HCM/New York, 119
Healthtex, 223, 227
Hearst Co., 134
Heiser Automotive Group, 353
Hell ScriptMaster, 385
Herbalife, 199, 553
Hewlett- Packard, 110, 315
HGTV (magazine), 124
Hoffman/Lewis, 126
Holiday Inn Express, 177, 375
Holland America Line-Westours cruises, 200
Home Box Office (HBO), 52, 431
Home Depot, 450
Home Shopping Network, 440, 560
Honda, 75
Honda Civic, 244
Honeywell, 405
Hoot Suite, 503
Houston Astros, 598
H&R Block, 107
HTML, 342
Hulu, 52
Hulu Plus, 447
The Hunger Site, 128
Hush Puppy, 182
Hyundai Advantage, 429

Hyundai Assurance, 430
Hyundai Genesis Coupe, 429
Hyundai Motor America, 429

I

IAB (Interactive Advertising Bureau), 93, 468,
    469, 475, 485, 488
IAG Ad, 227
Iams, 453
IAPI (Institute of Advertising Practitioners in
    Ireland), 439
IBM, 26, 75, 115, 143–144, 163, 364, 433,
    483, 607
The Ice Storm (film), 540
ICR, 583
IEG Inc., 594, 597
IEG Network, 596
IEGSR, 598
IFAW, 352
IGN, 489
IKEA, 483
Il Giornales, 189
Illusion (magazine), 476
Imperial Cruise Lines, 348
InDesign, Adobe, 343
Industry Guides and Trade Regulation Rules, 87
InformationWeek (magazine), 423
InfoScan, 219
Initiative Media, 532
Inside Edition (TV program), 438
Inside PR (magazine), 582
Instagram, 4, 25, 466, 494, 497, 498,
    499, 509
Institute of Advertising Practitioners in Ireland
    (IAPI), 439
Intel, 596
Interactive Advertising Bureau (IAB), 93, 468,
    469, 475, 485, 488
International Advertising Festival, 604
International Association of Fairs and
    Expositions, 596
International Data Group, 423
International Herald Tribune (newspaper), 422
International Paper, 607
International Telecommunications Union, 465
Internet Explorer, 464
Internet World Stats, 465
Interpublic Group, 117, 118, 127, 163
iPad, Apple, 144, 149, 150, 180
iPhone, Apple, 65, 144, 153, 488, 498
iPod, Apple, 65
iTunes, 467
iTunes, Apple, 157
Ivory soap, 115
Ivy League, 511
IW Group, Inc., 600–601

J

J. D. Powers and Associates, 429, 495
J. Walter Thompson (JWT), 115, 196, 214,
    215, 359
Jack in the Box, 363
James Ready Brewing Company, 515–516, 519
Japan Weather Association, 177
Japan-VALS, 180
JC Penney, 582
JCPenney, 107, 178, 186, 453
Jell-O, 46
Jenny Craig, 324, 405
Jeopardy (TV program), 438
JetBlue, 157, 507, 583
Jiffy Lube, 218
Johnson & Johnson, 110, 497, 585–586
Joomla, 396
Jupiter Research, 219
JWT (J. Walter Thompson), 115, 196, 214,
    215, 359

K

Kaiser Aluminum, 592
Karamel Sutra ice cream, 581
Katholische Hofkirche (Dresden), 605
Katz Radio, 451
KDWB, 93
Kellogg, 46, 115
Kenmore, 195
Kentucky Fried Chicken (KFC), 27, 228
Kessels Kramer, 63
Ketchum Advertising, 361
KFC (Kentucky Fried Chicken), 27, 228
KHJ, 448
Kia, 158
kibu.com, 591
Kimberly-Clark, 266–267
King World Productions, 438
Kinko's, 107
Kirshenbaum, Bond & Partners, 564, 565
KKDA, 452, 453
KLBJ, 93
Kleenex, 65, 506
Kmart, 305
Kodak, 115, 596, 597
Kraft Foods, 200, 405
Kraft General Foods, 126
Kraft Singles, 214, 215
Kroger, 195
KSDO, 93

L

L. J. Market Research, 537
La Opinion, 418

Ladies Home Journal (magazine), 72
Lamborghini, 156, 352
Land Rover, 202
Lands' End, 559
Las Vegas Convention Center, 531
Late Night with David Letterman (TV
    program), 215
Lay's Potato Chips, 352
Leap Partnership, 320
Lego, 371, 519
Leo Burnett, 116, 118, 121, 124, 126, 128, 130,
    310, 318, 326, 515
Leonard/Monahan, 167
Levi Strauss, 186, 187
Levi's, 89, 132, 154, 184, 187, 188, 189, 191,
    193, 195
Levi's Dockers, 154
Levi's Jeans, 132
Levi's Signature, 189
Levy's bread, 56
Lexis-Nexis, 219
Lexus, 13, 174, 370, 527, 600
Libby Owens-Ford, 70
Library of Congress, 84, 89–90
Life Savers, 48
Lifetime, 431
LightCMS, 396
Like.com, 473
Lincoln , Abraham, 607
Lindsay Olives, 447, 448
Linens 'n Things, 305
LinkedIn, 135, 497, 498, 502, 508
Lipton, 249
Literary Digest, 234
Live Aid, 597
Livefyre, 499
L.L.Bean, 559
London Organising Committee of the
    Olympic and Paralympic Games
    (LOCOG), 584
Lord, Dentsu & Partners, 52
Lord & Thomas, 28–29, 46
The Lord of the Rings (film), 472, 535
L'Oréal International, 17, 198
Los Angeles (magazine), 409, 415
Los Angeles City Council, 529
Los Angeles Times (newspaper), 45, 94, 415,
    418, 529
Lowe Worldwide, 136
Lubriderm, 359

M

Macbook Air, 146, 193. *see also* Apple
Macintosh computer, 143–144, 156. *see also* Apple
MacLaren/Lintas, 119
Macromedia, 396

Macy's, 111, 415

Macy's Department Store, 450

Mad Dogs & Englishmen, 413, 417

Mad Men (television program), 34, 72

MADD (Mothers Against Drunk Driving), 107

Magazine Publishers Association, 411

Mail Boxes Etc., 107, 202

MAIP (Minority Advertising Internship Program), 163

Make-a-Wish Foundation, 560

Marie Claire, 425

Market Design, 348

Marketing News (magazine), 135

Marketing Warfare (Ries and Trout), 245

Marks and Spencer, 463

Marlboro Man, 306

Married . . . with Children (TV program), 94

Martha Stewart Living (magazine), 423

Martha Stewart Living Omnimedia, 585

Martin Agency, 546

Mary Kay Cosmetics, 553

MasterCard, 14

MasterCard International, 541

Matchbox cars, 528

The Matrix (film), 540

The Matrix Reloaded (film), 540

Mattel, 233

Maxim (magazine), 94, 409

McCann Worldgroup, 14, 117

McCann-Erickson, 34, 79, 118, 119, 337–338, 339, 358

McClatchy Comp., 134

McCormick, 567

McDonald's, 38, 61, 103–104, 107, 108, 111, 112, 113, 115, 116, 118, 119, 120, 121, 128, 177, 178, 180, 202, 360, 416, 516, 522, 565, 600

McGraw-Hill, 138, 423

McGraw-Hill/Irwin, 569

MCI, 538

McNeil, 586

McNeil Products, 586

MDA (Muscular Dystrophy Association), 493

MECLabs, 572–573

Medgar Evers College, 163

Media Rating Council (MRC), 468

MediaCrossing, 299

Mediamark Research, Inc., 441

MediaNews, 134

Men's Wearhouse, 10

Mercedes, 370

Meredith Co., 134

Merkle, 549

Merrill Lynch, 607

Metro Trains, 337–338, 347

MGM, 463

Michelob Light, 353

Mickey Mouse, 195

Microsoft, 115, 194, 308, 423, 440, 464, 466, 468, 500, 511

Microsoft Office, 50

Microsoft Windows, 115

Miller Lite, 322–323, 357

Millward Brown Research, 215

MindBase, 181, 183

MINI, 405

Minority Advertising Internship Program (MAIP), 163

Minute Maid Company, 598

Mir PK Russia (formerly *PC World USSR*) (magazine), 423

MMA (Mobile Marketing Association), 488

Mobil Oil, 592

Mobile Marketing Association (MMA), 488

Money (magazine), 413

Montgomery Ward, 45, 305

Moroch Partners, 300

Mothers Against Drunk Driving (MADD), 107

Motorola, 136, 151

Motrin, 497, 504

Mountain Dew, 10, 11, 239–240, 244, 247, 259, 324, 517, 596

Moveon.org, 501

MRC (Media Rating Council), 468

MSNBC, 431

MSNTV2, 440

MTV, 72, 145, 294, 435

MTV.com, 299

Muscular Dystrophy Association (MDA), 493

MWWPR, 583

MySpace, 494, 498, 511

MySpace.com, 596

N

N. W. Ayer & Sons, 46

NAA (Newspaper Association of America), 420

Nabisco, 598

Nabisco SnackWells, 160

NAD (National Advertising Division), 92

NAICS (North American Industry Classification System), 185

NARB (National Advertising Review Board), 92

NARC (National Advertising Review Council), 92

NASCAR, 594

National Advertising Division (NAD), 92

National Advertising Review Board (NARB), 92

National Advertising Review Council, 92

National Advertising Review Council (NARC), 92

National Association for Female Executives, 411

National Association for Prevention of Alcoholism and Addiction (ANPAA), 49

National Association of Broadcasters Television Code, 93

National Cherry Festival, 596

National CineMedia (NCM), 538–539

National Consumer League, 95

National Council of Senior Citizens, 95

National Enquirer (newspaper), 415, 423

National Football League (NFL), 437

National Geographic (magazine), 135

National Guard, 593

National Panel Diary (NPD), 223

National Philanthropic Trust, 493

National Public Radio (NPR), 215

National Research Council, 89

National Rifle Association, 165

National Society for the Prevention of Cruelty to Children (NSPCC), 547

National Stigma Clearinghouse, 95

National Stuttering Project, 95

Nature (magazine), 410

Navistar International, 608

NBC, 72, 89, 135, 430, 436, 461, 494

NBC Outdoor, 532

NBC Universal, 463

NCM (National CineMedia), 538–539

NCN (Newspaper Co-op Network), 420

Near Field Communication (NFC), 524

Neil Cooper LLC, 92

Nestlé, 233, 252

Netflix, 52, 447, 470, 579–580, 581, 585, 586, 587

Network Advertising Initiative, 84

Network Radio Audiences, 451

New Coke, 34, 38

New England Journal of Medicine, 229

New Idea (magazine), 422

New York (magazine), 409

New York City Commission on Human Rights, 163

New York Daily News (newspaper), 415

The New York Times, 134, 203, 219, 401, 416, 464, 582

The New York Times Index, 219

New Yorker, 93

News Corp., 134, 463

News Feed, 509, 528

Newspaper Advertising Association, 94

Newspaper Advertising Bureau, 420

Newspaper Association of America (NAA), 420

Newspaper Co-op Network (NCN), 420

Newspaper National Network, 420, 421

Newspaper Rates & Data, 94

Newspaper Society in London, 353

Newsplan, 418

Newsweek (magazine), 93, 409, 412

Nextel, 531

Nextel Pavilion and Theater, 531

NFC (Near Field Communication), 524
NFL (National Football League), 437
Nielsen, 70, 178, 187, 204, 210, 219, 234, 295, 434, 435, 441, 444, 446, 464, 489
Nielsen Media Research, 441, 442
Nielsen Television Index (NTI), 441, 442
Nielsen//NetRatings, 464, 468
Nielsen-Online, 467
Nielsen's BuzzMetrics, 495, 508
Nike, 38, 61–62, 95, 173, 195, 312, 313, 315, 352, 360, 504, 530, 594, 595, 596, 603
Nikken, 199, 553
99designs.com, 510
Nintendo, 466
Nissan, 111, 227
Nissan 240SX, 244
Nissan Motor Company, 149
Nokia, 379, 540, 559
Nordstrom, 10, 563
North American Industry Classification System (NAICS), 185
Norwegian Cruise Lines, 168–169
Novartis, 87
NPD (National Panel Diary), 223
NTI (Nielsen Television Index), 441, 442
NYPD Blue, 94

O

OAAA (Outdoor Advertising Association of American), 518, 519, 527, 529
Office Depot, 85
Ogilvy & Mather, 118, 246, 332, 607
Ogilvy.com, 318
OgilvyOne Worldwide, 549
Oil Doctor, 540
Old Coke, 34
Old Spice, 152, 172–174, 175
Olympics, 592, 593, 594, 596
Omnicom, 117, 163
Omniture, 468
On War (Clausewitz), 245
1-800-Flowers.com, 528
Onslaught (advertising campaign), 332
Opinion Research Corp., 607
Oprah (TV program), 438
Orange County Register (newspaper), 353
O'Reilly Auto Parts, 450
Organic Crop Improvement Association, 357
Orient Express, 193
Osborne Clark, 353
Outdoor Advertising Association of American (OAAA), 518, 519, 527, 529
Outside (magazine), 62
Overstock.com, 500
Oxford Health Plans, 597

P

Packaging World (magazine), 409
PageRank, Google, 474
PageRank system, 582
PAL media planning system, 446
Palm Springs Life (magazine), 135, 409
Pampers, 115
PANTONE Matching System (PMS), 380, 385
Papa John's Pizza, 69
Parade (magazine), 415, 423
Paramount, 436
Parents Institute, 357
Partnership for a Drug-Free America, 20, 169
Party Pride, 195
Passenger, 509
Patent and Trademark Office, 84, 89–90
Payne Heating and Cooling, 567
PayPerPost, 582
PC Magazine, 500
PCH (Publisher's Clearing House), 421
Penske Motorsports, 594
People (magazine), 405, 423
Pepsi, 61, 69, 96, 507, 594, 596, 597
Pepsi Cola Company, 17, 72, 96, 517
PepsiCo, 189, 200, 240
Pepsi-Cola Company, 239–240
Pepsodent, 195
Perfect Pitch (Steel), 169
Peta, 244
Pew Internet & American Project Life Study, 465–466, 467
Pew Research Center's Project for Excellence in Journalism, 401
Pfizer, 440, 487
P&G (Procter & Gamble), 163, 165, 318
Pillsbury Doughboy, 17
Pinterest, 505, 509
Pitney Bowes, 549–550
Pizza Hut, 69, 154, 538, 540
PlayStation, 512, 596, 600
Please Be Ad-Vised, 80
PMS (PANTONE Matching System), 380, 385
PointRoll, 485
Polaroid, 167
Pondimin (fenfluramine), 228
Pontiac, 594
Porsche, 168–169, 195
Portable People Meter (PPM), 442, 451
Power Magazine, 561
PowerPoint, 591
PPAI (Promotional Products Association International), 537
PPM (Portable People Meter), 442, 451

Prairie Farmer (magazine), 409
Predictably Irrational: The Hidden Forces that Shape our Decisions (Ariely), 146
Premiere Radio Network, 448
President's Choice, 195
Prevention (magazine), 219
Prezi, 591
Priceline.com, 362, 559
Pringles, 115
Printer's Ink, 90
Prizm, 178
Procter & Gamble (P&G), 16, 49, 89, 110, 112, 115, 130, 163, 165, 173, 178, 200, 226, 233, 310, 415, 434, 495
Prodigy, 464
Productivity Products International, 608
Progressive Farmer (magazine), 409
Progressive Grocer (magazine), 135, 409
Promotion Marketing Association Coupon Council, 205
Promotional Products Association International (PPAI), 537
ProQuest, 219
Proximity, 549
Prudential, 501
Public Information Service Bulletin, 219
Publicis Group, 119, 163
Publicis Groupe, 117
Publisher's Clearing House (PCH), 421
Purchasing (magazine), 411
Pure Food and Drug Act, 57

Q

Qantas Airline, 79
Qatar Foundation, 594
Quaker Oats, 67, 72
Quantcast, 468, 485
Quick Burger, 570
Quicken Loans Arena, 597
Qwikster, 580

R

RADAR (Radio's All-Dimension Audience Research), 451
Radio Times (magazine), 422
Radio Usage, 451
Radio's All-Dimension Audience Research (RADAR), 451
Ragú, 475
Rapp, 549
Ray-Ban, 22, 405
RCA computers, 48
Reader's Digest, 93, 134, 138, 205, 422, 423
Reader's Guide to Periodical Literature, 219
ReadWriteWeb.com, 582

Red Cross, 18, 55
Reddit, 498, 502
Redux (dexfenfluramine), 228
Regal CineMedia Corporation, 538
Regal Entertainment Group, 538
Regular Strength Tylenol, 586
REI, 153
Reporters Without Borders, 354
The Return of the King (video game), 472
RISC, 181
Road & Track (magazine), 412
Rolex, 13, 176, 199
Rolling Stones, 487
The Rolling Stones, 201
Rolls-Royce, 352, 405
Ronald McDonald, 180
Ronald McDonald House, 122, 135
Roper Starch Worldwide, 181, 593
RSCG, 49
Rubio, 105
Rubio's Baja Grill, 105
Ruder Finn, 583

S

Saatchi & Saatchi, 49, 130, 315, 357,
    379, 395
Safeco Field, 200
Salvation Army, 320, 325
Sample, 49
Samsung, 467
Samsung Mobile, 596
San Diego Magazine, 409, 410
Sandra Salcedo clothing, 178
Santa Claus, 41, 180
Sara Lee Corp., 405, 608
SAS, 231
SBC, 110
Scarborough Research Corp., 418
Scentstrip, 405
Schering-Plough, 222
Schlitz, 29
Scientific Advertising (Hopkins), 29, 46, 56
Scientific American (magazine), 422
Scientific Certification Systems (SCS), 587
Scion, Toyota, 174
Scitex, 385
Scottrade, 470
SCS (Scientific Certification Systems), 587
Sea World, 168
Sears, 107, 165, 305, 415, 607
Sears Roebuck, 45
Seattle Times (newspaper), 419
Sega, 168–169
Seinfeld (TV program), 438
Self-Regulatory Guidelines for Children's Advertising
    (CARU), 83

7UP, 48, 319
Shaklee, 199, 553
Shalek Agency, 353
Sharper Image, 305, 559
Shell, 607
Shelter Pet Project, 71
Sheraton Hotels, 163
ShipShapes, 555
Shoebaloo, 63
Showtime, 52, 431
Silicon Graphics, 385
Siméus Foods International, 184
Simmons Market Research Bureau, 204, 295,
    418, 441
Simmons' Study of Media and Markets, 219
The Simpsons (TV program), 439
SiriusXM satellite radio, 93, 453
Ski (magazine), 423
Sky Channel, 424
Slideshare.net, 508
SlimFast, 453
Smart Water, 87
SmartPlus, 446
SnackWells, 160
Snapchat, 466, 494, 499, 506, 509, 510, 512
Snapple, 194, 564–565
Snapple Diet Iced Tea, 447
Snapple Mango Madness, 564–565
Snapple Natural Beverages, 447
Sony, 136, 375–376, 377, 404, 466, 596
Sony Bravia, 375
Sony Pictures Television, 463
South Beach diet, 228
Southern California Honda dealers, 110
Southern Living (magazine), 409
Southwest Airlines, 479
Sperry, 608
Spike TV, 70, 431
SPINE, 587
Splenda, 453
Sports Illustrated (magazine), 94, 153, 409, 423
Sprint, 111, 531
Sprint Nextel Corporation, 415, 470
Sprint Wireless, 450
SPSS, 231
SRDS (Standard Rate & Data Service),
    410, 557
SRI Consulting Business Intelligence
    (SRIC-BI), 180
SRIC-BI (SRI Consulting Business Intelligence),
    180
St. Mungo's, 405
Stand Out Designs, 554
Standard Directory of Advertising Agencies (the Red
    Book), 118
Standard Oil of New Jersey, 607
Standard Rate & Data Service, 219

Standard Rate & Data Service (SRDS), 410, 557
Standards for Advertising Motor Vehicles, 86
Star (newspaper), 415
Star Markets, 200
Star Trek, 319
Star TV, 424
Starbucks, 189, 199, 200, 203, 367, 509, 583
Starbucks DoubleShot, 189, 200
Starbucks Liqueurs, 189
Starcom Mediavest, 119
State Farm Insurance, 487
Statistical Abstract of the United States, 219
Stepstone, Inc., 608
Stihl, 68
STRATA Marketing, Inc., 413
Strategy (magazine), 332
Stumbleupon.com, 502
Sub-Zero, 164
Successful Farming (magazine), 409
Summer Olympics (2008), 148
Sunkist, 21, 149
Sunkist vitamins, 195
Sunset (magazine), 409
Super Bowl, 144, 153, 209, 212, 213, 239, 396,
    430, 433, 483, 507, 509, 594
Superchannel, 424
Supermarket News, 134
SurveyMonkey, 50
Sybase, 136

T

Taco Bell, 308, 538, 596
Tacoda, 471
TagHeuer, 61
Takara, 233
Take a Break (magazine), 422
Target, 10, 189, 305–306, 307, 308, 311,
    312, 314, 315, 319, 320, 328–329,
    331, 453
Targus Info, 502
Taster's Choice, 364
TAXI, 603
Tazo, 189
TBS, 72, 523
TBWA, 49
TBWA Chiat/Day, 124, 130, 168
TBWAParis, 460
TD Ameritrade Holding Corp., 470
TeAchnology, 483
TeamOne, 527
TechMart, 166
Ted Bates Agency, 48
Ted Bates Worldwide, 49
Telecite, 531
Teletubbies (TV program), 439
Tennis (magazine), 294

TenUnited, 163
Tesco, 353
TGI Friday's, 115
The Economist (magazine), 352
Thickburger, 180
3M, 536
Tiazzi, 189
Tide, 115, 197
Tier One, 584
Time (magazine), 93, 135, 138, 332, 409, 413, 511
Time Gold (magazine), 413
Time Inc., 421
Time Warner, 110, 134, 415, 422
The Tipping Point, 182, 500
TiVo, 487, 551
T-Mobile, 596
T-Mobile Wireless, 450
TNT, 72
Total Gym, 559
Touch-Screen Greetings, 569
Toyota, 26, 38, 111, 174, 227, 379, 538, 596
Toyota Corolla, 244
TransAmerica, 405
Tribal DDB, 128
Tribal Worldwide Shanghai, 128
Tribune Co., 134
TripAdvisor, 510
Truth, Lies & Advertising (Steel), 169
Tumblr, 498
Tumblr.com, 502
Tupperware, 553
Turn, 502
TV Choice (magazine), 422
TV Guide (magazine), 410, 423
The 2wenty, 538
TWICE/Campaigners, 195
Twitter, 4, 25, 135, 366, 466, 485, 494, 498, 500, 505, 507, 509, 580, 582
Twitter Power, 367

U

Ulster Orchestra, 597
Ultranoir, 476
Umbria Communications, 495
Under Armor, 567
Under Armour, 62
Understanding Media: The Extensions of Man, 532
Underwriters Laboratories, 95, 357
UNICEF, 424
Unilever, 173, 195, 581, 605
Unistar, 449
United Airlines, 126
United Way, 8, 55, 588
Univision, 454
UPN, 436

UPS, 557
UPS Store, 202
Urban Outfitters, 186
U.S. Army, 160, 161, 332
U.S. Census Bureau, 165, 433
U.S. Drug Enforcement Administration, 229
U.S. Environmental Protection Agency (EPA), 587
U.S. Federal Trade Commission (FTC), 567, 587
U.S. Food and Drug Administration (FDA), 84, 87–89, 534, 581, 586, 658n
U.S. News (magazine), 410
U.S. Olympic Committee, 594
U.S. Postal Service (USPS), 557, 569
U.S. Sales Corp., 421
U.S. Supreme Court, 658n
USA, 72, 135
USA Today, 134, 209, 323, 401, 415, 582

V

Vagrant Records, 596
VALS, 180, 181, 183
Value America, 85
ValueScope, 181
Van Houtte, 476
Vance L. Stickell Memorial Student Internship Program, 45
Vanity Fair, 404
Vans Warped Tour, 596
Verizon Communications, 10, 111, 136, 415, 470
Vespa, 559
Viacom, 511
Vietnam War, 57
Village Voice (newspaper), 413–414, 416, 417
Vimeo.com, 508
Virgin America, 495
Virgin Media, 501
Visa, 594
Vodafone, 501
Vogue (magazine), 480
Volkswagen (VW), 48, 56, 227, 246, 306, 318, 319, 352, 441
Volleyball (magazine), 410
Volvo International, 594
Voom, 440
Voyages-SNCF, 460
VW (Volkswagen), 48, 56, 227, 246, 306, 318, 319, 352, 441

W

WA W2O Group, 583
Waggener Edstrom, 583
Walgreens, 204
Walgreens Drug Store, 450
Walker's Sensations, 353
The Wall Street Journal, 34, 94, 97, 134, 357, 401, 416, 422, 424, 532

Wall Street Journal Office Displays, 532
Walmart, 8, 111, 130, 189, 305, 309, 511, 583, 600
Walt Disney, 415, 470
Warhol Factory X Levi's, 189
Warner Bros., 436, 438
Warners TrueFit, 453
Washington Post (newspaper), 215
Washington State Ferry system, 200
Washington Times, 552
Watergate scandals, 57
WB, 436
Weather Channel, 177, 215
WebTrends, 468
Welch's Grape Juice, 405
Wells Fargo, 596
Wells Rich Greene (WRG), 163
Western States Advertising Agency Association (WSAAA), 118
Westwood One, 449
Westwood One Radio Network, 452
What's Cooking (magazine), 405
What's on TV (magazine), 422
Wheel of Fortune (TV program), 438
Why Man Creates (film), 592
Wieden, 174
Wieden+Kennedy (W+K), 173, 174
Wikipedia, 466
Wilkinson Sword, 17
Willy the Hillbilly, 239
W+K (Wieden+Kennedy), 173, 174
Woman's Day (magazine), 409, 422
Wonderbra swimwear, 347
WordPress, 499
Words with Friends, 512
World Almanac and Book of Facts, 219
World Book, 553
World Cup, 593
World of Warcraft, 512
World Wildlife Foundation (WWF), 407, 525
World Wildlife Fund, 604
Worldwide Partners Inc., 80
WPP Group, 49, 117, 163, 169, 213
Wrangler, 258
WRG (Wells Rich Greene), 163
WSAAA (Western States Advertising Agency Association), 118
Wunderman, 549, 558
WWD. com, 582
WWF (World Wildlife Foundation), 407, 525
Wyeth-Ayerst, 228

X

Xbox, Microsoft, 447, 512
Xerox, 115, 193, 433, 437

Xhilaration, 306
XM satellite radio, 453

Y

Yahoo!, 134, 219, 485, 489, 500, 511
Yelp.com, 512

Yik Yak, 494
Young & Rubicam (Y&R), 29, 49, 72, 117, 118, 125, 126, 130, 213, 214, 234, 266
YouTube, 135, 338, 366, 466, 494, 500, 506, 508
Y&R (Young & Rubicam), 29, 49, 72, 117, 118, 125, 126, 130, 213, 214, 234, 266

Z

Zappos.com, 496, 505, 507, 509, 512
ZenithOptimedia, 486
Zeno Group, 583
Zubi Advertising, 118, 204
Zynga, 496, 512

subject index

A

AAAA Service Standards, 120
Abbreviations in television copy, 365
ABC (Audit Bureau of Circulations), 410
Absence of externalities, 63
Abundance principle, 67–68
Access to Internet, 466
Account(s)
    management, 121
    planning, 121
    reviews, 126–127
    supervisors, 121
Accountable relationship, 10
Account executives (AEs), 121
Account planning, 121
Account supervisors, 121
ACNielsen's ScanTrack, 223
Action
    close, in body copy, 357
    in creative pyramid, 325
    DAGMAR marketing objective setting
        system, 243
    in IMC pyramid, 253
    as result of advertising, 6, 18
    television commercial production process,
        389–391
Action advertising, 19, 27; see also Direct-response
    advertising
Actual consumers, 15, 17
Adapt technique to transform concepts, 318
Added value
    defined, 65
    Internet packages, 483
    tools, 565
Added-value services, 412
Addressable media, 9
Ad Lab
    advertising agencies, 117
    artist, role of, 342
    color, psychological impact of, 313
    consumer behavior application to ad
        creation, 167
    co-op marriage, 111
    corporate advertising, 578, 608
    creative gymnasium, 327
    creative pyramid, 325
    direct mail packages, 558
    economic effect of advertising on
        sales, 263

editorial or advertising, 94
green advertising, 587
GRP and TV market selection, 445
innovations in magazine advertising, 405
Internet ratings, 469
legal counsel, 80
literary form, advertising as, 17
magazines and creative mix, 404
market segmentation, 199
media selection, 295
needs and utility, 146
newspapers and creative mix, 417
off-the-wall media, 275
out of home advertising, 520–521
place element, 199
product elements, 189
product label, 197
product slogans, 53
promotion element, 202
push/pull strategies, 566, 569
radio, creative ways to sell
    on, 362
reports that make or break radio
    stations, 451
Starbucks, 188, 199, 203
strategies of marketing warfare, 245
television film vs. digital video
    decision, 392
TV ratings, 442
typography, 380
unfair and deceptive practices, 70
utility and needs, 146
Ad networks, 471
Adoption, social media, 496–498
Ads, for adidas, 185
AdSense, Google, 482
Ad tracking, Internet, 468
Advertisers (clients), 105–116; see also Advertising
    agencies
    client-agency relationship, 127–132
        accountability, 126
        client obtainment, 127–128
        factors affecting, 130–132
        stages, 128–130
    cooperative, 109–110
    expenditures on advertising
        1994-2005, 51–52
        direct mail, 554
        online advertising, 462
        as percentage of GDP, 64

public relations, 596
television, 430, 433
Hispanic media, 178
local, 105–109
national, 110
regional, 110
social responsibility, 74–75
transnational, 114–116
understanding, 106
Advertiser-supported syndication, 438
Advertising, 200, 210; see also specific topics
    campaigns
        Activia, 3–4
        AIDS.gov, 271–272
        Apple, 56, 143–144
        celebrity-based, 61–62
        Coca-Cola, 32–34
        GEICO, 545?
        Hewlett-Packard, 315
        Hyundai, 429–430
        Ikea, 483
        IMC; See My IMC Campaign
        McDonald's, 103–104
        Mountain Dew, 239–240
    to children, 82–83
    classification, 19
    color, 420
    as communication form, 8
    contemporary, 2–30
        communication dimension, 15–18
        ethical issues, 19
        learning objectives, 2
        marketing dimension, 18–28
        relationship marketing, 9–14
    controversies, 62–63
    definition, 8
    described, 7–9
    economic impact, 64–68
    ethical responsibility, 75–78; see also Ethics and
        ethical issues
    evolution
        Coca-Cola, 32–34, 40–43
        direct marketing, 548–549
        ethical issues, 45
        free markets, 34–54
        Golden Age (1946 to 1970s), 47–49
        industrial age, 44–47
        Internet, 45
        learning objectives, 32
        Portfolio Review: Coca-Cola, 32–34, 40–4

Advertising—*Cont.*
  postindustrial age, 49, 51–52
  preindustrial age, 44
  social issues, 54–55, 57
  timetable, 39
  21st century, 52–54
 expenditures on, 4
  1994-2005, 51–52
  direct mail, 554
  online advertising, 461, 462
  as percentage of GDP, 64
  public relations, 599
  television, 430, 433
 global; *see* Global advertising
 green, 587
 growth of, 595
 Hispanic media, 178
 Holiday Inn Express, 213–214
 as literature, 17
 local; *see* Local advertising
 management, 112–114
 mass/nonpersonal selling, 202
 for new business, 128
 objectives, 279
 offensiveness in, 72–73
 online sharing, 4
 persuasion and, 8
 proliferation of, 70–71
 vs. public relations (PR), 8–9, 580–581
 scope of, 102–139
 sex in, 322–323
 social impact of, 68–73
 stereotypes in, 71–72
 strategy for
  creative briefs, 309–310
  formulating, 308–311
  marketing mix, 189–191
  market segmentation, 174–188
  media objectives and strategies, 293
  message strategy (rationale),
    310–311
  research, 211, 212
  writing creative brief, 309–310
 as structured form, 8
 unfair and deceptive practices, 70
Advertising agencies
 administration, 123
 birth of, 44–47
 business-to-business, 118–119
 compensation, 125–126
 creative boutiques, 119
 defined, 104, 116
 departmental system, 123–124
 entrepreneurial, 118
 full-service, 118–119
 full-service advertising agency, 118

 general consumer agency, 118
 group system, 124–125
 in-house agency, 126–127
 interactive, 119
 international, 118
 media-buying services, 119
 national, 118
 people in, 120–123
 regional, 118
 role of, 15, 116
 specialized service agencies, 119–120
 structure, 123–125
 types, 116–117
Advertising allowance, 568
Advertising art, 44
Advertising development
 categories of research, 212
Advertising impressions, 282, 469
Advertising industry, 104–105
 organizations in, 104–105
 people in, 105
Advertising message exposure, 286
Advertising response curve, 286
Advertising services, 118
Advertising specialty, 537
Advertising strategy research, 211, 212
Advertising success, 203
Advertising text, 15
Advertorials, 607
Advocacy advertising, 607
AdWords, Google, 474–475, 482
Aerial banners, 275
Aerial lights, 275
AEs (account executives), 121
Affidavit of performance, 446
Affiliate marketing program, 471
Age groups
 product usage patterns, 177
Agency creatives, 121
Agency of record, 119
Agency review consultants, 128
Aggregating, 174
Aggregating market segments, 187
Aggressive sales promotion, 565
Agricultural advertising, 21
Aided recall, 226
Allocation of time, production
    management, 376
Allowances, for trade promotions,
    566–568
Ambush marketing, 595
American Express, 226
Analog proof, 386
Animatic, 366
Animation, 365
Animation advertisements, 390

Annual events, 596
Annual report, 591
Answer print, 393
Aperture, 392
API (application protocol interface), 498
Appearance of typography, 380
Application protocol interface
    (API), 498
Appropriateness of typography, 380
Approval in print advertising, 343
AQH (average quarter-hour audience)
    persons, 452
Art
 artistic concepts development for electronic
    media, 360–361
 creation in print production phase,
    379–384
 defined, 321
 formats in electronic media, 361–365
 sponsorships and events, 596–597
Art direction, 321
 for international markets, 371
Art directors, 122, 306, 342
Artist, 317–325
 big idea development, 317–321
 creative blocks, 319–321
 defined, 317
 implementing big ideas, 321
 role of, 342
Art studios, 132
AT&T, 178
Attention
 in creative pyramid, 322–323
Attention value, 296
Attitudes
 defined, 157
 as part of culture, 164
 produced by learning, 157
 tests of, 225, 226
Attitude test, 226
Audience
 aggregation of, 174
 characteristics, 295
 defined, 295
 fragmentation, 274, 276, 434
 impact on, 307–308
 Internet, 465–466
 magazine advertising, 403
 market segmentation, 190
 market segmentation process, 174
 objectives, 281–282
 radio, 448–450
 ratings
  television, 283
 reach, 283–284
 resonance, 307

secondary target audience, 308
size and message weight, 282–283
target
    advertising classification, 19
    analysis of, 555
    cost per point (CPP), 297
    in creative strategy, 308
    defined, 19, 308
    identification of, 19–21
    IMC strategy, 256
    Internet, 471–472
    transnational (global) markets,
        150–151
    as type of consumer, 16
    types, 19–21
television, 283
    trends, 432–435
types, 415
unduplicated, 453
Audience composition, 444
Audience objectives, 281–282
Audio, 358
Audio console, 388
Audiovisual materials, 592
Audit Bureau of Circulations
    (ABC), 410
Authenticity, 504
Authors of communication, 15
Autobiographical messages, 16, 17
Availability, need for awareness of, 145
Availability heuristic, 154
Avails, 444
Average quarter-hour audience
    (AQH persons), 452
Average quarter-hour rating, 452
Average quarter-hour share, 452
Awareness; *see also* Perceptions
    advertising classification, 19
    DAGMAR marketing objective setting
        system, 243
    in IMC pyramid, 253
    of product, creating, 26–27
Awareness advertising, 19, 26–27
Aware nontriers, 176
Ayer No. 1, 344

B

Bait-and-switch offers, 70
Balance, design principles, 345
Banners
    Internet, 471, 482–484, 556
    mobile (cell-phone), 488, 560
Barter syndication, 438
Base art, 384
Basic bus, 530

Basic transactional relationship, 10
B2B; *see* Business-to-business (B2B)
BBB (Better Business Bureau), 91–92
BDI (brand development index), 289
Behavior, consumer
    Apple, 143–144
    defined, 151
    habitual nature of, 157–158
    IMC strategy, 151–152
    interpersonal influences, 151, 161–165
        cultural and subcultural influence,
            164–165
        family influence, 161
        societal influence, 161–164
    learning and persuasion, 154–155
    learning objectives, 142
    motivation, 158–161
    nonpersonal influences, 165–166
        defined, 151, 165
        environment, 165–166
        place, 165
        time, 165
    perception, 152–153
    personal influences, 151–169
        consumer motivation process,
            158–161
        consumer perception process,
            152–153
        defined, 151
        information processing, 154–155
    postpurchase evaluation, 151, 166–167
    psychological processes, 152–161
    purchase decision process, 151,
        166–167
    summary, terms, and exercises, 170–171
Behavioral targeting, 469
BehaviorGraphics, 181
Behavioristic, 175
Behavioristic segmentation, 175
Benefit headlines, 352
Benefits, 177
Benefit segmentation, 177
Benefits sought, 175
Benefits-sought variables, 177
Berlin Wall, 49
Better Business Bureau (BBB), 91–92
Big idea
    creative blocks to, 319–321
    creative search for, 310
    defined, 317
    developing, 317–325
    implementing, 321
    incubating concepts, 321
Bleed, 386
Bleed pages, 403
Blimps, 275

Blinking, 298
Blogosphere, 503
Blogs; *See also* Social media
    corporate, 588
    defined, 499–500
    uses of, 507
Blue-Chip Blues social classes, 162
Blueline proof, 386
BMW, 179
Board, 380–389
Body copy, 354–357
    defined, 354
    formatting, 356–357
    styles, 354–356
Boldface subheads, 354
Books and publications, 588
"Boom" in advertising, creativity for,
    313–314
Boosted post, 509
Booths, 535
Bottom-up marketing, 245, 247–248
Brainstorming, 317
Brand, 195
BrandAsset Valuator, 213
Brand Capital, 213
Brand character statement, 310
Brand development index (BDI), 289
Brand equity, 195, 196
Brand interest, 157
Brand loyalty, 195
    Coca-Cola and, 34, 38
    defined, 157
    development, 158
    habits and, 157–158
    learning leads to, 157–158
    trade deals and, 566–567
Brand manager, 115
Brand meaning, 435
Brand messages, 4
    sources of, 13
Brand monitoring, 508
Brand partnership, 184
Brands and branding
    brand loyalty
        defined, 157
        development, 158
        habits and, 157–158
        learning leads to, 157–158
        trade deals and, 567
    character statement, creative brief, 310
    interest as action motivator, 158
Brand trains, 531
BRANDZ, 213
Briefs, creative, 309–310
Brite Lites Li'l City social classes,
    161, 162

Broadband, 466
Broadcast media; *see also* Electronic media
    direct-response advertising, 559
    production, 122
    types, 19
Broadcast TV
    commercial stations, 430–431
    defined, 430
    digital television (DTV), 431–432
    national advertising, 430
    number of hours watched, 433
    pros and cons, 433
    top ten advertisers, 430
Broadsides, 556
Brochures, 556
Budget buildup method, 266–267
Budgets and budgeting
    IMC approaches, 259–268
        developing, 264–268
        methods, 264–268
        sales to profit relationship, 259, 263
Bulk discounts, 418
Bulletin boards, 591–592
Bulletins, 519
Bulletin structures, 519
Bundle of values, 191
Bursting, 298
Business advertising, 20
    pull strategy, 566
    push strategy, 566
Business cycle, 67
Business magazines, 409
Business marketers, 187
Business markets, 174, 184
    defined, 149
    as key marketing participants, 149
    targets, 20–21
Business people, 116
Business reply mail, 556
Business-to-business (B2B)
    advertising, 20–21
    marketing, 149
Business-to-business agency, 118–119
Bus-o-rama signs, 531
Buttons, Internet, 482
Buyback allowance, 566
Buying advertising and media
    direct mail, 555–556
    Internet, 471–486
        added-value packages, 483
        ad networks, 471
        AdSense, 475, 482
        AdWords, 475, 482
        banners, 475, 483
        classified ads, 484

        e-mail advertising, 484–485
        Google, 475, 481–482
        pricing, 470–471
        search engine marketing, 473–474,
            484–485
        sponsorships, 483
        targeting, 471
        types of Internet advertising,
            471–473
    organizational buyer behavior, 151
    print media
        buyers, 402
    purchase patterns, 293

C

Cable TV
    audience demographics, 436
    defined, 430
    digital television (DTV), 431–432
    pros and cons, 436
Camera ready, 422
Camera-ready art, 342, 381–384
Cameras, television commercial production
        process, 389
Campaign creative process, 310
Campaigns; *see* Advertising: campaigns
Car-end posters, 530
Car seller AutoTrader, 179
CARU (Children's Advertising Review
        Unit), 83
Cash discounts, 412
Casting brief, 360
Catalogs, 557–559
Category development index (CDI),
        289–290
Category manager, 115
Cause marketing, 593
Causes, sponsorships and events, 592
CDI (category development index),
        289–290
Celebritie
    endorsements, 61–62
Celebrities
    entertainment sponsorships and
        events, 595
    interviews as sales tool, 362
    as opinion leaders, 164
Centers of influence, 149, 308
Central Hudson Gas v. *Public Service*
        Commission, 81
Centralized advertising department, 113
Centralized networks, 462
Central location test, 225
Central location tests, 225

Central route to persuasion, 155–156
Cents-off promotions, 570
Challenges, in plans book development, 555
Changes, in client-agency relationships,
        130, 132
Channels
    for messages, 14, 18
Charitable fundraising, 588
Chemistry, in client-agency relationships, 130
Children's Advertising Review Unit
        (CARU), 83
CHR (contemporary hit radio), 448
Chromalin (analog proof), 386
Cinema advertising, 537
Cinematographers, 391–392
Circulation
    defined, 282
    magazines
        added value services, 412
        controlled circulation, 411
        delivered circulation, 410
        guaranteed circulation, 410
        horizontal publications, 411
        merchandising services, 412
        paid circulation, 411
        primary circulation, 411
        secondary readership, 411
        subscription sales, 411
        vendor sales, 411
        vertical publications, 411
    media planning, 282
Circulation audit, 410
City-dwelling boomers, 223
Clarity, design principles, 345
Class, social, 161–162
Classical conditioning, 154
Classified ads, 417
Classified advertising, 108
    Internet, 483
Classified display ads, 417
Cleaned mailing lists, 550
Clearance advertising, 107–108
Click rate, 469
Click-through rate, 469–470
Click-through rates (CTRs), 510
Click-throughs, 471
Click to website, 509
Client-agency relationship, 127–132
    accountability, 126
    client obtainment, 127–128
    factors affecting, 130–132
    stages, 128–130
Client presentations, 591
Clients; *see* Advertisers (clients)
Close, in body copy, 357

Closing date, 380, 412
Clutter
    direct marketing, 553
Clutter test, 225
Clutter tests, 225
CMSs (content management systems), 499
Cognition, 153–154
Cognitive dissonance theory, 166
Cold-set inks, 385
Cold War, 49
Collaboration in Internet content, 466
Collateral materials, 27, 205
Color
    media planning, 292
    out of home advertising, 520–521
    print production process, 385
    psychological impact, 313
Color advertising, 420
Color key, 386
Color separation, 385
Color strip, 405
Column inch, 415
Combination offers, 571
Combination rates, 418, 420
Comedian power, 362
Command headline, 354
Commercial advertising, 19
Commercial producer, 389
Communication
    advertising as form of, 8; *see also* Advertising
    application in advertising, 15–18
    client-agency relationship and, 130
    in creative strategy, 308–311
    defined, 8
    direct, 546
    human communication process, 14–15
    interactive model, 15
    in marketing mix, 247
    mass communication, 8
    process, 12, 15–18
    of product utility, 145
    Stern model, 15, 16
    strategy, in plans book development, 555
Communication element, 202
Communication media, 212
Communication objectives, 241
Communications media, 257, 308
Communications mix, 202
Community involvement, 586
Community relations, 128
Company's marketing strategy, 198
Compare technique to transform concepts, 319
Competent researchers, 233

Competition
    effect on, 66
    media planning, 277
Competitive strategies, budget considerations, 290
Compiled direct-mail lists, 555
Complete information, 68, 69, 78
Composed commercial text, 15
Composed communication, advertising as, 8
Composition of target audience, 466
Comprehension
    DAGMAR marketing objective setting system, 243
    in IMC pyramid, 253
Comprehensive layout (comp), 341
Computers, media selection and scheduling, 299, 301
Conceptualization, 317
Conditioned stimulus, 154
Conditioning theories of learning, 154–155
Conduct, in client-agency relationships, 130
Confirm messages, 14
Connectors, 182
Connect technique to transform concepts, 318–319
Conquest sales, 67
Consumer(s)
    actual, 15, 17
    behavior of, 151–169
        Apple, 143–144
        cultural and subcultural influence, 164–165
        defined, 151
        family influence, 161
        habitual nature of, 157–158
        IMC strategy, 151–152
        influences on, 152–166
        Internet behavioral targeting, 469
        interpersonal influences, 151, 161–165
        learning and persuasion, 154–155
        learning objectives, 142
        motivation, 158–161
        nonpersonal influences, 151, 165–166
        perception, 152–153
        personal influences, 151–161
        postpurchase evaluation, 151, 166–167
        psychological processes, 152–161
        purchase decision process, 151, 166–167
        societal influence, 161–164
        summary, terms, and exercises, 170–171

    choice, 67
    decision process, 151
    defined, 8, 20
    demand by
        pull strategy, 566, 571
    implied, 16
    jeans, 189
    knowledge of, 151
    motivation process, 158–161
    perception process, 152–153
    privacy, 83–84
    sales promotions, 565–566
        cents-off promotions, 570
        combination offers, 571
        contests, 574
        convenience cards, 570
        coupons, 569–570
        defined, 566
        electronic coupons, 570
        point-of-purchase (P-O-P) materials, 568–569
        premiums, 570–571
        rebates, 570
        refunds, 570
        sampling, 571
        sweepstakes, 571, 574
    sponsorial, 16
    types, 16–18
Consumer accounts, 118
Consumer advertising, 19, 20
Consumer advocate, 95
Consumer appeal
    in packaging, 197
Consumer behavior, 151–169
    Apple, 143–144
    defined, 20, 151
    habitual nature of, 157–158
    IMC strategy, 151–152
    influences on, 151–169
    Internet behavioral targeting, 469
    interpersonal influences, 151, 161–165
        cultural and subcultural influence, 164–165
        family influence, 161
        societal influence, 161–164
    learning and persuasion, 154–155
    learning objectives, 142
    motivation, 158–161
    nonpersonal influences, 151, 165–166
        defined, 151, 165
        environment, 165–166
        place, 165
        time, 165
    perception, 152–153

Consumer behavior—*Cont.*
  personal influences, 151–169
    defined, 151
    perception, 152–153
  postpurchase evaluation, 151, 166–167
  psychological processes, 152–161
  purchase decision process, 151, 166–167
  summary, terms, and exercises, 170–171
Consumer-centric perspective, 6
Consumer decision process, 151
Consumer demand
  effect on, 66–67
  pull strategy, 566, 571
Consumer income
  and tastes, 199
Consumer information networks, 95
Consumerism, 95
Consumer magazines, 409
Consumer markets
  defined, 149
  marketing to, 19, 149
Consumer packaged goods, 44
Consumer sales promotion, 566, 568
  cents-off promotions, 570
  combination offers, 571
  contests, 574
  convenience cards, 570
  coupons, 568–570
  defined, 566
  effectiveness, 570
  electronic coupons, 570
  point-of-purchase (P-O-P) materials, 568–569
  premiums, 570
  rebates, 570
  refunds, 570
  sampling, 571
  sweepstakes, 574
Consumers' brand attitudes, 210
Consumers' motives, 216
Consumption
  Internet content, 462–463
Contemporary advertising, 2–30
  communication dimension, 15–18
  ethical issues, 19
  introduction, 4–7
  learning objectives, 2
  marketing dimension, 18–28
  relationship marketing, 9–14
Contemporary hit radio (CHR), 448
Content
  Internet, 463–466
  magazines, 405, 409
  of media and audience, 295
Content management systems (CMSs), 499

Content marketing, 23
Contests, 574
Continuity
  defined, 285
  design principles, 345
Continuous schedule, 298
Continuous-tone photographs, 382
Continuous tones, 381
Contract rates, 418
Contrast, design principles, 345
Control, of production process, 376
Controlled circulation, 411
Control room, radio, 388–389
Controversies, 62–63, 81–82; *see also* Economic aspects
Convenience cards, 568, 570
Conversion rate, 475
Convex advertising response curve, 286
Conviction
  creating for product, 5
  DAGMAR marketing objective setting system, 243
  in IMC pyramid, 253
Cookie/gobo advertising, 275
Cookies
  defined, 467–468
Cooperative (co-op) advertising, 109–110, 201
  sales promotion, 564
Cooperative (or co-op) programs, 417
Coordinated marketing communications, 12
Copy, 122, 321
  for electronic media, 358–360
Copy cast, 380
Copyfit, 380
Copy platform, 309–310
Copy points, 196
Copyright, 89–90
Copy strategy document, 309–310
Copywriters, 122, 306
Copywriting; *See also* Writing
  for electronic media, 358–360
  formats for print advertising, 361–365
  for print
    body copy, 354–357
    headlines, 351–354
    subheads, 354
  for radio, 358
  for television, 359–360
Corporate blogs, 587, 588
Corporate identity advertising, 599, 607
Corporate/institutional advertising, 599
  corporate identity advertising, 599, 607
  David Ogilvy on, 607
  defined, 19, 26, 599
  Portfolio Review, 602–606

  public relationship advertising, 597
  recruitment advertising, 608
Corporations
  conventions and dealer meetings, 568
Cost
  expenditures on advertising
    1994-2005, 51–52
    direct mail, 554
    online advertising, 462
    as percentage of GDP, 64
    public relations, 592, 598
    television, 430, 433
  increasing, 276
  Internet advertising, 471–473
  paper, 378
  production, 376–379
    digital media commercial production process, 378
    electronic production, 378–379
    print production process, 376–377
    radio commercial production process, 387
    television commercial production process, 389
  sales promotion, 564
  sponsorship fee, 592
Cost, of professional research, 220
Cost efficiency, 297
Cost per point (CPP), 297, 445
Cost per thousand, 276
Cost per thousand (CPM), 296–297, 412, 445
Coupons, 569–570
Cover date, 412
Cover papers, 380
Cover position, 403
CPM (cost per thousand), 296–297, 412, 445
CPP (cost per point), 297, 445
Creative boutiques, 119
Creative concept research, 212
Creative concepts, 122
Creative director, 122, 306
Creative execution, 336–373
  electronic media, 357–360
  international markets, 367, 370–371
  Internet, writing for, 366–367
  learning objectives, 336
  print layouts, designing, 339–347
  radio advertising, 360–366
  television advertising, 360–366
  Websites, writing for, 366–367
Creative message, 212
Creative mix
  advertising objectives and strategy, 279

IMC strategy, 256–258
   magazine advertising, 402–405,
      404, 409
   newspapers in, 413–417
Creative people, 116
Creative process
   Artist role, 317–325
   defined, 316
   ethical issues, 322
   Explorer role, 316–317
   Judge role, 326
   Warrior role, 326–327, 332–333
Creative pyramid
   action in, 322, 325
   vs. advertising pyramid, 321
   attention in, 322–323
   credibility, 322, 324
   defined, 321
   desire in, 322, 324–325
   elements, 322–325
   interest in, 322, 323–324
Creatives
   Artist, 317–325
   defined, 306
   Explorer, 316–317
   Judge, 326
   Warrior, 326–327, 332–333
Creative strategy
   big idea development and implementation
      (Artist Explorer role), 317–325
   creative team, 306, 308
   decision making (Judge role), 326
   elements of great advertising, 306–308
   enhanced by creativity, 311–316
   ethical issues, 322
   formulating, 308–311
   gathering information (Explorer role),
      316–317
   learning objectives, 304
   overcoming obstacles (Warrior role), 326–327,
      332–333
   Portfolio Review: creative director's
      outstanding ads, 328–331
   resonance and relevance dimensions,
      307–308
   summary, terms, and exercises, 333–335
Creative teams, 306, 308
Creative thinking, 314–316
Creativity
   blocks to, 319–321
   defined, 311
   IMC role, 311–314
   importance, 311–312
   thinking and, 314–316
Credibility
   advertising ethics and, 19
   in creative pyramid, 324

interior paragraphs, 356
   newspaper, 416
Crisis communication management,
      585–586
CRM (customer retention and relationship
      management), 484
Cross-tabulations, 231
Crowdsourcing, 510
CTR Market Research, 180
CTRs (click-through rates), 510
Cultural symbol positioning, 246
Culture and cultural differences
   interpersonal influences on consumer behavior,
      151, 164–165
   sponsorships and events, 597
Cume persons, 453
Cume rating, 453
Current customers, 148
Cursive type, 383
Customer lifetime value (LTV), 549
Customer relationships; *see also* Consumer(s);
      Market(s)
   categories of, 148–149
   importance, 9–10
   importance of ethical advertising, 19
   levels, 10–12
   lifetime customer value (LTCV), 9–10
   product utility and needs of, 146
   satisfaction as goal, 148
Customer retention and relationship management
      (CRM), 484
Customer(s)
   cost of acquiring, 10
   interviews, 362
   as key marketing participants, 148–151
   lost, 9–10
   loyalty, 9, 10
   needs of, 146
   perceptions, 145, 146–148
   satisfaction, 148
Customer satisfaction, 148
Customer satisfaction studies, 211
Customer service, social media, 505–506, 509
Custom magazines, 404
CYMK printing, 384–385

D

3-D ads, 405
DAGMAR (defining advertising goals for
      measured advertising results), 243
Daily Estimated Circulation
      (DEC), 527
Daily newspaper, 414–415
Data
   access to, 550
   explosion, 502

interpreting and reporting, 220
   management of, 550
Data access, 550
Database marketing, 547
Databases
   defined, 547
   direct marketing impact, 547–548
Data collection methods
   comparison of, 224
Data management, 550
Daypart mix, 443
Dayparts, 451–452
DBS (direct broadcast satellite), 446
Deadlines (closing dates), 380
Dealer meetings and company
      conventions, 568
Dealer premiums and contests, sales
      promotion, 566
DEC (Daily Estimated Circulation), 527
Decentralized system, 114
Deception in advertising, 68–69
Decision making process, 461
Deck, 488
Decline stage, 192
Decoding, 14
Defensive warfare, 245
Defining advertising goals for measured advertising
      results (DAGMAR), 243
Delivered figure, 410
Demand
   pull strategy, 566, 571
Demarketing, 49, 158
Demographic editions, 413
Demographics and population
   Internet access, 466
   as sales tool on radio, 362
   segmentation, 178
Demonstration, 362–363
   false, 70
Departmental system, 123
Design
   defined, 339
   principles, 345
   print layouts, 339–347
   storyboard, 365–366
   style, 339
Designated market areas (DMAs), 441
Desire
   creating, 6
   in creative pyramid, 324–325
   in IMC pyramid, 253
   interior paragraphs, 356
Desktop meter, Internet, 467
Development stage, 129–130
Device copy, 356
Dialogue/monologue copy, 356
Digital interactive, 135

Digital interactive media, 460–461
  history of, 460–461
  interactive TV, 486
  learning objectives, 458
  mobile advertising
    advantages, 295
    expenditures on, 486
    types, 486–490, 560
Digital media, 9
  cost of electronic production, 378–379
  defined, 376
  direct-response advertising, 560
  interactive media, 458–490
    history of, 461
    interactive TV, 486
    learning objectives, 458
    mobile advertising, 295, 488–490, 549
  producers, 395
  production process, 395–396
  trends, 393–395
Digital proof, 386
Digital television (DTV), 431–432
Digital video effects (DVE) units,
    390–391
Digital video recorders (DVRs)
  as interactive TV, 486
Direct broadcast satellite (DBS), 446
Direct close, in body copy, 357
Direct distribution, 199
Directing the production process,
    376–379
Direct mail (action) advertising, 138,
    554–556
  advantages, 295
  appearance, 558
  buying, 556–557
  defined, 554
  direct marketing *vs.,* 547
  disadvantages, 556
  in media mix, 556
  message, 558
  types, 19, 554–560
Direct-mail tests, 225
Direct marketing, 203, 547–548
  closing sales, 145
  database impact on, 549–551
  defined, 546–547
  direct-response advertising,
    554–560
  drawbacks to, 551–553
  evolution of, 548–549
  IMC role, 548–550
  types, 553–560
Direct marketing technique, 204
Director, 388
Directories, 517

Direct questioning, 224, 225
Direct-response advertising, 27, 554
  defined, 554
  growth of, 549
  types, 554–560
    broadcast, 559–560
    catalogs, 557–558
    digital, 560
    print, 563
Direct-response agencies, 120
Direct-response television, 439–440
Direct-sales strategy, 553
Direct selling, 553
DisABILITY believes, 216
Discount users, 176
Display advertising, 416
Display allowance, 567
Display type, 382
Distributed networks, 461
Distribution
  direct mail, 556
  in marketing mix, 247
  message objectives
    audience reach, 283–284
    audience size, 282–283
    exposure frequency, 284–285
    message weight, 282–283
Distribution channel, 199
Distribution costs, 198
Distribution element, 199
Distribution objectives
  audience reach, 283–284
  audience size, 282–283
  continuity, 285
  defined, 282
  exposure frequency, 284–285
  message weight, 282–283
Diversity representation, 163
Diverting, 567
DMAs (designated market areas), 441
Domestic scope for advertising, 288
Dominance concept, 213
Donut, 363
Drama messages, 16
Drive times, 452
DTV (digital television), 431–432
Dubs, 389
Dummy, 341
Dupes, 393
DVE (digital video effects) units,
    390–391

E

Early adopters, 192
Early advertising, 44

Earned rates, 418
"Eat like you mean it," 180
E-commerce, 461, 471
Economic aspects
  abundance principle, 67–68
  business cycle, 67
  competition, 66
  consumer choice, 67
  consumer demand, 66–67
  controversies of, 62–63
  free-market principles, 34–54, 65
  learning objectives, 60
  prices, 65
  product value, 65
  summary, review, and exercises,
    99–101
Economic conditions, 199
Economy
  print production, 380
EDGAR Online, 219
EDI (electronic data interchange), 437
Editing genius, 362
Effective exposures per dollar, 286
Effective frequency, 285–286
Effective reach, 285
Effective survey questions, 230,
    231, 232
e-fluentials, 366
Elaboration Likelihood Model, 155
Electronic billboards, 275
Electronic coupons, 570
Electronic data interchange (EDI), 437
Electronic media
  copywriting for, 358–360
  defined, 135
  developing artistic concepts,
    360–361
  electronic production, cost of,
    378–379
  Internet; *see* Internet
  radio; *see* Radio
  television; *see* Television
Electronic production, 378–379
Electronic signs, 531
Electronic sound, 362
Eliminate technique to transform
    concepts, 319
E-mail, 50
  buying, 484–485
  direct-response advertising, 559–560
Emphasis of typography, 380
Empirical research method, 268
Em space, 383
Encoding, 14, 316
Endorsements
  by celebrities, 61–62

Engraver, 377–378
Enhanced tracking, Internet, 467–469
Entertainment, 512
Entertainment sponsorships and events, 594–595
Entrepreneurial agencies, 118
Environment
    influence on consumer behavior, 151
    nonpersonal influences on consumer behavior, 151, 165–166
    political advertising, 551
    public relations, 580
    traditional *vs.* online, 463
EOI (Eyes On Impressions), 527
Equipment-based service, 193
Ethical dilemmas, 45, 278
Ethical lapses, 45
Ethical responsibility, 75–78
    levels, 77
Ethics and ethical issues
    accounting for account reviews, 126
    agency compensation, 278
    children, advertising to, 439
    commercial speech, 76–77
    dilemmas *vs.* lapses, 45
    diversity representation, 163
    overview, 19
    sex in advertising, 322–323
    similarities in print advertising, 353
    social responsibility, 75–78
    spillover, in outdoor media, 529
    subliminal persuasion, 248
    sweepstakes, 421
Evaluation and selection, consumer decision process, 151
Evaluation of alternatives, 151
Evaluative criteria, 166
Evoked set, 166
Evolution of integrated marketing communications
    Coca-Cola, 32–34, 40–43
    direct marketing, 548
    ethical issues, 45
    free markets, 34–54
    Golden Age (1946 to 1970s), 47–49
    industrial age, 44–47
    Internet, 45
    learning objectives, 32
    Portfolio Review: Coca-Cola, 32–34, 40–43
    postindustrial age, 49, 51–52
    preindustrial age, 44
    social issues, 54–55, 57
    summary, review, and exercises, 57–59
    timetable, 39
    21st century, 52–54

Exaggeration, 362
Exchanges, 145–148
Exclusive distribution, 201
Exhibitive media, 517, 531–536
Exhibits, 535, 592
Expenditures, advertising, 4
Expenditures on integrated marketing communications; *see also* Cost
    direct mail, 554
    by medium, 276
    online advertising, 461, 462
    as percentage of GDP, 64
    public relations, 598
    television, 430, 433
Experimental method, 224
Explorer, 316–317
Exposure frequency, 284–285
Exposure value, 295
Externalities (social costs)
    absence of, 63
    offensiveness, 72–73
    stereotypes, 71–72
    unfair advertising due to, 85
    value system, 69
Eyes On Impressions (EOI), 527

F

Fact-based thinking, 314–315
Factually false, 69
Fairs, 595
False advertising, 19, 45
False comparisons, 70
False demonstrations, 70
False promises, 70
False testimonials, 70
Families, interpersonal influences on consumer behavior, 151, 161
Family brand, 195
Farm advertising, 21
Farm publications, 409
Fatty trap, 387
FCB (Foote, Cone & Belding) grid, 159, 160
FCC (Federal Communications Commission), 89
FDA (Food and Drug Administration), 87–89
Feature articles, 590
Federal Communications Commission (FCC), 89
Federal restraints and regulation
    Bureau of Alcohol, Tobacco and Firearms (ATF), 567
    Environmental Protection Agency (EPA), 587

Federal Trade Commission, 567–568, 587
Federal Trade Commission (FTC), 84–87, 567, 587
Fee-commission combination, 125–126
Feedback, 14, 18
Festivals, 596–597
Film houses, 132
Finishing phase, radio and television, 389
First cover, 403
First-run syndication, 438
Five Ms (5Ms) methodology of media mix, 287, 291
Flanking marketing warfare, 245
Flat rates, 418
Flats, 384
Flexibility, 235
Flighting, 298
Focus group, 222
    show-and-tell, 222
Focus groups, 225
Folders, direct mail, 556
Font, 383
Food and Drug Administration (FDA), 87–89
Foote, Cone & Belding (FCB) grid, 159, 160
Foreign media
    defined, 139
    economics of, 297
    in media plan, 288
    print production cost, 377
Formal balance, design principles, 345
Forums, 499
Forward buying, 567
Four-color process, 384
Four Ps (4Ps), 21, 26–27, 191
Fourth covers, 403
Fourth dimension, 362
Fragmentation of audiences
    broadcast networks, 434
    increasing media options impact, 274, 275
Fragrance strips, 405
Framework for media planning, 279–281
Franchising, 202
Free association, 317
Free markets economy, 34–54
    brand, 37–38
    functions and effects, 35–37
    principles of, 35
Freestanding inserts (FSIs), 569
Frequency
    defined, 284
    effective, 285–286
    message exposure, 284–285
    optimal, 286

Frequency discounts, 412, 418
Frequency of delivery, newspapers, 414–415
FSIs (freestanding inserts), 569
FTC (Federal Trade Commission), 84–87
Full position, 420
Full-service advertising agency, 118–119
Fundraising, public relations (PR), 588

G

Games, 512, 574
Gamification, 512
Gatefold, 404
Gender
    Internet use, 464–466
General consumer agency, 118
General Motors, 178, 226
Generational differences, 146
Geodemographic segmentation, 178
Geographic, 175
Geographic editions, 413
Geographic segmentation, 178
Geography
    advertising classification, 19
    magazines, 409–410
GfK MRI Starch, 227
Global advertising, 26; *see also* International advertising
    markets, 150–151
    media, 138, 290–291
Global marketers, 115
Global markets, 150–151
Global media, 138, 290–291; *see also* Media
Global media vehicles, 138
Global positioning systems (GPSs), 527
Gobo/cookie advertising, 275
Golden Age (1946 to 1970s), 47–49
Goods, 8
Google's Keyword Planner, 217
Government markets
    defined, 150
Government regulation and restraints
    federal regulation
        Bureau of Alcohol, Tobacco and Firearms (ATF), 567
        Environmental Protection Agency (EPA), 587
        Federal Communications Commission (FCC), 89
        Federal Trade Commission (FTC), 84–87, 567, 587

Food and Drug Administration (FDA), 87–89
        Library of Congress, 89–90
        Patent and Trademark Office, 89–90
    international advertisers, 78–79
    learning objectives, 60
    local government regulation, 91
    nongovernmental regulation
        Better Business Bureau, 91–92
        by consumer groups, 95
        by media, 93–95
        National Advertising Review Council, 92
        self-regulation by advertisers, 95, 98
    state regulation, 90
Government regulations, 199
GPSs (global positioning systems), 527
Grades awarded, 195
Graphic designers, 342
Great Depression, 46–47
Green advertising, 587
Green marketing, 197
Grocery receipts, 275
Gross impressions, 282
Gross rating points (GRP), 282, 283, 444, 452
100 gross rating points daily, 521
Group system, 123, 124
Growth stage, 192
GRP (gross rating points), 282, 283, 444
Guaranteed circulation, 410
Guerrilla marketing warfare, 11, 245

H

Habits, 157–158
Halftone plates, 382
Halftones, 382–384
Halftone screen, 382–384
Halo effect, 226
Hard thinking, 314
Harmony of typography, 382
HD (high definition) digital program, 431
Headlines
    creation, 344
    defined, 351
    role of, 351–352
    in search ads, 354
    types, 352, 354
Heat-set inks, 385
Heuristics, 154

Hidden differences, 194
Hierarchy of needs, 158, 160
High definition (HD) digital program, 431
High-speed Internet connectivity, 466
Hispanic media, 178, 179
Historical fantasies, 362
History
    Coca-Cola, 32–34, 40–43
    digital media, 461
    direct marketing, 546
    ethical issues, 45
    free markets, 34–54
    Golden Age (1946 to 1970s), 47–49
    industrial age, 44–47
    Internet, 45, 461
    learning objectives, 32
    postindustrial age, 49, 51–52
    preindustrial age, 44
    social issues, 54–55, 57
    timetable, 39
    21st century, 52–54
Holiday Inn Express, 214
Hook, 363
Horizontal cooperative advertising, 110
Horizontal publications, 411
Hot property, 362
House direct-mail lis, 556
Households using TV (HUT), 443
House organs, 556, 591
HTML (HyperText Markup Language), 396, 464
Human communication process, 14–15
Humor
    fake interviews, 362
HUT (households using TV), 443
Hyperbole statements (exaggeration), 362
HyperText Markup Language (HTML), 464

I

Ideal structure, 116
Ideas, 8
Identification
    of sponsor, 8
    target audience, 19–21
Illustrators, 342, 346
Image, product, 65
Image advertising, 21
Imagery transfers, 362
Imagine technique to transform concepts, 318

IMC; *see* Integrated marketing communications (IMC)
IMC campaign, 221
   posttesting methods, 226
   pretesting methods, 225
IMC message; *see also* Message(s)
   defined, 258
   examples, 309
   types, 18–28
IMC plans
   defined, 252
   IMC strategy, 256–258
   marketing plan reviews, 253
   objectives, 253–256
   secrets to successful, 258
IMC pyramid, 253–254
IMC research, 212, 213
   defined, 211
   important issues, 228
Imc research, 211
IMC strategies, 174
IMC strategy, 214
   communications media, 257–258
   consumer behavior, 151–152
   developing creative concepts, 215
   IMC message, 258
   product concept, 257
   target audience, 256
IMC strategy research, 212
Imc strategy research, 212
Immersive advertising, 531
Impact dimension, 307–308
Impersonal reference groups, 162
Implied consumers, 16, 17
Improvisations, 362
IMS (Interactive Market Systems), 299
Inadequate planning, as budget buster, 377
Incentive system, 126
Incomplete description, 70
Independent production houses, 132
Independent research companies, 132
Independent shopping guide, 415–416
In-depth interview, 222
Individual brand, 195
Induced differences, 194
Industrial age, 44–47
Industrial customers, 185
Industrial markets, 149, 184
Industrial Revolution, 44
Inferred messages, 13
Inflatables, 275
In-flight ads, 275
Influentials, 584

Info graphics, 312
Infomercials, 439–440, 559
Informal balance, design principles, 345
Informal research, 218
Information
   awareness of availability of, 145
   complete, 68, 69, 78
   gathering for creative process, 316–317
   perception of equal exchange and, 148
   personal influences on consumer behavior, 154–161
   providing compelling, 152
   purchasing decision and, 5
   search for, consumer decision process, 151
Informational (negatively originated) motives, 160, 308
In-house agency, 126–127
In-house cable TV systems, 225
In kind sponsorship fee, 592
Innate factors, 153–154
In-pack premium, 571
Inquiry test, 228
Inquiry tests, 226, 228
Insert, 403
Insertion order, 421–422
Inside card, 530
Insight outlooks, development of, 316
Institutional advertising
   defined, 108, 599
   purpose, 19
Institutional copy, 356
In-store sampling, 571
Intangible services, 8
Integrated commercial, 361
Integrated communications, 12
Integrated marketing communications (IMC)
   concept, 12
   creative process, 316
   creativity, 311–314
   defination, 5, 12
   dimensions of, 14
   direct marketing, 548–553
   evolution of, 12
      Coca-Cola, 32–34, 40–43
      ethical issues, 45
      free markets, 34–54
      Golden Age (1946 to 1970s), 47–49
      industrial age, 44–47
      Internet, 45
      learning objectives, 32
      Portfolio Review: Coca-Cola, 32–34, 40–43

      postindustrial age, 49, 51–52
      preindustrial age, 44
      social issues, 54–55, 57
      timetable, 39
      21st century, 52–54
   importance of, 6–7, 28
   local advertising, 108–109
   as marketing tool, 144–148
   messages
      defined, 258
      examples, 309
      types, 18–28
   Mountain Dew example, 239–240
   My IMC Campaign
      personal selling, 560–564
   planning approaches
      bottom-up marketing, 247–248
      DAGMAR, 243
      ethical issues, 248
      IMC approach, 248–268
      learning objectives, 238
      marketing strategy, 243–247
      marking objectives, 241, 243
      mission statement, 240–241
      situation analysis, 241
   process, 12
   public relations, 580
   relationship marketing, 546
   sales promotion, 564
   strategy
      consumer behavior, 151–152
   tactics, 12
Integrated product, 12
Integration triangle, 14
Intellectual property, 89
Intensive distribution, 200
Intensive techniques, 221, 222
Interaction design, 460–461
Interactive advertising, 19
Interactive agencies, 119, 120
Interactive customer relationships, 11
Interactive marketing, 574
Interactive Market Systems (IMS), 299
Interactive media, 118
   defined, 15
   described, 15
   digital interactive media, 548–549
      learning objectives, 458
      mobile advertising, 295, 488–490, 549
   direct marketing, 548
   history of, 460–461
   interactive TV, 486
   kiosks, 487, 569, 570
   types, 19

Interactive model of communication, 15
Interactive store fronts, 275
Interactive TV, 487
Interactivity, 18
Interest
  in brands, 157
  in creative pyramid, 323–324
  produced by learning, 157
Interior paragraphs, 356
Interlock, 393
International advertising
  consumer behavior, 151
  defined, 19, 26
  foreign media
    defined, 139
    economics of, 297
    in media plan, 288
    print production cost, 377
  Internet, 466–468
  media plan, 288–289
  print production cost, 376
International agencies, 118
International marketers, 232
  art direction for, 371
  creating ads for, 367, 370–371
  legal restraints on, 371
  primary data collection, 232
International media, 138
International structure, 115
Internet, 45, 461–466
  advantages, 295
  audience, 466–470
    access to Internet, 466
    demographics, 466, 468
    described, 465, 466
    measuring, 466, 470
    vs. television viewers, 465–466
    use of Internet, 466
  buying time and space, 471–473
    added-value packages, 483
    ad networks, 471
    AdSense, 482
    AdWords, 475, 482
    banners, 482–483
    buttons, 482
    classified ads, 484
    e-mail advertising, 484–485
    Google, 475–481
    pricing, 470–471
    search engine marketing, 484
    sponsorships, 483
    targeting, 472–473
    types of Internet advertising, 471
  connectivity, 466
  cookies
    defined, 467
    cost, 470–471

defined, 462
as digital interactive media, 460–461
e-mail
  buying, 484–485
  direct-response advertising, 560
history of, 462
impact of, 460
integrated marketing communications (IMC),
  485–486
landing pages, 471–473
media planning tools, 466
microsites, 471
penetration, 465
Portfolio Review: challenges and creativity,
  476–484
problems with, 485
public relations and, 580
traditional *vs.* online environment,
  462–464
trends, 393–395
Websites
  advertising on, 474–476
  classified ads, 484
  defined, 474
  production, 395–396
  top ten most visited, 465
  writing for, 366–367
Internet advertising, 484
Internet Protocol Television
  (IPTV), 446
Interpersonal influences on consumer behavior,
  161–165
  cultural, 164–165
  defined, 151
  family influence, 161
  opinion leaders, 162, 164
  reference groups, 162
  societal influence, 161–164
  subcultural, 164–165
Interstitials, 482
Interviews, as radio sales technique, 362
Introductory phase, 192
Inventory, 438
iPhone, 488
IPTV (Internet Protocol
  Television), 446
Iron Curtain, 49
Island halves, 403
Italic subheads, 354

J

Japan Weather Association, 177
Jingles, 363
John Posey, 394
Judge, 326
Junior panels, 519

Junior posters, 519
Junior unit, 403

K

Kerning, 382
Key influentials, 308
Keyword, 470–471
Kicker, 354
Kiosks, 275, 487, 569, 570

L

Lady-scented body wash, 175
Landing pages, 471
Lavatory advertising, 275
Layout
  creating
    tools and formats, 343–345
  defined, 339
  designing, 339–347
  use of, 339
Leading, 382
Lead-in paragraph, 356
Learned factors, 153–154
Learning
  attitudes produced by, 157
  brand interest produced by, 157
  brand loyalty, 157–158
  in consumer decision process, 151
  defined, 154
  habits produced by, 157–158
  mental files, 154
  needs, 158–159
  repetition, 157
  theories, 154–155
  wants, 158–159
  Website production phase, 395
Legal announcements, 8
Length of message, and media planning,
  291–293
Letter shop, 557
Levels, relationships, 10–12
Library of Congress, 89–90
Licensed brands, 195
Lifestyle technique, 365
Lifetime customer value (LTCV),
  9–10
"Lightning Bug," 253–254
Lights, television production,
  391–392
Line art, 381
Line film, 382
Line plates, 382
Linkage media, 548
List brokers, 557
Literary form, advertising as, 17

Live action television, 390
Lobbying, 587
Local advertising
  advertisers
    cooperative (co-op) advertising,
      109–110
    integrated marketing communications,
      108–109
    types, 107
  creating, 109, 110
  defined, 19, 26
  example of, 105–107
  media plans, 288
  national *vs.*, 110–112
  types, 107–108
Local agency, 116–117
Local city magazine, 409
Local time, 451
Local TV advertising, 440–441
Location-based advertising, 527–528
Location shooting, 393
Logotypes *(logos)*, 17, 33, 357
Long-term macro criticisms, 68
L'Oréal, 198
Lost customers, 9–10
Lot, 392
Loupe, 386
Low-Rise Living social classes, 162
Loyalty
  Coca-Cola and, 34, 38
  customer, 9
  value of, 10
Loyalty programs, 550
LTCV (lifetime customer value), 9–10
LTV (customer lifetime value), 549

M

Macro model, IMC, 250
Magazines
  advantages, 295
  audience, 403
  buying space
    circulation, 410–412
    rates, 412–413
    reading rate cards, 412–413
  categorization, 405–409
    by content, 405, 409
    by geography, 409–410
    by physical size, 410
  circulation
    added value services, 412
    controlled circulation, 411
    delivered circulation, 410
    guaranteed circulation, 410
    horizontal publications, 411
    merchandising services, 412

  paid circulation, 411
  primary circulation, 411
  secondary readership, 411
  subscription sales, 411
  vendor sales, 411
  vertical publications, 411
consumer, 409
creative mix and, 402–405,
  404, 409
custom, 404
direct-response advertising, 559
innovations in, 405
local city, 409
national, 410
Portfolio Review: outstanding ads,
  406–408
pros and cons of, 402, 403
special possibilities with, 402–403
Mailing house, 557
Mailing lists, 556
Mail-response list, 556
Maintenance stage, 130
Makegoods, 446
Management (or account)
  supervisors, 121
Managing the production
  process, 376
  costs of production, 376–377
  directing and controlling, 377
  planning and organizing, 376
  print production manager, role
    of, 376
  producer, role of, 376
Manufacturer's brands, 195
Market concentration, 186
Market demand, 198
Marketer-centric perspective, 6
Marketers, 104, 151, 233; *see also* Advertising
  agencies
Marketers group, 175
Market expansion, 192
Marketing
  advertising professionals' views
    of, 582
  affiliate marketing program,
    Internet, 471
  communications
    integration; *see* Integrated marketing
      communications (IMC)
    media menu for integrated, 274
  defined, 18, 144
  direct, 145
  4Ps, 21, 26–27
  IMC message determination, 18–28
  IMC role, 144–148
    customer needs and product
      utility, 145

  exchanges, 145–148
  perception, 145, 146–148
  satisfaction, 148
key participants in process,
  148–151
learning objectives, 142
mix of
  marketing objectives, 279
objectives, 279
process, 18, 19
relationship; *see* Relationship marketing
relationships, importance of, 9–10
role of, 18, 144
strategy
  implementing, 21, 26–27
  marketing objectives relationship
    to, 279
  target audience determination,
    19–21
summary, terms, and exercises,
  170–171
Marketing communications
  advertising; *see* Advertising
  defined, 4, 7, 26
  integration; *see* Integrated marketing
    communications (IMC)
Marketing costs, 199
Marketing information system
  (MIS), 218
Marketing information system
  (mis), 218
Marketing mix, 191, 247
  determination, 247
  marketing objectives, 279
  in perspective, 205
  price element, 197
Marketing objectives, 241, 243
Marketing plan, 240
Marketing public relations (MPR),
  27, 583
Marketing research, 210
Marketing researchers, 198
Marketing research online community (MROC),
  508–509
Marketing research process, 218
Marketing research techniques, 187
Marketing strategy, 200, 243–247
  defined, 243
  4Ps, 21, 26–27
  marketing mix determination, 247
  marketing objectives relationship
    to, 279
  product positioning, 245–247
  selecting target market, 244–245
  tactics, 247
  warfare model, 245
Market prep corporate advertising, 608

Market research firms, 235
    Internet, 235
Markets, 216
Market(s)
    defined, 149
    identification of, 19–21
    in media mix (5Ms), 287, 288,
        289, 294
    sales potential of different, 289–290
    target
        defined, 19
        identification of, 19–21
    types, 148–151
Market segmentation, 48, 174, 184
    audience, 190
    business and government markets, 185
    challenge of, 187
Market share, 219
Market volume, 565
Markups, 125
Maslow's hierarchy of needs, 158, 160
Mass communication, 8
Mass media, 9; *see also* Media
Master tape, 389
Maturity stage, 192
Mavens, 182
McDonald's, 178
MDS (multipoint distribution system), 446
Measurement
    Internet audience, 466
    sponsorship results, 598
Mechanicals
    defined, 377
    in print advertising, 342
    print production process, 379
Mechanics in media mix (5Ms), 287,
        291, 294
Media; *see also specific forms of media*
    audiences, 295; *see also* Audience
    buyers, 402
    computers in selection and scheduling,
        299, 301
    defined, 105
    digital interactive, 135
    direct-mail advertising, 138
    electronic media, 135
    foreign
        defined, 139
        economics of, 297
        in media plan, 288
        print production cost, 377
    fragmentation of, 274, 276
    global, 138, 290–291
    increasing complexity, 276–277
    international media, 138
    mass, 9
    mix

    direct mail in, 554, 555
    elements of, 287
    methodology of media mix (5Ms), 287,
        288, 291, 294
mix of
    direct mail in, 554, 555
    nontraditional, 9
    objectives for, 281–286
        audience objectives, 281–282
        developing, 293
        message-distribution objectives,
            282–285
        reach, frequency and continuity
            optimization, 283–285
        review by planners, 294
    off-the-wall media, 275
    other media, 138
    out-of-home media, 135
    planning and buying, 122
    print media, 134–135
    print production cost, 379
    social media, 135, 138
    spillover, 291
    synergy of mixed, 297–298
    types, 9
    vehicles
        advantages by type, 295
        attention value, 296
        cost efficiency of, 296–297
        criteria for selecting, 294–301
        exposure, 286
        exposure value, 295
        motivation value, 296
Media agency, 119
Media buyers, 402
Media-buying services, 119
Media categories, 217
Media classes, 217
Media commission, 125
Media expertise, 116
Media kits, 588
Media mix
    direct mail in, 555
    elements of, 287
    methodology of media mix (5Ms),
        287, 291
Media-only agency, 277
Media planning, 270–303
    audience
        fragmentation, 274, 275
        objectives, 281–282
        reach, 283–284
        size, 282–283
    budget considerations, 290
    buyer purchase patterns, 293
    buying media, increasing complexity,
        276–277

    challenges, 272–278
    competition, 277
    continuity, 285
    cost increases, 276
    defined, 272
    defining media objectives,
        281–286
    ethical issues, 278
    Internet advertising, 469
    learning objectives, 270
    marketing framework role, 279
    markets' sales potential, 289–290
    media mix development, 287–294
    media objectives, defining,
        281–286
    message
        mood and medium, 291
        size, length, and position, 291–293
        weight, 282–283
    plans book development, 555
    purpose, 272
    questions involved in, 272
    scope of media plan, 288–289
    selling media, increasing complexity,
        276–277
    summary, terms, and exercises, 301–303
    tactics for
        economics of foreign media,
            297–299
        mixed media approach,
            297–298
        scheduling methods, 298–299
        vehicle selection, 294–301
    toolbox, 282
    written rationale for, 294
Media research, 213, 214
Media scheduling, 217
Media subclasses, 217
Media units, 217
Media vehicle, 217
Media vehicles, 217
    advantages by type, 295
    attention value, 296
    cost efficiency of, 296–297
    criteria for selecting, 294–301
    exposure, 286
    exposure value, 295
    motivation value, 296
Medium; *see also* Media
    advertising classification, 19
    as channel in communication
        process, 14
    defined, 9
Megamerger, 49
Membership drives, 587
Memory, 154
Mental files, 154

Merchandise, 216
Message(s), 216
   in advertising, 13, 16
   in communication process, 16
   decoding/encoding, 14
   defined, 14
   dimensions, 16
   distribution objectives
      audience reach, 283–284
      audience size, 282–283
      continuity, 285
      defined, 282
      exposure frequency, 284–285
      message weight, 282–283
   handling, 274
   IMC
      defined, 258
      examples, 309
      types, 18–28
   literary forms, 16
   objectives in creative strategy,
      308–309
   planned, 13, 14, 26
   product, 13, 14
   public service, 8
   receiving, 274
   service, 13, 14
   strategy, 310
   unplanned, 13, 14, 585
Message-distribution objectives,
   282–285
Message handling, 274
Message posttesting, 212
Messages, 216
Message strategy (or rationale), 310
Message testing, 224
Message weight, 282
Methodology of media mix (5Ms), 287,
   291, 294
Metrics, plans book development, 555
Microblog postings, 500
Microblogs, 500
Microsites, 472
Microsoft, 194
Middle class social classes, 161
Middleman, 199
Millward Brown Research, 215
MindBase, 181
MindBase Segments, 183
Misleading advertising, 45
Misleading comparisons, 70
Mission marketing, 586, 597
Mission statement, 240–241
Mixed interlock, 393
Mixed-media approach, 297
MMS (multimedia message service), 560
Mnemonic device, 364, 391

Mobile advertising
   advantages, 295
   expenditures on, 486
   types, 488, 559
Mobile App Installs, 510
Mobile billboard, 531
Mock magazines, 225
Models, IMC approach, 248–251
Mommy bloggers, 497
Money in media mix (5Ms), 287, 288,
   289, 294
Motivation
   brand interest as, 157
   in consumer decision process, 151,
      158–161
   defined, 158
   media vehicle value, 296
   personal influences on consumer behavior,
      158–161
   research on, 157
   understanding, in campaign
      design, 158
Motivation research, 221
Motivation value, 296
Motives, 216
   informational, 160, 308
   negatively originated, 160, 308
   positively originated, 160–161, 308
   relief, 160
   reward, 160
   transformational, 160–161, 308
Movement, design principles, 345
MPR (marketing public relations),
   27, 583
MROC (marketing research online community),
   508–509
Multicasting, 431
Multilevel marketing, 199
Multimedia production and
      presentations, 395
Multinational corporations, 115
Multipoint distribution system
   (MDS), 446
Musical commercials, 363–364
Musical logo, 363
My IMC Campaign
   agency review, 129
   assignment, 78–79
   client presentation, 591
   consumer needs and motivations, 159
   corporate blogs, 588
   creating local advertising, 110
   creating radio commercials, 359
   creating TV commercials, 360
   creative brief, 318
   design principles, 345
   headline creation, 344

   IMC budgets, 264
   IMC objectives, 255
   interactive media, 485
   magazine advertising, 403
   media objectives and strategies, 293
   newspaper advertising, 416
   out-of-home, exhibitive, and supplementary
      media, 532
   overview, 6
   plans book development, 554
   print media, 423
   producing ads, 386
   product facts for creatives, 340–341
   radio, planning and buying, 432
   radio advertising, 450
   situation analysis development, 242
   social media, 508
   television, planning and buying, 432
   tools for teamwork, 50
   understanding your client, 106
   ways to be a better client, 131
   writing effective copy, 355

N

Narrative copy, 356
Narrative messages, 16
National advertisers, 26, 110
National advertising
   defined, 19, 26
   Internet use, 465
   local *vs.,* 110–112
   media plans, 288
National agencies, 118
National brand, 195
National magazines, 410
National rate, 418
National rep system, 437
National rollout, 224
Needs, 158–159
   defined, 158
   hierarchy of, 158, 160
   learning's role in defining, 158
   product utility, 145
   understanding, in campaign design, 158
Negative effect on brand value, sales
      promotion, 564
Negatively originated motives,
   160, 308
Negative reinforcement, 155
Negs, print production prepress
      phase, 385
Net cost of space, 46
Network advertising, 436–437
Networking, 128
Network marketing, 199
   organizations, 553

Networks
    Internet, 462
    remarketing, 508
    television
        advertiser's expenditures, 430
Network television
    advertiser's expenditures, 430
News/information headline, 352
Newspaper bags, 275
Newspapers
    advantages, 295
    buying space, 417–422
        circulation
        rates, 418–420
        categorization
            audience, 415
            frequency of delivery, 414–415
            physical size, 415
            Sunday newspapers, 415–416
    in creative mix, 413–417
    direct-response advertising, 559
    pros and cons, 414, 416
    types, 416–417
    user, 414
Newsprint, 384
News releases, 584, 588, 589
Next to reading matter
        (NR), 420
NLEA (Nutritional Labeling and Education
        Act), 88–89
Noise, 14, 18
No media advertising, 199
Nonadvertising functions, 118
Noncommercial advertising, 19, 26
Nonfinal art, 339
Nonpersonal communication, 8, 202
Nonpersonal influences on consumer behavior,
        151, 165–166
    defined, 151, 165
    environment, 165–166
    place, 165
    time, 165
Nonprobability samples, 230
Nonproduct advertising, 19, 26
Nonproduct facts, 69
Nontraditional media, 9
Nonverbal component of message
        strategy, 310
North American Industry Classification System
        (NAICS) codes, 185, 186
North american industry classification system
        (naics) codes, 185
NR (next to reading) matter, 420
Nutritional Labeling and Education Act (NLEA),
        88–89

O

Obama campaign, 8
Objectives
    audience, 281–282
    marketing strategy relationship
        to, 279
    media, 281–286, 293
    message-distribution, 282–285
    plans book development, 554
Objective statement, 310
Objective/task method, 266–267
Observation method, 223
Offensive warfare, 245
Off-network syndication, 438
Off-the-wall media, 275
Old Glories social classes, 162
Old Spice, 175, 176
On camera presentation, 361
Online sharing, advertisement, 4
On-pack premium, 571
On-premise signs, 516
On-sale date, 412
OOH; see Out-of-home (OOH) media
Open rates, 418
Operant conditioning, 154–155
Opinion leader, 162, 164
Opinions, 512
Opinion sampling, 584
Opportunities, in SWOT
        analysis, 279
Opportunity to see (OTS), 282
Optimal frequency, 286
Order fulfillment, 562
Order-of-merit tests, 225
Organizational buyers, 151
Organizations, advertising industry,
        104–105
Original equipment manufacturers
        (OEMs), 199
Ornamental type, 383
Orthographic film, 382
OTS (opportunity to see), 282
Outbound telemarketing calls, 553
Outdoor advertising
    advantages, 295
    bulletins, 519
    buying, 520–521, 527–528
    defined, 135
    location, 527
    Portfolio Review: out-of-home advertising,
        522–526
    regulation of, 528
    standardized, 518
    technology in, 527–528

    types, 519–520
        bulletins, 519
        junior posters, 519
        spectaculars, 520
Out-of-home (OOH) media
    breakdown of, 516
    buying, 520–521, 527–528
    color and type in, 520–521
    defined, 135
    described, 516–517
    electronic signs, 531
    learning objectives, 514
    mobile billboard, 531
    outdoor advertising
        advantages, 295
        bulletins, 519
        buying, 520–521, 527–528
        defined, 135
        location, 527
        Portfolio Review: out-of-home advertising,
            522–526
        regulation of, 528
        standardized, 518
        technology in, 527–528
        types, 519–520
    parking meters, 531
    public phones, 531
    spillover, 529
    transit advertising, 528–531
        buying, 530–531
        defined, 528
        types, 528–530
    types, 19
Outside posters, 530
Overlay, 384
Overprint, 387
Overtime, as budget buster, 377
Owned properties, 503

P

Packaging
    change in, 535
    consumer appeal, 197
    defined, 532
    environmental issues in, 533–534
    government impact on, 534
    package manufacturing, 534–535
Page likes ads, 509
Pagerank, Google, 474
Paid-circulation, 411
Painted vehicles, 275
Paired comparisons, 225
PANTONE Matching System
        (PMS), 385

Paper
  categories of, 380
  cost of, 378
Parking meters, 531
Parody technique to transform
      concepts, 319
Partial disclosure, 70
Participation basis, 437
Particular market, 210
Partnership relationship, 10
Pass-along readership, 411
Pasteup, 342
Pasteups, 377
Peer influence, 161, 162
Pennysavers, 415–416
People-based service, 193
People Behind the Ads
  Albert Lasker, 28–29
  Alex Bogusky, 368–369
  Claude Hopkins, 28–29
  Cliff Marks, 538–539
  Edward Boyd, 96–97
  Joe Uva, 454
  Jon Steel, 168–169
  Ken Cervantes, 300
  Mark Zuckerberg, 511
  Nancy Berger Cardone, 425
  Samantha Avivi, 266–267
  Tim Piper, 332
  William Bernbach, 56
People meters, 441
Perceived equal-value exchange, 146
Percentage of sales method, 264–265
Perceptible differences, 194
Perceptions
  brand loyalty, 157
  cognition, 153–154
  in consumer decision process, 151
  defined, 152
  importance of, 145, 146–148
  learning and persuasion, 154
  marketing communications, 12
  mental files, 154
  model of, 152
  perceptual screens, 154
  as personal process, 152–153
  psychological process, 152–153
  stimuli, 153
Perceptual files, 154
Perceptual meaning studies, 225
Perfume brands, 195
Peripheral route to persuasion, 155, 156
Personal audience venue, interactive
      media as, 470
Personal communication, 202

Personal direct selling, 553
Personal influences on consumer behavior,
      151–169
  consumer motivation process, 158–161
  consumer perception process, 152–153
  defined, 151
  information processing, 154–161
  interpersonal, 151, 161–165
  nonpersonal, 151, 165–166
Personal processes, 151–161
  in consumer decision process, 151
  defined, 151
  learning and persuasion, 154–155
  motivation, 158–161
  perception, 152–153
Personal reference groups, 162
Personal selling, 26, 560–564
  advantages and drawbacks,
      561–562
  defined, 560
  as direct sales strategy, 553
  fulfilling orders, 563
  IMC role, 562
  information, gathering and providing,
      562–563
  relationship building, 564
  vs. telemarketing, 553–554
  types, 561
Personal video recorders, 487
Persona of communication, 15
Persuasion
  advertising's goal, 8
  in consumer decision process, 151
  defined, 155
  Elaboration Likelihood Model, 155
  repetition, 157
  structural, 327
  subliminal, 248
Philanthropy, 593
Photographers, 342, 346
Photographs and photography
  camera-ready art, 381–384
  cameras, television commercial production
      process, 389
  public relations (PR), 588
Phrase research questions, 232
Physiological screens, 153, 196
Pica, 382
Picture-window layout, 344
PLA (program-length advertisement), 439
Place
  influence on consumer behavior,
      151, 165
  nonpersonal influences on consumer behavior,
      151, 165

Place element, 200
Planned messages, 13, 14, 26
Planning; see also Media planning
  bottom-up marketing, 247–248
  communications objectives in, 241
  DAGMAR, 243
  ethical issues, 248
  IMC approach, 248–268
    budgeting, 259, 263–268
    IMC plans, 252–258
    importance to study of advertising,
      251–252
    models, 248–251
  learning objectives, 238
  managing the production process, 376
  marketing strategy, 243–247
  marking objectives, 241, 243
  mission statement, 240–241
  print production, 380
  public relations (PR), 584–592
  situation analysis, 241
  summary, terms, and exercises,
      268–269
  television production, 397
Plans book, 555
Plants, 518
Plates, print production, 381–382
PM (push money), 568
PMS (PANTONE Matching
      System), 385
Point (type), 383
Point-of-purchase (P-O-P) materials,
      568–569
Polished presentation, 327
Political advertising, 551
Polybagging, 571
P-O-P (point-of-purchase) materials,
      568–569
Pop-up ad, 405
Portfolio Review
  Activia, 23–25
  art director layout styles, 348–350
  Coca-Cola, 40–43
  corporate advertising, 602
  creative director's outstanding ads,
      328–331
  creative mix, 260–262
  Internet challenges and creativity, 475
  out-of-home advertising, 522–526
  outstanding ads, 406–408
  Ray-Ban campaign, 22
Portfolio tests, 225
Position, 193
Positioning, 14
Positioning strategy, 48

Position of message, and media planning, 291–293
Positive effect on brand value, 565
Positively originated motives, 160–161, 308
Positive reinforcement, 155
Postcards, 555–556
Poster panel, 519
Posters, 591
Poster-style format, 344
Postindustrial age, 49, 51–52
Postproduction phase, radio and television, 393
Postpurchase behavior, consumer decision process, 151
Postpurchase dissonance, 166
Postpurchase evaluation, 151, 166–167
Post-sale activities, 10
Posttesting, 215
PR; *see* Public relations (PR)
Preferred-position rate, 420
Preindustrial age, 44
Premium-priced brands, 198
Premium rates, 413
Premiums, 537
Premiums, consumer, 570, 571
Prepress graphic services, 377
Prepress (or production art) phase, 339
Prepress phase, print production, 384–385
  animation, 390
  color printing, 384–385
  copy casting, 380
  defined, 384
  four-color separation, 385
  live action, 390
  planning production, 391
  planning the job, 380
  print process, 379–380
  quality control, 385–387
  radio process, 387
  special effects, 390–391
  television process, 389–393
  typography, 380
Preprinted inserts, 417
Prerelationship stage, 129
Preroll, 483
Presentations, 128, 591
Presenter commercial, 361–362
Press agentry, 585
Press kits, 589
Press proof, 386
Pretesting, 215
  challenge of, 226

Price, 203
  effect on, 65
  Internet, 471–472
  in marketing mix, 247
Price advertising, 21
Price currents, 45
Price element, 197
Primary circulation, 411
Primary data, 218
Primary demand, 67, 192
Primary demand trend, 187
Primary market, 308
Primary motivation, 180
Primary quantitative research, 229
Primary research, 220
Primary resources, 180
Prime time, 443
Printed materials in public relations (PR), 591
Printers, 132
Print media
  copy formats, 351–357
    body copy, 354–357
    headlines, 351–354
    subheads, 354
  defined, 134–135
  direct-response advertising, 559
  layouts, 339–347
    creating, tools and formats, 343–345
    defined, 339
    designing, 339–347
    use of, 339
  learning objectives, 400
  logos, 357
  magazines; *see* Magazines
  newspapers; *see* Newspapers
  planning and evaluating, 423
  print media buyer, role of, 402
  production; *see* Print production process
  seal, 357
  signature cuts, 357
  slogans, 357
  software for buying, 413
  summary, terms, and exercises, 426–427
  technologies and, 424
  types, 19
  visuals in, 346–347
  worldwide medium, 422–424
Print media buyers, 402
Print production manager, 376
Print production process, 379
  costs, 377–379
  defined, 377

prepress phase: stripping, negs and plates, 384–385
  color printing, 384–385
  defined, 384
  four-color separation, 385
  quality control, 386–387
preproduction phase: project planning, 379–380
  copy casting, 380
  defined, 379–380
  planning the job, 380
  typography, 380
production phase: artwork creation, 380–381
  camera-ready art, 381
  halftones, 382–384
  mechanicals, 381
  quality control, 385
  visuals, 381
quality control, 385–387
  described, 386
  prepress phase, 384
  production phase, 386
Privacy, 553
Privacy rights, 83
Private-labeling strategy, 195
Private labels, 195
Proactive relationship, 10
Problem recognition, consumer decision process, 151
Process, defined, 18
Procter & Gamble, 178, 226
Procter & Gamble's Bonux detergent campaign, 233
Producers, 39, 376, 389
Product(s)
  defined, 8
  demos, 362
  in marketing mix, 247
  packaging; *see* Packaging
  perception of, 145, 146–148
  songs, 362
  usage rates vary for, 177
  utility, 145
  value of, 147
  value of manufactured products, 186
Product advertising, 26
  adapting to meeting marketing objectives, 279
  celebrity endorsements, 61–62
  concept of
    creative strategy, 308
  defined, 107
  product value effects, 65
  purpose, 19

unique selling proposition (USP), 48
usage-rate variables, 176–178
user-status variables, 176
Product attribute models, 211
Product attribute positioning, 246
Product classifications, 193
Product class positioning, 246
Product competitor positioning, 246
Product concept, 191, 213
   creative strategy, 308
   defined, 257
Product differentiation, 47, 194
Product element, 189, 191
Production artists, 342
Production luxuries, as budget buster, 377
Production of advertising, 374
   digital media process
      cost of electronic production, 378–379
      direct mail, 557
      producers, 395
      production process, 393–396
   electronic production, 378–379
   learning objectives, 374
   managing the process, 376
      costs of production, 377–379
      directing and controlling, 376–377
      planning and organizing, 376
      print production manager, role of, 376
      producer, role of, 376
   print process, 379–385
      costs, 377–378
      defined, 379
      preproduction phase: project planning, 379–380
      production phase: artwork creation, 380–384
      quality control, 385–387
   radio, 387–389
      cost of electronic production, 378
      postproduction phase, 389
      preproduction phase, 387
      production, 388–389
   television, 389–393
      commercial producer, role of, 389
      cost of electronic production, 378
      postproduction phase, 393
      preproduction phase, 390–391
      production phase, 391–393

Production phase
   print process, 380–384
      camera-ready art, 381–384
      defined, 380
      halftones, 382–384
      mechanicals, 381
      quality control, 386
      visuals, 381
   television process, "the shoot," 389, 393
      action, 392–393
      cameras, 392
      lights, 391–392
      sound, 391
      staging and talent, 378, 392–393
Product life cycle, 191
Product messages, 13, 14
Product news, 352
Product packaging, 196
Product placement, 540
Product positioning, 193, 245–247
Product user positioning, 246
Professional advertising
   defined, 21
   target audience, 19
Profession of advertising, 46
Profit margin, 11–12
Program-length advertisement (PLA), 439
Programming formats, 448
Program rating, 443
Projective techniques, 221, 222
Promotion, 203, 205
Proof copy, 422
Proofing print advertising, 386–387
Proportion
   design principles, 345
Prospective customers, 148–149
Protocols, 461
Provocative headlines, 352
PSAs; see Public service announcements (PSAs)
Psychographic, 175
Psychographics, 180
Psychographic systems, 183
Psychological processes, 152–161
Psychological screens, 153, 196
Psychology of color, 313
Public affairs, 586–587
Publications, 588
Publicity, 205, 584–585
Public notices, 417
Public phones, 531
Public relations (PR), 580–584
   vs. advertising, 581
   advertising vs., 8–9
   audiovisual materials, 592

   bulletin boards, 592
   community involvement, 586
   corporate blogs, 588, 589
   corporate public relationship advertising, 598
   crisis communications management, 585–586
   defined, 27, 580–581
   exhibits, 592
   feature articles, 589–591
   fundraising, 588
   IMC role, 581
   lobbying, 587
   membership drives, 588
   Netflix crisis, 579–580
   news releases, 584, 588, 589
   photographs, 589
   planning and research, 584–585
   posters, 591
   press agentry, 585
   press kits, 589
   press releases, 584, 589, 590
   printed materials, 591–592
   public affairs, 587
   publications, 588
   publicity, 584–585
   reputation management, 584–586
   role of, 580, 582–583
   social media, 588
   special-events management, 588
   speechwriting, 588
   stakeholders, 581
   tools, 589–592
   top firms, 583
Public relations activities, 27
Public relations advertising, 27
Public relations advertising, defined, 599
Publics, 27, 580
Public service announcements (PSAs)
   defined, 19
Public service messages, 8
Puffery in advertising, 44, 69
Pull strategies, 566, 569
Pull strategy, 192
Pulsing, 298
Purchase occasion, 175, 177
Purchase-occasion variables, 177
Purpose, as advertising classification, 19
Push money (PM), 568
Push strategies, 565, 568
Push strategy, 192

Q

QR (quick-response) bar codes, 560
QSR (quick-serve restaurant), 180
Qualitative research, 220, 221
Qualitative research methods, 221
Qualitative *vs.* quantitative research, 220
Quality
    control of, print production
            process, 385
    print production, 379
Quantitative research, 220, 223
Question headline, 352

R

Race and ethnicity
    Internet use, 465
    subcultures, 164–165
Radio, 46, 447–455
    advantages, 295
    artistic concept development,
            360–361
    audiences, 448–450
    copy, 358
    creating radio commercials, 359
    formats of commercials,
            361–365
    in IMC, 447–448
    learning objectives, 428
    planning and buying, 432
    production process,
            389–390
        cost of electronic production, 378
        postproduction phase, 389
        preproduction phase,
            387–388
        production, 388–389
    pros and cons, 450
    sales techniques, 362
    schedule, 453, 455
    summary, terms, and exercises,
            455–457
    terminology, 451–453
    testimonials, 362
    time, buying, 450–453, 455
    uses, 447
Radio personality, 362
Random combination table, 284
Random probability samples, 230
Ranking, 154
Rate base, 410
Rate card, 418
Ratings, 441, 443
    defined, 283
    Internet, 468
    television, 283, 444
Rating services, 441

Rational appeals, creative
            brief, 309
Reach
    defined, 283
    effective, 285
    of message, 283
    TV, 430
Reach potential, 453
Reactive relationship, 10
Readability
    typography, 382
Reader's Digest, 138
Readers per copy (RPC), 282
Reading notice, 416
Really Simple Syndication
            (RSS), 501
Rebates, consumer, 570
Recall test, 227
Recall tests, 227
Receivers
    communications process role,
            16–18
    defined, 14
    dimensions of, 16–18
Recency planning, 286
Recruiting, 211
Recruitment advertising, 608
Reference groups, 162
Referrals, 128
Refunds, consumer, 570
Regaining, 211
Regional advertisers, 110
Regional advertising
    defined, 19, 26
    media plans, 288
Regional agencies, 118
Regional publications, 409
Regular price-line advertising, 107
Regulation and restraints
    federal regulation
        Bureau of Alcohol, Tobacco and Firearms
            (ATF), 567
        Environmental Protection Agency
            (EPA), 587
        Federal Communications Commission
            (FCC), 89
        Federal Trade Commission (FTC), 84–87,
            567, 587
        Food and Drug Administration (FDA),
            87–89
        Library of Congress, 89–90
        Patent and Trademark Office,
            89–90
    international advertisers,
            78–79
    learning objectives, 60
    local government regulation, 91

nongovernmental regulation
    Better Business Bureau, 91–92
    by consumer groups, 95
    by media, 93–95
    National Advertising Review
            Council, 92
    self-regulation by advertisers,
            95, 98
    state regulation, 90
Relationship building, 546
    corporate/institutional advertising,
            599–608
        corporate identity advertising, 607
        David Ogilvy on, 607
        defined, 19, 598
        Portfolio Review, 602
        public relationship advertising, 598
        recruitment advertising, 608
    direct marketing, 546
        database impact on,
            549–553
        defined, 547–550
        direct-response advertising,
            554–560
        drawbacks to, 551–553
        evolution of, 548–549
        IMC role, 548–553
        types, 553–560
    learning objectives, 544, 578
    personal (face-to-face) selling,
            560–566
        advantages and drawbacks,
            561–562
        defined, 560–561
        as direct sales strategy, 553
        fulfilling orders, 563
        IMC role, 562–564
        information, gathering and providing,
            562–563
        vs. telemarketing, 553–554
        types, 561
    public relations (PR),
            580–592
        vs. advertising, 581–582
        audiovisual materials, 592
        bulletin boards, 592
        community involvement, 586
        corporate blogs, 588
        corporations, 598
        crisis communications management,
            585–586
        defined, 580–581
        exhibits, 592
        feature articles, 589–591
        fundraising, 588
        IMC role, 581
        job of, 583–592

lobbying, 587
membership drives, 588
Netflix crisis, 579–580
news releases, 584, 589, 592
photographs, 589
planning and research, 584–585
posters, 592
press agentry, 585
press kits, 589
press releases, 584, 589, 590
printed materials, 591–592
public affairs, 586–587
publications, 588
publicity, 584–585
reputation management,
    584–586
role of, 580
social media, 588
special-events management, 588
speechwriting, 587–588
stakeholders, 581
tools, 588–592
top firms, 583
relationship marketing, 9–14
    defined, 9
    importance of, 9–10
    integrated marketing communications,
        546–548
    levels of, 10–12
sales promotion, 564–565
    brand value impact, 565
    consumer promotions,
        568–574
    defined, 564–565
    IMC role, 565
    strategies and tactics, 565–574
    trade promotions, 566–568
sponsorships and events,
        592–599
    annual events, 596
    arts, 596–597
    benefits and drawbacks,
        593–594
    causes, 596
    cultural events, 596–597
    defined, 592–593
    entertainment, 595–596
    festivals and fairs, 596
    growth of, 592–593
    measuring results, 598
    methods of, 597–598
    philanthropy, 593
    sports marketing, 593–594
    types, 594–595
    venue marketing, 597
summary, terms, and exercises,
        574–575, 608

Relationship marketing,
        9–14, 54
    aim of, 9
    defined, 9
    importance of, 9–10
    integrated marketing communications, 546
    levels of, 10–12
Relevance dimension, 308
Reliability, 229
Reliability-validity diagram, 230
Relief motives, 160
Remarketing, 508
Reminding function, 312–313
Repertoire users, 176
Repetition, 157
Reputation management,
        585–586
    community involvement, 586
    crisis communication management,
        585–586
    defined, 584
    press agentry, 585
    publicity, 584–585
Research
    goal of, 145
    marketing and IMC, 210
    public relations (PR), 583–585
Research companies, 132
Research objectives, 219
Research revenues
    top 10 research companies by
        U.S., 211
Research statistics, 228
Reseller, 184, 199
Reseller markets, 149
Resellers, 184
Residual fee, 378
Resolution, 383
Resonance dimension, 307
Resources, local *vs.* national advertisers, 112
Resources (axis), 180
Retail advertising; *see also* Local advertising
    defined, 19, 20, 107
Retailers
    trade deals, 567
Retainer method, 126
Retention, 10
Retention programs, 550
Return on investment (ROI),
        210, 283
Reverse knockout, 387
Reverse technique to transform
        concepts, 318
Reviews, 512
Reward motives, 160
RFM (recency, frequency, monetary) formula,
        550, 551

Rich mail, 482
Rich-media advertising, 482
Roadblocking, 298
ROI (return on investment), 283
Role models, celebrities as, 61–62
ROP (run-of-paper) advertising
        rates, 420
ROS (run-of-station), 452
Rough cut, 393
Rough layout, 340
RPC (readers per copy), 282
RSS (Really Simple Syndication), 501
Run-of-paper (ROP) advertising
        rates, 420
Run-of-schedule positioning,
        435–436, 446
Run-of-station (ROS), 452

S

SaaS (software as a service), 502
Sale advertising, 21, 107
Sales letters, 555
Salesmen, 182
Sales promotion, 192,
        205, 564
    brand value impact, 565
    consumer, 568–574
        cents-off promotions, 570
        combination offers, 571
        contests, 574
        convenience cards, 568–570
        coupons, 569–570
        defined, 566
        effectiveness, 571
        electronic coupons, 570
        point-of-purchase (P-O-P) materials,
            568–569
        premiums, 570
        rebates, 570
        refunds, 570
        sampling, 571
        sweepstakes, 574
    defined, 27, 564
    growth of, 595
    IMC role, 565
    potential of different markets,
        289–290
    spiffs, 568
    strategies and tactics, 565–566
    trade deals, 567
    trade promotions, 566
        allowance, 566–568
        company conventions and dealer
            meetings, 568
        co-op advertising, 568
        defined, 564

Sales promotion agencies, 120
Sales promotion department, 123
Sales-target objectives, 241
Sales test, 226
Sales tests, 226, 228
Sample, 230
Sample unit, 230
Sample units, 230
Sampling, 571
Sampling methods, 230
Sans serif type, 382
Satellite master antenna television
    (SMATV), 446
Satellite radio, 453
Satisfaction, 148
SAU (standard advertising unit)
    system, 415
Savvy psychology, 326
Scale, 378
Schlock approach, 109
Scope of advertising, 102–139
    advertisers, 105–116
    advertising agencies, 116–127
    advertising industry, 104–105
    client-agency relationships,
        127–132
    ethical issues, 126
    learning objectives, 102
    local advertising, 105–109
    McDonald's, 103–104
    media, 134–135, 138–139
    national advertising, 110
    newspaper advertising, 108, 109,
        125, 134
    regional advertising, 110
    summary, review, and exercises,
        139–141
    suppliers, 132–133
    transnational advertising,
        114–116
Scope of media plan, 288–289
Screens
    halftone, 382–384
    physiological, 153
    psychological, 153
Script, 358
Script type, 383
SD (standard definition) digital
        programs, 431
Seal, 357
Search engines, 473–485
Search-results page, 473
Secondary data, 218
Secondary (or pass-along)
        readership, 411
Secondary target audience, 308
Second covers, 403

Segmenting consumer markets, 175
Selective demand, 67, 192
Selective distribution, 200
Self-concept, 154
Self-interest, 116
Self-liquidating premium, 571
Self-mailers, 556
Self-selects, 550
Self-service, 569
Semi-sole users, 176
Sensory gratification as transformational
        motive, 159, 160
Serif type, 383
Service, 193
Service messages, 13, 14
Services
    defined, 8
Sessions, 388
Sex in advertising, 322–323
Share, 444
Shared characteristics, 174
Share of market/share of voice
        method, 265
Sheets, 519
Shopper experience research, 224
Short Message System (SMS),
        488, 560
Short rates, 418
Short-term manipulative criticisms, 68
100 showing, 521
Signature cuts (sig cuts), 357
Simplicity
    design principles, 345
    of habit, 157
Situation analysis, 241
    plans book development, 555
Size
    audience and message weight,
        282–283
    magazines, 410
    message, and media planning,
        291–293
    newspapers, 415
Skinny trap, 387
Slice of life, 364
Slogans, 357
Slotting allowances, 566–567
Small-print qualifications, 70
SMATV (satellite master antenna
        television), 446
SMS (Short Message System),
        488–490, 560
Social advertising, 509
Social approval as transformational
        motive, 162
Social bookmarking, 501–502
Social class, 161–162

Social cognitive theory, 155
Social epidemics, 182
Social impact
    controversies over, 63
    deception, 68–69
    offensiveness, 72–73
    proliferation of advertising,
        70–71
    stereotypes, 71–72
    value system impact, 69
Social issues, 54–55, 57
Social listening, 508
Social media, 135, 492–513
    adoption of, 496–498
    application of, 507–512
    building social authority,
        503–507
    corporate, 588, 589
    customer service in, 505–506
    defined, 496
    introducing, 494–496
    learning objectives, 492
    managing, 502–503
    by the numbers, 506
    other, 510
    peronas, 495–496
    production process, 393–396
    public relations, 588
    public relations and, 582
    rise of, 496–502
    summary, terms, and exercises, 513
    transforming business, 507
    types, 499–502
        blogs, 499–500
        data explosion, 502
        forums, 499
        microblogs, 500
        RSS, 501
        social bookmarking, 501–502
        social networking, 502
        wikis, 501
    use of, 499
    viral marketing, 484
    writing for, 366–367
Social networking, 502
Social responsibility
    of advertisers, 74–75
    defined, 73
Social trends, 498
Society
    divisions in, 161–162
    interpersonal influences on consumer
        behavior, 151, 161–164
Sociologists, 8
Soft thinking, 314
Software, buying print media, 413
Software as a service (SaaS), 502

Sole users, 176
Soliciting, 128
Sorrell v. IMS Inc., 81
Sound
    radio, 388
    television, 391
Sound pictures, 362
Sound studio, 388
Sources, in communication process, 14
Spam, 484
Special effects, television commercials,
    390–391
Special equipment, as budget
    buster, 377
Special events, 205, 588
Specialized equipment, 193
Specialized service agencies,
    119–120
Spectaculars, 520
Speculative presentation, 128
Speechwriting, 587–588
Speed, typography in preproduction
    phase, 380
Spiffs, 568
Spillover media, 291
Split runs, 420
Split-run test, 228
Spokespersons, 15
Sponsored links, 474
Sponsorial consumers, 16
Sponsors
    advertising identifying, 8
    advertising paid for by, 8
    communication process,
      15–16
    consumer advertising, 20
    dimensions of, 15–16
Sponsorship, 436–437
Sponsorship and events, 592–599
    annual events, 596
    arts, 597
    benefits and drawbacks, 594
    causes, 597
    cultural events, 597
    defined, 592
    entertainment, 596
    festivals and fairs, 596–597
    growth of, 592–593, 595
    Internet, 482
    measuring results, 598–599
    methods of, 598
    philanthropy, 593
    special-events management, 588
    sports marketing, 594–596
    types, 594–598
    venue marketing, 597
Sports marketing, 594–596

Spot announcements, 437
Spot radio, 450–451
Spots (radio), 387
Square serif type, 383
SRI Consulting Business Intelligence
    (SRIC-BI), 180
S-shaped advertising response curve, 286
Staging and talent, electronic production, 378,
    392–393
Stakeholders
    defined, 9
    number of, 10
    public relations (PR), 581
    reputation management, 585
Standard advertising unit (SAU)
    system, 415
Standard billboard, 519
Standard definition (SD) digital
    programs, 431
Standardization, 235, 471
Standardized approach, 115
Standardized outdoor advertising, 518
Standard-size newspaper, 415
Statement stuffers, 556
Stay Smart campaign, 213
Stereotypes in advertising,
    71–72
Stern model of communication,
    15, 16
Stimuli
    comprehension, 153
    defined, 153
Stock posters, 519
Store choice and purchase, consumer decision
    process, 151
Storyboard
    defined, 365
    design, 365–366
Storyboard roughs, 360
Straight announcement, 361
Straight-fee, 126
Straight-sell copy, 355
Strategic issues
    advertising strategy
      creative briefs, 309–310
      formulating, 308–311
      media objectives and strategies, 293
      message strategy (rationale),
        310–311
      writing creative brief, 309–310
    creative strategy
      big idea development and implementation
        (Artist Explorer role), 317–325
      creative team, 306, 308
      decision making (Judge role), 326
      elements of great advertising,
        306–308

      enhanced by creativity, 311–316
      formulating, 308–311
      gathering information (Explorer role),
        316–317
      learning objectives, 304
      overcoming obstacles (Warrior role),
        326–327, 332–333
      Portfolio Review: creative director's
        outstanding ads, 328–331
      resonance and relevance dimensions,
        307–308
      summary, terms, and exercises,
        333–335
    IMC strategy
      communications media,
        257–258
      consumer behavior, 151–152
      IMC message, 258
      product concept, 257
      target audience, 256
    media planning; *see* Media planning
    relevance dimensions, 308
    sales promotion, 564–574
      consumer promotions,
        568–574
      push *vs.* pull strategies, 566
      trade promotions, 566–568
Strategic precision, 326
Strategic square, 245
Street marketing, 11
Strengths, in SWOT analysis, 279
Stripping, 384
Structural persuasion, 327
Structured communication, advertising
    as, 8
STV (subscription television), 446
Style, 339
Styles
    body copy, 354–356
Subcultural interpersonal influence on consumer
    behavior, 164–165
Subheads, 354
Subliminal advertising, 63, 248
Subscription television
    (STV), 446
Suitable structure, 116
Sunday supplement, 415
Supers, 393
Superstations, 431
Supplementary media
    advertising specialty, 537
    ATMs, 540–541
    business-to-business specialties, 537
    cinema advertising, 537
    emerging media, 537
    premiums, 537
    product placement, 540

Suppliers, 105, 132–133
Support statement, 310
Surface Pro 3, 194
Survey, 224
Survey questions
    open-ended, dichotomous, multiple-choice,
        and scale, 230
    personal questionnaire, 231
Sweepstakes, 574
SWOT analysis, 241
    marketing objectives, 279
    plans book development, 554
Syndication, 438–439
Synergy, 12, 297

T

Tabloid newspaper, 415
Tactics, 247
Taglines, 357
Take-ones, 530
Talent, 378, 393
Tangible goods, 8
TAP (total audience plan), 452
Target audience, 212
    advertising classification, 19
    analysis of, 555
    cost per point (CPP), 297
    in creative strategy, 308
    defined, 19, 308
    identification of, 19–21
    IMC strategy, 256
    Internet, 471
    transnational (global) markets,
        150–151
    as type of consumer, 16
    types, 19–21
Target market, 188
Target marketing process, 188
Target markets
    defined, 19
    identification of, 19–21
    selecting, 244–245
Target market selection, 188
Taxicab exteriors, 530
Tearsheets, 422
Technical component of message
        strategy, 310
Technology
    Internet connectivity, 466
    in outdoor advertising,
        527–528
    print media and, 424
Telemarketing, 204, 553
Teleprompter, 392

Television, 430–447; *see also specific television
    programs in company, brand &
    organization index*
    advantages, 295
    artistic concept development,
        360–361
    audience trends, 432–435
    broadcast TV
        commercial stations, 430–431
        defined, 430
        digital television (DTV),
            431–432
        national advertising, 430
        number of hours watched, 433
        pros and cons, 433
        top ten advertisers, 430
    buying television time
        avails, 444
        electronic media for buying
            software, 446
        negotiating prices and contracts, 446
        program selection, 445
    cable TV
        audience demographics, 436
        defined, 430
        digital television (DTV),
            431–432
        pros and cons, 436
    copy, 359–360
    creating TV commercials, 360
    formats of commercials, 361–365
    in IMC, 435
    vs. Internet users, 464–465
    learning objectives, 428
    planning and buying, 432
    production process, 389–393
        commercial producer, role
            of, 389
        cost of electronic production, 378
        postproduction phase, 393
        preproduction phase, 390–391
        production phase: the shoot,
            391–393
    ratings
        described, 283, 444
        gross rating points (GRPs), 282, 283
    summary, terms, and exercises, 455–457
    testimonials, 362
    time, 441, 443
    types, 435–441
Television households (TVHH),
        283, 443
Television production process, 389–393
    commercial producer, role of, 389
    cost of electronic production, 378

    postproduction phase,
        389, 393
    preproduction phase, 390–391
        animation, 390
        defined, 389
        live action, 390
        planning production, 391
        special effects, 390–391
    production phase: the shoot,
        391–393
        action, 392–393
        cameras, 392
        defined, 389
        lights, 391–392
        sound, 391
        staging and talent, 392–393
Terminal posters, 530
Termination stage, 130
Testimonials
    defined, 362
    false, 70
    radio and television, 362
Test market, 224
Text, 14, 15, 354
Text papers, 380
Text type, 382
Themelines, 357
Theory of cognitive dissonance, 166
The shoot, television commercial production
        process, 391–393
Thickburger TV spots, 180
Thinking
    creative thinking, 314–316
    fact- *vs.* value-based, 314–315
    hard *vs.* soft thinking, 314
    styles, 314
Third covers, 403
Third-party ad servers, 468–469
Threats, in SWOT analysis, 279
Thumbnail, 340
Time
    consumer behavior and,
        151, 165
    length of message, and media planning,
        291–293
    nonpersonal influences on consumer behavior,
        151, 165
Time orientation, 112
Timetable, 39
Tobacco advertising controversy,
        81–82
Tone or brand character statement, 310
Tools
    added value, 565
    media planning, 282

for public relations (PR), 588
sales tools, 362
value-added services, 565
Total audience, 444
Total audience plan (TAP), 452
Total bus, 531
Tracking, 215
Trade advertising
aim, 20, 21
deals and sales promotion, 567
defined, 565
target audience, 21
trade concentration, 566
Trade characters, 17
Trade concentration, 566
Trade deals, 567
Trademark, 89
Trade promotions
allowance, 566–568
company conventions and dealer meetings, 568
co-op advertising, 568
defined, 564, 565
spiffs, 568
trade deals, 567
Trade shows, 535
Traffic management, 122, 379–380
Train cars, 275
Transactional marketing, 9
Transformational (positively originated) motives, 160–161, 308
Transit advertising, 528–531
advantages, 295
buying, 530–531
defined, 135, 528
types, 528–530
Transit shelter advertising, 529–530
Transit terminal domination, 275
Transnational advertisers, 114–116
Transnational markets, 150–151
Transparency, 504
Traps, 386
Trash receptacles, 275
Trending, 498
Trial close, in body copy, 356
Trial/rejectors, 176
TVHH (television households), 283, 443
TV spots, 215
21st century, 52–54
TWICE/Campaigners, 195
Two-way brand communication, 504–505

Type families, 383
Typography
defined, 380
print production process, 380

U

UGC (user-generated content), 503
UHF (ultrahigh frequency) channels, 430
Ultrahigh frequency (UHF) channels, 430
Unaided recall, 226
Unconditioned response, 154
Unconditioned stimulus, 154
Unduplicated audience, 453
Unique selling proposition (USP), 48
Unity, design principles, 345
Universal Product Code (UPC), 223
Universe, 230
Unplanned costs, as budget buster, 377
Unplanned messages, 13, 14, 585
Upper Crust social classes, 161, 162
Urban Achievers social classes, 161, 162
U.S. Patent and Trademark Office, 89–90
Usage rate, 175
Usage rates, 176
Usage-rate variables, 176–177
Use/application positioning, 246
User-generated content (UGC), 503
User status, 175, 176
of prospective customers, 176
User-status variables, 176
USP (unique selling proposition), 48
Utility, product, 145
UX, for short, 223

V

Valentine v. Christensen, 80
Validity, 229
VALS classification system, 181
VALS typology, 180
Value-added packages, 277
Value-added services
Internet packages, 483
tools, 565
Value-based thinking, 314–315
Value systems
effect on, 69
in subcultures, 165
VCN (visual communication network), 531

Venue marketing, 597
Verbal component of message strategy, 310
Vertical cooperative advertising, 109–110
Vertical marketing system, 202
Vertical marketing system (VMS), 202
Vertical marketing system (vms), 202
Vertical publication, 411
Very high frequency (VHF) channels, 430
VHF (very high frequency) channels, 430
Video houses, 132
Video news releases (VNRs), 592
Videos, viral, 393, 395
Viral marketing, 484
Viral video, 3–4, 23–25, 393, 396
Virginia State Board of Pharmacy v. Virginia Citizens Consumer Council, 81
Visual communication network (VCN), 531
Visual distortions, 70
Visualization, 317
Visuals
defined, 346
focus for, 346
in print advertising, 346–347
in print production process, 379
purpose of, 346
selecting, 346–347
VNRs (video news releases), 592
Voice-over, 361
Voice power, 362
Volume discounts, 412
Volume segmentation, 176

W

Walmart, 189
Wang-Schultz planning model in IMC, 249–251
Wants, 158–159
Warrior, 326–327, 332–333
Warsaw Pact, 49
WCMS (Web content management system), 395
Weaknesses in SWOT analysis, 279
Web 2.0, 498
Web browsers, 464
Web content management system (WCMS), 395
Web designers, 342
Web design houses, 132
Weblogs, 499–500
Web pages, 464
Websites, 213, 223
advertising on, 473–474
classified ads, 484

Websites—*Cont.*
  defined, 474
  production, 395–396
  top ten most visited, 465
  writing for, 366–367
Weekly newspapers, 415
White space (isolation), 345
Wholeness, 12
Wikis, 501
Wireframe, 395
Wireless Internet connectivity, 466
Within the text, 15, 16
WOM (word of mouth),
    504–505

WOM (word-of-mouth) advertising, 9
Word of mouth (WOM), 504–505
Word-of-mouth (WOM) advertising, 9
Word pictures, 321
Work plan, 309–310
Work print, 393
World, world's top 10 values, 181
World Wide Web (WWW), 464; *See also* Internet
Writing; *see also* Copy
  composed commercial text, 15
  creative briefs, 309–310
  effective copy, 355
  media strategy planning, written rationale
    for, 294

  news releases, 584, 589
  papers, 380
  press releases, 584, 589, 590
  radio copy, 358
  television copy, 359–360
  websites and social media, 366–367
Writing papers, 380
WWW (World Wide Web), 464; *See also* Internet

Y

Yogurt, advertising, 3
Youngest Target Market, 182
Young Influentials social classes, 161, 162